LET'S GO

EUR

W9-AJQ-927

3 4028 09961 2823
HARRIS COUNTY PUBLIC LIBRARY

914.045 Bun 2019
Bunte-Mein, Julia,
Let's go Europe 2019 /
$19.99   on1054829818

"The writers seem to have experienced every rooster-packed bus and lunar-surfaced mattress about which they write."
— *The New York Times*

WITHDRAWN

NORWAY

North
Sea

DENMARK

IRELAND

GREAT
BRITAIN

THE NETHERLANDS

GERMANY

BELGIUM

Rhine

LUXEMBOURG

Atlantic
Ocean

Seine

Mosel

Danube

LICHTENSTEIN

Loire

SWITZERLAND

Bay of
Biscay

Dordogne

FRANCE

Rhône

Po

MONACO

Duero

ANDORRA

CORSICA

PORTUGAL

SPAIN

MENORCA

MALLORCA

SARDINIA

Guadalquivir

IBIZA

GIBRALTAR (U.K.)

CEUTA
(SPAIN)

MELILLA
(SPAIN)

ALGERIA

TUNISIA

MOROCCO

CONTENTS

MEET THE TEAM

MASTHEAD

Laura Wilson, Publishing Director

A sophomore concentrating in Applied Math who loves linear algebra (so much so that she spins around in her chair and squeals with glee when describing its application to differential equations), Laura adores a good cup of coffee and the word "amazing." She also appreciates minimalist outfits and pastel colors. Originally from Dallas, Texas, Laura did ballet in another life, and her spoken-word play incorporating both math and dance has wowed people the world over. She has also infected her coworkers with her continued usage of the word "y'all." (Editor's note: we don't mind. It's very efficient.)

Cassandra Luca, Editor-in-Chief

A font enthusiast with a penchant for blurting out incomplete phrases in French and Spanish at odd moments, Cassandra is a sophomore originally from Newton, MA. (Relocating to Cambridge was an ordeal requiring a lot of adjustment, as moving ten miles away from anywhere often does.) As someone who really likes words, she actually enjoys editing Researcher-Writer copy, her friends' papers, and basically anything else she can get her hands on; if you couldn't tell, she's an English concentrator. Outside of *Let's Go,* she reports for *The Harvard Crimson's* News Board. Her hobbies include learning foreign languages, buying outrageously expensive stationery—the kind with thick, smooth paper, not the ones filled with wannabe flimsy sheets—writing in her bullet journal, gushing about nineteenth-century literature, biking on crowded (read: dangerous) Boston streets, finding new types of granola, and comparing all the aforementioned granola she's ever had the good fortune to consume. She loves the color red, poached eggs, Paris, skincare that does what it says it does, cream cheese frosting, and late-night conversations.

Danielle Eisenman, Associate Editor

Danielle is a sophomore originally from New York. She lives in Mather House and studies History and Literature. Outside of *Let's Go,* Danielle DJs for WHRB Harvard Radio's Record Hospital and writes about music and films for The Harvard Crimson. Her favorite color is iridescent, her favorite milkshake flavor is strawberry malt, and her favorite art form is the coming-of-age high school dramedy. Talk to her if you're curious to see how far someone can stretch a joke that never really made sense in the first place.

RESEARCHER-WRITERS

Julia Bunte-Mein

Brace yourselves for an intense gastronomical experience featuring wine, cheese, and tapas in Eastern Spain and Southern France, courtesy of world nomad extraordinaire: Julia. A proud foodie, linguaphile, art-lover, and fitness aficionada, catch Julia doing early-morning yoga in the most obscure of places, scouring cities for little-known art galleries, and going to the most extreme lengths to sample the local cuisine. When she's not getting lost in European countries, Julia studies Government and Environmental Sustainability at Harvard.

Margaret Canady

This summer, Margaret found herself in Greece and the region of Tuscany, Italy, quite far from her tried and true Texas roots. Armed only with a terrible sense of direction and a half-empty travel sized bottle of suntan lotion, she braved the difficulties of Mediterranean traveling, which included having too many sunsets to watch and too much good art to review. Adventures included eating her weight in gelato, pretending to know the difference between regional wines ("This is supposed to taste like smoky blueberries? I'm getting hints of...red wine"), and convincing the Greeks that yes, she really is from Texas, cowboys come in all shapes, genders and sizes, and unfortunately no, she doesn't ride a horse to school. When not working on her Chaco tan or pretending she knows how to pronounce the Greek language, she studies psychology and dance, which have nothing (or everything) to do with world traveling, depending on your perspective.

Eric Chin

Warm Mediterranean sun on the back of his neck, the feeling of sand between his toes on an Italian beach, champagne on a tiled French portico... Wait—Eric's going where? Iceland and Scandinavia? *Shit.* He may have to trade in sandals for hiking boots and survive on a diet of sheep's head and "putrescent" shark meat (seriously, look it up), but at least he'll get to take advantage of the free education, right? Oh, it's summer? Well what about the free healthcare? Hopefully not? Okay, fine. He'll just have to settle for climbing behind waterfalls, kayaking through fjords, hiking on glaciers, and fulfilling his mission of finding as much IKEA furniture as he possibly can.

Emily Corrigan

Emily prepared for her travels in France, Belgium, and the Netherlands this summer in a *Rocky*-esque training montage: speed-eating croissants, running up hills wearing comfortable walking sandals, and bench pressing her 30-liter Osprey travel backpack. However, she realized the intense training may have been getting to her when she drop-kicked a box of macaroons off the Eiffel Tower, injuring three. For the rest of the summer, she recovered by playing chess with nice Flemish people. She ate *frites*. She took a silly yet endearing picture intentionally missing the point of the Louvre pyramid with her finger. She is now fully rehabilitated.

Austin Eder

A junior at a small liberal arts college just outside of Boston, Austin spent her summer city-hopping in Spain. An avid reader and a lover of the performing arts, she felt right at home on the cobblestone streets of Granada's Albaicín. Here, the scents of tanned leather and cured meats mingle in the air, and the sounds of guitar and castanets reverberate through rickety wooden doors and crumbling mud walls. When not reviewing museums, restaurants, bars, and the like, Austin spends her time discussing domestic and international affairs at Harvard's Institute of Politics and doing freelance copywriting and marketing work for real estate, tech, and law firms based in Los Angeles, Boston, and Chicago, respectively. In her free time, she enjoys jamming to indie rock, studying art and literature, Wikipedia deep-diving, contemplating life's larger questions, and exploring the greater Boston area on foot.

Lucy Golub

Navigationally challenged to a fault, Lucy has no idea what she's doing. But she's an expert at faking-it-til-you-make-it. Follow along as she discovers hidden gems and alleys throughout Great Britain and Ireland, often truly by accident. Yet these accidents help her befriend locals in a desperate attempt to get back on a familiar street. Getting lost (sometimes on purpose) results in discovering hole-in-the-wall restaurants and colorful murals off the beaten path. Other than being bad with directions, Lucy's other talents include an ability to eat anyone under the table when cheese is involved (and probably get some mouth-watering pictures while doing it @OurLifeInFood.) In the classroom, she studies Social Studies, which means she's got the being-social-in-a-hostel thing down. Or that's what she keeps telling herself as she struggles to understand Irish accents. A New York City native, Lucy's an expert on making the most of a city and exploring new neighborhoods. You can probably find her singing musical theater after checking out a local performance, breaking her third pair of sandals, or trying to convince Brits she meets at the pub that she doesn't hate beer.

Nick Grundlingh

Nick Grundlingh is going to spend the summer traveling through Germany, Poland, and the Czech Republic. He's looking forward to—*Sorry, what was that? What's Nick wearing?* That's his fanny pack. Anyway, Nick is looking forward to meeting—*Look, Nick really doesn't see what's so funny about it, unless you think keeping your valuables safe is some sort of joke. Now, where was he?* Oh yeah. Nick can't wait to meet new people and—*Seriously, guys. Knock it off. You know, in Europe, people make fun of you if you don't wear one.* At least Nick assumes they do. He hasn't actually been yet. But it's probably very similar to how he just described it.

Kristine Guillaume

Kristine traded her editor's desk at Let's Go HQ for an even more unglamorous life: a pack stuffed to the brim with extra underwear, much-needed shower shoes for grimy hostel bathrooms, and ridiculously rationed quantities of body lotion and hair product to tame the frizz (her efforts, however valiant, proved unsuccessful). Once packed, she took her set of extra fine pens and trusty Moleskine to the south of France, where she sampled *bouchons* in Lyon, strolled along *le promenade* in Nice, and swirled countless glasses of wine in Bordeaux. When Kristine isn't consuming ungodly amounts of *beurre, pain, et vin,* she enjoys writing for the News Board of *The Harvard Crimson,* drinking English Breakfast tea, and indulging her terrifyingly intense addiction to television.

Adrian Horton

Hailing from Cincinnati, Ohio, Adrian will be honing her bakery-finding skills in Greece and southern Italy this summer. Prior work experience: ranch-hand, gardener, fruit bat cage cleaner, one-time contributor to her hometown's Wikipedia page. Her current interests include distance running, 90s music, and convincing people she has seen *Game of Thrones* Seasons 1-5 (she hasn't, but oh my god wasn't the Red Wedding in Season 3 BANANAS?!). When she isn't watching movie trailers on YouTube, she studies History and Literature at Harvard and sometimes writes about pop culture.

Alejandro Lampell

Continuing with a desire to explore new places that stems from his time living in six different countries, Alejandro has set off on a new adventure in France and Switzerland, in which he will try to discover how much solitude he can handle while carrying all the clothes he needs for eight weeks in one hiking backpack. Not one to shy away from a challenge, Alejandro will explore the mountains of Switzerland and the beaches of Southern France, and indulge in the exquisite cuisine both countries have to offer. While not daydreaming about studying abroad, Alejandro likes to spend his time trying to learn to play the guitar or in the library, nestled between towers of books.

Gavin Moulton

In spite of a crippling Croatian supermarket crisis and the tragedy of a truffle hunting dog with an injured paw, Gavin was generally successful in covering Croatia from top to bottom - quite literally, he hiked to the summit of a mountain and went scuba diving. While he may have stayed in a hostel room of seven Canadian girls, another hostel room of five French girls, and another of four British girls, he somehow managed to stay focused on the important things: Dubrovnik's best castrated rooster soup, gin-treehouse-bars in Zagreb, and award winning mausoleums in Cavtat. Did his trusty headlamp come in handy? You betcha! Did his blond hair lead to locals thinking he was Croatian? Da! Did he fall asleep on a beach and have to run four miles because he missed a bus? Yes, just don't tell his mom who is under the impression that he only went to museums and other Croatian cultural sites.

Antonia Washington

Antonia is spending her summer pretending she knows a lot about wine and collecting tourist keychains she has no use for throughout Austria, Hungary, Slovakia, and Germany. Originally from Portland, Oregon, she spends much of her time schlepping through the wilderness and enjoys backpacking, kayaking, and low-pressure longboarding (because she's just not good enough to brake efficiently so crowds make her nervous). Catch Antonia eating carbs, looking fly in white Crocs (Crocs is the most innovative company in the world), and pleading for her mom's REI dividend.

Joseph Winters

Meet Joseph: junior, Earth and Planetary Science concentrator, vagrant vacationer. He spent eight weeks this summer in search of the Iberian Peninsula's best veggie burger, but en route discovered a bunch of famous monuments, museums, and cultural landmarks—coincidentally, enough to cover a whole section of *Let's Go 2019!* From *petiscos* in Porto to *siestas* in Salamanca, Joseph's travels took him up the Portuguese coast and across northern Spain before depositing him in bustling Madrid. According to his Garmin, he walked just under one million steps while navigating from far-flung bullrings to slaughterhouses-turned-cultural centers. A trip so varied, the only real constant was the Nutella-and-toast breakfast combo at every hostel. When he's not investigating tapas restaurants, Joseph enjoys distance running, playing piano, cooking, specialty coffee shops, and occasionally finishing a Thursday NYT crossword puzzle. He also writes for the Harvard Political Review and the Crimson, but the acme of his writing career was undoubtedly a blog post titled "What is Your Spirit Tapa?" His pet peeve is ambiguous museum signage.

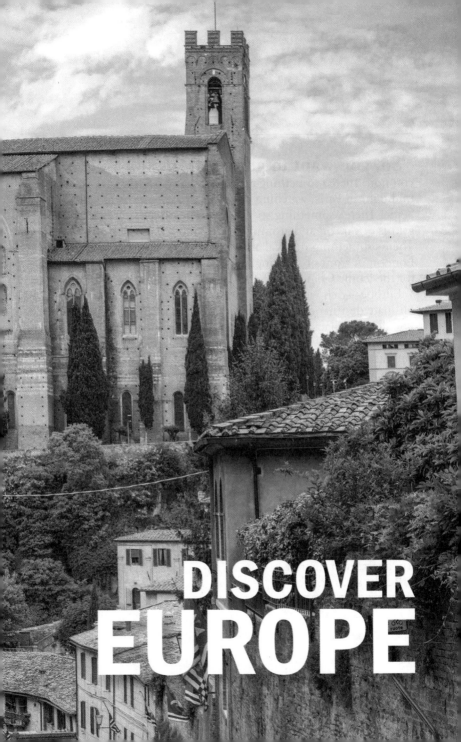

DISCOVER
EUROPE

So, you want to go to Europe? But how could you not? There's something awfully romantic about spending midnight in Paris, watching the lights glisten on the famed La Seine. There's something special about hearing the growls and grunts of cars on and around the *vias* and *piazzas* of Rome. There's something magical about walking on the streets of London in front of Buckingham Palace as the roads close down for the iconic Changing of the Guard.

Europe—rich with history, culture, art, and adventure—is the ultimate destination for any backpacker from any background. For all the hullabaloo around this small continent, the fairytale-like legends that you hear from old men in parks, friends, and parents are, for the most part, true stories. Well, maybe all except Uncle Marty's story claiming he found an old manuscript of *Ulysses* on a Dublin bar crawl..

Pub crawls and pretentious reading material aside, Europe awaits you. Paraglide above the Swiss Alps, shimmy your way into Berlin's most exclusive clubs, or scuba dive between two tectonic plates in Iceland. When in Dubrovnik, find love on Lokrum Island and, in Athens, find your Adonis or Aphrodite. Get blown away by the beat of Pamplona's Running of the Bulls and cheer on European sports teams in Munich's beer gardens. Europe has been, and will likely continue to be, the starting point for the adventures of students all around the world. Join the company of your fellow wanderlust-stricken adventure seekers and set your trip apart from the rest.

Ready, set, *Let's Go*!

WHEN TO GO

Summer is the most popular time to travel to Europe, meaning that if you take a trip during high season, thousands of backpackers will be right there with you. It's the perfect opportunity to meet students from around the world in hostels of varying social degrees, restaurants with communal tables, and in the long lines for incredible churches and monuments (small talk is a real thing, especially if you're alone). While it is very possible to complete a budget trip in the summertime, it's important to note that the season's many festivals can jack up prices for accommodations, restaurants, and general sightseeing. Keep an eye out for huge summertime events such as Pamplona's Running of the Bulls, Dublin's Bloomsday, Lisbon's Festas de Lisboa, and Edinburgh's Fringe. You'll need to plan ahead—like way ahead—if you intend to travel while these world-renowned events take place. They're definitely worth the extra effort (and perhaps even the extra cash).

If you're not into the summer backpacking experience, late spring and early autumn attract fewer tourists, meaning that you can save a bit on airfare and bookings, but it can be difficult to take time off during these seasons. Unfortunately, spring break isn't quite long enough to do a full tour.

For those looking to celebrate the holidays in Venice or shred the slopes of the Italian Alps, winter travel is also a viable option. However, this isn't the best time to hit the clubs of Ibiza or take a walking tour of Prague. You'll also find that some hotels, restaurants, and sights have reduced hours or are on vacation…from you.

SUGGESTED ITINERARIES

THE GRAND TOUR (40 DAYS)

For the travel-hungry soul who wants to see the most famous highlights of Europe—buckle up, you're in for a wild ride. We highly recommend tackling this bad boy with the trusty help of budget airlines or a rail pass.

- **LONDON** (4 days)—God save the Queen. Your first stop on your full-fledged adventure begins in an English-speaking country (baby steps). Make London your cup of tea by delving into its music culture and royal history. Here's hoping you'll catch a glimpse of the Queen (no, no, no not Elizabeth, J.K. Rowling). **(see p. 258)**
- **COPENHAGEN** (2 days)—It's time to venture north, as in Nordic. Blond people, Viking history, a whole soap opera of feuds with Sweden, and, of course, insane taxes await you in Denmark. Time to immerse yourself in Copenhagen's *hygge*. **(see p. 121)**
- **AMSTERDAM** (3 days)—Amsterdam has it all: imperial history, artistic pedigree, and killer music. Burn some calories in one of the most bike-friendly cities in the world and see some classic Dutch windmills. Let's not forget crossing over to the dark side either; if you so choose, the coffeeshop scene is out there—just keep this part of the trip to yourself (Mom doesn't want to know). **(see p. 462)**
- **PARIS** (4 days)—Go ahead, be romantic. This is the quintessential European destination for artists, lovers, tourists, foodies, and romantics alike. If you don't go here on your Grand Tour, you didn't go to Europe. Paris, *enchanté*. **(see p. 173)**
- **BARCELONA** (3 days)—Get your Gaudí on in one of the hottest (and we mean searing hot) parts of Europe. Architecture geeks will be awestruck by the beauty of La Sagrada Familia, foodies will triumph in the exquisite Catalan cuisine, and soccer fans will rejoice in the buzz of one of the world's most beloved teams at the Camp Nou. Let's get Messi. **(see p. 542)**
- **LISBON** (2 days)—Part of the beauty of Lisbon is that it's largely undiscovered. This hidden gem is bound to blow your mind with its seafood delights and geographic wonders. It's time for leg day, so gear up to hike as you soak up the sun and culture in Lisboa. **(see p. 521)**
- **MADRID** (2 days)—The Spanish capital reigns with the promise of pitchers of sangria, one of the most poppin' nightlife scenes on the globe, and countless opportunities to explore Spanish history from the Age of Exploration to present day. Madrid loves you already and you will fall for it even harder. **(see p. 571)**
- **ROME** (4 days)—Hop on that vespa, baby. It's time to talk fast, move your hands fast, and drive even faster. Get the best of the old Roman Empire and the new Roman paradise in the Eternal City. Gelato will cool you down as you climb Palatine Hill and pretend to be a gladiator in The Roman Colosseum. **(see p. 429)**
- **FLORENCE** (3 days)—Travel back in time to the Renaissance and get #cultured in this epicenter of art. This is Michelangelo's hometown, but today it is a modern hotspot for art, music, shopping, and gelato-mongering. **(see p. 394)**

- **PRAGUE** (3 days)—Prague's Old Town looks like a fairytale and it's time to make your dreams come true. This often-overlooked gem boasts must-sees like the Charles Bridge and castle, but the young and grungy bars, beer gardens, and galleries are more eager to see you. **(see p. 100)**
- **MUNICH** (2 days)— Munich is the quintessential German city, layered in tradition. Munich is a little quieter than other cities, but you can still appreciate its Bavarian roots as you tour its high-quality beer gardens. **(see p. 230)**
- **BERLIN** (3 days)— Pick up the pace and head to a city that never sleeps. Riddled with the history of a war-torn city and trendy, exclusive club scenes, Berlin is a true cosmopolitan center. Make sure you say, "Hallo!" to Merkel for us. **(see p. 202)**
- **ATHENS** (3 days)— Make your way back down south and turn up the temperature. Climb Mount Olympus, walk around the ruins of the Acropolis, and find your Adonis or Aphrodite under the sweet, Greek sun. Apollo, is that you? **(see p. 296)**
- **SPLIT** (2 days)—Top it all off in the Balkans. Split is the place to cool down, relax, and enjoy the beach as you dance the night away. **(see p. 81)**

ISLAND HOPPING (14 DAYS)

Does Europe even have any islands, you ask? That's preposterous. Tons of lively ones eagerly await you on your European adventure. We're talking palm trees, sand, pebbly beaches, bumping party beats, and master DJs. Tell Corona we've found our beach.

- **IBIZA** (2 days)—Kick it off with superstar DJs like David Guetta and show Mike Posner you can handle a rager better than he can in the nightclubs of this iconic Spanish island. **(see p. 563)**
- **MALTA** (3 days)—Combine cliff-jumping with clubbing in this 122-mile archipelago. The best part? You can mix the history of repeated conquest by the Phoenicians and Romans and the colonial rule of the British into your island vacation by visiting limestone temples, ancient ruins, and monumental forts. **(see p. 404)**
- **MYKONOS** (3 days)—Party animals all around the world hear the word "Mykonos" and know it's the holy grail of fun. Skip the architectural wonders of Ancient Greece and head straight here for nights to remember. **(see p. 316)**
- **HVAR** (3 days)—Hvar are you doing today? Not good? Swing by this Croatian island on the iconic Riva of Hvar. You've got nothing but clubbing, beach parties, and cheap alcohol ahead of you. **(see p. 75)**
- **VENICE** (3 days)—Okay, well Venice isn't exactly one island. Think more like 118. Venice is connected by a series of foot bridges that cross over the city's 170 boat canals. Close out your trip with a little culture on the glass-making island of Murano and with the lace-specialists in Burano. **(see p. 450)**

STOP AND SMELL THE ROSES (23 DAYS)

If you've got a green thumb, then you'll be glad to know Europe has much for you to see in the form of extravagance. The Romans, for example, were fixated with controlling nature and, as a result, created beautiful gardens with immaculately manicured plants in the strangest of shapes. We're not quite sure of the origins of the other gardens around the continent, but these are feats of man and nature that would make even the most talented gardener jealous. What do *you* have? Tomato vines? Growing upside down? Amateur.

- **FLORENCE** (3 days)—The Boboli Gardens at Florence's Palazzo Pitti are truly a sight to behold. Climb lots (and we mean lots) of stairs as you walk through what feels like the gardens of Sleeping Beauty's castle—without Maleficent trying to keep the prince out. (see p. 394)
- **VIENNA** (4 days)—The gardens of Schönnbrunn Palace await your royal highness. And, if that doesn't entertain you, the Hapsburgs also have gardens at the Belvedere for your pleasure. (see p. 37)
- **PARIS** (5 days)—The Jardin des Plantes lies in the fifth arrondissement and is the main botanical garden in France. (see p. 173)
- **BARCELONA** (4 days)—Parc Guëll. Garden? Outdoor space? Architectural wonder of Antoni Gaudí? All of the above. (see p. 542)
- **MALMÖ** (2 days)—*Aah* Slottsträdgården, complete with orderly, manicured hedges and multiple plots including a Steppe Garden and Japanese Garden that will make your jaw drop. (see p. 624)
- **LONDON** (5 days)—The Royal Parks are undoubtedly majestic. Hyde Park and Regent's Park are full of green spaces in an urban setting while the famed Kensington Gardens serves as the front yard for a king, situated right in front of the stunning palace. (see p. 258)

CALL OF THE WILD (12 DAYS)

We get it—you're Wilderness First-Aid Certified, you've spent every summer as a camp counselor in the middle of the forest, and you've hiked 111 miles solo. You're coming to Europe for the outdoor adventures—to get in touch with nature, if you will. In that case, we've got you covered. Lace up your hiking boots.

- **REYKJAVIK** (3 days)—Reykjavik is an excellent place to set up camp to do outdoorsy day trips in Iceland. Some of our favorites include the Blue Lagoon and Golden Circle. (see p. 350)
- **OSLO** (2 days)—Oslo Sommerpark is guaranteed to put the overeager kid spirit back in you, featuring a wicked obstacle course that allows you to climb 20 meters into the trees. Tarzan who? (see p. 480)
- **GIMMELWALD** (3 days)—This secluded mountain town in the Alps is a hidden gem: paraglide in the mountains, watch glaciers collide, and hike difficult, pristine trails. (see p. 644)
- **SPLIT** (2 days)—Get a drink on the rocks and then cliff jump off the rocks (into the Mediterranean). Note: *Let's Go* does not endorse drinking and jumping. (see p. 81)
- **LAGOS** (2 days)—If outdoor adventures at the beach are what you seek, opt for a change of pace in southern Portugal, kayaking off the coast in the Iberian Peninsula. (see p. 515)

HOW TO USE THIS BOOK

CHAPTERS

Let's Go Europe 2019 covers 22 countries in its 20 chapters. Each chapter contains comprehensive content that is designed to make your trip easy to plan. Chapters are organized in alphabetical order by country, so the book kicks off with Austria and culminates with Switzerland. The countries covered in this book are Austria, Belgium, Croatia, Czechia, Denmark, France, Germany, Great Britain, Greece, Hungary, Iceland, Ireland, Luxembourg, Malta, Montenegro, The Netherlands, Norway, Poland, Portugal, Spain, Sweden, and Switzerland.

Each chapter has been written by at least one *Let's Go* **Researcher-Writer.** Researcher-Writers (RWs) are students at Harvard College who spend a maximum of eight weeks of their summer covering a pre-planned route of cities for publication in *Let's Go Europe.* Credits are given after the name of each city.

Within a chapter, cities are arranged in alphabetical order, so don't be alarmed when you see the France chapter begins with Avignon instead of Paris. We promise we did not forget Paris; we did our due diligence.

Structure of a Chapter

Each chapter begins with a country introduction and, from there, it is divided into city sections. The first section in a city always consists of an **introduction** followed by an **orientation** and **city essentials,** which includes all of the important information you should know—the location of tourist offices, police stations, hospitals, a list of BGLTQ+ resources, and numbers to call in the event of an emergency—before traveling to a given place. Although Google Maps is a fantastic resource that can be downloaded on your phone and accessed offline, it is important to pick up a paper map from a tourist office in case of emergency.

On to the fun stuff: city chapters include several sections, each of which will help you plan your days. These sections are also in alphabetical order, with our *Let's Go* Thumbpicked™ establishments listed first and followed by all of the other wonderful things we've covered:

> **Accommodations:** *Let's Go's* accommodation listings consist of budget options, which are often hostels. In smaller cities, accommodation options are often limited, so we have included some B&Bs and budget hotels to ensure you have a comfortable stay without breaking the bank.
>
> **Sights:** Our "Sights" section is further broken down into four categories—Culture, Landmarks, Museums, and Outdoors.
>> ***Culture:*** These listings cover everything from churches to theaters to markets to interesting bookstores.
>> ***Landmarks:*** These are your Eiffel Towers, Colosseums, and Buckingham Palaces. All of the biggest sights and attractions are listed here.
>> ***Museums:*** Fairly self-explanatory, but here's where you'll find Prague's Dox, Paris' Louvre, and Madrid's Prado.
>> ***Outdoors:*** Here's where you'll find listings of a city's green spaces, beaches, and outdoor activities.
>
> **Food:** You need to eat when you're abroad, right? For your convenience, we have included restaurants that cater to a backpacker's budget with a few splurge options interspersed. Treat yo' self.

Nightlife: Sleep all day, party all night, sightsee all day, party all night—whatever your travel lifestyle is, we've got the right bars, clubs, and cafés to ensure your evenings are well spent.

Listings—a.k.a. reviews of individual establishments—constitute the majority of *Let's Go's* content, and consist of essential information (address, phone number, website, and hours), a review of a given establishment, followed by any miscellaneous information that may be useful.

ESTABLISHMENT NAME ($-$$$)
Address; phone number; website; hours
Review goes here.
Miscellaneous information such as prices, cash/card, dietary restrictions, whether or not an establishment is certified BGLTQ+ friendly, wheelchair accessibility, etc.

Every piece of content in *Let's Go Europe 2019*—the introductions, the orientations, the essentials, the listings, and the features—was researched and updated during the summers of 2017 and 2018.

The end of each country chapter contains a **country essentials** page in which we detail information that is applicable to the entire country. This includes the country code, regulations and laws surrounding drug and alcohol use, and country-wide safety and health information. This also contains information about attitudes toward BGLTQ+ travelers and minorities.

The *Let's Go* Thumbpick™

is an icon you will see a lot in this book. Whenever a listing has a Thumbpick™ next to the establishment name, it indicates that it was a favorite of the Researcher-Writer who visited that city. These are, in other words, our top-choice accommodations, sights, and food and nightlife establishments.

Price Diversity

Another set of icons in the book corresponds to what we call our "price diversity" scale, which approximates how much money you can expect to spend at a given establishment. We have noted price diversity in our Accommodations and Food listings only. For accommodations, we base our range on the cheapest price for which a single traveler can stay for one night. For food, we estimate the average amount one traveler will spend in one sitting. Keep in mind that no scale can allow for the quirks of all individual establishments.

BEFORE YOU GO

Planning a good trip takes a lot more effort than you think it will. The worst thing you can do is get off the plane in Warsaw, for example, and not know what you want to do or what resources are available to you. Each chapter of this book includes a list of country-specific resources that will help you out in a pinch, but this chapter contains overarching information for all of Europe. We've condensed the knowledge we've acquired over 59 years of travel to ensure you have a safe, enjoyable experience in Europe. Planning your trip? Check. How to get around? Check. Safety and health resources? Check. There is also a phrasebook at the back of the book for your convenience.

PLANNING YOUR TRIP

DOCUMENTS AND FORMALITIES

There's a lot of country-specific information when it comes to visas and work permits, but don't forget the most important piece of documentation: your passport.

Passport

You cannot board a plane to another country without a passport. If you do not have a passport, you should apply for one several months in advance, as the process can take a long time. US citizens can apply for a passport online at www.travel.state.gov or at a local United States Post Office. Adult passports are valid for 10 years while children's passports are valid for five. If you already have a passport, check the expiration date of your document before booking any flights or accommodations. **Your passport must be valid for at least six months after you return from your trip in order to travel to Europe. Your passport should also have at least two blank pages, depending on your destination.**

Visas

Those lucky enough to be EU citizens will not need a visa to travel throughout the continent. Being an EU citizen has other perks too, such as shorter security lines. Citizens of Australia, Canada, New Zealand, United States, and various other non-EU countries, however, do not need a visa for a stay of up to 90 days. This three-month period begins upon entry to any of the EU's **freedom-of-movement zones.** Those staying longer than 90 days may apply for a longer-term visa; consult an embassy or consulate for more information.

Double check entry requirements at the nearest embassy or consulate for up-to-date information, as political situations can make it easier or more difficult to move between countries. US citizens can also consult www.travel.state.gov. Keep in mind that admittance to a country as a traveler does not include the right to work, which is authorized only by a work permit. You should check online for the process of obtaining a work permit for the country in which you are planning to work.

THE EUROPEAN UNION: HOW IT WORKS

The European Union is a union of 28 countries within the continent of Europe based in Brussels, Belgium. This number still includes the United Kingdom. The countries covered in this book that are not part of the European Union are Iceland, Norway, Montenegro, and Monaco.

The European Union's policy of freedom of movement means that most border controls have been abolished and visa policies harmonized. This treaty, formerly known as the Schengen Agreement, means you still have to carry a passport (or government-issued ID card for EU citizens) when crossing an internal border, but, once you've been admitted to one country, you're free to travel to other participating states. Iceland and Norway are members of the Schengen Agreement, meaning that the rule extends to those countries as well.

It is important, however, to note that recent fears over immigration have led to calls for suspension of this freedom-of-movement and strengthening of borders. One of the most covered situations is **Brexit,** the vote by the citizens of the United Kingdom to leave the European Union. Lawmakers from the United Kingdom and the European Union, as of August 2018, are still in conversation about the new border restrictions and rules between the United Kingdom and European Union, so it is important to inform yourself about the situation before planning travel to the UK.

TIME DIFFERENCES

Most of Europe is on Central European Time, which is 1hr ahead of Greenwich Mean Time (GMT) and observes Daylight Savings Time in the summer. This means that, in summer, it is 6hr ahead of New York City, 9hr ahead of Los Angeles, 1hr. ahead of the British Isles, 8hr behind Sydney, and 10hr behind New Zealand. In winter, it is 10hr behind Sydney and 12hr behind New Zealand. However, the UK, Ireland, and Portugal are on GMT, also known as Western European Time, which means they are 1hr behind the Central European Time countries. In addition, Greece and some parts of Eastern Europe are on Eastern European Time, which means they are 1hr ahead of Central European Time countries.

MONEY MATTERS

BEFORE YOU GO

Call your bank. The first thing you should do is alert your bank that you will be abroad for a period of time. You should be prepared to give the bank representative the exact dates of your travel and where you will be if you plan to use your debit card in that country. Keep in mind that there may be a foreign transaction charge from your bank whenever you use your card. If your bank is a local US bank that does not have branches outside of a given city, you may want to consider changing your bank or opening a new account to one that is more widespread so that you can access customer service lines with larger networks in case of emergency.

Before you go, you should decide which credit cards to use before packing. It is advisable to pack credit cards that are widely accepted in Europe to avoid being caught in a pinch where you do not have any form of payment. Call your credit card company before going to alert them you will be abroad. As with banks, be prepared to give the representative the exact dates of your travel. Some credit card companies have online systems in which you can input the dates of your travel to skip the step of calling ahead.

CURRENCY BREAKDOWN

Nineteen countries in Europe use the euro, which is the currency of the European Union, meaning you will not have to worry about changing currencies when you hop from country to country. If you are traveling outside of the eurozone, however, you should be aware that you will need to convert once you leave. Countries outside the eurozone in the European Union are Croatia, Czechia, Denmark, Hungary, Sweden, and the United Kingdom. For an up-to-date list, check a currency converter (such as www.xe.com).

GETTING MONEY FROM HOME

Things happen and, if they do, you might need money. The easiest and cheapest solution to get you out of a pinch is to have someone back home make a deposit to your bank account directly. If this isn't possible, consider one of the following options:

Wiring Money

Arranging a **bank money transfer** means asking a bank back home to wire money to a bank wherever you are. This is the cheapest way to transfer cash, but it's also a slow process, taking several days. Note that some banks may only release your funds in local currency, potentially sticking you with a poor exchange rate; you should inquire about this in advance.

Money transfer services like **Western Union** are faster and more convenient than bank transfers—but also much pricier. Western Union has many locations worldwide. To find one, visit www.westernunion.com or call the appropriate number:
- Australia: 1800 173 833
- Canada: 800 235 0000
- UK: 0808 234 9168
- US: 800 325 6000
- France: 08 00 90 01 91

Money transfer services are also available to American Express cardholders and at selected Thomas Cook offices.

US State Department (US Citizens Only)

In serious emergencies only, the US State Department will help your family or friends forward money within hours to the nearest consular office, which will then disburse it according to instructions for a $30 fee. If you wish to use this service, you must contact the Overseas Citizens Services division of the US State Department (+1 202 501 444 or, from the US, 888 407 4747)

WITHDRAWING MONEY WHILE ABROAD

ATMs are readily available throughout Europe, excluding some rural areas, so you should also check ahead of time if you will be able to withdraw money in a given country. To use a debit or credit card to withdraw money from a cash machine (ATM) in Europe, you must have a four-digit Personal Identification Number (PIN). If your PIN is longer than four digits, ask your bank whether you can just use the first four digits or whether you'll need a new one. If your PIN includes a 0, you may need to make a new PIN, as some ATM machines in Europe do not have that key.

Travelers with alphabetical rather than numerical PINs may also be thrown off by the absence of letters on European cash machines. Here are the corresponding numbers to use:
- QZ = 1
- ABC = 2
- DEF = 3
- GHI = 4
- JKL = 5
- MNO = 6
- PRS = 7
- TUV = 8
- WXY = 9

It is also important to note that if you mistakenly punch the wrong code into the machine multiple (often three) times, it can swallow up your card for good.

Credit cards do not usually come with PINs, so if you intend to use ATMs in Europe with a credit card to get cash advances, call your credit card company before leaving to request one.

DEBIT AND CREDIT CARD FRAUD

If you check your account and notice that money has been stolen or is missing, you should call your bank immediately to remedy the situation and file a claim for the missing money. Many credit card companies have similar help lines and some online applications will allow you to automatically freeze your account. For this reason, we recommend that you always have some form of hard cash on you at all times.

TIPPING

Unlike in the United States, Europe does not have some unwritten universal tipping code of conduct. No one in the world tips like Americans, so tipping might just be a giveaway that you are a tourist. Although you are not required to tip, you can still leave one; even just 10% will seem quite generous.

TAXES

Members of the EU have a value-added tax (VAT) of varying percentages. It is most often between 19-21%. Non-EU citizens have the opportunity to be refunded this tax if you are taking these goods home. When shopping, make sure to ask for a VAT refund form that you can present with the goods and receipts at customs upon departure. Note: you must have the goods with you in order to be refunded.

GETTING AROUND

BY PLANE
Commercial Airlines

For small-scale travel on the continent, *Let's Go* suggests budget airlines for budget travelers, but more traditional carriers have begun to offer competitive deals. We recommend searching on www.cheapflights.com for the most affordable flights to Europe. You should look to book flights months in advance.

Budget Airlines

No-frills airlines make hopscotching around Europe by air remarkably affordable, as long as you avoid their rip-off fees. The following airlines will be useful for traveling across the pond and hopping from country to country:
- EasyJet: www.easyjet.com
- Eurowings: www.eurowings.com
- Iceland Air: www.icelandair.com
- Norwegian: www.norwegian.com
- Ryanair: www.ryanair.com
- Pegasus: www.flypgs.com
- Transavia: www.transavia.com
- Wizz Air: www.wizzair.com

BY TRAIN

European trains are generally comfortable, convenient, and reasonably swift. You should always make sure you are in the correct car, **as sometimes trains split midway through route to dock at different destinations.** Towns in parentheses on European train schedules require a train switch at the town listed immediately before the parentheses.

You can either buy a **railpass,** which, for a high price, allows you unlimited, flexible travel within a particular region for a given period of time, or buy individual **point-to-point** tickets as you go. Almost all countries give students or youths (under 26, usually) direct discounts on regular domestic rail tickets and many also sell a student or youth card that provides 20-50% off all fares for up to a year. Tickets can be bought at stations, but most Western European countries offer big discounts to travelers booking online in advance.

Check out the following sites to get discounts on train tickets and book trips in advance:

- www.raileurope.com
- www.railsaver.com
- www.rome2rio.com

BY BUS

Although train travel is much more comfortable, it may be cheaper to travel via bus from city to city. There are numerous operators across the continent, but Eurolines is the largest company running international coach services (www.eurolines.com). Inquire about 15- or 30-day passes when you book. For a higher price tag, Busabout offers numerous hop-on-hop-off bus circuits covering 29 of Europe's best bus hubs (www.busabout.com).

With that in mind, it is highly advised that you avoid travel at night via bus at all costs. It is much safer to book an early morning trip than it is to leave in the dead of the night, as drivers can be exhausted and many roads are narrow and unsafe to navigate in the dark. *Let's Go* has a policy with our Researcher-Writers in which we do not allow them to travel via bus at night.

PLACES TO STAY

For the budget traveler, accommodations options are limited, as expensive hotels are out of price range. That means hostels will be your best friend. All of the hostels in *Let's Go Europe 2019* have been visited by a Researcher-Writer and are therefore verified by this guide.

You should, at least for the first few nights of your stay, book a hostel before departing, that way you do not land without a place to stay. We recommend using HostelWorld (www.hostelworld.com), Homestay (www.homestay.com), or Booking.com (www.booking.com) to make reservations.

There are a few red flags to look out for before deciding to stay at a hostel, even if you have already made a reservation online. We advise looking at the area or neighborhood surrounding the hostel to see if it feels and looks safe. If it does not, we recommend finding another hostel in a more suitable area. Many a time there are hostels with little lighting in front of the establishment, which is a signal that it is not completely safe. Many hostels have 24hr security and lockout times, which can be reassuring. In addition, you should avoid hostels where you see pests, bedbugs, or signs of rampant uncleanliness. If you feel uncomfortable talking to staff members or if staff members make sexual advances, this is also a concern and you should find another place to spend the night.

SAFETY AND HEALTH

In any crisis, the most important thing to do is **keep calm.** In every chapter, we have included the address of the nearest US embassy or consulate so that you can seek help in an emergency; your country's embassy is your best resource in precarious situations. The following government offices can also provide travel information and advisories.

- Australia: Department of Foreign Affairs and Trade (+61 2 6261 3305; www.smartraveller.gov.au)
- Canada: Global Affairs of Canada (+1 800 267 8376; www.international.gc.ca)
- New Zealand: Ministry of Foreign Affairs and Trade (+64 4 439 8000; www.safetravel.govt.nz)
- UK: Foreign and Commonwealth Office (+44 20 7008 1500; www.fco.gov.uk)
- US: Department of State (+1 888 407 4747 from the US, +1 202 501 4444 from abroad; www.travel.state.gov)

PRE-DEPARTURE HEALTH

Matching a prescription to a foreign drug equivalent is not always safe, easy, or even possible. Remember to take **prescription drugs** with you and carry up-to-date prescriptions or a statement from your doctor stating the medication's trade names, manufacturers, chemical names, and dosages. Be sure to keep all your medication in your carry-on luggage.

Immunizations and Precautions

Travelers over two years of age should make sure that the following vaccinations are up to date:
- MMR (for measles, mumps, and rubella)
- DTaP or Td (for diphtheria, tetanus, and pertussis)
- IPV (for polio)
- Hib (for Hemophilus influenzae B)
- HepB (for Hepatitis B)

For recommendations on other immunizations and prophylaxis, check with a doctor and consult the **Centers for Disease Control and Prevention (CDC)** in the US (800 232 4636; www.cdc.gov/travel) or the equivalent in your home country.

KEEPING IN TOUCH

BY EMAIL AND INTERNET

Wireless hot spots (Wi-Fi) make internet access possible in public and remote places. Unfortunately, they can also pose security risks. Hot spots are public, open networks that use unencrypted, unsecured connections. They are susceptible to hacks and "packet sniffing"—the theft of passwords and other private information. To prevent problems, disable "ad hoc" mode, turn off file sharing and network discover, encrypt your email, turn on your firewall, beware of phony networks, and watch for over-the-shoulder creeps. **Data roaming** lets you use mobile data abroad, but it can be pricey. If you refuse to "later 'gram" and hyperventilate at the idea of losing access to Google, first consider that you are many hours ahead of the United States and can post when you return to your hostel and remember that Google Maps is available offline. If that doesn't placate you, though, you should get an international travel plan with your carrier or consider getting a local phone.

BY TELEPHONE

If you have internet access, your best (i.e. cheapest, most convenient, and most tech-savvy) means of calling home are probably Skype, FaceTime, or whatever calling app you prefer. **Prepaid phone cards** are common and a relatively inexpensive means of calling abroad. Each one comes with a Personal Identification Number (PIN) and a toll-free access number. Call the access number and follow the subsequent directions for dialing your PIN. To purchase prepaid phone cards, check online for the best rates (www.callingcard.com).

Another option is a **calling card,** linked to a major national telecommunications service in your home country. Calls are billed collect or to your account. Cards generally come with instructions for dialing both domestically and internationally. Placing a collect call through an international operator can be expensive but may be necessary in case of an emergency. You can frequently call collect without even possessing a company's calling card just by calling its access number and following the instructions.

How to Make a Call
1. Dial the international dialing prefix,
   - Australia: 0011
   - Canada or the US: 011
   - Ireland, New Zealand, and most of Europe: 00
2. Then the country code of the country you want to call,
   - Australia: 61
   - Austria: 43
   - Belgium: 32
   - Canada: 1
   - Croatia: 385
   - Czech Republic: 420
   - Denmark: 45
   - France: 33
   - Germany: 49
   - Greece: 30
   - Hungary: 36
   - Ireland: 353
   - Italy: 39
   - The Netherlands: 31
   - Norway: 47
   - New Zealand: 64
   - Poland: 48
   - Portugal: 351
   - Spain: 34
   - Sweden: 46
   - Switzerland: 41
   - UK: 44
   - US: 1
3. Followed by the city/area code,
4. And finally the local number.

Cellular Phones
The international standard for cellular phones is the **Global System for Mobile Communication (GSM).** To make and receive calls in Europe, you will need a GSM-compatible phone and a **SIM (Subscriber Identity Module) card,** a country-specific, thumbnail-sized chip that gives you a local phone number and plugs you into the local network. Most SIM cards will work in any country, but the charges for this can vary wildly, so check with your carrier and decide whether it might be cheaper to get a new SIM at your destination. Many European SIM cards are prepaid, and incoming calls are frequently free. You can buy additional cards or vouchers (usually available at convenience stores) to "top up" your phone. For more information on GSM phones, check out www.telestial.com. Companies like Cellular Abroad (www.cellularabroad.com) and **OneSimCard** (www.onesimcard.com) rent cell phones and SIM cards that work in a variety of destinations around the world.

BY SNAIL MAIL

Sending Mail Home

Airmail is the best way to send mail home from Europe. Write "airmail," "par avion," or the equivalent in the local language on the front. For simple letters or postcards, airmail tends to be surprisingly cheap, but the price will go up sharply for weighty packages. Surface mail is by far the cheapest, slowest, and most antiquated way to send mail. It takes one or two months to cross the Atlantic, which may be ideal for heavy items you won't need for a while, like souvenirs you've acquired along the way and the dresser you bought from that antique store that deep down, you know you don't need.

Receiving Mail in Europe

There are several ways to arrange pickup of letters sent to you while you are abroad, even if you do not have an address of your own. Mail can be sent via **Post Restante** (General Delivery). Address Poste Restante letters like so:

First and Last Name
Poste Restante
City, Country

The mail will go to a special desk in the city's central post office, unless you specify a local post office by a street address or postal code. It's best to use the largest post office, since mail may be sent there regardless. Bring your passport (or other photo ID) for pickup; there may be a small fee. If the clerk insists there is nothing for you, ask them to check under your first name as well. *Let's Go* lists post offices in the **Essentials** section for each city we cover. It's usually safer and quicker, though more expensive, to send mail express or registered. If you don't want to deal with Poste Restante, consider asking your hostel or accommodation if you can have things mailed to you there. Of course, if you have your own mailing address or a reliable friend, that is the easiest method.

CLIMATE

Europe may be the smallest continent in the world, but it has a surprisingly diverse climate. Some of its countries border the seas while others are landlocked. Some have mountains and glaciers, others have valleys and sandy ruins. Here's how it works: Southern Europe is known for warm weather surrounding the Mediterranean Sea. This area has mild, wet winters and hot, dry summers. Northern and Eastern areas are marked by temperate forests, where cold Arctic air contrasts with hot, warm summers and rain whenever the universe feels like mocking you. In between sits the exception: the mile-high Alps, where things are generally colder and wetter.

MEASUREMENTS

Like the rest of the rational world, Europe uses the metric system. The basic unit of length is the meter (m), which is divided into 100 centimeters (cm) or 10000 millimeters (mm). One thousand meters make up one kilometer (km). Fluids are measured in liters (L), each divided into 1000 (mL). A liter of pure water weighs one kilogram (kg), the unit of mass that is divided into 1000 grams (g). One metric ton is 1000kg. Gallons in the US and in Britain are not identical: one US gallon equals 0.83 Imperial gallons. Pub aficionados will note that an Imperial pint (20 oz.) is larger than its US counterpart (16 oz.)—we'll drink to that!

AUSTRIA

Arguably the world capital of classical music, Austria is home to many of history's greatest musical minds. Mozart is, of course, the country's favorite son, and his homes throughout Salzburg and Austria are remarkable tourist destinations—but the musical landmarks don't stop there. The Vienna State Opera is world famous, the Haus der Musik demonstrates the creation of music down to the scientific mechanisms of sound reverberation, and Salzburg's ball season offers dancing until the early morning in the birthplace of the waltz.

This music scene comes into the modern age with a visit to the country, where melodies old and new seem to hang in the air like electricity. You may find public outdoor symphony concerts in Vienna that draw attendees of all ages to stand, sway, chat with neighbors, and pop open bottles of wine. Classical music has never felt more enveloping yet casual. In Salzburg, side effects of *The Sound of Music* setting may include running, skipping, and spinning with arms outstretched. Here, the city does indeed seem to be alive with the sound of music, and visitors may find the voice of Queen Julie Andrews (this title is legitimate, just ask the people of Genovia) rattling around their heads, seemingly without end.

Meanwhile, Austria is a sight to behold, a stunning vision of mountains and man-made edifices wishing they could be mountains, too. Cities boast architectural works that reach for the skies, from the towering Gothic spires of the Rathaus and St. Stephen's Cathedral in Vienna to the clunky hilltop fortress of Salzburg that cradles the clouds in its own right. In Hallstatt, hillside churches and sharp, elongated steeples sit alongside a glistening lake, nestled between mountains. Home to its own corner of the Alps, the road through Austria winds among jagged peaks and sparkling bodies of water. Here, you'll find the air fresh, the language German, and the living easy.

SALZBURG

Coverage by **Antonia Washington**

The name Salzburg translates to "mountain of salt," and it was this very resource—known colloquially as "white gold"—that made this city great (and the archbishops that reigned incredibly rich). With the spoils from mining, the members of the ruling class built opulent state rooms and concert halls. The city took shape within just a few decades, and is now considered one of the most exemplary showcases of Baroque architecture in the world. Salzburg's city center is arguably the best preserved in Central Europe with tall domes peeking over the rooftops of Old Town and hillside fortresses looming overhead. Additionally, Salzburg is notable for its exquisite cultural composition. Once the social and governmental seat of its region, Salzburg was an independent state for nearly 300 years, after breaking from Bavaria and before becoming part of Austria in the early 1800s. It is also the birthplace of Wolfgang Amadeus Mozart (and the von Trapp family—can't forget about them), whose work is emblematic of the region's musical legacy.

ORIENTATION

Salzburg is a relatively small city built up on either side of the **Salzach River,** a right tributary of the **Inn River** and your number-one tool for orienting yourself. The city center spans both sides of the river. To the east you will find the **Mirabell Palace and Gardens**, the main train station, and Mozart's residence. Areas to note include **Linzer Gasse,** a major pedestrian street, and **Mirabellplatz,** a major square just in front of Mirabell palace and a frequent rendezvous site for tour groups and open-air markets. To the west lies Salzburg's **Old Town.** Here, pedestrian streets bustle with people from all walks of life, and most of the city sights, including Mozart's birthplace and the **Salzburg Cathedral** in the DomQuartier, stand in all of their former glory. Areas to note on this side of the river include **Judengasse,** Linzer Gasse's western counterpart, **Residenzplatz,** a main square in the middle of the **Residenz Palace,** the Salzburg Cathedral and the **Salzburg Museum.**

ESSENTIALS

GETTING THERE

The airport, named for Wolfgang Amadeus Mozart, can be reached on flights from most major cities in Europe and many major cities around the world, though the latter requires a connecting flight. If you are coming from elsewhere in Europe, travel via train is often the most convenient, as the Salzburg Hauptbahnhof train station is situated just on the northeast corner of the city center, easily within a bus ride or walking distance of many sights and accommodations.

GETTING AROUND

Salzburg does not have an underground metro, but buses go just about anywhere you may wish to go, and 1hr tickets cost just over €2. Once in the city center, Salzburg is very walkable, and, in fact, you will often be forced to walk, as much of Old Town consists of pedestrian streets. Bikes are also a popular method of transportation. Rental stores can be found throughout the city.

PRACTICAL INFORMATION

Tourist Offices: Located in Old Town in Mozartplatz, a smaller square right off of Residenzplatz (Mozartplatz 5; 66288 98 70; www.salzburg.info/en; open daily 9am-6pm).

Banks/ATMs/Currency Exchange: Most establishments in Salzburg only accept cash, but banks and ATMs are widely available to withdraw money.

Post Offices: There are many post offices throughout the city, one central location is listed (Residenzplatz 9; 0800 010 100; open M-F 8am-6pm).

Internet: Internet access is fairly standard at most accommodations in Salzburg, but worth checking ahead on.

BGLTQ+ Resources: The brochure "Austria Gay Guide" includes information about gay resources and establishments in cities including Salzburg. Find more information online at www.gayguide.me.

EMERGENCY INFORMATION

Emergency Number: 112

Police: Police stations are located throughout the city. Listed below is the information for the station located in Salzburg's town hall (Rudolfskai 2; 059 133 55 88100).

US Embassy: Austria's US Embassy is located in Vienna (Boltzmanngasse 16; (+43-1) 31339-0; open M-F 8am-4:30pm). In case of emergencies, the US consulate in Munich, Germany may be easier to access (Königinstraße 5; 8928880).

Hospitals: Unfallkrankenhaus (Doktor-Franz-Rehrl-Platz 5; 059 3934 4000; open daily 24hr)

Pharmacies: Pharmacies in Salzburg are widespread. Pharmacies are called *apotheke,* and are marked with a red symbol that looks like a cursive "L" or the number four. Engel-Apotheke (0662 87 32 21) is the most central pharmacy.

ACCOMMODATIONS

NATURFREUNDEHAUS STADTALM ($)

Mönchsberg 19c; 0662 84 17 29; www.stadtalm.at; reception open daily Sep-Apr 10am-6pm, May-Aug 10am-11pmt

You'll find this hostel on the second floor of a restaurant, housed inside a castle, and sitting on top of a mountain. Amid a combination of stone and wooden décor, you'll feel like fairytale royalty, though in real life you'll probably be a lot dirtier and sweatier, especially because getting up to the hostel on foot means hiking up the hill. Once you make it to the top, however, the recently renovated rooms and bathrooms will welcome you warmly. Another perk: the price of the room includes breakfast.

i Dorms from €24.50; reservation required; no wheelchair accessibility; free breakfast

YOHO INTERNATIONAL YOUTH HOSTEL ($)

Paracelsusstrasse 9; 066 2879649; www.yoho.at; reception open 24hr

Yoho International Youth Hostel is one of the youngest, most centrally located, and cheapest options in Salzburg. The rooms are clean, simple, and spacious, and communal areas like a bar and a lounge with daily *Sound of Music* screenings make Yoho a fun place to hang out with your new hostel friends. Plus, as a family-run establishment, staying here can mean sticking it to the man. Our only complaint is the name, which reminds us of Yoo-hoo chocolate milk (which we are missing dearly while abroad).

i Dorms from €20; reservation required; max stay 1 week; Wi-Fi; limited wheelchair accessibility; towels €0.50; laundry €2.50 per wash/dry; breakfast buffet €4, dinner from €3.50

SIGHTS
CULTURE

🏛 SALZBURG CATHEDRAL

Domplatz 1a; 662 80477950; www.salzburger-dom.at; open May-Sept M-Sa 8am-7pm (subject to change for worship)

The Salzburg Cathedral is a massive seventeenth-century Baroque edifice where **Mozart** once served as the church organist. If the exterior looks large, the interior feels even larger, with a nave that seems impossibly vaulted and a series of orange frescoes that heighten the intensity of the white walls. The decorative moulding inside is accented by unpainted groove-work, creating a stark aesthetic severity that may make you feel meek in comparison. It's exactly the kind of self-esteem booster you were looking for.

i Cathedral free, museum admission €12, students €10; limited wheelchair accessibility

NONNBERG ABBEY

Nonnberggasse 2; 662 841607; www.bene-diktinerinnen.de/index.php/adressen/2-un-categorised/26-nonnberg; open daily 7am-dusk (7pm in summer), visits not permitted during worship

The Nonnberg Abbey in Salzburg, established during the beginning of the eighth century, is one of the oldest continuously active nunneries in the world. Created in the late gothic style, the abbey is also known for its smaller works of art and murals. Its true claim to fame, however, may be its role as the abbey of Maria soon-to-be-von-Trapp, whose story was brought to the global stage in the smash 1965-hit, *The Sound of Music.* When the von Trapps married in 1927, they wed at the church of Nonnberg Abbey, though the movie filmed the scene elsewhere. Today, there are 21 nuns living at the abbey.

i Free; limited wheelchair accessibility

ST. PETER'S ABBEY

St. Peter Bezirk ½; 662 8445760; www.erzabtei.at; church open daily Apr-Oct 8am-9pm, Nov-Mar 8am-7pm; cemetery open daily Apr-Sept 6:30am-8pm, open daily Oct-Mar 6:30am-6pm; catacombs open daily May-Sept 10am-6pm, Oct-Apr 10am-5pm

One of the oldest continuously-employed monasteries in German-speaking Europe, St. Peter's Abbey was founded in the seventh century, more than a millennium before its female counterpart, the Nonnberg Abbey. Long connected to the likes of musical geniuses such as **Johann Michael Haydn** and the **Mozart** family, St. Peter's possesses some 100 autographs of the former and two dozen manuscripts of the latter. Haydn and the sister of W. A. Mozart are also buried in St. Peter's cemetery. The monastery is a large complex with much to see, but the cemetery—famous for its beautiful gravesites—is certainly a highlight.

i Catacombs €2, students €1.50; limited wheelchair accessibility

LANDMARKS

🏛 RESIDENZ PALACE

Residenzplatz 1; 662 80422109; www.dom-quartier.at; open M 10am-5pm, W 10am-8pm, Th-Su 10am-5pm

Touring through the Residenz Palace will give you an insight into the Salzburg line of prince-archbishops, who dominated oth poltical and religious life until the early nineteenth century. Because of the region's hugely successful salt mining industry, the prince-archbishops had no shortage of funds and were constantly renovating and redecorating the residence, creating lavish series of rooms that are now open for visitors to explore. Come see ceiling frescoes featuring images of **Alexander the Great** (even supreme rulers need role models), intricately woven tapestries with interpretations of the months of the year—a trending topic at the time—, and works of stucco that will make you say stucc-no you didn't!

i Admission €12, students €10; wheelchair accessible

HOHENSALZBURG FORTRESS

Mönchsberg 34; 662 84243011; www.festung-salzburg.at; open daily May-Sept 9am-7pm, Oct-Apr 9am-5pm

As the largest fully-preserved castle in Central Europe, this mountainside fortress is one of the most important sights in Salzburg. Today, it consists of expansive castle grounds, a restaurant, and walkways along the outer walls with incredible views of the city. The central building has been converted to a museum, where visitors can learn about the fortress' military history, the use of torture on prisoners, and more generally what life was like in the Middle Ages. There is a funicular that shuttles visitors from the base of **Festungsberg Hill** to the entrance of the fortress, but expect the line for this option to be downright insanity. We recommend choosing to hike the hill, so long as you're okay spending the rest of the day dripping with sweat.

i Basic tickets €12, standard tickets €15.20, discount from €2 (without lift); guided tours available; last entry 30min. before close; limited wheelchair accessibility

MIRABELL PALACE AND GARDENS

Mirabellplatz; open daily 8am-6pm

The Mirabell Palace and Gardens are, we think, the most significant sight in Salzburg east of the **Salzach River.** The palace itself does not factor significantly into this because, though the **Marble Hall** is open to the public, the rest of the building is used for office space. The gardens, on the other hand, are a sight to behold. Covered in roses, trees, fountains, and tourists, the gardens include the site upon which *The Sound of Music's* iconic "Do-Re-Mi" scene was filmed and provide the perfect opportunity to run down a tunnel of vines with your arms outstretched skipping and weaving about wildly.

i *Free; wheelchair accessible*

MUSEUMS

🏛 MOZART'S GEBURTSHAUS (MOZART'S BIRTHPLACE)

Getreidegasse 9; 662 844313; www.mozarteum.at; open daily 9am-5:30pm

The museum at Mozart's Birthplace is more personal than many accounts you'll find of the great musician's life. Of course, plenty of attention is paid to his career and compositional genius, and exhibits of his child prodigy will make you wonder what the hell you've been doing with your life. But, we truly appreciated the displays dedicated to the people who formed the man. See where Mozart spent the first 17 years of his life, learn about his family's involvement in his musical upbringing, and speculate on whether his ex-wife's marriage to his biographer was awkward because they were both in love with the guy. If you're into fetish history, you may also like the several locks of Mozart's hair the museum has managed to preserve.

i *Admission €11, students €9; no wheelchair accessibility*

SALZBURG MUSEUM

Mozartplatz 1; 662 620808700; www.salzburgmuseum.at; open Tu-Su 9am-5pm

Voted Europe's best museum in 2009—a title that we are still loving a decade ago—the Salzburg Museum houses exhibitions celebrating Salzburg itself. Many of the exhibitions focus on the artistic development of the city itself through a variety of media, including literature, science, craftsmanship, and archeology, among others. The museum is housed in the **Neue Residenz,** across from the **Residenz Palace,** which once belonged to the prince-archbishops of the city.

i *Admission €8.50, students €4; wheelchair accessible*

FOOD

🍴 CAFÉ LATINI ($$)

Judengasse 17; 662 842338; cafelatini.at; open summer M-Sa 9am-10pm, Su 10am-10pm; winter M-Sa 9am-7pm, Su 10am-6pm

Drawn by the promise of a Latini Panini (they don't call them this, but they should), we gravitated to this café after a tiring stint in the **DomQuartier museums.** The café name may have "Latin" in it, but Café Latini still offers Austrian foods at an affordable price, like goulash and a pastry (€5.70) or sausages with mustard and horseradish (€4.80). Often, the specials board includes an offering of paninis (€6.80), piled high with salami, bacon, tomato, and mozzarella.

i *Entrées from €4; vegetarian options available; limited wheelchair accessibility*

HALLSTATT

Describing Hallstatt as "a picturesque lakeside town" as we, admittedly, were about to do, would be a huge understatement. Compared to the reality of the scene, the adjective "lakeside" is about as lackluster as it gets. Standing on the shore of Hallstätter See, surrounded by stone cliffs and beautiful wooden structures that somehow, despite enduring centuries of harsh weather, are just as vibrant as they were when first constructed, is an experience that no image, no matter how enhanced, can truly capture. Hallstatt's nested configuration is accented by the towers of the Lutheran Protestant and Catholic Parish Churches, which draw the eye upward along the steep slopes of the Alps to the sky above. The town is indeed closely linked to the mountains themselves, as its history was shaped by the salt mining industry. Check out the history of salt mining at the Hallstatt Museum or take a cable car up to see the salt mines themselves.

Hallstatt sits on the southwestern bank of **Hallstätter See,** which itself is located in southwestern part of Austria. The small town hugs the lake pretty closely, with the city center and promenade—the most tourist-dense region— literally sitting on its shore. For this reason, the water is the simplest way to orient yourself in town. It is almost always visible between buildings, above buildings, or right in front of you. Hallstatt's main street, **Seestraße,** intersects with major thoroughfare **Hallstättersee Landesstraße** (and by major we mean you'll maybe pass a dozen other cars while following it) near **Marktplatz,** the town's main square.

GETTING THERE

Getting to Hallstatt is easiest by train. Trains stop at many towns surrounding the lake; Hallstatt's station is across the lake from the town itself. A ferry runs back and forth between the station and the center of town, and is both a convenient and fun way to start your visit (€2.50 one-way). Buses also loop from Hallstatt back and forth between Obertraun and Bad Goisern.

GETTING AROUND

Walk! Apart from bus and ferry services to get in and out of town, walking is your best option, and it's half the fun of visiting the town. Bicycles are a hassle to navigate in the city center, but can be great options for exploring the promenade, nearby beaches (the best are on the southernmost tip of Hallstätter See), or surrounding region.

Swing by...

LUTHERAN PROTESTANT CHURCH OF CHRIST IN HALLSTATT
Oberer Marktplatz 167; 613 48254; hours vary

A place of worship since 1863, the Lutheran Protestant Church is an interesting cultural sight, sure. Upon entering, you'll be greeted by an understated interior and a note written by the church's pastor encouraging visitors to take whatever words of encouragement they may need from bible verses on display and to have a pleasant visit to the region. But the real reason we love this sight (and the reason we think of it as a crucial landmark) is its tall steeple, which reaches far above all but the highest hillside buildings in town and defines the Hallstatt skyline.

i Free; limited wheelchair accessibility

MUSEUM OF HALLSTATT

Seestraße 56A; 6134 8280 15; www.museum-hallstatt.at; open daily 10am-6pm

The Museum of Hallstatt tells the history of the region, beginning in 7000 BCE and reaching the current day, through exhibits of archaeological artifacts uncovered at excavation sites in the region (some of the findings can also be seen at the **Natural History Museum** in Vienna). The most important part of the region's history is its relationship with salt mining, which the museum explains in detail. In our opinion, the highlights of the museum were the interactive videos that accompany each exhibition, some of which are even in 3D.

i *Admission €10, students €8; last entry 5pm; no wheelchair accessibility*

Grab a bite at...

CAFÉ ZUM MÜHLBACH

Oberer Marktplatz 53; 067 65348519; open Tu-Su 10am-7pm

Just slightly off **Seestraße,** Café zum Mühlbach offers a handful of quick-seller menu items—burgers, pizza, pastries, and beer—alongside fish, caught fresh from the lake daily. The patio seating spans the width of multiple buildings, creating its own de facto square on the small, quiet street. As for the pizza, the crust is fluffy and delicious, but for a cheese pizza, the amount of cheese is borderline paltry, not the gooey cheese-laden dairy swamp we prefer.

i *Entrées from €5.50, fresh fish from €18; cash only; vegetarian options available; limited wheelchair accessibility*

Don't miss...

HALLSTÄTTER SEE

Boat rental hours in season 6am-8pm

The best part about visiting Hallstatt is the Hallstätter See, so use it! Of all of the outdoor activities available, we recommend hitting the beach or renting a boat. Beaches can be found on the south rim of the lake, between Hallstatt and Obertraun, and are free to use. Signs for boat rentals are visible all over **Seestraße.** If you're traveling in a small group, we recommend the paddle boats, an age-old tourist classic, but small motor boats are also available.

i *Boat rentals from €10, depending on boat type and time*

CAFÉ TOMASELLI ($$)

Alter Markt 9; 662 8444880; www.
tomaselli.at; open M-Sa 7am-7pm, Su
8am-7pm; summer open M-Sa 7am-9pm,
Su 8am-9pm; summer kiosk open M-F
11am-6pm, Sa 10am-6pm

Established in 1705 as Café Staiger,
this charming establishment was once
frequented by members of the Mozart
family and is now one of Salzburg's
most famous cafés. It takes great pride
in the tradition of Austrian coffee
houses and serves a food menu of
Austrian breakfast classics: eggs, ham,
and toast with jam. Though many
of the options are admittedly out of
the backpacker price range, some
egg dishes won't break the bank, and
you can enjoy one on a second-floor
balcony overlooking a courtyard
next to the **Residenz Palace.** Café
Tomaselli is worth a visit for its
history alone, so if you're hungry but
not willing to splurge, grab a bite at
nearby Kiosk Tomaselli.

i Entrées from €5; vegetarian options
available; wheelchair accessible

FUCHSHOFER BAKERY ($$)

Linzergasse 13; 6769 352551; open
M-Sa 9am-7pm, Su 11am-6pm

A quaint café on a main pedestrian
street on the east side of the river,
Fuchshofer serves light breakfasts,
smoothies, and refreshments. Its true
draw, however, lies in the pile of fresh-
made pastries sitting in the storefront.
When we visited, the display case
was literally overflowing with sweet,
breaded treats. Walking past it takes
an inconceivable amount of will-
power. Better to just give in, we'd say,
and opt for a plate-sized sticky bun.
Though it won't last long in your
hands, it'll last long in your stomach,
giving you the kick in the ass (more
like sticking to your ass, are we right?)
needed to get up off your chair and on
your way.

i Breakfast from €4, cakes and pastries
from €2; vegetarian options available;
limited wheelchair accessibility

GASTHAUS WILDER MANN ($$)

Getreidegasse 20; 662 841787; www.
wildermann.co.at; open M-Sa 11am-9pm

Nestled in an alleyway that took us
way too long to find (seriously, we
walked right past it five times—turns
out it's the alley next to **Café Mozart**),
Gasthaus Wilder Mann is a local
favorite for regional cuisine. As such,
you should be aware that "Salzburg's
calf's lights" refers to calf lung and
heart, which we found out when we
tried to order it and the waiter was
like, "Um, I don't think you have
any idea what that is. You're getting
your advice from experts here," and
that salad refers to a small bowl of
sauerkraut topped with shredded
carrots and a few leaves of lettuce. A
menu section of light fare items also
provides options at a lower price.

i Entrées from €9; limited wheelchair
accessibility

NIGHTLIFE

AUGUSTINE BREWERY AND BEER HALL

Lindhofstraße 7; 662 431246; www.
augustinerbier.at; open M-F 3pm-11pm,
Sa-Su 2:30pm-11pm

If you are a human visiting Salzburg,
we recommend a trip to the
Augustinian Brewery. The beer hall
includes a range of food vendors
covering all five food groups: ham,
sausage, salami, pretzels, and strudel.
Beer is sold only by the liter or half
liter. Where the beer is always flowing,
there is little time to fret about the
timid naïveté of novice travelers,
so when you get to the taproom
entrance, fall in line and do what
the person in front of you is doing.
Soon you'll have a cold beer thrust
#unfabulously into your hands by a
grumpy bar-keep in a rush to fill the
next pint. Take your bounty to one
of the cafeteria halls or hang out in
the massive beer garden, packed with
people drinking their weight in the
liquid gold.

i No cover, half-liter €3.10, liter €6.20

CITY BEATS

Griesgasse 23; 0664 149 10 00; www.citybeats.at; open Th-Sa 9pm-5am

One of Salzburg's only real nightclubs, City Beats doesn't get busy until around 1am, making it the perfect last stop for a night full of cocktails and dance battles. Depending on the night, you may be greeted at the door by glittering shirtless gladiators or women on stilts—a ploy, we're convinced, to distract you from the three bouncers lumbering at the door. A big part of getting into City Beats is making sure you look the part. If you arrive dressed head to toe in workout clothes, regardless of the fact that you made the conscious decision to wear all black in hopes that your travel-wear could pass for club-wear, you will not make the cut.

i *Cover up to €10, drink prices vary; cash only; upscale club attire recommended*

MENTOR'S BAR KULTURE

Gstättengasse 3; 664 9133810; open M-W 4pm-1am, Th-Sa 4pm-2am

"Trendy" is the word that first comes to mind when describing Mentor's Bar. There's so much hip shoved into such a small space that it's easy to feel suffocated by it, but it'll also make you feel way cooler than you normally are. Clad in skinny jeans, suspenders, facial hair, and manicured button-downs that scream Los-Angeles hipster, the bartenders serve up a variety of drinks, including originals concocted on the spot. If you like gin, you'll get a kick out of the **Cranberry Cobbler** and **Torino Smash,** mixed with homemade cranberry syrup and mint, respectively. Mentor's serves some damn good cocktails, so go ahead, sip yours slowly and experience some Urban-Outfitters-circa-2013-euphoria.

i *No cover, cocktails from €9; BGLTQ+ friendly; limited wheelchair accessibility*

VIENNA

Coverage by **Antonia Washington**

With a look and feel like a cross between Paris and Manhattan, Vienna is a dream in the heart of Central Europe. One of the most open and fun-loving cities in the area, the "City of Dreams" is quite possibly the music capital of the world, boasting a proud history of operatic and orchestral music. Its claim to fame stems from its ties to great composers, from Mozart to Beethoven to the guy who was super jealous of Mozart (what was his name again? Oh yeah, Salieri). Take some time to soak up the city's spirit—sit endlessly in cafés sipping cappuccinos and eating strudel, stroll along major shopping streets, or relax in one of Vienna's many parks. A haven of chic, fashion-forward sun-seekers (who are a bit less stuffy than their Parisian counterparts), Vienna is the place to take a risk. Break out those mustard-yellow trousers, wear beige from head to toe like a Kardashian, or try to bring back flare jeans. We still, however, caution against wearing a fedora, as we would with any other time or place in the world. (Possibly the only exception is if you are in Cuba, under very specific circumstances. In that case, we think you should be Cuban, wearing white linen pants, and your name should not be Pitbull because something about that guy just pisses us off. If you're playing someone Cuban for a movie, like Vin Diesel in *The Fate of the Furious,* that's probably fine. You didn't even wear a fedora in that movie, but you're eternally off the hook, Vin.) With that digression, enter Vienna, land of culture, land of fashion, land of modern European living. Think New York City, if it were sunnier and more pedestrian-friendly.

ORIENTATION

Vienna rests on the **Danube River** (known as *Donau* in German), but it is not particularly useful for navigation. Instead, we suggest orienting yourself in relation to the **Ring Boulevard** (the name of this street changes in its different segments, but "Ring" is always in the name, and it is easy to identify on a map because of its circular shape). This street encircles the inner city, running the approximate route of the former city walls. Within the ring is the historic city center, including the **Hofburg Imperial Palace** and **St. Stephen's Cathedral.** Rimming the ring to its southern and western edges are many important public buildings like **City Hall,** the **Vienna State Opera,** and **Maria-Theresien-Platz,** which ties the city center to the **Museumsquartier.** Within the city center, major streets include **Kärntnerstraße** and **Herrengasse.** Another important neighborhood in the city is **Neubaugasse,** situated southwest of the city center in the seventh district. The neighborhood centers around **Neubaugasse** and **Mariahilfer Straße,** especially to the northeast of their intersection.

ESSENTIALS

GETTING THERE

Vienna is accessible by plane or train from just about anywhere. Trains come right into the city at Wien Mitte (city center), Wien Westbahnhof, or Vienna Central Station. Planes fly into the Vienna International Airport ("Flughafen Wien"). Be aware that the airport is not actually that close to the city. From the airport, the fastest public transport to the city is the C.A.T. train to Wien Mitte (€12). The S7 train (€4) also runs from the airport to Wien Mitte, although it makes several stops. Wien Mitte is a metro transfer station to metro lines U3 and U4. Taxis are expensive, but may cost less than the C.A.T. if you are traveling in a group.

GETTING AROUND

Public transport in Vienna is easily navigable. If you need to go a significant distance within the city, the metro is often the simplest way to travel. Metro stops are demarcated by a "U" and each line is associated with a number and a color. For example, the first metro line is called "U1" and is always marked in red. Single-ride tickets for the metro are €2.20. Within the historic city center, most destinations tend to be reachable on foot. Bicycles are also extremely popular in Vienna. City Bike in Vienna is free for the first hour, €1 for the second hour, €2 for the third hour, and €4 for every hour after.

PRACTICAL INFORMATION

Tourist Offices: There is one main tourist office in the city center called Tourist-Info Wien (Albertinaplatz S; www.wien.info/en; open daily 9am-7pm).

Banks/ATMs/Currency Exchange: Even in this large city, do not expect every business to accept cards. Cafés, especially, often only take cash. ATMs, however, are widely available; if at all possible, though, avoid using ATMs in major tourist areas such as St. Stephen's Cathedral due to increasing reports of ATM fraud.

Post Offices: There are post offices throughout the city. The post office website, with a branch locator, can be found at www.post.at. We have listed a central location (Fleischmarkt 19; open M-F 7am-10pm, Sa-Su 9am-10pm).

Internet: Many major attractions, plazas, and public transport stations have free Wi-Fi (look for networks like Freeware or Free Austrian Internet), though network connection and strength are often unpredictable. Free Wi-Fi access is also available at the tourist office.

BGLTQ+ Resources: The tourist information office of Vienna produces a pamphlet called the Gay & Lesbian Guide (and stocks others) with information on BGLTQ+-specific events, sights, bars, and more. Pick up a pamphlet in person or go to www. vienna.info/gay to learn more.

EMERGENCY INFORMATION

Emergency Number: 112

Police: There are police stations available all over Vienna, and most of them are marked on tourist maps. We have listed one central location (Brandstätte 4; open M-F 8am-6pm).

US Embassy: The US Embassy in Vienna is located on the north side of the city center (Boltzmanngasse 16; 1 31339 0; open M-F 8am-4:30pm).

Rape Crisis Center: If you have been a victim of sexual assault, you can reach out to Weisser Ring. They are not a sexual assault-specific crisis center, but they specialize in victim advocacy and their services are free (Nußdorfer Straße, 67, 1090 Wien; 01 712 14 05; open M-Th 9am-4pm, F 9am-3pm).

Hospitals: There are two main hospitals in Vienna. The first is Allgemeines Krankenhaus (AKH), which typically treats sickness and disease; if you contract Ebola, you should go here. The second is Unfallkrankenhaus (UKH), which typically treats traumatic injuries; if you're hit by a car, you should go here. In case of a life-threatening emergency, an ambulance will transport you to the nearest one; they are both well equipped to deal with a range of medical issues.

- AKH (Währinger Gürtel 18-20; 1 40400 0; open daily 24hr)
- UKH (Kundratstraße 37; 5 93 934 50 00; open daily 24hr)

Pharmacies: Pharmacies typically will say "Apotheke." They are marked with a red symbol that looks like a cursive "L" connected to a pillar, making a shape that looks sort of like a "4."

- Internationale Apotheke (01 512 28 25)
- Apotheke am Naschmarkt (01 586 51 59)

ACCOMMODATIONS

📛 HAPPY HOSTEL ($$)

Kurzgasse 2; 1 208 26 18; www.happyhostel.at; reception open 24hr

Happy Hostel offers a quiet, sleepy stay on the western edge of the **Naschmarkt district,** with small but homey rooms and facilities. All rooms are equipped with access to a kitchenette, but the hostel also provides breakfast. The hostel donates breakfast tips to their partner NGO Happy Africa, which works building schoolhouses and medical facilities in the Democratic Republic of the Congo. Unfortunately, the existence of dorms at the Happy Hostel is on the fritz because of noise considerations for the building's other tenants, but apartment prices are generally still affordable.

i Apartments with shared facilities single from €35, double from €24, triple from €22, quad from €21; other dorms from €20; reservation recommended; BGLTQ+ friendly; limited wheelchair accessibility; Wi-Fi; laundry €2 per wash or dry; breakfast served for tips

A&O WIEN HAUPTBAHNHOF ($$)

Sonnwendgasse 11; 1602 0617 3800; www.aohostels.com; reception open 24hr

A&O Wien Hauptbahnhof feels more like a hotel than a hostel, with wide tiled corridors and a lobby where kids run around or cling to their parents' legs waiting to check-in. Between the tile and the blue and orange color scheme, it somehow seems like a public pool doing its best to seem sterile. Large common areas provide opportunities to meet other solo travelers, but it may take a little extra effort. Our greatest critique is that A&O will nickel and dime you. Here, you'll pay for everything from using the foosball table (€5/hr) to renting sheets (€3.50).

i Dorms from €20; reservation recommended; max stay 14 nights; wheelchair accessible; Wi-Fi; €2.95 fee if paying with card; towels and linens not included

HOSTEL RUTHSTEINER ($$)

Robert Hamerlinggasse 24; 189 34202; www.hostelruthensteiner.com; reception open 24hr

Hostel Ruthensteiner sometimes feels like a commercial. Sitting in the common areas or sipping a beer in the garden, you will find groups of travelers planning their activities, meeting other backpackers for the first time, or breaking out a deck of Uno playing cards. Ambiguous rock music plays in the background and occasionally, someone pulls down a guitar or a ukulele from the wall and starts strumming out a familiar melody. With spacious, usually well-populated common areas and helpful staff, Ruthensteiner is a great place to meet other travelers.

i Dorms from €10, singles from €36; reservation recommended; BGLTQ+ friendly; no wheelchair accessibility; Wi-Fi; 3% charge if paying with card; laundry €2 per wash or dry; breakfast buffet €4.50

MENINGER HOSTEL CENTRAL STATION ($$)

Columbusgasse 16; 0720 88 14 53; www.meininger-hotels.com; reception open 24hr

Part hostel and part hotel, Meininger Central Station (Hauptbahnhof) has a clean, modern aesthetic. Meininger sometimes hosts large groups, and, in our few days there, we overlapped with a lacrosse team, a boys' choir, and a bunch of other people rubbing it in our face that they travel with friends. The group dynamic of travelers here can make it hard to meet people, so we recommend the hostel more to groups than to solo travelers. It is a convenient ride on the **U1** from the city center, which is ideal because the walk is not particularly exciting.

i Dorms from €20; reservation recommended; min stay 2 nights on peak weekends; wheelchair accessible; Wi-Fi; towels not included; breakfast €6.90; packed lunch €4.50

SEVEN HOSTEL ($)

Lindengasse 4A; 1070; 06908 012 813; www.bestlocation.at; reception open daily 9am-11:30am, 1:30pm-7pm, and 9-11pm

Seven Hostel Vienna will not be the cleanest hostel you have ever stayed in. But if all you need is a bed, it does the trick. The hostel isn't insurmountably dirty, but most of the time it smells just a little bit like sweat and urine, reminiscent of that one kid we all had in our high school PE class. The shower-stall floors are always wet and, on summer nights, when everyone gets in bed, it can become extremely humid. The perks of the hostel are few, but significant: the showers are hot and well pressured, the location is very central, and the beds are some of the cheapest in the city.

i Dorms from €10; reservation recommended; BGLTQ+ friendly; wheelchair accessible; Wi-Fi

SIGHTS
CULTURE

KARLS KIRCHE (ST. CHARLES CHURCH)

Karlsplatz; 1 505 62 94; www.karlskirche.at; open M-Sa 9am-6pm, Su noon-7pm

You'll find **St. Charles Church** looming over the plaza at **Karlsplatz,** where dogs splash nearby in the fountain and the sun beats down on the church's high, green dome. Inside, incense burns steadily, making the air is as thick as a Young Thug music video. Behind the haze, a huge altar shows off an opulent work of gold and stone meant to depict God's light. The dome of the church is 74m high and guests can visit the top, where there is a view of the city, though unfortunately it hides behind windows and fencing. The walk to the top will take you through a monstrous collection of scaffolding, giving you a rare personal look at the ceiling frescos, but if you drop your phone, you're so screwed.

i Admission €8, students €4; no wheelchair accessibility

MUSIK MÜLLER

Krugerstraße 4A; 01512 28 75; www.may-rische.at; open M-F 10am-1pm and 2pm-7pm

In the heart of Vienna lies a small storefront that reads "Musik Müller." Musik Müller is a sheet music store where you will find a selection ranging from orchestral classics to the score of *La La Land.* Our favorites are titles that claim to offer "The 14 Most Passionate Latin Songs," and "Love Songs from the Movies," with music from *Pretty Woman, Dirty Dancing,* and *Footloose,* among others. Maybe one day, they'll have sheet music written by you. Because in a city of music, the true magic is to play your own. The highest form of being is artistry; isn't that why Kanye claimed to be a god?

i Free; no wheelchair accessibility

NASCHMARKT

Naschmarkt; www.naschmarkt-vienna.com

Open air markets are often where cities show off their best selves. The Naschmarkt, at the confluence of Vienna's first, fifth, and sixth districts, pulls out all the stops. Picture this: aisles lined with colorful assortments of food from ripe red tomatoes to fresh baklava to Turkish

delight to dried fruit. Booths are stacked high with hundreds of bags of curry powder. Restaurants range from fish counters to bakeries. On Saturdays, a flea market sets up shop. Beware: excessive flirting with the young vendors along the walk may get you swindled into buying an absurd amount of candied nuts. Then again, who doesn't love candied nuts?
i *Stand prices vary; wheelchair accessible; flea market Sa 6:30am-6pm*

OPERA HOUSE

Opernring 2; 1514 442 250; www.wiener-sta-atsoper.at

Built in the mid-nineteenth century, the Vienna State Opera is a central feature in the "city of music." Though only the front portions of the opera house remain in their original form, having faced considerable destruction during WWII, it still feels like one of Europe's great opera houses (take that, Paris). Standing room tickets sell for a handful of euros, allowing you to explore the building and experience the opera for cheaper than a guided tour, though you may miss tidbits about the emperor drinking in his tea room instead of watching the show or figures on how much people spend for a table at the Opera Ball (let's just say it's a lot).
i *Tours €7.50, students €3.50, standing room at performances vary by show from €3; tours daily in English 2pm and 3pm (may vary by season); wheelchair accessible*

STEPHANSDOM (ST. STEPHEN'S CATHEDRAL)

Stephansplatz; 1 51552 3054; www.stephanskirche.at; open M-Sa 6am-10pm, Su 7am-10pm

This massive work of medieval Gothic style and home of the **Roman Catholic Archdiocese** is one of the most visited sights in all Vienna. At its highest point, the south tower of St. Stephen's Cathedral stands at 137m tall, making it one of the tallest built in the Middle Ages. The church's cavernous interior features an assortment of altars and ornamental characteristics of note, but our favorite part is the simple stained glass windows, which reflect glistening turquoise light off the massive stone-carved pilasters. Visiting the cathedral's towers is also essential, as they offer visitors expansive views of the city, though a view devoid of the cathedral

itself, a characteristic piece of the skyline.
i *Free; towers and catacombs from €4; wheelchair accessible; tour times and prices vary by sight at St. Stephen's, check the website for more information*

LANDMARKS

▨ BELVEDERE PALACE

Prinz Eugen-Straße 27; 1 795 57 134; www.belvedere.at; palace open daily 9am-6pm (21er Haus opens 11am), lower Belvedere and 21er Haus open W until 9pm, palace stables open daily 10am-noon

The Belvedere Palace, once home to nobility of the **Habsburg dynasty,** now houses the world's largest single collection of works by celebrated Viennese painter **Gustav Klimt.** Klimt's famous masterpiece, *The Kiss,* is the Belvedere's prized possession. Not only can you stand in front of the original, but you can visit the "selfie room" right next door where a poster board of the painting lets visitors pucker up and snap a picture alongside the lovebirds. Pick your favorite pose, but we like standing next to the couple and giving the classic "I knew I was going to be the third wheel" eye-roll. Make sure to experience the palace itself, which is said to be one of the most important Baroque structures in Austria, with gardens that you can peruse for free.
i *Upper Belvedere €15, students €12.50, Lower Belvedere €13, students €10, both Upper and Lower Belvedere €20, students €17; both Upper and Lower Belvedere with Winter Palace €26, students €22; include 21er Haus museum of contemporary art €23, students €19.50, audio guides from €3; gardens free; wheelchair accessible*

HOFBURG

Michaelerkuppel; www.hofburg-wien.at; open daily Sept-June 9am-5:30pm, July-Aug 9am-6pm

Hofburg Imperial Palace is an elegant monstrosity of Baroque architecture, gargantuan enough to count countless hours getting lost in the museum and surrounding palace grounds. The complex is so big that you may find yourself asking, "Why do rich people do this? They couldn't have just had a normal sized palace with one building and common sense hallways?" One of the most celebrated sights at the palace is the **Sisi Museum,** where you can view famous portraits of legend-inspiring **Empress Elisabeth.** The museum is by no means the only attraction on the grounds, though: check out the state hall of the **Austrian National Library,** the largest Baroque library in Europe.

i *Attraction prices vary; tours of Sisi Museum and Imperial Apartments €16.90, students €15.90; tours of Sisi Museum and Imperial Apartments daily 2pm; last entry 30min. before closing; wheelchair accessible*

PRATER

Prater 7/3; 1 729 20 00; www.praterwien. com; open daily Mar 15-Oct 31 noon-midnight

The Prater is an amusement park on the north end of the city where you will find Vienna's **Giant Ferris Wheel.** In its nineteenth century heyday, it was one of the largest ferris wheels in the world, and continues to offer incredible views of the city today. A staple of Vienna and a symbol of the city's fun-loving character, the ferris wheel was one of the first major restorations after WWII. Given its historic construction, the ride moves at a glacial pace, allowing for the perfect shot of Vienna, roller coasters, and children driven to the edge of madness by the ecstasy of sugar and adrenaline.

i *Park entry free, rides have individual prices, Giant Ferris Wheel €10; wheelchair accessible*

RATHAUS (VIENNA CITY HALL)

Friedrich-Schmidt-Platz 1; 1 525 50; www. wien.gv.at/english/cityhall

Vienna City Hall is a display of Gothic showmanship that made no attempt at conserving tax dollars. (Thank god our own city halls are sticking to the bare necessities.) The building's high gothic towers are reminiscent of the spires built on cathedrals, and we've heard of multiple people mistaking city hall for **St. Stephen's Cathedral** upon first glance. We don't think taking a tour of this landmark is necessary, but it's definitely worth checking out. The park out front is lined with benches squeezed tightly shoulder to shoulder if you need to rest in the shade.

i *Free; wheelchair accessible*

SCHÖNBRUNN PALACE

Schloß Schönbrunn; 181 11 30; www. schoenbrunn.at; open daily Apr-June 8am-5:30pm, July-Aug 8am-6:30pm, Sept-Oct 8am-5:30pm, Nov-Mar 8am-5pm; main gardens open daily 6:30am, closing times vary by season

Schönbrunn Palace, the summer residence of the **Habsburg monarchs,** is the largest and most ostentatious of the palaces in Vienna—enormous enough to house the industrious procreation of the Habsburg family (Empress Maria Theresa had 16 children, which we think sounds excruciatingly awful). Visitors can tour the palace rooms, visit the **Schönbrunn Zoo,** or spend time meandering the gardens. Built on more than 400 acres of land, the gardens are expansive, with extremely varied designs. Think, grass areas, rose gardens, an enormous fountain, and tunnels with mazes of vines. Bring a picnic or a book and spend some time enjoying what the Habsburgs once casually thought of as their backyard.

i *Palace tickets from €14.20, main gardens free, other garden attractions from €3.80, all-attraction pass €24; wheelchair accessible*

MUSEUMS

LEOPOLD MUSEUM

MuseumsQuartier, Museumsplatz 1; 1 52 57 00; www.leopoldmuseum.org; open daily M-W 10am-6pm, Th 10am-9pm, F-Su 10am-6pm

The Leopold Museum, one of the major institutions within Vienna's **MuseumsQuartier,** is known for its collection of works by painter **Egon Schiele,** who was inspired and advised by (guess who?) **Gustav Klimt.** The founder of the Leopold Museum, Rudolf Leopold, spent more than a half century compiling the collection of Schiele's work. (Can anyone say, um, stalker?) Though Schiele is particularly well-known for his self portraits, one of our favorite pieces is *House Wall on the River* (1915), which depicts a patchworked house. But in front of the cracked and graying concrete façade, a clothesline is strung with colorful shirts and fabrics. The oil paint is raised from the canvas especially on these fabrics, so that they seem to float in the foreground of the scene.
i Admission €13, students €9, audio guide from €4; wheelchair accessible

MUMOK

MuseumsQuartier, Museumsplatz 1; 1 52 50 00; www.mumok.at; open M 2pm-7pm, Tu-W 10am-7pm, Th 10am-9pm, F-Su 10am-7pm

You never can guess what'll be showing at mumok, the museum of modern arts, though it's sure to be something that piques your curiosity. With exhibitions curated by both the artists themselves and guest curators, the museum provides an uninhibited space for the curator's vision, allowing it to be completely transformed with the intention of display in mind. In effect, the museum itself becomes part of the exhibition. This is all very vague, we know, but mumok holds the true surprise in its **MuseumsQuartier** location.
i Admission €11, students €7.50; tours in English Sa 4pm; wheelchair accessible

WIEN MUSEUM KARLSPLATZ

Karlsplatz 8; 1040; 01 505 87 47; www.wienmuseum.at; open Tu-Su 10am-6pm

The Vienna Museum focuses on the history of the city itself. Though it displays many exhibitions from Viennese artists and features installments tracing the history of the city's nobility, our favorite pieces are those dedicated to the city's physical form. These include several large, wood-carved models of Vienna over time, which attempt to define the whole of Vienna, finding only that their image of the whole will never be objective or complete. It's all very "existential teen realizing there are no universal truths," but we're into it.
i Admission €10, students €7, free first Su of the month; free tours Su 11am; wheelchair accessible

OUTDOORS

THE CANAL

The Canal; open daily 24hr

In the summer months, the canal is the perfect place to see the city and the river come together. Wide walkways give lots of room for foot traffic, biking, and rollerblading. Friends and couples out for a stroll often sit on the edge of the canal wall and dangle their feet above the water. Check out the canal area next to **Schwedenplatz square.** Here, you'll find beverage and snack stands with sand areas and lounge chairs for reclining in the sun (somebody call Corona because it may be artificial, but we found our beach). Nearby, the **Badeschiff Wien** offers a pool above the river, a restaurant, and a sun deck. Be aware that more forested parts of the canal may be unsettling areas to walk alone at night.
i Pool day-pass at Badeschiff €5; stairs at most access points

FOOD

🔖 AMERLINGBEISL ($)

Stiftgasse 8; 1070; 15261660; www.
amerlingbeisl.at; open summer daily
9am-2am; winter M-Sa noon-midnight, Su
9am-midnight

The outdoor seating is major key when
it comes to Amerlingbeisl restaurant.
With garden and patio space, outdoor
seating is extensive but often full.
Tendrils of hanging vines dot the
garden, nearly tickling the heads of
guests walking through to find their
seats. Eat amid soft yellow light from
wall lamps that sit in vinyl records
molded into lampshades. The food is
mostly standard Austrian fare, and we
recommend the beef goulash with bread
dumplings, though this may be personal
bias because we are suckers for bread
dumplings.

i Entrées from €6; vegetarian options available; limited wheelchair accessibility

🔖 CAFÉ TIROLERHOF ($)

Führichgasse 8; 1010; 01 512 78 33; open
M-Sa 7am-10pm, Su 9:30am-8pm

A café house that feels a bit like a
Sherlock Holmes movie, Café Tirolerhof
features those old tea room style
booths that we don't know the name
of but find delightful and intriguing.
Take a seat at a velvety booth rounded
inward to hang out with friends, or at
one rounded outward to sit with your
back to your arch nemesis Moriarty
and inconspicuously whisper threats
to each other without ever seeing the
other's face. Serving Viennese breakfast
until 11am, it also has an all-day menu
consisting mostly of egg dishes.

i Entrées from €4; vegetarian options available; limited wheelchair accessibility

🔖 MOZART'S ($$)

Haidmannsgasse 8; 1150; 1892 08 78;
www.mozartsvienna.com; open daily M-Th
6pm-2am, F-Sa 6pm-6am, Su 6pm-2am

Mozart's is a dinner and late-night
restaurant serving delicious Austrian
cuisine. Grab a booth, hang your hat
on the coat rack, and take a seat on a
sheepskin rug covering the restaurant's
smooth wood benches. We recommend
the pan-fried dumplings and scrambled
eggs (€6.90), a savory scramble of
potato, egg, and onion that is comfort

food at its finest. For dessert, go for the
apple strudel (€4.20) or try the pulled
fluffy pancakes with rum-soaked raisins
and stewed plums (€6.80), which come
as easily-shareable, bite-sized poppers.
If that wasn't enough, put in an order
online and they'll deliver.

i Entrées from €6; vegetarian options available; no wheelchair accessibility

🔖 VOLLPENSION ($)

Schleifmühlgasse 16; 1585 04 64; www.
vollpension.wien; open Tu-Th 9am-10pm,
F-Sa 9am-midnight, Su 9am-8pm

In a brick basement, amid a soundtrack
of tunes from the golden oldies,
Vollpension has created an antique
living room café. You might recognize
it from *I Love Lucy* reruns, all the time
you spent obsessing over mid-century
aesthetics on Tumblr, or your actual
grandma's house. With offerings made
by a group of grandparents, watch an
80-year-old man bake cake after cake
right at the counter while you sip a
cappuccino or a wine spritzer. Live
a *Pink Lady* fantasy when you order
Gerti's Breakfast, a bun with butter
and homemade jam served with a
glass of prosecco, a tabloid magazine,
and pink nail polish (€4.80). Or
treat yourself to a tart (€3.90). Pastry
selections vary by chef, dictated by
which of their own family recipes they'd
like to share with the world.

*i Cake €3.20, tart €3.90, breakfast from
€4.80, other light dishes from €4; gluten,
vegan, and vegetarian vegetarian options
available; no wheelchair accessibility*

CENTIMETER II RESTAURANT ($$)

Stiftgasse 4; 1070; 1 470060 642; www.
centimeter.at; open M-Th 8:30am-midnight,
F-Sa 8:30am-1am, Su 8:30am-midnight

For those of you leaving the United
States out of devotion to the metric
system (probably the reason for most
of our expats, don't you think?), and
for the rest of you with a little metric
pride, this is the restaurant for you.
Centimeter Restaurant takes its name
seriously, with measuring tape decor,
"science experiment" beaker shots held
by a ruler stand, and even measurement
based foods! Try one of their specialty
bread pastries ordered by the centimeter
(€0.20-0.25/cm depending on warm
or cold). Treat yourself to two meters

of sausage (€9.20), or if you're with a group, get one Meter of Austria, a meter-long box with six different servings of traditional Austrian cuisine (€28).

i Entrées from €6; vegetarian options available; limited wheelchair accessibility .

FIGLMÜLLER ($$)

Wollzeile 5; 1512 61 77; www.figlmuller.at; open daily 11am-10:30pm

A popular restaurant in Vienna's central city, Figlmüller claims to be the home of the **schnitzel,** a massive, flat, breaded pork dish, which, from afar, looks something like a cross between fried chicken and an elephant ear dessert. The reality is a larger than life meat pancake. You can give it a go by yourself (€14.90), but it's large enough to split if you're not up for the commitment. This is usually paired with potato field salad (€4.70), but be warned that the dressing has a flavor we can only describe as a combination of mayonnaise and balsamic. If you plan to eat here for dinner you will need reservations, but you might be able to wiggle in for lunch.

i Entrées from €9; no wheelchair accessibility

WIENERWALD RESTAURANT ($$)

Annagasse 3; 1010 Wien; 15123766; www.wienerwald.at; open daily 11am-11pm

Our eyes see Wienerwald, but our brains see Wiener World. Think of the comedic potential; all the thinly veiled references to museums in Iceland. We were so ready to write, "Sorry, you'll have to go to Reykjavík for that." Sadly, the menu is surprisingly devoid of sausage; we only counted four schnitzel dishes. Mostly, there is a wide variety of breaded and fried meats. Pro-tip: skip the fried stuff (your cardiologist will thank you) and order the grilled chicken in garlic butter with a baked potato and sour cream (€11.90). With a portion size of one half chicken, once you get around the bones the meat is tender and the garlic butter gives it a soft, melt-in-your-mouth taste.

i Entrées from €8; vegetarian options available; limited wheelchair accessibility

NIGHTLIFE

1516 BREWING COMPANY

Schwarzenbergstraße 2; 1961 15 16; open M-Su 10am-2am

If you're in the market for a killer local beer, look no further than Vienna's own 1516 Brewing Company. Offering an array of unfiltered beers (mostly ales and lagers), it's hard to go wrong. Try one of their summer selections like an IPA spiced with earl grey tea, a lager and lemonade shandy, or an elderflower gose. We recommend coming with friends, ordering a round of different styles to pass around, and getting a big plate of bar snacks to split. Our favorite is the potato wedges with aioli and cheddar cheese melted on top, a slippery and cheesy delight that, similar to Totino's Pizza Rolls, will scald your mouth in all the right ways.

i No cover, drinks from €2.10, food from €4; BGLTQ+ friendly

DANZÓN

Johannesgasse 3; 676 5505 840; www.danzon.club; open daily Tu 6pm-2am, W-Th 6pm-4am, F-Sa 6pm-6am

If you need some Latin flavor in your Central European adventure (don't we all?), Danzón is a lounge for you. Here, you can expect to see some seriously spicy dancing, couples twirling around the dance floor to salsa, bachata, and rumba. Frankly, we need those couples to lower the barrier to entry for the rest of us. The club lends itself to stylized dancing more than downright clubbing, but the mood is light and receptive to veterans and beginners alike. Spanish-speakers may find a bartender dressed head to toe in white chatting them up about those family members who salsa way too aggressively.

i Cocktails from €8; cash preferred, card accepted

GRELLE FORELLE

Spittelauer Lände 12; www.grelleforelle.
com; www.grelleforelle.com; open daily F-Sa
11pm-6am

If you're looking for a place to dance
all night to live electronic music
performances, Grelle Forelle is the
place for you. A dark nightclub on the
canal, people come here to rage into the
morning hours. With rules explicitly
banning photo and video, the club hopes
to promote an atmosphere where people
are free to dance however feels right.
Though dancing here can take any form,
people really go for it, and we have seen
some stop to stretch between songs. As
one of our friends told us, "You just have
to close your eyes for like five minutes,
and then when you open them, you're
dancing way better."

i Cover €7, extra charge for live shows; card
minimum €30

RED CARPET BAR

Magdalenstraße 2; 676 7822966; www.red-
carpet.co.at; bar hours M-Th 9pm-4am, F-Sa
9pm-6am; club hours F-Sa 11pm-6am

Small bar on weekdays, dance club on
weekends, casually black-lit even when
the lights aren't fully down, Red Carpet
is a hangout catering mostly to gay and
lesbian patrons. Amid the neon lighting,
the DJ plays the hits of 2000s pop icons
like The Pussycat Dolls and Pink! (quick
pause for us all to wonder, where did Pink!
go?). A great place to bring a group of
friends and meet new people, you can also
come here to check up on community
news, as a TV in the corner cycles through
local BGLTQ+ news and events, a counter
in the back lounge offers pamphlets with
BGLTQ+ resources.

i No cover; cocktails from €5.50, beer from
€3.30; BGLTQ+ friendly

THE SIGN

Liechtensteinstraße 104-106; 66496 432 76;
www.thesignlounge.at; open daily 6pm-2am

If you're looking for fancy cocktails whose
cost might make you cringe momentarily,
The Sign offers a menu full of creative
combinations served in unexpected
presentations. Here, we sipped fruity
vodka drinks topped with fortune cookies,
and espresso and rum concoctions served
in ceramic, cigar-smoking chimp mugs.
If you're looking for something simple,
we recommend the **Special Pimm's Cup**
(€9.50), a gin and tonic with blackberry
and elderflower. Feeling extravagant? Get
the **Lei Lani Volcano** (€11), a pineapple
and Malibu combination served in a
bird-shaped watering can with a burning
cinnamon stick for incense.

i No cover, most cocktails from €9; BGLTQ+
friendly

TRAVEL SHACK VIENNA

Mariahilfergürtel 21; 0196 101 31; www.
travelshackvienna.com; open daily 4pm-4am

Travel Shack Vienna is a popular
destination for college students looking
to make mistakes on their spring break
trip to Europe. If you want to take your
top off and smoke out of every orifice of
your body, do that here. Go wild under
the disco ball or add your bra to the rack
hanging along the bar. Try their specialty
interactive drinks where the theme is self-
humiliation: the evidence is Snapchat and
the consequences are your friends never
letting you live it down. One of these is
called the "Cum Shot," which involves
liquor being poured into your mouth
from a dildo. Another is the "Tequila
Suicide," which involves snorting the
salt, tossing back the tequila, and
squirting lemon into your eye. Planning
to make it out with your dignity intact?
Good luck.

i No cover, specialty shots from €2; BGLTQ+
friendlyKehlsteinhaus (Eagle's Nest)

AUSTRIA ESSENTIALS

MONEY

Tipping: Tipping in Austria is common in interactions with most service workers. Generally, tip by simply rounding up to the next convenient number. Tipping about 5% is standard and a tip should not surpass 10%. It is common for a service charge to be included in the bill, so look on menus and bills to find out if the tip has already been included.

Taxes: Many goods in Austria are subject to a value added tax (VAT) of 20%, included in the purchase price of goods. The VAT is a standard rate, though it fluctuates based on the goods purchased, so you should ask the retailer for exact rates. Non-EU visitors taking these goods home unused can apply for a VAT refund for goods exceeding €75 at one retailer. To apply for this refund, ask the store for a VAT refund form and carry your passport with you as retailers may ask to see it. Present the refund form and be prepared to show the unused goods you are exporting at the customs office at your point of departure from the EU. Refunds usually must be claimed within 90 days of the original purchase.

SAFETY AND HEALTH

Local Laws and Police: Police in Austria are reliable if you need assistance, but always have your passport with you when interacting with police officers, as they may ask to see it. Under Austrian law, you must either have your passport with you, or be able to produce it within one hour.

Drugs, and Alcohol: The drinking age in Austria is 16 for beer and wine and 18 for distilled alcohols. Penalties for driving under the influence of alcohol tend to be stricter than in the United States. The legal blood alcohol limit for driving in Austria is 0.05%. Use or possession of illegal drugs in Austria can come with long prison sentences and harsh fines. Tobacco stores are the place for purchasing tobacco products in Austria and are marked with a sign depicting a cigarette. It is also common to purchase tobacco products in grocery stores and even occasionally restaurants. It is illegal to sell tobacco to persons under the age of 18.

Prescription Drugs: Austrian medical centers will not accept American medical insurance, so you will have to pay out of pocket for services and then seek a reimbursement from your insurer independently. Carry any prescription medications in their original packaging.

BELGIUM

Belgium tends to fall victim to misunderstanding: "Don't they all speak Dutch?" "Brussels is boring?" And, the dreaded "I thought (fill in the blank) was French." But this multifaceted nation is worth understanding. With its northern Flemish and southern Walloon influences, there is some cultural and political tension, but its people are primarily, and proudly, Belgian. The charmingly small cities and natural beauty of the Ardennes provide stunning scenery, while Brussels serves as home to the most important institutions of Europe. As the seat of the European Union and NATO, the nation's capital hosts tons of international professionals (who you can find looking to blow off steam after work). That said, its relaxed culture is so pronounced that the country was able to go 589 days in 2010 and 2011 without an elected government.

As far as Belgian specialties, it's not all chocolate, waffles, Belgian (not French) fries, and admittedly excellent beer. *Moules-frites, jenever, carbonade flamande,* and *waterzooi* provide more fodder for the imagination and the stomach. As far as art, the Dutch masters have nothing on the Flemish Primitives like Jan van Eyck and Bruegel, or surrealists like Magritte. Of course, we can't forget Tintin, the intrepid detective, and his dog Snowy, as well as Asterix and Obelix. And as far as cities, Belgium is home to some undiscovered gems— which are hipper, cheaper, and less touristy alternatives to the typical Eurotrip itinerary.

BRUSSELS

Coverage by **Emily Corrigan**

When you first arrive in Brussels, you may be confused to find that the streets have have names: one in Dutch and the other in French. Even the city itself has two different names—the Dutch *Brussel* and the French *Bruxelles*. This linguistic and cultural mélange speaks to the city's character as a true melting pot. Brusseleirs tend to be laid-back and welcoming, especially as Brussels is less of a tourist madhouse than many other European cities. Outside the city center, Brussels has an authentic feel, finding its roots in cafés and parks, where little old ladies sip from giant goblets of beer, couples make out, and joggers work off delicious, so-worth-the-calories fries. Even the parts that feel like tourist traps turn out to be satisfying: you're sure to see visitors and locals alike popping into chocolate shops or buying waffles from a cart. There is a vibrant energy here, with public murals and lively comic book stores constant reminders of the city's artistic passions. Brussels is full of wonderful restaurants, old breweries, and dynamic squares. You'll find yourself wondering how everyone seems to have so much time for just hanging out and drinking beer. Relax, you're in Brussels.

ORIENTATION

The Brussels city center is where you'll find the photo ops. **The Grand Place** dominates the tourist attractions while small streets and tall, narrow buildings give it a characteristic Belgian feel. The two **Sablon churches** (Grand and Petit) are the centerpieces of the historic **Salon** neighborhood just southeast of the center. Further southeast is **Ixelles,** bordered by the upscale **Avenue Louise,** which leads down to the forest of **Bois de la Cambre.** Attractive townhouses, European institutions, and the lovely **Parc du Cinquantenaire** define **Etterbeek** to the east. **Schaerbeek** to the north features wide avenues, lovely architecture, and a vibrant mix of international residents. The buses, trams, and metro lines make traversing the city efficient, but it's also easy to explore Brussels' various neighborhoods on foot.

ESSENTIALS

GETTING THERE

Brussels Airport lies northeast of the city center. The easiest way to get into the city is by bus, using the bus station a level below the arrivals. Bus tickets cost €4 at the station, but €6 if you buy them on the bus. Brussels also has a number of train stations throughout the city, making it easy to arrive fairly close to where you need to go.

GETTING AROUND

Bus, tram, and metro lines run across the city and are fairly easy to use. It's possible to use the same type of ticket for all three. Tickets cost €2.10 and are valid for one hour. The Villo! public bike service is free for the first half hour and has stations throughout the city. The basic rate for a day is €1.60.

PRACTICAL INFORMATION

Tourist Offices: Flanders and Brussels Information Office (Rue du Marché aux Herbes 61; 02 504 03 00; open M-F 8am-6pm, Sa-Su 10am-5pm)

Banks/ATMs/Currency Exchange: Bank of Baroda (Rue de la Loi 28; 02 285 00 40)

Post Offices: 5, Bd. Anspach 1; 02 201 23 45; open M-F 8:30am-6pm, Sa 10am-4pm

Internet: The city of Brussels offers free public Wi-Fi in many points around the city. It will prompt you to register with your name and email.

BGLTQ+ Resources: Rainbowhouse (Rue du Marché au Charbon 42; 02 503 59 90)

EMERGENCY INFORMATION

Emergency Number: 112
Police: Brussels Police Station (Rue du Marché au Charbon 30; 02 279 79 79)
US Embassy: There is a US Embassy in Brussels (Bd. du Régent 27; 02 811 40 00; open M-F 7:30am-5:30pm).
Rape Crisis Center: US State Department Rape and Incest National Network; 1-800-656-HOPE (4673)
Hospitals: Institut Jules Bordet (Bd. de Waterloo 121; 02 541 31 11)
Pharmacies: De Brouckere (02 218 05 75)

ACCOMMODATIONS

2GO4 HOSTEL CITY CENTER ($)

Bd. Emile Jacqmain 99; 022 19 30 19; www.2go4.be/qualityhostel; reception open 7:30am-1pm and 4pm-11pm

This hostel's lounge strongly resembles a vintage motorcycle shop owned by an eclectic, reclusive, horn-rimmed-glasses-wearing old man. Old go-karts hang from the walls alongside punching bags, a piano, and tiny chairs topped with potted plants. Confusing new treasures reside in every nook and cranny of the open space. The surrounding area is equally busy, perhaps even cluttered. The hostel is close to the shopping street **Rue Neuve** and the hustle and bustle of the **Grand Place.** Plus, if you burn through all your extra cash shopping, you can always cook at the hostel's fully stocked kitchen and grab coffee for free every morning. So GO4 it!

i Dorms from €21; reservation required; no wheelchair accessibility ; Wi-Fi; luggage storage; towels for rent

BRXXL 5 CITY CENTRE HOSTEL ($)

Rue de Woeringen 5; 02 5 02 37 10; www.brxxl5.com; reception open 24hr

A lively lounge area, complete with a pool table, sets the tone at this social hostel, located within walking distance of the city center and train station **Gare du Midi.** People congregate downstairs and in the outdoor courtyard to hang out, watch music videos, and use the Wi-Fi. It doesn't hurt that there are cute kitties living here, too. The service is top-notch, with free hot drinks, vending machines, and an attentive staff. The only drawback is the tiny beds, but we

doubt you'll be spending much time in bed anyway when there's fun to be had and kittens to be pet, amirite?

i Dorms from €23; reservation required; wheelchair accessible; Wi-Fi; linens included; towels for rent; luggage storage; lockers provided

HOSTEL BRUEGEL ($)

Rue du Saint-Esprit 2; 25 11 04 36; www.jeugdherbergen.be/en/youth-hostels/city-hostels/brussel-bruegel; reception open 7am-1:30pm and 2pm-1am

Walking out of Hostel Bruegel, you'll have to avoid running headfirst into the beautiful **Église Notre-Dame de la Chapelle,** located approximately six feet away. The church isn't all this hostel is close to though: it's within easy walking distance of many of Brussels' best sights and nightlife, too. If you're taking advantage of the latter, just make sure to put a deposit down for a late-night key, or else you'll get locked out when reception closes at 1am. Rooms with only a handful of beds and en suite bathrooms certainly trump the dozen-bed barracks of other hostels, and a free breakfast rounds out this comfortable and affordable lodging.

i Dorms from €23; reservation required; wheelchair accessible; Wi-Fi; luggage storage; free breakfast

SIGHTS
CULTURE

AVENUE LOUISE/BOIS DE LA CAMBRE

Open daily 24hr

With window shopping on the itinerary, Avenue Louise makes you wish you had a soul-sucking, six-figure job. On one end, near the **Louise tram stop,** is a ledge overlooking the entire city of Brussels (spot the **Atomium!**) and on the other end is **Bois de la Cambre,** a beautiful forest with a large pond. Walk along the road until you tire of not being able to buy every designer backpack that you see, and then take the #93 or #94 tram straight to Bois de la Cambre to reassure yourself that the simple pleasures of life are the most important.

i Establishment prices vary

ANTWERP

The people of Antwerp may be known for their big talk (especially in neighboring Ghent) but they have the city to back it up. From a castle on the river to a main square sprinkled with gold-plated guildhalls, Antwerp is certainly attractive. It boasts a train station widely considered the world's most beautiful, as well as the largest diamond district on this earth. Antwerp is closer in culture and language to the southern Netherlands than many of its fellow Belgian cities, yet a strong international community lends it a worldly vibe. Antwerp won't disappoint as a place to spend the day strolling (or biking) around, visiting its many museums, or just enjoying its relaxed Flemish lifestyle.

Arriving at the stunning **Antwerpen-Centraal train station** will find you on the eastern side of the city. The station is right near the zoo, Flemish painter **Peter Paul Ruben's house, the diamond district,** and the **Jewish quarter,** with a small **Chinatown** directly across from it. To the west, bordered by the scenic **Scheldt River,** you'll find the **Oude Stad,** or "old city" district, where the **Grote Markt** serves as the main square and the lovely churches define the skyline. Many streets here are reserved for pedestrians.

GETTING THERE

Antwerp has a small international airport. Antwerpen-Berchem train station is near the airport and provides national connections. Buses 51, 52, and 53 stop right in front of the airport and can take you to Antwerpen-Berchem in about 10min., where more bus lines are available. International trains and many national trains arrive at Antwerpen-Centraal, a beautiful train station on the eastern side of the city with easy connections to the bus and metro. Most buses also arrive at Antwerpen-Centraal.

GETTING AROUND

Bus and tram tickets can be purchased at newsstands, supermarkets, and machines located at many of the stops. An individual ticket costs €3, while a day pass costs €6. Antwerp's public bike rental service, Velo, has stations all around the city. Just look for the rows of red bikes. The first half hour is free, the second half hour is €0.50, the next is €1, and after that it's €5 per hour. A day pass costs €4.

Swing by...

GROTE MARKT
Old City Quarter; open daily 24hr

Without a doubt the most photogenic square (and there are many competitors for this title), the **Grote Markt,** located in the old medieval part of town, is a must-see. Featuring ornate guildhalls and an entrancing fountain, this gorgeous spot is close to the castle and the **Scheldt River,** the spire of the **Cathedral of Our Lady** towering over it. The land was originally donated to the city by **Duke Henry I of Brabant** way back in 1220, meaning you're hardly the first to have a beer in the surrounding cafés or scoff at the seven different restaurants with the "best mussels in the city." There, you'll the tourist office, the beautiful city hall, and the **Antwerp Jazz Club;** in the winter, you'll find a Christmas market.

i Free; wheelchair accessible

Check out...

ANTWERP ZOO

Koningin Astridplein 20-26; 03 224 89 10; www.zooantwerpen.be/en; open daily 10am-7pm

Even in their enclosures, the snakes of the Antwerp Zoo are masters of camouflage—it's certainly making us look over our shoulders more often in the forest. But these elusive creatures are far from the only ones to be seen. We're talking kangaroos. We're talking large cats. We're talking primates, zebras, giraffes, and a butterfly garden. This place has all the animals you know and love and plenty you never knew existed. Catch the sea lion shows, walk through the large aquarium, and marvel at koalas sleeping and monkeys grooming. The zoo is massive and the animals are allowed ample space to roam. It may be expensive, but it's a koala-ty zoo, we're not lion.

i *Admission €26, €24.50 if booked online, students €24; sea lion shows and feeding times can be found at the museum entrance; wheelchair accessible*

Grab a bite at...

BENI FALAFEL ($)

Lange Leemstraat 188; 03 218 82 11; www.benifalafel.be/en; open M-Th 11:30am-10pm, F 11:30am-2:30pm, Su noon-10pm

In the historic **Jewish Quarter,** this Israeli falafel restaurant boasts some of the most delicious and moist falafel in Belgium. See? We think it's even tasty enough to justify the use of the word moist! For a cheap and quick lunch, grab a thick piece of pita full of vegetarian and kosher delights, either for-here or to-go. Spicy sauces come alongside your meal, making it a flavorful, if not steam-out-the-ear inducing, lunch. Soup, sides, and desserts are also on the menu if you decide your falafel needs a friend.

i *Soup from €3, falafel dishes from €3; kosher and vegetarian options available; limited wheelchair accessibility*

Don't miss...

MUSEUM PLANTIN MORETUS

Vrijdagmarkt 22-23; 03 221 14 50; www.museumplantinmoretus.be/nl

Located in the historic former home of sixteenth-century printer **Christophe Plantin,** this gorgeous museum explores his famous printing business, the **Officina Plantiniana.** Aside from the beauty of the home itself, whose artwork and courtyard were frequented queens and princes, the museum holds Plantin's finest handiwork, libraries of books, and the printing room with the original printing presses (including the two oldest surviving presses in the world). Books are ubiquitous, from a manual of Arabic proverbs, to a Hebrew grammar book, to collections of delicate illustrations and colorful maps. Countless interesting objects await your discovery, like the old type cases holding over 90 fonts. And to think that from this rich, bibliophilic tradition emerged Comic Sans. Plantin would be rolling in his grave.

i *Admission €8, students €6; ground floor wheelchair accessible, no wheelchair accessibility on the top floor; keep your wristband to leave and return throughout the day*

PARC DE BRUXELLES AND THÉÂTRE ROYAL DU PARC

Rue de la Loi 3; 25 05 30 30; www.theatreduparc.be; open Tu-F noon-7pm

A few minutes in the Parc de Bruxelles will have you wondering why Belgium doesn't continually win all Olympic track and field events. (There are certainly enough joggers training here to warrant it.) But the park offers so much more than a prime running path—you can enjoy watching ducklings bob around an enormous fountain, recline in the shade under a canopy of vines, and daydream about the more attractive marble statues coming to life. The cultural experience, however, comes from enjoying a stage performance at the Théâtre Royal du Parc, a beautiful theater on the edge of the park.

i Show prices vary, park entry free; check online schedule for show times; wheelchair accessible

LANDMARKS

ÉGLISE NOTRE-DAME DU SABLON

Rue de la Régence 3; 320 25 11 57 41; www.upbxlcentre.be/eglises/notre-dame-du-sablon/; open M-F 9am-6:30pm, Sa-Su 9am-7pm

The church's history begins with a group of crossbowmen who obtained the land to build a chapel honoring the Virgin Mary. Of course, the statue commemorating her, currently inside the church, is *not* the original: that one got paraded around the edifice annually, which was a nice break from listening to organ music 24/7/364. Construction finally finished in the 1500s, more than century after they started the project. Now you can visit the fruits of their labors and see the stained glass windows decorated with the coats of arms of families who lost members in **World War II.**

i Free; no wheelchair accessibility; must cover shoulders and knees to enter; must observe silence in building

ROYAL PALACE

Rue Brederode 16, B; 25 51 20 20; www.monarchie.be/en/heritage/royal-palace-of-brussels; open July 21-Sept 1 Tu-Su 10:30am-3:45pm

Across from the **Parc de Bruxelles** and just around the corner from the **Royal Palace of Fine Arts,** this impressive palace is a necessary and convenient stop on your sightseeing tour of Brussels. It's the official home of the King and Queen of the Belgians. Even though visitors are only allowed inside from July 21st to the beginning of September, the palace is impressive enough from the outside to warrant a quick visit. Creatively trimmed shrubs line the courtyard and regal golden gates frame the front. Plus, you may be lucky enough to witness the changing of the solemn-faced guards or catch a glimpse of an important-looking person walking through a hallway. Riveting!

i Free

MUSEUMS

CENTRE BELGE DE LA BANDE DESSINÉE (BELGIAN COMIC STRIP CENTER)

Rue des Sables 20; 22 19 19 80; www.comicscenter.net/en/home; open daily 10am-6pm

Bande dessinée, or comic strips, hold an important place in Belgian culture. Humorous characters like **Tintin** and **Asterix** are household names, and we can see why. The medium casts a wide net, including everything from serious and painstakingly drawn dramas to wordless collections of short scenes. The Centre Belge de la Bande Dessinée (CBBD) is a tribute to the Belgian art form and proof of the seriousness of this national obsession. The museum showcases the entire drawing, script-writing, and production processes, culminating in countless displays of artists' funny and beautiful work. In addition to the museum, visitors can page through comic books in the library and bookstore. Any fan of the form cannot afford miss it.

i Admission €8, students €7; no wheelchair accessibility

🏛 MUSEUM OF MUSICAL INSTRUMENTS

Rue Montagne de la Cour 2; 25 45 01 30; www.mim.be; open Tu-F 9:30am-5pm, Sa-Su 10am-5pm

This might be painful to get through for the pun averse, but bEAR with us. We're not trying to harp on you, but the Musical Instrument Museum is a must-see. Pick up headphones at the ticket counter, and follow the audio guide through the four floors of musical exhibits. The earphones are no treble to use; numbers on the floor indicate what to press to hear songs from each instrument. Even though it may seem strange to stand around a room full of silent people looking at everything from pianos to Ukrainian *banduras* to wind-up music boxes, you'll be trumpeting this museum's praises by the time your visit is over. Plus, the €6 youth price will be music to your ears.

i Admission €8, students €6; wheelchair accessible

MAGRITTE MUSEUM

Rue de la Régence 3; 25 08 32 11; www.fine-arts-museum.be/en; open Tu-F 10am-5pm, Sa-Su 11am-6pm

René Magritte was either a brilliant artist who redefined what it means to paint a guy with the imagination of a six-year-old on psychedelics—we're not sure which. Either way, experiencing the world's largest collection of his works will leave you dazed and confused in the best way possible. In Magritte's world, a bird morphs into a leaf. Candles produce dark instead of light. And a painting of a carrot turning into a bottle can be titled "The Explanation" despite explaining absolutely nothing. Remember the *Mona Lisa?* Yeah, Magritte has one of those too, but instead of a half smiling woman, it's two red curtains suspended from thin air, a chunk of blue sky, and a strange white ball. This Belgian surrealist really got away with a lot.

i Admission €8, students €2; audio guide €4; wheelchair accessible

MUSEUM OF COCOA AND CHOCOLATE

Rue de la Tête d'Or 9; 25 14 20 48; www.choco-story-brussels.be; open daily 10am-5pm

A museum of chocolate isn't exactly a hard thing to sell. *There are free samples.* Yet even after you gorge yourself on them, it's worth sticking around. You'll learn about the ancient history of cocoa, like how Aztecs used cocoa beans as currency, regarding chocolate as the food of the gods. Posters with chocolate facts cover the walls, as well as decorated tins and special hot chocolate pourers. The museum traces chocolate's appearance in Europe, too, from its status as a symbol of wealth to its dissemination amongst the masses. Don't miss the machine where you can dip cookies into this liquid gold, or the chocolate-making demonstrations where you'll experience first-hand how this famous Belgian treat is crafted (with more free samples of course).

i Admission €5.50, students €4.50; last entry 4:30pm; no wheelchair accessibility

BRUGES

There's much to see in this small city, whose old architecture, fine art, quaint streets, and picturesque canals make it the perfect day trip from the area's larger cities. At different points in its history it's been an important harbor city, a significant European stock exchange, and a tourist attraction. (Guess which one it is now?) Its skyline is defined by the old tower of the Church of Our Lady, the belfry, and the spire of the St. Salvator Cathedral. While tourists may flock to the more well-known landmarks, dipping down lesser-known side streets can yield surprising discoveries like a second-hand book shop, a park that's home to dozens of swans, or a scenic place for a picnic. It would be hard to have an unpleasant day in Bruges.

There's not much orienting to be done in a town that's more or less the size of an American Super Walmart. The belfry borders the busy square right in the center of Bruges, with the **St. Salvator Cathedral** and the **Church of Our Lady** slightly to its south. A trip to the outskirts of the city will reveal parks and other small green spaces along the canals. Outside the city center are twisting medieval streets and more affordable restaurants and bars, and a bike trip farther north to **Zeebrugge** will take you to the beach. To get back to Brussels or Ghent, just find the train station to the southwest.

GETTING THERE

Getting to Bruges for the day from surrounding cities is simple. Just take a quick train ride to the city's only station. They run fairly often since it's a popular destination. On the southwest side of the city, the station is within walking distance of the city center and main sights.

GETTING AROUND

Public transport in Bruges is largely unnecessary because of its small size. Getting around by foot is easy, but bike rental is fairly cheap and may give you a better picture of the city beyond the main squares and tourist spots.

Swing by...

BELFRY OF BRUGES

Markt 7; 05 044 87 43; www.visitbruges.be/nl/belfort; open daily 9:30am-6pm

Belfries, common in Flanders and Northern France, were celebrated as symbols of municipal autonomy in the Middle Ages. The one in Bruges is stunning, even if getting to the top of the tall tower means €8, a potentially long wait, and 366 steps. At least the wooden structure that used to rest on top of the existing belfry is no longer there, finally abandoned after a couple rounds of getting struck by lightning and burned. Live and learn, as they say. If you make it to the top of this seven-century old building you'll be rewarded with gorgeous panoramic city views and an elevated heart rate that will delude you into thinking you did enough cardio for the day.

i Admission €10, students €8; no wheelchair accessibility

GROENINGEMUSEUM (MUSEUM)
Dijver 12; 05 044 87 11; www.visitbruges.be/nl/groeningemuseum; open
Tu-Su 9:30am-5pm

You may have seen statues of **Jan van Eyck** and **Hans Memling** around Bruges, but to see the artists' finest work you'll have to head to the Groeningemuseum. This museum features the largest collection of "Flemish Primitives" in the world ("primitive" as in the fifteenth and sixteenth century, not learning how to make fire and doing cave paintings). Don't miss the Jan van Eyck masterpiece *Madonna and Child with Canon Joris van der Paele*. A few things to keep in mind: you can access the museum until 4:30pm but you'll certainly want to have more than just half an hour here. In addition, if you try to go on Monday you'll be out of luck. Guess you'll just have to resort to the priceless Michelangelo masterpiece in the **Church of Our Lady.** Sigh, life is hard.

i *Admission €8, students €6; last entry 4:30pm; wheelchair accessible*

Grab a bite at...

SOUP ($)
Hallestraat 4; open daily 11am-3:30pm

The owner of this adorable little lunch spot must have a cat named "Cat" and a child named "Mistake" because the place's name really leaves no question about its nature. For some warm and filling comfort food on a budget, grab one of this restaurant's five soups with fruit—and not just those lackluster melon cups restaurants always seem to have. This €6 meal comes with bread, or pair your soup with half a panini for €8.50. A mural of rolling hills and some red-checked trays will make it feel like an indoor picnic, but to-go options are also available if you feel like riding off on your rental bike for a real one.

i *Soup with bread and fruit for €6, add half panini for €8.50; cash only; gluten-free, vegan, and vegetarian options available; limited wheelchair accessibility*

Don't miss...

⬛ RENT A BIKE!
Bruges and outskirts

Bruges is small enough that you can see most of it on foot in just a day. Having a bike, however, can lead you to small and off-the-beaten-path gems you probably wouldn't make it to on foot alone. Ride by the water at the city's edge and spot the handful of windmills to the north. Stop in at a plant-filled, abandoned house on **Botenmakersstraat** (at your own risk since the house is always on the verge of collapse). Pay a visit to some friendly sheep at **Hof de Jonge,** or ride north to **Zeebrugge's** beach. Or, get lost! Bruges is scenic everywhere! (Trust us.) There are bike rentals all around the city (for one hour, four hours, or the whole day), but make sure you ask for the student discount.

i *Daily rentals typically run €6-15, places further outside the city center have better deals*

OLD MASTERS MUSEUM

Rue de la Régence 3; 25 08 32 11; www.
fine-arts-museum.be/en/museums/
musee-oldmasters-museum; open Tu-F
10am-5pm, Sa-Su 11am-6pm

The **Royal Museums of Fine Arts of Belgium** are dominated by the Old Masters Museum, which takes up the upper section of the museum's great hall. The works shown here are masterpieces, and the museum offers interactive exhibits that detail the composition and meaning behind them. Particularly of note are the works of the sixteenth century Belgian painter **Pieter Bruegel I,** as well as those of his son **Pieter the Younger.** (It was quite a family business.) Here, you can see works that changed the course of Western art, and at a super cheap student price, there's no excuse to not get #cultured.

i Admission €8, students €2, seniors €6, free on every first W of the month after 1pm; last entry 30min. before closing; wheelchair accessible

OUTDOORS

PARC DU CINQUANTENAIRE

Av. de la Joyeuse Entrée; www.brussels. info/parc-du-cinquantenaire/

Sure, Paris has that one triumphal arch. Brussels, on the other hand, has a monument consisting of not one, not two, but *three* arches, dedicated to glorifying Belgium's independence. This massive structure, from which a huge Belgian flag flies, is the centerpiece of the Parc du Cinquantenaire. Behind it are a number of museums exploring everything from art to autos to the army. In front are dogs prancing, children playing, and Brussels' corporate titans picnicking on their lunch breaks. Just watch out for the impeccably manicured gardens: you could knock a tooth out on one of those perfectly square hedges.

i Free; wheelchair accessible

FOOD

🍽 DE NOORDZEE ($)

Rue Sainte-Catherine 45; 25 13 11 92; www.vishandelnoordzee.be; open Tu-Sa 8am-6pm, Su 11am-8pm

The only way to get fish soup fresher than that of Noordzee would be to drink your own goldfish straight out of its bowl. However, we can guarantee that Noordzee's option will be a lot tastier than poor little Goldie. This lunch spot in **Place Saint-Catherine** doubles as a fish market, so you know exactly where your deliciously grilled fish and expertly fried calamari come from. Eat at high standing tables in the square, with a view of **Saint-Catherine Church** to one side and the bustling activities of the fish sellers to the other. A filling bowl of fish soup goes for only €5, and you can pair it with a glass of wine for just another €2.75.

i Fish soup €5, other entrées from €6; gluten-free options available; wheelchair accessible

🏴 FANNY THAI ($$)

Rue Jules Van Praet 36; 25 02 64 22; www.fannythai.com; open M-F noon-3pm and 6pm-11:30pm, Sa-Su noon-11:30pm

The smell that greets you upon entering Fanny Thai is essentially the equivalent of tantalizing aromatic spices having a ménage à trois in your nose. We're convinced this is some of the best Thai food you can get outside Thailand, beating out the numerous other Thai restaurants at the fun and bustling **Place Saint-Gery.** The curries are warm and wonderful and the soup is full of complex flavors that will render you incapable of enjoying a can of Campbell's ever again. Try an entree for €12-13, or upgrade to a three-course fixed menu at around €18.

i *Three-course menus €18, curries and other entrées from €12; gluten-free, vegan, and vegetarian options available; wheelchair accessible*

BIA MARA ($$)

Rue du Marché aux Poulets 41; 25 02 00 61; www.biamara.com; open M-Th noon-2:30pm and 5:30pm-10:30pm, F-Su noon-10:30pm

When you think of fish and chips, you may think of greasy hunks of battered cod or British people in a sports pub. But Bia Mara does fish and chips its own way. First choose a batter, like the delicious lemon basil tempura. Next, pick from out-of-the-box sauces such as garlic truffle, thyme, or the classic tartar (they're not entirely insane). Finally, add sides like hot ink squid or popcorn mussels and a rhubarb ginger lemonade. The fresh and flavorful fish comes with thick seaweed-salted potatoes, too.

i *Fish and chips from €12; limited wheelchair accessibility*

LE CORBEAU ($)

Rue Saint-Michel 18; 22 19 52 46; www.lecorbeau.be; open M-Th 10am-midnight, F-Sa 10am-4am

Le Corbeau strikes us as the kind of place that has a lot of regulars: a large screen broadcasts sports in the back of the restaurant, the drinks are cheap, and there's a sign on the wall that says "free beer tomorrow." Old

Hmovie and beer posters decorate the establishment and give it a vintage feel. The real draw, however, is the daily lunch special. For only €9.50, guests can have the "plat du jour," which is an entrée, and a choice of either the daily soup or dessert.

i *Lunch special €9.50; vegan and vegetarian options available*

NIGHTLIFE

CAFÉ BELGA

Pl. Eugène Flagey 18; 26 40 35 08; open M-Th 7:30am-2am, F 7:30am-3am, Sa 8am-4am, Su 8am-midnight

You know that friend who never seems stressed out? They'd definitely go to Café Belga. This laid-back bar is always packed, inside and out, with beer-drinking students and young professionals pretending they don't have work tomorrow. The wide square of **Place Flagey** sprawls out next to the bar, its sides bordered by weeping willows and a tall church. By night, the indoor tables are removed and the bar turns into a packed nightclub. Luckily, the free entry and €4 draft beers are there to stay.

i *Beers from €3*

PLACE DU LUXEMBOURG

European Quarter; hours vary by venue

This square, known affectionately as "Place Lux" or even "Plux" by its dedicated fans, completely transforms on Thursday nights. The police even block it off for some government-sanctioned tomfoolery. That's because hundreds of young professionals from the surrounding European institutions, including the European Parliament, spill into it right after work to blow off steam. Some are even still wearing suits. Bars and clubs line the square, but if you really want to live like a local, buy some cheap beers from the convenience store down the street and claim a place in the grass. You'll find plenty of English-speaking friends, since much of the European Quarter's international crowd uses English at work.

i *Venue prices vary; limited wheelchair accessibility*

GHENT

Coverage by **Emily Corrigan**

Since people settled the area at the confluence of the Lys and Scheldt rivers, a long and fascinating heritage has unfolded. From a center for cloth trade during the Middle Ages, to the home of influential Flemish painters, to playing a hand in ending the War of 1812, this city has both history and modern-day appeal. Now a mid-sized northern Belgian city, Ghent boasts scenic inland waterways, old guild houses with stepped gables, a castle, and a skyline defined by the towering spires of a cathedral. It's a charming place to visit, but seems like an even more charming place to live. Local life buzzes around you, on bikes and in waterside cafés. Toss in some niche bars, historic squares, and fascinating museums and this city has the whole package.

ORIENTATION

The waterways that first drew people to the area curve through the city, acting as a guide throughout and drawing you to many of the city's cafés and restaurants. On the northern side of the city center, you'll find the castle, **Gravensteen,** right on the water. Just south are the three buildings making up Ghent's distinct skyline in a line from west to east: **St. Nicholas's Church,** the **bell tower,** and **St. Bavo's Cathedral.** Heading northeast from there will take you past the graffiti street and **St. Jacob's Church,** just past which is the historic **Vrijdagmarkt Square.** Finally, outside the city center to the south is **Citadelpark,** the home of the city's noteworthy art museums.

ESSENTIALS

GETTING THERE

If traveling from an international destination, Ghent is located 45min. away from the international airport, Zavantem (Brussels Airport). From there, you can take a train to Ghent. The Brussels South/Charleroi airport is located 70min. from Ghent; you can connect to Ghent via train. There are nine shuttles from Brussels South airport to Ghent's main train station. Ghent is perhaps easiest to reach via train, as it has two main stations: the Gent-Sint-Pieters Station and Dampoort Station. Take the tram #1 from the former to reach the city center and, from the latter, hop on buses #3, 17, 18, 38, or 39.

GETTING AROUND

Buses and trams are the methods of public transportation in Ghent, although you can easily walk to everything you want to see. Purchase tickets from Linjwinkels at main bus terminals and railway stations.

PRACTICAL INFORMATION

Tourist Offices: Sint-Veerleplein 5; 09 266 56 60; open daily 10am-6pm
Banks/ATMs/Currency Exchange: Steendam 108 (09 269 17 20; open M-F 8:30am-5:45pm, Sa 9:30am-4:30pm)
Post Offices: Bpost (Franklin Rooseveltlaan 2; 02 201 23 45)
BGLTQ+ Resources: This website is a good link for members of the BGLTQ+ community traveling in Ghent: www.stad.gent/over-gent-en-het-stadsbestuur/stadsbestuur/wat-doet-het-bestuur/uitvoering-van-het-beleid/welzijn-gezondheid/holebis-en-transgenders

EMERGENCY INFORMATION

Emergency: 100 for ambulance; 101 for police
Police: Politie Commissariaat Gent Centrum (Belfortstraat 4; 09 226 61 11; www.lokalepolitie.be/5415)
US Embassy: The nearest US Embassy is located in Brussels (Bd. Du Régent 27, 1000 Bruxelles; 02 811 40 00; open M-F 7:30am-5:30pm)

Rape Crisis Center: RAINN (800 646 4673) and National Coalition Against Domestic Violence (303 839 1852)
Hospitals: Ghent University Hospital (De Pintelaan 185; 09 332 21 11).
Pharmacies: Small green crosses mark pharmacies. Pharmacy Denys (Kasteellan 74; 09 225 20 69; open M-F 8am-12:30pm and 2pm-6:30pm)

ACCOMMODATIONS

🏨 HOSTEL UPPELINK ($)

Sint-Michielsplein 21; 92 79 44 77; www.hosteluppelink.com; reception open 7:30am-11pm

The location of Hostel Uppelink really couldn't be better. Right across from **St. Christopher's Church,** the hostel's sitting area and bar overlook the city's inland waterways, an area accompanied by countless other bars and restaurants. In addition to offering Belgian beer tastings every Tuesday and Thursday (they know what the people want), the hostel also conducts free walking tours and assists with convenient kayak rentals. A word of advice: beer tastings and kayak rentals do not mix well.
i Dorms from €19; reservation required; max stay 7 nights ; limited wheelchair accessibility; Wi-Fi; linens included; towels for rent; laundry €5; free breakfast

HOSTEL DE DRAECKE ($$)

Sint-Widostraat 11; 92 33 70 50; www.jeugd-herbergen.be/en/youth-hostels/city-hostels/gent-de-draecke; reception open 7am-11pm

Hostel de Draecke offers the small perks that every weary traveler rejoices to see. En suite bathrooms, an included breakfast (no stale-and-hurriedly-eaten-on-the-way-to-a-landmark muffins here), and a free walking tour make you appreciate the little things in life, like not wearing flip flops in the shower. The neighborhood, right across the water from the castle, is surprisingly secluded and quiet, although all the main sights and activities of the city center are still just a stone's throw away.
i Dorms from €23; reservation required; wheelchair accessible; Wi-Fi; lockers available; free breakfast

SIGHTS
CULTURE

GRAFFITI STREET

Werregarenstraat; open daily 24hr

Even if your only experience with graffiti was writing "Fill in the blank was here" on some wet cement or drawing penises in your friends' notebooks when they weren't looking (don't deny it, we've all done it), you'll appreciate this colorful alleyway. On this small street, it's legal for artists to paint as much as they want, and the result is a vibrant and constantly evolving public work of art. It has everything from ultra-realistic whales and giant heads to complicated signatures and messages on the floor. If you're feeling bold, grab some spray paint and give it a go. We just hope you've matured past phallic symbols.
i Free; wheelchair accessible

VRIJDAGMARKT

Vrijdagmarkt; open F 7:30am-1pm, Sa 11am-6:30pm

The Vrijdagmarkt is a square surrounded by eighteenth-century guildhalls that house cafés, bars, and restaurants. However, it's also the site of one of Ghent's old traditions: since 1199, the square has transformed into a market on Fridays (hence its name,

meaning "Friday market"). Now, there's also a market on Saturday, but "Vrijdagenzaterdagmarkt" doesn't have the same ring to it. After perusing the market stalls, check out the statue of **Jacob van Artevelde,** who was murdered at the market, and grab one of the 250 Belgian beers from the menu at **Tavern Dulle Griet.**

i Stand prices vary; wheelchair accessible

LANDMARKS

BELFRY OF GHENT

Sint-Baafsplein; 92 33 39 54; www.belfort-gent.be; open daily 10am-6pm

The construction of Ghent's belfry began around 1313. A visit to the bell tower today will take you through the cloth halls (relics from Ghent's textile-trading glory days) and the hidden "secrecy room," where a German command center was concealed with a false floor during World War II. Taking the stairs or elevator up into the tower will reveal the enormous drum and bells still used to mark the hour, as well as panoramic views of the city. This **UNESCO World Heritage** site also displays various dragon vanes. Try to go around the hour, when you can watch the drum rotate and ring the bells like a giant city-sized music box.

i Admission €2.70; guided tours at 3:30pm for €3; no wheelchair accessibility

GRAVENSTEEN

Sint-Veerleplein 11; 92 25 93 06; www.gravensteen.stad.gent; open daily 10am-6pm

This medieval castle has been a count's residence, a cotton spinning mill, and the seat of the Council of Flanders. Walk along the ramparts for a stunning view of the city, and be sure to explore the dungeons and accompanying torture museum. English explanation cards offer cheery titles like "Case 5: Stabbing." Rows of bludgeons, spiky collars, and even a guillotine will have you flinching. Nevertheless, this giant castle emerging out of the middle of a modern city is sure to impress.

i Admission €10, students €6; no wheelchair accessibility

MUSEUMS

MUSEUM VOOR SCHONE KUNSTEN (MUSEUM OF FINE ARTS)

Fernand Scribedreef 1; 92 40 07 00; www.mskgent.be; open Tu-F 9:30am-5:30pm, Sa-Su 10am-6pm

The museum's centerpiece is the **Ghent Altarpiece** (also known as the Adoration of the Mystic Lamb) from the **Van Eyck brothers,** described by the museum as the "highlight of fifteenth-century Flemish panel painting." Cards with English explanations are scattered throughout, detailing everything from the composition of religious paintings from the Middle Ages to the symbolism behind a tapestry collection from Brussels. Don't miss the massive modern art installation in the center either, a piece that takes up the entire room, surrounded by water beds on which to relax and immerse yourself in the artwork.

i Admission €8, students €2; wheelchair accessible

STAM (GHENT CITY MUSEUM)

Godshuizenlaan 2; 92 67 14 00; www.stamgent.be; open daily 10am-6pm

Not many museums ask you to put on shoe covers to enter. It's not because the staff is made up of insane neat freaks; it's because the highlight of the museum is an enormous satellite map of the city spread across a huge floor. In the center is an astonishingly large and detailed scale model of the city center, and, throughout the museum, there are computers where visitors can click through tons of interactive exhibits about the city's history. The museum goes all the way back to Ghent's beginnings, demonstrating why people first settled at this relatively high point at the confluence of the **Lys** and **Scheldt rivers.**

i Admission €8, 19-25 years old €2, under 19 free; wheelchair accessible

OUTDOORS

CITADELPARK

Citadelpark; open daily 24hr

Citadelpark has historically been a site of great military defenses in Ghent. It takes its name from the citadel built here (though now demolished) by **King William** of the UK in 1819. Now instead of heavy fortifications, you'll find a small waterfall, hills and caves, and even a playground (although you may be too young for children of your own and too old to play on it without getting at least a few glances from concerned parents). It's also the home of city's modern and fine art museums, so the park is a great place to relax and reflect on the life changing Flemish masterpiece you just saw.

i Free; limited wheelchair accessibility

FOOD

🌿 SOUP'R ($)

Sint-Niklaasstraat 9; open Tu-Sa 11am-5pm

Despite the fact that its name is a total dad joke, this restaurant serves up soups far better than that canned chicken noodle soup Dad heats up at home. A crowd clusters around the door before lunchtime waiting for the place to open up, and it'll soon become clear as to why. The soups, ranging from Belgian classics to Thai and Vietnamese curries, are both soup'r delicious and soup'r affordable. Three sizes of soups with bread and butter can be garnished with your choice of free toppings or paired with a sandwich or salad. You may have some trouble deciphering the Dutch menu, but even if you point at something random, you're sure to end up with piping hot and flavorful soup on the table eventually.

i Soups from €4.50; gluten-free, vegan, and vegetarian options available; limited wheelchair accessibility

GREENWAY ($$)

Nederkouter 42; 92 69 07 69; www.greenway.be; open M-Sa 11am-10pm

The name is not only indicative of the green plants covering seemingly every surface of this healthy "fast food" spot's interior, but the vegetarian and vegan menu will also satisfy those seeking a quick green meal—even on the go. With everything from veggie burgers to salads to wraps to lasagnas, the menu is sure to accommodate diverse diets in a way that's satisfying and flavorful. Be sure to check the specials and soups of the day for the freshest additions.

i Salads from €12, burgers from €8.90, wraps, lasagna, curry from €12; gluten-free, vegan, and vegetarian options available; limited wheelchair accessibility

SELI'S NOODLE BAR ($$)

Limburgstraat 28; 92 23 58 88; www.selinoodlebar.be; open daily noon-9:30pm

There are some things you just don't want to see being made: sausage, cigarettes, and your brother. If you've never seen noodles being made, however, you need to sit inside at Seli's and watch as their own house-made noodles are stretched, cut, and prepared. The next step is crucial: get

these very same noodles in your belly. Order a big bowl of salty and delicious noodle soup, full of plenty of vegetables and your choice of meat. Sides like fresh spring rolls and gyoza are equally satisfying.

i Noodle soup from €10.50; gluten-free and vegetarian options available; limited wheelchair accessibility

NIGHTLIFE

'T VERLOOTJE

4, Kalversteeg 2; 92 23 28 34; open daily noon-3am

Trying to describe the strange and wonderful experience of having a beer at 't Verlootje is like Alice trying to describe Wonderland to your average Joe. You'll be greeted on the tiny street by Lieven, the owner, identifiable by his short shorts and fuzzy beard. An eccentric man with a welcoming spirit, he'll be happy to show you his bar-cum-house, where bikes hang from the walls and ceiling and cover just about every actual surface in sight. He even claims to have a bike from **Napoleon III.** Everyone at the place is encouraged to chat, get to know one another, and sign the thick guest book. It's not uncommon for everyone to hug their new friends before they leave. So, go ahead, fall down this amazing rabbit-hole! You'll be mad for it.

i Beers from €6; cash only; limited wheel-chair accessibility

HOT CLUB GENT ($$)

Schuddevisstraatje 2; 92 56 71 99; www. hotclub.gent; open daily 3pm-3am

At a place with a name like Hot Club, you would expect to find a slightly stuffy, dark nightclub where the only thing keeping you there is the fact that you already paid a cover to get in. Yet the actual Hot Club is a classy affair, not a nightclub at all, but rather a small jazz bar with live music five nights a week named after **Hot Club de France,** a jazz club in Paris founded in the 30s. After dipping down a tiny unassuming alleyway, you'll find a charming courtyard and a small stage with piano and drum set at the ready. Hot Club isn't meant for a party; the neighborhood quiet hours begin at 10pm, and guests are asked to be silent during the concerts. Grab your 1920s hat like the jazz cat you are and spend another night drinking—except this time, culturally.

i Long drinks from €7, beers from €3; cash only; limited wheelchair accessibility; silence required during performances

BELGIUM ESSENTIALS

VISAS

Belgium is a member of the EU, meaning that citizens of Australia, New Zealand, the US, and other European countries do not need a visa for a stay up to 90 days.

MONEY

Tipping: In Belgium, service charges are included in the bill at restaurants, so there is no need to leave a tip, as waiters are paid fully for their service. If you do receive excellent service though, leaving a 5-10% tip would be appreciated. Tips in bars are uncommon and cab drivers are typically tipped 10%.

Taxes: The marked price of goods in Belgium includes a value-added tax (VAT). This tax on goods is generally levied at 21% in Belgium, although some good are subject to higher rates. Non-EU citizens who are taking these goods home unused may be refunded this tax. When making purchases, be sure to ask and fill out a VAT form and present it at a Tax-Free Shopping Office, found at most airports, borders, or ferry stations. Refunds must be claimed within six months.

SAFETY AND HEALTH

Drugs and Alcohol: Belgium has fairly liberal attitudes regarding alcohol with no legal drinking age. You must be 16 to buy your own alcohol (18 for spirits), but it's perfect legal for someone else to buy alcohol for someone under 16. Public drunkenness, however, is frowned upon. Belgium's attitude toward even soft drugs is traditional and conservative. Marijuana is illegal and not tolerated.

CROATIA

This is the country that gave the world both the necktie and the parachute, so unsurprisingly it's a bit like James Bond—sexy, elegant, but not afraid to down *rakija* shots at 2am before going hiking, sailing, and cliff jumping the next morning. Plus, a location smack dab in the middle of Europe means that Croatia combines everything we like about the western and eastern halves of the continent, not to mention easy access to major European cities. It's a place where you can go out with friends for pizza before belting out Croatian pop hits at a locals-only club or lounge on one of its many island like you're ballin' at St. Tropez, but instead on a Balkan budget.

Don't be fooled by the country's communist past: while less than 30 years ago Croatia was a key part of Yugoslavia, the scars of communism and the subsequent wars of independence seem to be almost repaired. Traveling across Croatia you'll see that the country's L-shape creates two distinct sides: the coast and the hinterland. Zagreb falls in the latter category, showing strong influence from Austria in both its architecture and cuisine. Here you'll see churches with onion domes and try gastronomic specialties such as *štrukli,* a savory version of baked strudel with cheese. The coast, however, historically had stronger connections with Italy, so brace yourself for Roman ruins, seafood, and risotto galore. And the best part: though Croatia is well-established as a tourist destination, its location in the Balkans translates to ideal prices. Oh, and did we mention the islands? Croatia's got over 1000 of 'em. So take your pick: Hvar-ever you like it, there's an island for that. Welcome to budget-traveler heaven. Cliff jump in Split, appreciate the art of Ivan Meštrović in galleries across the country, and sip ridiculously good coffee in one of Zagreb's ubiquitous cafés. And remember, you can't spell formerly part of Yugoslavia without U, so make sure you catch yourself along those Instagram jealousy inducing, pristine, and party-filled coastlines. *Živjeli,* my friends.

DUBROVNIK

Coverage by **Gavin Moulton**

Your grandma loves Dubrovnik. Your second cousin twice-removed won't shut up about his trip here. Your ex-girlfriend's uncle's stepfather's in-laws are still posting photos on Facebook from their time in the city. What's with the all the hype? Dubrovnik is drop-dead gorgeous. After just one day, you'll start looking up study-abroad options and figuring out how to get a work visa until you can become a citizen. There are beaches, bars, Baroque architecture, and those are the only b's we need besides beautiful babes. Prices in the city are more expensive, but cheap supermarkets, ice cream shops, and bakeries make budget life bearable. Outside of the old town there are plenty of outdoor activities: climbing Mt. Srd is a definite favorite. But, let's be real, you came here for the coast—so pack your suntan lotion, it's Croatian Riviera time.

ORIENTATION

Dubrovnik is located on a peninsula jutting into the Adriatic Sea. It's surrounded by massive medieval walls, so the only entrances to the **Old Town** are through the city gates. The main ones are the **Pile** (west side) and **Ploče** (east side) gates. The bus station and port are located a 20-minute bus ride to the west of the city and the airport is 30 minutes to the south. The main street is the **Stradun,** but the rest of the city is dominated by narrow alleyways and stairs, punctuated with the occasional piazza. The city center is walkable, and public transit is only needed for daytrips or rides to the airport. The airport shuttle shop is next to the cable car station, and tickets are 30-40 kn.

ESSENTIALS

GETTING THERE

Both international and domestic airlines land at Dubrovnik Airport. For budget prices, look at carriers such as Norwegian, Croatia Airlines, and Easyjet. You can also get to Dubrovnik by ferries from Bari, Italy or from neighboring Croatian islands.

GETTING AROUND

Dubrovnik's Old Town is small and easily navigable by foot. You will most likely not be staying in the Old Town, but 99% of what's interesting in Dubrovnik is located there. Buses regularly connect the various parts of Dubrovnik to the Old Town; if you exit the Pile Gate, you'll find a major hub for buses. Pro tip: if you're staying outside the city, walk to the Old Town and take a bus home (otherwise, you'll likely be walking uphill).

PRACTICAL INFORMATION

Tourist Offices: Turistička Zajedica Grada Dubrovnika (Brsalje ul. 5; 20 323 887)

Banks/ATMs/Currency Exchange: Addiko Bank-Poslovnica Dubrovnik (Vukovarska ul. 15; 1 603 000)
Post Offices: Hrvatska pošta (Široka ul. 8; 20 362 842; open daily 24hr).
Internet: There are a lot of cafés, but few public spots, with Wi-Fi available in Dubrovnik.
BGLTQ+ Resources: A good resource for members of the BGLTQ+ community is www.gaywelcome.com/gay-dubrovnik.php.

EMERGENCY INFORMATION

Emergency Number: 112
Police: Dubrovnik Police Department (Ul. Dr. Ante Starčevića 13; 20 443 777).
US Embassy: The US Embassy in Croatia is located in Zagreb (Ul. Thomasa Jeffersona 2; 1 661 2200; open M-F 8:30am-4:30pm)
Hospitals: Opća bolnica Dubrovnik (Dr. Roka Mišetića 2; 20 431 777; open daily 24hr)
Pharmacies: Ljekarn (Ul. Mata Vodopića 30)

ACCOMMODATIONS

HOSTEL AND ROOMS ANA ($)

Kovačka Ul. 4; 098 674 188; reception open daily 8am-1am

"Communal" can only begin to describe the vibe at Hostel and Rooms Ana. An inordinate number of people squeeze into what essentially amounts to the attic that Ana inhabits with her son. But don't judge a book by its cover: the close quarters build community. Or, on second thought, it might be the free alcohol that Ana provides. Regardless, a night spent around the wooden table drinking homemade *rakija* with newfound friends is reason enough to stay here.

i Dorms 185 kn; reservation recommended; Wi-Fi; kitchen available

HOSTEL CITY WALLS ($$)

Svetog Simuna 15; 917 992 086; www.city-wallshostel.com; reception open 8am-10pm

Bright blue walls await you at this hostel located next to the old city walls. A far walk from both the attractions of downtown as well as the **Ploče** and **Pile gates,** the hostel is typical of Dubrovnik options. The rooms are overpriced, but we all need a place to crash, we guess—probably a better plan than sleeping in a public park to the west of town to save money. For all it's worth, though, the lobby is a nice space to hang out.

i Dorms from 245 kn; reservation recommended; Wi-Fi

OLD TOWN HOSTEL ($$$)

Ul. od Sigurate 7; 20 322 007; www.dubrovnikoldtownhostel.com; reception open 8am-11pm

Sometimes you splurge unnecessarily. Sometimes you splurge on basic necessities. Old Town Hostel fits into the latter category. This place is kind of like paying extra for organic milk when it tastes exactly the same as the pumped-full-of-artificial-hormones full-fat store brand. But at least the **Old Town** location is ideal and the exposed stone walls and wooden floors are a nice touch. Console yourself for overpaying while gorging yourself on the free breakfast.

i Dorms from 300 kn; reservation recommended; Wi-Fi; breakfast included

SIGHTS

CULTURE

LAZARETI

Ul. Frana Supila 1

In order to prevent the spread of disease, the Lazareti was established as a quarantine for foreigners and goods passing through the city. Today, the complex has been converted into a restaurant, several shops, and a nightclub. Pro tip: for one of the best (read: most romantic) views of the city, head down the staircase in the middle to the rocks by the water.

i Prices vary; limited wheelchair accessibility

STRADUN

Stradun; open daily 24hr

This is *the* street in Dubrovnik. See and be seen on this expensive and tourist-infested stretch of stone-paved glory that crosses town to connect the **Ploče** and **Pile gates.** On the Pile side is **Onofrio's Fountain,** one of the city's most important landmarks (with potable water!). The street is flanked on the other end by the **City Hall Bell Tower,** which is home to two sculpted copper boys who strike the bells every hour.

i Free; wheelchair accessible

LANDMARKS

🖼 CITY WALLS

Gundulićeva Poljana 2; 020 324 641; open daily Jan 1-Feb 28 10am-3pm, Mar 1-Mar 31 9am-3pm, Apr 1-May 31 9am-6:30pm, June 1-July 31 8am-7:30pm, Aug 1-Sept 15 8am-7pm, Sept 15-Oct 31 9am-6pm, Nov 1-Dec 31 9am-3pm

From the window to the two-kilometer walls, there is plenty of walking to do. Forget swashbuckling pirates or armies though; these days the walls only protect Dubrovnik against thousands of cruise-ship tourists. There's really nowhere else in Europe like this. The city walls are still almost entirely intact, completely encircling the city. With the number of steps, if you don't bring water you'll surely die—if not from dehydration, then from the absurd prices that the bars in the walls charge.

i Admission 20 kn; no wheelchair accessibility

CATHEDRAL OF DUBROVNIK

Ul. kneza Damjana Jude 1; open Apr 4-Nov 1 M-F 9am-5pm, Sa 11am-5pm, winter M-Sa 10am-noon and 3pm-5pm, Su 11am-noon and 3pm-5pm

While you won't see Sean Connery or Robin Hood, the Cathedral of Dubrovnik was founded by **Richard the Lionheart** himself, according to legend. Whether or not you believe in the legend, however, the since-renovated cathedral is a must-see sight in Dubrovnik due to the **Titian polyptych** located above the main altar. The church was constructed in Baroque style and occupies a prominent place with *piazzas* on three sides. At night, the illuminated dome of the church is particularly beautiful.
i Free

CHURCH OF ST. IGNATIUS

Poljana Rudera Boškovića 7; 020 323 500; open daily 8am-7pm

As any Georgetown student will tell you, the Jesuits don't mess around. So, it's not really a surprise that their church occupies one of the most prominent vantage points in the Old City. The church is based on earlier Jesuit churches in Rome, but we can forgive the plagiarism for the innovative Lourdes Grotto. To us heathens, that basically means there's a manmade cave with a statue of the Virgin Mary that was built in the late seventeenth century.
i Free

FORT LOVRIJENAC

Ul. od Tabakarije 29; open daily 8am-7pm

This is the sans-CGI Red Keep from *Game of Thrones,* and it might be a bit less impressive than the show. But it's also less expensive than the **City Walls,** and the views are not to be missed. There is a small internal courtyard with three stories worth of steps, cannons, and ramparts. Beware that if you stay past closing time, you will get locked inside (we speak from experience). After closing time, the steps outside make a nice spot for a BYO drink.
i Admission 50 kn; no wheelchair accessibility

MUSEUMS

DOMINICAN MUSEUM

Ul. Svetog Dominika 4; open daily summer 9am-6pm, winter 9am-5pm

Slightly more off the beaten path than the **Franciscan Pharmacy** is the Dominican Monastery, home to the best religious art collection in Dubrovnik. The church is currently closed to the public, as it is undergoing renovations, but the small museum with a **Titian** painting of St. Mary Magdalene makes up for the church's closing. Smack dab in the center of it all is the **cloister,** objectively the most beautiful in the city.
i Admission 30 kn, students 20 kn

AQUARIUM

Kneza Damjana Jude 12; 020 0323 978; open daily 9am-8pm

Sure, you've been to aquariums before. Sure, you've been to medieval towers before. Sure, you've been to modern art museums before. But have you been to a combination of all three? That's right, you haven't. Painfully fork over that 60 kn and saunter through this pretty piscatorial place. What the museum lacks in size, it makes up for in ambience. The stone walls are impressive, especially with the projections and reflections of the water. Be sure to say "hi" to the dancing octopus and sea turtles for us. We miss them already.
i Admission 60 kn

FRANCISCAN MONASTERY AND PHARMACY

Placa 2; open daily summer 9am-6pm, winter 9am-5pm

This is the seventeenth-century version of CVS. Forget endless aisles and industrial fluorescent lighting, and instead think of painted *majolica* jars and homemade remedies. But this isn't your average old pharmacy. If that's what you're looking for, you can stop next door at the functioning pharmacy that the Franciscans continue to run. The main attraction of the complex, however, is the cloister. Columns topped with Gothic quatrefoils stand in the picturesque setting. Rooms leading off the cloister feature religious art from the history of the complex.
i Admission 30 kn, reduced 15 kn

MUSEUM OF MODERN ART DUBROVNIK

Put Frana Supila 23; 020 426 590; open Tu-Su 9am-8pm

Take me to the beach beach let's go get away way, to the Museum of Modern Art which is conveniently located above **Banje Beach.** Situated in an old palace, the museum is dedicated to nineteenth-century and contemporary art from the Dubrovnik area, which means you won't know anyone or anything here. Jury's still out on whether English language descriptions would help with understanding the abstract art that dominates the museum. Regardless, the terrace is easier to appreciate with its stunning views of **Old Town** and a few sculptures by our homeboy, **Ivan Meštrović.**

i Admission 20 kn

OUTDOORS

🏔 MT. SRĐ

Ul. kralja Petra Krešimira IV; 020 414 355; www.dubrovnikcablecar.com; open daily Jan 9am-4pm, Feb-Mar 9am-5pm, Apr 9am-8pm, May 9am-9pm, June-Aug 9am-midnight, Sept 9am-10pm, Oct 9am-8pm, Nov 9am-5pm, Dec 9am-4pm

Beached out? Hike **Mt. Srđ,** the giant hunk of rock located just behind the city. There's a cable car that goes to the top, but we recommend buying a one-way ticket and hiking the way down. The cable car company purposefully doesn't mark the mountain trail—attempting to scheme you into a roundtrip ticket. So insider tip, find the path behind the concrete fort, located just west of the top cable car station, if you want to avoid paying for the trip down. The view from the top of the mountain does not disappoint. On a clear day, you can see **Montenegro and Bosnia and Herzegovina.** You might not be able to check them off your bucket list, but at least you saw them.

i Round-trip 130 kn, one-way 80 kn, children under 4 free; limited wheelchair accessibility

BANJE BEACH

Ul. Frana Supila 10

Go east, young man! Fulfill your Dubrovnik version of Manifest Destiny by claiming a spot at Banje Beach. For the real homesteaders out there, the eastern part of the beach is free. The beach has great views of Dubrovnik, but then again, where doesn't? It's an easy five-minute walk to the east of the city.

i Free; beach chair rental 100 kn

LOKRUM ISLAND

Lokrum Island

Lokrum Island seems like an ideal romantic getaway with its heart shaped gardens and azure waters. That is, until middle-aged tourists start mimicking the peacocks that roam freely on the island. If you can overcome those terrifying, soul-crushing sounds, trek over from the small harbor to the old **Benedictine Monastery.** Legend has it that when the monks were kicked off the island, they left a curse on all those who come to Lokrum to seek pleasure. So instead, come as a *Game of Thrones* pilgrim to see an exact copy of the **Iron Throne** located in the visitors' center. On the top of the island is an **old fort** with panoramic views.

i Round-trip ferry 120 kn, island entrance 90 kn with self-provided transportation; last ferry departs at 7pm; limited wheelchair accessibility

# KOTOR

Thought Europe's only fjords were located in Norway? Think again. Montenegro is home to one of 'em. And boy, it is pretty grand. Kotor is located on the eastern part of the fjord's interior. For centuries, this was an important port town in the conflict between the Venetians and Ottomans. Although not caught between those empires anymore, Montenegro is at the crossroads of Russia and Europe. In the summer months, you'll quickly notice the many Russian tourists, on vacation from their miserable sunless country for the near constant sunshine and glorious beaches. Aside from gawking at the worst sunburns this side of Vladivostok, there are walls to climb, orthodox icon screens to admire, and plenty of places to take a dip in the clear waters. Welcome to the Russian Riviera.

Kotor is a triangle-shaped town hypotenused against **Sveti Ivan** (St. John's) mountain, smack dab on top of which is the town's fortress. To the north of the historic center is the **Škurda River**, which feels like a moat due to Kotor's massive walls. Continuing north is a small beach and large modern shopping center. Southwards is a small inlet of the **Bay of Kotor.** The cruise ship terminal where many tourists arrive is located due west from downtown. The historic center is quite small with minimal streets and *piazzas*—you can get lost but it is easy to reorient yourself based on the tall cathedral towers, mountain, and city walls.

GETTING THERE

Getting to Kotor from Dubrovnik is fairly easy. The approximately two-hour bus ride runs at just €15. Book a bus ticket after looking at the schedule at the Dubrovnik Bus Station.

GETTING AROUND

Kotor itself is small and best navigated on foot. Cars cannot get into the old town regions, although some golf carts are used as taxis or city tour transportation devices. Renting a bike is also a viable option for navigating your way around the city.

Swing by...

CATHEDRAL OF ST. TRYPHON
Pjaca Sv. Tripuna

Romanesque to the bone, or baptistery rather, this is the largest church in the city. Historically, Kotor had a mostly Catholic population and this is still an operational Catholic church. Due to the large influx of Orthodox Christians in the city, however, several of the city's other churches have since converted. Immediately after entering the cathedral, take note of the remaining frescoes on the soffit of the arches. Admission to the cathedral museum, located beyond the left side aisle, is included in admission to the church. Climb the steps to the small reliquary chapel, the most evocative spot in the cathedral.

i Admission €2.50; limited wheelchair accessibility

Check out...

FORTIFICATIONS
Put do Svetog Ivana; open daily 24hr

"City walls" fails to describe the straight-up-the-face-of-a-mountain fortifications that protected the city of Kotor for centuries. We're not quite sure how horses and soldiers made their way up the steep grades of the mountain, because it's near impossible to walk straight up the switchbacks without using the steps on the side. Should you survive, halfway up the mountain lies a small chapel dedicated to the Virgin Mary. You'll need divine help to hike all the way up to the fortress at the top, where there are even better views of the surrounding mountains. Be sure to bring water—midday can get quite hot in the summer.

i Admission €3; no wheelchair accessibility

Grab a bite at...

BOKUN ($)
Ul. 1; 69 290 019; open daily winter 8am-11pm, summer 8am-1am

Many people come here for the live music, the exposed stone walls, or the wine. We come here for the sandwiches. Hold the jazz, please, we want the arugula and prosciutto goodness served on a wooden platter. Prices are reasonable and there is plenty of seating both outside and in the trendy interior. The sandwiches themselves are not only delicious, but also made for Instagram. Make all your followers jealous and add a splash of food from Bokun to your feed.

i Sandwiches from €4.50

Don't miss...

MARITIME MUSEUM
Trg Bokeljske Mornarice 391; 32 304 720; www.museummaritimum.com; open Apr 15-July 1 M-F 8am-6pm, Su 9am-1pm; July 1-Sept 1 M-F 8am-11pm, Su 10am-4pm; Sept 1-Oct 15 M-F 8am-6pm, Su 9am-1pm; Oct 15-Apr 15 M-F 9am-5pm, Su 9am-noon

This ain't Seaworld. We're at the Maritime Museum, that's as real as it gets. While T-Pain might not agree with our evaluation of the museums of Kotor, this is the place to go for model ships (or model boats rather). There are old naval uniforms, trade documents from Venetian times, and maps on maps on maps. Many of the written documents seen here would commonly be housed in archives in other cities; it's neat to look at them up close. For the landlubbers out there, the nineteenth-century rooms of a noble family may be easier to appreciate.

i Adult €4, students €1, children €1.50

FOOD

▨ TRATTORIA CAPRICCIO ($$$)

Ul. Kneza Damjana Jude; 020 454 433; open daily 11am-midnight

Should you happen to be in Dubrovnik with your girlfriend's grandparents and want to pull off that sophisticated-man-of-the-world charm, look no further than Trattoria Capriccio. Run by a husband-and-wife team, the trattoria specializes in Italian food sourced entirely from local merchants and made fresh in the kitchen. The results do not disappoint. This place will impress your future in-laws enough for them to love you more even than your girlfriend. The prices are a bargain for the quality of food you'll eat, but considerably more than standard backpacker fare.

i Entrées from 100 kn

DOLCE VITA ($)

Nalješkovićeva 1a; 989 449 951; open daily 9am-midnight

While you can't live the suite life in your hostel dorms, enjoy the sweet life at this combo crêpe and ice cream parlor. The 10 kn prices are lower than the Dubrovnik average for a scoop and trust us, there was a thorough investigation (we may or may not have spent the equivalent of $100 on various ice cream retailers in the area). While we cannot not condone consumption of the crêpes (which are typical of the overly sweet varieties usually served in trendy places in eastern Europe), if you're into that kind of thing, you can find it here, too.

i Scoops from 10 kn

RESTAURANT KOPUN ($$$)

Poljana Rudera Boskovica 7; 020 323 969; www.restaurantkopun.com; open daily 11am-midnight

We're not joking, **castrated rooster** is quite literally the specialty of this place. How do we feel about it? Tastes like chicken. After a trip to Europe, you can out-gastronome all your friends with your adventurous new palate. (For major props, tell them you castrated the rooster yourself.) Travel is all about new experiences; this one is for the brave. If you need to convince a friend to come with you, they can order other milder local specialties such as risotto or various seafood options.

i Entrées from 100 kn

TAJ MAHAL ($$)

Nikole Gučetića 2; 020 323 221; www.tajmahal-dubrovnik.com; open daily 9am-1am

Forget India and instead take a culinary trip to neighboring Bosnia, the kind of cuisine that Taj Mahal actually specializes in. After all the fish options that are typical of the Croatian coast, these massive meat platters are a welcome relief for carnivorous backpackers. While the prices are average, the portion sizes are not. Bowls of fresh-out-of-the-oven bread accompany dishes with plenty of hearty sides such as *kumpir,* or traditional stuffed potatoes. Other options include shish kebabs and *pljeskavica,* which is essentially a hamburger without the bun that's large enough to satisfy all of your homesickness for America.

i Entrées from 90 kn, soups from 45 kn, beer from 35 kn; reservation recommended

NIGHTLIFE

▨ DODO BEACH BAR

Od Kolorine; 914 432 826

Don't try this at home kids: Dodo replaces bar stools with swings. Although alcohol and swings make for an unsettling combination, what really puts this place over the edge is its cliffside location above a beach. The views are drop-dead gorgeous: just don't fall over the edge or you might actually drop dead. For those late nights, Dodo has toast sandwiches, perfect for attempting to stop a hangover before it starts. And in the Balkans, that's probably a good idea.

i Cocktails from 60 kn, shots from 30 kn, sandwiches from 35 kn; no wheelchair accessibility

BUZZ BAR

Prijeko 21; 020 321 025; open daily 8am-2am

No bees here, the buzz at this bar is fueled by alcohol. And why not? With quotes on the wall from Ernest Hemingway convincing you to drink, there's no reason not to imbibe (not that we really needed one in the first place). After all the tourist places on the **Stradun,** the lowkey vibes and soccer matches on the TV give this bar a homier feel. While no place in Dubrovnik is truly a local joint, this is about as close as it gets.

i Cocktails from 5 kn

CULTURE CLUB REVELIN

Svetog Dominika 3; 020 436 010; www.clubrevelin.com; open daily 11pm-6am

There's nothing cultured in this club: not even its medieval tower location can make up for the stripper poles and dancing cages. That said, not too many fortifications get lit like the Revelin does. Expect giant glowing balls hanging from the ceiling, roaming photographers, and working your way through massive drunk crowds on the smoky dance floor—that is, if you can afford the hefty cover fee or sneak your way in through the glitzy VIP entrance.

i Cover 130 kn, beer from 35 kn

SKYBAR NIGHTCLUB

Ul. Marojice Kaboge 1; 914 202 094; open daily 10pm-6pm

Walking the stairs down into Skybar Nightclub is a bit like descending through Dante's layers of hell. The levels gradually shift from semi-chill hang-out spaces to the final floor where you'll physically feel the bass speaker five feet over your head send shock waves pulsing through your body. Drinks are expensive, but the location outside the Pile gate is easily accessible. Best to drink before coming to this place, not just to save money, but also to forget about the night the next day.

i Cover 30 kn, prices vary nightly; no wheelchair accessibility

HVAR

Coverage by **Gavin Moulton**

Hvar are you doing today? Let's be real, you'd probably be better off in Hvar. At least, that's the mentality of the celebrities, bohemian backpackers, and jet-set elites who vacation here. All that money and energy means that Hvar has the wildest nightlife anywhere on the Adriatic coast. For those rare moments when you're sober, there's plenty of other stuff to do too, with all of Hvar's beaches and sea caves. And even if you're not the adventurous type, the Venetian architecture and year-round sun make this a nice place to just relax. Hvar is *the* holiday destination of Croatia.

ORIENTATION

Hvar Town is the largest tourist destination on the island of Hvar, which consists of other cities such as **Stari Grad.** The central point of the city is the **Pjaca,** the main square. The square marks the location of the eighteenth-century **St. Stephen's Cathedral of Hvar.** This is pretty hard to miss and, if you don't see it, you're really not looking. The **Riva** area, which is near the coast and the location of much of the nightlife in Hvar, can be found west of the Pjaca. If you're looking to do more sightseeing, the **Franciscan Monastery** is south of the Pjaca and the **Fortica Spanjola** is north.

ESSENTIALS

GETTING THERE

If traveling internationally, the closest international airports are in Split and Dubrovnik. From there, you'll need to take additional transportation to Hvar via ferry. You can take a ferry from Split or a cross-island ferry from Korčula, Vis, or Brac to get to Hvar. There is also an international ferry line that runs from Italy that stops in Hvar. Most ferries will dock at Stari Grad, from which you'll have to take a 20min. bus to Hvar Town.

GETTING AROUND

Hvar Town is pretty small and easily walkable, so you won't need to worry about using public transportation or taxis. To get to other cities on the island, there are buses to connect you. The bus to Stari Grad is a 20min. ride.

PRACTICAL INFORMATION

Tourist Offices: Main tourist office (Trg. Svetog Stepana 42; 021 741 059; www.tzhvar.hr; open July-Aug daily 8am-2pm and 3pm-9pm)

Banks/ATMs/Currency Exchange: Privredna Banka (Fabrikia b.b.; 021 421 413; open M-F 9am-2pm, Sa 9am-noon)

Post Offices: Hrvatska pošta (Riva b.b.; 021 742 588)

Internet: The tourist office offers free Wi-Fi in Hvar, but otherwise, your best bet is accommodations.

EMERGENCY INFORMATION

Emergency Number: 112

Police: Police headquarters (Ive Milicica 5; 021 504 239; www.splitsko-dalmatinska.policija.hr)

US Embassy: The nearest US Embassy is located in Croatia's capital, Zagreb (Ul. Thomassa Jeffersona 2; 016 612 200; open M-F 8am-4:30pm).

Hospitals: Health Center Hvar (Ul. biskupa Jurja Dubokovića 3)

Pharmacies: Ljakarna Lakoš-Marušic (Trg. Sv. Stjepana 18; 021 741 002).

ACCOMMODATIONS

EARTHERS HOSTEL ($)

11 Martina Vučetića; 099 267 9889; reception open 24hr

Earthers Hostel is what happens when a location 15min. outside of town forces its guests to bond with each other. The result borders on a cult: Earthers has a strong community vibe and a stunning garden terrace, with a view to boot. Oh, and did we mention the hammocks? Kick back after a long day of sightseeing in one of these babies. For your more practical needs, unlike the other hostels in Hvar, Earther's has in-house washing and a drying rack.

i Dorms from 100 kn, privates from 350 kn; reservation recommended; Wi-Fi; luggage storage; linens included; towels included; laundry facilities

HOSTEL MARINERO ($)

Sveti Marak 9; 091 410 2751; reception open 9am-1am

The rooms are new and clean; some even have in-suite bathrooms (gasp). The dark secret of Hostel Marinero, though, is that the only common space is the stairs that they put pillows on. Be warned, if you come here with a big backpack you may accidentally knock out a fellow traveler who is j-chilling on the steps.

i Dorms from 100 kn; reservation recommended; Wi-Fi; luggage storage

WHITE RABBIT HOSTEL ($)

Stjepana Papafave 6; 021 717 365; reception open 24hr

You don't need a rabbit foot to be lucky at White Rabbit Hostel. Wacky name aside, the rooms are clean and showers have good water pressure, and that's about all we ask for. The rooftop bar is a nice gathering space for "interaction with fellow travelers" (i.e. drinking games), except the roof closes at 11pm due to the hostel's location in **central Hvar's** residential area. It's not a terrible trade-off for White Rabbit's proximity to all Hvar has to offer.

i Dorms from 100 kn; reservation recommended; Wi-Fi; luggage storage; meals available

CULTURE

ARSENAL

Trg Sv. Stjepana; hours vary by show

Located on the main square of Hvar, there's not much one can do here besides take a selfie. In its heyday, Hvar's Arsenal was used to service the Venetian navy before being converted into a theater. Times have changed, though, and now the building itself is under renovation. But its location on the terrace right by the water makes this a nice place to chill with gelato and enjoy views of Hvar.

i *Show ticket prices vary; wheelchair accessible*

RUINS OF ST. MARK'S CHURCH

Trg Sv. Stjepana

Although it's apparently too dangerous to enter the church itself, the guardian may be kind enough to let you into the courtyard outside the church, which houses old graves. Not your typical graveyard, the space feels ethereal with palm trees, marble tombstones, and old stone pavement. If you don't catch such a stroke of luck and nothing is open, hop on up the steps to the concrete walkway with stellar views of the church bell tower and Hvar Town.

i *Free; no wheelchair accessibility*

LANDMARKS

FORTICA ŠPANJOLA

Ul. Higijeničkog Društva; 021 741 816; open daily 8am-9pm

Forget romantic sunset pictures on the beach: Fortica Španjola is the place to go. This fortress protected Hvar over the centuries of rule by the Byzantines, Venetians, and French, just to name a few. While it's a bit of hike to get up here (read: stairs galore), the views make it all worth it and your legs will thank you for the unintended workout later. If you don't feel like paying for the fortress itself, you can always walk around below, where the views are still stunning. We recommend visiting the fortress right at sunset, so you can watch Hvar glow when the pink rays hit the tan stone.

i *Admission 40 kn; no wheelchair accessibility*

ST. STEPHEN'S CATHEDRAL OF HVAR

Trg Sv. Stjepana; 099 576 3019; open 9am-noon, 4pm-6pm

It's impossible to miss the Cathedral of Hvar, as it lies on the main piazza and dominates the city's skyline. The white stone façade is typical of Dalmatian churches and dates from the late Renaissance. The church is dedicated to **St. Stephen,** who is unsurprisingly the patron saint of Hvar. Expect to see artwork inside created by Venetian artists who worked on the cathedral when Hvar was part of the Republic.

i *Admission 10 kn; wheelchair accessible*

MUSEUMS

BENEDICTINE CONVENT AND HANIAL LUCIC MUSEUM

Kroz Grodu bb; 021 741 052; open M-Sa 10am-midnight

Your vegan friends know agave syrup as a healthy alternative to sugar. Our cloistered Benedictine nun friends have been using agave to make lace for hundreds of years. This method of lace production is unique to Hvar. In a small part of the nun's convent is a museum that displays examples of agave lace as well as artwork and artifacts from the history of the convent itself.

i *Admission 10 kn*

FRANCISCAN CHURCH AND MONASTERY MUSEUM

Šetalište put 13; 021 741 193; church open daily 24hr, museum open M-Sa 9am-3pm and 5pm-9pm

The world's most famous *Last Supper* may be in Milan, but Hvar's own rendition in the old refectory of the Franciscan Monastery is nothing to scoff at. Inside, there is a small cloister with the church entrance on the right. The church is an agglomeration of different styles with both Baroque and Gothic influences. For more artwork and Roman artifacts, the museum has a medium-sized collection. Don't miss the massive Last Supper painting and the works by none other than **Ivan Meštrović.**

i *Church admission free, museum admission 35 kn; limited wheelchair accessibility*

STARI GRAD

If your World War II history is a little mixed up, let us set the record straight for you. Stari Grad is not Stalingrad. The only battles waged here are wealthy French tourists competing over a bill at a restaurant. This is the type of town where wine is served by the liter over dinners that last long into the night. It's where the lowkey yachters and upper-middle-class Western European tourists come to get away from the hubbub of their real lives. They're attracted like moths to a light to the historic architecture, relaxed nightlife, and plentiful vineyards, but in numbers much less than neighboring Hvar. So don your striped sailor shirt and do as the yachters do: visit the many breathtaking churches, bike through Ancient Greek vineyards, and stroll along the stone corniche.

GETTING THERE

Stari Grad is on the island of Hvar, which is commonly reached by boats. The Port of Stari Grad is the largest island port on Hvar and is not far from Stari Grad itself. It receives frequent ferries from Split. If you are traveling to Stari Grad from Hvar, you can also take a 20min. bus.

GETTING AROUND

Stari Grad is best explored by foot and you can easily walk to all of the town's sites on foot. The town is situated at the end of an inlet and has characteristically narrow streets.

Swing by...

DOMINICAN MONASTERY OF ST. PETER THE MARTYR
Ul. kod Svetog Petra 1P; open daily 9:30am-12:30pm and 4pm-6:30pm
Art history nerds should know two things about **Tintoretto:** he was Venetian and he's famous. How did one of his paintings end up in this obscure Dominican monastery on a remote Croatian island? Well, a few centuries back this part of the world used to be controlled by Venice under the rule of the Doge (and most definitely not by a doggo or pupper). Beyond Tintoretto's *Pietà*, the church and courtyard of the monastery are beautiful, complete with flower-covered columns and arches. The museum, included with admission, lacks significant English descriptions, but displays important Greek and Roman artifacts from the nearby **UNESCO World Heritage site, Stari Grad Plain.**
i Admission to church and museum 20 kn

Check out...

TVRDALJ CASTLE
Priko b.b.; 922252391; open daily 10am-7pm
Tvrdalj Castle is an innovative take on the cliché rich-people-building-whimsical-castles theme. We expected lots of Renaissance faire kitsch, but were instead rewarded with the melodious poetry of Petar Hektorović and an ethereal fish pond. Without a doubt, ten minutes in this fifteenth-century palace will turn you into a true Andrea Bocelli-loving troubadour ready to sing longingly about your days in this most beautiful of Croatian villas. But we're warning you: inspired locals and travelers alike have written many a poem about this place, so the bar is pretty high.
i Admission 15 kn

Grab a bite at...

CAFÉ BAR ANTIKA ($)
Donja Kola 34; 021 765 479; open daily Feb-Oct noon-3pm and 6pm-1am

Tucked in a side street near the main square, Antika is everything you'd expect from a restaurant in a town called "Old Town." Vintage pepper mills, traditional foods, and plenty of wine are exactly what you'll get here. Grab a wooden menu and squeeze into the dining room or sit outside and enjoy the company of smokers on wooden benches. The offerings are similar to most restaurants in Dalmatia with fish, meat, and pasta.

i *Starters from 25 kn, entrées from 80 kn*

Don't miss...

STARI GRAD PLAIN
Open daily 24hr

It's all Greek to me—at least at Stari Grad Plain, that is. After creating the first settlement at Stari Grad (Pharos), the Greeks divided up the nearby fields into small family plots that have been used continuously for 24 centuries. Within the fields, there is a grid system of roads and dirt trails that connect chapels and ancient ruins that makes hiking or biking easy. Alternatively, you could check out the village of Doland and the Church of St. Michael Archangel for a view of the entire plain. Bike rentals start at 60 kn for half a day. A detailed guide to the ruins and sights of the plain is available from the tourist office.

i *Free; limited wheelchair accessibility; bike rentals from 60 kn*

Top it off at...

EREMITAŽ ($)
Obala hrvatskih branitelja 2; open daily noon-3pm and 6pm-midnight

With the best waterfront views in town and a location in a sixteenth-century hermitage, we're unsure how Eremitaž stays in business with entrees starting at 80 kn. But when something's good, don't question it. Eremitaž is across from the main part of town and a relaxing walk (or dare we suggest, Vespa ride) will get you there in 10 minutes (or less…we didn't actually take a Vespa).

i *Starters from 25 kn, entrées from 80 kn*

OUTDOORS

HVAR'S BEACHES

Open daily 24hr

Walking to east of the Riva, past the ferry landing, you'll find a small pebble beach. If you continue to walk east, there are plenty of rocks and ladders that make swimming and sun-tanning effortless. Another option is to take the 40 kn water taxi to one of the beaches on the **Pakleni Islands.** But why pay, when the water is just as crystal clear in Hvar?

i Beach entry free; water taxi 40 kn; limited wheelchair accessibility

FOOD

🖾 MIZAROLA ($)

Vinka Pribojevica 2; 098 799 978; open daily 11am-11pm

Eating on a budget in Hvar is hard. Eating good food on a budget is damn near impossible. Fortunately, Mizarola is here to help with 55 kn pizzas and 80 kn pastas, which makes it as friendly to the wallet as it is to the stomach. But don't get us wrong: we'd come here even if the prices were the same as the rest of Hvar. The terrace is next to the red-tiled roof of an old chapel and the food is blissfully well-seasoned. Plus, the servers are genuinely nice human beings.

i Pizza from 55 kn, pasta from 80 kn, other entrées from 90 kn; vegetarian options available

ALVIŽ ($)

Dolac 2; 021 742 797; www.hvar-alviz.com; open M-F 6pm-midnight, Sa-Su 6pm-1am

Is the secret to Alviž's pizzas in the tomato garden on the terrace? Years of experience? The local water? We'll never know, but we do know that they quickly churn out pies straight from the oven. Plus, at low prices, it's a sweet relief from the higher priced seafood and meat that most Hvar Town digs serve. If you're not feeling pizza tonight, there are plenty of savory entrées at similar prices, such as vegetable risotto and mussels *alla Buzara*.

i Entrées from 70 kn, pizza from 50 kn; vegetarian options available

GURME TAPAS BAR ($$$)

Ul. Marije Maričić br. 9 predio Groda; 098 192 4150; open daily 6pm-midnight

Traditional yet cool and trendy, Gurme is kind of like the Justin Trudeau of Croatian tapas bars. Sleek bar lights hang next to legs of ham and antique horseshoes. But just like in politics, you might not get everything you want here: portion sizes are small, although the tapas are relatively inexpensive. There are, however, tasting menus with a glass of wine and multiple tapas that make a better value.

i Tapas from 20 kn, tapas tasting with wine 70 kn, wine from 30 kn

RESTAURANT "ROOFTOP LUVIJI" ($$)

Jurja Novaka 6; 091 519 8444; open daily 6pm-1am

Since you'll be paying for overpriced food in Hvar, might as well do it with a view and polka-dotted tablecloths. Rooftop Luviji is located in an alleyway behind the cathedral, which is convenient, but also off the beaten path from the easily spotted restaurants on the **Riva** and **Pijaca.** The food is typical and not outstanding, but the real reason to come here is the picturesque view of the fortress and cathedral.

i Entrées from 100 kn

NIGHTLIFE

🖾 KIVA BAR

Fabrika b.b.; 091 512 2343; open daily summer 9pm-2:30am

We're pretty sure Croatia is in the EU and even surer that the EU bans smoking inside buildings, but Bar Kiva doesn't give a shit. Wild stuff happens here. People are packed into small spaces where strangers will grind on you—not out of attraction, but instead by being pushed by other strangers trying to get a drink from the bar. Don't be surprised to see fiery sparklers, girls dancing on the bar, and spilled alcohol. If you're looking for an experience akin to fighting your way through a mosh pit, though, look no further than Bar Kiva.

i No cover, cocktails from 50 kn

CAFÉ BAR ALOHA

Fabrika 15; 91 514 27 66; bar open daily 5pm-2am

Café by day, bar and wannabe club by night, Café Aloha is typical of the nightlife on the **Riva**. It's overpriced, there are gimmicky cocktails, and, if you can afford it, you can order literal fishbowls of alcohol. While the bar is acceptable, do not come for the coffee, as they're the only café in Croatia that didn't give us water with our cappuccino. We have standards.

i No cover, cocktails from 50 kn

CARPE DIEM

Riva 32; 021 742 369; www.carpe-diem-hvar.com; open daily 9am-2am

Rain drop, drop top, where that Dom Perignon pop pop? That would be at Carpe Diem, where the luxe yachters come to walk on the literal red carpet and pretend that Hvar is the French Riviera. Drinks are priced accordingly. In high season, the club goes until late in the morning. Outside there is a nice lounge with ridiculously comfy wicker sofas for those who would like a more relaxed party.

i No cover, drinks from 50 kn; may need reservations in high season

KONOBA KATARINA

Kroz Grodu 22; 095 547 5438; open daily 10am-11pm

This is the Croatian family wine cellar you never had. We're talking stone floors and ceilings, demijohns, and homemade wooden seating. There are even family photos. The place has old-world vibes, which happens to be our kind of vibes. Though the appetizers are limited and expensive, the glasses of wine are some of the cheapest in Hvar. Enjoy a glass on the steps or inside as you turn back time and savor a quiet, laid-back night on the island.

i Wine from 8 kn, appetizers from 50 kn

SPLIT

Coverage by **Gavin Moulton**

Thoughts about Balkan cities don't typically conjure images of palm trees, but then again Split is far from your average Balkan city. There are plenty of Roman monuments to gawk at, cliffs to jump off, and works of art to admire. But, in reality, you don't need to make much of an effort to enjoy Split. This is a place to do one of two things: relax and party. Split is where everyone goes to pregame for their individual island vacations. That said, let's be real. If your idea of a good time happens to be dancing at the Ultra music festival or partying on the beach until 6am, Split has much in store for you.

ORIENTATION

Split is easily walkable and therefore not really divided into separate regions. If we were to Split it, though, we'd say there are two main parts: **Old Town** and the waterfront **Riva.** To be frank though, the entire city could fit inside **Diocletian's Palace,** which is front and center in Old Town. Weave through the tiny, compact streets of Old Town Split to uncover all its nooks and crannies, including but not limited to shops, restaurants, and museums. Just south of Old Town lies the renowned **Riva,** best known for its breathtaking views of the Dalmatian coast and lively nightlife scene. If you're looking to escape, the neighborhoods flanking Old Town, **Veli Varos** and **Manus,** offer a quaint reprieve.

ESSENTIALS
GETTING THERE

If flying, you'll have to get transport to Split from either Zagreb Airport or Dubrovnik Airport. There are daily flights by Croatia Airlines between these cities and Split. We highly recommend flying from Dubrovnik (or taking a 14hr bus... the choice is yours). From Zagreb, Split is approximately a 7hr bus or train ride. Bus schedules and tickets are available at Zagreb Bus Terminal. The best way to book a train is to look up schedules for Croatia Railways. Split also has a massive ferry port that connects to several Croatian islands; the only international connection is, however, to Italy.

GETTING AROUND

The attractions in Split's Old Town are easily walkable; the streets are so narrow that car or rail travel is impossible and illogical. Public buses connect the Split city center with the suburbs, as well as neighboring cities like Omis (Bus #60) and Trogir (Bus #37). Tickets can be purchased at Tisak kiosks or on the bus.

PRACTICAL INFORMATION

Tourist Offices: Main tourist office (Peristil; 02 134 80 74; open M-Sa 8am-9pm, Su 8am-8pm)
Banks/ATMs/Currency Exchange: ATMs are located throughout the town. There are plenty located on the Riva such as Splitsha Banks ATMs. ATMs in Croatia typically dispense cash in 100 and 200 kn bills, which can get annoying.
Post Offices: Papandopulova Ul. 1; 02 134 80 74; open M-F 7am-8pm, Sa 7am-1pm
Internet: There are several cafés with free Wi-Fi in Split. There are other public hotspots like the Riva and Fish Market.
BGLTQ+ Resources: LGBT Center Split (Ul. kralja Tomislava 8; 91 620 8990)

EMERGENCY INFORMATION

Emergency Number: 112
Police: Mike Tripala br.6; 192
US Embassy: The US Embassy is located in Zagreb at Ul. Thomasa Jeffersona 2; 1 6612 200; open M-F 8am-4:30pm
Hospitals: Hospital Firule (Spinčićeva 1; 21 556 111)
Pharmacies: Bačvice Kralja Zvonimira 2; 21 482 830

ACCOMMODATIONS

🏠 SPLIT WINE GARDEN HOSTEL ($)

Poljana Tina Ujevića 3/3; 098 480 855; reception open 24hr

Sweet, sweet air-conditioning. If you've been missing this American staple, Split Wine Garden Hostel will hook you up. Their recently renovated rooms and relaxed wine terrace vibes are a nice break from the ubiquitous Split party hostel. Located on the **Marjan** side of Split, it's a longer haul from the train-ferry-bus station and not ideal for a late arrival. Regardless, the staff is friendly and the vine-covered terrace is a perfect space to get to know fellow travelers.

i Dorms from 160 kn; reservation recommended; Wi-Fi; linens included; towels included; luggage storage

DESIGN HOSTEL GOLI+BOSI ($$)

Morpurgova Poljana; 021 510 999; www.golibosi.com; reception open 24hr

What is a design hostel? We sure don't know and we doubt that Goli+Bosi knows either. But it's got futuristic lockers that open with a keypad, optical-illusion-style hallways lathered in yellow, and a swanky restaurant-bar combo. The hostel is ultra clean and the ensuite bathroom and shower are a definite plus. The downside is that Goli+Bosi feels more like a hotel than a hostel with hella impersonal staff and a lack of community bonding spaces.

i Dorms from 200 kn; reservation recommended; Wi-Fi; linens included; towels included

HOSTEL KISS ($)

Stari Pazar 2; 095 838 4437; reception open 9am-1pm and 3pm-9pm

That moment when you run out of money but your plane doesn't leave until next week is the kind of desperation that should lead you to Split's budget king: Hostel Kiss. Though not major, the general mustiness may worsen any allergies, colds, or stuffy noses you arrived with and you'll have to hold the shower head yourself, but it's survivable as long as you don't forget your keys after 9pm. If that happens you'll be stuck with a locked door and forced to sleep on the streets of Split until the police make you move—all hypothetically speaking of course. But granted, it's half the price of every other hostel in town and has a helpful staff.

i Dorms from 140 kn in summer, 100 kn during off-season; Wi-Fi; linens included; towels included

SIGHTS
CULTURE

🖼 CROATIAN NATIONAL THEATER

Trg Gaje Bulata 1; 021 306 908; www. hnk-split.hr

The performances at the Croatian National Theater are truly straight out of *Amadeus*. The 1893 theater itself was constructed in **Neoclassical style** and its interior is reminiscent of the great opera houses of Europe, down to the red velvet chairs and gilded box seating. Throughout the year, the theater puts on operas, ballets, and concerts—all at dirt cheap prices. So don your cleanest, least wrinkled shirt and try not to be intimidated by the elegantly dressed and music-loving locals as you take a break from the sun and soak up some culture.

i Tickets from 25 kn; wheelchair accessible; dress code semi-formal

LANDMARKS

CATHEDRAL OF ST. DOMINUS

Ul. Kraj Svetog Duje 5; open M-Sa 8am-7pm, Su 12:30pm-6:30pm

Split's center fits entirely within the former **Palace of Diocletian,** and, within what was Diocletian's mausoleum, is the Cathedral of Split. This must-see is one of the most important monuments remaining of the Roman Empire and a **UNESCO World Heritage Site** (casual, we know). From the many parts of the complex, we recommend seeing the cathedral itself and the bell tower. Not for the faint of mind, body, or spirit, prepare yourself for the hike up remarkably small steps and be rewarded with stunning city views. The main building of the cathedral dates back to the time of Diocletian, but has undergone extensive renovation, with architectural elements from the Romanesque and Baroque periods.

i Admission 45 kn; limited wheelchair accessibility

PROKURATIVE (TRG REPUBLIKA)

Trg Republika; open daily 24hr

The Prokurative is St. Mark's Square minus all the pigeons. The Republic Square, built in the 1880s, is heavily inspired (read: plagiarized) from Venetian sources. Located just outside the confines of **Diocletian's Palace,** the reddish-pink buildings frame the ocean in a three-sided *piazza* filled with cafés. During the summer season, be on the look-out for concerts and other public events frequently held here.

i Free; wheelchair accessible

MUSEUMS

🖾 GALERIJA MEŠTROVIĆ

Šetalište Ivana Meštrovića 46; 021 340 800; www.mestrovic.hr; open Tu-Sa 9am-4pm, Su 10am-3pm

Ivan Meštrović is the one Croatian artist you've never heard of, but really should have. He's essentially Rodin, minus most of the fame. The little celebrity status that Meštrović enjoyed, however, was enough to afford a giant villa and, once you're that rich, does fame truly matter? Ponder this philosophical question while gazing at Meštrović's mesmerizing secessionist sculptures located inside the villa, out in the surrounding garden, and in a chapel 200m down the street. The artist's works were influenced heavily by religious and classical themes, so you can finally put those years of high school Latin (and Sunday school) to use.

i Admission 15 kn

MUZEJ GRADA SPLITA (SPLIT CITY MUSEUM)

Papalićeva 1; 021 360 171; www.mgst.net; open M-Su 8:30am-9pm

The Split City Museum is a giant guide to all the history you'll experience but fail to fully understand in downtown Split. Something we learned, for example: locals used to fear the **Egyptian sphinxes** brought by our homie, **Emperor Diocletian,** because they thought the sphinxes cast bad luck. The museum's collection covers Split's history from present and the building is an attraction in itself. The second floor's Gothic ceiling, for example, is one of the few remaining pieces of **Gothic architecture** in the city.

i Admission 20 kn, students 10 kn

OUTDOORS

🖾 PARK MARJAN

Obala Hrvatskog narodnog preporoda 25; open daily 24hr

While you can't have stacks on stacks on stacks because Split will drain your wallet, you can have stairs on stairs on stairs at Park Marjan. Overlooking Split, Park Marjan is the giant mountain (okay, maybe not giant, but large enough to substitute for leg day at the gym) topped with a cross and the Croatian flag. The heavily forested area offers splendid views as you huff and puff and blow your house down… or just breath heavily while working off a week's worth of risotto. **Pro tip:** bring water and food as after **Teraca Vidilica,** there is only one water pump and nowhere to purchase sustenance.

The stairs to the park are located on the western side of Split; just keep going uphill and you'll get there eventually, we promise.

i Free; no wheelchair accessibility

BAČVICE BEACH

Šetalište Petra Preradovića 5; open daily 24hr

This is the most popular beach in Split due to its convenient location and over 20 feet of clear knee-deep water. More importantly, it's also the home of *picigin,* a game of group hacky sack played with a racquetball that will put your family beach volleyball tournaments to shame. The falls of players here are more dramatic than an Italian soccer player trying to get his opponent a red card. The beach is also **blue flag certified,** meaning it's one of the cleanest in Europe. At night, the many bars and restaurants on the beach come to life with parties in the high season lasting until the wee hours of the morning.

i Free; wheelchair accessible

FOOD

KONOBA GREGO LEVANTE ($$$)

Radovanova 2; 021 488 488; www.pizzeria-bakra.com; open daily 9am-11pm

Grego Levante should really make their own rendition of the classic "What Would I Do For A Klondike Bar" jingle, because we would seriously do some crazy shit for anything on the menu here. This is the food you will dream about, Instagram about, and then dream about again. What's not to like with an emphasis on fresh and local ingredients, the friendliest servers in Split, and prices better than competitors. The menu focuses on specialties of the region such as *pastičada,* a typical meat dish with gnocchi.

i Entrées from 60 kn

ARTIČOK ($$)

Bana Josipa Jelačića 19; 095 670 0004; open M-Th 9am-11pm, F-Sa 9am-midnight

Artichoke puns aside, there are art puns. The interior walls of this restaurant are covered in murals that would fit perfectly in a modern art museum. Adding to the cultured theme is the jazz music that's as smooth as the tomato sauce they put on their oh-so-good homemade gnocchi. Prices are slightly lower compared to the bland tourist trap restaurants in **Diocletian's Palace,** but what makes Artičok a gem is a more authentic gastronomic experience that includes dishes outside of traditional Dalmatian cuisine.

i Entrées from 60 kn

LUKA ICE CREAM & CAKES ($)

Ul. kralja petra svačića 2; 091 908 0678; open daily 9am-midnight

With the exception of **Gelateria Spalato,** the quality of ice cream in the rest of Split pales in comparison to Luka. Luka, however, undoubtedly takes the cake for the best value with their massive (and we mean *massive*) scoops. Its charming café vibe and seasonal flavors are also major game changers. If you're lucky enough to summer in Split, enjoy your ice cream at an outdoor shop around the corner from the main café under the gaze of a giant mural of a Roman emperor. I scream for Luka's ice cream; *et tu, Brute?*

i Scoops 8 kn

RESTORAN ŠPERUN ($$)

Šperun ul.; 021 346 999; open daily 9am-11pm

The Croatia of yesteryear may not survive in the straight-off-the-cruise ship swamped **Riva,** but it does at Restaurant Sperun, located in the less touristy Varoš neighborhood. The vibe is pure *Roman Holiday:* checkered tablecloths, old prints, and model ships. Only the *bocca della verità* hasn't come out to play. Soups and pastas are well within even the most constrained backpacker's budget, while splurge options include grilled meats and fish. If Audrey Hepburn doesn't show up, you can console yourself with the highly recommended *zuppa inglese* dessert. Either way, you're #blessed.

i Soups from 30 kn, pasta from 60 kn, meat and fish entrées from 100 kn

NIGHTLIFE

BAČVICE

5 Šetalište Petra Preradovića; 091 883 3710; www.zyhdi-munisi.com/zbirac; open M-Th 7am-1am, F-Sa 7am-2am, Su 7am-1am

If you go where the night takes you in Split, you're bound to end up at Bačvice. When all else fails and the downtown bars shut down, Bačvice will be faithfully waiting for you with its clubs and alcohol flowing and going late into the morning. Yes, it's a bit of a walk from downtown. Yes, the clubs could be a little bit nicer. And yes, it's easy to fall into the water because the sidewalks don't have guardrails. But that might not be the worst thing—after a long night of drunken debauchery, there's nothing like a sunrise swim to cure a hangover.

i Cocktails from 30 kn

ACADEMIA GHETTO CLUB

Dosud 10; 091 197 7790; open Tu-Th 4pm-midnight, F-Sa 5pm-1am, Su 4pm-midnight

People come here to rage, but not in the all-you-can-drink-pub-crawl kind of way. It's more like the, "Let's have stimulating intellectual conversation while dancing and drinking gin" kind of way. Thus, it's not super surprising that this is one of the few places in Split well stocked with absinthe. Never fear: should absinthe not suit your taste, but another niche alcohol would, go for the specials on Armenian brandy and then head outside to Academia's spacious courtyard to talk like Hemingway.

i Beer from 20 kn, cocktails from 50 kn

CAFFE BAR SKALINA

Obala Hrv. Nardnog preporoda 20; 021 344 079; open daily 9am-11pm

Lying on the **Riva**, Split's landscaped limestone path that rings the harbor, is a series of bars with overpriced drinks and over-eager tourists. One of those bars is Caffe Bar Skalina. Typical of the variety on the Riva—bars that are slightly less classy than their bougier cousins in France—most drinks are in the 60 kuna range. It wouldn't be our first choice, but, for the Riva, it does the trick.

i Drinks from 60 kn, gelato from 30 kn

PARADOX WINE & CHEESE BAR

Bana Josipa Jelačića 3; 021 787 778; open daily 8am-midnight

With a selection of wines that range from the affordable (26 kn) to the ungodly priced (120 kn) per glass, Paradox Wine & Cheese Bar is a great place to test out if you can actually fake your way through a wine tasting. Take this as an opportunity to learn about the rich varieties of Croatian wine, as Paradox's offerings are arranged by type on the extensive menu. While we're not whining about the wine selection, the cheese and bread sides can be a bit pricey. Pro tip: this isn't the place to end your night, but rather a spot to kick it off.

i Wine from 26 kn, starters from 50 kn

ZAGREB

Coverage by **Gavin Moulton**

Ever wondered what it would be like to live somewhere where everyone was just zen? Look no further than Croatia's capital: Zagreb, otherwise known as the epicenter of chill. What do the one million inhabitants of Zagreb do for fun? Banter in cafés or hang at bars. We recommend you follow their lead—take part in the laid-back lifestyle as you let your taste buds savor melted cheese, let your eyes take in both contemporary and ancient art, and let the night take you to some of the most interesting bars Europe has to offer. Zagreb is the perfect antidote to the high prices of Vienna and an oasis after the party scene of Berlin. With the world's shortest funicular, good craft coffee, and brewery startups, we're not complaining.

ORIENTATION

Zagreb is Croatia's capital, located in the northwestern region of the country. If you count the surrounding Zagreb country, Zagreb is the only Croatian city with a population of over one million people, but, that said, it doesn't feel that large. The city center, known as **Upper Town,** is famous for landmarks such as the **Zagreb Cathedral** and the very photogenic **St. Mark's Church.** In Upper Town lies **Trg bana Jelačića** (Governor Jelačić Square), the home of crowds and the largest tram stop in Zagreb. Many tourist destinations are concentrated in this area, which is also characterized by Austro-Hungarian architecture that lends it a charming old-timey feel. On the northern end of Upper Town is **Gradec,** the oldest region of Zagreb that is easily accessible via the funicular. Just south of **Upper Town** (and perhaps a bit obviously) lies **Donji grad** (Lower Town). This area has a more modern feel than its northern neighbor with more urban spaces and office buildings.

ESSENTIALS

GETTING THERE

The best way to get into Zagreb is by plane. Franjo Tuđman Airport, more commonly known as Zagreb Airport, is the largest airport in Croatia and serves many airlines, both domestic and international. From within Europe, travel to Zagreb by train, docking at Zagreb Central Station (Trg kralja Tomislava 12). Like the airport, the train station is the largest and busiest in all of Croatia, making it the main hub of the Croatian Railways network. Traveling in and out of Zagreb is also possible via bus at the station located at Avenija Marina Držića 4.

GETTING AROUND

Zagreb has a functioning tram system with major hubs at Ban Jelačić Square and by the Zagreb Central Station. Tickets (10 kn during the day) are valid for 90min. If you don't want to walk to Upper Town, you can take the funicular (4 kn); Zagreb's funicular is the shortest inclined railway in the world. At the city outskirts, you must make the switch to Zagreb's buses.

PRACTICAL INFORMATION

Tourist Offices: Tourist Information Centre (Trg Bana J. Jelčića 11; 01 481 40 51; open M-F 8:30am-9pm, Sa 9am-6pm, Su and holidays 10am-4pm)
Banks/ATMs/Currency Exchange: ATMs are located throughout the city, but most ATMs will dispense money in 200 and 100 kn bills. An exchange office is located at the bus station.
Post Offices: Hrvatska pošta (Jurišićeva ul. 13; open M-F 7am-8pm, Sa 7am-2pm)
Internet: The many coffee shops and cafés of Zagreb serve as Wi-Fi hotspots. Trg bana Jelačića also offers free public Wi-Fi.
BGLTQ+ Resources: Iskora (Petrinjska ul. 27; 091 244 4666)

EMERGENCY INFORMATION

Emergency Number: 112. The American Embassy in Croatia also maintains an emergency number for American citizens: 01 661 2400.
Police: Petrinjska ul. 30; 192
US Embassy: There is a US Embassy in Zagreb (Ul. Thomasa Jeffersona 2; 1 6612 200; open M-F 8am-4:30pm).
Rape Crisis Center: Centre for Women War Victims - ROSA (Kralja Drzislava 2; 1 4551 142; open daily 10am-6pm)
Hospitals: Clinical Hospital Center Zagreb (Šalata 2; 1 49 20 019)
Pharmacies: Gradska Ljekarna Zagreb (Trg Petra Svačića 17; 01 485 65 45)

ACCOMMODATIONS

⬛ SUBSPACE HOSTEL ($)

Ul. Nikole Tesle 12; 1 481 9993; www.sub-spacehostel.com; reception open 24hr

Subspace is not subpar, unless you're claustrophobic, that is. Instead of bunks, this newly opened hostel has space capsules stacked on top of each other. Each one is soundproof and comes equipped with a mirror, blue mood lighting, and a TV. The space theme extends to the bathrooms where you shower inside a "regeneration unit" that, in reality, is a large repurposed industrial pipe. The ceiling glows with a mural of the stars and the whole hostel is covered with sci-fi themed art. We're still trying to figure out why the bathroom doors are so damn hard to close and why you have to unlock the hostel door before you exit—rookie errors we suppose.
i Dorms from 170 kn; reservation recommended; Wi-Fi

HOSTEL CHIC ($$)

Pavla Hatza 10; 1 779 3760; www.hostel-chic.com; reception open 2pm-11pm

Chic is a word that describes a Parisian fashion show, not a budget hostel with purple and green walls. If you can overlook this poor usage of the French

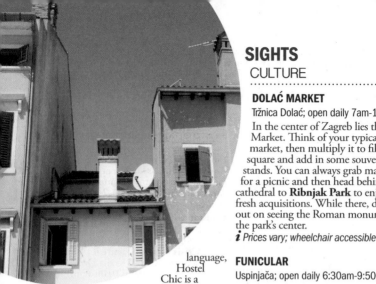

SIGHTS
CULTURE

. . . .

DOLAĆ MARKET

Tržnica Dolać; open daily 7am-1pm

In the center of Zagreb lies the Dolać Market. Think of your typical farmer's market, then multiply it to fill a city square and add in some souvenir stands. You can always grab materials for a picnic and then head behind the cathedral to **Ribnjak Park** to enjoy your fresh acquisitions. While there, don't miss out on seeing the Roman monument in the park's center.

i Prices vary; wheelchair accessible

FUNICULAR

Uspinjača; open daily 6:30am-9:50pm

When you have an opportunity to ride the world's shortest funicular for 75 cents, go for it. Although built in the late nineteenth century to practically connect the **Uper** and **Lower Towns,** today it's used more by tourists than locals. Like all of Zagreb's public transit, the funicular is blue and easily spotted on the hillside. But if you're not one to roll out those 4 kuna, there are steps located parallel to the funicular.

i Ride 4 kn; funicular runs every 10min.; wheelchair accessible

KAMENITA VRATA (STONE GATE)

Kamenita ul; open daily 24hr

The Stone Gate is the only surviving gate from Zagreb's medieval heyday when walls defended the Upper Town against attack. Today, the gate is most notable for the small chapel dedicated to an icon of Mary. Although a street runs through the gate, there are pews on one side and a small shop sells candles to the faithful. At almost any hour of the day, several members can be found praying at the shrine.

i Free; wheelchair accessible

language, Hostel Chic is a comeback kid, as it's a solid, centrally located budget option. Many of the rooms have balconies, which is a definite plus considering the hostel's social spaces are relatively small. Unlike the other comeback kid, Joe Montana, however, "The Catch" to Hostel Chic is not positive: namely, the small kitchenette (emphasis on the -ette) is *très petite* indeed.

i Dorms from 85 kn, privates from 260 kn; reservation recommended; Wi-Fi; kitchen

HOSTEL SWANKY MINT ($$$)

Ilica ul. 50; 1 400 4248; www.swanky-hostel.com; reception open 24hr

You shouldn't need any encourage-mint to stay at this establish-mint, but, in the rare case that the "Best Hostel in Croatia" commend-mint isn't convincing, let the free towels, locks, and welcome shot of *rakija* do the job. While we wish there were more bathrooms, the proximity to Zagreb's center makes it worth the stay. Swanky, boasting an added cool factor of being converted from an old laundry factory, has a bar-pool complex frequented both by locals and tourists. Although that disrupts the traditional hostel community vibe, if it turns out you're mint to be with someone, you can always upgrade to a private room, no judge-mint.

i Dorms from 150 kn, privates from 520 kn; reservation recommended; Wi-Fi

ST. MARK'S CHURCH

Trg Sv. Marka 5

The colorful tiles on the roof of the thirteenth-century church depicting the coat of arms of Zagreb and Croatia make the perfect photo op to show everyone back home that you are indeed in Croatia. St. Mark's, located across from the **Croatian parliament building** is one of the oldest churches in the city. Its south entrance is particularly notable for its impressive **Gothic portal,** with sculptures.

i Often closed, but the portal may be open to peek inside; wheelchair accessible

LANDMARKS

TUNEL GRIČ

Tomićeva ul; open daily 9am-11:30pm

Need to update your Instagram with James Bond-style dramatic photos of yourself? Tunel Grič is Zagreb's very own air raid shelter turned subterranean pedestrian passageway. Translation: a long tunnel with surprisingly good lighting and dramatic cavernous spaces. If we haven't convinced you yet, where else in the world can you go and walk in a tunnel for fun? (Put your hand down, Montréal. We're in Europe.) Enter the tunnel just to the west of the **funicular,** as there is an art exhibition before the entrance.

i Free; wheelchair accessible

ZAGREB CATHEDRAL

Kaptol ul. 5; 1 481 4727; www.zg-nadbisk-upija.hr

This Cathedral is to Zagreb what St. Stephen's is to Vienna, albeit a smaller, less impressive version, kind of like the city in general. But don't worry, your visit to the tallest building in Croatia is rewarded with gothic architecture and cultural insights. Take, for example, the **Glagolitic script** on the back wall immediately to its right entrance. And, if you didn't know what that was, Glagolitic script is an alphabet that was used for centuries in Croatian religious texts after being introduced by St. Cyril in the ninth century, before he teamed up with his brother, St. Methodius, to create the more widely used Cyrillic.

i Free; wheelchair accessible

ZAKMARDIJEVE STUBE (ZAKMARDI STAIRS)

Zakmardijeve Stube; open daily 24hr

Paris has the Pont des Arts and Rome the Ponte Milvio, and Zagreb the Zakmardijeve Stairs to express their affection through a lovelock. Why stairs, you may ask? These boast the most breathtaking and most romantic view of the city. More than just a set of stairs, they connect the lower town to the upper town and lead to the **Gradec Plateau,** next to **St. Catherine's Church,** which is also a highly recommended viewpoint. So, if the **Museum of Broken Relationships** isn't working with your significant (or soon-to-be significant) other, maybe this will do the trick.

i Free; no wheelchair accessibility

MUSEUMS

🖼 MUSEUM OF CONTEMPORARY ART

Av. Dubrovnik 17; 1 605 2700; www.msu.hr; open Tu-Su 11am-6pm, Sa 11am-8pm

Maybe it's the violins hanging from the ceiling or the museum's Brutalist concrete architecture, but the Museum of Contemporary Art feels like a scene from a dystopian nightmare. The wacky exhibits waiting inside don't help either. We're talking naked women laying on trees, optical illusions, and giant piles of coconuts. But the real reason to take the 15-minute tram out to **Novi Zagreb** is the **three-story slide.** It does not disappoint. Should you want to see Croatian modern art but don't want to make the trek out south, check out the **Moderna Galerija** for similarly mind-bending pieces.

i Admission 30 kn; students, seniors, disabled, groups 15 kn; wheelchair accessible

ARCHAEOLOGICAL MUSEUM

19 Nikola Šubića Zrinskog; 1 487 3100; www.amz.hr; open Tu-W 10am-6pm, Th 10am-8pm, F-Sa 10am-6pm, Su 10am-1pm

The world's longest text written in Etruscan? Cremated human remains sitting in the open with no glass? An American sports bar in the middle of a courtyard with Roman sculptures? No, this is not just a natural history museum, funeral home, or restaurant—it's the Zagreb Archaeological Museum. For an entrance fee of a mere 15 kuna, gain access to the best collection of

Egyptian and **Roman artifacts** in Croatia. The renovated first and second floors feature stellar English descriptions, while the **Stone and Bronze Age** content on the third floor is translated in orange notebooks found throughout the exhibits. And, if reading all these historical facts stresses you out, relax with a beer in the courtyard restaurant while sitting next to a Roman sarcophagus.

i *Admission 30 kn, students 15 kn, families 50 kn; wheelchair accessible*

MUSEUM OF NAÏVE ART

Sv. Ćirila i Metoda 3; 1 485 1911; www. hmnu.hr; open M-Sa 10am-6pm, Su 10am-1pm

Ever looked at a piece of art and thought "I could paint that"? That's the entire idea behind **naïvism,** the most important movement in twentieth-century Croatian art. Not quite as bizarre as the Museum of Contemporary Art, the **Museum of Naïve Art** keeps it real with a small, but interesting collection. What is naïvism you ask? It's when artists without formal training or experience create works of art. The results may reinforce the value of art school, but they also make for a treasured experience. Expect giant roosters and multicolored cathedrals.

i *Admission 25 kn, students 15 kn*

MUZEJ MIMARA

Rooseveltov trg 5; 1 482 8100; www.mimara.hr; open Oct 1-June 30 Tu-W 10am-5pm, Th 10am-7pm, F-Sa 10am-5pm, Su 10am-2pm; July 1-Sept 30 Tu-F 10am-7pm, Sa 10am-5pm, Su 10am-2pm

The Mimara Museum is Zagreb's response to New York's Frick Collection, as it is entirely composed of works from the collections of **Ante Topić Mimara,** Croatia's most famous art collector. It's also where we go for the best non-contemporary art in Zagreb. **Renoir?** Got two of 'em. **Rubens?** You betcha. Strong holdings in impressionist painting and medieval sculpture round out the collection. English descriptions are lacking, but there is a free Wi-Fi guide that works in some galleries.

i *Admission 40 kn, reduced 30 kn; wheelchair accessible*

FOOD

🏠 LA ŠTRUK ($$)

Skalinska 5; 1 483 7701; open daily 11am-10pm

We're never okay with missing an opportunity to eat melted cheese. And if you're like us and didn't grow up with a Croatian grandma, *štrukli* will be a game changer. It is a specialty of the Zagreb region and the only item on the menu at La Štruk. Think cheese strudel baked like lasagna with cheese on top. While the most typical version is baked, the restaurant also has variations—try it in soup or boiled. La Štruk gets major bonus points for the picturesque garden terrace hidden around the corner where you can dine under the warm Croatian sun.

i *Strudel from 30 kn*

🏠 STARI FIJAKER ($)

Mesnička 6; 1 483 3829; starifijaker.hr; open M-Sa 11am-10pm, Su 11am-9pm

If Zagreb were Pawnee and restaurants were people, Stari Fijaker would be Ron Swanson: unapologetically traditional, meat loving, and a little over-the-top—but we aren't complaining. Stari Fijaker will care for your physical, emotional, and spiritual (yes spiritual) needs, with its large portions of hearty Balkan food, comfortable chairs, and large crucifix. (Who doesn't need a bit more Jesus in their life after a week of partying on the Croatian coast?) The menu, with English translations, consists of traditional dishes such as shepherds stew: think goulash with gnocchi, which clearly shows the historical influences on local gastronomy due to its location between Hungary and Italy.

i *Entrées from 80 kn*

BISTROTEKA ($$)

Nikole Tesle 14; 1 483 7711; www.bistroteka.hr; open M-Th 8:30am-midnight, F-Sa 8:30am-1am

Bistroteka is the incarnation of the word "aesthetic." We're talking exposed brick, faux *majolica* floors, and chalkboard walls. Even better than the aesthetic are the reasonably priced starters (30 kuna). Perhaps even more impressive than that is the multi-functionality of the place. Brunch spot? Check. Café? Check. Bar? Dinners, lunches, birthday cakes? Check, check, check, and check. If only we could multitask as efficiently, and deliciously, as Bistroteka.
i Starters and sandwiches from 30 kn, meat entrées from 100 kn

COGITO COFFEE SHOP ($)

Varšavska 11; www.cogitocoffee.com; open M-F 8am-10pm, Sa 9am-7pm

Ditch the ubiquitous street cafés of central Zagreb for the holy grail of coffee. Welcome to Cogito, the pilgrimage destination of in-the-know Zagrebian hipsters, yuppies, and the otherwise cool. This coffee bar is the brainchild of Cogito Coffee Roasters, a 2014 startup dedicated to bringing quality, in-house roasted coffee to the Croatian capital. As you enjoy your artisanal flat white, elderflower juice, or homemade iced tea, don't be jarred by the seemingly eclectic décor: modern art, a vintage map of Africa, and a potted plant. We admit this is a bit over-the-top, but there is additional seating in a non-decorated exterior courtyard.
i Coffee from 10 kn, cappuccino from 14 kn

NIGHTLIFE

🏚 A MOST UNUSUAL GARDEN ($)

Horćanska 3; 091 464 6900; open daily 8am-midnight

A sculpture of an octopus with a giant cucumber in a bathtub is the first thing you'll see at A Most Unusual Garden. This bar is truly unlike anything else in Zagreb, or the world

for that matter. Part-gin bar, part-treehouse, part-wall murals, this joint, frequented by locals, will make you feel like you're a character in *Alice in Wonderland*. Aside from the steampunk décor, there is a large outdoor seating area with steps, tables, and you guessed it, a treehouse—all underneath string lights and empty bottles of gin lit with candles. *i No cover, drinks from 20 kn*

CLUB ROKO

Jarunska 5; 097 659 2000; open daily 8pm-3am

"You can go there, but they play trashy Croatian pop from the 90s," said the university students. "If you want to get lit on a Wednesday, it's the only place," said our bartender. "It's the sole club in the area," confirmed a stranger on the street. And they were all right. Club Roko, a locals-only joint south of the city center, gets going around 1am on weekday nights. No worries if you don't speak Croatian; with live music and the entire club belting out the chorus, you'll learn fast. Those willing to brave the smoke-filled interior will be rewarded with an authentic Zagreb experience and clothes that smell like a chain smoker's.
i No cover, drinks from 25 kn

RAKHIA BAR

Tkalčićeva 45; 098 964 0587; open daily
8am-midnight

The first word you'll learn in Croatia
is probably *rakija*. Found throughout
the Balkans, it's the national drink of
Croatia. And Rakhia Bar has every
type of this brandy imaginable. The
plum flavor is the strongest, but our
favorite was the walnut. But, with
over fifty options, why not find your
personal pick? Just not too many,
otherwise the steampunk interior
might make your stomach turn. If all
fails and Rakhia Bar is full, try out
Bar 45 or the many
other options on **Tkalčićeva Street.**
i No cover, shots from 11 kn

TOLKIEN'S HOUSE

Opatovina 49; 1 485 2050; open daily
8am-midnight

A pub with walls covered in swords,
maps of Middle Earth, and maces?
Now that's what we're Tolkien about.
Note: do not confuse Tolkien's House
with a hobbit house. For those, you'll
have to go to New Zealand. But,
if a small pub with lots of *Lord of
the Rings* paraphernalia and a solid
selection of beers sounds like a good
alternative, check it out on Opatovina
ul., the cooler and more local cousin
of the main bar drag, **Tkalčićeva ul.**
i No cover, beers from 20 kn

CROATIA ESSENTIALS

VISAS

Croatia is a member of the European Union. Citizens of Australia, Canada, New Zealand, the US, and many other non-EU countries do not need a visa for stays of up to 90 days. Citizens of other EU countries may enter Croatia with only their national identity cards. Passports are required for everyone else. Despite being part of the EU, Croatia is not in the Schengen Area, however holders of a Schengen visa are allowed to visit Croatia for up to 90 days without the need of an additional visa.

MONEY

Despite being a member of the EU, Croatia is not in the Eurozone and uses the Croatian kuna (HRK or kn) as its currency.

Tipping: Tipping is not always expected, but often appreciated in Croatia. For bars and cafés, tips are not expected, but it is common to round up the bill. So, if the bill comes to 18 kn, leave 20 kn. Tipping in restaurants is much more common, and you should tip your server about 10% and 15% for really exceptional service. Taxi drivers also do not expect tips, but customers generally round up the bill.

SAFETY AND HEALTH

Drugs and Alcohol: The minimum age to purchase alcohol in Croatia is 18, though technically there is no minimum age to drink alcohol (cheers!). Remember to drink responsibly and to never drink and drive. The legal blood alcohol content (BAC) for driving in Croatia is under 0.05%, significantly lower than the US limit of 0.08%.

Travelers with Disabilities: Croatia is largely not wheelchair accessible, as many of the sights require climbing stairs to reach the main attraction and elevators are not often provided. Streets themselves in Croatia often do not lend themselves to wheelchair travel, as they are not evenly paved and many are cobbled.

BGLTQ+ Travelers: Homosexuality has been legal in Croatia since 1977. It is also illegal to discriminate on the basis of sexuality and production of homophobic material can result in up to one year of imprisonment. There is still controversy, however, and homosexuality is still not widely accepted. Public displays of affection between same-sex couples may be met with hostility.

CZECHIA

Whether it's called Bohemia, Czechoslovakia, the Czech Republic, or now, as of a 2016 government initiative, Czechia, is the golden child of Eastern Europe. But, on the surface, the country's history follows the same old Eastern European sob story: it was part of big, fancy imperial powers (the Holy Roman Empire and the Austro-Hungarian one) from the Middle Ages until the First World War, independent until the Germans crashed the party in 1939, Nazi-occupied until the USSR said otherwise in 1945, Soviet-occupied despite Czech attempts to say otherwise, and otherwise enjoying this whole democracy thing since 1989. But dig a little deeper and some idiosyncrasies begin to pop up. From 1335 until 1437, the Kingdom of Bohemia wasn't just part of the Holy Roman Empire; Prague was the home of its imperial court. During the Second World War, it wasn't just any Nazi-occupied territory, but the only one to successfully assassinate a senior Nazi. When communism fell, it wasn't the result of any old revolution, but the Velvet Revolution, which implemented democracy without the loss of a single life.

Walking through the fairytale streets of Prague, the kaleidoscopic valley of Karlovy Vary, the rolling mountains of Bohemian Paradise Nature Park, or the skull and bone-laden chapel of Kutna Hora, you, like a person looking through movies filed under "Children's Fantasy" on Netflix, will find yourself enchanted. Spawning the likes of Franz Kafka, Antonin Dvořak, Sigmund Freud, and Ivana Trump, Czechia is a collection of many pretty faces, and over the years, it's attracted a formidable number of backpackers, beer-drinkers, outdoor enthusiasts, elderly tour groups, and bachelor parties.

KARLOVY VARY

Coverage by **Nicholas Grundlingh**

Unless you're a connoisseur of the world's hot springs, you've probably never heard of Karlovy Vary. But if you're a James Bond fan, you've probably already seen it. The home of the titular casino in *Casino Royale,* Karlovy Vary, with its thermal springs, architectural beauty, and walking trails, is the ideal place for a secret agent to kick back and relax while simultaneously thwarting evil in a high-stakes poker game. Although just two-hours west of Prague, this quaint spa town feels a million miles away from the city's bachelor parties. But the spa isn't the only place where you'll find some peace and quiet. A sense of serenity unspools itself as you walk amongst the gorgeous neo-this and art-that buildings that line the Tepla River, the grandest and largest of which is the 132-meter-long Mill Colonnade, while the most out of place of which is the brutalist Soviet-era Hotel Thermal. When you're in need of a pick-me-up, take a hike or funicular ride up Friendship Hill and meet someone new. It would be too generous to say the town has a young, trendy feel. It really only comes to life during the first week of July, when Eastern Europe's biggest film festival draws over 10,000 hipsters, cinephiles, and celebrities to Karlovy Vary for a week-long party. If you have even the smallest cinematic bone in your body, you would be wise to join them. After visiting one tourist-overrun European capital after another, a couple of days in Karlovy Vary is the perfect way to rejuvenate.

ORIENTATION

The **Ohře River** divides the greater region of Karlovy Vary into two parts, and the majority of the town's action (see: spas, colonnades, accommodations, restaurants, bars, museums) takes place south of it. This small southern area is itself split into two sections—north and south of the **Mill Colonnade.** If you're traveling from Prague via the more convenient bus option, you'll arrive north of the Mill Colonnade, either at the Tržnice bus terminal just north of the town's center or **Dolní nádraží,** the main bus station located a few minutes to the west. The former station serves most of the local bus lines, which travel to Moser glassworks factory, **Loket Castle,** and other surrounding areas. Following **T. G. Masaryka** street to the east will lead you to the **Tepla River.** Walking south along the river, you'll pass the best examples of the town's stunning architecture, the **Metropolitan Theater,** the **Karlovy Vary Museum,** as well as many historic landmarks, such as the **Hotel Thermal,** and the **Mill and Spring Colonnades.**

ESSENTIALS

GETTING THERE

The most convenient way to get to Karlovy Vary from Prague is via bus, which will disembark at either the Tržnice bus terminal or Dolní nádraží, the main bus station, which is a 5min. walk from the center. A map of the bus stops in Karlovy Vary can be found online. Alternatively, if you're arriving via train, you will arrive at Horni Nadrazi, located north of the city center across the Ohře River. It's a 10min. walk from the station to the city center, but it's much more convenient to wait for bus #1 or 13, both of which are one stop away from Tržnice bus terminal.

GETTING AROUND

Karlovy Vary is very walkable, and it takes around 25min. to walk along the Tepla from the bottom of the town to the Grandhotel Pupp at the top. A bus system (a map of the stops can be found at www.dpkv.cz/cz/mapa-zastavek-mhd) can take you around the main town as well as to places in the greater Karlovy Vary region (bus #1, 16, 22, and 23). Ticket options include: single trip (18Kč), 24hr (80Kč), 7-days (220Kč). Two night bus lines run from 10:30pm into the early hours of the morning. Intercity buses that run across Czechia can be taken to the Loket Castle, a 30min. journey.

PRACTICAL INFORMATION

Tourist Offices: T.G. Masaryka street Tourist Office (T.G. Masaryka 53; 355 321 171; open M-F 8am-1pm and 1:30-6pm, Sa-Su 9am-1pm and 1:30-5pm)

Banks/ATMs/Currency Exchange: Many ATMs are found on or nearby T.G. Masaryka street. South of Dvořákovy sady (Dvořák Park), ATMs can be found along the east bank of the Tepla. Try UniCredit Bank (Zeyerova 892/7; 955 959 823; open M -Tu 9am-5pm, W 9am-6pm, Th 9am-5pm, F 9am-4pm). Chequepoint currency exchanges should be avoided; we recommend withdrawing cash from ATMs.

Post Offices: Czech Post (T. G. Masaryka 559/1; 954 330 304; open M-F 7:30am-7pm, Sa 8am-1pm, Su 8am-noon).

Internet: Free Wi-Fi can be found in most cafés in Karlovy Vary.

BGLTQ+ Resources: Czechia is generally considered one of the most liberal Central European nations in terms of BGLTQ+ rights, legalizing same-sex partnerships in 2006. While Czech society is accepting and tolerant, however, BGLTQ+ individuals do not yet have full legal equality. For counseling for BGLTQ+ individuals in Karlovy Vary, try (Palackého 8; 731 549 171; www.ss-po.cz).

EMERGENCY INFORMATION

Emergency Number: 112
Police: 158; The City Police station (Moskevská 913/34, 353 118 911).
US Embassy: The nearest US Embassy is in Prague (Tržiště 365/15; 257 022 000; open M-F 8:15am-11:30pm).
Rape Crisis Center: There is no Rape Crisis Center in Karlovy Vary, but there is one located in Prague.
  • Elektra (Chomutovická 1444/2; 603 812 361; www.centrumelektra.cz; open W, F 9am-4pm).
Hospitals: The general emergency number is 353 115 640.
  • Karlovarská krajská nemocnice (Bezručova 19; 353 115 111; open daily 24hr)
  • Policlinics (náměstí Dr. M. Horákové 1313/8; 353 112 213; open M-F 6:30am-6pm)
Pharmacies: Dr. Max (Horova 1223/1; 353 233 900; open M-F 7am-7pm, Sa-Su 8am-8pm)

ACCOMMODATIONS

⬛ HOTEL KAVALERIE ($$)

T. G. Masaryka 53/43; 353 229 613; www.ka-valerie.cz; reception open daily 7:15am-6pm

If Karlovy Vary is indeed Coolio's fabled "Gangsta's Paradise," it's no wonder the song never mentions any hostels, seeing as the town has none. Thankfully, Karlovy Vary is home to a few, very affordable three-star hotels, of which Hotel Kavalerie is among the cheapest. Its location along **T. G. Masaryka** positions it smack dab in the middle of the town's nightlife hubs, and only a five-minute walk from the **colonnades.** For a hotel, the amenities are pretty basic—a clean and comfortable room and a free breakfast, but that's about it. That said, after you've spent your whole day walking through what Coolio describes as "the valley of the shadow of death," it will feel like the Ritz.

i Twin from 703Kč; reservation recommended; BGLTQ+ friendly; no wheelchair accessibility; linens included; free breakfast

A. DALIA ($$)

5.Kvetna 1; 222 539 539; www.adalia. hotels-karlovy-vary.com; no reception, check-in from 2pm

With its homey rooms, manicured garden, and friendly owners, A. Dalia is one of the best backup options you could ask for. Yet, while nowhere in Karlovy Vary is ever more than a 10-minute walk away, this B&B, peacefully secluded atop a hill overlooking **Hotel Thermal,** will probably be one of the more strenuous 600-second walks you'll take. Luckily, a nearby bus, which runs to the town center every five minutes, will save you the trouble.

i Singles from 750Kč, twins from 1000Kč; reservation recommended; BGLTQ+ friendly; no wheelchair accessibility

SIGHTS
CULTURE

⬛ KARLOVY VARY INTERNATIONAL FILM FESTIVAL

Ivana Petroviče Pavlova 2001/11; 221 411 011; www.kviff.com

If you had told us that one of Central Europe's biggest and most prestigious film festivals was situated in a small, Czech spa town where drinking hot, blood-tasting water was considered a treat, we would've called you a fat, stinking liar! But look who's got egg on their face now! The Karlovy Vary International Film Festival is as real as it gets. Held in the first week of July, the KVIFF screens over 200 films from nearly 50 countries and attracts around 15,000 visitors. It's by the far the most exciting time to visit the town—clubs, bars, and restaurants pop up everywhere (keep a lookout for something called Aeroport), while the area surrounding **Hotel Thermal**—a brutalist structure built specially for the festival—is full of things to do and drink.

i *Festival pass 1200Kč, reduced 900Kč; one-day pass 250Kč, reduced 200Kč; limited wheelchair accessibility*

🦇 MUNICIPAL THEATRE

Divadelní náměstí 21; 353 225 621; www.karlovarske-divadlo.cz; hours and show times vary

If there's one place in Karlovy Vary that we can't stand, it's the Municipal Theatre. This is partly because it's full of seats, but also because we can't bear its stunning Neo-Baroque beauty. Built in 1884 along the **Vltava River,** the theater is considered one of the country's most magnificent with its interiors painted by a couple of goofy Austrian twenty-somethings named **Gustav and Ernst Klimt.** Their greatest contribution is the incredibly intricate, hand-painted curtain that hangs in front the stage. As far as we can tell, the theater doesn't put on any English-language productions, but it often hosts orchestras, ballets, and operas.

i *Ticket prices vary; wheelchair accessible*

SPRING COLONNADE

Divadelní nám. 2036/2; 353 362 100; open daily 6am-6pm

Karlovy Vary's spring water is probably what a vegetarian vampire would drink, because even though it's 100% natural, it still retains that lovely blood taste. But where would this vampire go to get his fix? The Spring Colonnade, of course! The Colonnade's three natural geysers pump out water at 30°C, 50°C, and 70°C, and hordes of tourists stomach the water's bloody tang in exchange for its abundance of nutrients and minerals. Bring your own water bottle or purchase the traditional spa cups (120-190Kč), which also serve

as a thoughtful souvenir to give to your favorite bloodsucker back home. The floor above functions as a gallery of locally-produced glassworks, while the area below is home to the thermal springs that you can tour every half hour.

i *Free; wheelchair accessible*

LANDMARKS

MILL COLONNADE

Mlýnské nábř.; open daily 24hr

If you walk along the **Tepla River,** you will inevitably come across the Mill Colonnade. It's the *de facto* symbol of Karlovy Vary and one of the most beloved structures in town. In 1871, **Josef Zitek,** the architect behind Prague's National Theatre and Rudolfinum, designed this Neo-Renaissance colonnade, which let spa guests enjoy the spring waters come rain, shine, or one of those pesky nineteenth-century plagues. Pretty cool, right? This next one's even cooler. The structure is 132-meters long and it features 123 columns and an impressive five mineral springs.

i *Free; wheelchair accessible*

MUSEUMS

🦇 MOSER FACTORY AND MUSEUM

Kpt. Jaroše 46/19; 353 416 132; www.moser-glass.com; museum open daily 9am-5pm, factory tours 9:30am-2:30pm

Moser makes glassware like Mercedes Benz makes cars. Yes, in a factory—but also to an insanely high standard. Founded in 1857, this factory has produced some of the most celebrated luxury glassware in Europe, used by everyone from the saint-like Whoopi Goldberg to the hilarious Pope Pius. Most exhibits follow the same basic structure of "Moser did 'x' collection in 'y' year, and it was interesting because [insert uninteresting reason] and owned by 'z' dynasty/celebrity." We highly recommend a 30min. tour of the factory, during which you'll see 1200°C furnaces and sweat-drenched men blowing bubbles of glass.

i *Museum and factory tour 180Kč, reduced 100Kč; factory tour 120Kč, reduced 70Kč; museum 80Kč, reduced 50Kč; wheelchair accessible*

KARLOVY VARY MUSEUM

Nová louka 23; 736 650 047; www.en.kvmuz.
cz; open May-Sept W-Su 10am-6pm, Oct-Apr
10am-5pm

What's the deal with all the spas? Why are there so many colonnades? Did **Goethe's** love affair with a girl 55 years his junior have anything to do with his frequent visits? Did melting butter have anything to do with 97% of the town burning down in 1604? A visit to the Karlovy Vary Museum, which covers the town's modern and prehistoric past, will answer all these burning questions. The highlights include a large model of the town, parts of which you can illuminate to learn more, and an interactive screen with anecdotes about the town's famous visitors, including **Sebastian Bach, Karl Marx,** as well as **Sigmund Freud** and his mother.
i *Regular 100Kč, reduced 60Kč; wheelchair accessible*

OUTDOORS

◪ DVOŘÁK PARK

360 01 Karlovy Vary; open daily 24hr

Nowadays, when someone does something cool, the mayor will give them the key to the city. But back in the day, cool people had a park named in their honor, and the notoriously cool Czech composer **Antonín Dvořák** was no exception. Given that Dvořák was one of the most celebrated late-romantic composers of the nineteenth century, it's no coincidence that the park is one of the most romantic spots in the city. The ornate Neo-Renaissance Park Colonnade forms the southern perimeter, inside which are lush lawns, vibrant flowerbeds, cherry blossoms, and perhaps most romantic of all, a statue of Dvořák himself. The colonnade often hosts concerts during the summer, but you really don't need an excuse to sprawl yourself in the shade of these 200-year-old trees.
i *Free; wheelchair accessible*

FOOD

◪ DOBRA CAJOVNA TEA HOUSE ($)

Bulharská 2; 608 822 827; www.tea.cz/
obsah/27_dc-karlovy-vary; open daily 2pm-
11pm

Whether it's an actor-singer-dancer like Gene Kelly or a talking animal-comedian-corporate spokesperson like the Geico Gecko, we love a triple threat. That's why this vegetarian restaurant-tea house-hookah bar is near the top of our list for places to eat in Karlovy Vary. Inconspicuously located in a basement on **Zeyerova street,** Dobra Cajovna is conspicuously adorned in Middle Eastern and Himalayan décor, with Nepalese prayer flags draped along the ceiling, Islamic geometric patterns covering the walls, and rugs and cushions on the floor. The food menu dabbles in hummus, falafel, and cheese and the drinks menu makes it possible to go around the world in 80 teas.
i *Entrées from 98Kč; vegetarian options available; no wheelchair accessibility*

PANOPTIKUM ($)

Bělehradská 1004/3; 728 520 822; open M-Th 11am-2am, F-Sa 11am-3am, Su 11am-midnight

If you're near the bottom of town and desperate for some authentic Czech goulash/soup/schnitzel/whatever, you better tie yourself to the mast of your ship and resist the siren song of the touristy, restaurant-lined **Zeyerova street** as you make your way to Panoptikum. Just a three minute-walk away from the city center, this pub has portions fit for a future Weight Watcher and drafts on tap fit for a beer connoisseur or current alcoholic. The wooden walls are decorated with old-timey photos that document Czech history, and although there's no outdoor seating, for those of the nicotine-persuasion, there's a smoking area where you can indulge yourself as well as a non-smoking area where you can irritate the nerds who won't shut up about their precious lungs.
i *Entrées from 93Kč; vegetarian options available; limited wheelchair accessibility*

REPUBLICA COFFEE ($$)

T. G. Masaryka 894/28; 720 347 166; www.e-restaurace.cz/u-krizovniku; open M-F 7am-7pm, Sa-Su 8am-7pm

Republica Coffee is a contender for the best café in town, especially if this accolade went to the café with the most tables covered in comic book panels or the comfiest leather armchairs. The coffee is drip, both in the brewing sense and in the-shaking-the-cup-above-your-mouth-to-make-sure-every-last-delicious-drop-drips-into-your-mouth-sense, and the hot chocolate is just the right mixture of creamy and thick. Once you collect your drink, sandwich, or pastry, chillax in the courtyard, or head upstairs and luxuriate in the aforementioned leather chairs.

i Coffee from 45Kč; vegetarian options available; wheelchair accessible

RESTAURACE U KRIZOVNIKU ($)

Moravská 2093/2a; 353 169 500; www.e-restaurace.cz/u-krizovniku; open daily 11am-11pm

Flannery O'Connor might've thought that a good man is hard to find, but finding a tasty, well-priced restaurant south of the colonnades might be even harder. While most places aren't bad per se, they'll leave your wallet at least 250-300Kč lighter. Luckily, this traditional Czech cuisine pub serves good meals and will save you some money. Its paintings on the walls and medieval torches hanging from the ceilings give it an authentic feel, and its location—just to the east of the **Spring Colonnade**—means it's nearby tourist spots but not crawling with them.

i Food from 105Kč; vegetarian options available; limited wheelchair accessibility

NIGHTLIFE

BARRACUDA CARIBBEAN COCKTAIL BAR

Jaltská 7; 608 100 640; www.barracuda-bar.cz; open M-Th 7pm-1am, F-Sa 7pm-3am

After waiting half an hour for the friends you met at the sauna earlier in the day to return from the bathroom downstairs, you might assume you've been abandoned—a feeling that you're all too accustomed to. Seeing as things can't get any worse, you might use the five straws sticking out of the Cuba Libre bucket in front of you to make a giant straw and finish the whole drink in one giant slurp. But don't do that! Your friends haven't abandoned you. They've just discovered the small club hidden downstairs, which, replete with tiki masks and fishnets, echoes the above bar's beachy aesthetic. It's a cozy and slightly cheesy space that can be a ton of fun. But if you're less of a dancer and more of a drinker, the bar's 14-page cocktail menu will make you forget all about your abandonment issues.

i Cocktails from 80Kč, beer from 25Kč; cash only

KLUB PEKLO

Ivana Petroviče Pavlova 2001/11; 728 496 978; open M-Sa 9pm-6am

Occupying the basement of the brutalist high-rise **Hotel Thermal,** Klub Peklo is a monument to Western garishness—a tourist-filled, EDM-blasting space where your level of enjoyment is directly proportional to the number of shots consumed. The club is one large, low-ceilinged room. The bar bananas around a third of the club's perimeter while the center is cluttered with sleek rolling leather chairs and glowing green prisms. A multigenerational melting pot of land dads, and their female equivalents, populate the dance floor, which is presided over by a DJ backlit by an LED screen of someone doing the worm. I

i Cover up to 50Kč; cash only

PRAGUE

Coverage by **Nicholas Grundlingh**

So you want to experience the beauty of Paris, but don't think buying a cappuccino should require taking out a bank loan? You love the edginess of Berlin, but wish that—by virtue of you being a tourist—you weren't immediately excluded from it? You dream of a city that is basically a "Now That's What I Call Music!"-esque compilation of the best architecture from the last thousand years. Where culture and history flood every street, bridge, fortress, and castle, yet despite this, never takes itself too seriously, while also being one of the best places to party in Europe? Why, that sounds an awful lot like Prague! Of course, if you're planning on traveling to Prague, you already know this. You know that the Old Town looks like an illustration from a fairytale, but you'll soon find out that it's one of those fairytales full of tourists. You know that the Charles Bridge and the Prague Castle are indisputable must-sees, but you'll soon find out, with everything else the city has to offer, they certainly won't be your highlights. Get lost amongst the bars, beer gardens, and galleries of the young and grungy Holesovice and Zizkov areas, bask in the unmatched tranquility of the Vysehrad fortress and park, and discover hidden gems in the heart of the city like the underworld bar Vzorkovna, the majestic Wallenstein Gardens, or the magical Karel Zeman Museum.

ORIENTATION

Just like the skull of some punk who got into a fight with the star of *Stand by Me*, Prague is split by a river, which, in this case, is the Vltava River rather than the late River Phoenix. **Josefov** (Jewish Quarter), **Stare Mesto** (Old Town), and **Nove Mesto** (New Town) line the east bank of the river, and **Mala Strana** (Lesser Town) and **Hradcany** (Castle District), line the **West Bank.** Numerous bridges connect the two banks, the most famous of which is the **Charles.** These areas are often populated by hordes of tourists, but you can escape them by heading further inland east to the more local and residential **Zizkov** and **Vinohrady** neighborhoods, or crossing the Vltava north of Stare Mesto, where you'll find the grungy and artsy **Holesovice** district. What these less-touristy areas lack in sights, they make up for in cafés and dangerously chill vibes. The central bus and train stations are located just east of Stare Mesto in the **Florenc District,** while the Vaclav Havel Airport is found about an hour to the west.

ESSENTIALS

GETTING THERE

No direct train or bus lines run from the airport to the city center, but there are buses that connect to metro lines, which will take you into the city. Bus #119 runs from the airport to Veleslavín metro station on the green Line A. Bus #100 runs from the airport to Zličín metro station on the yellow line B. Both these lines will take you into the city center. The total journey is around 40min. Purchase tickets from Public Transport counters in Terminals 1 and 2 from 7am-10pm. Alternatively, use the coin-operated vending machines at the bus stop. Note that drivers usually accept small notes and change. You may need to purchase a half-price ticket (10Kč) for large pieces of luggage. Remember to validate tickets in the yellow machines before boarding any public transport. If you're arriving by train, you'll most likely disembark at Praha Hlavní Nádraží, the main railway station, located between Nove Mesto and Zizkov. The railway station is connected to the metro system (red line C). One stop north will connect you to the yellow line B, and one stop south to the green Line C; both will take you to the city center. Trains along the Berlin-Prague-Vienna/Bratislava route may disembark at the Praha Holešovice station, which is located in the north region of Prague. This station also connects to the metro via red line C. Most international buses disembark at Florenc Bus Station, which is just east of the Old Town.

GETTING AROUND

The public transport system is convenient and consists of three metro lines (green line A, yellow line B, red line C), trams, and buses. The same ticket is used for all forms of public transportation. Ticket options include: 30min. (for tram rides only, or metro journeys up to five stops, 24Kč), 90min. (32Kč), 24hr (110Kč), and 72hr (310Kč). Be sure to validate your ticket in the yellow machines on buses and trams or at the base of escalators in metro stations. Plainclothes police officers will often inspect tickets. They are notoriously strict and will fine you up to 1000Kč if you have not validated your ticket. The metro runs from 5am-midnight, and buses and trams operate from 4:30am-12:15am. Night buses and trams operate less frequently from 12:15am-4:30am. The central point of nighttime transfers is Lazarska in Nove Mesto. Be wary of potential pickpockets on crowded trains, trams, and buses, especially on trams #22 and 23. The minimum taxi fare is 28Kč/km. We recommend that you order a taxi through a dispatch office, where you can get information on fares in advance. Dispatch services that speak English include AAA radiotaxi (222 333 222; aaataxi.cz), Citytaxi Praha (257 257 257; www.citytaxi.cz) and Modry andel (737 222 333; www.modryandel.cz).

PRACTICAL INFORMATION

Tourist Offices: Old Town Hall Tourist and Information Center (Staroměstské náměstí 1; open daily 9am-7pm)
Banks/ATMs/Currency Exchange: ATMs can be found in the city center and tourist areas, belonging to local and international banks. Many are located in or around Wenceslas Square and can generally be found in shopping centers and metro stations. In the city, beware of currency exchanges that charge high commission fees. Exchange (Kaprova 14/13; 800 22 55 88; open M-F 9am-10pm, Sa-Su 9am-8pm) is found in Josefov and known as one of the most reliable currency exchanges.
Post Offices: Czech Post (Jindřišská 909/14; 221 131 445; open daily 2am-midnight)
Internet: Free Wi-Fi can be found at nearly every café, hostel, and most restaurants also provide free Wi-Fi.
BGLTQ+ Resources: Czechia is generally considered one of the most liberal Central European nations in terms of BGLTQ+ rights, legalizing same-sex partnerships in 2006. However, while Czech society is accepting and tolerant, BGLTQ+ individuals do not yet have full legal equality. Here are some resources:
- Gay Iniciativa (gay.iniciativa.cz/www/index) offers a 24hr hotline (476 701 444).
- GLBTI Counseling Center (Cílkova 639/24; 775 264 545; glbtiporadna.unas.cz)

EMERGENCY INFORMATION

Emergency Number: 112
Police: 156; the police headquarters are located directly at the bottom of Wenceslas Square (Jungmannovo nám. 771/9; 974 851 750, 24hr hotline).
US Embassy: The US Embassy (Tržiště 365/15; 257 022 000; open M-F 8:15am-11:30pm) is located in Mala Strana, near Malostranské náměstí).
Rape Crisis Center: There are two rape crisis centers located in Prague, which provide national crisis helplines.
- Elektra (Chomutovická 1444/2; 603 812 361; www.centrumelektra.cz; open W, F 9am-4pm)
- proFem o.p.s (Plzeňská 846/66; 608 222 277; www.profem.cz; open Tu 9am-noon, W 5:30-8:30pm)
Hospitals:
- The University Hospital in Motol (V Úvalu 84; 224 431 111)
- Nemocnice Na Momolce (Roentgenova 37/2; 257 271 111)
Pharmacies: Pharmacies in Prague are known as "Lékárnas."
- Lékárna Palackého (Palackého 720/5; 224 946 982; open daily 24hr)
- Lékárna U Svaté Ludmily (Belgicka 37; 222 513 396)

ACCOMMODATIONS

▨ ART HOLE HOSTEL ($$$)

Soukenická 1756/34, Staré Město; 222 314 028; www.artholehostel.com; reception open 24hr

Art Hole feels more like a communal living area than a hostel. The reception and kitchen areas function as social spaces and the staff prepare nightly dinners that'll make you realize the true meaning of *ohana* (meaning "family"). Like many hostels in Prague, Art Hole only allows 18-to-35-year-olds to stay in its dorms, which injects the place with a youthful energy. The wall murals are a hodgepodge of twentieth-century art, and you'll find the minimalism of **De Stijl**, the maximalism of Warhol, or the mickeyism of Walt Disney in nearly every room you enter. Even though the bathroom space is a little cramped, Art Hole's positives, such as its 5-minute walking distance from the **Old Town Square,** outshine such negatives.

i Dorms from 450Kč during summer; reservation recommended; linens, towels included; laundry facilities; free breakfast

▨ SIR TOBY'S HOSTEL ($)

Dělnická 1155/24, Holešovice; 246 032 610; www.sirtobys.com; reception open 24hr

If you're interested in staying in the hip part of Prague, making friends with fellow travelers, and sleeping in spacious rooms with debunked beds, then Sir Toby's hostel is your knight in shining armor. Found near the bottom of **Holešovice,** Sir Toby's is a short walk away from fantastic cafés, galleries, clubs, and bars, the nearest of which is found in their brick cellar basement. Whether you're participating in a nightly event (game nights, beer tastings, BBQs) or enjoying the 25Kč per beer happy hour, you're guaranteed to meet fellow guests. The **Prague Castle** and **Old Town** are just 10 to 15 minutes away by tram.

i Dorms from 250Kč, singles and twins from 768Kč; reservation recommended; BGLTQ+ friendly; wheelchair accessible; lockers provided; linens included; laundry facilities

ADAM AND EVA ($$)

Zborovská 497/50, Mala Strana; 733 286 804; www.adamevahostelprague.com; reception open 8am-10pm

We have two theories about how this hostel got its name. 1) It possesses the peace and tranquility of the Garden of Eden. 2) It was built using a man's ribs. But then again, these are just theories—why don't we look at the facts? Composed of just two floors, Adam and Eva is as cozy as a cloth you drape over your nether regions. Each floor has a small balcony area that overlooks a courtyard, the reception has a map that points out all the best things to do in the area, and each bottom bunk bed is fitted with a curtain, which gives a sense of professionalism to any puppet shows you might want to put on for fellow guests.

i Dorms from 312Kč, twins from 390Kč; reservation recommended; no wheelchair accessibility; Wi-Fi; linens included; laundry facilities

AHOY HOSTEL ($$$)

Na Perštýně 10, Stare Mesto; 773 00 4003; www.ahoyhostel.com; reception open 24hr

Everyone always talks about how "size matters," but we think location matters more. After all, a penis on an elbow is not sexy. Ahoy Hostel understands this, with its location in the swankier region of **Stare Mesto. Wenceslas Square** is a five-minute walk away. **Charles Bridge** is only double that. The proximity is prime, and while there aren't too many landmarks in the immediate vicinity, tram and metro stations are practically on the hostel's doorstep. Although the hostel's dorms are scarce on charging outlets, its rooms are big on cleanliness and comfort.

i Dorms from 492Kč, twins from 1378Kč; reservation recommended; no wheelchair accessibility; linens included; laundry facilities

CZECH INN ($)

Francouzská 240/76, Vinohrady; 267 267
612; www.czech-inn.com; reception open
24hr

Check in at the Czech Inn and you'll
be overwhelmed with things to check
out! The only Prague member of the
prestigious Europe's Famous Hostels
group, Czech Inn boasts 36-bed dorms
(a budget traveler's dream), a large
and vibrant bar downstairs, as well as
a series of nightly events. Every week,
the basement bar hosts live music
performances as well as one of the few
English-language comedy nights in
Prague, the latter of which is worth
checking out even if you aren't staying
at the hostel. While **Vinohrady** is
a 15min. tram ride away from the
city's main attractions, the hip and
trendy area is littered with less-touristy
restaurants and cafés.
i *Dorms from 125Kč, twins from 975Kč;
reservation recommended; BGLTQ+
friendly; no wheelchair accessibility; linens
included; laundry facilities; breakfast
150Kč*

MOSAIC HOUSE ($$$)

Odborů 278/4, Nove Mesto; 221 595 350;
www.mosaichouse.com; reception open
24hr

"Mosaic House" doesn't just refer
to the assortment of sculptures and
installations that adorn its façade and
entrance, but also its myriad purposes.
A hostel, hotel, restaurant, trendy bar-
lounge, and green building all in one,
this place is truly the Swiss Army knife
of accommodations (by the time this
is published, we assume *Dunkirk* will
have launched Harry's acting career
and he'll be recognized for versatility).
Mosaic House has the feel of a chic
hotel, and as such, prices higher than
those of your average hostel. While
there's a common area in the main
building for hotel and hostel guests
alike, you have to exit the building
to access the kitchen/common room
specific to the hostel, which remains
open until 9pm.
i *Dorms from 416Kč, twins from 3126Kč;
reservation recommended; wheelchair
accessible; Wi-Fi; linens included; laundry
facilities; breakfast buffet 40Kč*

SOPHIE'S HOSTEL ($)

Melounova 2, Nové Město; 246 032 621;
www.sophieshostel.com; reception open
24hr

Although the name may indicate
otherwise, this place is really a hostel of
the people. With nightly events, a 24hr
bar and a 25Kč per beer happy hour,
it's almost impossible not to befriend
fellow guests, which makes it perfect
for solo travelers and a nightmare for
misanthropes. The rooms, like the rest
of the hostel, have a modern and chic
feel. They come mercifully equipped
with a fan, making hot summer nights
bearable. Located in the center of
Nové Město and thus in the center
of Prague, the hostel is near tram and
metro stations.
i *Dorms from 250Kč, double from
1200Kč; reservation recommended;
BGLTQ+ friendly; no wheelchair accessibility; linens included; laundry facilities*

SIGHTS
CULTURE

BIO OKO

Františka Křížka 460/15, Holešovice; 233
382 606; www.biooko.net; show times vary

People get homesick in different ways.
While some tend to miss their mother's
home-cooked meals, others long for
their country's independent cinema.
Bio Oko primarily caters to the latter,
but its café might just have something
to offer the former as well. Screening
three films a day during the week and
five a day on weekends, the movie
theatre showcases local, international,
and American art-house films. When
we visited, Bio Oko was holding a
Christopher Nolan retrospective (or
maybe we just dreamt that it was?) as
well as outdoor summer screenings at
the **Prague Exhibition Grounds.** Even
by Czech standards, the tickets are
extremely affordable, and your options
for reclining are leather chairs, beach
loungers, or giant bean bags.
i *Tickets from 100Kč; wheelchair accessible*

JATKA78

Jatečni 1530, Holešovice; 773 217 127; www.jatka78.cz; open M-F 10am-midnight, Sa 9am-midnight, Su 6pm-midnight

A circus in a slaughterhouse. While it could be the name of some angsty emo band you liked as a teen, it's actually a pretty accurate description of Jatka78. In 2015, a group of performers successfully crowdfunded the conversion of an abandoned slaughterhouse into two theatre halls and a gallery-café space. Throughout the year and more intermittently during the summer, Jatka78 puts on performances as often as once a day. But even if you can't make it to a show, the space alone is worth a visit, with its large snake-like wooden structure that twists and coils itself around the inside of the building.
i Tickets from 250Kč; wheelchair accessible

MEETFACTORY

Ke Sklárně 3213/15, Smíchov; 251 551 796; www.meetfactory.cz; open daily 1pm-8pm, evening programs run later

A night at MeetFactory will drive you up the wall. Not just because of the two red cars vertically hanging above its entrance, but also due to the frustration you'll feel that your middle-of-nowhere hometown doesn't have a concert venue-art gallery-theater space-outdoor cinema as cool as this. The brainchild of "the Czech Banksy" David Cerny, MeetFactory is an industrial space that consistently attracts the biggest names in indie and electronic music, hosts a week-long summer film program, and curates three art galleries.
i Event ticket prices vary; wheelchair accessible

SHAKESPEARE AND SONS

U Lužického semináře 91/10, Malá Strana; 257 531 894; www.shakes.cz; open daily 11am-8pm

Normally, even the best English-language bookstores in non-English-speaking countries pale in comparison to your average Barnes and Noble back home. However, Shakespeare and Sons, which is unaffiliated with but of a similar quality to the famous Shakespeare and Co. in Paris, breaks this trend. The store's selection, while not as large as a Barnes and Noble, is incredibly well curated, meaning that you're just as likely to find the debut novel of the latest literary sensation as you are works by every big name in the Western canon. The poetry, philosophy, and second-hand collections are particularly impressive, and the Czech section is impressively particular, containing almost the entire bibliographies of national sweethearts, **Kafka** and **Kundera.**
i Books from 200Kč; limited wheelchair accessibility

LANDMARKS

 SS. CYRIL AND METHODIUS CATHEDRAL

Resslova 9a, Nove Mesto; 224 920 686; open Tu-Sa 9am-5pm

Quentin Tarantino would have you believe that Brad Pitt was the most notorious Nazi killer of the Second World War, but in truth, it was a group of Czech paratroopers, who, in May 1942, assassinated the architect of the Holocaust, **Reinhard Heydrich.** Unfortunately, the Czechs didn't have much time to celebrate. Three weeks later, the

Germans, who had launched a vicious retaliatory attack on the Czechs, found the assassins hiding out in the crypt of the Ss. Cyril and Methodius Cathedral, and after a heated battle, the remaining paratroopers, in order to avoid capture, took their own lives. Today, the bullet-hole ridden crypt serves as an exhibition and memorial dedicated to the heroes of the assassination. The cathedral represents a part of Czech history that tourists often overlook.

i *Admission 75Kč, reduced 35Kč; no wheelchair accessibility*

🏛 VYSEHRAD

V Pevnosti 159/5b, Vinohrady; 241 410 348; www.praha-vysehrad.cz; open daily Nov-Mar 9:30am-5pm, Apr-Oct 9:30am-6pm

Recommended by nearly every local we met, Vysehrad, a tenth-century fortress, sits atop a rocky promontory overlooking the **Vltava River,** and is the most idyllic spot in the city. Vysehrad served as the royal seat of Bohemia for a glorious 40 years before its role was usurped by **Prague Castle.** Today, the castle building itself no longer exists, but the infinitely tranquil parks and what, in our opinion, is the most stunning church in Prague still do. The fortress walls also contain the eleventh-century **Rotunda of St. Marti,** which is one of the city's oldest surviving buildings, the underground Casements, which store six of the original **Charles Bridge** statues, and a cemetery, home to the graves of **Antonin Dvořak** and **Alfons Mucha,** and the **Slavin tomb.**

i *Free entry to Vysehrad fortress; Church of St. Peter and St Paul 50Kč, reduced 30Kč; The Brick Gate, Casemates, Gorlice Hall and Permanent Exhibition 60Kč, reduced 30Kč; last entry 30min. before closing; limited wheelchair accessibility*

CHARLES BRIDGE

Karlův most, Staré Město; www.prague.cz/charles-bridge; open daily 24hr

During the high season, a walk across the Charles Bridge is not so much a walk as it is a struggle through a sea of bodies, so the perfect time to visit is early in the morning after a night out. At 5:31am on July 9, 1357, the Czechs' beloved King Charles IV laid the first stone of the bridge, doing so at that exact time because it formed an auspicious "numerical bridge" (1357 9/7 5:31). The bridge once served as the royal passageway from the **Old Town** to the **Prague Castle,** but nowadays it's occupied by street vendors and caricature artists. Impressive Baroque statues line the sides of the bridges but these statues are actually replicas and the originals can be found at the **Vysehrad fortress.** Oh, we forget to mention that the bridge is allegedly the pickpocket capital of Europe, so if you're looking for a good place to pickpocket, you should probably choose somewhere less mainstream.

i *Free; wheelchair accessible*

JEWISH QUARTER

Josefov, Stare Mesto; 222 317 191; www.jewishmuseum.cz; open summer Tu-Sa 9am-6pm, winter 9am-4:30pm

Just north of **Old Town Square,** the Jewish Quarter is one of the most historic sites in the city, home to five synagogues and the Old Jewish cemetery. A standard ticket (Ticket B, 330Kč) will give you access to most of the sights, including the cemetery as well as the **Pinkas and Spanish synagogues,** but access to the **Old-New Synagogue**—the oldest synagogue in Europe—can only be secured through the purchase of Ticket A+B (500Kč). The Old-New Synagogue isn't much to look at, and thus, if you're on a budget, Ticket B will suit you just fine. The Pinkas Synagogue's walls are covered in the names of the 78,000 Czech-Jews who died in the Holocaust, and the exhibits upstairs showcase drawings created by children from the Thereseinstadt concentration camp.

i *With Old-New Synagogue 500Kč, reduced 340Kč; without Old-New Synagogue 330Kč, reduced 220Kč; limited wheelchair accessibility*

JOHN LENNON WALL

Velkopřevorské náměstí, Malá Strana; open daily 24hr

A visit to the John Lennon Wall is obligatory. Created in the late 1980s as a rebuke to the country's communist regime, which had banned western music, the wall symbolized the desire amongst Czech youth for "Lennonism, Not Leninism." Following the fall of communism, however, the wall transformed from a counterculture icon to a fun spot for tourists and locals to spray-paint messages of peace and love, the most memorable of which is a mural of an Ewok doing the black power salute, captioned "Fuck Wars." It's just a minute from Charles Bridge, which means you really have no excuse for not checking it out, unless, of course, you are virulently pro-war.

i Free; wheelchair accessible

OLD TOWN SQUARE AND ASTRONOMI-CAL CLOCK

Staremêstská náměstí, Staré Mêsto; 236 002 629; clock tower open M 11am-10pm, Tu-Su 9am-10pm

Old Town Square is effectively the heart of Prague, and the area's history and architectural beauty make it a compulsory visit. In the middle of the square sits a memorial dedicated to the Czech hero **Jan Hus,** who was one of the first people to do the now unthinkable act of giving the Catholic Church a hard time. You'll also find the double-towered, **Gothic Church of Our Lady before Týn,** as well as the one and only Astronomical Clock, in front of which hundreds of people gather outside to watch puppets representing Death, Vanity, Greed, and Pleasure jump out of the clock face and stiffly move a few limbs for a couple of minutes each hour. It's not worth the hype, but something you might as well see if you're in the square.

i Clock tower 120Kč, reduced 70Kč; wheelchair accessible

PRAGUE CASTLE

119 08 Prague 1, Hradcany; 224 373 368; www.hrad.cz; castle complex open daily Tu-Sa 6am-10pm, historical buildings 9am-5pm

Castle, castle on the hill, do you provide visitors with a thrill? Visitor, visitor down below, the answer is yes and no. Yes, because Prague Castle—which isn't so much a castle as a collection of palaces, churches, and towers—contains **St. Vitus Cathedral,** whose stained-glass windows make it one of the most stunning structures in Prague. No, because from an aesthetic perspective the other buildings in the castle don't offer much, which given that regular tickets cost at least 250Kč (we recommend the Circuit B option) and a half hour of queuing, leaves us on the fence.

i Circuit A (350Kč, reduced 175Kč), Circuit B (250Kč, reduced 125Kc), Circuit C (350Kč, reduced 175Kč); last entry at 4:40pm; limited wheelchair accessibility

MUSEUMS

DOX CENTRE FOR CONTEMPORARY ART

Poupětova 1, Holešovice; 295 568 123; www.dox.cz; open M 10am-6pm, W 11am-7pm, Th 11am-9pm, F 11am-7pm, Sa-Su 10am-6pm

With a façade that functions as a work of art, a 42-meter-long blimp suspended in the courtyard, and a giant crucifix made out of sneakers hanging from a wall below it, DOX is arguably just as interesting a space as it is a gallery. But that argument would be shut down quickly given the quality of the center's exhibits. Aiming to provide a "critical reflection on current social topics," DOX's constantly changing exhibition spaces deal with topics such as big data, capitalism, "the cage of one's own mind," and many other cheerful things, none of which, at least when we visited, featured a single painted canvas, but one of which contained three VR headsets. The regular tickets are pretty reasonably priced.

i Admission 180Kč, reduced 90Kč; last entry 1hr before closing; wheelchair accessible

KAFKA MUSEUM

Cihelná 635/2b, Malá Strana; 257 535 373; www.kafkamuseum.cz; open daily 10am-6pm

Kafka, perhaps more than any other writer, explored what it meant to be a cockroach, and this museum, certainly more than any other museum, explores what it meant to be Kafka. The museum is filled with Kafka's own letters, manuscripts, sketches, and diary entries, as well as critical commentaries that help make sense of his life and work. What's more, the dimly lit rooms, eerie background music, and unsettling exhibit layouts work together to produce an atmosphere that can only be described by the term named after the writer himself: Kafkaesque. The museum is worthwhile, as it provides the perfect starting point for learning about a writer that everyone should know how to pretentiously reference.

i Admission 200Kč, reduced 120Kč; wheelchair accessible

KAREL ZEMAN MUSEUM

Saská 80/1, Malá Strana; 724 341 091; www.muzeumkarlazemana.cz; open daily 10am-7pm

Karel Zeman is one of the most celebrated animators and Czech filmmakers of the twentieth century, having inspired everyone from Monty Python to Wes Anderson. But, unless you grew up in Czechia during the Cold War, you've probably never seen his work. Zeman's films embody a rare combination of artistic brilliance and childlike innocence, and walking through the museum—where you'll encounter props, costumes, puppets, and most prominently, video clips from his films— you'll likely be overcome with the same wonder and awe that you'd get from Pixar movies, which—surprise, surprise—owe a great debt to Zeman.

i Admission 200Kč, reduced 140Kč; last entry 1hr before closing; wheelchair accessible

NATIONAL GALLERY

Sternberg Palace (Hradčanské náměstí 15), Trade Fair Palace (Dukelských hrdinů 47), Kinsky Palace (Old Town Square 12); 224 301 122; www.ngprague.cz; open Tu-Su 10am-6pm

Prague's National Gallery comprises many individual galleries scattered throughout the city. The most popular galleries include the **Sternberg Palace** in Hradcany, which showcases European art from the fourteenth to eighteenth century, and the **Trade Fair Palace** in Holesovice, which is the largest exhibition and focuses on contemporary works. Skip the **Alfons Mucha museum** and head to the Trade Fair Palace, if you're content with seeing just a few works by Prague's prodigal Art-Nouveau son. In Old Town Square, **Kinsky Palace** houses an interesting, but inessential Asian art exhibition.

i Admission 150Kč, reduced 80Kč, students free; wheelchair accessible

OUTDOORS

BOAT RENTAL ALONG VLTAVA RIVER

Janáčkovo nábř, Staré Město; open10am-sundown (varies)

Whether you're pedaling a car-shaped boat or rowing a boat-shaped boat, an hour on the Vltava River is one of the best ways to spend an afternoon in Prague. Boat rental companies are scattered along the **Staré Město bank** between the **Charles** and **Legií bridges,** with many found on Slovansky ostrov island. Once you've paid 200-300Kč (depending on the kind of boat), you are free to roam anywhere between the **Charles** and the **Jiráskův** most bridges. While most kiosks remain open until sundown, some offer the option of renting an oil lamp-lit boat at night, which makes for a great date idea. What's more, if the date goes badly, you can just push the other person into the river.

i *Boat rental from 200Kč; limited wheelchair accessibility*

LETNÁ PARK AND METRONOME

Badeniho; www.prahazelena.cz/letenske-sady. html; open daily 24hr

Why spend 10 bucks on the latest Drake album when you could get #views like this for free? That's a question we asked ourselves many times as we sat in Letná Park overlooking the entire city, feeling like fools as we stared at Drake's face on the cover of the CD we bought. The optimum viewing point is, without a doubt, on a ledge under the giant **Prague Metronome,** which occupies the former spot of the reviled Stalin monument and serves as a reminder of the city's past. When the sun's about to set, there's no better place to be. But there's more to this park than just breathtaking vistas and historically-significant landmarks. Walk west and you'll encounter one of the most idyllic beer gardens in Prague.

i *Free; limited wheelchair accessibility*

NAPLAVKA RIVERBANK

Rašínovo nábřeží, Vinohrady; open daily 8am-3am

It would be trippy if we told you that the best beer garden in Prague wasn't a garden, wouldn't it? Well, we hope you don't suffer from vertigo, because the best garden in Prague isn't a garden, or even park, but a riverbank. Woah! Every summer evening, locals and in-the-know tourists swarm the stretch of the Vltava riverbank between **Palackého most** (Palacký Bridge) and **Železniční most** (Railway Bridge). The area is lined with beer-serving barges, hole-in-the-wall cocktail bars, food stalls, as well as a Captain Morgan-sponsored club in the hull of a pirate ship. Hunt down a 25Kč pilsner and find a spot on the edge of the river, or hunt down a few and you might just fall in.

i *Free; limited wheelchair accessibility*

PETRIN HILL AND TOWER

Petřínské sady, Mala Strana; 257 320 112; www.muzeumprahy.cz/198-petrinska-rozhledna; funicular open daily 9am-11:20pm; tower open daily Nov-Feb 10am-6pm, Mar, Oct 10am-8pm, Apr-Sept 10am-10pm

France's best-kept secret for over a hundred years, the Eiffel Tower first received international exposure in the 2000 box-office smash Rugrats in Paris. Prague, too, decided to build its own in 1891. The Petrin Tower is a 60-meter-tall structure that, when you take into account the hill it sits atop, is nearly as tall as the 324-meter original. Take a 30-minutes walk from the base of the hill to its peak, a 299-step hike to the tower's viewing platform for stunning panoramic views of the city. Alternatively, use your public transport ticket for a ride up in a funicular.

i *Funicular free with public transport ticket, tower 150Kč, reduced 80Kč; wheelchair accessible*

FOOD

⚑ CAFÉ LOUVRE ($$)

Národní 22, Nove Mesto; 224 930 949; www. cafelouvre.cz; open daily 8am-11:30pm

Café Louvre is fantastic, but don't just take our word for it—take Albert Einstein's and Franz Kafka's. Back in the day, this café was a favorite amongst Prague's intellectual community, and when these geeks and nerds weren't discussing nuclear physics and the futility of man, they were most likely chomping on some very reasonably priced traditional Czech food. Enter under the "Café Louvre" marquee, follow a long hallway and head upstairs, where you'll encounter a scene straight out of your *Gatsby* nightmares. The ceilings are high, the tablecloths white, the lighting fixtures unusual, and the walls covered in a mix of old-school advertisements and black-and-white photos.

i *Entrées from 139Kč; vegetarian options available; no wheelchair accessibility*

🖳 PARALLEL POLIS ($)

Dělnická 475/43, Holešovice; 702 193 936; www.paralelnipolis.cz; open M-F 8am-8pm, Sa-Su noon-9pm

Parallel Polis is the world's first bitcoin café, which means you can only pay with, you guessed it, bitcoin. If you're some kind of Luddite who doesn't have a healthy stash of bitcoins already saved in the cloud, don't worry. There's a bitcoin ATM inside the café that'll sort you out. What's with this café's obsession with bitcoin anyway? Is it, like, run by some sort of crypto-anarchist hacking collective? Yes. Yes, it is. Above the café is the **Institute of Cryptoanarchy,** which aims to promote personal privacy, liberty, and all those other things that make people enemies of the state. But don't let all this cyber mumbo-jumbo distract you from that fact that the café, equipped with fancy V60 and aeropress filters, knows how to make a damn good cup of joe.

i Coffee from 40Kč, cash and credit cards accepted for bitcoin exchange; vegetarian options available; wheelchair accessible

CHOCO CAFE ($)

Red Chair, Liliová 250/4, Staré Město; 222 222 519; www.choco-cafe.cz; open daily 10am-8pm

If you gave this hot chocolate its own Instagram account, you'd be guaranteed to have at least one hundred dudes commenting "thicc af (peach emoji)" on every single post. But when a drink's this creamy, rich, and, yes, thick, what else would you expect? Even calling it a drink is a bit of a stretch. It has much more in common with a chocolate bar left in your pocket on a summer's day. If this is your first rodeo at Choco, stick to the most basic options, lest you risk a cardiac arrest of the senses. But if you think a trip to your sensory cardiologist is long overdue, then go for one of the chili, ginger, or alcoholic varietals.

i Hot chocolate from 59Kč; wheelchair accessible

CRÊPERIE "U SLEPE KOCICKY" ($$)

M. Horákové 600/38, Holešovice; 233 371 855; www.slepakocicka.cz; open daily 11am-11pm

While any restaurant with the word "crêpe" in the title will inevitably catch our eye—which, in the past, has led to heartbreak and stomachache—these crêpes are a cause to celebrate. With a comprehensive range of both sweet and savory pancakes and crêpes at very affordable prices, you can order everything from salmon, sour cream, and chicken to banana, chocolate, nuts, and eggnog. Beyond the food, the restaurant looks like it's straight out of a fairytale about a nice, old woman who's obsessed with cats. The wood-paneled interiors are decked out with feline-themed paintings, statues, and lampshade decorations. Luckily, the flowerpots dangling from the ceiling provide a merciful counterbalance to the cat-holism.

i Savory crêpes from 139Kč, sweet crêpes from 69Kč; wheelchair accessible

FERDINANDA ($)

Karmelitská 379/18, Mala Strana; 257 534 015; www.ferdinanda.cz; open M-Sa 11am-11pm, Su 11am-5pm

If your money's about as tight as a nun's budget to buy school supplies for the poor orphans she looks after, look no further than Ferdinanda. The restaurant's underground setting deprives it of the street-side seating common to most **Mala Strana** eateries, but when a bowl of goulash and a half pint of beer cost a mere 148Kč, we couldn't care less. The locals and tourists that regularly pack the place don't either. The menu also includes a vegetarian section, which isn't always guaranteed in most Czech cuisine places. Seeing as most of the nearby restaurants in **Malostranske Nam.** charge 200Kč or more per main, it's best to remember the unofficial Trump motto of "When they go high, we go low" and seek out the budget-friendly underworld of Ferdinanda.

i Entrées from 85Kč; vegetarian options available; no wheelchair accessibility

FOOD OF LOVE ($$)

Nerudova 219/32, Mala Strana; 736 633 098; www.foodoflove.cz; open daily 11am-10pm

With the overabundance of meat-heavy Czech cuisine restaurants, being a vegetarian in Prague can sometimes make you feel like the only free-range chicken in an industrial slaughterhouse. Thankfully for everyone who found that simile in poor taste, there's Food of Love, a quaint vegetarian restaurant situated in a courtyard just below **Prague Castle.** Beyond the vegetarian options, the menu is loaded with raw vegan and gluten-free meals. It also offers vegetarian goulash and over 20 varieties of tea. To find the restaurant, walk up Nerudova street, and about 20 meters before a more obnoxiously signposted vegan restaurant, turn into a small art gallery to the right and continue into the courtyard.

i *Entrées from 165Kč; gluten-free, vegan, and vegetarian options available; wheelchair accessible*

LOKÁL DLOUHÁÁÁ ($$)

Dlouhá 33, Staré Město; 222 316 265; www. lokal-dlouha.ambi.cz; open Su-F 11am-1am, Sa 11am-midnight

While most people are rightfully suspicious of **Old Town** restaurants that make a big deal about their local cuisine, you can let your guard down at Lokal. A huge beer hall populated by locals and tourists alike, this restaurant serves a wide array of traditional Czech cuisine that's as tasty as it is filling. After one plate of fried cheese and a helping of sausages, we felt simultaneously at one with the universe and practically comatose. The Old Town location is just one of many scattered across Prague, but thankfully the fact that it's a chain doesn't detract from the quality of the food or the restaurant's authentic feel, the latter of which is bolstered by the 40Kč mugs of beer.

i *Entrées from 115Kč, starters from 85Kč; wheelchair accessible*

THE CRAFT ($)

Náměstí Míru 1221/4, Vinohrady; 306 577 4230; www.thecraft.cz; open Su-F noon-midnight, F-Sa noon-2am

When your beers are microbrewed and you treat burgers as an artisanal practice, there's no better name for your restaurant than The Craft, which, just off **Namesti Miru** (Peace Square), is a go-to-place for the young **Vinohrady** crowd. Each burger has a juicy and tender patty between a warm and toasty bun, both of which are impaled with a giant steak knife instead of a measly toothpick. We found the tiger-prawn-topped Surf and Turf burger to be a revelation. The bathrooms are stocked with cotton wool and Q-tips, which may or may not come in handy for a less-than-clean backpacker such as yourself.

i *Burgers from 209Kč; wheelchair accessible*

NIGHTLIFE

NEONE

Bubenská 1477/1, Holešovice; 723 063 209; open F-Sa 10pm-6am

Devoid of drunken tourists and trashy music, Neone is an electronic music lover's dream and a British bachelor party's worst nightmare. Originally created as a temporary venue, Neone was so popular amongst the more artsy and hip locals that it became a permanent fixture of Prague's nightlife scene. Found at the bottom of **Holešovice,** the club occupies an unsuspecting, office-like building, identifiable by the façade's green neon "N." It draws the most cutting-edge electronic DJs and producers from across Europe, and mesmerizing visual art projections usually accompany their sets. With its DIY-attitude and communal feel, Neone is possibly the closest thing you'll find to a Berlin-esque club in Prague.

i *Cover 130Kč; cash only, limited wheelchair accessibility*

CLUB ROXY

Dlouhá 33, Stare Mesto; 608 060 745; www. roxy.cz; open daily 11pm-5am

Karlovy Lazne, the five-story club next to **Charles Bridge,** is the symbol of the trashy side of Prague's nightlife and, unless you're the kind of person who likes doing things "for the experience," should be avoided. However, for those wanting to experience Prague's mainstream clubbing scene without a tourist trap reputation and a 200Kč entrance fee, Club Roxy is a worthy alternative. Near the north of **Stare Mesto,** the club boasts a massive, techno/house-heavy dance floor and a crowd of tourists and locals alike. People of all ages flock here as if it's Macy's Thanksgiving Day Parade. If you like minimal entry fees and, by club standards, cheap drinks, you'll have a lot to be thankful for.

i *Cover up to 250Kč, beer from 50Kč, wine from 45Kč, shots from 65Kč, cocktails from 95Kč; cash only, limited wheelchair accessibility*

CROSS CLUB

Plynární 1096/23, Holešovice; 736 535 053; www.crossclub.cz; open daily 2pm-5am

Cross Club evokes Optimus Prime deciding to go steampunk and, due to violating the sleek Autobot aesthetic, being subsequently broken down into his constituent parts, which were then sold to the villain from *Mad Max* and used to furnish a local resto-bar-club. Once you've figured out how to navigate the multiple floors of this labyrinthine complex, you'll find it full of punks, hippies, locals, and tourists, all of whom are looking for something more alternative than Prague's mainstream nightlife offerings. The music spans several genres and is blasted out of one of the best sound systems in the city.

i Beer from 22Kč, cocktails from 66Kč; cash only; BGLTQ+ friendly

KLUB UJEZD

Újezd 422/18, Mala Strana; 251 510 873; www.klubujezd.cz; open daily 2pm-4am

Klub Ujezd must be on a sea monster diet, because as soon as you step inside this bar, you see monsters. Sea monsters. The Loch Ness monster protrudes from the yellow walls, while other mythical creatures hang from the ceiling and coil around the light bulbs. Play some foosball, and shout your drink order across the steampunk-y barrier that separates you from the bartender, or venture down into the stone-cobbled basement where things get a little grungier. Regularly hosting live music, DJs, and art exhibitions, Klub Ujezd is one of the most beloved spots west of the **Vltava River.**

i Beer and spirits from 30Kč, shots from 49Kč; cash only, limited wheelchair accessibility

VLKOVA 26

Vlkova 699/26, Zizkov; open Tu-Sa 8pm-3am

The cool kids of Prague wouldn't touch a lot of the bars and pubs in **Old Town** with a ten-foot pole. So where are the bars they touch? Well, of course, there's Holešovice, but there's also the even more local and residential neighborhood of **Žižkov,** in the heart of which you'll find Vlkova 26. A minimal and candle-lit space, replete with concrete walls and leather couches, you'll find an indie/hip hop/electronic-spinning DJ. During the weekdays, the bar is vibrant, but not crowded. But when the weekend comes around, Vlkova 26's bar is full and the dance floor is FULL (Fun, Underground, Lively, Life-affirming).

i Cocktails from 100Kč; cash only

VZORKOVNA

Národní 339/11, Nové Město; open M-F 5pm-3am, Sa-Su 6pm-3am

In both the below street level-sense and the shabby and coolsense, Vzorkovna is an underground playground. You'll pass a circle of swings suspended from the ceiling, walk through a brightly-lit room with three back-to-back foosball tables and leather seats nailed to the wall, eventually stumbling on a series of grimy rooms plastered in graffiti and strewn with antiques with the only source of light coming from the string of fairy lights snaking around the exposed pipes overhead. You'll encounter shirtless punks, 20-something hipsters, bachelorette parties, and a comically large dog. The drinks aren't half bad either. One bar specializes in craft beers served in mason jars while another brews tea.

i Beer from 30Kč

CZECHIA ESSENTIALS

VISAS

Czechia is a member of the EU and the Schengen area. Citizens from Australia, Canada, New Zealand, the US, and many other non-EU countries do not require a visa for stays up to 90 days. However, if you plan to spend time in other Schengen countries, note that the 90-day period applies cumulatively to all of them.

MONEY

Currency: Although Czechia is a member of the EU, it is not in the Eurozone and uses the Czech Koruna (Kč or CZK) as its currency. ATMs can be found in shopping malls, banks, and most public spaces. Avoid currency exchanges at airports and use ATMs instead. The best currency exchanges are those that advertise the "buy" and "sell" rates, which allow you to calculate exactly how much you will receive and don't charge a commission fee. To find out what out-of-network or international fees your credit or debit cards may be subjected to, call your bank.

Tipping and Bargaining: In restaurants, tips are usually not included in the bill, so it's customary to tip 10-15% for good service. Another way to tip is to round your bill to the nearest 10Kč and then add 10% of the total. When you pay the bill, include the tip. A 10% tip for taxis is acceptable. It is not customary to leave tips on the table before you leave. Bargaining is only done in open-air markets or antique shops.

SAFETY AND HEALTH

Local Laws and Police: Czech police have a reliable reputation and you should not hesitate to contact them if needed. Be sure to carry your passport with you, as police have the right to ask for identification. However, police can sometimes be unhelpful if you're the victim of a currency exchange scam, in which case it's best to seek advice from your embassy or consulate.

Drugs and Alcohol: If you carry insulin, syringes, or any prescription drugs on your person, you must also carry a copy of the prescription and a doctor's note. The drinking age is 18. There is a zero-tolerance policy for people who drive under the influence, meaning that the legal blood alcohol content (BAC) is zero. The possession of small quantities of marijuana (less than 15g), 40 pieces of magic mushrooms, 5 grams of hashish, five LCD-laced papers or other materials with LSD, 1.5 grams of heroin, 1 gram of cocaine, and 2 grams of methamphetamine were decriminalized in 2009. However, carrying any of these drugs is still a misdemeanor, which could result in a fine up to 15,000Kč. Carrying drugs across an international border—drug trafficking—is a serious criminal offence.

Petty Crime and Scams: A common scam in bars and nightclubs involves a local woman inviting a traveler to buy her drinks, which end up costing exorbitant prices. The proprietors may then use force to ensure the bill is paid. In bars, never open a tab and instead pay for each drink as you order it, as the tab bill may include drinks you never ordered, and once again, the proprietors will force you to pay. Check the prices of drinks before ordering. Con artists may also pose as police officers in metro stations and tell you your ticket is invalid, demanding that you pay large fines. To avoid this, make sure you buy a ticket and validate it, in which case you know you are in the right. Another scam involves one person approaching you in Old Town Square and asking if you'd like to hear a riddle. While you're distracted, an accomplice may try to steal your personal belongings.

Credit Card Fraud: Credit card fraud is also common. If you think you've been a victim of this, contact your credit card company immediately. Children may also approach you asking to sign a petition and provide a donation. These petition sheets are often fake, and the children are in cahoots with con artists.

Pickpockets: Pickpockets are common in crowded tourist areas such as Old Town Square, Prague Castle, and the Charles Bridge, as well as on public transport. Avoid too-crowded public transit and always keep an eye on your personal belongings.

DENMARK

The Scandinavian countries are Rand Paul's worst nightmare. They're the ultimate "nanny states"—overly taxing their people (most of whom are pretty okay with it), and giving back something more akin to a safety king-sized bed than a net. Denmark has characteristically high taxes and significant benefits for its people, but compared to Sweden and Norway, Denmark really plays it fast and loose. The Danes love to drink all day (and all night), still allow smoking indoors in some places, and, best of all, don't have a ridiculous government monopoly on alcohol (looking at you, Sweden and Norway). Whatever's going on over there seems to be working, though. The Danes are routinely ranked the happiest people in the world, thanks largely to a cultural mindset that is equal part bemusing and unpronounceable (see: *hygge*). Long story short, the Danes just think happy, and it works. For the whole country. Incredible. Denmark straddles the border between Scandinavia and the rest of Europe. Like its northern neighbors, it is still obsessed with Vikings and you'll find at least one museum exhibition dedicated entirely to furniture, but Denmark also contains the Renaissance castles of France, the picturesque canal-side waterfront of Italy, and the bike-friendliness of Amsterdam. Don't worry, though: with typical Scandinavian prices, you won't mistake Denmark for Germany any time soon. Your dollar won't take you as far here as, well, pretty much anywhere else, but, as Socrates once said, "you get what you pay for." In Denmark, that means "hostels" that are more like four-star hotels and "street food" markets reminiscent of premium food courts. But, if you're okay setting a budget, trying to stick to it, and quickly realizing that your bank account is emptying faster than Copenhagen during the summer vacation season (seriously, it's so damn long), experiencing Denmark is worth every *krone*.

AARHUS

Coverage by **Eric Chin**

Aarhus has come a long way since it was founded in the eighth century as a Viking settlement. Over the centuries, buildings rose, buildings burned, Christianity and the plague arrived with mixed results, and people came—so many people that Aarhus is now Denmark's second largest city. Today, Aarhus is trying out a bold new look—one with apartment buildings designed to look like icebergs and libraries and playgrounds under the same roof – but it hasn't forgotten its origins. The oldest part of the city, Latinerkvarteret, remains a cultural center for shops and restaurants, and despite several new high-rise buildings, the towering spire of Aarhus Cathedral remains still stands as the tallest point in the city. Despite this rich history, Aarhus is Denmark's youngest city demographically, thanks to a large student population. Combine that with a bustling tourism industry, and the result is everything from budget hostels to grand hotels, burgers and Vietnamese to Michelin-starred restaurants, and Irish pubs to Bond-style cocktail bars. Copenhagen may be the city to visit in Denmark, but you'd be remiss not to give Jutland a try, and there's no better place than Aarhus.

ORIENTATION

Aarhus doesn't have neighborhoods that are as distinct as in, say, **Copenhagen,** there are certainly distinct areas. The area known as **Aarhus C** is sometimes also called **Midtbyen,** and stretches north from **Aarhus H** to several streets past **Aarhus Cathedral.** Here you'll find almost all the major sights in the city, including restaurants, museums, and the busy nightlife streets **Aboulevarden, Skolegade,** and **Frederiksgade.** The area between Aarhus Cathedral and the **Ring 1 Road** to the north is known as **Latinerkvarteret** (The Latin Quarter), and is the oldest part of the city. To the west of the city center is **Vesterbro,** a largely-residential neighborhood that includes cultural attractions like the **Botanical Garden** and **Den Gamle By.**

ESSENTIALS

GETTING THERE

Aarhus Airport (AAR) is a tiny airport located about 35mi. northeast of the city. Departures mostly go to Copenhagen. There is an airport bus between Aarhus Central Station and Aarhus Airport scheduled for each flight. Tickets can be purchased on the bus for DKK 115. The easiest way to get to Aarhus is by train via Copenhagen, a journey of 3-4hr. Aarhus's main train station is Aarhus Central Station (Aarhus H), and there are many trains between Aarhus H and Copenhagen Central Station (København H) each day, often more than one per hour. Train service in Denmark is operated by DSB. Tickets (DKK 400) can be purchased at either station.

GETTING AROUND

Most attractions are within walking distance. To go beyond the city center (to the Moesgaard Museum, for example), Aarhus has a system of buses run by Midttrafik with several ticket options. Single tickets can be purchased with cash at a kiosk on the bus for DKK 20 for two zones, which covers the city center and immediate suburbs. Tickets can also be purchased for 24hr (DKK 80), 48hr (DKK 120), or 72hr (DKK 160) at the Aarhus bus station (Aarhus Rutebilstation, Fredensgade 45). The Danes are famous for loving their bicycles, and Aarhus is no exception. The city has a free city bike system for use October-April. There are a few important rules, though. Lights must be used at night, and you have to provide your own. You also need a 20 DDK coin to unlock a bike, which is returned to you when you return the bike. There are bike stands near many important cultural and recreational sites, and can only be used in the city center.

PRACTICAL INFORMATION

Tourist Offices: Dokk1 (Hack Kampmanns Plads 2; 87 31 50 10; open M-Sa 10am-4pm, Su 11am-2pm)

Banks/ATMs/Currency Exchange: Credit and debit cards are widely accepted in Aarhus, though you may have to pay a small fee to use an international card. Currency exchange and ATMs (sometimes called "pengeautomat") can be found at Aarhus Central Station or on main streets Sønder Allé and Store Torv.

Post Offices: The Danish postal service is run by PostNord (Posthus Superbrugsen; Vesterbro Torv 1; 70 70 70 30; open M-F 1pm-5pm).

Internet: Free internet is widely available in Aarhus, and can be found in hostels, museums, and most cafés and coffee shops. Many shops and restaurants will advertise free Wi-Fi with window stickers.

BGLTQ+ Resources: LGBT Aarhus is available on Thursdays 6pm-8pm at Café Sappho (Mejlgade 71; 86 13 19 48; lgbt. dk; Facebook @LGBTAarhus).

EMERGENCY INFORMATION

Emergency Number: 112. The police can be reached at 114 in non-emergency situations.

Police: The police headquarters in Aarhus can be found near Dokk1 (Ridderstræde 1; 87 31 14 48; open daily 9:30am-9:30pm and 24hr for emergencies).

Rape Crisis Center: The Center for Rape Victims can be found in the emergency department of Aarhus University Hospital (Nørrebrogade 44; 78 46 35 43; open daily 24hr).

Hospitals: The main hospital in Aarhus is Aarhus University Hospital. In an emergency, call 112. In urgent, non-emergency situations, call the emergency doctor service at 70 11 31 31. Emergency Department (Nørrebrogade 44; open daily 24hr).

Pharmacies: Pharmacies (called apotek in Denmark), can be found on main streets. Løve Apoteket is located near Aarhus Cathedral and is open 24hr (Store Torv 5; 86 12 00 22).

ACCOMMODATIONS

CITY SLEEP-IN ($)

Havnegade 20; 86 19 20 55; www.citysleep-in.dk/en; reception open M-F 8am-11am and 4pm-10pm, Sa-Su 8am-11am and 4pm-11pm

This place is truly a budget hostel; the dorm rooms are cramped, top-bunk ladders are a bit rickety, and, much like your grandfather's old house, there's sometimes a subtle hint of stale cigarettes. It's not the Ritz, but you knew that already. Luckily, the kitchen and dining area are clean and well-equipped. There's an outdoor courtyard with ample seating, and the lobby and hallways are covered with charming murals to add a homey touch. Expect to encounter some families and more than a few random old hostel guys (you know the type), but it's a small price to pay for... well, a small price to pay.

i Dorms DKK 190, doubles DKK 460; reservation recommended; BGLTQ+ friendly; wheelchair accessible; Wi-Fi; linen DKK 50; laundry facilities DKK 40; breakfast DKK 70

SIMPLEBED HOSTEL ($$)

Åboulevarden 86; 53 23 21 89; www.simplebedhostel.com; reception open 24hr

This is a very basic, small hostel with a great location right on **Åboulevarden,** one of Aarhus's main streets. The entire hostel is an apartment with just a few rooms: one six-bed dorm, a small kitchen, a common room, and a single bathroom. There's also a double with a private bathroom, but don't expect to see much of whoever is staying there. The bunk beds are huge (near to queen-size), and are fitted with mattress toppers, which guarantees you the best night's sleep of your trip.

i Dorms DKK 250, private doubles DKK 550; reservation required; cash only; BGLTQ+ friendly; no wheelchair accessibility; Wi-Fi; linens and towels included

SIGHTS
CULTURE

ÅBOULEVARDEN

Åboulevarden; venue hours vary

Åboulevarden, named for the **Aarhus River** (*Aarhus Å* in Danish) that it follows, is one of the busiest streets in the city, all day and all night. The pedestrian-only street is lined with establishments from shawarma shops, to dawn-to-dusk café-bars and full-on, weekend-only nightclubs. Tables line the buildings and waterfront, equipped with enough heat lamps when the sun goes down to make up for the savings of that sustainable Danish energy sector. Meals on Åboulevarden can be somewhat pricey and the nightlife a bit more exclusive, but even if you don't want to dress up or pay out, it's still a great place to people watch and remind yourself that you really don't need to spend half a day's paycheck on brunch.

i Venue prices vary; limited wheelchair accessibility

MUSIKHUSET

Thomas Jensens Allé; 89 40 40 40; www. musikhusetaarhus.dk/en; foyer open daily 11am-6pm, box office open M-Sa noon-5pm

Musikhuset Aarhus is the largest concert hall in Scandinavia, with over 1600 seats in its largest hall. It's home to the **Danish National Opera,** the **Aarhus Symphony Orchestra,** and **Comedy Zoo Aarhus,** an organization for Danish stand-up which, despite the promising name, is sorely lacking in squirrels, monkeys, cats, and other similarly funny animals. There are events every week, including concerts, operas, theater performances, and comedy shows, and, while most will be out of reach on a backpacker's budget, Musikhuset also puts on several free performances (mostly concerts) each month.

i Show prices vary; wheelchair accessible

LANDMARKS

AARHUS CATHEDRAL

Store Torv; 86 20 54 00; www.aarhusdom-kirke.dk/english; open M 9:30am-4pm, Tu 10:30am-4pm, W-Sa 9:30am-4pm

Aarhus Cathedral has changed its look more often over the years than Britney Spears has changed hers. Since construction began in the twelfth century, the cathedral has been built up, burned down, expanded, restyled between Romanesque, Gothic, and Baroque numerous times, always adding to its collection of tombs of old white men. The vast interior is packed with everything you've come to expect out of an old cathedral: paintings, statues, gravestones, gold leaf, and pipe organs (yes, plural). Tall windows provide natural light to illuminate the vaulted Gothic arches, decorated with white-based murals that can only be described as minimalist when compared to other great cathedrals of Europe.

i Tower admission DKK 20; wheelchair accessible

DOKK1

Hack Kampmanns Plads 2; 89 40 92 00; www.dokk1.dk/english; open M-F 8am-10pm, Sa-Su 10am-4pm

Dokk1 is a cultural hub in Aarhus—an incredibly Danish place where art, architecture, and of course, blond children, come together. This modern behemoth of a building sits on the harbor, clad in steel, glass, and concrete. Inside, Dokk1 serves many purposes: it's home to the city's public library and tourist information center. It also houses a café and small performance hall. Outside, it's practically a playground, with slides and climbing walls that resemble sculptures more than toys. All these attractions draw all kinds of people, from coffee-chugging students working in private study rooms to stroller-pushing soccer moms to children running everywhere. Stop for a drink, grab a book, or watch somebody's dad make a fool of himself on the playground. Seriously, whose mans?

i Free; wheelchair accessible

MUSEUMS

 AROS AARHUS KUNSTMUSEUM

Aros Allé 2; 87 30 66 00; www.en.aros.
dk; open Tu 10am-5pm, W 10am-10pm,
Th-Su 10am-5pm

Start in the basement with a gallery
called *The 9 Spaces* (an allusion to
Dante's *Inferno*), containing works
from a seemingly-infinite room
composed of mirrors to a simulation
of a whole day compressed into eight
minutes. From there, ARoS stretches
high with ten floors of concrete,
steel, and glass, culminating in *Your
rainbow panorama,* a circular rooftop
skywalk with rainbow-tinted walls
that affords vast, if a little green, view
of the city. Exhibitions range from
Human Nature, which asks the viewer
to consider the difference between
nature and landscape to *No Man is
an Island,* which has a 4.5 meter-tall,
hyper-realistic statue of a crouching
boy to another statue simply titled,
Fucked. You don't even need to own a
turtleneck; there's something here to
interest even the casual art critic.
i Admission DKK 130, students under
28 DKK 100, under 18 free; wheelchair
accessible

MOESGAARD MUSEUM

Moesgård Allé 15; 87 39 40 00; www.
moesgaardmuseum.dk/en; open Tu
10am-5pm, W 10am-9pm, Th-Su 10am-
5pm

This museum of archaeology and
ethnography is built into a grassy
hillside in a suburb of Aarhus like
some sort of concrete and glass
Little House on the Prairie. The
collection is vast, including
everything from Viking
swords to Roman pottery to
Egyptian gold jewelry. There
are also a slightly disturbing
number of human remains
on display, including a
2000-year-old corpse,
incredibly preserved after
spending two millennia
buried in a peat bog.
Looking at rusty farm tools
and dead bodies doesn't
sound like the most exciting
way to spend a day, but the
entire museum is modern and
interactive, with video presentations
mixed in, and a "laboratory" where
you can pretend to be an archaeologist
and actually do something with your
life.
i Admission Apr 8-Oct 22 DKK 140, students DKK 110, Oct 23-Apr 7 DKK 120,
students DKK 90; wheelchair accessible

OUTDOORS

MOESGAARD STRAND

Strandskovvej 2; 8270

Moesgaard Strand is a large stretch
of sandy beach along the coast,
just south of Aarhus itself. It has
earned **Blue Flag** status for having
exceptional water quality, meaning
it's especially clean and safe. How
Danish. The beach is a bit far
from the city center, but it is easily
accessible via city bus #31. It's also
just a short walk from the **Moesgaard
Museum,** so you can go relax in the
sun after a long morning of getting
#cultured while looking at skeletons.
i Free; wheelchair accessible

SURF AGENCY

Fiskerivej 2; 60 89 05 15; www.surfagency.dk; open Tu-Th 10am-6pm, F 10am-8pm, Sa 9am-8pm

SUP. No, not the favored salutation of ninth graders who wear baggy jeans. We're talking stand-up paddle boarding, the watersports craze that's sweeping Instagrams worldwide. This conceptually silly but aesthetically pleasing activity has spread from sunny California to stormy New England to Aarhus. Surf Agency is a watersports hub located right on the harbor specializing in SUP classes and rentals. If you're a newbie on the water, you can sign up for a somewhat expensive introductory course or you can just throw yourself right off the deep end with an hourly rental. For the health nuts out there, Surf Agency also offers SUP yoga classes led by an instructor. Unfortunately, artsy photos are not included.

i No wheelchair accessibility

FOOD

🍜 PHO C&P ($)

Sønder Allé 14; 86 16 16 42; www.pho-cp.dk; open M-Th noon-8:30pm, F-Sa noon-9:30pm, Su noon-8:30pm

Good morning, Vietnam! Well, maybe not, since Pho C&P doesn't serve breakfast, but this popular spot will definitely serve up a good lunch or dinner. The menu is inspired by Vietnamese street food, (arguably the best in the world), and Pho C&P does it justice, from traditional *bánh mì* sandwiches to *pho,* the world's most mispronounced soup. And though the authenticity doesn't quite translate into Ho Chi Minh City prices, the place is definitely a bargain in Aarhus. Located just off of one of the city's main shopping streets, Pho C&P is no secret, so try to eat during off-peak hours, or order takeout.

i Bánh mì from DKK 45, pho and other entrées from DKK 75, beer from DKK 25; vegan and vegetarian options available; no wheelchair accessibility

AARHUS STREET FOOD ($$)

Ny Banegårdsgade 46; www.aarhusstreetfood.com; open M-Th 11:30am-9pm, F-Sa 11:30am-10pm, Su 11:30am-9pm

Imagine if a huge fleet of food trucks all simultaneously got flat tires and jacked up their prices to pay for new ones, and you pretty much have Aarhus Street Food. Located in an old warehouse, food stands are designed to look like anything from corrugated metal shipping containers to plywood, cartoon-lemonade-stand-style shops. There's even greater variety in the cuisine, so you'll find everything from Afro-Caribbean jerk chicken and fries cooked in duck fat to Danish classics like *rugbrød* and *flæskesteg.* Smaller entrées like sandwiches go from DKK 50, but the price for a more substantial meal with a side and drink can quickly top DKK 100.

i Entrées from SEK 50; gluten-free, vegan, and vegetarian options available; wheelchair accessible

BILL'S COFFEE ($$)

Vestergade 58; 20 74 71 96; open M-F 7:30am-6pm, Sa 9am-6pm, Su 9am-5pm

Try to hop on the Wi-Fi at Bill's and you'll be greeted with a locked network called "BILLS is NOT an office," which is a not-so-subtle request for you to get your millennial head out of the sand (and more specifically, off your phone) and into a book or mug of Bill's coffee. So, have a seat at the counter, on a bench outside, or at a table underneath one of the strange, corrugated cardboard-esque lamps with a cappuccino poured by a denim-apron-clad barista, and take a minute to appreciate the eclectic reggae-jazz mix playing in the background. Or wonder how Bill's manages to make a needlepoint pillow look modern. Your phone battery will appreciate it.

i Coffee and espresso drinks from DKK 25, pastries and cakes from DKK 15; wheelchair accessible

NIGHTLIFE

📷 FATTER ESKIL

Skolegade 25; 21 35 44 11; www.fattere-skil.dk; open W 8pm-midnight, Th 8pm-2am, F 4pm-5am, Sa 8pm-5am

Fatter Eskil is one of Aarhus's top live music venues with concerts most Wednesday through Saturday nights. Performances range from rock and metal, to R&B and dance music, and even after the concert is over, a DJ often comes on to keep the party going. Admission to **Thursday Jam Nights** is free, where you can show up and hop on stage for a song or two, or just sit and enjoy the cheap beer and live music. If you're not feeling the vibe, or if the place dies down after the show is over, Fatter Eskil is located on **Skolegade,** which is also home to a number of other bars and nightclubs that are popular with the kids.

i Cover DDK 40-80 depending on night, drinks from DKK 25; BGLTQ+ friendly; limited wheelchair accessibility

THE TAP ROOM

Frederiksgade 40; 86 19 19 10; www.tirnanog.dk; open M-Th noon-3am, F-Sa noon-5am, Su 1pm-3pm

If you want the perfect pint of Guinness or glass of whiskey on the rocks, look no further. There are several Irish pubs in Aarhus (turns out the Irish know a thing or two about drinking), but The Tap Room is one of the best. The bartenders are Irish (or British or Australian), the whiskey is Irish, and the music is… American? The crowd is a great mix of young, not so young, Danish, Irish, American, and more, and the playlist contains everything from Arctic Monkeys to the Strokes. Thursday at 9pm is **quiz night,** but you can expect rugby or football (sorry, "soccer") on the televisions during the week, and live music late into weekend nights.

i Draft beer from DKK 50, cocktails from DKK 70, shots from DKK 30; BGLTQ+ friendly; wheelchair accessible

COPENHAGEN

Coverage by **Eric Chin**

There are a few things that generally hold true of Scandinavian cities: they're small (Stockholm, Scandinavia's largest, tops the list with just under one million people living in the city proper), they're expensive (can't argue there), and they're obsessed with Vikings. In short, they're great places to travel, but get a bit sleepy after a few days. Copenhagen is different. It's not just the capital city of Denmark; it feels like the cultural capital of all of Scandinavia. Between the city itself and the many towns within reach via commuter rail, Copenhagen boasts truly impressive Renaissance castles, Baroque gardens that would make Louis XIV raise an eyebrow, and one of the best food and microbrewery scenes in the north. You'll feel right at home in Copenhagen's vibrant young population, filled with starving art majors and wingtip-clad startup founders alike. There's something for everyone here, from the casual nightclubs of the Meatpacking District and the smoky bars of Nørrebro, to the bohemian paradise of Christiania with its alternative architecture and open marijuana trade. The discerning diner will love Copenhagen's massive food halls and local delicacies. Don't miss the *smørrebrød* or the greasy, crunchy goodness of *flæskesteg*. The casual cyclist will be amazed both by the sophistication of the city's bike lanes, and by how uncharacteristically aggressive a Dane on a bicycle can be. It won't be cheap (nothing in the Nordics ever is), but Copenhagen is one of the only Scandinavian cities where you could spend a week and still not have scratched the surface. It's small but busy, modern but timeless, and of course, it's very, very *hygge*.

ORIENTATION

The city center of **Copenhagen** (also known as **Indre By** or **København K**), extends from **Copenhagen Central Station** all the way to the northern end of the city. Like city centers everywhere, it's touristy, crowded, and expensive. It's also where you'll find many of Copenhagen's main attractions, including **Strøget** (one of Europe's longest pedestrianized shopping streets), a number of museums and palaces, and the people-watching meccas of **Kongens Nytorv** and **Nyhavn.** Just to the east is **Christianshavn,** a network of islands and canals constructed by **Christian IV** in the style of **Amsterdam.** Within Christianshavn is the offbeat community (and favorite of twenty-somethings from all over the world) of **Christiania,** famous for its open marijuana trade. North of the city center is **Østerbro,** an upscale residential neighborhood with plentiful parks and high prices. Just west is a funkier alternative: **Nørrebro,** a classic example of a once-heavily-immigrant neighborhood overtaken by broke hipsters and art students. Directly west of the city center is **Frederiksberg,** another wealthy neighborhood filled with parks and baby strollers (**Frederiksberg Have** and the **Cisterns** are worth a visit). South of **Frederiksberg** is **Vesterbro,** home to the **Meatpacking District** and old **Carlsberg Brewery.** Copenhagen is also a great hub for exploring other cities on the island of **Zealand,** Denmark's largest (except Greenland). To the west is **Roskilde,** one of Denmark's foremost Viking cities, and to the north are **Helsingør** and **Hillerød,** home to famous Renaissance castles.

ESSENTIALS

GETTING THERE

Copenhagen Airport, Kastrup (CPH), known as Københavns Lufthavn in Danish, is Scandinavia's busiest airport. The metro is the easiest way to get to the airport; Copenhagen's main train station is Copenhagen Central Station (København H), which connects to the rest of Scandinavia and other major European cities.

GETTING AROUND

Copenhagen's public transportation system includes buses, a metro, and trains, which are all covered under the same ticket. The capital region is divided into zones, with ticket prices varying accordingly. Tickets can be purchased at metro stations and at 7-Elevens, but you can also buy them on buses (with cash). A 24hr pass is DKK 80, and a 72hr pass is DKK 200. Copenhagen has a city bike program, but they're expensive (DKK 30 per hour) and bulky since they're equipped with unnecessary electric motors. Renting from a shop or company like Donkey Republic is a better option. With so many bikes on the road, know that Danes bike with a purpose and don't tolerate slow cyclists or pedestrians clogging up the bike lane, so make sure to stay clear. Additionally, city bus stops are often set up so that dismounting passengers step right into the bike lane, so look both ways before you get off the bus.

PRACTICAL INFORMATION

Tourist Offices: Copenhagen Visitor Service (Vesterbrogade 4; 70 22 24 42; check www.visitcopenhagen.com for monthly hours, but generally 9am-5pm or later during high season).

Banks/ATMs/Currency Exchange: Credit and debit cards are widely accepted in Copenhagen, though some places may charge a small fee for using an international card. ATMs (often called *pengeautomat,* or some variation thereof) can be found on the street and outside most banks. A branch of Forex Bank can be found inside Copenhagen Central Station (33 11 22 20; open daily 8am-9pm).

Post Offices: There is a centrally located post office on Pilestræde (Pilestræde 58; 70 70 70 30; open M-F 8:30am-7pm, Sa 8:30am-2pm).

Internet: Internet is widely available in Copenhagen. Most cafés and many museums provide free Wi-Fi, as do Copenhagen Central Station and the visitor center.

BGLTQ+ Resources: Denmark is one of the most gay-friendly cities in the world and in Scandinavia, and that's saying a lot. It's home to Denmark's oldest gay bar, Centralhjørnet, and a number of guides, and even an app (GAY CPH) is dedicated to BGLTQ+ travel. LGBT Denmark is the national organization for BGLTQ+ advocacy (Nygade 7; 33 13 19 48).

EMERGENCY INFORMATION

Emergency Number: 112. In non-emergency situations, call 1813 for a nurse or doctor, or 114 for police.

Police: Politigården, the Copenhagen Police Headquarters, is located near Copenhagen Central Station (open M-F 8am-9pm, Sa-Su 10am-5pm).

US Embassy: There is a US Embassy in Copenhagen (Dag Hammarskjölds Allé 24; 33 41 71 00; telephone open M-F 8:30am-5pm, appointments from M-Th 9am-noon).

Rape Crisis Center: The Centre for Victims of Sexual Assault at Rigshospitalet in Østerbro has a 24-hour crisis center and hotline (Blegdamsvej 9; 35 45 50 32).

Hospitals: Always call 1813 before visiting an emergency room, or you may not be admitted. The doctor or nurse you talk to will also help you find the nearest hospital (Bispebjerg Hospital; Bispebjerg Bakke 23; 35 31 35 31).

Pharmacies: Pharmacies (called apotek in Danish) are common on the street. Steno Apotek near Copenhagen Central Station is open 24hr (Vesterbrogade 6C; 33 14 82 66).

ACCOMMODATIONS

🏨 GENERATOR HOSTEL ($$)

Adelgade 5-7; 78 77 54 00; www.generatorhostels.com/copenhagen; reception open 24hr

Generator has built arguably the most successful hostel franchise in Europe, and its Copenhagen location doesn't disappoint. It feels like the kind of place a Saudi prince might stay—you know, if Saudi princes stayed in hostels and not five-star hotels. Most dorms have ensuite bathrooms, the bar has two happy hours each night, and the lounge area has arcade games, pool tables, and plenty of plush couches for lounging. Its location near Copenhagen's largest square is close to the lively nightlife along **Gothersgade,** and provides easy access to **Nørrebro.** The one downside: there's no guest kitchen. But Saudi princes don't cook for themselves anyway.

i Dorms from DKK 250, privates from DKK 600; reservation recommended; BGLTQ+ friendly; wheelchair accessible; Wi-Fi; linens included; storage lockers provided; laundry DKK 50; breakfast DKK 75

COPENHAGEN DOWNTOWN HOSTEL ($)

Vandkunsten 5; 1467; 70 23 21 10; www.copenhagendowntown.com; reception open 24hr

Copenhagen Downtown is a bustling, loud, whirlwind of a hostel smack in the middle of the city center. It's a place for the weekend and weekday warrior alike with a lobby bar always filled with booming music covering everything from "Macarena" to "Africa," and an outdoor seating area packed with people enjoying an afternoon beer or four. Live music twice a week, cheap beer (especially during happy hour from 8pm-9pm), and events like quiz nights and pong tournaments make this the best choice if you're the kind of person who wonders why people limit themselves to just two nights of partying a week.

i Dorms from DKK 200, privates from DKK 400; reservation recommended; BGLTQ+ friendly; wheelchair accessible; Wi-Fi; storage lockers provided; linens included; laundry DDK 40; breakfast buffet DKK 70

URBAN HOUSE ($)

Colbjørnsensgade 11; 33 23 29 29; www.urbanhouse.me; reception open 24hr

Urban House is massive, loud, and just as raucous as you'd expect a hostel next to a strip club to be. This hostel-hotel hybrid has every type of room from singles to family rooms and ten-bed dorms, drawing a varied crowd accordingly. Though it can often be difficult to meet people in such a large setting, Urban House gives you plenty of opportunities. There's a large guest kitchen and lounge area, and the restaurant and bar in the lobby are busy every night of the week. There are even events like walking tours and salsa dance nights, all free for guests. Each room has a private bathroom, but don't worry if it's occupied in the morning—there are extra showers on the third floor.

i Dorms from DKK 190, singles from DKK 650; reservation recommended; BGLTQ+ friendly; wheelchair accessible; Wi-Fi; linens included; towels included; breakfast DKK 75

SIGHTS
CULTURE

🖼 ROSENBORG CASTLE

Øster Voldgade 4A; 33 15 32 86; www.konger-nessamling.dk/en/rosenborg; open Jan 2-Feb 11 Tu-Su 10am-2pm, Feb 11-Feb 26 daily 10am-3pm, Feb 26-Apr 10 Tu-Su 10am-2pm, Apr 11-Apr 17 daily 10am-4pm, Apr 18-June 15 daily 10am-4pm, June 16-Sept 15 daily 9am-5pm, Sept 16-Oct 31 daily 10am-4pm, Nov 1-Dec 22 Tu-Su 10am-2pm, Dec 26-Dec 30 daily 10am-4pm, Dec 31 10am-2pm, closed Jan 1, Apr 24

Don't let Bernie Sanders come to Rosenborg and see what wealth inequality looked like in the Middle Ages. Rosenborg was built in the early 1600s by **King Christian IV** and became a place to showcase the Danish royal family's wealth, mostly in the form of lavishly-decorated rooms and excessively ornate artifacts. See chess sets made of amber, Christian IV's porcelain-paneled privy, and an entire model ship made of ivory. Downstairs in the windowless, concrete vault sit the most important artifacts from Danish royal history, from **Christian III's Sword of State**, to **Christian IV's** crown and the **Danish Crown Jewels.** The **King's Garden** outside is a wonderful park in which to relax, after frantically googling how you can marry into the royal family.
i Admission DKK 110, students DKK 70; guided tour DKK 45; guided tours daily at 2:10pm in summer season (check website for dates); no wheelchair accessibility in castle

CHRISTIANSBORG PALACE

Prins Jørgens Gård 1; 33 13 44 11; www.kongeligeslotte.dk/en; Royal Reception Rooms May-Sept

This is actually the third Christiansborg Palace erected here and there were two castles even before that. Today, it's the seat of the Danish government, and, while the royal family no longer lives here (not since 1794, when the first Christiansborg burned down), one wing holds the **Royal Reception Rooms**, which are still used for official business. This area is open to the public, where you can see lavish marble-floored and velvet-curtained rooms in which **Queen Margrethe II** greets her guests. Blue, surgeon-style shoe covers are provided to protect the floors from the filth on your commoner shoes.

Underneath the palace, visit the ruins of the first two buildings that existed here, **Absalon's Castle** (which was knocked down for fun by the Germans) and **Copenhagen Castle** (which simply went out of style).
i Combination ticket, including Royal Reception Rooms, Royal Kitchen, Ruins, Royal Stables DKK 150, students DKK 125; tour of Royal Reception Rooms daily at 3pm, Royal Kitchen Sa 4pm, Ruins Sa noon; wheelchair accessible

NYHAVN

Open daily 24hr

Nyvavn is Copenhagen's prime people-watching area. Its name literally means "new harbor" in English, but there's nothing new about this place. It's one of the most historic areas of the city with ancient wooden sailboats moored along the docks and steep-gabled, brightly-colored buildings on both sides of the canal. The streets are lined with cafés, ice cream shops, and even a gentlemen's club, but don't bother with any of them unless you're into getting ripped off; there are plenty of places to get better food and cheaper beer. Instead, bring your own, or just enjoy the boats and buildings of this little slice of Copenhagen.
i Prices vary; wheelchair accessible

TIVOLI GARDENS

Vesterbrogade 3; 33 15 10 01; www.tivoli.dk/en; open summer M-Th 11am-11pm, F 11am-midnight, Sa 10am-midnight, Su 10am-11pm

Tivoli Gardens is the second-oldest amusement park in the world, and it's thriving. There are copies all over Scandinavia, like **Gröna Lund Tivoli** in Stockholm and **Tivoli Friheden** in Aarhus, but they can't hold a candle to the king. See, Tivoli is a true cultural hub, with top notch rides, fine dining restaurants, and live music in every genre from big band swing to hard rock. And unlike Trix, Tivoli's not just for kids. Sure, there are plenty of stroller-pushing dads, but you'll also find elderly couples swinging away on the dance floor and teenagers just looking for a good place to rip through a pack of cigarettes.
i Admission DKK 120, Friday after 7pm DKK 160, DKK 23 ride ticket; wheelchair accessible

VISIT CARLSBERG

Gamle Carlsberg Vej 11; 33 27 10 20; www.visitcarlsberg.com; open daily May-Sept 10am-8pm, Oct-Apr 10am-5pm

"Probably the best beer in the world," is Carlsberg's famous tagline. Try the Carlsberg "exbeerience" (yikes). This museum and temple to all things Carlsberg is housed in the original brewery, where you can learn about the history of the company, including how the original beer was a flop and that there was a the long and incredibly petty feud between the founder, **J. C. Jacobsen,** and his son. The museum also holds the world's largest collection of unopened bottles—to the confusion of every college kid, because why wouldn't you just open the bottle? Best of all, every admission ticket includes a free beer!

i *Admission (includes one beer) DKK 100, students DKK 70; beer tasting DKK 75; guided tour DKK 50; beer tastings daily on the hour noon-6pm; guided tours daily on the hour 11am-6pm; last entry 30min. before closing; wheelchair accessible*

LANDMARKS

CHURCH OF OUR SAVIOUR

Sankt Annæ Gade 29; 32 54 68 83; www.vorfrelserskirke.dk; church open daily 11am-3:30pm, tower May-Sept open 9:30am-7pm, Su 10:30am-9pm, Jan-Apr, Oct-Dec M-Sa 10am-4pm, Su 10:30am-4pm

Staying in shape is tough while traveling. Gym access is pretty much zero, so if you're craving leg day, try climbing the tower of this church. It's one of the most recognizable of Copenhagen's many spires with its gilded staircase that spirals up outside the tower. There are over 400 steps in all, and the climb, while worth it, is not for the faint of heart. Be sure to arrive right at opening or risk long lines. For the aerially challenged, the church itself is also fantastic, with an altar featuring marble columns and life-sized statues. The facade of the massive pipe organ on the back wall is carved in Baroque style, and features a bust of **King Christian V.** Who else?

i *Admission M-Th DKK 40, students DKK 30, F-Sa DKK 45, students DKK 35; church wheelchair accessible, no wheelchair accessibility in tower*

KRONBORG CASTLE

Helsingør; 49 21 30 78; www.kongeligeslotte.dk/en; open Jan-Mar T-Su 11am-4pm, open daily Apr-May 11am-4pm, June-Sept 10am-5:30pm, Oct 11am-4pm, Nov-Dec T-Su 11am-4pm

Kronborg is probably etched somewhere in the back of your mind, even if you've never heard the name before. Located north of Copenhagen in the town of **Helsingør,** this famous Renaissance castle was **William Shakespeare's** inspiration for Elsinore, the Danish castle in every high school student's worst nightmare, *Hamlet.* The castle was built so the Danish kings could control trade in the Baltic Sea (read: tax the absolute shit out of just about everyone). Kronborg incorporates *Hamlet* differently each year, from offering guided tours from the prince himself (that must be depressing) to using a full cast to act out scenes. If you don't want scarring flashbacks to English class, explore the casemates, an underground network of tunnels with a statue of the local legend Holger Danske.

i *Admission June-Aug DKK 140, students DKK 130; off-season DKK 90, students DKK 80; tours June-Aug daily noon, 1pm, 3pm, and 4pm; last entry 30min. before closing time; limited wheelchair accessibility*

MUSEUMS

🖼 LOUISIANA MUSEUM OF MODERN ART

Gammel Strandvej 13; 49 19 07 19; www. en.louisiana.dk; open Tu-F 11am-10pm, Sa-Su 11am-6pm

Despite the name, you won't find any creole or crawfish at Louisiana (so-named by the original owner of the estate, who married three different women, all named Louise). What you will find is Denmark's most-visited art museum, breathtaking panoramic views of the **Øresund,** and some of the strangest galleries you've ever seen. Past exhibitions have involved live, naked models, hallways filled with speakers projecting the sound of machine guns, and shoes made of rocks. It's all very confusing, but luckily there are also more traditional galleries featuring well-known artists like **Andy Warhol** and **Picasso.** Overlooking the Øresund is a beautifully landscaped sculpture garden, with works by **Alexander Calder** and other prominent sculptors. **Humlebæk** is near **Helsingør,** so consider pairing Louisiana with a visit to **Kronborg** or the **Maritime Museum.**

i Admission DKK 125, students DKK 110; wheelchair accessible

DESIGN MUSEUM

Bredgade 68; 33 18 56 56; www.designmuseum.dk/en; open Tu 10am-6pm, W 10am-9pm, Th-Su 10am-6pm

The Danes are a famously beautiful people and Danish design is no different. The world of design is underappreciated, essential to daily life, and often completely ridiculous to normal people, and the Design Museum displays every aspect of Danish design, from the practical to the absurd. Consider, for instance, the Danish chair. Here, you can walk through a tunnel of 110 different chairs and watch the evolution of simple wooden stools into steel recliners and behemoths of oak and leather. Other exhibits showcase modern Danish designs with a focus on sustainability, with objects like bamboo bikes and Wi-Fi routers so good-looking you'd want to hang them on your wall.

i Admission DKK 100, students under 26 free; guided tours Su 2pm; last entry 30min. before closing; wheelchair accessible

NATIONAL MUSEUM OF DENMARK

Ny Vestergade 10; 33 13 44 11; www.en.natmus.dk; open daily 10am-5pm

This is Denmark's premier museum of cultural history, and damn does it cover a lot. It's definitely a history museum, but there's some pretty cool stuff in here. You'll find golden hunting horns for bougie Vikings, a room dedicated entirely to the "art" of cosplay, and one of the world's largest collections of rune stones (they actually exist). On the second floor, there's an exhibit called **Ethnographical Treasures,** which contains an incredible collection of artifacts from all over the world, including a case full of fur anoraks and entire suits of samurai armor. If that's all a bit too cultured for you, there's also an entire exhibit dedicated to toys, which might be more up your alley.

i Admission DKK 75; tours July-Sept daily at 11am and 1pm; wheelchair accessible

THE CISTERNS

Søndermarken; 30 73 80 32; www.cisternerne.dk; open May Tu-Su 11am-7pm, June-July Tu-Su 11am-8pm, Aug Tu-Su 11am-7pm, Sept Tu-Su 11am-6pm, Oct Tu-Su 11am-5pm

The Cisterns are dank (in the literal sense—grow up). This massive, manmade cavern underneath **Søndermarken,** a park in **Frederiksberg,** used to hold fresh drinking water for the city, but thanks to modern technology it has been repurposed into a contemporary art exhibition. The Cisterns are dark, cool, and damp, and the exhibitions are similar, often focusing on themes of light, darkness, and water. Be prepared to walk over boardwalks and through clouds of mist, all in near-darkness. The exhibitions can be quite confusing, but at least it's nice and cool down there!

i Admission DKK 60, students DKK 50; no wheelchair accessibility

OUTDOORS

CANAL BOAT TOUR

Nyhavn or Gammel Strand; 32 96 30 00; www.stromma.dk/en

Copenhagen is a city on the water, but a lot of that water is man-made. The canals that make up **Nyhavn** and **Christianshavn** were constructed by **King Christian IV,** who was trying to design the city to look more like

Amsterdam to attract wealthy Dutch merchants. Spoiler alert: it didn't work. The Dutch aren't stupid and have no interest in Danish taxes, but the canals remain. That said, a canal boat tour is a great way to explore the city. Multiple tours leave daily from a few spots, including Nyhavn, and pass by multiple sights, including the **opera house,** the famous *Little Mermaid* **statue,** and **Paper Island.** Just remember to duck going under the low bridges, or risk the wrath of the captain and a nasty knock on the head.

i Most tours DKK 80; tours at least every 30-45min., starting at 9:30am, last tour varies, but as late as 9pm in the summer high season; no wheelchair accessibility

FOOD

🍚 GRØD ($)

Jægersborggade 50; 50 58 55 79; www. groed.com/en; open M-F 7:30am-9pm, Sa-Su 9am-9pm

Grød's claim to fame is that it's the world's first porridge restaurant. Now, that may not sound exciting unless you're a bear or a curly-haired blonde girl lacking common sense, but Grød is a big deal. The morning menu (served until 5pm) mainly consists of the oatmeal-type breakfasts with toppings like homemade caramel sauce, fresh fruit, or *skyr* (everyone's favorite Icelandic pseudo-yogurt product), but the afternoon menu (served from 11am) is practically gourmet. Try fried risotto with apples, roasted nuts, and mustard vinaigrette, or Asian congee with ginger and peanuts. As you might expect from a porridge restaurant, Grød has the whole coffee-in-mason-jar vibe going and emphasizes its use of seasonal and organic ingredients.

i Morning menu from DKK 45, afternoon menu from DKK 65; gluten-free, vegan, and vegetarian options available; no wheelchair accessibility

🍚 NEXT DOOR CAFÉ ($)

Larsbjørnsstræde 23; 27 12 08 18; www. nextdoorcafe.dk; open M-F 7am-6pm, Sa-Su 9am-6pm

Too often, city center cafés are overpriced and underwhelming, filled with middle-aged tourist couples, reheated pastries, and generic jazz tracks. Not so with Next Door Café. This place is authentic, fun,

and always hopping. The basement café is painted entirely in different shades of purple, and the young, tattooed staff bounces the music between pop and hip-hop favorites like Latch and Jason Drool (wait, is he still considered a favorite?). Grab an American-style breakfast of pancakes or a lunch sandwich on homemade bread, and squeeze in at one of the glass-topped tables proudly displaying a wild selection items like banknotes from around the world, hotel room keys, and boarding passes. Enjoy the youthful energy, but don't get carried away and join in by accidentally leaving behind something important!

i Breakfast plates from DKK 40, lunch sandwiches from DKK 50, coffee and espresso drinks from DKK 20; gluten-free, vegan, and vegetarian options available; no wheelchair accessibility

PALUDAN BOG & CAFÉ ($)

Fiolestræde 10; 33 15 06 75; www.palu-dan-cafe.dk; open M-Th 9am-10pm, F 9am-11pm, Sa 10am-11pm, Su 10am-10pm

Picture an aspiring author, furiously scribbling away on a yellow legal pad, surrounded by books and empty coffee cups, and you already have a good idea of what Paludan is like. It's an all-day café and book store right in the heart of downtown Copenhagen filled with textured acrylic paintings, tables and decorations that toe the line between retro and shabby chic, and of course, books. All kinds of books, from paperback leaflets to leather-bound tomes, probably containing old secrets of alchemy, or unlikelier still, a proper English translation of *hygge*. The ground floor restaurant serves three meals a day, as well as a wide selection of coffee and espresso drinks, and since Paludan is right next to **Copenhagen University,** everything is reasonably priced.

i Coffee and espresso drinks from DKK 20, brunch plates from DKK 60; gluten-free, vegan, and vegetarian options available; wheelchair accessible

NIGHTLIFE

⬛ BAKKEN

Flæsketorvet 19; www.bakkenkbh.dk; open W 9am-3am, Th-Sa 5pm-5am

Bakken is a no-nonsense, unpretentious nightclub in Copenhagen's meatpacking district in **Vesterbro,** home to some of the city's best nightlife. It's the kind of place where the bouncer gives you the once over, and then remembers that Bakken lets just about everyone in. Energy levels are high, thanks to the soul-shaking electronic and dance music pumped out by weekend DJs, and even the bartenders want in on the fun, often drinking with the customers, each other, or just about anybody who will join them. Don't expect to debate the finer points of philosophy here, but if you're looking for a place that will blow out your eardrums, Bakken is a go-to.

i No cover, beer from DKK 30, mixed drinks from DKK 60, shots from DKK 25; BGLTQ+ friendly; wheelchair accessible

⬛ MIKKELLER BAR

Viktoriagade 8; 1655; 33310415; www.mikkeller.dk; open M-W 1pm-1am, Th-F 1pm-2am, Sa noon-2am, Su 1pm-1am

There are lots of microbreweries in Copenhagen, but Mikkeller is the darling of them all. It gained fame as a "gypsy" brewery (these guys are better at beer than at political correctness), meaning that it

didn't actually own its own brewery and relied mainly on collaborations. Today, it has locations all over the world, including several in the US, but the original is still its **Vesterbro** location. This basement bar has 20 ever-changing craft brews on tap. The whitewashed brick beer mecca is the place where people come for a drink after a long, six-hour Danish work day, whether they want to talk about beer, or simply enjoy it.

i Beer from DKK 55, bar snacks from DKK 30; BGLTQ+ friendly; no wheelchair accessibility

NØRREBRO BRYGHUS

Ryesgade 3; 35 30 05 30; www.noerrebro-bryghus.dk; open M-Th noon-11pm, F-Sa noon-1pm, Su noon-10pm

The clink of glasses and murmurs of light chatter filter their way downstairs, where candlelight flickers across exposed brick walls. It's Nørrebro Bryghus, a microbrewery. This place isn't just for the casual beer lover, though. It's for people who love drinking good beer, and don't mind feeling classy while they do it. The whole place is dimly lit, in a somehow classy way, by bare, incandescent bulbs, and the ultramodern exposed ventilation ducts balance the retro feel of brick in the basement.

i Beer from DKK 65; BGLTQ+ friendly; no wheelchair accessibility

TEMPLE BAR

Nørrebrogade 48; 35 37 44 14; open M-W 3pm-2am, Th 3pm-3am, F-Sa 3pm-5am, Su 3pm-1am

Surprisingly, smoking indoors is not completely prohibited in Denmark; it's legal in establishments smaller than 40 square meters. These bars have become local favorites all over Copenhagen, and Temple Bar is one of the best in **Nørrebro.** It's a dive bar in the middle of one of the city's hip neighborhoods that flatly rejects the maddening principles of Scandinavian simplicity. Cheap drinks, a student special on beer, and a pool table on the smoky second floor draw crowds of young people looking for a low-key place to drink and smoke. If you don't want to smell like an ashtray, the first floor is smoke-free.

i Beer from DKK 40, shots and mixed drinks from DKK 25; BGLTQ+ friendly; no wheelchair accessibility

DENMARK ESSENTIALS

VISAS

Denmark is a member of the European Union and is part of the Schengen Area, so US citizens can stay in Denmark for up to 90 days without a visa.

MONEY

Denmark's currency is the Danish krone, officially abbreviated DKK and locally used interchangeably with kr.

Credit/Debit Cards: Like in Sweden and Norway, cards are accepted at the vast majority of establishments, and some are even cash free. However, in Denmark, you are more likely to be charged a small fee for using an international card. The fee is usually small (no more than 3-4% of the value of the transaction), but consider cash if you're worried, though it's worth noting you could be charged a similar fee for withdrawing from a foreign ATM. Check with your bank about foreign fees.

Tipping: Tipping in Denmark is neither expected nor required; in fact, a service charge is normally included in the bill at most restaurants. As always, a tip is appreciated, so if you feel you received exceptional service, feel free to round up the bill or tip 5-10%.

Taxes: Like it's Scandinavian neighbors, Denmark has a sky-high VAT rate of 25%, which is included in all prices. Tip: Some stores in Denmark, specifically those with a "Tax Free Worldwide" or "Global Blue" sticker, will refund the VAT for goods leaving the country. Be sure to ask at the counter for specifics, and to save receipts for any goods for which you hope to claim a refund.

SAFETY AND HEALTH

Drugs and Alcohol: Though there is technically no drinking age in Denmark, there are purchasing ages, as well as laws aimed at preventing minors from getting alcohol. You must be 18 to be served in a bar or restaurant, or to purchase anything stronger than 16.5% ABV in stores. To purchase beverages weaker than 16.5% in stores, you must be 16.

BGLTQ+ Travelers: Denmark (and Copenhagen in particular) is very liberal in terms of BGLTQ+ rights. Hostels, restaurants, and nightlife establishments are very friendly towards the BGLTQ+ community, and cities like Copenhagen and Aarhus have extensive BGLTQ+ nightlife scenes.

FRANCE

France is like the popular student with prime real estate on the third page of the high school yearbook. The nation has been involved in so many of the major world events you learned about in world history that you can't turn a corner in either its vibrant metropolises or idyllic country villages without bumping into something historic. World War II comes to life in Normandy, the extravagance that provoked the French Revolution can be found at Versailles, and the jaw-dropping wealth of the upper class in the South is extremely prominent. The French capital, Paris, is renowned around the globe for its fashion and food. In more recent years, Paris has been affected by the tragedies of the 2015 Charlie Hebdo shootings and 2017 attacks at Notre Dame and the Champs-Élysées. France has been at the center of global news networks battling political unrest, inequality, and international conflicts. The nation, throughout its conflicts and challenges, preserves its pride in being a center of history where life revolved around family, friends, food, and other simple pleasures that make life worth living. *En bref,* as the French would say, they work to live instead of living to work.

In the world's yearbook—not just your high school's—France would win superlatives like "Best Dressed" and "Most Likely to Become a Movie Star." It's a center for all the finer things in life: art, music, film, and food. It's a country that made the definition of chic from the cosmopolitan center of Paris to the beaches of Saint-Tropez to the small towns of Aix-en-Provence. Explore the beautiful country from the misty farms and orchards of the north to the dramatic cliffs and crystal blue water of the Riviera. To travel in France is truly to wish you were French.

AVIGNON

Coverage by **Julia Bunte-Mein**

Avignon is a tranquil, medieval city in the Provence region of southern France that is a calm respite from the more bustling cities in France. Take a deep breath in this lavender-smelling walled destination and explore the Palais des Papes, Gothic cathedrals, and other Roman relics (all the sightseeing will, admittedly, take no more than one afternoon in this quaint town). You may be quick to say that you only need one day in Avignon, but its charm will grow on you and, if you stay a few nights, you'll experience its wild side. Avignon changed hands from conqueror to conqueror for thousands of years and once held an extreme amount of power as the seat of the Catholic Church in the fourteenth century. Today, the town is definitely tamer; there's no threat of the Roman or French empires invading, but you might have to look out for the breezy winds of Provence, known as *le Mistral,* which are fierce, unruly, and biting. Stay for a while, discover the history, and get to the nitty gritty of the subtle, understated culture of Avignon.

ORIENTATION

The medieval, walled city of Avignon is dense and easily navigable on foot. **Le Gare Avignon Centre,** the main train station, sits just outside the towering wall. To enter the city, simply walk through the gates, **Porte de la République.** The main street, **Rue de la République,** runs straight through the city and is lined with commercial stores. At the end of the street lies **Le Place de l'Hortage,** the largest (but still pretty small) square in Avignon. Keep going up from there, past the carousel, to the massive **Palais des Papes**. This is a huge complex that connects in the back to the beautiful gardens, **Les Rocher des Doms.** At the far end of the gardens is a lookout that has a steep staircase down to ground-level where you can access **le Pont d'Avignon** over the **River Rhône.**

ESSENTIALS

GETTING THERE

Avignon has a small international airport (AVN), but flights may be cheaper out of nearby Marseille (MRS) or Montpellier (MPL). From Marseille, you can access Avignon via an easy train or bus ride. Trains arrive at Gare d'Avignon-Centre, which is just across the street from Avignon's old-city gates. TGV high-speed trains service the city from Gare d'Avignon TGV, which is a 5min. train ride from Gare Centre (€1.30).

GETTING AROUND

Avignon has local buses running along the outskirts of the medieval walls, but everything you want to see is inside the walls and easily walkable. Use the blue line (#5) to get to the Fort Saint-André, which is 3km outside the city (€1.40 single journey).

PRACTICAL INFORMATION

Tourist Offices: 41 Cours Jean Jaurès; 04 32 74 32 74; open M-F 9am-6pm, Su 10am-5pm; www.avignon-tourisme. com.

Banks/ATMs/Currency Exchange: BNP Paribas (39 Rue de la République; 0 820 82 00 01; open T-F 8:15am-12:15pm and 1:30pm-5:30pm, Sa 8:15am-12:30pm)

Post Offices: La Poste (4 Cours Président Kennedy; open M-W, F 9am-6pm, Th 9am-12:15pm and 2pm-6pm, Sa 9am-noon)

Internet: There is free Wi-Fi in tourist offices, as well as many surrounding cafés and restaurants.

BGLTQ+ Resources: www. gay-provence.org has tips on accommodations, restaurants, events and nightlife.

EMERGENCY INFORMATION

Emergency Number: 112

Police: For non-emergencies, call the local police at 04 90 16 81 00.

US Embassy: The closest US consulate is in Marseille (12 Bd. Paul Peytral; 04 91 55 09 47; M-F 9am-noon and 2pm-5pm).

Rape Crisis Center: Rape Crisis Network Europe (www.inavem.org; 01 45 88 19 00).

Hospitals: Avignon Central Hospital (Centre Hospitalier Général, 305 rue Raoul Follereau; 04 32 75 33 33)

Pharmacies: Pharmacie Des Halles (52 Rue de la Bonneterie; 04 90 82 54 27; open M-Sa 8:30am-12:30pm and 2pm-7:30pm)

ACCOMMODATIONS

AUBERGE BAGATELLE ($)

25 Allée Antoine Pinay—Ile de la Barthelasse; 04 90 86 71 35; www.auberge-bagatelle.com

First things first, Bagatalle is primarily a campground, where many families stay in RVs or young people pitch tents. The hostel is definitely a large step up from sleeping outside, but it only comes with the bare minimum (no large storage lockers or blankets). White linoleum floors, happy-go-lucky murals, and bright bubble lettering on the walls makes it feel like it's designed for young kids, but many ignore this because of the ridiculously cheap prices. From its location across the river, you'll have great views of the old city at night.

i Dorms from €13; towels included; wheelchair accessible

POP' HOSTEL ($$)

17 Rue de la République; 04 32 40 50 60; www.pophostel.fr; reception open 24hr

Right in the heart of Avignon, Pop will make your stay in Avignon convenient and pleasant. They offer clean, spacious bathrooms with individual toilets and showers, which is major key. The air-conditioned, carpeted dorms have modern bunks, each equipped with a privacy curtain, reading lamp, and two outlets. The balconies look right over the **Rue de la République** and the airtight windows do a good job of blocking out noise. Skip the €5

breakfast and instead come for the €1 wine during happy hour from 5pm-8pm in their colorful and modern bar-lounge area on the first floor. The one caveat is the strange and very dysfunctional Wi-Fi system, which involves a complicated process to get online.

i Dorms from €24; reservation required during the Festival of Avignon in July; BGLTQ+ friendly; wheelchair accessible; Wi-Fi; towels for rent

SIGHTS
CULTURE

🖾 CATHÉDRALE NOTRE-DAME DES DOMS D'AVIGNON

Pl. du Palais; 04 90 82 12 21; www.cathedrale-avignon.fr; open summer M-Sa 7:30am-8:30pm, winter M-Sa 8am-8:30pm; mass M-Sa 7:30am-8:30am, Su 10am-11:30am

This pristine cathedral is like a twelfth-century Plaza Hotel. Built in three successive phases and renovated again in 1838, the cathedral underwent a major restoration in 2013, bringing it to tip-top condition. After 30 months of work, the dazzling structure, also known as the **Basilique Metropole,** was reopened in March 2016. The steadfast efforts clearly paid off, as the Romanesque nave, Gothic chapels, and ceiling frescos are truly marvelous. Check out the Baroque balconies, covered with angels and delicately carved leaves.

i Free; last entry 20min. before closing; wheelchair accessible

LANDMARKS

🖾 PALAIS DES PAPES

Pl. du Palais; 32 74 32 74; www.palais-des-papes.com; open daily July 9am-8pm, Aug 9am-8:30pm, Sept-Oct 9am-7pm, Nov-Feb 9:30am-5:45pm, Mar 9am-6:30pm, April-Jun 9am-7pm

Let's be honest: Palais des Papes is most likely the reason you're in Avignon. And yes, it's expensive. And yes, you've already seen ten other Gothic buildings on your European tour. But a visit here is simply non-negotiable. Built in 1335, this colossal fortress, now a **UNESCO World Heritage site,** is the largest

Gothic palace in Europe and attracts over 650,000 visitors a year. With over 25 rooms decorated in beautiful frescoes and faded wall paintings, its visuals are stunning with contemporary African art that creates a juxtaposition of eras and cultures. We recommend snagging the audio guide for €2, so you can learn about what the palace looked like in its prime and hear about its drama-filled history, soon to be adapted into the reality TV show: *Nine Popes, One Palace: Who Will Survive?*

i Admission €11, students €9; combined ticket with Pont d'Avignon €13.50, students €10.50; audio guide €2; last entry 1hr before closing; wheelchair accessible

PONT D'AVIGNON

Pont d'Avignon, Bd. de la Ligne; 04 32 74 32 74; www.avignon-pont.com/fr; open daily July 9am-8pm, Aug 9am-8:30pm, Nov 9am-7pm, Mar 9am-6:30pm, Apr-Jun 9am-7pm

The Pont d'Avignon, also called the **Bridge of Saint-Benezet,** wins the award for having the most confusing audio guide ever. As you walk on the old stones of this bridge to nowhere, listen to the legend of how a young shepherd, Benezet, received a divine order from God at age 12 to build a bridge in Avignon. The legend consists of Benezet developing superhuman strength to complete the project. When completed, the bridge stood, but the river eventually washed it away, which prompted an effort from Avignon locals to rebuild it, and the cycle continued. In all honesty, you cannot get a good view of the bridge while standing on it, but, the history lesson is interesting.

i Admission €5, students €4, combined ticket with Palais des Papes €13.50, students €10.50; free audio guide

MUSEUMS

MUSÉE DU PETIT PALAIS

Palais des Archevêques, Pl. du Palais; 04 90 86 44 58; www.petit-palais.org; open M, W-Su 10am-1pm and 2pm-6pm

This **UNESCO World Heritage** museum is home to one of the world's greatest collections of medieval art. Its permanent collection includes over 300 Italian pre-Renaissance religious

paintings, containing works by **Botticelli, Carpaccio,** and **Giovanni di Paulo,** as well as Gothic and Romanesque pieces from the fine arts school of Avignon. Juxtaposed against the towering **Popes Palace,** this small palace looks like a dollhouse, but, once you step inside, the two inner courtyards and airy main gallery give it an inexplicably majestic feel. Admire the frescoed ceiling and the ginormous sculptures and pottery (we swear we saw a sculpture taller than Michael Jordan). The highlight, however, is Botticelli's *La Vierge et L'enfant* (1470).

i Admission €6, students €3; last entry 45min. before closing; guided tours available upon request; wheelchair accessible

FOOD

⬛ L'AMISTA ($)

23 Rue de la Bonneterie; 06 19 24 15 47; open daily noon-10pm

At this small bistro in the heart of the old village, you can find traditional Catalan tapas like house favorite *patatas bravas con chorizo, pan con tomate,* and *gambas persillades.* Avignon's location in the south of France places it close to Catalonia, giving this place a more authentic vibe. Their most exciting offering is the *caissette de tapas,* which is a huge selection of tapas to share (minimum two people) that is served in a wooden crate. The terrace seating, just next to an ancient archway, is lovely, but take a moment to peek inside where there are decorations in a theme of the French children's book series "Martine." The bathroom is covered in pages from the picture book.

i Tapas from €3, charcuterie boards €8.50, large salads from €14, sangria €3; happy hour Th-Sa 6:30pm-8pm; vegetarian options available; wheelchair accessible

E.A.T. ESTAMINET ARÔMES ET TENTATIONS ($$)

8 Rue Mazan; 04 90 83 46 74; www. restaurant-eat.com; open daily noon-2pm and 7pm-10pm

This lovely, secluded French restaurant is hidden on a tiny alleyway (follow the signs once you get to **Place Crillon**) and has only about a dozen tables, so you'll be lucky if you even score a seat. Their a-la-carte menu, which changes on the regular, serves hearty and homey dishes, usually a balanced composition of a protein, grain, and some fresh, seasonal veggies. The cozy and neutral-tone interior reflects their simple, but very tasteful menu. Try the tender veal braised with rosemary or asparagus wrapped in a blanket of prosciutto, sprinkled with sliced almonds and poached cherry tomatoes.

i Entrées from €10, dessert from €6; reservation recommended; vegetarian options available; wheelchair accessible

LE VINTAGE ($$)

10 Rue Galante; 04 86 65 48 54; open daily 11:30am-2:30pm and 6:30pm-10:30pm

Le Vintage boasts quality *bistronomie Provençale,* serving traditional and modern French dishes of fresh and in-season produce. Serving over 60 types of regional wines, Le Vintage pairs its drinks perfectly with food of the highest quality made with only in-season fresh produce. We recommend coming for their set lunch menu, which is a bargain for the amount of food you get; the portion sizes are truly huge. If you're lucky, you'll snag a seat in the minuscule triangular square just outside the restaurant, although the air-conditioned interior is a nice break from the mid-August heat or windy fall days of Southern France.

i Entrées from €12; vegetarian options available; wheelchair accessible

NIGHTLIFE

AOC

5 Pl. Jérusalem; 04 90 25 21 04; www.aocavignon.fr; open M-T noon-2pm and 6pm-10:30pm, F-Sa noon-2pm and 6pm-11pm, Su noon-2pm and 6pm-10pm

AOC is a fabulous wine bar in the heart of Avignon. AOC allows you to play the best game of pretend wine-connoisseur of your life. Here's how to play: 1. Listen to the waiter describe the subtle notes of honeysuckle in such-and-such regional wine. 2. Pick up your glass (cup it from the bottom for red and hold it by the stem for white). 3. Stick your nose inside, gracefully. 4.

Swirl it, take a small sip, don't swallow, but instead swish it in your mouth. 5. Watch the waiter's respect for you go up tenfold, we promise. Correctly pair your wine (red with meat, white with seafood), or your effort will go to waste.

i Appetizers from €10, main courses from €15, lunch special €14.90; vegetarian options available; wheelchair accessible

LALOGÈNE

1 Pl. Pie; 04 86 81 60 76; open daily 7:30am-1:30am

Lalogène is a lovely terrace café by day and the closest thing Avignon has to a club by night. Tourists are in the minority in this stylish, clean bar with blue bumping beats and extremely affordable drinks. Situated on the lovely **Place Pie,** either party inside or chill on the outdoor terrace, which is one of our favorite spots to spend a warm summer evening with old and new friends. The best part? Waiters constantly swing by to clear tables outside, so you won't have to worry about empty beer bottles lying around as you're trying to have a fun rendezvous at Lalogène.

i Beer and wine from €2.50, coffee from €1.10

ARLES

Picture sunbaked houses on narrow cobbled streets with off-kilter wooden window shutters and pink and green flower boxes. Fade-in on Arles and that's exactly what you get. Arles looks straight out of a nineteenth-century impressionist oil painting. And, hey, now that we think of it, we're feeling a little déjà vu because we actually have seen this scene before on a Van Gogh canvas. Van Gogh painted over 200 works around Arles, capturing its shady squares, Roman monuments, and lovely countryside. And, if you, for some reason, still aren't sold, Arles also boasts a famous Roman arena where gladiators once fought to their deaths. The ruins of the amphitheater are quite well-worth a daytrip. The historic center of Arles is bordered by **Boulevard Georges Clemenceau**, which morphs into **Boulevard des Lices,** in the south. **Boulevard Emile Combes** constitutes the western border and the River Rhône runs on the northeastern edge of the city. The train station in the north is just a 15-minute walk from the entrance to Arles, which you will enter by passing a large roundabout and through **La Porte de La Cavalerie.** The main street from the gates leads you directly to the Roman Amphitheater (it's ginormous—you can't miss it). Continuing down **Rue de la Gallade** will take you right to **L'Eglise de Saint-Trophime. Place du Forum** is just a street away on your right, and the rest of sights are all within a few blocks from there.

GETTING THERE

There is a shuttle bus between Arles and Marseille-Provence Airport. Other nearby airports include Nîmes-Alès-Camargue and Montpellier-Mediterranee Airports. The Gare d'Arles (Av. Paulin Talabot) accepts high-speed (TGV) and regional (TEV) trains. The TGV is on the line from Paris-Lyon to Marseille-Saint-Charles train station. Paris-Arles direct trains connect Arles and Avignon (20min.), Marseille (50min.) and Nîmes (20min.). The fastest way to arrive from an international destination is via airplane to Marseille and connection to a train to Arles. The main bus station on is Bd. des Lices.

GETTING AROUND

Arles is easily walkable and requires no public transportation whatsoever. The tourist office provides maps that point out the best walking routes through the city to pass all the major sights. If walking isn't your thing, there is a train that offers a 40min. tour of all the sites with commentary in six different languages from April to October. You could rent a bike, but roads in Arles lend themselves to bumpy rides.

Swing by...

LES ARÈNES (ROMAN AMPHITHEATRE)
1 Rond-Point des Arènes; 08 91 70 03 70; www.arenes-arles.com; open daily May-Sept 9am-7pm, Nov-Mar 10am-5pm, Apr-Oct 9am-6pm

Welcome to the arena. You're in the middle of an enclosed sand pit and the stadiums are filled with 21,000 spectators. Let's hope you brought your strappy leather sandals and metal vest because today you'll be fighting against a fellow tourist to the death for an acceptable Instagram shot. The Roman amphitheater is where, centuries ago, gladiators fought bloody battles with wild animals before it became a fortress in the fifth century CE. Climb up the four towers added to each side of the oval for a great look down at the area and view of Arles on the opposite site.

i *Admission €9, students €7; limited wheelchair accessibility*

THÉÂTRE ANTIQUE (ROMAN THEATRE)
8 Rue de la Calade; 04 90 18 41 20; open daily Jan 9am-noon, Feb 10am-noon and 2pm-5pm, Mar-Apr 9am-noon, May-Sept 9am-7pm, Oct-Dec 9am-noon and 2pm-6pm

Eager for more oval-shaped, tiered Roman relics? You're in luck! Just around the corner from Les Arènes is the less visually impressive, but still historically fascinating Roman Theatre. The theatre—not to be confused with its neighboring relic—was built in the time of Augustus and had 33 tiers to hold 8,000 spectators. Unlike its amphi-counterpart, this theatre has had a much harder time holding up over the years, mainly because it was employed as a quarry in the Middle Ages to provide stone for the surrounding town wall. Save two, all the columns are mere stumps, giving the ruins an ancient Stonehenge feeling.

i *Admission €9, students €7, with Liberty Pass admission €12, students €10; wheelchair accessible*

Grab a bite at...

L'HUILE FAD'OLI
44 Rue des Arènes; 04 90 49 70 73; open daily noon-midnight
If you're looking for a delicious meal that won't break the bank, Fad'Oli is the spot. Just on the corner of Place du Forum, this brightly-colored, petite restaurant with four red and yellow tables outside serves gourmet baguette sandwiches, large "Fadola" sandwiches, and (perhaps strangely) sushi. Around the restaurant there are giant barrels of olive oil on tap since, if you couldn't tell from the name, olive oil is their specialty. Drizzled on top of salads and sandwiches (and let's hope not the sushi), this liquid gold adds rich flavor to even the simplest of ingredients. Inside, you can read the descriptions of each gold-medal winning oil (yes, there are competitions for these things), and you can even buy a bottle to-go.

i *Sandwiches from €4, salads from €6, sushi from €10; vegan and vegetarian options available*

Don't miss...

FONDATION VAN GOGH
35 Rue du Dr Fanton; 04 90 93 08 08; open daily Apr-Sept 11am-7pm; open Mar Tu-Su 11am-6pm
In 1888, when the renowned artist left Paris behind for the South, Van Gogh welcomed the light, sun, and rugged landscapes of Provence. Here, he painted like wildfire, producing over 200 works in just a few years. Every year, the Fondation Van Gogh exhibits a rotating selection of his works. Only about ten are on display at once, but the small number allows you to really take in each one at full value as you stare at each saturated color, unusual perspective, and evidence of compositional genius. After you pay your respects, tour the sleek, white galleries of Van-Gogh's contemporaries before heading to the geometric rooftop terrace.

i *Admission €9, students €4; last entry 45min. before closing; 75min. guided tours daily at 11:30am and 3pm €4; wheelchair accessible*

BIARRITZ

Coverage by **Julia Bunte-Mein**

This getaway in France's Basque country is aware of its elite status. When Napoléon III and his Spanish wife, Empress Eugénie, started summering here in the mid-nineteenth century, it became the go-to beach resort for European royalty. Not much has changed. Today, the Hôtel du Palais still glimmers in the sunlight, and linen-clad Europeans shop at Goyard and Hermès. Despite its glamorous (read: expensive) reputation, Biarritz has at least one free source of entertainment: the ocean. Young travelers from all over the world come to cruise the swooping waves, filling up bars and clubs that would otherwise be empty.

ORIENTATION

Biarritz has four main beaches that stretch from the **Pointe Saint Martin Lighthouse** to **La Plage de Milady.** The downtown area is located along these beaches, and is the hub of activity in the immediate region. The seaside trail, **Le Circuit Bord de Mer,** will take you from the lighthouse to **La Grande Plage,** Biarritz's most popular beach, passing the **Hôtel du Palais.** If you continue along the coast, past the **Port du Pecheûr** (Fisherman's Port), you'll run into the **Pointe Atalaye,** from which the Virgin Rock extends. On the southern side of the Virgin Rock lie the aquarium, **Plage Port Vieux, Plage de la Côte de Basques** (home to the best waves in town), **Plage de la Marbella, Plage Milady,** and finally **La Cité de L'ocean,** the ocean-themed interactive museum. A few more miles south are the towns of **Bidart** and **Saint-Jean-de-Luz.** Just inland of the coast is **Rue Gambetta,** Biarritz's main drag, which leads to **Les Halles,** the central market. Just beyond that is **Place Georges Clémenceau,** a neighborhood known for its great restaurants and exciting nightlife scene.

ESSENTIALS

GETTING THERE

Biarritz has its own airport situated just outside of town that receives international and domestic flights. From there, you can take Bus #6 into the city center. Gare de Biarritz is the town's central train station. From there, it is about a 10min. drive or 20min. bus ride (#8) into the city center. Regional buses connect Biarritz to neighboring destinations like Saint-Jean-de-Luz, Hendaye, and San Sebastian.

GETTING AROUND

The city center of Biarritz is quite compact, and easily navigable on foot. However, the town is very hilly, and if you're not one to enjoy hiking up hills all day, consult the bus schedule. The public buses (1hr ticket €1; 24hr ticket €2; purchase directly from driver), called Chronoplus, are the cheapest and most reliable way to get around Biarritz and the surrounding towns of Anglet and Bayonne. Bus #8 takes you from the train station to the center.

PRACTICAL INFORMATION

Tourist Offices: Square d'Ixelles; 5 59 22 37 00; open daily 9am-7pm
Banks/ATMs/Currency: Barclays Bank (7 Av. Edouard VII; 5 59 22 44 44; open M-F 9am-noon, 2pm-5pm)
Post Offices: Correus (17 Rue de la Poste; open M-F 9:30am-5:30pm, Sa 9:30am-12:30pm)
Internet: Free, functional Wi-Fi is available in most restaurants and cafés.

EMERGENCY INFORMATION

Emergency Number: 112
Police: The local police station is located 1 Av. Joseph Petit (5 59 01 22 22l; open 24hr).
Rape Crisis Center: Rape Crisis Network Europe (01 45 88 19 00; www.inavem.org)
Hospitals:
• Clinic Aguilera (21 Rue de l'Estagnas; 825 13 50 64; open daily 24hr)
Pharmacies: Pharmacie de L'Océan (7 Pl. Georges Clemenceau; 5 59 24 00 08; open M-Sa 8:30am-8pm)

ACCOMMODATIONS

⬛ NAMI HOUSE ($$)

14 Rue de Tartilon; 05 40 48 02 82; www.
nami-house-anglet.fr; reception open daily
8am-noon and 2pm-5pm

Part Japanese Zen garden, part Hawaiian
bungalow, part Australian surfer
hostel, Nami House feels more like a guest
house than a dormitory. Nami's interior—
decorated with orchids, succulents, paper
lanterns, bamboo cabinets, and large
murals to create an tranquil ambience—is
quite a welcome surprise compared to
its relatively unassuming exterior. Enjoy
a glass of wine in a chaise lounge on the
terraced veranda before heading upstairs
for a comfortable night in one of Nami's
spacious bunks.

i Dorms from €28, private rooms available;
reservation recommended; min. stay 2 nights;
BGLTQ+ friendly; wheelchair accessible; Wi-Fi;
lockers available; free breakfast

SURF HOSTEL BIARRITZ ($$$)

27 Av. de Migron; 06 63 34 27 45; www.
surfhostelbiarritz.com; reception open Apr-Oct
daily 8am-noon and 2pm-5pm

Providing its guests with a restful night of
sleep, filling continental breakfast (none
of that meager bread and jam bullshit),
and a complimentary board, Surf is more
B&B than hostel. As its name implies, this
establishment is really made for surfers,
but don't be deterred if you lack shredding
experience. Surf Hostel Biarritz recently
partnered with a surf school; opt into
taking a lesson or pester one of your surfer
bunkmates enough and you'll be on your
feet in no time.

i Dorms from €38; reservation recommended;
min. stay 3 nights; Wi-Fi; laundry facilities; free
breakfast; kitchen

SIGHTS
CULTURE

CHAPELLE IMPÉRIALE (PARISH OF NOTRE DAME DU ROCHER)

4 Rue Saint Martin; 05 59 23 08 36; www.
paroisse-biarritz.fr/eglises/chapelle-imperiale.
php; open Jun-Sept Th, Sa 2pm-6pm; Sept-
Dec Sa 2pm- 5pm; Mar-Jun Sa 2pm-6pm

Built in 1864 near Napoleon III's summer
villa, the *chapelle* has a deep purple
exterior that encases a Hispano-Moorish
interior, decorated with wooden paneling
and ornately-painted and tiled walls.
Known as the "Jewel of Biarritz," the
chapel was designed by French architect
Émile Boeswillwald and can be toured by
appointment only. The limited hours are
tricky to navigate, so make sure to plan
accordingly in advance of your trip.

i Admission €3; wheelchair accessible; guided
tours available by appointment

LANDMARKS

PHARE DE BIARRITZ

60 B Espl. Elisabeth II; 05 59 22 37 10; open
daily 2pm-6pm

The Phare de Biarritz, which was
constructed in 1834 and is still
operational, stands a whopping 73-meters
above sea level, offering stunning views
of the Basque coast and Atlantic Ocean.
The plot of the lighthouse is crawling with
hydrangeas (and tourists, especially during
sunset), peppered with tamarisk trees,
and crisscrossed by a network of pebbled
pathways. Pro-tip: arrive early to beat the
lines.

i Admission €2.50; no wheelchair accessibility

PORT DES PÊCHEURS

Allée Port des Pêcheurs; open daily 24hr

Biarritz's Port des Pêcheurs dates back to
its humble fishing-village days. The port
was rebuilt in the nineteenth century
but it still has its original *crampottes,* the
picturesque fisherman houses outfitted
with wooden doors and colorful shutters.
At low-tide, the port completely drains
out, leaving a huge stretch of tide pools
kids flock to with nets to catch crabs.
To the right of the port is a small beach
that provides a great alternative to the
crowded **Grande Plage,** as well as a
selection of delicious seafood restaurants.
Before you leave, make sure to check
out Crampotte 30, a tapas and wine
bar housed in one of the original
crampottes.

i Free; limited wheelchair accessibility

ROCHER DE LA VIERGE

Allée Port des Pêcheurs; 05 59 22 37 10;
open daily 9:30am-7pm

The Virgin Rock is the emblematic
symbol of and largest tourist attraction
in Biarritz. It's no Eiffel Tower, but
the metal footbridge was designed

SAINT-JEAN-DE-LUZ

Just a 15-minute train ride from Biarritz, the small fishing port of Saint-Jean-de-Luz is more relaxed, humble, and charming than its northern counterpart.
This is an exclusive holiday destination, but the wealth is so nearly as in-your-face. Buildings are beautiful, but not luxurious, and streets are busy but not overflowing with tourists. It has a certain… *douceur de vivre,* with its picturesque port, golden-sand beach, narrow pedestrian streets, traditional *baserris* (farmhouses) and glorious history. Saint-Jean-de-Luz was founded as a fishing and whaling port, but rose up to the level of aristocracy after King Louis XIV and wife Maria Theresa wed here in 1660. Only 10km from the Spanish border, this small beach town has a Basque vibe. It shares a bus and train station **(Gare St. Jean de Luz-Ciboure)** with the city of Ciboure. The center of Saint-Jean-de-Luz is found between the fisherman's port to the southwest and **La Baie de St. Jean de Luz et Ciboure** around the northwest bend, and is pressed up against **Le Grande Plage. Place Louis XIV** is the main square and **Rue Léon Gambetta,** running parallel to the beach and lined with specialty stores, is the town's main pedestrian thoroughfare. During your visit, walk down **Promenade Jacques,** which starts at the lighthouse and continues down to a sprawling beach.

GETTING THERE

The town shares a train station with Ciboure and receives local trains from surrounding towns, including Biarritz and Bayonne, and is included on the SNCF Bordeaux-Irun and high-speed TGV Paris-Madrid train lines. Buses run frequently between Saint-Jean-de-Luz and neighboring Bayonne, Biarritz, and Hendaye. Ouibus, TCRB, and Basque Bondissant are the major bus companies. Saint-Jean-de-Luz is only a 20min. drive from Biarritz and a 30min. drive from San Sebastian. It is located off highway A-63.

GETTING AROUND

You can walk from one side of Saint-Jean-de-Luz to the other in less than 20min., so your feet are all you need! If you want to check out the neighboring town of Ciboure, however, a shuttle bus named Itzulia runs between the two towns year-round (tickets €1). There is also a free shuttle that arrives every 30min. during the summer months connecting the Chantaco and Parc des Sports parking lots in the outskirts of the port to the town center.

Swing by...

MAISON LOUIS XIV

6 Pl. Louis XIV; 05 59 26 27 58; www.maison-louis-xiv.fr; open July- Aug daily 10:30am-12:30pm and 2:30pm-6:30pm; daily visits Sept-Oct, Apr-June at 11am, 3pm, 4pm, and 5pm

Designed by ship-builder **Joannis Lohobiague** and originally known as Lohobiague-Enea, the house changed its name after the king visited in 1660. Here, Louis signed the **Treaty of the Pyrenees** in 1659 to end the ongoing conflict with Spain, and also married the Spanish Infanta Maria Teresa. If only we could solve all of our twenty-first-century problems by joining together warring nations through marriage. Take a 40-minute guided tour to see the seventeenth-century furniture, splendid painted beams, and poodle-haired family portraits. In the bedroom, notice the table with human-like legs as well as the ridiculously short bed. Apparently, Louis XIV used to sleep half-sitting out of fear of suffocating to death while lying under his sheets!

i *Admission €6, students €3.80; guided visits only; tours every 40min. July-Aug, last tour 30min. before close, arrive 5min. before tour; no wheelchair accessibility*

Check out...

L'ÉGLISE SAINT JEAN BAPTISTE
Rue Léon Gambetta; 05 59 26 08 81; open Apr-Sept M-Sa 8:30am-6:30pm,
Su 8am-7:30pm; Oct-Mar M-Sa 8:30am-6pm, Su 8am-7:30pm

Just off the commercial pedestrian street **Rue Gambetta,** you'll find the
historic church where Louis XIV and Maria Theresa tied the royal knot.
Although the outside isn't that special, the interior is definitely fit for an
imperial marriage. As soon as you enter, your eyes will be drawn to the
front of the church, where the central nave is decorated with intricate
floral patterns, ornate carvings, and golden statues. Look up at the red and
gold ceilings, stained-glass skylight, and fleur-de-lis-adorned side chapels.
In stark contrast to the front of the church, the back has a clear traditional
Basque influence. There, you'll find three-tiered balconies of dark wood
and a giant sailboat hanging from the ceiling.

i *Free; limited wheelchair accessibility*

Grab a bite at...

LA TAVERNE BASQUE
5 Rue de la République; 05 59 26 01 26; open Tu-Sa noon-2pm and 7pm-
10pm, Su noon-2pm

Rue de la République, the little street between **Place Louis XIV** and **La
Grande Plage,** is the place to go for traditional Basque food, and of the
many restaurants that line it, La Taverne Basque is the obvious choice.
Enjoy a bowl of toro soup, split a Serrano ham charcuterie board, and
savor a grilled duck with honey-balsamic glaze, and wash it all down with
a pitcher of sangria. The portions are large and the food is relatively inexpensive, but, if you find yourself craving more, stop in one of the street's
many pastry shops to try a *gâteau Basque,* an almond-based cake filled
with vanilla, rum, or cherry-flavored cream.

i *Three-course meal €19.90; vegetarian options available; limited wheelchair
accessibility*

Don't miss...

LA GRANDE PLAGE
Promenade Jacques Thibaut

While Saint-Jean-de-Luz's port and pedestrian streets are admittedly adorable, it is the town's sandy shore that attracts thousands every summer.
Unlike Biarritz, where you have a plethora of fantastic beaches to choose
from, this is the beach to visit in Saint-Jean-de-Luz and, accordingly, it is
usually packed during the summer months. Also, unlike Biarritz, it's as flat
as a pancake. Nestled in a protected bay, you'll see lots of paddle boarders,
swimmers, and motor boats gliding over the smooth water. La Grande
Plage is the picture of summer in France: a mosaic of striped rainbow
beach umbrellas, topless women, and men in speedos framed by turquoise
water.

i *Free; limited wheelchair accessibility*

by the landmark's namesake, which is close enough. Located between **Port-Vieux** and **Port des Pêcheurs** on the promontory of Atalaye, the bridge joining the rock formation to the mainland was originally wooden, built on the orders of **Napoleon III,** who decided to drill a tunnel through the formation and use it as an anchor point for the sea wall of the **Port du Refuge.** Despite enduring centuries of damage by the Atlantic, the monument, consecrated in 1865, still stands strong today. Walk across and behold the beauty of the ocean before you, statue above you, and city behind you.

i Free; no wheelchair accessibility

MUSEUMS

▨ PLANÈTE MUSÉE DU CHOCOLAT

14 Ave. Beau Rivage; 05 59 23 27 72; www.planetemuseeduchocolat.com; open July-Sept daily 10am-7pm, Oct-June M-Sa 10am-12:30pm and 2pm-6:30pm

You could be like everyone else and go to the aquarium or **Cité de L'ocean,** but if you aren't feeling particularly aquatic, we recommend heading to this adorable and hilarious chocolate museum. Upon arrival, you'll be handed a bag of chocolates (if that's not already enough of an incentive, we don't know what is). The tour begins with an educational video of the cacao bean, tracing its history from legend of the Aztec deity Quetzalcoatl to King Louis XIII obsession's with hot chocolate. All of the descriptions are in French, but the close-up shots don't need translation. The second half of the visit includes a trip to a sculpture gallery, some of which are quite scandalous (read: a chocolate rendition of *Désir* by Rodin), and cabinets full of bizarrely-shaped chocolate molds (read: rifles and llamas. How appetizing!).

i Admission €6.50, students €5, guided tour groups of 15+ €4.50; ticket office closes at 6pm; wheelchair accessible

OUTDOORS

BIARRITZ BEACHES

Open daily 24hr (weather permitting)

You already know that Biarritz is famous for its beaches, but you may not know which one is best for you. **Le Grande Plage,** the closest one to the center of town, is popular among surfers and bathers alike for its easy access, broad swatch of sand, and huge waves. There is a narrow swimming area delineated by two flags; if you venture outside of it, lifeguards will yell at you and chase you down (believe us, we tried). To the northeast is **Plage Miramar,** close to the rocky area just south of the **Phare de Biarritz.** Plage Miramar is also great for surfing, but a little more dangerous. Sandwiched between of the **Port des Pêcheurs** and Le Grand Plage is the quiet, small **Plage Port Vieux.** This protected spot is popular for families because it has no waves or wind, and it also boasts a convenient location adjacent to Biarritz's diving clubs and seafood bars. Around the Pointe Atalaye is the long, open **Plage Côte des Basques**—the ultimate surfing beach where you can rent a board or take a lesson. Note that during high tide, the beach is not open for lounging as the water brushes up against the cliffs.

i Free

FOOD

EDEN ROCK CAFÉ ($$)

6 Pl. Port Vieux; 659681824; open daily 11am-2am

Located just north of **Le Plage Port View,** this cliff-side restaurant dangles right over the shimmering ocean, with direct views of the **Rocher de la Vieux.** Eden Rock Café's menu is simple—chipirons (cuttlefish), chili, fries, beer, sangria—but extensive, and the food is much cheaper than other restaurants in the area. The true draw of Eden Rock, however, is not the food, but its canopied outdoor patio. Arrive early enough and you'll be able to snag a table on its perimeter, one of the best places, in our humble opinion, to watch the sun set in Biarritz.

i Sangria from €3, cocktails from €7.50, appetizers from €8, entrées from €12; vegetarian options available

IL GIARDINO ($$$)

5 R. du Ctre; 05 59 22 16 41; www.ilgiardino-biarritz.com; open Tu-Sa noon-2pm and 7pm-11pm, Su 7pm-11pm

Come to Il Giardino to treat yourself to an exquisite meal that won't break the bank. This Italian restaurant serves homemade, melt-in-your-mouth pasta, along with all sorts of freshly-prepared meat, fish, and vegetable dishes. Take your pick of linguini, spaghetti, gnocchi, or risotto—we loved the *linguine nero di sepia* (squid in its ink)—in the "simple" or "complete" size. For dessert, soothe your sweet tooth with the tiramisu and panna cotta—they're both delicious.

i *Appetizers from €6, entrées from €14, wine €5; vegetarian options available; wheelchair accessible; reservation recommended*

MIREMONT SALON DE THÉ ET PATIS-SERIE ($)

1bis Pl. Georges Clemenceau; 05 59 24 01 38; www.miremont-biarritz.fr; open daily 9am-8pm

This tearoom and pastry shop is truly the king of all bakeries. Dating back to the nineteenth century, the shop was frequented by European royalty like King Edward VII of England and King Alphonso XIII of Spain, the latter of which loved it so much that he appointed its founder to the country's Royal House. And the pastries truly do live up to their royal heritage. Miremont's display case features layered *millefeuilles, macarons,* lemon tarts, chocolate mousse delicacies, *éclairs,* and more, all topped with edible gold and Miremont's confectioner crest. The interior of the shop is equally over-the-top, featuring baby pink walls, crystal chandeliers, and *grand siècle* ceilings. Pastry prices are a bit steep, so we recommend ordering yours to-go, which will automatically knock €2 off the top.

i *Cakes to-go from €3.50, to-stay €5.50*

NIGHTLIFE

DUPLEX

24 Av. Edouard VII; 05 59 24 65 39; www.nightclub-biarritz.com; open daily 7pm-6am

The population in Biarritz consists of two very distinct crowds: posh vacationers and young surfers. As its name suggests, Duplex accommodates both by leaning into the city's naturally-occurring dichotomy, funneling anyone above the age of 25 upstairs to the "Cotton Club" and anyone below that age downstairs to "Pulp." Despite their absurd names, both floors are surprisingly lit. Cotton Club may be more chic with its arched ceilings, glowing blue bar, and VIP lounges, but Pulp is where the real party happens. Here, you can order a vodka and orange juice concoction that's almost as sugary as the daddies upstairs, and dance the night away to the rapid thumping of house music.

i *Cover €12 (includes one free drink), cock-tails from €1; wheelchair accessible*

NEWQUAY BAR

20 Pl. Georges Clemenceau; 05 59 22 19 90; open daily 9am-midnight

A student hideaway in the middle of glitzy Biarritz, Newquay Bar is consistently packed with English-speaking Australians, Americans, South Africans, and tons of non-French-speaking Europeans. Unlike its neighbors, this pub is unpretentious, serving cheap beers, salty food, and ciders imported from Cornwall, England. It's the perfect a relaxed environment to meet other travelers, listen to live music, or watch the latest football match.

i *Beer from €2, drinks from €5; wheelchair accessible*

BORDEAUX

Coverage by **Kristine Guillaume**

Welcome to Wine Country. A city loaded with culture and, perhaps obviously, wine, Bordeaux has truly earned its place as the epicenter of beauty and sophistication in southwestern France. Years ago, when the city rose to fame for its bustling Chartons district, where wine merchants perfected blends of reds and whites, merchants and owners of the renowned *châteaus* wrote about the port, calling it the Port of the Moon, for its stunning, ornate architecture along the Garonne River. Today, the glistening reflections of landmarks such as Place de la Bourse and unmistakable Belle Époque architecture in the water make it impossible to question the Bordeaux's status as a UNESCO World Heritage Site. Yet, even with its ancient Roman and French history, the city has transformed from the *Belle au Bois Dormant* (Sleeping Beauty) to a bustling, cosmopolitan center with a trendy student nightlife scene and outdoor concert venues on the river. Not too far from the main city are Atlantic beach towns just a bus ride away if you're looking to enjoy the surf and sun. Let's make a toast—of Merlot, Claret, or Chardonnay— to Wine Country. Here's to Bordeaux.

ORIENTATION

The Garonne River divides Bordeaux in two parts**,** with its center on the western bank. **Les Quais,** the riverfront boardwalk, stretches between the two main bridges, **Pont de Pierre** and **Pont Jacques Chaban Delmas.** Along Les Quais, you'll find everything from skate parks to green spaces to restaurants. The main attraction along the boardwalk, however, is the city center at **Place de la Bourse,** in front of which is **Miroir d'Eau.** The city center, also called **Vieille Ville** (Old City) opens up to **Promenade Sainte-Catherine,** the longest pedestrian street in Europe lined with cafés, restaurants, and boutiques. To the north of Vielle Ville is the **Triangle D'Or** neighborhood, the wealthiest area in all of Bordeaux, where you'll find three main boulevards at have vertices at **Le Grande Théâtre, Place Gambetta,** and **Place Tourny.** North of Vielle Ville is the famous **Chartrons district,** known for its former status as a port city and even farther north is an industrial area, which is home to **Base Sous Marine** and the decanter-shaped **Cité du Vin.** South of Vielle Ville is the **Saint Michel** neighborhood, known for having the highest concentration of ethnic food in Bordeaux. On the eastern bank of the Garonne is the **Bastide** area, where you can find outdoor spaces like **Darwin Ecosystème.**

ESSENTIALS

GETTING THERE

If flying, you'll land at Bordeaux-Mérignac Airport, which is 9km from the city center. The Jetbus (€7) runs directly between the airport and the main train station, Gare Saint Jean, every 30min. The ride itself is 30min. To save money (like the responsible budget-conscious backpacker that you are), you can take the Line 1 bus (€1.40) to Gare Saint-Jean. If arriving by train, you'll dock at Gare Saint-Jean, which is a 15min. tram ride away from the city center. Take tram line C to Place de la Bourse (€1.60).

GETTING AROUND

The tramway is the most convenient mode of public transportation in the city. Trams depart roughly every 5min. from street-side stops (single ride €1.60). The most essential tram lines are Line C, which runs to the city center (Place de la Bourse) and Line B, which runs to Cité du Vin and Cathédrale Saint-Andre. Another option is to use Bordeaux's city bikes, VCub, with docking stations throughout the city (24hr pass €1.60). Take the ferry (€2) acro, which runs from the Stalingrad station on the eastern bank to Quinconces on the eastern. Also, the Transports Bordeaux Métropole (TBM) operates over 80 bus lines that serve the greater urban Bordeaux area.

PRACTICAL INFORMATION

Tourist Offices: 12 Cours du 30 Juillet; 05 56 00 66 00; www.bordeaux-tourisme. com; open M-Sa 9:30am-1pm and 2pm-7pm

Banks/ATMs/Currency Exchange: There are BNP branches with accessible located near the Opéra and in the Chartrons district (BNP Paribas Bordeaux: 40 Cours du Chapeau-Rouge; 820 82 00 01; open M-F 9am-5:30pm).

Post Offices: La Poste Bordeaux (29 Allée de Tourny; open M 9am-6pm, Tu 10am-6pm, W-F 9am-6pm, Sa 9am-noon)

Public Restrooms: You can easily find public restrooms, labeled "Toilettes," along the banks of the Garonne River. There is one located just in front of Place de la Bourse.

Internet: Bordeaux is covered with public Wi-Fi spots. Simply click "Wifi Bordeaux" on your phone network. Free Wi-Fi is also offered in all municipal buildings, including the tourist office.

BGLTQ+ Resources: LGBT Association of Aquitaine; www.le-girofard.org

EMERGENCY INFORMATION

Emergency Number: 112

Police: Hôtel de Police, Commissariat Central (23 Rue François de Sourdis; 05 57 85 77 77; open daily 24hr)

US Embassy: There is a US consulate in Bordeaux (89 Quai des Chartrons; 01 43 12 48 65).

Rape Crisis Center: Rape Crisis Network Europe (www.inavem.org; 01 45 88 19 00)

Hospitals: Hôpital Saint André (1 Rue Jean Burguet; 05 56 79 56 79; open daily 24hr)

Pharmacies: Pharmacie (30 Pl. des Capucins; 05 56 91 62 66; open daily 24hr)

ACCOMMODATIONS

🏠 HOSTEL 20 ($$)

20 Rue Borie; 06 65 52 16 80; www.hostel20. fr; reception open 24hr

Staying at Hostel 20 feels like you're staying at someone's house. And that's kind of because you are. The hostel allows young 20-somethings from across the globe to volunteer their time working in exchange for free extended lodging. As a result, Hostel 20 creates a quirky, homey,

and social atmosphere, complete with regular beds (read: no bunks!), cheap rental bikes (€3-5), and nightly hostel home-cooked dinners (€5). Meals include paella, pasta, and breakfast for dinner at a much-cheaper price than any restaurant in the surrounding **Chartrons district.** The hostel boasts a great location and provides a surge protector to every bed in the rooms, but loses points since the doors of the actual dormitories don't actually lock, so be sure to lock your valuables in the small lockers in each individual room.

i Dorms from €27; reservation recommended; BGLTQ+ friendly; no wheelchair accessibility; Wi-Fi; linens, towels included; lockers available; laundry €4; breakfast €2

AUBERGE DE JEUNESSE BORDEAUX ($$)

22 Cours Barbey; 05 56 33 00 70

It may come as a surprise that there are only two hostels in Bordeaux, but Auberge de Jeunesse was the only one until Hostel 20 sprouted in 2015. An organized and functional place to stay, the hostel provides comfortable lodging with an expansive kitchen in which you can prepare your own meals to avoid steep restaurant prices. Although the hostel boasts bright pink and lime green common areas and a balcony, it is less social than its budget-accommodation counterpart, but makes up for this with its convenient location, which is just 10 minutes from the city center on foot.

i Dorms from €24; reservation recommended; Wi-Fi; linens included; lockers available; full kitchen

SIGHTS
CULTURE

LA CITÉ DU VIN

134 Quai de Bacalan; 05 56 16 20 20; www.laciteduvin.com/fr; open daily 9:30am-7:30pm

La Cité du Vin is an impressive architectural feat: the structure itself is modeled after a decanter, so you already know that this glitzy, brand-spanking-new sight isn't going to disappoint. Established in 2016, Cité du Vin quickly overshadowed its younger sister, **Musée du Vin et du Négoce,** with its extensive exhibits about wine, modern features, and wine tastings. At the end of the day, we appreciated the smaller sibling a little bit more. Call us old-fashioned, but we'd rather have the three wine tastings in the **Chartrons district** than the two Cité du Vin offers (more is better, especially when it comes to wine). Plus, the entrance to La Cité du Vin is steep at €20. Yeah, you heard us. €20.

i *Admission €20, reduced €14; limited wheelchair accessibility*

PALAIS GALLIEN

Rue du Docteur Albert Barraud; 33 5 56 00 66 00; open daily

Bordeaux is just under 1000 miles from Rome, but, even with that distance, you're bound to find a piece of Roman history. Located just a few blocks away from the **Jardin des Plantes**, Palais Gallien is a Gallo-Roman amphitheatre that holds the very prestigious title of the oldest Roman ruin in Bordeaux. Although it serves today as a shelter for French pigeons, it has managed to keep its majesty throughout the centuries of wear and tear by even the most unsuspecting of guests (rumor has it that Palais Gallien was a hang-out spot for prostitutes and witches in the seventeenth century). Walk by at night to see the structure lit up courtesy of the bright lights implanted in the ground.

i *Free; daily tours €3 June 1-Sept 30 10:30am-3:30 pm, evening visits €5 Sa 9:30pm in July-Aug; wheelchair accessible*

LANDMARKS
....

BASILIQUE SAINT-MICHEL

Pl. Meynard; 05 56 94 30 50; open daily 8am-noon and 1pm-6pm

The city of Bordeaux may be a **UNESCO World Heritage Site,** but the Basilique Saint-Michel is one all on its own. This fourteenth-century basilica, although a bit of a walk from the city center, is well worth a trip to the **Saint-Michel** area. The interior is typical of a gothic European cathedral, bearing some similarity to the nearby **Cathédrale Saint-André,** but it has an older, more lived-in feel. Take a walk around the basilica and then climb its bell tower, the **Fleche de St. Michel,** for a leg workout and fantastic view of the city below. On Fridays and Sundays, you'll find an outdoor market of the antique and produce varieties in the adjacent square.

i *Free; tower and crypt €5, students €3.50; last entry 30min. before closing; limited wheelchair accessibility*

CATHÉDRALE SAINT-ANDRÉ

Pl. Pey Berland; 05 56 52 68 10; open daily June-Sept 10am-1pm and 3pm-7:30pm (until 7 pm on Su in July and Aug); daily Oct-May 10am-noon and 2 pm-6 pm (until 7 pm on M, W, Sa); closed on M mornings year-round

Take a deep breath because you're about to have it taken away. The Cathédrale Saint-André, also known as the Bordeaux Cathedral, stands tall in the middle of Place Pey-Berland with its magnificent gothic architecture of the Aquitaine region. The inside is an absolute masterpiece first constructed in the fifth or sixth century. Over many years, the Bordelaise have made improvements to the structure, elevating the nave with pointed arches, restoring the giant organ, and opening the royal portal. The cathedral, apart from serving as a religious center, was formerly an animal feed store during the French Revolution (which is kind of gross when you think about it) and was destroyed during WWI. Since then, it has been restored to its former glory with intricately decorated chapels dedicated to various saints and stunning biblically-inspired works of art.

i *Free; last entry 30min. before closing; wheelchair accessible*

PLACE DE LA BOURSE

Quai du Maréchal Lyautey; open daily 24hr

Perhaps the first thing you see when you Google "Bordeaux" is red wine. But the next thing that pops up will be, without a doubt, Place de la Bourse, the city's main square. Built in the eighteenth century in a neoclassical style, the square was erected for King Louis XIV and his obscenely lavish tastes. Within the square itself is the **Bourse,** the stock exchange, a fountain of the Three Graces, and the Customs Museum. In front of the square, you'll find the tram line C, which takes you to **Gare Saint-Jean** and the famous **Miroir d'Eau,** the world's largest water mirror, which spans a whopping 37,000 square feet. If you happen to be on the eastern bank of the **Garonne** in the evening, look out onto the square to see Bordeaux in all its glory, when the façades glow with soft, yellow light.

i *Free; limited wheelchair accessibility*

TOUR PEY-BERLAND

Pl. Pey-Berland; 05 56 81 26 25; www.
pey-berland.fr; open daily Jan-May 10am-
12:30pm and 2pm-5pm, daily June-Sept
10am-1:15pm and 2pm-6pm, daily Oct-Dec
10am-12:30pm and 2pm-5:30pm

Forget the StairMaster; the Tour Pey-
Berland has your leg workout covered.
The 233-step gothic structure is the bell
tower of the **Cathédrale Saint-Andre**
and offers the most incredible panoramic
360-degree view of Bordeaux. Built in
the fifteenth century, the tower lacked
bells until 1853 and just served as a
towering structure for a few hundred
years. Now, though, you can climb up the
tower and read about the history of every
neighborhood of Bordeaux, including the
Saint-Michel and **Chartrons** districts,
on the descriptive plaques on the first
landing. Pro-tip: bring water on your
trek up the bell tower, as the climb is
remarkably dizzying.

i Admission €6, free for EU residents and EU
students 18-25 years old; last entry 30min.
before closing; no wheelchair accessibility

MUSEUMS

✎ MUSÉE DU VIN ET DU NÉGOCE

Cellier des Chartrons; 41 Rue Borie; 05 56 90
19 13; www.museeduvinbordeaux.com; open
daily 10am-6pm

Don't overlook this museum for the glitzy
La Cité du Vin. This small museum,
located in the **Chartrons district,** is
designed like the wine cellars where the
merchants of the district used to produce
the highly prized Bordeaux wines. The
first hallway is a history lesson, while the
second explains how the wine was made,
with the actual barrels and machines.
After you walk through the museum,
enjoy tasting two wines as a museum
guide gives you an introduction to the
specific wine regions of Bordeaux.

i Admission €10, students €5; limited wheelchair accessibility

CAPC MUSÉE D'ART CONTEMPORAIN DE BORDEAUX

7 rue Ferrère; 05 56 00 81 50; www.capc-bor-
deaux.fr; open Tu 11am-6pm, W 11am-8pm,
Th-Su 11am-6pm

Contemporary art is weird. And the
CAPC is no exception. This museum
takes weird to the max, exhibiting videos
of a naked man desperately trying to
straighten his sheets, a female doll lying
face down on the ground, and abstract
rows of rocks. There's an interesting
room on the upper level with seaweed-
like strings hanging from the ceiling
spelling out the words *displaisir* and
plaisir, complemented by an eerie blue
light spelling out fragments of caveat-like
sentences. It's safe to say this is the stuff of
nightmares and yes, after visiting, we had
quite a few.

i Admission €7, students €4; wheelchair
accessible

MUSÉE DES BEAUX ARTS

20 Cours d'Albret; 05 56 10 20 56; www.
musba-bordeaux.fr; open M, W-Su 11am-6pm

Bordeaux's Musée des Beaux Arts is what
you'd expect: rows of art with pictures
of Jesus and Jesus' mom. The museum
is separated into two wings: fifteenth
to seventeenth century and eighteenth
to twentieth century. While the first
contains mostly the aforementioned
variety of paintings, the second contains
works by many Bordelaise artists. The
museum boasts a fair amount of works by
renowned artists, including masterpieces
by **Matisse, Monet,** and **Renoir** in its
high-ceilinged exhibits.

i Admission €4, students €2; wheelchair
accessible

OUTDOORS

✎ DARWIN ECO-SYSTÈME

87 Quai des Queyries; 05 56 77 52 06; open
M-F 8:30am-6pm

The *Rive Droite* of Bordeaux seems to
always live in the shadow of its left-
leaning sibling. But to ignore this side of
the **Garonne** would be a huge mistake,
especially when Darwin Eco-système
dwells just across from the **Chartrons
District.** Darwin, a repurposed
military barrack, is part of Bordeaux's
rejuvenation as a modern city. Come
here to enjoy drinks on the banks of the

river, complemented with a filling meal surrounded by vintage décor. This is *the* hub of urban culture in Bordeaux, complete with co-working spaces, an art gallery, and a skate park called the Hangar (we swear it was inspired by Avril Lavigne's 2002 hit "Sk8ter Boi," but that's just our opinion. Who knew the French were into angsty teen pop?).

i Free, hangar €5; limited wheelchair accessibility

BASE SOUS-MARINE

Bd. Alfred Daney; 05 56 11 11 50

If World War II history is your thing, then you came to the right place. Venture to the outskirts of Bordeaux to see the submarine base tucked away just steps from the **Cité du Vin** tram stop. Base sous-marine was one of five bases built on the Atlantic coast for fleets of German and Italian U-boats during the German occupation. The 42,000-meter structure, which was built between 1941 and 1943, looks like a huge hunk of rock from afar, but portions of it are open to the public. When we last visited, the submarine base was undergoing renovations and therefore closed to visitors, but will be open in 2019.

i Admission €5, reduced €3, free first Su of the month when open to the public; tours €3 with ticket, tours on W 5pm-6pm, Sa 4pm-5pm; limited wheelchair accessibility

FOOD

L'AGNEAU À LA BRAISE ($$$)

13 Rue du Pas-Saint Georges; 05 56 52 24 89; www.lagneaualabraise.com; open M-Sa 7pm-11pm

Don't get us wrong: we're all for solo travel and solo eating. After all, taking yourself out for a meal is on every single one of those "Ten Steps to Your 'Eat, Pray, Love' Experience" Buzzfeed lists. But L'Agneau à la Braise probably isn't the place to do it. It is, however, the place to treat yourself to a nice dinner. Serving typical French fare, this restaurant in the **Saint Pierre** neighborhood of Bordeaux provides an intimate setting for you and your backpacker friends. We recommend trying their rib-eye steak or their leg of lamb, both cooked perfectly to make your dinner delicious and flavorful (and you'll get to watch the chefs cook your meat from the dining room). Pair your meat with wine straight from the famous Bordelaise *châteaus* you've been hearing about to round out a meal you'll reminisce about forever.

i Entrées from €20, wine from €10; vegetarian options available; wheelchair accessible

FUFU BORDEAUX ($$)

37 Rue Saint-Rémi; 5 56 52 10 29; www.restaurantfufu.com; open M-F 11:30am-3pm and 6:30pm-11pm

Locals and tourists alike have heard of FuFu, and the crowds lining up at its door are living proof that this small, Japanese noodle bar has a cult following. With a wide selection of everything from ramen to stir fry to dumplings, FuFu's specialty is delicious noodles with perfectly salted broth and eggs. Choose from a basic ramen with pork or spice it up with a miso flavor. If noodles aren't your cup of tea, go for a spicy, flavorful wok dish and watch the skilled chefs prepare them right before your eyes as you wait eagerly at the counter for your lunch. FuFu has a second location not too far off from the first, where you can stop by for your second noodle dish (trust us, you'll want it)

i Entrées from €9, side dishes from €4, sake from €4, soft drinks from €3; vegetarian options available; wheelchair accessible

CAFÉ NAPOLEON ($)

6 bis Cours du 30 Juillet; 05 56 81 52 26; open daily 7am-9pm

Located steps away from the grand opera, Café Napoleon is the place to stop for your morning coffee. The seats spill onto the sidewalk. The café's interior, however, is a grand, mint-green wallpapered space featuring life-sized mirrors with ornate frames—perhaps a testament to its namesake: Napoleon. Like all its counterparts, this café boasts a delicious, flavorful espresso (paired with a biscuit) for just €2, but you'll find yourself coughing up at least €5 for a cup of tea (along with some coughs thanks to the lady chain-smoking next to you).

i Espresso from €2, other drinks from €3; vegetarian options available; wheelchair accessible

FRANCE BORDEAUX

NOM D'UNE CRÊPE ($)

32 rue Saint Remi; 05 56 06 46 81; open daily noon-2:30pm and 7pm-10:30pm

Just a few blocks away from **Place de la Bourse** lies the perfect destination to satisfy your craving for a French crêpe. Nom d'Une Crêpe offers a series of deals on both savory and sweet crêpes, ranging from your classic *fraise* to *oeufs avec jambon.* (That's strawberries and eggs with ham, respectively, for those of you who haven't picked up on French yet.) The interior of the restaurant resembles that of a wine cellar, which seems to be a common theme in Bordeaux. Order a cup of tea for a midday refresher and leave enough room in your stomach for at least two delectable crêpes: you won't want to miss out.

i Menu classique €11.90, crêpes from €9, coffee and tea from €2

LE REGENT ($)

6 Cours Georges Clemenceau; 05 56 44 90 00; open 11:45am

If we wanted to pretend that we were Blair Waldorf and Serena Van Der Woodsen prancing around France for an entire month (when they should have been prepping for their SATs), we would probably go to Le Regent. A café situated just steps away from the regal **Bordeaux Opéra,** Le Regent is the perfect place to grab an espresso in a posh chair while listening to pumping beats that belong in the background of *Gossip Girl.* Be warned that the chairs are strangely small, probably designed for skinny French people or those under 5'5". But the rich flavor of the coffee, whether you choose a classic espresso or a *café noisette,* is worth the tight squeeze.

i Espresso from €2, other coffee drinks from €4, entrées from €11; vegetarian options available; wheelchair accessible

NIGHTLIFE

BAD MOTHER FUCKER ($)

16 Cours de l'Argonne; 09 86 50 94 68; open daily 5pm-2am

If you're looking to meet some strange characters that won't have their nose stuck in a glass of wine that smells "oaky," swing by this bar to say *enchanté* to some bad motherfuckers. We're not quite sure what word to use to encapsulate the atmosphere of this pub:

Grungy? Alternative? Punk? Whatever it is, you're bound to enjoy a wild night consisting of Rolling Stones' hits, a wide selection of beers, billiards, and—if you're lucky—live music. So drop your wine glass and pick up a pint. Embrace the intensely red walls of this joint and grow a mullet: it's time to be a bad motherfucker (but even better to be one during happy hour from 5pm-8pm).

i Beer and wine from €5, shots from €3; wheelchair accessible

LA CONSERVERIE-CONSERVERIE ($)

18 Rue Notre Dame; 05 56 81 49 17; www.laconserverie-bordeaux.fr; open Tu-W 11am-8:30pm, Th-Sa 11am-10pm

Bordeaux is the city of wine and La Conserverie-Conserverie doesn't disappoint. This wine bar serves high-quality Bordelaise wines in a charming space geared toward an almost exclusively local crowd. Although there is a terrace courtyard, we recommend kicking back on one of the cozy armchairs and admiring the Moroccan rugs. If you've grown tired of wine, La Conserverie-Conserverie offers an expansive selection of other drinks, including Aperol spritz and a wide array of beers along with small plates to pair with your beverage of choice.

i Wine from €4, small plates from €10; wheelchair accessible

THE STARFISH PUB ($)

24 Rue Sainte Colombe; 05 56 52 88 61; open M-F 4pm-2am, Sa 2pm-2am, Su 2pm-midnight

For the love of all that is good in the world, you can finally put away your wine connoisseur alter-ego and let loose at this popping underground club and warm red and yellow-walled bar. This hotspot is a big draw for young backpackers, Erasmus students, and locals from all walks of life. If you're lucky, you'll be able to belt out a classic French song on karaoke night or listen to local musicians during Starfish's jam sessions. Pro tip: come during happy hour (5:30pm-8:30pm) before the bar gets really crowded for sweet deals on all your favorite drinks (wine included).

i Drinks from €3; wheelchair accessible

SYMBIOSE ($$)

4 Quai des Chartrons; 05 56 23 67 15; open M noon-2:30pm, Tu-F noon-2:30pm and 7pm-2pm, Sa 7pm-2am

At first blush, Symbiose looks like a hippie café joint that probably serves from the organic-only, grass-fed variety. Wrong. Located in the **Chartrons** district, Symbiose features a lovely fusion of tapas cuisine using meats such as chicken and duck in flavorful combinations only *Ratatouille's* Remy could have come up with. But the surprise about Symbiose and its welcoming wood-paneled interior doesn't end there. Behind the grandfather clock at the back of the restaurant is a secret door, transforming this unassuming joint into a speakeasy right in the historical wine district.

i Lunch entrées from €13, dinner entrées from €20, plates from €8, drinks from €5; reservations recommended; wheelchair accessible

CAEN

Coverage by **Emily Corrigan**

Caen made a name for itself in the annals of history long before students invaded the city, their backpacks and travel guides in tow. It especially gained fame as the former home of William the Conqueror (known as William the Bastard to some), and his castle and other constructions still dominate the city's architecture. In more recent history, Caen played an important role in World War II. Not far from the landing beaches on the coast of Normandy, it's the perfect base for exploring the region and understanding its harrowing past. In the city, medieval streets lined with bars and restaurants mingle with massive cathedrals and shops in modern buildings that were constructed after the city's near-complete bombardment during the war. Add some regional cheese and speciality cider and you'll feel yourself transported back to medieval times.

ORIENTATION

The city of Caen spreads over five main districts. Near the center of the city is **Caen Castle,** surrounded by the main hustle and bustle of the town. **Le Vaugueux,** the medieval district full of restaurants, lies just below it to the southeast, while the shop-lined pedestrian streets of **Saint-Sauveur** flank the castle to the southwest. The **Jardin des Plantes** district to the northwest showcases impressive nineteenth-century townhouses, while the **peninsula district** to the southeast is perfect for an evening stroll along the water. Don't miss the hippodrome towards the city's southern edge, or the historical beaches just a few miles north.

ESSENTIALS

GETTING THERE

Caen has its own small regional airport with some international flights from a limited number of other European cities. It's about 3mi. north of the city, so take a taxi. SNCF also runs high-speed trains out of Caen station.

GETTING AROUND

Caen has a tram system that spans over two lines. Tickets cost €2 but depend on how far you're traveling. Caen has a convenient bus system that can also travel to other nearby towns. The main hub is Gare de Caen. Tickets are €1.50.

PRACTICAL INFORMATION

Tourist Offices: 12 Pl. Saint-Pierre; 02 31 27 14 14

Banks/ATMS/Currency Exchange: Currency can be exchanged at the Bureau de Change (115 Rue Saint-Jean; 02 31 30 18 87; www.change-caen.com; open M-F 9:15am-12:30pm and 2:15pm-6:30pm, Sa 9:15am-12:30pm and 2:15pm-5pm).

Post Offices: La Poste (2 Rue Georges Lebret, open M-F 8:30am-6:30pm, Sa 9am-12:30pm and 1:30pm-4:30pm)

Internet: Free public Wi-Fi is provided in six areas, listed here: caen.fr/capitale-vivre/wifi-en-acces-libre.

BGLTQ+ Resources: Centre BGLTQ de Normandie (74 Bd. Dunois, 06 89 49 40 56; www.centrelgbt-normandie.fr)

EMERGENCY INFORMATION

Emergency Number: 112
Police: Police Nationale (10 Rue du Dr Thibout de la Fresnaye; 02 31 29 22 22)
Rape Crisis Center: In case of a crisis, call RAINN (800 656 4673).
Hospitals: Hospital Center University De Caen (Av. de la Côte de Nacre; 02 31 06 31 06)
Pharmacies: Pharmacy Hastings (24 Rue Lanfranc; 02 31 74 75 24).

ACCOMMODATIONS

HÔTEL DU HAVRE CAEN CENTRE ($$)

11 Rue du Havre; 02 31 86 19 80; www.caen-hotel.fr

Beds as soft as baby sheep covered in butter. Wi-Fi that works faster than the speed of light. The privacy of your own bathroom. In short, a weary traveler's oasis. This is how you will feel when you check in at Hôtel du Havre. Although Caen isn't exactly a young traveler's hub, the hotel provides the most comfortable and affordable accommodations near the city center. The staff is professional and knowledgeable, not just a teenager on summer vacation, and the fluffy (and *free*) towels feel like clouds compared to your average hostel sandpaper.

i Rooms starting at €55; reservation required; wheelchair accessible; Wi-Fi

SIGHTS

CULTURE

🏛 HIPPODROME DE LA PRAIRIE

Bd. Yves Guillou; 02 31 27 50 80; www.letrot.com/fr/hippodrome/caen/1400; hours vary

Experience authentic French horse-racing culture at Caen's very own hippodrome. The track features exclusively trotting races, meaning either the horses will remain in the trotting gait (if you know anything about horses) or it'll just look really weird (if you don't). Whether you want to bet on a horse, or just root for whichever one has the prettiest tail, one thing is certain: the fast-talking horse race announcing is even less comprehensible in French.

i Admission €3; wheelchair accessible

LANDMARKS

🏛 CAEN CASTLE

02 31 30 47 60; www.musee-de-normandie.caen.fr/application-chateau; open daily 9:30am-6pm

The Castle of Caen looms over the city like a basketball player looms over an oompa loompa. Its construction began in 1060 by none other than William the Conqueror, who resided there when he wasn't launching conquests on England. It remains one of the largest fortified enclosures in Europe, with 800 meters of ramparts (on which you can walk, of course, but we know you'll mostly pretend to shoot arrows out of small slits and pose comically with large cannons). The castle has a moat, drawbridges, dungeon ruins—the whole nine yards. If that's not enough to pique your interest, you can still visit the fine arts museum and the Museum of Normandy for free, provided you're under 25. That's ageism at its finest.

i Castle admission free, museum admission free under 25; tours Tu and F 11am and 4pm; wheelchair accessible

ABBAYE AUX HOMMES

Esplanade Jean-Marie Louvel; 02 31 30 42 81; www.caen.fr/node/457; open daily 24hr

We've all been there. You went and married your cousin (despite what Dad said) and now you have to get yourself some insurance just in case the old man upstairs isn't too pleased with your incestuous behavior. William the Conqueror's solution for this all-too-relatable problem was to construct the enormous Abbaye aux Hommes (mens' abbey). Much larger and more resplendent than the womens' abbey—1063 was a little early for feminism—this abbey features a beautiful cloister with a manicured garden, as well as the tomb of the famed conqueror himself. It would be a lovely place for a wedding to, say, your cousin.

i Admission €7, reduced €5.50, under 18 free; tours M-F at 10:30am and 2pm; wheelchair accessible

MUSEUMS

☒ MÉMORIAL DE CAEN

Esplanade Général Eisenhower; 02 31 06 06 44; www.memorial-caen.fr; open daily 9am-7pm

You would be hard pressed to find a more personal, inspiring, haunting, and devastatingly sad take on **World War II** history than this memorial, which emphasizes the costly human toll the war exacted from France. Caen was one of the cities in Normandy occupied by Germans for the longest and was later hit by Allied bombardment during its liberation. Not only does the museum explore combat, strategy, and politics, but it focuses on massacres, extermination, and the effects of waging total war on all of its fronts. It would be difficult to leave the Mémorial de Caen without both a nuanced understanding of an event that altered the course of human history and a heightened sense of your own humanity.

i *Students €17; wheelchair accessible*

OUTDOORS

☒ ÉTRETAT

Étretat; www.etretat.net

There should be a reality TV show called "Keeping Up with the Cliffs" because the cliffs at Étretat are as dramatic as they come. Turquoise water laps at the bottom of white cliffs topped with lush, green grass as well as a spattering of handsome cows and a quaint church building. As if these gargantuan striped walls weren't enough, there are a number of physics-defying natural archways carved into the stone that you have to see to believe. Be sure not to miss the small trail beginning just past the church and leading down to the beach, as it will take you to a long tunnel cutting straight through the stone.

i *Free; wheelchair accessible*

SWORD BEACH

Colleville Plage, Ouistreham; www.ouistre-ham.mobi/en/today/sword.html

Sword Beach has a number of draws that nearly necessitate a trip from Caen to stroll the sandy shoreline. First of all, it's a beautiful, wide beach where locals dig for clams, dogs with lolling tongues sprint by, and friendly locals sell cheap crêpes from beachside stands. It's also the most easily accessible **D-Day beach** to visit from Caen. A British landing beach near the strategically important **Pegasus Bridge,** the fighting that took place at this beach played a significant role in the outcome of the June 6, 1944 operation. To get there, just take the #61 bus about 25 minutes toward Ouistreham and get off at Colleville Plage.

i *Free; wheelchair accessible*

FOOD

☒ Ô CHATO ($$)

28 Rue du Vaugueux; 02 31 94 35 70; open M-Th noon-2pm and 7pm-10pm, F-Sa noon-2pm and 7pm-10:30pm, Su noon-2pm and 7pm-10pm

Situated in the medieval part of town, Ô Chato boasts both food and views that you probably can't find anywhere else. It lies at the end of a busy restaurant-filled street directly beneath Caen Castle, meaning you'll be living the fantasy of middle-aged moms everywhere: drinking wine and eating cheese with an unobstructed view of a French castle. And, presumably, you won't be accompanied by any screaming kids! The restaurant serves Italian food alongside irresistible local specialties. Just a few miles from the beach, Caen suffers no shortage of mussels, and Ô Chato is the perfect place to try *moules frites,* the traditional Norman dish of mussels with fries. The fondue starter is another regional gem, as Norman cheese is difficult to beat.

i *Moules frites €12, dinner menu €15; vegan and vegetarian options available; wheelchair accessible*

L'ATELIER DU BURGER ($)

27 Rue Ecuyere; 02 31 50 13 44; www.latelier-duburger.fr; open daily noon-2:30pm and 7pm-11:30pm

It may seem counter to your authenticity-seeking, off-the-beaten-path, traveler's attitude to come all the way to Caen and then go to a burger joint. I mean, come on, you have a "Not all who wander are lost" sticker on your guitar case and your Instagram bio is "I haven't been everywhere, but it's on my list." But L'Atelier du Burger isn't your average burger joint. They keep it simple: their menu consists of only five delicious burgers, one featuring the establishment's signature secret sauce. The only other option on the menu is to add fries and a drink for €3.

i Burgers from €7.50, combo add €3; vegetarian options available; no wheelchair accessibility

SA-SE-SU ($)

156 Rue Saint-Jean; 02 31 91 83 43; www.sasesu14.fr; open M-Sa noon-2pm and 7pm-11pm, Su 7pm-11pm

Caen, at only 10,122 km away from Vietnam, is the perfect place to have fresh and authentic Vietnamese food! Don't let our sarcastic tone fool you; Sa-se-su actually validates this statement. Light salads at the outdoor tables are refreshing on hot summer days, but the bo bun (beef and noodle soup) is the winner for a hearty meal, for as little as €6. Snacking on amazing starters doesn't get cheaper than at Sa-se-su either, with appetizers topping off €5.

i Starters from €3, entrées from €6; gluten-free, vegan, and vegetarian options available; wheelchair accessible

NIGHTLIFE

LE VERTIGO

14 Rue Ecuyère; 02 31 85 43 12; open M-Sa 11:30am-1am

This gritty, cider-slinging pub seems like the bar version of a Dungeons and Dragons club with the added advantage of being right down the street from a real life dungeon (dragons sold separately). Decorated like the inside of a castle, complete with swords and suits of armor, Vertigo hosts ye olde happy hour from 7pm-9pm, when ciders are only €2.10 and signature beer cocktails start at €5 for a hefty 50cl pour. If this spot doesn't fit your vibe, never fear. The bar is on Rue Ecuyère, one of Caen's most animated nightlife streets.

i Beer cocktails from €5 for 50cl, happy hour ciders €2.10; wheelchair accessible

LE WHAT'S

1 Bis Av. de Tourville; 02 31 93 57 76; www.lewhats.com; open W-Sa 11pm-6am

A night at Le What's is like hanging out with a cool exchange student: it's foreign and exciting but you're never 100% sure you understand what's going on. Unlike in larger French cities, this place plays real French music, and unlike in some cities that think they're too cool *cough* Paris *cough,* everyone actually dances too. Everyone else there will seem like they've been a hundred times (and they probably have), so to avoid sticking out as the tourist you are, keep a few things in mind: don't come before midnight (or better yet 1am or 2am), keep the receipt from entry to redeem two included drinks, and just smile and nod.

i Entry €10 with two drinks included; wheelchair accessible

CANNES

Coverage by **Alejandro Lampell**

Take out your only pair of clean slacks, unpack the button-down shirt that's been sitting in the bottom of your bag for weeks, straighten out the creases of your giant pack, for you are now in Cannes—a household name synonymous with affluence, extravagance, and class. Unlike tourist-friendly Nice or metropolitan Marseille, Cannes—the ritziest city in the Côte d'Azur—caters almost exclusively to, well, an exclusive clientele. You need only take a stroll along the yacht-filled Old Port or the diamond-encrusted storefronts at the

Boulevard de la Croisette to understand what we're talking about. Home to the infamous annual Film Festival, visiting Cannes in May entails rubbing elbows with A and B-list celebrities. The real draw of Cannes, however, is not the possibility of bumping into your celebrity crush while walking along one of the city's sandy beaches, but the sandy beaches themselves. They're a hot commodity in the French Riviera, and explain, in part, why it's virtually impossible to find a place to stay for less than €40 a night. That said, if you do it right, Cannes is actually a very manageable city, and with our recommendations, you'll be able to survive—thrive even—on a traveler's budget.

ORIENTATION

Cannes' city center hugs the coastline of the Mediterranean, with suburbs stretching inland towards the French Alps. It's just a 30-minute train ride west from **Nice,** making it a great day trip destination for those who don't want to break the bank on accommodations. **Vieux Port** marks the true center of town; here, you'll find the **Palais des Festivals et des Congrès,** the venue of the **Cannes Film Festival.** Just west of the Vieux Port is the **Old Town,** called **Le Suquet.** East of the city center lies the famous nightclub area and yet another yacht-packed port. Connecting these two areas are the **Boulevard de la Croisette,** a major thoroughfare that runs along the shore and is lined with name-brand stores, upscale restaurants, and art galleries, and **Rue d'Antibes,** Boulevard de la Croisette's inland counterpart.

ESSENTIALS

GETTING THERE

The nearest major airport is the Côte d'Azur Airport in Nice, located approximately 20 mi. east of Cannes. The smaller Cannes-Mandelieu airport, located 4 mi. from the city center, is much closer, but frequented exclusively by smaller private aircrafts. From the Côte d'Azur Airport, you can take a 20min. train ride to Cannes (€6). Cannes has two train stations, Cannes and Cannes la Bocca. Make sure to get off at the former, as the latter is several miles east of the city center.

GETTING AROUND

For us plebeians who cannot afford the luxury of wasting away our days bobbing on yachts on the Mediterranean, the most efficient means of exploring Cannes is by foot. Crossing the city from east to west takes 40min., tops. Cannes also has a public transportation system called Palm Bus, which consists of five bus lines. All five lines pass through the main Hôtel de Ville stop, adjacent to the Vieux Port. You can purchase tickets on the bus (single ride €1.50), from *tabac* shops, or from the tourist office on Boulevard de la Croisette (24hr ticket €4, 3-day ticket €7, 7-day ticket €13.50, 10-trip ticket €12). Buses run daily from 6am-9pm, but there is also a night line called Palm Night, which runs from 9pm-2am.

PRACTICAL INFORMATION

Tourist Offices: Cannes' main tourist office (1 Bd. de la Croisette; 04 92 99 84 22; open daily Mar-Oct 9am-7pm, Nov-Feb 10am-7pm, July-Aug 9am-8pm) is located near the Palais des Festivals et des Congrès.

Banks/ATMs/Currency Exchange: Banks, ATMs, and exchange houses litter the city, but most are located close to the Palais des Festivals et des Congrès.

Post Offices: Cannes Croisette (22 Rue Bivouac Napoléon; 04 93 06 26 50; open M-F 9am-1pm and 2pm-6pm, Sa 9am-12:30pm). The postal code is 06400.

Internet: There is free Wi-Fi at the train station and central tourist office. You can rent a personal hotspot box at the Cannes Tourist Office (€7.90 per day, additional €3 upon return).

BGLTQ+ Resources: Centre BGLTQ Côte d'Azur (123 Rue de Roquebillière; 09 81 93 14 82; www.centrelgbt06. fr; open M 9:30am-8pm, Tu 9:30am-5:30pm, W 9:30am-8pm, Th 9:30am-5:30pm, F 9:30am-8pm, Sa 2pm-8pm)

EMERGENCY INFORMATION

Emergency Number: 112

Police: Police Municipale (2 Quai Saint-Pierre; 0 800 11 71 18; open daily 24hr)

US Embassy: The nearest US Consulate is located in Marseille (Place Varian Fry; 01 43 12 48 85).

Rape Crisis Center: Institut National d'Aide aux Victimes et de Médiation (14 rue Ferrus; 01 45 88 19 00; open daily 9am-9pm)

Hospitals: Hôpital de Cannes (15 Av. des Broussailles; 04 93 69 70 00; open daily 24hr)

Pharmacies: Anglo-French Pharmacy Cannes (95 Rue d'Antibes; 04 93 38 53 79; open M-Sa 8:30am-8pm)

ACCOMMODATIONS

☒ HÔTEL PLM ($$$)

3 Rue Hoche; 04 93 38 31 19; www. hotel-plm.com; reception open daily 9am-1pm and 3pm-7pm

Hotel PLM is the clear winner in the race for value housing in Cannes. This small yet modern two-star is located on **Rue Hoche,** a popular pedestrian area, and is within walking distance of some of the city's best restaurants and nightlife. The well-lit rooms are clean and welcoming (unlike the staff, unfortunately), outfitted in sleek grey and white furniture—a sharp contrast from the décor of PLM's slightly more upscale neighbor, **Hotel Villa Tosca.**

i Basic single from €30, basic single with ensuite shower from €46, double from €59; reservation recommended; BGLTQ+ friendly; no wheelchair accessibility; Wi-Fi; linens and towels included; laundry facilities

HÔTEL ATLANTIS ($$$)

4 Rue du 24 Août; 04 93 39 18 72; www. hotel-atlantis-cannes.cote.azur.fr; reception open 24hr

Frequented by seasoned beach-goers, Hôtel Atlantis' rooms come equipped with air conditioning. The décor is uplifting, and although Atlantis doesn't offer a communal vibe like most European hostels, it has a communal eating area that lends itself well to conversations with other travelers

i Rooms from €44; reservation recommended, especially during high season (May-June); wheelchair accessible; Wi-Fi; linens included; laundry; breakfast from €7

SIGHTS

CULTURE

☒ MARCHE FORVILLE

12 Rue Louis Blanc; 04 92 99 84 22; www. cannes.com/fr/decouvrir-cannes/visiter-cannes/marche-forville.html; open Sept 15-June 14 Tu-F 7am-1:30pm, Sa-Su 7am-2:30pm; June 15-Sept 14 T-Su 7am-2:30pm

The Marche Forville is a vestige of a foregone past: a time when fishing vessels lined the coastline instead of mega-yachts, and quaint shops lined **Boulevard de la Croisette** instead of internationally-recognized stores. This market unites local fisherman and gardeners to sell their wares and evokes the Provençal, small-town feel you've been longing to find in the French Riviera. Walk along the wide lanes of the covered market, organized into different sectors according to produce type. If you are looking for something already-made, the market also offers seasonal *socca, paella,* and hamburgers.

i Market prices vary; cash only; wheelchair accessible

BOULEVARD DE LA CROISETTE

Bd. de la Croisette; street open daily 24hr, shop hours vary

The path to fame is lined with palm trees, brand-name stores, chic gallerias, and crêperies—if by fame you're referring to the horde of A-list celebrities slinking along the red carpet at the **Palais des Festivals et des Congres** and by path you're referring to Boulevard de la Croisette. Stretching from the **Old Port** to the **Cap de la Croisette,** this renowned street is not only the city's biggest thoroughfare, but also your best bet for ~casually~ running into your favorite celebrity. Stroll past the local branches of star-frequented Armani and Dolce and Gabbana; when you inevitably get tired of window-shopping (read: walking into a store and becoming the subject of passive-aggressive stares), take a breather on one of the street's iconic blue chairs.

i Free; wheelchair accessible

LANDMARKS

🏛 FORT ROYAL & MUSÉE DE LA MER

Saint-Marguerite Island; 04 89 82 26 26;
open daily Oct-Mar 10:30am-1:15pm and
2:15pm-4:45pm; Apr-May 10:30am-1:15pm
and 2:15pm-5:45pm; Jun-Sept 10am-
5:45pm

After spending a few hours walking
around Cannes, you'll see that the city
offers relatively few sources of affordable
entertainment—on the mainland, at
least. Enter **St. Marguerite Island,** a
tree-covered, yacht-flanked oasis located
15 minutes off Cannes' sandy shores by
boat. Upon it rests **Fort Royal,** a citadel
built just before the Spanish occupied the
island in 1635 and which was extended
in 1637 under the direction of French
military architect **Vauban.** The citadel
itself offers astonishing views of the
Mediterranean and the mainland, and
is just a short walk away from the **State
Prison,** which held notorious felons such
as the Man in the Iron Mask. Also within
walking distance is the **Musée de la Mer,**
which offers a comprehensive overview
of the island's history as a Roman trading
post.
i Admission €6, reduced €3; students under
26, children under 18, and disabled persons
free; limited wheelchair accessibility; last entry
5:30pm; guided tours available upon request
(04 93 38 55 26)

PALAIS DES FESTIVALS ET DES CONGRÈS

1 Bd. de la Croisette; 04 92 99 84 00

The Palais des Festivals et des Congrès
is truly a spectacle to behold, especially
in May when movie projectors and
camera flashes set it aglow, transforming
the structure into a beacon for artists,
cinephiles, and A-list celebrities alike.
Designed by architect and visionary
Sir Hubert Bennett and completed—
initially—in 1949, this six-story glass
complex is the venue of (you guessed
it) the **Cannes Film Festival** and the
**Cannes Lions International Festival of
Creativity.** In the intervening months
between the two festivals, the Palais hosts
a slew of cultural events, some of which
are open to the public. The interior of the
building is accessible only by guided tour
and slots fill up quickly, so be sure to book
well in advance.
i Admission €6, children under 16 free, half
price for disabled persons; reservation recommended; wheelchair accessible

OUTDOORS

🏖 PLAGE DU MIDI

Bd. Jean Hibert; open daily 9am-6pm

Can't bear to see one more damn yacht?
Looking for a classic, packed, semi-
nude beach that's basically the human
equivalent of a can of sardines? Then look
no further than the Plage du Midi, the
perfect place to spend an afternoon on
a hot summer day. The 20-minute walk
from Cannes' city center may seem like a
trek, but the tan sand, clear coastal water,
and surrounding hills make up for it.
i Free; limited wheelchair accessibility

FOOD

🖌 LA CRÊPERIE DE LA CROISETTE ($)

82 Bd. de la Croisette; 04 93 94 43 47; www.
creperiedelacroisette.com; open high season
daily at 9am, low season daily at 10:30am; by
reservation only

Located on the infamous **Boulevard de
la Croisette** and serving up a variety of
sweet and savory crêpes, this lavender-
clad locale is perfect for any meal. Each
crêpe comes with a side salad, dollop of
ice cream, or caramel drizzle. If you don't
identify as a crêpe aficionado, La Croisette
offers a small assortment of salads, cheese
plates, snack-style pastas, sandwiches, and
burgers as well.

*i Crêpes from €4, main plates from €8; card
minimum €10; vegetarian options available;
wheelchair accessible*

LE TROQUET À SOUPES ($)

Prom. De la Pantiero; 04 93 38 43 4; open
daily 9:30am-7pm

This small locale is run entirely by one
woman, Sylvie, who's a jill-of-all-trades.
Part owner, part manager, part waitress,
and all chef, she'll set up the umbrellas
on the patio, take your order, cook your
food, and still find time to chat about
life. We recommend starting your meal
with a hearty bowl of soup and splurging
on the plate of the day. A well-traveled
woman herself, Sylvie likes to experiment,
concocting dishes reminiscent of other
cultures, including *chili con carne* and
ceviche.

*i Soups from €6, salads from €7, main plates
from €10, plate of the day from €13; vegetarian options available; limited wheelchair
accessibility*

PHILCAT ($)

Promenade de la Pantiero; 04 93 38 43 4;
open daily 9:30am-7pm

A €4 panini in Cannes? At a restaurant
located two minutes from the **Palais des
Festivals?** No, you're not hallucinating.
Philcat, a white and blue shack serving up
a variety of sweet and savory sandwiches,
stands defiantly on the expansive **Pantiero
Promenade** and is truly a backpacker's
blessing. Don't let the small interior
dissuade you, as there is almost unlimited
seating surrounding the **Old Port.**

*i Sandwiches from €3; minimum card charge
€15; vegetarian options available; wheelchair
accessible*

NIGHTLIFE

GOTHA CLUB

Pl. Franklin Roosevelt; 04 93 45 11 11; www.
gotha-club.com; open daily midnight-7am

Recognized by nearly every Sperry-
clad Hamptons crew as one of the best
nightclubs in the world, Gotha is, well,
an experience. It has a tight window
of opening from midnight until about
12:30am, during which the bouncers pay
little attention to attire, company, and
level of intoxication. Arrive after 12:30am,
however, and your chances of getting in
will dwindle. Inside, the entrance soon
gives way to a dimly-lit dance floor,
strobe lights, large sofas, and VIP lounges.
Drinks start at €12 and venture into
the quintuple digits, so if you plan on
drinking, it'd be best to do so beforehand.
Don't go too hard, however, or you may
be coaxed into splitting a €500 bottle
of champagne with the son of a Russian
billionaire.

*i Beer from €12, alcohol from €15; dressy
attire recommended*

QUAY'S IRISH PUB

17 Quai Saint-Pierre; 04 93 39 27 84;
open M-Sa noon-2am

This English-speaking pub located on the
banks of the **Old Port** is the perfect place
to stop before spending an evening in
one of Cannes' exorbitantly-priced clubs.
Quay's interior is completely decked out
with wooden planks, signed dollar bills,
Irish flags, and sports memorabilia, and
will effectively bring you back down
to earth. And not just in the figurative
sense! The drinks are so cheap (relatively
speaking) that you'll be on your ass before
you get the chance to sing along to a live
cover of Billy Joel's "Piano Man."

*i Beer from €4, shots from €5; minimum card
charge €7; happy hour 5pm-8pm*

LYON

Coverage by **Kristine Guillaume**

It's all too easy to overlook Lyon as a random city smack in the middle of Paris and the French Riviera. Skipping over it may seem, at first blush, like a small sacrifice for the beaches of Nice or the mélange of culture in Marseille. But to do so would be a grave mistake. Lyon, the gastronomic capital of France, has much to offer in the form of delectable *bouchons,* hearty meat-centric dishes paired with all your French favorites: bread, cheese, and wine. Here, you can spend each night trying a different edible part of a pig or cow after a day of climbing Roman ruins, admiring masterpieces in the city's many museums, or roaming the cobblestone streets of Vieux Lyon—a UNESCO World Heritage Site in itself. Gear up for *bouchon* after *bouchon,* and get ready to immerse yourself in the vibrant culture of Lyon—influenced by its importance in the Roman Empire, its deep ties to Catholicism, and its status as an epicenter of intellectual development throughout the years.

ORIENTATION

Lyon is a city in the southeastern part of France, located just two hours south of Paris. The city itself contains two rivers: the **Rhône** and the **Saône.** The two rivers converge at the southern tip of the city, creating the famous peninsula **Presqu'île.** In the northern part of Presqu'île are many famous landmarks including **Hôtel de Ville** and **Place Bellecour.** In addition to the rivers, the city of Lyon is bounded by two hills: **Fourvière,** the site of **Vieux Lyon** (Old Town) and **La Basilique de Notre Dame,** and **Croix-Rousse,** the part of town where the silk workers resided during Lyon's economic prime. There are nine arrondissements in the city; the first and second arrondissements, the site of **Place des Terreaux** and **Place Bellecour,** contain the most attractions. **Vieux Lyon** makes up the fifth arrondissement while **Parc de la Tête D'Or,** on the eastern side of the Rhône, makes up the sixth. The **Part-Dieu** train station is located in the third arrondissement, along with **Les Halles de Lyon—Paul Bocuse.**

ESSENTIALS

GETTING THERE

If flying, Lyon St-Exupéry airport is the closest to the city center. From the airport, there is a 30min. express tram called Rhône express to Lyon Part-Dieu train station (€15, students €13). The tram runs daily from 4:25pm to midnight every 15-30min. We recommend purchasing your ticket ahead of time (www.rhoneexpress. fr), but there are ticket machines for purchase upon arrival at the airport. If traveling by train, there are two main train stations: Part-Dieu, located in the third arrondissement, and Perrache, located on the southern tip of Presqu'île. Both stations are located about 20min. away via metro from the city center. The cheapest way to get into Lyon is via bus. Most arrive in Part-Dieu station.

GETTING AROUND

The best way to get around Lyon is to walk. If you'd like to bike, you can rent one with Velo'v service. The first 30min. of each ride are free and every additional 30min. costs €1 for a maximum of 24hr. A day-long ticket is €1.50 (which makes 10 times more sense). For the city's public transit (metro, bus, and tram), 1hr tickets are €1.80. There is also a ticket called Soirée that allows for unlimited travel from 7pm until the end of that day's service for just €3. The metro runs from 4am-12:30am and the buses from 5am-midnight. To get up to Fourvière and the Musée Gallo-Romain, there is a funicular at the Vieux Lyon Metro Station (round-trip €2.80).

PRACTICAL INFORMATION

Tourist Offices: Office du Tourisme et des Congrès du Grand Lyon (Pl. Bellecour; 04 72 77 69 69; open daily 9am-6pm)

Banks/ATMs/Currency Exchange: BNP Paribas (5 Rue de la République; 08 20 82 00 01; bank open Tu-Sa 8:30am-12:30pm and 1:45pm-6pm; ATMs open daily 24hr)

Post Offices: The main post office is located by Place Bellecour (10 Pl. Antonin Poncet; 08 99 23 24 62; open M-F 9am-7pm, Sa 9am-noon).

Public Restrooms: Most of Lyon's tourist offices have public toilets.

Internet: You can rent out a pocket Wi-Fi from the Tourist Information Office for €4 with Lyon City Card (regular price €8).

BGLTQ+ Resources: Ligne Azur is an organization that provides information and support to BGLTQ+ individuals (08 10 20 30 40; daily 8am-11pm).

EMERGENCY INFORMATION

Emergency Number: 112

Police: Commissariat de police, second arrondissement (47 R. de la Charité; 04 78 42 26 56; open daily 24hr)

US Embassy: US Consulate of Lyon (1 Quai Jules Courmont; 01 43 12 48 60; open M-F 9:30am-5:30pm)

Rape Crisis Center: National Federation Women Solidarity (3919), not an emergency number. In case of emergency, call the police.

Hospitals: Hôpital Edouard Herriot (5 Pl. d'Arsonval; 08 25 08 25 69; open daily 24hr)

Pharmacies: Look for the green cross to find a pharmacy. There are plenty throughout the city.
• Great Pharmacie Lyonnaise (22 R. de la République; 04 72 56 44 00; open M-Sa 8am-11pm, Su 7pm-11pm)

ACCOMMODATIONS

🏚 AWAY HOSTEL AND COFFEE SHOP ($$)

21 Rue Alsace Lorraine; 04 78 98 53 20; www.awayhostel.com; reception open 24hr

If Urban Outfitters were a hostel, this would be it. Boasting boho-chic vibes, high ceilings, and wooden floors, Away Hostel features spacious rooms with lockers large enough to fit your entire backpack and then some. The hotel has a café on the ground floor that serves breakfast and strong lattes at affordable prices. Attached to the café, you'll find a common room filled with bean bags and books perfect for a mid-afternoon breather. The only downsides? The hostel is located right next to a busy street, so you'll hear cars zooming by throughout the night (pro tip: pick up a pair of free earplugs at the front desk). It's a small price to pay for the warm duvet, great air-conditioning, and welcoming atmosphere during your entire stay.

i Dorms from €21, privates from €65; reservation recommended; no wheelchair accessibility; Wi-Fi; linens included; towels not included; laundry €5 for wash and dry, detergent €1; breakfast €4, 7am-11am; kitchen

HO36 OPÉRA ($$)

9 Rue Sainte-Catherine; 04 78 28 11 01; www.ho36hostels/lyon-opera; reception open 24hr

The key when it comes to this hostel is location. Steps away from the **Parc National de L'Opéra, Hôtel de Ville,** and the **Musée des Beaux Arts,** Ho36 Opéra offers a convenient option with ensuite bathrooms, an open patio, and a spacious common bar-café area with tables and chairs reminiscent of a hipster's living room. While the hostel is comfortable, it does have some drawbacks: the bathroom doors inside the rooms lack locks (so you might find yourself becoming closer to your roommate than you ever expected), the lights tend to flicker, and there were only two open outlets in our room. In the end though, the hostel makes up for it with budget prices and a free welcome drink of beer or wine upon arrival.

i Dorms from €25, privates from €85; cash only; reservation required; BGLTQ+ friendly; no wheelchair accessibility; Wi-Fi; linens included; towels included; breakfast €8

SLO LIVING HOSTEL

5 Rue Bonnefoi; 04 78 59 06 90; www.slo-hostel.com; reception open 24hr

With an open courtyard, hammocks, and twinkly fairy lights, Slo Living Hostel truly encourages you to take a deep breath and live *slo*. This hostel is a great place to meet fellow travelers as you

OPÉRA NATIONAL DE LYON

Pl. de la Comédie ; 04 69 85 54 54; www.opera-lyon.com; ticket office open Tu-Sa noon-7pm; opera runs Sept-July

Situated right behind the grand **Hôtel de Ville** is the (arguably) grander Opéra National de Lyon, a massive glass-topped building. Throughout the year, the opera hosts dance performances, concerts, plays, special events, and, oh yeah, operas. Tickets don't come cheap for a place as fancy as this, but, if you're lucky, you can snag one for just €5 right before the show. Even if you're not seeing a performance, though, you can sit on the steps and listen to musicians perform or watch young teenagers practice dance performances on the opera's steps.

i *Tickets from €16, €5 tickets on sale 1hr before a show (if available); minimum age 5 years old; wheelchair accessible*

VIEUX LYON

69005 Lyon 5ème; 04 72 10 30 30; hours vary by store

Yeah, you're not in Paris, but that doesn't mean you can't have your perfect *Les Mis* moment. On the **Fourvière** side of the **Saône** lies **Vieux Lyon,** the Old Town. Walk through its cobblestone streets, which strongly resemble the set of *Les Mis,* or, perhaps more accurately, eighteenth-century France. There's even a little dip in the middle of the sidewalk that looks like a "drainage system" for sewage thrown out the window. It's kind of gross when you think about it… or even if you don't. Flat walking shoes are highly recommended for your stroll through the winding streets lined with *bouches authentiques* and local boutiques. In the center of Vieux Lyon is the metro station, which gives you full access to funiculars going up **Fourvière.**

i *Free; last funicular back to Vieux Lyon from Fourvière 10pm; no wheelchair accessibility*

pause in the courtyard or indoor common areas after a long day of sightseeing in Lyon. With spacious rooms, clean communal bathrooms, and relatively comfortable beds (which is saying a lot for a hostel), Slo gives you the chance to feel at home, even if you're traveling alone. And if you can splurge on a private room, you won't be disappointed by the lively, bright décor on the walls.

i *Dorms from €20, privates from €90; reservation recommended; max stay 7 nights; wheelchair accessible; Wi-Fi; linens included; breakfast €5*

SIGHTS
CULTURE

LES HALLES DE PAUL BOCUSE

102 Cours la Fayette; 04 78 60 32 82; www.halles-de-lyon-paulbocuse.com; open Tu-Sa 7am-10:30pm, most restaurants close around 6-7pm

Here lies the answer to all your food cravings. The holy grail of all things food, wine, and spirits, Les Halles de Paul Bocuse has everything you could imagine: *boulangers, fromagers, charcutiers, pâtissiers,* and so on. Walk through stall after stall of delicious and delectable aromas and pick up some of your favorite French staples. Although there are several restaurants for you to choose from, they might be a little out of your backpacker budget. Instead, stop by in the mid-afternoon and pick up a personalized assortment of fine wines, mouthwatering cheeses, and flavorful sausages to go.

i *Stall prices vary; wheelchair accessible*

LANDMARKS

LA BASILIQUE NOTRE-DAME DE FOURVIÈRE

8 Pl. de Fourvière; 04 78 25 86 19; www.four-viere.org; basilica open daily 8am-6pm, Mass daily 7:30am, 9:30am, 11am, 5pm, museum daily 10am-12:30pm and 2pm-5:30pm

This nineteenth-century church stands tall atop **Fourvière Hill.** Decked out in gold and ornate patterns in greens, pinks, and teal blues, the basilica's magnificence commands respect. Check out the detailed paintings of scenes from the Bible, but don't stop there: head down to the **crypt,** a space just as ornately decorated as the basilica itself. Once you've finished, walk to the back of the building, where you'll find a perch from which you can view the entire city of Lyon and the **Saône River.** Apart from the views, the basilica bears historical significance, as it is dedicated to the Virgin Mary, who is said to have protected Lyon during the Franco-Prussian wars.

i Free; discovery tour free Apr-Nov 9am-12:30pm and 2pm-6pm; discover roof and places of basilica June 1-Sept 30 M-Sa 11am, 2:30am, 4pm, Su 2:30pm and 4pm €10, youth €5, with Lyon City Card free; last funicular back to Vieux Lyon 10pm; wheelchair accessible

CATHÉDRALE SAINT JEAN DE BAPTISTE

Place St Jean; 06 60 83 53 97; www.cathe-drale-lyon.cef.fr; open M-F 8:15am-7:45pm, Sa 8:15am-7pm, Su 8am-7pm

In the middle of **Vieux Lyon** stands the Cathédrale Saint Jean de Baptiste, the seat of the archdiocese in Lyon, considered by some to be the seat of the French church, making it a pretty big deal. The cathedral is a beautiful sandstone color with distinctive red doors, high ceilings, and intricately decorated stained-glass windows. Inside the left nave of the church, check out the *horloge astronomique,* a clock that mirrors the movement of the stars. The **treasury** of the church holds artifacts from the Byzantine Empire for your crash course in Lyonnais history. Behind the church is **Palais St. Jean,** which has a library just in case you're looking for more books about Lyon's ties to Catholicism.

i Free; wheelchair accessible

PASSAGE THIAFFAIT

Between Rue René Leynaud and Rue Burdeau; store hours vary

Passage Thiaffait used to be a crime-infested alley, but, today, you need not fear anything so much as a stray cat. Named after **Monsieur Thiaffait,** the alley, which connects Rue René Leynaud and Rue Burdeau via two white staircases, is lined with chic boutiques, cafés, and artist workshops. Peruse the shops' offerings on your way to lunch in the **Croix-Rousse** district, but don't budget more than 20-30 minutes for this significant, yet small sight. The surrounding pastel-colored buildings do make for a good Instagram post, though.

i Free; no wheelchair accessibility

PLACE BELLECOUR

Place Bellecour; 04 72 77 69 69; open daily 24hr

Place Bellecour holds the title of the largest square in Lyon and the largest pedestrian square in all of Europe. Today, it doesn't seem like much, except for an expanse of Mars-red pavement, a statue of Louis XIV in the middle, a tourist office, and a Ferris wheel for kids and adults who haven't quite grown up. Back in the day, however, the square itself held much more significance: it was the sight of royal parades for the king and executions via the guillotine during the French Revolution. Although the square isn't too spectacular in the daytime, give it another try in the evening when the Ferris wheel lights up in a display of vibrant colors.

i Free; wheelchair accessible

MUSEUMS

☒ MUSÉE DES BEAUX ARTS

20 Pl. des Terreaux; 04 72 10 17 40; www.mba-lyon.fr; open M, W-Th 10am-6pm, F 10:30am-6pm, Sa-Su 10am-6pm

At last, the chance to hang with our artistically inclined pals: **Monet, Picasso,** and **Gauguin.** It feels like centuries since we've last gotten together! Probably because their art is from around a hundred years ago. Man, walking through all these carefully curated wings with art from Impressionists, Modernists, and Renaissance art really takes us back to Monet's fascination with landscapes, that time Pablo discovered Cubism, and Paul's trip to Tahiti that he won't stop painting about! When we're finished with our *rendez-vous*, we're going to the extensive sculpture hall featuring works by **Rodin,** as well as the antiquities wing with **Ancient Egyptian, Greco-Roman, Muslim,** and **Ottoman relics.**

i Permanent collection admission €8, students €4; temporary exhibition admission €12, students €7; last entry 5:30pm; audio guide €1 in French, English, Italian, free downloadable app; wheelchair accessible

LUGDUNUM: MUSÉES GALLO-ROMAIN DE FOURVIÈRE

17 Rue Cleberg; 04 72 38 49 30; www.museegalloromain.grandlyon.com; museum open Tu-F 11am-6pm, Sa-Su 10am-6pm; archaeological site open daily Apr 15-Sept 15 7am-9pm, daily Sept 16-Apr 14 7am-7pm

If we had to name one thing Lyon is proud of, it would have to be its importance during its time as Lugdunum, a city of the Roman Empire founded in 43 BCE. Now, we agree, it's kind of weird to look back fondly on practically being colonized and ruled by an outside power (Stockholm Syndrome, anyone?), but Lugdunum was a powerhouse that laid the groundwork for the city Lyon became. The museum, which details everything about the ancient city—from its religious practices to palace structures to stunning mosaics—is expansive, spanning four descending floors. As cool as all this is, walking between artifact after artifact can get a little dusty and dry. Thankfully, you can actually climb the steps of the Gallo-Roman theatre outside. Just don't fall—it's steep!

i Permanent collection admission €4, students under 26 €2.50, free under 18; temporary exhibitions admission €7, students under 26 €4.50; last entry 5:30pm; wheelchair accessible

MUSÉES GADAGNE

1 Pl. du Petit Collège; 04 78 42 03 61; www.gadagne.musees.lyon.fr; open W-Su 11am-6:30pm

This museum is actually two museums in one: the **Lyon History Museum (MHL)** and the **Puppetry Museum (MAM).** Why these two museums are housed together in a stunning seventeenth-century building is beyond

us, but what we can say is that they are both carefully curated and informative. The Puppetry Museum, although a bit creepy, features hundreds of puppets including **Guignol,** a beloved puppet who symbolizes the speech and *la vie quotidienne* of the Lyonnais. The history museums take you through 30 rooms of Lyonnais history, including its rise as the Roman city of Lugdunum to the rise of Catholicism to the city's importance as an economic and intellectual hotspot. Our favorite part was the room from the eighteenth-century describing how the elite developed a love for decorative arts. (Because what else do rich people have to do?)

i Admission €6, students €4, free under 18; temporary exhibition admission €8, students €6; last entry 6pm; tours M, W-F 10am-noon, 2pm-4pm, Tu 2pm-4pm, must book in advance, adults €3, children €1; wheelchair accessible

OUTDOORS

PARC DES HAUTEURS

Montée Nicolas de Lange; 04 72 69 47 60; open daily 24hr

Directly meaning "park of heights," the Parc des Hauteurs is more a hiking trail than anything else. The park, or trail, rather, connects the top of **Fourvière Hill** to the **cemetery of Loyasse.** There's a gold rose petal path that you can follow towards the **La Basilique Notre-Dame de Fourvière** or explore the rosary garden within the park. We recommend packing a lunch before coming up so that you can enjoy the views of Lyon's orange-tiled rooftops and the **Sâone River.**

i Free; last tram to Fourvière at 10pm; no wheelchair accessibility

PARC DE LA TÊTE D'OR

69006 Lyon; 04 72 69 47 60; www.loisirs-parcdelatetedor.com; mid-Apr-mid-Oct 6:30am-10:30pm, mid-Oct-mid-Apr 6:30am-8:30pm

On the east side of the **Rhône** lies a massive green space in the middle of Lyon's urban landscape: Parc de la Tête D'Or. Comparable to New York City's Central Park (although perhaps not as grand or expansive), the 117-hectare plot has everything you could want in a day outdoors: a lake filled with geese, a rose garden, and a zoo. For those of us that prefer the wonders of the great indoors, the northern side of the park houses the **Musée d'Art Contemporain.** But, honestly, why wouldn't you appreciate a leisurely stroll in the greenery for a respite from the chaos of the otherwise bustling city?

i Free; wheelchair accessible

FOOD

ATHINA ($)

3 Rue Romarin; 04 78 72 86 61; open Tu-Su noon-2pm and 7pm-10pm

There's a certain charm about small places, and Athina definitely has it. With only about six or seven tables, Athina boasts fast service and not-to-miss deals on Greek staples, including flavorful pork and chicken pitas with a side of scrumptious fries. Pair your meal with Greek beer and sit back as you enjoy your meal in the airy space, complete with inviting teal walls that make you feel like you're by the Mediterranean.

i Entrées from €6; cash only; vegetarian options available; wheelchair accessible

L'AUBERGE DES CANUTS ($$)

8B Pl. Saint Jean; 09 86 50 89 66; www. auberge-des-canuts.com; open daily 8am-midnight

If you're looking for a taste of *bouchons Lyonnais* on a budget, you've hit the spot. Located just steps away from the **Cathédrale Saint-Jean de Baptiste** with walls reminiscent of the cobblestone streets of **Vieux Lyon,** L'Auberge des Canuts serves traditional dishes such as pork sausages in a red wine sauce on its convienent prix-fixe menu (€15.90). The staff only begins to prepare your next course once you've finished the one in front of you, so take your time. They're in no rush and you shouldn't be either. When you finally make it to dessert after savoring pork sausages in red wine sauce, and your server asks you if you want your *fromage blanc* with fruit sauce, say *oui* without hesitation. It's truly a treat.

i Entrées from €14, prix-fixe menu from €16; card minimum €20; vegetarian options available; wheelchair accessible

CAFÉ 203 ($$)

9 Rue de Garet; 04 78 28 65 66; www. moncafe203.com; open noon-1am daily

If you're looking for a place for the perfect *rendez-vous,* look no further than Café 203. This bustling restaurant, although not an official *bouchon,* serves up traditional Lyonnaise dishes and then some. If you've had one too many sausages on your trip thus far, don't shy away from ordering one of Café 203's burgers or risottos for a good dose of familiarity. While you munch on your meal, in either the non-smoking or smoking area of the restaurant, look around at the tavern-like décor and listen to the friendly conversations of the locals and fellow tourists dining around you. And while the beer and wine are cheaper than the water on the menu, Café 203 will give you complimentary tap water with your meal (a rare occasion in Europe). Drink up!

i Entrées from €13, burgers from €12, beer and wine from €2.50; vegetarian options available; wheelchair accessible

A CHACUN SA TASSE ($)

2 Rue du Griffon; open M-Sa 8am-7pm

For a quick bite or *petit déjeuner,* swing by this tea shop, located a few blocks away from **Place des Terreaux.** Decorated in a warm orange with framed paintings hung on the walls, this café offers a wide array of teas, including green teas, black teas, and rooibos. The teas are steeped to perfection before being served. While you wait for your flavorful brew, pick up a French magazine on the café's bookshelves to brush up on your language skills or look smart as you attempt to read a piece on the EU's economic policy. For just €5.50, we were able to get a pot of delectable rose black tea and a plain croissant to start our day off on the right note.

i Pots of tea from €3.50, pastries from €2; vegetarian options available; wheelchair accessible

DIPLOID ($)

18 Rue de la Platière; 04 69 67 58 93; open M-F 9am-7pm, Sa 10am-7pm, Su 11am-7pm

An open space just a few blocks away from **Place des Terreaux,** Diploid is the perfect place to catch your breath with a cup of perfectly roasted coffee or freshly brewed tea. Diploid boasts a bright and welcoming atmosphere complete with calming teal blue walls, lights hanging from the ceiling, and wooden floors. Take your cappuccino with the locals as they work on their laptops using the café's free Wi-Fi, or converse with friends as upbeat English indie tunes play in the background. Diploid also offers a lunch menu that changes every now and then. Choose from a sandwich, entrée, or salad of the day and take a seat in the back room to enjoy your meal.

i Lunch from €10.50, coffee and tea from €3; vegetarian options available; wheelchair accessible

NIGHTLIFE

◾ THE MONKEY CLUB ($$)

19 Pl. Tolozan; 04 78 27 99 29; www. themonkeyclub.fr; open M noon-2pm, Tu-W noon-2pm and 6:30pm-1am, Th-F noon-2pm and 6:30pm-3am, Sa 6:30pm-3am, Su 11am-4pm

This is the kind of place Don Draper would go for after-work drinks on a particularly stressful day. Or perhaps any day he can find an excuse for a drink, which means every day. Straight out of the set of *Mad Men,* The Monkey Club features a deep red interior with armchairs and dim lighting to set the mood for recovering from a long day of work. The bar is mostly frequented by locals, who order quality wines or shots that the bar aptly names prescriptions. Sadly, the drinks are relatively pricey, so save this venue for a planned splurge on the town or if you somehow find yourself a job to whine—we mean wine—about.

i Cocktails from €11, shots from €5, beers from €5: BGLTQ+ friendly; wheelchair accessible

BOMP! ($)

1 Pl. Croix-Paquet; 09 73 18 78 43; open M-W 10am-1am, Th-F 10am-3am, Sa 4pm-3am

Café by day, restaurant in the afternoon, and bar by night, you could probably spend the whole day at Bomp! and never leave. Like most French shops and restaurants, the kitchen does close in the middle of the day though, so that's probably not the best idea. Bomp! has a space for every occasion: tables that spill onto the narrow sidewalk, an open, well-lit café area with round tables to chill with old friends and new, and an upstairs bar area complete with foosball tables. With happy hour deals selling drinks for just three or four euros, swing by for a lively night to meet locals (who are probably smoking outside) late into the night.

i Entrées from €10, beer and wine from €3, mixed drinks from €5; limited wheelchair accessibility

GROOM ($$)

6 Rue Roger Violi; www.groomlyon.com; open Tu-W 7:30pm-1am, Th 7:30pm-2am, F-Sa 7:30pm-4am

Tucked away under **Away Hostel and Coffee Shop** lies the new, hip kid on the block: Groom. With a dark interior and bright, popping lights—mostly the pink and white variety—Groom boasts a menu full of out-of-the-box cocktails intended to spice up your night. The cocktails, which start at around €12, are pricey, so if you're looking for something more budget-friendly, choose from their selection of beer and wine. Groom also has mocktails for those who want to stay sober, making it a perfect place for all kinds of party animals. And to make sure you party safe, there are empanadas on the menu to make sure those cocktails don't go down alone. Check out their online schedule of events before selecting a night to go— the club frequently hosts live concerts, often with no cover.

i Beer and wine from €5, cocktails from €12, empanadas from €4; vegetarian options available; wheelchair accessible

NICE

Coverage by **Kristine Guillaume**

Let's be honest. You came to Nice for the sunny beach days on the unfathomably blue waters of the French Riviera. And that's not such a bad idea. Nice is one of the most affordable cities along the Côte d'Azur, which may sound strange because it's hard on the budget-conscious backpacker wallet. But compare the city to its more bougie neighbors like Cannes and Monaco and you'll see what we mean. Nice boasts the picturesque Promenade des Anglais lined with many public beaches for you to perfect your tan. It's also centrally located among the other cities in the area, making it the ideal home base for daytrips to places such as the aforementioned Cannes and Monaco as well as Antibes, Menton, and Eze. Some backpackers even claim that those cities are nicer than Nice itself. But let's not make the mistake of thinking Nice is just for the coast and sun. The city has boatloads of culture for you to discover, including the works of Henri Matisse, Marc Chagall, and Russian orthodox aristocrats. When you've had enough sun, take a moment to discover the more artsy side of the city. It's nice, we promise.

ORIENTATION

Nice is one of many cities on the renowned **Côte d'Azur,** otherwise known as the French Riviera. The city center is located on the **Bay of Angels,** a long stretch of beach that starts at the airport and culminates in **Colline du Château (Castle Hill),** which is obviously a hill just in front of **Vieux Nice,** the old part of the city located southeast of the city center. To get to the city center from **Gare Nice Ville,** you'll most likely walk down the boutique-lined **Avenue Jean-Médicin,** which ends in the city's largest pedestrian center: **Place Masséna.** From Place Masséna, you can walk straight onto the **Promenade des Anglais** for an incredible view of the Bay of Angels. **The Port,** located east of Castle Hill, is less touristy than Vieux Nice, but still has some of the best cheap restaurants in town. Slightly north of the city center is **Cimiez,** site of the former Roman city, *Cemenelum,* which is now filled with villas, including the **Matisse Museum.**

ESSENTIALS

GETTING THERE

If flying into Nice, you will land at Aéroport de Nice-Côte D'Azur, from which you can take express buses #98 and 99 into the city center (€6). The buses run every half hour from 6am-midnight. Alternatively, you can walk 10min. to a train station, Saint-Augustin, and take it one stop to Gare Nice Ville, Nice's main train station. The train ticket costs €1.60 and it is the same train that runs to Monaco and the Italian city of Ventimiglia. If traveling via train, you will dock at Gare Nice Ville, which connects to multiple cities along Côte D'Azur, Lyon, and Paris. Train tickets are usually expensive (€70 from Lyon, €100 from Paris), so it might be better to take a bus. We recommend Ouibus.

GETTING AROUND

Nice is easily walkable. The main train station is a 10min. walk from the city center and Vieux Nice (Old Nice). The city does have an extensive public transport system called the Ligne d'Azur consisting of over 130 bus routes that extend to villages in the Maritime Alps and a tram line that makes a U-shape through the city center and Vieux Nice running from 4:35am-1:35am. A solo-ticket for one journey costs €1.50 and a 24hr pass costs €5. Be sure to validate your ticket each time you board a bus or tram to avoid paying hefty fines. In the summer, it's a great idea to bike along the Promenade des Anglais. For that, use Velo Blue, which costs €1.50 with the first 30min. of travel free.

PRACTICAL INFORMATION

Tourist Offices: Promenade des Anglais Office du Tourisme (2, Promenade des Anglais; 08 92 70 74 07; www.nicetourisme.com)

Banks/ATMs/Currency Exchange: Banks and ATMs are ubiquitous throughout the city, but this branch of BNP Paribas is not too far from Place Masséna (2 Bd. Victor Hugo; 820 82 00 01; open M-F 9am-12:30pm and 2pm-7pm).

Post Offices: The main post office, called La Poste, is located across from the main train station (21 Av. Thiers; open M-F 8am-7pm, Sa 8am-12:30pm).

Public Restrooms: There are public restrooms on the Promenade des Anglais. One of them is located right outside Plage Beau Rivage (107 Quai Etats-Unis).

Internet: The city offers free Wi-Fi at certain tourist offices and parks. There also are various cybercafés. You can also rent out a Wi-Fi hotspot at the Tourist Office for €7.90 per day.

BGLTQ+ Resources: Centre BGLTQ+ Côte d'Azur (123 Rue de Roquebillière; 09 81 93 14 82; www.centrelgbt06.fr; open M, W, F 9:30am-8pm, Sa 2pm-8pm)

EMERGENCY INFORMATION

Emergency Number: 112

Police: Central Police Station (1 Av. Maréchal Foch; 04 92 17 22 22; open daily 24hr, foreign visitor reception desk open daily 9am-5pm) For lost and found, go to Police Municipal (42 Rue Dabray 3906; open M-Th 8:30am-5pm, F 8:30am-3:45pm).

US Embassy: The nearest US consulate is in Marseille (Pl. Varian Fry; 01 43 12 48 85).

Rape Crisis Center: In case of all problems, call 115.

Hospitals: Many of the medical centers are located on the outskirts of the city. The Tourist Office recommends heading to Hôpital Pasteur in case of an emergency, although children would be better served at Lenval Hospital.

- Hôpital Pasteur: 30 Voie Romaine; 04 92 03 77 77; open M-F 8am-6pm, Sa 9am-5:45pm

Pharmacies:
- Pharmacie Masséna: 7 Rue Masséna; 04 93 87 78 94; open daily 24hr

ACCOMMODATIONS

⚑ HOSTEL ANTARES ($$)

5 Ave. Thiers; 04 93 88 22 87; reception open 6am-3am

When Mowgli and Baloo sang about the bare necessities, they must have been talking about Hotel Antares. Conveniently located five minutes from the train station, Antares provides air-conditioned rooms and ensuite bathrooms cleaned by staff daily with replenished soaps, towels, and shampoo. The noise from the trains at night can make its way into your room, but it's a small sacrifice for the security that the hostel offers featuring a 3am curfew and cages under the beds large enough to fit your backpack. It's not the prettiest or most entertaining hostel in the world, but it does share a common room with neighboring Hostel Baccarat to provide for ample socializing on beachy summer nights.

i Dorms from €17, privates from €60; max stay 7 nights; Wi-Fi; BGLTQ+ friendly; wheelchair accessible; linens, towels included; lockers available

HOSTEL BACCARAT ($$)

39 Rue d'Angleterre; 04 93 88 35 73; reception open 7am-3am

Baccarat offers affordable, basic accommodations with cages under every bed to ensure the security of each guest's belongings. Located just a 10min. walk from Place Masséna, the hostel creates a social environment for every kind of backpacker with its spacious shared common room, which has a kitchen, Internet room, and lounge where you can meet your fellow travelers before retiring to a good night's sleep.

i Dorms from €24, doubles from €80, singles from €60; reservation recommended; Wi-Fi; BGLTQ+ friendly; no wheelchair accessibility; laundry facilities; linens, towels included

HOSTEL VILLA SAINT EXPÉURY BEACH ($)

6 Rue Sacha Guitry; 04 93 16 13 43; reception open 24hr

Hostel Villa Saint Expéury's main selling point is that it's closest to the **Bay of Angels** and seafront. Located just off **Avenue Jean Médecin,** this hostel is just steps away from **Place Masséna** with a sauna, ping pong table, and happy hours for party-hungry backpackers. For solo-travelers, this is a great place to stay since the staff coordinates events such as pub crawls, sailing excursions, and daily yoga to keep things social and entertaining—even away from the pebbly beaches of Nice. So take advantage of the spacious common areas and comfortable rooms on your hours away from the **Promenade des Anglais**— you're bound to have a fun and wonderful stay.

i *Dorms from €18, privates from €40; Wi-Fi; wheelchair accessible; linens included; lockers, laundry; luggage storage*

SIGHTS

CULTURE

CATHÉDRALE SAINT-NICOLAS DE NICE (RUSSIAN ORTHODOX CATHEDRAL OF NICE)

Av. Nicholas II; 09 81 09 53 45; www.sobor.fr; open daily 9am-6pm, access restricted from noon-2pm for celebrations

One of the few remaining structures from Byzantine times, the Cathédrale Saint-Nicolas is a marvel of Russian architecture. Candy-style cupolas that could've been uprooted from Saint Petersburg adorn the cathedral, and bells ring every half hour. Do a full 360-degree walk around the grounds to fully examine the building's blends of red, teal, white, and gold before heading inside to admire the arguably more gorgeous interior. Russian icons and gold motifs decorate the interior. Be sure to cover your knees and shoulders before heading in—even if it is one of those hot summer days. Women should bring some sort of scarf as a head covering if they plan to walk inside the cathedral.

i *Free; wheelchair accessible*

MARCHÉ AUX FLEURS COURS SALEYA (COURS SALEYA FLOWER MARKET)

Cours Saleya; 04 92 14 46 14; open Tu-Sa 6am-5:30pm, Su 6am-1pm

Make sure to pack those OTCs in your backpack, although we're not sure if any dose of Claritin, Allegra, or Zyrtec can save you from the pollen-fest of the Marché aux Fleurs in **Vieux Nice,** the city's old quarter. Just steps away from the waterfront, the market is filled with refreshing aromas of every flower imaginable. Besides flowers, the stands offer everything from scented soaps to fresh vegetables to ripe fruits, so you can solve your backpacker BO and get your daily dose of vitamins in one shot.

i *Prices vary by stand; wheelchair accessible*

PALAIS LASCARIS

15 Rue Droite; 04 93 62 72 40; Jan 2-June 22 M, W-Su 11am-6pm, June 23-Oct 15 M, W-Su 10am-6pm, Oct 16-Dec 31 M, W-Su 11am-6pm (closed Jan 1, Easter Sunday, May 1, Dec 25)

In the middle of the winding paths of **Vieux Nice** (Old Nice) lies Palais Lascaris, a seventeenth-century aristocratic building that serves as a musical instrument museum. The unassuming exterior opens up into a lavish and ornate interior, complete with beautifully decorated ceilings and gold-painted walls. Palais Lascaris is home to the second-largest collection of musical instruments in all of France, including cigar box guitars, harps with intricately painted flowers, and more oboes and clarinets than Squidward could ever imagine. Built in the sixteenth century by the family of Jean-Paul Lascaris, the house still has much of the furniture (including paintings of fat men) you'd expect of a French aristocratic family. Word to the wise: don't budget too much time for this museum, as your visit will be under an hour.

i *Admission €6, students and under 18 free, part of Municipal museums day ticket €10; last entry 5:30pm; guided tours F at 3pm €6; no wheelchair accessibility*

LANDMARKS

PLACE MASSÉNA

15 Pl. Masséna; 06 29 64 10 12; open daily 24hr

What makes Place Masséna so unmistakable? Is it the red Pompeiian buildings on all its sides? The brightly lit Ferris wheel that can be viewed from a mile away? The perhaps overly massive fountain of the Greek god Apollo on the checked black and white patterned pavement? Or maybe it's just the fact that it's smack in the middle of Nice and you will, without a doubt, walk through it on your way to the waterfront every day. Just after sundown, statues of seven naked men light up on raised poles in every color of the rainbow. It's kind of like a PG Burlesque show that kids can watch, but only adults really understand. Cher and Christina, where you at?

i *Free; wheelchair accessible*

COLLINE DU CHÂTEAU (CASTLE HILL)

Montee du Chateau; open daily Oct 1-Mar 31 8:30am-6pm, Apr 1-Sept 30 8:30am-8pm

Get in some cardio by climbing this 300-foot hill for an aerial view of the coastline you won't get anywhere else. The site of the former **Château de Nice,** the Castle Hill today is, for lack of a better word, crumbling, but there is a certain charm in its age that you'll discover as you navigate through the maze of paths, many (many) stairs, and stunning array of greenery. Before making your way to the summit, stop

by **Bellana Tower** for the view of the **Bay of Angels** and you'll forget all about how your thighs hurt from the countless flights of stairs. If cardio isn't your thing, there is an elevator that will take you up to the top, where you'll find a playground, a man-made waterfall, and views of the port.

i *Free; limited wheelchair accessibility*

MUSEUMS

MUSÉE MATISSE

164 Av. des Arènes de Cimiez; 04 93 81 08 08; open daily Jan 2-June 22 11am-6pm, June 23-Oct 15 10am-6pm, Oct 16-Dec 31 11am-6pm

It'll take you a bus ride to get here, but once you arrive at this gorgeous red Genoese villa, you won't think twice about the commute. This small museum houses many of **Matisse's** earliest works, including paintings, sculptures, and cutouts. Although the museum doesn't house his most famous works (you'll find those throughout the rest of France and the world), it does offer an in-depth look into Matisse's life and the time he spent in the French Riviera, most significantly in Nice. When you've finished with your daily dose of artist trivia, take a walk around the surrounding **Arènes de Cimiez,** the ruins of a Roman amphitheatre.

i *Municipal museums day ticket €10, 7-day ticket €20, day group ticket €8 per person, free (children under 18, students, unemployed, disabled civilians, journalists); last entry 5:30pm; tours upon request; wheelchair accessible*

MUSÉE MARC CHAGALL

6 Av. Dr Ménard; 04 93 53 87 20; www.muse-chagall.fr; open Nov 1-May 1 M, W-F 10am-5pm, May 2-Oct 31 M, W-F 10am-6pm (closed Jan 1, May 1, Dec 25)

There's something perfectly soothing about the modernist's collection, which is housed in an expansive, open space with natural light. Fun fact: Chagall claimed that the "universe of light" is necessary to truly appreciate his artwork, which we don't exactly understand, but, whatever it is, it's working. When you've finished examining the stained glass windows and 17 biblically inspired paintings, check out the olive garden in which the museum is situated and yeah sure, then you can make your way back to the beach.

i Admission €10, reduced €8, under 18 free, free admission first Su of month; last entry 5:30pm; audio guide available; wheelchair accessible

MUSÉE D'ART MODERNE ET D'ART CONTEMPORAIN DE NICE (MAMAC)

Pl. Yves Klein; 04 97 13 42 01; www. mamac-org; open Jan 2-June 22 Tu-Su 11am-6pm, June 23-Oct 15 Tu-Su 10am-6pm, Oct 16-Dec 31 Tu-Su 11am-6pm

So abstract. So confused. Those are perhaps the two thoughts running through our minds as we climbed the many lit-up stairs of MAMAC. The building has magnificently open and airy galleries featuring everything from American pop art to the work of **Yves Klein,** painter and performance art pioneer, including his monochrome collection with works solely in the color blue. Some of our favorite pieces include a pile of trash, a pile of rocks, and a pile of boxes—all reminders of why our parents are terrified of us suddenly deciding to drop everything and become artists. The museum's true highlight is, however, the top floor, where you can walk around the terrace and admire views of Nice, including the **Tete Carée.**

i Admission €10, groups €8, students free; wheelchair accessible

OUTDOORS

PLAGE PUBLIQUE DE PONCHETTES (PONCHETTES BEACH)

70 Quai des États Unis; lifeguards on duty June 1-Sept 3 9am-6pm

You'll have the perfect beach day at any beach along **Promenade des Anglais,** but we recommend Ponchettes. This beach boasts a prime location just to the side of **Castle Hill,** a military citadel, and in front of **Vieux Nice,** the city's old quarter. Be warned that the beaches in Nice aren't exactly the sandy seafronts you might have imagined. Instead, you'll be walking through smooth pebbles, which is a surprising relief, since you won't get sand stuck in places sand

should never be. Join the sunbathers, beach volleyball players, and swimmers by the shore to enjoy the ever-present sun on the Côte d'Azur.

i Free; no wheelchair accessibility

PROMENADE DES ANGLAIS

Promenade des Anglais; 07 12 34 56 78

Usually, Tinder bios that mention long walks on the beach are a red flag. But walks along the Promenade des Anglais are a different story. This expansive stretch of seafront sidewalk, complete with chairs and benches to admire the unbelievably blue water and pebble beaches of the French Riviera, is filled with beach-goers, annoyingly over-eager children, topless women, joggers, and everyone in between. You could easily spend an entire day hopping from beach to beach with sporadic walks on the Promenade des Anglais, but we also recommend renting a bike and using the cyclists' lanes for some exercise down by the sea.

i Free; wheelchair accessible

FOOD

🍽 SOCCA D'OR ($)

45 Rue Bonaparte; 04 93 56 52 93; www.restaurant-soccador-nice.fr; open M-Tu 11am-2pm and 6pm-10pm, Th-Sa 11am-2pm and 6pm-10pm

An authentic local hang, Socca D'Or is just steps away from the pier and offers a chance to try the Niçoise specialty: *socca* (duh). *Socca,* a chickpea pancake from Genoa, and we recommend getting a demi-plate along with a large pizza or salad. When in doubt, just order what the person next to you is having. You'll be in luck if it happens to be one of the restaurant's scrumptious desserts, like a caramel crêpe. On particularly hot days, sit inside and admire paintings of the port, or brave the heat and sit on the restaurant's sidewalk terrace for a true Nice experience.

i Socca from €3, pizzas and salads from €8, beer and wine from €3; cash only; vegetarian options available; wheelchair accessible

MONACO

Monaco seeks to disprove those who say "size matters." Second to none in class and style, the tiny, two square kilometer Principality of Monaco is an independent city-state surrounded by French territory. Known as a private getaway for the affluent, mainly due to the no-income-tax rule for residents, Monaco calls to mind stacks of dollars, euros, pounds, pesos, or rupees. Housing the famed casino, Hôtel de Paris, and pavilions abundant with designer brand storefronts, the Monte Carlo neighborhood is the glam capital of the world. Stick to the army of tourists, avoid unwanted glances, and do a lot of eyeballing. They can't charge you for looking inside, right? Aside from Monte Carlo and the accompanying Grand Prix, however, Monaco has a stunning Old Town with a royal palace built on Le Rocher, which overlooks the Mediterranean Sea. The entire city-state can be knocked out in one day, if done properly. Get prepared, dear budget backpacker: you're entering high roller town.

Monaco is divided mostly into four different areas. Towards the western part of the city-state, on the **Rock of Monaco,** is **Monaco-Ville,** the old, fortified part of the city. Here, you'll find the Prince's palace and some of the cheaper restaurants and shops. To the west of Monaco-Ville is **Fontvieille,** the newest areas, that houses the stadium of AS Monaco (yes, even this city-state has a football team. This is Europe). North of Monaco-Ville is **La Condamine,** which is right at **Port Hercule.** This is the starting point of the famed Grand Prix. Finally, east of Condamine is **Monte-Carlo.** Popularized by Selena Gomez, Monte-Carlo is the most luxurious and famous area of Monaco where you'll find the famous **Monte-Carlo Casino** and **Hôtel de Paris.**

GETTING THERE

Getting to Hallstatt is easiest by train. Trains stop at many towns surrounding the lake; Hallstatt's station is across the lake from the town itself. A ferry runs back and forth between the station and the center of town, and is both a convenient and fun way to start your visit (€2.50 one-way). Buses also loop from Hallstatt back and forth between Obertraun and Bad Goisern.

GETTING AROUND

Given Monaco's small size, you can save a ton by walking. Some parts of

the city—like the palace—are built on a rock, so you'll spend a good portion of your day on an incline. Monaco does have a transport system for people who don't own private helicopters or yachts. The public bus transportation consists of five bus lines. A one-way ticket is €2 on-board the bus and €1.50 if purchased in advance at a machine. The buses usually run from 6am-9pm. A night bus operates from 10pm-4am. There is also a boat bus that crosses the harbor for €2.

Swing by...

CASINO DE MONTE CARLO
Pl. du Casino; 92 16 20 00; www.fr.casinomontecarlo.com; tours open 9am-1pm, gambling open 2pm-4am

Luxurious casinos frequented by millionaires isn't what comes to mind when you hear the word "backpackers." But we'll be damned if we don't try. Here's how to get in: Pass the fortified barrier of Ferrari and Lamborghinis parked outside. Avoid the snarky glances of doormen as they check your bag. You belong here. Act the part. Be Jay Gatsby. Be James Bond. Once you've played this small melodrama in your head, realize you're surrounded by mobs of tourists like yourself who want to see how the 1%

lives. So, come early to explore the golden-clad walls, marble pillars, and magnificent chandeliers all while listening to the history of the casino with an audio guide. From 2pm onwards, the casino is 18+ and the gambling commences in a different renowned salle.

i *Admission from €12, children 13-18 from €8, children 6-12 from €6; audio guide available; wheelchair accessible*

Check out...

OCEANOGRAPHIC MUSEUM

Av. Saint-Martin; 93 15 36 00; www.oceano.mc; open daily Jan-Mar 10am-6pm, Apr-Jun 10am-7pm, Jul-Aug 9:30am-8pm, Sept 10am-7pm, Oct-Dec 10am-6pm

Monaco is strangely filled with families and children who are young enough to be reckless, but not old enough to gamble. Meet the middle ground: the aquarium on the bottom floor of the Oceanographic Museum. The fluorescent corals, lion fish, and Mexican salamanders were pretty dope, but we actually enjoyed the upstairs museum Prince Albert envisioned as being a palace worthy of the ocean's treasures. This museum was also built into the side of the **Rock of Monaco** and therefore has a killer view of the ocean. See old time oceanographer's paraphernalia, including preserved ginormous and freaky-looking creatures. But, yeah, we'll go see the aquarium too because, you know, we're all kids inside.

i *Admission from €11, children 13-18 from €7, children 4-12 from €5, students from €7; last entry 5:30pm; limited wheelchair accessibility*

Grab a bite at...

CRÊPERIE DU ROCHER ($)

Oberer Marktplatz 53; 0676 534 85 19; open Tu-Su 10am-7pm

When you're this close to Italy and France, the cheapest foods around are easily going to be either pizza or crêpes. Accept and embrace it. Luckily for us, Crêperie du Rocher specializes in these foods, as well as pastas, salads, and ice cream for good measure. Right near the **Royal Palace** in the narrow streets of **Old Town,** the restaurant has tables on the patio so you can people-watch while enjoying a pizza. Break your preconceived notions of "thin pancakes" by trying the large variety of savory and sweet crêpes ranging from salmon to the classic Nutella and bananas. It's the perfect way to not break the bank in Monaco.

i *Pizzas from €6, crêpes from €5 ; vegetarian options available; no wheelchair accessibility*

Don't miss...

JARDIN JAPONAIS

5 Av. Princesse Grace; 93 15 22 77; open Apr 1-Oct 31 9am-6:45pm, Nov 1-Mar 31 9am-5:45pm

The extravagance, the cars, the casinos. They can get tiring. And there's no better place to recharge and refuel than in this small, serene (read: less ostentatious) Japanese Garden. Filled with a tiny red bridge, stone paths, and blossoming flowers, this free (key word: free!) garden transports you to a simpler place. After walking through the pavilions and getting rejected from the Hôtel de Paris, it's great to feel welcomed somewhere with open arms. Walk around for a couple minutes admiring the precision of the garden and characteristic Zen. You've now recharged enough to enter high-end stores and not care what people think. Or maybe you've decided you're better off without them. Good for you.

i *Free; wheelchair accessible*

MALONGO ($)

39 Av. Jean Médicin; 04 93 85 95 01; www.malongo.com; open daily 7:30am-7pm

The stereotypes are true: the French begin their day with an espresso, a croissant, and a cigarette (or four). Malongo is the perfect place to see these stereotypes in action. A decently sized café with bright orange walls on **Avenue Jean Médecin,** Malongo is a necessary stop on your way to the city center. Grab a carefully prepared warm drink and a pastry to kickstart your day. If espresso isn't your thing, the café offers a selection of green and black loose teas, cappuccinos, and lattes. Join the locals quickly ordering their *pétit dejeuner* and watch the fast-moving barista prepare everything from coffee to croissants with cheerfulness and ease. Whoever said the French had to be grumpy?

i Coffee and tea from €4, pastries from €2; wheelchair accessible

PLANET SUSHI ($$)

3 Av. Malaussena; 04 93 16 10 10; open daily 11:30am-10:30pm

In Nice, you spend so much time with the fish in the sea that you might as well eat them. Just off of **Place Masséna,** Planet Sushi offers the chance to take a break from heavy Italian cuisine. And worry not: this Niçoise take on Japanese cuisine is perfectly solid. For lunch, get a €12 sushi platter and try the salmon nigiri. You can dine at the sushi bar, where a futuristic-looking conveyor belt of sushi displays options priced according to plate color, or from the menu, where you choose from a selection of creative rolls topped.

i Sushi platters from €12 for lunch, €16 for dinner, rolls from €8; wheelchair accessible

PORTOVENERE ($$)

12 Rue Halévy; 04 93 88 24 92; www.portoverenerestaurant.fr; open daily noon-3pm and 7pm-11pm

Nice is just 18 miles from the French-Italian border, which explains why there are so many Italian places. Portovenere, located just a few blocks from the **Promenade des Anglais,** is perfect for traditional Italian dishes.

The restaurant's head chef walks around in colorful, patterned hats and chef pants, making sure all his customers are stuffed and satisfied. Choose your favorite pasta, whether that is spaghetti or tagliatelle, drown it in sauce, and you're home free. If you're feeling something a little heavier, go for a seafood or meat dish—we highly recommend the mussels.

i Entrées from €14; vegetarian options available; wheelchair accessible

LA STORIA ($)

1 Cours Saleya; 04 93 80 95 07; open daily 9am-11pm

The restaurants along **Marché aux Fleurs Cours Saleya** are tourist traps to be avoided. If you walk to the end of the marketplace, however, you'll stumble upon more reasonably priced restaurants just steps away from the **Promenade des Anglais,** like La Storia. Serving up Niçoise specialties like socca with parmesan and tomatoes (€8.50), the restaurant has both an indoor and outdoor area with chairs spilling onto the sidewalk. La Storia also offers a large selection of pizzas (€9.50) that can feed two—split with a fellow beach bum to get bang for your buck. Pro-tip: sit outside, but specify if you'd like to be seated away from smoking patrons, as the staff do make an effort to make you comfortable.

i Pizzas from €9, pastas from €12, other entrées from €9, beer and wine €7, during happy hour €5; wheelchair accessible

NIGHTLIFE
HIGH CLUB ($$)

45 Promenade des Anglais; 07 81 88 42 04; www.highclub.fr; open Th-Su 11:45pm-5:30am

It's no secret that you came to Southern France to party and everyone knows the clubs are exclusive. High Club is no different. With themed nights such as "We Are High" Saturdays, High Club boasts an energetic club atmosphere with crowds of the young and restless dancing and bumping to the beats pounding through the speakers. Our caveat is that a poorly planned night will result in a *high* bill. There's a €10 cover, and, once inside, you'll have a Ted and Marshall moment where you realize the drinks cost more than the experience is worth. Stop at pubs before coming to High Club so you only need to worry about the cover.

i Cover €10, beer and wine from €12, cocktails from €16; limited wheelchair accessibility

MA NOLANS IRISH PUB ($)

5 Quai des Deux Emmanuel; 04 92 27 07 88; www.ma-nolans.com; open daily 11am-2am

Ma Nolans Irish Pub has a cult following and three locations in the Côte d'Azur area: one in **Vieux Nice** (Old Nice), one near the port, and one in the nearby ritzy city of **Cannes.** Open practically all day, Ma Nolans is a lovely place to stop midday for a Guinness before walking through the pollen attack that is the **Marché aux Fleurs Cours Saleya** or a relaxing setting after a day on the seafront. Take a seat either inside or on the bar's sidewalk terrace to enjoy a drink or participate in one of many themed events, like live music nights, quiz nights, and game watch parties. If you're not the biggest sports fan, we recommend picking the team of the person next to you and making a friend over a pint.

i Beer from €4, cocktails from €8, shots from €5

WAKA BAR ($)

57 Quai des États-Unis; 04 93 87 94 61; open daily 9:30am-2am

Situated right on the **Promenade des Anglais,** Waka Bar is the ideal place to come after a long, restful day on the beach if you're looking to liven up your evening. The bar boasts a great menu, complete with a wide selection of cocktails and delicious pub grub choices, and a balcony that overlooks the **Bay of Angels.** Arrive just before the sun sets and join the crowd bumping to the reggae tunes as you enjoy the unparalleled view of the Côte d'Azur.

i Cocktails from €6, food from €10; wheelchair accessible

WAYNE'S BAR ($)

15 Rue de la Préfecture; 04 93 13 46 99; wwwlwaynes.fr/fr/accueil; open daily 10am-2am

We know you didn't come to Nice to go to an English-speaking bar, but Wayne's is an exception to the rule. Arguably the most popular bar in the area, Wayne's has a crowd at all hours for its busy dance floor filled with beach goers galore. There's no escaping their enthusiastic head-bopping and swaying to live music from British bands and local DJs as you kick back another pint or shot (€6). Perhaps the liveliest part about Wayne's is the irresistible allure of and eventual obligation to dance on top of the sturdy wooden tables after a long day of lying on the pebble beach.

i Shots from €6, cocktails from €8, beers from €3; BGLTQ+ friendly

PARIS

Coverage by **Emily Corrigan**

To the rest of the world, Paris can be surrounded by enigmas: where are people buying all those blue and white striped shirts? Why are their hats flat? How is that tower so sexy? The city seems at once nostalgic and *à la mode,* classic and modern. Yes, well-dressed people sip espresso in wicker café chairs, buy baguettes at *boulangeries,* and kiss each other on both cheeks, but a more dynamic view of the city reveals neighborhoods with distinct characters and plenty of people who are not too chic to laugh when someone trips, spill drinks while singing karaoke, let their dog just go right there on the sidewalk, or eat chicken McNuggets. Paris hasn't been blissfully left in some golden age of the past; it faces contemporary challenges of globalization and immigration and confronts social issues like from wealth to race to religion. These factors combine with its rich history and tradition, creating a diverse city that's livable, evolving, and exciting. So, while its landmarks reflect ancient influences, its museums house works from old masters, and its wineries take advantage of thousands of years of knowledge, there are always new and unique parts of the city to meet and explore. *Enchanté,* Paris.

ORIENTATION

They say that Paris is laid out like one of its famous escargots: unlike New York's its rigid grids, Paris's winding *rues* are divided into blob-shaped **arrondissements,** starting in the center and spiraling outward like a snail's shell. You'll always be able to tell which arrondissement an address comes from by looking at the last digits of its zip code (750 are the first three, followed by the number of the neighborhood). Arrondissements are also noted with the number and suffix -ème or -e (e.g. 8ème or 8e). The Seine River bends through the city's center, providing a frame of reference and historically separating the city into the **Rive Gauche** and **Rive Droite.**

The first arrondissement begins in the center of the city just north of the river. It's home to the big guns: the **Louvre,** the **Tuileries Gardens,** and **Place de la Concorde,** along with beautiful but bank-breaking shops. To its eastern end near **Les Halles,** however, you'll start to encounter more affordable living. Just north is the second, a small and trendy neighborhood defined by **Rue Montorgueil,** a street lined with cafés, cheese shops, produce stands, butchers, clothing stores—you name it. The third and fourth arrondissements make up **Le Marais,** whose youthful and slightly hipster crowd means it can always be counted on for unique restaurants and bars.

Before crossing the river to the fifth, you'll encounter **Île de la Cité** and **Île Saint-Louis,** two islands in the middle of the Seine which hold **Sainte Chapelle** and **Notre Dame,** and are some of the oldest parts of the city. Students from high school (*lycée*) and university (like the area's **Sorbonne**) crowd into the fifth arrondissement, or the **Latin Quarter.** The **Museum of Natural History** and its surrounding **Jardin des Plantes** make up its eastern edge while the beautiful **Jardin du Luxembourg** defines its western boundary with the sixth. The sixth itself, **Saint-Germain-des-Prés,** is host to the old haunts of celebrated writers and intellectuals, making it a fashionable and expensive area with famous cafés and plenty of bookstores. The seventh is the stuff of postcards: clean, quiet, picturesque Paris streets, in some parts mixed with the grand display of the **Eiffel Tower** and **Champ de Mars.**

Back across the river to the north is the eighth, where stereotypes of impossibly sleek, black-clad, high-heeled Parisians come to life. The district is bisected by the famous wide avenue of the **Champs-Elysées,** with its endpoints at the **Place de Charles de Gaulle** (where the **Arc de Triomphe** stands) and the **Place de la Concorde** defining two of its corners and the lovely **Parc Monceau** lining its northern boundary. East of the eighth, you'll find the **Grands Boulevards** neighborhood of the ninth, where young people can find thriving nightlife on even the slowest of nights and large department stores attract shoppers in droves. The tenth, where many hostels are located (along with the 18th), reveals a grittier side of Paris, but still doesn't lack in beautiful waterside views along the **Canal St-Martin.** The 11th has scores of small brasseries, hidden gems, and lively side streets, while the **Bastille** area in the 12th has more crowded bars. The 13th, 14th, and 15th are more residential neighborhoods, each with their own character: the 13th reflects significant Asian influences, the 14th has both cute sleepy streets and lively energy near Montparnasse, and the 15th holds hidden charm behind 1970s high-rises. Continuing to spiral outward to the west, the 16th feels upscale, full of young professionals with seemingly important business. On the side facing the Seine you'll find interesting museums and the **Trocadéro,** from which you'll find one of the best views of the Eiffel Tower the city has to offer. While the 17th is a haven for artists seeking pretty cafés, the 18th's **Pigalle** area is chock-full of sex shops and peep shows, and houses the **Red Light District** of *Moulin Rouge* fame. The 18th also features **Montmartre,** where **Sacré Coeur** beckons from the highest point in Paris and artists do sketches and portraits around **Place du Tertre.** Finally, **Parc des Buttes-Chaumont** is the highlight of the 19th, and the **Père Lachaise** cemetery makes a daytrip out to the 20th worth your while.

ESSENTIALS

GETTING THERE

Fly into either Charles de Gaulle or Orly airports. From Charles de Gaulle, take the RER Line B into the city. Some trains go directly to Gare du Nord, which is close to many of the city's hostels in the tenth arrondissement and connects to multiple other metro lines. The journey should take about 40min. and costs €10. From Orly, you can take RER Line C into the city for about €6, which will take approximately 30min. Most trains arrive at Gare du Nord or Gare de l'Est, both located in the 10th arrondissement. From there, you can take the metro to where you need to go.

GETTING AROUND

The metro, SNCF, is definitely the easiest way to get around Paris. Tickets can be purchased in the stations, and get cheaper the more you purchase. Navigo passes can also be purchased at many stations for €5, and are valid on the metro, bus, and RER (the larger commuter trains). They can be charged with the weekly fare, about €22, or the monthly fare, about €73. Buses are also easy to take and provide an opportunity to get acquainted with the layout of the city above ground. Vélib, the Parisian bike sharing service, also has stations all over the city and bikes are available daily 24hr. Passes can be bought by the day for only €1.70 or by the week for €8. The first 30min. of a ride are always free.

PRACTICAL INFORMATION

Tourist Offices: The main tourist office can be found at 25 Rue des Pyramides, 1e (open daily 10:15am-7pm).
Banks/ATMs/Currency Exchange: Major French banks include BNP Paribas, Banque Populaire, Société Générale, Crédit Mutuel, and more. ATM fees will apply.
Post Offices: The La Poste Paris, Louvre location is open all night at 16 Rue Étienne Marcel, 2e. Other locations include 18 Bd. de la Chapelle, 18e and 11 Rue des Islettes, 18e.
Internet: Many businesses in Paris don't offer free Wi-Fi, so McDonald's is going to become your best friend when you're in a pinch. Free internet access is also provided at nearly all of the city's most frequented museums.
BGLTQ+ Resources: The Centre BGLTQ Paris-ÎdF (63 Rue Beaubourg, 3e; 01 43 57 21 47; open M-F 3:30pm-8pm, Sa 1pm-7pm)

EMERGENCY INFORMATION

Emergency Number: 112
Police: Direction de la Police Judiciaire (36 Quai des Orfèvres, 1e; 01 53 71 53 71)
US Embassy: There is a US Embassy in Paris (2 Av. Gabriel, 8e; 01 43 12 22 22; open M-Th 7:30am-5pm, F 7:30am-12:30pm).
Rape Crisis Center: Institut National d'Aide aux Victimes et de Médiation (14 Rue Ferrus, 14e 01 45 88 19 00; 0884284637; helpline open every day 9am-9pm)

Hospitals:
- Hôtel-Dieu de Paris (1 Pl. du Parvis de Notre-Dame, 4e; 01 42 34 82 34)
- Hôpital Saint-Louis (1 Av. Claude Vellefaux, 10e; 01 42 49 49 49)

Pharmacies:
- Pharmacie de Garde Auber Paris Opéra (01 42 65 88 29)
- Pharmacie Monge (01 43 31 39 44)

ACCOMMODATIONS

◪ MIJE FOURCY FAUCONNIER MAUBUISSON ($$)

6 Rue de Fourcy, 4e; 01 42 74 23 45; www.mije.com/en/accueil; reception open 24hr

Staying at MIJE is a true French experience; you'll be living in one of its three seventeenth-century buildings in the **Marais**, one of Paris's most centrally located and trendy districts. There are plenty of picturesque cafés nearby, but it will be hard to leave the hostel with its free breakfast, lunch buffet, and full-service dinner. In true homey Parisian style, the front door opens onto a beautiful courtyard full of flowers and white tables. So say "bonne journée" to your elderly neighbor, grab your motor scooter keys and grocery bag and—wait, you're forgetting you don't actually live here.

i Dorms from €30; reservation recommended; Wi-Fi; luggage storage available; free breakfast 7am-10am

◪ OOPS! DESIGN HOSTEL-LATIN QUARTER ($$)

50 Av. des Gobelins, 13e; 01 47 07 47 00; www.oops-paris.com; reception open 24hr

You may pull an "oops" by forgetting to come back to the hostel since its location in the fun-filled Latin Quarter means you won't want to spend any more time cooped up inside. The hostel is tucked between cafés on a busy flower-filled street, within walking distance of attractions like the **Panthéon** and **Luxembourg Gardens.** As much fun as you'll find in the area, though, the hostel provides plenty of services itself. Pick up groceries across the street to cook in the kitchen or rent a board game to play in the colorful common room. Despite its name, staying at Oops! is no mistake (unlike using its TV to watch a Nicholas Cage movie).

i Dorms starting at €32; reservation recommended; cash only; Wi-Fi; linens included; luggage storage; lockers provided; free breakfast; kitchen

AUBERGE INTERNATIONALE DES JEUNES ($)

10 Rue Trousseau, 11e; 01 47 00 62 00; www.aijparis.com; reception open 24hr

"AIJ" is a true student hostel: there are no guests over 30, it's cheap as can be, and coffee is free. Even with some of the best rates in the city, this hostel still doesn't sacrifice its quality. A warm and inviting staff makes you feel at home, and the rooms are completely comfortable. The four-person maximum dorms and in-suite bathrooms are thoroughly cleaned between 11am and 3pm daily, but you'll have no trouble finding something to do outside the hostel during those hours. The **Bastille** area is full of bakeries, cafés, and shops, and there's even a small produce market just a block away.

i Dorms from €15; reservation required; no wheelchair accessibility; Wi-Fi; towels for rent; luggage storage; free breakfast

GENERATOR HOSTEL ($$)

9-11 Pl. du Colonel Fabien, 10e; 01 70 98 84 00; reception open 24hr

Located in the tenth arrondissement, this hostel features a rooftop terrace with views of **Sacré Coeur** in the foreground and **La Défense** in the distance. After watching the sunset, retire to your clean and comfortable dorm room or take advantage of the first-floor club open until 2am.

i Dorms from €35; reservation recommended; wheelchair accessible; Wi-Fi; café open daily 24hr, terrace 4pm-10pm, downstairs club 10pm-2am; laundry; lockers available

LE VILLAGE HOSTEL MONTMARTRE ($$)

20 Rue d'Orsel, 18e; 01 42 64 22 02; www.villagehostel.fr; reception open 24hr

You'll have to wade through the countless colorful fabric stores of **Montmartre** to get to this hillside hostel, but you'll get a free shot upon check-in at the pub next door. The location allows you to explore the historic neighborhood, and the terrace features a view of **Sacré Coeur.**

i Dorms from €33; reservation recommended; Wi-Fi; kitchen, hairdryers and towels for rent, breakfast €4.50

SMART PLACE GARE DU NORD ($$)

28 Rue de Dunkerque, 10e; 01 48 78 25 15; www.smartplaceparis.com; reception open 24hr

Smart Place isn't just book smart (although they do have a book exchange). It's smart in a plays-the-guitar, wears-horn-rimmed-glasses kind of way, too. The human embodiment of these characteristics can often be found casually playing foosball in the lobby, whipping up dinner in the common kitchen, or making moves on your girlfriend in the spacious dorm rooms. It's so smooth it'll even buy you a drink.

i Dorms €35; reservation recommended; BGLTQ+ friendly; wheelchair accessible; Wi-Fi; laundry; lockers available; reservation recommended

VINTAGE HOSTEL AND BUDGET HOTEL ($)

73 Rue Dunkerque, 9e ; 75009; 140161640; www.vintage-hostel.com; reception open 24hr

The handyman of hostels, Vintage offers an array of services inspire jealousy. Directions to famous monuments, restaurant recommendations, weather information, museum hours and prices: there's nothing Vintage can't provide. Plus, as one of the rare hostels with a gym, it offers the opportunity to offset at least some of what the backpacking lifestyle is doing to your body.

i Dorms from €25; reservation recommended; Wi-Fi; reservation recommended; laundry; towels for rent

SIGHTS
CULTURE

◪ MARCHÉ AUX PUCES

30 Av. Gabriel Péri, Saint-Ouen; www.marcheauxpuces-saintouen.com; open M 11am-5pm, Sa 9am-6pm, Su 10am-6pm

Marché aux Puces, the largest antiques market in the world, combines a coppery vintage feel with unexpected gems like garden gnomes giving you the finger and life-sized silver sharks to suspend from your ceiling. You wouldn't be surprised to see a boy in a newsboy cap and suspenders yelling something like "R2D2 coffee tables! Get your R2D2 coffee tables here!" With over 1700 vendors, the outdoor market is like a small city, with neighborhoods of plant shops, art dealers, and general collections of, for lack of a better word, stuff. Located just north of Paris, the market is a metro ride away, the ideal place to escape the city and spend a weekend day trying to find that perfect lampshade made of peacock feathers.

i Stand prices vary

AVENUE DES CHAMPS-ÉLYSÉES

8e; open daily 24hr

This famous avenue began as an extension of the **Tuileries Gardens,** but by the eighteenth century, it became a fashionable street for shopping, strolling, seeing, and being seen. Stretching between the **Place de la Concorde** and the **Arc de Triomphe,** it has a parallel garden on its northeastern side. Events such as the annual Bastille Day parade and the final stage of the Tour de France draw huge crowds to the Champs-Élysées. In the winter, the avenue adopts a ferris wheel and an extensive Christmas market. On a daily basis, tourists flock to the Tiffany and Co. shop, check out French styles from Zadig & Voltaire and Maje, or nibble dainty pastries at famous bakeries like the macaron shop **Ladurée.**

i Free

CHOPIN AU JARDIN

2 Rue Gazan, 14e; open summer Su 5pm-6pm

If you've ever fantasized about laying in a meadow with music softly caressing your eardrums and gentle horses nuzzling your face, you're not alone. While this dream may seem somewhat out of reach for those who don't live on a ranch in Candyland, Chopin au Jardin is certainly the next best thing. Every summer, renowned pianists give a series of free performances in **Parc Montsouris,** a beautiful green area on the southern edge of the city. Listeners crowd onto the nearby hill, shaded by large trees and featuring a beautiful view of the park's pond, to recline and relax. Children on stubborn ponies idle by periodically, but for the most part the audience is hushed, captivated by the beautiful music.

i Free; wheelchair accessible

GALERIES LAFAYETTE

40 Bd. Haussmann, 9e; 01 42 82 34 56; www.galerieslafayette.com; open M-Sa 9:30am-8:30pm, Su 11am-7pm

Do you ever get frustrated that your mink scarf is no longer in season? Do you hate it when your Prada boots get a little scuffed? What about when you can't decide between colors of Gucci sunglasses so you have to buy all of them? No??

Well then, you won't have much in common with many of the shoppers perusing the designer racks at Galeries Lafayette, Paris's most famous department store. Visitors flock by the busload to throw euros at shoes, bags, suits, perfumes, just about anything that will scream, "My parents own a boat." But there's lots to see even if you're not being crushed under the weight of your expendable income. Winter window displays draw crowds, cafés serve steaming hot chocolate, and the rooftop offers a beautiful view of the city.

i Prices vary; wheelchair accessible

JARDIN DES PLANTES

57 Rue Cuvier, 5e; 01 40 79 56 01; www.jardindesplantes.net; open daily 7:30am-8pm

It may seem repetitive to name a garden the "garden of plants." Here, though, it really is all about those beautiful rectangular-celled beings. Paris's own botanical garden features greenhouses growing tropical trees, shallow ponds full of water lilies, and gardens overflowing with beautiful flowers. A host of animals like leopards and wallabies lives in the menagerie, while a maze leads up to a small pagoda. Entrance to the garden is free, but its different components may have their own fees. If you're looking to relive your *Night at the Museum* fantasies, enter the **Museum of Natural History** housed in the garden to stare expectantly at life-like dioramas.

i Garden entry free, other areas of the garden for under 25 €9; wheelchair accessible

MARCHÉ DES ENFANTS ROUGES

39 Rue de Bretagne, 3e; 01 40 11 20 40; open Tu-Th 10am-8pm, F-Sa 8am-8:30pm, Su 8:30am-5pm

Despite the concerning literal translation (read: market of the red children), this outdoor market is innocent and charming. Among stalls selling meat, cheese, produce, and flowers are multiple excellent restaurants with outdoor seating. Although it's crowded at peak lunch hours, the wait is worth it. Don't miss the couscous royal (€12) from the Moroccan restaurant **Le Traiteur Marocain.** An entertaining connoisseur at a shop just behind it painstakingly crafts excellent sandwiches, if you're willing to wait. And, to calm your fears, the name's roots lie in the clothing worn by children cared for at an orphanage nearby.

i Stand prices vary

PLACE DES VOSGES

Pl. des Vosges, 4e; open M-F 8am-6pm, Sa 8:30am-6pm, Su 9am-6pm

Formerly **Place Royale** (the home of the French monarchy), Place des Vosges is now surrounded by some of the best art galleries of **Le Marais.** With beautiful architecture, the omnipresent aroma of the shady linden trees, and a stunning fountain, it's a relaxing spot that you would never guess was the site of King Henri IX's untimely death (by a lance through his eye; brutal). Step through the courtyard of the Hôtel de Sully, lunch at a neighboring café, or enter (for free) the former home of **Victor Hugo,** author of *The Hunchback of Notre Dame* and *Les Misérables.*

i Free; last entry 5:40pm; wheelchair accessible

LANDMARKS

LES CATACOMBES

1 Av. du Colonel Henri Rol-Tanguy, 14e; 01 43 22 47 63; ; www.catacombes.paris.fr; open Tu-Su 10am-8:30pm

After waiting in line until you're almost ready to join the ranks of the skeletons, you'll be welcomed into the chilly labyrinthine underground tunnels. Beginning in the late eighteenth century, as graveyards closed for public health reasons, remains were moved to the Catacombs. Millions of skulls and bones are stacked in arrangements that are surprisingly pleasing to the eye, until you remember that they were once living breathing humans. It begs the question: how does one get into the bone-arranging line of work? Do you have to have an internship, or just be one of those kids that burned a lot of ants? In any case, underground Paris is not for the faint of heart.

i Admission €13, under 17 free; last entry 7:30pm; no wheelchair accessibility

NOTRE DAME

6 Parvis Notre-Dame, Pl. Jean-Paul II, 4e; 01 42 34 56 10; www.notredamedeparis. fr/en; open M-F 7:45am-6:45pm, Sa-Su 7:45am-7:15pm

"A long time ago" to some means when their dog was a puppy. To others, it means when Patricia stole their juice box in kindergarten. But the construction of the Notre Dame cathedral began a really long time ago, far before the development of modern juice box technology. Its first stage began in the 1160s and the façade was finally completed in 1215. Its French Gothic style incorporates flying buttresses, impressive stained glass rose windows, and a gallery of 28 statues of kings demonstrating the privileged relationship between the era's monarchy and the Church of Paris. Pro tip: check out the cathedral's crypt (located down a stairway outside in the square), the site of Paris's first fortifications from 308 when the city was still called Lutetia.

i Free entry to cathedral, audio guide €2, towers €10, treasury €5, crypt €8; wheelchair accessible

PÈRE LACHAISE CEMETERY

16 Rue du Repos, 20e; 01 55 25 82 10; open M-F 8am-6pm, Sa 8:30am-6pm, Su 9am-6pm

The Père Lachaise Cemetery, established in 1804, is the most visited cemetery in the world for a few reasons. First, as the largest green space in Paris, it's incredibly beautiful and serene. Signs claim that 4134 trees of 76 species grow there. Secondly, more than one million bodies have been buried there over the years, making navigating the elaborate and numerous headstones and monuments an interesting journey through time. Finally, seeing the graves of famous people like **Oscar Wilde, Edith Piaf, Frédéric Chopin,** and others will allow you opportunities to boast that you've "always loved the work of Delacroix" or suggest that you "discuss Proust's *In Search of Lost Time,* shall we?"

i Free entry; wheelchair accessible

CHURCH OF SAINT-SULPICE

2 Rue Palatine, 6e; 01 42 34 59 98; open daily 7:30am-7:30pm

Despite terms like "French kissing" and *ménage à trois*, it's impossible to forget France's more pious traditions. With its age-old Catholic tradition, it's no surprise to find this church in the heart of the **Saint-Germain-des-Près** district. With foundations from as far back as the twelfth century, it has stood the test of time as one of Paris's largest churches. Additions from the 1800s include famous paintings from Eugène Delacroix in its interior and an enormous organ spanning the length of the back wall. Today, you may recognize parts of the church from its use in the film *The Da Vinci Code.*

i Free; no wheelchair accessibility; must cover shoulders and knees to enter

EIFFEL TOWER

Champ de Mars, 5 Av. Anatole, 7e; www. toureiffel.paris/en/; open daily 9:30am-11pm, mid-June to Sept 9am-midnight

The Eiffel Tower was supposed to be destroyed six months after its use for the **1889 World's Fair,** but a vote by Parisian citizens to keep it determined its fate as a setting for wedding photos, the site of the highest concentration of selfie sticks per capita in the world (we're assuming), and a source of inspiration for the more creative sex shops around the **Moulin Rouge.** Enjoy a picnic in the surrounding park if you're not willing to wait up to one hour amongst the engaged couples, selfie-takers, and sex toy designers to actually get into the tower and see its incredible panoramic views. Just watch out for dangerously high wind levels caused by thousands of moon-eyed romantics collectively sighing.

i Lift to 2nd fl. €11, stairs to 2nd fl. €7, lift to top €17; last 2nd fl. lift 11pm, last summit lift 10:30pm, last stairs entry 6pm; wheelchair accessible; reserve tours online

L'ARC DE TRIOMPHE

Pl. Charles-de-Gaulle, 8e; 01 55 37 73 77; monuments-nationaux.fr; open daily 10am-11pm

Assuming you played Little League, you are probably familiar with the concept that when you win something, you get a trophy. Usually it's a plastic statue in some sort of athletic stance, but add Napoleon to the mix and you get a 50-meter high tribute to military victory. L'Arc de Triomphe honors the achievements of the Grande Armée and memorializes the **Unknown Soldier** with an eternal flame. It was built in what was originally named Place de *l'étoile* (meaning star) after the 12 large avenues that radiate from it, including the famous **Champs-Élysées.** The top of the arch has one of the best views in Paris, especially since it's open late for the sunset. Someone give this arch a plastic statue.

i Admission €9; wheelchair accessible

LE PANTHÉON

Pl. du Panthéon, 5e; 01 44 32 18 00; par-is-pantheon.fr/en; open daily 10am-6:30pm (closed Jan 1, May 1, Dec 25)

Originally intended by Louis XV as a dedication to Geneviève, the patron saint of Paris, this large domed structure eventually became the secular national pantheon. It pays homage to writers who died for France in WWI and WWII, and it hosts the tombs of scientists like **Marie Curie** (who was the first female professor at the neighboring **Sorbonne** university) and thinkers like **Voltaire** and **Rousseau.** Although her spotlight was stolen, Geneviève is still featured in many of the massive paintings covering the walls, ensuring that she's still on Paris's side. In the center of the transept you'll find **Foucault's**

pendulum, which he used to prove that the Earth rotates around itself. Funny, we always thought it rotated around chocolate croissants.

i *Admission €9; last audio guide issued 5:15pm; wheelchair accessible; tours of upper levels available*

PALAIS GARNIER: OPÉRA NATIONAL DE PARIS

8 Rue Scribe, 9e; www.operadeparis.fr/en; open Sept 12-July 16 10am-4:30pm, July 17-Sept 11 10am-5:30pm

Charles Garnier undertook this architectural feat in 1861 at the request of **Napoleon III,** building what is now considered one of the world's most beautiful theaters. The elite opera-goers of years past and present have mingled in the **Grand Foyer** outside the most expensive boxes, admiring its high painted ceilings. Less elite civilians have just taken pictures of the chandeliers and called it a day. The ballets and operas still taking place here. are expensive, but those under 25 can see the theater and its museum and library with costume jewelry, set designs, books, and paintings for only €7.

i *Admission €11, ages 12-25 €7; guided tours daily 11am and 2:30pm; last entry 4:30pm; wheelchair accessible*

SACRÉ COEUR

35 Rue de Chevalier de la Barre, 18e; 01 53 41 89 00; www.sacre-coeur-montmartre.fr; basilica open daily 6am-10:30pm; dome open May-Sept 8:30am-8pm, Oct-Apr 9am-5pm

From the laying of the first stone in 1875, Sacré Coeur has had at least one person praying inside at all times, day and night, for over 125 years. Its construction began after France's defeat in the 1870 war against Germany, a response to thoughts that France's troubles had spiritual roots. Signs prompting you to dress respectfully and be silent reinforce the solemn mood and religious history, but the touristy souvenir shops of the **Montmartre** neighborhood have permeated even the basilica's interior. Here, have a souvenir coin with your dazzling mosaics and enormous angel sculptures.

i *Basilica admission free, dome admission €6; no wheelchair accessibility*

SAINTE-CHAPELLE

8 Bd. du Palais, 1e; 01 53 40 60 80; www. sainte-chapelle.fr/en; open daily 9am-7pm

Most stains require the tough, grease-fighting cleansing power of a Tide pen. But in the thirteenth century, King Louis IX threw caution to the wind and hired some guys to just stain the living hell (pun intended) out of some glass, Gothic style. A reliquary and place of worship, this two-story chapel is home to a stunning collection of stained glass windows, each telling its own story. The mammoth windows, including an impressive rose one, flood the place with light, which glints off chandeliers and golden decorations inside. The chapel often holds cultural events such as concerts in the summer months, so be sure to check the schedule before you go.

i *Admission €10, under 26 free; guided tours daily 11am-3pm; last entry 30min. before closing*

MUSEUMS

🖼 CENTRE GEORGES POMPIDOU

Pl. Georges-Pompidou, 4e; 01 44 78 12 33; www.centrepompidou.fr/en; open M, W-Su 11am-9pm, Level 6 open Th until 11pm

Your first indication that the Pompidou is going to get weird and wild is the fact that you enter the museum through a large transparent tube and your next indication is that the art is bananas. We mean that in a figurative sense, but, after an hour at the Pompidou, you would no longer be skeptical if you were to see a bunch of bananas wearing little jackets with a sign that read something like "Costumed Fruit. 2011. Reinterpretation of light, fabric, and organic energy. Medium: bananas, polyester." As the largest collection of modern and contemporary art in Europe, works by **Matisse** and **Picasso** are displayed alongside sideways urinals and stained folding tables. Ahh, art.

i *Admission €14; tours Sa at noon; last entry 8pm; wheelchair accessible*

⬛ MUSÉE DU QUAI BRANLY - JACQUES CHIRAC

37 Quai Branly, 7e; 01 56 61 70 00; www.
quaibranly.fr/en/; open T-W 11am to 7pm,
Th-Sa 11am-9pm, Su 11am to 7pm

We know, we know. All these museums are great but there are just not enough Yemeni feast dresses for your taste. Look no further: at this museum, you'll walk through a large display hall housing indigenous art from Africa, Oceania, Asia, and the Americas. Screens play footage of cultural ceremonies while visitors peruse Maori dugout canoes, Bedouin camel litters used in the Syrian steppes, Persian ceramics, Ethiopian prayer scrolls, and elaborate masks from all over the world. (And to think, we've just been using a brown paper bag!) Make sure to look up the temporary exhibits, since they take up almost half of the museum's space.

i Admission €10, access to temporary exhibitions €10; wheelchair accessible

⬛ MUSÉE DE PICASSO

5 Rue de Thorigny, 3e; 01 85 56 00 36; www.museepicassoparis.fr; open Tu-F 10:30am-6pm, Sa-Su and French holidays 9:30am-6pm (closed Dec 25, Jan 1, May 1)

For the artist with perhaps the most widely recognized name in the world, Picasso sure loved to paint in his underwear. We know this because the Picasso Museum, providing photo evidence, focuses as much on the master's life and influences as on his art. A well-crafted narrative guides visitors through the museum, with each step demonstrating chronologically how Picasso's relationships, setbacks, and passions (especially in his marriage and subsequent affair) manifested in his work and developed his artistic alter ego: a minotaur. It'll be difficult to leave, but, once you do, spend some time wandering through the small art galleries surrounding the museum.

i Admission €12.50; tours €7; tours Saturday at 2pm; wheelchair accessible

FONDATION LOUIS VUITTON

8 Av. du Mahatma Gandhi, 16e; 01 40 69 96 00; www.fondationlouisvuitton.fr; open M noon-7pm, W-Th noon-7pm, F noon-9pm, Sa-Su 11am-8pm

The "museum of man" explores how humans have evolved, organized ourselves, migrated to colonize continents, and developed our own languages and cultures. It incorporates archaeological history, art, models, and nature, but in fun and interactive ways. You can squash your face to look like a Neanderthal, pull rubbery tongues sticking out of the wall to hear different languages, look at brains in jars, and press buttons that give off the scents of various cuisines. See the Peruvian mummy that inspired the famous painting *Scream*. And don't forget to grin smugly to yourself knowing that of all species of the Homo genus, we Sapiens are the last ones standing. Suck it, erectus.

i Admission €14, students €10; wheelchair accessible and free entry to disabled visitors

LE LOUVRE

Rue de Rivoli, 1e; 01 40 20 50 50; www.louvre.fr/en; open M 9am-6pm, W 9am-10pm, Th 9am-6pm, F 9am-10pm, Sa-Su 9am-6pm

The Louvre. Oh, you've heard of it? Big glass pyramids, that one lady that doesn't smile with her teeth, people in scarves looking thoughtfully at things. We're guessing you have the basic info down, so here are some insider tips. Go in the morning or buy a Paris museum pass ahead of time to avoid lines. When viewing the famous sculpture *Winged Victory*, stand on the stairs from a three-quarters angle on the left, the vantage point from which its artist originally intended it to be viewed. Go to the **Pavilion to l'Horloge** to walk in what used to be the moat of the royal palace. Plan ahead: the massive museum can be overwhelming if you don't do your research. Unless, of course, you're just there to see our gal Mona.

i Admission €15; tour €12 and tickets can only be purchased at the museum the day of; wheelchair accessible

MUSÉE DE L'ORANGERIE

Jardin des Tuileries, Pl. de la Concorde, 1e; 01 44 77 80 07; www.musee-orangerie.fr/en; open M, W-Su 9am-6pm

The highlight of the museum, located at the edge of the **Tuileries Gardens,** is the collection of eight huge water lilies paintings by **Monet.** The rooms in which the *Nymphéas* series are installed were specifically designed with input by Monet himself. The paintings curve around oval rooms, encircling the viewer and inviting them into the beautiful natural scene. The other 145 paintings by famous artists like **Renoir, Matisse,** and **Picasso** are located two floors down. You know your museum is pretty important when you have to toss the Matisse in the basement.

i Admission €9; tours €6, M 2:15pm and Sa 11am; last entry 5:15pm; wheelchair accessible

MUSÉE D'ORSAY

1 Rue de la Légion d'Honneur, 7e; 01 40 49 48 14; www.musee-orsay.fr/en/home.html; open daily 9:30am-6pm, except Th 9:30am-9:45pm (closed May 1, Dec 25)

Housed in an old train station, the Musée d'Orsay takes advantage of an enormous main hall to display the largest collection of Impressionist masterpieces in the world. Between the huge landscapes, a polar bear sculpture, and masterpieces like **Degas'** *Petite Danseuse,* the museum's scale can be overwhelming. Luckily, enormous clocks occupy some of the fifth-floor windows if you need to take a gaze-romantically-over-the-rooftops-while-imagining-you-lived-in-the-mid-nineteenth-century break.

i Admission €12; tours €6 from 9:30am onward; last tickets entry 5pm, Th 9pm; wheelchair accessible

MUSÉE RODIN

79 Rue de Varenne, 7e; 01 44 18 61 10; www.musee-rodin.fr; open Tu-Su 10am-5:45pm

Rodin was a controversial sculptor in his day. Sometimes too provocative and erotic, he offended many and gained the loyalty and support of others. His statue of **Balzac** was first met with outrage, but is now considered the starting point for modern sculpture; who knows, maybe one day we'll realize that *Fifty Shades of Grey* was in fact the dawn of a new era of literature. Rodin's works are spread around a beautiful garden of roses and trees, from which the Invalides dome and the Eiffel Tower are both visible. An elegant mansion where Rodin once lived is also open to the public, although his most famous sculptures like *The Thinker, The Kiss,* and *The Gates of Hell* can all be found outside.

i Admission €10, audio guide €6; last entry 5:15pm; wheelchair accessible

GIVERNY

Giverny is only a 45-minute train ride from Paris, but it's an entirely different world. Vines entirely cover medieval buildings, lazy green streams meander through fields of cattle, and life seems much simpler than usual— kinda like in Disney Channel Original Movies. The small village, about 15-kilometers from Vernon, claims fame as the former home of Impressionist master Claude Monet. Visitors can walk through Monet's house and gardens, visit an Impressionist museum, and enjoy fantasies of being able to paint masterpieces rather than pathetically attempt shading in stick figures. Water lilies and floral compositions dot the landscape, making it clear why many famous American painters followed the lead of Monet, who discovered his love for the place out the window of a passing train. A visit to this magical spot is an ideal way to spend a dreamy long afternoon.

Vernon lies in the region of **Normandy,** northwest of Paris about halfway to **Rouen.** The Seine makes its way along the northeast edge of the city, with the old mill across the river from the city's historic center, and just southwest, the train station at **Place de la Gare.** The village of Giverny lies to the southwest, across the river from the city. About 15-kilometers away, the journey will take you past farms where ostriches, llamas, horses, and cows roam over the lush green landscape. Once in Giverny, you'll find the main street, **Rue Claude Monet.** The painter's house and gardens take up its eastern end, while walking further west will bring you to the tourist office, cafés, and eventually the **Museum of Impressionism.**

GETTING THERE

From Paris, take the train from Paris St-Lazare station to Vernon-Giverny. The trains run approximately hourly, and take about 45min. Allow extra time to buy your tickets (about €15-20) at the station if you can't print them at your hostel. Save time and trouble by buying the return ticket at the same time. You will probably want to spend at least a few hours in Giverny.

GETTING AROUND

Shuttles to Giverny depart from the train station in Vernon shortly after each train arrives. The round-trip costs €8. You can either take the large air-conditioned buses or a smaller "train" service that will pass sights in Vernon as well and provide some historical narrative along the way. Make sure to check the return shuttle times in order to make it back to the train station on time. In Giverny, everything is within walking distance.

Swing by...

MONET'S HOUSE
Rue Claude Monet

We like to believe that if we had lived in Monet's former home and had been able to stroll the beautiful aromatic gardens surrounding it, we too would have become famous artists instead of resorting to the lowly life of travel writing. In any case, entry to the property is only €5.50 for students, and you'll have access to the famous Impressionist's personal home of over 40 years and his main sources of inspiration. In the house, Monet's own collections of Japanese prints hang in colorful sunlit rooms, and his former studio holds replicas of 59 of his paintings, displayed exactly how they once were in the room in which they were painted. The gardens are both a treasure trove of beautiful flowers and a dream come true for any Monet fan. The lily ponds, framed by weeping willows, seem like old friends, familiar from the artist's most well-known paintings. You won't want to miss such an unbelievable indulgence.

i Students €5.50

Check out...

VERNON

Vernon is like Beyoncé's sister: amazing in its own right, but usually overshadowed by its close relation. A visit to Giverny necessarily takes you through this medieval town, whose history likely reaches as far back as the twelfth-century. Give yourself some time before heading out of its train station to marvel at the old buildings with exposed wooden beams, the large church **Notre-Dame of Vernon,** and the old mill that stretches into the Seine itself right next to the ruins of the city's formerly impressive bridge. You'll find cheaper food and drink options in the town than near the tourist-frequented sites of Giverny, and you'll experience the bucolic charm of an authentic medieval French city.

Grab a bite at...

TERRA CAFE

99 Rue Claude Monet, 27620 Giverny; 02 32 51 94 65; www.giverny.org/restos/ terra; open daily 10am-6pm

There's something irresistible about shady trellises covered with vines, and something even more irresistible about sweet, sweet air conditioning. It can get hot in Giverny during peak summer months, and the café at the **Museum of Impressionism** provides a cool spot to take a break from wandering the gardens and cool off with a cold beverage or a scoop of ice cream. It's just a stone's throw from Monet's house. If you have time to kill before a shuttle brings you back down to Vernon, grab lunch or a crêpe here and peruse the next-door gift shop and a small free art exhibit downstairs. The museum itself is, of course, an option as well, at only €4.50 for students.

i Meals from €13, beverages from €3, crêpes from €6; vegetarian options; wheelchair accessible

PALAIS DE TOKYO

13 Avenue du Président Wilson, 16e; 01 81 97 35 88; www.palaisdetokyo.com/en

Nobody can claim that Palais de Tokyo isn't an immersive experience. The huge modern art museum just across the river from the **Eiffel Tower** displays enormous video screens in dark rooms, complicated dioramas viewed from multiple angles as you follow the path of the exhibit, and light displays accompanied by music. What is subjective, however, is the art itself. The video screens depict strange silver robot animals speaking German, the dioramas have live fish that look like something you've only seen in episodes of *Planet Earth,* and the lights and music are jarring and discordant. You'll likely leave being somewhere between inspired, dazed, and thoroughly confused.

i Admission €12, for under 25 €9; tours conducted in French; wheelchair accessible

OUTDOORS

JARDIN DU LUXEMBOURG

Rue de Médicis, Rue de Vaugirard, 6e

The Luxembourg Gardens stretch out in front of Luxembourg Palace, once the home of King Henry IV's widow Marie de' Medici but now the home of the French Senate. Hundreds of statues are scattered throughout the gardens along with tennis courts, greenhouses, cafés, ponds, and plenty of painters and writers. The greenery ranges from perfectly manicured in some areas to more natural in others, and there seems to be an unwritten code of conduct for where you can and cannot walk on the grass. A good rule of thumb: if it looks like that golf course your stepdad took you to once, you should probably find somewhere else to picnic.

i Free; wheelchair accessible; hours subject to change

PARC DES BUTTES-CHAUMONT

1 Rue Botzaris, 19e; 01 48 03 83 10; open daily summer 7am-10pm, winter 7am-8pm

Paris' more touristy gardens achieve a manicured "wow" factor, but you may feel as if you have to hold your breath to prevent accidentally stirring a leaf from its rightful place. At Parc des Buttes-Chaumont, however, locals play soccer in the tall grass, people make out on blankets, giggling children try to outrun sprinklers, and nobody uses a measuring tape to make sure the bushes are all at regulation height. The site of a former gypsum quarry, the park was created by **Napoleon III** in 1867, complete with a waterfall, a cave, and a cliff with a white temple perched atop it. It's a more easygoing park for an easy-going traveler.

i Free entry; wheelchair accessible

TUILERIES GARDEN

113 Rue de Rivoli, 1e; open daily 24hr

When the **Louvre** was still the royal palace, long before that large glass pyramid became the subject of countless gimmicky photos, the Tuileries were the gardens of kings, queens, courtiers, and the ever-present ducks. A wide white gravel path stretches from the Louvre all the way to the **Place de la Concorde,** punctuated by large round fountains and hundreds of marble statues. While the main pathways can be packed, groves of trees on the sides provide more seclusion and a respite from the heat and dust of the day. Tons of green metal chairs let you relax in comfort, especially if you can snag one of the reclining ones. There's no doubt it's one of the most picturesque parts of Paris.

i Free; wheelchair accessible

FOOD

LA CRÊPERIE ($)

12 Rue Soufflot, 5e; 1 43 54 22 80; open M-Sa 7am-midnight, Su 8am-midnight

Picture this: you've just arrived in Paris, luggage in tow. You've finally taken a shower to wash off all that plane grime and rid yourself of children's germs and coughs that just circulate throughout airports with nowhere to go. You're tired, and you just want a meal that will stuff you so fully that you'll have to walk like a penguin for the rest of the day. This *crêperie,* my friends, is the place to have the meal you're craving. Savory crêpes made from buckwheat come with every filling imaginable, ranging from eggs, cheese, spinach, tomatoes, chicken, sausage, and ham, while the sweet crêpes (we recommend any of the ones with Speculoos) will leave you wondering if the waiter will judge you for ordering another. It *is* a crêpe place, but we also love the tiramisu *au caramel au beurre salé*—order it to find out why it's the stuff of dreams.

i Buckwheat crêpes from €4.20, sweet crêpes from €4.20, waffles from €4.70; gluten-free, vegan, and vegetarian options available

CAVE LA BOURGOGNE ($)

144 Rue Mouffetard, 5e; 01 47 07 82 80; open daily 7am-2am

There's no better place for traditional French staples *(croque monsieur, confit de canard, charcuterie)*. Mountains of delicious salads (especially the warm goat cheese and honey one) are surprisingly a bargain. Aside from the top notch food, the ambiance is *très français* as well. Tables spill onto the lovely rue Mouffetard, overlooking a fountain surrounded by flowers. In the summer, Cave la Bourgogne is packed with locals looking for typical French fare. In the back of the restaurant, cozy booths make the restaurant great for a chilly evening too.

i Entrées from €10; gluten-free and vegan options available; wheelchair accessible

CHEZ JANOU ($$)

2 Rue Roger Verlomme, 3e; 01 42 72 28 41; www.chezjanou.com; open M-F 10am-3pm and 7pm-midnight, Sa-Su 7am-midnight

Ever since that Disney movie you've always wanted to try ratatouille, huh? Well, Chez Janou is the place to do it. We're pretty sure that their chef is a person and not a small rodent, too. Serving traditional **Provençal** cuisine, they use plenty of fresh, light ingredients like crisp tomatoes, basil, and olive oil (not to mention the 80 or so different kinds of *pastis*, a typical Provençal alcohol). Try the duck, rabbit, or a beautiful goat cheese salad while you sit outside on a tree-lined **Marais** street corner. You'll want to go on the early side, though (meaning before 8pm), since the excellent food tends to draw crowds of locals later in the evening.

i Entrées from €16; vegetarian options available; wheelchair accessible

DERRIÈRE ($$$)

69, Rue des Gravilliers, 4e; 01 44 61 91 95; www.derriere-resto.com/restaurant/paris/derriere; open M-Sa noon-2:30pm and 8pm-11:30pm, Su noon-4pm and 8pm-11pm

Sometimes you just have to wrap yourself in a silk, diamond-studded bathrobe, put some cucumbers over your eyes, and get a hot stone massage. But then you remember that you're still slightly in touch with reality. A dinner, or just appetizers or a drink, at Derrière is the perfect way to treat yourself, and you don't even have to have parents that own exotic pets and summer in Capri. The restaurant is located in its own little courtyard in the **Marais,** where guests sit at colorful tables or around beds upstairs. A hidden passage through a mirrored armoire in the upstairs hallway leads to an extra bar area with a foosball table. High prices may deter more thrifty travelers, but then again, you're in Paris. Treat yo 'self.

i Appetizers from €12, entrées from €22, lunch starter and main course €25; vegan options available; wheelchair accessible

SOURIRE ($$)

27 Rue Galande, 5e; 01 42 01 06 43; www.sourire-restaurant.com; open Tu-Su noon-2:30pm and 7:30pm-10:30pm

The staff at Sourire, a French tapas restaurant near the trendy **Boulevard Saint-Germain,** suggests you start with two plates and see what happens. And like going on a date at an oyster restaurant, it's hard not to let one thing lead to another. You won't want to stop ordering until you've sampled all the unique and complex miniature dishes: mint risotto, Thai chicken, French cheeses, and all the other magical wonders your heart doesn't know it wants yet. Pair these plates with some well-crafted cocktails and a young, hip ambiance and you'll find out why the restaurant's name means "smile."

i Cocktails from €9, tapas from €8; vegetarian options available; wheelchair accessible

BOLLYNAN ($)

12 Rue des Petits Carreaux Montorgueil, 2e;
01 45 08 40 51; open M-Sa 11am-11:30pm

Bollynan has all the understated charm
of a common Parisian café: small outdoor
tables spilling onto a lively pedestrian
street, chic people smoking cigarettes, and
a relaxed atmosphere. But you won't find
any crêpes or croissants here. Unlike a
Parisian café, this restaurant features more
flavors than "bread" and "slightly sweeter
bread." It's known for its variety of savory
and sweet naan, going for just €2-4, as
well as its other flavorful staples of Indian
cuisine. For just over €10, build a combo
with your choice of curry, rice, and sides
like sweet potato or lentils.

i Naan from €2, other dishes from €8; vegetarian options available; wheelchair accessible

CAFÉ DES CHATS ($$)

9 Rue Sedaine, 11e; 09 73 53 35 81; www.
lecafédeschats.fr; open Tu-Th noon-10:30pm,
F-Sa noon-11pm, Su noon-10:30pm

Café des Chats is a cat-lover's dream (and
a dog-lover's nightmare). We're willing
to bet that you've never seen so much
tacky feline-themed artwork in one place
before, but the real highlight is the pack
of kitties dozing in the sun, snoozing on
the furniture, and, well, pretty much just
sleeping everywhere as you sip rich hot
chocolate and sample some cheesecake.
The cats are docile, friendly, and amenable
to being petted and sometimes held.

i Hot drinks from €5, lunch from €10

LE BRAQUE ($$)

11 Rue de Braque, 3e; 01 40 27 86 63; www.
lebraqueparis.com; open M-W 7pm-2am,
Th-Sa 6pm-3am

The interior of Le Braque is where
Beauty and the Beast meets Parisian chic.
Candelabras decorate the tables while cool
wallpaper lines the walls and a painting
on the ceiling dares guests to "trust me,
love me, fuck me." The owner, Chris, will
make your meal as much of an experience
as the delicious and beautifully presented
food and signature cocktails. Once you're
done with your meal, head downstairs to
the restaurant's club, where the floor is
made of sand and the DJ plays throwback
tunes that will get you moving. Son of a
beach, this is a great place.

i Salads from €10, entrées from €16, cocktails from €11; vegetarian options available

MIZNON ($)

22 Rue des Ecouffes, 4e; 01 42 74 83 58;
open M-Th noon-11pm, F noon-3:30pm, Su
noon-11pm

This Israeli restaurant in the heart of **Le
Marais** serves the best pita sandwiches
around. Heck, they even have specially-
made pita sandwich holders on the tables.
But forget greasy kebab—Miznon's dishes
taste fresh and complex. Self-serve sauces
add interesting flavor to your meal. On
the side, you can snack on a whole ear
of corn, a garlicky artichoke, or a giant
head of charred cauliflower. Piles of raw
vegetables decorate every surface (because
apparently perishable interior design is
now a thing). A casual vibe accentuated
by 80s tunes and friendly staff members
makes Miznon a perfect lunch stop.

i Pita sandwiches from €6, vegetables from €3; vegan and vegetarian options available

PÉNICHE MARCOUNET ($$)

Port des Célestins, au pied du Pont Marie, 4e; 06 60 47 38 52; open M-Sa 10am-1am, Su noon-9pm

What do a woman on roller skates walking a dog, a tourist on a Seine cruise, and a French man who shouldn't be wearing a Speedo (but nevertheless is) have in common? They can all be seen from your vantage point at Péniche Marcounet. It's the perfect people-watching position: half of the restaurant's tables are on a boat on the Seine, meaning you'll mingle with those taking advantage of the river's cooling breeze and scenic view. Higher prices reflect the prime location, but a refreshing drink before you join the

ranks of Speedo-clad men yourself is well worth it.

i Entrées from €15, cocktails from €10; vegetarian options available; wheelchair accessible

NIGHTLIFE

CANDELARIA

52 Rue de Saintonge, 3e; 01 42 74 41 28; open daily 6pm-2am

Upon first glance, Candelaria has the same basic features as any tiny taco place: greasy meat, fluorescent lights, people covered in hot sauce. But go beyond the store's front through an unmarked white door, and there you'll find a bumping bar full of Paris's "bobos" (read: hipsters). The music is electric, played by a DJ standing in a tiny corner with an impressive mustache and the walls are decorated with unidentifiable animal wool. Once you get to the bar (it might take a while), a tasty Summer Wish will be well worth it. So, while you're welcome to scarf down a beef tongue taco on your way in, let's just say there's more than *meats* the eye.

i Cocktails from €10, tacos from €3.80

FAUST

Pont Alexandre III, Rive Gauche, 7e; 01 44 18 60 60; www.faustparis.fr; open M-Th 10am-2am, F-Sa 10am-6am, Su 10am-2am

You know it's been a fun night out when the only time you stopped dancing was when you tripped on a pineapple. At this large and populated late-night club under the bridge **Pont Alexandre III,** moving with the masses is a must. You'll return home from Faust with a sweaty shirt, a ketchup stain from the inside

hot dog stand, and a revised definition of "bedtime." You'll also hold onto the memories of the mesmerizing light displays, the hypnotizing techno DJs, and the energetic crowd with as much strength as the cigarette smoke from the crowded outdoor smoking area will cling to your clothes.

i Cover from €20, cocktails from €12, shots from €5

LITTLE RED DOOR

60 Rue Charlot, 3e; 01 42 71 19 32; www. lrdparis.com; open M-W 6pm-2am, Th-Sa 6pm-3am, Su 6pm-2am

Beer? Never heard of it. Wine? Nope. Vodka Red Bull? Well yeah, but that's beside the point. At Little Red Door, nothing else flies. You *must* have one of their 11 extremely unique cocktails. Each one was developed and then blind-tasted by a different artist who created a visual representation of its flavor. Pick whichever picture speaks to you the most. You can check the description of the ingredients, but that doesn't exactly clear things up when the ingredients are things like fermented banana, panama wood, and green coffee. Its location can be difficult to find at first since it's unmarked, but just look for the little red door, Sherlock.

i Drinks from €13

BACARDI MOJITO LAB

28 Rue Keller, 11e; 01 75 77 23 95; www. mojitolab.com; open Tu-Th 6pm-2am, F-Sa 6pm-3am

At Bacardi Mojito Lab, get the alcoholic equivalent of dinner and a show. First, you'll pick one of the multitude of creative mojito variations on their photo-illustrated menu. These include twists like the smoky mojito, which looks like a middle school science experiment, the spicy mojito, and the *Star Wars* mojito, whatever that means. You'll then be able to watch the servers create fizzy rum spectacles in front of your eyes; the trio requires the simultaneous pouring of three separate flavors from a series of stacked glasses, and the *mojito aux effluves* entails a tube plopping bubbles of smoke onto the top of the drink and creating a giant bubble dome.

i Mojitos from €10; no wheelchair accessibility

VERSAILLES

The estate at Versailles has come a long way since it became a symbol of monarchical splendor and the catalyst for the separation from the French people in the 1600s. It was first established by Louis XIII as a hunting lodge, but eventually grew under the reign of the three successive Louises. The Sun King, Louis XIV, moved the court to Versailles, making it home to about 10,000 family members, court members, servants, and the like. In October 1789, Louis XVI and Marie-Antoinette were finally forced to leave Versailles for the last time as the revolutionaries took control of the country. Remarkably, the palace survived the Revolution and became a museum in honor of French glory. Now a popular tourist attraction, the vast estate is the perfect place to spend a day away from Paris learning about the history of the nation, wandering the gardens, or playing a game of "I Spy" in which every turn starts with "I spy something gold."

If you thought the Louvre was large, think again. With the main chateau, **Grand Trianon, Petit Trianon,** stables, and gardens it's nearly impossible to see everything at Versailles in a day. A good place to start is either the tourist office between the stables or the info desk and ticket office to the left as you enter the palace. After proceeding through the chateau, make your way outside to the gardens. The beautiful **Latona's Fountain** is directly ahead, but it's worth making a diversion to your left to look out across the **Lake of the Swiss Guards** before heading deeper into the gardens. An efficient way to see a lot is to head down the right-hand side of the gardens and groves and visit the **Grand Trianon, Petit Trianon, Queen's Hamlet,** and **Marie-Antoinette's estate** on the northwest side before heading back to the château on the other side. Once you leave the main palace, stop at the stables just across the parking lot from the Honour Gate if you have any gas left in the tank. From there, the train stations are just a short walk away (the Versailles-Château Rive Gauche station is to the east).

GETTING THERE

From Paris, take the RER Line C to Versailles-Château Rive Gauche. There are also two slightly further train stations, Versailles-Chantiers (departing from Paris Montparnasse), and Versailles-Rive Droite (departing from Paris Saint-Lazare.) You can also take Bus RATP #171 to Versailles Place d'Armes (departing from Pont de Sèvres).

GETTING AROUND

It's easy enough to get around the grounds on foot, but there's also a mini train going between the main palace and the Trianon Estate for €4.

Swing by...

PALACE OF VERSAILLES

The chateau has played an important role in the history of both the French monarchy and the rise of the Republic. Louis XVI and Marie-Antoinette were married there in 1770. A museum dedicated to the glories of France was opened there in 1837, years after the court left for Paris following the French Revolution. Today, visitors can see the rooms of Louis XIV, the State Apartments, the Gallery of Battles, and the Mesdames' Apartments. The extravagance of the gold façade and the chandeliers of the Hall of Mirrors leave no questions as to why the peasants had no qualms about beheading their former rulers. There's a room called the "Abundance Salon," for heaven's sake. Make sure to pick up a free audio guide; you won't want to miss such an unbelievable indulgence.

☒ TRIANON ESTATE

Made up of the **Grand Trianon, Petit Trianon, Queen's Hamlet,** and **Marie-Antoinette's estate,** this area to the northwest of the palace is a can't-miss. Far less crowded and equally historic and beautiful, it served as the quarters of the visiting Peter the Great and later as the separate residence of Marie-Antoinette. It makes sense: when your husband is Louis XVI, you want as much alone time as you can get. More natural gardens and meandering paths make this area magical to explore. You go, Marie.

Grab a bite at...

CRÊPERIE LA PLACE

17 rue Colbert, 78000, Versailles, France; 01 39 49 09 52; open M-F 10am-3pm and 7pm-11pm, Sa-Su 11am-11pm

Versailles is so huge it can swallow you up and not spit you out until hours later when you've seen 146 different gold statues and made circles around the same fountain 16 times. It can be easy to get sucked into the expensive Angelina cafés and pond-side restaurants, but getting a meal outside of the chateau will both save you money and remind you that actual people live in this town right next to a giant palace. La Place is still within sight of the chateau, so you can sit outside with a savory or sweet crêpe and continue to imagine yourself as Marie-Antoinette. Let them eat crêpes!

i Savory crepes from €8, sweet crepes from €6, salads from €9; vegetarian options; wheelchair accessible

THE GALLERY OF COACHES

On the ground floor of the Great Stables is an impressive display of coaches, sedans, chariots, and all other kinds of horse-drawn transportation that can be gold-plated, embellished, and generally fancified. If you need any more convincing that these royal families lived ridiculously and extravagantly, just go watch some dressage and know that the place they built for their horses is probably nicer than any home you ever will own.

i Boat rentals from €10, depending on boat type and time

BESPOKE

3 Rue Oberkampf, 11e; 01 58 30 88 59; open Tu-Su noon-2am

Even though spiky cacti greet you through the window, Bespoke could not be warmer or more inviting. Small tables line candlelit walls and a collage of rich brown leather belts sets the mood. Not in a *Fifty Shades* way, more in a romantic and rustic way that makes you wish your family owned a saddle-making business. A cocktail menu full of unique infusions and ingredients beckons you, and weekly specials mean you can visit again and again. Even better, though, is to tell the expert bartenders what you like; they're more than happy to craft a custom-made drink.

i *Cocktails from €8*

DIRTY DICK

10 Rue Frochot, 9e; 01 48 78 74 58; open daily 6pm-2am

Formerly a… umm… "hostess bar," this laid back lounge in **Pigalle** gives a nod to its former use in its name. These days, though, the bartenders wear Hawaiian shirts, tiki torches decorate the perimeter, and a large mural of a bikini-clad woman in the sunset dominates one wall. The drinks, however, are the highlight, hands down. Like a contestant on *Hell's Kitchen,* Dirty Dick understands the importance of presentation. You can order a conch shell decorated with flaming limes and sugary sprigs of mint, but the bar is renowned for their volcanoes. The bartender lights flames all along it with his own finger before pouring in the delicious frozen "magma."

i *Volcanoes and shells from €45 (for four people), other cocktails from €10; no wheelchair accessibility*

LA FOURMI

74 Rue des Martyrs, 18e; 01 42 64 70 35; open M-Th 8am-2am, F-Sa 8am-4am, Su 9am-2am

It's difficult to sit down in **Pigalle** without making yourself susceptible to a lap dance. La Fourmi is a safe haven for those located in the neighborhood who would rather chat with friends over some affordable beers than yell to each other over Nelly's "Hot in Here." Don't fear if you skipped dinner; La Fourmi serves food even past midnight, so you'll be able to snack on fries or a burger while you play foosball or

hang at the bar. Just consider that those down the street are probably trying to figure out how this whole dollar-bill-in-the-underwear thing works with €1 coins.

i *Beers from €3*

LES BLOUSES BLANCHES

186 Rue du Faubourg Saint-Antoine, 12e; 01 43 73 70 58; open M-Sa 7am-2am, Su 7am-midnight

Grabbing drinks at this café-turned-hangout-spot feels like going over to your friend's basement when you were in high school. You know, the friend who was popular and had arcade games and chill parents. With a very loose (and cheap) definition of "happy hour" and a great taste in music, Les Blouses Blanches attracts all the neighborhood cool kids with its €5 cocktails like the Zombie, Nurse, and Firefighter—and its abundance of comfortable leather couches doesn't hurt either. All you need to complete the vibe is a rousing game of Spin the Bottle.

i *Cocktails €5 at happy hour; wheelchair accessible*

MOONSHINER

5 Rue Sedaine, 11e; 09 50 73 12 99; open daily 6pm-2am

Just this bar's name conjures up images of moonlit nights spent in secluded locations, where alcohol and adrenaline flow freely with the thrill of secrecy. The bar itself surpasses these expectations. An unassuming red-painted pizza restaurant called **Da Vito** marks its entrance. You'll have to weave through a sea of families splitting pepperoni pies and couples debating adding olives to push through a refrigerator door and come out on the other side in a dimly lit, jazz-playing, gin-serving cocktail lounge. It's probably the first time "crossing the Red Sea" could apply to marinara sauce. Although you'll physically remain in the 11th arrondissement, you'll suddenly feel transported to Prohibition-era Hollywood.

i *Cocktails from €10; wheelchair accessible*

RAIDD BAR

23 Rue du Temple, 4e; 01 53 01 00 00; open
M-Th 6pm-4am, F-Sa 6pm-5am, Su 6pm-4am

The high-energy crowd at RAIDD always
comes out in full force, pun only slightly
intended. You'll constantly be bumping
up against the almost entirely-male
clientele, but only because everyone is
dancing, chatting, and engaging with
people around them. That is, until the
shower show begins and all eyes turn.
Yes, that's exactly what it sounds like. The
drinks are a little pricey, but what can
you expect when they have to constantly
replenish their supply of body wash? Go,
dance, drink, have fun, and then go home
and take a shower; you'll need it.
*i Shots €5, cocktails from €10; limited wheel-
chair accessibility*

YELLOW MAD MONKEY

8 Rue de Lappe, 11e; 01 43 38 30 20; open
M-Th 5pm-2am, F-Sa 5pm-5am, Su 5pm-2am

Located on a bar-lined street, Yellow
Mad Monkey is the star of the constant
show that is the **Bastille** area. It tends
to stay open later than its neighbors and
cultivates a rowdy dancing atmosphere
with top hits. The décor is fun and
unique: a large artificial tree is the bar's
centerpiece, and the branches extend
across the ceiling over chalk writing while
assorted bras hang from a birdcage in the
center, like a chandelier at Lady Gaga's
house.
i Drinks from €5

TOULOUSE

Coverage by **Julia Bunte-Mein**

Toulouse, France's fourth largest city, is one of the most beautiful, historic, vibrant,
and underrated cities in France. It is known as "La Ville Rose" (the Pink City) for its
ochre rooftops, blushing brick basilicas, and rose-tinted storefronts. Like a glowing
pink jellyfish, its historic center is dense, pulsing with life and light—but its tendrils
still stretch into a sprawling metropolis of residential areas. On every corner, you'll pass
an exquisite southern French restaurant, ethnic food stand, *bar à vin,* or overflowing
jazz, techno, or rock club. Home to one of the largest universities in France, Toulouse
is an extremely young city, and on weekends, La Place Saint-George explodes with
students at late-night clubs. While Toulouse surely knows how to have fun, it has a
tranquil ambiance and likes to get its beauty sleep on weekdays. That means from
lundi to *jeudi,* you'll find more pleasure in enjoying many a morning croissant in the
coral-colored Capitole square, indulging in lazy afternoons in green spaces, or having
a glass of wine while watching the sun set over the illuminated Pont Neuf on the
Garonne. The welcoming and friendly residents of Toulouse walk through life wearing
rose-colored glasses, drinking rosé, and enjoying life's pleasures. Here, you too can live
la vie en rose.

ORIENTATION

Le Vieux Quartier (Old Quarter) is situated between the mighty **Canal du Midi** and bend in **Garonne River**. The entire Vieux Quartier is bound by an octagonal ring of streets, with **Boulevard de Strasbourg** at the top and flanked by **Saint-Michel** and **Catalans** on either side. In the middle, **Pont Neuf** and **Le Pont St. Pierre** form the main entrances to the heart of the city. The **Gare de Matabiau**, Toulouse's main train station, is just across the Canal du Midi and a 15-minute walk to the entrance of the old city. The majestic **Place du Capitole** and **Charles de Gaulle Square** mark the center of Toulouse, from which narrow cobblestone streets extend. Almost all of the major sights are within 10-minutes walking distance from here. Nearby you'll find **Rue de Saint-Rome** and **Rue d'Alsace-Lorraine** lined with stores and a smattering of restaurants and cafés. **Place Wilson, Place Saint-Georges,** and **Place de la Trinité** are best for nightlife.

ESSENTIALS

GETTING THERE

Domestic and international flights arrive at Blagnac Airport, 11km west of Toulouse. To get to the city from the airport, you can take the airport shuttle bus to the Gare Matabiau (one-way €8, round-trip €15). Purchase tickets at the desk in the airport or on the bus. Alternatively, you can take the tramline T2 and then change to Metro red line A at Arenes station (single ticket €1.60). This takes approximately 40min. Buy a ticket at the machine or in the airport ticket office. A taxi will cost about €20-25. Both SNCF, the regional intercity train in France, and TGV trains go to Gare Matabiau. Ouibus and Megabus are popular options for bus travel.

GETTING AROUND

Toulouse is a large city, but the historic downtown center is quite small and best visited on foot. We also recommend renting a bike from any one of the 253 VeloToulouse bike stations. For only €1.20, you get 24hr of bike-riding; the catch? You have to return the bike within 30min. to avoid small fee. A €150 hold is taken on credit cards, but is only charged if the bike is not returned. The metro is made up of two lines going east-west and north-south. It operates from 5am-midnight during the week and until 3am on Friday and Saturday nights.

PRACTICAL INFORMATION

Tourist Offices: Tourist Offices: Donjon du Capitole, Square Charles; 0 892 18 01 80; open M 10am-7pm, T-Sa 9am-7pm, Su 10am-6pm

Banks/ATMs/Currency Exchange: Société Générale (536 Rue de Metz; open M-F 9am-12:30pm and 1:30pm-5pm)

Post Offices: La Poste Toulouse Capitole (9 Rue Lafayette; 0 810 82 18 21; open M-F 8:30am-6:30pm, Su 9am-12:30pm)

Internet: Cyber Copie (5 Pl. Peyrou; 05 61 21 48 80; open M-F 8:30am-7pm, Su 10am-7pm)

BGLTQ+ Resources: Arc en Ciel Toulouse (l'Espace des Diversités, 38 Rue d'Aubuisson, 05 81 91 79 60; www. acetoulouse.fr)

EMERGENCY INFORMATION

Emergency Number: 112

Police: Central Police Station (23 Bd. de l'Embouchure; 05 61 12 77 77)

US Embassy: Consulat des Etats-Unis d'Amérique (25 Allée Jean Jaurès; 05 34 41 36 50; www.fr.usembassy.gov/fr/ ambassades-et-consulats/toulouse-fr; open M-Th 7:30am-5pm, F 7:30am-12:30pm). Visit by appointment only, does not issue Visas.

Rape Crisis Center: Rape Crisis Network Europe (www.inavem.org; 01 45 88 19 00)

Hospitals: Centre hospitalier universitaire de Toulouse (170 Av. de Casselardit; 05 61 77 22 33; www.chu-toulouse.fr; open daily 24hr)

Pharmacies: Pharmacie de Nuit (76 Allée Jean Jaurès; open daily 8pm-8am. 00 33 5 61 62 38 05)

ACCOMMODATIONS

LA PETITE AUBERGE SAINT SERNIN ($$)

17 Rue d'Embarthe; 07 60 88 17 17; www.
lapetiteaubergedesaintsernin.com; reception
open 10am-12:30pm and 2:30pm-7pm

This hostel may not seem like much
when you arrive at its metal gate, see the
small terrace with garden tools and empty
paint cans, and drop your bags in the
packed white-tiled dorms. But unless a
new five-star hostel opened up since this
was published, it's your best hostel option
in Toulouse. Each dorm has its own
kitchenette, including a stove, fridge, and
microwave, but it's quite cramped, so we
advise not venturing past microwaveable
couscous. The rooms are cleaned daily, but
make sure to pack your shower shoes.

*i Dorms from €22; reservation recommended;
locks provided; kitchen; wheelchair accessible*

THE FRIENDLY AUBERGE ($$)

32 Rue Gilet; 05 61 42 24 92; www.friendsau-
berge.com/hotel; reception open 24hr

This boutique hostel in the recently-
renovated **Parc Hotel** pushes the limits of
what you'd consider a hostel. Located in a
beautiful white house outfitted with a lush
green garden and wood-planked kitchen,
The Friendly Auberge provides a homey
and luxurious atmosphere that couldn't be
more welcoming. It even has an attached
bar and restaurant that serves traditional
southwestern French cuisine. The only
downside: it's really far from the city
center. The facilities are pristine, though,
so we consider the 20-30 minute ride via
public transport to and from Toulouse's
center a small price to pay. You'll come
home to a communal dinner (€14) and
comfortable bed waiting for you.

*i Dorms from €18, triple from €25, double
from €50; Wi-Fi; linens, towel included; laundry
available; shared dinner €14*

SIGHTS

CULTURE

BASILIQUE SAINT-SERNIN DE TOULOUSE

Pl. Saint-Sernin; 05 61 21 80 45; www.
basilique-saint-sernin.fr; crypt open June-Sept
M-Sa 10am-6pm, Su 11:30am-6pm, Oct-May
M-Sa 10am-noon and 2pm-5:30pm; basilica
open June-Sept M-Sa 8:30am-7pm, Su 8:30-
7:30pm, Oct-May M-Sa 8:30am-6pm, Su
8:30am-7:30pm

This fifth-century church and now
UNESCO World Heritage site was built
in memory of Saint Saturnin, the first
bishop of Toulouse, who died by being
dragged through the streets by a sacrificial
bull and was subsequently named a
martyr. This church is one of the main
stopping points on the **Pilgrimage of
Saint-Jacques de Compostelle.** Restored
in the nineteenth century by **Eugène
Viollet-le-Duc,** a mid-eighteenth-century
Baroque dome picturing a night sky
crowns the church's central nave.

i Free; crypt admission €2.50, students €2

COUVENT DES JACOBINS TOULOUSE

Rue Lakanal; 05 61 22 23 82; www.jacobins.
toulouse.fr; open daily 10am-6pm

Visiting the Convent of Jacobins is like
eating at a restaurant and expecting just
one course and instead being treated with
an eight-course meal. You'll enter the
majestic church with geometric stained-
glass windows of brilliant oranges and
fiery reds that project onto the stone
floor. To the right is *le palmier,* a soaring
92-foot tall column, which holds up
the apse and branches out with red and
green brickwork. In the center are the
relics of **St. Thomas Aquinas.** Next, visit
the cloister, where you can hang in the
tranquil interior courtyard. To finish off,
head into the large chapterhouse room
where monks used to meet, the adjacent
Chappelle Saint Antonin, and the
large refractory where contemporary art
exhibits take place.

*i Church admission free, cloister admission
€4, large groups €2students free; wheelchair
accessible*

LANDMARKS

LA CAPITOLE DE TOULOUSE AND THE HENRI IV COURT

Capitole de Toulouse; 05 61 22 21 43;
Capitole open daily 8:30am-6pm

La Place Capitole is the pulsing heart of the city. While the square is a sight in itself, there are a bunch of interesting things to check out here at varying times. During the day, it's filled with street performers and covered markets, but at night it comes alive with terrace restaurants facing the illuminated pink façade of the magnificent Capitole. Blue and gold windows peek out from behind wrought iron balustrades, and eight pink marble columns symbolize the eight members of the municipal council. The sprawling brick Capitole acts like the Buckingham Palace of Toulouse, and is home to the city's **Town Hall, Théâtre de Toulouse,** and the **Court of Henri IV;** this last area is by far the best part. Inside, take *le grand escalier* to sumptuously decorated rooms and prepare yourself for some of the most beautiful frescos and murals you've ever seen.

i Free; wheelchair accessible

PLACE DAURADE AND LA GARONNE

1 Bd. de la Croisette; 04 92 99 84 00

Just left of **Le Pont Neuf,** Place Daurade, the previously twelfth-century fortified Pont Daurade, is an absolute must-visit when in Toulouse. The square and boardwalk accompanying it are right next to the **Garonne River,** from which you will have the best view of the sunset in all of Toulouse. Bring a bottle of wine, a picnic blanket, and food to settle down for the night. Starting in the early evening, young couples and friends flock to the banks to set up camp for sunset, so be sure to arrive a little early to snag a good spot. Watch as the towering **Dôme de la Grave** and giant Ferris wheel across the river become black silhouettes against a lilac sky and the water turn from dark indigo to shimmering gold.

i Free; in the summer months, lights illuminated at 9:45pm

MUSEUMS

🖼 LES ABBATOIRS

76 Allées Charles de Fitt; 05 34 51 10 60;
www.lesabattoirs.org; W noon-6pm, Th noon-8pm, Su noon-6pm

Prepare yourself for possibly the strangest sensory experience of your life. Open since 2000, Les Abattoirs has earned the renowned title of "Musée de France," and if being trippy earns you titles like that, we're truly astounded. Walk under the arched brick main gallery (into what used to be a slaughterhouse) to enter the museum, which consists of three floors of over 34,000 pieces from the twentieth and twenty-first centuries. Check out the internal monologues of a paralyzed turtle and Barack Obama reconstructed as an automaton: in short, art you won't be able to begin to understand in one visit.

i Admission €7, students €4, Th night "nocturne" visit €2; last entry 30min. before closing; guided tours included with entry ticket W 2:30pm-4pm, Sa 3pm-4:30pm, first Su of the month 12:30pm-2pm; wheelchair accessible

MUSÉE DES AUGUSTINS DE TOULOUSE (MUSÉE DE BEAUX-ARTS DE TOULOUSE)

21 Rue de Metz; 05 61 22 21 82; open M 10am-6pm, W 10am-9pm, Th-Su 10am-6pm

Housed in the former **convent of the Augustins of Toulouse,** le Musée des Augustins is a prime example of what we like to call *artception:* amazing works of art inside an amazing work of art. This fourteenth-century convent includes Romanesque sculpture galleries, a voluminous church, a cloister, and an interior courtyard. This museum boasts over 4000 works and is considered to have the richest collection of **Romanesque sculpture** in the world. Highlights include the gallery of Romanesque capitals suspended between blue-and-red-striped pillars and brightly colored lamps (yes, you should take a panorama), the thirteenth-century howling gargoyles adjacent to the courtyard, and the majestic red brick Darcy Staircase.

i Admission €5, reduced €3; guided tours €3; W evening visit includes a free organ concert in the church with entry ticket; wheelchair accessible

OUTDOORS

JARDIN ROYAL AND JARDIN DES PLANTES

Jardin Royal: Rue Ozenne; 05 62 27 48 48; open daily 7:45am-7pm; Jardin des Plantes: 31 Allée Jules Guesde; 05 62 27 48 48; www.jardindesplantes.net; open daily 7:45am-9pm

In the northwest corner of Toulouse's **Vieux Quartier,** just below **Canal du Midi,** are Toulouse's expansive green spaces, including the Jardin Royal and the Jardin des Plantes. The former is small and quaint, featuring a duck house, mossy bridge, and a statue of **St. Exupéry** holding the Little Prince. Stop here on your way to the impressive Jardin des Plantes. The latter features an arched bridge, large roundabout with a fountain, the **Natural History Museum,** and the **Henri Gaussent Greenhouse** in the botanical gardens. Check out the merry go-rounds, bumper cars, ice cream stands, and by the duck bond.

i Free entry, Grande Serres (Greenhouse) €7, students €5; wheelchair accessible

FOOD

🍽 LA FAIM DES HARICOTS ($$)

3 Rue du Puits Vert; 05 61 22 49 25; open daily noon-2:30pm and 7pm-10:30pm

Cassoulet, foie gras, Toulouse sausage, beef tartare: all delicious, signature dishes of southern France. But if you need a break from the typical, head to La Faim des Haricots, an all-you-can-eat vegetarian buffet where you can get your entire trip's worth of veggies. You won't find a better deal anywhere else when you can take advantage of enormous salads, delectable pasta, and a grain bar. Check out the wide selection of quiches and savory tarts, soups, and a full dessert display. It's easy to spend a few hours in this warm and inviting restaurant—enough time so you can get hungry enough for round two. But, if you're not into the all-you-can-eat aesthetic, you can also take a box to go for just €1.25 per kilo, choosing from among all the buffet options.

i One buffet €11, two buffets €12, three buffets €13, to-go box €1.25 per kilo

AU POUSSIN BLEU ($)

45 Rue du Languedoc; 05 61 52 01 70; open M 10am-1:30pm and 3pm-7pm, Tu-Sa 8am-7pm, Su 8am-12:30pm

Whether you pass the dark blue awning by chance or you came to Toulouse specifically for this one pastry shop, once you see its storefront filled with a forest of *macaron* trees, you won't be able to resist succumbing to this sugary temptation. Nor should you, because this is the best *pâtisserie* in Toulouse. Known throughout the city as home to the cake, pastry, and chocolate experts, all of their homemade desserts and melt-in-your-mouth *macarons* live up to their reputation. The hardest part of coming here is deciding whether to try the fruit tarts, chocolate pastries, pralines, or buttery frangipane tarts. Better yet, don't choose. Just buy all of them! Embrace obesity. Just kidding—whatever you choose will be a treat, and even Michelle Obama will forgive you for racking up those calories.

i Pastries from €1.80, cakes from €3

LE PETIT OGRE ($$)

1 Rue des Pénitents Gris; 06 95 33 33 18; www.restaurant-petit-ogre.com; open M-Th noon-11pm, F-Sa noon-midnight, Su noon-11pm

Like Shrek's moss-covered house, Le Petit Ogre can't fit more than a dozen people, has tree trunks stuck inside it, and is full of green (foods). This hippie eatery boasts all-natural, local, and in-season produce bought fresh from the market each morning. For only €10 at lunch or €15 at dinner, you'll get nicely-sized portions of meat and vegetarian dishes served with warm grains and fresh salads. For a drink, try their artisan lemonade, *délicieuse* fresh juices, or regional wines and local beers. With only one chef and one waitress, the food and service have a warm, personal touch. Dine at one of the three little tables by the wooden bar or on the floor at one of the low tables in the upstairs "Moroccan living room."

i Lunch €10, dinner €15; vegetarian, vegan, and gluten-free options available

NIGHTLIFE

🏴 LA CALE SÈCHE

41 Rue Léon Gambetta; open M-F 6:45pm-2am, Sa 6:45pm-3am

This all-rum bar is a great stop for all young travelers in Toulouse. It's the exact opposite of a terrace bar, as it looks and feels like a shoebox, containing all the noise and rambunctiousness in tinted-glass walls. From outside, you can just make out the outline of many dark forms and muffled noise. But, once you open the door, it'll hit you: rock music, skull and bones flags, and young people yelling *tchin tchin* as they clink their shot glasses together. Walk through a hollowed-out beer barrel into the dark, wooden bar and take your pick of one of their signature fruity, sweet, or spicy rums. Our favorites? Caramel, papaya, or lychee. You can also just point randomly and see what the bartender decides might fit your fancy.

i Rum shots from €2.50, cocktails from €5, beer from €3; card minimum €10

LE PETITE VOISIN

37 Rue Peyrolières; 05 61 22 65 22; open M-F 7:30am-2am, Sa 9:30am-3am

This student bar in the heart of **Vieux Quartier** is renowned for having over 50 different types of shooters, which are beefed-up mixed drinks taken as a shot. Start the night off with a classic Kamikaze (vodka, Triple Sec, and lime juice), pay homage to Europe's transportation system with the **TGV** (tequila, gin, vodka), and then venture into some signature recipes as the night gets wilder. We recommend the **Tsunami** (tequila, grapefruit juice, vodka, red hot chili pepper), but remember to check the blackboard for the cocktail of the night and shooter deals (6 shooters for €15!).

i Shooters €3, cocktails from €6, tapas, sandwiches, and charcuterie boards from €5

THE GEORGE AND DRAGON

1 Pl. du Peyrou; 05 61 23 16 22; open daily 5pm-1:30am

This lively, classic Irish pub, which is almost too classic (read: rugby on the telly, bartenders wearing vintage tweed hats, quiz nights, and "chips" with artisan IPA craft beers and draft ciders), is a hit for young English-speaking

travelers. Their flipbook beer menu features banana bread beer, special London ale, and something called a "double chocolate stout." Although the drinks are a bit pricey, the bottles are twice the size of a regular beer, so it's worth it. So make your way on over here, order a pint, and play beer pong at the table inside the bar. You know you want to.

i Beer from €4, cocktails from €6, wine from €3

FRANCE ESSENTIALS

VISAS

France is part of the European Union, so US citizens can stay in the country for up to 90 days without a visa.

MONEY

France uses the euro and is a part of the "freedom of movement" zone of the European Union.

Tipping: By law, a service charge, known as "service compris," is added to bills in bars and restaurants. Most people do leave some change in addition to this (up to €2) for sit-down service and, in more upscale restaurants, it is not uncommon to tip 5% of the bill. For other services, such as taxis, a 10% tip is acceptable.

Taxes: The quoted price of goods in France includes value-added tax (VAT). This tax on goods is generally levied at 19.6% in France, although some goods are subject to lower rates. Non-EU visitors who are taking these goods home unused may be refunded this tax for purchases totaling over €175 per store. When making purchases, request a VAT form and present it at a Tax-Free Shopping Office, found at most airports, road borders, and ferry stations, or by mail. Refunds must be claimed within six months.

SAFETY AND HEALTH

Drugs and Alcohol: There is no drinking age in France, but restaurants will not serve anyone under the age of 16. To purchase alcohol, you must be at least 18. Though there are no laws prohibiting open containers, drinking on the street is frowned upon. The legal blood-alcohol level for driving in France is 0.05%, which is less than that of the US, UK, and Australia. Possession of illegal drugs (including marijuana) in France could result in a substantial jail sentence or fine.

GERMANY

Germany was once your high school's star quarterback, if your high school had a quarterback that was also the nexus of the Prussian Empire. You see, this was back in the mid-to-late nineteenth century, when things were going great for the young hotshot—it became a global power and produced some incredibly important art and thinkers. But then, Germany went to college, and things got out of control. World War I was the gateway, then it started moving onto the harder stuff: World War II. Soon enough, Germany hit rock bottom. Goodbye World Cup career. Hello Cold War. Nowadays, Germany's back on its feet, and it's arguably doing better than ever. (Seriously, have you seen its economy? So robust.) Nonetheless, it's undoubtedly seen some stuff, and it's all the tougher—and stranger—because of it. While you'll see reminders from all periods of its history wherever you go, Germany is determined not to let its more recent and painful past define what it is today. Instead, the nation looks hopefully towards the future, paving a new path for other countries to trod down. The remnants of the Cold War also inject a punk attitude into Germany's metropolises. Berlin, Munich, Hamburg, and Frankfurt are young, vibrant, and multicultural cities, each with its own individual and artistic flair. Berlin, in particular, boasts an almost "poor but sexy" chic and practically frigid coolness. Some, however, might argue that the young and grungy Leipzig isn't too far behind. Locals are generally pretty helpful, and most have a working knowledge of English, making it easy to find someone who can recommend the best local beer and someone else who will immediately disagree.

BERLIN

Coverage by **Nicholas Grundlingh**

Nearly everyone says that Berlin's the coolest city on the planet, but honestly we just don't see it. Sure, if you like history, Berlin can be cool, what with its Prussian palaces, World War II museums, and defining landmarks of the Cold War. But besides having been the center of not just European, but world history for the last 200-odd years, the city really doesn't have much going for it. Yeah, okay. Maybe it has one or two or twenty clubs that run non-stop from Friday at midnight to Monday at noon. But who would want to go to them? They're all old industrial plants and abandoned buildings overrun by the best DJs in the world. Thanks, but no thanks. And don't even get us started on the food. Every neighborhood is just a complete and utter wasteland full of cheap, delicious, and diverse dining options. In other words, prepare to starve. What about the city's celebration of liberalism and multiculturalism, you ask? Well, what about it? Berlin's multicultural and liberal identity is just one of the many countless features that make it a place unlike anywhere else in the world, in the sense that no other city is this bland and forgettable. Look, if you don't have anything better to do, it's worth a visit.

ORIENTATION

Berlin, situated in the northeastern region of Germany, is a city full of cities, like a Russian nesting doll or a giant Transformer composed of many smaller Transformers. No single neighborhood is alike, and you could easily spend at least a week discovering the quirks and charms of each. As a general rule of thumb, the east side of the city, separated from the west by the **Spree River,** is younger, artsier, and has more of a gritty, industrial feel. This is where you'll find the best clubs, vintage stores, and cheap-eats. But if you're more interested in Berlin's famous landmarks, historical towns, or monstrously large **Tiergarten park,** the slightly more upmarket and touristy west is the place to be. In the likely situation that you're equally interested in gritty industrialism and large parks, however, and thus unable to decide which side sounds more appealing, head over to **Mitte,** the city center, which is split into two distinct districts. While a map of the public transport system may look like a pair of earphones that's been left in your pants pocket for 20 years, if you're equipped with Google Maps or a natural maze-solving ability, you'll be able to get wherever you want within a half hour.

ESSENTIALS

GETTING THERE

While the Capital Airport Berlin Brandenburg International (BBI), likely to be opened in 2020, undergoes construction, Tegel Airport will serve most international travelers. Schönefeld Airport is a smaller, second international airport serving mostly budget airlines. International trains pass through Berlin's Hauptbahnhof and run to nearby countries. Prices vary, depending on how far in advance tickets are booked, but typically range from €39 (advance) to €130-200 (standard). ZOB is the central bus station that links to all big cities in Germany and many regions in Europe.

GETTING AROUND

The two pillars of Berlin's metro are the U-Bahn, the underground trains, and the S-Bahn, the above-ground trains. Trams and buses (U-Bahn) scuttle many of the city's corners. The U-Bahn runs from 4am-1am and the S-Bahn from 4:30am-1:30am. These lines run with 30min. intervals on Friday and Saturday night. When the train stops running, night buses take over, indicated by the "N" preceding the bus number. Berlin is divided into three transit zones. Zone A is central Berlin and the rest of Berlin is Zone B. Zone C covers the larger state of Brandenburg, including Potsdam. An AB ticket is the best deal, but a one-way ticket is good for 2hr after validation (Zones AB

€2.80, BC €3.10, ABC €3.40). Within the validation period, the ticket may be used on any S-Bahn, U-Bahn, bus, or tram. If you have a ticket but don't validate it, plainclothes policemen, who occasionally ride the BVG, will fine you €7. If you are caught without a ticket or with an expired one, you will be charged €60.

PRACTICAL INFORMATION

Tourist Offices:
- Tegel Airport (Am Gate 1 Terminal A Flughafen Tegel; 030 25 00 25; open daily 8am-9pm)
- Schönefeld Airport (Terminal A, main hall, ground floor; 0331 200 47 47; open M-F 9am-6pm)

Banks/ATMs/Currency Exchange: Although not fantastic, the best rates are usually found at exchange offices with Wechselstube signs outside, at most major train stations, and in large squares. Provided that your overseas bank has a partner bank in Germany, however, it is best to withdraw from the ATM. For money wires through Western Union, use ReiseBank (M: Hauptbahnhof 030 204 53 761; open M-Sa 8am-10pm).

Post Offices: Post (Frankfurter Allee 1; 228 4333112; open M-Sa 9am-1pm and 2pm-6pm)

Internet: Free internet with admission to the Staatsbibliothek. During its renovation, Staatsbibliothek requires €10 month-long pass to the library. (Potsdamer Str. 33; 030 26 60; open M-F 9am-9pm, Sa 10am-7pm.) Most hostels and restaurants, and cafés, including Starbucks, provide free Wi-Fi.

EMERGENCY INFORMATION

Emergency Number: 112
Police: 112; Polizeirevier Abschnitt 53 (Friedrichstaße 219; 30 4664553700)
US Embassy: Embassy of the United States of America Berlin (Pariser Platz 2; 30 83050; open M-F 8am-5:30pm)
Rape Crisis Center: LARA offers counseling for victims of sexual assault (Fuggerstr. 19; 030 216 88 88; www.lara-berlin.de; open M-F 9am-6pm). Frauenkrisentelefon is a women's crisis line (030 615 4243; www.frauenkrisentelefon.de/en/home; open M 10am-noon, Tu 3pm-5pm W 7pm-9pm, Th 10am-noon, F 7pm-9pm, Sa-Su 5pm-7pm).

Hospitals: DRK Klinken Berlin Mitte (Drontheimer Str. 39-40; 30 30356000; open daily 24hr)
Pharmacies: Brandenburger Tor Apotheke (Under den Linden 69D; 30 39887448; open M-F 8am-7pm, Sa 9am-7pm, Su 10am-6pm)

ACCOMMODATIONS

🏨 GRAND HOSTEL BERLIN ($)

Tempelhofer Ufer 14, Kreuzberg; 30 20095450; www.grandhostel-berlin.de/en; reception open 24hr

If Wes Anderson had known about this place, everyone would be raving about Ralph Fiennes' performance in *The Grand Kreuzberg Hostel*. And there would probably be some chatter about the lovely hostel interiors, as well. "There's no way bedrooms that nice could belong to a hostel," Peter Travers would write in his *Rolling Stone* review. And he'd be right. The high-ceilinged rooms are 100% bunk-bed free, and, as a result, extremely capacious—a word that we don't use lightly. What's more, each room comes equipped with an old nineteenth-century heater, which is as much a functional piece of machinery as it is a steampunk sculpture. The hostel's nightly events and inviting library-bar area make meeting people an easy and organic experience.
i Dorms from €10, singles from €20, doubles from €49; reservation recommended; BGLTQ+ friendly; wheelchair accessible; Wi-Fi; laundry facilities

🏨 KIEZ HOSTEL ($)

Marchlewskistrabe 88; 30 12036240; kie-zhostel.berlin; reception open 9am-10pm

Kiez Hostel feels more like a boutique hotel than a hostel. Each room has its own theme, which, as opposed to being kitschy and gimmicky, lend them an understated and elegant touch. Furthermore, the rooms' large windows, which allow for ample sunshine, and spacious floor plans, give them a bright and airy feel. Every bed has its own light and electric outlet. Although the staff will do your laundry at a cost (€5), they'll recommend events to check out each day for free. Kiez Hostel is also ideally located, with **Berghain** and the **East Side Gallery** both within arm's reach (if you have 550-yard long arms).
i Dorms from €22.50, doubles from €49; reservation recommended; min stay 3 nights; BGLTQ+ friendly; Wi-Fi; wheelchair accessible

vending machines might lead you to think that you'd got the wrong place entirely. Of course, Aletto Kudamm consequently lacks the charm of a smaller hostel, but you'll be surprised by how trivial such an observation looks when viewed from the hotel's seven-story high rooftop bar.

i *Dorms from €19, singles from €49, doubles from €59; reservation recommended; BGLTQ+ friendly; wheelchair accessible; Wi-Fi; laundry facilities available, linens included*

EASTERN COMFORT HOSTELBOAT ($)

Muehlenstr. 73; 30 66763806; www.eastern-comfort.com; reception open 24hr

At first, the Eastern Comfort Hostel Boat might sound a little too good to be true. It floats on the gorgeous **Spree River.** It's located smack in-between **Friedrichshain** and **Kreuzberg.** And its boat, which not only adds a whimsical touch to the stay, gives guests the coveted opportunity to join the mile-low club. Although space is a little tight in the dorms, the rooms are clean and cozy. What's more, the boat hardly rocks, so the only reason you'll feel queasy at night is from drinking one too many drinks at the on-deck bar, which shares a bathroom with some of the dorms—not that it's too much of an inconvenience. Also, if camping's your thing, you can stay in a tent (€15 per night) on the boat's upper deck.

i *Dorms from €19, singles from €44, doubles from €50; reservation recommended; BGLTQ+ friendly; wheelchair accessible; Wi-Fi; linens not included, towels for rent*

HAPPY GO LUCKY HOTEL AND HOSTEL ($)

Stuttgarter Pl. 17, Kreuzberg; 30 32709072; www.happygoluckyhotel.com; reception open 24hr

We try not to judge a book by its cover (we prefer to do it by the author photo on the back), but when the cover is a graffiti-plastered five-story high façade, it's hard not to. The hostel's bubbly atmosphere continues in the reception area, which bustles with travelers and friendly staff. Although the €50 key deposit will send shivers down of the spine of the book you bought written

◼ BAXPAX DOWNTOWN HOSTEL ($)

Ziegelstraße 28; 30 27874880; www.baxpax.de/en/downtown; reception open 24hr

(To the tune of Fall Out Boy's "Sugar, We're Going Down.") Am I more than a bargain yet? / I've been dying to sell you another beer or coffee/'Cause that's what we do at our café-bar / Lie in our dorms* next to Museum Island / I'm just a conveniently-located hostel / But you're just a member of our typically younger clientele / Drop down in / Our bean-bag chairs / You're always hanging out, hanging out at our outdoor lounge / You're staying downtown at the Baxpax Hostel / Sugar, our downstairs club is popping / I'll change the Wi-Fi code every day** / A dorm that's not in suite,*** find it and book it.

i *Clean and comfortable but with no reading light or bedside plug points.*

ALETTO KUDAMM ($$)

Hardenbergstraße 21, Charlottenburg; 30 233214100; www.aletto.de/en; reception open 24hr

As both a hotel and a hostel, Aletto Kudamm gives you the best of both worlds. When it comes to your dorm, you'll get the affordable prices of a hostel but the housekeeping services of a hotel. In fact, if you arrived wanting to check into the hostel, the lobby bar, lounge, pool table and by the handsome author, the quality of the rooms—basic, yet comfortable—will set you at ease.

i Dorms from €16, singles from €37, doubles from €52; reservation recommended; BGLTQ+ friendly; no wheelchair accessibility; Wi-Fi; laundry facilities; linens included

U INN BERLIN HOSTEL ($)

Finowstraße 36; 30 33024410; www.uinnberlinhostel.com; reception open 8am-11pm

U-Inn Hostel is everything a good hostel should be. The rooms are clean and comfortable. The reception sells snacks and essential travel amenities (read: toiletries and beer). Although the scarcity of electrical outlets in the rooms means you're likely to wake up to 0% battery after a big night out, you'll at least be able to recharge your body with €4 breakfast. Because the area between the hostel and the center of **Friedrichshain** can be quiet and poorly lit at night, if you're heading back alone, it's best to walk along Frankfurter Allee until you can turn right down **Finowstraße.**

i Dorms from €15, singles from €28, doubles from €25; reservation recommended; BGLTQ+ friendly; wheelchair accessible; Wi-Fi; linens not included, towels for rent

SIGHTS
CULTURE

⬛ VABALI SPA

Seydlitzstraße 6, Mitte; 30 9114860; www.vabali.de; open daily 9am-midnight

A spa? You're telling us to go to a spa? We came here to immerse ourselves in this one-of-a-kind city and now you're telling us to go to a freakin' spa? We, too, were skeptical at first. But after two different locals recommended this place as an authentic German experience, we threw caution and our clothing to the wind (Vabali is "textile-free") and decided to check it out. While the prices may make your eyes do that thing in cartoons where they spring out of a person's skull in shock, if you've got the cash to splash, the spa is an unforgettable experience. The 15 saunas, each of which is gender-neutral save one that's women-only, fall under the categories of hot, organic, steam,

aromatherapy, or "Banja." And once you've rid your body of the toxins accumulated from successive nights out, take a dip in the pool. Vabali Spa isn't quite to Germany what bath houses are to Turkey, but the locals, young and old alike, seem to enjoy it all the same.

i Tickets 2hr €20.50, 4hr €27.50; wheelchair accessible

KINO BABYLON

Rosa-Luxemburg-Str. 30; 30 2425969; www.babylonberlin.de; open daily 5pm-midnight

Kino Babylon is one of, if not the premier arts house cinema, in Berlin. Kino Babylon features national cinemas from around the world, cult classics, legendary directors, animation, shorts, and, of course, German film, making it Berlin's go-to place for film lovers and people who want to impress their dates from the nearby **Berlin Art Institute.** It boasts three theaters, most notably a 450-seat hall with a nearly 90-year-old organ that is still used to accompany free weekly midnight screenings of silent films. Keep a look out for the film festivals, as well. When we attended, Kino Babylon was scheduled to host Cuban, Southeast European, and Italian festivals all within the same month.

i Tickets from €7; wheelchair accessible

RAW FLOHMARKT

Revaler Str. 99; 17 78279352; raw-flohmarkt-berlin.de; open Su 9am-7pm

The RAW site used to be the largest train repair facility in **Friedrichshain,** but nowadays it's known as a nightlife district that embodies Berlin's infamous "poor but sexy" attitude. Every Sunday, however, this labyrinth of derelict and graffiti-covered warehouses blossoms into a flea market full of vintage goods and multicultural food. Selling everything from clothes and vinyl to action figures and Buddhist ornaments, the stalls are mostly family-run and attract locals and tourists alike, which really make the market feel like a tiny microcosm of the city as a whole. Even if you decide not to buy anything.

i Free; no wheelchair accessibility

SPACE HALL

Zossener Str. 33, Kreuzberg; 30 53088718; spacehall.de; open M-W 11am-8pm, Th-F 11am-10pm, Sa 11am-8pm

While techno purists journey to Hard Wax—a fantastically curated, albeit small, collection of electronic vinyl—people interested in finding both the latest "12 from Berghain's Ostgut Ton" label as well as the new Carly Rae Jepsen LP (or, in our case, just the latter) head to Space Hall. With three large sections roughly divided between CDs, indie and rock vinyl, and electronic records, you're unlikely to be singing U2's smash-hit "I Still Haven't Found What I'm Looking For" any time soon, unless, of course, that song is on a record you bought. And if you're worried about how you're going to get a boatload of vinyl back home, you're wasting your time: Space Hall will ship it for you!

i LPs from €10, CDs from €10; wheelchair accessible

LANDMARKS

🖼 EAST SIDE GALLERY

Mühlenstraße; 17 23918726; www.east-sidegallery-berlin.de; open daily 24hr

The East Side Gallery, a 1.3km-stretch of the Berlin Wall covered in over 100 murals by artists from around the world, is a testament to Berlin's uncanny ability to turn painful reminders of the past into

contemporary symbols of hope and peace. Converted into the world's largest open-air art gallery following the fall of the wall in 1989, the Gallery is probably the most tourist-heavy spot east of the **Spree River,** but that's only because it's an absolutely essential component of any Berlin trip. The walk up and down the wall takes roughly 45 minutes, but it can last an hour depending on the time it takes to find someone willing to recreate "the socialist fraternal kiss" in front of the famous mural.

i Free; wheelchair accessible

BRANDENBURG GATE

Pariser Pl.; open daily 24hr

You're going to see this, regardless of what we say. It's big and impressive and the defining landmark of Berlin. It would be crazy if you didn't. While the Acropolis-inspired architecture is, indeed, striking, it's perhaps the gate's history that makes it such a permanent fixture in every tourist's schedule. Built by **Friedrich Wilhelm II** in the late eighteenth century as part of a system of city gates, the Brandenburg Gate is the only one that survives, although it's had a few close calls. Allied attacks inflicted significant damage during WWII, East German tinkering altered its quadriga (the thing on top) during the Cold War, and we accidentally bumped into a pillar during our visit. If you want to avoid the daytime infestation of tourists, pay a visit during the night, or better still, stop by on your way back from the club and watch the sunrise.

i Free; wheelchair accessible; private guided tours can be booked

CHARLOTTENBURG PALACE

Spandauer Damm 20-24; 33 19694200; www.spsg.de/en/palaces-gardens/object/schloss-charlottenburg; open Apr-Oct Tu-Su 10am-6pm, Nov-Mar Tu-Su 10am-5pm

An old wise man once told us, "If you've seen one palace, you've seen them all." But the Charlottenburg Palace proves what we suspected all along: that old guy's an absolute kook. Inside the palace, you might find yourself in the **White Room,** staring at the golden rococo patterns on the walls and ceiling, and think, "Wow, it doesn't get much better than this." But then you'll get to the **Golden Gallery** and hate yourself for being so foolish and naïve: the intricate, satin-covered walls in the private apartments and the collection of silverware, porcelain, and crown jewels will make you hate the Hohenzollern dynasty out of jealousy. Stroll through the sprawling palace gardens and visit the mausoleum, where various Prussian monarchs are buried in tombs that are works of art in themselves.

i Admission €12, reduced €9; free audio guide; last entry 30min. before closing; ground floor and park are wheelchair accessible; guided tours by appointment only

MUSEUMS

HAMBURGER BAHNHOF

Invalidenstraße 50-51, Mitte; 30 39783439; www.smb.museum/en/museums-institutions/hamburger-bahnhof; open Tu-W 10am-6pm, Th 10am-8pm, F 10am-6pm Sa-Su 11am-6pm

Housed in an old train station, Berlin's premier contemporary art museum is filled with permanent exhibits showcasing twentieth-century powerhouses such as **Warhol** and **Beuys.** It'll take a good three hours to fully absorb everything here, even counting the time saved by skipping the giant exhibit that attempts to dismantle capitalism by placing an axe next to a piano. Nonetheless, the most intriguing section of the museum is the adjacent warehouse full of nothing but installations. It's an area that invites intense contemplation as you walk through a football field-sized space. Because contemporary art reflects the contemporary world, and since the contemporary world is... complicated, today's art has to communicate that. That's why, although you probably won't comprehend the meaning behind half of the art in Hamburger Bahnhof, you'll find yourself unsettled by nearly all of it.

i Admission €14, reduced €7; guided tours in English Sa-Su at noon; limited wheelchair accessibility

PERGAMON MUSEUM

Bodestraße 1-3; 30 266424242; www.smb.museum/en/museums-institutions/alte-nationalgalerie; open Tu-W 10am-6pm, Th 10am-8pm, F-Su 10am-6pm

If you were stuck on a desert island and that island had a lot of museums on it, and you could only pick one to visit, which would it be? If you answered with anything but the Pergamon, you're wrong. Even though its crown jewel—the **Pergamon Altar**—is under renovation until 2023, the museum still contains some truly awe-inspiring exhibits. 2,500-years-old and 100-foot-tall, the **Ishtar Gate** is comprised of some of the most miraculous tilework we've ever seen—and trust us, we've seen some tiles. Come for these exhibits, but stay for the **Museum of Islamic Art,** which, with its beautifully ornate and intricate artifacts, might just be the most pleasant surprise of Museum Island.

i Admission €12, reduced €6, all exhibits on Museum Island €18, reduced €9; last entry 30min. before closing; wheelchair accessible

ALTE NATIONALGALERIE

Bodestraße 1-3; 30 266424242; www.smb.museum/en/museums-institutions/alte-nationalgalerie; open Tu-W 10am-6pm, Th 10am-8pm, F-Su 10am-6pm

Life is full of sad, unavoidable truths, but perhaps the saddest of them all is that, when you spend a day at **Museum Island,** there are only so many ancient relics you can see without wanting to plant your butt one of those oh-so-tempting benches in the center of each exhibit and just stay there. Luckily, the Alte Nationalgalerie is full of enough gorgeous nineteenth-and twentieth-century art to keep your booty high and tight as you hop from gallery to gallery. The collections of German Realism and Modernism are also highlights that might even inspire you to jot down the names of specific artists into your phone, which you will definitely refer back to and not forget about as soon as you leave to check out some more relics.

i Admission €10, reduced €5, all exhibits on Museum Island €18/€9; last entry 30min. before closing; wheelchair accessible

BERLINER DOM

Am Lustgarten; 30 20269136; www.
berlinerdom.de; open M-Sa 9am-8pm, Su
noon-8pm

Visiting a church? On a day that's
not a Sunday, Christmas, or Easter?
Why, what an absolute treat! But, it
gets better. The Berliner Dom isn't just
any old church, it's one of the most
breathtaking cathedrals in Europe. And
once you've retrieved your breath, guess
what else you can do? You can hike up
a seemingly endless flight of stairs, walk
around the very dome itself, and marvel
at another breathtaking sight—the city
of Berlin! At this point, if you're not
writhing on the floor gasping for air,
you're probably at the wrong church.
We mean, Kaiser Wilhelm II built this
thing to rival St. Peter's Basilica. He also
buried his family right beneath it. Swing
by their crypts on your way out!

*i Admission €7, reduced €5, audio guide
€3; last entry 1hr before closing; wheelchair
accessible*

C/O BERLIN

Hardenbergstraße 22-24, Charlottenburg;
30 28444160; www.co-berlin.org/en; open
daily 11am-8pm

With three exhibitions running
simultaneously, which usually feature a
mix of world-renowned, local, and up-
and-coming photographers, you're sure
to find yourself struck by something in
C/O Berlin. So, in short, photography
nerds, come—it's a no-brainer. C/O's
retrospectives (there's usually one
going on at any given time) alone are a
reason to visit for anyone: they not only
present an overview of an important
figure's work, but also do it in a way
that allows you to understand why they
were so important, and by extension,
why photography is an important art
form.

*i Admission €10, reduced €6; weekly
guided tours in English Sa 6pm; limited
wheelchair accessibility*

DDR MUSEUM

Karl-Liebknecht-Str. 1; 30 84712373; www.
ddr-museum.de; open Su-Fri 10am-8pm, Sa
10am-10pm

If you've ever wanted to know what
life was like under Communist rule,
but have never spent a weekend at my
mother-in-law's, the DDR museum has

you covered. Focusing on the public
and private lives of Eastern Germans
during the latter half of the twentieth
century as well as the practices of
DDR government, the museum uses
interactive and detailed exhibits to
make the past relatable today. In about
90 minutes, you'll walk through a
kindergarten, cinema, Stasi prison cell,
and even a full-scale replica of a typical
East German apartment—far and away
the museum's highlight.

*i Admission €8.50, reduced €7.50; limited
wheelchair accessibility*

MEMORIAL TO THE MURDERED JEWS OF EUROPE

Cora-Berliner-Straße 1, Mitte; 30 2639430;
www.stiftung-denkmal.de/en/memorials/
the-memorial-to-the-murdered-jews-of-eu-
rope; memorial open daily 24hr, information
center open Apr-Sept Tu-Su 10am-8pm,
Oct-Mar Tu-Su 10am-7pm

Just south of the **Brandenburg Gate,**
a sea of grave-like concrete slabs serves
as a memorial to the six million Jewish
victims of the Holocaust. Described by
the architect as representing "the innate
disturbances and potential for chaos
in all systems of seeming order," the
memorial is a quiet and contemplative
place. But once you reach its center and
the slabs begin to tower above you, the
memorial can become disturbing—
which, of course, is the point. While
it also provides a broad overview of
the Holocaust, the information center
focuses on telling the stories of the
individual victims. Learn about the lives
of families before the war, life inside the
camps, and the devastating experiences
of those who lost their lives. No two
stories are the same but all resonate with
an equally tragic weight.

*i Free entry, audio guide €4, reduced €2;
free guided tour in English Sa 3pm; wheelchair accessible*

NEUES MUSEUM

Bodestraße 1-3; 30 26 6424242; www.
smb.museum/en/museums-institutions/
neues-museum; open M-W 10am-6pm, Th
10am-8pm, W-Su 10am-6pm

Sure, everyone visits the Neues Museum
to see the **bust of Nefertiti**—one of the
world's most famous ancient artifacts.
But once you've seen the Egyptian lady's
clay head, have you seen everything

the museum has to offer? No. In fact, the museum's expansive collection of sarcophagi, located in a crypt-like hall, is arguably more intriguing, if only because it serves as a reminder of how cool it would be to get buried in a sarcophagus.

i Admission €12, reduced €6, all exhibits on Museum Island €18, reduced €9; last entry 1hr before closing; wheelchair accessible

OUTDOORS

▨ TIERGARTEN

Straße des 17; 30 901833101; open M-W 9am-6pm, Th-F 9am-3pm

Similar to Monaco in size, but used as a stress-free haven instead of a tax-heavy one, the Tiergarten used to be a hunting grounds for Prussian rulers. Nowadays, it is home to some of Berlin's most well-known landmarks. The **Reichstag, Brandenburg Gate, Memorial for Murdered Jews, Victory Column,** and **Berlin Zoo** can all be found in or around the park. But the Tiergarten hasn't let such success get to its head— deep down it's still just a regular park where you can picnic, rent kayaks, and watch teens drown their angst with fizzy alcoholic beverages. While the park's renown means it's the most crowded one in town, this is a reason to visit rather than avoid it—everyone simply knows that an afternoon at the Tiergarten is an unmissable element of any trip to Berlin.

i Free, limited wheelchair accessibility

STRANDBAD PLÖTZENSEE

Nordufer 26; 17 634418634; www.strand-bad-ploetzensee.de; open daily May-Sept 9am-7pm

Although we could spend all day praising the virtues of summer, we can only spend four words outlining its faults: it is very hot. Fortunately, when the sun becomes unbearable, Berliners have a contingency plan: they go to a lake, the closest and most convenient of which is the Plötzensee, a half-hour train ride from **Mitte.** While the lake has plenty of areas where you can swim for free, we recommend breaking out the ol' checkbook for the €5 (€3 reduced) entrance fee to Strandbad

Plötzensee. A small resort on the lake, Strandbad Plötzensee comes equipped with a lifeguard, a volleyball court, table tennis, and restaurants, as well as sunbed and beach chair rentals.

i Admission €5, reduced €3, sunbed €4, beach chair €3; wheelchair accessible

TEMPELHOF

Tempelhofer Damm; 30 700906616; open daily 6am-9:30pm

Tempelhof seems like it was designed in a lab focused on producing the most quintessential Berlin sight possible. Formerly an international airport until 2008, Tempelhof is now one of the most popular, and certainly the most interesting, parks in Berlin. Although it's still possible to receive tours of the building itself, most people are perfectly content to roam around the runway, which has since been converted into a wide walkway. For those who prefer to cycle, the nearby information center (open 10am to 7pm) makes renting a painless process. Since there's very little shade, a cool evening trip, equipped with a picnic blanket, dinner, and a portable speaker of sorts, is ideal.

i Free, limited wheelchair accessibility

TREPTOWER

Alt-Treptow; 30 25002333; open daily 10am-1am

There are two main reasons to visit Treptower. Of course, it covers the traditional aspects of a park without much fuss, but so do most Berlin parks. What makes Treptower special is that it's home to not just the intimidatingly large **Soviet War Memorial**, but also an abandoned amusement park. The former commemorates 6,000 USSR soldiers who fell during the Battle of Berlin, while the latter commemorates the poor financial prudence of Normann Whitte, whose bankruptcy in 2001 allowed Spreepark to become the dilapidated and endlessly fascinating sight it is today. You're technically not allowed into Spreepark without a guided tour, but if you manage to sneak in without alerting the patrol guards, hats off to you (not that we're advocating doing so).

i Free, limited wheelchair accessibility

VOLKSPARK FRIEDRICHSHAIN

30 25002333; open daily 24r

When it comes to large and central parks located east of the Spree, it doesn't get much larger, more central, and east of the Spree than Volkspark Friedrichshain. Beyond its centerpiece, the **Märchenbrunnen,** or "fountain of fairy tales," the space is more or less your typical park. Fun fact (well, not necessarily fun, but intriguing): the park's hills are actually landfills of rubble from bunkers destroyed during WWII. But the intrigue of this fact pales in comparison to that of the park's summer open-air-movie screenings (€7.50), which range from newly released German films to recent, yet acclaimed English ones.

i Free, limited wheelchair accessibility

FOOD

CAFE KALWIL ($$)

Motzstr. 30, Schöneberg; 30 23638818; www.cafekalwilberlin.de; open M, W-F 9am-7pm

On Wednesdays, you wear pink? Nice try, *Mean Girls*. Café Kalwil wears pink every single day. With pink drapes adorning the entrance, pink sequined pillows, and pink light bulbs intertwined with pink fairy lights running along

the awning, the café is impossible to miss. But let us be clear: Café Kalwil isn't tasteless or trashy. If you venture inside, you'll see it's less a Hello Kitty store vibe and more like an antique shop run by Hello Kitty. And it's not just a pretty face either: beside the usual café and breakfast fare, it has an incredibly detailed but pricey tea menu (€5.60 per pot), ice cream sundaes (€5), and a cake selection (€4) that made us question just how deadly our deadly gluten intolerance really is.

i Breakfast €10; vegetarian options available; limited wheelchair accessibility

CÔ CÔ - BÁNH MÌ DELI ($)

Rosenthaler Str. 2; 30 55475188; www.co-co.net; open M-Th 11am-10pm, Fri-Sa 11am-11pm, Su noon-10pm

Basically the Vietnamese-French version of Subway, Cô Cô - Bánh Mì Deli stuffs its sandwiches with liver patê, marinated pork, a homemade sauce that packs a punch, and traditional garnishes. To put it simply, it's the sandwich equivalent of a Vietnamese fresh spring roll, which is the spring roll equivalent of heaven, which is the Christian equivalent of Nirvana, the ultimate pinnacle of rock music. Sit inside surrounded by floral arrangements and jars of lemons, or outside amongst the vibrant goings-on of **Rosenthaler Platz.**

i Sandwiches from €5.50; vegetarian options available; wheelchair accessible

DAS EDELWEISS ($$)

Görlitzer Str. 1-3, Kreuzberg; 30 61074858; www.edelweiss36.com; open summer M-F 9:30am-last call, Sa-Su 9am-last call; open winter M 10:30am-last call, Tu 5pm-last call, Th-F 10:30am-last call, Sa-Su 10pm-open end

In any other city, the sight of an old, graffiti-plastered building might only excite amateur ghostbusters and professional old building-hunters. In Berlin, however, it's almost a guarantee that whatever's happening inside is worth checking out. Das Edelweiss is no exception. A breakfast joint, bar, café, traditional German dining experience, and weekly jazz club (Tuesdays at 10pm), Das Edelweiss is as versatile as James Franco and as enjoyable as he is insufferable. We could spend the rest of the book singing the praises of the restaurant's **Görlitzer Park** location, but we'd rather use that space to obsess over the tenderness and juiciness of its *Weißwürste* (traditional Bavarian sausage).

i Sausage from €5.90; vegetarian options available; limited wheelchair accessibility

INDIAN EXPRESS ($)

Kantstr. 74, Charlottenburg; 30 32301023; www.indiaexpress.de; open daily noon-11pm

Let's cut to the chase, and then we'll cut to the scene after the chase where we're all eating butter chicken at Indian Express. The thing is, Indian Express, at least from our experience, doesn't make the best naan bread. It's just a little undercooked, and when it comes to the cheese naan, you might as well be eating regular naan for all the difference it makes in taste. That said, we'll be damned if it doesn't make some of the most delicious butter chicken we've had. This chicken is so tender that it could be a Marvin Gaye song, which means that the Tandoori chicken and chicken tikka are definitely worth a try, as well. Of course, Indian food is much more than bread and chicken. And this family-run restaurant knows this, as proven by its 12-section menu that covers everything from duck specialties to vegan dishes. So what if the naan isn't great? You can literally order over 80 other things!

i Starter and entrée €10; vegetarian options available; limited wheelchair accessibility

MAROUSH ($)

Adalbertstraße 93; 30 69536171; www.maroush-berlin.de; open daily 11am-2am

We believe it's Webster's dictionary that defines "falafel sandwiches" as "delicacies perfected by Maroush." And after having eaten there ourselves, we have to say that those folks at Webster really did their research. As soon as you step into Maroush, you feel as if you've teleported to Beirut, in the sense that the restaurant seems like it has a population of 2,006,500 people. Not that this has any effect on your meal's preparation time. Within five minutes, three of which are spent grilling your order on a sandwich press, you'll

receive a piping-hot pita filled to the brim with falafel, mint, parsley, radish, cucumbers, and sesame sauce. Oh, and did we mention that it only costs €3?

i Entrées from €3; vegetarian options available; wheelchair accessible

GEMUSE KEBAB ($)

Mehringdamm 32, Kreuzberg; open M-Th 10am-2am, F-Sa 10am-5am, Su 10am-2am

O, Mustafa's! The most famous vendor of Berlin's favorite fast food: the *döner kebab!* How we wait in line for you! Your kebab, it is great and cheap! But your line, is it worth it? A 30-minute wait or more! O, Mustafa's! We have sights to see! We want not to doubt your greatness, nor to worship a false god! But we must ask: is there that great a difference between your kebab and that of another? Three kinds of sauces, O how they complement the chicken (or grilled vegetables)! And what is that taste? Feta salad? The warm bread? Potatoes? It weeps, my mouth, for it does not know where to focus! 'Tis o'erwhelmed. But is it worth the wait? If one's heart is set on this cultural icon, then yes! Alas, if one simply wants some good *döner kebab,* look elsewhere. For there are respectable rivals, with less fame but kebab of equal quality.

i Kebab from €3; vegetarian options available; limited wheelchair accessibility

PATTA ($)

Krossener Str. 16; 17 661918140; www.
patta-berlin.de; open daily 12:30pm-10pm

Question: What kind of restaurant has
the nerve to center its entire concept
around baked potatoes? Answer: Patta.
Patta has so much nerve that, when
your dish arrives, the potato itself
won't even be visible. Instead, it will be
submerged in what looks like Jackson
Pollock's best attempt at a salad. And
while you may be hesitant at first to
disrupt the work of art in front you,
your hunger will kick in and you'll
smash through the edible paint that is
the couscous, feta, roasted tomatoes,
and your choice of chicken or tofu
that smothers the potato canvas below.
Suffice it to say that, if you choose to
overlook Patta, we can only assume that
you have a baked potato for a brain.

i *Entrées from €6; vegetarian options
available; wheelchair accessible*

SCHEERS ($)

Warschauer Pl. 18; 15 788948011;
scheers-schnitzel.de; open Su-Th 11:30am-
10pm, F-Sa 11:30am-midnight

Not so much hole-in-the-wall as hole-
underneath-the-autobahn, Scheers is
an inexpensive, no-frills restaurant that
serves some, to borrow an old German
phrase, "gut schnitzel" ("good breaded
pork"). For just €5.50, get a paper
plate full of *schnitzel*, steak fries, and
coleslaw, and for a little extra, a range
of tasty toppings (go for the mushroom
sauce). If you choose to sit inside,
prepare yourself for an immersive visual
experience: the only wall spaces not
covered in crayon are plastered with
old concert posters. If you choose to
sit outside, prepare yourself for an
immersive auditory experience: the
sounds of cyclists whizzing by serves as
the perfect accompaniment to Scheers'
schnitzel-eating extravaganza.

i *Single schnitzel from €5, double from €9;
vegetarian options available; wheelchair
accessible*

SCHWARZES CAFÉ ($$)

Kantstraße 148, Charlottenburg; 30
3138038; www.schwarzescafe-berlin.de;
open daily 24hr except Tu 3am-10am

At midnight, Schwarzes Café is
relatively empty. But it's not winding
down for the night: it's just getting
started. A welcome respite from
the city's other 24hr falafel-centric
dining options, Schwarzes Café is
the kind of place you'll arrive at just
wanting to fill your stomach, but find
yourself unwilling to leave. Whether
it's packed with four people or 40,
the café manages to maintain a warm
and charming ambiance thanks to its
antique décor, background jazz, and the
general merriment that accompanies
drunk people in search of a meal. The
expansive menu, with nearly as many
sweet options as savory, has something
to satisfy anyone's cravings. However, if
you're in the mood for steak, *schnitzel,*
or salmon, you'd better be in the mood
to fork over upwards of €16.

i *Entrées from €5.80; vegetarian options
available; limited wheelchair accessibility*

THE BOWL ($$)

Warschauer Str. 33; 30 29771447; www.
thebowl-berlin.com; open M-Fri 11:30am-
11pm, Sa-Su 10am-11pm

Berlin's first ever clean-eating vegan
restaurant, The Bowl probably already
has you eagerly wondering what the
heck "clean-eating" even means. As
your waiter will be happy to tell you,
everything on the menu is 100%
natural—no artificial additives, sugars,
or fats here. Note, however, that this
doesn't mean your food will be lacking
in flavor. Once you finally reach the
bottom of your salad bowl, you'll feel
satisfied and stuffed, but, if your wallet
allows it, treat yourself to a smoothie, as
well. While The Bowl is a little pricier
than Goodies—the more casual vegan
option downstairs—its larger portions
and spacious dining area overlooking
the lively **Warschauer Straße** will make
you glad you chose something slightly
more upscale.

i *Bowl €11.90; vegetarian options available;
wheelchair accessible*

WAWA ($$)

Grunewaldstr. 10, Schöneberg;
3065774230; wawaberlin.com; open daily
5pm-11pm

Borat's catchphrase may be "Wawa-
wee-wa", but this Korean restaurant
has us saying "Wawa-we-want-more"!
While most good Korean food costs
an arm and a leg, Wawa is a relatively
inexpensive option in the heart of

Schöneberg, but doesn't sacrifice quality for affordability. The Wawa Spezial (marinated beef, which can be subbed for tofu, vegetables, and rice) was perhaps our favorite meal we've had in a city where every meal could've been our favorite. It's clearly a local favorite as well, since we didn't hear a word of English spoken the entire time. But if you want to avoid a wait, make a reservation, arrive outside of peak meal times, or steal someone's plate as you walk by. Seriously, it's that good.

i Entrées from €10.50; vegetarian options available; limited wheelchair accessibility

NIGHTLIFE

⧉ BERGHAIN

Am Wriezener Bahnhof; 30 29360210; www.berghain.de; open Th 10pm-6am, F-Su midnight-6am

A non-stop party from Friday night until Monday morning, Berghain is the most insane, mind-numbingly loud, grungy, wild, and clothing-optional place we've ever been. Here's how you get in: 1.Wear dark colors, but nothing too warm. 2. Forget about going at night. Arrive between 6am and 8am or 2pm and 4pm on a Sunday when the line is 15 minutes long. 3. Line up alone and act aloof. 4. When you get to the front, don't acknowledge the bouncers until they acknowledge you (unless they deliver a devastating burn as they turn someone away, in which case you have to give them credit). 5. Answer their questions politely and curtly. By now, chances are you've made it inside. And once you're in, you're in for good (stamps are good for reentry so you can return later at night without having to queue). What makes Berghain special isn't its exclusivity, cathedral-like dance floor, unrivaled sound system, or ice-cream bar; it's the club's ability to allow everyone to shed their self-consciousness and just be themselves. So go ahead, let loose and go crazy—we guarantee that everyone else will.

i Cover from €10, drinks from €2.50; cash only; BGLTQ+ friendly; closed-toed shoes, dark colors recommended

⧉ OHM

Koepenicker Str. 70; 17 78279352; ohm-berlin.com; open F-Sa midnight-late

Located in a small room not unlike a prison shower in the same abandoned power plant that houses Tresor, OHM is one of the best kept secrets of Berlin's clubbing scene. Unlike Tresor or Watergate, OHM attracts a younger crowd of locals purely interested in dancing to the most forward-thinking electronic music around, regardless of whether it's techno, house, or something a little more genre-defying and experimental. Although OHM lacks the brain-melting volume and lighting wizardry of larger clubs, the intimate, communal feel of the venue creates an environment where you can feel free to let loose. If you've grown tired of Berlin's more traditional techno clubs, a night at OHM will restore your faith in the city's nightlife scene.

i Cover from €5, drinks from €2; cash only; closed toe-shoes only

ABOUT BLANK

Markgrafendamm 24c; www.aboutblank.li; open W-Su midnight-8am

Located in a grimy shack-looking building, which almost seems a prerequisite for East Berlin clubs, About Blank is remarkable in that, without having any apparent hook (i.e., the space isn't particularly impressive and the line outside is of average length), it still manages to find itself consistently ranked among the best clubs in the city. But that's simply because it attracts a dedicated community of locals who, on most nights of the week, are willing to dance until the sun rises. When you arrive, the bouncers will expect you to know who's DJing, and if you can tell them, you'll spend the rest of the night gliding between three dancefloors.

i Cover from €10, beer and shots €3, mixed drinks from €5; cash only

GALANDER CHARLOTTENBURG

Stuttgarter Pl. 15, Charlottenburg; 30 36465363; www.stutti.galander-berlin.de; open daily 6pm-2am

It's all well and good to subsist on pilsner and vodka as you gallivant from club to club, but when you want a good, sturdy cocktail, where on earth do you go? Well, you follow the hordes of older, slightly better dressed adults into Galander, where you can sink into a red leather chair and pick your poison from a carefully crafted cocktail menu. The bar's smoky and old-fashioned feel may lead you to think that it's exclusively populated by "swag is for boys, class is for men" types, but thankfully such affectation is limited to its décor. While most of the crowd is 30+ years old, the atmosphere remains cozy and warm, rather than boring and unwelcoming—although your wallet may disagree.

i Cocktails from €8, long drinks from €7.50, beer from €3; cash only; BGLTQ+ friendly

KITKAT CLUB

Köpenicker Str. 76; 30 78718963; www.kitkatclub.org; open M, F-Sa 11pm-late, Su 8am-7pm

A night at KitKat isn't for the faint of heart, but it is for anyone who wants an unforgettable experience and/or their coat checked by a topless woman who might playfully ask you to refer to her colleague, a man who's dressed just as provocatively, as "Mr. President." Known as Berlin's most infamous "sex club," KitKat attracts a crowd that a) disregards clothes in favor of leather or nothing at all, and b) embraces sex with a sense of adventure and experimentation. But don't worry—regular, clothed tourists are welcome. As long as you come with an open-mind and have no qualms about dancing next to naked people, you're guaranteed to have a night out unlike any you've had before. That said, check the club's website beforehand to see if there's any dress code required on the night, because if you don't stick to it, you will, for better or worse, be turned away or forced to enter naked.

i Cover from €8; cash only; BGLTQ+ friendly; see website for event-specific dress codes

KNEIPE KLO

Leibnizstraße 57, Charlottenburg; 30 43727219; www.klo.de; open M-Th 7pm-2am, F-Sa 7pm-4am, Su 7pm-1:30am

People say you shouldn't poop where you eat, but they never mentioned anything about drinking, and Kneipe Klo (literally, "The Loo Bar") exploits this linguistic loophole to the fullest. At Kneipe Klo, your drinks will be served in urine collectors, which you can enjoy while sitting on a toilet and staring at the toilet-brush covered ceiling. Every inch of the interior not taken up by potty paraphernalia is plastered with a mix of Halloween decorations and nonspecific kitschy junk. The bar's a veritable madhouse—an impression only intensified by the mechanized tables and chairs that could, depending on the whims of the staff, give you quite the shock. The drink menu is nothing to write home about, but that's probably a good thing, since your family will be preoccupied with all your letters about the crazy toilet pub.

i Beer and liquor €4, long drinks and cocktails from €5; no shorts or sandals allowed

KUMPELNEST 3000

Lützowstraße 23, Wilmersdorf; 30 2616918; www.kumpelnest3000.com; open M-Th 7pm-6am, F-Sa 7pm-8am, Su 7pm-6am

It's pretty high praise to say that, out of all the places we've visited in Berlin, Kumpelnest 3000 is certainly the strangest. And it's not just because it's located in a former brothel. Here, that sort of quirky-risqué fact is virtually a given about any nightlife spot. What makes this disco-themed dive bar so weird and fascinating is the crowd it attracts. At least, in a place like the sex club KitKat, everyone you see broadly fits the archetype of "A Person Who Would Go to a Sex Club." But at Kumpelnest, there's no such consistency: underage teens, hipsters, 60-year-old hippies, lads on a pub crawl, tourists who look very confused to find that this isn't the Ritz Carlton—Kumpelnest welcomes everyone. And what's more, everyone seems to have a pretty good time.

i Beer and liquor from €2.50, mixed drinks from €5.50; cash only

COLOGNE

Coverage by **Antonia Washington**

Now the fourth-largest city in Germany behind Berlin, Hamburg, and Munich, Cologne dates back to the first century when it was established as a Roman territory. Fast forward almost 2000 years and Cologne was one of the most heavily bombed cities in Germany during World War II. By the end of the war, most of the city's population had fled and the vast majority of the city had been destroyed. At the time, Cologne was called the "world's greatest heap of rubble" by architect Rudolf Schwarz and the city then underwent some 50 years of rebuilding. About one million people now reside in the rejuvenated, reconstructed Cologne, which has a bustling city cafe. It boasts the largest BGLTQ+ community in Germany and is well-known for being one of the most socially open spaces in the country.

ORIENTATION

Cologne sits on the banks of the **Rhein River** (Rhine River), which runs through the city roughly from north to south. The city center is concentrated on the west side. Cologne has its own version of a ring boulevard, surrounding the city center in a semi-circle closed by the river on the east side. Along it, **Zülpicher Platz** and **Friesenplatz** tend to be good places to get a drink or hit the clubs, while the area around **Rudolfplatz** along **Hohenzollernring** is lined with restaurants. Further east, at the center of the ring, the plaza around the **Cologne Cathedral** is one of the most significant centers in the city. Moving south from the cathedral, **Hohe Straße** is the city's most prominent shopping thoroughfare. The **Old Town** is concentrated in the few blocks extending west from the river between **Hohenzollernbrücke** and **Deutzer Brücke bridges**

ESSENTIALS

GETTING THERE

The Cologne Airport, called Köln Bonn Airport, serves most European airlines and many others. The airport is located southeast of the city, so you will need to take some secondary form of transportation from the airport into town. There is an S-Bahn line from the airport to the city center. If you are headed into town from elsewhere in the region, we recommend traveling by train, as the central train station, Köln Hauptbahnhof, empties into a plaza linked to the Cologne Cathedral.

GETTING AROUND

Public transport in Cologne includes S-Bahn, U-Bahn, tram, and bus services, which all tend to be reliable. These can be very helpful getting to and from locations that are farther outside the city center. Within the city center, most things tend to be within about a 30min. walk. Much of the downtown area, especially the Old Town, is made up of pedestrian streets, so walking is often the best way to travel.

PRACTICAL INFORMATION

Tourist Offices: Köln Tourismus tourist office in Cologne (Kardinal-Höffner-Platz 1; 0221 346430; open M-Sa 9am-8pm, Su 10am-5pm)
Banks/ATMs/Currency Exchange: Expect to pay for most things with cash. There is an ATM around the corner from the tourist office, across the street from the McDonald's.
Post Offices: Go to the post office is in the city center (Marspfortengasse 10; open M-Sa 9am-8pm).
Internet: Wi-Fi tends to be standard in accommodations in Cologne. There is also Wi-Fi available in some major city centers, such as the plaza surrounding the Cologne Cathedral. Look for the network "hotspot.koeln."
BGLTQ+ Resources: Köln Tourismus and Cologne Pride put together a pamphlet called "A survival guide for Cologne visitors," which contains all sorts of tips, activities, and resources for gay visitors. Jugendzentrum Anyway is an BGLTQ+ youth center (Kamekestr. 14; 0221 5777760; anyway-koeln.de).

EMERGENCY INFORMATION

Emergency Number: 112

Police: Polizeiwache Stollgasse police station near the central train station (Stollgasse 47; 0221 2290).

US Embassy: The US Embassy in Germany is in Berlin, but there is a US Consulate near Cologne located in Dusseldorf (Willi-Becker-Allee 10; 40227 Düsseldorf; 211 7888927).

Rape Crisis Center: Frauen Gegen Gewalt runs rape crisis centers all over Germany. To find Cologne's nearest center to you, visit www.frauen-gegen-gewalt.de.

Hospitals: St. Marien Hospital (Kunibertskloster 11-13; 0221 16290; open daily 24hr)

Pharmacies: Dom Apotheke Köln (Bahnhofsvorplatz 1; 0221 20050500; open M-F 8am-6:30pm, Sa 9am-6:30pm)

ACCOMMODATIONS

◙ STATION HOSTEL FOR BACKPACKERS ($$)

Marzellenstraße 44-56; 221 9125301; www.hostel-cologne.de; reception open 24hr

The Station Hostel in Cologne is one of the city's more social accommodations, though the staff reminisces about the pre-smartphone days when the social scene was at its peak. This should be a hint that some of the hostel's staff has been around the block a few times—perfect if you're fishing for recommendations. Gather at the bar, in the beer garden, or in the lounge with cushy home-built looking sectionals and a string of rainbow pillows to kick back with your new hostel-mates. Downsides include toilets that sometimes smell a bit too removed from their last flush and the lack of a guest kitchen. The "pros" list, on the other hand, has one major factor working in its favor: no bunk beds.

i Dorms from €18; reservation recommended; max stay 7 nights; BGLTQ+ friendly; no wheelchair accessibility; Wi-Fi; linens included, towels for rent €1, laundry facilities €4

COLOGNE DOWNTOWN HOSTEL ($$)

Hohe Straße 30a; 22 12772950; www.downtownhostel.de; reception open 24hr

Cologne Downtown Hostel checks all the boxes: it's super clean, has spacious showers, and gives you towels. You don't have to make your own bed and reception is readily available round the clock. Still, there is something cold about the hostel (metaphorically as well as physically because sometimes the air-conditioning is really cranking in the rooms). Maybe it's the neutral color scheme with slate highlights or the insistence on going through the hostel rules at check-in, but socializing here often feels more difficult.

i Dorms from €20; reservation recommended; wheelchair accessible; Wi-Fi; linens, towels included; laundry facilities; kitchen

SIGHTS
CULTURE

COLOGNE CATHEDRAL

Domkloster 4; www.koelner-dom.de; open May-Oct M-Sa 6am-9pm, Su 1pm-4:30pm; open Nov-Apr M-Sa 6am-7:30pm, Su 1pm-4:30pm

The Cologne Cathedral is a humongous Gothic cathedral that pretty much no one expected to be so big. The cathedral towers over the city and distinguishes the city's skyline. On the site of original ancient church construction, the foundation for today's High Gothic cathedral was laid in the mid-thirteenth century. Though the cathedral was damaged by bombing in WWII, removing windows and sandbagging pieces in anticipation meant that no major works of medieval art were lost, yet minor damage to the cathedral's stone work can be seen even today. The cathedral also possesses the **Shrine of the Three Kings,** said to contain the remains of the Biblical magi.

i Free; English guided tours €8; tours M-Sa 10:30am and 2:30pm, Su 2:30pm, meet inside the main portal; tours M-Sa 10:30am and 2:30pm, Su 2:30pm, meet inside the main portal; wheelchair accessible

GROSS ST. MARTIN (GREAT ST. MARTIN CHURCH) ($)

Am Groß St. Martin; open daily 24hr

Another church shaping the city's horizon, Groß St. Martin is largely free of tourists, since most are drawn only to the cathedral. Fair enough—the interior isn't flashy by any standard. The true appeal of the St. Martin Church is the stone construction itself, which we know is ancient, but wow it really looks ancient. Today's Romanesque church building was constructed in the second half of the twelfth century on top of older Roman foundations, and, from within the chapel, visitors now can visit the Roman excavations underneath the church.

i Free; wheelchair accessible

LANDMARKS

🏛 HOHENZOLLERNBRÜCKE

50679 Cologne

This bridge crossing the **Rhine River** just behind **Cologne Cathedral** is one of the city's most romantic treasures. Constructed in the early twentieth century, the bridge carries rail traffic to the central train station and has pedestrian walkways on either side. Along these walkways, you'll find padlocks covering the bridge's fencing, affixed by couples to eternalize their love. The locks are especially concentrated on the south side of the bridge, and there are so many of them that they seem to cascade off of the fencing in waves. Giant locks and bike chains hang on the bridge and smaller locks hang on those, with still smaller locks attached to the second layer in turn. The wall of multicolored, drawn-on, and engraved padlocks are a beautiful sight for even the most jaded visitors.

i Free; wheelchair accessible

EIGELSTEINTOR

Eigelstein; open daily 24hr

The Eigelsteintor is one of the last remaining pieces of the city's ancient fortifications. Erected in the late twelfth century, it was the city's northernmost gate in medieval Cologne. With its towers and tall stone archway, the gate

stood guard around the city, protecting it from invaders. Though of course, **Napoleon Bonaparte** came through this very gate in his 1804 invasion of the city, so it's track record is a bit of a mixed bag (you can't win 'em all). And Napoleon was, like, a super-invader anyway, so that shouldn't even count.

i Free; wheelchair accessible

MUSEUMS

MUSEUM LUDWIG

Heinrich-Böll-Platz; 22 122126165; www. museum-ludwig.de; open Tu-Su 10am-6pm, 1st Th of month 10am-10pm

Cologne's Museum Ludwig is a major collection of modern and contemporary art from the turn of the twentieth century to the present day with a focus on the mid-century development of pop art. This style of art first bloomed in Great Britain and the United States as a commentary on mass production and consumerism in post-war society. Pop art's most famous contributor is **Andy Warhol,** and the museum has many of his works on display. All we have to say is that artists of this style did a lot of weird things with doll heads. All the depraved things you did to your little sibling's Barbies as a kid don't even begin to describe how dolls are often used in pop art displays.

i Admission €12, students €8, free under 18, first Th of month €7 from 5pm, tours €2; tour times vary, check the website; wheelchair accessible; audio guides down-loadable online

SCHOKOLADEN MUSEUM (CHOCOLATE MUSEUM)

Am Schokoladenmuseum 1a; 22 19318880; www.schokoladenmuseum.de; open M-F 10am-6pm, Sa-Su 11am-7pm

Chocoholics beware: binging ahead. The chocolate museum pulls out all the stops with exhibits that take visitors through cocoa's origins in the Amazon and its spread across the globe, a greenhouse room where you can suddenly find yourself in a humid tropical garden, and the museum's own small chocolate factory. Be on the lookout for free samples. Don't pass by the giant chocolate fountain at the factory's end without picking up a freshly dipped wafer. Keep your eyes peeled for a small monkey decal that looks like Curious George really let himself go; he marks children's exhibits which are often more hands-on that the adult plaques.

i Admission €11.50, students €9; can book guided tours in advance; chocolate production starts 30min. after opening, last entry 1hr before closing; wheelchair accessible

FOOD

📖 FRITES BELGIQUE ($)

Hohe Straße 96; 22 12 7121177; www. frites-belgique.com; open M-F 11am-8pm, Sa 11am-8pm

If you find it frustrating that you can't have french fries conveniently in hand at all times, you may find a kindred spirit in Frites Belgique. Here, they've implemented a cardboard cone, which puts their hand-cut French fries right in your hand as you amble through Cologne's busy shopping streets and pedestrian areas. Better yet, the cone has an attached mini-cone to hold Frites Belgique homemade sauce, meaning fries and sauce can be carried in one hand, without the risk of the delicious treat becoming soggy potato mush. The shopping area where this storefront is located typically isn't the place to find food other than fast food and French fry stands, but you should have an edible accessory while you shop.

i Fries from €2.90, sauces from €0.50, sausage from €2.50; vegetarian options available; wheelchair accessible

DON GELATI ($)

Am Hof 20; 22 127047950; www.don-ge-lati.de

If you have a breakfast sweet tooth, Don Gelati might be the place to soothe it. The café's specialty is, of course, gelato, so you can fill up on one of those towering monstrosities of gelato, fruit, chocolate, and candy that Europeans eat if they ever feel like slipping into a coma. The menu items that attract us most, however, are their waffles, crêpes and cannolis. Get a Nutella waffle with ice cream and whipped cream. Or order a panino if you feel like rubbing your health in everyone's face. Otherwise, the best part about Don Gelati is its location. Situated just across the street from **Roncalliplatz,** effectively the south plaza of the **Cologne Cathedral,** you'll get a great view while sitting outside.

i Paninis from €5.90, waffles and crêpes from €4, fancy gelatos from €5; vegetarian options available; wheelchair accessible

HANS IM GLÜCK

Hohenzollernring 38-40; 22 129892163; www.hansimglueck-burgergrill.de; open M-Th noon-midnight, F-Sa noon-2am, Su noon-midnight; kitchen open M-Th noon-11pm, F-Sa noon-1am, Su noon-11pm

If you go for burgers at Hans im Glück, you must sit indoors and take advantage of the magnificent and ridiculous ode to nature they have created within. The potted plant sitting inside a tray carved from a section of tree, which also holds a selection of the restaurant's homemade ketchup and sauces, is just the beginning. Apparently, the restaurant decided that it really ought to feel like you're eating inside of an alder forest, so the thin, white-barked trunks of the tree stretch from floor to ceiling inside, winding their way through aisles and separating tables from each other. Our favorites from their burger menu include the Als Dann (€8.30), with fried pear, mild gorgonzola sauce, and walnuts, and the Geissbock (€8.80), with goat cheese, bacon, and fig jam.

i Burgers from €7, lunch special of burger, drink, and side €5.50; vegan and vegetarian options available; wheelchair accessible

NIGHTLIFE

CENT CLUB

Hohenstaufenring 25; www.centclub.de; open Th-Sa 10pm-5am

Cent Club is a great place for a casual night out. We were told, "They let everybody in. The only thing they won't go for is athletic wear." While we think that's pretty unfair to the appropriate clothing genre athleisure (it's more than clothes really; it's a lifestyle), it means as long as your travel outfit looks intentional, you should be fine. The crowd is young enough to get wasted on free vodka energies and excited enough about each new song to yell out the opening lyrics in harmony. The club doesn't start to get busy until about midnight. If you show up earlier, you'll probably have plenty of space to yourself on the dance floor, and, depending on the night, it could also mean getting discounted or free drinks.
i Cover €5, drinks from €3, glass deposit €0.50; cash only; BGLTQ+ friendly; wheelchair accessible

DIAMONDS CLUB

Hohenzollernring 90; 17 85173273; www.club-diamonds.de; open Th-Sa 11pm-6am

Diamonds Club plays mostly hip-hop and reggaeton mixes, so if you're looking to drop it low and pretend you're Shakira, you made a great choice. In a haze of fog-infused air, get down in a t-shirt dress and your white Adidas sneakers (if that reference is dated by 2019 so be it: they made a comeback once, they can do it again) under the most arrogantly-sized disco ball we've ever seen. It's so big, it makes your mama look like a pygmy marmoset, and that's a size joke, not an ugliness joke, so if your mind went there, that's on you.
i No cover, minimum €5; cash only

FRANKFURT

Coverage by **Antonia Washington**

If you expanded Wall Street into an entire city, it would be Frankfurt. Best known as a hub, Frankfurt is home to the seat of the European Central Bank, the German Federal Bank, and the Frankfurt Stock Exchange, among other similar institutions. Frankfurt is among the primary financial centers of the European continent and that said, you might wonder why parallels to huge feature films like *Wolf of Wall Street* and *The Big Short* haven't taken place here. A friend we made in a hostel who moved to Frankfurt from the United States summed it up to us by comparing it to more commonly visited tourist destinations. "When you think of Paris," he told us, "Even if you've never been there, you have something in mind… the Eiffel Tower, pastries, baguettes, or people wearing scarves. But when you think of Frankfurt, most of us don't have a first thought." And, according to him, even after living in Frankfurt for a few years, he felt the same way. Frankfurt is a big city where there is always something going on, but you can be as seen or as anonymous as you want to be. It gives you the blank slate to springboard off into some adventure.

ORIENTATION

Frankfurt is split by the **Main River** (that's why you'll often see the city called "Frankfurt am Main"), which runs roughly east to west through the city, though in the city center it runs at more of an angle. To orient yourself, it helps to start with the **Frankfurt Hauptbahnhof,** the central train station. The train station sits north of the river and functions as the effective west end of the city center. If you walk east from the train station, you will find **Kaiserstraße,** a well-traveled area full of restaurants that runs through the heart of Frankfurt's Red Light

District. Further east, you will cross through a small park and find yourself in the city center, which is ringed by parks on the north of the river; these are small, green city blocks that do not typically mark a significant change in environment. Within this central city ring, you will find Frankfurt's main tourist sites, including the **Kaiserdom Cathedral.** On the south side of the river, directly across from this central city area is the Museumsufer where you will find many of the city's principal museums. Near the south side of the "Alte Brücke" bridge, around **Große Rittergasse,** there are many bars and clubs.

ESSENTIALS

GETTING THERE

Frankfurt is easily accessible due to its prominence in the business world. Frankfurt Airport is the largest international airport in Germany and services more passengers (read: men and women in suits) per year than any other airport in continental Europe. If you're coming into town from elsewhere in the region, we recommend travel by train to Hauptbahnhof because the train station's central location.

GETTING AROUND

Similar to elsewhere in Germany, Frankfurt uses an S-Bahn and U-Bahn; both rail lines tend to be easy to find and run efficiently. Together with bus lines, most parts of the city tend to be easily reachable. Within the city center, most places are within about a 30min. walk, so we recommend traveling on foot.

PRACTICAL INFORMATION

Tourist Offices: There is a tourist office inside Hauptbahnhof (Römerberg 27, 069 21238800; www.frankfurt-tourismus.de; open M-F 9:30am-5:30pm, Sa-Su 9:30am-4pm).
Banks/ATMs/Currency Exchange: Many places in Frankfurt do not accept cards. ATMs are most accessible at banks. There is a Wells Fargo in the city center (An der Hauptwache 7; 069 2980270; open M-F 8am-7pm).
Post Offices: Postbank Finanzcenter (Zeil 90, 60313 Frankfurt; 0228 55005500; open M-F 9:30am-7pm, Sa 10am-2pm)
Internet: Wi-Fi is generally available at accommodations. When in doubt, Starbucks has your back.

BGLTQ+ Resources: For an orientation to BGLTQ+ life in Frankfurt, check out http://www.germany.travel/en/ms/lgbt/culture/frankfurt-and-the-center/frankfurt-and-the-center.html. The tourist information office also publishes a pamphlet called Gay Frankfurt, which includes many BGLTQ+ resources and venues. Frankfurt also has a Lesbian Information Center, which you can find at www.libs.w4w.net.

EMERGENCY INFORMATION

Emergency Number: 112
Police: Polizeirevier Innenstadt (Downtown Police Station: Zeil 33; 069 755 10100)
US Embassy: Though the US Embassy in Germany is located in Berlin, there is a US Consulate in Frankfurt (Gießener Str. 30; 069 75350).
Rape Crisis Center: Frauen Gegen Gewalt, an organization from Berlin, has services available for victims of sexual assault in Frankfurt. Look into their locations and accessing resources at www.frauen-gegen-gewalt.de.
Hospitals: Burgerhospital Frankfurt (Nibelungen¬allee 37-41; 069 15000; open daily 24hr)
Pharmacies: Apotheke Hauptbahnhof (B-Ebene, at the central train station; 069; open M-F 6:30am-9pm, Sa 8am-9pm, Su 9am-8pm)

ACCOMMODATIONS

FIVE ELEMENTS HOSTEL ($)

Moselstraße 40; 69 24005885; www.5elementshostel.de; reception open 24hr

The Five Elements Hostel in Frankfurt has a nicely balanced social scene, where most evenings you can find groups crushing beers they picked up at the hostel bar and playing pool downstairs. Run by a young international staff, the hostel often puts on group activities, which range from movie nights to making crêpes or grilling burgers with the token (and often shirtless) American staffer on the Fourth of July. Plus, the breakfast buffet at the hostel includes seemingly endless Nutella, which is free when you stay at least three nights.

i Dorms from €15; reservation required; BGLTQ+ friendly; limited wheelchair accessibility; Wi-Fi; laundry €4.50; breakfast €4.50

FRANKFURT HOSTEL ($$)

Kaiserstrasse 74; 69 2475130; www. frankfurt-hostel.com; reception open 24hr

Frankfurt Hostel is another good place to make friends on the road, featuring a bar where we ended up for drinks when we weren't even staying there! There's also a small second common room for people who need a quiet place to work and perhaps brush up on their consulting interview skills. Plus, the hostel serves a daily free pasta dinner where travelers can come together over their love of noodles and dedication to free food (the most universal of human qualities). Their claim about having "live music" is a little sketch though (read: occasional piano-playing courtesy of some guests), but a little jazz never hurt anyone.

i Dorms from €18; reservation recommended; max stay 2 weeks; Wi-Fi; laundry facilities €5; towels for rent €1

UNITED-HOSTEL FRANKFURT CITY CENTER ($$)

Kaiserstraße 52; 69 256678000; www. united-hostel-frankfurt.com; reception open 24hr

The modern furnishings and panels of neon light in United-Hostel Frankfurt City Center give off a spaceship vibe—like that shirt American Apparel used to sell that changed color in heat (which was a cool idea until we realized it meant having constant and aggressive pit stains). Beds are built into their own nooks, giving you an added sense of privacy. There are plenty of large common spaces to crack open your own

supermarket beers and a gigantic TV in the lounge.

i Dorms from €17; reservation recommended; max stay 1 week; wheelchair accessible; Wi-Fi; towels €5; self-service laundry (wash €4, dry €2); breakfast buffet €4.50

SIGHTS
CULTURE

....

🏛 KAISERDOM (FRANKFURT CATHEDRAL)

Domplatz 14; 69 2970320; www. dom-frankfurt.de; tower access 9am-6pm

A grand red stone interior awaits visitors to the Frankfurt Cathedral, which today relies heavily on the Gothic style, but includes other architectural elements picked up over the church's centuries-long history. Visitors can also climb the 95-meter tower. The tower staircase is a seemingly endless spiral, wrapping in circles as it carries you upwards. It is a physically dizzying experience as much as it is an exhausting one (we all romanticize spiral staircases but also forget the strange lateral exertion that they actually require), but, at the top, you are rewarded with incredible views of the city, worthy of the 328 steps.

i Admission €3, students €1.50; wheelchair accessible

KLEINMARKTHALLE

Hasengasse 5-7; 69 21233696; www.
kleinmarkthalle.de; open M-F 8am-6pm, Sa
8am-4pm

This indoor market in Frankfurt operates rain or shine, meaning there are opportunities to stock up on novelty cheeses and sausages as big as your forearm no matter what time of the year it is. Pop in for fresh produce from papayas to teeny tiny blueberries you can eat by the handful. With a few cafés and butcher stands happy to slice cured meats straight into sandwiches, Kleinmarkthalle is also a reliable place to come for a midday bite. Whether you walk out with a fresh, meaty sandwich or a bag full of groceries, you made a good choice. Another bonus: several booths give free samples.

i Stand prices vary, some stands cash only; wheelchair accessible

LANDMARKS

FRANKFURT STOCK EXCHANGE

Börsenplatz 4; 69 21111515; www.frank-
furtstockexchange.de; open M-F 9am-5pm

To see one of the things that makes Frankfurt famous and lose yourself in an existential wormhole about how stocks really work, the Frankfurt Stock Exchange is a great place to swing by for a quick photo opportunity. Outside of the stock exchange there is a cool work of art posed for the world to see. No, not the trader in the gorgeous three-piece suit who spent the last 20 minutes chain-smoking and yelling into his cell phone. We're talking about the statues of the bull and the bear. Why are people drawn to the idea of placing metal sculptures, bulls in particular, in front of stock exchanges? We don't know, but we're into it.

i Free; plaza is wheelchair accessible

RIVERFRONT PROMENADE

Untermainkai 17; open daily 24hr

The promenade that extends on either side of the **Main River** in Frankfurt is one of our favorite ways to see the city. Start at the **Holbeinsteg pedestrian bridge** if you are staying at a hostel in the **Red Light District** and walk a loop along the promenade crossing **Eiserner Steg,** the city's other pedestrian bridge

further east. Eiserner Steg is known as destination where couples go to attach padlocks to the railings. The walk along the promenade is always well-populated with plenty of green spaces to stop and hang out by the river. This will lead you along the row of museums to the south of the river and **Old Town** to the north.

i Free; wheelchair accessible

RÖMERBERG (RÖMER SQUARE)

Römerberg 27; open daily 24hr

Römerberg is the lasting vestige of the old German town in Frankfurt's urban center. With the spire of the **Frankfurt Cathedral** looming in the background, fairytale apartment buildings stand precariously wedged side by side (it's unclear if they would all domino to the ground if not for the super glue holding them together, or if they are secretly all one building sliced into thin sections). Römer square sits at the center of the **Altstadt** (Old Town). Opposite the apartment buildings, you will find the **Römer,** which is the several hundred-year-old **City Hall of Frankfurt.** You'll also find restaurants, bustling pedestrian walkways, and a street performer who pretends to be a statue while gesturing at passersby.

i Free; wheelchair accessible

MUSEUMS

FILMMUSEUM

Schaumainkai 41; 69 961220220; www.
deutsches-filminstitut.de/en/filmmuseum;
open Tu 10am-6pm, W 10am-8pm, Th-Su
10am-6pm

The Frankfurt Filmmuseum boasts a small but modern collection that takes visitors through the history and evolution of film. Beginning with the development of technology, learn about the use of still photos to create moving video, and tinker around with kaleidoscopes and early flip-book style movie boxes. Next, take a look at the construction of narrative. Our favorite display is a four-projector ensemble where movie scenes are shown on alternating screens, while neighboring screens juxtapose clips from other productions using similar visual or thematic elements. Here, you can witness **Martin Scorsese** become legend with his avant-garde filming in

Mean Streets and rewatch the *Twilight* make out scene like never before.

i Admission €6, students €3, special exhibitions €7/€5; wheelchair accessible

STÄDEL MUSEUM

Schaumainkai 63; 69 605098200; www.staedelmuseum.de; open Tu-W 10am-6pm, Th-F 10am-9pm, Sa-Su 10am-6pm

The Städel Museum is Frankfurt's major art museum and houses one of the most important collections of art in Germany; the city's finance bros probably ignore it, but you shouldn't. Beginning with the Old Masters on the top floor, visitors will see pieces from **Rembrandt** and **Rubens,** as well as a significant display of early Dutch art, including pieces from **Jan van Eyck, Hieronymus Bosch** (though nothing as perverse as *The Garden of Earthly Delights*), and **Lucas Cranach the Elder.** In more modern sections, experience the transformation of art at the turn of the twentieth century, as artists like **Claude Monet** and **Max Liebermann** turned towards Impressionism.

i Admission €14, students €12; wheelchair accessible

OUTDOORS
....

FREIBAD ESCHERSHEIM

Alexander-Riese-Weg; 69 2710892300; www.bbf-frankfurt.de; open M-F 10am-8pm, Sa-Su 9am-8pm

If you need a day to unwind, a trip to the pool is the thing to do. This huge public pool is surrounded by equally massive grass areas, so while it doesn't have lounge chairs to recline on, it is the perfect place to bring a blanket or a towel and lay out with a picnic, alternating between the cool water and hot rays. In fact, the pool is unheated, so we advise visiting on a hot day or amping yourself up to take the plunge all at once. The edges are roped off, so you can't jump in, which we think is stupid, but relaxing beside an outdoor pool is always a net positive.

i Admission €4.80, students €3.20; wheelchair accessible

FOOD

✉ MEAT ROOM ($$)

Kaiserstraße 39; 69 87201927; www.meatroom.de; open M-F 11am-11:30pm

Amid furniture smoothed out of forklift crates and a blazing fire roaring on a flat-screen TV in the back corner, the Meat Room truly lives up to its name with an array of meat dishes and a few salads for the veg-heads among us. Choose between steak and seafood, including T-Bones, lamb chops, salmon, and lobster. Then, pick a side and add one of the restaurant's specialty sauces. Looking for more traditional food? Meat Room also has a menu of German specials, a long list of pork dishes where we counted "Frankfurter," the region's legendary sausage style, in the name of no fewer than five dishes. Try *handkäs with musik,* which translates to "hand cheese with music," a regional cuisine made of sour milk cheese.

i Entrées from €7; vegetarian options available; limited wheelchair accessibility

EBERT'S SUPPENSTUBE ($)

Grosse Bockenheimer Strasse 31; 69 20973877; www.ebert-feinkost.de; open M-F 11am-7pm, Sa 11am-6pm

This simple deli-style restaurant is a great place to stop in for the essentials, namely, soup and sausage, virtually the only things on the menu. Soups are Ebert's specialty; they did put "suppen" in their name. Still, their sausage is great and lots of their soups are sausage-based anyway, so, either way, you can't lose. The menu is not available in English, which can be daunting, but, when in doubt, simply ask for bratwurst. You'll be asked if you want beer or pork and then quickly handed your sausage in a bun, ready for mustarding at the self-serve pump. Soups are a little harder to navigate without being able to read the menu, but you can get clues from pieces of the names including wurst or *gulaschsuppe,* and vegetarian soups should usually say *vegetarische.*

i Sausage and soup €2.50-6; vegetarian options available; wheelchair accessible

URBAN KITCHEN ORIGIN FOOD ($$)

Kaiserstraße 53; 69 27107999; www.myur-bankitchen.de; open M-F 11am-midnight, Sa 11am-open end, Su 11am-11pm

Urban Kitchen Origin Food has a little bit of just about anything you could want. On the menu, you'll find burgers, pasta, pizza, steak, fish, ambiguous Asian food—and even sushi. We dove straight into their salad section because, after weeks on the road, we may be developing scurvy. Other menu highlights include ramen, an upscale wholesome version of everyone's favorite microwave lunch (we love you Cup Noodles, no shade), and pitas and skewers (€9.90-11.50), available with a variety of proteins, but also packed with veggies and tzatziki, both feel-good options for every occasion.

i *Entrées from €8, steaks and fish up to €30, card min €25; vegetarian options available; limited wheelchair accessibility*

NIGHTLIFE

⬛ SHOTZ

Große Rittergasse 40; www.shotz-bar.com/locations/frankfurt; open M-Th 8pm-1am, F 8pm-2am, Sa 8pm-3am

Shotz is the party spot for students in Frankfurt. With more than 150 specialty shots, choose one with an embarrassing title and see what happens. Favorites include the Google, with four layers of color, the Botox, with alcohol squirted from a syringe, the Psycho Killer, with a goldfish cracker swimming inside, and the Viagra, with a little blue pill (it's candy, don't worry). Try one of their action shots for a more involved experience with titles like the Bangcock, though the bartender made us swear we wouldn't divulge the stunt and ruin the surprise.

i *No cover, mixed shots from €2, straight shots from €2.50; cash only; BGLTQ+ friendly*

CITY BEACH

Carl-Theodor-Reiffenstein-Platz 5; 69 29729697; www.citybeach-frankfurt.de; open M-Th 11am-11pm, F-Sa 11am-midnight

City Beach combines two of our favorite things: rooftop bars and artificial urban beaches. We have no idea how they got sand on top of a six-story building, but we're thankful they did. At City Beach, you can recline on a lounge chair, drink in hand, and dig your toes into the sand looking out on the Frankfurt skyline feeling bad for all the sad financiers working away in their tall office buildings. Even if that's your work-week persona, you're on vacation now, so live it up. Take a dip in the pool and dry off in the unencumbered rooftop sun with a fruity cocktail on ice.

i *No cover, drinks from €5; cash only*

PLANK

Elbestraße 15; 69 26958666; www.barplank.de; open M-Th 10am-1am, F 10am-2am, Sa 11am-2am

Plank is a bar with an aesthetic that might be the material incarnation of a man-bunned IKEA designer wearing a charcoal suit with a white v-neck t-shirt and an Urban Outfitters scarf. The street-level chairs out front are almost always occupied, even in the bar's slowest moments. Gather at Plank for drinks and a relaxed place for conversation by their open floor to ceiling windows. Right around the corner from the restaurant strip on Kaiserstraß, the bar is a perfect after-dinner locale, but worth a late-night trip, when its dark walls seem to blend with the night.

i *No cover, drinks from €5; cash only; BGLTQ+ friendly*

HAMBURG

Coverage by **Antonia Washington**

Hamburg is the second-largest city in Germany, behind Berlin. Connected to the North Sea by the Elbe River, it gained prominence as a center of trade in Europe beginning in the Middle Ages. This Hanseatic port city, in fact, was once known as the "gateway to the world." The waterways permeate into the city's core, and because the city sits at the crux of a web of channels, it has bridges. A lot of them—Hamburg is home to more bridges than any other city in the world. With at least 2,300 and counting, the combined bridge totals of Venice, Amsterdam, and London doesn't even begin to approach this number. If you need more than this deluge of canals to entice you to Hamburg, consider its history as a rebounding city. Structurally, Hamburg has been through a lot. It was burned almost entirely to the ground in the nineteenth century, bombed heavily in WWII, and inundated by floods that killed hundreds of people as late as the 1960s. Through everything, Hamburg has always maintained the courage and the spirit to rebuild and look to the future—that's something worth experiencing.

ORIENTATION

The city center of Hamburg is a fairly small ring located north of the **Elbe River's** canals and just south of the **Außenalster lake.** A circular road winds around the area and the central train station borders it to the northeast. In the city center, you will find many of the historic sights, including the **Rathaus,** most of the historic churches, and many museums, as well as the corporate offices of modern companies like Google. To the west of the city center is the **St. Pauli district,** a hip, young neighborhood where it often feels like everyone could be a bassist in a punk band or a graphic designer. Important areas in St. Pauli include the **Reeperbahn** and surrounding streets, which are the center of the city's **Red Light district** and hotspots for nightlife. The Sternschanze area is in the north and, around **Schulterblatt street,** you will find tons of trendy restaurants and shops. To the east of the city center is the **St. Georg neighborhood,** the primary area for BGLTQ+ life in Hamburg.

ESSENTIALS
GETTING THERE

The Hamburg Airport is a major international airport north of the city. The airport is serviced by airlines from all over the world, so reaching Hamburg is simple by plane from just about anywhere. Direct flights to and from the United States tend to only be from New York City, so if you're flying from elsewhere, you may have a connecting flight. If you are traveling from elsewhere in the region, trains and buses are both great options for reaching Hamburg. The central train station, Hamburg Hauptbahnhof, and the central bus station, Hamburg ZOB, are right next to each other.

GETTING AROUND

Hamburg is surprisingly walkable, and things in the city center tend to be within about a 30min walk from each other. If you plan to move significantly between neighborhoods, it will be easier to use public transport. The S-Bahn and U-Bahn trains are both available as well as buses. We thought the U-Bahn was especially useful in Hamburg, particularly the U3, which essentially runs in a giant loop around the city center, with stops on the edges of the St. Pauli and St. Georg neighborhoods.

PRACTICAL INFORMATION

Tourist Offices: St. Pauli Tourist Office (Wohlwillstraße 1; 040 98234483; www.pauli-tourist.de; open M-Sa 10am-7pm)
Banks/ATMs/Currency Exchange: Most restaurants and many businesses in Hamburg only accept cash. Most ATMs are located in banks, which are readily available.
Post Offices: There are post offices throughout the city. The following is located in the city center (Alter Wall 38; 0228 4333112; open M-F 9am-6:30pm, Sa 10:30am-1pm).
Internet: Wi-Fi is fairly standard in accommodations in Hamburg, but not often elsewhere. Many coffee shops in the city center have Wi-Fi.
BGLTQ+ Resources: The Hamburg tourist office publishes a pamphlet called "Hamburger Queer" with resources and suggestions for BGLTQ+ visitors. Many of the establishments along Lange Reihe in St. Georg also have pamphlets and flyers with information on BGLTQ+ events.

EMERGENCY INFORMATION

Emergency Number: 112
Police: Polizeirevierwache Rathaus (Große Johannisstraße 1; 40 428 650)
US Embassy: The US Embassy in Germany is nearby in Berlin, but Hamburg also has its own US Consulate, listed here (Alsterufer 27/28; 040 411 71 100).
Rape Crisis Center: Emergency hotline for victims of sexual assault and rape (040 255566). Weißer Ring runs rape crisis centers in Hamburg. Call them at 040 2517680 or go online to www.hamburg.weisser-ring.de.
Hospitals: Universitätsklinikum Hamburg-Eppendorf (Martinistraße 52; 040 74100; open daily 24hr)
Pharmacies: Europa Apotheke (Bergstraße 14; 040 32527690; www.europa-apotheke-hamburg.de; open M-F 8am-8pm, Sa 9:30am-8pm)

ACCOMMODATIONS

🏨 MAC CITY HOSTEL ($$)

Beim Strohhause 26; 40 35629146; www.maccityhostel.de; reception open daily 8am-midnight

Rooms at the MAC City Hostel are clean and bright. They may be plain, but they are great places to wake up and stretch on a sunny morning before remembering that you're in a bunk bed and the guy sleeping above you is snoring. Still, it's great for a moment. The common areas at MAC City Hostel are small, but maybe you can start hanging out with friends in the incredibly spacious shower rooms, where showers are standard-sized but an unnecessary amount of floor space sprawls in front of the sinks. Don't try to lie and tell us you wouldn't love the space to just hang out in there with, like, any girl you've ever met in the bathroom at a party.
i Dorms from €25; reservation recommended; wheelchair accessible; Wi-Fi; linens included; towels €2.50 deposit; laundry €5; kitchen

BACKPACKERS HOSTEL ST. PAULI ($)

Bernstorffstrasse 98; 40 23517043; www.backpackers-stpauli.de; reception open Apr-Nov daily 8am-midnight, Dec-Mar daily 9am-10pm

Backpackers Hostel St. Pauli is not afraid of making a political statement. There's a small anti-Trump figurine standing atop a cabinet, and among the stickers plastering the bar, you'll find many with anti-racism slogans and things like, "refugees welcome," and "no human is illegal." The hostel believes in welcoming with open arms anyone who is willing to do the same. Common areas are limited, but the guest kitchen has a massive couch to compensate, and if you hang out around the bar or the small backyard patio, you're bound to encounter some friendly faces.
i Dorms from €15; reservation recommended; min stay 2 nights on weekends; no wheelchair accessibility; Wi-Fi; linens included; towels €1.50; locker deposit €5; breakfast buffet €5; kitchen

SIGHTS
CULTURE

🏛 ST. MICHAELISKIRCHE (ST. MICHAEL'S CHURCH)

Englische Planke 1; 40 376780; www.st-michaelis.de; open May-Oct daily 9am-8pm, Nov-Apr 10am-6pm

St. Michael's is a gorgeous Baroque church with a white and gold interior—in contrast to narrow Gothic churches, the body of St. Michael's opens up on wide balconies that extend the length of the nave into a bright and yawning space. These balconies are the seat of the church's several organs, so snag a spot on a balcony pew before service starts if you want a prime spot next to the DJ. Visitors to the church can also climb the church tower, one of Hamburg's most famous landmarks, and take a gander at the crypts.
i Free entry tower €5, students €4; crypt €4, students €3; combination ticket €7, students €6; unbooked church tours every second and fourth Su of month at 3pm; last entry 30min. before closing; wheelchair accessible; tours available daily but must be booked at least 2 weeks in advance

ELBPHILHARMONIE

Am Kaiserkai 62; www.elbphilharmonie.com; plaza open daily 9am-midnight

Newly opened in January 2017, the Elbphilharmonie is a dazzling demonstration of architectural imagination. A futuristic work of glass, the building reflects the sky while simultaneously evoking waves, an ode to its position on the water's edge, with a plaza observation deck that peers out over Hamburg's many ports. Inside the concert hall, custom-surfaced walls are designed to reflect sound in every direction and ensure acoustic perfection, making this one of the most advanced concert venues in the world in terms of acoustic technology. Visit the plaza for the city views or come to a concert to experience the superior orchestral sound.

i Free; wheelchair accessible; purchase concert tickets online or by phone at 040 35766666

LANDMARKS

🔯 PLANTEN UN BLOMEN

Planten un Blomen, St. Petersburger Straße; www.plantenunblomen.hamburg.de; open Apr daily 7am-10pm, May-Sept 7am-11pm, Oct-Mar 7am-8pm

This large park that sits between Hamburg's city center and the St. Pauli neighborhood stretches from the St. Pauli U-Bahn station at the east end of the **Reeperbahn** up past the north end of the city center. Here, you'll find open fields, flower gardens, and ponds meandering through the park where you can sit and read with your bike resting serenely against a park bench. We saw an old man doing just that when we visited. And even after an intense downpour, you'll find moms pushing strollers, kids running barefoot in the playground sand, and people dumping gravel out of their shoes.

i Free; wheelchair accessible

RATHAUS

Rathausmarkt 1; open daily 8am-6pm

The Hamburg Rathaus is the political center of the city, home to the office of the Hamburg mayor, and the places of meeting for the city's parliamentary and senatorial bodies. Built at the end of the nineteenth century, the exterior of the city hall is an exemplar of Neo-Renaissance style, made to display Hamburg's prosperity, especially at the time of its construction. The sandstone building is particularly ornate when compared to styles typical of the region. If you watched *Home Alone 2: Lost in New York* and identified most with the lady in the park who had a deep spiritual affinity for pigeons, the plaza in front of the Hamburg Rathaus would be a great place to start amassing your pigeon army.

i Free, tours €4; wheelchair accessible; call to book tours in English (040 4283124)

SPEICHERSTADT

Speicherstadt; www.speicherstadtmuseum.de; open daily 24hr

The Speicherstadt area is a small window into Hamburg's history as one of the world's great port cities. This warehouse district is the world's largest contiguous warehouse complex, designated as a **UNESCO World Heritage site** in 2015 and built on wooden piles in brick Gothic style. You might say, "you're literally raving about brick buildings," but they're special brick buildings, and their reflection off the canal waters feels like a real slice of history. If you're looking for historic neighborhoods to meander through and remark excitedly about the character of the buildings, the **Krameramtsstuben**, houses of the **Guild of Shopkeepers**, constitute the oldest lane of terraced houses in the world (Krayenkamp 10, 20459 Hamburg).

i Free; wheelchair accessible

MUSEUMS

🔯 KUNSTHALLE MUSEUM

Glockengießerwall 5; 40 428131200; www.hamburger-kunsthalle.de; open Tu-W 10am-6pm, Th 10am-9pm, F-Su 10am-6pm

The Kunsthalle Museum is Hamburg's greatest collection of art, stretching from the Old Masters to contemporary exhibitions. As you wander from room to room and through time periods, it may feel a bit like an art history lesson, where slowly your understanding of art movements will begin to take form. From the Enlightenment collection, keep an eye out for the understated *View of the Tiber and Fidenae at the Acqua Acetosa Spring* by **Johann Christian Reinhart,** a picturesque scene that could have come straight from *Westworld.* (But the TV show or the theme park itself? You'll never know. Ha! Set design inception.) And from the Romanticism collection, we loved **Caspar David Friedrich's** piece, *Wanderer Above the Sea of Fog,* with a nineteenth-century Instagram aesthetic to make everyone jealous.

i Admission M-F €12, students €6, Sa-Su €14, students €7, Th 5:30pm-9pm €8, students €4; tours €4; English tours Sundays at 11am; wheelchair accessible

MUSEUM FÜR HAMBURGISCHE GESCHICHTE (MUSEUM OF HAMBURG HISTORY)

Holstenwall 24; 40 428132100; www. hamburgmuseum.de; open Tu-Sa 10am-5pm, Su 10am-6pm

The museum, founded in 1908, walks visitors through the history of Hamburg from its early origins to the modern age. Of course, this has long been a port city, and you'll find plenty of ship reconstructions and dioramas here, documenting how industry flourished on its docks beginning with lumber milling and trade, filling barrels with all sorts of goods and stacking them in boats. Here, you'll also learn about the city's destruction in the **Great Fire of 1842,** life during the Baroque era, and even the history of the Jewish community in Hamburg. The museum itself is housed in a college-esque brick building overhung by trees, perfect to get you jazzed for learning!

i Admission €9.50, students €6; wheelchair accessible; tours can be booked in advance online at www.museums-dienst-hamburg.de or by calling 040 4281310

OUTDOORS

ALSTER LAKES

Alster Lakes; open daily 24hr, barring extraneous circumstances

At these lakes, you'll find inner city paradise in the form of sail boats, pedal boats, paddle boards (yes, "pedal" and "paddle" are different;

sometimes correct spelling is the bane of wordplay), and even inflatable rafts that people bring from home and plop down in the water. The **Binnenalster** is the smaller of the two lakes and sits within the city center, rimmed by cafés and marvelous city buildings reflecting off the water's surface. The **Außenalster,** the outer lake, is much larger, and it's here that you'll find the most boat activity. And even if you don't want to rent a boat, grab a soda or a snack at one of the boathouses or a dock-perched restaurant and dangle your feet in the water.

i Free; limited wheelchair accessibility

FOOD

◩ EDEL CURRY ($)

Große Bleichen 68; 40 35716262; www. edelcurry.de; open M-Sa 11am-10pm, Su noon-10pm

If you have any interest in sausage, Edel Curry is the place to go. It looks deceptively like it could be any random strip-mall chain restaurant. But no: its beef is sourced from local grass-fed cattle and sausage is prepared by a local butcher. The potatoes used to produce their french fries are also local and fresh, and their sauces are homemade. It's not all just yuppie obsession with locally-sourced ingredients; Edel Curry has the chops to back up the "philosophy" section of their menu. Named "best french fries in Hamburg" three times, the restaurant has also been crowned "best *currywurst* in all of Germany." We walked away with a stomach full of *currywurst,* French fries, and beer, all for under €10.

i Currywurst €3.80, bratwurst €3.50, fries from €2.80, specialty sauces from €0.50; limited wheelchair accessibility

FRAU MÖLLER ($)

Lange Reihe 96; 40 25328817; www. fraumoeller.com; open M-Th 11:30am-4am, F 11:30am-6am, Sa 11am-6am, Su 11am-4am; kitchen open M-Th 11:30am-1am, F 11:30am-3am, Sa 11am-3am, Su 11am-1am

One of our favorite restaurants in Hamburg, Frau Möller serves German cuisine in a restaurant that we would call a fun hodgepodge of antiquated items, from mismatched wooden furniture and intentional antiques like a wooden ship's steering wheel and old coffee cans to—perhaps even more dated—the CD collection behind the bar. But don't get your millennial knickers in a twist; if receding from the digital age tastes this good, we're all for it. Chow down on organic fried potatoes with onions, bacon, and three fried eggs (€5.90), or gobble up a chicken breast fillet with pepper cream sauce, fried potatoes, and salad (€8.50).

i Entrées from €5; vegetarian options available; limited wheelchair accessibility

BEAR CLAW ($)

Lange Reihe 1-5; 040 18040892; www.bearclaw.de; open daily 11am-11pm

If you love pulled pork, first, we completely agree with you, and second, your mind is about to explode. At Bear Claw, your meal starts with beef, pork, or chicken, all of which are slow roasted for eight hours to reach tender perfection. The meat is "clawed" from the roast, swirled in what we translated to "meat juices" but might actually be gravy, and doused in homemade sauce. Finally, it gets plopped onto bread and served as a sandwich, scooped into your desperate hands, and gulped down in a frenzy.

i Pulled-meat sandwiches from €8; no wheelchair accessibility

PAULINE CAFÉ ($)

Neuer Pferdemarkt 3; 40 41359964; www.pauline-hamburg.de; open M-F 8:30am-4pm, Sa 9am-6pm, Su 10am-6pm; Su brunch 10am-12:15pm and 12:30pm-3pm

Pauline Café is a great spot for breakfast in the **St. Pauli** neighborhood. Start the day feeling fresh with the "In a good mood" breakfast (€8.40), which includes yogurt with fruit and granola, vegetable sticks with guacamole, and herb cream cheese on whole-grain bread. Or order up something sweet with their french toast (€5.90), which comes dripping with maple syrup and piled high with fruit. If you're not a coffee drinker, we recommend ordering Pauline's sweet hot chocolate (€3), which is foamy and delicious. The whipped cream comes served on the side in a small metal cup and we've rarely felt so self-satisfied as we did when transferring our whipped cream into our cocoa with a parfait spoon. If you want to try Pauline for Sunday brunch, make sure to reserve a table ahead of time.

i Entrées from €6; vegan and vegetarian options available; no wheelchair accessibility

NIGHTLIFE

☒ KYTI VOO

Lange Reihe 82; 40 28055565; www.kytivoo.com; open M-Sa 5pm-varies, Su 2pm-varies

Kyti Voo is a large, chic gay bar. Too chic maybe, because their logo of a cat with a handlebar mustache and a bow tie takes the whole thing a tad too far. The bar specializes in craft beers and cocktails, and though you may not be able to read the menu, bartenders are more than happy to make recommendations. Plus, the best part is some drinks are served with glowsticks in the glass, and if you can move past the fact that your drink is holding a vessel of literal poison, that's an awesome touch! On the weekends, expect the crowd to get younger and the music louder.

i No cover, cocktails from €7; cash only; BGLTQ+ friendly

99 CENT BAR

Große Freiheit 31; www.bar-99.de; open M-Th 8pm-2am, F-Sa 8pm-4am

In a sea of night clubs in Hamburg's **Red Light District,** 99 Cent Bar stood out to us because, well, we're cheapskates at heart. This club is just a small room, and on busy weekend nights, there is no space for dancing. A fun-loving and social bar, there is only one real activity here, and that activity is drinking, because the bar's name is true. **All beers and shots are just €0.99.** (Longdrinks are €2, but we're not complaining.) Stop here to hang out with a rowdy and rambunctious crowd of students and gear up for a wild night at the surrounding clubs.

i No cover, drinks from €1; cash only; BGLTQ+ friendly

with friends, hostel-mates, or that guy with the short-on-the-sides, long-on-top haircut making eye contact with you from the bar. (What do you mean you don't know which one we're talking about?) Windows occupying most of the walls make the bar feel nicely linked to the street outside, and the vibe at the counter says young urban professional mingles with a young urban would-be-professional.

i No cover, drinks from €5; cash only

HERZBLUT ST. PAULI

Reeperbahn 50; 40 33396933; www.herzblut-st-pauli.de; open M-Th 5pm-varies, F 5pm-4am, Sa 1pm-4am, Su 1pm-varies

If you're looking to party on a weekday, do not come to Herzblut St. Pauli because it will feel like a sad Las Vegas with lots of empty seating and neutral tones. On the weekends, however, Herzblut St. Pauli transforms. Tables are cleared to create a dance floor and a young crowd comes to enjoy exotic cocktails and dancing with DJs and live music. So, if you're looking for a place to go out on the Reeperbahn, the street at the center of Hamburg's **Red Light District,** Herzblut St. Pauli isn't a bad choice. Just promise us that if you give them your bra, you'll spice things up with some bright colors or patterns.

i No cover, beers from €3, cocktails €9

GOLDFISCHGLAS

Bartelsstraße 30; www.goldfischglas.de; open daily 2pm-varies

If hipness and dim lighting are correlated, then we've hit max capacity. (Probably) named for everyone's favorite golden cracker, GoldFischGlas is lit by only a low orange glow that makes the bar feel a little like Halloween. Free-standing booths and cozy nooks along the walls make this a great place to chat over drinks

MUNICH

Coverage by **Antonia Washington**

Compared to those of its eastern neighbors, Germany's cities are much more cosmopolitan. Munich, one of the country's largest cities with a population of 1.43 million, is especially so. As such, getting a handle on it, especially if you've spent the last few weeks in the Austrian countryside, can be a bit tricky. If you feel like you're struggling to understand Munich, lean into its Bavarian roots, which truly remain its lifeblood. Lounge in a few beer gardens and you'll soon feel the city consolidating around you. If Vienna is the chic older sister of the German-speaking world and Berlin is the sister's edgy boyfriend who plays in a rock band and doesn't sleep before 4am, then Munich is the grandparent that gives you beer behind your parents' backs. Here, tradition matters. And as stereotypical as it may sound, we guarantee that while in Munich, you'll find plenty of people casually wearing lederhosen and subsisting on diet of beer (often cheaper than water) and pretzels.

ORIENTATION

When orienting yourself, start with **Marienplatz.** The area surrounding Marienplatz is a hub for restaurants and shopping. In the surrounding blocks, you will find many of Munich's historic sites. To the south of Marienplatz, sites include **St. Peter's Church** and **Viktualienmarkt.** To the north, sights include the **Residenz Palace.** The Residenz sits about equidistant between Marienplatz and the lower tip of the **Englischer Garten,** to the northeast. West of Marienplatz and ever slightly north is another square called **Karlsplatz.** Traveling south from Karlsplatz, along **Sonnenstraße,** you'll encounter many popular bars and clubs. The main train station is just west of Karlsplatz.

ESSENTIALS

GETTING THERE

Munich Airport is a major international airport with services from most major airlines worldwide and airlines of all kinds in Europe. The central train station (hauptbahnhof in German, often written "Hbf") is on the northwestern edge of the main historic city center. The central bus station in Munich, often called Munich ZOB, is in a similar area, on the west end of the train station. Both stations are connected to the S-bahn public transport lines. The name of the S-bahn stop at the central bus station is Hackerbrücke.

GETTING AROUND

Public transport is simple to use in Munich. It is important to keep in mind that if you plan to visit sites a little further from the city center, such as the BMW Welt and Museum, the Olympic park and stadium, or Dachau, you will likely need to use public transport. The S-Bahn and the U-Bahn are the primary subway train systems. Within the city center, the S-Bahn runs roughly northwest to southeast, and all the lines use the same route in this area.

PRACTICAL INFORMATION

Tourist Offices: The central tourist office is located in Marienplatz (Marienplatz 8; 089 23396500; www.muenchen.de; open M-F 9:30am-7:30pm, Sa 9am-4pm, Su 10am-2pm).

Banks/ATMs/Currency Exchange: Many businesses in Munich only accept cash, but ATMs are usually easily accessible.

Post Offices: Postbank (Sattlerstraße 1; open M-F 9am-6pm, Sa 9am-12:30pm)

Internet: Internet is generally available at accommodations in Munich. Additionally, you can find free Wi-Fi in major city areas, such as Marienplatz.

BGLTQ+ Resources: For BGLTQ+ resources, check out these websites: www.munich.international-friends.net/lgbt-guide-to-munich and www.angloinfo.com/how-to/germany/munich/family/lgbt/munich-gay-community along with the tourist office for information and resources.

EMERGENCY INFORMATION

Emergency Number: 112
Police: Ettstraße 2; 089 29100
US Embassy: The US Embassy in Germany is located in Berlin, listed here, but there are consulates in Munich and Frankfurt that may be more easily accessible (Clayallee 170; 30 83050). The US Consulate General Munich is located at Königinstraße 5 (8928880).
Rape Crisis Center: Frauennotruf München (Saarstraße 5; 89763737; www.frauennotrufmuenchen.de; open M-F 10am-midnight, Sa-Su 6pm-midnight).
Hospitals: Schwabing Hospital (Kölner Platz 1; 89 3304 0302; www.klinikum-muenchen.de; open daily 24hr)
Pharmacies: International Pharmacy Hauptbahnhof (Bahnhofplatz 2; 89 599 890 40; open M-F 7am-8pm, Sa 8am-8pm)

ACCOMMODATIONS

⬛ EURO YOUTH HOTEL ($$)

Senefelderstraße 5; 89 59908811; www.euro-youth-hotel.de; reception open 24hr

Housed in a wood building that looks like an awful lot like a pub, Euro Youth Hotel claims it blurs the line between hostel and hotel by providing both comfortable rooms and a hostel atmosphere. By the time we checked out, our vision was pretty hazy. You simply can't argue with complementary daily linen change, nor with weekly music performances. In the center of the in-house bar—the performance venue and location of most hostel-sponsored activities— a pillar is wallpapered with international currencies and hand-written notes.

i *Dorms from €30 in summer; reservation required; max stay 7 nights; wheelchair accessible; Wi-Fi; towels €1.50; laundry (wash €3, dry €1.50), detergent packs €0.50; breakfast €4.90*

GSPUSI BAR HOSTEL ($)

Oberanger 45; 89 24411790; www.gspusibarhostel.com; reception hours vary

A hip hostel aesthetic awaits at the Gspusi Bar Hostel, with a heavy emphasis on wood and metal décor. Even the bar area, a small space packed with seating from a picnic table to bar stools, is wallpapered with repainted metal roofing panels. In terms of amenities, Gspusi isn't trying too hard (if the early 2000s taught us anything, it's that trying hard is #lame). Instead, they provide the essentials: a place to sleep, to shower, and to get a drink before going out in earnest for the night. Because the bar is the central focus of the hostel, it's a great place to congregate and get to know other travelers. Situated just up the road from **Marienplatz,** the hostel is also exceedingly well located.

i *Dorms from €25; reservation recommended; wheelchair accessible; Wi-Fi; towels €2*

JAEGER'S MUNICH ($)

Senefelderstraße 3; 89 555281; www.jaegershostel.de; reception open 24hr

With a guest age limit of 18-35 years and a fleet of 260 beds, Jaeger's Hostel is a temporary home to slews of young travelers passing through Munich. Despite its massive size, the hostel still continues to expand. Friendly and helpful staff pour free welcome shots at the bar and occasionally organize hostel-wide activities. The rooms are simple and generally clean, but your locker may look like it's suffered through years of graffiti-crazed tweens.

i *Dorms from €30 in summer, €15 in winter; reservation recommended; max stay 7 nights per month; wheelchair accessible; laundry*

MEININGER MUNICH CITY CENTER ($)

Landsberger Straße 20; 89 54998023; www.meininger-hotels.com; reception hours vary

The Meininger hostel in Munich offers basic, clean accommodations. Although, like many chain hostels, the common areas are distant and quiet during the day, the crowd gets considerably more hostel-ish as the evening wears on. Groups of travelers often gather on the patio and around the hostel bar at night before going out. If you've come with a travel buddy or if you can round up friends in your room, we recommend ditching the hostel bar for **Augustiner Bräu** directly across the street, the perfect place to pop over for a beer and a pretzel. The hostel is a little further from the historic center than the others we reviewed, but it's close to the **Oktoberfest fairgrounds,** if you plan to splurge on the party of a lifetime.

i *Dorms from €20, privates from €55; reservation recommended; BGLTQ+ friendly; limited wheelchair accessibility; Wi-Fi; lockers, linens provided; laundry facilities; towels €1; breakfast €6.90*

SIGHTS
CULTURE

ALTER PETER (ST. PETER'S CHURCH)

Perersplatz 1; 89 210237760; www.erzbistum-muenchen.de/StPeterMuenchen; open summer M-F 9am-6:30pm, Sa, Su, and holidays 10am-7pm; open winter M-F 9am-5:30pm, Sa, Su, and holidays 10am-6pm

Unlike many old European churches, Alter Peter has bright, white walls that reflect the sun throughout the long center aisle. Ceiling frescoes painted in vibrant colors liven the dome and gleam down at parishioners, while the sides of the church are lined with tombs. After exploring the ground floor of the church, climb more than 300 steps to the top of the tower through narrow passageways to find a sweeping view over the city.

i *Free; last entry 30min. before closing; limited wheelchair accessibility*

ASAMKIRCHE (ASAM CHURCH)

Sendlinger Straße 32; 89 23687989

Though as intricate and ornate as the other churches we scoped out in Munich, the Asamkirche, originally constructed as a private chapel, is relatively small

in comparison. Sit in a pew and you may feel like the church is slowly closing in (in a cool way, not a you're-being-buried-alive way)—ornamental marble-work makes the walls feel heavy and balconies rounding the sides and nave of the church body narrow the space. Because the Baroque façade is built into the neighboring buildings, you may walk right by the church if you're not looking for it.

i Free; no wheelchair accessibility

FRAUENKIRCHE (MÜNCHNER DOM)

Frauenplatz 12; 89 2900820; www.muench-ner-dom.de; open daily 7:30am-8:30pm

As big as the Frauenkirche looks from the outside, the magnitude of its interior is downright confusing—its size amplified by the lack of ostentatious decoration. The cathedral's roof and massive towers are supported by smooth, white pilasters rather than darkened stone ones, and the simple webbed molding where the pilasters meet the ceiling makes the cathedral feel cavernous. Furthermore, Frauenkirche's large stained-glass windows don't resemble the typical Gothic windows of similar cathedrals, instead featuring a variety geometric shapes.

i Free; tours €6; tours May-Oct Tu, Th, Su 3pm; wheelchair accessible

VIKTUALIENMARKT

Viktualienmarkt 3; 89 89068205; www.viktualienmarkt-muenchen.de; open M-F 10am-6pm, Sa 10am-3pm

Viktualienmarkt is the major outdoor market where local vendors sell their wares every day of the week. Booths overflow with fresh fruits and vegetables, spices, floral arrangements, and even small potted plants. One of our favorite features are the booths selling arts-n-crafts-style home decorations. Run mostly by crafty-grandma entrepreneurs, these booths sell everything from magnets to baskets to lavender plants, but we especially like the emphasis on hanging knickknacks. Spend a wad of cash at these booths and you'll end up needing hooks and knobs so you have enough places to hang the many ornaments, wind chimes, lantern boxes, and wooden heart-shaped cutouts. Of course, in true Bavarian form, the market is also a decent place to pick up sausage and beer.

i Stand prices vary; wheelchair accessible

LANDMARKS

🖼 MARIENPLATZ

Marienplatz 1

Situated in the middle of the city center, the square is the crossing point of every person in Munich—visitors and locals alike. Named for its fountain, Marienplatz sits on the edge of **Neues Rathaus,** the new town hall, an imposing Neo-Gothic building with windows and archways often overflowing with flowers, and an 85-meter tower (with an observation deck accessible by elevator) and **glockenspiel.** Come here to grab some ice cream, eat at a slightly overpriced restaurant, stroll between groups of street performing musicians, or just hop on the public transport.

i Free; wheelchair accessible

DACHAU

Peter-Roth-Str. 2a; 81 31669970; www.kz-gedenkstaette-dachau.de

There is nothing cool or fun about visiting the Dachau concentration camp, but you would be remiss not to see the memorial site and museum during your time in Munich. The concentration camp in Dachau, a town just northwest of Munich, was the first such camp established under the Nazi regime, shortly after the election of Adolf Hitler in 1933. On this site, atrocities were committed which would proliferate throughout Nazi-occupied territories and lead to the murder and torture of millions of people. Today, the site holds tributes to the victims, remaining and reconstructed buildings from the camp, and a museum with an abundance of information on the history and events of the camp.

i *Free, audio guide €3.50; limited wheelchair accessibility*

ENGLISCHER GARTEN

Englischer Garten

The Englischer Garten is one of the largest urban parks in the world, filled with grass lawns, overgrown trees, and plenty of water. It offers 48.5 miles (78 kilometers) of paths to be taken advantage of by cyclists, walkers, and joggers. Frankly, we think Ann Perkins said it best on Parks and Rec when she said, "Jogging is the worst, Chris. I mean, I know it keeps you healthy, but God, at what cost?" But yes, people do jog here. If you have hay fever, you may need to arm yourself with plenty of Benadryl in the spring, but the FOMO of not hanging out at the park with your friends will probably kill you before your allergies will.

i *Free; limited wheelchair accessibility*

RESIDENZ MUNICH

Residenzstraße 1; 89 290671; www.residenz-muenchen.de

The seat of Bavarian rulership from 1508 to 1918, the Residenz is an expansive palace and garden complex on the northeast end of the city center, right between **Marienplatz** and the **Englischer Garten.** The present-day museum takes visitors through long hallways, past gold framed mirrors, and near walls covered in velvets and silks. It doesn't matter if wallpaper is long out of style, matching is always in. A throne room with over-the-top décor might make you think the throne itself looks like a small toy , but it's hard to be underwhelmed with the rest of the palace.

i *Admission €7, students €6; last entry 1hr before closing; wheelchair accessible*

MUSEUMS

◪ PINAKOTHEK DER MODERNE

Barer Straße 40; 89 23805360; www.pinakothek.de

One of four museums in the **Pinakothek museum complex,** the Pinakothek der Moderne is dedicated to contemporary and modern art of the twentieth and twenty first centuries, and includes exhibitions on architecture, design, and fine arts. When we visited, there was an installment of larger-than-life Russian nesting dolls and we got to sit among them, trying to look rolly-polly to blend in.

i *Admission €10, students €7; wheelchair accessible*

ALTE PINAKOTHEK

Barer Straße 27; 89 23805216; www.pinakothek.de

The Alte Pinakothek museum is a gathering of major works by the Old Masters, featuring European Renaissance paintings. With a substantial collection of works by **Rembrandt** and an impressive display of **Ruben's** pieces as well, be on the look-out for salient works in the history of Christian art. Here, you'll find one of our favorite **Albrecht Dürer** pieces, a self-portrait styled to appear like the image of Christ that looks like

a mix between Chris Hemsworth and long-haired Orlando Bloom. We would never wish to downplay the significance of this seminal work of art, but it's just a little *Snow White and the Huntsman,* if you know what we mean.

i Admission €4, students €2, Su €1; wheelchair accessible

BMW WELT & MUSEUM

Am Olympiapark 2; 89 125016001; www.bmw-welt.com/de/location/museum/concept.html

In a building seemingly from the year 3000, the museum is a tribute to the car company's development. The exterior construction of the BMW Welt was completed in 2006, which was the same year the Jonas Brothers' smash hit *Year 3000* was released. Coincidence? We don't think so. At the Welt, visitors can sit in Mini Coopers, wish they could sit in Rolls Royces, and shop the BMW lifestyle brand, while the museum presents exhibitions on the company's history, successes, and philosophies. That said, don't expect the museum to linger on its mistakes (including its darker history as an automaker for the Nazis).

i BMW Welt free, museum €10, students €7; last entry to museum 30min. before closing; wheelchair accessible

FOOD

◪ MARAIS GESCHMACKSACHEN ($)

Parkstraße 2; 89 50094552; www.cafe-marais.de; open Tu-Sa 8am-8pm, Su 10am-6pm

Serving cakes, croissants, and all sorts of coffee, Marais is a corner café frequented mostly by locals, with a menu entirely in German. But don't let that scare you off, "cappuccino" is the same in every language. Marais also offers paninis and other breakfasts, but our favorite part is the atmosphere, as it is also an antique shop. Almost everything in the café is for sale, so come here for coffee and you could end up buying a vintage tea kettle, dozens of new but old-looking postcards, or even the table where you sat down to enjoy your quiche.

i Entrées from €6.50, paninis €6.20; vegetarian options available; limited wheelchair accessibility

COTIDIANO ($)

Gärtnerplatz 6; 89 242078610; www.cotidiano.de; open M-Th 7:30am-10pm, F-Sa 7:30am-11pm, Su 7:30am-9pm

We ended up at Cotidiano when we were told that this was the best breakfast place in Munich. The café may be one more example of people abroad having no idea what an "American Breakfast" is, claiming that it's an oven-baked croissant filled with scrambled eggs and cheese, but we stuffed ourselves with that egg-filled croissant and loved every second of it.

i Entrées from €10; vegan and vegetarian options available; limited wheelchair accessibility

HACKERHAUS ($)

Sendlinger Straße 14; 89 2605026; www.hackerhaus.de; open daily 10am-midnight, kitchen closes at 11:30pm

Hackerhaus is the restaurant of Hackerbräu, a major brewery that dates back to the fifteenth century. The Hackerhaus has been burned down, rebuilt, bought and sold again, changing hands between the Hacker and Pschorr families for more than 200 years. Eventually, Hackerhaus was renovated and reopened by the Pongratz family in the 1980s. We recommend taking a look at their daily specials; that's where we found their homemade potato pancakes, served with thick, creamy apple sauce. To feel like you're sitting in a Bavarian hunting lodge, we recommend eating indoors.

i Entrées from €8; card minimum €15; limited wheelchair accessibility

LEDU HAPPY DUMPLINGS ($)

Theresienstraße 18; 89 95898460; www.ledu-dumpling.de; open M-Th 11:30am-9:30pm, F 11:30am-10pm, Sa noon-10pm, Su noon-9:30pm

A tiny storefront serving up big dreams, LeDU Happy Dumplings uses fresh ingredients to make Chinese dumpling concoctions that really will make you happy. Put in an order for 10 dumplings (€7.90), decide whether you want them steamed or pan-fried, and soon you'll have a pile of piping hot, puckered noodles steaming in front of you.

i 10 dumplings €7.90; vegan and vegetarian options available; limited wheelchair accessibility

ZUM FRANZISKANER ($)

Residenzstraße 9; 89 2318120; www.
zum-franziskaner.de

Just across the plaza from the **Residenz palace,** Zum Franziskaner is a little expensive for a casual meal, but a great place to stop for appetizers to share. Our favorite is the *weißbier-obatzda* (white beer obatzda), a Bavarian cheese delicacy and beer garden essential. The dish, made by mixing together an aged, soft cheese (Zum Franziskaner uses camembert, but we've seen recipes with others), butter, seasonings such as paprika powder, and a little bit of beer turns the concoction into a schmear. Spread the cheese over bread, pile it high with onions, and take a bite.
i Appetizers from €10, entrées from €11; cash preferred; vegetarian options available; limited wheelchair accessibility

NIGHTLIFE

⛩ CHINESISCHER TURM (CHINESE TOWER)

Englischer Garten 3; 89 38387327; www.
chinaturm.de; open daily 10am-10pm

The Chinesischer Turm is our favorite beer garden in Munich. Planted in the middle of the **Englischer Garten,** the Chinesischer Turm feels like a real garden, with immediate access to the park's many paths, swimming holes on the park's waterways, and expansive grass fields. The location encourages you to stroll through the park and take your time outdoors. The beer garden's namesake, the Chinese Tower, is a structure with pagoda-style architecture looming over the garden, built in the late eighteenth century. If you're headed for a picnic in the park, you might as well bring your food to the garden and add a fresh and frothy beer to the mix.
i No cover, liter from €6; cash preferred; wheelchair accessible

089 BAR

Maximiliansplatz 5; 89 59988890; 089-bar.
de; open Tu-Sa 9pm-7am

This bar is a great place to party with a young crowd, plus the occasional too-old-for-this dude trying his best to blend in. We came to the club sick of DJs who remix songs by slowing down the lyrics and speeding up the beat, a trend that we

hope dies soon, and we didn't have to put up with any of that here. We even heard Chris Brown remixed into House of Pain's "Jump Around," to which the crowd went wild. There's no need to dress up, but we'd ballpark that when we visited around 50% of the men were wearing black jeans and white Calvin Klein t-shirts, so keep that in mind.
i Cover €5; cash only; no wheelchair accessibility

HOFBRÄUHAUS

Platzl 9; 89 29013610; www.hofbraeuhaus.
de; open daily 9am-11:30pm

The Hofbräuhaus in Munich is one of the cities largest and most-frequented beer halls, packed with tourists, but worth a visit. Here, a lederhosen-clad band plays traditional Bavarian music while tourists clap along, swept up in the excitement of the accordion player, a relatable feeling, right? Although the beers are a little overpriced because of the tourist appeal, seeing the history of the famous beer hall that was open only to royalty until the late 1820s is worth a couple extra euros. A standard pour here is a full liter, and though they'll reluctantly serve you a half liter if you ask, you won't find smaller measures on the menu. The bigger, the better.
i No cover, beer liter from €8-10

MILCHUNDBAR

Sonnenstraße 27; 89 45028818; www.
milchundbar.de; open daily 24hr

Milchundbar is just large enough to fit a fully-stocked bar and just small enough that you'll get good and sweaty as soon as everyone starts moving. As you dance, steam is deployed through vents and descends to the dance floor, creating a colorful haze just thin enough to see the face of the person grinding next to you. If that's not enough, the DJ occasionally activates a smoke machine to cover the dance floor in a white cloud (hence the "milk" component of Milchundbar's name, which translates to "milk and bar"). Milchundbar is particularly popular on Wednesday nights and doesn't start getting busy until about midnight. Once it does, however, the party won't stop until 9am.
i Cover from €5

GERMANY ESSENTIALS

MONEY

Tipping: Service staff are paid by the hour, and a service charge is included in an item's unit price. It's customary and polite to tip your waiter normally. To tip, mention the total to your waiter while paying. If he states that the bill is €9, respond "€10," and he will include the tip, or just hand him a €10 and tell him to keep the change. It is standard to tip a taxi driver at least €1, and public toilet attendants around €0.50.

Taxes: Most goods in Germany are subject to a value-added tax or *mehrwertsteuer* (MwSt)—of 19%, which is included in the purchase price of goods (a reduced tax of 7% is applied to books and magazines, food, and agricultural products). Non-EU visitors who are taking these goods home unused may be refunded this tax for goods totaling over €25 per store. When making purchases, request a MwSt or tax-free form and present it at a Tax-Free Shopping Office. Refunds must be claimed within six months.

SAFETY AND HEALTH

Local Laws and Police: City regulations might seem weird and unusual. Drinking in public is perfectly acceptable while jaywalking is practically unheard of (it carries a €5 fine).

Drugs and Alcohol: The drinking age in Germany is 16 for beer and wine and 18 for spirits. The maximum blood alcohol content level for drivers is 0.05%. Although drinking in public is legal, it's smart to avoid public drunkenness; it can jeopardize your safety and earn the disdain of locals. Needless to say, illegal drugs are best avoided. Possession of small quantities of marijuana and hashish for personal use is legal in Germany. Each region has interpreted "small quantities" differently (anywhere from 5 to 30 grams). Carrying drugs across an international border is a serious offense that could land you in prison.

Prescription Drugs: Common drugs such as aspirin (*Kopfschmerztablette* or Aspirin), acetaminophen or Tylenol (*Paracetamol*), ibuprofen or Advil, antihistamines (*Antihistaminika*), and penicillin (*Penizillin*) are available at German pharmacies. Some drugs—like pseudoephedrine (Sudafed) and diphenhydramine (Benadryl)—are not available in Germany, or are only available with a prescription, so plan accordingly.

GREAT BRITAIN

Stop whatever you're doing and make a list of Great Britain-related things.

Keep going. Okay, stop. Were Liverpool's heartthrobs (aka the Beatles) on the list? What about football? No, not the kind that involves huge pads and smashing into other people, the kind that features grown men playing out a unique form of theatrical drama and graceful penalty kicks. Did you write down fish and chips, the heartiest of culinary creations and quite possibly your only source of sustenance as you visit the British isles? Plaid? Kilts? Blood sausage? Look it up. Sherlock Holmes, Ivanhoe, Middlemarch, Pride and Prejudice? Britain is a treasure trove for literature lovers. And, of course, we can't forget haggis. Great Britain is indeed all of these things, but is far more than the sum of its parts. Its long history means that you can walk through a museum to discover it, or walk through the streets of London or a small village to find the remnants of a time long past. Its political system is complicated enough that you have to do a lot of reading. Its cuisine is out-there yet comforting enough to appeal to many. And though its role in the world has changed over the course of hundreds of years, Great Britain somehow always makes itself known. From Elizabeth I's reign to the English Civil War and the execution of Charles I, to World War II, to today (Brexit, anyone?), the region has its own story to tell. Even now, it continues to evolve, as its place in the European Union appears precarious—yet one thing is certain: just like it always has, the world will continue watching every move it makes.

EDINBURGH

Coverage by **Lucy Golub**

A modern day city surrounding a twelfth-century castle built on an extinct volcano: Edinburgh sounds basically like an enchanting fairy tale. Edinburgh feels like a cross-hatching of time. Each stone is steeped in history. Home to thinkers like Adam Smith and David Hume who changed the way we live today, as well as countless other artists and figures, Edinburgh has the street cred to support the cultural name it's forged for itself. Combining stunning nature, history, and significant contributions to modern theatre (a month-long festival every year!), Edinburgh is a city that offers more to do the more you explore. Old-fashioned pubs offer pints while bagpipers in kilts busk on the street. Are we in 2019 or 1819? Edinburgh's beauty comes from the way it harkens to both. So climb those stairs, take your 10,000 steps, have a sip of whiskey, perhaps a bite of haggis (or not), and get ready to discover a time capsule of European history.

ORIENTATION

The Edinburgh Castle provides an almost-always visible guide to where you are. If you're close to the castle and the buildings around you look old, you're likely in the **Old Town,** the center of the city. **The Royal Mile** leads you past a bunch of souvenir shops to the castle. Almost parallel to the Royal Mile, **Grassmarket** and **Cowgate** house relaxed yet hip nightlife and restaurants. Between the old town and the new town, **Waverley Station** is a hub of train activity that can take you west towards **Haymarket** or east towards the airport. Nearby, **Princes Street** begins the **New Town,** home to more upscale shops, restaurants, and nightlife.

ESSENTIALS

GETTING THERE

The airport offers an easy tram service to multiple locations around the city for only £4.50 one way or £7.50 round trip. It runs 24hr and comes every 15min. You can buy tickets with cash or card when you board. There are also two central train stations connected to the Scotrail system: Edinburgh Waverley and Haymarket. Waverley is closer to New Town and Old Town, and Haymarket is best for trips outside the city center.

GETTING AROUND

Good news! Edinburgh has Uber. Even better news! You won't need it. The city is easy to walk when it's not too cold, and there's cheap public transportation. A tram runs through Princes Street, and 24hr bus services can take you anywhere you need to go. The Transport for Edinburgh app lets you buy tickets for the tram or bus on your phone—otherwise, they take exact cash for their £1.70 fare. An app named MyTaxi or old-fashioned hailing a cab in the street are both alternatives for evening travel after a night out. Day tickets for public transport are your best best if you plan on taking the bus or tram more than once.

PRACTICAL INFORMATION

Tourist Offices: Most information can be found online, but a few offices exist if you have any in-person questions. (Edinburgh and Scotland Information Centre, Visitscotland, 3 Princes Street, 131 473 3868; www.visitscotland.com; Apr 1-June 2 open M-Sa 9am-5pm, Su 10am-5pm; June 3-30 open M-Sa 9am-6pm, Su 10am-6pm; July 1-Sept 8 open M-Sa 9am-7pm, Su 10am-7pm; Sept 9-March 31 open M-Sa 9am-5pm, Su 10am-5pm).

Banks/ATMs/Currency Exchange: Bank of Scotland has branches in multiple locations, and so do HSBC, BNY Mellon, and Barclays (Bank of Scotland; 300 Lawnmarket; 131 470 2007; bankofscotland.co.uk; open M-Tu 9am-5pm, W 9:30am-5pm, Th-F 9am-5pm).

Post Offices: There are post offices in every neighborhood. (3 Princes Street; 034 5611 2970; open M 9am-5pm, Tu 9:30am-5:30pm, W-Sa 9am-5:30pm).

Public Restrooms: The city offers 61 public toilets spread throughout. (Castlehill Public Toilet; 131 608 1100; open daily 10am-6pm, summer open daily 8am-6pm).

Internet: Most of the city center has free public Wi-Fi, as do the buses. It is also widely available in cafés and other public spaces.

BGLTQ+ Resources: LGBT Health and Wellbeing (9 Howe Street; www.lgbthealth.org.uk; 131 523 1100; open M-F 9am-5pm)

EMERGENCY INFORMATION

Emergency Number: 999

Police: Police Scotland (14 St. Leonard's Street; 178 628 9070; open M-F 9am-12:30pm and 1:30-5pm)

US Embassy: Consulate General of the United States (3 Regent Terrace; 131 556 8315; open M-F 8:30am-5pm)

Rape Crisis Center: A hotline can be found at 08088 01 003 02, and you can go to Edinburgh Rape Crisis Center (17 Claremont Crescent; 131 556 9437; open M-F 9am-7pm).

Hospitals:
- Royal Infirmary of Edinburgh; 51 Little France Crescent; 131 536 1000; open daily 24hr
- St John's Hospital; Howden West, Livingston, West Lothian; 150 653 2000; open daily 24hr

Pharmacies: These can be found scattered throughout the city.
- Boots: 101-103 Princes Street; 013 1225 8331; boots.com; open M-W 8am-7pm, Th 8am-8pm, F-Sa 8am-7pm, Su 10am-6pm.

ACCOMMODATIONS

EDINBURGH BACKPACKERS ($)

65 Cockburn St.; 131 220 2200; www.edinburghbackpackershostel.com; reception open 24hr

Located directly at the center of **The Royal Mile** in **Old Town,** on a small curving road named Cockburn Street (pronounced "co-burn"—definitely don't pronounce that wrong) across from **The Baked Potato Shop** and loads of pubs, you won't find a better location. Clean and central with comfy enough beds and spacious lockers, Edinburgh Backpackers allows you to get a bang for your buck. While this hostel doesn't forge a super strong sense of community because of its vertical layout, they offer a kitchen, pool tables and darts, as well as Monday trivia nights. Dormitories range from five to 18 beds, with private rooms available in their four buildings. Reception checks for your key card when you enter—so no sneaking in new friends.

i Dorms from £11, private rooms from £57; no elevator; Wi-Fi; laundry; kitchen, game room

KICK ASS HOSTELS ($)

37-39 Cowgate; 131 226 6351; kickass-hostels.co.uk; reception open 24hr

Located right on **Grassmarket,** Kick Ass Hostels sits at the border of a fun nightlife scene and tons of restaurants, making it a centrally located and noisy option for travelers. Run by the same team as **Budget Backpackers Hostel** and boasting a bar and café for guests, Kick Ass emphasizes a social environment. You'll find travelers revving to go on their pub crawl (£5 for 4 shots and free entry all night). The linens are clean, the beds are cheap, and the people are friendly.

i Dorms from £12, private rooms from £60; reservation required; min 1 night; limited wheelchair accessibility; Wi-Fi; kitchen; towels, adapters, locks available for rent

ROYAL MILE BACKPACKERS ($)

105 High St.; 131 557 6120; royalmile-backpackers.com; reception hours 6am-3:30am

Royal Mile Backpackers, is, in one word, "cozy." With only six rooms, a small kitchen, and a homey common area with a fireplace right near the entrance, Royal Mile Backpackers feels like a friend's place rather than a big hotel. The steep and narrow steps walking up to reception could also be considered quite cozy, but luckily, all the rooms are located on the same floor of the building. Some dorms offer plants and seating, and each comes with a USB plug and light. Good for light sleepers, the bunk beds are wood, not metal, avoiding that inevitable creaky noise that comes from trying to sneak

up a ladder in the middle of the night. Royal Mile guests have access to the facilities at their sister hostels (**High Street Hostel** and **Castle Rock Hostel**) too, making this hostel an ideal place for a person seeking a warm and welcoming bed without a party vibe.

i Dorms from £12; cash only; reservation recommended; volunteers stay long term; no wheelchair accessibility; Wi-Fi; laundry service and breakfast for a fee

SIGHTS
CULTURE

🎨 DEAN VILLAGE AND WALK OF LEITH
Leith

After a busy day in the city, there's no better way to spend an hour on a sunny afternoon than a walk along the port on Leith's walkway and take a trip to Dean Village. A residential area outside of the city center, Dean Village comprises enchanting homes from the nineteenth century. The precious homes look like they're taken out of a storybook, making it hard to believe that people get to live there. Nearby **Mews** present picturesque homes to snap pictures of, but be sure to be respectful of the residents. Expect a leisurely walk to take about an hour. You can walk to the village from the **Royal Mile** (about 20min.), or take the bus (24, 29, or 42) to **Stockbridge,** and you can walk from the bridge of the Water of Leith to the **Modern Art Gallery** to embrace the full views.

i Free

GRASSMARKET
www.greatergrassmarket.co.uk; store and restaurant hours vary

Lively and bustling, Grassmarket provides an unparalleled view of the castle between the street's independent shops and restaurants. Some gems include **Oink** and **Mary's Milk Bar.** Next to Grassmarket, **Victoria Street**—the inspiration for J.K. Rowling's Diagon Alley—curves down from the hill. If you're trying to find a souvenir different from the kilts, shortbread, and whiskey at every tourist shop, Grassmarket's stores will answer your query. In the middle of the road, buskers play music on a central median, entertaining those eating at the restaurants outside. Steep staircases lead into the area from the castle, creating an air of centrality and reminding tourists that people used to be hanged right where they're currently enjoying lunch. Heartwarming.

i Free; store and restaurant prices; limited wheelchair accessibility

GREYFRIARS KIRKYARD
26A Candlemaker Row; greyfriarskirk.com/visit-us/kirkyard; open daily 24hr

Harry Potter fans rejoice—here you'll find the graves of a William McGonagall and Thomas Riddell, while some even claim the neighboring school **George Heriot** to be the inspiration for Hogwarts. For those not *Harry Potter*-inclined, the cemetery is still worth a visit. Estimations project over 100,000 bodies are buried in the hill of the cemetery, so you might occasionally find a bone. Yet as you walk through immaculately kept trees and flowers and families picnicking, you'll almost forget that the park is a graveyard. The cemetery is home to the legend of **Greyfriar's Bobby,** the most loyal dog there ever was, and his memorial can be found right outside the graveyard. Seemingly sacrilegious, high school-aged students have been heard to frequent the cemetery after dark with new friends made at the pub.

i Free; limited wheelchair accessibility

LANDMARKS

🏰 EDINBURGH CASTLE

Castlehill; 131 225 9846; www.edinburgh-castle.scot; open daily Mar 26-Sept 30 9:30am-6pm, Oct 1-Mar 31 9:30am-5pm

You can't come to Edinburgh without seeing the city's castle; after all, Edinburgh is practically in its shadow. To really experience its majesty, though, you've got to go inside. Cough up the fee and allot two hours to walk around and explore. The torture demonstration might curdle your blood a little bit, and the war memorials have caused visitors to shed tears. The real treasure lies with the crown jewels—but not the diamonds. No, the real treasure is found with the Stone of Destiny, which is basically a giant rock. It's said that wherever the stone lies, the Scots shall rule. Hundreds of years of history pack themselves into the castle, and stepping in feels like stepping back in time.

i *Admission from £17, student from £10.20; last entry 1hr before closing; limited wheelchair accessibility*

CALTON HILL

2 Regent Rd.; open daily 24hr

Hands down the best place to watch the sunset in Edinburgh. Overlooking the whole city with a view of Arthur's seat, golden hour makes the hills glimmer. The hill itself contains landmarks within it, like the **National Monument,** a half finished acropolis-like structure that looms over the skyline. In fact, the monument itself at the top of the hill provides the best vantage point of the glow reflected on the yellow Gorse flowers and the glinting snowy hills in Holyrood park, or even of the slowly sinking sun. Couples and families picnic to enjoy the view of the setting sun over the dreamlike city. No, our eyes aren't tearing up at the beauty—it's just the wind.

i *Free; no wheelchair accessibility; trails lead to Holyrood Park*

ST. GILES

High St.; 131 226 0674; www.stgilescathedral.org.uk; open April-Oct M-F 9am-7pm, Sa 9am-5pm, Su 1pm-5pm; Nov-Mar M-Sa 9am-5pm, Su 1pm-5pm

Stained-glass windows light up the room, and a hushed silence that comes from centuries of worship falls over the tourists who step inside. Each window tells a story, just like every name on benches and inscribed into walls. A cathedral of secret histories. A £2 photo doesn't really do the cathedral justice, but standing in the middle of the church under the flags of Scotland and the high arched ceiling creates tranquility. Services and concerts ring out on certain days of the week. A moment inside the church lets you forget the aggressive musicians outside on **the Royal Mile** and focus on Edinburgh's real draw: its history.

i *Free, photo permit £2; main cathedral wheelchair accessible*

MUSEUMS

🏛 NATIONAL MUSEUM

Chambers St.; 300 123 6789; www.nms.ac.uk/national-museum-of-scotland; open daily 10am-5pm

You could spend days in this museum and not see everything, so it's probably best not to try. But the highlights you shouldn't miss include the **Millennial clock** that animates every hour from 11am to 4pm, the Scottish history and archaeology galleries, the interactive screens, and machines (read: toys) in the science and technology galleries. If you're interested in literally anything in the world, this museum probably has information on it. Scottish pop music? Check. Festivals in Vietnam? Check. A giant stuffed alpaca next to a polar bear? Also check. And if you're unsure where to begin or tired of a paper map, check the museum's app.

i *Free; wheelchair accessible; tours at 11am, 1pm, and 3pm*

NATIONAL GALLERY OF MODERN ART

75 Belford Rd.; 131 624 6200; www.nationalgalleries.org/visit/scottish-national-gallery-modern-art; open daily 10am-5pm

Two majestic buildings provide hundreds of pieces of art for perusal, picturesque cafés, and outdoor areas for relaxation. Connecting the spaces is an outdoor sculpture gallery. Exhibits change every few months, but make sure to check out the reconstruction of sculptor Eduardo Paolozzi's studio in the Modern Two building, so you can drink up all the bright colors and learn about how the Edinburgh native (his parents were Italian immigrants, if you're confused) pioneered the pop art movement. Bus #13 offers an easy connection from Princes Street, but for the best route you should walk through **Dean Village.** Some exhibits charge, but most are free, and we recommend just skipping anything you have to pay for, because there's so much to see already between the two buildings.

i Free; wheelchair accessible; lockers £1; wheelchair accessible

SCOTTISH NATIONAL GALLERY

The Mound; 131 624 6200; www.nationalgalleries.org; open M-W 10am-5pm, Th 10am-7pm, F-Su 10am-5pm

The National Gallery hosts Scotland's greatest works on permanent display for free. On Scotland's cloudy days, this centrally located museum provides a crimson-walled spot for an afternoon at the museum. The first rooms hold the Bridgewater loan—some of the most prized art on the continent. (Island?) While art aficionados may flock to the **Rembrandt** and **Titian** pieces, those looking for interesting and funny works shouldn't miss Henry Raeburn's *The Skating Minister.* Even those with no interest in art can enjoy a stroll through the museum with rooms that are easy to navigate. The museum also hosts classes and other special events like tours, talks, live music and BSL interpretations, most of which are free to attend. Beware of the noisy bagpipers on the street walking in, though.

i Free; wheelchair accessible

OUTDOORS

ARTHUR'S SEAT

Queen's Dr.; open daily 24hr

Don't think you can hike? Try anyway. Reaching the summit of Arthur's Seat feels like the making it to the top of the world. All of Edinburgh sprawls below your feet. There are multiple routes, and our recommendation is the path that begins from **Queen Street** next to the **Holyrood Palace.** From there, follow the left path to the top. Various stopping points along the way encourage you to take in the juxtaposition of the extinct volcano's natural beauty and the city. If you go at sunrise or sunset, it's especially picturesque. But if the weather is good, you'll have to brave the crowds no matter the time. And hey, if that couple with gray hair can make it up to the very top, you can, too.

i Free; no wheelchair accessibility

FOOD

BRUNCH AND SUPPER ($$)

37-39 George IV Bridge; 131 225 6690; brunchandsupper.co.uk; brunch M-Sa 8am-4pm, Su 10am-4pm; dinner Tu-Sa 6pm-10:30pm

Once known as simply "Brunch," this restaurant has expanded to serve two meals. You can probably guess what they are. But it's not just a gimmick—the food is excellent. I mean, the brunch menu contains both sweet AND savory pancakes: what more could you want? Those looking for something healthy can get the veggie burrito or porridge, but why not just order a scone and live a little? They don't take reservations for brunch and get busy on the weekends, but the menu options provide something for everyone. And the portions are huge.

i Entrées from £7; vegan and vegetarian options available; reservations for dinner available

OINK ($)

34 Victoria St.; 077 7196 8233; www.oinkhogroast.co.uk; open M-Su 11am-5pm

If you don't like seeing a giant dead pig, this isn't the place for you. But if you're looking for cheap and delicious hog roast, Oink is a must. Once you step in the door, the smell of perfectly cooked pig will overwhelm you. Sizes range from a snack to a full meal. They go through a full pig everyday (plus a few extra "bums"), and when it's out, it's out. Choose your bread and you'll receive a heaping portion of pork. With four locations around the city, meat eaters can't miss Oink.

i Piglet from £3.10; no vegetarian options; limited wheelchair accessibility

NIGHTLIFE

🍸 LUCKY LIQUOR CO. ($)

39A Queen St.; 131 226 3976; www.luckyli-quorco.com; open daily 4pm-1am

Thirteen is the lucky number here. Thirteen homemade liqueurs complete 13 specialty cocktails that have a home on the menu for only 13 weeks. Way tinier than a typical bar, Lucky Liquor Co. feels intimate, with small drinks on small circular tables. Along the back wall, this season's colorful liquors glow. Because of their focus on limited liquors, the bartenders make every garnish and ingredient by hand, so you know the stone fruit shrub and dill-infused Akvavit cocktail you're getting is top notch. We don't know what those words mean either, but we do know the drinks are delicious and worth the price. With craft cocktails and a tiny space, you might assume that you'll be served by pretentious hipsters, but luckily that's not the case—the staff is down-to-earth and knowledgeable about their ingredients, adding the finishing touch to a pretty great bar.

i Drinks from £4, cocktails from £7; BGLTQ+ friendly; limited wheelchair accessibility

🍺 ST. ANDREWS BREWERY COMPANY ($$)

32-34 Potterrow; 131 662 9788; www. standrewsbrewingcompany.com; open daily noon-1am

Walking into St. Andrews Brewing Company feels like getting home after a long day. Musicians strum guitars and croon slow pop-punk songs on Thursdays, Fridays, and Saturdays. You'll find yourself surrounded by garden-themed decorations, but somehow it doesn't feel tacky. Big terracotta pots holding plants hang from the ceiling, and you can spot small buckets and shovels along the wooden walls and small booths as you sip on a £2.50 gin and tonic or a 2 for £8 house special cocktails or one of their many craft beers. Located near the **University of Edinburgh,** students chat, sing along, and enjoy their food, all the while lit by candlelight.

i No cover, drinks from £2.50, entrées from £13; BGLTQ+ friendly; wheelchair accessible; open mic on Th; live local musicians F-Sa

GLASGOW

Coverage by **Lucy Golub**

Glasgow's city motto can be read from the center square, where you'll find a bright pink sign emblazoned with the words "People Make Glasgow." And it's true. While often overlooked in favor of charming Edinburgh, Glasgow's thriving music scene, art venues, museums and shopping leave little to be desired. It takes a local to make you fall in love with the city, so when a friendly Glaswegian chats with you at a pub, listen. When they talk about what life is like for them, you'll hear about their version of the city, learn about the film festival of the week, and discover the latest gig in this UNESCO World Heritage music city. While the early twentieth-century **Charles Rennie Mackintosh** architecture in the city center creates a grand outer body for the city, the real bloodline comes from the people, who open your eyes to the creativity bubbling around every corner. Glasgow is *real*. The city isn't made for tourists, but since you're here anyway, let the people show you around. After all, the life inside is what makes it worth it.

ORIENTATION

This large city is split up into different areas, each with a distinct personality. The north part of the city above **The River Clyde** is home to the city center with **Buchanan Street, Merchant City,** and **St. Enochs Square.** Further north lies **Sauchiehall Street,** which contains much of the nightlife scene. To the west, **Kelvingrove Park** and the **West End** are home to greenery and cute cafés. Between the West End and the center, **Finnieston** is home to new trendy restaurants, the neighborhood a victim of recent gentrification. Finally, to the east, the **Glasgow Cathedral** and other attractions are only a 25min. walk from the center.

ESSENTIALS

GETTING THERE

Glasgow is easily accessible by bus (Citylink or Megabus) as well as train on the Scotrail, which stops at Glasgow Central and Glasgow Queen Street. The airport is about 15min. from the city, and buses can be caught from Buchanan Street. The Airport Express departs about every 10min. and is £7.50.

GETTING AROUND

Buses or walking are the easiest ways to get around the city. You can also hail taxis on the street, although students usually use Uber. Another option is Glasgow Taxis, a large taxi company. The subway is small and runs in a circle, and day tickets are available for £4.10 for an all-day pass. Bus passes can be purchased for £4.50 for all-day, otherwise they accept contactless credit cards or exact change.

PRACTICAL INFORMATION

Tourist Offices: VisitScotland Glasgow iCentre (156a/158 Buchanan Street; www.visitscotland.com/info/services/glasgow-icentre-p332751; Nov-Apr open M-Sa 9am-5pm; May-Oct open M-W 9am-6pm, Th 9:30am-6pm, F-Sa 9am-6pm, Su 10am-4pm; July-Aug open M-W 9am-6pm, Th 9:30am-6pm, F-Sa 9am-6pm)
Banks/ATMs/Currency Exchange: There are many banks and ATMs on the streets.
- Barclays ATM (5 George Square; 343 734 9354; open daily 24hr)
- Bank of Scotland (54-62 Sauchiehall St; 141 532 9204; open M-F 9am-5pm, Sa 9am-4pm)

Post Offices: Post offices are limited in the city. (136 West Nile St.; 354 611 2970; open M-Sa 9am-5:30pm)
Public Restrooms: Public restrooms are rare, but most restaurants and cafés have them (43 St Vincent Pl.; 141 287 9700; open daily 24hr)
Internet: Public Wi-Fi is available around the city, and many cafés and restaurants offer it as well.
BGLTQ+ Resources: LGBT Youth Scotland (30 Bell St (3/2); 141 552 7425; www.lgbtyouth.org.uk)

EMERGENCY INFORMATION

Emergency Number: 9990. The non-emergency medical number is 111.
Police: Baird Street Police (6 Baird St.; www.scotland.police.uk/police-stations/greater-glasgow/153070; open daily 8am-6pm, closed 12:30pm-1:30pm)
US Embassy: There is no US Embassy in Glasgow, but there is a Consulate General of the US in Edinburgh (3 Regent Terr.; 131 556 8315; open M-F 8:30am-5pm).
Rape Crisis Center: Rape Crisis Centre (30 Bell St.; 141 552 3201; www.glasgowclyderapecrisis.org.uk)
Hospitals:
- Glasgow Royal Infirmary (84 Castle St.; 141 211 4000; emergency room open 24hr)
- Queen Elizabeth Hospital (1345 Govan Rd.; 121 627 2000; open daily 24hr)

Pharmacies:
- High Street Pharmacy (128 High St.; 141 552 5929; M-F 9am-6pm, Sa 9am-5:30pm)
- Abbey Chemist (83 Trongate; 141 552 2528; M-Sa 9am-5:30pm)

ACCOMMODATIONS

🏠 EUROHOSTEL ($$)

318 Clyde St.; 8455 399 956; www.euro-hostels.co.uk; reception open 24hr

Big white bunk beds create an almost sterile appearance that's only partially countered by the red walls and smart TVs in each room. EuroHostel offers clean beds, a fun bar, and many en suite bathrooms. Save for a lack of easy-to-find lockers, Eurohostel was way more than "EH." The Wi-Fi is fast and every amenity is available for rent or purchase at reception. Although the bathrooms are small, EuroHostel is our top recommendation for a social, safe, and clean room in Glasgow. Near to the city center and **Buchanan Street** and on the edge of the **Clyde River,** the location is ideal as well.

i Dorms from £10; reservation recommended; wheelchair accessible; Wi-Fi; laundry room, towels and locks for rent; linens provided, luggage storage £1; breakfast available

GLASGOW YOUTH HOSTEL (SYHA HOSTELLING SCOTLAND) ($)

8 Park Terr.; 141 332 3004; www.syha.org.uk/where-to-stay/lowlands/glasgow/; reception open 24hr

All age ranges are welcome in this white building in a quiet area next to **Kelvingrove Park.** For a weary traveller looking for a quiet and relaxed place to rest, Glasgow Youth Hostel will not disappoint. Wi-Fi doesn't reach the rooms, but a lounge and another common room offer access. The reception stocks guides to the city, provides a daily "What's On" board, and offers super-knowledgeable and friendly staff. Wood staircases welcome you in, reminding guests that this grand building used to be an actual hotel. While the dorms are definitely not luxurious—it is a hostel, after all—Glasgow Youth Hostel offers a clean and relaxed atmosphere a little outside of the city center, and we have no complaints.

i Beds from £14; reservation recommended; max stay 21 days; limited wheelchair accessibility; Wi-Fi; laundry; linens provided, game room

HOT TUB HOSTEL ($)

62 Berkeley St.; hottubhostel.co.uk

Hot Tub Hostel offers a cheap, clean, no-frills accommodation—and a hot tub. With only eight rooms ranging from four-person to 10-person mixed dorms, as well as small bathrooms and showers, Hot Tub Hostel is a true backpacker's hostel. The hot tub sits beside the common room with sagging but comfortable couches. If inclined to cook, guests can use sister hostel Clyde Hostel's kitchen. The hostel is a 15min. walk from both the **West End** and the city center, and it's only a few minutes from the rowdy **Sauchiehall Street,** making it an ideal choice for a budget traveler looking to go out on the town.

i Dorms from £10; reservation recommended; limited wheelchair accessibility; Wi-Fi; linens provided; hot tub use free; age range 18-35 years old

SIGHTS
CULTURE

🏠 ASHTON LANE

Ashton Ln.; establishment hours vary

The cosmopolitan **West End** is filled with bars and restaurants that surround the cobbled streets, with vines hanging overhead. Ashton Lane brings a quaint air to an industrial city, briefly allowing you to forget the bustle only a few minutes' walk away. A small cinema connects to a bright and rustic themed restaurant called **The Gardener,** where you can order brunch and bring some of the menu items inside, or go for a bite then a show. (Trust us: the gnocchi bites are a must.) On Sundays, market stalls fill the street selling food and crafts. Although the street is small, it's lively and picturesque, and a perfect spot to have lunch before checking out the nearby **Hunterian Museum** or **Kelvingrove Park.**

i Prices vary; wheelchair accessibility varies

BUCHANAN STREET

Buchanan St.; establishment hours vary

A mile-long shopping street begins at **Sauchiehall Street** and spans the remaining length down to **St. Enoch Square.** If you're looking for a brand-name store, you'll find it here. From international powerhouses like H&M to random tacky tourist shops, if you're in a purchasing mood, Buchanan Street has your answer. You'll also find two Starbucks locations across the street from each other and a busker or magician every few steps. Busy businesspeople push past meandering tourists as they gawk at the architecture, and parents chase children keen on running away. If not to shop, Buchanan Street is the place to people-watch, reminding you that Glasgow is a living, breathing, thriving city.

i *Prices vary; wheelchair accessibility varies*

GLASGOW FILM THEATER

12 Rose St.; 141 332 6535; www.glasgow-film.org; box office open Su-F noon-15min. after start of final film, Sa 11am-15min. after start of final film

Glasgow Film Theater isn't a regular movie theater; it's a cool movie theater. They feature different flicks ranging from big-budget classics to to National Theater Live screenings to niche productions that the manager found at film festivals. Best of all, a bar upstairs serves Scottish snacks and drinks that guests are encouraged to bring into the theater. This is no AMC. Elegant stairs and walls made from dark wood highlight the upscale nature of the venue. If you're lucky, come for one of the film festivals hosted here and experience the true Glasgow artsy film scene. Or come to the Moana sing-along... who are we to judge?

i *Adults £10.50, students £7.50, shows on Tu and F £6.50; wheelchair accessible; captioned; autism-friendly, and dementia-friendly showings available*

LANDMARKS

CATHEDRAL AND THE NECROPOLIS

Castle St.; www.glasgowcathedral.org; open Oct-Mar M-Sa 10am-4pm, Su 1pm-3:30pm, lower church closes 3:15pm; April-Sept M-Sa 9:30am-5:30pm, Su 1pm-4:30pm, lower church closes at 4:45pm

Thousands of visitors have walked through and prayed in this stained-glass-filled stone church. The cathedral still hosts services, as well as recitals, amplified by the echo from the vast arches above. Nearby, 50,000 bodies lay to rest in the Necropolis, including a memorial to John Knox, even though he isn't buried here. The tombstones loom over the horizon, themselves works of art, and some of which were designed by **Charles Rennie Mackintosh.** It's a little creepy perusing the graves, but the expansiveness and intricacy of each makes the Necropolis worth a wander.

i *Free; tours available; last entry 30min. before closing; limited wheelchair accessibility*

GLASGOW CITY CHAMBERS

George Sq.; 141 287 4018; ww.glasgow. gov.uk/index.aspx?articleid=19136; open M-F 8:30am-5pm

You might want to consider running for Glasgow city government just to enter this building. Alternatively, you can take one of their guided tours to explore the inside of this massive icon, right in **George Square.** The definition of "City Chambers" remains unclear after the visit, but what we do know is that the building is stunning. Tall ceilings with aligning arches evoke images of castles, while long staircases complete with marble and detailed tile mosaics makes you wonder just how much money the government of Glasgow really has. The building hosts events and awards ceremonies, but is there an award for how stunning the building itself is? There should be.

i *Free; free 45min. tours at 10:30am, 2:30pm; wheelchair accessible*

GREAT BRITAIN GLASGOW

LIGHTHOUSE

11 Mitchell Ln.; 141 276 5365; www.thelighthouse.co.uk; open M-Sa 10:30am-5pm, Sun noon-5pm

The Lighthouse stands above much of Glasgow's (admittedly short) skyline. As Scotland's center for Design and Architecture, the building is home to galleries, studios, and a **Charles Rennie Mackintosh** exhibit, because, of course. But more importantly, the Lighthouse's tower has a beautiful panoramic vantage point of the city. 135 steps stand between you and the best views, so you can get that Insta caption that's worth the exercise and actually lives up to #views. For those not looking to visit the rotating exhibitions, you won't need too much time in this building; a half-hour should do the trick. Upstairs and outside, various significant people's favorite places in Glasgow are denoted on plaques that point your eye in their direction of choice.

i Free; limited wheelchair accessibility

THE WILLOW TEA ROOMS

97 Buchanan St.; 141 204 5242; www.willowtearooms.co.uk; open M-Sa 9am-6:30pm, Su 10:30am-5pm

Glasgow's original afternoon tea, tailored to the no-BS nature of a Glaswegian: big portions and a good deal. Although tea can sometimes feel stuffy, the vibe is just refined enough here. An afternoon tea includes four mini sandwiches, a scone, a pastry, and, of course, your choice of tea. The food is good, but the experience is the real draw. The servers, dressed a in classic black and white uniform, charm locals and tourists alike. Upstairs, in the China Tea Room, geometric turquoise walls and dividers brighten the room. Luckily, you can order afternoon tea in the morning, or breakfast at 5pm, so the Tea Rooms are perfect for a meal or snack and immersion in a **Charles Rennie Mackintosh**-designed room.

i Entrées from £5; no wheelchair accessibility; same-day reservations accepted

MUSEUMS

⬛ CENTRE FOR CONTEMPORARY ARTS

350 Sauchiehall St.; 141 352 4900; www.cca-glasgow.com; open M-Th 10am-midnight, F-Sa 10am-1am, Su noon-midnight; galleries open Tu-Sa 11am-6pm, Su noon-6pm

The Centre comprises a cinema, theater, offices, and galleries, as well as two late-night bars and a vegan restaurant. The most interesting part of the building is just standing there and taking it all in. An open skylit courtyard hosts comfy couches and dark tables, softly illuminated from the glow of string lights. Glasgow's most creative people gather here for a drink at the end of the day. At night, the Centre has shows whose titles range from "Pity Party Film Club: Assholes" to "Freedom to Run." We recommend checking out the resident artists in the galleries before they close, then hanging around to see who you meet.

i Tickets from £5; wheelchair accessible; BGLTQ+ friendly

HUNTERIAN MUSEUM AND HUNTERIAN ART GALLERY

University Ave.; 141 330 4221; www.gla.ac.uk/hunterian/; open Tu-Sa 10am-5pm, Su 11am-4pm

What do the world's smallest dinosaur footprint and paintings by Raphael have in common? You can find them both in the Hunterian Museum and Art Gallery. Enter the **University of Glasgow** campus and follow the signs for the Hunterian Museum, and you find five floors of displays on surgical tools, archaeology, fossils, and the life of William Hunter, the museum's namesake. A few minute's walk across the street lies the Art Gallery. Home to a sculpture garden and several rooms of masterpieces contrasting the light teal and deep red walls, the Art Gallery also offers entry (for a £5 fee) to an exhibit on Glasgow's own **Charles Rennie Mackintosh.**

i Free, some exhibits charge; free tours at 11am, noon, 2pm, 3pm; last entry to art gallery 4:15pm (Su 3:15pm); wheelchair accessible

FOOD

🍴 BREAD MEATS BREAD ($$)

104 St Vincent St.; 141 249 9898; www.breadmeatsbread.com; open M-Su 11am-10pm

Late night last night? Bread Meats Bread welcomes the hungover with its elaborate menu of delicious carb, meat, cheese, and fried combos. This place doesn't serve your average greasy hamburger. The name describes a burger, technically, and that's what you'll get at this restaurant. But what the name *doesn't* tell you is that here, you'll eat one of the best fried chicken burgers or grilled cheese sandwiches found in Scotland. Bread Meats Bread won multiple well-deserved "Best Burger in Glasgow" awards. Order a side to receive heaping piles of french fries, or try the vegan poutine. With chipper staff and large windows looking out onto the street and letting in sunlight, Bread Meats Bread is the carb-filled wonder you didn't know you needed. Around noon, people pack in, so try and get there earlier to avoid a wait.

i Entrées from £8; vegan and vegetarian options available; wheelchair accessible

'BABS ($$)

49 West Nile St.; 141 465 1882; babs. co.uk; open daily noon-10pm

This place is a little fancier than your typical side-of-the-street late-night joint. Be prepared to eat kebabs with a fork and knife. And we're *so* thankful. Customers who step in the door are immediately greeted by fragrant cooking, mosaic tiles, and a plethora of plants at this Mediterranean eatery. A small fountain bubbles in the corner, transporting guests away from Scotland. Founded by the same team as **Bread Meats Bread**, 'Babs offers kickass dishes with fresh and high quality ingredients. Don't let the fork and knife intimidate you—come in for a killer lamb or halloumi plated kebab, and enjoy.

i Entrées from £9; vegan and vegetarian options available; limited wheelchair accessibility

KELVINGROVE ART GALLERY AND MUSEUM

Argyle St.; 141 276 9599; www.glasgow-life.org.uk/museums/venues/kelvin-grove-art-gallery-and-museum; open M-Sa 10am-5pm, Su 11am-5pm

The foreboding brick walls of this massive museum can be seen from all over **Kelvingrove Park**, inviting tourists and locals alike to come in for a wander of the three floors and many exhibits. With displays ranging from the history of tartan cloth to rainforest biodiversity, you can spend an afternoon in the free museum and not get bored. We recommend the Glasgow-specific exhibits that detail Glasgow's rebirth in the 90s, rising from an old industrial hub to the art and music center it is today. Of course, there's an exhibit on **Charles Rennie Mackintosh** that you can't miss. Some exhibits charge, but even without them, the museum holds more than you can see through the naturally lit and decorated center areas—make sure to look up to see the floating heads—through the wings. The art gallery and museum take up separate sides of the same building, so it's easy to check out both.

i Free, some exhibits charge; free tours on weekends; wheelchair accessible

GREAT BRITAIN GLASGOW

MONO ($$)

12 King St.; 141 553 2400; www.mono-cafebar.com; open daily noon-9pm; bar open Su-Th 11am-11pm, F-Sa 11am-1am

When you enter, you'll spot their in house microbrewery to your right—that's where they make their own lemonade. *Shakes head* Classic hipster vegans. Don't let the intimidatingly cool staff deter you from this hip vegan bar and restaurant. With food options from mac n' cheese to pear, chickpea, and blue cheese dressing pizza, their menu provides something for the pickiest meat-eater *and* a well-versed vegan ordering seitan. In the corner, a live DJ spins records or a musician strums a guitar to provide live music ambiance. Outside, young Glaswegians sip their beer at wood tables, completing the casual hip, young, and welcoming aesthetic found throughout the place.
i Entrées from £7; vegan options available; wheelchair accessible; reservation recommended

NIGHTLIFE

SPEAKEASY

10 John Street; 845 166 6063; speakeasy-glasgow.co.uk; open W-Sa 5pm-3am

One of the least sneaky speakeasies we've ever seen, Speakeasy lets everybody in and prides itself on it. A gay bar in the center of **Merchant City**, Speakeasy welcomes guests with dark lights and red plush walls. On Saturdays, the upstairs level—called The Trophy Room—opens up for dancing to classic 80s cheesy music and super ballads. Thursdays host karaoke night, and if you're there on a Friday, you may be able to catch a drag show parade around the bar, ensuring that everyone has a good time. Grab a cocktail jug and open your heart for a rowdy night.
i Cover £3 on Sa, food from £8, drinks from £4; cash only; BGLTQ+ friendly; wheelchair accessible

SUPER BARIO

7 King St.; open daiy noon-midnight

Customers can let out their inner child while feeding their outer adult—you can sip a beer while playing pinball or Super Monkey Ball. Small enough that you might just miss it, this arcade-themed bar aptly titled Super Bario sits on a small street, identifiable by the bells and clicks of arcade games and yells of success (or defeat) that emanate into the street. Locals frequent the games, especially the free ones. Some of the games are even two player, giving you the perfect opportunity to meet a new friend. Go for the novelty; stay for the nostalgia.
i No cover, drinks from £7, games up to £1; BGLTQ+ friendly; limited wheelchair accessibility

WAXY O'CONNORS

44 West George St.; 141 354 5154; www.waxyoconnors.co.uk/index.php/welcome-to-waxys-glasgow; open M-Th noon-11pm, F noon-midnight, Sa 10am-midnight, Su 11am-11pm

Waxy O'Connors is is the beating heart of a giant tree. Three floors containing nine bars leave guests with endless opportunities throughout the maze of activity. Wood is everywhere. Flags hang from staircases adorned with stained glass, while massive tree branches stretch from the walls to the ceilings. Waxy O'Connors isn't just a bar; it's an experience. You can often find live music or locals and tourists yelling at the TV blaring the latest football match.
i Food from £8, drinks from £4; cash only; BGLTQ+ friendly; limited wheelchair accessibility

LIVERPOOL

Coverage by **Lucy Golub**

A city best known for its musical contributions to the world—namely the Beatles—Liverpool is also famous for its football. Yet, with the exception of a few streets, the city doesn't actually feel like a tourist hub. It feels like a living, breathing remnant of an industrial hub, a port that connects England to the world. But the city isn't just a vestige of the past; lively streets of restaurants shops and bars are home to a flourishing culture. People come from all over the world to visit and live in Liverpool, as seen by the different types of food dotting the sidewalks of Bold Street. The carnival-like Albert Docks and museums embody the different features of the city. Often overlooked in favor of bigger cities like London and Manchester, those who skip this gem are missing out. Although Brits may not be known for their friendliness, Scousers might just change your mind. Come for the music and the sports. Stay for the city itself.

ORIENTATION

Liverpool is on the water, and the west of the city comprises **Albert Docks** and the **Baltic Triangle.** To the east lies the picturesque **Georgian Quarter,** the **Liverpool Cathedral** and the University, as well as surrounding stores and nightlife on **Hope Street.** In the center of the city, you'll find more museums and nightlife encompassing **Bold Street** and **Ropewalks.** Nearby, **Chinatown** and the **Chinese Arch** welcome visitors. Further inland and slightly south, Liverpool's **South End** are the Beatles' childhood homes, including the now-famous **Penny Lane** and **Sefton Park.** To the north of the center, the football field draws crowds on game days.

ESSENTIALS

GETTING THERE

If you fly, you'll likely end up in the city's closest airport, John Lennon Airport. From the airport, the 80A and 86A buses run to the city centre with plenty of stops. The 86A runs 24hr, so no matter what time your flight gets in, you'll be able to leave the airport without a problem. You can use the Merseyside Travel Planner (www.jp.merseytravel.gov.uk) to plan your route if you come by train or bus. There's a bus stop right at Liverpool ONE in the city center, and a train station at Lime Street as well.

GETTING AROUND

Like other small cities in England, Liverpool is relatively walkable. To get to tourist attractions further from the city center, like the football fields or Penny Lane, Liverpool is well served by bus. You can read specifics online at www.merseytravel.gov.uk, but the buses take cash on board (around £2, less for students), and daily tickets are available for £4.80.

PRACTICAL INFORMATION

Tourist Offices: Tourist Information Centre (Anchor Courtyard Albert Dock; 151 707 0729; www.visitliverpool.com; open daily Oct-Mar 10am-4:30pm, Apr-Sept 10am-5:30pm)

Banks/ATMs/Currency Exchange: NatWest Liverpool ONE (2-8 Church St.; 345 788 8444; open M-Tu 9am-6pm, W 10am-6pm, Th-F 9am-6pm, Sa 9am-5pm)

Post Offices: Liverpool Post Office (1-3 South John St.; 151 707 6606; open M-Sa 9am-5:30pm, Su 11am-3pm)

Public Restrooms: Most shopping centers and cafés have restrooms. You can go to Liverpool Lime Street Station (Lime St.; open M-F 3:15am-12:40am, Sa 3:15am-12:35am, Su 7am-12:30am).

Internet: Most cafés, bars, museums, and hotels have free Wi-Fi.

BGLTQ+ Resources: The Armistead Project offers confidential support and information (Hanover St.; 0151 247 6560; www.merseycare.nhs.uk/our-services/physical-health-services/armistead/; open M-F 10am-6pm).

EMERGENCY INFORMATION

Emergency Number: 999

Police: Merseyside Police have locations all around the city. Headquarters at (Canning Pl.; non-emergency number 101; www.merseysidepolice.uk).

US Embassy: The closest U.S. embassy is in London (33 Nine Elms Ln., London; 20 7499 9000).

Rape Crisis Center: RASA Merseyside provides support for survivors of sexual assault. (2 and 3 Stella Nova, Washington Parade, Bootle; www.rasamerseyside.org; helpline staffed Tu 6pm-8pm, Th 6pm-8pm, F noon-2pm).

Hospitals:
- Royal Liverpool University Hospital (Prescot St.; 151 706 2000; open daily 24hr)
- Broadgreen Hospital (Thomas Dr.; 151 282 6000; open daily 24hr)

Pharmacies: Pharmacies are very easy to locate.
- Boots (18 Great Charlotte St., Clayton Sq.; 151 709 4711; open M-Sa 8:15am-7pm)

ACCOMMODATIONS

🏨 HATTERS ($-$$)

56-60 Mount Pleasant St.; 151 709 5570; www.hattershostels.com; reception open 24hr

Situated in an old Gothic building near the city center, Hatters feels like you're staying in a church—if, of course, the church had a games room, kitchen, and a bunch of dorms. Facilities are basic, but rooms have lockers for valuables and ensuite spacious bathrooms that are cleaned often. Thursday's night out includes free entry into **The Cavern Club** and Friday and Saturday have raging pub crawls, free shots included. And the hostel is only a few streets from **Bold Street**, so lots of restaurants and shopping are only a couple minutes away. A hot cooked breakfast can be added for only £5. There's not much else you could ask for.

i Dorms from £14 weekdays, weekends £20; privates £35 weekdays, weekends £100; reservation recommended; min weekend stay 2 nights, max stay 14 nights; BGLTQ+ friendly; no wheelchair accessibility; Wi-Fi; linens provided; laundry machines available; games room, nightly events

EMBASSIE HOSTEL ($$)

1 Falkner Sq.; 151 707 10 89; www.embassie.com; reception open daily 24hr

An old Georgian home used to be the location of the Venezuelan consulate, and was then converted into Liverpool's first hostel. Embassie is a family-run business; Kevin Sr. and his children personally ensure the comfort of all guests. He also runs a Beatles tour every Thursday, including free entry into the **Cavern Club.** The walls of the three-story home are covered with photos of previous guests, wedding announcements (apparently over 150 couples have met at the hostel), and postcards sent back from those who once stayed here. Inside the dimly-lit kitchen, free coffee, tea, bread, and jams are provided at all hours to the three-dorm rooms. Though perhaps not the most social of hostels, Embassie offers old-but-still-kicking accommodation and incredibly friendly hosts.

i Dorms from £19 weekdays, weekends £22; no wheelchair accessibility; Wi-Fi; linens, towels provided; kitchen

YHA LIVERPOOL

25 Tabley St.; 345 371 9527; www.yha.org.uk/hostel/yha-liverpool; reception open 24hr

Situated a few minutes from **Albert Docks,** YHA offers an ideal location for an arts-obsessed tourist looking to immerse themselves in museum, culture, and more museums. The hostel accepts guests of all ages, and although it has a café and bar, isn't a party hostel. But it is a quiet, clean, and accommodating place to sleep near all of the places you'll want to visit. Rooms have big lockers for your valuables and lots of power outlets. There's even a library if you forgot your copy of *Middlemarch* and need to brush up on some British literature while you're here.

i Dorms from £11, privates from £29; reservation recommended; max stay 14 days; BGLTQ+ friendly; wheelchair accessible; Wi-Fi in common areas; café and bar; linens provided; locks and towels for rent

SIGHTS
CULTURE

🖼 BOLD STREET
Bold St., store hours vary

Vintage stores. Buzzing bars. Vibrant cuisine. And it's all at your fingertips. Here, Liverpool's cultures converge—so much so that almost all visitors can find what they're searching for. If you're on the hunt for a hipster café full of green juice and vegan pancakes, look no further than **Love Thy Neighbor.** Craving something a little less Instagram-edgy? **Kabsah Café Bazaar** serves piping hot Moroccan food, fez hats included. Or if you're looking for some new threads, thrift shops line the streets—check out **Cow Vintage** or **Take 2.** Whoever said Liverpool wasn't trendy clearly never stepped foot onto this street. You could easily spend a day here alternating between eating and shopping—don't say we didn't warn you.
i Prices vary; wheelchair accessible

THE BLUE COAT
School Ln.; 151 702 5324; www.theblue-coat.org.uk; open M-Sa 9am-6pm, Su 11am-6pm

The Blue Coat—an art gallery with a community center attached—has it all. You can browse galleries and watch performances, eat at a café and sit in an outdoor garden, visit a tailor (if you bought a suit at one of the vintage shops only to realize it doesn't *actually* fit you) and get a new do at the hairdresser. Exhibits in the galleries change often—check the website for the most up-to-date information. Upstairs in the galleries, a large room offers couches, books, and an area to relax. Programming at night includes shows, workshops, and talks. The bulletin boards are covered in flyers advertising other performances and vintage sales. If you don't like food or getting a haircut, the building itself is incentive enough to visit.
i Free; wheelchair accessible

CAINS BREWERY VILLAGE
Stanhope St.; www.breweryvillage.com; store hours vary

A once-abandoned brewery received a new life once this mini-village sprang to life. Not your "typical" village (read: not situated in the countryside with roses climbing up the walls of cottages), Cain's is a collection of vintage and antique stores, food stalls, and, of course, bars. Make sure to check out **Red Brick Hangar,** another market filled with more than 50 local shops that offers wares like band t-shirts, hipster meal-prep services, random trinkets, and artsy photo prints. And if you're feeling spending money on a new tattoo to honor your time in Liverpool, they offer that too—walk-ins accepted. (Just don't accidentally do this while drunk, so you don't regret it the morning after.) Grab a beer at **Peaky Blinders,** a 1920s-inspired pub and walk around the **Baltic Market.** Then, head to **Ghetto Golf** (questionable name, much?) for a neon mini-golf game like no other.
i Prices vary; limited wheelchair accessibility

LANDMARKS

🖼 MENDIPS
251 Menlove Ave.; 1514277231; www.thenationaltrust.org.uk/beatles; visible 24hr

Imagine the room where John Lennon wrote his first songs—and then *imagine* the kitchen, dining room, and rehearsal room. From the outside, you can view the building's façade and a commemorative plaque. But to get the full experience, tickets are available via the National Trust, and they include both John Lennon and Paul McCartney's childhood homes, as well as the original windows (yeah, we know that's what you came for) and multiple stories about their childhoods. View the houses the way they were in the 50s—it's like entering a photograph. But no matter how much you love the Beatles, the tour guides ask that you do not steal things from the houses (for real, people do that) and just *Let It Be.* Okay, we'll show ourselves out now.
i Admission £24; online advance bookings preferred; no wheelchair accessibility

LIVERPOOL CATHEDRAL

St. James Mount; 151 709 6271; www.liverpoolcathedral.co.uk; open M-Sa 8am-6pm, Su service 8am-12:30pm, visits 12:30pm-6pm

Liverpool cathedral is *huge*. Like crane-your-neck-towards-the-ceiling-and-still-not-be-able-to-see-it-all huge. A pink neon sign by artist Tracey Emin randomly looms above the lower floor, firmly grounding the cathedral in this century, even though the church was constructed almost 100 years ago. For a great view of Liverpool, you can pay a small fee to go up to the **Vestey Tower;** you won't regret paying when you get the #prime view of the **Georgian Quarter.** The church doesn't try to shove its history down your throat, although there are some exhibitions along the walls and on the third floor. And if you're sick of all of Europe's churches (no, they're not all the same), the enormity of this one makes it worth a visit.

i Free; tower admission £5.50, students £4.50; wheelchair accessible

PENNY LANE

Penny Ln.; store hours vary

A barbershop still exists on Penny Lane, one of many shops to capitalize on the Beatles' famous song. Penny Lane Wine Bar, Penny Lane Surgery, Penny Lane Hotel: you get the picture. And if you're looking for a picture of the sign, check out the corner of Penny Lane and Elm Street, or walk down the lane to get to the Penny Lane Development Trust for a colorful Beatles mural and the classic sign. The 86, 80, and 75 buses all take you to nearby stop **Plattsville Road,** but to be honest, there isn't all that much to see on Penny Lane (other than the sign). It's just another pretty brick street. Definitely stroll along, listening to the song, pretending you're with your mates Paul and John. Also, we're sorry that we said Penny Lane so many times in this review; those two words probably appear more often here than in the actual song.

i Prices vary; wheelchair accessible

MUSEUMS

⬛ THE BEATLES STORY

Britannia Vaults; 151 709 196; www.beatlesstory.com; open peak days 9am-7pm; open super peak days 9am-8pm; check website for details

In case you couldn't already tell from the thousands of references to the Fab 4 all over the city, the Beatles originated in Liverpool. You can check out their stories at this museum. Inside, after a slightly hefty admission fee, you can follow their trajectory, passing through detailed replicas of significant locations like **Casbah Coffee Club, The Cavern Club, Nems Record Shop,** and their recording studios. Step into the set of the music video for Sgt. Pepper's Lonely Hearts Club Band and explore the **Yellow Submarine.** The audio guide helps lead you through the museum, and even if you're not a Beatles fan (unclear why you're in Liverpool then but ok, sure), you'll learn about the Beatles, their rise to fame, and their eventual separation.

i Admission £16.95, students £12.50; last entry 1hr before closing; wheelchair accessible

MERSEYSIDE MARITIME MUSEUM

Albert Dock; 151 478 4499; www.liverpoolmuseums.org.uk/maritime/index.aspx; open daily 10am-5pm

Liverpool was known as one of the world's most vibrant ports, and you can learn about its history here. Containing an exhibit on the *Titanic* and one on the *Lusitania,* as well as exhibits on Liverpool's maritime successes, the museum approaches boats and the sea from all angles. Be sure to check out the downstairs exhibit "Seized!" to hear of some ridiculous smuggling attempts and pretend to catch a drug dealing boat via simulation. The **International Museum of Slavery** is located on the third floor, where guests can read about England's role in the slave trade and the tragedies that accompanied it.

i Free; wheelchair accessible

FOOD

🍽 MOWGLI ($)

69 Bold St.; 151 708 9356; www.mowglistreetfood.com; open M-W noon-9:30pm, Th-Sa noon-10:30pm, Su noon-9:30pm

Higher-end Indian street food sounds like an oxymoron, but Mowgli provides high-quality small plates of traditional dishes you likely haven't had before if you're used to your regular Indian restaurant fare. Mowgli meshes zen and club vibes, creating a dimly-lit, trendy space with birdcage decorations overhead, complete with wood seats and tables. Dishes come out as soon as they're ready. If you're only going to get one thing, make it the chaat bombs—aka crispy bread filled with chickpeas, spices, and yogurt. It's best to come in a group, so you can share as many dishes as possible.

i *Plates from £4; vegan vegetarian options available; wheelchair accessible*

THE BAGELRY ($)

42 Nelson St.; 151 306 5723; www.the-bagelryliverpool.com; open Tu-F 9am-5pm, Sa-Su 9:30am-4:30pm

Europe really has good bread covered: we may not be in France enjoying a perfectly-baked *baguette,* but even British bread is *good.* Unfortunately, that baking skill doesn't always translate to bagels—which is where The Bagelry comes in. Serving 10 styles on eight different bagels (jalapeño cheddar stole our hearts) and novel cream cheese flavors like maple-pecan or spring onion, this sit-down restaurant kicks bagels up a notch. They even come with a fork and knife (which you can ignore). If you're on a tight budget, grab a "daygel" aka yesterday's bagel for half price. Nothing like a lump of carbs to start your day, amiright? Especially when it's served warm and heaped with toppings.

i *Bagels from £4, drinks from £2.40; vegan and vegetarian options available; wheelchair accessible*

WALKER ART GALLERY

William Brown St.; 151 478 4199; www.liverpoolmuseums.org.uk/walker; open daily 10am-5pm

A crash course in art history from the fourteenth century through today awaits you inside the doors of the Walker Art Gallery. You don't need to be an art expert; if you follow the rooms from one through 15, you'll see the chronological shift in art trends, grouped by room. Pretty easy to get, if you ask us. So start with a room of filled with multiple renditions of Madonna and Child, and end up in their current exhibition of modern art. If paintings confused you and you don't get what the fuss is all about when you look at Renaissance art, you can also visit the sculpture gallery. And if you've ever seen a picture of Henry VIII, it's likely the same one that's replicated in the gallery (coat and hat for photo op included).

i *Free; audio guide £2.50; wheelchair accessible*

DEATH ROW DINER

32 Hope St.; 151 345 6160; www.death-rowdiveanddiner.com; open M-F 5pm-11:30pm, Sa-Su noon-11:30pm

It could be called Death Row because of the dozens of animals this place likely goes through in a day. (Yikes.) Or maybe it's because every fried meat-loaded meal brings you closer to a heart attack. Morbid, we know. But where else can you get a fried chicken bacon burger called "I dream of Jesus?" You know what you're getting here. Lucky for carnivores, less so for vegans, you can add pastrami fries or chorizo waffles to any meal. Meaty, meaty heaven. Oh yeah, the burgers come stabbed with a lollipop, too. The restaurant's neon wall signs display slightly confusing phrases, and long wood tables are bathed in red light. We'd say it's pretty much the perfect atmosphere to gorge yourself on meat. Here, you'll forget about the concept of vegetables.

i Burgers from £9; no wheelchair accessibility

LOVE THY NEIGHBOR

108 Bold St.; 151 352 2618; www.love-thy-neighbour.co.uk; open M-Sa 8am-11pm, Su 9am-11pm

A café with pink walls, pink neon lights, succulents, and vegan food: yeah, it's your Instagram feed reincarnated. Sounds pretty typical. (Millennials and their avocado toast these days, smh.) Except at night—and all day, we don't judge—they serve killer gin and tonics in bowls, decorated with flower garnishes, because, of course. This is *the* place to brunch. Let's face it, the beer and chips diet of a Brit doesn't do the best thing for your waistline. Luckily, you can get a hearty açaí bowl or some spiced falafel to fill you up. (With actual nutrients!)

i Entrées from £6, drinks from £8; gluten-free, vegan, and vegetarian options available; wheelchair accessible; kitchen closes at 10pm

NIGHTLIFE

⌗ CAVERN CLUB

10 Mathew St.; 151 236 9091; www.cavernclub.org; open M-W 10am-midnight, Th 10am-1:30am, F 10am-2pm, Sa 10am-2am, Su 10am-midnight

Stepping down the three flights of stairs to the Cavern Club is like entering a time machine, especially when the resident Beatles Tribute band is playing. (Is everything in Liverpool Beatles-themed? Yeah, mostly.) But if you look around at the older crowd, the faces of the couples in their 70s reflect the impact of long-lasting Beatlemania. The space itself feels a little like a bunker—you are way underground afterall.

i No cover M-W, Th free until 7pm, then £4; F-Sa free until noon, £2.50 until 8pm, £5 until midnight; Su free until noon, £2.50 until 8pm, £4 until midnight; all-day and all-night passes available for £6 (£5 in advance); beer from £4, spirits from £3; wheelchair accessible

BAA BAR

43-45 Fleet St.; 151 708 8673; www.baabar.co.uk; open M-Th 8pm-4am, F-Sa 6pm-4am, Su 8pm-4am

This classic, cheap-drink, student club doesn't disappoint. Sickly-sweet shots are available in scores of flavors, including classics like Birthday Cake and Squashed Frog. Don't ask, just try them for yourself. The bass thumps to the latest pop and hip-hop music, and there are two floors with lots of room to dance. (And dance they do.) If you look around, you'll spot students in groups pop-lock-and-dropping it (or whatever kids these days do). Just embrace the cheap drinks and the young atmosphere to party until 4am, any day of the year except Christmas.

i No cover, drinks from £2; BGLTQ+ friendly; limited wheelchair accessibility; PIN and contactless cards only

THE PHILHARMONIC

36 Hope St.; 151 707 2837; www.nicholson-spubs.co.uk/restaurants/northwest/thephil-harmonicdiningroomsliverpool; open M-Sa 11am-midnight, Su 11am-11pm

Paul McCartney once said that the worst part about being famous was not being able to go for a pint at the Philharmonic. Luckily for you, you can! Steeped in history, wandering around inside this pub is akin to exploring a lavish museum. The men's restrooms (really) are works of art in themselves. Local students don't really hang here, since drinks aren't the cheapest, but the opulent atmosphere makes a classy pint (or two) worth it before a night out. Be sure to explore the multiple rooms and shimmering chandeliers, and you might even recognize a face or two in the portraits along the walls.

i No cover, beer from £3, spirits from £3; limited wheelchair accessibility

THE RED DOOR

21-23 Berry St.; 151 709 7040; www.reddoor.co.uk; open M-W 7pm-2am, Th 7pm-4am, F 5pm-4am, Sa 2pm-4am, Su 5pm-1am

Cheap shots and beer can only take you so far, especially if you're craving an expertly-crafted cocktail and ready to splurge. Considering a similar cocktail easily runs you £15 in London, let's call this place an expensive steal. Earlier on weekend nights, live music blasts from the speakers (and when we say blasts, we mean it), until around 10pm when a DJ comes to transform the bar into a club. Everything about the place feels high end but not snooty—brick walls and a giant red door (hence the name) always remind you where you are, while tall seats let you perch at a table as you sip your perfectly-balanced, steel-tin encased fruity drink. Plus, you'll notice being really hot is an employee requirement—everyone who works here is gorgeous. The Red Door is happily located near many of the other bars in the **Ropewalks,** so come for an early evening cocktail, go get drunk on cheaper liquor elsewhere, and come back to dance til 4am.

i No cover, cocktails from £8; BGLTQ+ friendly; limited wheelchair accessibility; live music Th-Sa, discounts if you register online

LONDON

Coverage by **Lucy Golub**

Red telephone booths and double decker buses. Beefeater guards and camera-happy tourists positioned in front of Buckingham Palace. Harry Potter inspiration and the West End. London is a city like no other, with more claims to fame than we can count. From the rich and glitzy Mayfair to the rock 'n roll punk grunge of Camden to the industrial and corporate City of London and hipster on-the-rise Hackney, London's essence can't quite be categorized. The city is booming and living, breathing and evolving—and changing every season. Overwhelming in both size and scale, London can be daunting. Boroughs spread for miles from the center. Yet the city has its quirks that make it feel familiar, like the way people align so expertly on the right side of a Tube escalator, or the chants that fill the streets after an English player scores during a football match. It's puzzling how a modern metropolis feels both so old and so new, when museums hold prehistoric artifacts and contemporary masterpieces just doors away. Between theaters are countless pubs and restaurants, many of which challenge the notion that British food isn't fine dining. And the city is home to a plethora of green spaces, perfect for when you feel overwhelmed by the hustle and bustle of a city that never stops moving.

ORIENTATION

London has well-defined neighborhoods (officially called Boroughs) and is also split into zones on the Underground that circumvent the center of the city. The zip codes are an easy indication of which section of the city your target location is in. **Zone 1,** also known as "central London," includes key tourist points like **Westminster,** home to the **Parliament, Westminster Abbey, the London Eye.** Also in central London are upscale **Chelsea & Kensington** and **Mayfair.** Towards the west and in **Zone 2** you'll find **Notting Hill** and **Portobello Road,** a charming market on the weekends, and a pastel-tinged residential area. Northwest of Zone 2 brings you to grungry and hip **Camden** (and of course, **Camden Market**) and **Hampstead Heath.** To the east of the city center, trendy **Shoreditch** lies on the border of Zone 1 and 2. Further east is **Hackney,** eclectic and quickly filling with hipsters. Between Shoreditch and the center you'll also find the **London Bridge** and the **Tower of London.** Finally, the **Thames River** cuts through the center of the city, and south of the river **Southwark, Shakespeare's Globe,** and **Borough Market.**

ESSENTIALS

GETTING THERE

London is serviced by multiple airports. Most US flights arrive to Heathrow International Airport, and from there you can take the Piccadilly Line into the city center. There's also a more expensive express train. From Gatwick Airport, the easiest route to central London is the Gatwick Express, which runs every 15min. and only takes 30min. to get to Victoria Station. EasyBus also runs an airport transfer service. Multiple routes run from Stansted Airport to the city center as well, like National Express buses that can cost as little as £5 when booked online in advance. Stansted Express trains are quicker to the city center, but they cost a little more. From Luton Airport, buses and trains run to the city as well. From other locations in the UK trains arrive at multiple train stations in London, particularly King's Cross and Victoria. International trains often arrive at St. Pancras.

GETTING AROUND

London's public transportation system is one of the largest and most organized, and is still one of most overwhelming. But don't panic! Public transport is split into the Underground (the Tube), buses, and, if you're going a little further than the center of the city, the Overground. Stations have charts and maps for you to double-check if you're heading in the right direction. If you're going to be using the Tube and bus a lot, you'll want to buy an Oyster card. It's a £5 investment, but it drastically reduces the fares you pay. Or, if you have a contactless credit card, you can use that and avoiding the fee. Bus fares are a flat £1.50, whereas tickets on the Tube depend on which zones you're visiting. You'll likely need an Oyster card for Zones 1 and 2, because that's where most tourist attractions are. If you pay as you go for an Oyster, you can go to any zone. Make sure you don't lose the card on your ride, as you'll need to tap in and out. The Tube doesn't run 24hr, but most buses do on weekends. If you're out late, you'll likely take the night bus, although Transport for London has expanded the Night Tube to include 24hr service with some stop changes on the weekends on the Victoria, Central, Jubilee, Northern, and Piccadilly Lines.

PRACTICAL INFORMATION

Tourist Offices: There are a few London Tourist Information Centres around the city. One is City of London Information Centre (St. Paul's Churchyard; 020 7332 1456; www.visitlondon.com; open M-Sa 9:30am-5:30pm, Su 10am-4pm).

Banks/ATMs/Currency Exchange: You should have no trouble finding ATMs, banks, and currency exchanges. It's usually better to withdraw pounds than to exchange due to fees.

Post Offices: Post offices are readily available.

- Camden High Street (112-114 Camden High St.; 0345 722 3344; open M-F 9am-6pm, Sa 9am-5:30pm)
- Great Portland Street Branch (54-56 Great Portland St.; 0845 722 3344; open M 9am-6pm, Tu 9:30am-6pm, W-F 9am-6pm, Sa 9am-12:30pm)

Public Restrooms: Many stores like Asda and Sainsbury's are open all day and have restrooms, and there are also some official public restrooms throughout the city. Some Tube stations also have toilets. There's one in the City of London (Monument St.; www.visitlondon. com/traveller-information/essential-information/toilets-in-london; open 24hr; 50p charge).

Internet: Most cafés, pubs, and restaurants have Wi-Fi. You can also find public Wi-Fi on the street thanks to the new modernized phone booths. Pret à Manger and Starbucks usually have Wi-Fi as well.

BGLTQ+ Resources: There's a BGLTQ+ Tourist Information Centre in Soho, where lots of gay nightlife is located (25 Frith St.; www.gaytouristoffice.co.uk). In June, London decks out in rainbow for Pride.

EMERGENCY INFORMATION

Emergency Number: 999

Police: Police stations are common and police are often visible in crowded tourist areas. A central station is Charing Cross Police Station (Agar St.; 101 for non-emergency; www.met.police.uk; open daily 24hr).

US Embassy: US Embassy (33 Nine Elms Ln.; 020 7499 9000; www.uk.usembassy. gov; open M-F 8am-5:30pm)

Rape Crisis Center: Rape & Sexual Abuse Support Centre and South London Rape Crisis provides support to women and girls who are victims of sexual assault. Their helpline is 0808 802 9999 (www. rasasc.org.uk; helpline available daily noon-2:30pm and 7pm-9:30pm).

Hospitals: London has multiple hospitals in many different areas. Here are two that have emergency care.
- Chelsea and Westminster Hospital: 369 Fulham Rd.; 020 8746 8000; www.chelwest.nhs.uk; open daily 24hr
- St. Thomas' Hospital: Westminster Bridge Rd.; 020 7188 7188; open daily 24hr

Pharmacies: Pharmacies can also be found on almost every street. Each of the following has multiple locations throughout the city.
- Boots: 11 Bridge St.; 020 7930 4571; www.boots.com; open M-F 8am-7pm, Sa 9am-5:30pm, Su 10am-4pm

ACCOMMODATIONS

🏨 HOSTEL ONE CAMDEN ($)

2 Southampton Rd.; 020 7813 6243; www. hostelone.com/camden; reception open 24hr

Daily activities for guests include visits to **The Science Museum** and **Hampstead Heath,** and every night, volunteers and guests head out to nearby **Camden Town.** While triple bunk beds and slightly cramped rooms are no one's favorite, the hostel's accommodations seem better with each passing day. The bathrooms are well-maintained with shockingly spacious showers. Our hearts broke just a little when it was time to say goodbye to all the new friends we had made. Something about this little building on a quiet street in **Camden** makes a big city like London feel easily manageable when you've got your Hostel One family with you.

i Dorms from £21, higher on weekends; reservation recommended; BGLTQ+ friendly; no wheelchair accessibility; Wi-Fi; linens, dinner included; laundry and kitchen available

ASTOR VICTORIA ($)

71 Belgrave Rd.; 020 7834 3077; www. astorhostels.com/hostels/victoria; reception open 24hr

White sheets in a hostel are underrated. Why? Because with a pure white sheet, you really know how clean the bed you're slipping into is. Here, the sheets are as white as a pristine sheet of paper. Beyond the clean sheets, they offer luxurious showers with strong water pressure, fun staff, and common rooms you'd actually want to spend time in. As a bonus, they offer discount tickets to nearby **West End** theater shows. As you may have figured out by now, we're big fans of a bargain, which is what you're getting with Astor Victoria.

i Dorms from £19; reservation recommended; no wheelchair accessibility; Wi-Fi; linens, towels, padlocks, adapters included; laundry facilities; breakfast £1

BARMY BADGER BACKPACKERS ($)

17 Longridge Rd.; 020 7370 5213; www. barmybadger.co.uk; reception open M-Th 7am-3am, F-Sa 7:30am-5am, Su 9am-8pm

"What's in a name?" asked our buddy William. Well, in this case, everything. How could you not fall in love with a place called the Barmy Badger? Although we didn't run into any badgers during our time here, we did see two adorable dogs who hang around. Staying in this hostel feels like staying in somebody's home. Gone are the sterile metal beds and generic neon common rooms of hostels yore, Barmy's common areas seem like they've been lived in and are waiting for you to join. With a lovely outdoor area in the back, we could see ourselves staying here for quite a while. The hostel recently celebrated its 20th anniversary, so looks like she's here to stay too.

i Dorms from £21.50; reservation recommended; no wheelchair accessibility; Wi-Fi; linens provided; laundry available; breakfast included

ST. CHRISTOPHER'S VILLAGE ($$)

161-165 Borough High St.; 0207 939 9710; www.st-christophers.co.uk/hostels/uk/london/london-bridge-village; reception open 24hr

You've just walked seven miles through London. Except—the sounds of your half-naked neighbor in the bunk bed next to you keep you awake all night. Luckily, you'll never have to worry about that here in London's first capsule room. Each pod comes with a curtain, an outlet, and personalized mood lighting. Although there's only one capsule room in the building, every room is air conditioned with big beds, and even the 33-bed dorm has individual curtains and space. St. Christopher's definitely costs more than other hostels, but in return you're getting the top-of-the-line treatment. The downstairs bar and lounge has events and fun people, so the only downside is the lack of kitchen.

i Dorms from £33, capsule room from £30 on weekends, privates from £79; reservation recommended; BGLTQ+ friendly; wheelchair accessible; Wi-Fi; breakfast, linens provided; laundry available

THE WALRUS ($)

172 Westminster Bridge Rd.; 0207 928 8599; www.thewalrusbarandhostel.co.uk; reception open M-W noon-11pm, Th noon-midnight, F-Sa noon-1am

As the joke goes: what do you call a walrus in a telephone booth? Stuck! Being stuck in this hostel certainly wouldn't be the worst fate. Dorms are basic but clean, and the kitchen is an added bonus. Although they could benefit from a few more outlets, the dorms don't hold more than eight beds, so you'll have more than enough space for your belongings. The bar downstairs doubles as a common room. Events like walking tours and yoga provide an easy opportunity to make friends to explore nearby **Westminster Abbey.**

i Dorms from £22; reservation recommended; BGLTQ+ friendly; no wheelchair accessibility; Wi-Fi; linens provided; kitchen available

WOMBATS ($)

7 Dock St.; 020 7680 7600; www.wombats-hostels.com/london; reception open 24hr

More hotel than hostel, Wombat's ensuite bathrooms, showers, and beds outfitted with outlets and lamps make the hostel feel luxurious. For a solo traveller, the lack of events and the hostel's large size can feel intimidating. But you might meet some rowdy Australians playing ping pong and end up clubbing til 5am. Or not. A coveted *Let's Go* insider tip: the lounge on the ninth floor (with a killer view of London) is available for anyone to use, not just the rooms attached. Just ask at reception!

i Dorms from £21; reservation recommended; BGLTQ+ friendly; wheelchair accessible; Wi-Fi; linens provided; laundry, towels available

YHA OXFORD ST. ($)

14 Noel St.; 0345 371 9133; www.yha.org.uk/hostel/yha-london-oxford-street; reception open 24hr

Like at most YHAs, you know what you're getting when you check in—basic but very well-kept rooms with spacious lockers and clean sheets. The dorms lack Wi-Fi, but you won't be doing much except sleeping here. The location of this hostel couldn't be better for someone looking to sightsee. Right near **Oxford Street,** the land of shopping galore, and close to many museums, someone seeking chill but comfortable stay will find a home. They book up quick, though, so making a reservation might be a good idea.

i Dorms from £20, higher on weekends and in summer; reservation recommended; BGLTQ+ friendly; no wheelchair accessibility; Wi-Fi only on ground floor; laundry, kitchen available; linens provided

SIGHTS
CULTURE

🏛 CAMDEN MARKET

Camden Lock; www.camdenmarket.com; market open daily 10am-late; KERB open M-Th 11am-6pm, F-Su 11am-7pm

We love Camden Market, especially for the food. But the market has more than just endless rows of different cuisines (ranging from fried cheese to lamb burgers). It's split into multiple sections, but know that the tourist-trap stalls of useless souvenirs and graphic tees assaulting your senses when you step off the Tube at **Camden Town** station are not the *proper* Camden Market. To find the actual market, you'll want to take the Tube to **Chalk Farm** and head to the Stables Market (literally, old horse stables) for vintage clothes galore, leather wares, tons of jewelry, glow in the dark mini golf, and of course, on the other side, the food stalls at **KERB Camden.**

i Establishment prices vary

BARBICAN CENTRE

Silk St.; 020 7638 8891; www.barbican.org. uk; open M-Sa 10am-8pm, Su 11am-8pm

If you're searching for a different kind of night out (a different kind of culture than beer, perhaps), then boy have we got a lucky find for you: the Barbican Centre. Here, you'll find a true center for the arts encased in giant concrete buildings. They've got a movie theater, they've got an art gallery, they've got **Shakespeare plays** and dance performances. They've even got the **Symphony,** so get ready for a classy night on the town. By the way, they also offer Young Barbican tickets to most shows and exhibits, accessible to anyone under 25 who registers!

i Free; show and exhibit ticket prices vary; Young Barbican tickets for £5; wheelchair accessible

BOROUGH MARKET

8 Southwark St.; 020 7407 1002; www. boroughmarket.org.uk; open M-Th 10am-5pm, F 10am-6pm, Sa 8am-5pm

You get a sample! And you get a sample! And *you* get a sample! Samples for everyone! Borough Market specializes in **produce, cheese, meat, and condiments,** in addition to the stalls cooking up fresh lunch. As you wander around the market, artisan mustards on display will call your name, begging to be tasted. Each cheese stall offers multiple types of samples, and (of course) you've got to try them all to determine your favorite. Olive oil? Why yes, of course we're interested in trying that truffle olive oil with this fresh bread next to it. And sure, the cheddar cheese, *mmm delicious,* I'll have to think about it, though. Oh, it costs £30? Nevermind, thank you for your time. You can likely nab enough samples to equal a small meal, but good luck resisting buying a chunk of cheese (we couldn't).

i Free, stall prices vary; limited wheelchair accessibility; limited market M-Tu

BOXPARK SHOREDITCH

2-10 Bethnal Green Rd.; www.boxpark. uk; fashion available M-W 11am-7pm, Th 11am-8pm, F-Sa 11am-7pm, Su noon-6pm; food and drink available M-Sa 8am-11pm, Su 10am-10pm

What's that long line of people on a Saturday night in Shoreditch? A new trendy bar? Some hipster restaurant hybrid pop-up? All of the above! Trendy food stalls are jammed together in shipping containers so you can try novel desserts at **Dum Dums Donutterie** or street fries from **Poptata.** Downstairs, different stores sell wares ranging from soft t-shirts and artsy cards to skincare (shoutout to **Deciem**). This must be the new hipster version of a mall. Don't millennials just ruin everything these days?

i Prices vary; limited wheelchair accessibility

BRICK LANE

Brick Ln.; www.visitbricklane.org; store hours vary

Isn't it funny how just one street can have so many restaurants that have been voted the "best curry in London?" Strange. Urban legend says that all the restaurants on Brick Lane are connected by one underground kitchen. While we think that's not true, it can be a little confusing when a restaurant owner calling out wine deals in front of a storefront leads you into a different restaurant. But embrace it and you might get some free appetizers. Once grungy, now hip and fully vibrant, Brick Lane serves up Indian food that ranges from the stuff of legends to airplane food. A walk along the street, experiencing the smell and sounds of the area provides an insight to the changing landscape—vegan cafés can be found next door to decades-old curryhouses. Street art aficionados, keep your eyes peeled, as some phenomenal **murals** coat the walls of Brick Lane itself and most of the side streets.

i *Establishment prices vary; wheelchair accessible*

LIBERTY LONDON

Regent St.; 020 7734 1234; www.liberty-london.com; open M-Sa 10am-9pm, Su noon-6pm

Founded in 1875, Liberty stands out from most of the **West End's** buildings with its white walls and half-timber facade. Inside, the luxury goods and clothing store could basically be called a museum. Fancy designer dresses decorated with ruffles and tulle hang on racks surrounding the open center. Upstairs, you can sample colognes and touch vibrant fabrics that super wealthy Brits buy for their arts and crafts. Or downstairs, you can sample cosmetics with unpronounceable ingredients promising a plethora of anti-aging properties. We certainly couldn't afford anything inside, but we still enjoyed browsing through the racks, imagining uses for a fluffy hot pink coat.

i *Item prices vary; wheelchair accessible*

LLOYD'S OF KEW

9 Mortlake Rd.; 020 8948 2556; www.lloyd-sofkewbooks.co.uk; open Tu-Sa 10am-5pm

There's something magical about bookstores. Especially ones where the books spill from the shelves onto piles on the floor and the titles can't be found in an average Barnes and Noble. Lloyd's offers vintage and antiquarian books, and call themselves an emporium of "literary delights for the discerning bibliophile." With free coffee available while you browse, it'd be easy to get lost in the bookstore forever, wandering among ceiling-high shelves, all while avoiding the piles on the floor. They specialize in botanical and horticultural books, which makes sense considering the **Botanic Gardens** are only a few minutes' walk away. So pick up a book before heading to the park.

i *Book prices vary; limited wheelchair accessibility; free coffee available*

NEAL'S YARD

Between Shorts Gardens and Monmouth St.; area open 24hr, establishment hours vary

Plants, fairy lights, and colorful walls encircle this tiny alley in **Covent Garden.** Although increasingly crowded with more tourists every year (and we're not exactly helping) Neal's Yard feels like a secret garden inside a busy city. Although it's compact, there's a plethora of culinary options at your fingertips. We recommend **Wild Food Café,** a vegan restaurant that could convert any meat eater (at least for a meal) or **Home Slice,** which has some *amazing* pizza (and long waits). **Neal's Yard Dairy** is also a moo-st (lolz) for any cheese fan. The yard looks like it's taken from a village a few hundred years ago (if you were to remove all the cell phones), and it's a gem.

i *Establishment hours vary; wheelchair accessible*

NOTTING HILL AND PORTOBELLO ROAD

Notting Hill Gate station; www.portobelloroad.co.uk/the-market; open 24hr, market open M-W 9am-6pm, Th 9am-1pm, F 9am-7pm (antique stalls), Sa 9am-7pm (main day)

Notting Hill, of the movie fame, draws flocks of tourists to **Portobello Road Market** and the picture-perfect white houses with pastel doors. The market offers antiques and jewelry, as well as food and fashion on Saturday. But the gems of Notting Hill can be uncovered in the side streets, not just on the main road. Light pink houses covered in flowers meet pure white streets and long façades on Victorian townhouses—Instagram everything to your heart's desire. We recommend starting at **Ladbroke Grove Station** and heading to **Portobello Road,** but you can veer down side mews if you see something that interests you. If you happen to visit in August, you'll see Notting Hill come alive with **Carnival,** a giant street party that celebrates Caribbean culture.

i *Establishment prices vary*

SHAKESPEARE'S GLOBE THEATRE

21 New Globe Walk; 020 7902 1400; www. shakespearesglobe.com; exhibition open 9am-5pm

William Shakespeare once wrote "be not afraid of greatness." History nerds, bibliophiles, and regular lay-people alike: come step foot into the Globe to experience Shakespeare's greatness. Stop by for a show, or just take a tour of one of the most influential theatres of all time. Although what stands on the **South Bank** today is just a mere replica, not the real thing (rip), the exhibit tells the story of theater in Shakespeare's time. It demonstrates his legacy, like the phrases he coined (which include "skim milk"). To truly taste the history, performance tickets entitle you to one standing-room only ticket, just like the peasants of yesteryear.

i Show ticket prices vary, cheapest from £5; tours £13.50, students £11; tours M 9:30am-5pm, Tu-Sa 9:30am-12:30pm, Su 9:30am-11:30pm; wheelchair accessible

LANDMARKS

ST. PAUL'S CATHEDRAL

St. Paul's Churchyard; www.stpauls.co.uk; open M-Sa 8:30am-4:30pm, galleries open 9:30am

No big deal. It's only 528 steps to the top of St. Paul's dome, our personal favorite view of the entire city. Huffing and puffing up stairs that feel more like ladders, you'll see the entire city sprawling before your eyes. Yes, the Cathedral costs you (call it penance?), but if you don't want to pay, come for **Evensong,** the evening prayer service. Some lucky visitors will be chosen to bask in daily Evensong from inside the nave. The angelic choir voices echo from the walls of the church as the sunbeams reflect off the glinting mosaics on the ceiling. If a religious service ever felt transcendent, even for someone not religious, it's here, in St. Paul's. Don't worry if the enormity of this testament to faith gives you an existential crisis; it happens to the best of us.

i Admission £18, students £16, free for worship only; last entry 4pm; wheelchair accessible (except towers); last entry to gallery 4:15pm

BIG BEN

Intersection of Parliament St. and Great George St.

Sure, you can walk around, but Big Ben will be closed until 2021 due to conservation efforts. This means that even the regular chimings at noon will halt, and this cease in sound will last for the longest time in the tower's history. Fun fact: the tower was renamed Elizabeth Tower after Elizabeth II. The more you know!

i Free; wheelchair accessible

BUCKINGHAM PALACE

Westminster; 3031237300; www.royal-collection.org.uk; State Rooms open July 21-Aug 31 9:30am-7pm, Sept 1-Sept 30 9:30am-6pm; Royal Mews open Feb 1-Mar 25 10am-4pm, Mar 26-Nov 3 10am-5pm, Nov 4-30 10am-4pm

The land of the tea and the home of the Queen, Buckingham Palace is popular with tourists who want to witness the iconic changing of the guard. But we're gonna be real with you: the Changing of the Guard just isn't that exciting after the first couple of minutes. It consists of jostling for space with hundreds of other people to watch guards switch lines in perfect unison. But of course, you gotta do it once. And it is pretty funny to watch kids' trying to get the Beefeaters to crack a smile by the palace. Don't expect to see the Queen, as she doesn't, in fact, invite every tourist in for tea. If you are however desperate to get inside, go online to book an expensive tour of the **throne room** and other state rooms.

i Admission £24, students £22; last entry 45min. before closing; wheelchair accessible

BRITISH LIBRARY

96 Euston Rd.; 0330 333 1144; www.bl.uk; open M-Th 9:30am-8pm, F 9:30am-6pm, Sa 9:30am-5pm, Su 11am-5pm

The library contains more than 150 million items, including 200 literary gems available to view for free in the Sir John Ritblat Gallery of treasures. England's own **William Shakespeare's folios** are on display inside the dark room, alongside Beatles memorabilia and the **Magna Carta.** Marxists, there's a shelf for you too, covered in original manuscripts and writings. A copy

of *Beowulf?* Check. **The Gutenberg Bible?** Check. Original **Mozart** sheet music? Triple check. The library also contains other exhibits that charge and a multitude of places to sit and reflect on the history you've just seen. Head to the website to book your tour
i Free, some exhibits charge; wheelchair accessible

DR. JOHNSON'S HOUSE

17 Gough Sq.; 0207 353 3745; www. drjohnsonshouse.org; open Oct-Apr M-Sa 11am-5pm, May-Sept M-Sa 11am-5:30pm

You've never heard of Dr. Johnson? That's a shame, because he literally wrote the dictionary. Some of the architecture inside makes you do a double take, like the sliding doors on the second floor, but you'll only need an hour or so here. The very thorough description cards scattered on the tables offer insight into Samuel Johnson's life, friends, and shenanigans. Go find out the reason why there are bars above the front door.
i Admission £7, students £6; no wheelchair accessibility

JEWEL TOWER

Abingdon St.; 0370 333 1181; www. english-heritage.org.uk/visit/places/jewel-tower; open Nov 1-Mar 31 daily 10am-4pm, Apr 1-Sept 30 10am-6pm, Oct 1-31 10am-5pm

Right by **Westminster Abbey** and the **Houses of Parliament,** the Jewel Tower generally has a shorter line and a cheaper entrance fee. This makes sense when you figure out the tower used to host King Edward III's royal treasure. Key phrase: used to. Today, the tower is one of the only remaining parts of **Westminster Castle,** and the building is super old. Upstairs, you can learn about the "Stuff in the Old Jewel House" like the history of weights and measures and old records from the **House of Lords.**
i Admission £5.40, students £4.90; last entry 30min. before closing; no wheelchair accessibility

HOUSES OF PARLIAMENT

Parliament Sq.; www.parliament.uk/visiting; visits available Sa and during recesses

The British government is confusing. So there's the House of Lords, but also regular Lords who aren't involved in the government. Then, the House of Commons are common people—except they're in the Parliament to help make laws. But, additionally, the Prime Minister's opinion matters for legislation. There's a lot going on. Luckily, the overly-informative guided tour (or more reasonable self-guided audio tour) can help you figure out what exactly is going on in these lavishly decorated government buildings. Imagine going to work in a building that looks like the child of a church and a palace, and that's the appearance of the inside. Book in advance and come for the tour, usually only available on Saturdays, and perhaps you'll leave with a better understanding.
i Tour £28, students £23; audio tours £20.50, students £18 (discounts for booking in advance); last entry 4:30pm; wheelchair accessible

KENSINGTON PALACE

Kensington Gardens; 8444827788; www. hrp.org.uk/kensington-palace; open daily 10am-6pm

Home to the Duke and Duchess of Cambridge (that's William and Kate) as well as the Duke and Duchess of Sussex (Harry and Meghan), Kensington Palace is more than just a place to spot your favorite royal couples. With all of the history and drama surrounding the crown, the palace tells the history of the crown but could just as easily be recounting an episode of *The Crown,* if that show were real. We'd totally watch it. On the tour, you can see the luxurious rooms of royalty, where they wine and dine guests and have important royal meetings. If **Buckingham Palace** is just too crowded but you want to enter a royal building, Kensington's a very solid choice, especially if you can see the **White Garden,** previously known as the Sunken Garden.
i Admission £19.50; last entry Mar 1-Oct 31 5pm, Nov 1-Feb 28 3pm; wheelchair accessible

CAMBRIDGE

Pint-sized and picturesque, Cambridge has its history is built into its very walls. Biking through the city, you can imagine yourself as one of the bespectacled and backpack-bearing University students studying science and literature. After all, the University of Cambridge has produced some of the world's most influential minds, like Isaac Newton and Charles Darwin. Theoretically, without the University, gravity might not exist (thanks, Isaac). Of course, the colleges look more like gothic cathedrals than typical university buildings. Walk around King's College to visit the cathedral or stop by Trinity College's green pastures. People lounge in parks and libraries, on the green spaces, amid massive shelves of books. Theater and art can be found just around the corner. The Cam River flows through the city as if it were taken out of a painting, bridges spanning the punting patrons. Like its well-known rival Oxford, Cambridge offers old-timey beauty and charm in its quaint streets, well-worth a weekend wander.

The train station is slightly outside of the city center, and it's an easy walk or bus ride. In the center are **King's College,** the tourist center, many chain and local restaurants, and many of the University buildings. **The University of Cambridge** is split up into multiple different colleges, which are spread out around the city. **The Fitzwilliam Museum** is southwest of the center. The city is split by a river (classic) called the **Cam River.** You can walk along the river, but if you're looking for punting in particular, your best bets are to travel southwest to **Mill Pond** or northwest to **Quayside.**

GETTING THERE

Multiple routes run between London and Cambridge. Additionally, you can take a train or bus from London Stansted Airport. Though they're less convenient National Express coach services between Heathrow or Gatwick Airports and Cambridge are still accessible. National Rail trains run between Liverpool Street or King's Cross and Cambridge. You can book in advance for a better fare; the trip is about 60-90min. There are also buses from London Victoria Station to Cambridge whose routes end at Drummer Street.

GETTING AROUND

Many of Cambridge's tourist attractions surround the University, which is located in the city center. Almost everything is easy to reach by foot, but students and visitors alike rely on bicycles. You can rent one at City Cycle Hire at 61 Newnham Road. You can also take the bus, but be aware that multiple different services run throughout the city. Some offer all-day tickets for as little as £3, but your best bet would be to purchase an all-day multi-bus ticket from the bus driver for £8 daily or £33 weekly.

Swing by...

KING'S COLLEGE CHAPEL
King's Parade; www.kings.cam.ac.uk; 01223 331212; during College terms open M-F 9:30am-3:30pm, Sa 9:30am-3:15pm, Su 1:15pm-2:30pm; otherwise open M-Su 9:30am-4:30pm

Cambridge is old and Cambridge is beautiful. Yet reigning supreme for peak grandeur is King's College. Over a century of work resulted in the stunning gothic architecture inside King's College Chapel. The ceilings alone are intricate enough to cause a crick in your neck while admiring their beauty. Don't worry, it's totally worth it. At night, choirs perform **Evensong,** a service that even non-religious people can embrace (plus it's free). When the chapel isn't in service, entering is essentially joining a tourist parade—you can walk through the nave and end up near the transepts that contain information about the chapel. Fun fact: Oliver Cromwell used to parade his troops inside on rainy days.

i *Admission £10, students £6; tours £6, students £4, run daily 11am, noon, 2pm, 3pm; last entry 1hr before closing; wheelchair accessible*

Check out...

FITZWILLIAM MUSEUM
Trumpington St.; 01223 332900; www.fitzmuseum.cam.ac.uk; open Tu-Sa 10am-5pm, Su noon-5pm

Step inside this museum to get lost in rooms of armor, Ancient Egyptian artifacts, and shelf upon shelf of British pottery. But, for real, you might actually get lost: we were stuck wandering through sarcophagi for quite a few minutes in search for the exit. The museum holds similar wares to the **Ashmolean Museum** in Oxford, meaning you can easily spend a few hours here and still not see everything. We'd recommend sticking to just a few rooms—the Gayer Anderson room and some of the **Matisse** and **Picasso** paintings found upstairs. Of course, you absolutely can't miss the suits full of armor.

i *Admission €10, students €8; last entry 5pm; no wheelchair accessibility*

Grab a bite at...

AROMI
1 Bene't St; 0122 330 0117; www.aromi.co.uk; open M-Th 9am-7pm, F-Sa 9am-10pm

Every college town needs pizza, and Aromi doesn't disappoint. Your best bet is to take the food to go, since the space isn't huge and seating is limited. No matter where you park yourself to consume your meal, the slices will blow your mind. They're huge, befitting a starving college student who needs fuel as they prepare to write papers due at midnight. They use fresh ingredients and carry staples such as margherita pizzas, focaccia, and even a cheesy basil creation that will make your mouth water. You might not be a student, but you're a starving tourist on a budget—if you come here, you'll should blend right in.

i *Pizza from £5; vegetarian options available; limited wheelchair accessibility*

Don't miss...

RIVER CAM
Runs along the city; www.visitcambridge.org/things-to-do/punting-bus-and-bike-tours; river open 24hr, company punting hours vary

Poring over old manuscripts in the library, sipping on coffee in a hundreds-of-year-old coffee places, strolling through the colleges of the University—all traditional options for a city steeped in history. But if you're looking for something a touch more athletic and aquatic, the River Cam holds another option: **punting.** Yes, England is known for its football, but this type of punting entails paddling down the moss-green river on what looks like a flat canoe. The concept is simple; one person stands on the boat and paddles while the others sit, eat, and drink. Floating along the river, you might just be able to convince yourself you're a student living in the 1600s. (Maybe that's just the champagne talking.) For the less athletic, you can take a chauffeur-led tour, or simply watch the people below from a vantage point like the famous **Bridge of Sighs.**

i *Prices vary; no wheelchair accessibility*

MARBLE ARCH

Northeast Hyde Park; open daily 24hr

The arch was designed to be the entrance to **Buckingham Palace** but was later deemed too small. If it draws to mind a similar arch in old Paris, that's no coincidence—part of the inspiration came from the **Arc du Triomphe.** You won't need to spend too long embracing the beauty of the arch, but clearly it's an important landmark because it has its own Tube station. Nearby are **Speaker's Corner** in **Hyde Park,** where legendary orators and random people with opinions spill their guts, as well as the **Tyburn Gallows,** a once-popular place of execution.

i Free; wheelchair accessible

MILLENNIUM BRIDGE

Thames Embankment; open daily 24hr

Since London has a river running through the middle, there are many bridges connecting the two sides. But not all bridges are created equal, and this footbridge stands above (well, literally next to, but hypothetically above) the rest. One of the best views of London comes from the top of **St. Paul's Cathedral,** and one of the best views of St. Paul's can be seen from Millennium Bridge. Walk over the **Thames River** at night to see the lit-up dome, or in the afternoon, it's an easy walk from the **Tate Modern** to St. Paul's. The bridge also appears in *Harry Potter and the Half Blood Prince,* but luckily it's still standing.

i Free; wheelchair accessible

OXFORD STREET

Oxford St.; www.oxfordstreet.co.uk; street open daily 24hr, store hours vary

Shopping on Oxford Street while surrounded by tourists with arms full of shopping bags is practically a London rite of passage. While neighboring **Regent Street** houses luxury retail stores like Chanel and Louis Vuitton, Oxford Street likely holds more affordable alternatives. The term "high street fashion" was practically invented here! With a plethora of options including Zara, Topshop, Primark, and H&M, you'll find what you need.

i Store prices vary; wheelchair accessible

PICCADILLY CIRCUS

London W1J 9HP; open daily 24hr

Not your typical circus with acrobats and clowns, Piccadilly Circus is a bustling roundabout in the center of London. People come from all over the world to hustle through, desperate to get out of the crowds of neon-vest-clad school children, flashing ads, and people who don't know how to cross a street. Take a moment to perch by the metal statue at the center of the circus. Watch the cars zoom by or honk, depending on the traffic. While it's not London's most quiet place to sit and hang, the Circus is the city's heartbeat. Undeniably alive, and most beautiful at night when the streets quiet down. The Victorian buildings and red buses could be taken from a postcard.

i Free; wheelchair accessible

TOWER BRIDGE

Tower Bridge Rd.; www.towerbridge.org.uk; open Apr-Sept daily 10am-5:30pm, Oct-Mar daily 9:30am-5pm

We hate to burst your bubble but the **London Bridge** of " falling down" fame is not this bridge. An exhibit inside explains the bridge's history, and visitors can witness the **Engine Room,** where the magic of bridge-raising happens—it still opens today for large ships. Thrill-seekers can get a ticket to walk on the glass floor rising 137 feet above the **Thames.** Oh bridges, how you thrill us. For a cheaper option, simply walk over it from the **Tower of London,** its namesake.

i Admission £9.80, students £6.80; last entry Apr-Sept 5:30pm, Oct-Mar 5pm; wheelchair accessible

TOWER OF LONDON

Tower of London; 020 3166 6000; www.hrp. org.uk/tower-of-london; open M 10am-5:30pm, Tu-Sa 9am-5:30pm, Su 10am-5:30pm

Multiple towers comprise the fortress that is the Tower of London. As visitors wait in long lines to enter the castle, they might just spot one of the ravens that is kept in the tower out of superstition. It's said if the ravens leave, "the kingdom will fall." Spooky. The crowds make it hard to grasp the weight and significance of the buildings, but this *is* the site of long-past tortures, imprisonments, and killings. The most recent execution occured in 1941, which makes history feel a lot closer.

While the history of prisoners are gory and slightly horrifying, other parts of the tower like the **Crown Jewels** glimmer with royal history.

i *Admission £22.70; guided tours about every 1.5hr; last entry 5pm; wheelchair accessible*

TRAFALGAR SQUARE

Trafalgar Sq.; open daily 24hr

Lions and tourists and stairs, oh my! Home to fine art museums and chalk art creators, Trafalgar Square receives thousands of tourists every day. Whether you're seeking the **National Gallery** or a floating Yoda street performer, you'll find it. (Although, sometimes, the pavement art competes with the masterpieces inside the museum.) Make sure to snap a selfie with the big bronze lions flanking **Nelson's Column** and the turquoise fountain nearby. Trafalgar Square is a real pedestrian plaza, home to marches and protests and different public events. You'll likely end up here without even trying.

i *Free; wheelchair accessible*

WESTMINSTER ABBEY

20 Deans Yd.; 020 722 5152; www.westminster-abbey.org; open M-F 9:30am-3:30pm (late nights W 4:30pm-6pm), Sa 9am-3pm (May-Aug), Sa 9am-1pm (Sept-Apr)

Wow. Wow to the lines snaking around the building from before the first entry time, wow to the ticket price, and finally, wow to the truly breathtaking inside of the buildings, making the wait and the price worth it. The soaring ceilings, intricate carvings, and famous tombs result in crowds that sometimes feel like a concert mosh pit. But you won't notice the jostling when exploring the Gothic Architecture where the majority of Britain's monarchs took the throne. And as of this year, the **Diamond Jubilee Galleries** are finally opened, (if the audio tour wasn't enough). These galleries look down on the Abbey from above, offering spectacular views of the **Palace of Westminster** from the **Weston Tower.**

i *Admission £22 (£20 online), students £17; tours Apr-Sept M-F 10am, 10:30am, 11am, 2pm, 2:30pm, Sa 10am, 10:30am, 11am; tours Oct-Mar M-F 10:30am, 11am, 2pm, 2:30pm, Sa 10:30am, 11am; all tours £5; limited wheelchair accessibility*

MUSEUMS

 BRITISH MUSEUM

Great Russell St.; 020 7323 8181; www.britishmuseum.org; open M-Th 10am-5:30pm, F 10am-8:30pm, Sa-Su 10am-5:30pm

This museum has the freaking **Rosetta Stone.** Not the language-learning program, but its namesake that enabled historians to decode hieroglyphics. Pretty sick. The criss-crossed glass ceiling and circular stairs could be works of art themselves. Although there's controversy over the Brits' laying claim to the carvings from the Parthenon, the sculptures reveal centuries of craftsmanship that still stun today. Since there's so much to see, you should focus in on key sections via free guided tour. Our only other suggestion is the **Africa Gallery,** filled with thousands of years of artifacts from countries in Africa. Highlights including the moving **Tree of Life** statue made of weapons from Mozambique, a demonstration of art's ability to make a statement.

i *Free; multiple tours throughout the week, updated information available online; wheelchair accessible*

MUSEUM OF LONDON

150 London Wall; 020 7001 9844; www.museumoflondon.org.uk; open daily 10am-6pm

Oh, another museum about England, you may think to yourself, stepping inside the high-ceilinged building. But wait! It's a museum about the history of London itself. From 450,000 BCE to today, visitors can trace London's history. Artifacts, movies, and interactive displays tell the story of the city that became one of the greatest in the world. You won't get to see everything in one visit, but particularly fascinating are the history from 1850-1940 when London really rose to prominence and the Victorian Walk, a recreation of a street from the mid nineteenth century. A little more gruesome but equally important in the city's history are the stories of the Great Fires (of 1666 and 1834) and the history of the plague. Your head will be spinning with names, dates, and a larger appreciation for the city by the time you leave.

i Free; wheelchair accessible

CABINET WAR ROOMS

Clive Steps, King Charles St.; 020 7416 5000; www.iwm.org.uk/events/cabinet-war-rooms; open daily July-Aug 9:30am-7pm, Sept-June 9:30am-6pm

Come, step into the bunker. Dark and dreary, kind of creepy, and maybe a few hours' wait if you don't book online, the Cabinet War Rooms delve deep into the history of **Winston Churchill's** leadership during World War II. You'll learn about spies and traitors, and see the cramped living quarters of those fighting to win the war. Inside, a mini-museum devoted to Churchill himself follows his life, his political rise, fall, and rise again. It's hard to believe, but they somehow built the bunker and cased it in concrete without anyone above-ground becoming suspicious. And that's just the tip of the iceberg. Just wait until you reach the map room with push pins for every target of a potential bomb.

i Admission £21 (£18.90 online), students £16.80 (£15.10 online); last entry July-Aug 5:45pm, Sept-June 5pm; wheelchair accessible

DESIGN MUSEUM

224-238 Kensington High St.; 020 3862 5900; www.designmuseum.org; open daily 10am-6pm

Often when we think of Europe, we think of old stone buildings, castles, and ivy. The Design Museum is the exact opposite. Full of contemporary design and art, from an exhibit on graphics and politics to immersive displays on the "home of the future," this museum emphasizes the here and now. While there are some historic parts, like the evolution of the Apple logo, everything inside results in a futuristic feel. As design shifts through practical and aesthetic changes, you might end up wondering what some of the objects even do. While we can't guarantee the function of the shiny blob-looking thing that's supposedly a light, we can promise that the museum will leave you thinking about how much design impacts everything in your life. From white sneakers to iPhone speakers, the temporary and permanent exhibits connect design to fashion, architecture, engineering, and education.

i Exhibition prices vary, generally from £12; last entry 5pm; wheelchair accessible

IMPERIAL WAR MUSEUM

Lambeth Rd.; www.iwm.org.uk/visits/iwm-london; open daily 10am-6pm

Tea, crumpets, and war: three of the things on which England was built, basically. So it's only fitting that the Brits have (multiple) massive museums dedicated to war, both informational and memorial. In the museum, you can learn about World War I and World War II's causes and impacts on the city today. Don't miss the **Holocaust Exhibition,** a heart-wrenching but informative exploration of the Holocaust and different countries' roles. The museum doesn't boast about winning wars; rather, it examines how different people were affected and how the country moved forward. Through a showcase of suspended airplanes and tanks, a visit to this museum might leave you shaken by the devastation that war can cause, but you'll definitely be more informed.

i Free; wheelchair accessible

MUSEUM OF BRANDS, PACKAGING, AND ADVERTISING

111-117 Lancaster Rd.; 0207 243 9611; www.museumofbrands.com; open M-Sa 10am-6pm, Su 11am-5pm

Step inside folks, for a time-machine-esque endless hallway of trinkets and toys. The museum presents time capsules from the 1800s to today, starting with vintage tins for tobacco and soaps and ending with laundry detergent and sugary cereal. It's like an antique shop combined with a grocery store and deli. Anything that has a cabinet for One Direction (and, okay, the Beatles) has our vote. The museum presents an almost sociological study about cultural norms like the role of women and children throughout the

years. Particularly interesting are the magazines that only begin to promote slimming down and toning up in the 70s, around the same time when packaged food made an appearance. While the main gallery isn't interactive, some exhibits in other rooms let you create your own brands. We made some liquid *Let's Go* hand soap—fruity with bursting bubbles, and, of course, all-natural ingredients.
i *Admission £9, students £7; wheelchair accessible*

NATIONAL GALLERY

Trafalgar Sq.; 020 7747 2885; www.national-gallery.org.uk; open daily 10am-6pm

Showcasing some of Britain and the world's greatest hits, the National Gallery is an album of winners. Room after room, the paintings begin to blur. You might find yourself lost in the rooms of masterpieces in a brain fog. "Is this Da Vinci or Monet?" you think to yourself. Oh you poor lost soul, you'll find both here! Of course, no art museum is complete without (probably) hundreds of paintings of Jesus and Mary, some beheaded soldiers, and mythical creatures. If you get all arted out after only a few rooms, we'd suggest the Impressionist rooms. But if you're looking for directions to **Water Lilies** or **Sunflowers**… good luck, Charlie.
i *Free; wheelchair accessible*

NATIONAL PORTRAIT GALLERY

St. Martin's Pl.; 020 7306 0055; www.npg.org.uk; open M-Th 10am-6pm, F 10am-9pm, Sa-Sun 10am-6pm

Walking through room after room of paintings of people could definitely be boring. And it is, usually. All those paintings of old kings start to blur together until you're standing in the middle of a gallery yelling "NO MORE I CAN'T TAKE IT!" But luckily, the gallery also holds portraiture in other mediums and some faces that you'll recognize. The contemporary portraits provide a breath of fresh air from the typical portrait styles of earlier centuries. The gallery might best be known for its annual BP Portrait Competition, a summer exhibit showcasing the winners and recognized artists for one of the most important portrait competitions in the world (apparently, there are many). Anyone over 18 can enter a painting for

consideration, but the 48 on display in the gallery every summer are breathtaking in scope, talent, and detail that can be appreciated by everyone.
i *Free, temporary exhibits charge; wheelchair accessible*

SCIENCE MUSEUM

Exhibition Rd.; 0332414000; www.sciencemuseum.org.uk; open daily 10am-6pm

When we reach a museum, we generally head for the interactive galleries (aka games). At the Science Museum, three hours wouldn't give you enough time to play every game or touch every screen—not by a long shot. The Wonderlab has a fee but has over 50 exhibits and demonstrations. Their target audience might be kids, but even adults will learn and enjoy. Also make sure to check out the "Who Am I?" Gallery, which was difficult to find, but worth it for the games where you make babies, control their lives, and learn about your own identity. #Science. Also featuring rockets, rocks, and the history of infectious diseases, this museum has everything you've ever wanted, and more.
i *Free; wheelchair accessible*

SERPENTINE GALLERY

West Carriage Dr.; 020 7402 6075; www.serpentinegalleries.org; open daily 10am-6pm

Strolling through **Kensington Gardens** in need of a restroom, you may wander into this melted building resembling a frisbee. The art can be a little *too* contemporary for our taste, but the building offers a welcome reprieve from inevitable London rain. The gallery is intimate, as in you can walk around the whole thing in three minutes if you really try. Every summer there's a new temporary exhibit, so you never really know what you might find.
i *Free; wheelchair accessible*

SHERLOCK HOLMES MUSEUM

221b Baker St.; 020 7224 36888; www.sherlock-holmes.co.uk; open daily 9:30am-6pm

Elementary, my dear *Let's Go* reader, this museum is only worth your time if you're a well-established Sherlock fan. In which case, you'll fit right in with the people sporting with Sherlock caps and 221b tattoos. The line is somehow *really* long, and the tickets are expensive to enter the actual house where the characters

TATE MODERN

Bankside; www.tate.org.uk/visit/tate-modern; open daily 10am-6pm

Three seconds into a virtual-reality-inverted-color-anime simulation, we figured out two things: first, we know nothing about modern art, and second, modern art is pretty freaking weird sometimes. But exploring the industrial brick rectangle that makes up the lobby of one of the two buildings, we realized that part of the experience is watching those art snobs take perfectly imperfect photos in the shadow of the windows and realizing everyone's faking it just a little bit. The museum's collection spans from "classic" modern art of the twentieth century like **Andy Warhol** through to avant garde video splicing and 3D art. Most of it will leave you wondering what it all means.

i Free, temporary exhibits charge; guided tours 11am, 11:30am, noon, 2pm, 2:30pm, 3pm, 3:30pm; wheelchair accessible

VICTORIA AND ALBERT MUSEUM

Cromwell Rd.; 020 7942 2000; www.vam.ac.uk; open M-Th 10am-5:45pm, F 10am-10pm, Sa-Su 10am-5:45pm

Where to begin with this massive museum? The V&A, the self-proclaimed world's leading museum of art and design, does not disappoint. We're often hesitant to pay extra for an exhibit, (it's budget travel after all), but the V&A's temporary exhibits absolutely give you bang for your buck. The museum combines ancient statues and tombstones with modern British design and some unexplainable art. If your feet and neck get tired of looking, take a breather in the stunning red courtyard, but beware of the babies playing in the fountain.

i Free, temporary exhibits charge; free tours 10:30am, 12:30pm, 1:30pm, 3:30pm; wheelchair accessible

Sherlock and Watson allegedly lived and worked. Most of the visit is self-guided up steep steps with little information. At the end of the day, you're in a fake house of a fictional character, so maybe we can suspend our disbelief and be spooked by the human like mannequins climbing out of the ceilings. Or not.

i Free; multiple tours throughout the week, updated information available online; wheelchair accessible

TATE BRITAIN

Millbank; 020 7887 8888; www.tate.org.uk; open daily 10am-6pm

The more mature and refined older sister of the **Tate Modern,** Tate Britain contains room upon room of many of England's most prominent artists, including **Henry Moore** and **Francis Bacon.** Tate Britain also holds some contemporary pieces, but the spectacle comes from the half-millennium of British art. Stepping into the building, you instantly know there's something special here. The circular staircases, massive marble, and stone Duveen Galleries play host to different visiting exhibits that emphasize the impeccable architecture.

i Free; guided tours 11am, noon, 2pm, 3pm; wheelchair accessible

OUTDOORS

🏞 HAMPSTEAD HEATH

Hampstead Heath; 020 8340 5260; www.
cityoflondon.gov.uk/things-to-do/green-spac-
es/hampstead-heath; open daily 24hr

Less than five miles from the center of the
city (and easily accessible via the Northern
line to Hampstead) lies an enormous
park. City life isn't for everyone, and if
you find yourself needing a breather, go
for a long walk through fields of grass
and meadows, hopefully following the
butterflies and not the snakes. Deeper
inside the park, **Parliament Hill** offers a
skyline view of London. On a nice day,
the park serves as London's version of a
beach, with a big pond that's surprisingly
pleasant to bathe in. Yes it's next to a lake
with that surprisingly toxic algae, but let's not
talk about that.

i *Free; limited wheelchair accessibility*

KENSINGTON GARDENS AND HYDE PARK

Kensington Gardens; www.royalparks.org.uk/
parks/kensington-gardens; www.royalparks.
org.uk/parks/hyde-park; Kensington Gardens
open daily 6am-9:15pm; Hyde Park open daily
5am-midnight

It makes sense that the backyard of
Kensington Palace is filled with flowers,
fountains, hedges, and delicately designed
nature. Inside the Gardens, the **Orangery**
provides charming afternoon tea inside a
greenhouse for the orange trees. Close to
Oxford Street, the gardens' tranquility
instantly calms frantic tourists. For
another culture hit on the way, stop by the
Serpentine Galleries. Nearby you'll find
the Gardens' larger neighbor, **Hyde Park,**
which provides enormous green space
in the center of the city. Swans in **the
Serpentine River** might look glamorous,
but watch out, some say they bite. Every
Sunday morning, **Speakers' Corner** hosts
citizens who want to make their opinions
known. It's like *Hamilton* except totally
not.

i *Kensington Gardens free; Hyde Park admission £16, students £14; wheelchair accessible*

KEW GARDENS

Accessible via District line; 020 8332 5655;
www.kew.org/kew-gardens; open daily 10am-
7pm

A train runs through the garden,
taking visitors all around the enormous
Botanical Gardens. They recommend
three to fours hours inside, and as soon as
you enter it's easy to see why. Any garden
that needs its own train clearly has a ton
to see. The **Temperate House** reopened
after an enormous renovation to become
a botanists' dream. To feel like you're in a
rainforest (excessive humidity included),
step inside the **Palm House** tropical
rainforest. Instead of a basic picture of
banana leaf wallpaper, you can snap a
selfie with real banana leaves! The garden
contains over 30,000 different types of
plants. The only thing it doesn't have is
reasonably-priced snacks, and eating the
grass is frowned upon, so you might want
to pack something before arriving.

i *Admission £16, students £14; last entry
6pm; wheelchair accessible*

REGENT'S PARK

Regent's Park; 0300 061 2300; www.royal-
parks.org.uk/the-regents-park; open
daily 5am-9:30pm

On one side, well manicured hedges
and sculptures could be taken from a
postcard of a pristine park. The other
half of the park has lots of dogs. Small
dogs, big dogs, fluffy dogs, barking dogs.
You get the picture. Laughing children
glide on scooters and throw tantrums
about wanting ice cream. Check out the
London Zoo because it has giraffes, and
you can even pay to feed them. If dogs
or giraffes don't do it for you, nearby
Primrose Hill has one of the best London
skyline views, and it's a gorgeous place
to watch the sunset. At night, you'll find
young people hanging around, often with
beer. Cheers to open container laws.

i *Free; wheelchair accessible*

ST. JAMES PARK

St. James Park; 0300 061 2350; www.royal-
parks.org.uk/parks/st-jamess-park; open daily
5am-midnight

A few minutes from sights like
Westminster Abbey and the **Churchill
War Rooms,** St. James Park contains
a large lake that reflects the three
surrounding palaces. It's perfect for a
stroll or a picnic (or a nap). For budding

fruit in it is a health food. The tapestries and carpets along the walls and floor set the scene: you're in Persia now, eating what just might be the best meal of your life. Grilled *halloumi*, *meze* platters, harissa eggs, and delectable daily specials can all be found here.

i Entrées from £4; gluten-free, vegan, and vegetarian options available; limited wheelchair accessibility; card minimum £10

THE CHEESE BAR ($)

Unit 93/94 Camden Stables, Chalk Farm Rd.; www.thecheesebar.com; open M-Th noon-10pm, F noon-1pm, Sa 11am-10pm, Su noon-8pm

Dairy dreamers can get their fix at this all-cheese based restaurant. Lactose-intolerant people might want to avoid it, since the menu contains mouth-watering mac and cheese, raclette, cheese fondue, cheeseburgers, and even some cheese sweets like cheesecake and goat-cheese-and-honey ice cream. Did we mention cheese? Basically, it's heaven for a mouse or a hungry cheese-addicted traveler. Some entrées veer on the expensive side for casual dining, but most are reasonable (one of London's best grilled cheese for around £6). So get ready to spend a little cheddar… on a lot of cheddar.

i Entrées from £7; vegetarian options available; limited wheelchair accessibility; last seating 30min. before closing

BEN'S COOKIES ($)

35-36 Great Marlborough St.; 020 7734 8846; www.benscookies.com; open M-Sa 10am-8pm, Su 11am-7pm

Ben's Cookies are famous for their giant chunks of toppings instead of the more traditional chips. You'll find stands everywhere: in the Tube, in markets, and of course, in bigger shops on the street. They price cookies by weight, which is a little weird, but as soon as one of the melty ooey-gooey cookies dissolves in your mouth, you won't care about paying the extra 20 pence for a chunkier cookie. If just one cookie won't satisfy your sweet tooth, why not be a little wild and indulge in the cookie monster: a cookie with gelato. C is for Cookie, and B is for Ben's. That's good enough for us!

i Cookies from £1.60; vegetarian options available; wheelchair accessible

ornithologists— bird scientists— more than fifteen species of waterfowl live in the lake. Be sure to note the pelicans. We heard one of them made a cameo in *Finding Nemo*. Just kidding, but their story is almost as cool. Pelicans have been around in the park since 1664, a gift from the Russian ambassador. These days, they're fed once a day so they don't snag the fish from the **London Zoo** as snacks. Feisty.

i Free; wheelchair accessible

FOOD

SNACKISTAN AT PERSEPOLIS ($)

28-30 Peckham High St.; 020 7639 8007; www.foratasteofpersia.co.uk; open daily 11am-8:45pm

London's best restaurant (in our humble opinion) hides at the back of a Persian market. Situated in **Peckham,** an area once considered unsafe but now undergoing the early touches of gentrification, Snackistan is kind of hard to get to. But the best things in life are worth fighting for, and certainly whoever first said that was talking about the bus situation you'll encounter on the way to this restaurant. The menu itself is full of jokes and dotty one-offs, adding to the quirky confusion. We do have to agree with the menu: a sundae that has nuts and

BREAKFAST CLUB ($)

12-16 Artillery Ln.; 020 7078 9633; www. thebreakfastclubcafes.com; open M-W 7:30am-11pm, Th-F 7:30am-midnight, Su 8am-10:30pm

Boasting walls decorated with egg-yolk yellow paint and neon "Sex, Drugs, and Bacon Rolls" signs, the restaurant's interior is quirky and a little bizarre. But the Bacon, Egg, and Cheese and Salted Caramel Banoffee Pancakes are enough to draw crowds even without the cute décor. Because the store has multiple locations around the city, you're bound to stumble upon one, but if you end up nearby, we'd recommend the **Spitalfields** location, for it's not-so-secret speakeasy. Step through a refrigerator after telling the hostess you're "here to see the mayor," and you'll end up downstairs at a hidden bar called **The Mayor of Scaredy Cat Town.**

i *Entrées from £5.50; vegan and vegetarian options available; wheelchair accessibility*

CHURCHILL ARMS ($$)

119 Kensington Church St.; 020 7727 4242; open M-W 11am-11pm, Th-Sa 11am-midnight, Su noon-10:30pm

One of London's most beautiful pubs, the Churchill Arms stands on a street in **Notting Hill,** a tall, proud, and stately building covered in flowers and flags. Take a deep breath, step inside, and inhale the scent of pad thai. Yes, this Winston Churchill memorabilia-loaded pub serves Thai food. In summer, the back conservatory is a little steamy, both because of the hot food and the sun shining through the windows. But if you can come around Christmas, the outside of the pub shines with lights and Christmas trees, a sight to behold. You won't find many locals, but you will find mouthwatering pad thai, which is sometimes even better!

i *Entrées from £9; vegetarian options available; limited wheelchair accessibility*

GAIL'S BAKERY ($)

128 Wardour St.; 020 7287 1324; www. gailsbread.co.uk; open M-Th 7:30am-7pm, F 7:30am-8pm, Sa-Su 8:30am-8pm

Freshly-baked breads and pastries line the stone counters at this soothing and artisanal bakery. With breakfast served until 3:30pm, Gail's wants to make sure everyone gets a taste of their baker's breakfast. Some locations serve lunch—mostly healthy options with salads and vegetables. Not only nutritious but also philanthropic, they partner with multiple charities to help homeless people and those facing hunger. So you can feel great about those scrambled eggs and toast you devoured inside this shop boasting a cornucopia of pastries.

i *Breakfast from £4; gluten-free, vegan, and vegetarian options available; wheelchair accessible; breakfast kitchen closes at 3pm*

GRANGER AND CO KING'S CROSS ($)

7 Pancras Sq.; 020 3058 2567; www. grangerandco.com/kings-cross; open M-Sa 7am-11pm, Su 8am-10:30pm

This restaurant's hotcakes (that's British for pancake, ya silly goose) are *mindblowing.* We tried the ricotta banana hotcakes, which came with a jug of maple syrup to pour to our heart's content. And honeycomb butter. Fluffy and thick, their hotcakes are substantial. We couldn't even finish the plate, which, for a hungry traveler, is a rarity. Though not listed on the menu, hotcakes sometimes come with a strawberry version, not just banana. Somehow, everyone here seems to be incredibly beautiful, and the natural light coming in through the windows only adds to the aspirational ambience.

i *Entrées from £7; gluten-free, vegan, and vegetarian options available; limited wheelchair accessibility*

HOME SLICE ($)

13 Neal's Yard; 020 3151 7488; www. homeslicepizza.co.uk; open daily noon-11pm

Pizza by the slice is a rarity in London. That might be for the best, because none can come close to Home Slice's giant slices. This pizza is like an ideal date: hot and cheesy, yet balanced with other fun and funky ingredients, and big enough to cover the entire table with deliciousness. Okay, maybe that's taking the analogy a bit far. On a nice night, you'd better order to go and sit on one of the benches in **Neal's Yard,** rather than wait for your perfect pie. No starters and no desserts—they cut to the chase.

i *Pizza slices £4, whole pizzas £20; vegetarian options available; limited wheelchair accessibility*

OXFORD

Famed for its university and famous graduates (scores of Prime Ministers and five kings, to name just a few), Oxford's petite and picturesque city calls out to visitors looking to explore centuries past. Bibliophiles and retrophiles alike will find solace in the stone-lined streets and majestic buildings, famous libraries like the Bodleian Library, and centuries-old structures like the Bridge of Sighs. Of course, while the history and academia compel thousands of tourists to Oxford's streets every year, the small city brims with its own life and culture, especially when the students are in session. So step inside the charming city and explore the magnificent architecture of the spired buildings. Stumble upon one of the many colleges and explore the legacy of students past, sometimes controversial political figures like Bill Clinton or Theresa May or imagine you're gallivanting with literary legends like Lewis Carroll (Alice and Wonderland), CS Lewis (The Chronicles of Narnia), and JRR Tolkien (Lord of the Rings). By the end of your stay, you'll likely wish you were studying here, if only to wake up and see the sunlight hit the buildings that look like magic. The city center is quite compact, and has access to the nearby train station, which is west of the city. **George Street** is one of the main avenues; found close by is **Broad Street,** where you'll find **Bodleian Library.** The Tourist Office is on the same street. Don't miss pastel-toned **Holywell Street** nearby. To the south is **High Street,** where you'll find lots of shopping. The University's 38 colleges are scattered throughout the city. Notably, **Christ Church College** is in the south. To the north you'll find the **Ashmolean Museum** and **Pitt Rivers Museum.** The **Cherwell River** runs along the east side.

GETTING THERE

Oxford is an easy train or bus away from London. Trains from Victoria Station and King's Cross are available about every 20min. Book in advance for cheaper fares. The X90 bus stops at Marylebone Rd, Marble Arch, and Victoria. The X90 is slightly cheaper. Fares run at £18 for a return fare for adults and £14 for 16-26 year olds, and the trip is about 100min. long.

GETTING AROUND

Oxford's city center is so tiny that it's almost impossible to get lost. There are also buses that take you everywhere you need to go, with fares ranging from £1.10 to £4.20 for an all-day pass. Return fares are usually around £3, so if you're taking multiple bus trips, your best bet is to invest in an all-day pass. Make sure you don't lose the receipt!

Swing by...

BODLEIAN LIBRARY

Broad St.; 01865 277162; www.bodleian.ox.ac.uk; open M-Sa 9am-5pm, Su 11am-5pm

We'll cut to the chase: to see most of the inside of this masterpiece of a library, you'll have to be a student or researcher. Or cough up extra cash for an extended guided tour. For free, you can, however, see the exterior of buildings in the seventeenth-century quadrangle, and entering the divinity school only costs a hefty £1. Fun fact: the divinity school made an appearance in *Harry Potter and the Sorcerer's Stone* as Hogwarts' infirmary. Another must-see comes in the form of a rotund and robust building: **the Radcliffe Camera.** The gated building near the main library appears in many Oxford postcards.

i Standard 60min. guided tour £8, extended 90min. tour £14, mini 30min. tour £6, audio tour £2.50, self-guided tour of divinity school £1; limited wheelchair accessibility

ASHMOLEAN MUSEUM

Beaumont St.; 01865 278000; www.ashmolean.org; open Tu-Su 10am-5pm,
last F of every month 10am-8pm

Much more traditional than the **Pitt Rivers Museum,** the Ashmolean Museum is still a clown car of a museum. And by that we mean when you think you've seen everything, you'll uncover yet another floor full of seemingly endless exhibits and artifacts. Once you've accepted that you won't see it all, check out our top recommendations: begin with the mummy of Meresamun and learn about Ancient Egypt. Another must-see is the Powhatan Mantle. England's oldest public museum holds half a million years of art and history, so yeah, it's a little overwhelming. If you're a plan-in-advance type of person, make sure to book a visit to the Western Print Room (it's free) to see Michaelangelo's and Raphael's sketches. No big deal.

i Free; wheelchair accessible

Grab a bite at...

COVERED MARKET ($$)

Accessible via Market St., High St., or the Golden Cross in Cornmarket St.;
www.oxford-coveredmarket.co.uk; open M-Sa 8am-5pm, Su 10am-4pm

What's a city without a market? At first, it seems the only vendors sell slightly tacky Oxford-branded tourist apparel. Head deeper (past the clothing stores) and you'll find a solid selection of places to eat. This is no Camden Market, but a smattering of food stands at the ready to greet visitors. In the mood for something healthy? We recommend **Alpha Bar,** which changes its salad and sandwich options daily. And then, of course, you should stop at **Ben's Cookies** for a chunky and melty cookie for dessert. You could even head to the butcher and the **Oxford Cheese Company** to buy picnic foods if you want to go punting on the river.

i Prices vary

Don't miss...

TURF TAVERN

4-5 Bath Pl.; 01865 243235; www.greeneking-pubs.co.uk/pubs/oxfordshire/
turf-tavern; open daily 11am-11pm

Tucked between two alleys, Turf Tavern is one of Oxford's hidden secrets. And we mean really hidden—we had to obsessively follow our phone's GPS function to find it. Luckily for you, we'll tell you where it is. Walk down **New College Lane,** right across from the **Bodleian Library** and under the **Bridge of Sighs.** On your left, there's a teeny alley called **St. Helen's Passage** that looks like its too small to fit anyone. Follow it (trust us), and you'll end up at the pub. Inside, you won't find the world's cheapest drinks, but people mostly come for the history. It used to be a prime location for cockfighting until there was a fire. While some of the Harry Potter movies were filmed, cast and crew would camp out in the pub on their breaks. Today, students and tourists lounge in the back garden, enjoying a pint.

i Drinks from £6, entrées from £10; limited wheelchair accessibility

KEU BANH MI DELI ($)

332 Old St.; 020 7739 1164; open M-W 9:30am-9:30pm, Th-Sa 9:30am-10pm

Banh Mi: a Vietnamese baguette sandwich with meat (usually pork), crispy vegetables and crunchy bread. This café serves big portions for less than a fiver. Score! Found in **Shoreditch,** it has the obligatory hipster element—in this case, boxy glass lamps hanging from the ceiling. At lunchtime, the restaurant fills up quickly, so we'd suggest takeaway, which saves you a hefty 50p anyway. (Unless you want to fight your way to the window seats to observe the almost uniformly trendy Shoreditch residents.) Other than the Keu Classic, they serve curries and other rice dishes, as well as a Kimchi BBQ Pork Banh Mi.
i Entrées from £6.50; vegetarian options available; limited wheelchair accessibility

MAC FACTORY ($)

152-156 North Gower St.; www.themacfactory.co.uk; open M-F 11am-8pm

Ooey gooey cheesy deliciousness awaits inside this small store. Customers choose from six varieties of mac including the classic Nostalgic (mature cheddar and mozzarella), or more fun and funky options like Hey Mac-Arena (beet chili, tortilla crisps, sour cream, jalepeño). This is not your average box of Kraft: crispy breadcrumbs and perfectly firm noodles make every bite an enlightening experience. The stand at **Camden Market** sometimes has quite a line, but the brick-and-mortar shop in **Euston Square** is big enough to satisfy all your cheesiest cravings.
i Entrées from £6; vegetarian options available; wheelchair accessible

NEW JOMUNA ($$)

74 Wilton Rd.; 078287509; www.thenewjomuna.com; open daily noon-3pm and 6pm-midnight

Here, he menu goes on for days. But be careful when you order, because those appetizers they push on you at the beginning will most certainly be tacked onto the bill at the end. Regardless, the immense variety of dishes on the menu means even the pickiest Indian food fan is bound to find a meal. The restaurant shines with their flavorful vegetarian meals. The nice hot towel after the meal adds just a touch of luxury that perhaps the fake chandeliers and neon ceiling decor might have conveyed.
i Entrées from £8.25; vegan and vegetarian options available; limited wheelchair accessibility

PILAU ($)

22 Noel St.; 079 5457 6380; www.pilaurestaurant.co.uk; open M-Tu noon-8pm, W-Sa noon-9pm, Su noon-4pm

Think Chipotle—but Indian food and very high quality. Pilau delivers quick and delicious plates, perfect for lunch. Their target customers are people on their lunch break, but who's to say a starving sightseeing won't want to wolf down a bowl of their butter chicken with a side of Naan balls? And if you want to do your good deed for the day: for every meal you buy at Pilau, one gets donated through Akshaya Patra to a hungry child in India. From the pleasant staff to the concept to the freshness of the food, Pilau's a hit for sure.
i Medium plates from £5, entrées from £6; gluten-free and vegetarian options available

MANDIRA ($)

78B Long Acre; 020 7836 9463; www.mandiralondon.com; open M-F 8am-7pm

Bio-live yogurt sounds like a scientific lab experiment, but it's a Turkish staple and found in most of the dishes at Mandira. Sweet or savory (don't knock it 'til you try it), the yogurt comes in bowls with a variety of toppings ranging from basic granola and strawberries to more adventurous hummus and za'atar. But we first fell for the Simit, a traditional turkish bagel that's crispier and less doughy than classic American bagels. They're fresh, cheap, and filling, and come with different toppings like Turkish pastrami or Anthotyro cheese, fig, and honey. Yes, that's right, Turkish food in London is way more than just kebabs! The stand in **Old Spitalfields Market** serves just the Simit Bagels.
i Large bowls from £5; gluten-free, vegan, and vegetarian options available

NIGHTLIFE

⚑ QUEEN OF HOXTON

1 Curtain Rd., Shoreditch; 0207 422 0958; www.queenofhoxton.com; open M-W 4pm-midnight, Th 4pm-2am, F-Sa noon-2am, Su noon-midnight

A four-seasons-themed rooftop bar: what more could you ask for? How about a two-story club with an upstairs game room, murals on the walls, and a basement bar with a bangin' bass system. Or a film club, drag bingo, and hip hop karaoke. With a plethora of bars in **Shoreditch** it can be hard to choose, but Queen of Hoxton's the queen of clubs. Come as you are. You never won't have a good night boogie-ing on down or stopping for an afternoon cocktail. Be warned, though: it can get hot, sweaty and very loud, but aren't the best things in life?

i Weekdays no cover, weekend cover varies; BGLTQ+ friendly; limited wheelchair accessibility

THE DRAYTON ARMS

153 Old Brompton St..; 020 7835 2301; www.thedraytonarmssw5.co.uk; open M 11am-11pm, Tu-W 11am-11:30pm, Th-F 11am-midnight, Sa 10am-midnight, Su 10am-11pm

If a speakeasy is a bar hidden behind something else, then what do we call a theatre hidden behind a bar? A watcheasy? Nah, we call it the Drayton Arms. The theatre's no secret, though, and is home to multiple monthly shows, including previews for shows heading to the **Edinburgh Fringe Festival.** It's a small black-box theatre, so there are no bad seats. When ticket prices on the West End get as high as the triple digits, a nice play for a tenner can be the remedy for a theatre-seeking tourist on a budget. Plus, the pub downstairs serves burgers almost too pretty to eat, along with other very high-quality modern British food. Your dinner will likely end up costing you more than the show.

i Entrées from £12, drinks from £5, show tickets from £12; limited wheelchair accessibility in theater

HEAVEN

17 Villiers St.; 020 7930 2020; www. heavennightclub-london.com; hours vary by gig, usually open until 4am

As we stood at the center of the bouncing stage, surrounded by intoxicated revelers screaming and jumping to the seminal classic "Since U Been Gone," we felt half at home and half sure we'd be instantly trampled. Sweating and singing, the crowd at Heaven embraces their policy of embracing everyone. The bouncers *have* been known to pick out those who've had a few too many pints to drink, so be careful when you get here. Upstairs, the hip-hop rooms hold even more shirtless men and some classic R&B jams. Downstairs, the cheesy pop palace blares divas from Lady Gaga to Carly Rae Jepsen, and stage dance floor space comes at a premium. Heaven is run by the same people as **G-A-Y** in **Soho** and hosts different events and concerts like drag and theme nights. We've found few places as fun to dance and not feel judged by anyone in the room.

i Cover £5 before 1am, £8 after, often free with guest list online or student card; BGLTQ+ friendly; no wheelchair accessibility; last entry 3am

RED LION

48 Parliament St.; 020 7930 5826; www. redlionwestminster.co.uk; open M-Tu 8am-11pm, W 9:30am-11pm, Th-F 8am-11pm, Sa 8am-9pm, Su 9am-9pm

Ah, the smell of beer. But not like, stale-frat-house-with-sticky-floors type of beer. No, the beer smell from this pub is pure class from the tap. In this old and well-maintained pub, you'll feel like a real true grownup sipping a pint after a long day's work. Or however British professionals feel. With no TVs or music, people rely on conversation to entertain them. (The horror!) Upstairs ,the dining rooms invite hungry people in, but we'd recommend sticking to the downstairs bar by the window so you can people-watch in **Carnaby** while getting drunk at the same time!

i Drinks from £4; limited wheelchair accessibility

THE SOCIAL

5 Little Portland St.; 0207 636 4992; www.
thesocial.com; open M-W 3pm-midnight, Th
3pm-1am, F 12:30pm-1am, Sa 6pm-1am

Clubbing in London can go one of
two ways: dressed up, your heels or
button-downs ready for a big night out
in **Mayfair,** or the beer-laden sticky
floors of clubs in **Camden.** The Social
blurs the lines between them. Since the
venue is owned by a record label, there's
a heavy emphasis on music here. Most
nights you'll find a live gig down by the
basement bar. With names like MGMT,
Adele, and Vampire Weekend having
graced the stage here, there's someone
worth seeing to appeal to everyone. You're
not getting the see-and-be-seen crowd,
nor are you getting aggressive musicheads
who don't want to meet people. The kind
of people who come here are, well, social.
i Ticket prices vary; BGLTQ+ friendly; limited
wheelchair accessibility

TRAPEZE

89 Great Eastern St.; 020 7739 6747; www.
trapezebar.co.uk; open Tu-Th 4pm-2:30am,
F-Sa 4pm-3:30am

"Welcome, locals and travelers, to the
greatest show on earth!" is what we
imagine the bartenders at Trapeze saying
to us (with their eyes) as they make
cocktails that are basically works of art.
This circus-themed bar has real trapezes
hanging from the ceiling (usually unused)
and a nightclub open on the weekends.
But even during the week, the bar
becomes a dance floor and DJs keep the
party going until 3am. Free fresh popcorn
fuels your thirst for another drink while
you're dancing your butt off. Yes, cocktails
are pricey, but that's the price you pay
for free beer pong tables, and circus tent-
themed boots. Embrace the experience (or
just pregame) for a night to remember.
i Beer from £5, cocktails from £9; BGLTQ+
friendly; limited wheelchair accessibility

YE OLDE CHESHIRE CHEESE

145 Fleet St., City of London; 2073536170;
open M-Sa 11am-11pm

At almost 500 years old, this pub is just a
little older than that leftover pizza you said
you were going to throw out yesterday.
In fact, according to the expert bartender,
the cellars downstairs where people
dine are from the 1300s. Legend says
Samuel Johnson and **Charles Dickens**
frequented this pub, and it probably still
looks exactly how it did then. There's
no music and no TV—just an old clock
that doesn't work. The pub draws visitors
with history, but keeps them there with
reasonably-priced drinks and a historic
atmosphere. And Polly, the taxidermied
parrot above the bar, makes for a story
too.
i Beer from £4, entrées from £11; BGLTQ+
friendly; no wheelchair accessibility

MANCHESTER

Coverage by **Lucy Golub**

The bee symbolizes Manchester—hardworking, industrious, and buzzing around
from one thing to the next. You'll find it emblazoned on walls, logos, and even the
trash cans on the street. And it fits. Manchester used to be known as Cottonopolis, the
textile hub of the world. Today it's known for music and art (ever heard of a little band
called Oasis?), vintage shopping and street murals, its football team, and countless
bars and clubs. Manchester is well on its way to London-level trendiness, but hasn't
lost its character in its quest to make it to the big leagues. It's not just a mini-London,
but rather an evolving creative hub full of history, working its way into the shells
of industry that used to occur there. And although they say Brits might not be the
friendliest people out there, Mancunians might just prove you wrong.

ORIENTATION

Manchester's neighborhoods are distinct but so small you'll be in the next without even realizing. In the center of the city you'll find the **Central Retail District** and **Civic Quarters.** To the east lies **Piccadilly Station,** where the tourist center and trains are located. The city's trendy **Northern Quarter,** home to vintage stores, coffee shops, and lots of nightlife can be found north of the station. West of Piccadilly Station are the **Gay Village** and **Chinatown,** more nightlife hubs. West and slightly south of the center, you'll find **Spinningfields,** home to the **Museum of Science and Industry** and the **People's History Museum,** as well as more restaurants and nightlife. Much further west are **Trafford,** home to **Old Trafford,** the football stadium, and **Media City,** where many TV programs are produced.

ESSENTIALS

GETTING THERE

Flying into Manchester Airport is easy, and trains run every 10min. from the airport to Piccadilly Station. Trains run to Piccadilly Station and Victoria Station from all over England. From there, a bus or tram take you around the city.

GETTING AROUND

Manchester is compact enough that most places are near enough to walk. If you're looking for public transportation, the metro shuttle bus offers multiple routes that can be viewed online at www.tfgm. com. Additionally, the tram has fewer routes but takes you to the areas you'll likely be going. There are taxis, but they are rather expensive. Public transportation runs late enough into the night to be serviceable at most hours.

PRACTICAL INFORMATION

Tourist Offices: The Manchester Tourist Information Centre (1 Piccadilly Gardens, Portland St.; 0871 222 8223; www. visitmanchester.com; open M-Sa 9:30am-5pm, Su 10:30am-4:30pm)
Banks/ATMs/Currency Exchange: Banks and ATMs are prevalent. One is Barclays Bank (88-86 Market St.; 345 734 6345; open M-Tu 9:30am-5:30pm, W 10am-4:30pm, Th-Sa 9:30am-5:30pm, Su 11am-3pm).
Post Offices: Piccadilly Plaza (F4, Londis Store, Portland St.; 161 237 1229; open M-F 10am-6pm, Sa 10am-4pm, Su 11am-3pm)
Public Restrooms: Town Hall Extension Public Toilet (Lloyd St.)
Internet: Most cafés, restaurants, and museums have Wi-Fi.

BGLTQ+ Resources: The Proud Trust provides BGLTQ+ resources and support (49-51 Sidney St.; 7813 981338; www. theproudtrust.org).

EMERGENCY INFORMATION

Emergency Number: 999
Police: Greater Manchester Police Headquarters (Northampton Rd.; non-emergency 101; www.gmp.police.uk)
Rape Crisis Center: The Manchester Rape Crisis Centre (60 Nelson St.; 0161 660 3347; www.manchesterraoecrisis. co.uk; phoneline available daily 9am-5:30pm)
Hospitals:
• Manchester Royal Infirmary (Oxford Rd.; 161 624 0420; open daily 24hr)
• North Manchester General Hospital (Delaunays Rd.; 161 624 0420; open daily 24hr)
Pharmacies: You'll have no trouble finding pharmacies.
• Boots (32 Market St.; 161 832 6533; boots.co.uk; open M-Sa 8am-8pm, Su 11am-5pm)
• Everest Pharmacy (80 Stockport Rd.; 161 273 4629; www.everestpharmacy. co.uk/; open M-F 9am-7pm, Sa 9am-3pm)
• Lloyds Pharmacy (Brunswick St.; 161 273 1327; www.lloydspharmacy. com; open M-F 8:30am-6:30pm, Sa 9am-1pm)

ACCOMMODATIONS

🔖 HATTERS ON NEWTON ($)

50 Newton St.; 161 236 9500; hattershostels. com/manchester-newton-street; reception open 24hr

Is Hatters the most luxurious hostel out there? No. Do the beds have fluffy pillows? Also no. But you won't find a

bed rather than in the bathroom. Every bed comes with a light and power outlet (thank you!) so all you'll have to worry about is the noise coming from the windows facing the rowdy streets of the northern quarter.

i Dorms from £13, privates from £42; reservation recommended; weekend min stay 2 nights, max 2 weeks; BGLTQ+ friendly; wheelchair accessible; Wi-Fi; linens provided; kitchen; locks and towels for rent

YHA ($)

Potato Wharf; 0345 371 9647; www.yha. org.uk/hostel/yha-manchester; reception open 24hr

Another city, another YHA. This one offers the same neon sheets and colorful common rooms with a pretty quiet atmosphere. There's a café and bar onsite and a large common room with games as well as a self-service kitchen and paid breakfast. We didn't see anyone hanging about when we got inside, though. If, however, you're looking for clean, spacious, and useful beds (USBs and outlets abound) in a quiet location, you won't find better. As a bonus, the hostel is near **Spinningfields**, home to the **Museum of Science and Industry** as well as lots of restaurants.

i Beds from £12, privates from £29; reservation recommended; max stay 2 weeks per month; BGLTQ+ friendly; wheelchair accessible; Wi-Fi; laundry facilities, café and bar onsite; linens provided; towels and locks for rent

better-situated room for the price. Dorms are basic: bunk beds and hall bathrooms, and you *might* be pushed to claim a power outlet for yourself. Those looking for more hotel vibes should perhaps seek out neighbor hostel **Hatters Hilton Chambers.** The community here, though, is unmatched, and events during the week ensure guests get to know each other. The common room's fairly outdated Tumblr-based QR code map is a good metaphor for the hostel itself—a tad old, a tad non-functional (outlets, we're looking at you), but it's got a lot of heart and is super convenient.

i Dorms from £13, privates from £40; reservation recommended; BGLTQ+ friendly; no wheelchair accessibility; Wi-Fi; linens provided; towels and locks for rent

HATTERS HILTON CHAMBERS ($)

15 Hilton St.; 161 236 4414; www.hattershostels.com/manchester-hilton-chambers; reception open 24hr

A slightly-nicer sister hostel to **Hatters on Newton,** Hatters Hilton Chambers provides more amenities and a cleaner space, but perhaps at the price of sociability. Guests can, however, head over to the other Hatters just down the street for their events like free food Tuesdays and weekend pub crawls. There's no breakfast, but guests get a discount at a nearby café and a bar. We must admit, the ensuite bathrooms are gems, but some rooms have the sink randomly next to a bunk

SIGHTS
CULTURE

ROYAL EXCHANGE THEATRE

St. Ann's Sq.; 161 833 9833; www.royalexchange.co.uk; open M-Sa 9:30am-7:30pm, Su 11am-5pm

The architecture of the suspended central theater in the middle of giant colorful marble pillars is a spectacle in itself. Yet on top of the breathtaking enormity of the space itself, the Royal Exchange Theatre hosts shows in their two-performance spaces almost every day. The center theater is the largest **theater in the round** in the country, and it resembles a Mars rover mixed with a robotic flower. You'll have to see it yourself to understand; the theatre offers different student and early-bird discounts, so you'll be able to watch some classic British theater as well as newer modern shows.

i Free; show prices vary, tickets from £10; wheelchair accessible

AFFLECK'S

52 Church St.; 161 839 0718; www.afflecks. com; open M-F 10:30am-6pm, Sa 10am-6pm, Su 11am-5pm

Don't be surprised when you run into goths sporting neon hair and giant boots buckled up to their knees. Affleck's contains 60 independent stores spread out over 4 floors, so you can take your pick of vintage denim, floral dresses, American candy, and classic punk rock record shops. And of course, lots of jewelry for obscure body piercings. All we're saying is that if you're looking for a very bedazzled wedding dress and leather gloves while shopping for bath products in the shape of cupcakes and classic Levi Mom Jeans, you've found your place. Come and browse the costumes and the characters of the people you'll meet here.

i Prices vary; wheelchair accessible

MANCHESTER ART GALLERY

Mosley St.; 161 235 8888; manchesterartgallery.org; open M-W 10am-5pm, Th 10am-9pm, F-Su 10am-5pm

Oh, art galleries. You're so cultured and highbrow. That's what we think of when we hear "art gallery," but if you're burned out and have no desire to stare at old paintings of dead people, then you're in luck, because this gallery holds way more than just the typical landscapes and portraits. Some of the best pieces of the gallery come from the re-done caption addendums from the gallery's first feminist takeover. So while you're reading a snooty art historian's interpretations of the juxtaposition of light and dark in the paintings of pre-Raphaelite artists (whose works are beautiful, we'll admit), you can also read a nice little paragraph roasting the men who refused to acknowledge female competency. Snaps. The gallery also hosts contemporary exhibits upstairs, often using multimedia to express political messages. Be sure to check out the

mindfulness exhibit. It's as if the art gallery had a rebellious teenage kid—the two different vibes you'll get from the gallery might not match, but they create a full experience (imagine the vibes of Banksy amid seventeenth-century paintings).

i Free; tours available Th, F, Sa, Su; wheelchair accessible

LANDMARKS

🏛 JOHN RYLANDS LIBRARY

150 Deansgate; 0161 306 0555; www.library. manchester.ac.uk/rylands; open M-Sa 10am-5pm, Su noon-5pm

The reading room of this library puts basically every American library to shame. Neo-Gothic architecture meets centuries-old books in an old but warmly lit banquet-hall-esque library. If you have any reading to get done, you might not want to do it here, because the room's details will keep your eyes focused on everything but your book. And yet it *is* an ideal place to work—hushed and somber except for the occasional echo of a step, a camera click, or the brush of pages turning. Make sure you look up (they provide mirrors to avoid sore necks—*nice.)* and look at the lights, which are indicative of John Rylands claim to fortune: cotton. His second wife created the library in his honor. Thanks Enriqueta! The books they have on display are not-quite page-turners but are historically important—as in, really old.

i Free; wheelchair accessible

ALAN TURING MEMORIAL

Sackville Park; open 24hr

Ah, Alan Turing: genius, inventor, world-changer. Yet too few know his story. We'll break it down quickly: the man basically invented the first computer and assisted the Allies in World War II. But Turing was gay, and when he revealed his identity during an investigation, he ended up losing his job. At the time, being gay was a crime, and his admission led to brutal physical punishment and his eventual suicide by cyanide poisoning. Honor his legacy and learn more about his life at this statue in a small park. There he sits in casual clothes, an apple in his palm.

i Free; wheelchair accessible

MANCHESTER CATHEDRAL

Victoria St.; 0161 833 2220; www.manches-tercathedral.org; open M 8:30am-5pm, Tu-Th 8:30am-6:30pm, F 8:30am-5pm, Sa-Su 8:30am-6:30pm

When tragedy struck Manchester in the summer of 2017, the city responded with a mural emphasizing the love and connections between people of all backgrounds. This mural was painted on one of the walls of the Cathedral, broadcasting a message of peace. Unlike others you might encounter on your travels, this church feels like a place people actually visit for worship, making it more than just a beautiful testament to the past. Especially intricate are the details on the center quire, which has looked basically the same since 1509. With only a £1 photo permit paid to a sometimes hard-to-find individual welcoming you into the cathedral, the structure is yours to explore and wander as you remember the city's resilience.

i Free; photography permit £1; wheelchair accessible

MUSEUMS

MUSEUM OF SCIENCE AND INDUSTRY

Liverpool Rd.; 0161 832 2244; www.msimanchester.org.uk; open M-Sa 10am-5pm

Manchester used to be called Cottonopolis—the world's hub for textile production. Today, that claim to fame has dimmed, but the Museum of Science and Industry clings onto its past life as an industrial city. Watch an engine demonstration, and learn about how cotton was spun. And when you get bored of that (it happens to the best of us), head upstairs to the interactive "Experiment!" gallery with 25 hands-on exhibits that feel like games. You can play a Dance Dance Revolution-style game to learn how about recycling, or pedal a bicycle to see your skeleton move. Although you might be playing some of these games with six year-olds, no one's judging. Go live your best life and learn a lot while having some arcade (or museum) fun.

i Free except for some exhibits; wheelchair accessible

PEOPLE'S HISTORY MUSEUM (SPINNINGFIELDS)

Left Bank; 0161 838 9190; www.phm.org.uk; open daily 10am-5pm

Do you hear the people sing? Singing the song of angry men. Well, kind of. This museum focuses on England's fights for equality for different groups of people—hint: usually the groups are not white French men. But the museum condenses hundreds of years of movements into three floors, and reminds you that there have always been ideas worth fighting for. While the panels, artifacts, and stories may overwhelm you with information, we left feeling angry at the injustice others have experienced, yet empowered and hopeful for progress. The first floor focuses on pre-1945 and the second follows movements from 1945 to the present day. You might just find your next passionate protest here or learn about a movement whose achievements you took for granted.

i Free; wheelchair accessible

NATIONAL FOOTBALL MUSEUM

Urbis Building, Cathedral Gardens; 0161 605 8200; www.nationalfootballmuseum.com; open daily 10am-5pm

Manchester's name instantly brings to mind the soccer team—excuse us, football team—**Manchester United.** Here, at the self-proclaimed best football museum in the world, you can learn all about it. The first floor showcases some fine memorabilia like jerseys and footballs. And if you turn around you'll find some jerseys and footballs. And, in the next room are some jerseys and footballs accompanied by videos. You get the picture. But upstairs you'll find interactive games you can (pay to) play, like shooting goals. For football fans, this place is surely a must-see. For those less sporty, the exhibits upstairs have some cool photography, and you can learn a fun fact or two to impress your more athletic friends.

i Free; visitor guide package £6, tours £3.50; guided tour part of package M-F 10:30am, 12:30pm, 2:30pm, Sa-Su 11am, 3pm; wheelchair accessible

FOOD

🏷 COMPTOIR LIBANAIS ($$)

18-19 The Ave.; 0161 672 3999; www.comptoirlibanais.com/locations/manchester; open M-Th 10am-11pm, F-Sa 10am-midnight, Su 10am-10pm

If we could eat every meal here, we would—and we'd probably never get sick of the Za'atar. Despite being one branch of a larger chain, Comptoir Libanais' offerings taste like perfectly thought-out Lebanese home cooking. The menu includes tons of options for meat eaters and vegetarians alike, and the mini shop inside the restaurant even sells some ingredients so you can cook your own version of the dishes! Unfortunately, we're not good at cooking, but that's why we leave it to the pros here. The food alone would be draw enough, but the decor and ambiance inside is another reason to visit—pastel tiles and mosaics cover the floors and the walls, while colorful chairs and lamps add pops of color that transport you across the world while enjoying some hummus or a cocktail.

i Entrées from £9; vegan and vegetarian options available; wheelchair accessible

COMMON ($)

39-41 Edge St.; 161 832 9245; www.aplace-calledcommon.co.uk; open daily 10am-late

We get it. Common called themselves common because they're just another random brunch place. Except they're totally not. Part hipster-vaguely-American café, part bar, part social club, Common has got it all. Signing up to be a free member online gives you BOGO burgers and different monthly rewards. Or you could stop in and check out their Not Mac 'n cheese (hint: there's corn) or Korean fried chicken. Sandwiches are cheapest weekdays before 5pm, but if you come later you might arrive in time for a trivia night or pub quiz. It's hard to capture the vibe, but think wood stools and staff with beards and cool hair welcoming you to the giant restaurant with what might be sheets hanging from the ceiling.

i Entrées from £5; gluten-free, vegan, and vegetarian options available

FIG & SPARROW ($)

20 Oldham St.; 0161 228 1843; www.figandsparrow.co.uk; open M-F 8am-7pm, Sa 9am-7pm, Su 10am-7pm

Half café, half design store (think £20 glasses), Fig & Sparrow is where a hipster goes to get a ~hipster drink~ after a day of thrift shopping or kombucha-brewing. But when you're craving avocado toast, there's no place like a hipster café. Vegan and veggie options abound, but don't worry, meat eaters can find an (organic and probably aquaponic-garden-originating locally-sourced) snack as well. Breakfast and people-watching all day—what more could you want? And believe us, the people who eat here are worth watching. We saw some of the most bizarre and mismatched clothing that still somehow looked super cool on these young and beautiful couples strolled into the cafe. Maybe drinking the ridiculously priced $4 (but oh so so good) latte can give us those superpowers, too.

i Entrées from £6, coffee from £4; gluten-free, vegan, and vegetarian options available

THE FISH HUT ($)

27 Liverpool Rd.; 0161 8390957; open M-Sa 10am-10pm

Nothing like fresh fish and chips and fresh wood-fired pizza? Yeah, we don't really get the mix either, but the pizza is top notch. The Fish Hut is like a drunk-food chippy except it's high quality and open during the day. So you'll get a killer Neapolitan pizza with any toppings or a gigantic plate of fish and chips. But like, from a restaurant, not a greasy imposter. Get your food to take away and eat outside or head upstairs to the (dining) room with a view.

i Pizza from £5.90, fish and chips from £6; vegetarian options available; limited wheelchair accessibility

NIGHTLIFE

🖼 NIGHT & DAY CAFE

26 Oldham St.; 0161 236 1822; www.nightnday.org; open M-Th 10am-2am, F-Sa 10am-4am, Su 9am-10:30pm

People flock to Manchester for the music. And Mancunians flock to Night & Day for the authentic up-and-comers, hazy fog, and obscure band posters. Many now-famous bands and artists performed here in their early days, and, if you're looking to discover some new music, there's often free gigs of relatively unknown or on-the-rise artists. If you're looking to see someone big, we recommend booking in advance. Oh yeah, and not only do they play rock and roll, EDM, and "umm what?" concerts, but they serve breakfast in the morning. Get the name now?

i Cover varies by concert, pints from £4.50, entrées from £8; BGLTQ+ friendly; wheelchair accessible

THE LIAR'S CLUB

19a Back Bridge St.; 0161 834 5111; www.theliarsclub.co.uk; open M-Sa 5pm-4am, Su 5pm-3am

England isn't known for its gorgeous Caribbean weather and beaches. But hey, we can dream. And at The Liar's Club, we can have our dreams come true. If you're craving a tropical drink or a reprieve from the rain, step on down into this tiki-themed paradise. Yes, it's underground, but that adds to the sense that maybe, just *maybe,* you might be on a beach. Palm trees and jungle-themed prints surround you in all directions. Their cocktails are strong and fruity—just the way we like them—and are two for £10 during happy hour. The Liar's Club is one of the only bars open until 4am every night, and if you get hungry, you can pop upstairs to **Crazy Pedro's Part Time Pizza Bar** and get one of their specials of the month (think creations like hot dog pizza). Don't judge—weird food tastes great when you're drunk.

i No cover, drinks from £8; BGLTQ+ friendly; no wheelchair accessibility

THE WASHHOUSE

19 Shudehill; 0161 839 5287; www.the-washhouse.co.uk; open M-Th 5pm-1am, F 5pm-3am, Sa noon-3am, Su 3pm-11pm

Behind a wall-height tumble dryer lies a hidden speakeasy, luxurious leather booths, mood lighting, and pricey cocktails to boot. The menu veers toward the bold, offering varieties including spicy chili peppers, Coco Pops cereal, and every spirit you can name. Call ahead (phone lines open at noon) to book your washing machine for the night, because they tend to be strict on reservations. Even if you're armed with the address, you'd still probably walk by the nondescript laundromat a few times. They know how to hide this secret. But once you find it, pick up the phone and press the button. You might feel silly and you might feel sneaky—we've been there, but it's a bar experience like no other.

i No cover, cocktails from £10; wheelchair accessible; reservation required

YORK

Coverage by **Lucy Golub**

Are you always reminiscing about "the good old days?" If the modern era doesn't quite cut it for you, York—where the past feels more real than ever—is calling your name. New York is lame. Pull up to the original. The effect of its buildings and cobblestoned streets give York an air of having been ripped from a storybook—albeit an old, regal European storybook. Castle walls surround the medieval city, whose history goes back centuries. From the chocolate trade to railroads to the monarchy, York's past is buried in its stones and dispersed through the air. The spires of York Minster, a church built over 250 years, can be seen from all over the city, reminding you of the passion, labor, and love it took to grow the metropolis. Literature aficionados will fall for Shakespeare's references—Richard III was the Duke of York, after all. The city's charm comes from well-preserved old streets, narrow lanes, timber-framed buildings, and plethora of churches. Yet despite the well-preserved setting, new life grows in York, with museums, nightlife, and arts all around. The present exists in the buildings of the past, calling out to tourists and locals to come see and come explore.

ORIENTATION

In the center of the city lies **York Minster,** the giant cathedral visible from all around the tiny city. Basically everything you'll want to see is in the same general area. The **River Ouse** runs through the center of the city, and multiple bridges connect the two sides. On the south side of the river are **York Station, the National Railway Museum,** and **Micklegate.** The north side holds most of the attractions. Slightly south of the Minster are **the Shambles,** and nearby is much of York's nightlife and restaurant scenes, although some bigger clubs lie on the south side of the river. Slightly east are **Clifford Tower** and **York Castle Museum.** The **Castle Walls** run along the outside of the city center, encircling the quaint town inside.

ESSENTIALS

GETTING THERE

Getting to York via train is a breeze; you'll end up at York Railway station, only about 15min. from the city center. The most convenient airports are Manchester Airport and Leeds/Bradford, and there are trains to take you directly into York from each one. The TransPennine Express will bring you from Manchester, Liverpool, or Newcastle.

GETTING AROUND

You could basically walk anywhere in less than 15min. from York Minster. There also are buses. Use a smartcard or pay cash on board (exact change preferred). All day passes are also available for £4.50. Many bus lines don't run 24hr, so be sure to check the return times.

PRACTICAL INFORMATION

Tourist Offices: 1 Museum St.; 01904 55 00 99; www.visityork.org; open M-Sa 9am-4pm, Su 10am-4pm
Banks/ATMs/Currency Exchange: TSB Bank (25 Parliament St.; open M-F 9am-5pm, Sa 9am-4pm).
Post Offices: York Post Office (22 Lendal St.; 0845 722 3344; open M 9am-5:30pm, Tu 9:30am-5pm, W-F 9am-5:30pm, Sa 9am-4pm)
Public Restrooms: Public Toilets Union Terrace (Clarence St.)
Internet: There is public Wi-Fi in many of the tourist attractions as well as most main streets.
BGLTQ+ Resources: The York LGBT forum ensures the rights and interests of LGBT people in the Yorkshire county and offers support and resources (15 Priory St.; 07731852533; www.yorklgbtforum.org.uk).

EMERGENCY INFORMATION

Emergency Number: 999

Police: Acomb Police Station (Acomb Rd.; non-emergency number 101; open M 10am-noon, Tu 2pm-4pm, W-Th 6pm-8pm, F 2pm-4pm, Sa 10am-noon)

Rape Crisis Center: Bridge House is a Sexual Assault Referral Centre that provides services for victims of sexual assault (48 Bridge Rd., Bishopthorpe; 0330 223 0362; www.bridgehousesarc. org; phone available daily 9am-5pm).

Hospitals: York Hospital (Wigginton Rd.; 01904 631313; open daily 24hr)

Pharmacies: There are many pharmacies in the city centre.
- Boots: 43 Coney St.; 01904 653657; open M-Sa 8:30am-6pm, Su 11am-5pm
- Monkbar: 3 Goodramgate; 01904 626181; open M-Sa 7:30am-10:30pm, Su 8:30am-6:30pm

ACCOMMODATIONS

🏨 FORT BOUTIQUE HOSTEL ($)

1 Little Stonegate; 01904 620 222; www.the-fortyork.co.uk; reception located at Kennedy's Bar and Restaurant next door, open M-Tu 8am-11pm, W-Th 8am-midnight, F-Sa 8am-2am, Su 8am-midnight

Luxury and hostels don't generally go hand in hand, but if five-star hostels were a thing, this would be it. After climbing mural-covered stairs, guests are greeted by a blow-dry bar, and every bed comes with (free!) towels. Hostels can often be stingy, but Fort Boutique Hostel lives up to its middle name. A large clean kitchen, individual power outlets, and specially decorated rooms complete the bougie that will surpass your perhaps-low hostel expectations. We'd probably live here, tbh. The hostel's located right in the middle of the city center, by the **Shambles** and a few minutes from **York Minster.** It's not the most social hostel, but the amenities are truly incomparable.

i Dorms from £15, privates available; reservation recommended; weekend min 2 nights, 1 night during week, max 2 weeks stay; BGLTQ+ friendly; no wheelchair accessibility; Wi-Fi; laundry and hair dryers available; linens and towels included

SAFESTAY YORK ($)

88-90 Micklegate; 01904 627720; www.safestay.com/york; reception open 24hr

This hostel houses travelers in an upscale sixteenth-century Georgian townhouse—historical plaques detailing the old uses of the rooms included. So while you're sharing a room with seven strangers, just remember that there used to be a stable right next door! As you climb a seemingly endless staircase to the top floors, take note of the jewel-toned carpet beneath your feet and the crystal chandelier hanging overhead. We can imagine the splendor the previous wealthy family tenants used to enjoy. Staying in a room on one of the higher floors will give you views of **York Minster** that are worth paying for, but luckily the hostel doesn't charge any extra for a window view. In the stone-walled basement common room and main reception, gilded frame portraits of crown-clad animals dot the walls: a little funky but definitely (somewhat) regal.

i Dorms from £12, prices higher on weekends; reservation recommended; BGLTQ+ friendly; limited wheelchair accessibility; Wi-Fi; laundry facilities; linens provided; bar onsite

SIGHTS
CULTURE

🏛 THE SHAMBLES

Shambles; 01904 550099; neighborhood open daily 24hr, store hours vary, market hours 9am-5pm

The most picturesque piece of a picturesque city, The Shambles' narrow paths and low-hanging timber-fronted buildings look like they're from a postcard. Three Harry Potter stores, and counting, join old-fashioned fudge shops and card-and-trinket stores galore. But the history of the streets holds a more grim story—the alleys used to be full of butchers with windows full of hanging animals, blood and guts included. Today, the street's appearance is much more pristine. At the market, locals shop for produce while tourists stock up on York-themed souvenirs, jewelry, and intricately decorated photo frames. Your best bet for an unobstructed view of the street would be to go in the evening, once the shops and the markets have closed.

i Store prices vart; wheelchair accessible

THE ORIGINAL GHOST WALK OF YORK

The King's Arms Pub, Ouse Bridge; www.
theoriginalghostwalkofyork.co.uk

We generally steer clear of ghost tours, which are usually just sneaky tourist traps, and not just because we're afraid of being haunted. This ghost tour proved us wrong. Theatrically telling stories while wearing an old-fashioned suit, our guide regaled us with stories of York's ancient haunters. The tour begins with the most beautiful ghost of York, a dark-haired woman clad in a wedding dress who stood outside of the **Church of All Saints,** and finishes near the **Minster** after a story about a field of soldiers. We won't spoil all the fun, but the tour is worth the five quid. It's not scary *per se,* but the captivating stories teach you more about York's hidden history without the usual gimmicks and scare-tactics of a typical tour.

i Admission £5, students £4; tours daily 8pm; limited wheelchair accessibility

SPARK:YORK

17-21 Piccadilly; www.sparkyork.org; open Su-Th 8am-10:30pm, F-Sa 8am-11pm; food available at noon

People don't often associate centuries-old York with up-and-coming trends. But if you're tired of the gorgeous old buildings that sometimes look like a movie set, Spark brings you back to reality. Here, you'll find the city's young and hip sipping on craft beers and picking at Thai food. Old shipping containers host shops that range from crafts to vintage clothes to food and drink. It's like a mini Camden Market but in the old streets of York. Colorful murals decorate the walls of the outdoor market's ground floor, and up the stairs you can get a drink and sit on a patio, all while quietly people watching.

i Store prices vary; limited wheelchair accessibility

LANDMARKS

CLIFFORD TOWER

Tower St.; 01904 646940; www.english-heritage.org.uk/visit/places/cliffords-tower-york; open daily 10am-6pm

What remains of **York Castle** today is mostly ruins, but Clifford's Tower stands tall above York. The tower itself has been around in one form or another for nearly 1000 years and was the site of the 1190 Massacre of the Jews, a horrific piece of oft-forgotten history. On a lighter note, the views from the tower are amazing, especially towards the **Minster.** Although the ticket fee is a little hefty for just a climb up some stairs, the tower marks an excellent starting point for the beginning of your days in York—you really can see everything from this "roofless ruin."

i Admission £5.40, students £4.90; last entry 15min. before closing; no wheelchair accessibility

YORK MINSTER

Deangate; 01904 557200; www.yorkminster.org; open M-Sa 9am-4:30pm, Su 12:45pm-3pm

Breathtaking in size and scope, York Minster is one of the most impressive cathedrals in the world, and the largest in Northern Europe. Light filters through the surrounding stained glass windows, illuminating the detailed carvings and intricacies in a rainbow of colorful rays. The organ's light notes and heavy undertones originate from the center of the cathedral, the highest of the notes twinkling and echoing to even the uppermost windows. Every stone is packed with history; the cathedral was built in 637, after all. The underbelly of the church contains an exhibit on its history, but if you're pressed for time we'd suggest buying a ticket to climb the tower for birds eye views of York down below. Even without the extras, the grandeur of the internal and external architecture draw hundreds of thousands of visitors each year.

i Admission £11, in advance £10, students £9; wheelchair accessible

YORK CASTLE WALLS

13 sections throughout the city; www.yorkwalls.org.uk; open 8am-sunset

A little over two miles long, the York Castle Walls are the oldest medieval walls in Europe. The walk itself is narrow, and you'll have to "excuse me" and elbow your way around tourists taking selfies with enormous DSLR cameras if you go at a crowded time. But where else can you walk around the fortress of an entire city? If you don't have time to walk the whole thing (understandable, there's pints to be drank), we recommend climbing up on **Goodramgate** to follow the walk that

YORK ART GALLERY

Exhibition Sq.; 01904 687687; www.yorkart-gallery.org.uk; open daily 10am-5pm

A recent redevelopment in this old city, York Art Gallery reopened its doors in the summer of 2015, with an eye for timeliness and attention to pertinent world events and how they relate to art. You'll find temporary topical exhibits throughout the entire gallery. During our visit, the highlight was an exhibition called "The Sea is the Limit," focusing on art surrounding refugees. Upstairs, what might as well be millions of ceramics sit on shelves in the Center of Ceramics. If you're a fan of pots, go take a look. In an area that focuses on the past, it's refreshing to wander through galleries containing new art, ranging from unclear representations in contemporary art to photography.

i Admission £7.50, ages 17-24 £3.75; wheelchair accessible

views **York Minster** and some large mansions behind it. You'll get a taste of the royal life from the time when the walls were built. If the weather is nice, a sunset walk and golden-hour light make for stunning photos.

i Free; no wheelchair accessibility

MUSEUMS

YORK CHOCOLATE STORY

King's Sq.; 01904 527765; www.yorkschocolatestory.com; open daily 10am-5pm

This museum traces York's chocolate-making history and its role as one of the world's chocolate capitals. Yes, the guided tour provides you with chocolate samples so you can snack the whole way, as well as information about the founding families, some chocolate samples, demonstrations of chocolate making, and even more chocolate samples. Did we mention there are chocolate samples? There's a different kind for every taste, ranging from sweet milk to cacao nibs. Yeah, there's lots of chocolate here. Learn about the Rowntrees, the Terrys, and the Cravens, and why the air in York sometimes smells like chocolate. Well-practiced tour guides engage their audience, creating a tour that's both informative and fun (and delicious). If that's not enough, you get to make and decorate your own chocolate lollipop at the end of the tour. Sweet!

i Admission £12.50, students £11.50; tours every 15min.; last tour 4pm; wheelchair accessible

FOOD

BREW AND BROWNIE ($)

5 Museum St.; 01904 647420; www.brewandbrownie.co.uk; open M-Sa 9am-5pm, Su 9:30am-5pm

Here's a pro tip that has been tripping us up for weeks—when Brits say pancakes they mean crêpes! Luckily, you can get your American pancake fix here, served with streaky bacon and blueberries, Nutella and bananas, or salted caramel. Count us in. *And* it's served until late afternoon: what more could you ask for from brunch? (Other than sandwiches, avocado toast, and eggs, which they also serve.) Top-notch quality, central location, and adorable decorations. If you're looking for more of a coffee shop vibe, we'd also suggest the delectable sourdough toasties from their sister store, **Brew and Brownie Bake Shop.**

i Entrées from £4.50; vegan and vegetarian options available; wheelchair accessible

LUCKY DAYS CAFE ($$)

1 Church St.; 01904 733992; open daily 9am-5pm

Almost too quaint to be real, the light green walls and wood tables remind us of our non-existent British grandmothers' homes. With three locations spread around the city, the café advertises itself as not the cheapest, but as definitely the best. We'd have to agree. We've tried our fair share of scones, and its famous mature cheddar scone takes the cake. Or takes their classic blueberry and orange zest scone, should we say? Main meals come with multiple sides, and every detail has been meticulously planned out. Even the butter for the homemade bread comes in a little wax paper: so rustic, so farmhouse, so delicious. If York itself were a restaurant, it would be Lucky Days Café—old, incredibly cute, maybe a little touristy, but ultimately worth it for the quality.

i Entrées from £8; gluten-free, vegan, and vegetarian options available; limited wheelchair accessibility

GREEK STREET FOOD SOUVLAKI ($)

Silver St.; 07478 258971; open Tu-F noon-4pm, Sa noon-5pm, Su noon-4pm

Gyros aren't hard to find in Europe—if you're walking down the street, by the time you figured out how to spell "souvlaki," you'd probably find one. But would you find a cheap, massive, freshly cooked, and delicious gyro or chicken souvlaki next to an equally delicious donut stand? We think not. So head over to **The Shambles Market** to pick up your meal. Follow your nose, and wash down the hearty Greek food with some freshly fried donuts from **The Donut Kitchen**. It may not be healthy, but it's good for your soul.

i Gyro and souvlaki from £5; vegetarian options available; wheelchair accessible

HUMPIT ($)

12A Church St.; 01904 620 066; www.humpit-hummus.com; open M-Sa 11am-8pm, Su noon-8pm

The restaurant owners either didn't think about the name, or they really knew what they were doing. Where do you get a fresh pita stuffed with healthy vegetables? Humpit. A quick and healthy lunch? Humpit. Homemade hummus? Humpit. If the name is still giving you pause, try and convince it: this is Mediterranean dining at it's finest. The restaurant is a classic fast-casual place with a counter where you order and generic tables at which to devour your meal. It's basically a vegan mediterranean Chipotle. What they lack in atmosphere (think Chipotle), they make up for in flavor and portion

size. They even offer white and brown pita bread, if you like having options or are particular about your pita. It's okay, we get it: it sets up the rest of the meal.

i Entrées from £4.50; gluten-free, vegan, and vegetarian options available; wheelchair accessible

NIGHTLIFE

🏴 FOSSGATE SOCIAL

25 Fossgate; 01904 628692; www.thefossgatesocial.com; open M-Th 9am-midnight, F-Sa 9am-12:30am, Su 10am-midnight

An all-day coffee shop turns into a bar at night. But when the bottles come out, the venue still retains the cosiness and comfort it has during the day. Upstairs you'll find a casual room with couches and small tables. It's homey inside, and the dim lights and cramped seating somehow help conversation flow (and help your drink of choice as well). We didn't hear a single American accent inside; it's a local hub. Head to the garden out back and mingle with York's young and artsy. Also, we're not kidding when we say the brownies they sell here (all day and night!) are the best we've ever had. And that's not the alcohol talking.

i Cocktails from £6, pints from £4; limited wheelchair accessibility

THE GOLDEN FLEECE

16 Pavement; 01904 620491; www.goldenfleecepubyork.co.uk; open daily 10am-midnight

If you're looking for spirits, the Golden Fleece has got you covered, both in the ghoul and alcohol senses. York's (self-proclaimed) most haunted bar might just send chills down your spine. Was that a ghost moving in the corner of your eye or just the skeleton perched at the bar sipping a cocktail? #spooky. If your chair starts to slide, don't panic. It's probably not a ghost, just the slanted floors and the narrow doors dating back to the 1503 birth of this bar. A ghost tour begins at the pub, but we suggest avoiding the tourists and seeing if you can find a local—we met a man who's been coming to the Golden Fleece for 40 years.

i Pints from £3.60; BGLTQ+ friendly; limited wheelchair accessibility; dog friendly

THE PUNCHBOWL

5-9 Blossom St.; 01904 666740; www.
jdwetherspoon.com/pubs/all-pubs/
england/north-yorkshire/the-punch-bowl-
york; open M-Th 8am-midnight, F-Sa
8am-1am, Su 8am-midnight

Spoons, spoons, how we love spoons.
The Punchbowl is consistently cheap
and consistently open. What more
could you ask from a bar? You know
what you're going to get: ages ranging
from just-out-of-high-school lads
looking for a cheap pint to full grey-
haired groups snacking on fish and
chips. The Punchbowl is an excellent
option for some classic pub-grub, and
they offer multiple meal deals and
specials. Wetherspoons overtook the
previous pub that used to be there
since 1770. So you're basically on a
historical tour of the city by drinking
here.
i Entrées from £5, pints from £1.99;
wheelchair accessible

GREAT BRITAIN ESSENTIALS

VISAS

Britain is not a signatory to the Schengen Agreement, which means it is not
a member of the freedom of movement zone that covers most of continental
Europe. EU citizens do not need a visa to visit Britain, and citizens of
Australia, Canada, New Zealand, the U.S. and many other non-EU countries
do not need a visa for stays of up to six months. Those staying longer than six
months may apply for a longer-term visa; consult an embassy or consulate for
more information. Because Britain is not a part of the Schengen zone, time
spent here does not count toward the 90-day limit on travel within that area.
Entering to work or study for longer than six months will require a visa. You
can learn more at www.ukvisas.gov.uk. Although there is a lot of uncertainty
surrounding the recent Brexit, this appears to only affect EU citizens living in
the UK and not those who are just visiting.

MONEY

Tipping and Bargaining: Restaurant servers are paid at least the minimum
wage, so tipping is slightly different. If you receive table service, there may be
a tip included in your bill. It will appear as a "service charge" and you do not
need to tip on top of it. If there is no service charge, you should tip around
10%. You do not need to tip if you order at the counter, or in bars or pubs.
If you are staying in a nice hotel (read: not a hostel), you should tip porters
£1-2, and tipping the housekeeper is up to your discretion. For taxi drivers,
it is customary to round up to the nearest pound, but you don't need to tip.
Bargaining is not common in the UK and should probably not be attempted.

Taxes:
The UK has a 20% value added tax (VAT), a sales tax applied to everything but food, books, and children's clothing. The tax is included on the amount indicated on the price tag, and all prices stated in *Let's Go* include VAT. Upon exiting Britain, non-EU citizens can reclaim VAT (minus an administrative fee) through the Retail Export Scheme, although the process can only be applied to goods you take out of the country. Participating shops display a "tax-free shopping" sign and have a minimum purchase condition, usually around £75. To claim a refund, you must fill out the form given to you in the shop (VAT 407) and this must be presented to customs when you depart. You must leave the UK for at least twelve months within three months of making the purchase to qualify.

HEALTH AND SAFETY

Drugs and Alcohol: The British pint is 20oz. as compared to the 16oz. U.S. pint. The legal age at which you can buy alcohol in the UK is 18; expect to be asked for I.D. if you look under 25. Sixteen- and seventeen-year-olds can drink beer or wine in a restaurant if they are accompanied by an adult and the adult makes the purchase. The use, possession, and sale of hard drugs is illegal and can carry a penalty of up to seven years in prison for possession alone. Do not test this. Penalties for cannabis are less severe, but police can issue a warning or on the spot fine of £90 if you're found with it. Smoking is banned in enclosed public spaces, including pubs and restaurants.

Local Laws and Police: There are two types of police offers in the UK: regular officers with full police powers and police community support officers (PCSOs), who have limited police power and focus on community and safety. The emergency number is 999, and the non-emergency number is 101. Find out more at www.police.uk.

Terrorism: The terrorist attacks of 2017 in Manchester Arena and London Bridge and Borough Market revealed that the UK is still susceptible to terrorism, despite the more stringent safety measures put in place after the 2005 London Underground Bombings. Expect thorough security checks in airports and do not pack any sharp objects in your carry-on luggage. Check your home country's foreign affairs office for travel information and advisories.

MEASUREMENTS

Brits primarily use the metric system of measurement, and metric must be used when selling packaged or loose goods—the exception to this is beer or cider, sold in pints. However, road distances are always given in miles, not kilometers.

GREECE

Made up of the Aegean blue, an ancient language, and a home with a story (or five), Greece is a country with so much history it almost doesn't know what to do with itself. Their myths are the original soap operas, featuring the flawed and fabulous Greek gods and goddesses. Their musings are the foundations of everything we know about Western civilization. Their olives decorate our martini glasses. Their vices are our vices. Once a conglomerate of city-states and different empires ruling over the country at various points in history, no two Greek landmarks are alike. Athens shines as the sprawling capital, mixing honking taxicabs and graffitied walls with the commanding sites of the Parthenon and Acropolis. To the north lies Thessaloniki, a seamless blend of modern living and ancient history. Southwest of Athens lies the Peloponnese, a peninsula of mythical legends and mountainous villages. Ferries will bring you to the Cyclades Islands, characterized by powerful winds, rocky islands, white stuccoed churches, and sunsets that will make your heart ache. No matter what is happening in the country, the Greeks think deeply, care intensely, and party so hard they give validity to the connotations of Greek life. A proud flag always waves fearlessly through their slice of the Mediterranean. Greece is ouzo, souvlaki, and mounds of pita. It's endless skies, lapping waves, and miles upon miles of sand. It's soaring Mt. Olympus, acres of olive groves, and a beach that is never too far away. It's a home, as long as you're up for an adventure (or five).

ATHENS

Coverage by **Margaret Canady**

According to Greek mythology, Poseidon, god of the oceans, and Athena, god of
wisdom, were vying for patronage over the then-unnamed city. Poseidon offered the
citizens saltwater, and Athena the first olive tree. In another instance of "girls rule boys
drool," the people chose the olive tree and Athena (I mean, come on Poseidon, the city
is literally right next to the sea, and regifting is *so* last millenia). Some 3,400 years later,
here lies the modern metropolis of Athens. The city, of course, immediately conjures
up images of antiquity. Plato and Aristotle walked the streets of ancient Athens,
creating some of the modern society's philosophical foundations, all while eating olives
(probably). Acropolis is known as the birthplace of Western civilization and democracy
and the Parthenon stands regal over the city. For anyone visiting Athens for the first
time, however, you might be surprised to find that not everything is colosseums and
marble. Athens is a car-honking, expletive-loving, graffiti-filled city. Stray cats intermix
with a vibrant nightlife where the clubs don't open until midnight and a local will have
nine favorite bars in one neighborhood. By day, fulfill your inner history buff, soaking
in the thousands of years of art, history, and knowledge. By night, grab a cocktail (or
five), hit a rooftop bar (or three), and soak up urban Athens life.

ORIENTATION

The Mediterranean Sea borders Athens to the west, while three mountain ranges
circle the cities on its other sides. The city is a 30min. metro ride away from the
Port of Piraeus, one of the busiest passenger ports in Europe. The pulse of Athens
can be found in two squares of the city center: **Syntagma Square** and, west a few
blocks, **Monastiraki Square.** To the south of Monastiraki is the **Acropolis,** which
stands on the top of a hill and can be seen from most places in the city center. At
the base of Acropolis lies **Plaka,** a picturesque historical neighborhood with flora
covered walkways and plenty of shops and restaurants. To the west of Monastiraki
is **Gazi,** a neighborhood with a high concentration of cool bars and late night clubs.
To the north of Monastiraki is **Psiri,** an area with traditional restaurants and bars
with live music such as *rembetika,* or Greek blues. Farther north will take you to
Omonia Square, a central metro stop and the oldest square in the city. To the north
of the historical city center is **Metaxourgeio,** a neighborhood with a strong sense of
community and fewer tourists.

ESSENTIALS

GETTING THERE

If flying, you'll arrive at Athens
International Airport (Eleftherios
Venizelos). From there, you can take the
metro or express bus downtown. The ride
will take about 45min. to 1hr and cost €5
or €6, respectively. A taxi to the city center
will cost €38 (set price during the day)
and will take about 25min. If arriving by
port, you'll most likely land at Piraeus
Port. To go downtown, take the green line
from Piraeus Port Station.

GETTING AROUND

Most of the sites and landmarks you'll
want to see are all within walking
distance, as are the major hostels. The
city is serviced by three metro lines and
an elaborate bus system. The metro has
stations in most major destinations and
neighborhoods and runs M-Th and
Su 5:30am to 12:30am, and F-Sa until
2:30am; check online for bus schedules.
Tickets range from €1.40 for a 1.5hr
ticket to €9 for a five-day unlimited ticket.

PRACTICAL INFORMATION

Tourist Offices: Athens Tourism Information (Dionysiou Areopagitou 18; www.visitgreece.gr/; open M-F 9am-7pm, Sa-Su 10am-4pm)

Banks/ATMs/Currency Exchange: ATMs can be found throughout the city, especially in tourist-heavy areas. We were particularly fond of this currency exchange place with no fees: Argo Exchange S.A. (Agiou Konstantinou 6; 21 0523 6636; www.argo-exchange.gr/; open M-Sa 8am-9pm, Su 9am-5pm).

Post Offices: Omonia Square Post Office (Koumoundourou 29; 21 0524 8551; www.athensconventionbureau.gr/en/node/4240; open M-F 8am-5pm, Sa 8am-2pm)

Public Restrooms: There are public restrooms in the underground station beneath Omonia and Syntagma Squares. Otherwise, you'll need to stop in a restaurant or café.

Internet: Most cafés and restaurants have Wi-Fi. There are internet cafes located around the city, check online for details (www.athensinfoguide.com/geninternet.htm).

BGLTQ+ Resources: Some resources can be found online (www.athensinfoguide.com/gay.htm).

EMERGENCY INFORMATION

Emergency Number: 112

Police: Dial 100 for emergencies. Athens Municipal Police (Agiou Konstantinou 14; 21 0521 0606; www.cityofathens.gr/)

US Embassy: US Embassy Athens (Leof. Vasilissis Sofias 91; 21 0721 2951; gr.usembassy.gov/)

Rape Crisis Center: WomenSOS (support number: 15900; administrative number: 213 1511113; www.womensos.gr/; support number open daily 24hr)

Hospitals: Dial 166 for an ambulance.
- Laiko General Hospital of Athens (Agiou Thoma 17; 21 3206 0800; www.laiko.gr/; open daily 24hr)
- Alexandra General Hospital (Lourou Athina 115 28; 21 0338 1100; www.hosp-alexandra.gr/; open daily 24hr)

Pharmacies: Pharmacies are located throughout the city; look for the green plus sign. Here are two:
- Pharmacy (near Monastiraki): Ermou 74; 21 0323 9616; open M-Sa 8am-11pm

ACCOMMODATIONS

☑ ATHENS BACKPACKERS ($$)

Makri 12; 21 0922 4044; www.backpackers.gr/; reception open 24hr

Athens Backpackers is arguably the most popular hostel for travelers, and for good reason. Cheap rooms at the base of the **Acropolis,** an abundance of common spaces, free breakfast and a free drink at the rooftop bar, a variety of different rooms, many of which offer private baths and balconies: how can you *not* love the place? They offer cheap walking tours of the city daily, so you before you hit Athens' nightlife with your new hostel friends, you'll already be able to tell the differences between the **Agora, Acropolis,** and **Ouzo.**

i *Dorms from €24; cash only under €50; reservation required; wheelchair accessible; Wi-Fi; luggage storage; laundry; linens included*

ATHENSTYLE ($$)

Agias Theklas 10; 21 0322 5010; athenstyle.com/en_GB/; reception open 24hr

Traverse Greece in style with Athenstyle. Located right off **Monastiraki Square,** convenience and hostel living converge at Athenstyle. Fun amenities include a cheap breakfast, a clutch laundry service, zen yoga lessons, and not one, but *two* bars. Our favorite place is the rooftop, which offers cheap alcohol and fantastic views of the **Acropolis.**

i *Dorms from €16, depending on season; reservation recommended; Wi-Fi; wheelchair accessible; laundry facilities available; breakfast from €3*

BEDBOX ($)

Poliklitou 11; 21 5555 9334; bedbox.gr/; reception open 24hr

Bedbox is the new kid on the block, and boy, are they coming in swinging. Their totally new take on hostel living makes affordable accommodations remarkably stylish and comfortable. (What a novelty!) Every bed is contained within a bento box cubby, with a personal curtain so you have *actual* privacy, which is another concept foreign to most hostels. It's small, but the warmth that exudes from the staff and owners more than makes up for it.

i *Dorms from €15; wheelchair accessible; kitchen, luggage storage, and linens included*

SIGHTS
CULTURE

🎦 THISION OPEN AIR CINEMA

Apostolou Pavlou 7; 21 0342 0864; cine-thisio.gr/; open last week of Apr-late Oct

Plush red seats, buttery popcorn, a good movie, and ... a view of the Parthenon? Located at the base of the **Acropolis,** Thision Open Air Cinemas is one of the best outdoor movie theaters on the planet. Where else can you watch international movies (English captions provided) underneath the stars, with a more than 2000-year-old monument casually just chilling in the background? With reasonable ticket prices and good vibes only, you can't miss this.

i Tickets M-W €6, Th-Su €8; tickets only available at cinema before movie, arrive 30min. early to reserve tickets; wheelchair accessible

CHANGING OF THE GUARD AT THE TOMB OF THE UNKNOWN SOLDIER

Syntagma Sq., in front of the Parliament Building

The Changing of the Guard definitely exceeds expectations, even though our only expectations were that they would occasionally move a little to the left and perhaps a smidge to the right. The 15-minute choreographed performance consists of perfectly-synchronized leg extensions that demanded as much core strength and stamina as a professional ballet dancer. Somehow, the two guards remain in sync, even when facing opposite directions, and never once fall or crack a smile. To top it off, they sport traditional Greek uniforms (which, frankly, makes us wonder how they fought in those dresses). The guards stand guard 24 hours a day at the Tomb of the Unknown Soldier, a cenotaph dedicated to Greeks killed in war.

i Free; wheelchair accessible; every 30min.; procession Su 11am

MONASTIRAKI FLEA MARKET

Monastiraki Sq., Ifestou 2; 694 608 6114; open daily 8am-6pm

This isn't your run-of-the-mill flea market all the time, but it's still pretty cool. Down the narrow street labeled "Athens' Flea Market," you'll find shop after shop of souvenirs and shoes. Adjacent to the fenced **Agora,** local artists and vendors set up their carts to sell handmade jewelry and crafts every day. Early on Sundays, the surrounding streets are filled with antique sellers and more flea market-type stuff.

i Free; limited wheelchair accessibility

THE GREEK KITCHEN

Athinas 36; 697 846 4701; greekkitchen-athens.com/; open M-Sa 9am-7pm

For those amateur chefs out there (and for those of you who ambitiously say you're going to learn how to cook but only bother to make instant ramen), come here to learn how to make traditional Greek food at the Greek Kitchen. Located four minutes north of **Monastiraki Square,** you'll be guided through four traditional dishes, including *dolmades* and *tzatziki.* Teach a man to fish, they say, but give him all of the ingredients, a kitchen, professional chefs, and free bread and wine, and you'll be eating well today (and possibly for a lifetime).

i Cooking class from €38; free for lone travelers; vegetarian classes only; limited wheelchair accessibility

LANDMARKS

🏛 ACROPOLIS

Acropolis Hill; 21 0321 4172; open daily 8am-8pm

The Acropolis needs no introduction. A universal symbol and iconic monument, it's one of the most prized gifts of Ancient Greece, which also includes some non-essential things: you know, like democracy, philosophy, theatre, and freedom of expression and speech. Created to celebrate their win over other city-states, the Acropolis, which consists of the **Parthenon,** the **Erechtheion**, the **Propylaia,** and the **temple of Athene Nike,** was completed in 438

BCE. The Parthenon has been used as a church, a mosque, and a bomb storage—which led to its partial demolition in 1687. 2500 years later, after a series of restorations, the Acropolis stills stands, imbued with the power and wisdom of the goddess for whom it was erected (Athena).

i Admission €20, students €10; last entry 30min. before closing; wheelchair accessible; special ticket package (admission €30, students €15) provides entry to many major sites, including Acropolis

ANCIENT AGORA AND THE TEMPLE OF HEPHAESTUS

Adrianou 24; 21 0321 0185; open daily 8am-8pm

Ancient Agora used to be the hub of ancient Athens, where city dwellers gathered to buy and sell goods, meet up with friends, and talk smack about Helena from down the block. Located northwest of the **Acropolis,** we can imagine toga-clad aristocrats walking down the mountain for a gyro in the Agora. Today, visitors can walk through the remnants of the agora to take in the sights for themselves. Make sure to check out the **Temple of Hephaestus,** the best preserved Doric peripteral temple of the ancient greek world. The Temple was made for the god of metalworking and fire, which is pretty lit if you ask us.

i Admission €8, students €4; last entry 7:45pm; wheelchair accessible

LYKAVITTOS HILL

www.lycabettushill.com/; open daily 24hr

Relative to Mount Everest, this 'mountain' is a dwarf. But, at 910 feet, it's still the tallest point in Athens. Located smack dab in the middle of the city, Lykavittos Hill will provide you with views galore of the city before you, so the 20-minute climb is well worth the sweat and potential heat stroke. and, with each zig, the view gets more and more beautiful (and your calves feel more and more sore). At the top, you'll find a bell tower, small church, and panoramic views. It's the perfect place to watch the sunset and crack open a cold one. We only found out after the hike that there's a cable car that transports people both up and down the hill, but we wouldn't have reached our targeted steps for the day had we known about this option before, so take your pick.

i Free; wheelchair accessible by cable car; cable car round-trip €7, runs every 30min.

SYNTAGMA SQUARE

Pl. Sintagmatos; 21 0325 4708; open daily 9am-11pm

At the hub of Athens life lies Syntagma Square. Along with peanut vendors and buskers, here (or across the street) you'll find the **Greek Parliament Building, National Garden,** and the **Tomb of the Unknown Soldier.** Syntagma Square has a rich history. A military uprising here in 1843 forced the king to grant the first constitution of Greece. From 2010 to 2012, protestors congregated in the square in reaction to the Greek debt crisis.But when the Greeks aren't fighting the government, they're also here catching a bus or train at the Syntagma metro station.

i Free; wheelchair accessible

GREECE ATHENS

MUSEUMS

🏛 ACROPOLIS MUSEUM

Dionysiou Areopagitou 15; 210 9000900; www.theacropolismuseum.gr/en; open Apr 1-Oct 31 M 8am-4pm, Tu-Th 8am-8pm, F 8am-10pm, Sa-Su 8am-8pm; open Nov 1-Mar 31 M-Th 9am-5pm, F 9am-10pm, Sa-Su 9am-8pm

Here's a sign you need to go to the Acropolis Museum: you accidentally keep saying "metropolis" or "apocalypse" instead of Acropolis. The museum, at the base of **Acropolis Hill,** is both informative and attractive. Informative, as it's geared towards those who flocked to Greece to take in Ancient Greek history. Attractive, since it opened in 2009, complete with modern gray shades, wall-to-wall windows that look out at (and, on the 3rd floor, imitate) the **Parthenon.** Translucent floors complement the old art and marble its there to uphold. It's also features well-preserved artifacts from the old Athena temple, such as *friezes* (marble sculptures) that adorned the Parthenon. We recommend going to the museum before the actual Acropolis, so that when you get to the famed landmark, you actually know what you're looking at.

i Admission €5, students €3; audio guides €3; last entry 30min. before closing; wheelchair accessible

BENAKI MUSEUM

Koumpari 1; 21 0367 1000; open W 10am-6pm, Th 10am-midnight, F 10am-6pm, Sa 10am-midnight, Su 10am-4pm

A man with a ridiculously nice white mustache by the name of Antonis Benakis donated his private collection to Greece. The museum has a broad range of artistic goodies with something for everyone: Byzantine icons, Greek busts, sculptures, gold wreaths, and wooden dolls. You'll have a blast looking through the three levels of art the Benakis' stashed away over the years.

i Admission €9, students €7; wheelchair accessible; Wi-Fi

MUSEUM OF CYCLADIC ART

Neofitou Douka 4; 21 0722 8321; cycladic.gr/en; open M 10am-5pm, W 10am-5pm, Th 10am-8pm, F-Sa 10am-5pm, Su 11am-5pm

Museum of Cycladic Art writes that its exhibits explore and appreciate the timelessness of the human figure and how it manifests itself in different ways through time. And it certainly succeeds, curating an informational and interesting display of both ancient and contemporary exhibits revolving around human experience and body. "Cycladic" refers to the islands and inlets that are found in the central and south Aegean Sea (not, as we originally thought, referring to cyclones or cyclops). Don't miss their contemporary art exhibit, which is a weird, but pleasant and welcome change from the previous exhibits of ancient art.

i Admission to permanent collection €3.50, permanent and visiting exhibit €7; last entry 15min. before close; wheelchair accessible

NATIONAL ARCHAEOLOGICAL MUSEUM OF ATHENS

28is Oktovriou 44; 21 3214 4800; www.namuseum.gr/; open Apr 1-Oct 31 M 1pm-8pm, Tu-Su 8am-8pm

It's hard to imagine what the world was like 20 years ago, let alone 2000. Their collection of artifacts is huge and old (very old), with skeletons dating back to 450 BCE, ceramic pots from the fourteenth century BCE, and sculptures of naked Greeks from any century in between. It's easy to lose a couple of hours wandering through the museum, and all the old stuff can start blending together. If this happens, try thinking about the people behind the artifacts: the child from 2500 years ago who played with those wooden dolls, the women who wore Byzantine jewelry 1500 years ago from now.

i Admission €10; galleries cleared 20min. before closing; wheelchair accessible

OUTDOORS

NATIONAL GARDEN

Amalias 1; 21 0721 5019; open daily
sunrise-sunset

Take some time out of your Athens
agenda to visit the National Garden,
a public park across the street from
Syntagma Square. One hundred and
fifty four square meters hold an oasis of
lush trees and shrubbery, curved white
gravel pathways, and plenty of benches
and ivy covered walkways. A couple
of wrong (or right) turns will take you
to the small petting zoo with billy
goats and ostriches, or maybe to some
random marble pillars. It's a great spot
to escape the ceaseless cycle of buses and
taxis, and we won't blame you if you
take a quick nap in the grass.
i Free; wheelchair accessible

FOOD

AISCHYLOU GRILL HOUSE PSIRI ($)

14-16 Aischylou St., Psyri Sq.; 210
3244117-8; grillhouse-psiri.gr/en

Hunger, heat, thirst, air: these are
the four elements that are sure to hit
you at *least* once on a hot summer's
day in Athens, so you'll want (no,
need) something cheap, tasty, and
filling. Aischylou Grill House Psiri is a
mouthful, pun intended. Located at the
fork between street 1 and street 2, you'll
be first attracted to the restaurant's ivy
canopy that extends across the street,
creating (blessed) shaded outdoor
seating. Next, you'll check out the
menu, where everything is less than
€10. Finally, your food will come, and
it will surely be a mouthful—they don't
skimp on the meat platters or the pita
sandwiches, and you'll more than likely
be taking leftovers home for post lunch,
pre dinner munchies.
i Entrées under €10; wheelchair accessible

ATLANTIKOS ($)

Avliton 7; 21 3033 0850; open daily 1pm-
1am

If you hadn't read this, you'd probably
would have walked by Atlantikos a
hundred times. Tucked in a side alley
off the main street in the **Monastiraki**
neighborhood, none of the hosts try
to sell you their food, and for the most

part this seafood restaurant sees only
locals. Just locals, and hopefully now
you, because Atlantikos serves some of
the best seafood in Monastiraki, if not
Athens. Both their fried and grilled
portions are large, filling, and fresh. And
what's more—the chefs cook up their
grilled tuna in the open kitchen, right
before your very eyes. Entrées range
from €6-8, so you have money left over
for *ouzo* (or maybe just more food).
i Seafood entrées from €6; wheelchair
accessible

ARCADIA ($$$)

Makrigianni 27; 21 0923 8124; www.greek-
taverna.gr/; open daily 8am-1am

After a hot and sweaty climb to the
Acropolis, (or an equally interesting
but less sweaty trip to the **Acropolis
Museum**) Arcadia is the perfect place
to get pampered with some really good
food. The restaurant, named after a
town in Greece symbolizing "simplicity,
beauty, and peace," hosts a bustling
business, probably because of their
prime location and appealing off-white
aesthetic. The antique-style moussaka
(€16.50) is a bit expensive but very
big, and will change your world: baked
lamb cocooned in roasted eggplant and
yogurt sauce. Yes *please.*
i Salads from €7.50, appetizers from €9,
entrées from €10.80; wheelchair accessible

CAFE "111" ($)

Ermou 111; 21 0323 7967; ermou111.
blogspot.com/; open M-Sa 8am-5am, Su
8am-midnight

With Cafe 111's wooden décor
and random hanging objects (read:
suspended bicycle from ceiling), we
kinda got grimy shipwreck vibes. This
café serves primarily appetizers and
drinks, and a fair amount of locals
stop here in the afternoon before going
elsewhere for dinner. Considering it
stays open until 5am, though, we're
curious to know what it's like post-
dinner or post-midnight, and if do the
people who work there ever get any
sleep. (We hope so?)
i Most drinks and appetizers under €10;
wheelchair accessible

LOTTE CAFE-BISTROT ($)

Tsami Karatasou 2; 21 1407 8639; open M-Sa 10am-2am, Su 10am-midnight

By day, Lotte is a hip coffee shop, with good R&B music, studious college students, and delicious coffee options. By night, it's a slinking, sexy bar option. The music slows, the sun sets, and beautiful people drink *ouzo* and cocktails. Sit inside at the antique window seats, or outside next to their small garden and random lamp and couch décor. The cafe boasts a friendly staff, free Wi-Fi, and an atmosphere that just screams "I'm cooler than you."

i Coffee from €2, snacks from €2.50; wheelchair accessible

MANI MANI ($$$)

Falirou 10; 21 0921 8180; manimani.com. gr/; open M-Sa 2pm-11pm, Su 1pm-11pm

If you've been saving up for a special dinner, or you're trying to impress that cute person from your hostel, grab your credit card and head to Mani Mani. This moderately upscale restaurant takes traditional Greek food and gives it a modern twist, using fresh ingredients and creativity to amaze your palette. They serve some of the best olives we've ever had, and the lamb was simply to die for. Your wallet groan in pain, but your stomach will be in heaven.

i Starters from €7, salads from €8, entrées from €12; no wheelchair accessibility

QUICK PITTA ($)

Mitropoleos 78; 21 0324 9285

With a name like "Quick Pitta," this restaurant offers you a simple expectation, and it's pretty easy to mess things up. Luckily, they don't. The corner restaurant offers both dine-in and speedy takeaway service (thanks to the friendly and attractive waiters), and, most importantly, cheap and delicious pita wraps. You can choose from a variety of meat options. Though we're not sure if it's the best pita in Athens, it's certainly better than anything we might've picked up in the States.

i Pita sandwiches from €2.10, entrées from €7.50; wheelchair accessible

YOGOLICIOUS ($)

Adrianou 48; 21 0323 7394; www.yogolicious.global/; open M-Th 10am-midnight, F-Sa 10am-1am, Su 10am-midnight

Frozen yogurt shops may have gone out of style a couple years ago, but that doesn't mean you shouldn't try *Greek* frozen yogurt. Made with Greek yogurt, this is the perfect sweet treat on a hot summer afternoon, and you don't have to feel guilty eating it—one sign read "1.5% fat = 50% calories = Greek yogurt," which is foolproof logic in our book. We got ours at Yogolicious in **Monastiraki Square,** where it's self-service. This means we probably cancelled out all the health due to all the extra toppings we added.

i Frozen yogurt €2 per 100g; wheelchair accessible

NIGHTLIFE

✂ DOS GARDENIAS

Navarchou Apostoli 17; 21 0323 5349; open daily 5pm-3am

Día de los muertos came early (and to the wrong country). Dos Gardenias is a great Latin-themed bar that always seems to attract a full house. Their cocktails are reasonably priced, and they serve high quality alcohol—we're talking glass bottles, people. After a couple of beers, you might pick up one of their decorative maracas and start to merengue in your seat. The only downside is that there's no dance floor to show off your Latin dance moves, but don't be afraid to move to the street.

i Beer from €4, cocktails from €6; wheelchair accessible

✂ SIX D.O.G.S

Avramiotou 6-8; 21 0321 0510; sixdogs. gr/; open M-Th 10am-3am, F-Sa 10am-7am, Su 10am-3am

We tried very hard to understand the meaning behind the name and aesthetics of six d.o.g.s, but gave up after our complimentary shot (maybe that was their plan all along). The perfect place to start the night, this place has a cool corner bar, two floors of outdoor seating, and a young and energetic ambience. Grab one of their beers on tap or (recommended) one of their specialty cocktails, creative concoctions that conjure images of tree fairy nymphs and other mythical creatures. You'll be ready to hit the party scene, yet also tempted to just spend the night under the multicolored string-lit green canopy; on Fridays and Saturdays they're open until 7am (!).

i Cocktails from €9, beer and wine from €5; wheelchair accessible

A FOR ATHENS 360 COCKTAIL BAR

Ifestou 2; 21 0321 0006; www.three-sixty.gr/; open M-F 9am-3pm, Sa-Su 9am-4am

360 Cocktail Bar has its own special elevator and colored LED lights on the floor and walls. It might be a little extra, but when you arrive at this rooftop bar, you really won't mind. The view of the **Acropolis** and the rest of Athens speaks for itself so, for prime seats, be sure to make a reservation. The drinks are reasonably priced—and they're definitely a good value for the view at this local hang-out.

i Cocktails from €9, wheelchair accessible; reservations recommended for best seating

CANTINA SOCIAL

Leokoriou 6; 210 3251668; open daily 24hr

Cantina Social is one is the most lowkey spot in Athens, we swear by it. This hole-in-the-wall bar is sandwiched between two chained-up shops, and to enter you have to go through a dark corridor that looks absolutely nothing like an actual bar. After a few moments, the dark corridor opens up to a pleasant courtyard, where locals drink and smoke under string lights and potted plants. The bar is self-service indoors, and everyone is very laid back. The bartender spent 25% of her time making whiskey sours and mojitos, and 75% DJ-ing. Cantina Social lets you get away from the hub of some of the main bars and streets, and provides the perfect setting for long conversations and good drinks with close friends.

i Beer from €4, spirits and cocktails from €6; wheelchair accessible

CORFU

Coverage by **Margaret Canady**

Corfu is the grandmother of Greek island destination vacations, a refuge for travelers. It's easy to see why: unlike the dry Cyclades or windy Dodecanese islands, Corfu is blessed with lush, fertile hills, stunning lookout points, white sandy beaches, and clear blue water. Here, Odysseus was given shelter and a new boat for his journey in Homer's *Odyssey*. In the 1960s, Corfu became one of Greece's first tourist destinations for international visitors, and remains one of the most popular islands to visit today. Not everything is fun in the sun, and the island's history has seen a wealth of battles and conquests, by the Venetians and the British Empire. The global influences can be seen in the island's architecture, food, and culture. In some of the more crowded destinations, you might get frustrated with the sheer amount of tourists milling around, but to best experience Corfu, you need patience, a car, and at least a week.

ORIENTATION

Corfu is a part of the **Ionian Islands** on Greece's northwest corner; as the farthest north of the islands, half of Corfu actually lies off the **coast of Albania**. The island is shaped like a sickled foot, with the concave side facing the mainland. **Corfu Town** lies in the center of the mainland facing side, and the port and airport lie slightly north and south, respectively, of the town. The rest of the main towns are scattered on various sides of the islands, historically claiming the coast for defense tactics, and today for tourist attractions. Some of the more popular beach destinations include **Kavos,** at the southern tip of the island, **Sidari,** on the northwest coast, **Paleokastritsa** on the northern east coast, and **Agios Gordios** on the lower east coast.

ESSENTIALS

GETTING THERE

Corfu International Airport (Ioannis Kapodistrias International Airport) serves the island. There are frequent daily flights between Corfu and Athens that take about an hour (from €50 one way), as well as flights between Thessaloniki and major European cities. Daily ferries connect Corfu to the mainland (at Igoumenitsa) and take about 75min. (€11). There are three daily KTEL buses between Corfu and Athens (€48), and two daily buses between Corfu and Thessaloniki (€39).

GETTING AROUND

There's no getting around it—to fully experience Corfu, the best option is to rent a vehicle. ATVs start at €30, cars at €60, and motorcycles or scooters somewhere in between, but be warned: many companies require an international driver's license, the minimum age for a car is typically 23, and motorcycles require a motorcycle license. Your options? Befriend someone at your hostel who fulfills one of these options and hitch a ride, or take the bus. Corfu is run by two lines: the blue line (which runs around Corfu Town and its surrounding suburbs) and the green line, which connects the major cities of the island. Both are reliable, have accurate schedules online (see greenbuses. gr/routes-en and www.astikoktelkerkyras. gr/indexeg.php), and cost anywhere between €1.40-€5.50 one way, depending on distance. Because of the size and hilliness of the island, it takes anywhere from 45min. to 90min. to get from Corfu Town to any of the coastal cities, so don't plan to see the entire island in a single day. Additionally, most of the green line buses only run out of Corfu Town, so if you're staying in Agios Gordios, for instance, and want to get to Sidari Beach, you have to go through Corfu Town, and the trip one way will take over 2hr.

PRACTICAL INFORMATION

Tourist Offices: Tourist information can be found at the Municipal Information Office outside of the entrance to the Old Fortress. Additionally, check out www.visitgreece.gr/en/greek_islands/ionian_islands/corfu for more information.

Banks/ATMs/Currency Exchange: ATMs are located throughout the island, and many banks can be found in the Old Town. Here is one: National Bank (Vrachlioti 56, Kerkira; 2661 083943; www.nbg.gr/; open M-Th 8am-2:30pm, F 8am-2pm).

Post Offices: Greek Post ELTA (Leof. Alexandras 26, Kerkira; 2661 025544; www.elta.gr/el-gr/home.aspx; open M-F 7:30am-8:30pm)

Public Restrooms: Restrooms can be found at national landmarks, and restaurants, and cafés.

Internet: Wi-Fi can be found at most restaurants and cafés.

BGLTQ+ Resources: Corfu is a relatively gay-friendly island. Check www.travelbyinterest.com/destination/2823/gay/guide for more information.

EMERGENCY INFORMATION

Emergency Number: 112
Police: Dial 100 in an emergency.
• Tourist Police Department (I. Andrea-di St, 1; 26610 29169)
US Embassy: The closest US Embassy is located in Athens (Leof. Vasilissis Sofias 91; 21 0721 2951; gr.usembassy. gov/). There is a US Consulate located in Thessaloniki (43 Tsimiski, 7th Floor; 2310 242 905; gr.usembassy.gov/).
Rape Crisis Center: WomenSOS (support number: 15900; administrative number: 213 1511113; www.womensos. gr/; support number open daily 24hr)
Hospitals:
• Corfu General Clinic (Corfu Town; 2661 036044; www.corfugeneralclinic. gr/?lang=en; open daily 24hr)
• Hospital Corfu (Kontokali 491 00; 2661 360400; www.gnkerkyras.gr/; open daily 24hr)
Pharmacies: Pharmacies are located in most major towns. Here are two:
• Pharmacy Kavvadia Diomedes, in Corfu Town (Polichroniou Kostanta 10, Kerkira; 2661 043339)

ACCOMMODATIONS

THE PINK PALACE ($$)

Agios Gordios; 26610 53103; thepinkpalace.com/; reception open daily 8am-8pm

The Pink Palace is the type of hostel that you'll remember forever, or, if you're doing it right (as some believe), perhaps you won't. First off, it's not called the Pink Palace for naught: their signature Pepto-Bismol shade of pink is splashed across every building on the sprawling grounds, you never get lost on the downhill path to the dorms. With daily parties at their 24-hour beach bar, booze cruises, quad and kayak safaris, as well as biweekly infamous pink toga parties (pink togas, free shots, and plates broken over heads all included), you'll wonder if you even knew what fun was before arriving here. Breakfast (including freshly-prepared fried eggs and bacon!) and a three-course dinner are included in the price, and you'll find yourself tanning on their beach on more than one lazy afternoon.

i Dorms from €28; reservation required; limited wheelchair accessibility; Wi-Fi in limited locations; linens provided; free pickup with min 2 night reservation; breakfast and dinner included; shuttles to Corfu Town, airport, and bus station available

ANGELICA'S BACKPACKER'S HOSTEL ($)

Agios Ioannis; 6944 96 2002; angelicashostel.com; reception open daily 24hr

If candy-colored walls and drunk college students aren't your cup of tea, Angelica's Backpacker's Hostel might just be the place for you. This home-turned-hostel is like visiting your granny's beach home, hospitality and doting included. Comfy beds, a lush backyard, kitchen access, and sweet staff will make you feel welcome and cozy. The only downside is its location; while conveniently located on the north coast (**Sidari Beach**), a long bus ride from Corfu Town: nearly 90 minutes.

i Dorms from €17; reservations required; wheelchair accessible; Wi-Fi; linens, towels included; kitchen; laundry; breakfast €3

SIGHTS
CULTURE

CANAL D'AMOUR

Sidari Beach

Rumor has it that if you swim through the Canal d'Amour, you'll have good fortune in your love life. If Cupid doesn't hit you with his love arrow after a trip here, you might just fall in love with the location itself. Located on **Sidari Beach**, two coves of steep, sandstone rock make up this natural wonder. The site is a popular destination for tourists, and you'll find a fair amount of people tanning on the yellow rock, cliff jumping into the rich blue sea, making face masks from the mud, and, of course, swimming for dear life.

i Free; no wheelchair accessibility; umbrella and chair daily rental €4

EASTER IN CORFU

Old Corfu Town; annually beginning on Palm Sunday

Watch out, Easter Bunny—Corfu's Easter traditions give yours a run for your money. People of the Greek Orthodox faith go all out for the holiday, and festivities start early. **The Philharmonics,** the island's local and widely celebrated brass bands, start off the celebrations on Palm Sunday, and throughout the week, families participate in a variety of traditions, including hymn singing, traditional baking, and dyeing eggs red. The festivities crescendo on Easter Saturday, and as the citizens of Old Corfu Town proclaim *Christós Anésti* (Christ has risen), they throw large clay pots filled with water to the streets below. While no injuries have ever been reported, don't be that person who forgets what day it is and stumbles outside only to be promptly drenched by the "downpour."

i Free; wheelchair accessible

CORFU DONKEY RESCUE

Paleokastritsa; 694 737 5992; www.corfu-donkeys.com/; open daily 10am-5pm

Do you think the TSA would be comfortable with us bringing a live donkey home to the States? About a 15-minute drive from **Paleokastritsa** will take you to Corfu Donkey Rescue. The rescue was opened for unwanted and abandoned donkeys of the islands. (Does this sound like Mamma Mia 2? Absolutely.) The rescue now welcomes cats and dogs, among others, and visiting the Rescue will tempt you to either take one home, or make Corfu your home and spend the rest of your days working on the rescue.

i Donations welcome; wheelchair accessible; volunteering options available

LANDMARKS

🏛 ACHILLEION PALACE

Achillion, Gastouri; 2661 056210; www. achillion-corfu.gr/default_en.html; open daily 8am-8pm

At one point in time, Corfu was the vacation spot only for the richest of the rich—basically, the royalty of the Western World (**Pink Palace** and your €30 bed wouldn't have cut it, sorry). Achilleion Palace was a summer home built for the Empress of Austria, Elisabeth of Bavaria (also known as "Sisi"), and was built with the intention of revering Ancient Greece and Achilles. As you walk through the truly *extra* palace, everything screams "this is expensive and my owner is rich," from the dramatic, ornate internal staircase, the open courtyard on the top floor, the 11.5-meter bronze statue of Achilles overlooking the island, the body-length mirrors... We could continue, but you probably get the picture. Sisi, you really got me in my feelings with this palace.

i Admission €8, students €6; wheelchair accessible; free audio guides in 11 languages

OLD CORFU TOWN

Corfu Town (or Kerkyra)

For travelers who have been to Venice, Corfu Town may seem oddly familiar. The historic city, now a **UNESCO World Heritage Site,** was under Venetian control for about four centuries, and the pastel buildings and narrow winding lanes are living proof of their time here. The city is the most populous town on the island, and, of course, is a popular site for tourists, too. The main streets are filled with quality dining, and tourist stores a dime a dozen. Smaller, narrower streets offer a quiet escape and a glimpse

into daily life via the colorful clothing hanging to dry. The city also offers a nice selection of museums, as well as many churches and landmarks, such as the **Old and New Fortresses.**

i Free; wheelchair accessible; admission fees for museums and fortresses

PALEOKASTRITSA

Paleokastritsa Beach

One of the most popular beaches on the island can be found in the village of Paleokastritsa. Visitors come early to stake out a spot on the coast, armed with suntan lotion and inner tubes for a full day of sun and sand. The clear blue waters are perfect for snorkeling, and you could spend a good couple of hours alone posing with the rocks and water. Canoes, paddle boats, and guided tours of **Paleokastritsa's caves** are available for cheap. Make sure to make the 15-minute hike up the hill to visit the **Paleokastritsa Monastery** and lookout point, which offers jaw-dropping, breathtaking, life-stealing views of what might as well be paradise.

i Free; limited wheelchair accessibility; monastery closes at 1pm

MUSEUMS

🏛 MUSEUM OF ASIAN ART OF CORFU

Palea Anaktora, Kerkira; 26610 30443; www.matk.gr/en/; open daily 8am-8pm

Perhaps the last thing you expected to see in Corfu is a Museum of Asian Art, especially when you learn that the man who spearheaded the museum's creation was the Greek ambassador to, of all places, Austria. All assumptions aside, the museum is set in a large neoclassical nineteenth-century palace, and hosts a superb collection of Chinese, Japanese, and Indian artwork, with select pieces from areas of northeast and southeast Asia. It's the only museum in Greece dedicated solely to Asian art, and their 11,000-odd pieces are paired with richly informative texts, making a trip to the museum worth your while and then some.

i Admission €6, students €3; wheelchair accessible

CASA PARLANTE MUSEUM

Nikiforou Theotoki 16; 2661 049190; casaparlante.gr/; open daily 10am-6pm

Casa Parlante prides itself on being Corfu's "living history museum." Perhaps you're thinking, *Ah that's nice! They're bringing history alive with a visit to their museum. Lovely!* Things are going well: Casa Parlante is a nineteenth-century private home, decorated in the aristocratic style, making it totally understandable that you're offered rose liquor when you start the private tour. Pure silver teapots, how chic! Just wait until you enter the living room and discover in shock (and perhaps a little fear) that there are literal human *robots* occupying the house. The mannequins have simple, repetitive movements: the countess brings her teacup to her lips (forever!); the grandfather turns his head to read the newspaper (forever!). We have to give Casa Parlante credit: it's an innovative idea, and the tour is extremely informative regarding the house, Corfu's history, and its culture. You just might not be able to get the image of the cook craning her head (forever!) out of your mind.

i Admission €6; private tour included with ticket; no wheelchair accessibility

MUNICIPAL GALLERY OF CORFU

St. Michael & St. George Palace; 2661 048690; www.artcorfu.com/; open Tu-Su 9:30am-3pm

Located in the Saint Michael & Saint George Palace (entrance is through the garden to the right of the building) is the small but comprehensive Municipal Gallery of Corfu. Works range from the rich oil painting of sixteenth-century Byzantine artwork to twentieth-century Impressionist-influenced landscapes. All of the work is representative of Corfu and other Ionian island artists. The garden, as well as a separate room in the palace, holds modern sculptures made by graduates from Corfu's School of Fine Arts.

i Admission €2, students €1; limited wheelchair accessibility

FOOD

🗹 STARENIO BAKERY ($)

Guilford 59, Kerkira; 2661 047370; open M-Sa 8am-7pm

In the center of **Old Corfu Town** lies a slice of heaven that sells slices of heaven: Starenio Bakery. Homemade sweet treats and savory pies await you, and there are a few table outside the flowered overhangings where you can sit and devour the glory of your selections. There are vegan options, too, making it savory sanctuary for all.

i Most pastries and pies under €3; cash preferred; vegan options available; wheelchair accessible

BARDIS GRILL HOUSE

Prossalendou 1; 2661 042970

Hidden on an alley connecting two main streets in **Corfu Town,** Bardis Grill House serves down-and -dirty traditional Greek food: salads, *gyros, souvlaki,* and the like. The overzealous waiter will recommend the *souvlaki* platter (€7.50), and we can't help but agree– they don't skimp on the well-seasoned rotisserie pork, and it's complemented with thick slabs of pita. Try to grab a table outside, as the small interior can get rather stuffy.

i Everything under €8; wheelchair accessible

PANE E SOUVLAKI ($)

Gkilford 77, Kerkira; 2661 020100; open daily noon-midnight

Pane e Souvlaki is in the heart of **Corfu Town** and popular among tourists, and it's easy to see why. With the cheerful decor vaguely reminding us of our grandma's flowered linens, the cheap traditional specials, and the English descriptions on the menu, you'll get a good meal for a reasonable price, and actually know what you're eating, too. It can get busy during peak hours, and waitstaff can be a little cool, but the food is worth it.

i Specials for €5, most entrées under €10; vegetarian options available; wheelchair accessible

PORTA REMOUNDA ($$$)

Moustoxidi 16; 2661 022658; portaremounda.gr/

When we asked our waiter at Porta Remounda what their daily specials were, he led us to the kitchen, where one of the chefs opened up metal ice containers and showed us the dead fish that must've been caught that morning. Porta Remounda doesn't play around with its seafood, and with the price you're paying for by the kilo, we're sure its worth it. But if you thought we were paying €65 for a kilo of fish, you. thought. wrong. The salmon salad (€11) was quite good though, and there are reasonable seafood appetizers and pastas available, too.

i Salads and pasta from €4, fish by the kilo from €16; wheelchair accessible

TAVERNA TROUMPETA ($$)

Troumpeta 490 83; 2663 022136

On the road between the towns of **Paleokastritsa** and **Sidari** lies a tavern perfect for a road trip pit-stop. Probably only frequented on happenstance (their business card has their longitude and latitude as opposed to a physical address), the tavern serves quality sit-down meals made up of various dishes, including juicy lamb chops, chunky *souvlaki*, and pasta. If you sit outside, every so often you'll be both entertained and awed as huge tour buses try to turn the corner on a narrow, one-way winding along Corfu's hillside. Dinner and a show!

i Appetizers from €3.50, traditional dishes from €8; vegetarian options available; wheelchair accessible

NIGHTLIFE

◪ 7TH HEAVEN CAFE

Above Logas Beach; 2663 095035; open daily 10am-midnight

No beach day or island vacation is complete without a gorgeous sunset to match, and Corfu certainly doesn't fail to produce. The best place to watch the sunset with a cocktail is 7th Heaven Cafe on the north coast of Sunset Beach (aka **Logas Beach**). Make sure to come early for a seat at a swing, table, or bar chair with cliff views of the beach, coast, and horizon. They offer your typical range of cocktails, but when blueberries are season,

ask for a fresh blueberry margarita (€8). Make sure not to miss the glass-bottomed platform that hangs over the cliff precipice and gives you stunning views of the beach below—it's the perfect place to take silhouette yoga poses against a cotton-candy sunset.

i Cocktails from €7.50, fresh juice from €4; restaurant reservations required; wheelchair accessible

◪ PINK TOGA PARTIES AT THE PINK PALACE

The Pink Palace; W and Sa nights

Given how difficult it is to get between towns in Corfu, the Pink Palace has taken care of everything you may need for a good time, including nightlife. Every person in the hostel seems to know and anticipate the (in)famous parties; we heard several backpackers say they extended their stay to make sure they could bear witness to at least one of the biweekly blowouts. It's truly a sight to behold: beautiful gods and goddesses (read: hot young people) decked in their finest attire (read: pastel pink sheets wrapped haphazardly toga-style) feast on ambrosia and love (read: alcohol and each other's faces). Is this an authentic Greek toga party? Perhaps the smashing of plates over people's heads, initiated by the hostel's staff, is supposed to make it such. The party goes until the crack of dawn, and luckily the dorms are only a few steps away for wobbling party goers. One word of wisdom: whatever you do, for the love of Zeus, don't go into the jacuzzi. You can probably guess why.

i Toga and 2 free drinks €20 (€10 if you return the toga the next morning); cash only; BGLTQ+ friendly; wheelchair accessible

POLYTECHNO

Scholemvourgou St 39; 26610 27794; open daily 8:30pm-3am

We're not actually sure what polytechno means, but if the upbeat house music and black-and-white musician portraits say anything, the bar likes its tech music and chic, sleek decor. Tucked in a street under the New Fortress, you can sit outside and enjoy a coffee or cocktail, or stay inside and listen to the occasional live DJ under glowing lights.

i Beer and wine from €4, cocktails from €7; wheelchair accessible

CORINTH

Coverage by **Margaret Canady**

The name "Corinthians" may ring a bell to you, especially if you're familiar with the New Testament. Located on the Isthmus of Corinth, the city is the gateway of the Peloponnese, and for this reason was an important trading city in Ancient Greece, and was, at one point, the center of early Christianity. Today, modern Corinth is a sleepy little city, and the inhabitants spend their days drinking coffee and lying on the beach. The preserved archaeological sites of Ancient Corinth and Acrocorinth are located on the outskirts of the town, and are worth a visit if you're passing through.

ORIENTATION

Corinth is located on the isthmus that connects **mainland Greece** with the **Peloponnese,** and can be found right on the **Gulf of Corinth.** The city is located about 48 miles west of Athens. New Corinth is relatively small, and most of the city center (which is found near the Gulf) follows a grid pattern. Many of the restaurants, cafés, and shops are on or near the streets of **Damaskinou, Eth. Antistaseos, and Apostolou Pavlou.** Residential neighborhoods are found farther away from the city center and on the hills surrounding the city. **Ancient Corinth** and **Acrocorinth** are found about seven kilometers southwest of the modern city.

ESSENTIALS

GETTING THERE

The easiest way to get to Corinth is via bus. Buses run hourly between Athens and Corinth; they take about 1hr and cost around €8. Main bus lines from all areas of the Peloponnese peninsula also run through Corinth. Corinth is served by the Isthmus KTEL Bus Station, which is about 15min. away from the actual city. A bus from the Isthmus bus station to Corinth runs on the hour and costs €1.20, and a taxi costs about €10.

GETTING AROUND

Getting around Corinth is very easy, and most things in town are about a 10min. walk away. To get to the coastal cities that are adjacent to Corinth, local buses run hourly. To get to Ancient Corinth from Corinth, a local bus station in town runs hourly until 2:30pm (except Su) and costs €1.80 one way; a taxi costs about €10.

PRACTICAL INFORMATION

Tourist Offices: Visit www.visitgreece.gr/en/destinations/korinthos for more city information.

Banks/ATMs/Currency Exchange: There are several banks and ATMs near the city center, one of which is National Bank (Pilarinou 42-50; 2741 078043; www.nbg.gr/; open M-Th 8am-2:30pm, F 8am-2pm).

Post Offices: Corinth Post Office (35 Adimantos St.; 274102 4122)

Public Restrooms: There are no public restrooms, but most cafés and restaurants have restrooms available with purchase.

Internet: Most cafés and restaurants have Wi-Fi.

EMERGENCY INFORMATION

Emergency Number: 112

Police: Corinth Police Station (27410 77250 or 27410 77263; call 100 in a police emergency)

US Embassy: The closest US Embassy is located in Athens (Leof. Vasilissis Sofias 91; 21 0721 2951; gr.usembassy.gov/).

Rape Crisis Center: WomenSOS (support number: 15900; administrative number: 213 1511113; www.womensos.gr/; support number open daily 24hr)

Hospitals: Corinth General Hospital (Athinon 53; 27413 61400; www.hospkorinthos.gr/; open daily 24hr)

Pharmacies: There are several pharmacies in the city center; look for the green cross.
• Giannou Konstantinos M (Papandreou Georgious 45; 2741076210)

ACCOMMODATIONS

ACROPOLIS HOTEL ($$)

Eth. Anexartisias 25; 2741 021104; acropolis-corinth.gr/en/

Down the street from the city center lies Acropolis Hotel, one of the several low budget hotel options in Corinth. The receptionists are friendly, and the rooms are cheerful, and come complete with bright blue carpets and small private balconies. It's simple, sweet, and perfect for a night in the city.

i *Privates from €29; wheelchair accessible; Wi-Fi; breakfast available; linens and towels included*

KORINTHOS HOTEL ($$)

Damaskinou 26; 2741 026701; www.korinthoshotel.gr/

Corinth isn't used to having lone youth travelers interested in exploring the city, so there are no hostels in the nearby area. Cheap hotels, however, are abundant, like Korinthos Hotel. Lilac-painted rooms and comfy beds make up the low-key accomodation, and if you've been roughing it in tents and hostel dorms, the privacy, good air-conditioning, minifridge, and other facilities will make you feel like you're in the Ritz.

i *Privates from €30; wheelchair accessible; breakfast €5*

SIGHTS
CULTURE

🏛 CORINTH CANAL

Korinth Bridge; open daily 24hr

Near the **Isthmus Bus Station** and about a 15-minute drive from Corinth lies the Corinth Canal, a spectacular structure that evokes both vertigo and the desire to pull out a camera. The canal really is stunning, though, and its steep rock walls stretch four miles in length and almost 150 feet high. You can stand on the pedestrian bridge and watch small boats pass through, as well as thrill (or death) seekers, who voluntarily plunge into the abyss held to life only by some rope. Yes, bungee jumping is available and extremely popular on the canal, but we'll let you sign the death consent form yourself.

i *Free crossing; wheelchair accessible*

LOUTRAKI THERMAL SPA

G. Lekkas St. 24, Loutraki; 2744 062186; www.loutrakispa.gr; open M-F 11am-7pm, Sa-Su 10am-9pm

One beach-residing town over from Corinth lies the city of **Loutraki,** along with the popular Loutraki Thermal Spa. Apparently even the Ancient Greeks were concerned with pore size and supple skin: the thermal baths of Loutraki have been around for nearly 3000 years. Today, with modern facilities and 5000 square meters of pools, saunas, steam rooms, and massage rooms, you too can dip your toe in the fountain of youth (or your entire body, depending on your desire).

i *Services from €10; limited wheelchair accessibility; visit with Spa Doctor required for entrance; visit the website to see if you're qualified to enter pools*

LANDMARKS

🏛 ANCIENT CORINTH

Ancient Corinth; 27410 31207; open daily Nov 1-Mar 31 8am-3pm, Oct 1-15 8am-7pm, Oct 16-31 8am-6pm; summer open daily 8am-8pm

As any person with siblings will know, information is power—the more dirt you have on them, the more they'll bend to your will. Ancient Corinth was kind of like Ancient Greece's middle child. Its prime location between the mainland and the **Peloponnese** made it an ideal trading city, and all the top names wanted control over the city. Today, the remnants of Ancient Corinth can be found a few kilometers southwest of modern day Corinth. Main features include the **Temple of Apollo** and the two main roads of the city that welcomed trade and transportation. Buses run between Corinth and Ancient Corinth (€1.80 one way) every day except Sunday, but make sure to go early—buses stop at about 2:30pm, and taxis cost about €10.

i *Admission €8, students €4; wheelchair accessible*

ACROCORINTH

Acrocorinth; 27410 31266; open daily 8am-3pm

While Acropolis in Athens gets all of the fame and glory, an *acropolis* is actually a common landmark in Ancient Greece; the word describes a settlement built upon elevated ground. Acrocorinth is Ancient Corinth's *acropolis* and was used as a fortress and defense system. What's left isn't much—just a bunch of medieval ruins on the top of a hill—but the view of the area is pretty awesome. Just like there's no elevator to success, there's no bus to the top of the hill, so you have three options: drive (if you have a car), hike (if you have strong calves and an hour to spare), or wait for some nice Greek people to offer you a ride.
i Free; no wheelchair accessibility

MUSEUMS

ARCHAEOLOGICAL MUSEUM OF ANCIENT CORINTH

Ancient Corinth; 27410 31207; www.corinth-museum.gr/en/; open daily 8am-7pm

The Archaeological Museum can be found in a building on Ancient Corinth's premises, and the first thing you'll notice when you step foot inside is how freaking *amazing* the air-conditioning is. As your sweat dries and your body returns to a comfortable internal temperature, the next thing you'll notice is that the museum is actually a big little place, filled with many remnants of graves and artifacts from the archaeological site right outside. Tiny vases, utensils, and coins stand among tombs and even a few conserved graves, bones and all. There's interesting information on the walls about Ancient Corinth and archeology in general, including a section about grave robbers and antiquity smugglers.
i Admission €8, students €4 (included with Ancient Corinth tickets); wheelchair accessible

FOOD

🍽 KANDAYLOS ($)

Pilarinou 64; 27410 74848; open M-Sa 11am-1am

When your food comes out on a plate that's twice the size of your face, you *know* it's gonna be good. Kandaylos serves some of the best traditional Greek food in Corinth, and we can't decide what we liked best the **freshly prepared chicken souvlakis,** the sheer amount of food you get per serving (this is no artisanal restaurant with small portions; that dinner plate was completely full), or the cheap prices. You'll be wanting to come back for more, but honestly you might have enough leftovers for at least another meal.
i Souvlaki and gyro platters mostly under €8, salads and burgers €4; gluten-free and vegetarian options available; wheelchair accessible; Wi-Fi

SABOR BY LEFTERIS ($$)

Agiou Spiridonos 1; 2741 072202; sabor-by-lefteris.business.site; open daily 8pm-1am

About a 10-minute walk from the **Korinthos Bus Station** lies Sabor, a hidden gem overlooking the city of Corinth. It's fine dining—that is, compared to the *souvlaki* and *gyro* fast food places in town—with a view of the sun setting over the gulf that will make your heart sing and your cameras click. Because Corinth isn't a big city, you're not paying the typical fine dining cost. The stomachable prices only make the exceptional Greek- and Italian-inspired cuisine go down even easier.

i Entrées from €10, appetizers from €4; no wheelchair accessibility

PASTEL

Kolokotroni St; 2741 081803; open M-Sa 9am-1am, Su 9am-midnight

The hub of city life in Corinth orbits around the streets between the city center and the coast, where a multitude of cafés and restaurants lines the streets. Corinth's inhabitants spend hours in the early morning and the evenings sitting with friends, talking, smoking, and drinking coffee or cocktails. Pastel was one of our favorite cafés in Corinth, with its quality coffee, comfortable indoor and outdoor seating, and friendly waitresses with really good makeup skills.

i Coffee from €2, cocktails from €8, beer from €3; wheelchair accessible; Wi-Fi

NIGHTLIFE

DOLCE E AMARO

Periandrou 2; 2741 025500; dolceeamaro. gr/; open daily 8am-2am

If you're looking to get completely hammered on a Friday night, Dolce E Amaro is not for you. Part café, part restaurant, and primarily a wine bar, Dolce E Amaro serves you upscale looks and a classy affair, all at super reasonable prices for wine by the glass. They'll bring you an iPad with an extensive wine list that displays each wine, where's it from, and what's it's supposed to taste like (oak, chocolate, etc). Each glass is served with tapas, and you'll feel quite fancy as you swirl, smell, and sip. When the waiter asks if you can taste the blackberries in your glass, smile and nod politely, even if all you taste is, um, red wine.

i Wine from €4; wheelchair accessible

ARTICHOKE

Pilarinou 68; 2741 084233; www.facebook. com/Artichoke.Corinth/; open daily 8am-3am

You're not going to find anyone over the age of 25 at Artichoke. The alternative bar is a popular spot for the young people of Corinth, and it's pretty easy to understand why: the aesthetic is very I'm-cool-and-at-a-bar (i.e. lowlights, lush couches, rock star décor), they serve cheap drinks, and live bands play on the weekends. A little immature, but definitely a solid choice for a night out on the town.

i Beer and wine from €2.50, cocktails from €7; no wheelchair accessibilit

KALAMATA

Coverage by **Margaret Canady**

There are two main types of olives that most people remember off the top of their heads: the black ones and the green ones. Kalamata's claim to fame, then, is the black Kalamata olive, grown exclusively in the Kalamata region and exported around the world. Despite the fact that it's a household name, the city itself doesn't see much traveler love, and many people pass through quickly to get to the rest of Messinia and the Mani Peninsula. If you give the city a chance though, you'll be pleasantly surprised by the amount of young people in Kalamata spending their days sipping *frappe* in one of the many cool cafés and spending their nights in the popular bars on the beach. For the culturally inclined, make sure to check out the diverse collection of museums in the Historic Center, the annual internationally recognized summer dance festival, and unique shopping finds—including silk scarves and, of course, olive products.

ORIENTATION

Kalamata is located on the **Peloponnese** with a coast on the Mediterranean Sea. It's the second-most populous city in the Peloponnese, as well as the capital of the region of Messenia. At the north end of the city is the **KTEL bus station.** If you cross the **Nedontas Potamos River** and head south of the station you'll find the **Historic Center** or **Old City of Kalamata,** which is home to a variety of museums and several landmarks. Heading south, you'll reach the modern city, characterized by a grid-like neighborhood structure with 3 main streets running north to south: **Akrita, Faron,** and **Aristomenous.** The north end of Aristomenous is a pedestrian only walkway that leads into **Central Square,** the area where many cafés and restaurants are situated. Continue south and you'll eventually reach the Kalamata coast, lined with restaurants, youthful nightlife, and several kilometers of beaches.

ESSENTIALS

GETTING THERE

The city is served by Kalamata International Airport, a small airport that is most active in the summer and sees flights from Thessaloniki and Athens, as well as several other European cities. A taxi from the airport to Kalamata is about €22, and there is also a local bus to the city. KTEL Messinia bus station has buses to and from many cities in Greece, including Athens (€25, approx 3hr), Thessaloniki, (€71, approx 11hr), and closer cities, such as Tripoli, Pyrgos, and Sparta. Check the website (www.ktelmessinias.gr/) for updated bus schedules. If driving, the city can be accessed from Athens and Corinth via the Moreas highway.

GETTING AROUND

Kalamata is a relatively small city, and you can easily walk to most places you need to get to. Everything is about a 10-20min. walk from Central Square. Many people in Kalamata also bike, and this could be ideal if you're staying in the north end of the city (where the only hostel is located) and want to get to the beach; a bike path runs down the center of town. Bike rentals cost around €7 per day. Additionally, there are four local bus lines that leave from the KTEL Messinia bus station. The most useful one is Bus 1, which has hourly departures and goes through the center of the city before heading east along the coast down to the edge of town. Tickets are €1.30 and can be bought on the bus.

PRACTICAL INFORMATION

Tourist Offices: Tourist Information Office (Agion Apostolon Square; 27210 90413; open M-Sa 9am-6pm)

Banks/ATMs/Currency Exchange: Banks and ATMs can be found down and around Aristomenous St. A popular ATM is Piraeus Bank (Polychronous 1 & Aristomenous 43 B; 2721 067000; www.piraeusbank.gr/el/idiwtes; open M-Th 8am-2:30pm, F 8am-2pm).

Post Offices: Hellenic Post Office Elta (Analipseos; 2721 022151; open M-F 7:30am-2:30pm)

Public Restrooms: No public restrooms, but all restaurants and cafés have a restroom you can use with purchase.

Internet: The city offers Wi-Fi in the city center.

BGLTQ+ Resources: Check out www.iglta.org/europe/greece/ and www.travelbyinterest.com/destination/1087/gay/guide for BGLTQ+ businesses and resources in Greece.

EMERGENCY INFORMATION

Emergency Number: 112

Police: Police Department of Kalamata (Iroon Polytechniou 24100; 27210 44653)

US Embassy: The closest US Embassy is located in Athens (Leof. Vasilissis Sofias 91; 21 0721 2951; gr.usembassy.gov/).

Rape Crisis Center: WomenSOS (support number: 15900; administrative number: 213 1511113; www.womensos.gr/; support number open daily 24hr)

Hospitals: The main hospital in Kalamata is Prefecture General Hospital. However, there are various other medical facilities nearby.

- Prefecture General Hospital of Kalamata (Antikalamos 241 00; 2721 046000; www. nosokomeiokalamatas.gr/**index. php; open daily 24hr)**

Pharmacies: There are several pharmacies in the city center; look for the green cross.

- Systegasmena Farmakeia Elissavet Alexidou (Aristomenous 47; 2721 022223; open M-F 8am-3pm and 5:30pm-9:30pm, Sa 8am-2:30pm)
- Pharmacyonclick (Platonos 8; 2721 023431; www.pharmacyonclick. gr/; open M 8am-2:30pm, Tu, Th 8am-1:30pm and 5:30pm-8pm, W 9am-2:30pm, F 9am-1:30pm and 5:30pm-8pm, Sa 8am-10pm)

ACCOMMODATIONS

HOTEL BYZANTIO ($$)

Railway Station 7; 2721 086824; www. byzantiokalamata.gr/

One of the best things about visiting Kalamata is that prices are extremely reasonable—the first example of which is Hotel Byzantio. The hotel is casual and lowkey, located right off the **Central Square,** and it's perfectly central to both the beach and **Historic Center.** What you might expect to pay for an average dorm in a big city will get you a large private room and bath, air-conditioning, and free breakfast.

i Dorms from €35; wheelchair accessible; Wi-Fi; breakfast, linens, and towels included

SIGHTS
CULTURE

🏛 KALAMATA DANCE FESTIVAL

Athinos 99; 2721 360700; kalamatadancefestival.gr/index.php/en/; mid-July, annually

Kalamata has gained international attention for its annual dance festival, and we think you should go. The festival has been around for over 20 years, and is held in several venues throughout the city, including the city's **International Dance Center** and the amphitheatre in the medieval **Kalamata Castle.** The festival attracts both Greek and

international dance companies, with a large focus on contemporary and modern dance performances; there are also workshops and masterclasses available to the public. Even if you don't know the difference between a *posse* and a *ponche,* the festival is designed to be accessible to anyone and everyone who's interested, so make sure to check it out when you're in town.

i Performance tickets from €12; limited wheelchair accessibility; see website for lineup

CENTRAL SQUARE

Central Sq., on Aristomenous; open daily 24hr

Life in Kalamata centers around, go figure, Central Square. At 13,500 square meters, the square is a marble paved rectangle (plot twist), lined with restaurants, cafés, and trees. While it can be pretty barren during the heat of the day, as the sun sets the square hums with life: children running and playing in the fountain at the south end of the square, teenagers showing off their bike tricks, moms with strollers, couples strolling. At Central Square, you're only a few minutes away from everything else in town.

i Free admission; wheelchair accessible

LANDMARKS

🏛 HISTORIC CENTER AND THE CHURCH OF YPAPANTI

Historic Center, Kalamata; 2721 022602

At the base of **Kalamata Castle** and just north of the modern city lies the Historic Center of Kalamata. There's a certain charm to this area; the streets, some strung with flags and lights, weave into one another, and you'll find a variety of cafés, local handmade stores, and small bakeries (we recommend **Chrysanthi's Bakery** with enthusiasm) with the best *koulourakias* (Greek butter cookies) you'll ever have. At the north of the historic center you'll find the Church of Ypapanti, a Byzantine-style Greek Orthodox church lushly decorated with twilight blue walls and not one, not two, but nine low-hanging chandeliers.

i Free; wheelchair accessible

▨ KALAMATA'S CASTLE

Spartis 28; 2721 083086; open Tu-Su 8am-8pm

Before you enter, an informational plaque will offer you a brief description of the thirteenth-century edifice. On this plaque, the castle is described by some ancient military man as "weak," which is, quite frankly, hilarious (but also kind of a good prime for what to expect). It's a rather small building, with a couple of floors for you to walk around. The top of the castle is flat and shaded with pine trees, providing a good escape from the heat, and offers a lovely view of the city down to the sea, as well as mountainous landscape behind Kalamata. Despite being weak af, the castle has been controlled by no less than the Byzantines, Franks, Slavs, Albanians, Venetians, and Turks.

i *Admission €2, students €1; limited wheelchair accessibility*

MUSEUMS

▨ ARCHAEOLOGICAL MUSEUM OF MESSENIA

Agiou Ioannou 3; 2721 083485; archmusmes.culture.gr/; open M 1:30pm-8pm, Tu-Su 8am-8pm

How old is too old to make use of a museum's activity rooms? Kalamata's Archaeological Museum is kid- and adult-friendly, with a main path that weaves through the museum like the Pamissus River, and four smaller roads that represent the four provinces of the **Messenia Area.** The artifacts are interesting and well-preserved, and include jewelry and figurines from tombs and other archeological excavations. And if you think the museum's activity roms have no age limit, you can join the third-graders in the museum's large, interactive activities room.

i *Admission €3, reduced €2; wheelchair accessible; free English guides available*

OUTDOORS

KALAMATA BEACH

Navarinou St.; open daily 24hr

Two kilometers south of the city lies Kalamata's beach, which is long enough to feel uncrowded and popular enough to have something for everyone. The beach is bordered by clear blue water, and dotted with restaurants, cafés, and tiki bars offering great drinks and free umbrella or beach chair use. There are also beach volleyball courts and floating inflatable play areas for kids. At night, the beach becomes a popular place for young people to hang out and grab drinks.

i *Free admission; beach umbrellas and chairs available with purchase at a bar/restaurant; wheelchair accessible*

FOOD

▨ BLOSSOM OWL / COFFEE SHOP / ROASTERY ($)

Valaoritou 7; 2721 060008; open M-Sa 8am-midnight, Su 9am-midnight

Maybe it was the eight hours we spent here writing, the option of cold brew and chemex coffee, the really good Wi-Fi, or some great combination of the three, but Blossom Owl was one of our favorite spots in Kalamata. A surprisingly hip place that gives off hipster-moves-to-gentrified-Brooklyn vibes, the coffee shop has two buildings and outdoor seating that connects the two. Blossom Owl is consistently full of young people, who often spend hours talking and slowly sipping *frappe* (cold coffee), as is the tradition in Kalamata. The coffee is exceptional, as are the breakfast options and the homemade sweet shop and its waffle, pancake, and pastry offerings. The items are listed in English, but the descriptions aren't, which (in our opinion) is the perfect blend of expectation and surprise.

i *Coffee from €1.80, waffles from €2.50, food from €4.40; wheelchair accessible; Wi-Fi*

◾ KARDAMO ($)

Sidirodromikou Stathmou 21; 2721 098091; kardamo.gr/?lang=en; open daily 1pm-1am

Kardamo puts a modern and personal twist on traditional Greek food, such as a beef liver *meze* in oregano and olive oil, or their handmade pasta dish with smoked pancetta. Their salads are not neglected, either, and the lettuce kinda tastes like the it was given a really good massage with olive oil. Elegant and modern doesn't mean expensive: 99% of the menu is less than €10.

i *Most entrées under €10; vegetarian options available; wheelchair accessible*

TA ROLLA ($)

Spartis 53; 2721 026218; www.ta-rolla.gr/; open M-F 8am-10pm, Sa 8am-7pm

If you were Greek and coming home for dinner, we imagine it would taste something like Ta Rolla. The family-owned restaurant on the northwest corner of the **Historic Center** has been around since 1924, and its a popular lunch spot with the locals. For lunch, choose from a variety of traditional Greek meats and vegetables; the *okra raguet* and

moussaka are to die for.

i *Most entrées under €10; vegetarian options available*

NIGHTLIFE

◾ TRICKY BAR

Navarinou 161; 2721 110437; open daily 9am-3am

Every beach town has its own version of the tiki bar, and Kalamata is no different. But unlike a lot of places, Tricky Bar's drinks match its thatched roof and Polynesian masks. They have an incredible selection of spirits—the best from Central America—and their exotic cocktails use fresh juice (which makes all the difference). The vibe isn't rager-friendly—come here for a relaxed and tropical feeling.

i *Cocktails from €8, spirits from €7, juice and smoothies from €3; wheelchair accessible*

LE JARDIN

Navarinou 202; 2721 098928; kalamatain.gr/new/le-jardin/; open daily 9am-3am

Le Jardin is like the PG-13 version of *The Secret Garden*. Le Jardin is a popular bar that gets its name from its lush tropical garden. Grab a cocktail and sit underneath a large tree decorated with glowing glass ornaments, or have fun with the hookah on their comfortable lounge chairs. Lush plants attract mosquitoes, but the bar also has beach access during the day, so you can switch between tropical paradise and... tropical paradise.

i *Cocktails from €8, wine from €4.50, entrées from €6.50; wheelchair accessible; free parking lot*

MYKONOS

Coverage by **Margaret Canady**

The island of Mykonos really has some *Dr. Jekyll and Mr. Hyde* themes going on. On the surface, there's classic "Mykonos," which is the stereotypical image of Greek island paradise: picturesque white-walled and blue-trimmed buildings, floral canopies, stunning seaside beaches and coves. Tourists of all ages (and A-listers) can be found enjoying the island that, during high season, is sunny, windy, and always bustling. A couple vials of magic potion later (read: your choice of alcoholic libations), and the island's twin sister "MYKONÓSSSSS" emerges. The underbelly of the island (literally—the best parties happen at the south end of the island) is home to a never-ending stream of college students, beat drops, and alcohol. (Did we mention this already?) The party lasts well into the morning, turns into a darty, and then transforms into a pregame for the night to come. Regardless of your alcoholic or party preferences, you're sure to find a good time in the party hub of the Aegean Sea.

ORIENTATION

Mykonos is part of the **Cyclades Islands** on the Aegean Sea. The island is relatively small, and most of the action of the island occurs on the west and southwest sides. **Mykonos Town** is located right in the middle of the island's west coast. Here, you'll find the majority of the hotels, landmarks, and restaurants—making it a guarantee that photo-ops will take place. To the north of the town is the **New Port of Mykonos,** located in **Tourlos,** where all ferries arrive. The airport is to the east of the town. On the south end of the island are **Paraga, Paradise,** and **Super Paradise Beach.** Here are the hostels and camping accommodations (read: the only cheap places to stay on the island), as well as the majority of young nightlife. Outside of these areas, the island consists of rocky terrain, less-populated beaches, and farmland.

ESSENTIALS

GETTING THERE

The island is served by Mykonos Airport (JMK). Buses between the airport and Mykonos Town run four times a day and cost €1.60, or you can grab a taxi for €29 at any time. Most people reach Mykonos by ferry. All ferries arrive at the Old Port in Tourlos. Many hotels and hostels offer free transport from the port. Otherwise, take a sea taxi between the Old Port and Mykonos Town for €2 (10min.), and land taxis are available 24/7.

GETTING AROUND

Mykonos Town is extremely walkable; it takes about 10min. to walk from one edge of town to the other. The island itself is not as easily walkable, and public buses provide hourly transport between Mykonos Town (Fabrika Square) and other popular destinations, such as Paraga Beach, Paradise Beach, and Elia. (The bus ride, is in itself, an adventure—the narrow, steep streets that curve through Mykonos were meant for donkeys, not tour buses, and you'll find yourself both in fear and in awe as the driver, with one hand on the wheel and the other lighting a cigarette, makes the unmakeable turns with grace). Tickets are €1.80 and can be purchased on the bus or at the ticket kiosk. Public buses stop around midnight, and make sure to check the schedule so you don't have to taxi, which can cost anywhere from €20-40. ATVs, cars, and motorbikes are available to rent, but most companies require an international driver's license and have age restrictions.

PRACTICAL INFORMATION

Tourist Offices: There's no physical tourist information center on the island, but information can be found at www.visitgreece.gr/en/greek_islands/mykonos. There are several private tourist agencies in Mykonos Town that offer services and information, such as Mykonos Tours & Travel (Mykonos Hora; 2289 079376; www.mykonos-web.com/; open daily 9am-9pm).

Banks/ATMs/Currency Exchange: There are several ATMs throughout Mykonos Town, and there's one at both the Paraga and Paradise Beach accommodations. Here's a bank in the city center: National Bank of Greece (Axioti 6; 2289 077011; www.nbg.gr/; open M-Th 8am-2:30pm, F 8am-2pm).

Post Offices: Post Office of Mykonos (Paralia Cyclades; 8011138000; open M-F 7:30am-2:30pm)

Public Restrooms: There are public restrooms located at the Old and New Port.

Internet: Most cafés and restaurants have Wi-Fi.

BGLTQ+ Resources: Mykonos is often ranked one of the top gay-friendly tourist destinations in the world. Check out nomadicboys.com/gay-mykonos-guide/ for more information.

EMERGENCY INFORMATION

Emergency Number: 112

Police: Dial 100 in emergencies. Police Department of Mykonos is located by the airport (22890 22716).

US Embassy: The closest US Embassy is located in Athens (Leof. Vasilissis Sofias 91; 21 0721 2951; gr.usembassy.gov/).

Rape Crisis Center: WomenSOS (support number: 15900; administrative number: 213 1511113; www.womensos.gr/; support number open daily 24hr)

Hospitals: Both of the following are private medical centers.
- Mykonian Hygeia (Agiou Ioanni-Agiou Stefanou; 2289 024211; www.mykonos-health.com/; open daily 24hr)

Pharmacies: Pharma Mykonos (Drafaki Mykonou, on the way to the airport; 2289 023900; www.pharmamykonos.gr/en/; open M-Sa 9am-11pm, Su 11am-10:30pm)

ACCOMMODATIONS

☑ PARAGA BEACH HOSTEL & CAMPING ($$)

Paraga Beach; 2289 025915; mycamp.gr/; reception open 24hr in summer

Paraga Hostel is, on the surface, perfect—almost too perfect. The hostel is cheap by Mykonos standards, and one of the friendly receptionists, once checked in, gives you a tour of their facilities: four bars, one restaurant, large pools that seem to melt into the sea, beach access, and a DJ. Once you look closer, however, the hostel starts to show its (tiny) flaws—slow Wi-Fi only available in a few common areas, basic tents with few outlets, no access to the pool lounge without a purchase. That said, it's still one of the best bangs for your buck on the island, and you're only a five-minute walk from the main party spot, **Paradise Beach**.

i Dorms from €30; reservation required; wheelchair accessible; limited Wi-Fi; free transport to and from port; linens included; free luggage storage day of check-in and check-out

PARADISE BEACH CAMPING ($$)

Paradise Beach; 2289 022129; www.paradisemykonos.com/; reception open 24hr

At Paradise Beach Camping, you probably won't get much sleep, and by "much," we mean "any." The tents are located directly behind two beach clubs, which is the perfect location for partiers to stumble to bed without getting lost. The hostel is less than ideal for anyone who dislikes loud bass and likes sleep. The tents are surprisingly nice, with floral sheets, windows you can open, and hardwood floors.

i Single cabins from €20; reservations recommended; wheelchair accessible; Wi-Fi available for purchase; linens included

SIGHTS
CULTURE

☑ CYCLADIC WINDMILLS OF MYKONOS

Kato Mili; 2289 360100; mykonos.gr/en/; open daily 24hr

Before Mykonos was known for its picturesque scenery and less-picturesque party scene, the island's main source of income came from its iconic windmills. Built in the sixteenth century, the windmills were used to process wheat, channeling the rocky island's fierce winds for good. Seven of the remaining 16 windmills of Mykonos are found on a hill in **Mykonos Town** overlooking the sea. The windmills in town are an iconic landmark, perfect for pictures and as a physical reference point for everything else in town.

i Free; wheelchair accessible; museum entrance at leftmost windmill

RARITY GALLERY

Kalogera 20-22; 2289 025761; www.raritygallery.com/; open daily 10am-midnight

A slew of contemporary art galleries adorn **Mykonos Town,** in the hopes that its rich tourists will come in and they'll purchase something for a pretty penny. The best one we saw was Rarity Gallery, with thrilling and carefully curated pieces that challenge today's art scene. You'll spend several minutes staring at hyperrealistic sculptures of a security guard and Carole Feuerman's ladies in swimsuits, 100 percent expecting them to blink or breathe. Captivating optical illusions play with your perception of color and distance. Entrance is free and the museum is small—we definitely recommend stopping in while in town.

i Free, artwork available for purchase; wheelchair accessible

LANDMARKS

🖾 CHURCH OF PANAGIA PARAPORTIANI

Kastro neighborhood, Mykonos Town; mykonos.gr/en/the-island/ekklisies-monastiria/

Of the 400-plus churches in Mykonos, the Church of Panagia Paraportiani is definitely the most photographed. A five-minute walk from the **Cycladic Windmills,** the fifteenth-century church consists of not one, but five churches built on top or next to one another, giving the edifice a look that resembles blotches of whipped cream. Its meringue (okay, we're hungry) white puff walls are delicious contrasts against the rich blue Aegean sea and sky. There's a rock stairway that leads to a small lookout between the sea and the church, but the plethora of used condoms makes it less than ideal, unless you're into that symbolic (and other) kind of stuff.

i Free; limited wheelchair accessibility

LITTLE VENICE

Between Kastro and Scarpa neighborhoods, Mykonos Town; mykonos.gr/en/the-island/axiotheata/

There aren't any canals, gondolas, or bridges that remind us of Venice in Mykonos, but this neighborhood is still named as such. Buildings with colorful windows and wooden balconies are suspended above the sea, making for an ideal background to watch the sunset. Additionally, along the narrow streets behind the seafront you can find a nice variety of artisan jewelry shops, tourist trinkets, and beachy fashion, as well as chic (read: expensive) cafés and restaurants. In this sense, it is a bit like Venice: a tourist-driven neighborhood with crowds and shops looking for some cold hard euros.

i Free; wheelchair accessible

MUSEUMS

🖾 MYKONOS FOLKLORE MUSEUM

Kastro neighborhood, Mykonos Town; 22890 22591; mykonos.gr/en/the-island/mousia/; open M-Sa 10:30am-2pm and 5:30pm-8:30pm

Mykonos Folklore Museum looks less like an organized museum and more like an antique collector's side gig. The house, possibly one of the oldest Byzantine era building on the islands, is a structure with an eclectic hodge podge of antiques and artifacts from the island. Mannequins dressed in original clothing are scattered throughout the house, lounging at an antique table or standing in the doorway. Downstairs, wooden boats and weapons from the nineteenth century are parked like cars in a garage. It's a cute treasure hunt of goodies, and seems to fit the vibe of Mykonos better than a regular museum.

i Free, small donation requested; limited wheelchair accessibility; English information sheet available

LENA'S HOUSE FOLK MUSEUM

Enoplon Dinameon; 2289 022390; myko-nos.gr/en/the-island/mousia/; open M-Sa 6:30pm-9:30pm, Su 7:30-9:30pm

Part of the Folklore Museum, Lena's House does the museum night shift in **Mykonos Town.** The house, a conserved nineteenth-century-style building, captures a moment older than anyone who visits. A living room and two bedrooms host old furnishings, reconstructed attire for Mykonos women in the early 1700s, decorated plates, and artwork. It's hard to believe that streets now lined with tourist shops and artisan fashion stores used to hold houses like these, and it's a gentle reminder that things used to be different (read: less commercial).
i Free, suggested minimum donation €2; wheelchair accessible

OUTDOORS

TRIP TO DELOS

Delos Island, ferry access at seashore of Mykonos Town (Gyalos); 22890 22218; mykonos.gr/en/dilos/; departures M 10am and 5pm, Tu-Su 9am, 10am, 11:30am, 5pm

Before Apollo rode his sun chariot across the sky or Artemis stood guardian over the hunt, they were born on the island of Delos, A 30-minute ferry ride from Mykonos takes you to this ancient rocky island, an archaeological treasure **in the middle of the Aegean Sea.** Delos consists completely of ruins from its peak in the ninth century BCE. In Ancient Greece, the city was considered one of the most sacred cities in Greece, and you can walk through the remnants of what's left of the city: the **Minoan fountain,** the **Doric Temple of the Delians,** and the **Terrace of the Lions.** Give yourself extra time to climb to the top of the mountain, where Apollo was born, and get a panorama view of the remnants of a dead city.
i Round-trip transportation €20; island admission €12, students €6; island tours from €10; limited wheelchair accessibility

FOOD

GIORA'S MEDIEVAL WOODEN BAKERY ($)

Agiou Efthimiou; 2289 027784

Giora's Bakery doesn't look *that* old. To get to this restaurant, tucked away in one of the winding streets of **Mykonos Town,** you'll descend into a white-walled cave heaven and be met immediately with the comfortable smell of coffee and sweets. Pastries are displayed on a table, and served on delicate glass plates, and they are *delicious.* Honey balls burst with sweet, sweet delight; powdery almond bites are so good you'll think the powdered sugar is something a *little* more addicting. The prices are perfect, and—sorry, this bakery has been here since 1420?
i Baked goods from €1.50, coffee from €3; cash only; no wheelchair accessibility; vegetarian options available

CAPTAIN'S—FOOD FOR SHARING ($$)

Mykonos Waterfront; 2289 023283; www.captainsmykonos.gr/; open daily 7am-1am

On the old dock in **Mykonos Town,** there are a slew of expensive restaurants on the seaside, all offering good food, Wi-Fi, AC, a free car, etc. One of our favorites was Captain's Food for Sharing, which has the same prices as other places but with shareable portions, so if you divide the price by two, it's not too bad. **The captain's salad** (€10) is the perfect fresh selection for a hot summer day. They also have a wide selection of local beer, including a brew of the week, a special homemade concoction made by the owner's brother.
i Appetizers from €6, seafood entrées from €11; vegan and vegetarian options available; Wi-Fi; wheelchair accessible

JIMMY'S GYROS ($)

Lakka, Mykonos Town; open daily noon-2am

While waiting for your food at Jimmy's, your eyes will wander to the décor: literally hundreds of pictures of a balding middle-aged man smiling and giving a thumbs up, posing with customer after smiling customer. Jimmy's might not be the definition of classy, but it's a quick place that serves hot food and (comparatively speaking) cheap prices. Most people get the chicken or pork *gyro* (€5), but there are also burgers (€5), mixed plates (€12), and more. If you're lucky, Jimmy himself might walk in to check on business, twisting rosaries and smiling at customers. You might just make it on the wall, right next to a Greek 2013 calendar of topless women.

i *Gyros from €5, entrées from €6; cash only; wheelchair accessible*

JOANNA'S NIKOS PLACE TAVERNA ($$)

Megali Ammos; 2289 024251; open daily noon-11pm

Restaurants with a seaview are usually major $$$$ moves, but Joanna's Nikos Place Taverna has managed to maintain reasonable prices on its oceanfront haven. Serving traditional Greek cuisine, the taverna has a slew of homemade platters that must've been cooked by Joanna herself. Make reservations though, especially if you want to sit in their outdoor seating. One note of warning: like mom's cooking, it sometimes can be a crapshoot, so make sure to stick with the seafood or the waitress' recs.

i *Pasta from €7.50, meat and seafood entrées from €10; vegetarian options available; no wheelchair accessibility; dinner reservations highly recommended*

TASOS TAVERNA ($$)

Paraga Beach; 2289 023002; open daily 10am-11pm

There probably isn't a reason to leave Paraga Beach Hostel. But, if you find yourself fed up with the shoddy Wi-Fi and drunk hostel-mates, head to Tasos Taverna, conveniently located two minutes down the beach. The restaurant serves seafood (duh) at fine prices, and there's beach chairs and umbrellas if you want to go for a quick dip between appetizers and entrées.

i *Appetizers from €5, entrées from €10; vegetarian options available; limited wheelchair*

NIGHTLIFE

🖼 CAPRICE BAR

Little Venice, Mykonos Town; 2289 023541; capriceofmykonos.com/; open daily 6:30pm-5am

There are way too many bars in **Mykonos Town** that have good music and plenty of space to dance, but everyone acts too cool to get out there and throw it around. Almost all hope was lost until we stumbled upon Caprice Bar, where almost every single person was dancing, drinks in hand. The crowd overflows onto the narrow street that looks into the sea. The crowd is slightly older than the likes of Paradise Beach, so the purpose of Caprice Bar is not to get laid, but simply to have a good time, regardless of if you can dance or not. Besides, their decorations consist solely of huge sunflowers and bowls of tropical fruit—what's not to love? (Except, maybe, the high prices.)

i *No cover, cocktails from €13, BGLTQ+ friendly; limited wheelchair accessibility*

🖼 PARADISE BEACH

Guapaloca (697 301 6311; guapalocamykonos.com; open daily 10am-4am); Tropicana (22890 23582; tropicanamykonos.com; open daily 9am-1:30am)

Paradise Beach is the unspoken holy grail for the best party scene on the island, if not all of Greece. Young 20-somethings from all corners of the globe travel to the island to drink a shit-ton of alcohol, get on one of the numerous dance club platforms, gyrate their bodies, and scream *MYKONOSSSSS* into the great Aegean Sea. Technically, there are two clubs, **Guapaloca** and **Tropicana,** which have completely different vibes, but partiers will find a hype DJ and hyper fellow partiers at either location. Paradise Beach is what you expected college to be like, and for a few nights on the island you too can ascend to Paradise.

i *No cover, cocktails from €11; BGLTQ+ friendly; limited wheelchair accessibility*

SANTORINI

Coverage by **Margaret Canady**

In the Miss Universe Pageant of World Geography, Miss Santorini is undoubtedly a top contestant. Take one step onto the island and you might feel as celestial as the ground you stand on; sensational steep cliffs line the crescent shaped *caldera,* and anywhere you find yourself on the island's inner precipice gives you views you've only dreamed of. The *caldera* is dotted with white stuccoed villages that look out into the sparkling Aegean Sea hundreds of feet below, and the sunsets stun even the most experienced of travelers. Besides this, there are multicolored beaches to be visited, ancient archaeological sites to be discovered, and exciting nightlife to be had. Santorini is a choose-your-own-adventure type of island, and the best news is there's no wrong choice (as long as you don't miss sunset).

ORIENTATION

Santorini, officially known along with its neighboring islets as **Thira,** is part of the **Cyclades islands** in the Aegean Sea. Though circle-shaped before a volcanic eruption 3600 years ago, the island is now shaped like a croissant, with crescent (or *caldera)* side facing west. Many of the major points are located on the caldera. The **port of Thira** is located in the middle of the crescent. Midway between the port and the northernmost point of the crescent is the cliff hugging town of **Fira,** the capital and main city in Santorini. Here you'll find a majority of the hostels, tourists, and nightlife. The northernmost point of the crescent is **Oia** with its famous sunset views. **Akrotiri** is found at the bottom of the crescent. On the opposite side of the island is the airport (center), **Ancient Thera** (south of the airport), and the black beaches of **Perissa.** Smack dab in the center is the mountain and village of **Pyrgos,** an often-overlooked mountain with stunning views of its own.

ESSENTIALS

GETTING THERE

Santorini is served by Santorini International Airport. Buses run between the airport and Fira approximately every 90min. between 7am-10pm. Tickets can be bought on board for €1.80. Most people arrive at Santorini via ferry, which dock at the port of Thira. Public buses run from the port to Fira approximately every hour and can be purchased for €1.80 on the bus. Private transport can be arranged to any location and will cost around €15-20, depending on the location, and will be approximately €20 cheaper than a taxi.

GETTING AROUND

The main towns of Santorini are connected by an extensive bus system with reliable time tables. Tickets can be bought on the bus and range from €1.80-€2.50, depending on the location. Buses run approximately between the hours of 7am-10pm daily. Check ktel-santorini.gr/ktel/index.php/en/ for exact time schedules, and call 228 6025404 or visit the main bus terminal in Fira for

questions. Otherwise, renting an ATV, car, or motorbike is highly recommended for exploring the island. Motorbikes can only be rented if you have a motorcycle license. Additionally, many rental services have an age minimum for car rentals (23), or require Americans to hold an international driver's license to rent vehicles. There are several services in Fira that do not require an international license, you may just have to look around. ATVs cost €30-35 for 24hr.

PRACTICAL INFORMATION

Tourist Offices: Information is available at www.santorini.gr/?lang=en. Additionally, there are a variety of private tour companies that can arrange tours or provide information, such as Santo-line (Myrtidiotissa 3 Kamari; 2286 032518; santo-line.com/; open daily 9:30am-10pm).

Banks/ATMs/Currency Exchange: There are many ATMs located on the island, especially in the more tourist-heavy hubs of Fira and Oia. The National Bank of Greece is located in Fira (Dekigala 303; 2286 021051; www.nbg.gr/; open M-Th 8am-2:30pm, F 8am-2pm).

Post Offices: Post Office Elta (Dekigala, Thira; open M-F 7:30am-2:30pm)

Public Restrooms: Some restaurants and cafés offer restroom access with purchase.

Internet: Almost all restaurants and cafés offer Wi-Fi.

BGLTQ+ Resources: Check out www.iglta.org/europe/greece/ and www.travelbyinterest.com/destination/1087/gay/guide for BGLTQ+ businesses and hotels in Greece.

EMERGENCY INFORMATION

Emergency Number: 112

Police: You can call the Department of Thira (Fira, 84700; 22860 22649) or Oia (22860 71954).

US Embassy: The closest US Embassy is located in Athens (Leof. Vasilissis Sofias 91; 21 0721 2951; gr.usembassy.gov/).

Rape Crisis Center: WomenSOS (support number: 15900; administrative number: 213 1511113; www.womensos.gr/; support number open daily 24hr).

Hospitals: Santorini Hospital (Karterados 84700; 2286 035300; www.santorini-hospital.gr/; open daily 24hr)

Pharmacies:
- Pharmacy Zacharopoulos Fira (Fira, across from the taxi stand; 2286 023444; open M-Sa 8am-10pm)
- Pharmacy Oia (Oia 847 02; 2286 071464; open M-F 8am-11pm, Sa 8:30am-10:30pm, Su 9am-10:30pm)

ACCOMMODATIONS

🏚 CAVELAND ($)

Karterados, Post Box 39; 2286 022122; caveland.com/; reception open daily 8:30am-1pm and 3pm-10:30pm

If the word "cave" doesn't elicit images of luxury, a resort, and free breakfast, that means you're perfectly normal, but that also means you need to stay at Caveland. In classic Santorini cave tradition, the sturdy structures were carved from the soft volcanic pumice stone. This former winery now hosts incredible lodging, including a six-bed dorm that has enough room for space between beds, a lounge area, and a large private bath, and it's *all* *in a cave.* Top it off with a luxury pool, rooftop (cavetop?) yoga lessons, and complimentary breakfast, and by the end of your stay you'll be feeling like a Cave King. It's a bit removed from **Fira** (about a 25-minute walk), but that's just another reason to rent an ATV.

i Dorms from €15 depending on season; cash only; reservation required; limited wheelchair accessibility; Wi-Fi; free breakfast; linens included; laundry

ANNY STUDIOS ($)

Perissa Beach; 2286 082669; www.annystudios.com/

On the opposite side of the caldera lies the black beach of **Perissa,** which is a relaxed and less-crowded alternative to the tourist towns of **Fira** and **Oia.** Anny Studios is a comfortable beach-side accommodation offering mainly private rooms, but also hosts several dorms too—all of which are clean, quiet, and comfortable. The hostel is owned by the same two brothers who own **Fira Backpackers** (one of whom used *Let's Go* when he was a wee traveler!); they'll be sure to help you answer any questions you might have about the island.

i Dorms from €15; reservation recommended; limited wheelchair accessibility; Wi-Fi; linens provided; laundry

FIRA BACKPACKERS PLACE ($$)

Downtown Fira, behind Coffee Island; 2286 031626; www.firabackpackers.com/; reception open daily 9am-9pm

Fira is the heart of Santorini's nightlife, and Fira Backpackers Place is a stone's throw away from the action. By day, it's perfectly situated near your essentials: the central bus station, ATV and car rentals, and popular restaurants and shops. By night, it's *still* perfectly situated near your essentials: the bar- and club-heavy streets are only a couple of blocks away from the hostel. The hostel has basic but comfortable bedding, and while it can get a bit pricey, especially during the summer season, you're sure to meet a bunch of new friends as groups from the hostel prepare to bar hop and club stumble.

i Dorms from €35 depending on season; reservations recommended; Wi-Fi; limited wheelchair accessibility; linens and locks included; cooking facilities available

SIGHTS
CULTURE

🖼 SANTO WINERY

Pirgos 84701; 22860 22596; www.santow-ines.gr/en/; open daily 9am-11pm

The majority of Santorini's residents is involved in one of two fields: tourism or wine-making. Santo Winery is a celebration of the latter by appealing to the former, and they sure do a damn good job. Part wine tour and part wine-tasting, you can appreciate both the process of making wine and the final product, although we're definitely a fan of appreciating the people's hard work. The wine tasting occurs on an outdoor terrace (with clear glass barriers) and lies smack dab in the center of the caldera—the view of the sea and the island is simply stunning. You'll be sipping wine in style, and the prices for wine flights certainly reflect that (from €31 per person). Hack the system by only getting a glass or two—you can pay as little as €2.50.
i Wine tastings from €2.50, full flights from €31, wine tours sans wine €11; 25min. tours multiple times daily; wheelchair accessible

ATLANTIS BOOKSTORE

Nomikos Street; 2286 072346; atlantisbooks.org/; open daily 10am-midnight

Once upon a time in 2004, a couple of chaps from the UK visited Santorini and, after discovering the island's lack of bookstores, decided to open one. Atlantis Bookstore is a whimsical wonderland for every bookworm visiting Santorini, and you can easily spend an hour in the small and usually crowded traditional cave edifice housing the bookstore. There are books in at least five languages, and each section has a wide but carefully selected collection of books, as well as recommendations written on index cards for each section. There's a surprisingly large collection of **rarities** and **first edition books,** too, like a first-edition *Great Gatsby* or English translation of Plato, which are hefty purchases that can reach €5000. The rooftop terrace has seats to read your new purchase, and you can also watch the sunset up here.
i Books from €12 (not including rare or first editions); cash preferred; no wheelchair accessibility

LANDMARKS

🖼 AKROTIRI

Thera 847 00; 2286 081939; open summer M-W 8am-8pm, Th 8am-3pm, F-Su 8am-8pm; open winter Tu-Su 8am-3pm

Akrotiri might lowkey be the lost city of Atlantis. Akrotiri, located on the southwest corner of the island, was a successful port and trading city until the seventeenth century BCE. The city was abandoned, probably due to severe earthquakes. Following its evacuation, the infamous volcanic eruption occurred in 1613, creating the island's caldera and covering and preserving Akrotiri in a thick volcanic ash. Excavations of the city still occur today, and visitors can explore the carefully preserved city, including multi-layered buildings and a drainage system. Plato wrote about Atlantis, and it's speculated that his inspiration might have been Akrotiri, if not the lost center of the island.
i Admission €12, students €6; archaeological special package admission €14, reduced €7; wheelchair accessible

🖼 ANCIENT THERA

Ancient Thera Road, on Mt. Mesa Vouno; 22860 23217; open Tu-Su 8am-3pm

Long after the dust settled at Akrotiri, a new city prospered on the island. Founded in the ninth century BCE, Ancient Thera, sitting atop steep **Mt. Mesa Vouno** gained importance in Roman and Byzantine eras. Today, you can walk through the ruins of the old *agora* and *stoa,* and the mountain offers panoramic views of the sea. There are a couple of options to get to the top: it takes about an hour to hike up from either side of the mountain (the **Perissa** side is an unpaved footpath; the **Kamari** side is a paved road); you can grab a bus to the top that leaves hourly, or you can drive up, which is kind of an experience in itself. The road zigzags at a steep angle, and with its staggering cliffside views without railings, it's not called the "Kamari serpentines" for nothing, and has been listed as one of the most dangerous roads in the world. We prefer the term "epic" as opposed to "dangerous," though.
i Admission €4, students €2; cash only; last entrance 2:30pm; no wheelchair accessibility; round-trip buses to summit €10, hourly 9am-2pm

GREECE SANTORINI

WATCH THE SUNSET AT OIA

Oia

Watching the sunset at Oia has been listed on many a bucket list on travel websites, and it really is a must-see while on the island. It will be exceptionally overcrowded, and we advise you to either come early (a couple of hours, honestly) to grab a spot on the white stucco cliffs, or you'll be watching the sun set behind some guy's head rather than actually see the horizon. There are less crowded places, too, such as a grassy overlook behind a parking lot, or leading down to **Amoudi Bay.** The explosion of oranges and golds and pinks as the sun descends is unlike any we've seen before. Some dad will ultimately start clapping, as if the sun is setting just for you and your hundred new Santorini friends.

i Free; limited wheelchair accessibility

MUSEUMS
....

🖼 FOLKLORE MUSEUM

Kontochori; 2286 022792; www.santorinis-folkmuseum.com/en/; open daily 10am-5pm

Folklore museums tend to be redundant, given their characteristic quality of looking eerily similar to your grandma's old attic. Santorini's, however, is the best one we've ever visited, and it 100 percent has to do with the private tour that's included with the ticket. You're led through the eight-part museum, and each part is explained in full: the cave home dating to 1861 and furniture owned by a family of nine; an original carpenter and shoemaker workshop and tools; a winery and underground cave showing evidence of the volcanic eruption from 36 centuries ago. You also learn a lot about the island, like how it didn't have electricity until the 1950s (!!) and the tradition of capturing and releasing songbirds that exists to this day. It's the best €5 you'll spend here, and it's the perfect predecessor to any of the other museums or sites you'll visit.

i Admission €5, private tour included; limited wheelchair accessibility

MUSEUM OF PREHISTORIC THERA

Downtown Fira; 2286 022217; www.santonet.gr/museums/prehistoric_museum.htm; open Tu-Su 8:30am-3pm

This small museum in the heart of **Fira** offers a glimpse at artifacts and life from the Neolithic era to the Late Cycladic Period. There are clay cooking pots, really incredible frescoes from excavations of **Akrotiri,** and—nipple vases? Not kidding, these ewers (yes, this is a word: it's a jug with a large mouth) from the seventeenth century BCE have nipples on them. It's a little bit boring, as museums can be, but really cool to connect the artifacts to the locations they came from, such as Akrotiri or **Ancient Thera.**

i Admission €6, students €3; cash only; wheelchair accessible

OUTDOORS
....

🖼 CLIMB SKAROS ROCK

Skaros Rock, Imerovigli; open daily 24hr

On this week's episode of *Xtreme Sports,* climb the majestic Skaros Rock. Located off of **Imerovigli,** this rock used to be home to one of the most important castles on the island, and was inhabited during medieval times because the rock and fortress offered protection from pirates. Not much of the fortress is left, but you can understand how it provided shelter when you ascend: rising high above the sea, the edges are steep and impossible to climb. To climb the rock, one first passes through the neighborhood of Imerovigli (feeling only slightly jealous of the tanning tourists in exorbitantly-priced hotels). Most of the climb is horizontal with an upward slope, but the final ascent onto the platform of the rock requires a vertical climb that looks scarier than it actually is. (They don't call it "Skaros" for nothing, amirite?)

i Free; no wheelchair accessibility

is deep—four steps in and you'll be underwater—but very refreshing, and a plethora of restaurants line the beach and offer free umbrellas and chairs with a meal.

i *Free; wheelchair accessible; beach chairs and umbrellas available with beach restaurant purchase*

FOOD

🍽 BRUSCO ($$)

Epar. Od. Pirgou Kallistis; 2286 030944; open daily 9am-12:30am

The mountain and village of **Pyrgos** is often overlooked by visitors to Santorini, although it definitely shouldn't be. The quaint town lies at the highest point of the island, and offers panoramic views smack dab in the center of Santorini, which is perfect for sunset and strolling. While there, stop into Brusco, a café with cute seating and cuter food. Their breakfast platter offers seven small servings of food that are served on a wooden plate.

i *Breakfast platter from €10, sandwiches from €2.50*

🍽 FISH TAVERN FRATZESKOS ($$$)

Perissa Beach, closer to Mt. Mesa Vouno; 2286 083488; open daily noon-11:30pm

One of the best restaurants on **Perissa Beach** is Fish Tavern Fratzeskos, a seafood tavern popular with Santorini locals. The tavern is family run, and the seafood is caught fresh daily. A lot of the menu is designed for large families (you can only buy the fresh fish by the kilo, and it ranges from €35 to €80), but there are plenty of other options that cost less and are single portions. Our favorite was the orzo pasta with seafood (€17), a pasta similar in size and texture to rice. It easily served two people and the seafood was so *clap* damn *clap* good *clap*.

i *Pasta from €6, fish from €35/kg; wheelchair accessible; beach access and seating*

🍽 OIA VINEYART ($$)

Sidearas, Oia; 2286 072046; oiavineyart.gr/homepage-en/; open daily noon-midnight

We'll look past Vineyart's relatively cheesy name given that it was the best restaurant experience we had in Santorini. Tucked away from the main strip in **Oia,** the

---

GREECE SANTORINI

🛵 RENT AN ATV

Check online for rental locations

There's no efficient way to discover Santorini by bicycle or on foot, and while the bus system is lovely, your time on the island is FLEETING, and you are an independent being who shall not be confined to the BUS SCHEDULE. Hence, your best option is renting an ATV for a couple of days. They comfortably hold two, so if you're traveling with a buddy you can split the price; they're fast, and they're, like, really, really fun. The streets in Santorini are relatively wide and smooth, but of course, always practice caution on turns and in traffic. Many places require you to have an international driver's license, but ask around; there are several in Fira that will rent to you without one.

i *From €35/day; many places require a deposit that they refund upon bike return*

PERISSA BLACK BEACHES

Perissa Beach; open daily 24hr

No island is complete without a trip to the beach, and Perissa Black Beach offers a relaxed spot to spend a day soaking up the sun and swimming. The beach is black from **eroded volcanic molten rock,** and pairs nicely with the blue sea and other visual wonders of Santorini. The water restaurant sees few tourists and gives off a very relaxed vibe, with its upstairs outdoor patio strung with lights and filled with honeysuckle. Vineyart offers 130 wines (aka literally every single wine that is produced on the island), while the staff is extremely well-versed in the subtle differences of each bottle and which local cheeses, meats, or smoked salmon will best match your wine of choice. Besides the superb food and wine, Vineyart also sells local art, and *oh!* Suddenly the name makes a little more sense. A must if you're in Oia, and a great way to experience local culture.

i Cold cuts from €5, cheese from €4, entrées from €12, wine from €6; vegetarian options available; limited wheelchair accessibility

◪ TAVERNA SIMOS ($)

25is Martiou; 2286 023815; www.tavernasi-mos.gr/; open daily noon-midnight

Authentic menu plus shaded rooftop garden plus reasonable prices equals happy eater. Taverna Simos is just a hair north of the main streets of Fira, close enough to get to on foot but far enough to be a quiet escape from the crowds. They have a wide selection of food, including a delicious eggplant paste appetizer that goes great with the free bread, the meat dishes from their charcoal grill, and their seafood fillets. The roof garden also has a fabulous view of the sea.

i Entreés from €8, appetizers from €3.70; limited wheelchair accessibility

POSIDONIA GREEK TAVERN ($$)

Imerovigli; 2286 023998; posidonia-santorini.gr/en/; open daily noon-10:30pm

Things we ask ourselves as we fall asleep at night: did Poseidon eat seafood? Seems like it would be problematic. Regardless, his name evokes the sea and its fishies, and the restaurant Posidonia was all up in that. Serving fresh seafood, including grilled fish and a variety of other Greek foods, you'll for sure find something fishy to love. The restaurant is located in Imerovigli, but behind all of the restaurants that have a view, which makes it more affordable and less crowded.

i Grilled dishes from €10.50, pasta from €9, appetizers from €5.20

SVORONOS BAKERY ($)

25is Martiou; 2286 023446; open daily 24hr

Svoronos Bakery is in a prime location. A strip of clubs exist right in the heart of **Fira,** and late at night you'll catch drunk partiers stumbling out into the street, and their only desire in that instant is food, cheap food, and they have a choice: McDonald's or Svoronos Bakery? We choose Svoronos: open all day every day, the bakery has a wide assortment of cream-filled pastries and croissants, as well as savory pies, sandwiches, and cheap coffee. Does it taste like a 24-hour bakery? Absolutely. But it's perfect for drunk you at 2am, hungover you at 11am, and hangry you at 3pm—besides, who wants to go to McDonald's when they're in Greece, anyway?

i Pastries from €1.50, coffee from €2; cash only; vegetarian options available; wheelchair accessible

NIGHTLIFE

◪ KIRA THIRA JAZZ BAR

Fira; 2286 022770; open W-Su 9pm-3am

Bars are a dime a dozen in Santorini, but Kira Thira Jazz Bar stands out like a saxophone solo in an improv jazz band (yes, that was a jazz joke). An upright bass is suspended above the bar, and a mannequin sits in the bar in a corner with hundreds of CDs and records, as if listening intently to the music playing over the speakers. The best part of Kira Thira, besides the drinks—which are exceptional because of the quality of liquor—might be the bartender. He's worked here for 22 years, and his energy is electric: he dances to the music and engages in conversation with everyone at the bar almost simultaneously. He's old-fashioned, and therefore not a fan of the new age fancy-schmancy cocktails, so don't expect a triple beach mojito with four different syrups. Turn off your phone, grab a classic drink, and enjoy some good energy and music.

i Drinks from €8

CASABLANCA SOUL BAR AND CLUB

Ypapantis 12, Fira Downtown; 2286 027188; www.casablancasoul.com/; open daily 8:45pm-5:30am

When a bar has a DJ, a live musician, *and* a drummer, you're almost guaranteed a good time (unless they're all playing different songs, in which case we suggest you find another bar). Casablanca practically oozes with coolness: an upstairs outdoors bar is complete with white lounge chairs, a large dance space, funky soul music, and, of course, all the people. It's like every attractive person on the island was given a special invitation to Casablanca, and they're ready to party. Come dressed to the nines and get ready for a noir night.

i Cocktails from €12, wine from €5; cash preferred; no wheelchair accessibility; reservations allowed

MOMIX

Marinatou 14, Caldera Fira; 693 61 777 83; www.momixbar.com/momix-santorini/; open daily 5pm-4am

MoMix was created by the boys in your high school chemistry class who really, really liked lab day and played around with chemicals haphazardly until something exciting happened. MoMix, short for "molecular mixology", is chemistry class for grown-ups, and the chemicals are (obviously) alcohol. The menu, shaped like a cube that lights up each time you flip it, has descriptions such as spherification, foaming, intense carbonation, and mouth tricks, just to name a few. There are cocktail bubbles that burst in your mouth, vials and shots of alcoholic concoctions, and "solids," too, such as a crème brûlée that they cook right in front of you. It's as visually entertaining as it is delicious, and come prepared to get some quality Snapchat story content.

i Cocktails from €9, macaron vodka shots from €3; wheelchair accessible

THESSALONIKI

Coverage by Margaret Canady

Throughout history, the city of Thessaloniki has always came in second place—the second biggest city in modern Greece, the second biggest city of the Byzantine Empire, and the same fate under the Ottoman Empire. No harm, no foul though, because the phrase 'second is the best' exists for a reason. Thessaloniki is an incredibly easy city to love. A laid-back attitude exists no matter where you turn, from the winding streets of the old neighborhoods in Ano Poli all the way down to the city's expansive sea front. It's a big city with a beach mentality, and the city pulses with a multicultural vibrancy that can be found in the cuisine, architecture, and people. Thessaloniki manages to integrate its history into its modern bustle in such a seamless way that you might overlook a 1700 year old monument without blinking an eye. You won't want to, though—there's no rush here.

ORIENTATION

Thessaloniki is located on the northwest corner of the **Aegean Sea** on the **Thermaic Gulf,** and has a popular waterfront that traces the shore. The city center along the shore is in a grid layout, rebuilt after the Great Fire of 1917. Some main streets that run parallel with the shore and cut through the city center include the shop-heavy **Egnatia, Tsimiski,** and **Agiou Dimitriou.** The city center is bounded by the nightlife neighborhood **Ladadika** on one end and the famous **White Tower** on the other; **Aristotelous Square** lies in the middle. Up the hills past the modern grid lies the old neighborhood of **Ano Poli,** conserved Ottoman architecture untouched by the fire. The airport and suburbs extend farther southeast of the city center on the coast.

ESSENTIALS

GETTING THERE

The city is served by Thessaloniki "Makedonia" International Airport and is linked to the other airport of Greece, as well as international cities. From the airport, bus lines X1, 78, or 78N will take you to the city center for €2. Buses and coaches to Thessaloniki arrive and depart from at Macedonia Intercity Bus Station, and connect the city to many cities in Greece and in surrounding countries.

GETTING AROUND

It's relatively easy to get around on foot, especially in the grid neighborhoods closer to the sea (not included in the easy description is the sweat inducing climb up to Ano Poli), and most things are a 20min. walk or less. Thessaloniki is served by a host of public bus lines running from 5am-midnight and cost €1-2 depending on the time and distance. Tickets can be bought on the bus or at the central bus station, but make sure to bring exact change unless you feel like tipping the ticket machine. For more information, visit www.ktelmacedonia.gr.

PRACTICAL INFORMATION

Tourist Offices: Information centers are located at the airport and Aristotelous Square. Tourist Information Office (Aristotelous Sq.; 2310229070; thessaloniki.travel/en/useful-information/addresses-phone-numbers/information-centers; open daily 9am-9pm)

Banks/ATMs/Currency Exchange: Banks and ATMs are located throughout the city. HSBC Bank (Tsimiski 8; 21 0696 0000; www.hsbc.gr/1/2/gr/; open M-F 8am-2:30pm)

Post Offices: Greece is served by ELTA. An ELTA Post Office can be found at Vasileos Irakleiou 38 (231 027 7434; open M-F 7:30am-8:30pm, Sa 7:30am-2:30pm, Su 9am-1:30pm).

Public Restrooms: Restaurants and cafés usually have restrooms available for use.

Internet: The city offers Wi-Fi hotspots in major squares and popular areas.

BGLTQ+ Resources: Thessaloniki offers a welcoming, gay-friendly atmosphere. Thessaloniki has been holding gay pride festivals since 2011, and the Panorama Gay Film Festival since 1996.

EMERGENCY INFORMATION

Emergency Number: 112
Police: Dial 100 in an emergency.
- Downtown Police Station (Aristotelous 18; 231 025 3341; www.astynomia.gr/)

US Embassy: There is a US Consulate located in Thessaloniki (43 Tsimiski, 7th Floor; 2310 242 905; gr.usembassy.gov/). The closest US Embassy is located in Athens (Leof. Vasilissis Sofias 91; 21 0721 2951; gr.usembassy.gov/).

Rape Crisis Center: WomenSOS (support number: 15900; administrative number: 213 1511113; www.womensos.gr/; support number open daily 24hr)

Hospitals: Dial 166 for an ambulance.
- Ippokrateio General Hospital of Thessaloniki (Konstantinoupoleos 49; 231 089 2000; www.ippokratio.gr/; open daily 24hr)
- General Hospital "St. Demetrios" (Elenis Zografou 2; 231 332 2100; www.oagiosdimitrios.gr/; open daily 24hr)

Pharmacies:
- Deligiorgis Pharmacy (Agias Sofias 23; 231 026 0163; www.deligiorgispharmacy.gr/; open M-F 8:30am-8:30pm, Sa 8:30am-5pm)
- Pharmacy128 (Agiou Dimitriou 128; 231 111 7000; www.pharmacy128.gr/; open M-Sa 8am-11:55pm)

ACCOMMODATIONS

🛏 LITTLE BIG HOUSE ($)

Andokidou 24; 231 301 4323; www.littlebig-house.gr/; reception open daily 8am-11pm

Little Big House is the hostel you didn't know you needed. This home away from home, located in the quiet **Ano Poli** neighborhood, welcomes you upon arrival with a free frappe from its sweet, cozy café. Next, they'll usher you to your apartment-style dorm that includes a full kitchen, private bath, working AC (!) and Wi-Fi (!!), and the comfiest bed and duvet you'll find this side of the Atlantic. Seriously, we haven't slept this well in Zeus knows how long.

i Rooms from €15; reservations recommended; limited wheelchair accessibility; Wi-Fi; breakfast included; laundry; lockers, locks, linens, towels included

⬛ STAY HYBRID HOSTEL ($)

Ionos Dragoumi 61; 231 124 4600; www.thestay.gr/; reception open 24hr

The only thing we like better than cheap hostels are *centrally located* cheap hostels. STAY Hybrid Hostel is only a few minutes' walk from some of the city's most popular areas, including the nightlife of **Ladadika** and **Aristotelous Square.** The hostel is new and impeccably clean, and you'll feel comfortable relaxing in the huge dorms or one of the welcoming common rooms. The best part of the hostel might be the bathrooms—we'd pay €10 alone just to stand in the huge showers (pass through a set of frosted doors to enter) and let the jet-like water pressure strip away months of travel grime.

i Dorms from €10; wheelchair accessible; linens and lockers included; Wi-Fi; kitchen

RENTROOMS THESSALONIKI ($)

Konstantinou Melenikou 9; 2310 204080; www.rentrooms-thessaloniki.com/en/

On the east side of the city center you'll find rooms to rent and a space to unwind at RentRooms. This hard-working hostel covers all of the basics: clean rooms with soft beds and private baths, good Wi-Fi, and a place to gather and socialize—in this case, at their cute outdoor garden café. Breakfast is included, and there are six different hot breakfast options to fill you up. After cuddling with the hostel cat, a short stroll around the neighborhood will take you to the **White Tower** and **Roman Agora.**

i Dorms from €14; reservation recommended; wheelchair accessible; Wi-Fi; breakfast included; linens included

THESSALONIKI STUDIOS ARABAS ($)

Sachtouri 28; 694 446 6897; www.hostelarabas.gr/; reception open daily 8am-11pm

Friends back home may ask you: how do you stay so fit on vacation? Well, it's called the backpacker workout, and you'll be doing reps getting to Studios Arabas: take one 600-pound backpack, 95-degree weather, and a climb up one of **Ano Poli's** steep hills—if you don't pass out, you'll have great calves once you reach the hostel. Anyway, Studios Arabas is toying with a rustic cowboy theme, which means you'll discover a wooden reception bar and smoky terrace upon arrival. The beds are pretty standard, but

the hostel offers Monday Movie Nights and there's a barbeque you can use, which is pretty cool, if you ask us.

i Dorms from €12; Wi-Fi; limited wheelchair accessibility; linens included

SIGHTS
CULTURE

⬛ ANO POLI

Ano Poli; open daily 24hr

Things that don't get easier with time: goodbyes, stagefright, and climbing up the steep hills of Ano Poli. You can distract yourself with the winding roads and pastel-colored surroundings, but at the end of the day it's still a sweaty feat to be conquered. And sure, you could take the bus, but then what would you complain about? It's worth it though: the neighborhood has maintained its Ottoman and Turkish influences, seemingly untouched by a twentieth-century fire. Notable landmarks in the neighborhood include **Vlatadon Monastery** and **Trigonou Tower,** which offer the best views of the city, the walls of the Ottoman fortress *Yenti Koule,* and the hostel **Little Big House,** which might as well be a landmark in our humble opinion.

i Free; limited wheelchair accessibility

ARISTOTELOUS SQUARE AND ATHONOS MARKET

Aristotelous Sq.; market open Tu-Su early mornings and afternoons

At the centrally-located, lamp- and rose-bush-lined Aristotelous Square, families, walkers, and elderly people sit at cafés and take in the sea-front location. In the surrounding streets of the square you'll find the popular central market. In the wee hours of the morning, chefs come to grab the best pick of seafood (there's nothing like the smell of raw fish to really get your blood pumping at 7am). Fish markets rub shoulders with the meat markets, which rub shoulders with fresh fruit stands and small shops. If you're not entirely keen on picking up some anchovies to bring back to the hostel, you can buy olive oil, fresh flowers, and cheap clothes, too.

i Market prices vary; wheelchair accessible

ROMAN FORUM

Olimpou 75; 231 022 1260; www.inthessa-loniki.com/el/romaiko-forum-arxaia-agora; open daily 8am-3pm

One of the things Thessaloniki does very well is integrating old stuff with new stuff. A good example is the **Roman Forum (Ancient Agora)** that lives smack dab in the middle of a popular restaurant and café neighborhood. The Forum features your typical Ancient Greek remains, including two pools and a theater that once sat 400 people. Underneath, there's a museum that gives a thorough history of the city and the site. An interesting tidbit: the square was occupied by the Germans during World War II and was used as a concentration site for prisoners. The best pictures of the large forum can be taken for free, and the admission price is primarily if you want to go to the museum.
i Admission €4, students €2; wheelchair accessible

LANDMARKS

CHURCH OF AGIA SOPHIA

Agias Sofia; 231 027 0253; www.agiasofia.info/; open M 1pm-7:30pm, Tu-Su 8am-7:30pm, siesta breaks possible

Greek Orthodox churches have a flair for the dramatic, but we're not mad about it. The Church of Agia Sophia (not the Istanbul one) in Thessaloniki is a prime example, featuring intricate wall decorations, shimmering gold mosaics, and a huge low hanging chandelier made of, we kid you not, golden fowl. The church was a once basilica, then a church, then a mosque, and then went back to being church in 1912. This church of a place for worship than a tourist destination, so cover those shoulders and bring your respect.
i Free; wheelchair accessible; appropriate clothing required

ROTUNDA AND ARCH OF GALERIUS

Egnatia 144; 231 331 0400; open Tu-F 8am-6:45pm, Sa-Su 9am-3:45pm

The Rotunda of Thessaloniki will spin your head right round as you gaze up at its large dome and rectangular reccesses. While it's gone through some serious wear and tear since 300 CE, there are still remnants of the mosaics and murals left on the concrete walls. Originally created as either a temple for ancient cult worship or as a royal mausoleum (not sure how those two can be confused, but whatever), the rotunda was converted to a Christian church, then to a mosque, and then again to a church (they really need to make up their minds). You might be tempted to lie on the floor to get as much of the dome in your photo as possible, but we recommend you don't from our personal, dirty experience.
i Admission €2, students €1; cash recommended; wheelchair accessible

THE WHITE TOWER

Thessaloniki 546 21; 231 026 7832; www.lpth.gr/; open Tu-Su 8:30am-3pm

The White Tower, in all its off-white, six-story tall glory, stands as the symbol of Thessaloniki at the city's waterfront. It's a highly photographed monument, and you're basically obligated to visit and photograph it while in the city. The tower, with its swirling steps to the top, short ceilings, and teeny-tiny doors, was once a prison and mass-execution site during Ottoman rule. Today, the tower hosts a museum, and each floor representing a different aspect of Thessaloniki's history. All the info boards in the tower are in Greek, so be sure to get the audio guide (although a word of warning: it might be hard to concentrate on the information because the man sounds like he needs three days of rest and a healthy amount of Nyquil).
i Admission €3, students €2; audio guides available; no wheelchair accessibility

MUSEUMS

🏛 JEWISH MUSEUM

Agiou Mina 13; 231 025 0406; www.jmth.gr/; open M-Tu 10am-3pm, W 10am-3pm and 5pm-8pm, Th-F 10am-3pm, Su 10am-2pm

Thessaloniki was once known as the "Mother of Israel," and Jewish history is virtually inseparable from the history of the city. The city became a safe haven for Jewish refugees from Spain, Portugal, Sicily, Italy, and North Africa, and by the late nineteenth century half of Thessaloniki's population was Jewish—nearly 70,000 people. In 1917, the Great Fire of Thessaloniki occurred, and most of the Jewish neighborhood was

destroyed, leaving 53,737 Jews homeless. On July 11, 1941, Axis Powers occupied the city; about 50,000 Jews lived here during this point. By the end of World War II, 99 percent of the city's Jewish population was lost in the Holocaust. This museum and Holocaust memorial is an incredibly sobering and critically important museum to visit, and we highly recommend that you do make the time to do so.

i *Admission €5, students free; wheelchair accessible; photography prohibited*

🏛 THE MUSEUM OF BYZANTINE CULTURE

Leof. Stratou 2; 231 330 6400; mbp.gr/en/home; open daily 8am-8pm

Byzantine is a word that's casually thrown around to describe various cultural things in Greece, particularly Thessaloniki. Yes, the church is from the Byzantine era. Mhm, Byzantine architecture in this neighborhood! I was eating some Byzantine food the other day—oops, make sure you know what you're talking about. Luckily, the Museum of Byzantine Culture is here to answer your questions and show you a wealth of Byzantine examples. This era was a continuation of the Eastern Roman Empire, and starts when Constantinople assumed control (from 330-1453 CE, approximately). The museum is well-curated and features huge rooms with thematic elements and helpful information that gives what the art you're looking at some context and meaning.

i *Admission €8, students €4; wheelchair accessible*

🏛 MUSEUM OF PHOTOGRAPHY

Port of Thessaloniki, Warehouse A; 231 056 6716; www.thmphoto.gr/; open Tu-Th 11am-7pm, F 11am-10pm, Sa-Su 11am-7pm

Contemporary art gallery in a warehouse? Perfect: all we need are our black turtlenecks, hipster glasses, and Mason jars filled with artisanally roasted coffee. Thessaloniki's Museum of Photography is Greece's only government-funded museum dedicated solely to photography, and with their rotating exhibits featuring a majority of Greek photographers, it's definitely worth a visit. There's a large collection of thoughtfully-curated photographs, so it's well worth a measly €1.

i *Admission €2, students €1; wheelchair accessible*

ARCHAEOLOGICAL MUSEUM OF THESSALONIKI

Manoli Andronikou 6; 231 331 0201; www.amth.gr/; open daily 8am-8pm

Before Ancient Greece there was *Ancient* Ancient Greece, and the Archaeological Museum of Thessaloniki sheds light onto the prehistoric human settlement of the area. You'll find everything from the Paleolithic to the Neolithic Age, as well as Macedonian and Hellenistic artifacts. This translates to spears, gold blossomed myrtle wreaths, a bunch of stuff from tombs, and a third century CE female skeleton with hair. Gnarly.

i *Admission €8, students €4; wheelchair accessible*

FOOD

🏛 ERGON AGORA ($$)

P. Mela 42; 231 028 8008; www.ergonfoods.com/restaurants/thessaloniki/; open daily 9am-midnight

A quick glance into Ergon Agora and you might think that it's just a cute coffee-to-go type of shop. Then you'll see a long hallway, walk through said hallway, and find yourself in a large room with a sit-down restaurant *and* specialty grocery store (!). Ergon Agora is the hippest of the hip, with its chic industrial vibes, hipster indie music playlists, and a wealth of homemade brunch and lunch options. Get gooey cream pies and a cappuccino, or specialty eggs with smoked ham, or even go browse the artisan pastas and wines and specialty meat and fish section. Whatever you do, you can't go wrong, and you'll feel as cool as a cucumber doing it.

i Brunch €7, lunch entrées from €4.50, coffee and pastries under €5; vegetarian options available; limited wheelchair accessibility

🍽 GARBANZO FALAFEL ($)

Agnostou Stratiotou 6; 231 307 5892; open daily 1pm-midnight

Light on the wallet and heavy on the flavor is the name of the game for the street food at Garbanzo Falafel. Located next door to the **Roman Agora,** the shop serves delicious falafel sandwiches and plates at unbelievable prices. All you have to do is choose your sauce and customize your flavors and toppings at the self-service salad bar. Take a seat at their window bar and try not to drop the lettuce and jalapeños you added to the falafel.

i Everything on the menu under €5; vegan and vegetarian options available; wheelchair accessible; Wi-Fi

🍽 TAVERNA TO IGGLIS ($)

Irodotou 32; 21 1311 5555; open daily 1pm-12:30am

A neighborhood favorite tucked quietly away in **Ano Poli,** To Igglis is a local tavern with some of the best Greek food in town. Their daily specials are cheap, their meats are well-seasoned, and their outdoor seating is bustling with high spirits of the human and alcoholic forms. When in season, you *must* try the tomato salad: fresh tomatoes are diced and tossed with feta, olive oil and basil… Our mouths are watering just thinking about it.

i Specials from €4, entrées from €6.50; vegan and vegetarian options available; wheelchair accessible

CAFÉ AITHRIO ($)

Dim. Tzachila 7; 231 024 5981; www.cafeai-thriothessaloniki.gr/; open M-Sa 10am-2am, Su 10am-midnight

If you're bold and decide to climb from the city center to **Ano Poli,** you'll be huffing and puffing all the way up, and you deserve a cold drink once you get there. Café Aithrio, located right next to the Ottoman fortress **Yedi Kule,** is the perfect place to catch your breath, and somehow all of its green and white tables

manage to fit perfectly under the shade of the large leafy tree nearby. The inside is elaborately decorated, Turkish lamps and all, and if you look touristy enough the waiter will offer you one of Thessaloniki's free guides to the city.

i Drinks from €3, light snacks from €3; wheelchair accessible

MASSALIA ($$)

Manousagiannaki 6; 231 400 3714; open daily 1pm-midnight

If you find yourself starving, dehydrated, and dying just a little in the middle of a hot Thessaloniki day, Massalia is a good refuge. Every item on the menu has pictures, so in your starved state you can haphazardly point to something that looks good that will, in fact, taste good. Prices are reasonable, the main flavor variety comes from the type of meat you choose, and for €1 you get bread with olive oil and fish roe, as well as a light dessert at the end of the meal.

i Entrées from €8; vegetarian options available; wheelchair accessible

ROOTS VEGETARIAN & VEGAN PLACE ($$)

Mpalanou 4; 231 026 8063; www.facebook.com/roots.vegan/; open daily 10am-2am

After spending any amount of time in Greece, you'll soon realize that most Greek dishes get their variety from the meat; this makes it a bit harder for the visiting leaf-lovers and vegetarians. Luckily, rOOTS (capitalization intentional but not understood) does a solid job of concocting creative vegan and vegetarian options for Thessaloniki. They have a monthly rotating kitchen, the menu is changed biannually, and on certain days they'll offer themed menus, such as their recent Thai food takeover. Veggies are fresh, and you can feel healthy and clean for at least one meal in Greece.

i Entrées from €7.50, coffee and iced tea from €3; vegan and vegetarian options available; wheelchair accessible

NIGHTLIFE

◪ THE HOPPY PUB

Nikiforou Foka 6; 231 026 9203; open Tu-Sa 5:30pm-1:30am, Su 5pm-1:30am

This hoppy-go-lucky pub will put a hop in your step. Hopportunity awaits you as soon as you sit down, and hop dog, do they have an great selection of artisanal beers! The beers have hop notch labels and IPAs, and even if you don't like beer, the 300ml on tap are cheap enough to try—and you might even end up liking it. This is the perfect place for a bar hop, or a hoppy ending to your night out on the town. Alas, this listing is over, and the hoppy puns have hopped out of the picture.

i Beer on tap and bottles from €3.50; wheelchair accessible

THE BLUE CUP

Salaminos 8; 231 090 0666; thebluec-up.gr/; open M-Th 8:30am-3am, F-Sa 8:30am-5am, Su 10am-3am

We like a man good who's with his hands—and the bartender at The Blue Cup knows how to make a damn good cocktail. Known first for its artisanal coffee, this cool-kid coffee joint turns into a cooler-kid cocktail bar as the sun sets. There's a set menu, but if you don't see something you like, the bartender will concoct something for your liking. The drinks flow well into the night, especially on the weekends, and you'll be hard-pressed to find outdoor seating. Maybe this is the alcohol talking, but the attractiveness of every waiter and bartender at Blue Cup starts at model status and only goes up from there.

i Cocktails from €8.50; wheelchair accessible

LA DOZE

Vilara 1; 231 053 2986; open daily 7pm-5am

The vibe of La Doze can be kinda hard to read: graffiti and stickers? Lone sad disco ball? A lit up palm tree? Eventually, we decided on urban house. This low-key bar is apparently most lit in the winter time, when the empty dance floors fills with shuffling youth. The bar is well-known for its honestly excessive amounts of spirits: they serve 200 whiskeys, and some 120 rums and tequilas. How? Why? Not sure which tequila our cocktail had, but it was pretty good nonetheless.

i Spirits and cocktails from €6; wheelchair accessible

YPSILON

Edessis 5; 231 053 0480; www.facebook.com/ypsilonproject/; open M-Th 9am-2am, F-Su 9am-3am

If an art gallery and a cocktail bar had a baby, that hipster newborn would be called Ypsilon. With its high ceilings, large rooms, white minimalist design, and live DJ, the café bar is photographic and almost too cool-looking to get comfortable in. The cocktails are creative, and ingredients include things like beefeater gin, mastic liqueur, red grapefruit syrup, and balsamic vinegar—and that's all in one drink.

i Cocktails from €7; beer, coffee, and juices from €3; wheelchair accessible

GREECE ESSENTIALS

MONEY

Currency: Few are keen to acknowledge that Greece is saddled in debt. This has led to much controversy over Greece's status in the eurozone. The country still uses the euro as of August 2018, but be sure to check the news before you go.

Taxes: Currently, the value-added tax (VAT) in Greece is 24%, with a 13% excise tax on tobacco, fuel, and alcohol.

SAFETY AND HEALTH

Local Laws and Police: Many parts of Greece, especially Athens and the popular vacation islands, are accustomed to tourists, but make no mistake—illegal behavior will not be taken lightly. Don't drink and drive or behave indecently, as these actions could result in fines or imprisonment. Purchase of pirated goods (CDs, DVDs) can result in heavy fines, as does stealing rock or material from ancient sites. Though Greece decriminalized homosexuality in 1951, it is still frowned upon socially in some areas of the country. In urban areas and some islands, especially Mykonos, attitudes towards the BGLTQ+ community have changed rapidly, and gay and lesbian hotels, bars, and clubs have a larger presence.

Drugs and Alcohol: Attitudes towards alcohol are fairly blasé in Greece, and most visitors can obtain it easily. Drugs are a different story. Conviction for possession, use, or trafficking of drugs, including marijuana, can result in heavy fines or imprisonment. Authorities are particularly vigilant near the Turkish and Albanian borders.

Demonstrations and Political Gatherings: Strikes and demonstrations occur frequently in Greece, especially during the ever-deepening debt crisis. Most demonstrations are peaceful but a few have escalated into more dangerous protests. If a demonstration or tense political situation does occur during your trip, it is advisable to avoid the area of the city where it is taking place and or head for the islands, where things are typically more peaceful.

HUNGARY

In Hungary you will find an amalgam of a place, constructed from the cultures that have collided here. At the end of the ninth century, a federation of Hungarian tribes, nomads united under Árapád—the single-named precursors to the world's Madonnas and Chers, whose progeny would rule Hungary for the next near-millennium—conquered the Carpathian Basin and established Hungary as their own. Next, the country came under Ottoman rule for just over 150 years in the sixteenth and seventeenth centuries, before being seized by the Habsburgs. The Habsburg monarchy tightened the country's relationship to Austria, as well as the other territories under Habsburg rule, which today number parts of at least 13 modern countries. Finally, the Austro-Hungarian Empire established by the Habsburgs defined the region until its dissolution following WWI. Each new culture left a legacy in Hungary. The Hungarian tribes established ethnic and cultural unity that gave form to early Hungarian identity; the Ottoman Empire left a land populated with Turkish bathhouses and thermal spas; and if not for trying to upstage the Austrians, the Hungarian State Opera in Budapest may never have been so opulent. These legacies also combined to have great influence on Hungary's architectural landscape. Historic forms sit beside works of modern design, skate parks, and several-story Coca-Cola super-billboards, so the country seems planted on a fault line between distant centuries. Walking the streets, you are as likely to stroll past old people smoking pipes and gossiping on benches as you are to pass trendy millennials with gauged ears and skateboards. Spend your days soaking in thermal baths or public fountains, your meals pounding goulash and renowned wines, and your nights partying in Budapest's ruin pubs, the ultimate culmination of this age collision which merges the club scene with the vestiges of past architectural lives.

337

BUDAPEST

Coverage by **Antonia Washington**

Budapest is a city that feels lived in: an urban center that isn't manicured, where the people you meet, even in the city center, are often as likely locals as visitors. It's a place where people unapologetically sit back and enjoy the summer, a city with an optimistic amount of gelato stands. Budapest is a city where entire crowds spontaneously climb up and lounge upon the massive steel beams of Szabadság híd (Liberty Bridge). After witnessing such a scene, we're tempted to say, "Enough!" with all of the liability nonsense espoused in other countries. But if people want to climb all over potentially dangerous public fixtures, then let the people climb! Spending a week scouting out Budapest's best places to kick your feet up and relax is the perfect way to start off a trip, for above all else, this city reminds you that every once in a while, it's okay to just stop and take a breath.

ORIENTATION

The rule of thumb for orienting yourself in Budapest is to know your position in relation to the **Danube River.** If you know this, it's impossible to get lost. Street names in Budapest are sometimes hard to find, but are usually written on white tiles on the sides of corner buildings. Underneath the street name, there is a series of numbers with an arrow. This indicates the address numbers found on this block. The city itself is split into two sides and is divided by the Danube River, with **Buda** located to the west and **Pest** to the east. While Buda contains popular tourist areas such as **Gellért Hill** and **the castle quarter,** Pest is truly the city center. **District 7** (in Pest) is home to much of the city's nightlife.

ESSENTIALS

GETTING THERE

Getting to Budapest is easy by plane, train, or bus. Planes fly into Budapest Ferenc Liszt International Airport, from which most city destinations can be reached via public transport. Routes change frequently depending on destination, so check ahead. Taxis from the airport give a price estimate before the ride, and generally take cash or card (though we recommend keeping cash on you just in case). The airport offers shuttle services to the city center through miniBUD (www.minibud.hu), which can be booked in advance.

GETTING AROUND

Budapest is a very walkable city, especially within the city center, and public transportation is fairly efficient. The city's public transportation authority BKV uses a ticket system, so each new ride requires a single ticket. Transfers between metro lines are free, but all other transfers are not. If you plan to travel by public transportation frequently, it may be worthwhile to purchase a 24hr or weeklong pass.

PRACTICAL INFORMATION

Tourist Offices: Budapestinfo is the city's official tourist office, with information available online at www.budapestinfo.hu. Tourism stands also can be found throughout the city center selling Budapest Cards, which provide unlimited public transportation and free or reduced admission to many of the city's museums. We wouldn't recommend purchasing one unless you intend to use more than a handful of public transport rides or visit the majority of museums in a brief window of time.

ATMs: ATMs are available throughout Budapest and typically have options to perform transactions in English. Many show the exchange rate and withdrawal equivalency in U.S. dollars before concluding transactions. Currency exchange booths are also widely available.

BLGTQ+ Resources: www.budapestgaycity.net provides updates on BGLTQ+-friendly businesses in the city and is a hub for information on BGLTQ+ activities and events.

Internet: Wi-Fi is available throughout the city in accommodations, as well as often in restaurants and bars. Some major squares and tourist attractions also provide free public Wi-Fi.

Post Offices: Post offices in Budapest are run by Maygar Post. Information regarding shipping mail internationally can be found online at https://posta.hu. You can translate the site from Hungarian to English by clicking on a button located in the top right corner of the home screen.

EMERGENCY INFORMATION

Emergency Number: 112

US Embassy: The American Embassy is located at Liberty Square. (Szabadság tér 12; 14754400; hungary.usembassy.gov).

Pharmacies: Pharmacies are marked with a green "+" sign. Many are not open 24hr, but Deli Pharmacy (Alkotás út 1/B) and Teréz Pharmacy (Teréz körút 41) are two reliable stops.

Hospitals: The majority of medical centers in Budapest have English-speaking staff. The US Embassy keeps a list of English-speaking doctors as well.

ACCOMMODATIONS

ADAGIO HOSTEL 2.0

Andrássy u. 2; 1 950 9674; www.adagiohostel.com

Adagio Hostel 2.0 is very proud of its Hungarian heritage. Each room in the hostel is named after a different important Hungarian thing —a person, a dish, an invention (did you know the Rubik's Cube was a Hungarian invention?). Near the reception desk, a computerized photo of **John von Neumann,** the conceptual inventor behind digital computing, hangs next to a photo of Mark Zuckerberg, who doesn't really have anything to do with Hungary (that we know of). Overall, it's a reliable hostel in a great location between **St. Stephen's Basilica** and **Erzsébet Square.**

i 8 and 10-bed dorms from €12; reservation recommended; BGLTQ+ friendly; Wi-Fi; reservation recommended; lockers provided; free beverages

HIVE PARTY HOSTEL

Dob u. 19; 3 082 66197; www.thehive.hu; reception open 24hr

If in visiting Budapest you hope to let loose with your friends and your friends happen to be named Jose Cuervo and Captain Morgan, Hive Party Hostel is the place for you. It's located in Budapest's party district and has recently installed a bar on the main floor that stays open late every night featuring live music and DJs. The accommodations are modern, but if you don't want to party, we'd recommend going with another option.

i 14 and 16-bed dorms from €9, from €15 on weekends; 6, 8, 10, 12-bed dorms from €10, double bed privates from €30, weekends €70; female-only dorms available; reservation recommended; BGLTQ+ friendly; Wi-Fi; lockers provided; in-house bar; hairdryers, irons available to borrow

MAVERICK HOSTEL

Ferenciek Tere 2; 1 267 3166; mavericklodges.com

Maverick Hostel seems to have thought of everything. It boasts a large luggage room, multiple common rooms, and kitchens for guests staying in rooms above the main floor. They hold events in the lobby every other night (past events include movie nights and wine tastings) and offer "intimacy kits" at the reception desk—not that we recommend picking up a stranger in a strange land. This hostel is comfortable, professional, and noticeably experienced.

i 10-bed dorm from €10, 5-bed dorm from €15, private suites from €50; reservation recommended; BGLTQ+ friendly; not wheelchair accessible; Wi-Fi; reservation recommended; lockers provided

SIGHTS
CULTURE

🖾 DAYTRIP TO SZENTENDRE

North of Budapest; establishment hours very

Take the H5 train line, change to the M2 metro line at Batthyány tér station, and you're there! (Just be sure to add a suburban railway extension ticket to your fare since they might check your ticket.) Once there, check out the

Catedral Beogradska Serbian Orthodox Church and **Szentendrei Képtár:** the former is a church that displays eighteenth-century art, and the latter is a modern art museum that's small enough to be interesting but not large enough to overwhelm you. Sit along the **boardwalk** before you leave—it's a great place to grab a snack and watch the people, and the river, go by.

i Establishment prices vary

HUNGARIAN STATE OPERA BUILDING

Andrassy u. 22; 1 814 7100, 1 332 8197; www.opera.hu, www.operavisit.hu; open daily 10am-8pm

Built in the late nineteenth century, the Hungarian State Opera is the birthplace of operatic rivalry between Hungary and Vienna. Said to be so beautiful that the Austrian king of the Austro-Hungarian Empire refused to attend after its opening night in 1884, the opera house is a sight to awe both the devoted supporters of the arts and the casual tour-taker alike. Opera fans, you're in luck. The Hungarian opera is heavily subsidized by the state, so book ahead of time and you could get tickets on the cheap for one of its 200 performances per season.

i Opera tickets vary; tour tickets 2990HUF, reduced 1990HUF; mini concert 690HUF; camera ticket 500HUF; tours daily at 2pm (English), 3pm, and 4pm (English and a handful of other languages); wheelchair accessible

MATTHIAS CHURCH AND FISHERMAN'S BASTION

Szentháromság tér 2; 1 488 7716, 2 095 94419; www.matyas-templom.hu; open M-F 9am-5pm, Sa 9am-noon, Sa 1pm-5pm

Matthias Church is a mosaic masterpiece that no Pinterest board could ever imagine in its wildest dreams. The inside is intricately painted, giving the walls a soft quality, almost like they're thinly carpeted. Tickets to the upper level of Fisherman's Bastion, the fortress-like terrace that rims the portico on the church's front façade, can be purchased with tickets to the church, but there are also great views from the ground (free).

i Church 1500HUF, reduced 1000HUF; bell tower 1500HUF, reduced 1000HUF; bastion 800HUF, reduced 400HUF

ST. STEPHEN'S BASILICA

Szent István tér 1; 1 311 0839; www.bazilika.biz

Another day, another church, another dollar. Actually, lots and lots of dollars, because the inside of this church is ridiculously beautiful. Visit to experience one of the essential cultural sights of Budapest. Marvel at the gold-leafed walls and wonder how in the world people painted such intricate ceilings. The steeple is also open for visitors to climb and see the city from on high. Although there's a museum, we recommend prioritizing the actual tower.

i Church free; panoramic tower 600HUF, reduced 400HUF; museum 400HUF, reduced 300HUF; wheelchair accessible

LANDMARKS

ERZSÉBET SQUARE

Erzsébet tér; 2 025 47818; erzsebetter.hu; open daily 24hr

Erzsébet Square is a great place to take a break and absorb all that laid-back Budapest has to offer. Because let's be honest, but being a tourist can be exhausting. So take off your backpack, take off your shoes, take off your socks, keep your pants on, and relax with your feet in the cool water of the park's central fountain. The square is also home to the country's largest seasonal Ferris wheel, the Budapest Eye (locally known as the **Sziget Eye**), which offers breathtaking views of the city below.

i Free; wheelchair accessible

HEROES' SQUARE

Hősök tere; 1146 Budapest; open daily 24hr

The monument at Heroes' Square is another public fixture literally crawling with people. Tourists flock here to see (and climb on) its statues, including the seven chieftains of Magyars and the **Tomb of the Unknown Soldier.** So you can do as the tourists do and whip out your selfie stick—the site's history will not disappoint.

i Free; wheelchair accessible

HUNGARIAN PARLIAMENT BUILDING

Kossuth Lajos tér 1-3; 1 441 4000; latogatokozpont.parlament.hu/en; open daily Apr-Oct 8am-6pm, Nov-Mar 8am-4pm

This is one of Budapest's few Gothic buildings. Daily tours provide a snippet of historical context on everything from the era of kings to that of communism. Gawk at the statues of chiefs and kings lining the walls and, if you're lucky, you'll catch a glimpse of the original Holy Crown of Hungary. Beyond the tour, stroll along the Buda side of the Danube after dark to watch the building—including its 96-foot-tall dome—come to life.

i EU adults 2400HUF, EU students 1300HUF, other adults 6000HUF, other students 3100HUF; last entry varies; wheelchair accessible (appointment necessary); Wi-Fi available in Kossuth Square

LIBERTY SQUARE

Szabadság tér; open daily 24hr

A visit to Liberty Square is a quick way to explore the war-torn history of Budapest, which has endured centuries of political tension. Here, a monument implying Hungary's innocence in WWII has seen three years of frequent protests. On the south end of the square lies a row of personal items, flowers, and photos placed by Holocaust survivors and their families. Towards the back, a Soviet monument stands in front of the American embassy along with a **statue of Ronald Reagan,** which was erected after the fall of the Berlin wall in 1989.

i Free; wheelchair accessible

SZÉCHENYI THERMAL BATH

Állatkerti krt. 9-11; 136 3210; www.szechenyibath.hu; open daily 9am-10pm

The Széchenyi Baths were the first of their kind. Originally called the **Artesian baths,** Széchenyi's hot spring wells were opened to the public in 1881. The baths quickly became popular, and in 1909, the city council broke ground on building **Széchenyi palace.** The palace itself is extraordinary, featuring nearly 20 indoor pools, three large outdoor pools ranging from 81 to 101°F (27-39°C), ample space for tanning, and several bars. There are several saunas and steam rooms. Pro tip: bring your own towel to avoid queues.

i Ticket and locker 4900HUF, weekends 5100HUF; last entry 6pm; wheelchair accessible

MUSEUMS

HUNGARIAN NATIONAL GALLERY

Szent György Tér; 1 201 9082; www.mng.hu; open Tu-Su 10am-6pm

If you only go to one art museum in Hungary, go here. Beginning in the medieval and renaissance periods, the permanent collections of the museum cover the history of Hungarian art in every medium. The museum has something for everyone: things to laugh at if you "don't get" art and things to ponder if you do. One of our favorites was Czimra Gyula's *Still Life in the Kitchen* (1962). Most of the galleries are housed in Buda Palace, and exhibits showcasing the building's rich history line the perimeter of the royal grounds.

i Permanent exhibitions 1800HUF, all exhibitions 2200HUF; wheelchair accessible

TERROR HOUSE

Andrássy u. 60; 6 137 42600; www.houseofterror.hu; open Tu-Su 10am-6pm

This museum takes visitors through the experience of the Nazi and Soviet occupations in Hungary, documenting the history of Nazi concentration camps, Soviet work camps, and Soviet prisons. The path of Terror House takes you progressively lower into the basement of the building, which has been converted into a reconstruction of Soviet prison cells. Fair warning: this is an intense and emotional experience, so we'd recommend preparing yourself accordingly.

i Adult 2000HUF, reduced 1000HUF (EU citizens); wheelchair accessible

OUTDOORS

GELLÉRT HILL

Paths begin on the Buda side of Erzsébet Bridge; open daily 24hr

For the outdoorsy and the athletically inclined, Gellért Hill offers a fun, short, and rewarding hike up the highest hillside in Buda. The park's many monuments are great places to stop and catch your breath. At the top, look upon the city from the citadel—but beware that the park is a web of paths, all of which lead to the same place, so continue uphill and you'll make it, we promise.

i Free; wheelchair accessible

FOOD

ALFÖLDI VENDÉGLŐ RESTAURANT ($)

Kecskemétu u. 4; 1053; 1 267 0224; open daily 11am-11pm

Hungarian in every regard, Alföldi Vendéglő is a dimly lit, relatively inexpensive dinner restaurant. The cool ambiance is accented by walls paneled with strips of thin dark wood that resemble stacked pretzel sticks. Also difficult to master: deep-frying cheese, which, to our surprise, Alföldi Vendéglő did with tremendous ease.

i *Entrées from 1890HUF; wheelchair accessible; Wi-Fi*

BONNIE ($$)

Ferenciek tere 5; 3 074 43555; bonnierestro.hu; open M-W 8am-1am, Th-F 8am-3am, Sa 9am-3am, Su 9am-midnight

For an establishment that's so clean-cut and industrial, Bonnie has surprisingly hearty, home-style food. Come here for a nice dinner that may push the budget boundary, but not by much. On the menu, you will find *goulash* (1550HUF), a traditional Hungarian stew, as well as more modern dishes such as bacon-wrapped chicken breast stuffed with mozzarella, basil, and roasted tomatoes (2890HUF).

i *Entrées from 1550HUF; vegetarian, or gluten-free options available*

BUDAPEST HOT DOG COLD BEER ($)

Zrínyi u. 14; 17921702; open M-Th 11am-3am, F-Sa 11am-6am, Su 11am-midnight

Outside of **St. Stephen's Basilica,** amid a sea of overpriced restaurants; there is a sign with a simple promise: Hot Dog Cold Beer. Pro tip: patrons with nose rings may want to remove them to better facilitate rapid consumption. If you feel like testing the limits of the human body, finish your meal with a sweet dog (790HUF) or choice of deep-fried candy bar covered in powdered sugar.

i *City dogs 990HUF, corn dog 790HUF, sweet dog 790HUF, cold beer 490-790HUF; wheelchair accessible*

FARGER KÁVÉZÓ ($)

Zoltán u. 18; 2 023 77825; www.farger.hu; open M-F 7am-9pm, Sa-Su 9am-6pm

Sandwiched between **Liberty Square** and the **Hungarian Parliament Building,** Farger is an affordable café with a specialty dish that we can get behind: sliders. The "Farger Plank" includes one of every variety that the restaurant offers and will leave you feeling more optimistic about the state of the world—until you remember that the beef industry is rapidly killing the planet. Pair your meal with beer and wine, or try Farger's fresh squeezed juice, but make sure to specify that you want orange juice. If you don't, they'll bring you Orangina instead.

i *Breakfast from 610HUF, sliders from 1190HUF; limited wheelchair accessibility*

NIGHTLIFE

⚑ SZIMPLA

Kazinczy u. 14; 2 026 18669; www.szimpla.hu; open M-Sa noon-4am, Su 9am-5am

Szimpla is one of the largest and most famous ruin pubs in Budapest. The eclectic mix of decorative collections strewn about the building looks like it came out of the garden of a hoarder clown who played in a punk band in his 20s and dabbles in local business and organic farming. Host to DJs and live bands all week long and a farmer's market on Sunday mornings, Szimpla's got a little something for everyone.

i *Beer from 400HUF; main floor is wheelchair accessible; Wi-Fi*

PONTOON

Id. Antall József Rakpart; 3 065 22732; www.pontoonbudapest.com; open daily noon-4am

Location, location, location. Situated on the **eastern bank of the Danube River,** Pontoon offers a stunning view of the **Széchenyi Chain Bridge** and ample outdoor seating. The drink menu is extensive; the food menu… not so much. What's offered *is* tasty, though. Sip your wine from a plastic cup to the muffled pulse of electronic music playing softly in the background and soak in the magnificence that is the Danube at dusk.

i *Beer and wine from 400HUF; BGLTQ+ friendly; wheelchair accessible*

GYÖR

Coverage by **Antonia Washington**

With its pedestrian streets, outdoor bistros, and fair share of river-front properties, Györ is like a quickly-expanding, small-scale Budapest. Construction crews hang out on seemingly every street corner—so who knows? Györ could be the next trendy town in Europe. The place is already covered in bookstores. Also, the ice cream portions here are bigger and cheaper per ounce than elsewhere in Hungary, so we're fans. As for the architecture: it's mostly baroque and often painted yellow. Think a combination of the life's work of a decorative molding devotee and the scene in Juno when Vanessa can't decide which shade of yellow to paint the nursery. You may not think there's a huge difference between paint swatches for custard and cheesecake yellow, but it's called nesting, it's especially important for adoptive mothers, and you would know that if you read the baby books and started pulling your fucking weight, Mark.

ORIENTATION

Györ is located in the northwest of Hungary, directly between **Budapest** and **Vienna** and an hour south of **Bratislava, Slovakia.** It sits at the intersection of the **Mosoni-Duna** and **Rába Rivers,** with the city center situated in the southeast portion of this intersection. The best places to orient yourself within the city center are **Széchenyi tér,** the main square with the **Benedictine church,** and **Baross Gábor út,** a major pedestrian street that runs roughly north to south and sits a couple of blocks west of the square. When we visited, some museums and landmarks were closed for construction, so before marking them down to visit when you arrive, check ahead to see if they have reopened.

ESSENTIALS

GETTING THERE

By train or bus, Györ is easily reachable from Budapest, Bratislava, and Vienna. The Györ train and bus stations are separate, but located next to each other at the south end of the city center. Most central accommodations are within walking distance. There is usually a taxi or two at the station, but if you plan to travel by taxi, calling ahead may be a good idea.

GETTING AROUND

Györ, especially the city center, is small, so the easiest way to travel is usually on foot. Beyond the city center, walking is generally still the easiest form of transportation for able bodied individuals. Otherwise, buses sometimes travel within the city from the Györ bus station, or visitors can call a taxi service to request a ride (the most frequently used taxis in Györ are Duna Tele-4 Taxi; 96 444 444).

PRACTICAL INFORMATION

Tourist Offices: There is a very helpful Tourinform office in the heart of the city center. (Baross Gábor u. 21; 96336817; open M-F 9am-5pm, Sa 9am-2pm)
Banks/ATMs/Currency Exchange: While there may not be ATMs on every corner like in Budapest, they are available and many businesses accept cards.
Post Offices: There are multiple post offices in Györ, but the post office closest to the city center is near the National Theater of Györ (Bajcsy-Zsilinszky u. 46; 96547600; open M-F 8am-6pm).
Internet: Most accommodations in the area provide free wireless Internet.

EMERGENCY INFORMATION

Emergency Numbers: 112

Police: Police in Hungary are safe to call, but they are allowed to ask for paperwork and identification, so make sure to carry yours with you. There are no police stations in the city center, but there is one across the river to the west (Köztelek utca 4-6; 96520083).

US Embassy: Györ is almost equidistant between Budapest, Vienna, and Bratislava, Slovakia, each of which have U.S. embassies. Information for the embassy in Budapest is as follows: (1054 Budapest, Szabadság tér 12; 14754400; open M-F 8am-5pm).

Hospitals: The main hospital in Györ is located substantially southeast of the city center (Petz Aladár Megyei Oktató Kórház: Vasvári Pál u. 2-4; 96507900).

Pharmacies: There are many pharmacies in Györ, but the most central one is run by the Benedictine church in Széchenyi square (Széchenyi Patika: Széchenyi tér 8; 96550348).

ACCOMMODATIONS

FEHÉR HAJÓ PANZIÓ ($)

Kiss Ernö u. 4; 9 631 7608; www.feherhajop-anzio.hu/; reception open 24hr

The Fehér Hajó Panzió is a good place to crash if all you're looking for is Wi-Fi and a bed (in that order). The rooms are small, it smells vaguely of cigarettes, and the toilet flushes by a pull-cord from the ceiling. All the fine comforts of home, no? The duds here are not flashy, but it's a short walk to the city center and you've probably been staying in hostels for a while now, so how much do you care?
i Single room from €25, room with double bed from €35; BGLTQ+ friendly; no wheelchair accessibility; Wi-Fi; reservation recommended; linens provided

HOTEL FAMULUS ($$)

Budai u. 4-6; 9027; 9 654 7770; www.famulushotel.hu

If you looked up Hotel Famulus without reading this blurb, you probably rejoiced about what a treat it was to be able to afford such a nice hotel. Well, you should have kept reading. The main hotel is not affordable at all, but they offer small apartment style accommodations—much like college dorms—with a much lower price tag. This is a popular option for students, especially those taking summer classes in Györ. Hotel Famulus offers short-term housing, which is a great deal if you can snatch it! Rooms are suite-style and very small, but include a kitchenette.
i One bed in 4-person suite 3300 HUF, personal suite 5700 HUF; reservation recommended; wheelchair accessible; Wi-Fi

SIGHTS
CULTURE

LOYOLAI SZENT IGNÁC TEMPLOM (BENEDICTINE CHURCH ST. IGNATIUS OF LOYOLA)

Széchenyi tér; 9 651 3020; bencesgyor.hu; open M-F 9am-5pm, Sa 9am-1pm, Sunday mass (time varies)

Though smaller than many European churches, it was built to impress, with carved wooden pews, ornate ceiling frescos, and an overwhelming amount of gold leaf. Visiting the church is free; however, because it is an active place of worship, it's recommended to double-check hours before entering.
i Free; limited wheelchair accessible

NATIONAL THEATER OF GYÖR

Czuczor Gergely u. 7; 9 652 0611; www.gyoriszinhaz.hu

Offering a smattering of performances in the classical arts and a slightly wider repertoire than other Hungarian theaters like the **Hungarian State Opera** in Budapest, the National Theater of Györ is a must-see for those who consider themselves art fanatics. The building itself dates to 1978 and reflects many of the architectural trends of the decade—brutally clean lines, lots of reinforced concrete, and a sweeping façade. It is an imposing cornucopia of creativity, serving as a striking antithesis to Györ's homogeneous cityscape. Catch one of their performances during the September to May season.
i Show prices vary; wheelchair accessible

LANDMARKS

ARK OF THE COVENANT STATUE
Gutenberg tér

A baroque sculpture with a healthy dose of gold leaf, the Ark of the Covenant statue in Györ was once a gate to the citadel. Today, it's a work of art for visitors to admire and a convenient place to sit and hang out—particularly important because of its close proximity to several ice cream shops. Take in the significance of historic monuments—with sweets.
i Free; wheelchair accessible

COLUMN OF ST. MARY AT SZÉCHENYI TÉR
Széchenyi tér

A towering structure standing watch over the main square in Györ, the column was erected in the late seventeenth century by the Bishop of Györ, and offers another opportunity to struggle to get a decent photo featuring a really tall thing (we all do this). Our visit to the fountain in front of the monument taught us that no matter how many times you've watched that three-year-old in his underwear clap his hands over the bubbling fountain and try to get the water to do what he wants, you will watch when he does it again 30 seconds later.
i Free; wheelchair accessible

THE BOATMAN FOUNTAIN
Baross Gábor u.

This statue and fountain, located right in the middle of Györ's major pedestrian street, gives a great sense of the spirit of the city. On nice days, musicians often sit on the rim of the fountain and play wonderfully accented versions of songs by The Beatles, Bruno Mars, and The Script. The songs they chose tend to be of a genre we call, "These haven't been relevant for a while, so maybe you won't notice when I don't actually know the words." A beloved genre overall, but we were 13 years old when The Script's "Breakeven" came out. We know all the words.
i Free; wheelchair accessible

MUSEUMS

BORSOS HOUSE
Király u. 17; 9 631 6329; open T-Su 10am-6pm

This art exhibition displays the work of Miklós Borsos, a Hungarian sculptor who worked in a range of mediums, creating figures, busts, and medals. His works explore grief, fertility, and perfection, as well as more abstract themes. If you're interested in contemplating the significance of an artist's not having fully carved the details of a woman's face, Borsos House is the place to do so.
i Admission 700 HUF, students 350 HUF; no wheelchair accessibility

KOVÁCS MARGIT PERMANENT EXHIBITION
Apáca u. 1; 9 632 6739; open T-Su 10am-6pm

There's a place in Györ where you can judge your amateur ceramics against one of the most celebrated ceramic artists in Hungary: Margit Kovács. Her permanent collection consists of a sizable number of small figurines (first floor) of everyone from soldiers to women with elegant up-dos. Move to the second floor to see some of Kovács' larger pieces. The gallery itself can be easy to miss, so look out for a marker above a door on the right side of the building.
i 700 HUF, student 350 HUF; no wheelchair accessibility

OUTDOORS

RÁBA RIVER
Center of Györ.

Running north to south through Györ is the Rába River, in the middle of which lies **Radó Island.** Both the island and the banks of the Rába feature extensive networks of walking paths which, barring the weather is nice, are a great means of checking out the city. The northern section of Györ (along the north bank of the **Mosoni-Duna River** and west of **Jedlik Ányos Bridge**) has a grassy shoreline and sandy beach complete with volleyball courts. Come lie out in the sun or lounge in a lawn chair in the shade of a big tree.
i Free; wheelchair accessibility varies by location

FOOD

DUNA DÖNER GYÖR ($)

Széchenyi tér 7; 9 631 0325; zeugmakebap.com; open Su-W 11am-10pm, Th 11am-11pm, F-Sa 11am-11:45pm

Duna Döner is one of the cheapest and most delicious take-out restaurants on Széchenyi tér. Their specialty is the *Döner* Box, which consists of a pile of French fries covered in spicy sauce, a hearty portion of freshly-carved meat (chicken or beef), and fresh slices of tomato, onion, and lettuce.

i Döner Box 990 HUF; vegetarian options available; wheelchair accessible

ISTAMBULDA ÉTTEREM ($)

Baross Gábor u. 30; 9 625 4761; open M-Th 10am-midnight, F-Sa 10am-4am, Su 10am-9pm

Despite the fact that Istambulda's only outward-facing signage features a picture of a hookah, tobacco in Hungary is highly regulated and only available at specific tobacco shops. So, while said hookah is a fun reminder of Turkish culture and of Hungary's multicultural history, you will not casually smoke with your lunch here. What you will find is a fast-food counter style restaurant that puts Turkish food in your hands right when you need it.

i Entrées from 700HUF; wheelchair accessible

PIZZA PICCOLINO ($)

Kazinczy u. 16; 9 631 4461; open daily noon-9pm

There are two kinds of abundant foods in Hungary: Hungarian food and pizza. Many Hungarian pizzerias, however, are sit-down restaurants, where you order full pizzas instead of by the slice. Pizza Piccolino is the first old-fashioned pizza counter we encountered on our trek, and we eagerly grabbed a slice (or three), paid in cash, and were on our way in a matter of minutes. Pizza varieties include (but aren't limited to) Hungarian favorites such as ham, corn, and ham with corn.

i One slice from 200HUF; vegetarian options available; wheelchair accessible

NIGHTLIFE

DIVINO GYÖR

Széchenyi tér 7; 9 631 0342; gyor.divinoborbar.hu; open M 4pm-midnight, Tu-Th 4pm-2am, F 4pm-4am, Sa 2pm-2am, Su 2pm-midnight

Visiting a wine bar basically anywhere can make you feel like a chic, urban 20-something. That said, DiVino Györ's clientele spans a fairly wide age range. In Hungary, wine is a crowd favorite. But fear not, the music gets louder and the crowd gets younger as the night wears on. Oh, and the wine only gets more delicious.

i No cover, drinks from 300HUF; BGLTQ+ friendly; wheelchair accessible

YOLO PUB GYÖR

Baross Gábor u. 5; 3 025 20100; open Tu-Th 8pm-1am, F-Sa 8pm-2:30am

Do not walk into the Yolo Pub at opening on a Tuesday and expect to see anyone but the bartender—weekdays tend to be slow. Every Friday, Yolo Pub's staff clears out all of the furniture to make space for a dance floor and cranks up the music, which ranges from old-school funk to current pop hits. Shrouded in neon light, Yolo Bar is an ideal place to embarrass yourself on the dance floor and debut those "signature moves" you rehearsed in the mirror at home. #Yolo.

i Drinks from 450 HUF; cash only; BGLTQ+ friendly; no wheelchair accessibility

HUNGARY ESSENTIALS

MONEY

Tipping: Tipping in Hungary is most common at restaurants, where it is standard to tip about 10% and not more than 15%. Often, the tip will be included in the bill, in which case the menu and/or bill will state that there is a 10% service fee. It will generally suffice to tip bartenders by rounding above the cost of your drinks to the next 100-forint denomination. In restaurants and bars, it is common to tell the server how much to charge total with the tip, or instruct them how much change you want back, instead of leaving a tip on the table. Usually taxis should be tipped 5-10%.Public restrooms often will charge a fee of 100-200 forints to pay restroom attendants as well.

Taxes: Most goods in Hungary are subject to a value added tax (VAT) of 27%, included in the purchase price of goods. The 27% VAT is a standard rate, though it fluctuates based on the goods bought, so you should ask the retailer for exact rates. Non-EU visitors taking these goods home unused can apply for a VAT refund for goods totaling more than 55,000 HUF at one retailer. To apply for this refund, ask the store for a VAT refund form, sometimes called a tax-free form, and carry your passport with you as retailers may ask to see it. Present the refund form and be prepared to show the unused goods you are exporting at the customs office at your point of departure from the EU, regardless of country. Once your paperwork has been approved by customs, present it at a Tax-Free Shopping Office, also at the point of departure, to claim the refund. Refunds must be claimed within 90 days of the original purchase.

SAFETY AND HEALTH

Local Laws and Police: Police in Hungary can generally be relied upon if you need help, but always have your passport with you, as they are entitled to ask for your documentation.

Tobacco, Drugs, and Alcohol: The drinking age in Hungary is 18. There is a zero tolerance policy on drinking in public, which is illegal to do in Hungary. If you are found driving with a BAC of even 0.001%, you could be in serious trouble. Tobacco is tightly regulated in Hungary. Only official tobacco shops are licensed to sell any tobacco products at all, though these shops are easy to find. They are marked by signs with the number 18 inside of a circle and labeled "Nemzeti Dohánybolt." The signs are brown with red and green. Persons under the age of 18 are not allowed to enter these stores.

HUNGARY GYŐR

ICELAND

Do Iceland wrong, and you'll find yourself languishing in an overpriced Reykavík hostel, struggling to fall asleep as the midnight sun streams through the paper-thin curtains and that middle-aged guy two beds over snores like an Icelandic horse. You'll head out to book a minibus tour to the South Coast and only then remember that you blew your last $50 on a few shitty beers at the bar last night. You'll aimlessly wander the streets of the capital, surrounded by super jeeps and backpackers, catching snatches of conversation about black-sand beaches and snow-capped mountains while you dream of the lands beyond the city. Do Iceland wrong and you'll spend a lot and see very little.

But do Iceland right, and you'll have the adventure of a lifetime. You'll stay up late to sit on the shore and watch the sun as it sets behind the distant mountains at 11:45pm. You'll feel the raw power and majesty of this planet as you swim in the frigid water between two tectonic plates sitting just meters apart. You'll drive up mountain roads that seem to ascend into the clouds and through fjords with slopes of scree on one side and boundless sea on the other.

This country develops further each year. Hotels and gift shops sprout up around once-unknown waterfalls, and camper vans and coaches cover every kilometer of the Ring Road. But drive long enough, and the buses will become few and far between; climb high enough, and the tourists will shrink like ants below you; walk far enough and you'll find yourself alone with the sand or the trail and the sky. Iceland's untouched beauty is still out there.

Do Iceland right, and you'll discover what so few have found.

REYKJAVÍK

Coverage by Eric Chin

Everything about Iceland's capital city just *feels* expensive and purposely built for tourists. Information and booking centers line the main streets, menus in restaurant windows showcase eye-opening cuisine (and eye-popping prices), and even the street art is in a league of its own. What's more, despite being Iceland's largest city by a big margin, Reykjavík doesn't even feel like the island's main attraction. Talk to fellow travelers and their primary question will not be "Have you tried fermented shark yet," but rather "What tours of the island have you done so far?" as if the only thing to do once you get to Reykjavík is leave it.

Was Reykjavík the artistic and cultural hub of Renaissance Europe? No (it wasn't even a city back in the days of Michelangelo). Did it command a vast global empire and help lead Europe into the modern era? Not really (it wasn't even fully independent until 1944). Does it have an entire museum about penises with almost 300 biological specimens? Absolutely. (Oh, so now you're intrigued?) Reykjavík is a different breed of city—one that is modern and completely unapologetic about its many oddities. It's the kind of city that you *actually* want to visit. The museums are unpretentious and genuinely interesting (sometimes shockingly so), the nightlife is thriving and without the usual pressures of dress codes and exorbitant cover charges, and, in the summer at least, daylight never fades.

Do take tours to see the astounding natural beauty of Iceland, and do plan for only a few days in the city itself, but don't overlook Reykjavík as nothing more than a gateway to the island. There is more here for you than meets the eye.

ORIENTATION

The **BSÍ Bus Terminal** is located at the very southern tip of the city center. Tourist information centers, shops, restaurants, and bars can be found on **Laugavegur**, which turns into **Bankastræti** and then **Austurstræti** as it stretches west. These streets are generally touristy during the day and are crowded late at night, especially on weekends. They also house the city's post office and many ATMs. Head uphill from Laugavegur to reach **Hallgrímskirkja,** Reykjavík's iconic church, and the statue of **Leif Erikson** which looks out over the city. North is the ocean, along which a paved walking and biking path runs west, past the statue **Sólfar, Harpa,** and the harbor at the northwestern end of the city.

ESSENTIALS
GETTING THERE

Iceland is, well, an island, meaning that air travel is inevitable. Most international journeys go through Keflavík International Airport (KEF). Your best bet is Icelandair, though WOW Air is always an option, provided you don't mind paying for a carry-on and a reserved seat in addition to your ticket. Keflavík is about 30mi. southwest of Reykjavík, so take a bus ("transfer," as it's called) to the main city. The Flybus will take you to Reykjavík's BSÍ Bus Terminal, about a 45min. trip, for 2500 kr, and has free Wi-Fi.

GETTING AROUND

Reykjavík is easily walkable; it's less than a 30min. walk across at its widest point. There is a city bus service, Strætó, but note that you must buy a ticket in advance (sold at a number of shops) or pay with exact change on the bus, in cash! If you plan to use the bus a lot, the 1-day (1560 kr) and 3-day passes (3650 kr) are a better value. Taxis are also available, and rates are standard. Try Hreyfill (588 5522) or BSR (561 0000). In such an expensive country, though, walking is a great way to save some money.

PRACTICAL INFORMATION

Tourist Offices: Reykjavík's official information center is located in City Hall (Tjarnargata 11, 101 Reykjavík; 411 6040; open daily 8am-8pm).

Banks/ATMs/Currency Exchange: Banks are mostly closed on weekends, but ATMs are common on main streets. You can exchange currency upon arrival at the airport or in any bank, but cards are accepted almost everywhere (Landsbankinn: Austurstræti 12, 101 Reykjavík; 410 4000; open M-F open 9am-4pm).

Post Offices: Pósthússtræti 5 (101 Reykjavík; 580 1000; open M-F 9am-9pm)

Internet: Free Wi-Fi is available at most cafés and public spaces, as well as at City Hall.

BGLTQ+ Resources: Iceland is one of the most progressive countries in the world with regard to BGLTQ+ rights and was the first country to openly elect a gay head of state. Reykjavík, like the rest of the country, is so well integrated that specific BGLTQ+ spaces are hardly necessary, though a few exist (Samtökin '78 is the National Queer Organization at Suðurgata 3, 101 Reykjavík; 552 7878; www.samtokin78.is; open M-F 1-4pm, open house 8-11pm).

EMERGENCY INFORMATION

Emergency Number: 112

Police: Icelandic police are known for being friendly and fun-loving. Check out their Instagram (@logreglan) to see how they've been cracking down on crime among the snowman population (113-115 Hverfisgata, 105 Reykjavík; 444 1000).

US Embassy: Laufásvegur 21 (101 Reykjavík; 595 2200 (595 2248 after hours and weekends); open M-F 8am-5pm)

Rape Crisis Center: A special emergency unit is located in the Emergency Department at Landspítali University Hospital, Fossvogur (108 Reykjavík; 543 2085; open daily 24hr).

Hospitals: The main hospital is located outside the city center. If urgent care is required, call 112 for an ambulance (Landspítali University Hospital, Fossvogur: Bráðamóttaka, Fossvogi; 543 2000; open daily 24hr).

Pharmacies:
- Lyfja (Laugavegur 16; 552 4045; M-F 9am-6pm, Sa 11am-5pm)
- Lyfja (Lágmúla 5; 533 2300; open daily 8am-midnight)

ACCOMMODATIONS

⌂ HLEMMUR SQUARE ($$)

Laugavegur 105; 105; 415 1600; www.hlemmursquare.com; reception open 24hr

Look, it's expensive to stay in Reykjavík. So, if you're going to spend the money anyway, treat yourself and book a room at Hlemmur Square. It's a hotel-hostel combo, and while dorm prices are average for this city, the amenities are top-notch. Dorm rooms are spacious and include couches and sinks. The restaurant in the lobby offers a special "Square Meal" (1100 kr) Tuesday through Saturday. Sit at a communal table with other travelers and enjoy a selection of Icelandic cuisine. Seating begins at 6pm, but come early as it's first come first served.

i Dorms from 4800 kr, private double with shower from 19000 kr, private quad from 32400 kr; reservation recommended; BGLTQ+ friendly; Wi-Fi; linens included; laundry facilities (1500 kr); breakfast 7:30am-10:30am (1800 kr); luggage storage

ODDSSON ($$)

Hringbraut 121; 101; 511 3579; www.oddsson.is; reception open 24hr

ODDSSON creatively markets itself as "Ho(s)tel." Dorm rooms are standard issue, but the common spaces are some of the best you'll find, including a lobby with bare neon lights, a yoga studio, and a rooftop with a hot tub. Located right next to Reykjavík's harbor, it puts long strolls on the coast and midnight sunset walks just outside your door. Although it's a little far from town, you'll love being right by the beach. When the tide is low, there may even be a few patches of black sand exposed on the rocky shore.

i Dorms from 5500 kr, private from 15000 kr; reservation recommended; BGLTQ+ friendly; Wi-Fi; linens included; lockers (500 kr); towel rental; laundry (1500 kr)

SIGHTS
CULTURE

HALLGRÍMSKIRKJA

Hallgrímstorg 1; 101; 510 1000; www.
en.hallgrimskirkja.is; open daily May-Sept
9am- 9pm, Oct-Apr 9am-5pm, closed for
Sunday mass

Situated high on a hill in the center of Reykjavik, Hallgrímskirkja stands tall and proud over the city. Finding this contemporary Lutheran church is easy, as its 74.5-meter tower can be seen from ground-level throughout the city. The design evokes Iceland's mountains, glaciers, and volcanic rock, and the result is what must be one of the world's most striking concrete structures. Inside, wander through the cavernous yet comfortable sanctuary, which contains **Iceland's largest instrument**: a 25-metric-ton organ composed of 5000 pipes. The church organist sometimes practices during the day, and you can listen for free. For a fee, take the elevator up to the top of the tower for a vertigo-inducing view of downtown Reykjavik and the ocean beyond.

i *Church admission free, tower 900 kr; tower closes 30min. before church; wheelchair accessible*

HARPA

Autobrake 2; 102; 528 5000; www.
en.harpa.is; open daily 8am-midnight

Outside, it looks like the Water Cube's trendy younger cousin. Inside, it's like standing in a giant kaleidoscope. Overall, it's the essence of Iceland (read: aesthetically pleasing) captured in stone and glass. Harpa is officially a conference center and concert hall, home to the **Iceland Symphony Orchestra** and the **Icelandic Opera,** but it also hosts many lesser-known artists, cultural performances, and comedy shows. For 4500 kr, try *How to become Icelandic in 60 minutes,* a production which promises to have you feeling "100% Icelandic." If only it were really that easy...

i *Free, show prices vary; paid guided tours available regularly in summer, winter M-F 3:30pm, Sa-Su 11am and 3:30pm; wheelchair accessible*

LANDMARKS

SÓLFAR (SUN VOYAGER)

Sæbraut; open daily 24hr

You're in Iceland. Expectations for your Instagram posts have never been higher, but there's already a 100-person line in front of **Leif Erikson** (Eiríksgata; open daily 24hr; wheelchair accessible)! Fear not, Sólfar delivers. The platform on which this dreamboat statue sits juts away from the otherwise uniform coastline, with the ship's bow extended proudly toward the sea and the mountains beyond. Though it looks something like a jungle gym, most viewers stay back, snapping clear shots from every angle. There's really no bad time to visit, but we'd recommend going at sunset.

i *Free; wheelchair accessible*

REYKJAVÍK CITY LIBRARY

Tryggvagata 15; 101; 411 6100; www.
borgarbokasafn.is/end; open M-Th 10am-7pm, F 11am-6pm, Sa-Su 1pm-4pm

Not the most interesting spot in the city—it is a library after all. But the City Library is a great spot for strong Wi-Fi access and outlets for your phone, laptop, portable battery, camera, and whatever other gadgets you're dragging around. The space is modern with lots of natural light and several types of seating (beanbag chair anyone?). The upstairs level houses the kids' section where you can let loose your inner child in play spaces with cushioned reading nooks, comic and picture books, and an entire shelf of board games

i *Free; wheelchair accessible*

MUSEUMS

▨ ICELANDIC PUNK MUSEUM

Bankastræti 2; www.thepunkmuseum.is; open M-F 10am-10pm, Sa-Su noon-10pm

The Icelandic Punk Museum has established itself below street level in an abandoned city restroom. Everything about the IPM screams "anarchy," and it's not just the anarchy symbols painted just about everywhere you look. It's also the punk music blaring from street-level speakers, eliciting disgruntled looks from patrons of a nearby seafood restaurant, and the child-sized blue M&M statue sporting a mohawk and an ammo belt. Travel through the history of this famously Icelandic genre from the first appearance of punk in 1974 through its current evolution. If you're feeling brave (or rebellious), listen to famous punk hits from the array of headsets or try out the electric guitar and drum kit for yourself.
i Admission 1000 kr

▨ THE ICELANDIC PHALLOLOGICAL MUSEUM

Laugavegur 116; 105; 561 6663; www. phallus.is

Now that you know it exists, you *have* to go, right? This well-endowed museum boasts a collection of over 280 specimens from more than 90 species (including species of "folklore," how Icelandic), ranging in size from a few millimeters to several feet. Yes, feet! If you're getting overwhelmed by penises dried, stuffed and mounted, or preserved in formaldehyde, check out the museum's even bigger (by quantity at least) assortment of penis art and "practical utensils." Prepare to learn more fun (or maybe not fun) phallus facts than you ever wanted from a series of panels in Icelandic and English. And while it can be difficult to stay composed when learning about the "surprisingly high motion control" that an elephant has over its member, please try to stay classy.
i Admission 1500 kr; wheelchair accessible

ÞJÓÐMINJASAFN ÍSLANDS (NATIONAL MUSEUM OF ICELAND)

Suðurgata 41; 101; 530 2200; www. thjodminjasafn.is; open T-Su 10am-5pm, closed Sept 16-Apr 30

If your parents are expecting to hear about museums, this one's a no-brainer. Iceland's National Museum covers over 1000 years of Icelandic history, from the first settlement of the island by the Norse to the establishment of the modern republic in 1944 and to present day events. Check out the collection of ancient drinking horns and gawk at an entire fishing boat annotated with complete, syntactically convoluted English translations. (Ever heard of an "unruly reformation" before?) For a break, head to one of the "Hands-On Rooms," where you can grab a comfy reading nook or try on a selection of traditional Icelandic clothing.
i Admission 2000 kr, students 1000 kr, seniors and under 18 free; tours only for groups of 10+ and booked in advance; audio guide 300 kr; wheelchair accessible

FOOD

BÆJARINS BEZTU PYLSUR (THE BEST HOT DOG IN TOWN) ($)

Tryggvagata 1; 101; 511 1566; www.bbp.is; open M-Th 10am-1am, F-Sa 10am-4:30pm, Su 10am-1am

That's right, this hot dog stand is open later than most bars in America. The menu is simple, too. Hot dog: 450 kr. Soda: 250 kr. So easy you'll still be able to understand it even after a few too many *brennivín* shots at the bar. This tiny hot dog shack's unassuming appearance belies its deliciousness and popularity; it's been around since 1937, giving its staff a lot of time to perfect their single item. Apparently, Bill Clinton was here once, and judging by his picture on the wall, they've done a damn good job.

i Hot dog 450 kr, soda 250 kr; wheelchair accessible

BRAUÐ & CO ($$)

Frakkastígur 16; 101; www.braudogco.is; open M-F 6am-6pm, Sa-Su 6am-5pm

You can't miss Brauð & Co, but by its appearance alone you won't recognize it as a bakery. What gave it away to us was the smell of freshly-baked pastries wafting out of the front door. The building's façade, just a short walk from Reykjavík's main shopping street, is painted in a kaleidoscopic rainbow that belongs on the set of a psychedelic Beatles music video. Inside, most of the square footage is behind the counter, where you can watch as the bakers mix, pour, knead, and shuffle trays full of warm buns, croissants, and their signature cinnamon rolls and sourdough bread in and out of ovens. The place is understandably busy, but don't be fooled by a long line; it's worth the wait for a delectable cinnamon bun or famous sourdough loaf.

i Individual pastries from 500 kr; vegetarian and vegan options available

OUTDOORS

THE BLUE LAGOON

240 Grindavík; 420 8800; www.bluelagoon.com; open Jan 1-May 24 8am-10pm, May 25-June 28 7am-11pm, June 39-Aug 19 7am-midnight, Aug 20-Oct 1 8am-10pm, Oct 2-Dec 31 8am-9pm

Along with large quantities of geothermally-heated water and steam, the Blue Lagoon oozes luxury. This pristine spa has everything from a steam cave to a man-made waterfall. It even has a bar in the lagoon itself where you can charge in-water drinks to your Star Trek-style wristband. None of this comes cheap, though, and it shows. You'll be sharing the enormous pool with wealthy couples, foreign tourists, and lots of families with kids (they get in free under 14). The Blue Lagoon is about an hour from Reykjavík, so you'll have to arrange bus transit as well. Depending on how early you schedule your trip, it can be cheaper and easier to book through an independent tour company.

i Book in advance; admission 6100 kr; price goes up during high season; from Reykjavík/airport 4500 kr; towel/bathing suit (700 kr); robe/slippers (1400 kr); last entry 1hr before close; wheelchair accessible

◪ CAFÉ BABALÚ ($$)

Skólavörðustígur 22; 101; 555 8845; www.babalu.is

Nothing in Café Babalú makes sense. The tables and chairs don't match, the advertised opening time is 11am, but it often opens earlier, and the music unexpectedly switches from Journey to polka. But, in a way, everything does makes sense: décor is so eclectic that nothing looks out of place, not even the entire shelf of *The Flintstones* merchandise. Babalú makes you think, "Well, why wouldn't there be a New York license plate hanging next to a clock made entirely of plastic forks?" Drinks are in the 500 kr range, and food varies from the sweet (the signature cheesecake, 990 kr) to the savory (traditional lamb soup, 1690 kr). Oh, and the bathroom is Star Wars themed and mysteriously playing the soundtrack when you enter.

i Tea from 400 kr, coffee from 500 kr, sweet crepes from 890 kr, cheesecake 990 kr; vegan and vegetarian options available; wheelchair accessible

NOODLE STATION ($$)

Laugavegur 103; 551 3198; www.noodlestation.is; open M-F 11am-10pm, Sa-Su noon-10pm

It's late, the grocery stores are closed, and the line for the hostel kitchen is way too long. How are you going to get the daily dose of ramen that college kids and budget travelers need for survival? Head east, away from downtown Reykjavík to Noodle Station. There's only one item on the menu: noodle soup (beef, chicken, or vegetable), and, at 1580 kr, it's one of the cheapest meals in town. You'll feel right at home among a crowd of younger travelers grabbing a quick meal before a night out. Select a spice level and then adjust to taste with fish sauce, hot chili oil, and salt.

i Soup from 920 kr, drinks 300 kr; vegetarian and vegan options available

ÍSLENSKI BARINN ($$$)

Ingólfsstræti 1a; 101; 517 6767; www.islenskibarinn.is; open M-Th 11:30am-1am, F-Sa 11:30am-3am, Su 11:30am-1am

If you find yourself with a little bit of extra cash (unlikely as that is) and want to try some strange Icelandic food in a decidedly not-strange setting, try Íslenski Barinn. The menu features all the greatest hits, including shark, fish stew, and meat soup. As a bonus, the bar is stocked with almost every alcohol produced in Iceland, you know, for when you get bored of Viking beer and *brennivín*. Retro décor, unlike in your grandmother's house, is done well, in a wallpaper-without-the-mold way.

i Beer from 900 kr, spirits from 800 kr, entrées from 2850 kr, burgers from 2500 kr; gluten-free, vegan, and vegetarian options available; no wheelchair accessibility

NIGHTLIFE

◪ KIKI QUEER BAR

Laugavegur 22; 101; www.kiki.is; open W-Th 8pm-1am, F-Sa 8pm-4:30am, Su 8pm-1am

In a country as progressive as Iceland in terms of BGLTQ+ rights, it's surprising that there's only one queer bar. Maybe it's because Kiki would drive any others out of business. Up the rainbow stairs are two small bars that fill up quickly on the weekends. Pro tip: show up before 11pm to beat the crowds and take advantage of one of the best happy hour deals around (beer and shots from 500 kr). Make new ones in a diverse crowd of people of all stripes: young, old, gay, straight, or somewhere in between. The atmosphere is a mélange of bar and club, but always upbeat thanks to a DJ who indulges all of your guilty pleasures (come on, you know "Take on Me" never gets old).

i No cover, beer 1000 kr, mixed drinks from 1500 kr; happy hour 8-11pm (500 kr beer/shots); BGLTQ+ friendly

HRESSÓ

Austurstræti 20; 101; 561 2240; www. hresso.is; open M-Th 9am-1am, Sa 10am-4:30am, Su 10am-1am

In America, people with man buns don't normally mix well with those who wear camo. At Hressó, the guys with man buns also wear camo. Hressó is a full-service restaurant during the day and a hot local venue at night. In the early hours of the evening, the courtyard is often bumping with locally produced hip hop mixtapes. After midnight, the party moves inside to a live DJ. It's a fantastic spot for feeling out the local scene or potentially scouting the next great Icelandic music star, but if you're after something upbeat, look elsewhere.

i No cover, beer 1250 kr, mixed drinks from 1650 kr; BGLTQ+ friendly

PRIKIÐ

Bankastræti 12; 101; 551 2866; www. prikid.is; open M-Th 8am-1am, F 8am-4:30pm, Sa 11am-4:30pm, Su 11am-1am

Don't be fooled by Prikið's daytime alter-ego of "oldest café in Iceland;" this place shines after dark (err, in the evening?). After the kitchen closes at 9pm, the tourists clear out and Prikið makes the typical Icelandic switch from coffee shop to late-night hangout. The DJ's loud hip hop selections keep the crowd casual, young, and quite local, and two bars and an outdoor courtyard provide ample space to mix, mingle, and marvel at the amount of sunlight present at 1am on a summer night. They also offer Jack Daniels-spiked milkshakes—marketed as a "hangover helper," we're not quite sure if it does what it says it does, or if it'll just add to your headache in the morning. Maybe one of their regular milkshakes will do the trick.

i No cover, mixed drinks from 1500 kr, happy hour 4-8pm (beers from 600 kr), burgers 2000kr; BGLTQ+ friendly

RING ROAD

Coverage by **Eric Chin**

"Hringvegur." "Þjóðvegur." "Route 1." Each of these names refers to the same 1332 kilometer stretch of asphalt and gravel winding its way in a lazy circle around Iceland. Most know it simply as the Ring Road.

Though its fame and popularity grow each year, a road trip on the Ring Road is still the ultimate way to experience as much of Iceland's raw beauty as you can at your own pace. Sure, a guide can explain what makes geysers erupt or why all the beaches have black sand, but no bus driver will pull off the road every 10 minutes to let you gawk at and photograph the newest scenery. Nor will any tour drive you through the most remote regions of the island least touched by society, like the East Fjords or the highlands of the north. Only getting behind the wheel yourself will enable you to immerse yourself in Iceland's glaciers and volcanoes, its black beaches and waterfalls, and its peaks and fjords.

But it won't be easy. You'll be jockeying with other tourists for the best photo angles one day and aching to see a fellow traveler the next. You'll cross a lifetime of one-lane bridges in a span of just days. You'll struggle to find accommodations priced so you can also afford to eat. The road will just wear you down. But if you want to have the adventure of a lifetime, it's all worth it. There's no better place and no better way. Here's how to do it.

BEFORE YOU GO

Renting a Car: If you're going to drive the Ring Road, you'll need a car—that much is non-negotiable. But you do have options. In the summer, when road conditions are good, just about any car will be suitable for the journey, and your cheapest option will be a subcompact. These tiny things are cheap to rent (under $500 for a week-long rental) and very fuel efficient. Here are a few technicalities:

- In order to rent a car in Iceland, you must be 20 years old and have held a valid driver's license for over a year. The minimum age for many companies is 21.
- Like in the United States, you will need a credit (not debit) card in the main driver's name.
- For any car rental, **make sure you have insurance. If your insurance does not cover you abroad, buy insurance.** This trip is long and hard on vehicles. Just get the insurance.
- Most cars in Iceland are manual transmission. Renting an automatic will probably be more expensive. (Get a friend to teach you to drive manual; it will save you a lot of money!)

Driving in Iceland: The vast majority of Route 1 is a paved, undivided highway with one lane traveling in each direction. Lanes are added near Reykjavík and in some larger towns. Most of the road has little or no shoulder, but there are frequent pull-offs where you can get out, stretch, and take pictures. One section of the Ring Road in East Iceland, and many of the roads branching off of Route 1, are gravel.

- Like in the United States, cars drive on the right side of the road in Iceland.
- The speed limit is 90 kph (about 56 mph) on paved roads and 80 kph (about 50 mph) on gravel roads.
- Your headlights must always be on and seatbelts are mandatory in all seats.
- Most towns have gas stations, but these can be few and far between, especially in the eastern region. Generally, refuel whenever your tank drops below half-full, but be warned: gas is expensive in Iceland—around $7 per gallon.

Navigation: The nice thing about driving on the Ring Road is that it's tough to get too lost; it's just one road! Okay, it's not quite that simple. While many stops are directly off Route 1, you will need to take other roads to get to some areas of the country. To avoid using international data (expensive) or renting a GPS (not worth it), the following strategy with Google Maps is usually plenty effective:

- Decide on your start/end points for the next day and star them in Google Maps.
- Star all the sights you might want to visit between those two points. Seriously, star everything!
- Google Maps will allow you download entire portions of maps for offline use. Download the area covering your two endpoints and the entire section of road in between. Most of Iceland is pretty empty, so downloads are generally a reasonable size.
- Most waterfalls, mountains, and other attractions are already labeled by name in Google Maps. If not, the coordinates can be looked up online and plugged in.

Accommodations: This is probably the piece of your trip that requires the most planning, and you have two basic options:

- **Camping.** There are designated campsites all over Iceland, allowing almost unlimited customization of your route. Campsites charge fees, but for 18900 kr the Camping Card (www.campingcard.is) gives you access to over 40 of these sites. If you don't want to lug your own gear all the way to Iceland, many companies in Reykjavík rent out tents, sleeping bags, and other supplies.
- **Not camping.** This is doable, but requires serious preparation to be cost-effective. True hostels are somewhat rare on the road, and the ones that exist aren't cheap. Failing hostels, Airbnb can be a good option, but be sure to book early.

Food: Eating out in Iceland is expensive, and it's no different on the road. To save money, it's a good idea to stock up on food in Reykjavík at Bónus or a similar discount store, as groceries are more expensive outside the city. If you're camping, it's not a bad idea to bring or rent a camp stove.

Trip Length: Driving the Ring Road is possible in five days, but only if you want to spend (even more) hours a day in the car, driving past beautiful sights you wish you could stop at. A week is more reasonable, allowing you to pull over and take photos when you want to, throw in a spontaneous extra stop or hike, and retain some semblance of sanity.

Packing: It probably shouldn't come as a surprise that a country called "Iceland" is cold. Summer temperatures often sit in the 50s during the day and can drop to the low 40s at night. If you plan on camping, thermal layers and a sleeping bag are a must. Rain is fairly frequent, and wind is almost constant outside Reykjavík, so a raincoat or light shell is a good idea, even if just to break the wind. A sturdy pair of hiking boots or shoes is also necessary.

Bring a friend! A solo trip of the Ring Road can be incredibly rewarding. It can also drive you insane. Going with a friend allows you to split up the driving, have some much-needed human contact during the loneliest times, and split the cost of the car, tent, campsite, and so on more effectively. Plus, Icelandic radio is great (if spotty in places), and you wouldn't want to have to sing along by yourself!

Iceland can be divided very roughly into six regions, one of which won't be covered here (the **Westfjords** are sparsely populated, tracked with rough roads, and seldom traveled). Here are the five regions of Iceland you should hit on your trip:

THE GOLDEN CIRCLE

The Golden Circle is, you guessed it, a circle. Starting from Reykjavík, it winds through West Iceland's landscape, hitting several of Iceland's most famous natural and historical landmarks before returning to the capital or continuing to other regions of the country. It's a logical first day for a Ring Road trip, but it can also be booked as a day trip through any of Reykjavík's tour agencies. The waterfalls and geysers are breathtaking, but be prepared to battle crowds all day.

SIGHTS

ÞINGVELLIR NATIONAL PARK

482 3613; www.thingvellir.is/english; visitor center open June-Aug 9am-8pm, Sept-Apr 9am-6pm

Þingvellir has something for everyone. History buffs will appreciate the fact that Iceland's parliament, the Alþing, was established here in 930 CE. Science and nature geeks will appreciate the fantastic natural phenomena created by Þingvellir's location on the edge of the North American and Eurasian tectonic plates. Everyone else will enjoy the easily accessible hiking trails that crisscross the park. For a truly unforgettable, if somewhat cold, experience, sign up for a tour to snorkel in Silfra, a crack between the tectonic plates found in Lake Þingvallavatn.

i Free admission, parking 500 kr per day; from Reykjavík, head north on Route 1 for about 35km. At traffic circle, turn right onto Þingvallavegur (Route 36), following signs for Þingvellir. Park will be about 30km on the right.

SILFRA

Þingvellir National Park

You don't have to be a scientist to know that tectonic plates are pretty damn big, and nowhere but Iceland gives you the chance to stand between them. In the **northern part of Lake Þingvallavatn** lies Silfra, a fissure between the North American and Eurasian plates. Water from a glacier melts and trickles through an underground aquifer of volcanic rock for decades before finally being released into the giant crack. The result is some of the clearest, purest water to be found anywhere on Earth. Oh, and it's also 2-4 degrees Celsius year-round, a temperature known in Iceland as "really fucking cold." But when has a little bit of glacial water stopped humans from appreciating the beauty of nature before, right? Your guides will layer you up in a puffy thermal suit before stuffing you into a thick drysuit. (Ever wondered what a hybrid of Iron Man and a marshmallow would be like? No? Well now you know.) It's hard not be anxious about the frigid waters, but once you're in, the view is all you'll be able to think about. The water is so clear and the colors so vibrant that it makes the air seem dull. The depths of Silfra are a deep blue, the jagged boulders that make up the walls of the tectonic plates seem to glow red and green, and the long strands of algae, affectionately called "troll's hair," stand out a vibrant green. The buoyant drysuits seal out the cold (er, mostly) and keep you afloat so you can enjoy the view as you drift through Silfra Hall and the majestic Silfra Cathedral (where the walls of the plates can reach 20 meters in depth) and end in the wide expanse of Silfra Lagoon. Head back to the parking lot (pro tip: keep your gloves on for this bit), where most tours will regroup with hot chocolate and cookies, or similar goodies.

i Book a tour in advance, most tours over 15000 kr, cheaper if you don't need transportation from Reykjavík

HAUKADALUR

Haukadalur is home to the famous Geysir. That's right, one of the first geysers known to Europeans, and the one that gave us the word "geyser" in the first place. Some sources say its spray can reach 80 meters high. Oh, and it's broken. Seriously, the Great Geysir has been dormant since the early twentieth century. Conveniently, though, a second geyser named Strokkur is right next door, and spouts to heights of 15- to 20 meters every five to ten minutes. The area also contains a number of steaming hot springs and fumaroles. When you can't bear the smell of rotten eggs anymore (nobody ever tells you how goddamn awful these things smell), head back to the visitor center, where you can join throngs of tourists at restaurants and peruse a gift shop.

i *From Þingvellir National Park, head northeast on Route 36. In 15km, stay straight onto Route 365. In 15 km, stay straight through roundabout onto Route 37, which becomes Route 35. Stay on Route 35 for 5 km and you'll arrive at Haukadalur.*

GULLFOSS

www.gullfoss.is

Gullfoss is the first of countless waterfalls you'll encounter along the Ring Road, and it starts things off with a bang. Easy hikes will take you from the parking lot to several viewpoints (ideal for picking the best Instagram angle). To hike the trail closest to the falls, bring raingear because the spray reaches high enough to soak the trail. Like every stop on the Golden Circle, Gullfoss is often overrun with tourists, but don't lose hope! You're driving the Ring Road! You'll leave these amateurs behind soon enough.

i *From Haukadalur, head east on Route 35 for about 9 km. Parking will be on your right.*

KERIÐ CRATER

Another great stop on the Golden Circle is Kerið Crater (55 km south of Gullfoss on Route 35), a collapsed volcano which now holds a strikingly blue lake. After touring the Golden Circle, spend the night in Reykjavík or at Midgard Adventure for a head start on the South Coast.

i *Admission 400 kr; from Gullfoss, drive 55 km south on Route 35, and the parking lot will be on the left.*

SOUTH COAST

The term "South Coast" most commonly refers to the region between Reykjavík and the southern city of Vík. This heavily traveled section of the Ring Road includes waterfalls, rock formations, and several of Iceland's famous sand beaches. Like the Golden Circle, tours of the south coast from Reykjavík are popular.

SIGHTS

SELJALANDSFOSS AND SKÓGAFOSS

Gullfoss was just the beginning. The south coast is home to these two popular waterfalls, each with a different claim to fame. At Seljalandsfoss, suit up in your raingear and take a very wet, if short, hike into a cave behind the pounding falls. Half an hour east is Skógafoss, where you can climb a man-made staircase to an aerial viewing platform. From here, you can escape the selfie stick-wielding crowd by taking a bit of a hike up the ridge for panoramic views of the ocean, snow-capped mountains, and, in all likelihood, a good number of sheep.

BLACK BEACH

Vík

It's a lot like any other beach you've ever visited, but the water is way too cold for swimming. Oh, and the sand is black, but you've probably figured that bit out by now. A good rule of thumb for any outdoor sight is that the farther you go from the parking lot, the fewer tourists you'll encounter, and it holds true here.

If you head all the way down the left side of the beach and around the point (accessibility changes based on the tide), you'll find another beach, just as beautiful, but significantly less crowded.

i *Take Route 215 from the Ring Road until you reach the beach parking lot.*

OTHER SIGHTS ON THE SOUTHCOAST

If you're looking for an incredible photo spot and are up for a hike, visit Sólheimasandur to see the wreckage of a United States Navy DC plane on the beach. If you plan on continuing around the Ring Road, try camping at Skaftafell Campground in Vatnajökull National Park, or finding other accommodations in the Skaftafell area.

EAST ICELAND

If you've made it this far, congratulations! Welcome to the solitude, the untamed wilderness, and the stunning beauty that is East Iceland. You've made it where even Reykjavík's endless tour buses can't reach. Just you, the sheep, and the road. And the road is glorious out here. It winds by the massive glacier Vatnajökull, past ethereal glacier lagoons, and through the majestic East Fjords. The drive is long and lonely, but you won't want to miss a mile.

SIGHTS

▨ VATNAJÖKULL NATIONAL PARK, SKAFTAFELL REGION

Route 998; 470 8300; www.vatnajokulsthjod-gardur.is/english; open Jan 10am-4pm, Feb-Apr 10am-5pm, May-Sept 9am-7pm, Oct-Nov 10am-5pm, Dec 11am-5pm

If you took up the mantle of driving the Ring Road, chances are you're into flannel, recycling, and nature. Well here's your big chance to get up close and personal with some of Iceland's best, all walkable from the Skaftafell visitor center. Svartifoss, a waterfall framed by sheer cliffs of columnar basalt, is one of the area's main attractions and a quick 5.5km loop. From there, trails feature every variation of length and difficulty, all the way up to a nearly-30km haul around the park. Another unforgettable (if a bit expensive) tour opportunity leaves right from the visitor center: a chance to hike on one of Europe's largest glaciers.

GLACIER HIKE

Vatnajökull National Park; tour leaves from Skaftafell

You've probably heard of glaciers before: they're basically just big ice cubes on mountains, right? But how big, exactly? Find out for yourself with this once-in-a-lifetime (seriously, they're disappearing at an alarming rate) chance to hike on one of Europe's largest glaciers, Vatnajökull. Included with your tour is a badass set of gear: crampons, ice axe, harness, and helmet (bring your own raincoat, rain pants, boots, food, and camera) to make you feel like the mountaineer you could never be. After a short bus ride and hike out to the tongue of the glacier, strap on your spikes and follow your guide up onto the ice. Oh right, the guides! They're incredibly friendly and knowledgeable about all things glacier, and each one carries an enormous, three-foot beast of an axe used to clear the trail. The path winds up the slope and down into crevasses (not "crevices;" this is the big leagues), some which are just a few feet wide. The longer, half-day tours go all the way up to the edge of the icefall, which is just as cool as it sounds—a jagged cliff of ice formed by chunks falling from the main glacier above. Your guide will show you arches and caves, as well as glacial clay—a fine black silt, reportedly excellent for the skin. Seriously, they sell mud masks of the stuff. Most tours will spend around 1.5 or 3.5 hours on the glacier itself, and it's impossible not to be awed and humbled by nature at its purest.

i Tours are frequent during the spring/summer season and generally start from about 10000 kr for 3-hour tours and 15000 kr for half-day tours.

JÖKULSÁRLÓN GLACIER LAGOON AND DIAMOND BEACH

About 50 km east of Skaftafell is Jökulsárlón Glacier Lagoon. It's basically a lake full of icebergs—big, scary, Titanic-sinking icebergs is what you're probably picturing. These are much more manageable, and unlike the Titanic, you can safely travel among them. Boat tours start at 5500 kr for large boats, or 9500 kr for a nimbler Zodiac. Just across the road from Jökulsárlón is Diamond Beach, a black-sand beach named for the tiny icebergs dotted across its shores like, well, diamonds. Walk among the smaller chunks higher on the beach; just don't try standing on them.

OTHER SIGHTS IN EAST ICELAND

The drive through the East Fjords is one of the most beautiful sections of the entire Ring Road, winding up the coast with sheer cliffs on one side and the vast ocean on the other. It's also the emptiest. The gravel roads are well-maintained, but use caution. Finding a place to spend the night out here can be tricky, so be creative. Your best bet is to look in the area around Alistair, the largest town in the region.

NORTH ICELAND

From Egilsstaðir, Route 1 turns west and away from the coast. You'll head up into the gorgeous highlands of Iceland's northeastern interior, before descending into the touristy Mývatn area.

SIGHTS

🏔 KRAFLA

If you're driving in from the east, this is the first big stop in the Mývatn region, and it's a can't-miss. Krafla is a volcanic crater (a caldera, to be pedantic) that still exhibits lots of geothermal activity, even though it hasn't actively erupted in a while. Yes, this sounds boring, but trust us, it's better for you that way. Check out Víti, another of those utterly-Instagramable crater lakes with impossibly blue water. The road leads right up to the edge, and it's a short hike around the lip of the crater. From the lower parking lot, a more substantial hike will take you to the Leirhnjúkur lava field. Walk among jagged spikes of cooled lava, many still spewing sulfurous steam, and look out over a milky blue hot spring.

HVERIR

Just past the road to Krafla is Hverir, a huge geothermal area that feels more like an artist's rendition of the surface of Mars than a naturally occurring landscape. Cracked yellow earth, bubbling pits of dark mud, and rock chimneys spewing steam so vigorously you can hear it all lie beneath the red mountain Námafjall. Great for a quick pit stop, but if you just can't get enough of the smell of rotten eggs (hey, no judgment) hike up Námafjall for an incredible view of the whole area.

MÝVATN NATURE BATHS

Office 464 4411; www.myvatnnaturebaths. is; open May 15-Sept 30 9am-midnight, Oct 1-May 14 noon-10pm

It would be a shame to come to Iceland and not bathe in one of the country's famed geothermal pools, but you also don't want to hurt your wallet or your reputation as a savvy traveler by going to the Blue Lagoon. Enter the Mývatn Nature Baths. It's like the Blue Lagoon's lowkey little brother who just wants to hang out. The warm, milky blue water gives you all the best parts of a hot tub without having to awkwardly squeeze yourself between wrinkly old men in "European-style" bathing suits. You know what we're talking about. It's certainly not a steaming pool out in the middle of the forest, but it's been a long trip. Don't you deserve a little pampering?
i Admission May 15-Sept 30 4300 kr, students 2700 kr, Oct 1-May 15 3800 kr, students 2400 kr, towel/swimsuit rental 700 kr each, bathrobe rental 1500 kr; last entry 30min. before close

OTHER SIGHTS IN NORTH ICELAND

The volcanic lake Mývatn was formed in the aftermath of an eruption, so it's no surprise that the surrounding landscape is rich in volcanic landforms like Dimmuborgir, a lava field with especially strange spires of rock, and the Skútustaðir pseudocraters, a field of craters formed not directly by volcanic eruptions, but by steam. Route 1 stays on the north side of the lake, while Route 848 loops around to the south before rejoining the main road. Akureyri, the first real city since Reykjavík, is a good spot to spend a night or two to recharge.

AKUREYRI

Akureyri's population of just under 20,000 people makes the city a thriving metropolis by Iceland's standards—the country's second-largest, in fact. It certainly doesn't have the attractions and landmarks of a major city, but it is an excellent spot to take a day to rest, resupply, and generally reconnect with civilization. There's a Bónus where you can restock on all your favorite Icelandic groceries at a reasonable (for Iceland, at least) price, and Akureyri Backpackers is an excellent hostel, with a restaurant and bar that serve as a hub for the whole town. Akureyri is the main tourist hub outside of Reykjavík, and some of the most popular offerings include whale watching and horseback riding.

ACCOMMODATIONS

🏨 AKUREYRI BACKPACKERS ($$)

Hafnarstræti 98, 600 Akureyri; +354 571 9050; www.akureyribackpackers.com; reception open M-F 7:30am-11pm, Sa-Su 7:30am-1pm (late check-in can be arranged)

They say that first impressions matter, and Akureyri Backpackers nails it by giving you a free drink at the bar when you check in. Everything that follows is similarly fantastic. The vibe is upbeat and energetic, the clientele tired from packed days yet adventurous and excited for what tomorrow will bring. Pro tip: stop by the tour desk to book a whale watch or super jeep trip. A prime location in the middle of "downtown" Akureyri (if such a thing exists) keeps the street-level restaurant and bar alive with a mix of backpackers and locals all day and into the evening. Akureyri, and indeed the entire north of Iceland, seems to live and breathe through this hostel.
i Dorms from 4500 kr, privates from 16000 kr; reservation recommended; Wi-Fi; BGLTQ+ friendly; pillow included but not duvet (1100 kr for whole stay); sleeping bags allowed; free sauna, continental breakfast buffet 1215 kr if booked in advance; laundry; security lockers

FOOD

DJ GRILL ($)

Strandgata 11, 600 Akureyri; 462 1800; open M-F 11:30am-9:00pm, Sa-Su noon-9pm

Sometimes the only thing to fill you up is a nice hot meal, especially if you've been pounding PB&Js on the road for the past few days. Whether you're in Akureyri for days or just a few hours, stop by Dj Grill for the greasy, delicious burger you've been dreaming of. A cheeseburger is just 690 kr, but you can add patties, toppings, and sides to bring the price into more familiar Icelandic territory. Just a short walk from the center of town, Dj Grill is also a convenient takeout spot, with locals popping in and out during dinner hours.
i Burgers from 690 kr, sides from 400 kr

SNÆFELLSNES PENINSULA

From Akureyri, it's a bit of a drive to the Snæfellsnes Peninsula, the last big stop on the Ring Road. Route 1 cuts inland a bit, only navigating one or two fjords before reaching Snæfellsnes. This area is sometimes called "Iceland in miniature" by various tour agencies, because it features many of Iceland's main attractions—waterfalls, volcanoes, beaches, and glaciers.

SIGHTS

🏔 KIRKJUFELL

Kirkjufell is one of the most photographed mountains in Iceland (that Dr. Seuss-like one that shows up in every search for "Iceland"). Sweet, sounds touristy, move on. Oh wait, you can climb it? Better switch out your fanny pack for a CamelBak—this is a proper adventure now. The ascent isn't long, but it's certainly not easy; the trail is ill-defined and without distinct markers, and features a fair bit of slippery scree on the way up. Oh, and the ropes. The locals have fixed (only slightly frayed) ropes to large boulders to help in the ascent and descent of three particularly dicey scrambles. If you're bold (or slightly stupid?) and reach the peak, the reward is huge. Though only 1500ft., a long ridge along the summit affords unobstructed views of the sea on one side and snow-capped mountains to the other.

i Park in Kirkjufellsfoss parking lot. Walk up the road toward Kirkjufell and turn right up a drive-way leading toward a few guesthouses. The trail heads up toward the front of the mountain before reaching the guesthouses.

🏔 RAUÐFELDSGJÁ

Fantasy novels abound with scenes of overgrown grottos buried deep under mighty mountains, but unless you're actually Gollum you've probably never been inside one. This is your chance. It's a huge fissure in the cliffs on the southern coast. Just inside the mouth of the gorge is a large, mossy chamber with plenty of standing room. Most people stop here, but if you're not afraid of a bit of water, the ravine goes much further. You may have to hike a bit through the shallow river and past a few bird carcasses, but eventually you'll find a waterfall you can climb with the help of, you guessed it, a sketchy rope! You'll get soaked, but you'll travel further into *Lord of the Rings* territory.

GATKLETTUR
Arnarstapi

Just minutes from Rauðfeldsgjá is the tiny fishing village of Arnarstapi, a town made relevant only by the fantastic rock formations carved out of its cliffs. The most famous, Gatklettur, is a huge, moss-covered stone arch, perpetually pummeled by waves on one side and flashbulbs on the other. Walk left along the paths to reach several smaller arches, which are not freestanding but part of the cliffs themselves. This means you can walk over them (cool!), but also that you can't actually get a good view of them (less cool). If the cliffs aren't enough, though, there's also a fish and chips food truck.

OTHER SIGHTS ON THE SNÆFELLSNES PENINSULA

Snæfellsnes has countless attractions beyond those listed here, including Snæfellsjökull National Park, where you can book a snowmobile or lava cave tour, the Lóndrangar rock pillars, and Skarðsvík Beach, a rare white sand beach. The Harbour Hostel, located in the town of Stykkishólmur on the northern coast of the peninsula, is an excellent place to stop for the night or to use as a base for an extra day of exploring.

This is the home stretch now! From Snæfellsnes, it's just a two-hour drive back to the capital. The road is busy in this last segment, and there's a tunnel under a fjord that requires a toll. But through the anticipation of arriving back in Reykjavík and returning to civilization for real, be sure to enjoy these last kilometers. Who knows what they'll look like if you ever return?

ICELAND ESSENTIALS

VISAS

Iceland is part of the Schengen Area, meaning that US citizens do not need a visa for visits of up to 90 days. Note that your passport should be valid for at least three months after your planned date of departure from the Schengen Area.

MONEY

Iceland's currency is the Icelandic króna, abbreviated as ISK officially and as kr locally. As an island, Iceland has to import a lot of goods, raising prices. The Icelandic króna has also gained strength in recent years relative to the dollar, driving prices even higher for American tourists. Long story short, this place is expensive!

Tipping: Tipping is not expected in Iceland. All prices, including at stores and on menus, include all service charges. That said, tipping is not rude or offensive, as is sometimes claimed. If you want to leave a tip for excellent service, more power (and an emptier wallet) to you.

Taxes: Bad news. Iceland's standard VAT rate is 24%. The rate is reduced to 11% for a number of relevant services, including hostel rooms, food, and travel agents. Taxes are always included in prices, so what you see is what you pay. You can have your VAT refunded for goods leaving the country with you, like souvenirs, as long as the total spent is over 6000 kr. You must present the goods for which you are claiming a refund, as well as the receipt from the time of purchase.

HEALTH AND SAFETY

Drugs and Alcohol: The legal drinking age in Iceland is 20. The only alcohol sold in grocery stores is low-alcohol beer (ABV 2.25% or below). Anything stronger can be purchased in state-owned liquor stores called Vinculin or at restaurants and bars. Drinking in the streets is legal and very common (especially on Friday and Saturday nights), being a drunken mess less so, you degenerate. Driving under the influence is a serious offense in Iceland. Drivers can be charged with a BAC as low as 0.05%. Just don't do it.

WEATHER AND CLIMATE

Iceland lies just south of the Arctic Circle, the implications of which are twofold. First, that means it's cold. Even in summer, temperatures rarely rise above the 60s. Second, it leads to the midnight sun. Through much of the summer, though the sun will set and rise (often just a few hours apart), it will never be truly dark. No matter how prepared you are for it, you may not get used to walking out of the bar at 1am into broad daylight.

LANGUAGE

Iceland's official language is Icelandic, but English is spoken almost everywhere. Avoid trying to pronounce Icelandic words at all costs. (Seriously, you'll just make a fool of yourself.) If you have to try and say a street name though, be aware that the non-English letters eth (Ð,ð) and thorn (Þ,þ) are both pronounced with a "th" sound, crudely speaking.

IRELAND

Ireland's hills hold thousands of years of history—yet the country only became independent in 1922. Most people know the classic images of lush emerald landscapes, and while those hills and mountains are part of Ireland's heart, there is much more to dive into. Rolling green countryside, craggy cliffs, and rocky hikes make up the nation's scenic landscapes, perfect for backpackers and nature lovers. The cities, far from being outdone by the natural world, are filled with books and music, melting pots of cultures once suppressed and now released. Of course, one can't talk about Ireland without mentioning the beer and whiskey that flow through its veins. (Is it a coincidence that both Guinness and Ireland use the harp as their symbol? We think not.) The Guinness, Jameson, and Teeling factories draw in those pining for a pint (or a shot), and the Cliffs of Moher and Connemara call out to those who would rather spend their life outdoors. Though today Ireland is mostly English-speaking, the people's Gaelic roots and traditions still shape the country's culture. (While you're here, try and learn a little Gaelic, if you can.) Ireland is more than its famed potatoes and Irish coffee: it is an island with spirit, a land of stories and tradition, a place where lore reigns true. The history still writes itself today, a merging of religion, arts, and good spirits, all splashed across the canvas of the country.

DUBLIN

Coverage by **Lucy Golub**

A mix of a modern big city and a quaint historical town, Dublin has everything you could ask for. The city still bears the scars of the country's fight for independence in 1919, so history buffs can find lots of places to see, stories to hear, and museums to explore. The city is the *queen* of literature, and you'll find many odes to great writers of the age in the names of streets, pubs, and museums. (And, of course, emblazoned on every tacky postcard in a tourist shop.) But this city doesn't live in the past. Today, it thrives, as shown by its new restaurants, bars, museums, arts, and nightlife. You won't run out of things to do, especially if you leave the tourist-filled central part and actually interact with locals. But embrace the live music, the old streets filled with new stores, and the Guinness. You're in Ireland's capital now.

ORIENTATION

Dublin is cut in half by the **River Liffey.** Today, the south side is considered more upscale, although this was not the case in the 1700s. The southern half includes tourist areas like **Temple Bar, Grafton Street, St. Stephen's Green,** and beyond that, **Portobello.** East of Temple Bar, you'll find the students that surround **Trinity College.** The north also has lots to see, like the **Garden of Remembrance** and the **Spire** and **O'Connell Street.** The sides of the river connect at many bridges, the most famous of which is called the **Ha'penny Bridge.**

ESSENTIALS

GETTING THERE

Dublin Airport is about 40min. from the city center via public transportation, and there are easy buses taking you right there. Take the Airlink (signs will direct you) to be dropped off at many of the key tourist areas. Tickets cost €7 one-way and €12 round-trip. Buses from other places in Ireland or Northern Ireland also have stops along the River Liffey, and the Irish Rail is another option.

GETTING AROUND

Dublin is very walkable, but if that's not an option for you, the city uses a bus system called Dublin Bus. The Transport for Ireland app can also be useful. Fares are €2-3. The tram system, Luas offers some mobility within the city as well, with Zone 1 tickets costing €2.10. Unlimited day tickets are also available for €7.20. They're supposedly working on an underground subway, as well. Until then, walking, buses, and Luas it is!

PRACTICAL INFORMATION

Tourist Offices: Dublin Visitor Center (17 O'Connell St.; 01 898 0700; www.dublinvisitorcentre.ie; open M-F 9am-5pm, Sa 9am-6pm, Su 9am-4pm)

Banks/ATMs/Currency Exchange: Banks and ATMs are all over and easy to find. Here's one: Ulster Bank (33 College Green; 01 702 5400; open M-Tu 9:30am-4:30pm, W 10am-4:30pm, Th-F 10am-4:30pm).

Post Offices: This post office has a special place in Dublin's history and can also send mail (O'Connell St.; 01 705 7000; www.anpost.ie; open M-Sa 8:30am-6pm).

Internet: Most restaurants and cafés have Wi-Fi, as do most stores.

BGLTQ+ Resources: Outhouse is a BGLTQ+ community center (105 Capel St.; 01 873 4999; www.outhouse.ie; open M-F 10am-6pm).

EMERGENCY INFORMATION

Emergency Number: 999 or 112

Police: Kevin Street Station (Kevin St. Upper; 01 666 9400; www.garda.ie; open daily 24hr)

US Embassy: US Embassy (42 Elgin Rd.; 01 668 8777; www.ie.usembassy.gov; open M-F 9am-5pm)

Rape Crisis Center: The national 24hr helpline can be reached at 1800 77 8888.
- Dublin Rape Crisis Center (70 Leeson St. Lower; 01 661 4911; www.drcc.ie; open M-F 8am-7pm, Sa 9am-4pm)

Hospitals:
- Beaumont Hospital (Beaumont Rd., Beaumont; 01 809 3000; open daily 24hr)
- St. James's Hospital (James's St.; 01 410 3000; open daily 24hr)

Pharmacies:
- Hickey's Pharmacy (55 O'Connell St.; 1873 0427; open M-F 8am-10pm, Sa-Su 9am-10pm)

ACCOMMODATIONS

◤ ABBEY COURT HOSTEL ($)

29 Bachelor's Walk; 01 878 0700; www.abbey-court.com; reception open 24hr

With a view of the **River Liffey** and **The Spire,** Abbey Court sits in the heart of Dublin's tourist center. Ensuite bathrooms and lockers make it easy to stay. They even have a hammock room where you can relax and an outdoor area complete with rainbow-patterned umbrellas to chill in—both of them right by the enormous kitchen where you can get your free breakfast. Our only complaint is a slight lack of plugs. But the price, the location, and the amenities will make your stay worth it.

i Dorms from €13.50; reservation recommended; no wheelchair accessibility; Wi-Fi; games room, laundry services, breakfast included; linens provided, towels for rent

GENERATOR HOSTEL ($$)

Smithfield Sq.; 1902 2222; www.generator-hostels.com/destinations/dublin; reception open 24hr

A mix of a chain hotel and hostel, Generator tries to create community through nightly events in its bar, but it ends up mostly catering to people traveling together. The hostel's 540 beds might intimidate a solo traveler, but hey, at least you're in the perfect environment to make friends. Many rooms have ensuite bathrooms; all have lots of plugs and lockers, and cleanliness

is clearly a priority. With no kitchen and a definite party vibe, however, backpackers looking for family-style accommodation or quieter quarters should probably steer clear. Young people looking to meet up with other groups and go out will find a throng of people to spend time with on evening pub crawls. You'll find the hostel in **Smithfield,** a quieter area of the city.

i Dorms from €14, private rooms from €50; reservation recommended; wheelchair accessible; Wi-Fi; female-only dorms available; laundry room; linens provided, towels for rent

KINLAY HOSTEL ($)

2-12 Lord Edward St.; 01 679 6644; www.kinlaydublin.ie; reception open 24hr

Located steps away from **Christchurch Cathedral** and near **Temple Bar,** the hostel's location puts you right near Dublin's key tourist attractions in an area that feels a little less touristy than across the river. Decorated with flags and featuring red- and green-colored walls, the hostel is huge, but a kitchen and common room create a smaller feel, making it feel welcoming. Free walking tours and a stocked game room complete our conception of an ideal hostel. If you get lucky, you might end up in one of the rooms with vaulted ceilings—how European. Contrast that with neon green bathrooms, and you've got an experience that blends the old and the new.

i Dorms from €15, weekends from €18, privates from €25; reservation recommended; max stay 28 nights; no wheelchair accessibility; Wi-Fi; free beverages; free walking tours; linens provided; towels and locks for rent

SIGHTS
CULTURE

◤ GUINNESS STOREHOUSE

St. James's Gate; 1408 4800; www.guinness-storehouse.com; open daily July-Aug 9am-8pm; Sept-June 9:30am-7pm

If you weren't already a Guinness expert from nights at the pub, here's your chance to become a professional. At the heart of the **world's largest pint-shaped building** lies all of the information you ever wanted to know about Guinness—

and more. Smell the barley roasting; feel the water; see the bubbles. This tour is as close to being inside a beer bottle as you can get. For the full experience, you can learn how to pour your perfect pint. They also teach you the best way to drink the beer (yes, this is a thing), samples included (hint: the Guinness-stache is a *must*). The skybar offers 360-degree views of the whole city, so even if you're not a beer drinker, it's worth it.

i Admission €20, students €18; prices lower if you book in advance; last entry 1hr before closing; wheelchair accessible; free drink with ticket

THE ABBEY THEATRE

26/27 Abbey St. Lower; 1878 7222; www.abbeytheatre.ie

The exterior doesn't reveal the Abbey's special place in Irish literary history, but, in fact, an exhibit at **The Writer's Museum** is devoted to this theater, founded in 1904 by **W.B. Yeats** and **Lady Gregory.** Controversy surrounds the opening of the theater: some works were banned for supposedly illicit content. *Scandalous.* Today, it sits in a city filled with other performance halls, and they perform a mix of classic Irish plays and new works. But the venue still seeks to bring theater to Ireland, and you should let it by going to see a show. We weren't allowed in, likely because rehearsals were happening, but read up on the history before you see a show to get the full experience.

i Early bird tickets from €10, regular tickets from €25, students from €16; wheelchair accessible

GEORGE'S ARCADE

George's St.; www.georgesstreetarcade.ie; open M-W 9am-6:30pm, Th-Sa 9am-7pm, Su noon-6pm

No city would be complete without a market selling vintage clothes, records, and … artisanal dried fruit? We weren't expecting this, but it's a market, so you're bound to find strange things that you never knew existed (but now desperately need). George's Arcade checks the above boxes and more. Grab a snack and stroll through the covered market, gawking at Irish tourist t-shirts and Italian food stalls. Many of the stalls are closed on Sundays, so your best bet is to avoid peak lunch hours during the week and stop

by in the afternoon. Nearby, boutiques like **Om Diva** sit along **Drury Street.** Window-shopping is likely the move here, as these stores tend to be expensive. Some of the vintage shops in the arcade have an occasional steal, though, so browse through denim jackets to your heart's content.

i Prices vary, wheelchair accessible

NATIONAL LIBRARY

Kildare St.; 1603 2300; www.nli.ie; open M-W 9:30am-7:45pm, Th-F 9:30am-4:45pm, Sa 9:30am-12:45pm

Picture enormous rooms of books and irritable people who shush you when you talk. That could only mean one thing: you're at a library. Home to the largest collection of Irish works in the world, Ireland's National Library stores the literary treasures of many a lifetime. Too bad you can't get past the front desk of the reading room unless you're a registered researcher—which is sad, because the room itself is painted a bright turquoise. You can, however, go in and look, explore the **Yeats** exhibit downstairs, or, if you have any Irish ancestry, stop by the family genealogy room to explore your roots. Lockers are available to store bags and coats (which they strictly enforce, so don't try to sneak anything in).

i Free; limited wheelchair accessibility; free lockers

TEMPLE BAR

47/49 Temple Bar; open 24hr

Step into *the* **Temple Bar** and prepare your ears. Live music rings out in this noisy bar at all hours of the day, and you'll hear more international accents than Irish ones. Temple Bar doesn't draw too many Dublin locals, and is more of a tourist watering hole, but that doesn't mean that you shouldn't at least drop in. Once you tire of the statue-filled beer bar, head out to the rest of the area. Whether you're on a pub crawl or just walking around, explore the nearby pubs and clubs, many of them complete with flowers in the windows and even more live music. You'll always have somewhere to go, and if you get lost, just follow the music (and the tourists).

i Prices vary; limited wheelchair accessibility

LANDMARKS

🏛 DUBLIN CASTLE

Dame St.; 1645 8813; www.dublincastle.
ie; open M-Sa 9:45am-4:45pm, Su noon-
4:45pm

We'll rip off the Band-Aid—you won't
find princes or princesses in this castle,
but you will find gorgeous apartments
and inauguration chambers. Basically
all of Ireland's history of governance has
taken place in this building. You could
take a guided tour, but we recommend
exploring on your own with the help of
the pamphlet they give you. And if you
happen to overhear bits of the person
leading the guided tour… well… you
can't help what your ears hear. Make sure
you look up! The intricately decorated
ceilings await. While here, you'll also
get to see a throne in the middle of a
city. While visiting, stop by the **Chester
Beatty** library.
i Admission €7, students €6; guided tours
€10, students €8; tours roughly every hour;
last entry 30min. before closing; wheelchair
accessible

CHRISTCHURCH CATHEDRAL

Christchurch Pl.; 1677 8099; www.christ-
churchcathedral.ie; open Jan-Feb M-Sa
9:30am-5pm, Su 12:30pm-2:30pm; Mar
M-Sa 9:30am-6pm, Su 12:30pm-2:30pm
and 4:30-6pm; Apr-Sept M-Sa 9:30am-7pm,
Su 12:30pm-2:30pm and 4:30pm-7pm; Oct
M-Sa 9:30am-6pm, Su 12:30pm-2pm and
4:30pm-6pm; Nov-Dec M-Sa 9:30am-5pm,
Su 12:30pm-2:30pm

At first, Christchurch Cathedral seems
like just another church. And then you
walk in and realize it *is* just another
church. Except it's a church with
hidden features that make it worth
exploring despite the price tag. It
might not be as impressive as some
of the larger European churches
at first glance, but you'll have to
walk around to fully appreciate
the gilded portraits and the
history. The cathedral has stood
in Dublin for over 1000 years,
and its nooks and crannies
contain books and small
paintings that can be easily
overlooked by rushed tourists
in a hurry to see the next thing
on their must-see list. If you can,
take one of the guided tours so

you get to explore the crypt (featuring
lots of gold plates and some mummified
animals). You might as well check out
the **Dublinia** next door, where they sell
combined tickets.
i Self-guided tour €7, students €5.50;
guided tours €11, students €9.50; cash only;
tours M-F 11am, 12:10pm, 2pm, 3pm, 4pm;
tours Sa 2pm, 3pm, 4pm for €4; last entry
45min. before closing; wheelchair accessible

GARDEN OF REMEMBRANCE

Parnell Sq. East; 1821 3021; open daily
8:30am-6pm

Mosaics of rusted weaponry line the
bottom of this cross-shaped pool, an
ode to a tradition symbolizing the end
of battle. This pool acts as a centerpiece
for this tranquil garden in the middle of
the city. Grassy elevated areas surround
the recessed pool in the Garden of
Remembrance, an area built to honor
those who lost their lives in the 700-year
fight for freedom. This fight ended
so recently that Ireland still bears the
wounds of battle. Stop by to pause and
to reflect, and be sure to check out the
statue at the top of the cross depicting
the myth of the Children of Lir. When
the Queen of England visited Ireland,
the first British monarch to do so, she
commemorated the men and women
who had fought against her own people.
i Free admission; wheelchair accessible

THE SPIRE

O'Connell St.; open daily 24hr

Lost? Look up. If you see a 120-meter (that's almost 400 feet) giant silver shiny needle, congrats! You've found the spire. Built in 2003 after the demolition of Nelson's monument, the spire makes a point about Ireland's transformation. You can't do anything except look at the big, pointy stick, but it's a pretty cool landmark to get a view of, especially at night. You can even see it from some points across the **River Liffey.** Fitting, as some locals call this baby the "Stiffy on the Liffey." Most likely, your Dublin explorations will bring you past the Spire, but if not, make it a point (gotcha again!) to see it.

i Free; limited wheelchair accessibility

TRINITY COLLEGE

College Green; 1896 1000; www.tcd.ie; open M-Sa 8:30am-5pm, Su 9:30am-5pm

Then-Queen of England, Elizabeth I founded Trinity college in 1592. Almost 500 years later, the college still holds some of the world's brightest minds. You can walk around on the green and sit, but in order to go inside, you'll have to take a pricey student-led guided tour. Probably more compelling, the tour lets you see the **Book of Kells,** an ancient book containing the four Gospels. Time it right and you can check out the cricket team practicing on the field. It's like it's a real school or something! But definitely go inside—otherwise it just feels like a park.

i Free, guided tour and Book of Kells €14, students €13; tours daily every 20min. from 9am-4pm; wheelchair accessible

MUSEUMS

🏛 EPIC

CHQ Custom House Quay; 1906 0861; www.epicchq.com; open daily 10am-6:45pm

If you only have time for one museum during your trip, then this is the one to visit. Once the friendly staffer hands you your "passport," you're free to explore the world of the museum and collect a stamp in each room. If you've ever wanted to learn about the influence of Irish emigrants in every single aspect of your daily life, then you've come

to the right place. Irish emigrants developed vaccines, starred in Broadway shows, and championed athletic events. Integrating interactive displays that feel like toys with important messages about Irish culture, EPIC's museum experience is truly epic. Seriously. Stop reading and go to this museum.

i Admission €14, students €12; last entry 5pm; wheelchair accessible

DUBLINIA

St. Michaels Hill; 1679 4611; www.dublinia.ie; open daily Mar-Sept 10am-6:30pm, Oct-Feb 10am-5:30pm

Ever wanted to know that the Vikings used moss as toilet paper? Neither did we. But you can learn that, and more, at this interactive museum. The first floor teaches visitors about the Vikings, and you can even dress up like a Viking wearing chainmail if that floats your boat. Upstairs, you can explore medieval Irish life through lifelike mannequins with leprosy and a scale model of Dublin in 1500. The third floor contains an archaeology lab where you can practice carbon dating. Then head on up to the tower with a view of Dublin. This museum has a little bit of everything, but don't let that deter you. Yeah, this museum's pretty weird, but it's kind of like popping a pimple: there's a lot of gross stuff going on here, and yet, you'll still want to keep going.

i Admission €9.50, students €8.50; last entry 1hr before closing; wheelchair accessible except the tower; combined ticket with Christ Church Cathedral available

NATIONAL GALLERY

Merrion Sq. West; 1661 5133; www.nationalgallery.ie; open M-W 9:15am-5:30pm, Th 9:15am-8:30pm, F-Sa 9:15am-5:30pm, Su 11am-5:30pm

Almost 700 paintings dating from the fourteenth century to the present fill this museum. Sounds like a lot of art. Which it is, but the layout makes it manageable and even fun to walk through. The building reopened in 2017 after years of refurbishment, and the result is a spacious gallery with lots of light, making it relaxing to explore. Highlights include the Irish Stained Glass exhibit and some of the greats on the 3rd floor like **Rembrandt, Vermeer,** and **Caravaggio.** Since it's around the corner from the **National Museum,** you might as well pop in and leave just a touch more cultured.

i Free; wheelchair accessible

NATIONAL MUSEUM OF IRELAND (NATURAL HISTORY MUSEUM)

Merrion St. Upper; 1 677 744; www.museum.ie/Natural-History; open T-Sa 10am-5pm, Su 2pm-5pm

Taxidermy enthusiasts rejoice! Here you can find two very packed floors of stuffed animals. Upstairs holds the animals native to Ireland. (Hint: there are a *lot* of birds and deer.) As you walk through different species of baboons interspersed with opossum babies and other rodents whose names we definitely can't pronounce, you'll marvel at the world's biodiversity and wonder how many species the earth *actually* has. This museum has occasionally been called the Dead Zoo. (You can imagine why.) Although the specific Dublin connection isn't all that clear, stepping foot inside feels like entering a very climate-confused jungle. Just go with it.

i Free entry; limited wheelchair accessibility

DUBLIN WRITERS MUSEUM

18 Parnell Sq.; 18722077; www.writersmuseum.com; open M-Sa 9:45am-4:45pm, Su 11am-4:30pm

A literary fanatic's heaven, Dublin Writers Museum boasts the history of Ireland's most prolific writers, with artifacts from their lives and panels describing their accomplishment. You're better off coming to this museum if you've already got some interest in literature or poetry—the exhibits aren't particularly interactive as much as they are informative. But hey, when in Dublin, a **UNESCO city of literature,** start cultivating your appreciation for literary greats like **James Joyce, George Bernard Shaw,** and **W.B. Yeats.** Plus, there's a little garden and some grand decorated rooms filled with—you guessed it—books.

i Admission €7.50, students €6.30; last entry 4:15pm; no wheelchair accessibility; free audio guide with entry

OUTDOORS

ST. STEPHEN'S GREEN

St. Stephen's Green; 1475 7816; www.ststephensgreenpark.ie; open M-Sa 8am-sunset

Dublin's a busy city—cars honk, people yell, pedestrians go places. But step into this green oasis for a moment's rest, and walk along the outer circle to get a moment of peace—here, the faint murmurs of moving cars get washed out by chirping birds and laughing kids. This park was central to parts of **The Rising,** which you can learn more about by walking around and seeing the statues. Or, you can just look at the statues as you go on a nice long romantic walk. In summer, people picnic in the park until the cops shoo them out at night (Ireland has pretty lax open container laws).

i Free; wheelchair accessible

FOOD

LEO BURDOCK ($)

4 Crown Alley; 1 611 1999; www.leoburdock.com; open M noon-8pm, Tu-W noon-11pm, Th noon-midnight, F-Sa noon-3am, Su noon-midnight

If the sign listing the 100+ celebrities who have dined at the iconic fish and chips shop is any indication, Leo Burdock's is basically a rite of passage. The menu lists only a few options—fish, chips, chicken, and burgers. Fishing and beach gear cover the walls in the back, somehow both touristy and traditional. Burdock's knows they're the best, so they make sure you can read all about their accolades. The price might seem steep until an entire steaming, freshly fried fish and a *box* of french fries appear before your eyes. And on weekend nights, when the drunchies come calling, Burdock's has your back until 3am.

i Entrées from €7; limited wheelchair accessibility

CORNUCOPIA ($$)

19-20 Wicklow St.; 1677 7583; www.
cornucopia.ie; open M-Sa 8:30am-10pm, Su
noon-10pm

Your parents always told you to eat
more vegetables. At this charming and
quaint restaurant, you can eat your
vegetables while feeling like you're at
Grandma's kitchen table. Soft floral
patterns and light colors provide a super
homey atmosphere that can be hard
to find while traveling. No Wi-Fi and
shared tables complete the farmhouse
grandparent and hipster convergence
vibe. Vegetarians and vegans: you're in
luck. We especially recommend coming
for breakfast, because here, the classic
Irish breakfast has gotten a makeover.
(Veggie sausage anyone?) And meat
eaters, you're gonna be alright. The food
is so hearty you won't even notice your
lack of animal flesh.

i *Breakfast from €6, lunch from €9, dinner
from €13; gluten-free, vegan, and vegetarian options available; limited wheelchair
accessibility*

GOOSE ON THE LOOSE ($)

2 Kevin St. Lower; 86 152 9140; open M-F
8:30am-5pm, Sa-Su 9am-5pm

Step inside and come face to face with
a goose in goggles, hanging from the
ceiling, standing between you and a
kitchen that perfectly mastered the art
of crêpe-making. Locals frequent this
all-day breakfast joint, so you know
this place is onto something. Close to
St. Stephen's Green, you can start your
day with a hefty (and not crazily priced)
omelette—or a Nutella-and-ice cream
crêpe (if we're being honest) then head
over to the park for a nice walk. We've
just planned the perfect date. You're
welcome.

i *Entrées from €4; gluten-free and vegetarian
options available; limited wheelchair accessibility*

NOLITA ($$)

64 South Great George St.; 01 478 1590;
www.nolita.ie; open M-Th noon-11:30pm,
F-Sa noon-2:30am, Su noon-11:00pm

If you're seeking something hip and
trendy (Would hip and trendy people
use those words? We're not sure.) look
no further than NoLIta. This New
York-inspired restaurant and bar will
make you feel like you're on *Gossip Girl.*

Except in Dublin, not the Upper East
Side. Anyway, the cocktails are amazing.
And if you don't see something you like,
ask away—the bartenders know their
way around the liquor cabinet. Later at
night on the weekends when they stop
serving food, the place gets a lot clubbier.
The pasta portions are shockingly huge
for a nice place, so leave room for the
cheesy goodness. Upstairs you can chill
in charming-yet-cool garden and discuss
how elegant you are now.

i *Entrées from €14, cocktails from €11,
drinks from €5.50; cash only; limited wheelchair accessibility*

PÓG ($$)

32 Bachelors Walk; 18783255; www.ifancy-
pog.ie; open M-F 8am-5pm, Sa 9am-5pm,
Su 10am-5pm

Crowded and bright, Póg's all-day
brunch creates healthier versions of
your favorite breakfast foods with a
vegan focus. And everything is perfectly
plated—in fact, the whole restaurant
is adorable. The millennial pink plates
contrast Insta-perfectly with the floor's
turquoise tiles. Their vegan fruit plate
draws eyes and cameras from the
restaurant-goers. Don't worry about
other people judging you: you gotta do
what you gotta do for that #fire pic. If
you've got a bit of a sweet tooth, the
protein pancakes come with your choice
of toppings ranging from Nutella to
berries to white chocolate chips. The
description on the menu doesn't include
how awesome the design-your-own
pancakes are, so you're gonna have to
trust us. Or stick with the green eggs (no
ham) and call it a day.

i *Entrées from €9, smoothies from €5; vegan
and vegetarian options available; limited
wheelchair accessibility; sharing tables
40min. max during peak hours*

NIGHTLIFE

☒ P.MAC'S

30 Stephen St. Lower; 14053653; open
M-Th noon-midnight, F-Sa noon-1am, Su
noon-11:30pm

The place is on fire—both literally
and figuratively. Here, you'll find red
candles dripping wax all over the tables
(be careful not to leave the candelabras
too close to the walls… trust us).
P.Mac's combines weird decorations,

board games, vaguely metal music, and a killer selection of craft beers to become the kind of place where last call actually makes you sad. They serve a grapefruit beer (one of many varieties) and have an arcade game on the way to the bathroom. It's hard to categorize the vibe, but it's not your typical stuffy pub full of old men drinking Guinness. Instead, you might find a hotel guest snacking away at the bar, mingling with a group of musicians, and pondering the beer choices. It's eclectic in the best way possible.

i No cover, drafts from €7; BGLTQ+ friendly; wheelchair accessible

DICEY'S GARDEN CLUB

21-25 Harcourt St.; 1478 4841; www.russellcourthotel.ie/diceys-garden; open M-Sa 4:30pm-2am

You just turned 21 and want to hit the dance floor to club remixes of your favorite 40 songs (otherwise known as Top 40 hits). Oh, do we have just the place for you. Dicey's ridiculous drink specials that change daily and (tbh) killer pop tunes make it a fun place to dance and get rowdy. You likely won't meet your future spouse here, but you can still meet people if you dance in the courtyard or order food from the grill. One thing to note: the bouncers really don't play. But as long as you don't show up smashed (that's what Tuesday's €1.50 pints and Jägerbombs are for) and don't try and bring your drink into the bathroom, you should be all set. Some people report being able to get around the age limit. (Whether you want to try for yourself is up to you.)

i Cover €10, daily drink specials from €2, cocktails from €8; limited wheelchair accessibility; Su-Th age 20+ only, Sa age 21+ only

37 DAWSON STREET

37 Dawson St.; 1902 2908; www.37dawsonstreet.ie; open M noon-11:30pm, T-Su noon-3am

When you walk in to the whiskey bar, you will immediately come face to face with a life-size sparkly zebra. Seems legit. Random but luxurious decorations adorn the walls and seating areas, including enormous anatomical posters, neon lights (#trendy), and lamps shaped like dogs. It somehow all blends together to feel like a cool-kids-only club—except their age limit is usually 23 and up. So it's a cool-twentieskids-only club? On some weekends, the back lounge opens up for only the most elite, but if you can sweet talk your way in, you'll find an intimate, dark space where every detail has been thought through, and though it's hard to explain why, the pieces just fit.

i Pints from €6; cash only; BGLTQ+ friendly; wheelchair accessible; age 23+ some nights

THE HAIRY LEMON

41-42 Stephen St. Lower; 1671 8949; www.thehairylemon.ie; open M-Th 11:30am-11:30pm, F-Sa 11:30am-1:30am, Su noon-11pm

There's no shortage of pubs to choose from in this city—if you threw a Guinness can at a random wall, you'd likely hit one (but don't do that). There's a reason The Hairy Lemon is filled with locals and packed tables, and it's not the appetizing name. For one, the Teeling whiskey taster lets you sample all your favorite whiskeys, if you can even tell the difference. The outdoor garden and smoking area also draw people to the bar. Mostly, the real attraction is the relaxed atmosphere where you can watch the game, have a meal, and sip on a pint in a true Irish pub.

i Drinks from €6; no wheelchair accessibility; live music Sunday nights

GALWAY

Coverage by **Lucy Golub**

People sometimes call Galway the graveyard of ambition, a moniker locals hold near and dear. The true meaning of the phrase isn't as morbid as you think it is, though. It actually means that people intend to come for a little while, but often end up staying. Rain or shine, Galway sucks you in and holds you captive. There's not much to do or that much to see, but, for some reason, visiting makes you want to stay forever. Only those who commit themselves to exploring this enchanting town the way those who live here do can understand why everyone seems so freaking happy. After a few nights at the pub with live music singing *Piano Man* with a group of strangers and a day "sparching" like the locals by the Spanish arch, you'll slowly fall in love with Galway. You might not notice it happen. But just wait. Soon when you look at the colorful façades of the very short Long Walk, you'll feel your heart swell just a touch and you'll know that Galway is part of you now.

ORIENTATION

The River Corrib splits the city. On the east of the river, you'll find the **Latin Quarter, Eyre Square,** and most of the tourist accommodations. To the West, the aptly named **West End** calls your name with its low-key restaurants and pubs. Along the river, a lovely walk takes you to the **Galway Cathedral,** past the university. If you ever get lost, just find **Galway Bay** to lead you back to the **Spanish Arch,** the beginning of **The Latin Quarter** and site of the **Galway City Museum.** The entire city is within reach of the river, though, because it's all so small.

ESSENTIALS

GETTING THERE

You can fly into nearby Shannon Airport or Knock Airport, but Dublin Airport is also an option. From each airport, take an easy bus transfer via Bus Éireann (from Shannon or Knock) or GoBus or Citylink (Dublin). You can pay on board, but the best fares come from booking early. Buses run at least once an hour and often every 30min. Galway Coach Station is a few steps from the center of the city, meaning the buses drop you off in the center of the action.

GETTING AROUND

Galway is a walkable city. The center is made up of a few easy-to-navigate streets. Otherwise, a bus service called Bus Éireann runs between Eyre Square and Salthill and other areas of Galway. Fares are between €2 and €3 depending on distance, and all-day tickets can be purchased for €4.70.

PRACTICAL INFORMATION

Tourist Offices: The Galway Tourist Office (Forster St.; 091 537 700; www.galwaytourism.ie; open M-Sa 9am-5pm)

Banks/ATMs/Currency Exchange: AIB ATM (18 Eyre Sq.; open 24hr)

Post Offices: An Post (3 Eglington St.; 091 534 727; www.anpost.ie; open M-Sa 9am-5:30pm)

Public Restrooms: (Eyre Sq.; open 24hr)

Internet: Most restaurants and cafes have Wi-Fi. Banks and other public spaces have available Wi-Fi networks that are easy to find.

BGLTQ+ Resources: Teach Solais LGBT+ Resource Center (Victoria Pl.; www.amachlgbt.com; open W 6pm-9pm, Sat 2pm-4pm); helpline at 1890 929 539

EMERGENCY INFORMATION

Emergency Number: 999
Police: Galway Garda Station (Mill St.; 091 538 000; www.garda.ie)

Rape Crisis Center: Galway Rape Crisis Center (Forster Ct.; 091 564800; www.galwayrcc.org); helpline available 800 355 355 (call M-F 10am-1pm)

Hospitals:
- University Hospital: Newcastle Rd; 091 524 222; open daily 24hr

Pharmacies: Galway doesn't have any 24hr pharmacies.
- University Late Night Pharmacy (1-2 University Halls; 091 520 115; open M-F 9am-9pm, Sat 9am-6:30pm, Su noon-6pm)
- Walsh's Pharmacy (Corrib Shopping Centre; 091 561 605; open M-W 9am-6pm Th-F 9am-8pm, Sa 9am-6pm, Su 11am-6pm)

ACCOMMODATIONS

🏠 GALWAY CITY HOSTEL ($$)

Eyre Sq.; 091 535878; www.galwaycityhostel.com; reception open 6am-3:30am

Perfect for solo travelers, Galway City Hostel understands the meaning of family-style, with daily events that encourage socializing. Before you know it, you'll have made best friends after sharing a €2 dinner and going on a pub crawl led by one of the hostel's entertaining and experienced volunteers. Free breakfast with fresh Irish soda bread and a social common area encourage mingling in the mornings for those less inclined to bar-hop at night. The pod-style beds feature curtains, plugs, and USB ports that almost let you forget you're staying in a room with a bunch of strangers. Almost. Fortunately, the travelers you'll meet at this hostel will turn your dorm room into a home.

i Dorms from €22; reservation recommended; min stay 2 nights starting F or Sa; BGLTQ+ friendly; no wheelchair accessibility; Wi-Fi; laundry facilities €8.50; towels €2; free printing

BARNACLES HOSTEL ($)

10 Quay St.; 91 568644; www.barnacles.ie; reception open 24hr

Barnacles Hostel is a labyrinth. Literally. Narrow hallways snake up and down multiple staircases in this 400-year-old building, making it almost impossible to find your way around. You'll probably find the kitchen since they have a pancake machine available for use—and breakfast is free. The rooms are nothing special and nothing terrible—they're a little cramped, but clean, and feature ensuite bathrooms. Surrounded by stores in the middle of the **Latin Quarter,** the hostel could not be more centrally located, but the noise of the streets can't be ignored. Overall, the rooms win no prizes, but the communal spaces and kitchen combined with its location make Barnacles a very solid bet.

i Dorms from €14, privates from €50; reservation recommended; no wheelchair accessibility; Wi-Fi; laundry; linens provided; locks and towels for rent

KINLAY ($$)

Merchants Rd., Eyre Sq.; 91 565244; www.kinlaygalway.ie; reception open 24hr

Kinlay's huge common rooms, cool murals, and fish tanks make it super social, even if the size of the building can intimidate those traveling alone. If you're coming with friends, Kinlay should be your #1 stop. Sister hostels with **Galway City Hostel,** the two do their nightly pub crawls together. The dorms upstairs are larger, while those downstairs have pod beds and ensuite bathrooms. The rooms are cleaned daily, the location is awesome, and the staff are fun as well. You really can't go wrong!

i Dorms from €21, privates from €88; cash only; reservation required; BGLTQ+ friendly; wheelchair accessible rooms available; Wi-Fi; laundry service €8.50; linens provided

SIGHTS
CULTURE

🏠 LATIN QUARTER

www.thelatinquarter.ie; neighborhood open daily 24hr; store hours vary

So we'll just get this out of the way: the Latin Quarter isn't Latin. It is, however, adorable. Old-fashioned pubs crop up between coffee shops, *Claddagh* jewelers, tourist trap-y souvenir shops, and upscale boutiques. You won't find too many locals spending time with the musicians playing guitar in the street singing "Galway Girl" or doing some Irish dancing. But at night, the area comes alive when throngs of people descend on the area to pub-hop in

like those by **George Bernard Shaw** and **W. B. Yeats**. Or you might feel like you're barely literate as you browse through Irish history sections detailing events and historical figures you probably haven't heard of. Either way, it's easy to get lost in the stacks of books, some of them even spilling off shelves and tables. If you're not sure what you want to read, check out the recommendation section towards the front. You might just leave with your new favorite novel.
i Book prices vary

LANDMARKS

🏛 SPANISH ARCH

2 The Long Walk; open daily 24hr

This arch is the last remaining part of a medieval wall, built in 1270, that once circled the city. It's neither big nor tall, but it reminds you of Galway's history—torn down and suppressed yet still standing. The Spanish Arch label, according to the locals, also extends to the nearby grassy areas along the **River Corrib,** and gets truncated to "Sparch." "Sparching" is a local tradition dating back hundreds of years which entails drinking (non-alcoholic beverages, of course) on the grass on a nice day. So, clearly, the Spanish Arch holds history both old and new.
i Free; wheelchair accessible

EYRE SQUARE

Eyre Sq.; open daily 24hr

The official name for the park is **Kennedy Park** due to JFK's visit to Galway in 1963. That was 50 years ago but okay, sure. Next to the park, a large rusty sculpture that supposedly looks like the Galway Hooker (a *fishing boat*, obviously), stands along your way to the **Latin Quarter.** In summer, you can't miss the bubble man, who dips ropes in soap to make giant bubbles that pop around the flags representing the 14 Galway Tribes, the families who contributed to the city's beginnings. Even when the weather is cooler people still congregate at this central point to walk their dogs, grab a pint at a bar, or just pass through.
i Free; limited wheelchair accessibility

search of the best live music. Yes, it's super touristy, but if you embrace it you'll enjoy it, and The Latin Quarter is definitely part of Galway's charms.
i Establishment prices vary

ATHENRY ANTIQUES

Sheehan House, Church St.; 086 600 8886; www.athentryantiques.ie; open T-Sa 10am-6pm

Yeah, we know, antiques can be boring. But this store's not. Come in to explore old rugs, vaguely creepy dolls, and memorabilia from World War I, including postcards sent bearing the SS seal. The woman who runs the shop has been there for 12 years, and her stories alone are reason enough to enter the store. The old photos and antique lighters in the back room, however, are relics of another time. When you step across the store's threshold, the smell of old books snakes up your nostrils and transports you to the past. Embrace it.
i Prices vary

CHARLIE BYRNE'S BOOKSHOP

Cornstone Mall, Middle St.; 9156 1766; www.charliebyrne.com; open M-Sa 9am-6pm, Su noon-6pm

Entering this massive bookshop could go one of two ways: you might feel enlightened by the thousands of books surrounding you, including Irish greats

GALWAY CATHEDRAL

River Corrib West Bank; www.galwaycathedral.ie; open daily 8:30am-6:30pm

This cathedral's marble floors and enormous walls forming the shape of a cross around a central marble pew almost make you forget that this church was built in the '60s. And by the '60s, we mean the 1960s, not the 1560s. In case you forget what time period you're in, the circular mosaic portrait of former president **John F. Kennedy** on the wall in the side chapel, next to a larger-than-life mosaic of Jesus's resurrection, will remind you. While the church isn't old, it is a beautiful work of architecture, and as music wafts from the speakers mounted on the walls, you can explore the wall panels explaining the church's history.

i Free; wheelchair accessible; services held weekdays 9am, 11am, 6pm and Su 9am, 10am, 11am, 12:30pm, 6pm

MUSEUMS

GALWAY CITY MUSEUM

Spanish Parade; 91 532460; www.galwaycitymuseum.ie; open T-Sa 10am-5pm; open Easter Sunday to Sept Su noon-5pm

Picture this: you're hanging out by the **Spanish Arch** and it starts to rain. You could go back home and get in bed, or you could pop into this free museum to learn about the history of Galway, Irish fishing, the Galway Hooker, and marine biology. Some artifacts of note include those lying in the glass cabinets at the center of each room. The panels along the wall explain oft-forgotten history like the **Irish Civil War.** For a history junkie, you'll find lots of things to explore. For someone looking for a game, check out the interactive submarine simulation upstairs. Thank us later.

i Free; wheelchair accessible

FOOD

🍽 THE PIE MAKER ($-$$)

10 Cross St. Upper; 91 513151; www.thepiemaker.ie; open daily 11:30am-10pm

Apple pie? Yum. Banoffee Pie? Yesss. Slow braised beef and eight degree stout pie? Yes—trust us on this one. This shop sells one type of food: pies. And they're fantastic. Savory pies can be ordered with either classic mash and mushy peas, or

(for the health conscious) a salad. But if you're eating at a pie place, we're not really sure that you're in the right place for a healthy meal. Regardless, the flaky crust and flavorful combination of ingredients make this classic Irish food a must-eat. The restaurant is tiny, surrounding you with the smell of freshly baked pies while random mirrors and candelabras emphasize just how *quirky* the store is.

i Sweet pies from €5, savory pies from €13; vegan options; wheelchair accessible

DELA ($)

51 Lower Dominick St.; 91 449252; www.dela.ie; open M-Th 11:30am-3pm and 6pm-10pm, F-Sa 10am-3pm and 6pm-10pm, Su 10am-4pm and 6pm-10pm

On every wood table in this airy and plant-decorated restaurant, there's a pamphlet advertising their **polytunnel,** aka a huge plastic tube in which the owners grow all their produce. So you know that this restaurant's food is super fresh. It also tastes delicious, and with extensive brunch hours, you can't come to Galway and *not* brunch here. The hashtag written on every chalkboard is #notallbrunchesarecreatedequal and we'd have to agree, because this meal was one of the best. The butterscotch pancakes are to die for, as is the adorable farm-house type aesthetic.

i Entrées from €9; vegan and vegetarian options available; wheelchair accessible

THE DOUGH BROS ($)

1 Middle St.; 087 176 1662; open M noon-9pm, Tu-Sa noon-10pm, Su noon-9pm

The Dough Bros started out as a food truck, and the counter at the back of the restaurant makes sure you don't forget it. A floral arch adorns the door, and a long line of hungry people greets you on the inside. This pizza is absolutely worth the wait if you want something like the Hail Caesar pizza. Cheaper than Domino's (for real) and freshly wood-fired, their pizza begs to be devoured. You can watch the dough being mixed in the machine in the open-air kitchen, in case you want to torture yourself while you starve waiting for your pizza. The expert technique of the cooks is something to admire, too.

i Pizza from €6; gluten-free, vegan, and vegetarian options available; wheelchair accessible

TUCO'S TAQUERIA ($)

6 Abbeygate St. Upper; 091 563 925; www.tuco.ie; open daily noon-10pm

When people think of Irish cuisine, Mexican food usually doesn't come to mind. *Pero,* Tuco's Taqueria might change the game. They use Irish meats like pork and sirloin steak in their concoctions. We'd recommend Tuco's as a casual dinner between the first and second pub visits of the evening... and you can get a beer at Tuco's too. So, if you really can't go a few days without a burrito, Tucos has your answer. They also serve "boxes," which are like a typical burrito bowl—but artsier. We don't judge. There's more seating upstairs in this tiny taco joint.

i Entrées from €6.95; vegetarian and paleo options available; wheelchair accessible

NIGHTLIFE

O'CONNELL'S

8 Eyre Sq.; 91 563634; www.oconnellsbargalway.com; open M-Th 10:30am-11:30pm, F-Sa 10:30am-12:30am, Su 12:30pm-11pm

Imagine a fancy pub combined with an outdoor beer garden that looks like its own small street full of other mini-pubs, and another bar outside open on the weekends. Add a pizza truck run by the owners of **The Dough Bros,** walls of whiskey and gin options, and nooks and crannies filled with glass displays of vintage toothpaste containers, cereal boxes, mice poison, and an old phone booth. With rooms connected by passageways, this bar is worth a visit just to take it all in. Add a classic whiskey ginger, get a little tipsy, and it might just feel like a magical cave of gold. Go during the day so you can fully experience the outdoor fun.

i Spirits from €6; BGLTQ+ friendly; limited wheelchair accessibility

THE QUAYS

11 Quay St.; 91 568347; open M-Sa 10:30am-2:30am, Su noon-midnight

The Quays (pronounced KEYS) is the giant pub you'll end up at at the end of the night, singing along to the live band from one of the three bars inside. They've got a restaurant as well, but we'd recommend coming after dinner for the drinks and atmosphere. In between pints, take a look around—and not just at the rowdy Irish football fans yelling at each other. The stone walls, stained glass and instruments on the wall give off a medieval vibe that doesn't seem like it would work with the glowing dance floor and alternative covers of "Hey Jude," but hey, it does.

i Beer from €5, mixers from €7; BGLTQ+ friendly; limited wheelchair accessibility; live music daily

RÓISÍN DUBH

9 Dominick St.; 91 586540.; www.roisindubh.net; open M-Su 5pm-2am depending on concert

It feels like it takes *years* to walk to this venue, but it's really only a 10-minute walk from the center of the **Latin Quarter.** Named after a centuries-old Irish song, it's only fitting that the bar hosts concerts almost nightly, as well as a silent disco on Tuesdays and stand-up comedy. When the weather's nice, the rooftop patio offers a reprieve from the noise, even though it's still super packed, ensuring you won't escape the people. The gigs range from up-and-coming bands to more obscure artists like Ed Sheeran. Maybe you've heard of him?

i Concert ticket prices vary, open mic nights free, silent disco €5; limited wheelchair accessibility

IRELAND ESSENTIALS

VISAS

Citizens of almost all first-world countries (including Australia, Canada, New Zealand, and the US) do not need visas to visit the Republic of Ireland for up to three months. Note that the Republic of Ireland is not a signatory of the Schengen Agreement, which means it is not part of the freedom of movement zone that covers most of the EU. Accordingly, non-EU citizens can visit Ireland without eating into the 90-day limit on travel in the Schengen area, but will be subject to border controls on entry.

Citizens from the aforementioned countries do not need visas for long-term study or work in the Republic of Ireland, although they must have proof that they are enrolled in a course or proof of employment, apply for permission to stay, and register with immigration authorities upon arrival. For more information on this, consult www.inis.gov.ie.

Citizens from the EU do not need a visa to come to Ireland—but it is unclear exactly how U.K. citizens wishing to stay in Ireland will be affected by Brexit. Since Northern Ireland is in the United Kingdom, its visa rules are the same as for Britain. For more information on these policies, see the Great Britain chapter.

MONEY

Tipping: Ireland does not have a strong tipping culture. In sit-down restaurants, there may be a service charge already figured into the bill. If not, you can tip 10-15 percent. In bars, tipping is not expected and even looked down upon. Tipping taxi drivers is also not expected, although it's standard to round up to the nearest euro. Hairdressers are generally tipped 10 percent.

Taxes: The Republic of Ireland had a standard 23 percent value added tax (VAT), although some good are subject to a lower rate of 13 percent. Northern Ireland shares the United Kingdom's 20 percent VAT. The prices in *Let's Go* include VAT unless otherwise noted.

SAFETY AND HEALTH

Drugs and Alcohol: Ireland is a land famed for its beer and pub culture, so it's not surprising that alcohol is a common presence in the county. The legal drinking age is 18 in both the Republic of Ireland and Northern Ireland, and this is more strictly enforced in urban areas. Both regions regulate the possession of recreational drugs, with penalties ranging from a warning to lengthy prison sentences. In the Republic, possession of cannabis can result in a quite hefty fine, and repeated offenses can result in imprisonment. Check the Great Britain chapter for more detailed information on drug laws in Northern Ireland.

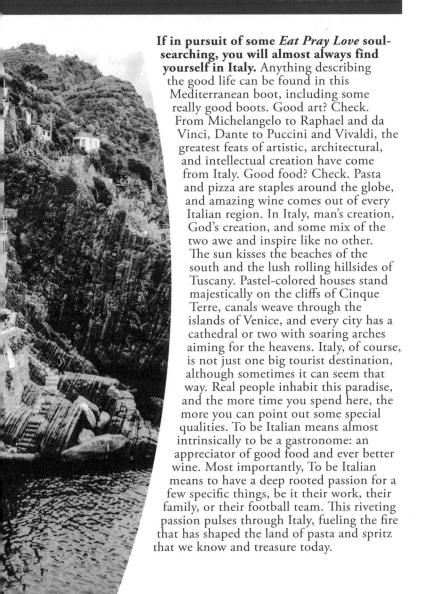

ITALY

If in pursuit of some *Eat Pray Love* soul-searching, you will almost always find yourself in Italy. Anything describing the good life can be found in this Mediterranean boot, including some really good boots. Good art? Check. From Michelangelo to Raphael and da Vinci, Dante to Puccini and Vivaldi, the greatest feats of artistic, architectural, and intellectual creation have come from Italy. Good food? Check. Pasta and pizza are staples around the globe, and amazing wine comes out of every Italian region. In Italy, man's creation, God's creation, and some mix of the two awe and inspire like no other. The sun kisses the beaches of the south and the lush rolling hillsides of Tuscany. Pastel-colored houses stand majestically on the cliffs of Cinque Terre, canals weave through the islands of Venice, and every city has a cathedral or two with soaring arches aiming for the heavens. Italy, of course, is not just one big tourist destination, although sometimes it can seem that way. Real people inhabit this paradise, and the more time you spend here, the more you can point out some special qualities. To be Italian means almost intrinsically to be a gastronome: an appreciator of good food and ever better wine. Most importantly, To be Italian means to have a deep rooted passion for a few specific things, be it their work, their family, or their football team. This riveting passion pulses through Italy, fueling the fire that has shaped the land of pasta and spritz that we know and treasure today.

CATANIA

Coverage by **Adrian Horton**

ITALY CATANIA

Some cities have loose lips about their drama; their streets openly bear the scars of the past, veering from medieval to ancient to modern in a single block. And then there are places like Catania, which has a smooth rhythm to its daily life—small *piazzas* with relaxed cafés, bars that hum in the evening, a castle to tour on quiet afternoons. This placid hub of Baroque architecture *will* divulge its secrets, if you look hard enough. Omnipresent flourishes of marble belie the fact that nearly the entire city was destroyed in a 1693 earthquake. Numerous dedications to Vittorio Emanuele II hint at Catania's early submission to Italian unification. And neighborhoods surrounding the Castello Ursino remind us that this fortress once overlooked the sea—until it was surrounded by lava. A blend of explosive and peaceful, easygoing and resilient, Sicily's second-largest city has emerged from the shadow of Mt. Etna as a worthy destination in its own right. Etna's lava oozes at the slow but steady rate of a meter or so per hour, and Catania operates at a similar pace. It won't reach out to grab you, but the city is used to playing a long game. Poke around the markets, in awe of the airy frescoes, and let Catania work its way with you one chapel, fish stand, and volcanic crater at a time.

ORIENTATION

Catania resides on the east coast of the island of **Sicily.** Its greater metropolitan area is bound by the Mediterranean on the east, its airport (Catania Fontanarossa) to the south, and by the smoldering **Mt. Etna** to the north. Trains arrive at **Stazione Centrale Catania,** on the city's east end, directly north of Catania's two main ports, **Porto Vecchio** and **Porto Nuovo.** The **Cattedrale,** marks the heart of the city center at the intersections of **Vittorio Emanuele II** and **Via Etnea (Etna).** Heading south from **Piazza Duomo,** you reach the old fish market and the imposing **Castello Ursino.** Via Etnea heads north from Piazza Duomo towards the rest of the city. Side streets from Via Etnea lead east to the **Teatro Massimo Bellini** and clubs and bars, or west to the **Via Crociferi** and its Baroque churches.

ESSENTIALS

GETTING THERE

The public bus, Alibus, runs from Catania-Fontanarossa Airport to the city center (near Piazza Duomo) every 20min. between 5am-midnight. Tickets cost €4 and can be purchased on board. Taxis to and from the airport cost around €20. Catania's main train station, Stazione Catania Centrale, is a manageable walk from the city's attractions. Most bus lines depart from the lot directly in front of Stazione Centrale's doors. If you want to walk to the city center, turn left outside the station and proceed down V. VI Aprile. When you reach a large roundabout (P. dei Martiri), turn right onto V. Vittorio Emanuele II (note: if you find a street with this name in Italy, it leads somewhere important). Follow Vittorio Emanuele II until it runs into the unmistakable P. Duomo.

GETTING AROUND

Catania has a bus system that reaches most of the city with tickets costing €1. Tickets last 90min. and can be purchased from *tabacchi* (tobacco shops) or ATM kiosks. If you're planning on traveling for more than 90min., you can purchase a day pass for €2.50. The subway system is the shortest metro system in the world, boasting a mere six stations. Tickets cost €1 and the trains run every 15-30min. daily from 7am-8:45pm. Radio Taxi Catania (095 330 966) operates daily 24hr and is a helpful resource that might help you get to Mt. Etna.

PRACTICAL INFORMATION

Tourist Offices: Tourist Info Stop (V. Etnea 63; 0957367623; open M, W, F 9am-noon, Tu, Th 3pm-6pm)

Banks/ATMs/Currency Exchange: ATMs are available throughout the city, particularly on main thoroughfares such as V. Etnea or V. Vittorio Emanuele.

Post Offices: Mail is handled by Poste Italia. Two post offices convenient for most accommodations can be found at V. Vittorio Emanuele II 347 (095 316955) and Corso Sicilia 25 (095 316 957).

Internet: Catania does not offer public Wi-Fi, but many restaurants and cafés offer a strong connection. Look for complimentary Wi-Fi advertisements.

BGLTQ+ Resources: Though rural areas in Sicily may have less tolerant attitudes, Palermo and Catania have thriving gay scenes and a popular pride parade in the summer (www.cataniapride.it). For additional resources and support, check out www.arcigay.it or Coordinamento Lesbiche Italiano (Italy's largest lesbian activist organization; www.clrbp.it).

EMERGENCY INFORMATION

Emergency Number: 112 (general emergency), 115 (fire brigade), 118 (ambulance)

Police: Polizia Di Stato Questura Catania (P. Santa Nicolella, 8; 095 736 7111)

US Embassy: The nearest US Consular Agency is in Palermo (V. G.B. Vaccarini, 1; 091 30 5857 (call between 10 a.m. and noon); USCitizensPalermo@state. gov)

Rape Crisis Center: Telefono Rosa, based in Rome, provides support and resources at telefonorosa.it as well as a help line at 0637518282.

Hospitals:
- Ospedale Vittorio Emanuele (V. G.Clementi; 0957431111)
- Ospedale Garibaldi Centro (P. S. Maria di Gesù, 5; 095 7591111; open daily 24hr)

Pharmacies: Farmacia Consoli (V. Etnea 400; 095 448317; open M-F 8:30am-2pm, 4-8:30pm, Sa 8:30am-1pm)

ACCOMMODATIONS

🛏 OSTELLO DEGLI ELEFANTI ($)

V. Etnea, 28; 952265691; www.ostellodeglielefanti.it; reception open 24hr

Ostello degli Elefanti picked an apt inspiration for its name, because the hostel hasn't forgotten anything. Complimentary breakfast with coffee cake fresh out of the oven? Check. Spacious rooms with the remains of an old palace fresco on the ceiling? Check. Access to the rooftop bar? Check, with five-euro cocktails coming right up. This guest house, located just north of the **Piazza Duomo** on Via Etnea, has the look and service of a hotel, with the laid-back air of a hostel. The common areas offer ample space to meet fellow travelers (or screen *Game of Thrones*), and the rooftop bar provides one of the best views in the city of **Mt. Etna.** Did we mention there's a 20 percent discount on drinks? Oh, we forgot? Well, Ostello degli Elefanti did not.

i Dorms from €23; reservation recommended; BGLTQ+ friendly; Wi-Fi; luggage storage; linens included; laundry; free breakfast; kitchen

CITY-IN HOSTEL B&B CATANIA ($)

V. Grimaldi 2; 95341450; www.cityinhostel.it; reception open 9am-11pm

There's nothing that stands out about City-In Hostel's name (do they mean "In the City?"), which is indicative of this indistinct hostel a short walk from the fish market. The rooms are fine—clean, colorful, with enough room to spread out—but unremarkable in character. City-In does provide a courtyard patio and second floor porch, though the space is quiet and not often used. To City-In's credit, the facilities are solid, the price one of the best in Catania, and the location convenient for the **Piazza Duomo** and other nearby sights. But memorable, it is not.

i Dorms from €16, private rooms from €20 per person; cash only; reservation recommended; BGLTQ+ friendly; no wheelchair accessibility; Wi-Fi; linens included; laundry; kitchen

SIGHTS
CULTURE

🏛 VIA DEI CROCIFERI

Via dei Crociferi; street open 24hr

Via dei Crociferi is Sicilian Baroque in concentrate form: ornate facades and marble-columned balconies bottled up and contained. This stretch of road has been designated a **UNESCO World Heritage Site** for its cluster of picturesque churches and obsessive detail. A short walk, beginning at the **Piazza San Francesco d'Assisi,** will cover enough ornamented pediments to last you a lifetime. First, you'll pass the **Church of St. Benedict,** with its adjoining monastery, then the **Church of St. Francesco Borgia.** Additional stops include the **Church of San Giuliano** and the **Basilica St. Camillus.** The stroll down Baroque lane ends with the **Villa Cerami,** once a lush mansion for Catania's aristocracy. Today, it's home to Catania's College of Law and is a popular outdoor study space.

i Free; limited wheelchair accessibility

BASILICA DELLA COLLEGIATA

V. Etnea 3; 95313447; hours vary

In 1693, a massive earthquake decimated Catania and the surrounding towns, reducing much of the existing architecture to dust. This was bad luck for the residents of eastern Sicily but fortunate for you, because the money of the aristocracy survived and funded the Basilica della Collegiata to rise as a phoenix from the ashes. This compact church represents the epitome of the Sicilian Baroque style, which flourished under the island's Spanish rule for a half century following the earthquake. Essentially, local architects modified the ornate style popularized in Rome with their own touch of concave façades, decorative *puttis* (Cupid figures, often supporting a balcony), and flamboyant sculptures. Basilica della Collegiata displays all of these elements in spades, as well as airy frescoes and gilded columns in the nave. **Mt. Etna** may be powerful, but it can't keep naked babies and marble balustrades down.

i Free; wheelchair accessible

LANDMARKS

DUOMO (CATTEDRALE DI SANT'AGATA)

V. Vittorio Emanuele II 163; 95320044; open daily 7am-noon and 4pm-7pm

It's not an easy time, living in the shadow of **Mt. Etna.** Thanks to the area's tectonic activity, Catania's Duomo, a cathedral dedicated to the patron Saint Agatha, has experienced almost as many reinventions as Madonna (the singer, not Jesus's mom). The OG Duomo, built in the eleventh century over the ruins of the **Roman Achillean Baths,** was reduced to rubble in 1169. The Duomo rebounded under the Normans, only to be struck down again by the famous 1693 earthquake. Today's Duomo was constructed in the Baroque style, as conveyed by the curved façade and marble figures. The interior of the church impresses with its tall cupola (dome) and distinct pulpit, which seems to surge from the heart of the building. Stare and admire, but don't call it a comeback.

i Free entrance to the cathedral, "terrace" view €1; wheelchair accessible

TEATRO MASSIMO BELLINI

V. Giuseppe Perrotta 12; 957306111; www. teatromassimobellini.it; open Tu-Th 9am-noon

It's not a Sicilian city without a lavish opera house, and it's not a Sicilian opera house without a story of delay, disruption, and funding issues. The plans for an opulent public theater in Catania began shortly after the devastating earthquake in 1693, but the municipality took their sweet time in hashing out the details; the cornerstone of the theater wasn't laid until 1812, and it took another 78 years to complete the structure. Today's Teatro Massimo seats 1,200 in plush red velvet, and takes its name from the local hero of opera, **Vincenzo Bellini.** The theater is open to the non-opera-attending public for limited hours each week, which reserves most of its energy for what really matters: the show.

i Ticket €6; guided tours available in English between 10am and 11:30am; wheelchair accessible

TEATRO ROMANO DI CATANIA (ROMAN THEATER AND ODEON)

V. Vittorio Emanuele II 266; 957150508; open daily 9am-1:30pm

Though long buried by earthquakes and eager church-builders, glimpses of Catania's Roman past still peek through the cobblestones, most prominently at the Roman Theater, just off Vittorio Emanuele II near the **Benedettini monastery.** Catania's theater, which likely held up to 15,000 people, is Roman ruins without makeup—casual, unkempt, still in clothing from the night (or couple centuries) before. Opening hours are sporadic but the weeds covering the old concrete are not. This Colosseum prototype lacks the crowds of its famous descendant, which makes visiting this theater an eerie tour through empty archways and abandoned seats. A note: the Teatro Romano, a semi-circular theater, can be confused with the remains of the Roman amphitheater farther north, off Via Etnea. Those ruins are mostly obscured by the street, though a portion (specially, one fourth) of the amphitheater, located below street level, is open to the public each day.

i Free; no wheelchair accessibility

MUSEUMS

MUSEO CIVICO AL CASTELLO URSINO

Piazza Federico di Svevia 24; 95345830; open daily 9am-7pm

Like any good humanities major, the Civic Museum in Castello Ursino has many great ideas but no idea who it wants to be. A museum of Greek vases and Roman sculpture? Perhaps—the museum has intriguing works from antiquity, particularly a collection of emotional grave inscriptions from the late Empire. A repository of Christian relics and medieval art? Maybe, as several rooms house more takes on the Madonna and Child and the plight of Saint Sebastian. A display for local talent? Potentially, part of the museum is devoted to local artists. The Civic Museum attempts combinations others would forego—ancient figurines and a provocative, modern painting titled "The Effects of Hashish." Not everything sticks, but you have to give Museo Civico credit for trying.

i Tickets €6, students €3; wheelchair accessible

MUSEO DIOCESANO CATANIA

V. Etnea 8; 95281635; open M 9am-2pm, Tu 9am-2pm and 3pm-6pm, W 9am-2pm, Th 9am-2pm and 3pm-6pm, F 9am-2pm, Sa 9am-1pm

Just off the **Piazza Duomo,** Catania's Diocesan Museum serves as a testament to the longstanding influence of the Catholic Church in Sicily. The museum displays a series of valuable church relics—altarpieces, antiquities, and commanding views of the city—but an understated presentation and lack of English subtitles obscures most of their significance. Visitors of a religious bent may find the Catholic treasures enthralling, but others will breeze through the rooms quickly. Tickets, however, recoup value for the secular with access to the **Achillian Baths,** the remains of a Roman-era thermal bath systems that resides beneath the museum.

i Tickets €6 (includes Achillian Baths); last entry 30min. before closing

OUTDOORS

CATANIA FISH MARKET

V. Pardo 29; open M-Sa 6am-1:30pm (restaurants and food counters open later)

Catania's fish market has learned a thing or two over the years. This outdoor series of shops, hawking the port's fish hauls since medieval times, knows how to chop up a swordfish. It knows how to drain buckets of octopi and scoop barrels of squid. And it knows how to shout at you in wildly gesticulated Italian, in a way that doesn't make you run for the hills. This fish market keeps it old-school, from the lack of decoration or printed labeling to the fishermen's calls that you *must* try this shrimp here or that sardine there. It's a fishy, briny jungle out there—an authentic and lively one that you want to at least stroll through for a taste (and smell) of Catania's mix of past and present.

i Free entry, prices vary; limited wheelchair accessibility

MT. ETNA

Etna Cable Car (Funivia dell'Etna, Stazione Partenza): Parco dell'Etna, Nicolosi, Piazzale Rifugio Sapienza, Nicolosi, CT; 95914141; www.funiviaetna.com; open daily 9am-4:15pm

Don't let the numerous "Etna" name drops and postcards fool you: this is not a casual mountain. Sicily's most famous volcano, which towers over Catania and the neighboring coast, has been very active throughout the centuries. It buried part of Catania in 1669, nearly scalded a town in 1993, and exploded on a BBC camera crew as recently as March 2017. It can also be climbed, if you have euro and a day to spare. Hiking on Etna requires advance planning and is subject to the whims of the mountain, so double check schedules ahead of time. First, take the AST bus from Catania's central station at 8:15am (buy from the station in advance). The bus will arrive at **Rifugio Sapienza,** the mountain's base camp (altitude 2,000 meters) around 10:15am. From there, you can hike the next 1,000 meters to the summit; or, you can ride the cable car to a stop 500 meters from the top. Be sure to bring a jacket, sunscreen, and a camera.

i Bus tickets €6.60 each way; cable car tickets €30; last ride 4:15pm; hiking essentials sold at Refuge Sapienza

FOOD

FUD ($)

Via Santa Filomena 35; 957153518; www.fud.it; open daily 12:30pm-1am

Most nights after 8pm, the narrow, quiet Via Santa Filomena transforms into a purgatory of people with flashing blinkers, waiting for their turn at FUD. This experimental kitchen has earned a reputation for its fresh ingredients and gargantuan portions. Despite the hype, FUD keeps its décor debonair—simple café tables lining the small patio, large family-style tables, barstools, and signs encouraging you to eat inside. What's not understated? The quality of their dishes, from skyscraping burgers to artfully-seasoned fries to Naples-quality pizza. The ingredients may be top-tier but your manners need not be; go ahead and smear the ketchup on your nose, pool the olive oil on your plate, and share a fry or two with your (elbow-bumping) neighbor—no one's here to judge you.

i Pizza from €8.50, paninis and burgers from €7, salads €10, chips from €3; vegetarian options available; wheelchair accessible

SCARDACI ICE CAFÉ ($)

V. Etnea 158; 95313131; open daily 11am-11pm

It's just too easy to end up in a gelato shop when strolling through Catania. The question is not if you will get gelato but where, and for what price. Scardaci Ice Café aces both of those queries, with its prime location (on Via Etnea) and unbeatable scoop-per-euro ratio. For a mere €1.90, you can try two of Scardaci's many flavors, including its signature "Etnea," a combination of pistachio and almond. The gelateria offers both indoor and patio seating, as well as coffee, pastries, and other frozen treats, but let's not get distracted from the main point: a medium cup (three scoops) of very good gelato for less than a specialty *gelateria's* kiddie portion. If you're not aiming for the *crème de la crème* of Catanian gelato (they're all good, if we're being honest), then gelato shopping means striking the perfect balance between quality.

i One scoop €1.90, three scoops €2.30; wheelchair accessible

NIGHTLIFE

LA CHIAVE

V. Landolina 70; 347 948 0910; open M-Sa 4pm-3am, Su 4pm-midnight

Most nights, the area surrounding **Piazza Bellini** resounds with club beats and amped up renditions of "Despacito." Out of the fray of neon lights and club promoters emerges La Chiave, a laid-back bar which, on the right night, puts on its own low-key show. There's one guy on the bass, one on the tuba, one stroking the ivories, one singing a scat mix of English and Italian into the mic. It's a down-home, real jazz show, witnessed by a small crowd with spritzes in-hand. Inside, La Chiave holds a trove of bottles and barstools, but that doesn't matter to most when the real attraction keeps the beat outside. On a summer night, try your luck at the patio; like the best improvisational jazz, some great things can't be planned, but it's worth a shot (and another spritz).

i Aperitivi from €3, cocktails from €5, beer from €3; BGLTQ+ friendly

RAZMATAZ

V. Montesano 17/19; 95311893; open M-Sa noon-4pm and 7pm-1am

Razmataz has a lot going on—rhythm in its name, cooks in its kitchen, people on its patio, frames on its walls. There's enough happening in this bohemian wine bar to make your attention zig from the French cartoon on the right to the full menu of daily specials on the left. Antique goods loom from the wooden railings above, while vintage Coca-Cola advertisements peer at you from the walls below. Cheerful, tipsy patrons pack the bar at night, sharing space with large plates, strong cocktails, and cheekily-censored sexual drawings. Anything goes here, whether you're looking for dinner, a rowdy pint, or a long evening of good conversation.

i Wine from €4, beer from €3, cocktails from €6; wheelchair accessible

CINQUE TERRE

Coverage by **Margaret Canady**

Welcome to paradise. Cinque Terre (pronounced cheen-kway tehr-ray) is a cluster of five villages and commonalities. The villages were sculpted out of the jagged coastline of the Ligurian Sea. The houses are pastel-hued; something about the burst of color paired with the fact that the creation seems impossible on this steep terrain leaves visitors stupefied and reaching for their cameras. And boy, are there a lot of cameras. While Cinque Terre sees about 2.4 million visitors a year, only about 4000 people live in all five cities combined. Cinque Terre has become an international tourist destination, and it can be overwhelming, especially during the summer season. This, of course, should not derail you from the villages, but inspire you to give back to the city and invest in it. For the best views and least tourists, take the time to hike anywhere uphill—the crowds disappear within minutes. When you go into a restaurant or shop, strike up a conversation with the shop owner, and ask about their village. We promise you'll love the city a little bit more if you do.

ORIENTATION

Cinque Terre is a 15-kilometer stretch of five villages located on the **Ligurian Sea.** The villages, from north to south, are as follows: **Monterosso, Vernazza, Corniglia, Manarola, and Riomaggiore.** Each village is small, with only one or two main roads and several side streets that are easy to navigate.

ESSENTIALS

GETTING THERE

The closest airport is Pisa International Airport, located about 87km south of the villages. The best way to access Cinque Terre is by train. You first have to take a train to either La Spezia Centrale or Levanto. With these two stations as endpoints, the Cinque Terre Express runs between the five villages.

Cars are not allowed in most areas of the villages. Paid parking lots are available in La Spezia and Levanto.

GETTING AROUND

The train is the most convenient way between cities and only takes about 3-5min. between each village. Trains runs very frequently and are reliable, averaging about 2 per hour both ways. One-way tickets cost €4 each. Visitors can also hike between the cities. There are several trails, some of which run along the coast, and some which run up behind the villages. It can take anywhere from 1-3hr to hike between cities. The sole means of traveling within a city is by walking. The villages offer day passes, which give you unlimited access to the trains, hiking trails, shuttles, restrooms, and station Wi-Fi. See the tourist center for more details.

PRACTICAL INFORMATION

Tourist Offices: There is a tourist office in every village. Here are two:
- Riomaggiore Tourist Information Office (P. Rio Finale, 26; 0187 920633; www.parconazionale5terre.it; open daily 8am-7:30pm)
- Monterosso Tourist Information Office (Monterosso Train Station; 0187 817059; www.parconazionale5terre.it; open daily 8am-7:30pm)

Banks/ATMs/Currency Exchange: There are ATMs in every village. Avoid the mobile ATMs near the train station since they have higher bank fees.

Post Offices: There is a post office in each village. Here are two:
- Riomaggiore Post Office (V. Pecunia, 7; 0187 920121; www.poste.it; open M-F 8:15am-1:45pm, Sa 8:15am-12:45pm)
- Manarola Post Office (V. Discovolo, 216; 0187 920198; www.poste.it; open M-F 8:15am-1:45pm, Sa 8:15am-12:45pm)

Public Restrooms: There are public bathrooms at each of the train stations, they cost €1 or are free with the purchase of a Cinque Terre pass.

Internet: There is Wi-Fi at each of the train stations, but can only be accessed with the purchase of a Cinque Terre pass. Many restaurants have Wi-Fi.

BGLTQ+ Resources: The closest physical resource is located in Pisa at Pinkriot Arcigay Pisa (V. Enrico Fermi, 7; 050 23278; pinkriot.arcigaypisa.it/; open Th 6-10pm).

EMERGENCY INFORMATION

Emergency Number: 112
Police: 113. The phone number for Monterosso Town Hall Police is 0187 817525.

US Embassy: The nearest US consulate is located in Florence (Lungarno Vespucci 38; 39 055 266 951; it.usembassy.gov/embassy-consulates/florence/). The nearest US embassy is located in Rome (V. Vittorio Veneto 121; 39 06 46741; it.usembassy.gov/embassy-consulates/rome/).

Rape Crisis Center: Telefono Rosa, based in Rome, provides support and resources at telefonorosa.it as well as a help line at 0637518282.

Hospitals:
- Sestri Levante Hospital: (V. Terzi Arnaldo, 37, Sestri Levante; 0185 4881; www.comune.sestri-levante.ge.it/polo-ospedaliero-di-sestri-levante; open daily 24hr)

Pharmacies: There is a pharmacy located in each village. Here is one in Monterosso: (Via Fegina, 42; 0187 818391; open daily 9am-7pm).

ACCOMMODATIONS

🛏 OSTELLO CINQUE TERRE ($)

V. Riccobaldi, 21, Manarola; 0187 920039; www.hostel5terre.it/en/home; reception open 4pm-7pm

You're not visiting Cinque Terre to stay inside all day, and the staff at Ostello Cinque Terre knows it. What they lack in extravagance, they make up with its surroundings: you're staying in, like, the prettiest place in Italy for an incredible rate. The shared dorm gives you the ability to make friends with other young people, all of whom are trying to figure out if they *really* have to pay for a train ticket (spoiler alert: you do). Be warned: the initial trek up the mountain to the hostel is a steep one, especially with a heavy backpack or any type of luggage. Our calves were begging for mercy.

i Dorms from €33; shared dorm and bath; reservation required; wheelchair accessible; Wi-Fi; breakfast 8am-9am; check-out before 10am, check-in 4pm-7pm; linens provided

MAR-MAR ($$)

V. Malborghetto, 4, Riomaggiore; 0187 920932; www.hostels.com/hostels/cinque-terre/mar-mar

There's a minimum two-day stay at Mar-Mar hostel, but we can guarantee that you'll want more than one day to explore Cinque Terre. Mar-Mar is a great hostel, with big enough rooms that you'll actually

have space between bunk beds and you won't stick your butt into someone else's sleeping face. One of the rooms also has a patio with a view of **Riomaggiore,** where you can lounge or dry your wet swimsuits.
i Beds from €30 night; min 2 day stay; check-in before 7pm; no wheelchair accessibility; Wi-Fi; free breakfast; linens included

SIGHTS
CULTURE

🖾 IL PRESEPE DI MANAROLA (THE NATIVITY SCENE OF MANAROLA)
Collina delle Tre Croci, Manarola; cinquet-erre.a-turist.com/presepe; 347 336 9187; early Dec-late Jan

When we visited Cinque Terre in the summer, every night we would gaze up at a single house on the **Manarola** mountainside that featured a Nativity scene, the white neon shining bright in the darkness. Christmas in summer, we thought. Exciting! Now, if you can, imagine dozens of nativity scenes lighting up the night sky. Every winter, almost every house on the iconic Manarola skyline features a nativity scene of their own to celebrate the holiday season. Baby Jesuses, angels, and Marys seem to float in the darkness.
i Free; wheelchair accessible

SAGRA DEI LIMONI (MONTEROSSO LEMON FESTIVAL)
Monterosso; 3477703718; www.cinqueterre.eu.com/en/monterosso; usually the 3rd weekend of May (lemon season dependent)

When life gives you lemons, make an endless supply of lemon desserts and call it Sagra dei Limoni. Every year **Monterosso** holds Cinque Terre's Lemon Festival, a weekend-long celebration in May that celebrates the village's famous fruit. If you make it here on this weekend, be prepared to be engulfed in a sea of yellow and to indulge in as much citrus dessert as your heart desires. Locals create desserts such as lemon cake, lemon cream pie, lemon marmalade, and limoncino. Pucker up!
i Free admission, product prices vary; limited wheelchair accessibility

LANDMARKS

🖾 CASTELLO DORIA
V. San Francesco, Vernazza; 0187 812546; www.tellaroitaly.com/castello_doria_vernazza.html; open daily 10am-9pm

Remember when you were seven and your treehouse was the backyard your kingdom? Castello Doria is like a real-life fortress amid the kingdom of your dreams. The tower offers arguably some of the best views in the entire area. Whip out that panorama mode on your cameras, friends, because this perch offers you a view of the ocean touching the horizon, an aerial view of the city of **Vernazza,** and glimpses of **Monterosso** and **Corniglia** among the mountains.
i Admission €1.50; cash only; last entry 8:45pm; no wheelchair accessibility

CONVENTO DEI CAPPUCCINI E CHIESA DI SAN FRANCESCO (CHURCH OF SAN FRANCESCO AND CAPUCHIN FRIARS MONASTERY)
Salita San Cristoforo, Monterosso; 0187 817531; www.conventomonterosso.it/

A quick climb out of **Monterosso** and suddenly you're transported to a serene world of trails, trees, and the sacred world of the Capuchin Friars. The church and monastery overlook **Monterosso Bay.** If you're lucky, you'll be able to hear the Gregorian chants echo through the valley. Past the monastery, you can find Monterosso cemetery decorated with fresh flowers and lit candles.
i Free; no wheelchair accessibility

MANAROLA
1km south of Corniglia

Manarola is like your rich aunt who has an impeccable sense of fashion and lives in a perfectly-decorated apartment. The village offers the best views in Cinque Terre. The **Manarola Overlook** gives you a perfect and unobstructed view of the city at any time of the day, and during sunset you can see the sun pass behind the mountains, perfectly framed by the sea. The city is very clean and empties out as soon as the sun sets.
i Limited wheelchair accessibility

MONTEROSSO AL MARE

Northern-most of the five villages

When we asked the tourist information center about museums, they looked at us incredulously and replied, "There are no museums in Cinque Terre." One simply does not go to Cinque Terre to spend time indoors, let alone in a museum. Monterosso is the quarterback of the football team. The largest of the villages, Monterosso has the most restaurants, hotels, and shops for visitors, as well as the most beaches. The village is probably the most walkable, too, with smooth paved roads that are more horizontal than vertical. The village is ideal for families and people who want to pay for beach chairs.

i Wheelchair accessible

RIOMAGGIORE

0.5km south of Manarola

Riomaggiore is like the little kid next door who kind of reminds you of the Tasmanian Devil. The village is always bustling, with a constant stream of people coming in from docked cruise ships and the train station (it's the first stop after La Spezia). It's easy to lose the crowd, though: climb through the smaller streets to reach better viewpoints and significantly fewer people. Some daredevils like to climb on the rock jetty that runs parallel to the city and offers a great view, but we're not entirely sure if that's legal.

i Limited wheelchair accessibility

SANTUARIO NOSTRA SIGNORA DI SOVIORE (SANCTUARY OF OUR LADY OF SOVIORE)

Localita Soviore, Monterosso; 0187 817385; www.santuariodisoviore.it/

Getting to the sanctuary from Cinque Terre is no walk on the beach. The hike from **Monterosso** to the oldest sanctuary in Cinque Terre is about an hour long, completely uphill, and consists almost entirely of narrow paths and uneven stone. When you get there, prepare to be amazed. When the weather is nice, you have an unobstructed view of the entire valley that cradles Monterosso. When we made the trek up, it was a rainy Saturday morning and fog obstructed the landscape before us, but we were greeted by choral singing from the sanctuary for Sunday mass.

i Free; wheelchair accessible if driving up the mountain; respectable clothing required in the sanctuary; café located on hilltop

OUTDOORS

HIKING CINQUE TERRE: THE BLUE PATH

01016890111; www.cinqueterre.it/en/content/il-sentiero-azzurro-n2;

For centuries, this path was the only road between the villages. Today, you'll walk through vineyards and wildflowers—your eyes, ears, and nose will be taking in the fresh mountain air, the gorgeous ocean views, and the sweet smell of wildflowers. We recommend going early in the day to beat the heat and the other hikers. Check with the tourist office to see if any sections of the trail are closed due to safety or repair.

i Admission €7.50 a day or included in Cinque Terre pass; no wheelchair accessibility

HIKING CINQUE TERRE: SENTIERO DEL CRINALE (THE HIGH PATH)

01016890111; www.cinqueterre.it/en/content/sentiero-del-crinale-n%C2%B0-1

High above the cities lies the High Path, the hiking path for #hardcore hikers and backpackers. Now, we're not saying you can't or shouldn't hike this path, but if you think your weekly hour-long yoga class has prepared you for this hike, you're wrong. The path is meant for advanced hikers. It's also over 40 kilometers and the walking time is something between 10-12 hours. If you conquer the path, though, you can look down (literally) upon all the weaklings taking the easy Blue Path.

i Free; no wheelchair accessibility; check tourist center for information about safety and hazards

FOOD

🍽 LA CANTINA DELLO ZIO BRAMANTE

V. Renato Birolli, 110, Manarola; 0187 920442; open M-W 10am-1am, F-Su 10am-1am

Not everything has to be fancy-schmancy to be a restaurant in Cinque Terre. La Cantina dello Zio Bramante is a late night place to grab a drink and some food, and its chill vibes welcome any and all. They have a live musician most evenings, and when we went, the guy had an affinity for playing the harmonica, which is always a plus in our book. They have some fun and cheap bruschetta options, and as you eat you'll be rubbing elbows with the people next to ya, so you might as well strike up a conversation.

i Entrées from €7, bruschetta from €4; limited wheelchair accessibility

🍽 IL PESCATO CUCINATO ($)

V. Colombo 199, Riomaggiore; 339 262 4815; website; open daily 11:30am-7:30pm

Eating seafood in Cinque Terre is a definite must, but you don't have to break the bank to experience local cuisine. Il Pescato Cucinato is a takeaway shop in **Riomaggiore** that serves fried fish, calamari, and fried veggies in convenient cones, which are deceptively large but miraculously inexpensive. The takeaway option allows you to eat fried anchovies with one hand, take a picture of the cone with the other, and attempt to walk around without running into anyone. We never figured out how to fit the tartar sauce on the rest of the cone, unfortunately.

i Small seafood cone from €6, large from €8; wheelchair accessible; benches available outside

🍽 LUNCHBOX ($)

V. Roma 34, Vernazza; 338 908 2841; open M-Th, Sa-Su 7am-9pm

LunchBox knows exactly what the people want and what they arguably need: perceived free choice and the perfect amount of guidelines. It's a delicious option for takeaway lunch or dinner, with a wide variety of paninis and freshly made juices available.

i Juices from €4, paninis from €4.50; gluten-free, vegan, and vegetarian options available; limited wheelchair accessibility; Wi-Fi

IL GIGANTE BEACH BAR ($)

V. Fegina, 138, Monterosso; 338 339 6036; open daily 8:30am-7:30pm

Il Gigante could charge twice as much as they currently do and probably still get the same amount of business, but lucky for us, they don't. Located right on the beach, they offer a variety of sandwiches for the hungry beachgoer. We got a salmon and avocado sandwich for only €4.50. Salmon *and* avocado? At any American restaurant, that would cost at least $14 and your first-born child.

i Sandwiches from €4.50; gluten-free and vegetarian options available; wheelchair accessible

PIZZERIA LA CAMBUSA DI ZAMPOLLI MATIA ALFIO

V. Renato Birolli, 114, Manarola; 0187 921029; open M-F 7:30am-1pm and 5-8pm, Sa-Su 7:30am-8:00pm

By now you've probably noticed a trend: we eat at a lot of takeaway places, mostly because we didn't want to pay for the high prices of sit down restaurants geared towards tourists. Pizzeria La Cambusa Di Zampolli offers up fat slices of focaccia with a variety of toppings, heated up and ready to take away.

i Takeaway €4; cash only; no wheelchair accessibility

NIGHTLIFE

🍽 BLUE MARLIN BAR AND CAFE

V. Roma, 61, Vernazza; 0187 812207; open M-Tu 7:30am-midnight, Th-Su 7:30am-midnight

The first thing the bartender asked we said hello was "What was the name of Michael J. Fox in *Back to the Future?*" "Um, Marty McFly?" We wondered if this was some sort of secret Italian game show or something. "Ahhhh, yes!" he exclaimed, and went to tell his coworker in the back. It was a weird encounter, but we ended up staying since Blue Marlin is a low-key bar that attracts people of all ages. Its open patio and easy access to the train station makes it popular by location for passersby and regulars alike. They also do takeaway, so we took our drink to watch the sunset in **Vernazza.** They make a damn good margarita, too.

i *Cocktails from €6, focaccia from €8; BGLTQ+ friendly; wheelchair accessible*

IL PORTICCIOLO

V. Renato Birolli, 96, Manarola; 0187 920083; www.ilporticciolo5terre.it/; open M-Tu noon-10pm, Th-Su noon-10pm

Every time we walked by, we heard live music and young people laughing and talking over drinks and tapas. When we finally went in, the bartender warmly greeted us and offered us tapas and drinks immediately. The bar puts a good amount of effort into its décor: exposed rock and walls the color of white sand mix with slow-fading colorful lights. Pretty awesome prices match the aesthetic. FOMO, you've been replaced with €5 cocktails.

i *Cocktails from €5, beer and wine from €3.50; wheelchair accessible*

FLORENCE

Coverage by **Margaret Canady**

Stendhal Syndrome was named after a French author who visited Florence and promptly went into an ecstatic frenzy, overwhelmed at the city's sheer existence. While his heart palpitations may have actually been sunstroke, we can't help but agree: Florence is undeniably breathtaking. Nearly a third of the world's art treasures reside in this ageless city, and Florence has been to some of the most influential minds and artists of human history. Da Vinci, Michelangelo, Brunelleschi, Dante, Raphael, and countless others once walked the same streets you'll find yourself wandering down. And if that's not enough for you, there's something simply indescribable about the magic of the city: the way the sun sets perfectly on the Arno, the terracotta buildings fill the gaps between churches. Florence is no well-kept secret, of course, and it's safe to assume thousands of people daily (especially in the summer) try to grasp a little bit of Florentine magic as well. There's something for everyone: streets filled with name-brand fashion, Medieval and Renaissance churches, Renaissance art, *chianti,* and bustling nightlife. If you can dodge and weave among the tour groups, Florence can become your city, too—you just won't get a disorder named after you.

ORIENTATION

Florence is the capital of the region of Tuscany. The city is built on the **Arno River,** with most of the city's landmarks and population found north of the river. **Piazza del Duomo** is the most central square and home to the impressive **Cattedrale di Santa Maria del Fiore.** Northeast of the Piazza is **Mercato Centrale, Basilica di Santa Maria Novella,** and **Santa Maria Novella Train Station.** To the north of the Piazza by several blocks is **Galleria dell'Accademia,** and farther north are many of the city's hostels. South of the the the Piazza lies remnants of the **Roman grid system,** as well as landmarks such as **Piazza della Signoria, Galleria degli Uffizi,** and finally the Arno. **Over the Ponte Vecchio** and across the river lie the expansive **Boboli Gardens.** East of the gardens is the popular lookout point **Piazzale Michelangelo.**

ESSENTIALS

GETTING THERE

Florence is served by two airports: Vespucci Airport, the international airport of Florence, and the Pisa International Airport, which is larger but farther away. There are shuttles that run from the airports to Florence's Santa Maria Novella

Train Station (Pisa €14, 70min., Florence €6, 20min.). The city is also a central stop on the Italian train system; a train from Rome is only an 1.5hr away and 2hr from Venice. The train station is centrally located with the city. If arriving by car, highway A1 runs north-south in Italy and has four exits into Florence.

GETTING AROUND

Walking is the suggested mode of transportation in Florence. Most of the things you'll be seeing and doing in the city are usually under a 30min. walk away, but if you're trying to get from one corner of the city to the other, it will take you about 1hr. Bikes are available for rent from Florence By Bike. The city center is a Limited Traffic Access Zone, and cars cannot pass unless they have a permit. Part of Florence's public transportation system is called "Le City Line de Firenze," a series of bus lines that run around the city center. Single-ride 90min. tickets are €1.20, four tickets are €4.70; make sure to validate your tickets on board. In late 2018, three new tramway lines will open, linking the airport, the hospital, the central railway station, and main tourist attractions.

PRACTICAL INFORMATION

Tourist Offices: There are four tourist offices. One is by the train station (P. Della Stazione, 4; 055 212245; www.firenzeturismo.it/en/; open M-Sa 9am-7pm, Su 9am-2pm).

Banks/ATMs/Currency Exchange: There are ATMs on most street corners. We were particularly fond of a currency exchange that has no extra fees: Change Exchange Marco Alunno (V. della Ninna, 9; 055 217611; open M-Sa 8:15am-7pm, Su 8:15am-6:30pm).

Post Offices: Poste Italiane (V. Pellicceria 3; 055 273 6481)

Public Restrooms: Public restrooms can be found throughout the city near landmarks. They cost €1. The Duomo location is Piazza San Giovanni, 7.

Internet: Almost all cafés have Wi-Fi. The city also offers Wi-Fi in many popular plazas.

BGLTQ+ Resources: Azione Gay e Lesbica (V. Pisana, 32; 371 3761738; www.azionegayelesbica.it/)

EMERGENCY INFORMATION

Emergency Number: 112
Police: Emergency police number 113. Here is a police station: Commissariato di Polizia S. Giovanni (V. Pietrapiana, 50r; 055 203911; open M-F 8am-2pm).
US Embassy: Florence houses the US consulate (Lungarno Vespucci 38; 39 055 266 951; it.usembassy.gov/embassy-consulates/florence/). The nearest US embassy is located in Rome (V. Vittorio Veneto 121; 39 06 46741; it.usembassy.gov/embassy-consulates/rome/).
Rape Crisis Center: RAINN; (202) 501-4444
Hospitals: For an ambulance or in case of a medical emergency, dial 118.
• Hospital of Santa Maria Nuova (P. Santa Maria Nuova, 1; 055 69381; www.asf.toscana.it/; open daily 24hr)
Pharmacies: There are many pharmacies located throughout the city. Look for the green plus sign. Here are two:
• Farmaceutica di Santa Maria Novella: V. della Scala, 16; 055 216276; www.smnovella.com/; open daily 9am-8pm

ACCOMMODATIONS

🏠 HOSTEL GALLO'ORO ($)
V. Camillo Cavour, 104; 055 552 2964; www.ostellogallodoro.it/index.php

When staying at a hostel, we usually expect, at best, a clean place to stay, some breakfast, and maybe a few new friends. Hostel Gallo'oro goes above and beyond, making a home out of a hostel. The apartment-turned-lodging provides big, comfortable beds, lotion and shampoo, free breakfast, snacks, *and* dinner, and receptionists genuinely care about your well-being. If we're ever back in Florence, we know who to call.

i Dorms from €24; wheelchair accessible; Wi-Fi; linens, breakfast, snack, and dinner included

🏠 PLUS FLORENCE HOSTEL ($$)
V. Santa Caterina D'Alessandria, 15; 055 628 6347; www.plushostels.com/; reception open 24hr

You might accidentally walk by Plus Florence, convinced that the sliding doors and marbled floors of reception lead to a fancy hotel and are not meant for you and your skimpy budget. Lucky for your sweaty, sticky self (and your sweaty wallet) those doors are indeed for you. Plus Florence strives for comfort, starting with its spacious rooms and private baths to its long list of amenities. There's a pool (and pool bar), a disco and karaoke dance floor, full-service restaurant, and, oh yeah, a sauna. This resort—whoops, hostel—will almost convince you that you're there for the pampering, not the beautiful city right outside.

i Dorms from €30; reservation required; wheelchair accessible; Wi-Fi; check-in from 2:30pm, check-out by 10am; laundry available

▨ WOW FLORENCE ($)

V. Venezia, 18/b; 055 579603; wowflorence. com/; reception open 24hr

Our spidey senses are always on high alert for the best hostels, and WoW Florence was definitely out of this galaxy. The superhero-decorated hostel likes its primary colors as much as it likes serving its guests, so expect free breakfast, a rooftop terrace, and comfortable bedding. You can use the kitchen if you feel like making yourself a meal, but with free breakfast and a whole city outside, you might not choose to stay in if you have other options. Each room has a private bathroom, and the lounge boasts yellow and orange-colored tiles to make your stay even more colorful. Holy Hostel, Batman!

i Dorms from €27; reservation recommended; wheelchair accessible; Wi-Fi; free breakfast; linens included

NEW HOSTEL ($)

V. Jacopo Peri, 3; 055 527 2220; www.ne-whostelsflorence.com/; reception open 24hr

Walking to New Hostel, you might be surprised to find that virtually all tourists fade from view, making it seem like you could be in any ordinary neighborhood. New Hostel is located a bit off the beaten path, about 10 minutes northwest of the train station and the central hub of the city. On the one hand, this could be somewhat inconvenient, but on the other, you gotta prep your body for all the gelato you're ingesting. The bedding is simple, but there's helpful staff and a lovely outdoor terrace—you'll get some awesome sleep in the quiet neighborhood. Coffee and tea is free for those eager to get out into the city.

i Dorms from €25; cash only under €50; reservation recommended; wheelchair accessible; Wi-Fi

OSTELLO CENTRALE

V. Faenza, 46r; 055 285960; ostellocentralefirenze.myadj.it/v/ostellocentralefirenze

Ostello Centrale doesn't look like much from the outside: tucked quietly in between a supermarket and a *gelateria,* it could easily be mistaken for someone's parking garage. Instead, a small, simple, yet comfortable hostel awaits its visitors. Though there are only three rooms to house guests, they all have large windows looking out into the common courtyard, *and* the beds are big (and no bunks, bless). The hostel lives up to its name and can be found a few seconds away from **Mercato Centrale.**

i Dorms from €24; cash only; reservation required; wheelchair accessible; Wi-Fi

SIGHTS
CULTURE

▨ MERCATO CENTRALE (CENTRAL MARKET)

P. del Mercato Centrale, V. dell'Ariento; 055 239 9798; www.mercatocentrale.it/; open daily 8am-midnight

Finally, we've found a place to buy your I Love Italia shirts, organic mushrooms, and artisanal pizza all at one quick convenient stop. If you couldn't tell by the name, Mercato Centrale is the **largest market in Florence,** but unfortunately only seems to attract tourists. Outside, the building's perimeter is surrounded by stand after stand of leather goods, which means you'll get an incredible sense of déjà-vu if you walk around long enough. On the first floor of the industrial-esque building are produce stands and meat or seafood vendors, as well as take-away food shops. Upstairs kinda reminded us of Whole Foods: chefs at artisanal restaurants serve their creations, and there's a large seating area for eating. It's a great place to buy a quick trinket and sandwich.

i Wheelchair accessible; Wi-Fi

⬚ PONTE VECCHIO

Ponte Vecchio; open daily 24hr

No postcard of the **Arno River** would be complete without the Ponte Vecchio smack-dab in the middle. The oldest bridge in Florence has always been a hub for merchants, and today is no different: you'll find an odd combination of cheap souvenir vendors and high-end jewelry stores here. A decent number of tourists take their picture with the iconic three arches found at the middle of the bridge, which is nice and all, but you want to see the bridge in your photos, right? The best place to get it is one bridge over, right of the Ponte Vecchio.

i Free crossing; wheelchair accessible; establishment hours vary

CHIANTI WINE TOUR

www.chianti.com/wine/chianti-winetasting. html; tours daily

Every region in Italy produces its own wine, and it's simply a necessity to try the local specimen (which locals say is the best in Italy). The region of Florence and Siena produce *chianti*, a fruity red wine that, of course, gets better with age. Chianti is available at every restaurant, but the best way to develop your wine palate is to go on a wine tour, which are not as expensive as one may expect. Done right, you can taste the wine of local producers, and get a glimpse of some incredible views too. It's definitely not the least grimy activity you'll ever do (the Tuscan roads were made for horses, not tour buses), but sometimes it pays to be a tourist—the local producers offer bottles for as cheap as €6.

i Guided tours from €49; wheelchair accessible; tour company prices vary

MERCATO SANT'AMBROGIO

P. Lorenzo Ghiberti; 055 234 3950; www.mercatosantambrogio.it/; open M-Sa 7am-2pm

If **Mercato Centrale** is six notches too high for your tastes or you're sick of seeing the same five leather purses, Mercato Sant'Ambrogio will more likely suit your fancy. The market is tucked away in the **Santa Croce** neighborhood, and the language of the signs, like the people who visit, are Italian. Next door is **Mercatino delle Pulci,** an antique market that has "Italian grandma" written all over it. The tourists haven't found it yet, so try to keep this gem a secret, yeah?

i Stand prices vary; wheelchair accessible

TEATRO DEL SALE

V. dei Macci, 111 r; 055 200 1492; www. teatrodelsale.com/; open Tu-Sa 11am-3pm and 7:30pm-11pm, Su 11am-3pm

A members-only club for wining, dining, and watching performances sounds like the type of party we normal folk usually aren't invited to, but Teatro del Sale is different. An annual membership is welcome to anyone for only €7, and while the dinners are a tad expensive (€35), you're being treated to unlimited food prepared daily by Florentine chef **Fabio Picchi** (co-owner and creator of the theater with his wife Maria Cassi), as well as nightly performances. Artists from all around the world have performed at the theater, and we're sure it's an experience worth having.

i Membership €7, dinner from €35, lunch from €15; wheelchair accessible

OFFICINA PROFUMO - FARMACEUTICA DI SANTA MARIA NOVELLA (SANTA MARIA NOVELLA PHARMACY)

V. della Scala, 16; 055 216276; www.smnovella.com/; open daily 9am-8pm

While pharmacy information is usually found elsewhere in this guidebook, Santa Maria Novella pharmacy is special. Before you think we've completely lost our marbles, (because who recommends a pharmacy as a cultural necessity?) hear us out. Dominican friars created this pharmacy after people kept dropping like flies during the Black Plague. The people who were left started going to the pharmacy, hosted in the monastery, for rosewater distillate, ladybug liqueurs, and other ointments and concoctions. Today, the pharmacy can be found in the monastery, and the recipes from 600 years ago are still used for many of the products. A wide variety of perfumes, soaps, candles, and more can be found under the frescoed domes of the monastery. Step aside, CVS: Your Extrabucks got nothing on this pharmacy.

i Prices vary; wheelchair accessible

LANDMARKS

🏛 BASILICA DI SAN LORENZO

P. di San Lorenzo, 9; www.operamedicealaurenziana.org/en/home-2/; open Mar 1-Oct 31 M-Sa 10am-5:30pm, Su 1:30pm-5:30pm; open Nov 1-Feb 28 M-Sa 10am-5:30pm

If you're reading this, here's a fun fact about churches: Renaissance architecture was designed with man at the center of importance. He used reason, math, and geometry to design churches and show off his intelligence. Basilica di San Lorenzo is an incredible example of this fun fact. The Medicis were members (and donors, *and* leaders) of the church, and all of the leading characters in the Medici family are buried here. The church's interior itself is rather minimalist for 1418, with tall, clean columns, circular windows, and shades of grey and white. Another fun fact: underneath the church lies a secret room where Michelangelo went into hiding for a couple of months and sketched on the walls of the room. You'll have to take our word for it; you can't go into the room, unfortunately (we tried, but apparently our status as "Best Travel Guide in the Universe" isn't sufficient).

i Admission €6, with library €8.50

🏛 PIAZZA DEL DUOMO

P. del Duomo; 055 2302885; www.museumflorence.com/; open daily 24hr

Let's not judge a city by its church, but if we did that for Florence, we wouldn't be disappointed. Piazza del Duomo is the hub of the city, the center of the historic district, and the main attraction for literally everyone in the world, it seems. Four monuments find their home in the Piazza and each one helps compose the iconic city center. **Cathedral Santa Maria del Fiore,** the third-largest church in the world, reigns large with its intricate facade, topped by Brunelleschi's octagonal dome. Next to the Cathedral are the **Baptistry of San Giovanni** and **Giotto's Bell Tower.** All three are clad in swirls of olive green and pastel pink, which (somehow) go together. We also noticed that you just can't get a bad photo of the Piazza, either.

i Piazza free; cathedral, baptistry and bell tower package ticket €18; limited wheelchair accessibility; reservations required to climb the Dome; monument hours vary

BASILICA DI SANTA TRINITA

P. di Santa Trinita; 055 216912; www.diocesifirenze.it/; open daily 7am-noon and 4pm-7pm

Nestled between outposts of Valentino and Dior quietly lies Basilica di Santa Trinita, a 900 year-old church. Repent for your shopping sins by stepping a foot in and taking a quick breather. Built in the Gothic style, the church features a large number of frescoes (most of which are faded, unfortunately), and offers access to its crypt. Basilica di Santa Trinita is quiet and free, in cost and from shoe temptations.

i Free; wheelchair accessible

PIAZZALE MICHELANGELO

Piazzale Michelangelo; open daily 24hr

To get to Piazzale Michelangelo, you have to cross the **Arno,** head uphill, walk up some steps, stop for breath, walk up some more steps, and then you're there. (Note: "some steps" is actually, like, a lot of steps.) You can thank us for the Charley horse and the incredible view when you get to the top. From there, you'll see the entire city of Florence, and there is perhaps no better place to watch the sunset. Maybe it's the view, or maybe it's the Spanish guitar playing softly in the background, but the lookout makes us want to pull our lovers close. Make sure you and your lover head up there early, though—it can be hard to get a spot on the edge to see the sunset.

i Free; wheelchair accessible with bus

SANTA MARIA NOVELLA

P. di Santa Maria Novella, 18; 055 219257; www.smn.it/en/; open M-Th 9am-7pm, F 11am-7pm, Sa 9am-6:30pm, Su noon-6:30pm

Santa Maria Novella has everything you'd expect from a church: high arches striped with black-and-white stone, important works of Renaissance art, a really big cross with our main man Jesus. This church features a stunning rose-gold altar, and the facade is simple but elegant. The church sits in a wide plaza that has surprisingly little people, but a lot of good shops and restaurants nearby to explore.

i Admission €7.50; last entry 45min. before closing; wheelchair accessible; hours vary based on season

MUSEUMS

🖾 MUSEO FERRAGAMO (SALVATORE FERRAGAMO MUSEUM)

Palazzo Spini Feroni, P. di Santa Trinita, 5/R; 055 356 2846; www.ferragamo.com/museo/it/ita; open daily 10am-7:30pm

If shoes are your best friends, then you'll find new friends at Museo Ferragamo. Underneath the original headquarters of international shoe designer **Salvatore Ferragamo,** the museum celebrates his work and other avenues of Italian fashion. Ferragamo was sought after by the glamour actors and actresses of the 1920s for the perfect shoe. After strolling through his original shoe designs, you'll exit through the gift shop—sells shoes more expensive than your trip to Europe.
i Admission €2; free admission first Su of every month

GALLERIA DELL'ACCADEMIA

V. Ricasoli, 58/60; 055 238 8609; www.galleriaaccademiafirenze.beniculturali.it/; open Tu-Su 8:15am-6:50pm

Ok, we know we said there's a lot of must-sees in Florence, but this one is a serious must. The museum is home to Michelangelo's *David*. It's hard to look away from the 17ft giant-slayer, who stands with his weight in his right hip and a #beastmode pose. You can walk completely around *David,* and make sure to take some time to soak up every little detail, from the bulging veins in his hands to his knee muscles and his incredibly ripped physique. We thought V-lines were a myth, but holy Old Testament, David is ripped. Besides the bod, the museum is actually pretty small and you'll breeze through it. Take some time to look at the Michelangelo's unfinished sculptures that lead to David; they provide an insight into the process of the artist's mind and technique.
i Admission €8, advance tickets €12; audio guide €6; last entrance 6:40pm; wheelchair accessible; reservations highly recommended

LE GALLERIE DEGLI UFFIZI (UFFIZI GALLERY)

Piazzale degli Uffizi, 6; 055 23885; www.uffizi.it/en/the-uffizi; open Tu-Su 8:15am-6:50pm

The Uffizi Gallery used to be the Medici's private gallery (we know, who would've guessed it?), and now is the most popular museum in Florence, if not Italy. Two levels of long U-shaped hallways are filled with full-figure statues and busts, and the long views and checkered floor are beautiful enough to be worth the visit. Attached to the hallways are rooms chock-full of magnificent works from magnificent men (food for thought, name a Renaissance woman who isn't nude). **Botticelli's** *Birth of Venus* and **da Vinci's** *The Baptism of Christ* and *Adoration of the Magi* are fan favorites.
i High season admission €20, low season €12; high season advance ticket €24, low season €16; last entry 6:35pm; wheelchair accessible; reservation recommended; free entrance on first Su of every month

MUSEO DI PALAZZO VECCHIO

P. della Signoria; 055 2768325; museicivicifiorentini.comune.fi.it/en/; open Apr-Sept M-W 9am-11pm, Th 9am-2pm, F-Su 9am-11pm

You'll probably walk through **Piazza della Signoria** a dozen times during your stay in Florence. Despite its imposing edifice and dominance in the square, the museum is surprisingly empty by Florentine standards (probably because

everyone is waiting in line for the **Uffizi** next door). The palace has been the center of public and civic life for centuries, and inside a mammoth hall encapsulates its importance—golden ceilings and huge wall-to-wall murals depicting Florence victory battles. The museum also hosts the private rooms of the Medici court, and, spoil alert, they lived in style.

i Admission €10, students €8; multimedia guide €5; last ticket sale 1hr before closing; wheelchair accessible; times and prices vary for tower, archeological site, and battlementss

PALAZZO STROZZI

P. degli Strozzi; 055 264 5155; www. palazzostrozzi.org/; courtyard open daily 8am-11pm

In a shocking turn of events, it turns out there is a museum in Florence that isn't Renaissance art- or Jesus-related, and that museum is Palazzo Strozzi. Run by an independent foundation of public and private donors, the Renaissance palace is home to a rotating schedule of temporary contemporary art exhibits. Recent works were Italian modern art that paralleled the divided nation in the twentieth century, as well as an interactive experiment testing the hypothesis if plants feel emotion. Hint: it involves you, a two-story slide, and a plant.

i Admission price varies based on exhibition, student prices available; wheelchair accessible

OUTDOORS

🏞 BOBOLI GARDENS

P. Pitti, 1; 055 229 8732; www.uffizi.it/en/boboli-garden; open daily Nov-Feb 8:15am-4:30pm, Mar 8:15am-5:30pm (6:30pm after daylight savings), Apr-May 8:15am-6:30pm, June-Aug 8:15am-6:50pm, Sept-Oct 8:15am-6:30pm

Across the river, you'll find the Medicis' private gardens, and, like everything else owned by the family, the question is never "go big or go home," it's "go big because the entire city is your home." The gardens are 111 acres of curated beauty. Your wanderings may take you by the lemon gardens, through arches greenery and

rolling hills, past a host of sculptures, and to the **Fountain of Neptune.** The hike up the hill is worth it for a view of **Pitti Palace** and the city. We can only imagine a couple of the Medicis lounging in their garden, surveying the city they literally owned and built.

i Admission €10; last entry 1hr before closing; limited wheelchair accessibility (enter from Pitti Square or Porta Romana Square); free ticket on the first Su of each month

BARDINI GARDEN

Costa S. Giorgio, 2; 055 2006 6233; www.villabardini.it/; open daily Nov-Feb 8:15am-4:30pm, Mar 8:15am-5:30pm, Apr-May 8:15am-6:30pm, June-Aug 8:15am-7:30pm, Sept-Oct 8:15am-6:30pm

Adjacent to the **Boboli Gardens** is the Bardini Garden, which may arguably have the best views of the city—even better than **Piazzale del Michelangelo.** Somehow, the majority of tourists haven't caught wind of this garden, and its smaller size makes it a perfect escape from the bustling streets. The garden is found along a steep hill, but the trail is very relaxed. The outlook, with its sweeping views of the city, also has a restaurant and café, so you can soak up the silence and beauty for a little bit longer than your tired legs will standing up. Make sure to walk down the vine and flowered covered archway: it's simply perfect.

i Admission €10, students €5, admission included with Boboli Garden ticket; last entry 1hr before closing; limited wheelchair accessibility; closed first and last M of each month

FOOD

🍴 ALL'ANTICO VINAIO ($)

V. dei Neri, 74/R; 055 238 2723; www. allanticovinaio.com/en/; open Su-F 10:30am-10pm

All'Antico Vinaio has our vote for best panini in Florence, and is a contestant for the best in Italy. They don't skimp on any ingredient that makes up their eight-item menu. For a summer special, they cut a third of a loaf of thick, soft bread, sliced half a ripe tomato, an entire mozzarella ball, a generous handful of basil leaves, and topped it off with several thick slices of ham. The bad news is that this is no hidden gem, and on any given summer day you can find all three (!) of their locations have a line at least 30 minutes long.

i Paninis from €5; cash only; wheelchair accessible

ANTICA TRIPPERIA NERBONE (DA NERBONE) ($)

Mercato Centrale, 1st floor; 055 219949; open M-Sa 8am-2pm

Cows have four stomachs, and da Nerbone makes sure no stomachs are forgotten. The traditional market stand has been serving Florence and **Mercato Centrale** since 1872, and it doesn't look like much has changed since then. The menu is in Italian, but basically the options are a variation on how many ways they can cook different parts and types of meat. Their most popular dish is *panini con bollito*, a boiled-beef sandwich dunked in the meat's juices. Da Nerbone's peak hours are during lunch, and the line can get pretty long, but do it for the beef.

i Sandwiches from €4, pastas from €6; cash only; wheelchair accessible

VIVOLI ($)

V. dell'Isola delle Stinche, 7r; 055 292334; vivoli.it/en/home-2/; open Tu-Sa 7:30am-midnight, Su 9am-midnight

If we could marry a business, we would get hitched to Vivoli's. Boasting the title of the oldest *gelateria* in Florence, it quite possibly might also be the best. Each batch of gelato is made fresh daily in the "laboratory" next door, and flavors alternate depending on which fruit and ingredients are available. The gelato is thick, not too sweet, and absolutely perfect.

i Gelato from €2; cash only; dairy-free options available; wheelchair accessible

CERNACCHINO ($)

V. della Condotta 38R; 055 294119; open M-Sa 9:30am-7:30pm

Cernacchino was one of the only places in Italy we visited that used mustard on their paninis, and for that (and more) we are ever so grateful. The restaurant is small but cozy, and if you decide to sit at one of their tables,

you'll be rubbing elbows with locals and travelers alike. The choose-your-pasta plates are nothing to write home about, but they make a mean panini—large slices of crunchy bread, thick slabs of meat, and a wide selection at a low cost make it the perfect pit stop for lunch.

i Paninis from €5, entrées from €6; wheelchair accessible

DAL BARONE ($)

Borgo San Lorenzo, 30; 055 205 2519; dal-barone-solo-cose-buone.business.site; open daily 11am-11pm

In general, you should expect to pay a little more for the restaurants in the surrounding area of **Piazza del Duomo.** One of the standouts that defied this trend was Dal Barone. Many visitors here do takeaway, grabbing a panini before running off again, but there's also a sit-down option that is cute and cozy while still being a part of the busy city outside. There's a huge range of options here, so it's almost guaranteed you'll find something for your tastes.

i Appetizers from €6, first entrées from €7.50, 2nd entrées from €5; vegan and vegetarian options available; wheelchair accessible

FOODY FARM ($)

Corso dei Tintori, 10/R; 055 242327; www. foodyfarm.it/en/; open daily 11am-2pm

Farmhouse chic décor plus organic and locally produced food? No, this isn't a new Brooklyn pop-up shop, but Foody Farm in Florence, a farm-to-table concept restaurant with fantastically fair fares. The restaurant works with about 10 farms in Tuscany to bring you fresh, local ingredients, and it really makes the difference. Their menu boasts food from the "pasture, barnyard, farmyard, garden, and granary," and it can be hard to know what to choose. Luckily, there are half portions, which is perfect for trying different things, sharing with friends, and being kind to your wallet.

i Entrées from €6; vegetarian options available; wheelchair accessible

OSTERIA PASTELLA ($$$)

V. della Scala, 17/r; 055 2670240; www.
osteriapastella.it; open daily noon-
2:30pm and 7pm-10:30pm

You don't know what you're missing
until you've watched pasta be made
before your very eyes, only to
have it land on your plate within
seconds. Osteria Pastella, along
with its handmade pasta and fancy
interpretations of Italian classics,
provides a type of entertainment to
its hungry customers and passerby.
A chef in the window kneads dough
and cuts slices of pasta to order, and if
you order the pasta *flambé,* the pasta
is prepared and flamed on a Grana
Padano wheel right at your table. It is
a bit of an expensive night out, but so
worth it.
i Pasta from €14, entrées from €18;
reservations recommended; vegan and
vegetarian options available; wheelchair
accessible

SHAKE CAFÉ ($)

V. degli Avelli, 2R; 055 215952; www.
shakecafe.bio/; open daily 7am-7:30pm

Shake up your carb-loaded Italian
diet with something that actually
resembles healthy eating at Shake
Café. This place is hip in the sense
that a hashtag using, white American
girl is going to absolutely love the
#cleanliving options on the menu
(conveniently, this is also the crowd
the café generally attracts). There
are smoothie bowls, smoothies, and
juices made fresh and with fresh fruits
and vegetables, and the wraps and
salads are large and filling. There's
also coffee, but not the Italian classics
you're used to (yes, that means you
can get flavored lattes, chai and
matcha included).
i Coffee from €1; cash only; vegan and
vegetarian options available; wheelchair
accessible

NIGHTLIFE

MAYDAY CLUB

V. Dante Alighieri, 16; 055 238 1290;
www.maydayclub.it/english.html; open
Tu-W 7pm-2am, Th 8pm-2am, F-Sa 7pm-
2am

Perusal of Mayday's website is quite
the read, seemingly coming straight
out a script for a romantic novel.
But at this luxury bar, your long-lost
lover is not a pirate or an Italian man
on a horse, but an artisanal cocktail,
concocted from ingredients and
liqueurs you've probably never
even of heard of. The bartenders
are called alchemists with a
passion for "chemistry, botany,
perfumery, and food science,"
and after all this hype, our
(high) expectations were
properly met. The drinks
are strong but complex,
which is more than we can
say for a lot of ex-lovers,
so maybe Mayday is our
true love.
i Cocktails from €8; cash
only; wheelchair accessible

KING GRIZZLY PUB

P. de Cimatori, 5; 328 775 6321; open daily noon-2am

King Grizzly Pub screams toxic masculinity. We mean, come on, the name is *King Grizzly,* wooden kegs are used as décor, and beer is the unanimously-chosen drink of choice. Walking in, we were expecting to be unimpressed, or even judged, but were pleasantly surprised. The bartenders are welcoming, and the weekend DJ plays good music. At one point, all the guys at the bar started dancing, and since the pub is located on a bustling piazza corner, passersby would often come in and out to dance or watch from the sidelines. You can't help but relax and smile here, and the casual atmosphere makes it welcome for anyone. So, come in, it's just boys being people.

i *Drinks from €4; wheelchair accessible*

THE FIDDLER'S ELBOW

P. di Santa Maria Novella, 7R; 055 215056; www.thefiddlerselbow.com/fiddlers_florence; open daily 11am-2am

A local Florentine described The Fiddler's Elbow as a place for expats and American transplants, so we had to check it out. It opened in 1990 and is now known as the first Irish pub in Florence, so it's exactly what you would expect: lots of Guinness, Irish accents, and a mix of chatting groups. The outdoor seating has a great view of **Santa Maria Novella,** and it's a good place to go with a group of people.

i *Food from €4, drinks from €3.50; limited wheelchair accessibility*

RED GARTER

V. de' Benci, 33/r; 055 248 0909; www.redgarter1962.com/; open M-Sa 4pm-4am, Su 11:30am-4pm

Take a college party and replace the red solo cups with real glasses and you've got yourself Red Garter. They boast that they're Italy's oldest American bar, which basically translates to getting American teens drunk in Italy since 1962. A raised stage features karaoke and a bunch of drunk sorority girls definitely not singing the right lyrics. There's also a restaurant adjacent to the bar where you can sit and watch American football or real football. Overall, if you're in the mood to get a little sloshy, the Red Garter is the place to do it. They'll call you a taxi when you're ready to go home, be it 10pm or 3:59am, and the nice security guards outside will help you in it.

i *Cocktails from €8; wheelchair accessible*

SE·STO ON ARNO ROOFTOP BAR

P. Ognissanti, 3 (6th floor of The Westin Excelsior); 055 27151; www.sestoonarno.com/; open daily noon-2am

When you open *Let's Go's* imaginary wallet, the only thing you're gonna find in it is a couple of euros and maybe a moth, so reviewing SE•STO is something out of the ordinary. But this rooftop bar is something spectacular, and it combines our two favorite things: great drinks and incredible views. From the luxury of this hotel bar/restaurant (read: plush sofa couches, waiters in white suits, chandelier lighting), you get an unbeatable view of entire city of Florence, and you can watch the sun set over the Tuscan mountains. As the color and light changes the city and landscape, the moment the sun sets will seem to be made from pure magic—or maybe that's just the artisan cocktail talking.

i *Drinks from €15, minimum €25 per person between 7pm-9pm; wheelchair accessible; walk-in only for bar, dinner reservations required*

MALTA

Malta plays a long game. This tiny island archipelago nation, a republic since only 1974, has withstood centuries of bombardment and besiegement. Before that, it weathered the Roman empire and the Phoenicians, who dotted the island with tombs. And even before that, this speck of land in the middle of the Mediterranean—lodged on a map between Sicily and Libya—supported some of the earliest human settlements known in the world, as evidenced by the limestone temples at Hagar Qim and Qrendi. Now, at only 122 square miles and 445,000 people, Malta has built a reputation for sun and sport, making it an ever more popular tourist destination. In Malta, you can float on the surface or dive deep.

The country's cinematic natural landmarks, such as the Blue Grotto or the Blue Lagoon, shimmer in the year-round sun, while some of Europe's best scuba diving rests just off the coast. The beaches, trendy restaurants, and thumping bars and clubs of Malta's active social scene live in the moment, while its temples and foundations pull you six thousand years back in time. The island's numerous pubs, coffee joints, and English-language signs point to its recent history as a strategic port in the British Empire, while the gargle of letters in Maltese relay the island's longstanding Arabic, Italian, and French influences. In densely populated Malta, everything swirls together like the ancient markings on its signature limestone. Take a meat pie with your Baroque churches, combine cliff jumping with clubbing, and a catch a fort with your beach trip. Through it all—and there's been a lot, as its long list of conquerors suggests—Malta plays it cool, but knows how to make an impression. Just don't expect to master its language anytime soon.

The tiny country of Malta consists of three main islands. From east to west: **Malta** (the big island), **Comino,** and **Gozo.** Gozo is a holiday resort island renowned for diving, and is accessed by ferry from Malta's **Cirkewwa port.** Comino has very few full-time residents; the island receives mostly day visitors there to see its famed **Blue Lagoo**n and sea caves. Most of the country's human action occurs on the island of Malta, which contains the capital, **Valletta,** and its airport, in **Luqa.** Most accommodations reside on shore of the hammerhead-shaped bay in and around Valletta. The capital itself lies along a peninsula on the island's northeastern side. The city is relatively small—its narrow streets, set along a grid, contain classic restaurants, churches, and white apartment buildings. To the northeast of Valletta is **Sliema,** a town full of more places to eat, drink, and sleep. (In any other place, Sliema would be a neighborhood of Valletta). The cheaper, livelier town of **St. Julian's** lies further up the coast from Sliema, and is popular with students. The northernmost part of St. Julian's, a peninsula known as **Paceville,** teems with clubs and bars, particularly on **St. Georges Street.** From Valletta, buses proceed to other notable towns on the island, including **Mosta** to the west, **Mdina/Rabat** to the southwest, and **Marsaxlokk** to the southeast.

GETTING THERE

From Malta Luqa International Airport LQA: The "X" bus lines (X1, X2, X3, and X4) run from outside the baggage terminal to Malta's hubs (Valletta, St. Julian's, Paceville, and Sliema). X4 heads directly to Valletta, X2 to St. Julian's and Sliema, and X1 to destinations across the island, including the ferry port (Cirkewwa) to Comino and Gozo. Tickets cost €3 and can be purchased on the bus. Though Valletta and the neighboring cities aren't far, in distance, from Luqa, the journey can take more than an hour, depending on traffic.

From Valletta waterfront (ferry dock): Ferries arrive at Valletta's eastern harbor, which is connected by bus to most points on the island. Check routes and schedules at www.publictransport.mt or call +356 212 2000. Tickets cost €3 and can be purchased on the bus.

GETTING AROUND

Though often incredibly inefficient, public transport does connect most of the popular destinations in Malta. Buses fan out from the central station in Valletta to stops across the island. Routes and schedules vary, but most run from about 8am until 10pm. Tickets cost between €1.50-3, depending on the route.

You can pay with cash on the bus or purchase a Tallinja card at the station. For more information, visit www.publictransport.com.mt or call +356 2122 2000. To get from Sliema to Valletta, it is most efficient to take the ferry, which runs every half hour from 7am until 11pm (on the 00/30 from Sliema, on the 15/45 from Valletta). Tickets cost €1.50 one way, €2.80 with return (prices are raised to €1.75/3.30 after 7:30pm).

Swing by...

FORTIFICATIONS OF VALLETTA
Surrounding Valletta

A summary of Valletta's history sounds pretty standard for a European city: fortified, invaded, convulsed with religious purpose, refortified, life goes on, etc. But Valletta—its shape, its creation, and its battle-scarred history—is far more unusual than what comes across on paper. For a visual understanding of Valletta's singularity, take a stroll along its fortifications, which still outline the upper end of its peninsula. First built in 1488, Valletta's outermost defenses have seen their fair share of defeat: first, in 1551, when the Ottoman toppled a tower, and again in 1565, when the Turks sieged the **Fort of St. Elmo** for four months. The current walls were built under the tutelage of Jean de Valette, who imposed a grid and his name on the new capital city. Today, the limestone walls spend far more time glowing in the sun than defending the city, which is great news for your Facebook album. The fortifications still have the military on their mind, though—a walk along the walls will lead you to Malta's **National War Museum** and to the secret **Lascaris War Rooms of WWII.**

i Malta's National War Museum: Fort St. Elmo, Valletta; 2123 3088; open daily 9am-6pm; Lascaris War Rooms: St. James Ditch, Valletta; 212 34717; www.lascariswarrooms.com; open daily 10am-5pm (last entry 4:15pm); tickets €10

HAGAR QIM TEMPLES
Triq Hagar Qim, Qrendi; 21424231; www.heritagemalta.org; open daily Apr-Sept 9am-6pm, Oct-Mar 9am-5pm

You'd expect Hagar Qim, at over 5,600 years old, to quake with age. Yet it stands resolute on Malta's southern edge, demonstrating that Stonehenge's status as the symbol of *the oldest of old* is merely great marketing. For those keeping score, this temple complex, built around 3,600 BCE, is the oldest religious site in the world, predating even the Egyptian pyramids. Without context, Hagar Qim looks as if a kindergartener built a parking garage out of dominoes. This is in part due to the ivory color of Malta's globigerina limestone, which composes most of the island and all of Hagar Qim. This is also due to the arrangement of the buildings, which consist of entrances and circular recesses made from large slabs. Visitors to the complex can stroll in and around the weathered remains of these devotional buildings, which have been studied and debated for—you guessed it—centuries. Most of the complex's treasures (statuettes, pots) now reside in the museum in **Valletta,** but a few decorative limestones are on display at the site. Bring water, a hat for shade, and an appreciation for the longevity of mankind.

i Entrance adult €10, students €7.50; audio guide €1; Apr-Sept last entry 5:30pm, Oct-Mar last entry 4:30pm; wheelchair accessible

MDINA

Only a Maltese city could take abandonment issues and turn them into a selling point. Mdina, Malta's former capital, has guarded its hilltop perch in the center of Malta for over 4000 years. First founded by the Phoenicians, Mdina once bustled with merchants, the island's 1% and the territory's provisional government, but declined when all the resources were diverted to **Valletta.** Now, only three hundred or so full-time residents live in the walled "Silent City," though the villas of the past's elite are still on view. Mdina is a place to wander—through cream-colored alleyways, around sixteenth-century corners, and into **Baroque St. Paul's Cathedral.** Mdina's subdued monasteries, palaces, and gardens seem trapped in a fantasy world. This isn't completely inaccurate, as Mdina played King's Landing in the first season of *Game of Thrones.* When you play the game of thrones, you either win, or you die—or, in Mdina's case, you keep on standing silently, raking in those photo ops.

i Free, excluding the cost of travel St. Paul's Cathedral admission €5

Grab a bite at...

MINT
Triq Windsor, Sliema; 2133 7177; www.mintmalta.com; open W-Su 8am-4pm

In a culinary world where "cheap" is often synonymous with fat, fried, or simply not filling, Mint appears like a healthy, affordable, delicious Narnia near the waterfront in **Sliema.** This nature-themed eatery, owned by a couple from New Zealand, tempts with two glass displays full of freshly-designed delicacies. The Chronicles of Mint cover most of your healthy-ish food cravings with items like tofu noodle salad (€4.90), a grilled chicken and mushroom quesadilla (€4), and a chicken and brie sandwich with homemade kiwi relish (€5.80). The play is simple, quick, and easy: order your combination of goodies from the counter, take a seat at their expansive patio, and enjoy a warm meal with a complimentary side salad. Mint also offers numerous vegan, gluten-free, and dairy-free baked goods, for those craving a dosage of oats and chocolate. But never fear, fans of the fat and filling—there's still our favorite, "mega double chocolate brownie with warm chocolate sauce and vanilla ice cream" (€5.80).

i Baked goods from €1, entrées from €4; gluten-free, vegan, and vegetarian options available; wheelchair accessible

CAFFE CORDINA
224 Republic Street, Valletta; 2123 4385; www.caffecordina.com; open M-Sa 7:30am-7:30pm, Su 7:30am-3pm

Caffe Cordina isn't modest about its status as a Maltese landmark. In business since 1837, this salon-style restaurant and bakery presides over one of Valletta's main streets, with an eye for business and self-promotion. "Buy Cordina to try Maltese," its advertisements implore, with pictures of their signature honey rings and savory pies. To its credit, Cordina's efforts—the slogans, the crisply attired wait staff, the excess of marble tabletops—contribute to a generally positive experience. The traditional pea-stuffed pie, at only a euro, is flaky and filling, and their selection of cakes, cookies, and various sweets is unparalleled in Valletta. It's a task to get beyond the options peering through the long glass counter, but those that do will find a menu stocked with sandwiches, salads, and savory appetizers. No matter your choice, Caffe Cordina, with its nineteenth-century flourishes, provides enough elegance to make any stop in its large hall look classy.

i Egg breakfast from €5.50, entrées from €7, platters from €10, ice cream sundaes from €2.50, pies from €1, cocktails €6; vegetarian options available; wheelchair accessible

HAVANA CLUB
St. Georges Street, Paceville; 2137 4500; open daily 24hr

On St. George's Street, the question is not where to go but what order to go in. Borderline underage kids start with pitchers at **Qube,** while mid-twenties folks mingle on the balcony at **Native.** But at one point or another, everyone passes through Havana. This dance club brings in everyone with its buy-one-get-one-free shot cards, from kids who may or may not have their driver's licenses to probably alcoholic old men. Not that you'll be taking in the crowd, though, when you're jiving to the latest "Shape of You" remix and or screaming "I love it!" about crashing your car into a bridge. Simply put, Havana is a textbook club, one with multiple bars, a "throwback" section for 90s hip-hop, and plethora of cheap tequila shots. Feel the beat, let your hair down, and forget all the people you need to email—at Havana, one must prioritize correctly to have a good time.

i *No cover, shots €2, mixed drinks €4, cocktails from €4; BGLTQ+ friendly; wheelchair accessible*

Rest your head at...

⬚ MARCO POLO HOSTEL
Triq Ross, San Ġiljan; 2700 1430; www.marcopolomalta.com; reception open 24hr

Opened a few years ago by the same management as **Hostel Malti,** Marco Polo is Malti's cooler, fashionable younger brother who gets invited to more parties. It's similar to its predecessor but with brighter colors, a bigger rooftop, and more socializing over cheap beers. Located closer to the nightlife in Paceville than Malti, Marco Polo's rooftop, with its pillowed lounge chairs and bar, has become a prime pre-game spot for both hostels. It's a development the management welcomes, hosting barbecues for all guests on Fridays and joining forces for excursions to nearby attractions. Marco Polo runs more expensive than its brother hostel for similar lodging, though its rooms are, to be fair, nicer—cleaner, larger, with outlets and privacy curtains, and arranged so everyone gets a quality dose of natural light. A little sibling rivalry doesn't hurt, though in the end, the choice between the two comes down to how much you're willing to pay.

i *Dorms from €27, private rooms from €90; reservation recommended; min stay 2 nights; BGLTQ+ friendly; wheelchair accessible; Wi-Fi; linens included; laundry; kitchen*

Don't miss...

⬚ THE BLUE GROTTO
Boat Service: Qrendi; 2164 0058; open daily 9am-5pm

Since the collapse of the **Azure Window** in March 2017, the Blue Grotto has assumed the position as Malta's most recognizable natural landmark. The Grotto resembles the departed Window, but with more rock and less *Game of Thrones* recognition. Located just southeast of the **Hagar Qim Temples,** the Blue Grotto frames the bright Mediterranean waters with a series of limestone sea caverns. You could just look up a picture, but why not snap your own? Visitors can get a glimpse of the Grotto from atop a lookout, or get a closer look through an official 20-minute boat tour. To get to the Blue Grotto, arrange private transport, rent a car, or take the 30-minute bus route #74 from Valletta.

i *Tickets for 20-minute boat ride €8; wheelchair accessible; weather permitting*

LUCCA

Coverage by **Margaret Canady**

The defining features of Lucca are, in no particular order, the walls, the streets, and the dogs. If you removed any one of these things, Lucca would not be the same. The majority of Lucca is contained within its magnificent walls—these walls help define the city and have preserved its magic for hundreds of years. The modern world is let in, yes, but under the condition that its entrance does not disturb the city's peaceful equilibrium. Throughout the city run dozens of criss crossing streets, most paved with cobblestones. Faded hues of orange and yellow paint the buildings hugging the streets. Every curve and turn you make will lead to another perfectly conserved road and new line of shops and restaurants. You'll stumble upon a monument or church after making a wrong turn or three. When you get lost, as you ultimately will, don't panic—eventually, you will run into a wall, or a friendly person with a map. It seems that every resident of Lucca has a dog, and all of them radiate pure joy. The dogs seem to be a reflection of the city—happy dogs equal happy city. Learn how to pronounce this: Posso per favore coccolare il tuo cane? (Can I please pet your dog?) Thank us later.

ORIENTATION

Lucca is located on the **Serchio River** at the base of the **Apuan Alps** in **Tuscany.** The majority of Lucca resides within the **Old Walls**. There are four entrances into the city: **Porta S. Pietro** (south entrance), **Porta S. Maria** (north), **Porta Elisa** (east), and **Porta S. Anna** (west). Streets, for the most part, run north to south and east to west within the city; the center of the city is **Piazza S. Michele**. The streets of Lucca can be confusing, as they all tend to look similar and there are many pedestrian paths that are not labeled on the map. The train station (**Lucca Stazione F.S.**) is located two blocks southeast of the south entrance, Porta S. Pietro.

ESSENTIALS

GETTING THERE

The closest airport to Lucca is Pisa International Airport, located about 34km south of Lucca. The city is most accessible by train, and has railway lines that run hourly and connect Lucca to Florence, Pisa, and Viareggio. Tre train station is located 1min. outside the walls. If traveling by car, Lucca can be reached via highway A11 (or A12 from the coast), and parking is available outside of the city walls.

GETTING AROUND

The city of Lucca is extremely walkable, and we suggest walking to maximize your experience; it can be difficult to bike around pedestrians on the narrow streets. If you're living outside of the walls, most accommodations are found within a 30min. walking distance of the city, but biking is also an option. Rentable bikes are available around the city starting at €12 per day. There's an extensive bus system for Lucca and the surrounding area, but full disclosure: it's rather confusing and often runs late due to traffic. There are three different coding systems (LAM Red, Blue and Green, urban bus 5/suburban bus 6, and VAIBus). Buses are €1.30 one way and can be bought at the train station.

PRACTICAL INFORMATION

Tourist Offices: Tourist Center Lucca Srl Unipersonale, located in the Railway Station Square (Piazzale Ricasoli, 203; 0583 494401; www.touristcenterlucca.com/; open daily 9:30am-7pm)

Banks/ATMs/Currency Exchange: There are several banks and ATMS located within the city. Here is one: Deutsche Bank (V. Fillungo, 78; 0583 9661; www.db.com/italia/index.htm; open M-F 8:20am-1:20pm and 2:40pm-4:30pm).

Post Offices: Lucca Centro (V. Antonio Vallisneri 2; 0583 433555; www.poste.it/; open M-F 8:20am-7:05pm, Sa 8:20am-12:35pm)

Public Restrooms: Most monuments and museums have restrooms available with ticket purchase.

Internet: Many cafés and restaurants have Wi-Fi.

BGLTQ+ Resources: The closest physical resource is located in Pisa at Pinkriot Arcigay Pisa (V. Enrico Fermi, 7; 050 23278; pinkriot.arcigaypisa.it/; open Th 6-10pm).

EMERGENCY INFORMATION

Emergency Number: 112

Police: Polizia Ferroviaria (V. Nottolini, 233; 0583 493008; www.poliziadistato.it/).

US Embassy: The nearest US consulate is located in Florence (Lungarno Vespucci 38; 055 266 951; it.usembassy.gov/embassy-consulates/florence/). The nearest US embassy is located in Rome (V. Vittorio Veneto 121; 06 46741; it.usembassy.gov/embassy-consulates/rome/).

Rape Crisis Center: RAINN; (800) 656-4673

Hospitals:
- San Luca Hospital (V. Guglielmo Lippi Francesconi, 55; 39 0583 970111; www.uslnordovest.toscana.it/ospedali/44-nuovo-ospedale-san-luca-lucca; open daily 24hr)

Pharmacies: There are several pharmacies in Lucca. Here are two:
- Alliance Municipal Pharmacies (P. Curtatone, 7; 0583 491398; www.alliancefarmacie.it/; open daily 24hr)
- Alliance Farmacia Comunale Monte S. Quirico (V. per Camaiore, 1156; 0583 341567; www.alliancefarmacie.it/; open M-Sa 8am-8pm)

ACCOMMODATIONS

📷 B&B VILLA SUNRISE ($)

V. di Vicopelago e di Pozzuolo, 403; 328 225 1807; www.villasunrisebeb.com/

After staying at B&B Villa Sunrise, you're going to think that you've always had long lost friends in Lucca. Run by a mother and son duo, this B&B will treat you with the hospitality and warmth you'd expect from neighbors, not strangers. Eduardo will give you a rundown of the best restaurants in Lucca, the must-see sites, and how to get there, as well as a map and a free bike. (Yeah, we were shocked too.) The house is about

a 30-minute walk away from the city, but it's located right next to a bus stop, and shoot—that's what the free bike is for. Besides, the view is worth it; the house is situated on a farmland, and the view out of your window is that of the Tuscany mountains. When you leave Lucca, we won't be surprised if you miss this B&B as much as the city itself.

i Singles from €35, season dependent; reservation required; private bath; limited wheelchair accessibility; Wi-Fi; free bikes available; breakfast included, served 8:30-10am

COUCHSURFING ($-$$)

Addresses vary; www.couchsurfing.com/

Couchsurfing is one of the more popular options for backpackers and solo travelers visiting the city. With over 950 hosts in Lucca, it's a great option to make a new friend, gain a local perspective of the town, and save money. While we did not use couchsurfing.com when traveling to Lucca, we were informed by a local resident that couchsurfing was a popular option for travelers, and based on the couchsurfing website, it seems to be a reliable, safe, and popular option. Be careful when choosing accommodations; make sure to request a couch from someone with reliable references.

i Free; gift to host expected

TROPICAL B&B ($)

V. Romana Traversa V Corte Camaldi, 89; 388 751 9555

When we arrived at Tropical B&B, hours before we were supposed to check-in, we discovered Italian rap music, mopped floors, and a surprised but welcoming host. Tropical B&B is indeed an oasis for the weary traveler, all the way from the multi-colored bricks to the warm homemade pancakes in the morning—and especially for your bank account. A moderately priced place to spend the night, perfect for any traveler who will trade conveniency (it's also a 25-minute walk from the city, but the buses are a little sporadic) for the price.

i Singles from €30, season dependent; cash preferred; limited wheelchair accessibility; shared bath, one per floor; Wi-Fi; breakfast included and served upon request

SIGHTS

CULTURE

⬚ LUCCA COMICS & GAMES INTERNATIONAL CONVENTION

P. San Romano, 1; 0583 401711; www.luccacomicsandgames.com/it/lcg/home; last weekend of Nov

Ah, Tuscany, home of breathtaking landscapes, incomparable wines, and... comic book festivals? Lucca Comics & Games is Europe's largest comic convention and the second-largest in the world. Every year on the **last weekend of November,** tens of thousands of cosplayers and comic lovers flock to Lucca, turning the old city into a world of fantasy. The convention has several components, including the exhibition area, shows, games, and reenactments. Gosh, what we would pay to see a hoard of Pikachus in line for gelato.

i Admission from €18; wheelchair accessible

⬚ LUCCA SUMMER FESTIVAL

P. Napoleone; 0584 46477; www.summer-festival.com/; several weeks throughout June-July

If we still haven't convinced you to visit Lucca, maybe the likes of **Macklemore, Imagine Dragons, Norah Jones,** and **Ringo Starr** can help you out. Lucca Summer Festival is highkey the hottest music festival of the summer, and big names come every year and perform in open air venues throughout the summer. Skip Coachella—the only cute pics you're going to get there are with trampled muddy grass. You could be posing with hundreds of years of Italian beauty *and* listening to good music!

i Admission from €28.75; wheelchair accessible

WINDOW SHOPPING ON VIA FILLUNGO

V. Fillungo; hours vary

All of the streets in Lucca look alike, so you'll probably lose your bearings more than a few times, but at some point you'll definitely find yourself on Via Fillungo. The main road that runs between the middle of town to the **Anfiteatro,** this street is a treasure trove for those with some money to burn. There's something for everyone: clothing boutiques, of course, for the wannabe fashionista (and their kids!); furniture and decor stores for the wannabe interior designer; and even a Gamestop for the—well, actually, 2007 called, and they want the Gamestop back.

i Prices vary; wheelchair accessible; some stores close in the afternoon and reopen in the evening

LANDMARKS

⬚ TORRE GUINIGI (GUINIGI TOWER)

V. Sant'Andrea; 0583 48090; www.lemuradilucca.it/torri/torre-guinigi; open daily 9:30am-6:30pm

Any monument that requires stairs better be worth it, and Torre Guinigi fits the bill. The 230 steps (did we count? Maybe.) give way to a tree covered rooftop and a panoramic view of the entire city and the **Apuan Alps.** If you're into the stair-climbing thing, we also recommend the **Torre delle Oro** (Bell Tower) two blocks away; combined ticket options are available and you'll get to add even more steps towards your Fitbit goal.

i Admission €4, students €3; combined ticket (Torre Guinigi, Torre delle Ore, and Orto Botanico) admission €9, students €6; last entry 20min. before closing; no wheelchair accessibility; closing time varies based on month, see website for details

BASILICA OF SAN FREDIANO

P. San Frediano, 16; 0583 53576; www.sanfredianolucca.com/; open daily 9am-6:30pm

As you walk into the open *piazza* that holds the Basilica of San Frediano, your eye will immediately be drawn to the well preserved mosaic at the top of the monument. You, like us, might make the mistake that the mosaic depicts Jesus Christ with two mermaids and be surprised at the artist's creativity, only to realize the mermaids are just angels in long twisty dresses. The Basilica of San Frediano, built in 1112, is rather dark and narrow, but it is quiet and a nice escape from the crowds. The Basilica also holds the chapel and body of **St. Zita,** a popular peasant girl-saint of the thirteenth century. Today, you can see her perfectly conserved mummy resting peacefully.

i Admission €3, students €2; cash only; last entry 30min. before closing; scheduled services Sept 2-July 1 Sa 5:30pm and Su noon (entrance visits not permitted 30min. before scheduled services until they finish)

PIAZZA DELL'ANFITEATRO

P. dell'Anfiteatro; 0583 4422; www.comune.
lucca.it/home; open daily 24 hr

Piazza dell'Anfiteatro was originally an arena for gladiators seeking blood and vengeance. Today, there's little evidence of the *piazza's* original intent, unless you count the ravenous hordes of tourists fighting for a spot in line at a *gelateria*. Still, the *piazza* is beautiful to visit and maintains its large oval structure. Above the restaurants and stores that surround the perimeter, signs of life can be spotted in the faded buildings above: flowers hung from window sills, laundry hung to dry. The residents seem undisturbed by the tourists below; like the gladiators, one day they too will be gone. But first, gelato!
i Free; wheelchair accessible

MUSEUMS

✪ PALAZZO PFANNER

V. degli Asili, 33; 0583 952155; www.palazzo-
pfanner.it/; open daily Apr-Nov 10am-6pm

If Italy were a monarchy, step one would be to marry Italian royalty, and step two would be to get married at the Palazzo Pfanner. The baroque palace is a building fit for only the cream of the crop, complete with a grand staircase and main central hall, but the attached garden is the main attraction. Maintained in pristine condition, the garden features lemon trees, rose bushes and huge statues of Greek gods and goddesses surrounding the pathways. An octagonal fountain lies at the center of the two main paths. We may have been imagining it, but we swear there were wedding bells coming from behind a corner.
i Garden admission €4.50, students €4; garden and palace €6, students €5; cash only; limited wheelchair accessibility

✪ PUCCINI MUSEUM

Corte S. Lorenzo, 9; 0583 584028; www.puc-
cinimuseum.org/en/; open daily May 1-Sept 30 10am-7pm, Oct 1-Nov 1 10am-6pm, Nov 2-Jan 7 10am-1pm and 3pm-5pm (closed Tu and Dec 25); Jan 8-Feb 28 10am-5pm (closed Tu); Mar 1-Apr 30 10am-6pm

The Puccini Museum is a definite must for music and opera aficionados. The museum, set in the house of opera composer **Giacomo Puccini**, features almost entirely original artifacts. Scan the original drafts, scores, opera costumes, and letters to his friends and family, and admire the piano he used to compose most of his greatest works. If you're unfamiliar with his work, don't worry—his opera compositions waft through the museum.
i Admission €7, students €5; wheelchair accessible; ticket office is located at Piazza Cittadella, 5

MUSEO NAZIONALE DI VILLA GUINIGI (THE VILLA GUINIGI NATIONAL MUSEUM)

Via della Quarquonia, 4; 0583 496033; www.
luccamuseinazionali.it/en/guinigi/museo-na-
zionale-di-villa-guinigi; open Tu-Sa 8:30am-
1:30pm

It's pretty hard to miss the influence of Italy's Catholic roots, and the perfect example is Museo Nazionale di Villa Guinigi. We have literally never seen more versions of Mary and baby Jesus than at this museum. There's crying baby Jesus and ugly baby Jesus (I really hope that isn't blasphemy), naked baby Jesus and baby Jesus with brown, blond, curly and thick hair. They really covered all their bases. There is, of course, more art than just baby Jesus. The museum is highly curated and directs your experience to be chronological; you start with **ancient ceramic artifacts** and end with the **Counter-Reformation movement** of the sixteenth century.
i Admission €4, students €2; 1hr tours at 3:30pm and 5:30pm; wheelchair accessible

MUSEO DELLE TORTURE (MUSEUM OF TORTURE)

V. Fillungo, 209; 0583 955788; www.tor-
turemuseum.it; open daily 10am-7pm

If you have some kind of masochistic fascination with torture, then you're going to love Lucca's Torture Museum. The museum is fully aware of its niche audience, and it definitely plays up that theme—dark red walls alternate with drawings demonstrating torture devices, and the Grim Reaper stands ready for you with an ax. Despite its dramatic inclinations, the museum is actually very meticulous in both its presentation of instruments and descriptions. There are translated labels and descriptions for each weapon, and the descriptions are well-written and perhaps the best part about the museum. To describe the garrotte, the museum writes that "an iron point penetrates and crushes the trachea against the fixed collar, thus killing, in theory, by both asphyxiation and slow destruction of the spinal cord." Fun!

i Admission €7; limited wheelchair accessibility; Wi-Fi

OUTDOORS

🖼 BIKE ON THE OLD WALL

V. delle Mura Urbane; 081 867 5234; www.lemuradilucca.it/; open daily 24hr

It's kind of hard to forget that a literal wall encloses Lucca. Unlike the other walled cities that we've seen (who are we kidding, the bar here is pretty low), Lucca's novelty lies in the walkability of the wall itself. Over 30 meters wide, the wall was declared a public walkway in the nineteenth century, and ever since people have strolled and biked the circumference of the city. Large trees on both sides create a canopy of green over the pathway, and beyond the walls you have a fantastic view of both the **Apuan Alps** and the buildings of Lucca. For 20 minutes of fun, we recommend biking during sunrise or sunset: not only is it golden hour, but you'll have a fantastic view as as the sun beams down upon the mountain range not far from the city.

i Free; limited wheelchair accessibility; bikes available for rental around the city

FOOD

🖼 DA GIULIO ($)

V. delle Conce, 45; 0583 55948; open M-Sa noon-2:30pm and 6:30-10:30pm

The bar has been set. Da Giulio is the perfect restaurant for families, businessman, cute old couples, and definitely you. Unlike a lot Lucca restaurants on the main roads, Da Giulio (located on the northwest edge of the city) attracts mainly locals, and for good reason. The prices are super reasonable, the wide open rooms are air-conditioned, and the staff is incredibly helpful and welcoming. Come early for both lunch and dinner—it fills up quickly.

i Entrées from €7; vegetarian options available; wheelchair accessible

🖼 LA CREMA MATTA GELATERIA ($)

V. Fillungo, 178; 0583 952012; www.lacremamatta.it/; open M-Th noon-9pm, F-Sa noon-9:30pm, Su noon-9pm

When visiting Italy, your dietary requirements will adjust. Your four new food groups are: wine, pizza, pasta, and gelato. While we can't say our gelato palette is the most refined, we still know good gelato when we see it, and La Crema Matta is *good.* Upon ordering, the inside of your cone is first rimmed with either pistachio or chocolate sauce. Next, you get your gelato (we won't tell you what to get, there is no wrong answer—although you can't go wrong with their namesake, *crema matta),* and finally it is drizzled with pistachio or chocolate sauce and topped with a wafer biscuit. Presentation is key, and execution is 10/10.

i Gelato from €2.30; wheelchair accessible

L'OSTE DI LUCCA

Corte Compagni, 2; 0583 164 6901; open daily 11am-midnight

L'Oste di Lucca's menu proudly boasts 30 years of ownership by the Del Magro family, and we think the Del Magro family must eat really well at home. Conveniently located near the **Anfiteatro** and the **Basilica,** they're open all day and serve classic Italian fare. We got the **farro soup,** a local Lucca-style classic with whole grains of farro that is hearty and perfect with the accompanying bread. Their outdoor seating serves as a great spot for people watching.

i Appetizers from €6, entrées from €8; vegetarian options available; wheelchair accessible

PEPEROSA RISTORANTE ($$)

P. dell'Anfiteatro, 4; 0583 082361; www.peperosaristorantebistro.it/; open daily 10:30am-2:30pm, 7-10:30pm

With the delicious array of restaurants in Lucca, it can be hard to pick one, especially when they're all poppin' and people appear happy at all of them. Peperosa is one of the better options if you're looking for a nicer dinner. Located smack dab in the **Piazza dell'Anfiteatro,** you can wine and dine with a view, and usually there's live music in the piazza. Dinner comes with a mini cocktail and sample cracker, and at the end they'll give you small artisanal candies. We felt underdressed—apparently people wear things other than leggings and tank tops, #lifeofabackpacker—but the staff was very friendly and made us feel super welcome.

i Lunch from €8, dinner entrées from €12; vegetarian options available; wheelchair accessible

PIZZERIA RUSTICANELLA 2 ($)

V. San Paolino, 32; 0583 55383; www. trattoriarusticanella2.com/; open daily 11am-3pm and 7pm-midnight

The waiters at Rusticanella 2 tease each other like brothers—their playful banter bounces between tables and infects even the grumpiest of customers. This pizzeria is a great option for an affordable sit-down meal. They have a wide variety of pizza and pastas, and it's all served with a goofy smile and a friendly wink. The house wine was the cheapest we found in Lucca (€2.50 for 0.25 liter!), and you'll leave feeling warm and fuzzy. A word of warning, though—we kinda just chose an appetizer without reading the fine print, and ended up with two fat raw sausages. They were good (their meats are curated in house), but we just weren't ready for something so #thicc.

i Pizza from €7, entrées from €8; gluten-free and vegetarian options available; wheelchair accessible

NIGHTLIFE

✍ FRANKLIN'33

V. S. Giorgio, 43; 328 467 7416; open M-Tu 7am-2pm, W-Sa 7am-2pm and 6pm-1am, Su 6pm-1am

If Franklin'33 were a movie, it would be the leather jacket-wearing, cigarette-smoking, badass cool kid. Everything about the bar exudes *cool*, from the twirling bar stools to the upstairs lounge and the rich amber walls. The cocktails are inspired by both Italian and American superstars; we had something with tequila which was delicious—so delicious, in fact, that we forgot the name... The drinks come with tapas, but go early if you want to find a seat; the bar fills up almost every night.

i Cocktails from €8; BGLTQ+ friendly; wheelchair accessible

REWINE BAR

V. Calderia, 6; 0583 050124; open daily 6pm-3am

If Franklin'33 is the cool kid, ReWine Bar plays the best supporting role as the quirky and loveable best friend. We were a big fan of the red and chrome theme, the early 2000s American rock music (what's up, Kings of Leon) and the free snacks at the bar. It's a great place to meet people—after all, you kind of have to be social when you're in such close proximity and snacking on the same chips.

i Wine and beer from €4, cocktails from €6; wheelchair accessible

MILAN

Coverage by **Joseph Winters**

If you accidentally packed those green velvet Prada sandals with the hand-embellished sequins instead of the calf leather Bottega Veneta ones with the *intrecciato* borders that you meant to grab, you'll probably be able to buy a new pair once you get to Milan. Industry, particularly fashion, lives side-by-side with history here, and the dynamic duo will permeate every part of your touristic experience. Go about your day, casually sightseeing your way from the grandeur of the fourteenth century Duomo to other marvels of the Renaissance, like Da Vinci's *The Last Supper.* At any point, look up and *voilà*—chances are, you'll be face-to-face with another ultra-fancy boutique. Just be sure to save some money for the real cultural experiences: a night of aperitivos (appetizers and tapas), creative cocktails, and the hottest beats in one of Milan's famous nightclubs.

ORIENTATION

Milan is roughly circular; it spreads outwards from the center, where most of the historic sites are located, like the **Duomo, Galleria Vittorio Emanuele II,** and **Teatro alla Scala.** Beyond those, there are many broad *piazzas* (plazas), each bringing a defining characteristic to their neighborhood. The most popular neighborhoods are **Brera, Centrale, Isola,** and **Navigli.** Isola is renowned for alternative culture, Navigli for nightlife, and Brera for high-end shopping. To get the full Milanese experience, we'd recommend spending at least a day in the historic **Duomo and Castello district,** then picking out a couple areas to really delve into for the remainder of your stay.

ESSENTIALS

GETTING THERE

Milan has two international airports: Malpensa Airport (MXP) and Linate Airport (LIN). The former carries more flights from areas outside of Europe while the latter mostly handles domestic and international flights within Europe. You can also take the train into Milan, docking at Milano Centrale. The station receives trains from both MXP and LIN every 20-30min. and cities such as Florence, Geneva, Paris, Nice, and Rome. It also has connections to Milan's metro system. Bus operators such as Ouibus also serve Milan, docking at the Autostradale Viaggi Lampugnano Coach Station.

GETTING AROUND

The metro will be your ever-faithful best friend in Milan. Tickets are €1.50 per ride within the urban city limits (you probably won't do much outside in the "hinterlands"—as the information sign calls it—anyway), but the best deals are either a 24hr or 48hr ticket, for €4.50 and €8.25, respectively. There's also a carnet of 10 tickets (€13.80), or a nighttime ticket for unlimited use between 8pm and the end of that day's service (€3). You can buy any of these ticket options inside the metro, but the carnets cannot be purchased self-serve. Pick those up at the ticket office. The metro consists of the M1 (red), M2 (green), M3 (yellow), and M5 (purple). There are easy-to-read signs at every station and in every metro car, so navigation should not be a hassle. While planning your Milanese adventures, plan your nights so you don't get stranded far from your hostel after the metro stops running; the M1, M2, and M3 run from 6am-12:30am, and the M5 goes from 6am-midnight. You can catch a night bus every 30min. while the M1, M2, and M3 are on break.

PRACTICAL INFORMATION

Tourist Offices: Galleria Vittorio Emanuele II, P. della Scala; 02 8845555; www.turismo.milanoit.com; open M-F 9am-7pm, Sa 9am-6pm, Su 10am-6pm

Banks/ATMs/Currency Exchange: There are ATMs throughout the city, so you should have no problem finding one. Here's the address of HSBC in Milan (V. Mike Bongiorno, 13; 02 7243741).

Post Offices: Poste Italiane (Milano Centrale, P. Duca d'Aosta; 02 6707 2150; open M-F 8:20am-7:05pm, Sa 8:20am-12:35pm)

Internet: There are Wi-Fi hotspots in public squares throughout Milan.

BGLTQ+ Resources: Centro di Iniziativa Gay—ArchiGay Milano (V. Bezzeca 3; 02 5412225; www.arcigaymilano.org)

EMERGENCY INFORMATION

Emergency Number: 112

Police: 112 for carabinieri or 113 for local police.
• Police headquarters (V. Fatebene-fratelli, 11; 02 62261; www.questure.poliziadistato.it/milano)

US Embassy: The nearest US Embassy is located in Rome (V. Vittotio Veneto 121; 06 46741). There is a US consulate in Milan (V. Principe Amedeo, 2/10; 02 290351).

Rape Crisis Center: RAINN (800 646 4673) and National Coalition Against Domestic Violence (303 839 1852)

Hospitals:
• Ospedale Niguarda Ca'Granda (P. dell'Ospedale Maggiore, 3; 02 64441; open daily 24hr)
• Milan Medical Center S.R.L. (V. Mauri Angelo, 3; 02 4399 0401; open M-F 9am-6pm)

Pharmacies: Della Cittadella (Corso di Porta Ticinese, 50; 02 832 1584; open M-Sa 7am-1am, Su 8pm-midnight)

ACCOMMODATIONS

🏨 OSTELLO BELLO ($$)

V. Medici 4; 236482720; www.ostellobello.
com; reception open 24hr

According to the counter staff, "this hostel
is more of a bar." Named the best hostel
in Italy by Hostelworld, Bello is truly
much more than just a hostel. Aside from
the bar, there's a big breakfast buffet, free
dinner, and a fridge stocked with food
for the taking. They even offer Wi-Fi
modems to take with you throughout
your days pedaling through Milan's streets.
Plus, it's the most centrally-located hostel
in Milan, just a few blocks away from
the Duomo, near a sort of Bohemian
neighborhood full of niche bookstores,
cafés, and nightclubs.
i Dorms from €45; reservation recommended;
wheelchair accessible; Wi-Fi; linens, towels
included; lockers provided; free breakfast

MADAMA HOSTEL AND BISTROT ($)

V. Benaco 1; 3663107485; www.madamahos-
tel.com/en; reception open 24hr

Something of an oasis in the middle of an
otherwise unremarkable part of Milan,
Madama Hostel and Bistrot makes up
for its location with the amenities it
provides. Free breakfast in the morning,
aperitivos in the evening, free entrance to
the affiliated club, morning yoga, African
dance classes, and poetry readings, just
to name a few. The staff are both friendly
and knowledgeable, which helps as the
bistrot gets surprisingly busy at night. It
serves hostel-goers, clubbers, and other
passersby who are up for some cheap eats
and maybe a final shot (of espresso) before
bedtime.
i Dorms €25; reservation recommended;
BGLTQ+ friendly; wheelchair accessible; Wi-Fi;
linens, towels included; lockers provided;
laundry (wash €3, dry €3)

QUEEN HOSTEL ($)

V. Regina Margherita, 9; 236564959; www.
queenhostel.com; reception open 24hr

Part hostel, part local college student
study spot, Queen Hostel is the new kid
on the block. The common areas, with
a pool, foosball tables, and punk rock
instruments strewn about, make you feel
like you're in an underground lounge.
This might be because you're so far from
most of the other notable nightlife in
Milan, although the metro isn't too far

away. Plus, whatever Queen Hostel
lacks location-wise, it makes up for in its
amenities: like daily events at the bar an
a stocked guest kitchen. They have a bit
of fun with the word "breakfast," though,
as they really mean a croissant, some
"rusks" (croutons in a bag), and coffee.
Thankfully, grocery stores abound in this
neighborhood.
i Dorms from €24; BGLTQ+ friendly; wheelchair accessible; Wi-Fi; linens, towels, lockers,
breakfast included

SIGHTS
CULTURE

FIERA DI SINIGAGLIA FLEA MARKET

Ripa di Porta Ticinese; open Sa 8am-3pm

When the Milanese aren't perusing the
Vittorio Emanuele Mall for a new pair
of diamond-studded, crocodile skin
stilettos, you might find them doing
normal people things, like haggling over a
head of cabbage at a street market. It can't
get more authentic than the market on
the edges of the **Parco Baravalle.** There
are killer deals on veggies, fruits, cheeses,
fish, and even some prepared delicacies
like *arancini di riso.* Pro-tip: swing by at
4pm when the vendors are almost done
packing up—lots of the fresh stuff can't be
resold at the next market, so often times
you can pick up food on the cheap.
i Stand prices vary; some stands cash only;
wheelchair accessible

NAVIGLI

Navigli District; open daily 24hr

Canals? In Milan? They aren't the canals
of Venice, but Milan has its own set of
boutique and restaurant-lined waterways
in the Navigli District, south of the
Duomo. Home to not one but three
universities, students and tourists flock to
the area after sunset for some cocktails and
aperitivos. Pros include quality seafood,
beautiful sunsets, and flea markets on the
weekends. Cons include having to discern
which places are the tourist traps and
which are the local joints. The best advice:
use your instincts; if a place is serving
"Tradishonal Milan Cuisine," chances are
it might not be as "tradishonal" as they'd
have you believe.
i Store prices vary; wheelchair accessible

PORTA VENEZIA

Porta Venezia; open daily 24hr

Navigli is generally the first place people think of when it comes to Milanese nightlife and culture, but Porta Venezia, on the opposite side of town, offers a different genre of entertainment. Unlike Navigli, which caters to larger hordes of unknowing tourists, you won't find as many Americanized places like "Pizzeria Manhattan" in Porta Venezia. Instead, look for tons of hipster cafés, ethnic restaurants, clubs, and a thriving BGLTQ+ nightlife scene. There's also an interesting park full of science-y attractions, like the **Museum of Natural History** and a **Planetarium,** which offers pretty much the only way to see the stars in Milan due to urban light pollution.

i *Store prices vary; wheelchair accessible*

LANDMARKS

🏛 THE DUOMO

P. del Duomo; 272022656; www.duomo-milano.it/en; church open daily 8am-7pm, museum open daily 10am-6pm

It's not like you're going to miss it, since it's pretty much the center of the whole city and reaches a gargantuan height of 158 meters, but the Duomo—the fifth largest cathedral in the world—is non-negotiable as far as tourist destinations go. It took nearly 600 years to build and has since attracted thousands of tourists on the daily, including Mark Twain and Ernest Hemingway (yes, celebrities can be tourists, too). The interior is breathtaking, but for the real deal, clamber onto the rooftop terraces for a panoramic view of Milan. Pro tip: there's little information to be found, so we advise that you buy an audio guide, tour the museum, or research its architectural style to give the Duomo historical context. Or, you know, there's also Wikipedia.

i *Admission to church, terrace, and museum €12, combo ticket with terrace access €16; tours every 90min.; wheelchair accessible*

🏛 THE LAST SUPPER

P. Santa Maria della Grazie, 2; 292800360; www.cenacovinciano.net; open Tu-Su 8:15am-7pm, closed Jan 1, May 1, Dec 25

For some reason, no one ever tells you that *The Last Supper* isn't some painting hanging on a curator's wall, but rather an enormous, **15-foot-high fresco** that completely covers one side of a Dominican monastery. **Da Vinci** used an avant-garde technique called "dry" painting in order to make changes as he went, but it actually ended up making the fresco really hard to preserve. Way to go, Leo. To get in, you'll have to book tickets online way in advance, or hope someone canceled their reservation. Best is to play it safe: your trip to Milan pretty much won't count if you skip *The Last Supper.*

i *Admission €25 plus €2 booking tax, EU citizens €5 plus €2 booking tax, under 25 free plus €2 booking tax, guided tours daily every 15min. €3.50; last entry 6:45pm; wheelchair accessible*

GALLERIA VITTORIO EMANUELE II

P. del Duomo; open daily 24hr

Instead of exhausting your brain through intense study of Renaissance painting or Gothic architecture, invest time into the history behind the world's oldest malls: the Galleria Vittorio Emanuele II. Crash course: the building, completed in 1877, was named after the first king and its architecture makes it a must-see. Stroll through two massive glass-paned hallways that meet in the centrally-located glass dome. Once you've snapped a few photos, there's plenty of perusing to do in high fashion stores. That isn't to say there aren't some trinket shops and cheap eats sprinkled here and there.

i *Store prices vary; wheelchair accessible*

L.O.V.E.

P. degli Affari; open daily 24hr

L.O.V.E. might seem an inappropriate name for a statue of a hand flipping the bird, but, in this case, it stands for *Libertà, Odio, Vendetta,* and *Eternità* (Freedom, Hate, Vengeance, and Eternity). It was provocatively added to Piazza Degli Affari, the center of the Italian stock exchange, in 2010. Ever since, hordes of tourists with Gucci handbags bursting with designer clothes and sunglasses have stopped by to snap a picture of this anti-capitalist symbol. The *piazza* itself is actually relatively quiet but it offers a worthwhile change of scenery from the more commercial piazzas that surround it.

i *Free; wheelchair accessible*

MUSEUMS

CASTELLO SFORZESCO

Museo

P. Castello; 288463700; www.milanocastello. it/en; open Tu-Su 9am-5:30pm

Castello Sforzesco Museo is an... eclectic mix of Italian art. Seriously, one second you'll be appreciating **Michelangelo's** *Pietà Rondanini,* and the next you'll be admiring a decorative set of silverware from the 1980s. There's the **Museum of Ancient Art, the Museum of Musical Instruments, an Egyptian Museum,** and so on. The best strategy is to select just a few areas, and explore them thoroughly, rather than try to hopelessly sprint through the entire museum to see everything in one shot (we found out the hard way). Don't miss the **da Vinci** museum, though—unfortunately, you won't see THE *Last Supper,* but there's an entire room full of replicas, some nearly as old as the original. You'll turn corner after corner, thinking, "this has got to be the last *Last Supper.*" It won't be.

i Admission €5, reduced €3; last entry 5pm; wheelchair accessible

MUSEO DI STORIA NATURALE DI MILANO

Corso Venezia, 55; 288463337; open Tu-Su 9am-5:30pm

Many, many years ago, before its conquest by the Romans in 222 BCE, and before being captured by the Celts in 400 BCE, and right around the years 1000 to 4.5 billion years BDG (before Dolce and Gabbana), Milan had a pretty rich natural history. The Museo di Storia Naturale di Milano showcases it expertly with an impressive density of dioramas featuring animals and skeletons by region of origin. They even have an entire section devoted to the wildlife of Italy—something often forgotten by the average city-going tourist. Granted, sometimes, the taxidermists were a little too ambitious in planning some of the dioramas; keep your eyes peeled for a particularly wonderful display of two marmosets in the midst of a fierce battle. *Nota Bene:* most of the exhibits are labeled only in Italian, so be prepared to admire the displays without really understanding what's going on.

i Admission €3, reduced €1.50; last entry 5pm; wheelchair accessible

MUSEO TEATRO ALLA SCALA

Largo Ghiringhelli 1, P. Scala; 288797473; www.teatroallascala.org; open daily 9am-5:30pm

Step into the shoes of the Milanese elite (like Armani or Prada) at the Museo Teatro alla Scala and look onto the stage, home to some of Italy's most renowned performing artists, from a third-story box. Imagine it's 1776 and you're settling down for a nearly endless showcase of supersonic arias and unintelligible cantatas. Thankfully, you can snap yourself out of that fantasy by checking out the museum's musical artifacts —of particular note is a copy of **Verdi's** *Requiem Mass* and **Franz Liszt's** piano, gifted to him by Steinway and Sons themselves in 1883.

i Admission adult €7, students €5, audio guide €7; wheelchair accessible

OUTDOORS

🖼 LAKE COMO

Como, Italy; open daily 24hr

A mere hour-long train ride away from **Porta Garibaldi** or **Cadorna Station** (€4.80), Como is a playground for the uber-rich. Prices are sky-high for everything, the streets are pristine, and the typical tourist carries a different pair of sunglasses for every hour of the day. If you make the trek to Como, do a quick walk-through of the streets, checking out some historical sites (like its own Duomo—much smaller than Milan's), and soak in some beautiful views of the water. You can take a ferry ride to one of the smaller villages further north. **Bellagio,** the "Crotch of Lake Como" (because Lake Como is shaped like a pair of pants) is very popular, but it's a whole notch (or three) more touristy than Como.

i Train from Garibaldi or Cadorna Station €4.80, speed ferry to Bellagio €14.80, regular ferry €10, bus round-trip to Bellagio €3.60; wheelchair accessible

PARCO SEMPIONE

V. Wolfango; open daily 6:30am-8:30pm

Just behind the grandiose **Castello Sforzesco** is Parco Sempione, Milan's largest urban park, home to lots of hidden gems like the **Arco della Pace** (Arch of Peace), an Arc-de-Triomphe-style tribute to Napoleon Bonaparte's victories; the **Arena Civica** (Civic Arena), a sports and music venue built in the early 1800s; the **Acquario Civico** (Civic Aquarium); the **Torre Branca,** a tower you can ride an elevator to the top of for €4; and the **Palazzo dell'Arte,** home of the **International Exhibition of Decorative Arts.** If none of that piques your interest, it's always nice to sprawl out in the grass and soak up the Milanese sun while locals walk their dogs through the park.

i Free; wheelchair accessible

FOOD

FLOWER BURGER ($$)

V. Vittorio Veneto 10; 239628381; www. flowerburger.it; open daily 12:30pm-3:30pm and 7pm-11pm

"Don't be a fool, nutrition is cool!" reads a sign on the wall at Flower Burger. Even though you may have come to Milan for the hunks of breaded meat fried in butter that they call *alla Milanesa*, it's not like that's what the Milanese eat at every lunchtime; if they did, they wouldn't fit into those teeny cars. At Flower Burger, however, the Milanese have struck a mouthwatering balance between health and flavor; the six burgers served are all vegan, cooked on black, yellow, or pink buns and slathered with delicious homemade "cheese" or "mayo" concoctions, spicy salsas, and—of course—topped with a hearty dose of veggies. There's no

Wi-Fi, but that's okay because you'll be too busy devouring your burger to check Facebook anyway.

i Burgers from €6.50, 10% lunch discount; wheelchair accessible

IL MASSIMO DEL GELATO ($)

V. Lodovico Castelvetro, 18; 23494943; www. ilmassimodelgelato.it; open Tu-Su noon-midnight

With a gelateria on literally every street corner, it can be hard to separate the fantastico from the average. Try to restrain yourself from the allure of the first one you spot and seek out Il Massimo del Gelato—the difference in quality is well worth the wait. Self-described as having been "created to conquer the eyes," Il Massimo offers "voluptuous" flavors like 100% dark chocolate, Aztec (chocolate with chili pepper), and classics such as pistachio and gianduja (hazelnut). A surprising favorite: the *limono,* which might just be more lemon-y than sucking on an actual slice of fresh lemon. There are a couple different locations—the original one in the northwest part of Milan has the most flavors, but there's a smaller store right by the **Duomo.**

i Scoops from €2; card minimum €10; vegetarian options available; wheelchair accessible

PAVÉ ($$)

V. Felice Casati, 21; 294392259; www. pavemilano.com; open Tu-F 8am-8pm, Sa-Su 8:30pm-7pm

"Sex, love, and *panettone"* are apparently the ingredients to a life of bliss, according to one of the many typographic posters adorning the walls of this hipster coffee joint. The *panettone* doesn't disappoint, and it's certainly served with a lot of love (but you'll need to look elsewhere to complete the happiness trio). Expect deliciously rich shots of espresso brewed with "traditional values" and "raw materials value." Bad translations aside, it's worth coming for the funky vibes and free Wi-Fi. You might even meet a fellow traveler at their communal table. Serendipitous meetings are encouraged, as Pavé's menu reads "By the way, you should know your greatest love was a stranger once." Maybe that bite of *panettone* really could lead to love, which could lead to... Well, you get the idea.

i *Entrées from €6, pastries €5, coffee from €1, wine €20; vegetarian options available; wheelchair accessible*

PIZZA AM ($$)

Corso di Porta Romana, 83; 25110579; www.pizzaam.it; open Tu-F noon-3pm and 7pm-11:30, Sa noon-3:30pm and 7pm-11:30pm, Su 7pm-11:30pm

The Italians know they're famous for pizza, and you'll get the feeling everyone is trying to jump on the pizzeria bandwagon whether it makes sense or not. Use your discerning eye and say no to "Kebab Pizzeria" or similar jack-of-all-trades places like "Pizzeria Restaurante Café Internet!"; there are better places out there, we promise. Pizza AM, with its bright colors, creepy marionettes, and world flags galore, boasts a mere six—but highly sought-after—flavors. In the evenings, hungry patrons form lines that extend down the street. Waiting may not be so bad, though, as the owner appeases hungry soon-to-be customers by offering them free beers and much-needed *aperitivos.*

i *Slices from €6; vegetarian options available; wheelchair accessible*

NIGHTLIFE
FRIDA

V. Pollaiuolo, 3; 2680260; www.fridaisloa.it; open M-F 10am-3pm and 6pm-8pm, Sa 6pm-2am, Su noon-1am

Just north of the ultra-polished shopping mall at **Piazza Gae Aulenti** is a grungier student hangout called Isola, where chain stores and clean-cut sidewalks are replaced with hole-in-the-wall bars and urban patches of greenery. Here, you'll find Frida, a café/bar/nightclub/shop hybrid with a lovely patio area surrounded by vine-covered walls and geometric graphic art. Frida boasts an ability to cater to all palettes, so whether you're looking for a simple Mai Tai or more creative creations like the "Puppa Puppa" with vodka, peach juice, and passion fruit, this is the place to be.

i *Small plates from €5, beer from €5, wine from €7, cocktails €7; wheelchair accessible*

VINILE

V. Alessandro Tadino 17; 02 36514233; www.vinilemilano.com; open Tu-Su 6:30pm-2am

Beyond wine, enjoy beer or "Mixing Desk Specials," as well as a Jazz Menu replete with Soul Salads, Rock Snacks, and Funky Sandwiches named after rock and pop legends like Beyoncé. If you're already dizzy from an overdose of eclectic-ness and groovy live music, try to avert your eyes from the disco ball that dimly illuminates the bar. Side note: pretty much every piece of Vinile's décor is for sale, so the fun doesn't ever have to end. If you buy the life-sized R2-D2 replica, our editorial staff would love a photo as proof.

i *Wine from €5, beer from €5, cocktails from €7; entrées from €7; vegetarian options available; wheelchair accessible*

GINGER COCKTAIL LAB

V. Ascanio Sforza, 25; 33 55690779; open Tu-Su 6pm-3am

Who said being vegan was supposed to be boring? At Ginger Cocktail Lab, a tiny bar adorned with car hoods and antique furniture, carnivores and herbivores alike can both nosh on traditional Milanese *aperitivos* gone animal-free while sipping on specialty cocktails with names like Jekyll and Hyde. There are also some more traditional drinks like caipirinhas or mojitos for the less adventurous. For the even less adventurous, there's a pharmacy across the canal where you can sip vitamin water or prepare for the next morning's epic hangover.

i *Drinks from €6; vegan and vegetarian options available*

NAPLES

Coverage by **Adrian Horton**

You've probably heard some rumors about Naples. "It's incredible!" some say, citing the city's energy, authenticity, and pizza. "It's so dirty!" others claim, put off by the port's crowded apartment buildings, overstuffed trash bins, and grit-stained sidewalks. Naples has a mixed reputation; churches and palaces abound in Naples but Rome, it is not. Rather, Naples has its own unpolished take on the living history museum—medieval buildings teem with people and televisions, apartments rest upon Roman ruins, and restaurants serve up recipes perfected over generations. Once a Roman resort city, later a jewel in the French and Spanish crowns, and formerly the second largest city in Europe, Naples wears its turbulent past on its sleeve. It also bears the scars of Italian unification, which decimated its economy. The twin thorns of poverty and pollution still burrow into Naples' side, though conditions have improved in the past couple decades. Don't be deterred by the word on the street, though—Naples doesn't hide, and neither should you.

ORIENTATION

Though on the west coast of Italy, Naples actually faces south; its coastline on the Gulf of Naples is bookmarked by the town of **Pozzuoli** to the west and the storied **Mt. Vesuvius** to the east. **Napoli Centrale Station** and the overrun **Piazza Garibaldi** greet visitors at the east end of the center city. The historic center of Naples, **Centro Antico,** lies just west of Piazza Garibaldi and is framed by two major streets. The first, **Via Tribunali** runs west from **Castel Capuano** to **Piazza Dante** and provides the main artery through which flow Centro Antico's towering apartment buildings, artisan shops, and most famous pizza joints. The second, **Via Toledo,** runs from Piazza Plebiscito on the harbor, through Piazza Dante and towards **Capodimonte** in the north. Across Via Toledo lies the **Spanish Quarter,** a maze of narrow streets, laundry lines, and scooters that do not look before they power around corners. The Spanish Quarter slopes upward towards the **Vomero Hill,** home to the star-shaped **Castel Sant'Elmo.** Along the coast to the south of Vomero is **Chiaia,** where many bars, upscale restaurants, and some clubs can be found.

ESSENTIALS

GETTING THERE

From Naples International Airport, "Alibus" connects the airport with Napoli Centrale Station. Buses run from 6:30am-11:50pm from the station just outside the terminal. One-way tickets cost €4. From Napoli Centrale Station (Piazza Garibaldi), trains from other cities and surrounding areas arrive at Napoli Centrale, also referred to as Garibaldi Station. Napoli Centrale is east of the city center, so most visitors will need to hop on the metro (downstairs in the station; follow signs from the train platforms) to reach their final destination.

GETTING AROUND

Naples is, for the most part, navigable on foot (though the hills are a challenge), but recent investment in public transportation provides visitors with several less strenuous options. Naples' metro caters mostly to suburban commuters, though the two main lines span large portions of the city. Line 1 connects Napoli Centrale to the east with the Vomero hill to the north, and weaves through popular stops such as Piazza Dante, Via Toledo, and the Archaeological Museum (Museo). Line 2 mirrors the coast, running from Centrale in the east to the Stadio San Paolo in the west. Single metro tickets cost €1.10 and are valid for 90min. A day-pass costs €3.10. The metro runs from 6am-11pm. Bus routes can occasionally provide efficient service to areas not as well-reached by the metro. Tickets cost

€1.20 and are valid on any changes for 90min. Naples's four funiculars serve the Vomero hill: Centrale, Chiaia, Mergellina, and Montesanto. The routes save you some walking (the average ride time is 10min.) and make for great pictures. All four are open daily 7am-10pm except for Chiaia, which remains open until 2am on Saturdays. Tickets cost €1.20.

PRACTICAL INFORMATION

Tourist Offices: There are numerous tourist information centers across the city, including Garibaldi Station (081268779), P. del Gesú (0815512701), and P. dei Martiri (0814107211).

Banks/ATMs/Currency Exchange: As in most large Italian cities, ATMs are common throughout the popular areas and deliver cash in euros.

Post Offices: Besides Poste Italiane centers, international stamps can be purchased at tourist information centers in Naples.

Internet: Naples does not offer reliable public Wi-Fi, but many restaurants and cafés do.

EMERGENCY INFORMATION

Emergency Number: 113
Police: Headquartered at the Palazzo della Questura, via Medina 75 (081 794 1111); call 112 for police (carabinieri) emergencies.
US Consulate: P. della Repubblica 2; 081 5838111; open daily 9am-8pm
Rape Crisis Center: For English-language support, contact RAINN (Rape, Abuse, and Incest National Network) at 1-800-656-4673. The hotline, supported by the American Victims Assistance Programs, is toll-free and available 24hr.
Hospitals:
- Cardinale Ascalesi (V. Egiziaca a Forcella 31, 80139; 081 254 2111; open daily 24hr; located near Garibaldi Station)
- Primo Policlinico di Napoli (P. Luigi Miraglia 2, 80138; 800 177 780; open daily 24hr; located near Garibaldi Station)

Pharmacies: As in most big cities, pharmacies are a dime a dozen in the heart of Naples.
- Farmacia Internazionale (V. Calabritto 6, 081 7643444)
- Farmacia Mezzocannone (Corso Umberto I, 43, 081 5517488)

ACCOMMODATIONS
🗒 GIOVANNI'S HOME ($)

V. Sapienza 43; 8119565641; www.giovannishome.com; reception open as long as Giovanni is awake (he will stay up for you but prefers to close shop at 11pm)

Giovanni doesn't mess around. When he says "home," he means it—the hostel is literally his house, a medieval building converted into cozy bunk rooms with bathrooms, a common area, a patio, and a kitchen. When he advertises hospitality, he means it—he will stay up late into the night to greet incoming travelers, arrange transportation for guests, and cook fresh pasta for new arrivals. (When asked if he likes to cook, Giovanni shakes his head firmly. "No," he says, "I like to eat.") And when he promotes Naples, he means it—travelers who reveal they've never been to the former capital city are treated to a 45-minute tutorial on its importance, complete with picture books and a Google Earth geography lesson.

i Dorms €16; reservation recommended; min stay 2 nights; BGLTQ+ friendly; no wheelchair accessibility; Wi-Fi; laundry; kitchen

NEAPOLITAN TRIPS HOSTEL AND BAR ($$)

V. dei Fiorentini 10, 18366402; www.neapolitantrips.com; reception open 24hr

Sturdy metal-frame beds? Check. High ceilings, complimentary lockers, and repurposed game tables? Naturally. Neapolitan Trips Hostel and Bar definitely took the intro class on the Art and Architecture of Modern Hostels, and earned all the cheeky posters, sleek style, and electronic key-card credentials needed for a good time. In fact, with a full-service bar, a piano, and a refurbished stone and wood interior, we'd say it aced the course. Extra credit points go to its local accents, such as the decorations documenting the history of Italian soccer (er, football), central location off of Via Toledo, and winning staff with the best food recommendations in town.

i Dorms from €22; reservation recommended; BGLTQ+ friendly; wheelchair accessible; Wi-Fi; towels included; laundry (€4 per machine); kitchen; free breakfast

SIGHTS
CULTURE

CAPPELLA SAN SEVERO
V. Francesco de Sanctis 19; 815518470; www.museosansevero.it; open M, W-Su 9:30am-6:30pm

Housed within the chapel of San Severo, built in 1590, this museum houses objects of the bizarre, otherworldly, and downright confounding. The chapel's sculpture collection astounds, with pieces that make a mockery of the limitations of stone. A man peeks out from under netting in one, and cloth clings lightly to a woman in another. The star of this stock-still show, and arguably of Naples' art collection, is **Giuseppe Sanmartino's** *Veiled Christ*, a virtuosic work that defies the weight of marble. If you're still not dumbfounded, head down to "anatomical exhibits" in the museum's basement. The two creepy skeletons that reside there have perfectly preserved (or constructed, it's still unclear) circulatory systems, and stare down at you from upright models. How? Why? We don't know, either.
i Tickets €7, under 25 €5; last entry at 6pm; wheelchair accessible

PIO MONTE DELLA MISERICORDIA
V. dei Tribunali 253; 81446944; www.piomont-edellamisericordia.it; open M-Sa 9am-6pm, Su 9am-2:30pm

A small, unassuming church from the outside—especially compared to the nearby **Duomo**—Pio Monte della Misericordia holds firm on its trump card: **Caravaggio's** *The Seven Works of Mercy*. This work is considered one of the most important religious paintings of the seventeenth century; or, in non-technical speak, another example of Caravaggio being an art celeb who mastered the compare/contrast concept better than anyone else. His beautiful rendering of a man who's clearly done a lot of push-ups (oh, and his use of light and shadow) cannot be ignored, though the church hangs the painting front and center, just in case. There's not a ton to see for the ticket price, but it does pay off to casually drop the word *chiaroscuro* in conversation.
i Tickets €7, reduced €5; audio guide €2; wheelchair accessible

LANDMARKS

CASTEL SANT'ELMO
V. Tito Angelini 22; 812294459; open daily 8:30am-6:30pm (access to Piazza d'Arma and Spalti on Tu only)

On a map, it's impossible to miss the star-shaped Castel Sant'Elmo. First built in the fourteenth century by King Robert of Anjou, then enlarged into its distinctive shape by the sixteenth century, the Castel Sant'Elmo looms over Naples from the **Vomero Hill.** It's role in past and present is more difficult to pinpoint, however. The defensive fortress witnessed little fighting, though it has seen death—a lightning-sparked explosion killed 150 people within its walls in 1587. Today, it rotates through temporary art and museum exhibitions of varying interest. The spectacular view of Naples from its ramparts (the Piazza d'Armi) remains a constant gem, and is accessible by lift.
i Tickets €5, reduced (EU residents 18-24) €2.50, combined ticket for the Castel Sant'El-mo, Museo di Capodimonte, Certosa e Museo San Martino, and Villa Pignatelli €10 (valid for 2 consecutive days); last entry 1hr before closing

NAPLES UNDERGROUND
San Gaetano 68; 81296944; www.napolisot-terranea.org; hours vary

A Naples underground tour, officially operated by the company Napoli Sotterranea, explores the vast network of tunnels and ancient remains that honeycomb the city about 35 meters below the current street level. Dating back to the Roman times, these streets, later tunnels, were in and out of use for centuries before being overhauled in WWII as a citywide bomb shelter for air raids. Visitors today have far less to fear when venturing down the steps (unless you don't like cool, dark spaces) and plenty to see, including the remains of a Greco-Roman theater, a water-filled Roman cistern, and the shelters themselves.
i 90min. tour €10.50; daily tours in English every 2hr from 10am-6pm; last tour begins at 6pm; no wheelchair accessibility

PALAZZO REALE

P. del Plebiscito 1; 815808255; open Th-Tu 9am-7pm

Though not associated today with the sumptuous tastes of kings and queens, Naples was once quite the coveted royal residence, as the Palazzo Reale reminds you. The Palazzo Reale, which dominates the **Piazza del Plebiscito** in central Naples has catered to the whims of rulers since the Spanish first built the sprawling building in the 1600s. Given that it was occupied for several generations by the same dynasty that commissioned Versailles (the Bourbons), it's unsurprising that Palazzo Reale's interior luxuriates in marble, exquisite draping, gold trim, more marble, and Baroque art. The ostentatiousness of royal spending habits—lots of frescoes, chandeliers, did we mention the marble?—assaults the senses at times.

i Admission €4, reduced €3 (includes audio guide); wheelchair accessible

MUSEUMS

MUSEO ARCHEOLOGICO NAZIONALE

P. Museo 19; 814422149; www.museoarcheologiconapoli.it; open M, W-Su 9am-7:30pm

It's an open secret—yet one that still escapes some tourists—that the best parts of Pompeii actually reside in Naples, in their renowned Archaeological Museum. Though not necessarily the best promoted nor the most streamlined, Naples' Archaeological Museum maintains one of the finest troves of Greco-Roman treasures in the world. Remnants of Pompeii's mosaics are given a second life; sculptural wonders such as the Farnese Bull marble finally secure their rightful space. The museum winds through masterful bronze figures (some with stirring inlaid eyes), Egyptian sarcophagi, marbles of Hercules and Atlas, and one sensual, semi-naked model of Venus. Don't miss the so-called "secret cabinet," the museum's collection of erotic art from **Pompeii and Herculaneum,** which has only been open to visitors since 2005. Turns out that the Romans were ahead of their time in raunch and R-ratings as well.

i Tickets €12, reduced (EU citizens aged 18-24) €6; last entry at 6:45pm; wheelchair accessible

MUSEO NAZIONALE DI CAPODIMONTE

V. Miano 2; 817499111; www.museocapodimonte.beniculturali.it; open M-Tu, Th-Su 8:30am-7:30pm

The folds of bedsheets in Titian's *Danaë* catch every possible beam of natural light. The hands in Parmigianino's *Antea* reflect the genteel steeliness of the woman's face. And the bulbous noses in numerous portraits of the Bourbons demonstrate that you did not need to be Prince Charming to be royal and very, very rich. The museum, one of the largest in Italy, fills vast gilded halls with collections ranging from thirteenth to eighteenth-century paintings to the Roman marbles of the famed Farnese collection. Many of the Renaissance and Baroque A-listers get a byline—**Raphael, Titian, Caravaggio, El Greco,** and **Botticelli,** to name a few.

i Tickets €8, age 18-24 €4, under 18 free; last entry 6:30pm (galleries begin closing at 7pm); wheelchair accessible; for guided tours, call 0639967050

OUTDOORS

▨ PARCO NAZIONALE DEL VESUVIO

V. Palazzo del Principe, Ottaviano; 818653911; www.vesuviopark.it; open daily 9am-4pm (until 6pm July-Aug)

One of the most famous volcanoes in the world, claimer of thousands of lives, and the hulking backdrop of Naples—all in a half day's hike! Mt. Vesuvius isn't as tricky to ascend as one might assume. The National Park Authority has established clear paths to the crater rim, which presents stunning views of both the volcano's hidden middle and the city of Naples beyond. Once at the Vesuvius park entrance, begin brainstorming Instagram captions. Assess your energy level and footwear situation. Select your path (treks range from an easy hour to a moderate three-hour excursion on "Il Gran Cono," the standard trail). Ascend! Determine what is harder: the hike or settling on a caption. Take photos. Descend. Find clever ways to boast about your adventurousness. Impress everyone. Just another day at the office, right?

i Tickets €8, issued by the Vesuvius National Park Authority for access to the crater; no wheelchair accessibility; bring layered clothing on spring and autumn days; no wheelchair accessibility

FOOD

🍽 L'ANTICA PIZZERIA DA MICHELE ($)

V. Cesare Sersale 1; 815539204; www.dami-chele.net; open M-Sa 11am-11pm

If you can endure the crowds long enough to snag a table at da Michele's or even just peek inside, you'll see a sparse white interior, a glowing oven, and a framed picture of Julia Roberts chomping down on a slice of pizza from *Eat, Pray, Love*. For some, that's enough to trust that this Neapolitan establishment, in business since 1870, represents the holy grail of pizza. If you're not persuaded by Hollywood or bestselling memoirs, well, we don't know what it will take to convince you. The small army of pizza soldiers who constantly tend the smoldering oven? The smiling man who kneads pizza dough with the finesse of a practiced craftsman? The simplicity of options—margherita or marinara?

i Pizza from €4, drinks from €2; limited wheelchair accessibility

PIZZERIA GINO SORBILLO'S ($$)

V. dei Tribunali 32; 81446643; www.sorbillo.it; open M-Sa noon-3:30pm and 7pm-midnight

In the *Game of Margherita Thrones* that is Neapolitan pizza, Gino Sorbillo is a fierce competitor. A celebrity within and now beyond Naples, Sorbillo's builds on a family legacy of pizza-making with award-winning pizza, global accolades, and crowds of hungry fans. Notoriety aside, they serve exceptional pizza—thin, flavorful, inventive, and defiant of any American imitation. The hype and wait time, which can be as long as a couple hours, is too much for some. But if the art of pizza is your calling, consider picking Sorbillo's, which manages to deliver despite having half of Naples eyeing its crown. Winter seems nowhere in sight here, though it will have to adjust to the colder temperatures of New York City, where Gino is set to open a location later this year.

i Pizza from €8; vegetarian options available; wheelchair accessible

SCATURCHIO ($)

P. S. Domenico Maggiore 19; 815517031; www.scaturchio.it; bakery open daily 8am-9pm, restaurant open W-Su 12:30-3:30pm

Naples has built a global reputation on savory, but it still knows how to sweet talk. Specifically, the city has developed its own signature pastry, *sfogliatella* (sfoy-AH-tell-uh), a mastery of light pastry and dense filling (usually orange-flavored ricotta cream or almond paste). *Sfogliatella* requires a delicate layering of dough, resembling a lobster's tail—a feat few perform better than Scaturchio. Open since 1905, this establishment in Naples' ancient center offers arguably the city's best iteration of *sfogliatella*—warm, flaky, and somehow light yet very filling. Scaturchio also specializes in its original *ministeriale* pastry, a medallion of chocolate-covered liquored cream that may have you leaving dough behind.

i Baked goods from €2.50, restaurant dishes from €6; wheelchair accessible

NIGHTLIFE

📱 L'ANTIQUARIO

V. Vannella Gaetani 2; 817645390; open daily
7:30pm-4am

Italy had the good sense to avoid America's experiment with Prohibition (we can't say the same for organized crime, though), but a speakeasy can still flourish in the land of pizza. L'Antiquario, run by celebrity bartender **Alex Frezza,** takes its cocktails as seriously as any bootlegger found in *Boardwalk Empire.* Frezza's colorful, generous, expertly-crafted drinks will make the transition back to rum and Coke difficult, as will the staggering array of alcohol bottles rising like the Great Wall above the bar. You might miss this swanky cocktail lounge, with couches upholstered in red, if you're not in the know; like any good speakeasy, L'Antiquario doesn't have any signage. You must ring the doorbell to gain admittance, which leaves ample time to ask yourself the question: "Am I cool enough to be here?" We cannot answer that for you, but knowing the difference between liquor and liqueur is a good start.

i Cocktails from €10; snacks and small plates from €7; BGLTQ+ friendly; cocktail attire recommended

DANTE 4

P. Dante 43; 3349578690; open daily-7am-midnight

Despite its reputation as the Italian version of happy hour, *aperitivo* is oftentimes hard on the wallet. This is not the case at Dante 43, where aperol spritzes go for a cool €3 for most of the evening. You won't be skimping on location, either; Dante 43 rings its eponymous piazza on main shopping drag Via Toledo, offering great views of the square. Just across the piazza lies the **Porta Alba,** a gate to the old city that dates from 1625 and now welcomes a secondhand book market. Whether or not you're on the hunt for vintage Italian children's literature, stop by Dante 43 in the early evening to take advantage of the price, before you move on to better cocktails and bigger bills.

i Aperitivi from €3, snacks from €5; wheelchair accessible

PALERMO

Coverage by **Adrian Horton**

On an island as quaint, traditional, and rustic as Sicily, Palermo strikes an odd note. The former capital city sprawls along Sicily's northern coast, paints the night with music and dancing, and bustles with cars, and is filled with weathered apartment buildings. Palermo is a modern city—Italy's fifth largest, with the requisite cafés and designer stores—that wears centuries of history on its sleeve. Massive wooden doors lead to the foundations of twelfth-century Norman structures. Markets tingle with the same energy (and fishy smell) that wafted through medieval times. Landmarks are tattooed with insignia from various cultural chapters—Arab, Norman, Spanish Gothic, French—lest you ever forget the trials and tribulations of this city. Palermo puts on a show, but doesn't put on airs. This lively and spontaneous mix of old and new finds the wizened local chatting with the eager traveler, the youth-filled piazzas layered with centuries-old dust, and three hundred-year-old shops hosting freshly caught octopus. Check your hat, your diet, a few of your inhibitions, and enjoy the ride.

ORIENTATION

The bay of Palermo takes a bite out of Sicily's northern shore, though the city itself faces the sea. Ferries dock at the port on the east side of the city, while trains arrive at **Stazione Centrale,** south of the city center. From Stazione Centrale, two main thoroughfares extend north to form the main arteries of the city: **Via Roma** and

Via Maqueda. Both streets cross the main east-west road, **Vittorio Emanuele,** in the center of Palermo's shopping district. The intersection of Maqueda and Vittorio Emanuele, known as "Quattro Canti," marks the center point of the city. From here, Albergheria forms the southwest quadrant with its narrow streets and Arab-style markets, including the famous **Ballarò street. Monte di Pieta** forms the northwest quadrant, just above the landmarks of **Palazzo Normanni** and **Cattedrale.** To the northeast is **Castellamare,** with its collection of restaurants, churches, and former castles. North of that is **Borgo Vecchio,** a more residential and shop-filled area. The southeast quadrant houses **Kalsa,** an older neighborhood that contains nightlife hub **Vucciria,** as well as smaller piazzas where people gather to mingle, eat, and drink. Popular day trips include beach ventures to **Mondello,** which is northwest of Palermo central, and to **Cefalú,** which is an hour east by train.

ESSENTIALS

GETTING THERE

Take the Prestia Comandé bus (€7) from outside the terminal, which leaves every 30min. and arrives at Palermo's Stazione Centrale.

Bus #139 runs from the ferry dock to Stazione Centrale. Tickets cost €1.40 and must be purchased in a *tabaccherie* or kiosk. Many accommodations are located within walking distance of Stazione Centrale. To reach the city center, follow Via Roma, which continues straight ahead as you exit the front of the station. Numerous bus lines also leave from the front entrance and lead to various parts of the city.

GETTING AROUND

Palermo is larger than you think, but by sticking to the main thoroughfares (Maqueda, Vittorio Emanuele, and Roma), most of it is accessible on foot. Palermo's AMAT provides bus transportation across the city and to nearby points of interest, such as Monreale and Mount Pellegrino. For a map of routes and schedules, check kiosks at major bus stations, or www.amat.pa.it. Tickets cost €1.40 and must be purchased before you board the bus at a nearby tabaccherie or small shop. Buses run from 6am-9:15pm. For questions or concerns, contact AMAT Palermo S.P.A. (Via Roccazzo 77) at 091 350 111.

PRACTICAL INFORMATION

Tourist Offices: Servizio Turismo Comune di Palermo (Via A. Salinas #3, Villa Trabia; 091 740 5924; www.turismo. comune.palermo.it)

Banks/ATMs/Currency Exchange: ATMs are dispersed throughout the city, particularly on main shopping streets such as Vittorio Emanuele, Maqueda, and Via Roma.

Post Offices: Poste Italia handles mail in Sicily. The central post office in Palermo is located at Via Roma 320 (open M-Sa 8:30am-7pm).

Internet: Palermo does not have strong public Wi-Fi. For Internet access, look for cafés or restaurants with complimentary Wi-Fi.

BGLTQ+ Resources: Though attitudes in rural areas may be less tolerant, Palermo and Catania both have thriving BGLTQ+ populations and large pride parades during the summer. For assistance, support, or resources, check out www.palermopride.it, www.arcigay. it, www.arcigaypalermo.wordpress.it, or call ArciGay Palermo's helpline at 344 0123880.

EMERGENCY INFORMATION

Emergency Number: 112

Police: State Police/Questura Palermo (Via Della Vittoria 8; 091 210111)

US Embassy: US Consular Agency (Via G.B. Vaccarini 1; 091 30 5857, call between 10 a.m. and noon; USCitizensPalermo@state.gov)

Rape Crisis Center: Telefono Rosa, based in Rome, provides support and resources at telefonorosa.it as well as a help line at 063 751 8282.

Hospitals: Ospedale Civico (Off Via Carmelo Lazzaro; 091 606 1111; open daily 24hr)

Pharmacies: Farmacia della Stazione Centrale (Via Roma 1, 90100; 091 616 7298; open 24hr)

ACCOMMODATIONS

A CASA DI AMICI ($)

Via Dante 57; 091 765 4650; www.acasa-diamici.com; reception open 24hr

On Google Maps, "A Casa di Amici" translates to "At Friend's Place," which is not linguistically correct, but accurate in spirit. This multi-story hostel and guesthouse, located a 10-minute walk northwest from **Teatro Massimo,** strikes a balance few hostels achieve: fresh and clean facilities that still feel personal and well-loved. The owner, Santos, doubles as a drum maker and has filled the hostel with his musical instruments—a unique touch that brings guests and staff together on the patio for impromptu concerts (with drinks from the hostel's bar, of course). A Casa di Amici exudes an easy, welcoming rhythm, from the pillowed lounge couches, from the free breakfast and tea area, to the informal group bar crawls that wind late into the night.
i *Dorms from €20; payment on arrival; reservation recommended; BGLTQ+ friendly; no wheelchair accessibility; Wi-Fi; linens provided; laundry; free luggage storage*

SUNSHINE HOSTEL ($)

Via Lincoln 97; 3238 327 9897; reception open daily 8am-11pm

Finished in 2017, Sunshine is Palermo's newest hostel and has put its best brightly-painted, well-priced foot forward. The facilities are small—only a few rooms and one common area—yet immaculate, with the courtyard patio offering extra seating away from the bustle outside. The staff, led by owner and manager Francesco, do their best to welcome you to Palermo by offering restaurant and day tour recommendations, complimentary breakfast, and free shots of limoncello. Sunshine Hostel's location near the **Botanical Gardens,** a five to 10-minute walk from **Stazione Centrale,** makes it easy to reach most of the city's sights, as well as Palermo's lively food and drink scene near the harbor.
i *Dorms from €15; reservation recommended; BGLTQ+ friendly; no wheelchair accessibility; Wi-Fi; laundry available; free breakfast, luggage storage; kitchen*

SIGHTS

CULTURE

🏛 MERCATO BALLARÒ

Via Ballarò; 091 616 1966; open daily 8am-2pm

Mercato Ballarò provides fish for 10 holiday dinners, a mess for your kitchen, and a feast for your eyes. This Arab-influenced street market, which dates to medieval times, is a visual cacophony. Sausages hang from the rafters and spill over counter. Raw octopus and chunks of fish dot the tables. A price list hangs from the nose of a recently beheaded swordfish. A man guts a shark before your eyes. Welcome to Sicily, where "fresh" means straight from the water bucket and into your bag. Ballarò occupies several blocks northwest of **Stazione Centrale,** and assaults your senses with the smell of seafood and the shouts of vendors hawking their wares. For the look, taste, smell, and song of authentic Sicily, wander through Ballarò's maze of counters.
i *Free; limited wheelchair accessibility*

TEATRO MASSIMO

Piazza Verdi; 091 605 3267; www.teatromassimo.it; open daily 9:30am-6pm

1870 marked the start of a pivotal decade for Palermo. Several years earlier, in 1861, the former Kingdom of the Two Sicilies was absorbed into the new Italian state. Palermo, the former capital, was still the second largest city in Italy (following Naples). The thriving arts and culture scene in Sicily demanded a venue of global import. Thus, Palermo's mayor commissioned Giovan Battista Filippo Basile to build the biggest opera house in Italy. It took 23 years and, sadly, Basile's life, but the Teatro Massimo finally opened as the third largest opera house in Europe in 1897. Since then, the Teatro Massimo has ridden a wave of artistic highs and corruption-riddled lows. Tickets to a show today can cost you an arm and a leg, but you can still tour all 1,350 of the theater's plush seats, as well as it's backstage area and posh cocktail lounge for a few euros.
i *Guided tours (30min.) €8, reduced €5, plus €5 for backstage tour; wheelchair accessible*

LANDMARKS

PALAZZO NORMANNI AND CAPELLA PALATINA

Piazza Indipendenza 1; 091 626 2833; www.fondazionefedericosecondo.it; Palatine Chapel and Royal Palace open M-Sa 8:15am-5:45pm, Su 8:15am-1pm; Royal Apartments closed Tu-Th

Pop quiz: when you successfully invade England and Sicily in the same decade, do you convert the existing Muslim palace into your own crib, transform said Muslim palace into a masterpiece of medieval Christian iconography, or all of the above? If you've learned anything in Sicily, you know the correct answer is, well, to ball out with conquered territory as much as possible. Which is exactly what the Normans did when they claimed Sicily in 1072. Today, you can walk through the rooms of the Norman Palace complex, which display a mix of architectural styles—Norman, Aragonese, Bourbon Renaissance—typical of Palermo. The main draw, however, is the **Palatine Chapel,** the best example of Norman-Byzantine church decoration in Sicily. Translation: gold on gold, a lot of Latin and geometric mosaics, and a bevy of important Christian figures staring down at you from the ceiling.

i Tickets €12, reduced (EU residents 18-24) € 10; €10, Tu-Th €8; last entry 5pm M-Sa, noon on Su; wheelchair accessible

CATTEDRALE

Piazza di Cattedrale; 091 334373 or 329 3977513; www.cattedrale.palermo.it; cathedral open daily 9am-5:30pm; tombs and roof open M-Sa 9am-5:30pm, tombs open Su 9am-6:45pm

Compared to its baroque counterparts in Rome, the Cattedrale's style is all over the place, from twelfth-century Norman towers to a Renaissance cupola to the Quranic inscriptions of an older mosque. This isn't due to a lack of taste but rather centuries of revisions and renovations at the hands of Palermo's many rulers. Today's Cattedrale dates principally to 1184, when the Normans reclaimed an existing mosque and put up the structure's original rectangular walls. Since then, the Spanish added Catalan Gothic porches, while Bourbon rulers furnished the interior with Renaissance-style frescoes. It takes time, a guide, and a discerning eye to work through the details, so come prepared. For a few euros, you can also visit the crypt, tour the collection of crowns, and trek up to the **Duomo terrace** for a panorama of Palermo.

i Cathedral free; roof access €5, treasury and crypt €2, royal tombs €1.50; combo ticket without roof access €3, with roof access €7; roof access scheduled for every 30min.; last entry at 5pm; roof and tombs not wheelchair accessible

MUSEUMS

🏛 PALAZZO CHIARAMONTE

Piazza Marina 61; 091 343616; open Tu-Su 10am-7pm

Many medieval palaces conceal sordid pasts—torture, incarceration, takeover, the usual—but Chiaramonte does not shy away from its demons. Rather, they are painted floor to ceiling on its former prison walls, accessible to you by guided tour. Constructed in the fourteenth century as a lavish home for a Sicilian lord, the palace was converted in the sixteenth century into the HQ of the Spanish Inquisition. Before the reign of terror ended in 1782, nearly 8,000 men and women were imprisoned in Chiaramonte. Today, the cell walls, stripped of plaster, reveal extraordinary hints of the souls lost to religious tyranny in the form of Christian imagery, poetry, and even explicit cartoons of the inquisitors.

i Tours depart every hour on the hour for €8, reduced €5; cash only; no wheelchair accessibility

FOOD

ANTICA FOCACCERIA SAN FRANCESCO ($)

Via Alessandro Paternostro 58, 90133; 091 320264; www.anticafocacceria.it; open daily 11am-11pm

There's a reason brides travel for miles to have their pictures taken in front of Antica Focacceria San Francesco's storefront. This institution of Sicilian cuisine, open since 1834, has built a reputation for serving some of the best food, fried and otherwise, in Palermo. Order a selection of street food (*arancini, focaccia,* fried things) from the counter, or dine *al fresco* with San Francesco's classier menu of pasta and meat dishes. The *piazza* seating area—

definitely one of the more picturesque in Palermo—and selection of salads cater to tourists, but that's hardly a complaint when faced with a plate of delectable swordfish pasta.

i *Street food from €3, entrées from €8; wheelchair accessible*

MOUNIR ($)

Via Giovanni da Procida 19, 90133; +39 091 773 0005; open daily 7pm-midnight

Nested in an alley between the main drags of **Via Roma** and **Via Maqueda,** Mounir attracts a large crowd of street revelers in Palermo with its killer portions and light price. Mounir makes its pizzas fresh to order and, in case you need a reminder that Palermo isn't Naples, loads them with toppings—prosciutto, capricciosa, and piles of cheese, to be specific. There's also Mounir's famous kebab pizza—literally, a kebab on a pizza (minus the stick) drenched in yogurt sauce. This monster makes pizza purists shudder but provides enough fuel to keep you dancing all night long.

i *Pizza and kebabs from €4; wheelchair accessible*

NIGHTLIFE

TAVERNA AZZURRA

Via Maccherronai 15; Vucciria; 091 304107; open M-Sa 9am-5am

Though cocktail lounges and wine bars pepper Palermo, the real party occurs on streets or in markets filled with music and the cheapest drinks you'll find in Italy. At the heart of **Vucciria,** Palermo's largest meat and fish market, lies Taverna Azzurra, a family-run establishment that hosts informal dance parties on its front stoop. Azzurra serves one euro beers and mixed drinks to a raucous, nightly crowd. The price is a godsend, because you'll need a few to loosen up for the impromptu limbo games you're bound to partake in later in the evening.

i *Beer €1, mixed drinks €2; cash only; BGLTQ+ friendly*

MONKEY PUB

Piazza Sant'Anna 19; Piazza Sant'Anna; open Tu-Su 8:15am-2am

It's late on a Saturday night, and the pounding stereo of **Vucciria** has your head spinning. You leave the house music and strobe lights behind in search of a more placid scene. Enter *Piazza Sant'Anna,* a large church square that teems with young people, plastic cups, and one guy playing music from a speaker rigged to his bike. Huddled in a corner of the fiesta is MONKEY Pub, a British-themed establishment that, despite its small size, manages to supply drinks to most of the party. Revelers fill the dark wood and bottle-cap adorned MONKEY to the brim, yet the bartenders keep a pace faster than the music playing in the background.

i *Beer from €2, mixed drinks €4; cash only; BGLTQ+ friendly*

ROME

Coverage by **Adrian Horton**

You know the legacy of Rome well, though you may not realize it. It's there when you check the date, or celebrate a birthday in October. It's there when you add "etc." to the end of a text instead of continuing *ad nauseam,* or take a sip from a public drinking fountain. And it's there when you see a fish fry during Lent, or say "when in Rome…" before doing something ill-advised. Rome looms heavily in the global imagination, and for good reason. The Eternal City—officially founded in 753 BCE but likely settled earlier—forms the bedrock of our concept of Western civilization. Rome's 2770-year-old résumé puts most other cities to shame, and includes casual stints as seat of one of the largest and most powerful empires the world has ever seen, patron saint of Baroque art, headquarters of one of the world's most popular religions, and now the destination for lovers of *la dolce vita* everywhere.

And those are just a few of the highlights. Rome has led more lives than there are enemies of Julius Caesar, and has enchanted visitors for centuries to study, eat, admire, pray, and wander in its well-trod streets. Today, modern Rome attracts millions of tourists every year, which results in the formation of daunting crowds—they're particularly dense near the big monuments, especially during the sweltering summers. Even if you can't handle the lines, though, Rome still charms with an extensive offering of museums, churches, excavation sights, galleries, and sorry, pasta repurposed remains. Oh, and the food—cafés, pasta restaurants, pizza joints, trellis-covered *trattorias,* and gelato stops galore. Go ahead and enjoy that third scoop, because if there's one place that understands indulgence, it's Rome. Take a deep breath and take in the sunset as it lights up the ochres, burnt oranges, and pinks of the city—you don't have to be an arts and culture buff to appreciate that.

ORIENTATION

Rome has been planned, built, re-planned, rebuilt, and revitalized continuously for over 2770 years, so it's no wonder that old and new meld together throughout the city. While other major cities possess a grid layout or distinct districts, in Rome, many of the neighborhoods flow together in a mix of marble, terracotta, tight streets, and churches. Though it's hard to get too disoriented, it can be difficult to discern where one neighborhood ends and another one begins, especially in the old-city area between **Termini Station** and **the Tiber.** To complicate matters, the official districts of Rome *(riones),* first delineated by Augustus and revised every couple centuries thereafter, don't correspond perfectly to common names for different sections of town. Technically, Rome has twenty-two *riones,* each with their own coat of arms. Knowing them makes for impressive trivia but, as a tourist, you're better off remembering the unofficial, colloquial terms for different areas, which usually refer to famous landmarks nearby or their geographic locations.

If Rome were the four-quadrant graph from sixth grade math, the **Foro Romano** (Roman Forum) would mark the origin point, which is fitting, since the Foro Romano was the heart of the ancient city. The area surrounding the Forum, known colloquially as the **Ancient City,** contains, unsurprisingly, the headliners of Imperial Rome: the **Capitoline Hill** and its world-class museum on the Forum's western edge, the **Palatine Hill** and its former palaces to the south, the Circus Maximus behind the Palatine, and the **Colosseum** to the east. Directly west of the Ancient City is the old historic center of Rome, known as **Centro Storico,** around which the Tiber River bends westward like an elbow. Centro Storico is Rome at its most classic and picturesque—cobblestone streets, buildings that glow in evening sunlight, apartment buildings and ristorantes that bump up against Baroque fountains and medieval churches. This area, about 14 square kilometers in total, breaks down further into neighborhoods focused on certain monuments: to the northwest, **Navona,** near the elliptical Piazza Navona and the **Pantheon;** to the south, the narrow streets and squares of **Campo de' Fiori;** to the southeast, the old **Jewish Ghetto;** and to the north, the luxury shops and crowds of **Spagna**.

Heading west across the Tiber on the **Vittorio Emanuele II bridge,** you reach the walled **Vatican City,** which is technically its own country (with its own post office!). To the north of the Vatican sprawls **Prati,** known for its cheaper accommodations and restaurants. To the south rests **Trastevere,** the former working-class neighborhood that is now a top tourist destination due to the area's quaint restaurants, centuries-old buildings, and ivy-lined streets.

Starting again from the Forum and heading south along the east bank of the Tiber, you reach the Aventine Hill, sight of beautiful sweeping views of the city, expensive homes, and not much to eat. Further south lies the neighborhood of **Testaccio,** known for its energy and collection of fine restaurants. Just north of the Forum lies **Monti,** a combination of the **Esquiline, Quirinale,** and **Virinale** hills that buzzes with hip cafés, popular *aperitivo* bars, and boutique shops. Continuing north from Monti is the **Borghese area,** near the **Borghese gardens** and several notable churches. **Termini Station,** Rome's main transportation hub, resides northeast of Monti and the Ancient City. Most of the city's hostels surround Termini and its nearby streets, as do cheap tourist shops, international chain restaurants, and mini-markets. The area in and around Termini marks a gritty break from the other districts of Rome (and is a frequent complaint of unprepared tourists). The streets heading northeast from Termini go toward the blocks with the most popular hostels. Heading southeast, you reach **San Lorenzo,** home to Rome's **Sapienza University,** bars with attitude, and affordable housing.

The list of areas may sound daunting, but don't worry—you will develop confidence in your navigational skills as your trip goes on. Rome was designed to be explored by foot (or Vespa, but that requires technique we cannot assume you possess), so strap on those €15 gladiator sandals and get walking. You're bound to find a Baroque *piazza,* narrow street, or enticing café that moves you.

ESSENTIALS

GETTING THERE

From Leonardo da Vinci Airport/ Fiumicino (FCO): Known commonly as Fiumicino, Rome's main airport resides on the coast, 19mi. southwest of the city. The Leonardo Express train runs between the airport and track 25 at Termini, Rome's main train station; the ride takes 30min. and costs €11. Another train, the FM1, stops in Trastevere.

From Ciampino Airport (CIA): Rome's other airport lies 9mi. south of the city center and mainly draws budget airlines. There are no direct train links from Ciampino to the city, but express buses leave every 30min. or so and run directly to Termini. Tickets cost €4.90 and can be purchased at the information desk to the right as you're walking out of the terminal. The ride takes approximately 50min., depending on traffic.

By rail: State-owned Trenitalia operates trains out of Termini, Tiburtina, Ostiense, and Trastevere stations. Termini is open 4:30am-1:30am and its bus stop at Piazza del Cinquecento connects with most bus lines in the city. For those arriving in the wee morning hours, the night bus #175 runs from Tiburtina and Ostiense to Termini.

GETTING AROUND

Rome is a relatively compact city, and the best way to explore its cluster of monuments, churches, and narrow streets is by foot. There are various options for public transportation, however, all operated through ATAC. One ticket costs €1.50 and is valid for 75min. on any combination of vehicles.

By metro: Though not comprehensive for the entire city, the most efficient way to travel to the most popular sights in Rome is by metro. Rome has two metro lines that intersect at Termini Station. Line A, the "tourist line," runs from Battistini to Anagnina and passes through Piazza di Spagna, the Trevi Fountain, and the Vatican Museums (Ottaviano). Line B runs from Laurentina to Rebibbia, and passes through the Colosseum, Ostiense station, and the Testaccio District. Stations are indicated by the red letter "M" on a pole. Tickets can be purchased inside; a single ride costs €1.50 (valid for 60min.) and a day-pass costs €7 (€18 for a 3-day pass and €24 for a week). The metro operates 5:30am-11:30pm and is open until 1:30am on Sa night.

By bus: Buses cover more of Rome than the metro, but are less straightforward to use. ATAC operates city buses 5:30am-midnight, plus a network of night buses (*notturno*). Check routes and schedules at www.atac.roma.it (on the site, look for the Italian flag in the upper right corner to change the language to English). Tickets, valid for 75min., cost €1.50 and can be purchased at tabaccherie, kiosks, and storefronts but NOT on the bus itself. Enter from the rear of the bus, immediately validate your ticket in the yellow machine, and proceed towards the middle.

By tram: The trams, also operated by ATAC, make more frequent stops than buses and can be useful getting to and from Trastevere. As on the buses, tickets cost €1.50 and must be purchased ahead of time (consider buying several to have on you, in case a ticket station is hard to find in a pinch). Useful lines include: #3 (Trastevere, Aventine, Piazza San Giovanni, Borghese Gallery), #8 (Trastevere to Largo Argentina), #9 (Piazza Venezia, Trastevere), and #19 (Ottaviano, Villa Borghese, San Lorenzo).

By taxi: Taxis should be reserved for emergencies or pressing situations. It is technically against the law to hail cabs on the street, but they may still stop if you flag them down. They also wait at stands and can be reached by phone (+39 066645, 063570, 064994, 065551, 064157). Only enter cabs with the marking "Servizio Pubblico" next to the license plate. Be sure to ask for your receipt *(ricevuta)* to confirm the price.

By bike: ATAC operates bike-sharing. Purchase a rechargeable card from any ATAC station in the city. The initial charge is €5, with a €0.50 charge for every additional 30min. Bikes can be parked at stations around the city. Alternatively, companies such as Bici & Baci (01683230567, www.bicibaci.com) loan bikes and mopeds and have stations by the major metro stops (Colosseo, Repubblica, Spagna).

By scooter: The honking, buzzing Vespa is ubiquitous in Rome, as are the daring yet helmeted people who ride them. You can join in on the chaos by renting a two-wheeler, provided you show a valid driver's license and can handle the stress of Rainbow Road on MarioKart. Rates vary by the company, but start at around €30 for 4-8hr.

PRACTICAL INFORMATION

Tourist Offices: Comune di Roma is Rome's official source for tourist information. Green PIT information booths, located near most major sights, have English-speaking staff and sell bus and metro maps and the Roma pass (V. Giovanni Giolitti 34; 060608; www.turismoroma.it; open daily 8am-8:30pm).

Post Offices: Poste Italiane are located throughout the city (800160000; www.poste.it), but the main office is located at Piazza San Silvestro 19 (0669737216; open M-F 8:20am-7pm, Sa 8:20am-12:35pm).

Luggage Storage: Termini Luggage Deposit (Termini Station, below Track 24 in the Ala Termini wing; 064744777; www.romatermini.com; open daily 6am-11pm; bags max 22kg; max 5 days; 5hr €6, €0.90/hr for hrs 6-12, €0.40/hr thereafter).

EMERGENCY INFORMATION

Emergency Number: 112, 118 (medical emergencies)
Police:
- Police Headquarters (V. di San Vitale 15; 0646861)
- Carabinieri have offices at V. Mentana 6 (near Termini; 0644741900) and at P. Venezia 6 (0667582800).
- City police (P. del Collegio Romano 3; 06468)

Hospitals:
- Policlinico Umberto I. (Vle. del Policlinico 155; 0649971; www.policlinicoumberto1.it; open 24hr; emergency treatment free)
- International Medical Center (V. Firenze 47; 064882371, 060862441111; www.imc84.com; call ahead for appointments)

Pharmacies: The following pharmacies are open 24hr.
- Farmacia Internazionale (P. Barberini 49; 064871195)
- Farmacia Risorgimento (P. del Risorgimento 44; 0639738166)

ACCOMMODATIONS

✷ THE BEEHIVE ($$)

V. Margherita 8; 644704553; www.the-beehive.com; reception open daily 8am-11pm

If the interchangeability of IKEA furniture and persistent odor of sweaty travelers has you down, then The Beehive should be your first stop out of **Termini Station.** With clean floors, wall of framed family photos, and warm staff, the Beehive layers on character with a personal touch few hostels can match (especially if you're lucky enough to be there for monthly storytelling night). The Beehive stretches the title of hostel well into the hotel realm, with a basement café (breakfast €2-7) and a clientele that favors families and couples more than rowdy students.

i Dorms from €25, private rooms from €70; reservation recommended; no wheelchair accessibility; lockers; linens included; laundry available; in-house café; massage and tour booking available at front desk

THE YELLOW ($$)

V. Palestro 51; 64463554; www.
the-yellow.com; reception open
24hr

If you tell a fellow backpacker
that you're headed to Rome,
there's a 50 percent chance
that they'll respond, "Oh,
you must be staying at the
Yellow!" The place has a
reputation, and not without
reason. A multi-building hostel,
bar, restaurant, and tour guide
service, the Yellow occupies nearly
an entire block in the **Termini
neighborhood** and is basically the
hostel version of an all-inclusive resort.
The Yellow has identified everything a
social traveler might want: 24hr bar, clean
rooms, cooking classes, comfy common
areas, cheerful staff with great party
recommendations, and friendly bartenders
who make American-style iced coffees
(€2). The Yellow can be a trap, but it's the
most fun trap in Rome (if you can afford
it). And even with all that space, the Wi-
Fi still works, although you won't need it
when you're so busy making friends.
i *Dorms from €30, private rooms from €120;
reservation recommended; limited wheelchair
accessibility; Wi-Fi; luggage storage; small safe
and towels provided; breakfast from €3; in-
house bar open 24hr; option to book cooking
classes and excursions*

ALESSANDRO DOWNTOWN HOSTEL ($)

V. Carlo Cattaneo 23; 644340147; www.
hostelsalessandro.com; reception hours vary

Night out on the river on Tuesday, sangria
night on Wednesday, wine happy hour
on Monday, Wednesday, and Friday, club
night in Rome on Saturday. Got it? Good.
You're ready for Alessandro Downtown.
Like its companion hostel on the other
side of **Termini Station, Alessandro
Palace,** the Downtown Hostel encourages
partying and makes sure you don't miss
one poster or promo video for it. With
its large dorm rooms and seating area
that rotates Top 40 music videos on a
flat screen, Downtown Hostel caters to
a younger crowd of backpackers—the
kind willing to shell out €20 upfront for
drinking games.
i *Dorms from €25, private rooms from €80;
lockers €2; breakfast €5; linens provided;
laundry; kitchen available noon-10pm*

FREEDOM TRAVELLERS ($)

V. Gaeta 23; 648913910; reception hours
vary

There's little that would distinguish
Freedom Travellers in a hostel lineup, but
when accommodations in Rome range
from questionably sanitary to nearly
€40 per night, that's not necessarily a
bad thing. Housed in an old apartment
building a stone's throw from **Termini
Station,** Freedom Travellers checks most
of the boxes for a quality hostel stay:
convenient location, lively neighborhood
(the party hostels are just around the
corner), high ceilings, showers with elbow
room, and a common garden space. The
hyper-social vibe found in nearby hostels
is missing, however, and there's a reason
why the complimentary wine at happy
hour is free. (It's poured from a bottle, but
is it really from a bottle?) What it lacks in
atmosphere, though, Freedom Travellers
recoups in affordability and location.
i *Dorms from €18, private rooms from €60;
reservation recommended; no wheelchair accessibility; linens provided; laundry available;
free croissant and coffee breakfast; outdoor
patio*

HOSTEL DES ARTISTES ($)

V. Villafranca 20; 64454365; www.hostelrome.com; reception hours vary

For those preferring a quieter, more private hotel feel rather than the communal parties of the neighboring **Yellow** and **Alessandro Palace,** Hotel Des Artistes offers tidy, two to six-person dorms and private rooms with the dignified air of the artists adorning its walls. The hostel section of Des Artistes sits atop the three-star Des Artistes hotel, which means the clientele here is more Disney movie than shots at midnight. But close proximity to a nice hotel has its perks—namely, very clean rooms, an expansive rooftop patio, and FaceTime-quality Wi-Fi at all times of day.

i Dorms from €22, private rooms from €80, with en-suite bath from €100; luggage storage available; linens included; laundry available; breakfast buffet €10

SIGHTS
CULTURE
....

BASILICA SAN CLEMENTE

V. Labicana 95; 67740021; www.basilicasanclemente.com; open M-Sa 9am-12:30pm and 3pm-6pm, Su 12:30pm-6pm

Ancient Rome consisted of thousands of buildings and palaces—a thriving city that Jupiter didn't just zap off the earth when he fell out of favor. Today's Vespa traffic drives on top of medieval ruins, which in turn rest on the streets and homes of the ancient city, buried some twenty to thirty feet underground. Basilica San Clemente takes a knife to this lasagna of history, if you will, revealing three distinct eras of Rome's past. The current basilica was built in the twelfth century, and contains typical Renaissance decorations. One floor down lies the original fourth-century church, with its ghosts of eighth-century frescoes. Another staircase leads down to the first century CE, with the remains of Roman homes, alleys, and spring water faucets. If you thought the ancient city surrounded the Colosseum, think again—it's snaking beneath you.

i Free entrance to the basilica; tickets for the excavation site €10, students €5; last entry M-Sa 12:15pm and 5:30pm, Su 5:30pm; limited wheelchair accessibility

BASILICA SANTA MARIA DELLA VITTORIA

V. 20 Settembre 17; 642740671; open M-Sa 8:30am-noon and 3:30pm-6pm, Su 3:30pm-6pm

Between the **Borghese Gardens** and the front of **Termini Station,** the Basilica Santa Maria della Vittoria showcases Bernini at his most whimsical. The church, considerably smaller than Santa Maria Maggiore or St. Peter's, was designed to resemble a theater, with dozens of flying naked babies and marble likenesses of the wealthy Cornaro family. Bernini's playfulness rises throughout the church—literally, the ceiling, which transitions seamlessly from wood pediment to fresco painting, appears to float away in a haze of pink clouds. Closer to earth, the front of Santa Maria della Vittoria holds the masterful *Ecstasy of St. Theresa,* Bernini's depiction of female pleasure disguised as religious symbolism.

i Free; wheelchair accessible

SISTINE CHAPEL

Musei Vaticani, Vatican City; 669884676; www.museivaticani.va; open M-Sa 9am-6pm

The Sistine Chapel is basically the sixteenth-century Olympics of Renaissance painting—you win just by being included, though the gold medal goes, of course, to Michelangelo's ceiling frescoes, whose technical virtuosity overshadows the other masterful works from **Pinturicchio, Perugino, Botticelli,** and **Ghirlandaio.** Begun in 1508, Michelangelo's defiance of gravity was intended to grace Pope Julius II's private chapel, but the Tuscan artist's stupidly impressive achievement has since gone viral—it's estimated that the Sistine Chapel's paintings are viewed by over 15,000 people *per day.* And a majority of those visitors do not follow the no talking rule (or no photos, for that matter). But no matter how packed the room or how weak people's attempts to hide their selfies, the Sistine Chapel will command your attention, and also leave you baffled by Michelangelo's ability to endure neck cramps.

i Access to the Sistine Chapel comes with a ticket to the Vatican Museums; adults €16, reduced €8; ticket office closes at 4pm; wheelchair accessible; proper dress (covered shoulders, clothes to the knees) required

⚜ ST. PETER'S BASILICA

P. San Pietro, Vatican City; 669882350; www.
vaticanstate.va; open daily Apr-Sept 7am-7pm,
Oct-Mar 7am-6pm

As one of the most important examples
of Renaissance architecture and one of
the most visited pilgrimage sites in the
world, St. Peter's Basilica needs no help
fighting for attention. Built over the
legendary tomb of the Christian martyr
whose name it bears, it's the culmination
of the Church's power and patronage in
the sixteenth and seventeenth centuries.
The basilica is the final-exam group
project of the biggest names in Baroque
art—**Michelangelo, Bernini, Maderno,
Bramante,** and whoever laid the
incomprehensible amount of precious
marble everywhere. It also exemplifies
Rome's commitment to recycling: some
of St. Peter's marble comes from the
Colosseum, while Bernini's stunning
baldacchino (altar piece) was cast using
927 tons of metal removed from the
Pantheon roof. Words fail to describe
the staggering impression of St. Peter's
interior, just as human eyes fail to process
the sheer amount of wealth and beauty
within it. Most days, you will need to
wait a crazy amount of time to witness the
excess of St. Peter's, though your chances
are better if you arrive before 9am or after
5pm.

*i Free, but up to 3-4 hr wait; wheelchair acces-
sible; covered shoulders, clothes to the knees
required for entry; audio guides available
(reserve at 0669883229); the dome can be
climbed daily 8am-6pm—entrance is at the
porch of the Basilica*

ALTARE DELLA PATRIA

Piazza Venezia; 6699941; open daily 9am-
5:30pm

This monstrosity of white marble (many
Romans refer to it derisively as "the
wedding cake" or "the typewriter") is
also known as the Monumento Vittorio
Emanuele II or "Vittoriano." It was
constructed in the late nineteenth century
as a testament to, you guessed it, **King
Victor Emmanuel II,** who was elevated
from King of Sardinia to the first ruler of a
unified Italy. More broadly, the bombastic
monument was erected to symbolize the
aspirations of the nascent Italian state,
which was riding the waves of intense
nationalism that swept across Europe in
the late nineteenth century. Regardless of

your aesthetic judgment of the building,
Vittoriano offers quality views from the
top and a chance to see Italy's version of
the Tomb of the Unknown Soldier. Inside
the monument and to the right is the
more reserved **Museo di Risorgimento,**
which traces the history behind Italy's
unification.

*i Adults €7.50, under 18 €3.50; wheelchair
accessible*

BASILICA DI SANTA MARIA MAGGIORE

P. di Santa Maria Maggiore 42; 669886800;
open daily 7am-7pm

You don't have to be a church person to
appreciate the magnificence and ambition
of Santa Maria Maggiore. It's not St.
Peter's, but the mind-clobbering attention
to detail and commitment to purple
marble (some of the most expensive in the
world—it's the signature of the popes in
stone) will leave you needing a seat in one
of the nave's temporary chairs. Between
gilded columns, a gold-pediment ceiling,
and another painted altar masterpiece,
Santa Maria Maggiore communicates all
you need to know about the spectacular
effort poured into Rome's churches during
the Renaissance. Santa Maria Maggiore
also features a museum of relics and an
archaeological excavation for a couple
extra euros, but the main show is free and
worth a good, long, air-conditioned sit.

*i Free; museum costs €3 for relics, €5 for
excavations; wheelchair accessible; shoulders
must be covered and clothes to the knees for
entry (wraps provided free at the entrance)*

PALAZZO VENEZIA

V. del Plebescito 118; 669994388; www.
museopalazzovenezia.beniculturali.it; open
Tu-Su 8:30am-7:30pm

It takes the eyes a second to adjust to
the Palazzo Venezia. Hard corners? No
marble? No columns? Where are we?
Venice? Well, close. The Palazzo Venezia
was indeed gifted to the Venetians in
1564 by **Pope Pius IV** (gotta keep
those relations tight), hence its medieval
style that looks nothing like any of its
neighbors. Located just north of the
Capitoline Hill, the Palazzo Venezia has
stood as a symbol of power for over 700
years. Mussolini adopted the palace as
his headquarters and office; you can still
see the balcony where he delivered most
of his speeches, including his declaration
of the Italian Empire on May 9, 1936.

POMPEII AND HERCULANEUM

Though nearly two millennia have passed, the story of August 24, 79 CE is still hard to fathom. That morning, the Roman city of Pompeii and resort town of Herculaneum went about their usual business—eating, trading, drawing erotic graffiti on the bathhouse walls. By the next morning, it was all gone, buried under meters of pumice, ash, and pyroclastic sludge. The two cities remained locked in time and molten earth—their locations and histories lost for generations—until excavations began in the eighteenth century. Today, the tale of Pompeii and Herculaneum still fascinates, though the sites themselves elicit mixed opinions. To enjoy your day trip to these archaeological wonders—and they are wonders—you should know what you're getting into ahead of time. First, remember that the most interesting artifacts from Pompeii and Herculaneum aren't there anymore; they're in Naples at its **National Archaeological Museum.** The sites themselves display the cities' skeletons—a framework of their previous shape and scope. Second, know that a visit to these sites involves a fair amount of walking, sun exposure, and imagination. Herculaneum, the smaller and better preserved of the two sites, displays colorful mosaics and an idea of how Romans filled their seaside villas. Pompeii is a vast maze of mundane buildings (homes, shops, toilets) and grand public spaces (the forum, an amphitheater). In short, the entire spread of a Roman city, calcified and emptied out for you to explore. Visit one on a whim, or combine the two for a full-day experience. If you intend to see both, buy the combined ticket (€20, reduced to €10 for EU citizens 18-24), which is valid for three days and also includes entrance to one of the other three "Pompeii Sites": Oplontis (a well-preserved mansion built in Rome's version of the Riviera), Stabiae (more villas—seriously, this was Rome's Riviera), and Boscoreale.

GETTING THERE

From Napoli Centrale: Follow signs for the Circumvesuviana line (www.vesuviana.it, trains run daily from 5am until 10pm). Make sure to check which train you board—not all follow the same route around Vesuvius. Take the train to Sorrento or Poggiomarino (via Pompei) and disembark at the station called Pompei Scavi. Tickets cost €2.80 each way and the journey takes approximately 45 min.

For Herculaneum (Ercolano): As with Pompeii, board a Circumvesuviana train to either Sorrento or Poggiomarino, but disembark at the station called "Ercolano Scavi." The entrance to the excavation site is about a 10min. walk downhill, along Ercolano.

GETTING AROUND

The entrance to the Pompeii excavations is right across from the train station, and can only be accessed on foot. To reach the modern city of Pompei, follow the road outside the Pompei Scavi station to the east.

POMPEII

First things first, get an audio guide. For a city with such an explosive history, the intrigue of Pompeii doesn't translate well to visitors. There are no guides throughout Pompeii's 163-acre spread, nor are there many signs (and the ones that do exist are mostly in Italian). Today's Pompeii is like a beetle's exoskeleton, or the skin of a snake—you can see the shape of the former inhabitants, but none of the color or vibrancy. Without an audio guide, Pompeii's story fades quickly into a monotonous route of bricks, arches, and uneven roads. The cost may seem steep on top of the entrance ticket, but an audio guide earns will tell you exactly where you are, what these rows of doorways mean, and why we care about the House of the Faun.

It is also important to note that in terms of food, the cheapest and possibly most satisfying option is to plan ahead and pack a lunch, as food options near the excavations are limited and overpriced. There is a cafeteria within the park that serves sandwiches, pizza, coffee, gelato, and other standard lunch foods for somewhere between eight and 15 euros. The street between Ercolano Station and the archaeological site is lined with typical restaurants and takeaway places, all similarly priced and geared towards tourists.

Don't miss...

THE HOUSE OF THE FAUN
One of the largest and most lavish of Pompeii's Hamptons-esque villas, the House of the Faun offers a glimpse of rustic luxury in the Imperial era. The famous faun statue fountain greets visitors to the sprawling complex, which contains mosaics, frescoes, and plenty of breathing room for Rome's 1%.

THE AMPITHEATER
It can be difficult to envision, but all of these empty rooms used to contain thousands of real, raucous people, and they enjoyed having a good time. Pompeii's amphitheater predates the Colosseum and could hold about 15,000 people. Mt. Vesuvius pummeled the former crowds here but did preserve some of the benches, which make for a nice resting place as you figure out how to get back to the entrance from this corner of the park.

THE GARDEN OF FUGITIVES
It's the question on your mind and on the lips of every over-eager child: "Where are the bodies? I thought there were plaster casts?" Yes, in this case, Google Images didn't lie; there are plaster casts of the unfortunate souls who perished hiding from the wrath of Vesuvius, and they're in the Garden of the Fugitives. If there's one part of the park that can bring the horror of the eruption to life, this is it.

HERCULANEUM

Don't miss...

THE HOUSE OF NEPTUNE AND AMPHITRITE
A beautiful gold and blue mosaic—still glowing in color despite enduring centuries caked in volcanic sludge—resides in this house-turned-shop. Many Roman homes during this period doubled as storefronts, a trend recalled here.

THE HOUSE OF THE WOODEN SCREEN
How can wood withstand a volcanic eruption whose heat wave instantly killed everyone within its radius? Good question. Science is weird, but seeing very old wood in its original location is, indeed, very interesting. The screen in the back hall of this house gives a better impression of how homes were styled in Pompeii than any other on-site artifact.

THE HOUSE OF THE BLACK SALON
Not everything in Campania is terracotta-colored. Though sleepier than Pompeii, Herculaneum attracted a crowd of glitzy Romans to its shores, which is reflected in this home's lavish decor.

Today, the balcony appears unadorned, as Rome downplays its fascist past. The focus is instead placed on the Palazzo Venezia museum, which houses frescoes, pottery, and sculpture from the early Christian years to the Renaissance.

i *Adults €14, reduced (EU citizens 18-25) €7; ticket also valid for the Museo Nazionale di Castel Sant'Angelo; balcony free, on the right side of the palace if you're facing with your back to the Altare della Patria; last entry 6:30pm; wheelchair accessible*

PORTA PORTESE

Piazza di Porta Portese; open Su 6am-2pm

Porta Portese provides a break from all of the lavish tourist attractions found throughout Rome. This outdoor market, open only on Sunday mornings, specializes in the cheap, eclectic, and unpolished—things with value in the eye of the beholder. Here, you can find antiques, knick-knacks, cards, figurines, souvenirs as cheap as €1, and racks on racks of clothing to replace the smelly, wrinkled shirts lumped in the bottom of your pack. Located along the **Tiber** to the south of the city center, Porta Portese lacks the glamour of Rome's monuments, but it attracts a mixed crowd of locals and visitors and will reveal aspects of the city that the Vatican will not.

i *Stand prices; limited wheelchair accessibility*

VILLA FARNESINA

V. della Lungara 230; 668027268; www.villafarnesina.it; open M-Sa 9am-2pm

When you're a rich banker from Siena, how do you make your presence known in Rome? Build a lavish summer villa and borrow the pope's favorite fresco painter **(Raphael)**, of course. **Agostino Chigi** completed his mansion at the peak of Renaissance style in 1511, complete with floor-to-ceiling frescoes, the typical marble showcases, and airy porticoes. Chigi further cemented his status as the Gatsby of Rome by throwing extravagant parties, during which he allegedly encouraged guests to toss their silver into the **Tiber** (which he then fished out with a net). These indulgences didn't work out so well for Chigi, as the home was sold to the Farnese family by the end of the sixteenth century. But it works out great

for you, old sport, as you can stroll through the still outlandishly-decorated halls and light-toned *loggios* like the Leonardo DiCaprio film extra you long to be.

i *Admission €6; last entry 2pm*

LANDMARKS

⬛ FONTANA DEI QUATTRO FIUMI (AND PIAZZA NAVONA)

P. Navona; open daily 24hr

Like your best night-out stories, the Fontana dei Quattro Fiumi (Fountain of the Four Rivers) is all drama and excess. Designed by **Bernini** for Pope Innocent X, the fountain features a skyscraping Egyptian obelisk atop a pyramid pattern of rocks, cascading water, one roaring lion, and four nude river gods. Bernini designed the fountain as a celebration of four continents, with each god representing the Ganges, the Nile, the Danube, and the Rio de la Plata. Apparently North America was not important enough in 1651 to warrant a shout-out, but judging by the number of English menus on the surrounding Piazza Navona, people today have taken note of America. Ochre-colored apartments, purplish shutters, and flowering window boxes ring the elliptically shaped Piazza Navona, making it one of the more picturesque piazzas in the city and a rewarding stop on any walking tour of Rome.

i *Free; wheelchair accessible*

⬛ THE COLOSSEUM

Piazza del Colosseo 1; open daily 8:30am-7:30pm

The Colosseum has over two thousand years of experience at keeping people entertained. It held naval battles, featured wild beasts, and absorbed the blood of thousands of gladiators. It contained 80,000 people and then spit them out in less time than it takes you to get dressed in the morning. It inspired your favorite sports team arena and one historically inaccurate but highly quotable Russell Crowe movie. And now it hosts upward of 9000 visitors a day, making it Rome's top tourist attraction. To visit the Colosseum, you can book a tour or skip-the-line pass from one of the numerous companies operating in or around it. Or, muster more patience than Emperor Joaquin Phoenix in *Gladiator* and brave the line. The games are long gone, but the Colosseum still captivates.

i Tickets €12, valid for 2 consecutive days at Roman Forum and Palatine Hill; limited wheelchair accessibility; last entry 1hr before sunset; tickets at Forum or Palatine Hill

THE PANTHEON

P. della Rotunda; open daily 9am-7:30pm

The Romans may have had the most powerful empire of their time, but it can be difficult to see the architectural genius through so much crumbling marble. And then there's the Pantheon, one of the best-preserved symbols of the Eternal City (thank you, very rich popes), here to remind you that the Romans really were ahead of their time. This marvel still dazzles with its enormous, perfectly proportioned concrete dome, which is still the largest in the world a whopping 1,890 years later. The optical illusion of the ceiling—a series of square pediments in concentric circles surrounding the oculus (opening)—will make your head spin (don't worry, there's free seating). The Pantheon's lavishly marbled ground-floor, consecrated today as a Catholic sacred space, also offers its fair share of treasures: **Rafael** is buried here (specifically, creepily exhumed, confirmed dead, and reburied), as well as national hero **King Vittorio Emanuele II.**

i Free; last entry 7pm; wheelchair accessible; entry may be restricted depending on crowd size

THE ROMAN FORUM

V. della Salara Vecchia; open daily 8:30am-7:15pm

On a surface level, the Forum appears to be a series of marble things at various stages of decay. Once the Times Square of Ancient Rome, the Forum has persevered through more than nine lives, including "stage for Cicero," "public looting ground," "Catholic Church reclamation area," "demolition zone for Mussolini," and now "the largest outdoor museum in the world." A visit to the Forum begins with the **Arch of Titus**—notable for its clear depiction of the sack of Jerusalem in the

first century CE—and weaves through the remains of temples, basilicas (public buildings), the **House of the Vestal Virgins,** and marketplaces. As most of what we see today forms only the corners, slices, or skeletons of the original buildings, a visit to the Forum requires some imagination to fully appreciate its significance. But as the epicenter of Ancient Rome's power and the heart of the old city, the Forum is a must-see in Rome.

i Tickets €12, valid for 2 consecutive days at the Colosseum and Palatine Hill; last entry 7pm; wheelchair accessible

PIAZZA DI SPAGNA

P. di Spagna; open daily 24hr

Despite its butterfly shape, the **Spanish Steps** is a monument of circular reasoning. Why see the Spanish Steps? Because they're famous and important, you say. Why are they famous and important? Because… they're the Spanish Steps? Yes, it's a set of steps (a very manageable 135 of them) leading from Bernini's least impressive fountain below to a church of moderate importance above. In the past, the Spanish Steps served a logistical purpose—connecting the Spanish Embassy with the church—and as a functioned as a symbol of the Bourbon family's wealth (the guys who also funded Versailles). Today, the money is housed in the luxury shops lining the Piazza di Spagna, while the steps have become a hub for the Senate and for people-watching. By Roman ordinance, you can't each lunch here, but you can take five on the smooth marble steps.

i Free; piazza is wheelchair accessible

THE ARCH OF CONSTANTINE

V. di San Gregorio; open daily 24hr

When you've consolidated power, drowned your rival in the Tiber, and paraded his head through the streets of Rome, what's the natural next step? Build a gigantic arch with no practical use, of course. Technically gifted by the (mostly defunct, at this point) Senate of Rome to the emperor **Constantine I,** Rome's largest triumphal arch still stands beside the Colosseum as a reminder of what would happen if Ancient Rome wanted your money. Though completed in 315 CE, the arch contains details from earlier works also dedicated to the military booty seized by emperors such as Hadrian and Trajan. See Constantine's Arch if you're interested in 3D friezes and the spoils of war, skip it if the coolest thing about an arch to you is walking through it (as this one is fenced off).

i *Free; wheelchair accessible*

THE CAPITOLINE HILL

P. del Campidoglio; open daily 24hr

Simultaneously the smallest of Rome's seven hills and its most sacred, the Capitoline Hill has upgraded over the years from the city's mint and political center to the home of two massive naked men and their horses (statues, of course). The pair boldly welcomes you to the **Piazza di Campidoglio,** designed by **Michelangelo** in the fifteenth century and the entrance to the **Capitoline Museums,** the world's oldest public collection of ancient art. The Capitoline today testifies to the egos of past Roman and Italian leaders—an impressive bronze statue of **Marcus Aurelius** dominates the *piazza*, though it is dwarfed by the neo-Baroque monument to **Vittorio Emanuele II** behind it. You can climb this "wedding cake" building for a heightened view, or look onto the **Forum** for free from the back end of the Capitoline

i *Free; limited wheelchair accessibility*

THE PALATINE HILL

Palatine Hill; open daily 8am-7:30pm

Once upon a time, a she-wolf rescued abandoned twin babies—Romulus and Remus—on the Palatine Hill, and nursed them in a cave. One of them (Romulus) went on to found the city of Rome, then killed Remus out of…let's call it brotherly love. Whether or not you believe the founding legend of Rome, it's fact that the Palatine Hill has been inhabited since at least 1000 BCE, and that people likely pulled a Romulus to live there in the years since. During its heyday as the Beverly Hills of Rome in the Republican and Imperial eras, the Palatine Hill was populated with the who's who of the city and adorned with mansions for the emperor and his family (hence, the word "palace"). Visitors today can use their combined Colosseum-Forum-Palatine ticket to visit the **Palace of Domitian,** the remains of **Augustus's house,** and the

beautiful frescoes in his wife's villa.

i *Tickets €12, valid for 2 consecutive days at the Colosseum and Roman Forum; last entry 1hr before sunset; wheelchair accessible; entrance on V. San Gregorio, as well as through the Roman Forum*

THE TREVI FOUNTAIN

P. di Trevi; open daily 24hr

You know you need to see the Trevi Fountain, but you're not sure why until you're there. It is impressive. It is massive. It commands the square. It is Baroque architecture at its finest, in that it's beautiful and knows it and will beat you over the head with it (not that you'll mind). By day, the Trevi Fountain, completed in 1762 as a celebration of Agrippa's ancient aqueducts, is a spectacle of excess—money (popes again!), marble, symbolism, people, selfies. By night or dawn, however, the smaller details of Nicola Salvi's artistic triumph trickle through—the precise definition of Poseidon's horses, the strategic pour of water over the rocks, the still edges of the pool, and of course the sound of running water filling the square. Close your eyes, toss a coin, and wish for fifty first dates with Fontana di Trevi. You'll meet a different fountain each time.

i *Free; wheelchair accessible*

THEATER OF MARCELLUS

V. del Teatro di Marcello; www.tempietto.it; open daily 24hr

Rome displays a constant contradiction between past and present, and few buildings in the Eternal City demonstrate this odd symbiosis better than the Theater of Marcellus. Inaugurated by **Augustus** in 12 BCE, the Theater of Marcellus has been confusing tourists ever since with its passing likeness to the Colosseum. To be fair, it is a large entertainment venue—older and better preserved than the **Colosseum,** at that—but it is semi-circular whereas the Colosseum is 360 degrees, and your taxi driver will know the difference. Over the years, the structure has served as an apartment building, fortress, quarry, inspiration to Christopher Wren, and glory project for Mussolini. Today, the Theater of Marcellus straddles the gaps between public and private, ancient and modern; the bottom half of the structure—restored in recent years—hosts live musical performances in the summer (check online for schedules), while the top half is composed of privately owned and occupied apartments. Thus, you have two options to access the theater: see a show outside its walls, or somehow befriend the person who reportedly shelled out $10 million last year to live there.

i Free; wheelchair accessible

TRAJAN'S COLUMN

V. dei Fori Imperiali; open daily 24hr

A short walk from the Colosseum, Trajan's column in the Imperial Forum seems a bit unimpressive at first, especially compared to the **Vittorio Emanuele II monument** across the street. But this 126-foot-tall stone spire is actually one of the most important artifacts from Ancient Rome, and has stood for over 1900 years. Spiraling around the column from bottom to top are 155 friezes depicting Emperor Trajan's victory in the Dacian Wars (in present day Romania), a story which goes like this: Trajan musters thousands of soldiers to cross the Danube, destroys the Dacians, then uses all of their money to build a gigantic column in which he appears as hero/conqueror 58 times. Trajan is not renowned for his subtlety, but his column (seriously, not subtle) is highly regarded today for its detailed depictions of second-century war.

i Free; wheelchair accessible

MUSEUMS
....

◪ BORGHESE GALLERY

Piazzale Scipione Borghese 5; 68413979; www.galleriaborghese.it; open Tu-Su 9am-7pm

The Borghese Gallery, located at the northeastern end of the **Borghese Gardens,** imparts a few inescapable lessons, including that money makes the seventeenth-century art world go 'round, **Caravaggio** was the original master of shade, and Bernini knew a thing or two about rippling muscles (and marble, too). Housed in Scipione Borghese's former party villa (because you're nobody until you have a papal party villa on the edge of town), the private collection is now a must-see museum for Baroque art, with notable works from **Caravaggio, Bernini, Titian, Rubens,** and other titans of excessive detail. Finding a time to visit can get tricky; technically, ticket reservations must be made online for two-hour visiting

slots, but they can also be purchased onsite if there are any left-over (though don't expect the staff to be pleased about this). The Borghese Gallery is worth the hassle, though, for a chance to witness what Google Images still can't capture: the virtuosity of Baroque A-listers.

i Adults €15 (including €2 reservation fee), reduced (EU students only) €8.50; though you can try your luck with buying tickets at will call, visiting the Borghese Gallery requires a ticket reservation, which can be bought online or by phone (+39 06 32810); the Gallery admits 360 ticket holders every 2hr starting at 9am, and all guests are required to leave the Gallery after their 2hr tour is up; first entry 9am, ticket office closes at 6:30pm; wheelchair accessible

◪ CAPITOLINE MUSEUMS

P. Campodoglio; www.museicapitolini.org; open daily 9:30am-7:30pm

As you have probably figured out by now, Imperial Rome was not subtle about its accomplishments (see: **Colosseum, Trajan's Column,** every marble frieze of military takeover). As the house of some of the greatest hits of Roman art, the Capitoline Museum puts on a show of size. Visitors are welcomed by the massive feet of Constantine, whose marble toe is the size of your head (because big feet, well... you know). The museum winds through the large (bronze she-wolf of Rome, exquisite statue of Venus), the huge (remains of Greek bronzes, entrancing bust of Brutus), and the downright colossal (bronze of Marcus Aurelius on a horse, Constantine's head). The classic **marble statues** and **bronze casts** steal the show, but you can get your dose of Renaissance and Caravaggio in the Capitoline's picture gallery and rooms furnished by, you guessed it, the popes.

i Tickets €15, video guides €6; last entry 1hr before closing; wheelchair accessible, call 0667102071 for directions and assistance

◪ PALAZZO MASSIMO (MUSEUM OF ROME)

Largo di Villa Peretti 1; 639967700; www.archeoroma.beniculturali.it; open Tu-Su 9am-7:45pm

Today, Ancient Rome is often summed up by its monuments, mighty ruins, and impressive concrete. But there would be no Colosseum, Forum, or aqueducts without the many ordinary people who worked, wined, dined, shopped, and lived in the city, a fact showcased in the exceptional Palazzo Massimo, a segment of the Museum of Rome next to the entrance of **Termini Station.** A visit to the Palazzo Massimo conjures the recognizably human ghosts of Ancient Rome: take in the colors of the restored full-room fresco from the **Villa of LiV,** then see how busts depict the change of style over time (beards only became a thing because of Hadrian, for example). Don't miss the outstanding **"Boxer at Rest" bronze,** marked with cuts and bruises from an exhausting fight. In the basement, an extensive collection of coins traces the flow of commerce in Italy over centuries, while a display of jewelry confirms that chokers have been going in and out of style for millennia.

i Admission €7, free for visitors under 18; ticket valid at all National Roman Museum sites (Baths of Diocletian, Palazzo Altemps, and Balbi Crypt), ticket office closes 1hr before closing; tickets can be booked at www.coopculture.it; wheelchair accessible

MUSEO DELL'ARA PACIS

Lungotevere in Augusta; en.arapacis.it; open daily 9:30am-7:30pm

While most celebratory arches in Rome are all about the "booty booty booty booty rockin' everywhere" (the spoils of war, that is), the Ara Pacis marks a change of pace. Literally translated to "Altar of Peace," the Ara Pacis was commissioned by Augustus in 13 BCE to commemorate an era of uncharacteristic peace and prosperity for Rome. With its scenes of bounty, fertility, and the Imperial family, the Ara Pacis also worked to visually establish a new civic religion for the recently imperialized Roman state (because if you're Augustus, it's not enough to be military conqueror and emperor—you must be father of the people, as well). Restored and now displayed in the Museo dell'Ara Pacis next to the Tiber, the Ara Pacis demonstrates that it was possible for Rome to produce exquisite sculptures without crushing another state first (actually, that's a lie, Augustus was fresh off a campaign in Gaul. But it's the thought that counts?).

i Admission €10.50; last entry 1hr before closing; wheelchair accessible

THE BATHS OF DIOCLETIAN

NV. Enrico de Nicola 79; www.archeoroma.benicultuali.it; open Tu-Su 9am-7:30pm

Across the street from **Termini Station,** the remains of Diocletian's baths remind you that public nudity was all the rage back in Ancient Rome, at least in the bathhouse. Today, this mega-complex of personal hygiene, part of the National Roman Museum, houses an exhibit on the written communication of Rome, a room on inscriptions from the Roman republic, and **Michelangelo's Cloister,** a garden lined with sculptures of various quality. The baths themselves are difficult to find within the museum—you have to go left from the bookstore, not out the back door of the Cloister that locks behind you and won't let you back in.

i Admission €7, free for under 18; ticket valid for 3 consecutive days at all National Roman Museum sites (Palazzo Altemps, Palazzo Massimo, and Balbi Crypt); last entry 1hr. before closing; wheelchair accessible

THE VATICAN MUSEUMS

V.le Vaticano; 669884676; www.museivaticani.va; open M-Sa 9am-6pm, last Su of every month 9am-2pm

A visit to the Vatican demands preparation. You can reserve tickets to skip the line, bring an umbrella to weather the heat, and wear proper shoes to endure the nearly 7km of exhibits. But for all your thinking ahead, nothing can deflect the overwhelming power of the Vatican's opulence. The Vatican has zero chill when it comes to wealth, with over 70,000 works of art (20,000 on display)—including some of the most recognizable pieces in the world—and an exorbitant amount of rare marble. Follow the crowd through the **Pinacoteca,** down the intricately tiled and painted hallways and past the map collection. Take in what you can. This is the one of the most extensive and significant collections of art in the world, and even a sliver of it will impress.

i Adults €16, booked ahead €20, reduced (students, religious seminaries, disabled persons) €8, booked ahead €12, free last Su of the month; tickets include entrance to Sistine Chapel, and are only valid for the date and time issued; book online to avoid waiting in line for 2-3hr; tours begin every 30min. starting at 9am; last entry 4pm; wheelchair accessible

OUTDOORS

AVENTINE HILL

V. di Santa Sabina; open daily Apr-Sept 7am-9pm, Oct-Mar 7am-6pm

According to legend, **Romulus'** settlement on the Palatine defeated **Remus'** camp on the Aventine for the founding of Rome, but the Aventine has since recouped its losses in the form of views of the city and sun-kissed gardens. A 10-to 15-minute hike from the path along the Tiber, the Aventine features the **Giardino degli Aranci** (Orange Garden), which smells of pine and flower blossoms and offers one of the best sunset perches in the city. From the balcony at the edge of the park, just past the evergreen trees and peaceful fountains, you can see sun-drenched Rome stretch before you, from the Altare della Patria on the right, to the **Vatican** beyond, to **Trastevere** on the left. You may also see some serious PDA, a few selfie sticks, and perhaps a guitar player welcoming the evening with an acoustic rendition of U2's "One."

i Free; wheelchair accessible

GIANICOLO HILL

Open daily 24hr

Gianicolo Hill is to the seven hills of Rome what Lake Champlain is to the Great Lakes—too far away to ever be included, but with enough perks to make a claim. Across the Tiber from the actual hills of Rome (which, really, is not far away at all), Gianicolo is the second-tallest hill in the city, and arguably its greatest vantage point for views of the ancient center, if you can find a spot to look between the trees. Though outside the limits of the Imperial city, Gianicolo has since been embraced by Rome, as signified by its Baroque fountain (the **Fontana dell'Acqua Paola**) and its church. Getting to the top of Gianicolo requires some focus, but if you can manage the roadblocks, confusing street signs, and allure of bar patios, the *piazza* provides a worthwhile peek at the pink-tan city sprawled across **the Tiber.**

i Free; wheelchair accessible

VILLA BORGHESE GARDENS

Open daily 24hr

The Villa Borghese Garden is not a destination, but a place to wander. The Garden's maze of gravel paths, less official dirt paths, steps, and occasional roads were designed to get you lost, but that's not at your expense. First designated by Cardinal Scipione Borghese in 1605, and thus the oldest public park in Rome, the Villa Borghese Garden has since filled in with towering trees, overgrown grasses, villas, too many fountains to keep straight, and of course the **Borghese Gallery.** Casual wanderers will also stumble upon some of the lesser known yet still intriguing sights, such as a group of high school kids up to no good, several elderly ladies yelling colorful Italian at their dogs, and a couple of brave joggers attempting to work off the day's pasta lunch.

i Free; wheelchair accessible; entrances include: Porta Pinciana, V. Belle Arte, V. Mercadante, and V. Pinciana

FOOD

▩ BARNUM CAFÉ ($)

V. Del Pellegrino 87; 64760483; open M-Sa 9am-2am

Open for the better part of the day, Barnum Café shapeshifts from trendy breakfast spot to studious work café to popular *aperitivo* bar over the course of your waking hours. Like its eponymous circus entertainer, Barnum has many acts, but it always remains a full-time creative space and frequent hangout for Rome's freelancers, alternative types, and internationally-minded crowd. Situated in the heart of the rose-tinted **Centro Storico neighborhood,** Barnum specializes in artful salads, cocktail creations, and actually cold iced coffee (served in a martini glass, no less). Go for a snack, go for a spritz and a bruschetta, or go for an hour of focused laptop time—regardless, you'll feel cooler for doing so.

i Daily specials from €6, coffee from €1.50, juices €4, desserts €5, cocktails from €7; vegan and vegetarian options available; wheelchair accessible

BISCOTTIFICIO ARTIGIANO INNOCENTI ($)

V. della Luce 21; 65803926; open M-Sa 8am-8pm, Su 9:30am-2pm, closed Aug

Though its exterior beckons to no one, the one-room interior projects all the signs of serious bakery business: a huge oven, baskets of cookies in the window, a large scale to accurately weigh your haul of cookies, and store plaques plastered on top of American political campaign signs from the 1970s. The vintage look isn't a show: the bakery has been operated by the same family for over 50 years, and is subject to the usual non-corporate whims (such as closing the whole month of August for vacation). Innocenti delivers on a wide range of baked goods, but specializes in traditional Italian nut cookies, such as hazelnut bites *(brutti ma buoni)* or almond wedges (some with chocolate). Running about €2 for six or so, you can afford to try a few (or 20).

i Biscuits and cookies by weight (about 6 cookies per €2); vegetarian options available; wheelchair accessible

BONCI PIZZARIUM ($$)

V. della Meloria 43; 63974516; www.bonci.it; open M-Sa 11am-10pm, Su 11am-4pm and 6pm-10pm

Sure, the Vatican contains the wealth of a country a hundred times its size, but the real treasure might be just outside its walls. We're talking about Bonci Pizzarium, arguably the best take-away pizza in Rome. Founded by famed pizza connoisseur **Gabriele Bonci,** the Pizzarium seems more like a pizza art museum than a fast food joint, as the crusts are loaded with Willy Wonka-style portions of toppings—mounds of mozzarella, piles of sautéed veggies, and even heaps of seared tuna. (Haven't you heard? Margherita was *so* last season). A word of warning: some gourmet slices (yes, that tuna one) can run several euro more per slice, so check the labels before you accidentally end up with a €15 takeaway pizza bill.

i Pizza from €4 per slice, from €7 per slice for gourmet varieties; vegetarian options available; wheelchair accessible; take-away only; small counter space provided

GELATERIA DELLA PALMA ($)

V. Della Maddalena 19-23; 668806752; www.dellapalma.it; open daily 8:30am-12:30am

Gelateria Della Palma's rainbow palm tree logo doesn't scream "GOOD GELATO," but don't be fooled by the neon: this shop takes gelato as seriously as the color spectrum. Della Palma, on the corner of the Pantheon plaza, specializes in the wacky and wonderful, with over 150 flavors ranging from Kiwi Strawberry to Kit Kat to Sesame and Honey. Yes, it's swimming with people all taking too much time to make a flavor decision, but the quality of gelato and heaping portions render the hassle irrelevant. Plus, there are numerous soy or rice milk and yogurt options for those challenged by dairy and full fat. If you're going to ball out on gelato in Rome (and you should), this is center court.

i Gelato from €2.30; wheelchair accessible

PIANOSTRADA ($$)

V. della Zoccolette 22; 689572296; open Tu-Su 1pm-4pm and 7pm-11:30pm

Recently relocated from Trastevere to a quiet corner of **Monti,** Pianostrada puts a fresh spin on familiar Italian staples. Their menu presents a tour de force of re-energized dishes, from refined street food (i.e., fried everything), to stir-fried veggies with pine nuts and raisins, to the best damn focaccia in Rome. The old trattoria provides inspiration for Pianostrada's pizzas, focaccias, and small plates, but their salads, fried dishes, and flavor combinations defy classification. Ristorante, this is not. And though it occupies the tail end of the student budget spectrum, Pianostrada's daring take on Italian cuisine, sprightly interior, and spacious back patio justify the cost.

i Primi from €12, secondi from €12, sides from €8, wine from €6 per glass; vegan and vegetarian options available; wheelchair accessible

FORNO CAMPO DE' FIORI ($)

Vicolo del Gallo 14; 668806662; www.forno-campodefiori.com; open M-Sa 7:30am-8pm

There are numerous *fornos* (bakeries) throughout Rome, which can make it difficult to choose one that doesn't hand you a bag of dried-out cookies or surprisingly charge you €4 for a couple biscotti. And then there's Il Forno Campo de' Fiori, which catches your gaze with its bright sign, yet soothes you with sweet, sweet sugar (specifically, a hefty bag of lemon cookies and biscotti for under €2). Il Forno Campo de' Fiori can also tempt you with savory treats, as its paninis, *piadinas,* and various other combos of sliced things and bread are delicious, filling, and mercifully cheap. No seating for this meal; you can pace yourself to all the nearby monuments one chocolate-dipped almond biscuit at a time.

i Biscuits and cookies by weight, sandwiches from €3; vegan and vegetarian options available; wheelchair accessible

LA CARBONARA ($$)

V. Panisperna 214; 64825176; www.lacarbonara.it; open M-Sa 12:30pm-2:30pm and 7pm-11pm

La Carbonara strikes a hard pose against the games of tourism, starting with a "No TripAdvisor" sign on the door. It's a bold play for a dining scene that runs on reputation and recommendations, but judging by the walls filled with notes and signatures of satisfied patrons, La Carbonara has earned enormous confidence. This no-frills trattoria on one of Monti's wider streets keeps its memories close—a case of used wine corks over here, a framed moon chart from a decade ago over there—and its pasta secrets closer. TripAdvisor or no, the reviews are in: the *cacio e pepe* under this framed record and shelf of wine bottles earns five stars (or, perhaps more appreciated, a sincere *grazie* to the waiter).

i Primi from €6, secondi from €8; vegetarian options available; wheelchair accessible

QUE TE PONGO? ($)

V. Della Dogana Vecchia 13; 668803029; open M-Sa 9am-8pm

"Que te pongo? What would you like?" A small, understated "salmoneria" around the corner from the Pantheon asks you. *Hmm...a sandwich, you think, one that is not 80% bread and has some flavor and enough protein to fuel these 16,000-step days.* "We've got you," the smile from behind the counter seems to say, and the menu confirms it. There are no slim prosciutto pieces here. Specializing in fish of the smoked, pickled, or marinated variety, Que Te Pongo? delivers in taste and quantity where other sandwich shops skate by on a baguette. Their extensive list of sandwich options—combinations

of fish, vegetables, and homemade sauce. There's minimal seating, so opt for takeaway between monument stops.

i Sandwiches from €5, salads from €7.50, platters from €10; wheelchair accessible

NIGHTLIFE

🖼 BAR DEL FICO

P. Del Fico 34/35; 668861373; www.bardelfico.com; open daily 7:30am-2am

In Rome, nightlife is smooth, easy, and continuous—good food, soothing drinks, fun company, and establishments that shift from café to restaurant to bar throughout the day. Bar del Fico represents the best of these multitasking hangouts, with a consistent crowd of young professionals from morning espresso, to early evening spritzes, to late night cocktails. Taking up half a square in **Centro Storico,** Bar del Fico's packed wrap-around patio sets the tone for nights out in the surrounding restaurants and bars: not rowdy, but definitely not quiet, with plenty of drinks and fresh food to go around.

i Beer from €4, cocktails €8, food from €6; wheelchair accessible; serves Su brunch

🖼 BLACKMARKET

V. Panisperna 101; 3398227541; www.blackmarketartgallery.it; open daily 7:30pm-2am

BlackMarket is Rome's angsty art school student who matured into a retro hipster with some business sense. Behind a heavy door and curtain on one of Monti's busier streets, this combo bar and art gallery keeps things dark—shaded lamps, mahogany-polished furniture, and the pitch black of late nights. It's too moody, from the outside, for some tourists, but its creative cocktail menu has stirred enough buzz to draw both visitors and some locals. A little edgier than your standard wine bar and a little more rebellious than your classy patio cocktail, BlackMarket marks the second or third stop on a night out, when you're ready to upgrade from a small café table to a swanky velvet couch (cocktail glass delicately in hand, of course).

i Beer from €4, cocktails €10; limited wheelchair accessibility

🏮 FRENI E FRIZIONI

V. del Politeama 4-6; 645497499; www.
freniefrizioni.com; open daily 6:30pm-2am

If you're walking along **the Tiber** outside
Trastevere on any given summer night,
you'll inevitably be stopped by the sight
of a square full of people, mostly mid-20s,
lounging outside a restaurant. People
drape over the stone walls and down
the steps. A man breaks out some John
Lennon on his guitar. Plates and wine
glasses dot the tables. "I have to be a
part of this," you say, without thinking.
Welcome to Freni e Frizioni, Trastevere's
go-to spot for aperitivos, drinks, and
blending into the scene. There's beer,
wine, and croquettes aplenty, but Freni
e Frizioni sets a new standard with its
cocktails—please see the print-out menu
of their creative creations, disguised as
album covers. You know what's far cooler
than being a Green Day fan in middle
school? Sipping a Green Day cocktail
on a *piazza* in Rome while watching the
sun brighten every reddish paint job in
Trastevere.

i Beer €6, long drinks €7 (decrease by €1
after 10pm), cocktails from €8; aperitivo
(7pm-10pm): wheelchair accessible; casual,
hip attire

CELESTINO

V. degli Ausoni 62; 645472483; open daily
7:30am-2am

At Celestino, the glass display of old
liquor bottles and array of psychedelic
rock posters celebrate the hard drinking
of days past, but the crowd only knows
Jimi Hendrix from their parents
(or grandparents). Located a short
walk from the **Sapienza University**
campus, Celestino draws a youthful,
predominantly local crowd, at prices
friendly to students. Celestino serves
coffee and sandwiches throughout the
day, as well as beer (€2.50) and aperitivos
(€3.50), but concentrates in cocktails.
Take your pick from creations featuring
whiskey, gin, rum, and coffee, or try your
chances with "The Long Drink," (€3.50)
marked with a skull and crossbones and a
long-legged woman falling into a martini
glass.

i No cover; coffee from €0.60, cocktails from
€4, shots from €1.50, sandwiches from €2,
beer from €2.50; wheelchair accessible

CUL DE SAC

P. di Pasquino 73; 668801094; www.enote-
caculdesac.com; open daily noon-4pm and
6pm-12:30am

If you thought "go big or go home" was
confined to America, then you haven't
seen Cul de Sac's wine selection. Some
wine bars offer a booklet; Cul de Sac
ups the ante to encyclopedia. The phone
book-thick wine list here ranges from
Italian, of course, to American and
French, and manifests in an extensive
collection of bottles lining the walls of Cul
de Sac's narrow interior. Come for cured
meat and cheese *aperitivos*, stay for an
education in the global expanse of wine
and the indulgent ambiance of an Italian
evening.

i No cover, wine glasses from €4, cured meat
and cheese from €7, primi from €8, secondi
from €7; wheelchair accessible

EX DOGANA

Vle. dello Scalo S. Lorenzo 10; 3343849185;
www.exdogana.com; open Tu-W noon-10pm,
Th-F noon-1am, Sa 10am-1am, Su 10am-
10pm

The former 1920s train depot in **San
Lorenzo** is more complex than nightclub,
which requires navigation. It's a mostly
local, university-student hangout, which
requires either understanding Italian or
accepting you're the only one who doesn't.
It's located southeast of the **Termini**
hostel neighborhood, which means you'll
be trekking a good 20 minutes through
Rome's less picturesque streets to get there.
And the venue hosts primarily live music
events, which requires knowing what is
going on and when. If you think you can
hang, then check the lineup of acts online
and hit up the electronic dance floor or
themed parties. Congratulate yourself on
infiltrating one of Rome's unapologetically
coolest night spots, though it's probably
still too cool for you. Congratulations on
infiltrating one of Rome's coolest clubs.

i Free, depending on event; some areas
reportedly charge €12 for entrance; wheelchair accessible; check online for upcoming
concerts or music festivals

SAN GIMIGNANO

Coverage by **Margaret Canady**

San Gimignano has been called the Manhattan of the Medieval, and it's hard to believe that something so antiquated can still thrive in the modern world. The small town, built in the third century, is known for its numerous towers and preserved wall. Situated atop a hill, it looks out over a land of vineyards from its position. We half-expected to see knights on white horses galloping down the cobblestoned streets to save a damsel in distress stuck in Torre Grossa, the tallest tower in the city. But this is 2019, and things have changed—including gender norms and the city's culture. The town is actually a hub for cutting-edge contemporary art and artists, and you'll find several galleries with one-of-a-kind modern art. A day trip to San Gimignano is definitely worth the effort, and it's light-years better than anything Medieval Times Dinner Theater can give you.

ORIENTATION

San Gimignano's shape resembles a rose with only a stub of a stem left over. Most travelers enter from the south of the city (the stem), where you can find **Piazzale Martiri Montemaggio** and the main entrance, **Porta San Giovanni.** The city's main street, **Via San Giovanni**, runs north from the entrance, and if you follow it you'll reach the heart of the city, at which point lies **Piazza della Cisterna** and **Piazza Duomo.** The main entrance leaving Piazza Duomo is **Via San Matteo**, which curves north-west and take you to the north entrance of the city, **Porta San Matteo. Via delle Romite** is a street north of and runs parallel with Via San Matteo and leads to **Piazza Sant'Agostino**. A medieval wall surrounds the entire city.

ESSENTIALS

GETTING THERE

The closest airports are in Pisa (Pisa International Airport) and Florence (Aeroporto di Firenze). The easiest way reach San Gimignano is by car. If arriving from Florence or Siena, you'll take SS2 to Poggibonsi. From here, go along SS68 east and follow the signs to San Gimignano. There are parking lots available on the edge of the city (€2/hr or €20/day). If traveling by train, train lines do not stop at San Gimignano, but it is relatively easy to get to the city. Train lines from Florence and Rome stop at a train station called Poggibonsi. From here, there is a bus that takes you directly to San Gimignano. Tickets for the bus are €2.50 one way and can be bought at the Poggibonsi train station tobacconist.

GETTING AROUND

Cars are forbidden in San Gimignano, so once you park or get off the bus, you'll be walking through the walled city. This is the best way to experience the city, and due to the fact that there are virtually only two main roads, you (almost certainly) won't get lost. There is also an electric shuttle bus between Porta San Giovanni, Piazza della Cisterna, and Porta San Matteo. The bus is €1 and tickets can be bought at the Tourist Information office.

PRACTICAL INFORMATION

Tourist Offices: Associazione Pro Loco San Gimignano (P. del Duomo, 1; 0577 940008; www.sangimignano.com/en/; open daily 10am-1pm and 3pm-7pm)

Banks/ATMs/Currency Exchange: There are several ATMs located around the city. Here is a bank: Banca Cambiano 1884 S.p.A. (V. S. Giovanni, 3; 0577 942235; www.bancacambiano.it/; open M-F 8:30am-1:30pm).

Post Offices: There is one post office in the city (P. delle Erbe; 0577 90 77 35; open M-F 8:20am-1:35pm, Sa 8:20am-1:35pm).

Public Restrooms: There are several restrooms located around the city, which cost €0.50 to use. Grab a map from the tourist office for specific details.

Internet: There is Wi-Fi in the three squares of the old town center. Many cafes also have Wi-Fi.

447

BGLTQ+ Resources: The closest physical resource is located in Pisa at Pinkriot Arcigay (V. Enrico Fermi, 7; 050 23278; pinkriot.arcigaypisa.it; open Th 6-10pm).

EMERGENCY INFORMATION

Emergency Number: 112

Police: Police Headquarters (Via Mario Lalli, 3; 050 583511; questure. poliziadistato.it/pisa)

US Embassy: The nearest US consulate is located in Florence (Lungarno Vespucci 38; 39 055 266 951; it.usembassy.gov/embassy-consulates/florence)

Rape Crisis Center: RAINN: (800) 656-4673

Hospitals: The closest hospital is located in Poggibonsi.
• Hospital Campostaggia (Loc. Campostaggia; 0577 9941; open daily 24hr)

Pharmacies: Here are two pharmacies:
• Municipal Pharmacy (P. della Cisterna, 8; 0577 990369; open daily 9am-1pm and 4pm-8pm)

ACCOMMODATIONS

🖾 PALAZZO BUONACCORSI ($$)

Palazzo Buonaccorsi; 349 807 9349 or 0577940908; www.palazzobuonaccorsi.it/

Owning a palace is *just* out of our price range, unfortunately. Luckily, Palazzo Buonaccorsi exists to indulge our wildest dreams, if only for a night. The palace dates back to the thirteenth century and has been passed down from family to family. Today, it is used as luxurious accommodation for visitors of San Gimignano, and you can tell how much pride the owner, Pierluigi, has for his family, his home, and his heritage. Immaculately kept, the palace houses a variety of large and decorated rooms truly fit for the elite. There's a pristine living room where breakfast is served each morning, as well as an outdoor patio shielded from the street by the tall stone walls.

i *Private room with shared bath from €30; reservation preferred; no wheelchair accessibility; Wi-Fi; breakfast €7; linens included*

SIGHTS
CULTURE

🖾 GALLERIA CONTINUA

V. del Castello, 11; www.galleriacontinua. com/; open daily 10am-1pm and 2pm-7pm

If you showed someone Galleria Continua out of context, they would probably assume it was a contemporary art gallery in the heart of New York, San Francisco, or some other city with a big arts scene. Instead, Galleria Continua is pushing the boundaries of modern art in a small, secluded Medieval town. It doesn't make any sense, and yet it works perfectly. The Gallery opened in San Gimignano in 1990 in a former cinema, and has woven its way into the folds of the city since. The constantly-rotating exhibits activate the energy of the ancient city, which inspires the art and artists who find themselves here.

i *Free; limited wheelchair accessibility*

SAN GIMIGNANO 1300

V. Costarella, 3; 327 439 5165; www. sangimignano1300.com/; open daily 10am-5pm

Current obsession: those Facebook videos featuring miniature scenes and dollhouse cooking. So, imagine our excitement when we stumbled upon San Gimignano 1300, a free museum that features a miniature version of the city as it was in 1300. The mini-city, conceived and executed by brothers **Michelangelo** and **Raffaello Rubino** (not the famous guys, these are just some dudes from *our* lifetime), is made entirely from ceramics. The re-creation is meticulously designed, the details of windows and roofs inspiring joy. We may have enjoyed it more than the little kids who dominated the population of museum-goers.

i *Free; wheelchair accessible*

LANDMARKS

🏛 PIAZZA DEL DUOMO AND PIAZZA DELLA CISTERNA

P. del Duomo and P. della Cisterna; 0577 940008; www.sangimignano.com/en/; open daily 24hr

The connecting Piazzas del Duomo and della Cisterna are the center of San Gimignano and where you'll find the most hustle and bustle in the city. If coming from the south, you'll first enter through the grandiose archway **Arco dei Becci** into Piazza della Cisterna. Although the plaza was originally used as a market and festival stage, today restaurants and gelaterias line the street, and people sit on the steps of the octagonal well that resides in the center of the plaza. Walking straight through the Piazza, you'll immediately enter Piazza del Duomo, which is equally grandiose, if slightly smaller. This Piazza holds a lot of the main landmarks, including the **Church of Collegiate, Torre Grossa,** and the **Twin Towers.** Long story short, in the thirteenth century, two competing families built two sets of towers to assert their dominance and importance in the city. Just a hunch, but we think it must've been the men who decided this was a good idea. Comparing tower length is such a boy thing.
i Free; wheelchair accessible

TORRE GROSSA

V. di Sant'Andrea, 121; www.sangimignano.com/en/; 0583 977048; open daily Apr 1-Sept 30 10am-7:30pm; Oct 1-Mar 31 11am-5:30pm

In our pursuit of good views, we've climbed more than the average person's fair share of towers. Torre Grossa is a pretty standard one, and on a scale of 1 to "I can't feel my thighs," the climb lands at a 2.5. As you walk up the wide metal staircase, a projection in the center of the bell tower entitled "Medieval Vertigo" gives you a dramatic history of the tower, which felt a little off putting in the 700 year old edifice. The price is a little steep, too—if we're paying €9, we want to sweat like we would in an extreme Soulcycle class. The views from the top, however, are truly breathtaking. It's only when you're at the top that you realize how secluded the town is from the rest of the world. Surrounded by green vineyards, lush farmlands, and the **Apuan Alps,** there's not much to give away the fact that it's 2019 and not 1619 (other than the parking lot on the outskirts of town).
i Admission €9; last entry 30min. before closing

MUSEUMS

🏛 DUOMO DI SAN GIMIGNANO (COLLEGIATE CHURCH OF SAN GIMIGNANO)

P. del Duomo, 2; 0577 940316; www.duomosangimignano.it/; open Apr 1-Oct 31 M-F 10am-7:30pm, Sa 10am-5:30pm, Su 12:30pm-7:30pm; Nov 1-Mar 31 M-Sa 10am-5pm, Su 12:30pm-5pm

If this is the sixth (or 18th) Italian church you've seen on your trip thus far, you should know the drill by now: frescoes and murals, high ceilings and stained glass—and, of course, disdain for your blasphemously exposed shoulders, for shame! The Collegiate Church, located smack dab in the middle of **Piazza del Duomo,** fits nicely into this stereotype, but that doesn't take away from the awe we feel upon stepping into a place of worship. Along the walls, frescoes tell the

stories of Creation, Heaven and Hell; on one panel, the church offers detailed descriptions of Hell's punishment for each of the seven cardinal sins. We hope exposed shoulders wasn't one of them. The church also holds the sarcophagus of **Saint Fina,** the Saint of San Gimignano. Saint Fina died at 15, and when she passed, the wooden board upon which she lay is said to have burst in blooms of violet.

i Admission €4, students €2; wheelchair accessible; covered shoulders and respectable clothing to enter; free audio guide

PALAZZO COMUNALE

P. Duomo, 2; www.sangimignano.com/en/; 0577 286300; open daily Apr 1-Sept 30 10am-7:30pm, Oct 1-Mar 31 11am-5:30pm

Before checking out the Palazzo Comunale, give the site's Wikipedia page a brief skim (for that matter, do this before going to literally any monument anywhere, and you'll feel much more informed and #cultured if you do). Attached to **Torre Grossa,** the Palazzo Comunale consists of two parts: the outside courtyard and stepped gallery with stone arches, and the indoor civic museum and gallery. The civic authority used to address the crowd from this stepped gallery, and inside, would discuss important business stuff in the council chamber. Today, you can view some old Italian art, and that's about it.

i Admission €9, included with ticket to Torre Grossa; no wheelchair accessibility

OUTDOORS

⚔ LA ROCCA DI MONTESTAFFOLI

V. della Rocca, 13; 0577 940008; www.sangimignano.com/en/san-gimignano/guide-to-the-town/rocca-di-montestaffoli.asp; open daily 24hr

For the perfect picnic or a stroll during sunset, head over to La Rocca di Montestaffoli. Flora and greenery overrun the ruins of the town's fourteenth-century fortress, and there's usually a musician and/or painter there to entertain and enjoy the view. In the corner there's a fortress tower, and a short walk gives you a sweeping view of the vineyard valleys around the town. Look out for the picture-perfect doorway to the right of the

tower: surrounded by lush purple flowers, the doorway will give you a view out and over the city.

i Free; limited wheelchair accessibility

FOOD

🍨 GELATERIA DONDOLÍ ($)

P. Della Cisterna, 4; 0577 942244; www.gelateriadondoli.com/; open daily 8am-11:30pm

Gelateria Dondolí has been crowned the **world's best gelato** several years in a row. So, of course, in pursuit of the truth, we had to try it. To avoid a line, go early or late in the day; we went around 12:30pm and the wait was short. There's an overwhelming number of flavors: you can stick with the classics (pistachio, chocolate, ya know) or try some of their specialities (eggnog, grapefruit, etc). After grabbing your gelato, you can take a seat at the octagonal well in the *piazza* or walk around the city. What's our verdict, you ask? Well, it was some pretty damn good gelato. We're basically experts now.

i Gelato from €2.50; non-dairy options available; wheelchair accessible

DAL BERTELLI ($)

V. Capassi, 30; 39 348 318 1907; open M-Th 11am-7pm, F-Su 11am-midnight

This panini shop gets straight to the point: you're hungry, and they have food. There are literally three things on the menu: a panini with one type of meat, a panini with another type of meat, or a panini with meat and cheese. Mr. Bertelli, the passionate and jolly owner whose family has owned the shop for two generations, spoke only in Italian, but with free samples and gestures, we communicated pretty effectively. Not sure what their secret is, but the sandwich was *so good.* No condiments, nothing fancy, yet the smoked cheese and cured meat on fresh bread still made our day. As we munched contentedly, the Bertelli patriarch looked on fondly from the framed picture.

i Paninis from €4; wheelchair accessible

VENICE

Coverage by **Joseph Winters**

Within minutes, you'll realize why it's the romantic capital of the world. Couples abound, cuddling on guided gondola tours, sipping glasses of wine at canalside trattorias, or hugging tight while taking a vaporetto ride across the lagoon. And you? Well, your backpack will have to be company enough.

The romanticism of Venice is evidently present in the minds of those who visit: with 20 million visitors each year, Venice is one of the most popular tourist destinations in Italy (and the world—Venice is even considering instituting a tourist cap to limit the number of annual visitors), making many of the city's squares feel alarmingly like mosh pits rather than the far-flung getaways they were designed to be. In fact, the city was established by Romans for the very purpose of being inaccessible and inconvenient: they were fleeing from Barbarians (specifically, the Huns), and, upon reaching the area that would become Venice, they decided to start building on top of a seemingly-uninhabitable lagoon. By pressing wooden posts into the marshy wetland, they created the foundation of what would become one of the most powerful cities of the Middle Ages.

Thankfully for you, you're not in danger of an Attila attack, but you may still need to flee from other tourists. Strolling through St. Mark's Square is a must—the Palazzo Ducale, the Royal Palace, and the Campanile are unquestionably the city's most awe-inspiring landmarks—but you'll need to do a bit more digging to discover what it is that makes Venice so special. Put your map away and roam, far away from the crowds. You may find it in the twisting alleys of Cannaregio, on the nearly-uninhabited island of Tronchetto, or on a lagoon-side park near the Arsenale.

ORIENTATION

You (and everyone else) will enter Venice from either the **Ferrovia** (the train station) or **Piazzale Roma** (the bus stop) in the part of Venice called **Santa Croce.** From there, there are signs clearly marking the route to the two major hubs of the city: **Per Rialto** ("to Rialto") and **Per San Marco** ("to San Marco"). Follow these, or just let yourself be carried by the river of tourists flowing towards these tourist-dense destinations. The **Rialto Bridge** neighborhood is called **San Polo,** and the **St. Mark's Square** area is, believe it or not, **San Marco.** Venice wraps itself around the Grand Canal, which serves to connect all its major islands. To the south of these areas is **Dorsoduro,** where you'll find the **Gallerie dell'Accademia** and the **Peggy Guggenheim Collection,** as well as some lovely lagoon-side restaurants facing the island of **Giudecca.** This is a good spot to get away from tourists (except for those staying in Giudecca's famous five-star resort).

To the northwest is **Cannaregio,** the historic Jewish Ghetto (the first official ghetto, actually); this is your best bet for what little nightlife can be found in Venice, as well as local restaurants and *cicchetti* (the Venetian equivalent of bar food). On the northeasternmost reaches of the island you'll find **Castello,** home to the Biennale's world-renowned art pavilions, the Byzantine shipyard, cheaper accommodations, and cheap eats (and a much sparser tourist density).

There are three main island destinations for Venice's tourists: **Lido, Murano,** and **Burano.** Lido, to the east, has a small airport and is known for good beaches (the island is really just a massive sandbar). Murano, a ten-minute *vaporetto* ride from **Fondamente Nove,** is the island most famous for its glass production: all of Venice's glass-blowing factories were moved here in 1295 to prevent the spread of fires throughout the rest of Venice. Burano is a bit more far-flung and is known for lace-making and brightly-colored pastel houses. When you're getting ready to leave Venice, the same helpful signs helping you navigate "Per San Marco" will help you find your way back to the Piazzale Roma or the Ferrovia.

ESSENTIALS

GETTING THERE

If you're flying into Marco Polo airport, you have a few options. Taxis take around 15min. (Radiotaxi Venezia, 041 936222, €35) to get to Piazzale Roma. There are also two bus services. ATVO buses are more expensive, leaving the airport every half hour (5:20am-12:20am daily, €15), whereas ACTV buses (the public buses, Line 5) go for €8,and there is an option to get an extended ticket that will let you use the public transportation system in Venice for an extended period of time. If you're coming in by train, you'll get off at the Santa Maria Lucia station (not Venezia Mestre), which is just steps away from the Venetian canals. There's also luggage storage just left of the station, open daily 6am-midnight).

GETTING AROUND

Maps will be your best friend in Venice: the city of canals was obviously not designed for intuitive navigation. Just try to look up every now and again to appreciate the cityscape. It is highly recommended that you spend at least some time exploring Venice by foot—it's the best way to escape the most touristy areas. Another option is to take a water taxi. Apparently, there are 159 kinds of watercraft that paddle the canals of Venice, all operated by ACTV (the biggest public transportation provider). City Center lines (1 and 2) leave from Tronchetto and Piazzale Roma, and crisscross the main parts of Venice along the Canal Grande and the Giudecca Canal. City Circle lines (3, 4.1, 4.2, 5.1, 5.2, and 6) go to slightly more far-flung destinations like Murano and Lido, and the Lagoon lines (12, 13, 14, and 19) can get you as far as Chioggia, Fusina, San Giuliano, Punta Sabbioni, Treporti, and Marco Polo airport. You can buy a 1-, 2-, 3-, or 7-day unlimited water taxi pass (one day starts at €20) at www.veneziaunica.it/en/.

PRACTICAL INFORMATION

Tourist Offices: Tourist offices are just about as plentiful as tourists, so you should have no trouble finding one regardless of which island you happen to be on. Check www.turismovenezia.it for more information. Stazione Ferroviaria (Santa Lucia, 30121, open daily 8am-6:30pm); Piazzale Roma Tourist Office(Piazzale Roma Garage ASM, 30135, open daily 9:30am-3:30pm); San Marco Tourist Office (71/f, San Marco, 30124, open daily 9am-3:30pm).

Banks/ATMs/Currency Exchange: Venice wants you to spend your money. A lot of it. It shouldn't be too hard to find a bank, ATM, or currency exchange center in any of the city's neighborhoods.
- BNL Venice (Rio Terà Antonio Foscarini, 877/D, 30123; 060060; M-F 8:35am-1:35pm and 2:45pm-4:55pm)

Post Offices: Look for Poste Italiane throughout the islands (bright yellow and blue signage).
- Poste Italiane Dorsoduro (Dorsoduro, 1507, 30123; 041 520 3218; open M-F 8:20am-1:35pm, Sa 8:20am-12:35pm)
- Poste Italiane San Marco (Merceria S. Salvador, 5016, 30124; 041 240 4149; open M-F 8:20am-7:05pm, Sa 8:20am-12:35pm)

Internet: There is a Wi-Fi network called VeniceConnected that works throughout the five main neighborhoods of Venice. You can purchase a special code for 24hr (€5), 72hr (€15), or a week (€20) at www.veneziaunica.it. A 24hr pass is also included with the Rolling Venice three-day public transportation package (students 26 and under €29).

Wheelchair Accessibility: Venice's streets are especially narrow and its many canals require climbing flights of occasionally steep stairs. This is an important note for travelers who require a wheelchair, as they will need assistance navigating around Venice's islands.

EMERGENCY INFORMATION

Emergency Number: 113

Police: As in other Italian cities, there are both the local police and the Carabinieri. Either can help in case of an emergency.

- Carabinieri Piazzale Roma (Piazzale Roma; 041 523 53 33)
- State Police, Santa Croce (Sestiere di Santa Croce, 500, 30135; 041 271 5586; open M-F 8am-10pm, Sa 8am-2pm)

U.S. Embassy: There is no US consular embassy in Venice; the nearest ones are in Milan (V. Principe Amedeo, 2/10, 20121 Milan; 02 290351) and Florence (Lungarno Vespucci, 50123 Florence 38; 055 266 951).

Hospitals: Venice has two good options for hospitals, one of which is open for 24hr emergency care. Your next best bet is the hospital in Mestre, a bus ride away from Piazzale Roma or a train ride away from Santa Lucia station.

- Ospedale SS. Giovanni e Paolo (Castello 6777; 041 5294111, open M-F 3pm-4pm and 7pm-8pm, Su 10am-11:30am and 3pm-7pm)
- Ospedale San Raffaele Arcangelo (Fatebenefratelli)(Dell'orto,30100, Campo Madonna, 3458, Venice; 041 783111; open daily 24hr)

Pharmacies: There aren't any 24hr pharmacies in Venice, but there are a few that are open 9am-7pm daily. For pharmacies open on Su, check the updated roster compiled at www.farmacistivenezia.it.

- Baldisserotto al Basilico (Castello): 041 5224109.
- Marangoni Internazionale, Lido (041 5260117).
- Zamboni San Francesco, Santa Croce (041 5286936).

ACCOMMODATIONS

⛺ BACKPACKERS HOUSE VENICE ($)

Campo Santa Margherita, Dorsoduro 2967/a; 3294724966; www.backpackershousevenice.com; reception open 24hr

If you want to stay in Venice proper, your euros won't get you the fancy schmancy accommodations you might be used to in less popular destinations like Bologna or even Milan. At Backpackers House Venice, you're paying for an incredible location—**Campo Santa Margherita** is pretty much in the heart of the residential part of the city, minutes away from the **Rialto Bridge** or the **Gallerie dell'Accademia.** But the charming college grad manager/receptionist comes for free (just beware of his nap schedule). Despite the lack of free breakfast, laundry, or personal space, the hostel's 24 beds fill up really quickly. Best to book well in advance.

i Dorms in the summer €45, winter €20; reservation recommended; Wi-Fi; no wheelchair accessibility; towels included; free locker storage

⛺ GENERATOR VENICE ($$)

Fondamenta Zitelle, 86; 418778288; www.generatorhostels.com/destinations/venice; reception open 24hr

Self-described as an "experience and design-led hostel," Generator Venice feels more like Venice Beach, California, than Venice, Italy. Between the vegan bagel sandwiches and **throwback karaoke nights,** the whole place feels remarkably modern. Behind the reception counter is a spacious common area where nightly events are held, bringing the late-night scene into an otherwise quiet part of town. Sometimes it seems like they're trying too hard ("Make some *noise! Get craaaaazy!*" the guitarist yells one night to an audience of six 40-year-olds who are clearly busy making light conversation amongst themselves at the bar counter), but they're well-intentioned. Compared to the lobby and café, rooms are pretty basic, but your eyes are closed while you sleep anyways, right?

i Dorms summer from €40; Wi-Fi; wheelchair accessible; linens, towels included; free luggage storage, locker storage €1; laundry (wash €3.50, dry €3.50); breakfast from €4

PLUS CAMPING JOLLY ($)

V. Giuseppe de Marchi, 7; 041 920312; reception open 24hr

When you see how expensive the most basic accommodations in Venice are, you may end up fleeing the city to the far-flung PLUS Camping Jolly.

If you can say its name with a straight face, the €12 per night for a bed in a "tent" is probably the best deal you'll get around Venice. Don't worry—it's not real camping, and the tents' flimsy doors lock completely if you back into them. There's also a giant pool, two hot tubs, a bar/restaurant, and a supermarket all owned by PLUS, so you won't feel like you're depriving yourself too much. Just make sure you calculate the cost of getting to and from Venice every day—€3 total by public transport or €5 total by PLUS's private bus.

i Tents from €12, private bungalows from €65; Wi-Fi; wheelchair accessible; linens included; laundry (wash €5, dry €4.50), buffet breakfast €6.50, free computers

SIGHTS
CULTURE

⬛ JEWISH GHETTO

Cannaregio; open daily 24hr

In the year 1516, the Venetian Doge forced the city's Jewish population to move the northwesternmost corner of the island, in the area today known as **Cannaregio.** The result: the world's first official ghetto (the word "ghetto" comes from *geto* from the Venetian dialect), closed off from the rest of the city. Today, it's just another Venice neighborhood (Napoleon incorporated it in 1797), but the area still retains certain characteristics that differentiate itself from the rest of Venice. Apart from the five synagogues and the annual conference on Hebrew Studies, the area boasts some of the best food and nightlife in Venice. Look for the classic Venetian *cicchetti* and wine (at a reasonable price, too), but keep an eye out for the international flair in its streets.

i Free; prices vary by establishment; wheelchair accessible

⬛ MURANO

Murano Island; open daily 24hr

If Venice had a suburbia, this might be it. But instead of cookie-cutter picket fences, they have glass-blowing furnaces (which is way cooler). Due to Venice's unlucky history with fires (that's what you get when you combine tightly-packed wooden buildings with glass factories), in 1295, the city decided to move all of its glass-blowing production to the island of Murano. Today, Murano is world-famous for the glass it produces; just walk through the town and you'll see *fornace* after *fornace* (furnace), as well as an entire museum devoted to the art of glass. Murano is also a little more real than the mainland; here, you can escape the tourist traps and walk through real neighborhoods, cemeteries, and parks where real Venetians play pick-up soccer games.

i Free; vaporetto from Fte. Nove roundtrip €15; wheelchair accessible

⬛ TEATRO LA FENICE

Campo San Fantin, 1965; 41786511; www.festfenice.com/en; open daily 9:30am-6pm

The name "The Phoenix" is both appropriate and ironic—yes, the sumptuous theater rose from the ashes of devastating fire (1774) to live again, but fire also ravaged the theater in 1836, and yet another fire completely destroyed the theater in 1996. Since then, it has been rebuilt (all over again) to look exactly as the previous one did—solid gold-lined parapets and all. Thanks to this painstaking restoration, the history of the theater has been largely preserved, and you can now walk through the grand foyer, the reception areas, and even the theater itself. Musicians like **Rossini, Stravinsky,** and **Verdi** have all written works specifically for La Fenice, and it is still a world-renowned opera house.

i Admission €10, reduced €7; free audio guide; book "Walk to the Theater" tour in advance via phone or email (visite@festfenice.com); wheelchair accessible

LANDMARKS

⬛ BASILICA DI SAN MARCO

San Marco, 328; 412708311; www.basilicasanmarco.it/?lang=en; open M-Sa 9:45am-5pm, Su 2pm-5pm

When they say San Marco, they're talking about none other than the Saint Mark. He's kind of important to the Christian religion, as he casually helped write the Christian Bible. His bones were brought from Alexandria (stolen?) in 828, and they helped put Venice on the map, giving the city power and prestige. Since then, the Byzantine-style building has experienced influence from the ages it has lived through, from the height of the Gothic era's popularity to the emergence of

Renaissance painting, making the basilica one of the most complex and magnificent in all of Italy. It's free to admire the interior, but make sure to bring some extra money in with you if you want to see the **museum**, the **loggia**, and the **Pala d'Oro** (which contains the relics).

i *Free; St. Mark's Treasure €3, reduced €1.50; Pala d'Oro €2, reduced €1; Museo, Cavalli, and Loggia €5, reduced €2.50; free tours M-Th 11am in basilica atrium; last entry M-Sa 4:45pm, Su 4:15pm; wheelchair accessible*

⬛ PALAZZO DUCALE

S. Marco, 1; 412715911; www.palazzoducale.visitmuve.it; open daily 8:30am-7pm

The history of the Palazzo Ducale alone makes it a must-visit Venetian landmark and museum. First built in the tenth century, its primarily gothic architecture shows hints of Renaissance and Napoleonic influence. It had a specific room for every body of the Venetian government, which you can walk through yourself on the museum's pre-planned itinerary. The most impressive is the **Chamber of the Great Council:** a 53m by 25m room fit to hold 2000 noblemen. It's one of the biggest rooms in all of Europe, and it's home to the longest canvas painting in the world, **Jacopo Tintoretto's** *Paradiso*. From there, cross the **Bridge of Sighs** and enter the medieval prison, which feels like finding yourself onstage during a production of *The Merchant of Venice*.

i *Admission €20, reduced €13; last entry 6pm; wheelchair accessible; tours must be booked in advance online for €20, English tour at 11:45am, "Secret Itineraries" tour at 9:55am, 10:45am, 11:35am*

BASILICA DEI FRARI

San Polo, 3072; 412728611; www.basilicade-ifrari.it

If you haven't gotten sick of basilicas yet, the Basilica dei Frari in the **San Polo** district is one of the city's most impressive. It even has its own **campanile** (not as high as the St. Mark one, though). Since the façade is done in the Gothic style, it might seem a little plain from the outside, but once you enter you'll be able to see the stunning gilded choir stalls. Singers, along with the basilica's multiple organs, occasionally fill the church with ghostly Italian chorales (they don't take song requests, so don't bother asking). Also,

Titian—one of Venice's most famous Renaissance painters—is buried here, which means you can check out his artwork and his monument.

i *Admission €3, reduced €1.50; 5:30pm; wheelchair accessible; book tours in advance via email at basilica@basilicadeifrari.it*

RIALTO BRIDGE

Sestiere San Polo; open daily 24hr

Chances are, you'll cross the Rialto Bridge at some point during your stay in Venice. It's one of four bridges that crosses the **Grand Canal**, connecting the **San Marco** neighborhood to the **San Polo** neighborhood. It's also one of Venice's most popular landmarks—so get ready to wade through a sea of other tourists. The current stone structure was built in 1588, but there were other previous iterations of a bridge, including a floating bridge (1181) and a wooden one (1255). Take note of the ultra-expensive diamond and jewelry shops along either side. Fun fact: these kinds of shops aren't there only to take advantage of the hundreds flush tourists that clamber over the bridge; rather, the high rent for the bridge's coveted location helps pay for the bridge's maintenance.

i *Free; limited wheelchair accessibility*

MUSEUMS

⬛ GALLERIE DELL'ACCADEMIA

Campo della Carità, 1050; 415222247; www.gallerieaccademia.it; open M 8:15am-2pm, Tu-Su 8:15am-7:15pm

This is classic museum material: pre-nineteenth century artwork, airy rooms, full of roaming bespectacled fine art students with sketchbooks in hand. Housed in one of the ancient *Scuole Grandi* ("big schools"—founded in 1260) of Venice, the Accademia is an important center for art restoration and preservation. If you aren't sick of them yet, take some time to stroll through the triptychs of the Virgin Mary, a giant *Last Supper* that was deemed heresy by the Church, and works by **Bellini, Tintoretto,** and **Titian.** Or, you know, you can just book it for Da Vinci's *Vitruvian Man* and call it quits; no one's judging you.

i *Admission €12, reduced €6; last entry 45min. before closing; wheelchair accessible*

🎨 LA BIENNALE DI VENEZIA

A Campiello Tana, 2169/F; 415218711; www. labiennale.org/en/biennale/index.html; open Tu-Su 10am-6pm, F-Sa 10am-8pm

Every two years, La Biennale di Venezia coordinates a monumental showcase of the world's best modern art and design. In between art years, the association organizes a similarly groundbreaking collection of modern architecture. From May to the end of November, the Biennale takes over nearly the entire northeastern corner of Venice in the **Arsenale** and the **Giardini.** Walking through all the exhibits is a hike in itself; wear a comfy pair of shoes because you'll be doing a lot of shuffling. It might be good idea to wear the froofiest getup you packed; lots of inconvenient lace and ridiculous sunglasses will help you blend in with the other locals. No guarantees that it'll help you understand the artistic significance of a video showing a man slicing an apple with a MacBook Air, though.

i 48hr ticket €30, reduced €22; 24hr ticket €25, reduced €15 ; last entry 15min. before closing; wheelchair accessible

MUSEO CORRER

Piazza San Marco, 52; 412405211; www. correr.visitmuve.it; open daily 10am-7pm

It doesn't mean "to run" (that's *correre*), but you might need to run if you plan on getting through the Museo Correr's massive collection of Venetian art and historical artifacts in a timely manner. Housed in the palatial building that encircles **San Marco Square,** a walking tour will take you through the gluttonously posh life of the Venetian elite, from the cream-colored *marmorino* of the Emperor's bathroom to the **"Dining Room for Weekday Lunches."** There's also a picture gallery that highlights the emergence of international Gothicism in Venice, as well as some really intriguing Venetian artifacts, like an early form of high-heeled shoe that *did* have a functional purpose: to keep women's feet clean as they strolled the muddy streets of Venice.

i Admission €20, students €13; last entry 6pm; wheelchair accessible

PEGGY GUGGENHEIM COLLECTION

Dorsoduro, 701-704; 412405411; www. guggenheim-venice.it; open daily 10am-6pm

The Guggenheim Collection is one of those museums that makes you question what exactly defines art. Is a blank canvas art? Does *Curved Black Line's* curved black line count? What about *The Way West,* which is literally "uncarved wooden blocks"? Either way, the museum is one of Venice's most popular tourist attractions. The building used to be Peggy Guggenheim's house, so it has a sort of quaint, homey feel. That is, if you consider a mini-mansion on the banks of the Grand Canal to be quaint. Whether you go to ponder the avant-garde art (or should we say "art"?) or to say you saw works by **Picasso, Jackson Pollock,** and **Joan Miró,** the Collection is definitely an unmissable Venetian attraction.

i Admission €15, students under 26 €9; 90min. tours for €75 booked in advance via email at prenotazioni@guggenheim-venice.it; last entry 5:30pm; wheelchair accessible

OUTDOORS

🎨 GIARDINI DELLA BIENNALE

Sestiere Castello; 415218711; open Tu-Sa 10am-6pm

If you stick to the **San Polo** and **San Marco districts,** you might think all of Venice is devoid of trees. But the northeastern Giardini della Biennale (Gardens of the Biennale) more than make up for chlorophyll-deprived city center. First set up during **Napoleon's** reign, the gardens have been a key part of the Biennale di Venezia's biannual international art exhibition since 1895. Inside the ticketed area are 29 pavilions, each devoted to groundbreaking artwork from a single country. But the gardens' reach extends far beyond the international pavilions; there are public spaces where you'll find people sprawled out on the grass, walking their dogs, or tossing frisbees. It may not sound like much, but this kind of public space is a rarity in Venice, making the Giardini quite special.

i 48hr ticket €30, students under 26 €22; 24hr ticket €25, students under 26 €15; tours must be booked in advance via email at booking@labiennale.org; wheelchair accessible

FOOD

ACQUA E MAIS ($)

Campiello dei Meloni, 1411-1412, San Polo; 412960530; www.acquaemais.com; open daily 9:30am-8pm

Despite the "Pizza Kebab" places at seemingly every street corner, there actually is a more traditional Venetian street food. Called *scartosso*, it's named for the paper cone that the dish is served in. At Acqua e Mais (literally "Water and Corn"), they fill the *scartosso* with polenta and heap crispy veggies, cod, or black cuttlefish on top—your choice. There's also a cold bar with mixed seafood salad or the no-frills but classic *baccalà*, which is just salted fish whipped with oil to form a pasty cream (it sounds grosser than it is). Perfect for a speedy (and cheap) lunch.
i *Cones of polenta with toppings from €3.50, polenta and wine €10; gluten-free, vegan, and vegetarian options available; wheelchair accessible*

CANTINE DEL VINO GIÀ SCHIAVI ($)

Dorsoduro, 992, Fondamenta Nani; 415230034; www.cantinaschiavi.com; open 8:30am-8:30pm

Whether you're feeling pecking or penniless on your Venetian adventure, Cantine del Vina già Schiavi (literally "Wine Cellars Already Slaves") is worth a visit. They are legendary for serving dozens of kinds of Venice's famous *cicchetti* (basically mini bruschettas) on the daily, all of which are painstakingly prepared by a little old lady with a penchant for salty cheeses and buttery purees. On any given day, you might find flavors like pumpkin-ricotta-parmesan, tuna-tartare-cocoa, or dried cod cream with garlic and parsley. At €1.20 a pop, a nice-sized plate of these *cicchetti* won't break the bank. Plus, you can take your plate outside and eat on the banks of the canal, just to the side of a high bridge.
i *Cicchetti €1.20, sandwiches from €3.50; vegetarian options available; wheelchair accessible*

LE SPIGHE ($)

Castello Via Garibaldi, 1341; 415238173; open M-Sa 10:30am-2:30pm and 5:30pm-7:30pm

Although you probably couldn't call her cooking "traditional," Doriana Pressotto's organic-vegetarian-fair trade dishes come with a hefty serving of traditional Italian attitude, completely free of charge. "This system, this is brainwashing us!" she'll exclaim, pointing dramatically to the grocery store across the street while loading your plate with her own, less virtuous vittles. To Pressotto, it's all about the *ennergia* of the food, which is why she's been serving wholesome, affordable, and delicious meals in the vegetable-starved **Castello** area since 2008. Every morning, she prepares around eight different dishes and serves them deli-style until the end of the evening. You can also take your meal to go and have a picnic in the park next door.
i *Small plates from €6, medium plates from €8, large plates from €10; gluten-free, vegan, and vegetarian options available; wheelchair accessible*

GELATERIA ALASKA ($)

Santa Croce, 1159; 41715211; open daily 11am-7pm

Finally, a gelato place serving more than just a cup of ice cream. At Gelateria Alaska, gelato comes with a smile (imagine that!) and a story (sometimes a very long one). Mr. Pistacchi, the owner of this 26-year-old creamery, is passionate about quality. All of his flavors are made with seasonal ingredients collected from the Venetian street markets; for example, when he finds apricots, apricot gelato appears on the menu. He doesn't use any artificial ingredients, either (so don't expect green pistachio gelato). Mr. Pistacchi also likes to experiment with off-the-wall flavors like "rocket salad" or "asparagus," which are highly recommended, although Rose Water is a good bet as well, with the flower petals coming from his own garden.
i *Scoops from €2.50; vegan and vegetarian options available; wheelchair accessible*

NIGHTLIFE

☒ AL TIMON

Cannaregio, 2754; 415246066; open daily 6pm-1am

Don't be alarmed if the bartender gives you a *bacio* or two when you walk into this **Cannaregio** area establishment; kisses on the cheek are the Italian equivalent of the handshake. They happen all the time at Al Timon, because the staff seems to know everyone who walks in. Customers line up for a heaping plate of *cicchetti* (€1 each, and you can choose up to ten per group—which works out great if you're solo or coming with a single friend) and a glass of wine, and then migrate outside to sit on Al Timon's two boats. The soulful Italian jazz, wooden barrels, and melting Venetian sun make for quite a romantic atmosphere.

i No cover, cicchetti €1 (max of 10 per group), wine by the glass from €3

☒ BACARO JAZZ

San Marco, 5546; 415285249; www.bacarojazz.com; open M-Th noon-2am, F-Sa midnight-3am, Su noon-2am

In a city where nightlife is sparse, Bacaro Jazz fills the late-night void with a bizarre mix of classy cocktails and autographed bras. Lots and lots of bras. For 13 years, this cocktail bar-restaurant-jazz club has encouraged visitors to leave behind signed bras as souvenirs, which are then hung from the ceiling in tightly-packed rows. Not all the bras are deemed suitable to go up, though. "These aren't even all of them," the bartender explains. It's anyone's guess where the unhung bras go. As for the food and drink, Bacaro Jazz is more of a bar than a restaurant, serving lots of cocktail-seeking Americans classic and signature drinks for a fair price. Plus, there's BOGO happy hour from 4pm-6pm.

i No cover, pastas and soups (primi piatti) from €12, cocktails from €4

VENICE JAZZ CLUB

Dorsoduro, 3102, Ponte dei Pugni; 415232056; www.venicejazzclub.com; open M-Sa 7pm-11pm

Is there anything more authentically Venetian than a night of spicy bossa nova and smooth Charlie Parker? Probably, but the Venice Jazz Club is still one of the city's nightlife gems. The club has its own quartet of musicians who play international jazz standards, often joined by musicians and groups from around the world. The €20 cover fee pays for your place at a table, as well as your first drink. The space is pretty small, making this a cozy place to spend a relaxing night out (this also means no space for dancing, though). So, if seventh chords and esoteric jazz lingo are your thing, we'd definitely recommend getting down in this crib so you can hear these 18-karat cool cats and finger zingers get crazy with...uh, their instruments?

i Cover €20 (includes first drink), aperitivos €5, beer from €4, long drinks €8, liquor from €5, wine €4; semi-formal dress; wheelchair accessible

ITALY ESSENTIALS

MONEY

Banks and ATMs: To use a debit or credit card to withdraw money from a *bancomat* (ATM), you must have a four-digit PIN. If your PIN is longer than four digits, ask your bank whether you can use the first four or if they'll issue a new one. If you intend to use just a credit card while in Italy, call your carrier before your departure to request a PIN. The use of ATM cards is widespread in Italy. The two major international money networks are MasterCard/Maestro/Cirrus and Visa/PLUS. Most ATMs charge a transaction fee, but some Italian banks waive the withdrawal surcharge.

Tipping: In Italy, a 5% tip is customary, particularly in restaurants. Italian waiters won't cry if you don't leave a tip; just be ready to ignore the pangs of your conscience later on. Taxi drivers expect tips as well, but luckily for oenophiles, it is unusual to tip in bars.

Bargaining: Bargaining is appropriate in markets and other informal settings, though in regular shops it is inappropriate. Hotels will often offer lower prices to people looking for a room that night, so you will often be able to find a bed cheaper than what is officially quoted.

SAFETY AND HEALTH

Local Laws and Police: In Italy, you will encounter two types of boys in blue: the *polizia* (113) and the *carabinieri* (112). The *polizia* are a civil force under the command of the Ministry of the Interior, whereas the *carabinieri* fall under the auspices of the Ministry of Defense and are considered a military force. Both, however, generally serve the same purpose: to maintain security and order in the country. In the case of an attack or robbery, both will respond to inquiries or requests for help.

Drugs and Alcohol: The legal drinking age in Italy is 16. Remember to drink responsibly and to never drink and drive. Doing so is illegal and can result in a prison sentence, not to mention early death. The legal BAC for driving in Italy is under 0.05%, significantly under the US limit of 0.08%.

Travelers with Disabilities: Travelers in wheelchairs should be aware that getting around in Italy will sometimes be extremely difficult. This country predates the wheelchair—sometimes it seems even the wheel—by several centuries and thus poses unique challenges to disabled travelers. Accessible Italy (378 941 111; www.accessibleitaly.com) offers advice to tourists of limited mobility heading to Italy, with tips on subjects ranging from finding accessible accommodations to wheelchair rentals.

THE NETHERLANDS

Anything beyond a bike ride to the supermarket is traveling a great distance in the Netherlands. Yet, this small country much more than its legal substances, The Fault in Our Stars reference, bicycles, and jokes about "your mom's nether-lands" (grow up, by the way). Each city and neighborhood within them is exquisite with its own distinguishable accent, customs. This heritage makes for a wealth of regional festivals, cultural events, and local specialties. That's not to mention the country's impressive line-up of influential artists from Rembrandt to Van Gogh to M.C. Escher.

Beyond the rich history and thriving traditions, experiencing the fun and carefree student life here is easy. The country has small and navigable cities with blissfully flat bike paths, crowded cafés, and canal-side bars. Its filled with plenty of young people with progressive and easygoing attitudes (and impressive fluency in English). While the Dutch are straightforward and practical, a visit during King's Day, the Amsterdam Dance Event, or, well, pretty much any weekend for proof that everyone from rural farmers to university students are the world's more passionate partiers. Even though only about half the country is a meter above sea level, there's no better place to get high on life.

AMSTERDAM

Coverage by **Emily Corrigan**

When you say you're going to Amsterdam, a lot of people raise their eyebrows, smile knowingly, and say "oh Amsterdam huh?" It's a city known for its legal prostitution, "coffee shops" selling selling plants more popular than mere coffee beans (marijuana, for those who need it spelled out), and its wild nightlife. With an annual tourist population larger than its actual population, Amsterdam can be subject to misrepresentation by the weekend-trip frat bros, the nearly adulterous bachelorette parties, and the "I've never done it, but it's Amsterdam!" crowd. Amongst the madness, though, is a city with much more real character than first meets the eye. In terms of culture, practicality and efficiency meet relaxed social attitudes and an unmatched ability for leisure and fun. Scenic canals flanked by narrow buildings and a constant stream of bikes make up the cityscape. Cafés, tons of electronic music festivals, and a surprising number of all-you-can-eat sushi restaurants join the ranks of the "coffee shops" as gathering places. World-renowned art museums are tucked next to shops selling Dutch snacks out of cubbies in the wall, like *frikandel* and *kroketten* (find these at the Febo chain). Amsterdam is perhaps best described by the non-translatable Dutch word which describes something cozy and easy to relax into, a warm feeling, a nice day with friends or a date gone well: It's gezellig.

ORIENTATION

Arriving at **Centraal Station,** you'll be on the northern side of the city. A ferry across the harbor to the north will bring you to **Amsterdam Noord,** an neighborhood featuring the new **Eye Film Institute** and a multitude of cafés overlooking the harbor. South are some of the more touristy parts of town: the **Red Light District** is a center for nightlife, popular among tourists for its more debaucherous reputation ("red light" comes from the red lights that indicate the windows of prostitutes). In the city center, you'll find **Leidseplein,** the site of many clubs and restaurants, and the first location of the **Bulldog,** Amsterdam's oldest coffee shop. **Rembrandtplein,** Leidseplein's even more touristy counterpart, is also close by. The city center is where you'll find many quaint canals and terraces on narrow houses, the classic Amsterdam views. East of the city center are the "nine streets," full of cute shops and small restaurants. Southwest in **Oud-Zuid** lies **Vondelpark,** the city's largest park, as well as **Museumplein,** a large grassy area with a stunning view of the Rijksmuseum as well as two of the city's other most famous museums. Oud-Zuid is also home to some of the city's wealthiest residents, leafy streets, restaurants, and boutiques. **Jordaan** is the home of cool traditional bars frequented by longtime Amsterdammers, and in **De Pijp** you'll find upscale young hipster places along like restaurants and chatty bars, as well as one of the city's most famous markets. **Amsterdam Oost** in the east is spacious and green. Finally, visit **Amsterdam West** for an up-and-coming nightlife scene, trendy design stores, excellent restaurants, and hip hangouts.

ESSENTIALS

GETTING THERE

Buses, taxis, and trains are all available from the international airport, Schiphol. The airport's train station is just below it and buses leave from directly outside the arrivals area. On the train, you'll arrive at Centraal Station, the metro system's main stop. From there it's easy to walk into the city center.

GETTING AROUND

Amsterdam has excellent public transport, including buses, trams, ferries, and the metro. All public transportation in Amsterdam can be accessed with an OV-Chipkaart or temporary travel card, which can be purchased at vending machines in the main stations. A variety of options are available, from personalized rechargeable chip cards to single-use or 24hr tickets. You can also consider purchasing the "i amsterdam" City Card, which provides free entry to the top attractions, a canal cruise, and free public transport. It can be purchased for 24hr, 48hr, 72hr, and 96hr durations on www.iamsterdam.com. Bikes are also a popular way to get around Amsterdam. Bike rental shops are all over the city, the most popular being MacBike (red bikes) and Yellow Bike (obviously yellow bikes).

PRACTICAL INFORMATION

Tourist Offices: Stationsplein 10; 020 702 6000; open M-Sa 9am-5pm
Banks/ATMs/Currency Exchange: Damrak 86; 020 624 6682; open M-Sa 9am-8pm, Su 11am-6pm
Post Offices: PostNL (Overtoom 8; 900 0990)
Internet: There are internet cafés and Wi-Fi hotspots available to the public throughout Amsterdam.
BGLTQ+ Resources: A complete list of Amsterdam's BLGTQ+ resources can be found here: www.iamsterdam.com/en/see-and-do/whats-on/gayamsterdam/resources.

EMERGENCY INFORMATION

Emergency Number: 112
Police: Politiebureau Centrum-Jordaan (Lijnbaansgracht 219; 0900 8844)
US Embassy: US Consulate General (Museumplein 19; 020 575 5309; open M-F 8:30am-4:30pm).
Hospitals:
• OLVG, location Spuistraat (Spuistraat 239; 020 599 4100; open M-W, F 8:30am-4:30pm, Th 8am-7:30pm)
• Amsterdam Tourist Doctors (Nieuwe Passeerdersstraat 8; 020 237 3654; open daily 24hr)
Pharmacies:
• Leidsestraat Pharmacy (020 422 0210; open M-F 8:30am-8pm, Sa 9am-8pm, Su 11am-8pm)
• Amsterdam Central Pharmacy (020 235 7822; M-W, F 7:30am-9pm, Th 7:30am-10pm, Sa-Su 10am-8pm)

ACCOMMODATIONS

🏨 COCOMAMA ($$)

Westeinde 18; 1017 ZP Amsterdam; 206272454; www.cocomamahostel.com; reception open 9am-9pm

At Cocomama, you'll feel like it truly is your mama's house. From family dinners to the social activities, the sweet staff, and the adorable cat, Joop, this place is easy to call home. The dorm rooms are clean, comfortable, and Dutch-themed, while the outdoor garden and living room are cozy places to hang. A non-smoking hostel, this is the place to find the laid-back crowd that's in for the real Amsterdam, not just the party scene. Breakfast, cheap dinner nights, and a fully-stocked kitchen will save you money on food, especially if you shop at **De Pijp**, the nearby market. With such a warm atmosphere, you would never guess that this place used to be a brothel.
i Dorms from €39; reservation required; no wheelchair accessibility; Wi-Fi; laundry; towels for rent; free breakfast

🏨 THE FLYING PIG DOWNTOWN HOSTEL ($)

Nieuwendijk 100; 1012 MR Amsterdam; 204206822; www.flyingpig.nl; reception open 24hr

If you said you'll love a hostel when pigs fly, this place makes it possible. It's a social backpacker's heaven: a bar open until 3am hosting activities like quiz nights, a pool table, a communal kitchen and included breakfast as well as a smoking lounge. A fun and laid-back staff greets you at the door, which is off one of Amsterdam's busiest shopping streets. It's a busy area with lots of tourists, but the more easygoing Amsterdam is always accessible by foot and the security at the hostel is top notch. It's truly a great place to stay, regardless of our all-too-obvious flying pig joke.
i Dorms from €32; reservation required; no wheelchair accessibility; Wi-Fi; towels for rent; lockers provided; free breakfast

THE BULLDOG HOTEL ($)

Oudezijds Voorburgwal 220; 1012 GJ Amsterdam; 206203822; www.hotel. thebulldog.com; reception open 24hr

Maybe you're telling people you're coming to Amsterdam for art, culture, and a picture of yourself wearing clogs in front of a windmill. Or maybe you just want to get high and engage in shenanigans. If the latter is more your style, you need to stay at the Bulldog Hotel. The Bulldog is the oldest and most famous "coffee shop" in Amsterdam, and its various locations now dominate the **Leidseplein** and the **Red Light District.** The hotel is next door to one of the "coffee shops," and even has its own smoking lounge and bar. Even if your stay isn't all about the Devil's lettuce, the complimentary breakfast, security, and location make this hotel worthwhile.

i Dorms from €38; reservation required; min stay 2 nights; wheelchair accessible; Wi-Fi; laundry; luggage storage; free breakfast

SIGHTS
CULTURE

⬛ EYE FILM INSTITUTE

IJpromenade 1; 1031 KT Amsterdam; 205891400; www.eyefilm.nl; open daily 10am-7pm

The Eye is all about films: their development, creation, and projection, as well as stunning examples of color, editing, and music. The building itself is a striking work of architecture and features a gorgeous café on the water and four large cinemas. It highlights influential directors and a permanent presentation in the Panorama explores the creation and history of film. Visitors can sit in the mini cinemas, make their own flip books, create a film on the green screen, and sift through the institute's enormous film archives.

i Film tickets online €10, students €8.50; at the door €10.50, students €9; exhibitions and permanent presentation €13, students €11.50; wheelchair accessible

⬛ GEITENBOERDERIJ RIDAMMERHO-EVE (GOAT FARM)

Nieuwe Meerlaan 4; 1182 DB Amstelveen; 206455034; www.geitenboerderij.nl

No kidding around, nothing bleats a visit to the **Amsterdamse Bos** when you goat to get way from the chaos of the city center. All caprine jokes aside, at this working farm set in a picturesque forest, you'll get a taste of real rural Dutch farm life. Visitors can pet friendly pigs, cows, and baby goats, hold chickens, and sit on tractors (for free)! The farmers are happy to let you watch them milk the goats, and you can even buy fresh goat cheese and homemade goat's milk ice cream in the farm's store. Whether you're an animal lover or a city slicker, this farm will make you fall in love with the pastoral side of the city.

i Free; limited wheelchair accessibility

BOOM CHICAGO

Rozengracht 117; 1017 LV Amsterdam; 202170400; www.boomchicago.nl/en; hours vary

This fun comedy club is beloved by Dutch locals and humor-loving visitors alike. Reserve a small table beforehand and grab a bucket of Heinekens to loosen your giggles and you'll find yourself in tears of laughter. **Improv nights** in English involve the audience, and some routines by the expat comedians poke fun at the particularities of Dutch culture as well as American and Dutch current events. Stick around at the bar afterward to chat with the comedians themselves.

i Tickets €15, students €7.50, pre-order beer buckets (6 beers) €15; shows at 8pm, check website for details; wheelchair accessible

LANDMARKS

⬛ NEMO SCIENCE MUSEUM ROOFTOP

Oosterdok 2; 1011 VX Amsterdam; 205313233; open daily 10am-5:30pm

While we would equally recommend a visit to the inside of the NEMO Science Museum on Amsterdam's eastern harborside, it's worth the trip just for the roof. The top of the building is long and slanted, making it easy to walk up the flat steps to the top. Water features cascade down the stairs, and binoculars let you closely examine the spectacular view of the harbor and the city. Purchase lemonade or a snack from the cool café at the top and sit on the benches or the rotating circular pods. Check out the many sailboats and ships below but don't be deceived; the large old-looking ship that you see across the water is actually a replica made of concrete. Not as effective as an actual boat.

i Free; no wheelchair accessibility

BLOEMENMARKT

Singel; 1012 DH Amsterdam; open M-Sa 9am-5:30pm, Su 11am-5:30pm

Stereotypes have never been more pleasant and colorful. The world famous Dutch tulips and clogs abound at this floating flower market that stretches along a canal between **Muntplein** and **Koningsplein.** Flower bulbs fill the stalls along with seeds, souvenirs, and plenty of other plants like succulents and cacti. You may not be able to bring dozens of live plants home on the plane—and you shouldn't try to pack a cactus next to your sweater anyway—but a walk along the market to peruse the plants is certainly time well spent anyway.

i Stall prices vary; wheelchair accessible

WESTERKERK

Prinsengracht 279; 1016 GW Amsterdam; 206247766; www.westerkerk.nl/english; open M-Sa 11am-4pm

Westerkerk can often be found telling people that it "isn't like other churches." Unlike the totally not-chill European cathedrals, Westerkerk knows how to keep it classy and has been doing so since 1631. Simple white walls divert all attention to the church's organ, which is used for free concerts every summer on Fridays at 1pm. The church also features a tall tower that can be accessed for €8 in small groups of six. From the top, you'll find a panoramic view including the **Prinsengracht canal** and surrounding **Jordaan**.

i Church admission free, tower admission €8; tower tours every 30min.; church wheelchair accessible, tower no wheelchair accessibility

WINDMILLS AT ZAANSE SCHANS

Schansend 1; 1509 AW Zaandam; 756810000; www.dezaanseschans.nl/en/; open daily 24hr

Many visitors to the Netherlands are taken with the idea of nostalgic windmills surrounded by happy, round-faced people wearing wooden shoes. "Ah, simpler times they were," they might sigh after buying a souvenir tulip bulb. The windmills at Zaanse Schans are bound to satisfy these idyllic dreams with a classic Dutch landscape. The windmills, mostly originals from the area, date as far back as the sixteenth century and were relocated here in the sixties, to a neighborhood of **Zaandam** that's been made to look like the typical Dutch village of old. Note the oil mill **De Bonte Hen** of 1693 that has survived multiple lightning strikes in its long life.

i Free; limited wheelchair accessibility

MUSEUMS

◪ ANNE FRANK HOUSE

Prinsengracht 263-267; 1016 GV Amsterdam; 205567105; www.annefrank.org; open daily 9am-10pm

The voice of Anne Frank has touched millions of people around the world. Her diary, written while hiding in Amsterdam during Nazi occupation is a reminder not to forget the atrocities of the **Holocaust** and the many innocent lives that it touched. Even though Anne's life was eventually claimed, her father Otto made sure her diary was published in order to illuminate the horrifying reality of life under Nazi rule. At the Anne Frank House, visitors can see the small annex that concealed the Frank family for two years before their discovery and arrest in 1944. This museum will not only give you a new perspective on Anne Frank, but also deliver a powerful message that you won't be able to ignore.

i Admission €9; last entry 30min. before closing; limited wheelchair accessibility; from 9am-3:30pm the museum is only open to people with online tickets for a specific time slot. After 3:30pm tickets can be purchased at the museum entry; online tickets become available two months in advance.

MOCO MUSEUM

Honthorststraat 20; 1071 Amsterdam; 203701997; www.mocomuseum.com; open daily 10am-6pm

The Moco Museum, set in a townhouse in **Museumplein,** has displayed exhibitions from famous yet anonymous street artist **Banksy** and artist **Salvador Dalí,** whose surrealist work is only rivaled by his iconic mustache and his quote "I don't do drugs, I am drugs." The Moco Museum highlights specific artists, focusing on those who have carved new paths in their fields and approach society with a fresh voice and with a sense of irony. Banksy, for example, is cynical toward capitalism and once sold pieces of his artwork, each worth tens of thousands of dollars, on the streets of New York City for $60 a piece. At the Moco Museum, you're sure to find niche art and artists, curated well and displayed in an intimate setting.

i Admission €12.50, students €10, under 16 €7.50; audio guide €2.50; purchase tickets to skip line; limited wheelchair accessibility

VAN GOGH MUSEUM

Museumplein 6; 1071 DJ Amsterdam; 205705200; www.vangoghmuseum.nl; open M-Th 9am-6pm, F 9am-10pm, Sa-Su 9am-6pm

With his bold and colorful work, it's hard to imagine Van Gogh as a tortured artist plagued by inner turmoil and, eventually, the author of his own death. Not only does this museum display around 200 of his paintings, more than 500 drawings, and almost all of his letters, but it acquaints you with the Dutch painter's eventful life as well. It traces his studies in Antwerp and Paris, his friendships with other artists, and the extremely productive period (averaging a painting per day) that occupied the few months before his death. Be sure to buy your tickets online the day before in order to bypass the long ticket line.

i Admission €17, under 18 free; wheelchair accessible; no photography allowed

RIJKSMUSEUM

Museumstraat 1; 1071 XX Amsterdam; 206747000; www.rijksmuseum.nl; open daily 9am-5pm

With more than 8,000 artifacts of art and history, the Rijksmuseum is one of Amsterdam's finest attractions. It houses paintings from **Vermeer, Lucas van Leyden, Van Gogh,** and **Rembrandt** (including the masterpiece *Night Watch,* painted with no preliminary drawings). A centuries-old Shiva statue, an elaborate model of a warship, and a dollhouse with marble floors and real china commissioned by the **Dutch East India Company** (costing as much as an actual house on the **Herengracht** at the time) are all on display as well. In order to really delve into the artwork, download the free Rijksmuseum app, full of virtual guided tours of varying lengths and themes.

i Admission €17.50, under 18 free, multimedia tours €5; wheelchair accessible

OUTDOORS

VONDELPARK

West from the Leidseplein and Museumplein; www.amsterdam.info/parks/vondelpark; open daily 24hr

Vondelpark takes up a good portion of the southwest side of Amsterdam. Ponds and weeping willows make for scenic lunches in the grass. 'T Blauwe Theehuis, a nice tea house and café, can be found closer to the center if you're looking for a fresh mint tea. Go further southwest away from the city center for a more natural, less crowded part of the park. Watch out for all the bikes, especially during rush hours when the paths running through the park are regular bicycle highways. One of the summer highlights of Vondelpark is the free concert series that takes place at its open-air theater on weekend afternoons. The events are popular, so check online for the schedule. For a less famous but equally beautiful outdoor experience, head to Oosterpark instead, where locals play soccer, jog, bike, and do yoga.
i Free; wheelchair accessible

FOOD

🍴 RESTAURANT THT ($)

Silodam 386; 1013 AW Amsterdam; 204422040; www.tht.nl; open daily 11am-4pm and 5:30pm-10pm

This trendy restaurant and bar lies across the water from the city center, making it accessible by ferry. A large outdoor patio overlooks the harbor, so you can watch the steady flow of boats trundling by from your vantage point above the water. The interior walls are covered in live plants while succulents and cacti rest on the colorful outdoor tables. Apart from the out-of-the-box location and design, the food itself also makes this place appealing. At lunch, THT serves sandwiches, salads, excellent soups, and Dutch specialties. Their menu elucidates the sources of their fresh ingredients and nearly everything can be made gluten-free.
i Entrées from €6.50; card only; gluten-free, vegan, and vegetarian options available; no wheelchair accessibility

BULLS AND DOGS ($)

Van Woustraat 58; 1073 LN Amsterdam; open M-W 4pm-10pm, Th noon-10:30pm, F-Sa noon-11pm, Su noon-10pm

This restaurant's name is both a nod to Amsterdam's most famous coffee shop, The Bulldog, and a play on words. Elaborate hot dogs (beef, pork, veggie, and more) make up the menu, from the Dutch Delight to the Spicy Texas Dog. Fries on the side can be topped with truffle sauce or feta, and you can add a specially selected beer to complete the combo. The restaurant is hip and unique, and its food is as yummy as it is photogenic. You may have to make another trip back for their incredible milkshakes; you'll need to whip out the trampoline and the lawn furniture because they will bring the boys to your yard.
i Hot dogs from €5; vegetarian options available; limited wheelchair accessibility

SIR HUMMUS ($)

Van der Helstplein 2; 1072 PH Amsterdam; 206647055; www.sirhummus.nl; open Tu-F noon-8pm, Sa-Su noon-5pm

This isn't your average "we needed a vegetarian option at our barbecue so we put out some celery sticks and hummus" hummus. Sir Hummus makes only one meal, done extremely well: the delicious vegan Middle Eastern classic with chickpeas, veggies and pickles, warm pita bread, and your choice of topping. A small version is a perfect afternoon snack while a large will quell the tempers of even the hangriest guests. The free "secret sauce" (also vegan) on the communal tables knocks the spice up a notch. For cheap and healthy eats in De Pijp, this is the place to go.
i Large bowl €7.50, small bowl €6.50, toppings from €1; card only; gluten-free, vegan, and vegetarian options available; limited wheelchair accessibility; will sometimes close earlier if supply runs out

NIGHTLIFE

COOLDOWN CAFE ("KLEINE COOLDOWN")

Lange Leidsedwarsstraat 116 3 BG; 1017 NN Amsterdam; 204212284; open M-Th 10:30pm-4am, F-Sa 10:30pm-5am, Su 10:30pm-4am

Known affectionately to locals as the "Kleine Cooldown" or just the "Kleine," this place beats any famous touristy club for a crazy night. With wild bartenders flipping between hit songs, Dutch folk songs, and electronic music every thirty or so seconds, ringing loud bells, and passing out Santa hats regardless of the month, this is where real Amsterdammers go. A true Kleine Cooldown experience means showing up super late on a weekday, dancing like crazy, dousing your clothes in beer, and not leaving until you've ensured that the next day (or, more accurately, later that day) is thoroughly ruined. If you're lucky, you'll even wake up in a Santa hat. A free souvenir!

i *Free; limited wheelchair accessibility*

VOLKSHOTEL

Wibautstraat 150; 1091 GR Amsterdam; 202612100; www.volkshotel.nl/en; open Su noon-6pm

Things young budget travelers usually don't come across too often: free stuff, luxury rooftop bars, hot tubs. Things that Volkshotel has: all of the above. Normally the rooftop hot tub and bar areas are restricted to guests, but entry is free to the public on Sundays from noon to 6pm, so grab your swimsuit and towel and head up for the spectacular views, tasty drinks, and a little sauna. The hot tubs are small, so you'll get a chance to bump shoulders with real Amsterdam residents. After your relaxation time, you can easily transition to dinner or a drink at the hotel's restaurant, where live DJs play, or later on, head to its nightclub. This gem of a spot is one of the city's best kept secrets.

i *Free entry; limited wheelchair accessibility; bring your own towel and swimsuit, showers*

WATERKANT

Marnixstraat 246; 1016 TL Amsterdam; 207371126; www.waterkantamsterdam.nl/nl/index.html; open M-Th 11am-1am, F-Sa 11am-3am

Waterkant has perfected the recipe for attracting trendy young people: start with a beautiful but odd location, mix in a bunch of picnic tables, and top it off with plentiful beers. Dutch locals pack this cool waterside bar, even during the week, to hang their legs over the picturesque canal, watching the sunset in a friendly and chatty atmosphere. As the night wears on, it gets increasingly lively, making it a great place for pre-drinks and snacks or a stand-alone spot for a night out. The coolest part? Tourists tend to miss it because it's underneath a parking garage.

i *Beers from €2.75; limited wheelchair accessibility*

PIANOBAR MAXIM

Leidsekruisstraat 33; 1011 CR Amsterdam; 630364965; www.pianobarmaxim.com; open M-Th 9pm-3am, F 5pm-4am, Sa 9am-4am, Su 9pm-3am

Pianobar is fairly straightforward: it's a bar with a piano. The performer can do it all; request a classic song by writing it on a coaster and soon the whole bar will be singing and dancing along. By "the whole bar" we mean a cluster of people of all ages, drunk moms out with their friends and rowdy teens coming from nearby clubs alike. Whether you're starting the night off with some live music or you feel like yelling out some familiar songs after exploring other bars is of little importance. There is a cover but don't let it deter you. It's only €1, a small price to pay for the amount of times you'll request "The Piano Man."

i *Cover €1, beers €3.50; wheelchair accessible*

UTRECHT

Coverage by **Emily Corrigan**

Though often overshadowed by its larger neighbor Amsterdam (remember, even Beyoncé has a sister), Utrecht is a can't-miss stop for students who love the relaxed and honest Dutch culture, beautiful canals, and fun cafés, but not the tourist-filled madness. This medieval city was once considered the most important city in the Netherlands, and continues to be a religious center as well as the host of countless cultural events. It holds the tallest church tower in the country, shopping areas and markets, boats gliding over flat water, and stair-accessible canal-side restaurants. It has small-town charm and the relative scarcity of tourists makes it feel traditional and authentic. The presence of Utrecht University also means there are always plenty of young people biking through town and packing the popular bars.

ORIENTATION

The medieval city center is dominated by **Dom Tower** and the neighboring cathedral. Surrounding **Dom Square,** you'll find many of the city's shops and restaurants, as well as **Utrecht University.** East of the city center are a number of small parks and green walking paths along the large canal, which also bends around its northern end and to the south past the observatory. Near the observatory, you'll find a number of the city's other popular museums and the beautiful neighborhood of **Lange Nieuwstraat.** Farther west is the train station, **Utrecht Centraal.** Finally, a trip farther east will take you to the university's beautiful botanic gardens and historic buildings.

ESSENTIALS

GETTING THERE

To get to Utrecht by plane, you will have to fly in to Schiphol Airport in Amsterdam. Trains leave directly from the airport to Utrecht Central Station. The train station is located within walking distance of most accommodations and sights in the city center.

GETTING AROUND

Most attractions in Utrecht are within walking distance. Buses and trams also run throughout the city. Tickets cost €2.70 either on the bus or tram or at a vending machine in the station. One-day passes can be purchased for €6. There are also numerous bike rental shops around the city.

PRACTICAL INFORMATION

Tourist Offices: Domplein 9, 3512 JC Utrecht; 0900 1288732; open M noon-5pm, Tu-Sa 10am-5pm, Su noon-5pm
Banks/ATMs/Currency Exchange: Western Union (De Lessepsstraat 59, 3553 RJ Utrecht; 030 244 4333; open M-F 8:30am-6pm)
Post Offices: Voorstraat 3 (Open M-Sa 8:30am-5pm)

Internet: The city of Utrecht provides free Wi-Fi nearly everywhere.

EMERGENCY INFORMATION

Emergency Number: 112
Police: Politie Utrecht Bureau Kroonstraat (Kroonstraat 25, 3511 RC Utrecht; 0900 8844)
Rape Crisis Center: Centrum Seksueel Geweld Utrecht (Postbus 85090, 3508 AB Utrecht; 88 755 5588)
Hospitals: University Medical Center Utrecht (Heidelberglaan 100; 088 755 5555; open daily 24hr)
Pharmacies: Apotheek Binnenstad (Van Asch van Wijckskade 30; 030 232 6010; open M-F 8am-6pm)

ACCOMMODATIONS

⬛ HOSTEL STROWIS ($)

Boothstraat 8; 3512 BW Utrecht; 302380280; www.strowis.nl; reception open 8am-1am

Staying at Hostel Strowis feels much more like crashing at a friend's house than renting a hostel bed. A large and secluded garden with a long picnic table encourages a friendly social scene, as do the communal kitchen and cozy living room with bright colors and plenty of light streaming through tall windows. You're greeted with a cup of coffee or tea and a host of amenities at your disposal—think free earplugs, books, and games. The hostel's excellent location makes it super easy to explore the center. If that's not enough, there are free concerts in the garden every Sunday.

i Dorms from €20; reservation required; no wheelchair accessibility; Wi-Fi; lockers available; laundry

STAYOKAY UTRECHT ($$)

Neude 5; 3512 AD Utrecht; 307501830; www.stayokay.com/nl/hostel/utrecht-centrum; reception open 24hr

Walking into Stayokay you'll think you're in the wrong place. That's because it looks more like a large hipster café—we're talking plants, strange artwork, copper pipes, exposed bulbs, people wearing glasses—than it does a hostel lounge. The bar is professional, and you can grab a fresh snack from the small restaurant area. The hostel is on the edge of the **Neude,** one of Utrecht's nicest squares. Even with such a central location, the hostel offers bicycle rentals for enjoying the rest of the city.

i Dorms from €32; reservation required; wheelchair accessible; Wi-Fi; laundry; lockers provided; towels for rent

SIGHTS
CULTURE

SONNENBORGH OBSERVATORY

Zonnenburg 2; 3512 NL Utrecht; 308201420; www.sonnenborgh.nl/page=site.home; open Tu-F 11am-5pm, Su 1pm-5pm

Even if you didn't planet, a trip to the Sonnenborgh Observatory is sure to be an out-of-this-world experience. While much of the museum portion of the observatory seems to cater to Dutch children, you'll still be able to find highlights like footage of the 2012 Curiosity landing on Mars, enormous telescopes, and a 115-kilogram meteorite. Better yet are the star-watching and sun-viewing events held at the observatory. On summer "Sun Sundays," a guide can help you view the sun through a special telescope

that protects your eyes, and from September to April, you can view stars with the help of one of the pros.

i Admission €7, students €4.50; sun viewings Su 2pm and 3:30pm; no wheelchair accessibility

VREDENBURG MARKET

Vredenburg; 3511 AG Utrecht; open W 10am-5pm, F 10am-5pm, Sa 8am-5pm

On Wednesdays, Fridays, and Saturdays, in a square surrounded by busy stores, you'll find the Vredenburg Market. Here you can find everything from fresh fish to shampoo to books, records, cheese, and food stands selling tasty snacks. Local vendors often offer free samples of their goods, making it fun and filling to wander the stalls. For a jam-packed Saturday, check out more of Utrecht's street markets, like the colorful and aromatic **Janskerkhof Flower Market** or the **Breedmarkt Fabric Market.**

i Stall prices vary; wheelchair accessible

LANDMARKS

DOM TOWER

Domplein 21; 3512 JC Utrecht; open M noon-5pm, Tu-Sa 10am-5pm, Su noon-5pm

The people of Utrecht really wanted to make a statement back in 1321 when they started work on Dom Tower, the highest tower in the Netherlands. *Compensating for something?* The tower, once attached to the neighboring church, is over 112 meters tall, making for a long climb to the top for #views. Buy your tickets at the tourist office in the square before joining a tour. You'll be able to stand right under the enormous bells, many dating back to 1505, and watch the upper musical bells chime out a melody. For a tower experience even from the ground, just hang around the area on Monday at 8pm; the city's carillon player gives bell concerts of anything from David Bowie to Radiohead.

i Tickets (with guided tour included) €9, students €7.50, student combination ticket €16; tours every hour on the hour; no bags allowed inside, but lockers are provided for free; no wheelchair accessibility

SAINT MARTIN'S CATHEDRAL

Achter de Dom 1; 3512 JN Utrecht;
302310403; www.domkerk.nl; open M-Sa
10am-5pm

This stunning cathedral is located at
the heart of a Roman fort founded
around 43 CE. Originally Catholic,
it became Protestant during the
Reformation of 1580, and that's not
the only change that has occurred since
its construction. It was once connected
to Dom Tower via a nave, which was
destroyed in a tornado in 1674 and
never rebuilt. Citizens even waited
about 150 years to clear out the rubble,
like teenagers hoarding dirty dishes in
their rooms. Don't miss the gorgeous
fifteenth-century courtyard, where
the life story of Utrecht's patron saint,
Saint Martin, is told through reliefs.
i *Free; tours available upon request;
wheelchair accessible*

MUSEUMS

CENTRAAL MUSEUM

Agnietenstraat 1; 3512 XA Utrecht;
302362362; www.centraalmuseum.nl;
open Tu-Su 11am-5pm

Centraal Museum has it all, in a
thrilling and confusing way. It starts
with a huge fashion collection,
including some clothes that you have
to already know are clothes in order to
recognize them as such. One moment
you can be looking at a panel painting
from 1363 and then turn around
and see a room full of modern chairs,
lifesize sculptures made of molten
plastic, or a sweater made of human
hair. Tucked in the basement almost
as an afterthought is an enormous,
thousand-year-old ship found by
archaeologists.
i *Admission €12.50, students
€5; wheelchair accessible*

MUSEUM SPEELKLOK

Steenweg 6; 3511 JP Utrecht;
302312789; www.museumspeelklok.nl;
open Tu-Su 10am-5pm

Having a guided tour of clocks and
organs may not immediately sound
appealing to a young and adventurous
traveler. Yet, this museum of self-
playing instruments is about much
more than just those creepy music
boxes with spinning clowns. The tour
guide will demonstrate instruments
from moving-picture clocks to the
ancestor of the karaoke machine to
enormous traditional Dutch moving
organs, which people would roll
between neighborhoods to start
impromptu block parties. One
instrument even automatically plays
multiple violins. The tickets are on the
pricey side, but it's impossible to have
a bad time at this cheerful museum.
i *Tickets €12, museum and Dom Tower
combination tickets €16; tours every hour
on the half hour; wheelchair accessible*

OUTDOORS

⬛ UTRECHT UNIVERSITY BOTANIC GARDENS

Budapestlaan 17; 3584 HD Utrecht; 302531826; www.uu.nl/botanischetuinen; open daily 10am-4:30pm

Walking through these extensive botanic gardens, you'll find yourself wondering why birds aren't tying bows in your hair and small doe-eyed forest critters aren't singing to you about love. That's because this place is truly magical. It holds a butterfly house, a solitary bee apartment complex, a vegetable garden, massive orchids, and a section of particularly aromatic flowers and herbs. Even a cannabis plant has made its way into the gardens for "research." Visiting the gardens is like strolling through an entire world of vastly different ecosystems: alpine plants, bamboo forests, tropical greenhouses, a rock garden. Plus, €2.50 is a small price to pay to spend hours amongst flowers the size of dinner plates.

i Admission €7.50, students €2.50; wheelchair accessible

FOOD

⬛ VISJES ($)

Twijnstraat 24; 3511 ZL Utrecht; 302333944; www.kokenmetvisjes.nl; open M noon-7pm, Tu-F 10am-7pm, Sa 9am-5pm, Su noon-5pm

Kibbeling is a traditional Dutch snack consisting of battered and fried chunks of fish smothered in a delicious special sauce. And nobody does *kibbeling* better than Visjes; they even won the 2017 Utrecht-area **Kibbeling Cup** (a competitive and prestigious honor). Other Dutch specialties like herring are served alongside seafood paellas, fried mussels, shrimp, and more. You can also purchase raw fish, the fresh goods that the restaurant uses itself. Even though it's such an acclaimed spot, you would have to search hard to find anything on the menu over €5.

i Kibbeling from €2.75, other entrées under €5; wheelchair accessible

'T OUDE POTHUYS ($$$)

Oudegracht 279; 3511 PA Utrecht; 302318970; www.pothuys.nl; open M-Tu 3pm-2am, W-Sa noon-3am, Su noon-midnight

This candlelit, wine-cellar-esque restaurant placed classily along a romantic canal could easily fall under "food" or "nightlife." That's because a late dinner transitions easily into live musical performances, many by students from **Utrecht's Conservatorium.** A small, intimate stage is the focal point of the restaurant, whose walls are decked out with all kinds of instruments. Prices are on the slightly higher end for budget travelers; after all, they include dinner and a show. If you're not up for the full dinner menu, grab some less-expensive snacks or starters at the beginning of the performances.

i Snacks and starters from €3.50, entrées from €14; vegetarian options available; no wheelchair accessibility

NIGHTLIFE

⬛ FEESTCAFÉ DE KNEUS

Nobelstraat 303; 3512 EM Utrecht; 302318799; http://www.feestcafedekneus.nl/; open daily 8pm-5am

Feestcafé de Kneus is where sobriety goes to die. You'll only find Dutch students in this late night "party café," where everyone knows the bartenders, each other, and the mostly Dutch songs (hip hop, electronic, or folk, with the occasional appearance of crowd-pleasers like "Unwritten" or "Breaking Free" from *High School Musical*). It's not a glamorous place—tacky lights and a smoking area make it look like an alley where people leave unwanted furniture, but, boy, does it have character. You won't find any attention-seeking bottle buyers, confused tourists (except for you), or meek and self-conscious dancers here. Here, nobody cares if you're a terrible singer or you keep spilling beer on them. They probably won't remember anyway.

i Beer and shots €2.50; no wheelchair accessibility

BELGIAN BEER CAFÉ OLIVIER

Achter Clarenburg 6a; 3511 JJ Utrecht; 302367876; www.cafe-olivier.be; open M-W 11am-midnight, Th-Sa 10am-2am, Su 11am-midnight

For some, "church" means a place where their mother gets mad at them for texting. For others, it's a place of religious devotion or just another building. At Café Olivier, it's a place to drink beer. Under the high ceilings of this former Catholic Church and the watchful eyes of the statue of Mother Mary, the bartenders proudly serve more than 200 Belgian beers to a predominantly older crowd. At first, you'll keep expecting to hear music from the giant organ and be shushed, but soon you'll get accustomed to the large bar's poppin' atmosphere. All it takes is a Belgian beer and a healthy sense of irony.

i Beers from €3.60; limited wheelchair accessibility

NETHERLANDS ESSENTIALS

MONEY

Tipping: In The Netherlands, a service charge of usually 5% is often included in menu prices, so there is no need to worry about tipping extra. If you received really good service, it might be nice to round up the bill or leave a small tip, but you are not expected to do so even if there isn't a service charge included. A service charge is sometimes included in taxi fares, but drivers will appreciate if you round up the bill as well. Paying the exact amount, however, is never offensive.

Taxes: The marked price of goods in The Netherlands includes a value-added tax (VAT). This tax on goods is generally levied at 21%. Non-EU citizens who are taking these goods home unused may be refunded this tax at the end of their trip. When making purchases, be sure to ask and fill out a VAT form and present it to a Tax-Free Shopping Office, found at most airports, borders, or ferry stations. Refunds must be claimed within six months.

SAFETY AND HEALTH

Drugs and Alcohol: The Dutch are liberal towards alcohol, with the drinking age set at 16 for beer and wine and 18 for hard liquor. Public drunkenness, however, is frowned upon. When it comes to drugs other than alcohol, consumption of marijuana and things like hallucinogenic mushrooms (which fall under "soft drugs") are legal. Consumption isn't limited to coffee shops and smart shops, just purchasing is.

BGLTQ+ Travelers: The Netherlands are accepting of homosexuality and Amsterdam is a center thought of as a haven of homosexual tolerance. It was the first capital city to legalize gay marriage, and there are many parts of the city with BGLTQ+ nightlife establishments.

Minority Travelers: Despite Amsterdam being known for its openness, there's a lot of conversation around ethnic minorities coming into the Netherlands. Immigrants are not always welcomed with open arms. Although foreign tourists might be approached with suspicion, regardless of background, non-white visitors might encounter more hostility.

NORWAY

At first glance, Norway seems like another one of those Scandinavian utopias that always lands near the top of those "World's Happiest Countries" rankings. And it's easy to see why when you look at the country's extensive welfare state, featuring universal healthcare and free public universities—not to mention a ridiculously high standard of living. But things are a bit more complicated than that; society in Norway today is far from harmonious. While it's true that the country makes impressive use of renewable energy, especially of hydroelectric power, Norway also has enormous fossil fuel reserves, which are a considerable source of revenue for the government. Though Norwegians are willing to pay the sizable taxes levied by a bureaucracy often labeled as socialist, they are unwilling to buy into the biggest bureaucracy of all: the European Union. The best way to figure it out the ins and outs of Norway is to pay a visit yourself. Its rich cultural history is inextricably tangled with nature, from the fearsome Vikings who used the sea to discover North America centuries before Columbus to the snow-capped mountains that lead to the country's dominance in winter sports. While its cities can't quite rival the vibrancy of Stockholm or Copenhagen, Norway boasts national treasures you can't afjord to miss. Ditch your movie conceptions of Norway. Contrary to public opinion, there's more to this Nordic paradise than vikings, the laboratories of evil scientists, and friendly talking snowmen. Whether you come here for midsummer parties till dawn or some of Europe's best scenery, it's not a surprise that Norway consistently tops the list of the globe's happiest countries. Oslo is where most begin their adventures. This clean, green, capital city machine is chock full of art. Even if you don't spend Munch time in the city, The Scream is a must-see. But let's be real, you can't afjord to to miss out on the nature. Head north to Bergen, and use the city as a base to explore plentiful options for hiking and swimming (and to give your insta a wanderlust boost). With all Norway has to offer, it won't take listening to Kygo to put you on *Cloud Nine,* Norway is *Here for You.*

BERGEN

Coverage by **Eric Chin**

If you're sick of hordes of tourists mindlessly riding Segways, look no further. Bergen is not your typical Scandinavian city. Sure, it's a popular tourist destination, especially in the summer. But it's the kind of city where the woman behind the counter at the coffee shop will watch you stare vacantly at the Norwegian menu, prompt you a few times in Norwegian, and then ask, feigning surprise, "Oh, you don't speak Norwegian, do you?" It may seem stiff, but it's honestly a refreshingly authentic experience. Since prices in Bergen are somewhat lower than in Oslo, use the extra cash to experience the surprising sights the small city offers. Take to the high seas to see why Bergen is called "The Gateway to the Fjords," or splurge on some of the freshest seafood (a lot) of money can buy at the Fish Market. If hiking is more your thing, The Seven Mountains, within which Bergen rests, offer trails to suit all abilities, and views to impress anyone.

ORIENTATION

Downtown Bergen is situated around the main square, **Torgallmenningen,** where you'll find expensive stores and chain restaurants. Just north is Bergen Harbor, where the **Fish Market** and **Tourist Information Center** sit on the east end of the harbor. North of the harbor is the historic **Bryggen district** and **Bergenhus Fortress,** which is the sight of **Rosenkrantz Tower** and **Haakon's Hall.** Just east of Torgallmenningen is **Byparken,** a large green with walking trails around a lake. The **KODE art museums** can be found along one side of the park. And to the south is the **University of Bergen.** The area between the square and the university is a hotspot for student nightlife.

ESSENTIALS

GETTING THERE

Bergen Lufthavn, Flesland (BGO) is Bergen's international airport, which receives regular flights from many European cities. From the airport, the easiest way to get to the city center is the Flybussen (www.flybussen.no, NOK 100, students NOK 80) to Bergen bus station (20min.). The train between Oslo and Bergen, a journey of almost 7hr, is famously one of the most scenic rides in Europe (NOK 950, students NOK 713). Trains arrive at Bergen Station.

GETTING AROUND

Bergen is an easily walkable and compact city. Most hostels and guesthouses are also centrally located, so public transportation is often unnecessary. Skyss is Bergen's public transportation system, consisting of buses and light rail. Single tickets can be bought in advance (NOK 37), on board (NOK 60), or for periods of 24hr (NOK 95), 7 days (NOK 245), or longer. Tickets can be bought at transportation stops. Bergen Taxi (07000, bergentaxi.no) is the largest taxi company in the city. Rates vary wildly, depending on the day of the week and the time of day.

PRACTICAL INFORMATION

Tourist Offices: Bergen Tourist Information Center (Strandkaien 3;55 55 20 00; open daily June-Aug 8:30am-10pm, May and Sept 9am-8pm, Oct-Apr M-Sa 9am-4pm)

Banks/ATMs/Currency Exchange: You can use a credit or debit card almost everywhere in Bergen, but if you need cash, ATMs, known as Minibanks, can be found on the street and in stores like 7-Eleven in the Fish Market area.

Currency Exchange: It's often best to withdraw cash directly from an ATM, but you can change currency at the Bergen Tourist Information Center.

Post Offices: Bergen Sentrum Postkontor (Småstrandgaten 3; 91 23 35 11; open M-F 9am-8pm, Sa 9am-6pm)

Internet: Free Wi-Fi is widely available around Bergen at cafés, bars, and the Tourist Information Center. Internet is also available at the Bergen Public Library (Strømgaten 6; 55 56 85 00; open M-Th 10am-6pm, F 10am-4pm, Sa 10am-3pm).

BGLTQ+ Resources: Bergen Pride (Strandgaten 6; 40 45 65 00; open M-F 9am-3pm www.bergenpride.no)

EMERGENCY INFORMATION

Emergency Number: 112

Police: Bergen Sentrum Politistasjon (Allehelgens gate 6; for emergencies call 112, for non-emergencies call 02800)

US Embassy: The nearest US Embassy is in Oslo (Morgedalsvegen 36, 0378; 21 30 85 40).

Hospitals: Haukeland University Hospital (Haukelandsveien 22; for emergencies call 113, for non-emergencies call 05300; open daily 24hr)

Pharmacies: Apoteket Nordstjernen (55 21 83 84; open M-Sa 8am-11pm, Su 1pm-11pm)

ACCOMMODATIONS

BERGEN YMCA HOSTEL ($)

Nedre Korskirkeallmenning 4; 556 06 055; www.bergenhostel.com/en; reception open 7am-midnight

If this was an episode of *House Hunters,* Bergen YMCA's selling point would be "Location, location, location!" It's a two-minute walk to the **Fish Market,** five minutes from **Bryggen,** and less than 10 minutes from some of Bergen's best nightlife, all at a price that's hard to beat. Oh yeah, about the price. How is it so low? Well, what Bergen YMCA has in location, it lacks somewhat in amenities. The comfortable rooms, are small, so don't expect a hot tub or anything crazy. Overall though, it is indeed fun to stay at the YMCA.

i Dorms from NOK 215, singles 600 NOK; reservation recommended; BGLTQ+ friendly; wheelchair accessible; Wi-Fi; linens included; lockers available

MARKEN GJESTEHUS ($)

Kong Oscars gate 45; 553 14 404; www.marken-gjestehus.com/home; reception open daily May-Sept 9:30am-11pm, Oct-Apr 9:30am-4:30pm

Marken is located a bit farther from the city center, just distant enough to be in a quiet area while still feeling very much downtown. The building itself shows signs of age (the elevator has an upholstered bench, what?), but the rooms and common spaces are very clean and well-kept. Dorms include storage lockers

big enough to hide a body, but outlets are somewhat scarce. If you're arriving late at night after reception is closed, reach out about late check-in before your arrival; your credit or debit card will then work seamlessly as a key card, so you can pass out on freshly-starched sheets. Goodness, what will they think of next?

i Dorms from NOK 250, singles NOK 575; reservation recommended; Wi-Fi; linens included; towel rental NOK 20; lockers provided; kitchen

SIGHTS
CULTURE

🐟 FISH MARKET

Bergen Harbor; hours vary

Never been to an open-air market before? Head over to Bergen's famous Fish Market for a welcoming, if somewhat tame, experience. The atmosphere is busy but relaxed, vendors aren't too pushy, and samples of caviar, reindeer sausage, and a mysterious jam made from cloudberries are plentiful. If you've been saving room in your stomach for some of Norway's best fresh fish, you won't be disappointed. Take your pick of salmon, shellfish, and live king crab or lobster, and the vendors will cook it and serve you at a table overlooking the harbor. How's that for farm (er, sea?) to table?

i Stand prices vary; wheelchair accessible

BRYGGEN

Bergen Harbor

Want to feel cultured without having to set foot in a museum? A walk through Bryggen is your best bet. This historic district on the north side of the harbor is immediately recognizable by its traditional red and yellow wooden buildings. The buildings were originally used by traders of the **Hanseatic League** as storehouses. Today, they're mostly shops, where modern merchants loosely adhere to the Hanseatic tradition, peddling not stockfish and cereals, but Norwegian flags and Christmas sweaters. You can walk through the front row of buildings and into the alleyways of Bryggen for more interesting and authentic options, like a moose leather shop.

i Shop prices vary; wheelchair accessible

LANDMARKS

HÅKONSHALLEN (HAAKON'S HALL)

Bergenhus; 479 79 577; www.bymuseet.no/
en; open daily summer 10am-4pm, winter
noon-3pm

Haakon's Hall is the other major
building in the **Bergenhus Fortress**
complex, and it's perfect if you're tired
of poking around the dingy, cobweb-
filled rooms of **Rosenkrantz Tower.**
Originally a banquet hall constructed
in the thirteenth century, the building
suffered damage from several major
fires (seems to be a recurring theme in
Bergen), and has been restored more
than once. The dimly-lit rooms are
decorated with colorful tapestries, and
the cavernous great hall is set with a
high table. Today, Haakon's Hall still
hosts official dinners and events, for
which the dress code includes battle axes
and horned helmets (we think).
*i Admission NOK 80, students NOK 40;
guided tours NOK 20; tours at 10am and
2pm June 24-Aug 15*

ROSENKRANTZ TOWER

Bergenhus; 479 79 578; www.bymuseet.
no/en; open daily summer 9am-4pm, winter
noon-3pm

Rosenkrantz Tower is the most visible
piece of **Bergenhus Fortress,** sitting
proudly at the entrance to **Bergen
Harbor** like a shorter, slightly stubbier,
less humanoid Statue of Liberty. The
tower was originally a thirteenth-
century keep, but has expanded since
into its present form. Inside, you can
tour the whole building starting with
the basement, where the dungeon
sits empty, except for an original,
thirteenth-century electric dehumidifier.
From there, climb through the tower's
many rooms: guard rooms, bedrooms,
chapel rooms, rooms with cannons, you
get the point. Learn about the single
battle in which Bergenhus Fortress was
involved before stepping out onto the
roof and taking in views of Bergen and
the harbor.
*i Admission NOK 80, students NOK 40,
guided tours NOK 20; tours at 10am
and 2pm June 24-Aug 15; no wheelchair
accessibility*

MUSEUMS

KODE 4

Rasmus Meyers allé; 530 09 704; www.
kodebergen.no/en; open daily 11am-5pm

Art museums are confusing; they're
huge, overwhelming, and it's impossible
to see everything. Bergen's art museum,
KODE, is different. It's composed of
four smaller buildings, KODEs 1, 2,
3, and 4 (not a very creative naming
scheme for a bunch of art people), each
with different galleries and exhibitions,
so check the website to pick the best
one for you. Each bite-sized museum
is easy to walk through in an hour or
two. KODE 4 starts off in classic form:
lots of oil paintings of landscapes and
church figures. But don't worry, the
top floor is devoted to contemporary
"art" like a box lined with seal teeth
and a giant, plush model of the female
reproductive system suspended from the
ceiling. Avant-garde?
*i Admission NOK 100, students NOK 50;
tour times vary, check website for details.;
wheelchair accessible*

OUTDOORS

◩ MOUNT ULRIKEN

Open daily 24hr

What's that? Oh, you really like hiking,
but you're allergic to cable cars? Good
news! For true outdoorsy types, it's
possible to walk to the base of Mount
Ulriken, though it may take over 45
minutes. There are multiple routes to
the top of varying difficulty, and, on
clear days, the trails will be packed with
active types of all sorts. Once you reach
the peak, enjoy panoramic views of
Bergen or grab a snack at the summit
restaurant. If you still haven't broken
a sweat, there are more trails from the
cable car station, the king of which is
a 13-km haul over to the summit of
Mount Fløyen. This is a challenging
hike, so if you want to attempt it,
consider using the cable car after all.
You deserve it.
i No wheelchair accessibility

NORWAY BERGEN

FOOD

⬛ HORN OF AFRICA ($$)

Strandgaten 212; 954 25 250; www.hornofafrica.no

For almost all of human history, we have eaten with our hands. Why this sudden fascination with utensils? It's probably just a phase. Stay ahead of the curve at Horn of Africa, an Ethiopian/Eritrean restaurant that eschews fork and knife in favor of nature's own finely-crafted utensil: your ten fingers. Choose from a selection including sinus-tingling beef tips and buttery chicken wet, and get ready to get down and dirty. The concept of eating with your hands seems pretty self-explanatory, but, just to be sure, the host will demonstrate the nuances of scooping up the spiced meat stews and vegetables with *injure,* a spongy and slightly sour bread that accompanies all entrées.

i Entrées from NOK 150, combo platters from NOK 215, beer from NOK 60; vegetarian options available; wheelchair accessible

⬛ PINGVINEN ($$)

Vaskerelven 14; 556 04 646; www.pingvinen.no

Pingvinen means "penguin" in Norwegian, and that's just about the only animal you won't find on the menu. This gastropub feels like a low-key bar, with ugly wallpaper on one wall and exposed brick on another, but you won't find nachos and wings here. If you can grab a table, ask for an English menu and choose from potato dumplings with mashed *swede* (a root vegetable, not a jab at Norway's neighbor to the east), wild boar, and even reindeer neck, all prepared to perfection. If you have a bit of extra cash to spend (in the name of cultural immersion, of course), go full-on Norse with a beer from Pingvinen's impressive spread of local brews.

i Entrées from NOK 169, beer from NOK 80; wheelchair accessible

TREKRONEREN ($)

Kong Oscars gate 1; hours vary

Bergen doesn't have much of a street food scene, especially outside the Fish Market. Trekroneren is the one, juicy exception. It's a counter-service sausage stand in the heart of downtown, and an establishment in its own right. Select from over ten varieties, from the familiar *bratwurst,* to the slightly enigmatic "wild game" sausage. But nothing can top the **reindeer sausage,** topped with mustard, crispy onions, and lingonberry jam. Somehow it works, okay? Just stay away from Rudolph at the Christmas store for a while. It's still a bit of a sore subject for him.

i 150g sausage NOK 60, 250g sausage NOK 90; wheelchair accessible

NIGHTLIFE

🏴 GARAGE

Christies gate 14; 553 21 980; www.garage.no; open M-F 3pm-3am, Sa 1pm-3am, Su 5pm-1am

Some of Norway's most famous musical exports are in the rock and metal genres, and Garage is the place to tap into that scene. It feels like one of the first venues you perform at in *Guitar Hero*—dim lighting, album covers and old setlists plastered on the walls, and an eclectic crowd composed of middle-aged men trying to relive the glory days and college kids hopelessly lost in the wrong decade. Look out for live shows on the weekends, but, even if there's nothing happening on stage, the bar has a great spread.

i No cover, beer and shots from NOK 70; BGLTQ+ friendly; wheelchair accessible

🏴 KVARTERET

Olav Kyrres gate 49; 555 89 910; www.kvarteret.no; open M-W 11:30am-10pm, Th-F 11:30am-3:30am, Sa 2pm-3:30am

If you want to find the best local spots and cheapest drinks in any city, it's never a bad idea to follow the local students. In Bergen, they all head to Kvarteret, the city's student culture house. It's run by student volunteers and attracts young people from both near and far. Drinks are reasonably priced in the warehouse-style bar where you'll probably walk into special events like quiz nights, concerts, wine and cheese shindigs, or poetry readings. If you're bold (or bored) enough to go out on a Monday night, swing by Kvarteret's Mikromandag (Micro-Monday) to try local Norwegian microbrews at reduced prices.

i No cover except for special events, drinks from NOK 50; BGLTQ+ friendly

OSLO

Coverage by **Eric Chin**

Of the three Scandinavian capitals, Oslo is definitely the youngest child. While Stockholm and Copenhagen were busy inventing dynamite and opening the world's best restaurant, Oslo was crashing and burning (literally) with a fair amount of sailing and hiking thrown in the mix. The result is a cultural diversity all its own. Oslo's museums are interesting, but not pretentious; its landmarks are grounded, not extravagant. The river running through the middle of the city separates wealthy, established houses and cultural landmarks from the young, international neighborhoods to the east. And within just a few kilometers of it all are mountains for skiing, *fjords* for sailing, and islands for exploring. All this variety doesn't come cheap, though. Since Oslo isn't Scandinavia's go-to destination for young travelers and backpackers, the hostel scene is sparse and high prices can make it difficult to experience all there is to offer. At the same time, crowds are smaller overall, making it easy to make the most of every museum, sculpture, and restaurant.

ORIENTATION

Oslo's city center sits right on the **Oslofjord,** into which jut the piers in front of City Hall. Just to the east is the **Opera House,** which is easily the most recognizable building in the city. The main street, **Karl Johans gate,** runs straight through the middle of downtown, from the **Royal Palace** on its eastern end to **Oslo S** and the **Tiger statue** to the west. Along **Karl Johans gate** are landmarks like the National Theater, and the seat of Norway's Parliament. A short bus ride to the west brings you to **Bygdøy,** a large peninsula with beaches, walking and biking trails, and several of Oslo's most famous museums. The **Akerselva River** runs north from the city center, effectively dividing the rest of Oslo in two. To the west are parks and wealthier residential neighborhoods. To the east are younger, more diverse areas that house most of Oslo's nightlife, including **Grønland,** and a little farther north **Grünerløkka,** a veritable hipster's paradise. Far to the northwest is **Holmenkollen,** home to the only steel ski jump in the world.

ESSENTIALS

GETTING THERE

Oslo Airport, Gardermoen (Oslo Lufthaven) is Norway's main international airport. The airport is about 50km north of the city itself, and the easiest way get to the city center is the Flytoget Airport Express (20min. to and from Oslo S), which leaves from Oslo Sentralstasjon, better known as Oslo S, the main train station, every 10-20min. (NOK 180, students NOK 90). Tickets kiosks are located at the airport and Oslo S. The Flybussen also travels between downtown Oslo and Oslo Lufthaven, but the journey is closer to 40min. from Oslo Bus Terminal, which is behind Oslo S (adults NOK 160, students NOK 90). Trains to other Norwegian cities from Oslo S are operated by NSB (www.nsb.no). SJ also operates express trains between Oslo and Stockholm. The station is open daily 3:45am-1:30am.

GETTING AROUND

Public transportation in Oslo is operated by Ruter, consisting of buses, trains, ferries, and the metro. The system is divided into zones, but you should be set with Zone 1, as it covers the city center as well as the whole metro service. Tickets can be purchased at stores including Narvesen, 7-Eleven, and at kiosks at some stations (single ticket NOK 33 in advance, onboard NOK 55). If you plan on using public transportation frequently, consider a 24hr pass (NOK 90) or a 7-day pass (NOK 240). Your ticket is not active until you validate it. When you buy a new ticket, make sure you scan it the first time you use it or it doesn't count. Ticket officials will board random trains or buses and check tickets. The fine for being caught without a valid ticket is NOK 1150 (NOK 950 if paid on the spot).

PRACTICAL INFORMATION

Tourist Offices: The Oslo Visitor Center is located in Østbanehallen, next to Oslo S (81 53 05 55; open daily May-June 9am-6pm, July-Aug M-Sa 8am-7pm, Su 9am-6pm, daily Sept 9am-6pm, Oct-Dec M-Sa 9am-6pm, Su 10am-4pm)
Banks/ATMs/Currency Exchange: Credit and debit cards can be used almost everywhere in Oslo, but, if you need cash, currency exchange and ATMs (called "Minibanks") can be found in Oslo S and on Karl Johans gate (Forex Bank: Oslo S; 22 17 22 65; open M-F 7am-9pm, Sa 9am-6pm, Su 10am-5pm).
Post Offices: Tollbugata 17; open M-F 7am-5pm
Internet: Wi-Fi is widely available in Oslo, both in cafés and restaurants, and in public settings like the Opera House and museums. Some networks may require a code sent via SMS.
BGLTQ+ Resources: FRI is the national BGLTQ+ organization in Norway (Tollbugata 24; 23 10 39 39; open M-F 10am-3pm).

EMERGENCY INFORMATION

Emergency Number: 112
Police: Grønlandsleiret 44, 0190; 22 66 90 50
US Embassy: Morgedalsvegen 36; 21 30 85 40; check no.usembassy.gov for details
Rape Crisis Center: DIXI is a free and confidential resource for victims of sexual assault (Arbins gate 1; 22 44 40 50; Weekdays 9am-3pm).
Hospitals: Oslo Emergency Ward is open daily 24hr (Storgata 40; 113 (emergencies only), 116117 (non-emergencies)).
Pharmacies: There are pharmacies all over the city center. Pharmacies are called apotek in Norway.
- Jernbanetorvets Apotek (Jernbanetor-get 4B; 23 35 81 00; open daily 24hr)
- Apotek 1 (Storgata 40, 22 98 87 20; open daily 24hr)

ACCOMMODATIONS

SAGA POSHTEL OSLO ($$)

Kongens gate 7; 231 00 800; www.saga-hoteloslocentral.no; reception open 24hr

One of Saga Poshtel Oslo's claims to fame is that it's the first hostel in Oslo to call itself a "poshtel," and it's easy to see why. If you can get past the ridiculous name and the somewhat-higher prices, you'll find that the poshtel is one of the best accommodations in Oslo. Included are linens, towels, and a breakfast buffet; you'd have to take out a second mortgage to afford an all-you-can-eat, hot breakfast elsewhere in Oslo. The brand new building also has a great location downtown, just a few minutes from the **Opera House, Karl Johans gate,** and **Oslo S.**

i Dorms from NOK 395; reservation recommended; BGLTQ+ friendly; wheelchair accessible; Wi-Fi; linens, towels included; laundry facilities NOK 30; free breakfast

EKEBERG CAMPING ($$)

Ekebergveien 65; 221 98 568; www.eke-bergcamping.no/en; open June-Aug

If you have your heart set on camping but turn up your nose at the anarchy of **Langøyene,** Ekeberg Camping offers a professional, structured option. The campsite has about 600 sites, so you shouldn't have a problem finding a place, even though reservations aren't allowed. Facilities include drinking water, restrooms, and paid showers, but they don't come cheap. By the time you pay for a tent site, snacks, and a shower, you're looking at the price of a hostel.

i 2-person tent NOK 200, shower (6min.) NOK 15; reservation recommended; BGLTQ+ friendly; wheelchair accessible

LANGØYENE CAMPING ($)

Langøyene Island

Camping on Langøyene Island is free. That's right, free! But as they say, you get what you pay for. There's no source of clean drinking water on the island and compost-style outhouses may not be your preferred option for restrooms. (Nor is there Wi-Fi.) The house rules are simple enough (yes there are rules; what do you think this is, *Lord of the Flies?*): clean up after yourself, don't light fires (that hasn't worked out well for Oslo in the past), and don't be an asshole to your fellow campers (paraphrasing, of course). Easy, and as long as you don't mind roughing it a bit, Langøyene has lots to offer, including a nude beach, hiking trails, and easy ferry access to the mainland.

i Free; reservation recommended; BGLTQ+ friendly; wheelchair accessible; bring your own tent, food, and drinking water; accessible via the B4 Ferry, which leaves from City Hall Pier 4

SIGHTS
CULTURE

NOBEL PEACE CENTER

Brynjulf Bulls Plass 1; 483 01 000; www.nobelpeacecenter.org/en; open daily May-Aug 10am-6pm, Sept-Apr Tu-Su 10am-6pm

Two interesting facts about the Nobel Peace Prize: it's the only one of the five annual prizes not presented in Sweden and it was established by funds from the invention of arguably unpeaceful dynamite. The **Peace Prize** is awarded each year in Oslo's **City Hall,** just across the street from the Nobel Peace Center. This museum features exhibitions about the most recent laureate as well as about worldwide current events. The heart of the museum is The Nobel Field, an exhibit dedicated to all past laureates. A sea of waist-high lights interspersed with tablets are dedicated to every winner of the Nobel Peace Prize. Occasionally, the ethereal music pauses as an excerpt plays from a **Nobel Lecture.**

i Admission NOK 100, students NOK 65; tours daily 2pm, 3pm; wheelchair accessible

OSLO FREE TOUR

The Tiger, Jernbanetorget; www.freetouroslo.com

Yeah you perked right up when you saw the word "free," right? It's an uncommon term in Scandinavia, but this tour is a gem. The meeting point is the **Tiger statue** next to the Ferris wheel in front of **Oslo S.** From there, your guide will lead you around to all the major landmarks and historical sites in downtown Oslo, including the **Opera House, Akershus Festning,** and **City Hall.** Along the way, you'll hear stories of the devastating fires that forever robbed Oslo of wooden buildings and how a ridiculous royal moved the city center on a whim. Though the whole thing is technically free, you'd have to be stingier than Scrooge not to tip after this two-hour tour.

i Free, though tipping expected; tours M, Th-Su 10am and 4pm; wheelchair accessible

ROYAL PALACE

Slottsplassen 1; www.royalcourt.no; changing of the guard daily at 1:30pm

Among the great palaces of Europe, Oslo's Royal Palace is something of an imposter. Sure there's a resemblance to Versailles and Buckingham Palace—it stares imposingly down a long gravel drive, has a big statue of a guy on a horse, and is surrounded by guards in funny costumes—but it doesn't take itself too seriously. The gardens are open for sunbathing (though it is allegedly the only park where you can't do so topless), and you barely have to try to get the guards to move. Slottsparken, the large park surrounding the palace, is free, but if you want to see inside, you'll have to pay for a guided tour.

i Park admission free; guided tours NOK 135, students NOK 105; tours daily at noon, 2pm, 2:20pm, 4pm June 24-Aug 17; wheelchair accessible

LANDMARKS

🔖 HOLMENKOLLEN

Kongeveien 5; 229 23 200; www.skiforeningen.no/en/holmenkollen; open Jan-Apr 10am-5pm, May 10am-5pm, June-Aug 9am-8pm, Sept 10am-5pm, Oct-Apr 10am-5pm

Norway has many proud traditions that have stretched back centuries: seafaring, not joining the European Union, and skiing. If you've ever watched the Winter Olympics, you're likely familiar with Norway's dominance on snow, and Holmenkollen, Oslo's ski jump, is where the magic happens. Situated on a high hill, the jump serves as a training ground during the winter and a tourist attraction in the summer, where visitors flock to jump. At the ski museum, learn about the history of skiing. An elevator goes to the top of the jump tower, where you'll find a zip line (expensive) and a viewing platform that looks out over Oslo and the fjord beyond (priceless).

i Ski Museum/jump tower admission NOK 130, students NOK 110, zip line NOK 600; wheelchair accessible

OPERA HOUSE

Kirsten Flagstads plass 1; 214 22 121; www.operaen.no/en

In a city that was once built mostly of brick in fear of fire, Oslo's Opera House sticks out. Designed to resemble a glacier, the angled marble structure seems to rise right out of the fjord like the real glaciers did millennia ago. But, like the rest of Oslo, it's not too uptight; you can literally walk all over it. The roof is open for visitors, and serves as the perfect place for views of the Oslofjord and the many tourists who continuously get in your pictures.

i Free admission; tours NOK 100, students NOK 60; M-F, Su 1pm, Sa noon; wheelchair accessible

MUSEUMS

🖼 KON-TIKI MUSEUM

Bygdøynesveien 36, Bygdøy; 230 86 767; www.kon-tiki.no; open daily Jan-Feb 10am-5pm, Mar-May 10am-5pm, June-Aug 9:30am-6pm, Sept-Oct 10am-5pm, Nov-Dec 10am-4pm

The Kon-Tiki Museum follows the journey of Thor Heyerdahl, who sailed ("floated" is more accurate) from Peru to Polynesia in 1947 on a balsa raft. It's a lot like *Moana,* but instead of an intrepid Polynesian girl setting off to fight the evils of the world, the protagonists of Kon-Tiki were six white guys and a parrot who wanted to spite a bunch of ivory-tower academics. The main hall features the original Kon-Tiki raft, along with panels about the expedition itself, from how the food was stored to Thor's fear of water and surprising lack of swimming skills. Downstairs, check out *Ra II,* a boat made of Papyrus reeds that Thor captained across the Atlantic, because, you know, the Pacific was just too easy.

i Admission NOK 100, students NOK 60, joint ticket for Kon-Tiki, Fram, and Norwegian Maritime museums NOK 270, students NOK 100; wheelchair accessible

🖼 NATIONAL GALLERY

Universitetsgata 13; 219 82 000; www.nasjonalmuseet.no/en; open Tu-W 10am-6pm, Th 10am-7pm, Sa-Su 11am-5pm

It certainly isn't the prettiest building on the outside (no glass pyramid or marble columns like you'll find at the Louvre or the British Museum), but inside, the National Gallery is a manageable museum with works you'll recognize even if you don't own a beret. Does *The Scream* ring a bell? There's even a bench in front of a cast of *The Thinker,* where you can sit and, well, think. But where the National Gallery really shines is in its organization. It's not a labyrinth of hallways that split in two or lead to dead ends; the rooms are arranged chronologically (and numbered) to show you art from the earliest Greek and Roman sculptures to the movements of Romanticism and Realism, and everything in between.

i Admission NOK 100, students NOK 50, free under 19 and every Th; audioguide NOK 50; wheelchair accessible

NORWAY'S RESISTANCE MUSEUM

Akershus Festning; 230 93 138; www.forsvaretsmuseer.no/hjemmefrontmuseet; open June-Aug M-Sa 10am-5pm, Su 11am-5pm; Sept-May M-F 10am-4pm, Sa-Su 11am-4pm

Germany had a habit of invading neutral countries during World War II, and Norway was no exception. The Nazis came knocking in 1940 and, probably enamored with the high standard of living, decided to stay for awhile. As Norway's Resistance Museum shows, though, their occupation was anything but easy. The museum details every bit of Norway's involvement in the war, from life during the five-year German occupation, to the inner workings of the Norwegian resistance movement. Check out the huge collection of news clippings, artifacts (including the remains of an actual Tallboy dropped by the Allies), and painstakingly constructed dioramas of specific battles. The exhibit is fairly short, but packed with information on every facet of the war.

i Admission NOK 60, students NOK 30; wheelchair accessible

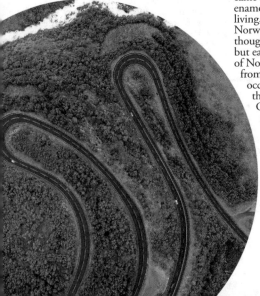

OUTDOORS

OSLO SOMMERPARK

Tryvannsveien 64; 221 43 610; www.
oslosommerpark.no; hours change over the
course of the summer; be sure to check the
website

Not content to sit at the top of
Holmenkollen and just look at the view,
but too cheap to crack open the piggy
bank for the zip line? Head north on the
1 train to Oslo Sommerpark instead. It's
a huge aerial ropes course with enough
elements and routes to make Tarzan
jealous. Climb as high as 20 meters
into the treetops on a combination of
bridges, ladders, and steel cables before
swinging from one tree to the next on a
network of zip lines. This is a must for
any adventure-seeker looking to ditch the
city and remember what those opposable
thumbs were for in the first place.
*i Admission NOK 375; last entry 2hr before
closing; wheelchair accessible*

VIKING BIKING

Nedre Slottsgate 4; 412 66 496; www.viking-
bikingoslo.com; open daily 9:30am-6pm

Biking is always an excellent option for
seeing a lot of city in minimal time,
but honestly, city bikes are the worst!
Fortunately, the aptly/unfortunately
named Viking Biking has you covered.
Full-day rentals for students start at just
NOK 140 (NOK 160 for adults) for
a real bike (with gears!), and a horned
helmet. Not kidding. Wander the city
and the surrounding area on your own,
or, if you need a little more structure in
your life, consider joining one of Viking
Biking's guided bike tours, which include
a variety of routes.
*i Guided tours from NOK 350, students NOK
280; limited wheelchair accessibility*

FOOD

🍽 MATHALLEN ($)

Vulkan 5; 400 01 209; www.mathallenoslo.
no/en; open Tu-W 10am-7pm, Th-F 10am-
8pm, Sa 10am-7pm, Su 11am-6pm

"Mathallen" translates to "food hall," and
that could not be more accurate. The
real treat is inside Mathallen; restaurants
run the gamut from sushi stands to
microbreweries, and market stalls sell
fresh fish and Scandinavian sausages and
jams (look out for free samples). Sitting
down for a full meal can get pricey
(surprise!), but there are plenty of great
options for under NOK 100, like Ma
Poule's duck confit sandwich (NOK 89),
or the pulled chicken from Strangeriet
(NOK 85).
*i Prices vary, sit-down meal from NOK 100;
gluten-free, vegan, and vegetarian options
available; wheelchair accessible*

🍽 TUNCO ($$)

Bjerregaards gate 2a; 400 98 690; www.
tunco.no; open M-F 11:30am-10pm, Sa-Su
1pm-10pm

It's always tough to find a restaurant
with quality food and a great atmosphere
at a reasonable price, but TUNCO
does it all and adds a global awareness
that most restaurants don't. This new
concept restaurant serves up delicious
woks, with a selection of proteins and
noodles large enough to satisfy even the
pickiest eater. Pick a sauce to match your
spice tolerance, but what will really give
you the warm and fuzzies is TUNCO's
"Meal for Meal" program. For every meal
purchased, TUNCO donates money to
charity to give a meal to a child in need.
It's like the TOMS of the Oslo food
scene, and it's sure to become just as
popular.
*i Entrées from NOK 150, beer from NOK 79;
gluten-free, vegan, and vegetarian options
available; wheelchair accessible; card only*

ILLEGAL BURGER ($$)

Møllergata 23; 222 03 302; open M-Th 2pm-11pm, F-Sa 2pm-1am, Su 2pm-10pm

Illegal Burger is exactly the kind of place you want to go when you just can't take another day of the Scandinavia traveler's diet of herring, grocery store sushi, and regret. The burgers are juicy and generously portioned, the prices reasonable (or at least competitive), and the menu full of teenage angst (featuring a tomato wearing a bandit mask). Keep it simple with the Cheese Royale, or branch out with the Hot Mama (barbecue sauce and jalapeños) or the Illegal Spessial (chorizo and guacamole). Seating is limited, but you can sit under the watchful gaze of a David Bowie poster while you wait for takeaway.

i Single burgers NOK 100, double burgers NOK 140, potatoes NOK 42; gluten-free, vegan, and vegetarian options available; no wheelchair accessibility

PASTEL DE NATA ($)

Kongens gate 10; www.pasteldenata.no; open M-F 11am-6:30pm, Sa-Su 11am-4:30pm

Your first instinct when you see the price for individual pastries at Pastel de Nata (NOK 35) will be to run as fast as you can, but don't be so hasty. The coffee prices are some of the best around, and for a reasonable NOK 55, you can get a coffee and pastry of your choice. That, and you get to hang out in the airy café for a while. The pastries are also top-notch, especially their namesake *pastel de nata,* a traditional Portuguese egg tart.

i Pastries from NOK 35, coffee/espresso drinks from NOK 20; wheelchair accessible

NIGHTLIFE

CROWBAR AND BRYGGERI

Torggata 32; 213 86 757; www.crowbryggeri.com; open M-F 3pm-3am, Sa 1pm-3am

No need to lock up your valuables; Crowbar has nothing to do with armed robbery. It's a bar and microbrewery in Grünerløkka with a slightly wacky theme: crows. The beer is excellent in terms of taste, variety, and naming (try the 3.7% ABV "Featherweight"), but Crowbar isn't just for middle-aged guys with a knack for misusing the word

"hoppy." It's the kind of place where the bartender drinks kombucha, and it attracts a young crowd to match. The multi-floor venue is packed on the weekends, both downstairs at the bar and upstairs where the kitchen serves all your drunk favorites like kebab wraps, quesadillas, and pork cracklings.

i Beer from NOK 80; BGLTQ+ friendly; wheelchair accessible; age limit 23 F-Sa

SCHOUSKJELLEREN MIKROBRYGGERI

Trondheimsveien 2; 213 83 930; www.schouskjelleren.no; open M-Tu 4pm-1am, W-Th 4pm-2am, F 3pm-3:30am, Sa 4pm-midnight

Sure, PBR must have won that blue ribbon for something, but haven't you ever wondered what it's like to try beer that you can't buy in a 30-pack? Schouskjelleren, one of Oslo's best microbreweries, is your place. The bartenders know every hop and spice that goes into the selection of brews on tap. To top it all off, the bar is in a vaulted brick cellar that feels like a Viking banquet hall, complete with stained glass windows. There really is something for everyone here, from IPAs like "No Means No," to stouts so rich they taste like chocolate syrup.

i Draft beers from NOK 80; BGLTQ+ friendly; no wheelchair accessibility

DATTERA TIL HAGEN

Grønland 10; 221 71 861; www.dattera.no; open M 11am-midnight, Tu-W 11am-1am, Th 11am-2am, F-Sa 11am-3am, Su noon-midnight

Club going up on a Tuesday? Probably not in Oslo, but, if it were, it would definitely be this one. Located in the young, diverse Grønland neighborhood, Dattera is a favorite among locals and tourists alike. The two floors and courtyard provide something for everyone, regardless of whether you'd prefer to get (maybe a bit too) cozy on the upstairs dance floor in front of a live DJ or sit in the courtyard to marvel at the sea of Norwegian man buns.

i Cover NOK 10, drinks from NOK 80; BGLTQ+ friendly; wheelchair accessible

NORWAY ESSENTIALS

VISAS

Norway is not part of the European Union, but it is part of the Schengen Area, so US citizens can stay in Norway for up to 90 days without a visa.

MONEY

Tipping: Norway's currency is the Norwegian krona, officially abbreviated NOK or kr. Tipping in Norway is not usually expected or required, though if you have received excellent service in a restaurant, it is not uncommon to round the bill to the nearest NOK 10, or leave a tip of 6-10%.

Taxes: Norway's standard VAT rate is an eye-popping 25%, with a few patently Norwegian exceptions like raw fish, which is taxed at only 11.11%. However, tax is included in all advertised prices. Pro-tip: Some souvenir shops in Norway, specifically those with Global Blue or Tax Free Worldwide stickers, will refund the VAT for goods leaving the country with you. The protocol can vary, so ask at the store for instructions to claim your refund.

SAFETY AND HEALTH

BGLTQ+ Travel: Like most of Scandinavia, Norway is very liberal in regard to BGLTQ+ rights. In 1981, Norway became the first country in the world to explicitly ban discrimination in places of employment based on sexual orientation, and that momentum can still be felt today.

Drugs and Alcohol: The legal drinking age is 18 for beverages below 22% ABV and 20 for anything higher. Drinking in public is technically illegal, but it's not uncommon to see beer and wine outside, especially in parks. Grocery stores only sell alcoholic beverages below 4.75% ABV; everything else must be bought from government-owned liquor stores called *Vinmonopolet*. Norway's taxes on alcohol are extremely high.

WEATHER/CLIMATE

As you may have noticed, Norway is pretty far north. Much of the northern region lies within the Arctic Circle, leading to long hours of daylight during the summer and seemingly endless night during the winter, even in southern cities like Bergen and Oslo.

POLAND

When it comes to being occupied or destroyed by other countries, Poland's had a pretty rough time. Only receiving full independence following World War I, Poland enjoyed a couple of decades of sovereignty before the World War II, during which it was invaded by Germany. They carved it up and split it with the USSR, which was soon forced out by the Germans, who then unleashed carnage on a scale unlike anything seen elsewhere. After Germany declared defeat in 1945, Poland was finally able to savor the sweet taste of freedom for a year or two before the USSR barged in and set up a puppet government (nowhere near as cute or endearing as it sounds), which lasted for over 30 years until a radical MTV ad campaign convinced the world that communism wasn't cool anymore. Given its tumultuous past, today's Poland isn't doing too badly at all. The once-ravaged country is now a vibrant cultural center. Kraków, medieval yet young-at-heart, is quickly becoming an essential destination for history buffs and partiers alike. Idyllic mountain and seaside towns are popping up faster than you can say "Gdańsk." Boasting the dangerous combination of extreme affordability and a national cuisine that emphasizes dumplings and pancakes, what once was modeled as a socialist paradise is now a backpacker's dream. You'll get by with English in any tourist-friendly establishment, but as soon as you start heading into the more local areas, you'll have to rely on sign language, assuming you don't have a Rosetta Stone to decipher the phonetics of your "Useful Polish Phrases" book. Polish people are generally helpful and approachable, but don't expect them to invite you to their birthday party after they've told you what you need to know.

GDAŃSK

Coverage by **Nicholas Grundlingh**

When naming this town, did the King of Poland accidentally add a "g" at the start and an "s" near the end? Probably not! Nonetheless, if you're into medieval streets, World War II history, Soviet-era Poland, seafood, Ferris wheels, and using words like "dank," you'll undoubtedly find Gdańsk to be very dank, indeed. A small naval town founded in the tenth century, Gdańsk became decisively less boring when its Westerplatte region witnessed the first shots of WWII. In the wake of the war and during the dawn of communism, large shipyards were established in the town. Shipyard strikes in the 70s and 80s were pivotal to the Polish independence movement and the collapse of the Eastern bloc. The town looks back upon these events with its Museum of the Second World War and European Solidarity Center, both of which are undoubtedly some of the finest museums in Europe. Today, Gdańsk's historic Old Town is teeming with tourists, particularly young students and elderly tour groups. But that's not to say it lacks excitement. Bars and clubs are everywhere, and the nearby town of Sopot boasts a vibrant nightlife scene as well. The town also hosts many music and theater festivals on an annual basis, so make sure you keep an eye on a local events calendar, unless you deliberately want to look like an uncultured yahoo.

ORIENTATION

Unless you traveled via a pirate ship or pirated a ship of your own, your first taste of this idyllic, seaside town will be its unimpressive and landlocked central railway and bus station. But before you become disappointed and catch the next train out, fear not—the medieval **Old Town,** the one plastered across Polish travel brochures, is just a 10-minute walk away. Thankfully, this will be one of longest walks during your stay. With the exception of a few museums and landmarks, you'll find everything you need in the Old Town. **Ul. Piwna** and **ul. Dulga,** lined with cafés and restaurants, are the town's busiest streets. On the former, you'll find the tallest structure in the region, **St. Mary's Basilica,** and along the latter, you'll run into **Fontana di Neptune,** Gdańsk's own Trevi fountain. Both roads, among many others, will lead you to the harbor front, which contains the expected number of seafood restaurants as well as Gdańsk's unofficial symbol, the Crane. In between the Old Town and the more modern and residential area across the harbor lies an island, which is only significant thanks to its sizable Ferris wheel. Buses that run along **ul. Olawska,** which marks the end of the Old Town, will take you to the **Westerplatte ruins** as well as the nearby towns of **Sopot** and **Gdynia.**

ESSENTIALS

GETTING THERE

Trains and buses arrive at Gdańsk Glowny station, a 15min. walk from the center of the Old Town. From the station, Bus #111 or Trams #8 or 9 will take you along the western and southern perimeters of the Old Town. Planes arrive at Gdańsk Lech Walesa Airport, 15km (9mi.) west of the Old Town. Trains from the airport travel to Gdańsk Glowny (3.80zł), taking around 30min. A taxi from the airport costs around 60zł.

GETTING AROUND

If you're spending most of your time in and around the Old Town, you should be able to walk to any given destination in less than 15min. But, if you're choosing to explore the tri-city area, then Gdańsk's public transport system will be more than adequate. The public transport system is comprised of buses and trams, respectively known as the ZTM and ZKM, and serves the tri-city area of Gdańsk, Sopot, and Gdynia. Google Maps hasn't yet incorporated the local public transport into their navigation system, but this website (www.jakdojade.pl/trojmiasto/ trasa) allows you to select a start point and destination and shows you the best bus/tram route to take. The ticket options include: single (3.20zł), single on night or fast services (4.20zł), 1hr (3.80zł), 1hr on night or fast services (4.80zł), and 24hr (13zł). Local trains run between the three cities every 15min. from 5am-7pm, and less frequently from 7pm until 4am. Prices range from 4.20zł to 6.20zł. Be sure to validate your tickets in the yellow boxes. Plainclothes police officers will fine you if you're caught traveling without a validated ticket. Elite Airport, Hallo, Monte, and Neptun are reliable taxi companies.

PRACTICAL INFORMATION

Tourist Offices: The three main tourist information centers are found in ul. Długa (Długi Targ 28/29, 58 301 43 55; open daily summer 9am-7pm, winter 9am-5pm). The official tourism site is www.visitGdańsk.com.

Banks/ATMs/Currency Exchange: ATMs can be found all around the Old Town. ING Bank branches are located inside Madison Shopping Gallery (Rajska 10; 571 203 119; open M-Sa 9am-9pm, Su 10am-8pm). The Old Town is full of currency exchanges, known as "kantors." We recommend using ATMs, but if you have to exchange cash, avoid doing so at airports, any exchanges labeled "change" instead of "kantor," and any exchanges that remain open until late. A safe option is the Poczta Polska post office that also exchanges money, located a third of the way down Ul. Długa (Długa 23/28; 58 301 80 49; open daily 24hr).

Post Offices: Poczta Polska (Ul. Długa 23/28; 58 301 80 49; open daily 24hr)

Internet: Most cafés, restaurants, and fast food restaurants have free Wi-Fi.

BGLTQ+ Resources: Although Poland's government doesn't offer many legal rights and protections for the BGLTQ+ community, the people of Gdańsk are generally open-minded and all the accommodations and nightlife locations listed are BGLTQ+ friendly. Here are some resources.

- Campaign Against Homophobia Warsaw Headquarters (22 423 64 38)
- Poland-wide BGLTQ+ helpline Lambda Warszawa (22 628 52 22; open M 6pm-10pm, Tu 6pm-9pm, W 6pm-10pm, Th 6pm-10pm, Tu, F 6pm-9pm)

EMERGENCY INFORMATION

Emergency Number: 112; Poland Tourist Emergency Hotline (22 278 77 77, 608 599 999; open daily Oct-May 8am-6pm, Jun-Sept 8am-10pm)

Police: 997; headquarters (ul. Nowe Ogrody 27; 58 321 62 22; open daily 24hr)

US Embassy: The nearest US Embassy is in Warsaw (22 504 2000; open M-F 8:30am-5pm).

Rape Crisis Center: The Feminoteka Foundation (helpline: 731 731 551; admin: 720 908 974; open Tu-Th 1pm-7pm)

Hospitals:
- Copernicus Podimiot Leczniczy (Copernicus Hospital) (Nowe Ogrody 1-6; 58 764 01 00; open daily 24hr)

Pharmacies: Pharmacies are identifiable by the green cross on or protruding from their façade, and are known as aptekas. Most operate daily from around 8am-8pm.
- Apteka Dr. Max (Pańska 6; 58 778 90 37; open M-F 8am-8pm, Sa 9am-4pm)

ACCOMMODATIONS
MIDTOWN HOSTEL ($)

Podwale Staromiejskie 105/106/1; 587 105 057; www.midtownhostel.pl; reception open 24hr

Small and quaint. Simple but elegant. Quiet and clean. Modern yet homey. Any of these descriptions could easily apply to Midtown Hostel, and god dammit, we're gonna apply them! Tucked just inside the Old Town, the hostel makes what's already a painless place to navigate even easier. With only eight rooms, the largest of which is a six-person dorm, it's also a reprieve from the crowded and busy streets surrounding it.

i Dorms from 45 zł, doubles from 115 zł; reservation recommended; BGLTQ+ friendly; no wheelchair accessibility; Wi-Fi; linens included; laundry facilities available

SIGHTS
CULTURE

GDAŃSK SHAKESPEARE THEATRE

Wojciecha Bogusławskiego 1; 583 510 101; www.teatrszekspirowski.pl

As much a historical site as it is an architectural landmark, the Gdańsk Shakespeare Theatre stands on the same site that hosted traveling English theater troupes in the seventeenth century. It was the only Shakespearean theater outside of England in existence at the time. Four hundred or so years later, this 95 million zł fortress-like structure is home to one of the most renowned Shakespeare festivals in the world, held in the first week of August. When it's not telling the tales of a brooding prince that wants to get with his mom, it's a popular local theater and concert space.

i Tours 14 zł, reduced 8zł; wheelchair accessible; daily English tours at 3pm

MARKET HALL

Pl. Dominikański 1; 583 463 133; www.teatrszekspirowski.pl; open M-F 9am-6pm, Sa 9am-5pm

An old Dominican monastery turned railway station turned food and clothing market, Market Hall is a wonderland of all things good and cheap. Inside, you'll find food on the first floor—meats, cheeses, chocolates—and clothing—mostly women's—on the second. The **outdoor fresh produce** area, however, is where the magic really happens. Blueberries, strawberries, cherries, kiwis and nectarines—you name it and some vendor will inevitably be selling it, and you can almost guarantee that "it" will be fresh, juicy, and delicious. Because most vendors can't speak English, your purchases will probably be made through pointing and typing numbers into a calculator, but this isn't too inconvenient, especially given the satisfaction you'll get from looking at your too-good-to-be-true prices on a digital screen.

i Stand prices vary; limited wheelchair accessibility

GRAND HOSTEL ($)

Świętojańska 43/44; 666 061 350; www.grandhostel.pl; reception open 24hr

Even the world's most brilliant city planner couldn't have found a better location for Grand Hostel. It's not only right on the harbor front, but also within a very impressive long-jump's distance of the town's iconic and profoundly peculiar **Crane**. The hostel's décor matches its nautical location. Each room is painted in a baby blue and includes nice touches like posters of naval designs and an old sea captain who could tell you a tale or two about the South China Sea. If you're looking for a place to stay in Gdańsk, Grand Hostel—with a buffet breakfast included as well as a small art gallery and bar forthcoming—is a pretty unbeatable choice.

i Dorms from 39 zł, doubles from 120 zł, singles from 120 zł; reservation recommended; BGLTQ+ friendly; no wheelchair accessibility; Wi-Fi; linens included; laundry available

LANDMARKS

ST. MARY'S BASILICA AND NEPTUNE'S FOUNTAIN

Podkramarska 5; 583 013 982; www.bazylikamariacka.Gdańsk.pl; open M-Sa 8:30am-6:30pm, Su 11-noon and 1pm-6:30pm

St. Mary's Basilica and Neptune's Fountain, together with the **Crane,** make up the "Terrific Trio of Gdańsk"—a term we just made up for the town's famous landmarks. The tallest structure in the tri-city area, **St. Mary's Basilica** is particularly impressive. The view from the top is absolutely breathtaking, not that you'll have much breath left after climbing 400-odd steps. The church's astronomical clock is also a sight to behold, although not for its creator, whose eyes were gouged out so he'd never be able to design a better clock (yikes!). The nearby Neptune Fountain is the center of **Długi Targ,** or the Long Market.

i Church admission 4 zł, reduced 2 zł, viewing tower admission 8 zł, reduced 4zł; limited wheelchair accessibility

ZURAW (CRANE)

Szeroka 67/68; 583 016 938; www.en.nmm.pl/crane; museum open Tu-Su 10pm-4pm

Zuraw, or the Crane, is probably Gdańsk's most famous landmark. At the very least, it's certainly its weirdest. Resembling a gigantic bat perched along the harbor, the Crane looms over passersby, giving it a rather sinister feel that belies its actual history and purpose. Built in the middle of the fifteenth century, the Crane used to transfer cargo to and from ships but today houses the **Polish Maritime Museum.** The museum's exhibits are exclusively in Polish, but if you fancy checking out the inside of the crane, the 8 zł entrance fee isn't anything to lose sleep over.

i Observation free, museum admission 8 zł, reduced 4 zł; limited wheelchair accessibility

MUSEUMS

EUROPEAN SOLIDARITY CENTER AND MONUMENT TO THE FALLEN SHIPYARD WORKERS OF 1970

Pl. Solidarności 1; 587 724 112; www.ecs.gda.pl; open daily winter 10am-5pm, summer 10am-7pm

Before you reach the European Solidarity Center, you'll come across a statue of three enormous crosses with anchors attached to each of their intersections. You'll quickly discover that the edifice before you is in fact the Monument to the Fallen Shipyard Workers of 1970, but many questions will continue to linger. *Who were the workers? How did they fall? Why did they fall?* If you walk towards the huge rust-colored structure behind it, all these questions (and more) will be answered. The European Solidarity Center focuses on Poland under communist rule and the resistance movement that eventually led to the country's liberation. Its immersive exhibits engage you in a subject that you likely knew or cared little about beforehand.

i Admission 20 zł, reduced 15 zł; wheelchair accessible

MUSEUM OF THE SECOND WORLD WAR

Pl. Władysława Bartoszewskiego 1; 587 600 960; www.muzeum1939.pl; open Tu-Su 10am-7pm

You'd need a museum the size of a football stadium to even begin to provide a comprehensive overview of World War II. Luckily, Gdańsk has one. Covering everything, and we mean everything, from the end of the First World War to the post-WWII climate that ushered in the Cold War, the museum still manages to shine a light on how the war affected both Poland and Gdańsk. It's so chock-full of highlights that it's almost futile to single out any specific ones. All we can say is that the two to three hours you'll spend here will probably be the some of the best you've spent inside a museum ever.

i Admission 23 zł, reduced 16 zł, audioguide 5 zł (recommended); last entry 2hr before closing; wheelchair accessible

FOOD

NOVA PIEROGOVA ($$)

Szafarnia 6; 516 414 200; open daily noon-10pm

What dumplings are to China, *pierogies* are to Poland, which is pretty obvious considering *pierogies* are just traditional Polish dumplings. You'll see them on the menu at just about any Polish restaurant, but it'll be tough to find a place that does them better than Nova Pierogova. Nestled on the harbor front on the less historic side of town, the nautical-style restaurant specializes in an exhaustive range of delectable meat and vegetarian *pierogi*. Ten will be more than enough to fill you up, which means you'll somehow need to find some extra stomach space for the sweet varietals. We can't stress how important this is—the **apple and cinnamon pierogi** was one of the best desserts we've had in Europe.

i 6 pierogi from 16 zł, 12 pierogi from 18 zł; vegetarian options available; wheelchair accessible

TURYSTYCZNY BAR MLECZNY ($)

Szeroka 8/10; 583016013; www.bartu-rystyczny.pl; open M-F 8am-6pm, Sa-Su 9am-5pm

Of all the corrupting effects *A Clockwork Orange* has wrought upon society, the worst is undoubtedly the perception that a milk bar is a bar that specializes in milk, when, in reality, it's a Soviet-era cafeteria-style restaurant that specializes in traditional Polish cuisine. And while some may find the idea of a commie canteen unappealing, it's perhaps the most cherished kind of culinary institution in Poland. Once you reach the front, point at the menu until the old Polish woman behind the counter understands your order. After having paid, rejoice that your wallet is (at most) only 14 zł lighter. Besides having your country destroyed by Germany and the USSR, visiting a milk bar is the quintessential Polish experience.

i Entrées from 6 zł; vegetarian options available; wheelchair accessible

NIGHTLIFE

PUB LAWENDOWA

Lawendowa 8; 531 194 277; www.lawen-dowa8.ontap.pl; open M-W 3pm-1am, Th 3pm-2am, F-Sa 3pm-3am, Su 3pm-1am

Pub Lawendowa doesn't look too different from your average "cool" bar. It's got gritty exposed brick walls, David Bowie blasting out of the speakers, and an arcade machine—the holy trinity of hip. It undoubtedly fits a certain aesthetic, especially with its emphasis on craft beer, but it isn't necessarily a place you'll remember based on looks alone. Who needs looks when you've got the kind of drinks and service that'll make folks weak at the knees. The range of craft beers on tap is stellar, and if you're having any trouble deciding what to drink, your bartender will go out of their way to ensure that you make the right choice.

i Beers from 6 zł; BGLTQ+ friendly

BUNKIER CLUB

Olejarna 3; 531 711 207; www.bunk-ierclub.pl; open M-Th 7pm-1am, F-Sa 7pm-5am, Su 7pm-1am

An old air-raid shelter built in 1942, Bunkier Club looks like a hulking concrete monolith. Once you waltz through the entrance, paying the bouncers nothing except a courteous smile (there is no cover fee), you'll discover five whole floors of madness that would give any military general worth their salt a heart attack. The venue plays your typical Top-40 fare with Eurotrash bangers slipped into the mix, and its general accessibility attracts all kinds of people. Wander around and you'll find decorative motorcycles, tables set up inside prison cells, and numerous sculptures of naked women's torsos. On weekend nights, the club gets so full that you might not have the luxury of doing so.

i No cover, beer from 6.50 zł, spirits from 10 zł; BGLTQ+ friendly

KRAKOW

Coverage by **Nicholas Grundlingh**

Your grandmother visits Kraków for the medieval architecture. Your grandfather? For the Wawel Castle and its medieval history. Your UNESCO World Heritage site-obsessed sister? She can't wait to check out the Wieliczka Salt Mine. Your brooding teenage cousin who believes the only salvation in life is art? He should be left at the hostel so you can enjoy the city's numerous galleries and museums in peace. Kraków, as small as it seems, has something to offer everyone. If you're into your facts and figures, you'll find yourself astonished that Kraków was named after a lowly peasant who slayed a fearsome dragon. And if you're a fan of myths and legends, you won't help but be amazed that Kraków once served as the Polish capital back when kings ruled and peasants drooled—a period that most historians agree ranges from the fourteenth to seventeenth century. The city, and the Old Town in particular, is populated with all kinds of historic landmarks, such as the world's oldest shopping mall (in Main Market Square), Europe's largest golden altar (found in St Mary's Basilica), and Poland's only fire-breathing dragon (the Wawel Dragon Statue). Auschwitz-Birkenau, the largest of the former Nazi concentration camps, lies an hour and a half outside of Kraków, and Schindler's Factory can be found in the city's Podgórze district. Widely regarded as the new Prague, Kraków hasn't been this hot since the days of that fearsome dragon.

ORIENTATION

You should be familiar with two areas, the medieval **Stare Miasto** (Old Town) and the more rugged and hip **Kazimierz district.** The Old Town is bound by a ring made of grass called **Planty Park.** In the center, you'll find' the **Main Market Square.** A walk down **ul. Grodzka** will lead you to **Wawel Castle.** A tram line, which borders the east side of Planty Park, will take you into Kazimierz, either via **Stradomska** or **Starowiślna,** the latter of which is closer to the **Jewish Quarter.** In between these two streets lies **Plac Nowy**—a hotbed of bars and restaurants. **Schindler's Factory** and the **Museum of Contemporary Art** both share the same complex and are located across the river from Kazimierz in the **Podgórze/Zabłocie district.** Northeast of the Old Town, **Kraków Główny**—the main railway and bus station—awaits, ready to transport you out of the city to the **Wieliczka Salt Mine** (by train) or **Auschwitz** (preferably by bus).

ESSENTIALS
GETTING THERE

Kraków Airport is 15km (9mi.) west of the city, and trains run every 30min. from 4am-midnight from the airport to Kraków Glowny, the main train and bus station, which is a 10min. walk north of the Old Town. The journey is 17min., and tickets (9zł) can be purchased on the platform or on-board. Buses #208 and 252, and night bus #902 (4zł) run from the airport to the city center and take around 40min. If you're traveling to Kraków by bus or train, you will arrive in Kraków Glowny. The bus

terminal is on the east side of the station, and you should exit on the west side to walk to the Old Town.

GETTING AROUND

Kraków's public transport system consists of buses and trams. Regular service runs from 5am-11pm, with night buses and trams continuing less frequently afterwards. You can plan your journeys using www.jakdojade.pl/Krakow/trasa. 20min. (2.80zł), 40min. (3.80zł), and 1hr. (5 zł) tickets are available, as well as 24hr (15zł), 48hr (24zł), 72hr (36zł), and 7-day (48zł) options. Tickets can be purchased at bus and tram stops, and 1hr. tickets can be purchased from the driver. Tickets must be validated on-board, and inspectors will fine you if they find you have not done so. No public transport runs within the Old Town, but the area is very walkable and can be crossed by foot in about 20min. Trains to the Wieliczka Salt Mine and buses to Auschwitz-Birkenau run from Kraków Glowny. Train tickets for the Salt Mine can be purchased at ticket machines or onboard the trains, which means you do not need to queue in line for domestic tickets.

PRACTICAL INFORMATION

Tourist Offices: InfoKraków is the official city information network run by Kraków (hotline 124 320 060; open daily 9am-5pm), with five information centers in the Old Town (ul. Św. Jana 2; open daily 9am-7pm).

Banks/ATMs/Currency Exchange: ATMs are found throughout the city, especially in the Old Town. In the city, currency exchanges are known as "kantors," some of which give better rates than ATM machines. Avoid kantors with English names, such as Western Union and Interchange, and those in touristy areas, such as the Old Town Square and ul. Florianska. Kantors along ul. Slawkowska usually provide reasonable rates.

Post Offices: The main office is just outside the eastern perimeter of the Old Town (Westerplatte 20; 12 421 44 89; open M-F 8am-8:30pm, Sa 8am-3pm).

Internet: Most cafés, restaurants, hostels, and fast food restaurants provide free Wi-Fi. Public libraries, identifiable by the phrase "Biblioteki Publicznej," also provide free Wi-Fi.

BGLTQ+ Resources: Although Poland's government doesn't offer many legal rights and protections for the BGLTQ+ community, Kraków is generally considered an BGLTQ+ friendly city. Here are some resources:
- The Campaign Against Homophobia can be reached for any BGLTQ+ queries (22 423 64 38) and provides a list of therapists in Kraków online (kph.org.pl/pomoc/pomoc-psychologiczna).
- Poland-wide BGLTQ+ helpline Lambda Warszawa (22 628 52 22; open M, W, Th 6pm-10pm, Tu, F 6pm-9pm).
- Poland's first transgender member of Parliament Anna Grodzka offers free psychological consultations in her Deputies' Office for transgender people (biuro@annagrodzka.pl).

EMERGENCY INFORMATION

Emergency Number: 112; Poland Tourist Emergency Hotline (22 278 77 77 and 608 599 999; open daily Oct-May 8am-6pm, Jun-Sept 8am-10pm)

Police: Rynek Główny 27; 12615 73 18

US Embassy: US Consulate General is located east of the Old Town Square (Stolarska 9; 12 424 51 00; open M-F 8:30am-5pm).

Rape Crisis Center: The Feminoteka Foundation serves as Poland's primary rape crisis helpline, providing legal and psychological support to victims of all kinds of violence (731 731 551 (helpline/support), 720 908 974 (admin); open Tu-Th 1pm-7pm).

Hospitals: The following 24hr hospitals have emergency wards that are obliged to help anyone who arrives regardless of nationality or health insurance.
- University Hospital of Kraków (Mikołaja Kopernika 36; 12 424 70 00)
- Health Care Ministry of Internal Affairs and Administration (Kronikarza Galla 25; 12 662 31 50)

Pharmacies: Pharmacies are identifiable by the green cross on or protruding from their façade, and are called aptekas in Polish.
- DOZ Apteka (Mikołajska 4 12 431 10 19; open M-Sa 8am-8pm, Su 10am-6pm)
- Apteka Pod Złotym Lwem (Długa 4l 12 422 62 04; open M-Sa 8am-8pm, Su 8am-2pm)

ACCOMMODATIONS

🏠 SECRET GARDEN HOSTEL ($$)

Skawińska 7; 124 305 445; www.thesecret-garden.pl; reception open 24hr

Although we never found the secret garden (we spent most of our time in the one right by the entrance), we did find plenty to enjoy about our stay at this hostel. Let's talk about the rooms—each is assigned a theme like "Frozen Cranberry," which gives this relatively large hostel a personal feel. The location is (insert fire emoji); the hostel's a leisurely stroll or a short tram ride to the **Old Town.** A single traveler in need of a bed in a dorm will have to search elsewhere, but a single traveler looking to bring back a hot date to a chic-looking room will feel right at home.

i Singles from 90 zł, twins from 150 zł; reservation recommended; wheelchair accessible; linens included; laundry; kitchen

BUBBLE HOSTEL ($)

Basztowa 15; 500 498 100; www.bubble-hostel.krakówhotels.net; reception open 24hr

Unlike the housing market circa '08, this bubble is something we hope will never burst. While the hostel's fifth-story view of **Planty Park** is a treat in itself, the real cause for celebration lies just behind the park, where the **Old Town's** best cheap restaurants and bars can be found. The hostel's rooms are basic, yet clean and comfortable, and the fact that the entire establishment occupies just a single floor gives it a cozy and intimate feel. And if you like your hostels how you like your trains (near a train station), then you're in luck—the main Kraków station is just a five-minute walk away.

i Dorms from 45 zł, doubles from 160 zł; reservation recommended; limited wheelchair accessibility; linens included; laundry; kitchen

CRACOW HOSTEL ($)

Rynek Główny 18; 012 429 11 06; www.cracowhostel.com; reception open 24hr

If you're looking to stay in a fourteenth-century building right in the heart of Kraków, look no further than this hostel. Because of its superb location, the hostel attracts backpackers from around the world, which imbues it with a vibrant atmosphere and makes it an easy place to meet people. The bathrooms are clean, the clientele young, the Wi-Fi strong, and the views of **Main Market Square** spectacular—all factors that ensure Cracow Hostel isn't only a place to rest your head, but also an unforgettable part of your trip. Only potential downside: because of its killer location, Cracow's dorms can get quite noisy.

i Dorms from 45 zł, twin from 160 zł; reservation recommended; Wi-Fi; BGLTQ+ friendly; no wheelchair accessibility; linens included; laundry

SIGHTS
CULTURE

UNSOUND FESTIVAL

www.unsound.pl; occurs early to mid-Oct

For about a week in October, Kraków's cathedrals, factories, cinemas, salt mines, and brutalist Soviet-era hotels are overtaken by the world's most forward-thinking electronic DJs and producers. Since its creation in 2003, Unsound has transformed from a small underground festival to one of the most respected electronic music events in the world. It emphasizes collaboration between the international acts and the Polish arts community, so it's not uncommon to see a Kraków ballet company dancing to dubstep, or a local symphony orchestra backing a techno set. With a week-long pass roughly $123 USD, the festival is unlike any other you've ever attended and engenders a cult-like loyalty from fans across Europe.

i Week pass 470 zł, event-specific tickets also available

LANDMARKS

⬛ WIELICZKA SALT MINE

Daniłowicza 10; 12 278 73 02; www.
wieliczka-saltmine.com; open daily 7:30am-
7:30pm

Attracting over a million tourists per
year and listed as a **UNESCO site,** the
Wieliczka Salt Mine certainly has a bit
of a reputation. But does it live up to the
hype? At first, a 90-minute guided tour of
the mine might sound like a trade-off. But
luckily, the engaging guides, animatronic
exhibits, and small-scale mine replicas
make salt-mining more interesting than
it frankly has any right to be. The **Chapel
of St. Kulga,** far and away the tour's
highlight, is breathtaking and contains a
salt replica of *The Last Supper* and a salt
statue of **Pope John Paul II,** as well as
majestic salt chandeliers. The **Tourist
Route** is a favorite, but if you're feeling
brave, a Miners' Route, which takes you
deep into the darkness of the mine's oldest
shaft, is also available.

i *Tours 84 zł, reduced 64 zł; last tour 7:30pm;
limited wheelchair accessibility*

⬛ GHETTO WALL FRAGMENT AND
GHETTO HEROES SQUARE

Wall: Lwowska 29/Limanowskiego 60/62; pl.
Bohaterow Getta; Wall and Square open daily
24hr

The **Podgorze district** is home to
two important symbols relating to the
persecution of Cracovian Jews during
World War II—a fragment from the wall
surrounding the Jewish Ghetto and the
Ghetto Heroes Square memorial. In 1941,
the Nazis imprisoned nearly 20,000 Jews
in Podgorze, and over the next few years,
plac Zgody became the Ghetto's social
hub as well as the site of deportations and
executions. The Ghetto Wall Fragment
located along ul. Lwowska isn't as
significant, but a longer stretch of wall can
be found nearby behind the school at ul.
Limanowskiego 60/62, providing an eerie
contrast to its playground setting. The
Ghetto Heroes Square is located closer to
the river on plac Zgody. Here, you'll find
33 empty bronze chairs representing the
absence of the Ghetto's victims.

i *Free; wheelchair accessible*

AUSCHWITZ

1.5hr from Kraków

Auschwitz-Birkenau is the largest, and
most well-known Nazi concentration
camp. The name "Auschwitz" refers to
three camps: **Auschwitz I,** which greeted
prisoners with the message of "Arbeit
Macht Frei" ("Work Sets You Free")
looming above its entrance; **Auschwitz
II-Birkenau,** whose "Gate of Death"
and railway have become symbols of the
Holocaust; and **Auschwitz III,** which is
not open to the public. Nazi authorities
at these camps murdered approximately
1.1 million people, the majority of which
were Jewish, but also included Sinti and
Roma Poles and other political prisoners.
Since 1947, Auschwitz I, and, to a lesser
extent Auschwitz II-Birkenau, has served
as a museum, documenting the Nazi
occupation of Poland, the establishment
of Auschwitz-Birkenau, life at the camps,
the horrific experiments carried out on
prisoners, and many personal accounts
of the prisoners' suffering and courage.
Auschwitz II-Birkenau is primarily the
site of the monument to the victims of
Auschwitz. The site represents one of
the greatest tragedies in human history,
and although everyone's experience at
Auschwitz is personal, it is an emotionally
charged visit.

i *Free; recommended 3.5hr guided tour
40zł, reduced 30zł, book online in advance,
tour available 10am-3pm; self-guided tours
available 8am-10am and 3pm-8pm (no ticket
needed), 1-2hr wait possible; self-guided visit
of Auschwitz I: begin at Block 4, continue in
clockwise direction*

ST. MARY'S BASILICA

Pl. Mariacki 5; 124 220 737; www.mariacki. com; basilica open M-Sa 11:30am-6pm, Su 2pm-6pm; Mariacki Tower open M-Sa 9:30am-5:30pm, Su 1pm-5:30pm

The church's ostensible highlight is its golden Gothic altarpiece, the largest of its kind in Europe, but we found ourselves more impressed by its starry, deep blue ceilings, which wouldn't look out of place in a Van Gogh painting. You have to pay a small fee to look inside the church, and an additional one to ascend the **Mariacki Tower,** which overlooks the **Main Market Square.** You could just wait outside the church to hear the famous **Hejnał Mariack**—the hourly bugle call that commemorates the thirteenth-century trumpeter, who was shot in the neck while warning the city of an impending Mongol attack.

i Admission 10zł, reduced 5zł; last entry 15min. before closing; limited wheelchair accessibility

MUSEUMS

MUSEUM OF CONTEMPORARY ART IN KRAKÓW

Lipowa 4; 122 634 000; www.en.mocak.pl; open Tu-Su 11am-7pm

MOCAK provides a fascinating insight into Polish culture that is difficult to find elsewhere, as well as serving as a meta-critique of art itself. And while we can already hear the retching noise that the phrase "meta-critique" is likely to incite, the exhibits—which include a painstakingly recreated work of nineteenth-century realism ripped to pieces and a real-life video recording of an artist trying to steal the *Mona Lisa*—are (mostly) devoid of pretension and just plain hilarious. We can assure you, even the most uncultured Neanderthal can find something to appreciate about a blown-up photo of an anonymous person wearing nothing but a pair of EU flag-print underwear.

i Regular 14zł, reduced 7 zł; last entry 1hr before closing; wheelchair accessible

NATIONAL MUSEUM IN KRAKÓW

Al. 3 Maja 1; 124 335 500; www.mnk.pl/ branch/main-building; open Tu-Sa 10am-6pm, Su 10am-4pm

When in a place as historic as Kraków, it might seem like a waste of a precious few hours to visit an art museum, which, in a broad sense, contains the same kind of work you're likely to find in similar museums around the world. And if your interest in expressionism is solely limited to expressing how boring expressionism is, this museum won't change your mind. That said, any art-lover or art-curious individual will find this assortment of late eighteenth, nineteenth, and twentieth-century Polish art unquestionably worth their time. The galleries focusing upon Polish impressionism are particularly stunning.

i Main building admission 11 zł, reduced 6 zł; all-branch pass 35 zł, reduced 28 zł; free on Su; wheelchair accessible

OUTDOORS

KOSCIUSZKO MOUND

Al. Waszyngtona 1; 124 251 116; www.kop-ieckosciuszki.pl; open daily 9am-dusk

Kosciuszko Mound is one of the most beloved spots in the city, but we're not sure if this is because of or in spite of the fact that it looks like an enormous grassy nipple. Following the death of Tadeusz Kosciuszko, leader of the Polish army and soldier in the American Revolutionary War, in 1817, citizens from across the country flocked to Kraków to build this mound in tribute to their hero. A few decades later, Austrian authorities constructed a brick fortress around the mound, which, today, makes your visit to the mound feel like a kind of invasion. Once you reach the top of the mound, any imperial guilt will be replaced with an imperial enjoyment of the magnificent views of the **Old Town** and **Wawel Castle.**

i Admission 12 zł, reduced 10 zł; wheelchair accessible

FOOD

🍴 POD WAWELEM ($$)

Świętej Gertrudy 26-29; 012 421 23 36; www.podwawelem.eu; open M-Sa noon-midnight, Su noon-11pm

As close as you'll come to a Polish feast without traveling back in time to **Wawel Castle** c. 1200, Pod Wawelem is one of the best dining experiences you'll have in Kraków. If you arrive around peak time (7-9pm), don't be deterred by the waiting time—it's worth it. The restaurant serves delicious Polish cuisine that, once you take into account the enormous portions, is an absolute steal. Although the inside is perfectly nice, the outside veranda looking out onto **Planty Park** is nothing short of idyllic, and you should absolutely demand to be seated there. And while the in-house jazz trio is a nice touch, you'll wish the restaurant had spared the expense and bought each of its customers a larger pair of pants for optimal post-consumption comfort instead.

i Entrées from 23 zł; vegetarian options available; wheelchair accessible

KAWIARNIA LITERACKA ($$)

Krakówska 41; 513 158 167; www.kawiarnia-literacka.pl; open daily 11am-11pm

After a long, exploratory stroll from the **Old Town** through the **Kazimierz district,** you'll feel exhausted—physically (from all the walking), mentally (from the all the sights), and spiritually (from being a person living in a twenty-first-century world). Chances are, you'll need a drink. And this café's selection of beer, wine, liquor, and coffee might just do the trick. If it doesn't, its cozy suede couches and bean-bags chairs certainly will. You can also grab a book from one of Kawiarnia Literacka's many bookcases to take your mind off things.

i Coffee from 10 zł, alcohol from 8 zł; vegetarian options available; no wheelchair accessibility

ZAPIEKANKI KROLEWSKIE ($)

Plac Nowy 4; open daily 10am-2am

We've said it once and we'll say it again: after sundown, **Plac Nowy,** the beating heart of the Kazimierz district, is the place to be. But while it's criminally easy to find a good bar, where can you find a hearty meal? Truthfully, there are quite a few sit-down places that'll get the job done, but every Pole on planet earth knows that it's not even a discussion: Zapiekanki is the way to go. Essentially a 15-inch toasted baguette covered in mushrooms, cheese, and your choice from an exhaustive list of toppings, Zapiekanki is the Subway-pizza combination that you didn't know was missing from your life. **The Royal** (bacon, chicken, lettuce, sweet corn, tomato and chives, 10zł) is the crowd favorite, and with good reason—it tastes good!

i Zapiekanki from 7 zł; wheelchair accessible

POLAND KRAKOW

NIGHTLIFE

ALCHEMIA ($)

Estery 5; 012 421 22 00; www.en.alchemia.
com.pl; open M 10am-2am, Tu-W 9am-2am,
Th 9am-3am, F-Sa 9am-4am, Su 9am-2am

Even if Alchemia weren't **the most lively
and vibrant bar we visited in Kraków,**
we'd recommend it purely based on its
gritty bohemian furnishings, candlelit
ambiance, and eclectic food menu, which
includes fish and chips, falafel, pad thai,
and everything in between. You'll struggle
to find a table on most nights of the week,
but if you're lucky enough find a seat
or smart enough to steal someone else's,
you're likely to have a memorable night,
provided that you can still remember
it in the morning (less a consequence
of drinking, and more of falling off the
tables, which double as a dance floor). The
cellar regularly hosts DJs and live music
acts—guaranteed all-night long affairs.
i Beer from 7 zł, cocktails from 10 zł, food
from 19 zł

PROZAK 2.0

Pl. Dominikański 6; open Su-Th 10pm-6am,
F-Sa 10pm-8am

If you want the proverbial "big night
out," head straight to Prozak 2.0, which,
on any weekend night, is packed to the
gills with what seems like the entirety of
Kraków's local and tourist population.
Your typical brick-walled, black-ceilinged
basement space—save for the neon signs
all over the place—Prozak won't be a
nightlife experience, but it will be fun.
With four bars, three dance floors, and
the best sound system money can buy, it
caters to music-purists, party-pedants, and
fast food enthusiasts (it's directly below a
McDonald's) alike. The bar doesn't have a
menu, so make sure you know the prices
before you order. On the big nights, the
lines seem to have no end, so make sure you
arrive early, get stamped, and come back
later.
i Cover 10 zł, beer 10 zł, cocktails 20-30 zł

WARSAW

Coverage by **Nicholas Grundlingh**

Warsaw won't make you go back home to report, "It's one of the better-looking places
I saw." But what the Polish capital lacks in architecture it makes up for in history and
a relaxed, vibrant atmosphere. A city that was effectively leveled during World War
II and lost nearly 30% of its population in the Holocaust, the Warsaw you see today
is a replica of its former self, reconstructed and ruled, along with the rest of Poland,
by a communist government until 1990. Institutions such as the Warsaw Rising and
History of Polish Jews museums remember the war, and many of the buildings, most
noticeably the Palace of Culture and Science, serve as relics to the period of Soviet
influence. With over a thousand years of history but only around three decades of
independence, Warsaw is an exciting blend of old and new. Spend your days roaming
around museums, parks, and cafés, your nights along the Vistula River, and the
months afterwards thinking how stupid you were to judge this place by its looks.

ORIENTATION

Just like your guidance counselor in high school, nearly every neighborhood in
Warsaw is worth visiting at least once. Along the west bank of the **Vistula River**—
which separates the more metropolitan part of the city from the grungy, less glamorous
(but arguably cooler) **Praga district**—you'll find the **Old Town** (entirely rebuilt after
WWII), the **Powisle district** (the student district), and **Lazienki Park** (filled with
palaces, Chopin, and an art museum). **Powisle,** contains some of the best restaurants
as well as **Plac Zabaw,** a bunch of bars and food trucks on the river. Head further west
into the city from Powisle to enter the city center, which subtly announces itself with
the towering **Palace of Culture and Science.** If you follow **ul. Marszałkowska** south
in the direction of hipster haven **Plac Zbawiciela,** restaurants and bars jump out as
if you're walking through a very un-scary haunted house. Trams run horizontally and
vertically along most main roads, and two metro lines, one adjacent to the river and
the other perpendicular to it, intersect at **ul. Swietokrzyska.**

ESSENTIALS
GETTING THERE

From Chopin Airport Terminal A, take the SKM S2 train to the Środmieście station and the S3 to Warszawa Centralna station (single-trip public transport tickets 4.40zł). From the budget airline-friendly Warsaw-Modlin Airport, take one of the green or yellow shuttles to Modlin Train Station, from which trains run into Warszawa Centralna station. If you're traveling by train, you'll likely disembark there as well. A bus journey into Warsaw will drop you off at the main bus station along Aleje Jerozolimskie, which is either a 15min. train ride from the nearby Warsaw West station or a 12min. bus ride (#127, 158, 517) east into the city center.

GETTING AROUND

The public transport system consists of trams, buses, and two metro lines running north-south (blue line M1) and east-west (red line M2). A night bus runs 11pm-5am, and the metro runs from 5am-11am on weekdays, and until 3am on Friday and Saturday. Public transport tickets (single ride 4.40zł) are valid for all three modes of transport, and can be purchased from green and yellow kiosks or anywhere with a "Bilety" ("ticket") sign. Unless you're traveling to the outskirts of Warsaw, you'll only need a Zone 1 ticket, which includes the Chopin Airport. 24hr (15zł), 72hr (36zł), and weekend (24zł) tickets are also available. You cannot board the metro without validating your ticket, but this isn't the case when riding a bus or tram. If a plainclothes police officer catches you without a validated ticket, you will be fined 266zł. Ubers are available in the city, and reliable taxi companies like Glob Cab Taxi (666 009 668).

PRACTICAL INFORMATION

Tourist Offices: Old Town (Rynek Starego Miasta 19/21/21a; open daily May-Sept 8am-7pm, Oct-Apr 8am-6pm)

Banks/ATMs/Currency Exchange: ATMs are found throughout the city at most banks and by the arrival terminal at the airport. Use ATMs instead of currency exchanges at the airport. In the city, currency exchanges are known as "kantors," some of which give better rates than ATM machines. Avoid kantors with English signs and those in touristy areas. The kantors in Złoty Tarasy and Arkadia shopping malls offer reasonable rates.

Post Offices: Poczta Polska, and two branches are located near to aleje Jerozolimskie, right next to the Palace of Culture and Science.

Internet: Most cafés, restaurants, and fast food restaurants have free Wi-Fi available. This website (www.wifispc.com/poland/mazowieckie/warsaw) provides a map of all the available Wi-Fi hotspots in the city.

BGLTQ+ Resources: Although Poland's government doesn't offer many legal rights and protections for the BGLTQ+ community, Warsaw is generally considered an BGLTQ+ friendly city. Here are some resources:

- Counseling for BGLTQ+ people at the offices of the Campaign Against Homophobia (ul. Solec 30A; 22 423 64 38; kph.org.pl; bezpieczny@kph.org.pl)
- Poland-wide BGLTQ+ helpline Lambda Warszawa (22 628 52 22; open M, W, Th 6pm-10pm, Tu-F 6pm-9pm)

EMERGENCY INFORMATION

Emergency Number: 112; Poland Tourist Emergency Hotline (22 278 77 77 and 608 599 999; open daily 8am-6pm, June-Sept 8am-10pm)

Police: Komenda Główna Policji (Puławska 148/150; 22 621 02 51)

US Embassy: There is a US Embassy in Warsaw (al. Ujazdowskie 29/31; 22 504 2000; open M-F 8:30am-5pm).

Rape Crisis Center: The Feminoteka Foundation serves as Poland's primary rape crisis helpline, providing legal and psychological support to victims of all kinds of violence (731 731 551 (helpline/support), 720 908 974 (admin); open Tu-Th 1pm-7pm). The foundation is based at ul. Mokotowska 29a, nearby plac Zbawiciela (open M-F 11am-7pm).

Hospitals:
- Lux Med. Al. Jerozolimskie 65/79 (Nowogrodzka 45; 22 33 22 888 (general hotline); open M-F 7am-8pm)

Pharmacies: Pharmacies are identifiable by the green cross on or protruding from their façade, and are called aptekas in Polish.
- Apteka Mirowska (pl. Mirowski 1; 22 620 02 66; open daily 24hr)

ACCOMMODATIONS

▨ OKI DOKI HOSTEL ($)

Pl. Dąbrowskiego 3; 22 828 01 22; www.okidoki.pl; reception open 24hr

Although it's the only hostel in Warsaw to be recognized as a member of Europe's Famous Hostels, Oki Doki doesn't have any airs about it whatsoever. The rooms are homey, the bar, where you'll find 5 zł (!) beers during happy hour, is always packed and in high spirits, and the nightly events are well-attended and welcoming. What's more, when you check in, you'll receive an Oki Doki wristband that entitles you to discounts at restaurants, bars, and sights across the city. Suffice it to say, the hostel, which is just a street away from a metro station, is a backpacker's wet dream.

i Dorms from 29 zł, doubles from 128 zł, singles from 100 zł; reservation recommended; Wi-Fi; BGLTQ+ friendly; no wheelchair accessibility; linens, towels included

EMKA HOSTEL ($$)

Kopernika 3; 22 657 20 04; www.emkahostel.com; reception 24hr

Unlike the famed astronomer, Nicolaus Copernicus, whose initials (MK in Polish) give the hostel its name, EmKa won't change the way you think about the universe, but it will provide you with a comfortable stay and a rather convenient location. Although not unique, the hostel does have clean bedrooms, a large common space, and incredibly spacious bathrooms—what more could you ask for? The hostel also makes navigating Warsaw a trouble-free experience, with the **Nowy Świat metro,** the cheap eats-lined **ul. Foksal,** and the alternative nightlife strip **Smolna** all just a 3min. walk away.

i Dorms from 50 zł, doubles from 200 zł, singles from 140 zł; reservation recommended; Wi-Fi; BGLTQ+ friendly; limited wheelchair accessibility; linens, towels included

WARSAW DOWNTOWN HOSTEL ($)

Wilcza 33; 22 629 35 76; www.warsaw-downtown.pl; reception open 24hr

You can tell a lot of effort has been put into this place to make it as warm and inviting as possible. In the common spaces, blackboards display the schedule of daily hostel-organized events, posters highlight staff recommendations for things to do in the city, and two separate maps document the hometowns of previous guests as well as those of current ones. The rooms are clean and each has a view of a quaint courtyard. It's very difficult to fault this hostel, but thanks to our millennial cynicism, not impossible: the rooms are just a little small.

i Dorms from 42 zł; reservation recommended; BGLTQ+ friendly; no wheelchair accessibility; Wi-Fi; reservation recommended; linens, towels included; kitchen

CULTURE

CHOPIN CONCERTS IN ŁAZIENKI PARK

Chopin Statue in Łazienki Park; 22 506 00 24; www.lazienki-krolewskie.pl/en/wydarzenia/koncerty-chopinowskie-2; summer concerts Su at noon and 4pm

While women around the world be shoppin', Varsovians be Chopin. More specifically, they be Chopin in Łazienki Park, which, every Sunday at noon and 4pm, hosts a free Chopin concert to celebrate the city's prodigal son. Appropriately held right next to the park's Chopin monument, the concerts are packed with people eager to hear some of the freshest beats and dirtiest drops in all of classical music. You can come and go as you like, although if you want a good place to sit, it's best to arrive early. And if you find such a place, it's likely that there won't be much shade, so definitely bring some sunblock, a hat, and a book of Chopin insults so you can throw some shade of your own.

i Free; wheelchair accessible

SOHO FACTORY

Mińska 25; 22 323 19 00; www.sohofactory.pl; hours vary

Frustrated by the lack of a dedicated artistic area in Warsaw, a group of creatives decided to repurpose an old manufacturing plant and turn it into a cultural hub. Today, SOHO Factory is the permanent home of many design, film-production, and publishing firms, and holds a variety of cultural events on a biweekly to monthly basis. The factory's center is often used as a gallery space, most famously displaying a 21m nude balloon sculpture of famed Polish artist Pawel·Althamer in 2012. With the exception of the **Neon Museum** and a few modern art sculptures scattered around the place, there isn't much to see if you're not here to check out a specific event. Keep an eye on the SOHO Factory Facebook page for all the latest goings-on.

i Events may be ticketed; limited wheelchair accessibility

LANDMARKS

PALACE OF CULTURE AND SCIENCE

Pl. Defilad 1; 22 656 76 00; www.pkin.pl; observation deck open daily 10am-8pm

As if a Soviet puppet government weren't enough, Stalin also decided to gift Poland the enormous Palace of Culture and Science. Constructed in the early 1950s, the building is the tallest in the country, the center of the city, and a source of mixed feelings among locals. Some see the palace as a painful reminder of communism—others are willing to say "history shmistory" and simply enjoy its malls, cinemas, theaters, and museums. Nonetheless, just about every person in Poland would agree that a trip to the Palace's observation deck is a must. From the 42nd story, you'll receive panoramic views of the city that make even a place as ordinary-looking as Warsaw seem spectacular.

i Admission 20 zł, reduced 15 zł; wheelchair accessible

ROYAL CASTLE

Pl. Zamkowy; 22 355 51 70; www.zamek-kro-lewski.pl; open summer M-W 10am-6pm, Th 10am-8pm, F-Sa 10am-6pm; Su 11am 6pm; winter Tu-Sa 10am-4pm, Su 11am-4pm

Destroyed by the Germans during World War II, the Royal Castle, while still containing many of its original furnishings, is almost entirely reconstructed. It still looks impressive, but you can tell that it's just not the real deal. The castle's most memorable rooms involve either exceedingly opulent rococo décor or gigantic paintings in ornate, gilded frames. Additionally, the series of video exhibits on the castle's turbulent twentieth-century-existence—like the two Rembrandts downstairs—is deeply fascinating. But beyond such features, you'll find that many rooms are quite ordinary. But if this isn't the first palace you've seen in Europe, then t you won't lose any sleep over passing.

i Admission 30 zł, reduced 20 zł, free on Su; audio guides 17 zł, reduced 12 zł; last entry 1hr before closing; wheelchair accessible

MUSEUMS

⬚ CSW ZAMEK UJAZDOWSKI (UJAZDOWSKI CASTLE CENTRE FOR CONTEMPORARY ART)

Jazdów 2; 22 628 12 71; www.u-jazdowski.pl; open Tu-W noon-7pm, Th noon-9pm, F-Su noon-7pm

Situated on a hill overlooking Łazienki Park, this sixteenth-century Baroque castle turned contemporary art gallery emphasizes interdisciplinary forms of art, hosting everything from video installations to experimental theater performances. When you purchase your ticket, you're given a guidebook that contains at least a paragraph worth of information on every single piece in the gallery. The book's effect on your experience at the gallery is transformative. As soon as these challenging and abstruse works are contextualized and explained by critics and sometimes the artists themselves, the gallery becomes an immensely different invaluable experience.
i Admission 12 zł, reduced 6 zł; wheelchair accessible

POLIN MUSEUM OF THE HISTORY OF POLISH JEWS

Anielewicza 6; 22 471 03 01; www.polin.pl; open M 10am-6pm, W 10am-8pm, Th-F 10am-6pm, Sa-Su 10am-8pm

Built on the site of the former **Warsaw Ghetto,** this museum provides a comprehensive look at the history of the Jewish community in Poland. Consisting of eight galleries, the core exhibition not only gives insight into the evolution of social, political, and religious components of Jewish life, but also explores the nature of the anti-Semitism and persecution that Jews faced for centuries prior to the **Holocaust.** The exhibits are often confusing to navigate, making the audio guide (10 zł) a very worthwhile expenditure. While some may find the museum a little dry and overwhelming, anyone with an active interest in Jewish or European history will find themselves endlessly engaged.
i Admission 25 zł, reduced 15 zł; audio guide 10 zł; last entry 2hr before closing; wheelchair accessible

OUTDOORS

THE FILM SUMMER CAPITAL

Various locations across the city; 22 826 83 11; www.filmowastolica.pl; occurs daily late June-late August

It's common knowledge that the only people who like watching movies indoors are agoraphobes and those whose faces are too hideous to be seen in the light of day. With this in mind, Warsaw's annual Film Summer Capital festival is the perfect opportunity to prove that you don't have any intense fears and that your face is, at the very least, not hideous, but just plain old ugly. From late June until the end of August, various parks around the city will host free film screenings daily. Historically, the festival has had an incredibly diverse program, ranging from cult classics to animation to various subgenres of Chinese cinema.
i Free; wheelchair accessible

FOOD

KROWARZYWA BURGER ($)

Hoża 29/31, Marszałkowska 27/35A; www.
krowarzywa.pl; open daily noon-11pm

It says something about the quality of
Krowarzywa that it's not only one of the
top vegan restaurants in the city, but one
of the best burger joints as well. Now
if we could only figure out what it says
about the quality, then everything would
make sense. But we're tempted to guess
that it means that these vegan burgers are
really, really good. At least, our experience
there would indicate as much. With six
different kinds of patties available, four of
which are gluten-free, vegans, for possibly
the first time in their lives, are spoilt for
choice. Beyond the vegan components,
the burger buns are toasted and warm,
and once the patty is in place, dolloped
with a healthy dose of fresh garnishing.

i Entrées from 13.50 zł; vegan and vegetarian
options available; wheelchair accessible

ZAPIEKANKI REGIONALNE AND
BUBBLE WAFFLE ($)

Chmielna 2; www.bubblewaffle.com; ZR open
M-Th 11am-11pm, F-Sa 11am-2am, Su
noon-2am; BW open M-W 9am-10pm, Th-Su
9pm-midnight

Hey wise guy, you want the perfect fast
food-dessert combo? Well then, listen
up and listen good, because what you're
going to do is this: head down ul. Foksal
until you find a place called Zapiekanki
Regionalne. Bright rainbow colors on
the awning—you can't miss it. Once
you're in, order a traditional Polish pizza
kind of dish. A toasted baguette, some
mushrooms, cheese, some toppings—
bada bing bada boom, it's a *zapiekanki*.
Then without even giving it a moment's
thought, go next door to Bubble Waffle—
and guess what, genius? You're going to
order a bubble waffle. It's ice cream inside
a waffle with bubbles on it. But what do
you think's inside the bubbles? Whatever
you want. Chocolate sauce, strawberries,
bananas—the sky's the limit. Are the
calories worth it? Buddy, these things
could give me a freakin' heart attack and
they'd be worth it.

i Large zapiekanki from 10 zł, small from
7, bubble waffle from 15 zł; wheelchair
accessible

BAR PRASOWY ($)

Marszałkowska 10/16; 666 353 776; www.
prasowy.pl; open M-F 9am-8pm, Sa-Su 11am-
7pm

One of the few communist-era relics that
people cherish, milk bars are no-frills
canteens that serve the cheapest Polish
cuisine in town. They're a requisite
experience for any visitor to Warsaw and
thus the question remains, which is the
best one to visit? And while we're no
experts, the common consensus amongst
Varsovians is that Bar Prasowy is the
milkiest bar of them all. Although recently
revamped, it retains its original charm,
possessing a similar atmosphere to a classic
American diner. And with everything
under 10 zł, you could eat three very
filling meals for the price of a single dish
at most restaurants in the city.

i Entrées from 5 zł; vegetarian options available; wheelchair accessible

GOŚCINIEC POLSKIE PIEROGI ($$)

Podwale 19; 22 400 79 23; www.gosciniec.
waw.pl; open M-Th 11am-10pm, F-Sa 11am-
10pm, Su 11am-10pm

There's a famous statistic that states,
in New Zealand, there are four sheep
to every person. And in Poland, we
imagine that something similar is true of
dumplings, which, over here, are known
as *pierogies*. You'll find these little guys
everywhere, and truthfully the quality
is fairly consistent. After all, they're
just different combinations of meat,
vegetables, and potatoes steamed inside
a dough casing. That being said, if you're
interested in chomping on some 'rogis in
a scenic setting, then Gosciniec, a quaint
place with walls featuring murals, is tough
to beat.

i Nine pierogies from 19.90 zł; vegetarian options available; limited wheelchair accessible

NIGHTLIFE

▨ PLAC ZABAW AND BARKA

Podgórska 16; 796 122 108; PZ open M-Sa 11am-2am, Su 11am-midnight; BarKa open M-Th 11am-midnight, F-Sa 11am-6am, Su 11am-midnight

There aren't many better ways to spend a summer's night than at Plac Zabaw and BarKa. Right next to the **Vistula River,** Plac Zabaw is a beer garden-esque area filled with bars and food trucks, which overlooks **BarKa,** a floating café-club on the river itself. Both places are operated by the same people who run the perennially hip **Plan B,** and although the crowd's a little more diverse in terms of age, the atmosphere's just as lively and vibrant. Start off your night at Plac Zabaw, sitting on the riverbank with a beer in one hand, a burger in the other. Once you're sufficiently well-fed and tipsy, head down to BarKa, where the DJ's warm, tropical house will take care of you until sunrise.

i Beer 10zł, cocktails from 15 zł

CLUB LUZZTRO

Aleje Jerozolimskie 6; www.luzztro.com; open W-Th 10pm-10am, F-Sa midnight-2pm

A more alternative option to the mainstream clubs that line **Mazowiecka,** Luzztro is a dark and grimy venue filtered through pulsing red hues. A comically large disco ball hangs above the main house-focused dance floor—a Persian-carpeted platform. Head upstairs to find various nooks and crannies fitted with red leather couches, or slip off to the side and enter a no-frills, black-walled room blasting punishing techno. It's not for everyone, but if you're tired of dancing to radio pop while surrounded by a bunch of dudes who looked like they just stepped off the set of *Entourage,* then Luzztro might just be the place for you.

i Cover 20 zł, shots 10 zł, cocktails from 22 zł

POLAND ESSENTIALS

VISAS

Poland is a member of the European Union, and the Schengen area. Citizens from Australia, Canada, New Zealand, the US, and many other non-EU countries do not require a visa for stays up to 90 days. However, if you plan to spend time in other Schengen countries, note that the 90-day period applies to all Schengen countries.

MONEY

Poland uses the złoty (zł or PLN as currency). Currency exchanges are known as "kantors," and those with signs in English, often located in airports or touristy areas, should be avoided. The best are those that advertise the "buy" and "sell" rates, which let you calculate exactly how much you will receive. To find out what out-of-network or international fees your credit or debit cards may be subjected to, call your bank.

Tipping: In restaurants, tips are not included in the bill, so it's customary to tip 10% or 15% if the service was exceptional. Be careful with saying "Thank you" to the waiter when they collect the bill, as it means that you don't want any change back. In taxis, tipping is not expected, but you can tip 10% for good service. ATMs in Poland can be found in shopping malls, banks and most public spaces in urban areas.

SAFETY AND HEALTH

Drugs and Alcohol: The minimum age to purchase alcohol is 18. The legal blood alcohol content (BAC) for driving is under 0.02%, which is significantly lower than the US limit of 0.08%. The possession of any quantity of drugs, including marijuana, is penalized with up to 3-years imprisonment.

PORTUGAL

Although it's not even half the size of Idaho, Portugal crams thousands of years of rich history—from the Celts to the Romans to the Moors—into its 500-mile sliver of paradise on the westernmost edge of Europe. Medieval cathedrals rub shoulders with Islamic architecture and Roman ruins crumble beneath Neoclassical palaces, all scattered along the country's craggy coastlines and otherworldly forests. Less clogged by tourists than its Spanish neighbor— and really all of Western Europe— Portugal is the unsung hero of the Iberian Peninsula, a budget traveler's dream. Lisbon and Porto stand out as the country's self-confident cultural capitals, but every region of Portugal has its own special charms. Bask in the somber fado music of the capital, revel in the legendary Lagos nightlife, and soak in the colorful turrets of Sintra's epic hillside palace. Wherever you find yourself in Portugal, the country's saltwater cuisine will be waiting—salt cod, fried eel soup, seafood stew, and the ubiquitous can of sardines will follow you everywhere. Of course, there are other options like Porto's infamous *francesinha* (a "sandwich" with half a dozen kinds of meat, cheese, and an egg, all drenched in a gravy-like sauce) and Lisbon's high-demand *pastéis de nata* (mini egg custards). Just remember to wash it all down with a glass of the Douro's silky port wine. With a full belly and happy heart, find yourself a romantic *miradouro* (viewpoint) and allow yourself to be enveloped by the plucky, glamorous, irresistible heart of Portugal.

CASCAIS

Coverage by **Joseph Winters**

Leave it to the king to spoil a perfectly good secluded summer getaway. In the early nineteenth century, Cascais was a rural fishing village with rugged character, wild and scenic beaches, and lots of local commerce. Then, when King Luís I decided to make the city his summer hideaway, outfitting the village with opulent mansions and luxurious gardens, Portuguese nobility—and later, mere mortals—began flocking to the city in the hopes of finding their own slice of "the king's beach." Cascais remains one of the most popular destinations for Lisbon daytrippers, who descend upon the city to sunbathe, inhale the sea breeze, and slurp up dozens of açaí bowls (we counted at least six açaí joints within a minute of each other). Visitors can spend the day exploring the cozy historic center, sauntering through the peacock-filled Parque de Marechal Carmona and visiting the park's many museums, or biking between far-flung beaches like the Praia do Guincho. The combination of history, fantastic infrastructure, and nature make Cascais an obligatory stop for tourists looking for something a bit more laid-back than the bustle of cosmopolitan Lisbon.

ORIENTATION

From the Cascais train station, it's a short walk southwest towards the beach to arrive in the historic city center. En route to the ocean, you'll pass through the historic city center, filled with lots of restaurants, souvenir shops, and a several options for accommodations. Along the water is an esplanade that wraps around the coast, all the way west to the scenic **Praia do Guincho** and east towards Lisbon, passing through **Estoril** and beyond (a good walking half-daytrip). West of the historic city center, just above the esplanade and north of the Cascais marina is the **Bairro dos Museus** (museum district) and the **Parque Marechal Carmona,** Cascais' central green space and home to a handful of small museums, including the Museu das Histórias Paula Rego and the Museu do Mar. The central **Pr. 5 de Outubro** (on the Av. Dom Carlos I) is where the **Cascais Visitor Center** is, as well as several late-night dining and drinking options.

ESSENTIALS

GETTING THERE

The easiest way to get to Cascais is via train. Take the metro green line to Cais do Sodré and from there, switch to the rail network (Comboios de Portugal) towards Cascais (40min., €2.50 on a Viva Viagem card—you'll pay €0.50 if you don't already have one). You'll be deposited at the Cascais train station, just northeast of the city center, and a 3min. walk from the city center. You can also drive to Cascais—more of a hassle than the train, but convenient if you want to tour the remoter regions of the Sintra-Cascais National Park. From Lisbon, take the meandering N6 route or the A5 westward. And, if you're committed to taking the bus, it runs between Lisbon and Cascais, but takes longer than the train (1hr) and tickets are comparably priced. Look for the orange Linha de Cascais signs in departing from Pr. Martim Moniz.

If you're coming from Sintra-Cascais National Park, buses are good for traveling within the park. From Sintra, Colares, Cabo da Roca, and other origins north of Cascais, look for route 403, which stops frequently in every village between Sintra and Cascais, or take the more direct 417. The route takes less than an hour and costs €4.25.

GETTING AROUND

Cascais is easily walkable. The train station, the city center, a park, and beaches are all located within 10min. of each other. Some of Cascais' most beautiful beaches, however, are up to 8km from downtown—to reach these, it's best to rent a bike or take public transit. Look for the 415 or 405 buses from the Cascais bus station to reach the western Praia do Guincho. For the eastern Praia de Carcavelos, take the train headed towards Lisbon and get off at Carcavelos. For bike rentals, check Bicas Bike. From the Cascais Visitor Center, bikes can be checked out from 8am-7pm. Note that these bicycles have no gear switch or locks, and they do not come with helmets. Better bikes can be found at a rental service on the marina (€4.50/hr or €10/4hr).

PRACTICAL INFORMATION

Tourist Offices: The Cascais Visitor Center has a shop, a ticket office for some surrounding museums, an auditorium for cultural events and presentations, and an interactive table touchpad with information on what to do in and around the city (Pr. 5 de Outubro; 912 034 214; visitcascais.com; open daily May 1-Sept 30 9am-8pm, Oct 1-Apr 30 9am-6pm).

Banks/ATMs/Currency Exchange: ATMs in Cascais are clustered around the main shopping area and along Avenida D. Carlos I. There are also several options near the train station. Full banks are also concentrated near the train station. Look for BPI, Millennium BCP, or the handy-dandy Multibanco sign.
- Millennium BCP Cascais: R. Sebastião José de Carvalho e Melo 6; 21 112 6990; millenniumbcp.pt; open M-F 8:30am-3:30pm
- Banco BPI: R. Dra. Iracy Doyle, 6B; 21 482 3580; www.bancobpi.pt; open M-F 8:30am-3pm

Post Offices: Your trusty CTT stop is a short walk north of the beach in a residential neighborhood. There is a smaller location nearer the train station, as well.
- CTT main branch: Av. Ultramar 2; 21 482 7281; www.ctt.pt; open M-F 9am-6pm
- CTT train station: Av. Marginal 9302; 214 827 273; www.ctt.pt; open M-F 9am-6pm

Public Restrooms: Rejoice! Unlike some Portuguese cities, Cascais is replete with bathroom options. Aside from the toilets you'll find in any of the inexpensive museums in the Bairro dos Museus circuit, you'll find a public WC in the shopping complex at the marina, near the Ponta da Bombeira, and on the western outskirts of the Parque Marechal Carmona.

Internet: Cascais generously offers over a dozen Wi-Fi hotspots throughout the city and on several of its beaches. Look for tall poles reading Cascais Wi-Fi. There's a convenient hotspot outside the Museu do Mar and another in the center of the Parque Marechal Carmona.

BGLTQ+ Resources: The nearest BGLTQ+ resource options are in Lisbon. Try ILGA, the city's oldest NGO fighting for equality without regard to sexual identity (R. dos Fanqueiros, 38; 218 873 918; ilga-portugal.pt; open M-F 10am-7pm).

EMERGENCY INFORMATION

Emergency Number: 112

Police: In case of an emergency, call the Portuguese emergency number (112) or get in touch with the local PSP. The police office is in the historic downtown, off the main road leading towards the water. Facing the water, look left while on Alameda dos Combatentes da Grande Guerra.
- Tourist square: Largo Mestre Henrique Anjos; 214814067; www.psp.pt

US Embassy: The nearest US Embassy is in Lisbon (Av. das Forças Armadas 133C; 21 727 3300; pt.usembassy.gov; open M-F 8am-5pm).

Rape Crisis Center: The nearest rape crisis center is in Lisbon, a part of APAV, the Portuguese Association for Victim Support.
- GAV Oeiras: Esquadra de Oeiras da PSP, R. do Espargal 18; 21 454 02 57; apav.pt; open M-F 10am-6pm

Hospitals: The closest large hospital is CUF Cascais, but a taxi ride to the more popular Hospital de Cascais Dr. José de Almeida might be worth the trouble.
- Hospital de Cascais Dr. José de Almeida: Estr. Militar, Alcabideche; 21 465 3000; www.hospitaldecascais.pt; open daily 24hr
- CUF Hospital Cascais: R. Fernão Lopes 60; 21 114 1400; www.saude-cuf.pt; open daily 24hr

Pharmacies: There is a 24hr pharmacy just west of the train station on the highway leading to the waterfront. Other than that, the historic city center is home to a number of smaller pharmacies offering daytime services.
- Farmácia Marginal Lda.: Pr. Dr. Francisco Sá Corneiro 1; 21 484 9440; www.farmaciamarginal.pt; open daily 24hr

ACCOMMODATIONS

🏨 LJMONADE HOSTEL AND SUITES ($)

R. Manuel Joaquim Gama Machado, 4-6; 916 880 056; www.ljmonade.com; reception open 8am-11pm

Despite questionable spelling skills, Ljmonade Hostel and Suites offers more services to guests than a quality mid-range hotel. Sunday night is Sunset Sunday: they offer free glasses of wine and a group field trip to the westernmost tip of Europe. There are bike trips on Fridays, occasional hikes in the **Sintra-Cascais Natural Park,** and Friday happy hours (more free wine). You can also pay for a kite surfing lesson, horseback rides, and more. Dorms are a bit unconventional—no bunks, just a barracks-style line of beds—but spacious, and come with plenty of charging space. And, true to their name, the buffet-style Ljmonade breakfast comes with fresh, tangy lemonade (made daily with fresh ljmons).

i *Dorms from €18, privates from €45; reservations recommended; BGLTQ+ friendly; no wheelchair accessibility; Wi-Fi; breakfast, linens, towels, lockers, luggage storage included; laundry available (wash €5, dry €5)*

CASCAIS BAY HOSTEL ($)

Largo Luis Camões, 38; 218 022 629; www.cascaisbayhostel.com; reception open 9am-9pm

It's not exactly beachside, but if you look closely you can definitely see the nearby **Praia da Ribeira** and maybe a volleyball or two floating through the air—which is close enough for us. Cascais Bay Hostel is right in the thick of the city's historic center, overlooking a popular plaza filled with tourist-trap restaurants. Entering into their second-floor reception (just past a laser hair removal center, in case you're not feeling swimsuit-ready), guests are immediately greeted by a cozy (small) common space, with only four dorm rooms split between two floors. It's a convenient launching point for adventures around Cascais, but visitors hoping to chill inside the hostel might find it a bit crowded. For a rare moment of solitude, enjoy a sea-themed common room with guitars and conga drums, or lounge around on the lush terrace.

i *Dorms from €25; reservation recommended; max stay 14 days; no wheelchair accessibility; Wi-Fi; breakfast, linens, towels, maps, luggage storage included*

SIGHTS
CULTURE

CIDADELA ARTS DISTRICT

Av. Dom Carlos I; 21 481 4300; www.cidadelaartdistrict.com/#cad; establishment hours vary

Part hotel, part ancient military stronghold, and part arts collective, the Cidadela Arts District is a little hard to figure out. As of 2014, the space—found in the courtyard of an ancient citadel—has sought to introduce art into the everyday. Surrounding the courtyard are several galleries, an art magazine's office and first showing room, and even a Portuguese pencil producer. Upstairs, visitors can glimpse the artistic process in one of many open studios. There's also an excellent used bookstore above one of the Arts District's restaurants, which has a surprisingly solid collection of English books in addition their Portuguese collection.

i *Prices vary; limited wheelchair accessibility*

MERCADO DA VILA (VILLAGE MARKET)

R. Padre Moisés da Silva, 29; 21 482 5000; www.cascais.pt; open daily 6:30am-midnight; fish and meat market open Tu 8am-2pm, W 6:30am-3pm, Th-F 8am-2pm, Sa 6:30am-3pm, Su 8am-2pm; flowers, fruits, and vegetables market open Tu 8am-3pm, W 6:30am-3pm, Th-F 8am-4pm, Sa 6:30am-3pm, Su 8am-4pm; mercado saloio (traditional market) open W-Sa 6:30am-2pm

This multi-purpose space west of the train station showcases the best of Cascais, from the fishermen's daily catch to fine dining. An enormous covered plaza is flanked by butchers, vegetable farmers, bakeries, and florists, and the adjacent open-air plaza houses a collection of casual restaurants and bars. The diversity of offerings means there's always something going on at the Mercado da Vila, from early morning to late(ish) at night. Check the market schedule for the best days to visit, as well as the monthly theme; in the summer, they've held special markets centered around chocolate, sardines, and even craft beer.

i *Prices vary; wheelchair accessible*

LANDMARKS

BOCA DO INFERNO (HELL'S MOUTH)

Av. Rei Humberto II de Itália, 642; open daily 24hr

"Hell's Mouth" may be a bit overkill, but this natural rock formation just over a kilometer away from the center of Cascais is an impressive sight. It's an outcropping of an arch carved from rock, formed by eons of waves crashing against the cliff. Summer visitors will see the water gently lapping at the opening, but winter storms unleash a fearsome force through the arch, launching powerful waves high into the air. Thankfully, modern visitors can enjoy the waves from the shelter of a classy restaurant, or at least from high above from a protected walkway. Fun fact: in 1930, a magician named Aleister Crowley faked his death at the Boca do Inferno, only to reappear three weeks later at an magic exhibition in Berlin.

i *Free; limited wheelchair accessibility*

MUSEU CONDES DE CASTRO GUIMARÃES (CONDES DE CASTRO GUIMARÃES MUSEUM)

Av. Rei Humberto II de Itália, Parque Marechal Carmona; 214 815 304; www.cascais.pt; open T-Su 10am-1pm and 2pm-5pm

As if the count couldn't make up his mind on a single style, Castro Guimarães included architectural influences from across the spectrum in his fanciful nineteenth-century mansion: Byzantine domes, Manueline arcades, Italian verandas, Indo-Portuguese cabinets, some Gothic inspiration, and a room painted with shamrocks just for good measure (actually by request from the original Irish owner). Found near the southern edge of the **Parque Marechal Carmona**, the Museu Condes de Castro Guimarães is less a museum and more of an open window into the life of some of the earliest elites to erect lavish vacation homes in Cascais. Be sure to check out the turret room, which holds a host of archaic weaponry, including a very rusty combat sword from the fifteenth century.

i *Admission €4, students €2; pre-book tours by phone (groups only); limited wheelchair accessibility; part of the Bairro dos Museus circuit (day pass €13, 3-day pass €19)*

MUSEUMS

MUSEU DAS ARTES PAULA REGO (PAULA REGO ART MUSEUM)

Av. da República, 300; 21 482 6970; www. casadashistoriaspaularego.com; open Tu-Su 10am-6pm

Housed in a building designed by Pritzker Prize-winning architect Eduardo Souto de Moura, this art museum in the heart of Cascais' **Bairro dos Museus** (Neighborhood of Museums) showcases the life's work of **artist Paula Rego.** Born in Lisbon in 1935, Rego has been showered with a multitude of decorations, including honorary doctorate degrees from eight universities like RISD and Oxford, as well as awards from the Queen of England and the President of Portugal. With a collection of over 500 paintings, etchings, and drawings, the Museu das Artes Paula Rego showcases the artist's passion for Portuguese culture, storytelling, and reinterpreting history through art. The engravings are especially impressive, with three-dimensionality that borders on lifelike.

i *Admission €5, students €2.50; last entry 5:30pm; limited wheelchair accessibility*

MUSEU DO MAR REI D. CARLOS (KING D. CARLOS OCEANIC MUSEUM)

R. Júlio Pereira de Mello; 21 481 5906; www.cascais.pt; open Tu-F 10am-5pm, Sa-Su 10am-1pm and 2pm-5pm

Long before it was a hip summer residence for Portuguese royalty, Cascais had a history intertwined with the sea. The Museu do Mar digs way back into this background, combining oceanic natural history with firsthand portraits of fishermen who helped build Cascais. Named in honor of D. Carlos I, who was himself an avid fisherman and admirer of the sea, the small museum includes a diverse array of water-themed exhibitions. There's a History of the Ocean room with stuffed seabirds and the 15-foot-long jaw bone of a fin whale, a Seafaring and Navigation collection with scale models of eighteenth-century fishing vessels, and a room dedicated to D. Carlos that features a frightening—but aptly-named—goblinfish.

i Admission €3, students €1.50; pre-booked tours only; wheelchair accessible

OUTDOORS

◩ PRAIA DO GUINCHO (GUINCHO BEACH)

Parque Natural Sintra-Cascais; www.cascais.pt; open daily 24hr

Full of thrashing waves, strong winds, and jagged rocks, the Praia do Guincho isn't exactly a tranquil sunbathers' beach. In its heyday, this remote strip of sand was the host of the World Surfing Championships; most of its current visitors come with long hair and wetsuits, their surfboards under one arm, ready to ride some waves, bro. Grab a board for yourself, or enjoy the entertainment as newbies try (unsuccessfully) to find their balance. To get there, we highly recommend biking; there's a single-use bike lane the whole 8km between Cascais and Praia do Guincho, and the views along the way may be even more breathtaking than the beach itself. Sign up online for MobiCascais (€4/day) or try one of the city's rental services (usually €10/day). The 405 or 415 bus from Cascais also makes frequent trips to Praia do Guincho (€1).

i Free; no wheelchair accessibility

PARQUE MARECHAL CARMONA (MARECHAL CARMONA PARK)

Av. Rei Humberto II; www.cascais.pt; open daily Nov-Mar 8:30am-5:45pm, open daily Apr-Oct 8:30am-7:45pm

Watch your feet—you'll find roosters and peacocks while wandering through Cascais' central public park. Since the sixteenth century, the grounds currently making up the Parque Marechal Carmona have passed through many wealthy hands, with each owner adding additional flourishes of romanticism to the space. Today, the park has rose gardens, children's play areas, a duck pond, and half a dozen museums (part of the **Bairro dos Museus** network of Cascais museums). If you're lucky, you may get to watch a traditional round of *petanca* or *chinquilho* in an area reserved specifically for these games. On Saturday mornings, the Parque Marechal Carmona hosts an organic farmer's market (8am-2pm).

i Free; limited wheelchair accessibility

FOOD

◩ CAFÉ GALERIA HOUSE OF WONDERS ($$)

Largo da Misericordia, 53; 911 702 428; open daily 8am-10pm

We usually don't use words like "crave-worthy" or "creative" or even "good" to describe buffet dinners, but Cascais' House of Wonders is all that and more: their spread of vegetable-heavy sides (roasted sweet potato salad, smoky mushroom pilaf, pomegranate baba ghanouj) and seasonal mains (eggplant curry, sweet potato falafel) may make for your best meal in Portugal—for under €15 (€9.75 if you go for lunch). The "Café Galeria" takes has four dining spaces within two adjacent buildings (rooftop terrace, café, buffet room, and an additional sit-down dining room), each decorated with handwritten messages. "All about sharing and tasting," reads one sign near the buffet. In a country where salad usually means dry lettuce (sometimes with a tomato slice!), House of Wonders is a beacon of hope for foodies everywhere. Pro tip: get yourself a plate of the silky-smooth hummus, served with *chapati*, baked in-house daily.

i Entrées from €9.75 (café) or €14.75 (restaurant); gluten-free, vegan, and vegetarian options available; limited wheelchair accessibility

CRÊPES DA VILA ($)

Trav. Afonso Sanches, 12b; 21 483 3472;
open Tu-Th 10am-10pm, F 10am-10:45pm,
Sa 10:30am-10:45pm, Su 10:30am-10pm

It's a tough call whether crêpes or açaí bowls dominate as Cascais' #1 cheap lunch fare, usually served up in a beach-themed, Habana-style eatery offering one or the other. Right on the main drag, the locals' choice for crêpes in Cascais is Crêpes da Vila. In addition to the ubiquitous strawberry-Nutella, they also serve cheese and mushroom crêpes, savory ham waffles, granola, muesli, and omelets stuffed with couscous and vegetables. By far the favorite option is a lunchtime special: €5.45 for a soup of the day, their signature savory crêpe, and a house-made drink of choice (usually fruit juice or a smoothie).

i Entrées from €5.45; gluten-free, vegan, and vegetarian options available; no wheelchair accessibility

NIGHTLIFE

SPICY LOUNGE

R. Marques Leal Pancada, 16A; 916 304 983;
open daily 10pm-4am

We're not sure what "#1 Warm-Up Bar" means, but the folks at Spicy Lounge can toot their horn as much as they want, because they've undoubtedly got some of Cascais' best late-night partying. From their small space below a pizzeria, Spicy Lounge puts on loud and sweaty dance parties, featuring local artists and DJ sets, while they serve up a flaming hot selection of craft beers and cocktails (some of which are literally on fire). Check their Facebook page to see when they're hosting their Suruba Music night, a monthly jam session, open to all interested artists.

i No cover, drinks from €4; limited wheelchair accessibility

CROW BAR

Trav. da Misericórdia, 1; 21 403 9164; open Tu-Su 2:30pm-2am

Although nightlife in Cascais is bizarrely dominated by Irish pubs, Crow Bar stolidly holds its ground as a pure metal and rock n' roll bar—no funny business (or shamrocks) allowed. A sign above the bar informs visitors that music requests aren't accepted, "but if you insist, €2 metal, €50 pop, and €100 all the other crap." The menu is similarly intense, including selections like the Valhalla Painkiller (jaeger, fireball, mead) or the Crow Bar Acid Trip (jaeger and pineapple juice), although they may be best known for their comparatively tame espresso martinis. Best plan of action: take whatever the bartender recommends and drink up, no questions asked. And remember to leave a tip; the bartender apparently needs a new tattoo.

i No cover, cocktails from €5; limited wheelchair accessibility

LAGOS

Coverage by **Joseph Winters**

Despite its reputation for raucous nightlife and alluring beaches, Lagos has a lot of important, but easily-overlooked history. Beginning with the Carthaginians, Lagos fell into Roman hands, then to Visigoths, Byzantines, Moors, the Spanish, and finally back to the Portuguese in the 1600s. In its glory days, Lagos was a powerhouse of European trade. It was also home to colonial Europe's very first slave market, found in the downtown Praça do Infante Dom Henrique. The building now houses a museum acknowledging this history. In 1755, a massive earthquake and tsunami leveled most of Lagos, so most of what you'll see downtown has been reconstructed since then. But that doesn't make Lagos's architecture any less impressive: there's Baroque architecture, cobblestone streets, and zigzagging alleyways galore. Perhaps the most exciting part of Lagos lies outside its ancient walls: several of Lagos beaches are world-famous for their crystal waters and natural rock formations. No visit would be complete without taking a walk along the Avenida dos Descobrimentos to the string of beaches starting with the Praia da Batata and culminating in the breathtaking Ponta da Piedade. This sheltered collection of underwater grottos and hidden caves is Lagos's crown jewel, and 40+ tour companies (who, like predatory animals, lie in wait for unwitting tourists as they disembark the regional train) suck in umpteen thousands of tourists here per year. Even still, this is required sightseeing—you'll thank yourself when friends at home ask which edition of Nat Geo your travel photos are from.

ORIENTATION

Walking westward along the beachside **Avenida dos Descobrimentos**, Lagos's largest road, you'll pass the bus terminal and eventually arrive at the **Praça Gil Eanes**. This is the Times Square of Lagos, full of high-end shopping, restaurants, and cafés. From here, sidestreets branch off in every direction, many of which are pedestrian-only, leading to yet more shopping and dining opportunities. A bit further along the Avenida dos Descobrimentos puts you at the **Praça do Infante Dom Henrique**, home to the **Igreja Santa Maria** and the **Mercado de Escravos**, Europe's oldest slave market. Just up the hill from here is Lagos's nightlife neighborhood, roughly along the **Rua Gil Vicente**. Outside the city, continue walking along the Avenida dos Descobrimentos to arrive at Lagos's white sand beaches like the **Praia de Dona Ana** and the **Praia do Camilo.** Eventually the road meets the **Estrada da Ponta da Piedade,** which will lead to—you guessed it—the **Ponta da Piedade,** a group of rock formations along Lagos's coastline: the city's most famous tourist attraction.

ESSENTIALS
GETTING THERE

From the eastern Algarve, trains to Lagos are inexpensive (about €10 from Faro) and reasonably reliable. There are also trains arriving from the north (€24, 5.5hr from Lisbon; €42, 7-8hr from Porto). Surprisingly, fares and travel times by bus from the north are similar.

GETTING AROUND

The easiest way to navigate the historic city of Lagos is by foot, although you'll see some bikes wobbling along the uneven streets. The beaches to the west of the city center are easily accessible by foot, and even the Ponte da Piedade is less than an hour's walk away. If needed, bikes can be rented from many sports shops downtown (try COAST Supply Co. on the R. Cândido dos Reis 58), or you can hire a taxi for around €5 to take you to any of the handful of beaches up to the Ponta da Piedade.

PRACTICAL INFORMATION

Tourist Offices: Praça Gil Eanes (Antigos Paços do Concelho); 282 763 031; www.visitalgarve.pt/en)

Banks/ATMs/Currency Exchange: Banks are plentiful in Lagos, and you'd have to try pretty hard to avoid running into an ATM. Try the Praça de Gil Eanes or Praça do Infante Dom Henrique, or look for the blue and white Multibanco sign.
- Av. dos Descobrimentos 39; 282 770 940; www.bancobpi.pt/particulares; open M-F 8:30am-3pm
- R. da Porta de Portugal 19; 282 770 940; www.santandertotta.pt; open daily 9am-3pm

Post Offices: Look for the red and white of CTT in Lagos' cultural center, surrounded by patches of greenery and public fountains.
- R. da Porta de Portugal 25; 282 770 251; www.ctt.pt; open M-F 9am-6pm

Public Restrooms: In Lagos? A pipe dream. Your best bet is to give in and buy an Americano somewhere. Almost all cafés and restaurants offer free restrooms for customers.

Wi-Fi: There is no public Wi-Fi available in Lagos, but almost all cafés, restaurants, and hostels have their own private networks that you can use after buying something. A cheapskate alternative is to skulk around some of the banks along the Avenida dos Descobrimentos or in the Praça Gil Eanes, trying to find a free network. Word on the street is that Santander Totta is a good bet for password-free internet.

EMERGENCY INFORMATION

Emergency Number: 112
Police:
- PSP: Sítio da Horta do Trigo; 28 278 02 40; www.psp.pt
- GNR: Largo Convento da Glória; 28 277 00 10; www.gnr.pt

Hospitals: Should you need the hospital, it's hard to miss: the Hospital Distrital de Lagos takes up some prime waterfront property at the south end of historic downtown.
- Hospital S.Gonçalo: Av. Dom Sebastião 129; 800 224 424; www.hsglagos.pt; open daily 24hr
- Hospital Distrital de Lagos: R. do Castelo dos Governadores 14; +351 282 770 100; www.sns.gov.pt; open daily 24hr

Pharmacies: Check for pharmacies near the Praça Gil Eanes, as well as along the R. Candido dos Reis. Here are a couple 24hr options:
- Farmácia Ribeiro Lopes: R. Garrett 22; 282 762 830; www.farmacia-barral.com/farmacia-ribeiro-lopes/; open M-Sa 8:30am-midnight, Su 9am-7pm
- Farmácia Silva: R. 25 de Abril 9; 282 762 859; www.sns.gov.pt; open M-F 9am-8pm, Sa 9am-1pm

ACCOMMODATIONS

🏨 OLIVE HOSTEL ($)

R. da Oliveira 67; 915 296 129; reception open 8am-midnight

Not only does Olive Hostel look like someone's home, it actually *feels* like home. Olive Hostel invites you to take *pasteis de nata*, or egg pastries, as well as donuts, wine, beer, chips, and more from their private stash, writing your name on "Honesty" sheets. At the end of your stay, you pay for what you've taken, along with the fee for your room. Other notable features of Olive Hostel include its charming and eclectic décor, featuring lots of potted plants, wooden shoes, and quirky art; two fully-equipped kitchens; and its rooftop Hatha yoga (offered daily for €8).

i Dorms from €15, privates from €45; cash only; reservations recommended; laundry €0.50/garment excluding underwear; Wi-Fi; breakfast, linens, luggage storage, and lockers included; limited wheelchair accessibility

ORANGE3 HOSTEL ($)

R. dos Ferreiros, 34; 928 022 810; reception open 8am-6pm, receptionist on call via WhatsApp

With its serene, green atmosphere, Orange3 offers a more reserved experience than your typical party hostel. But really, who needs a wild night in when you can kick back in the backyard garden, featuring the hostel's very own namesake orange tree? Perched on a hill above Lagos's busiest square, Orange3 offers small but comfortable rooms, lots of private bathrooms, and a small kitchen stocked with all the necessary tools. In a word, staying at Orange3 is downright cozy; despite its petite size, the hostel packs quite a punch in terms of charm.

i Dorms from €16; reservations recommended; BGLTQ+ friendly; Wi-Fi; breakfast, linens, luggage storage, and lockers included; no wheelchair accessibility

SIGHTS
CULTURE

🏫 LAGOS FARMERS MARKET

R. Mercado de Levante 9; open Apr-Oct W 6pm-10pm, Sa 7am-1pm

If you want to see a bit of the real Lagos, head to the Saturday morning market, located in a large warehouse next to the Lagos bus station. Here, farmers and artisans congregate for a few hectic hours of browsing, sampling, and bargaining—it's a foodie's paradise. Among the avocados, mangos, lettuce, onions, and other typical fare, you'll find Algarvian specialties like *nêsperas* (plum-like fruits called "loquats" in English), live snails, roasted figs, fava beans, and much more. Starting in the summer of 2018, there's a second weekly market on Wednesday evenings, highlighting small producers and specialty farmers. Many vendors are certified *biológico* (organic), and several local vendors showcase products like homemade Echinacea extracts or—our favorite—*kombuchá artesanal.*

i Prices vary; wheelchair accessible

MAR D'ESTÓRIAS (SEA OF STORIES)

R. Silva Lopes 30; 282 792 165; www.mardestorias.com; open M-Sa 10am-midnight

"Buy local, buy Portuguese!" reads a sign at the entrance to this three-story treasure trove of Portuguese culture. Instead of the ubiquitous dog tags (unquestionably the worst souvenir known to man), this shop is all about highlighting Portuguese craftspeople. The first and second floors stock handmade soaps, ceramics, baskets, towels, artwork, photography—all made by homegrown artists. We're talking goat milk soap neatly packaged in a sardine tin, small-batch and locally-roasted chocolate bars (also in sardine tins), and gorgeous marble coasters (often depicting sardine tins). On the rooftop terrace, Mar d'Estórias highlights Portuguese food in much the same way. Taste fresh mollusks *Bulhão Pato* style, or try a dessert made from Alcagoita de Aljezur (locally-grown peanuts).

i Restaurant petiscos from €7, entrées from €12; limited wheelchair accessibility

LANDMARKS

🏫 FORTE DA PONTA DA BANDEIRA (FORT OF THE TIP OF THE FLAG)

Cais da Solaria; www.cm-lagos.pt; open Tu-Su 10am-12:30pm and 2pm-5:30pm

In its prime, the Forte da Ponta da Bandeira was one of the most advanced military forts in the Algarve. Along with the Porta da Vila and Governor's Castle bulwarks, it protected the quay of Lagos from invasion. To enter the fort, you'll use a drawbridge that crosses a small moat. Inside is the chapel of Santa Bárbara, coated with tiles from the 1600s. Other rooms house exhibitions honoring everyday military figures whose stories would otherwise be lost to history. While you visit, be sure to climb onto the roof for a great view of the **Praia da Batata (Beach of the Potato)** to the west and views of Lagos to the east. Pro tip: Forte da Ponta da Bandeira is part of the trio of museums including the **Museu Municipal** and the **Forte da Ponta da Bandeira**—buy a ticket for all three for €6.

i Admission €2, students €1; wheelchair accessible

IGREJA DE SANTA MARIA (CHURCH OF SANTA MARIA)

Pr. Infante D. Henrique; 282 762 723; www.paroquiasdelagos.pt; in the summer, open daily 9am-7pm, mass M-Sa 7pm, Su 11:30am

Compared to the gold-plated, marble-coated, diamond-studded churches you're probably familiar with, the Igreja de Santa Maria is on the austere side. Its plain white walls, unremarkable benches (instead of pews), and the modern announcement board at the entrance make it easy to forget that this church was founded in 1498 (although renovated post-earthquake of 1755). Unlike some of its neighbors, this church is used quite a lot (some would say it's used religiously), offering a unique view into the life of a Lagos resident beyond the gelato, seafood, and souvenir shop. Be sure to note the modern art behind the altar—the bright pinks and yellows patterns are almost psychedelic.

i Free; wheelchair accessible

MUSEUMS

🏛 MERCADO DE ESCRAVOS (SLAVE MARKET)

R. da Graça e Praça Infante D. Henrique; www.cm-lagos.pt/; 282 771 724; open Tu-Su 10am-12:30pm and 2pm-5:30pm

Portugal's slave history goes back to the fifteenth century, when slaves from West Africa were first brought to the country for household maintenance and heavy labor. When Brazil was discovered, the Portuguese slave trade boomed, and as many as five million Africans were uprooted and sent to the New World. The Mercado de Escravos is an attempt to engage with this history. Housed on two floors in the central **Praça Infante D. Henrique**, it's a museum with virtual recreations of slave-era Lagos, as well as historical artifacts documenting the creation of Lagos and its early dependence on slavery. The building itself is a part of this history, as it used to be an inspector's office and military prison where Africans were held before being sold.

i Admission €3; limited wheelchair accessibility

MUSEU MUNICIPAL DR. JOSÉ FORMOSINHO (MUNICIPAL MUSEUM OF DR. JOSÉ FORMOSINHO)

R. General Alberto Silveira; www.cm-lagos.pt; 282 762 301; open Tu-Su 10am-12:30pm and 2pm-5:30pm

This is Lagos's only "traditional" museum, and there's not much of a unifying theme: it's full of sacred art, paintings, archeology, minerals, and more. It was founded in 1932 by Dr. Jose Formosinho as part of an effort to raise awareness about Lagos's rich history. Perhaps the most exciting part of the museum is the baroque period **Igreja de Santo Antonio (Church of St. Anthony),** located at the museum's entrance. First built in 1707, it boasts lots of gold, wood carvings, and paintings depicting several strange legends about Santo Antonio, including one in which he reattached a devotee's severed foot (after all but telling him that his foot deserved to be cut off).

i Admission €3, students €1.50; no photography allowed

OUTDOORS

🏞 PONTA DA PIEDADE (MERCY POINT)

Ponta da Piedade

If you're in your Lagos hostel, chances are you've already been offered several dozen tour packages for the legendary Ponta da Piedade, an area just west of downtown Lagos made up of sandstone rock formations, hidden caverns, and ocean-carved tunnels. In fact, there are over 40 companies offering kayak trips and boat rides to the grottos. Taking a kayak or stand-up paddleboard tour is highly recommended, especially if they include add-ons like snorkeling—most tours will leave from central Lagos (buy tickets in advance from a tour company downtown for €15-30). If you're more comfortable on land, it's well worth walking to the Ponta de Piedade—it's less than a three kilometer trek, and will take you along beachside cliffs (there's a trail, don't worry) that offer panoramic views of the ocean before you.

i Ponta da Piedade free, from €15 for kayak/boat tours; no wheelchair accessibility

PRAIA DE DONA ANA (DONA ANA BEACH)

Praia de Dona Ana

The Praia de Dona Ana is one of the most spacious beaches in Lagos, although it's still sheltered enough to feel cozy. At least, you'll probably feel somewhat cozy (or maybe claustrophobic) while vying for an unclaimed patch of sand on this popular beach. Even with the stiff competition, the Praia de Dona Ana's majestic rock formations, vibrant waters, and silky white sand are worth the 2.5-kilometer trek along the **Avenida dos Descobrimentos.** Once you lay out your beach towel, snorkel, sunbathe, and swim to your heart's content. You can even pick up a refresco or two at the beach bar (or climb up the stairs for something more filling).

i Free; no wheelchair accessibility

PRAIA DO CAMILO (CAMILO BEACH)

Praia do Camilo

If you're en route to the Ponta da Piedade, you're unlikely to miss this popular beach (there's even a big restaurant at the top called O Camilo). It's definitely worth a stop—you'll descend a long wooden stairway to arrive at a quaint patch of sand, sheltered by sheer cliffs on both sides. There's a man-made tunnel in the rocks on the left, leading to Camilo Beach's not-so-hidden other half. During peak season, you may need to tiptoe over quite a few half-naked sunbathers to navigate this tiny beach, but if you can tune out your fellow tourists, you'll find Camilo quite serene. Pro tip: bring your own provisions unless you're into overpriced bottled water and food.

i Free; restaurant, bathroom, and parking available; no wheelchair accessibility

FOOD

🖼 CAFÉ GOLDIG ($)

R. Infante de Sagres; open Tu-Sa 9am-4pm

Perched above most of historic downtown Lagos, this tiny café is ideal for a mid morning snack, or pick-me-up espresso. Written in cursive on their awning is the message, "Thank you for being mindful," and it's clear that Café Goldig is also mindful in their food prep. As though transplanted straight from some Californian ecovillage, this café offers homemade and whole grain breads, fresh squeezed juices, vegan pastries, and daily lunch specials like zucchini lasagna or beetroot curry. If you're on the go, they can serve any dish as takeaway, too.

i Entrées from €5; gluten-free, vegan, and vegetarian options available; wheelchair accessible

DOIS IRMÃOS (TWO BROTHERS) ($$)

Tr. do Mar 2; 282 181 100; open daily 11am-midnight

Given its prime location on the **Praça do Infante Dom Henrique,** right on the water, Dois Irmãos isn't exactly what you'd call a "hidden" gem. But it's certainly a gem, if you want to try some of the Algarve's most famous dishes. Offering a long list of broiled, grilled, roasted, and however-else-prepared seafood, an obvious standout is the *Cataplana*. Dois Irmãos's version involves *amêijoas,* and a lot of them. For dessert, the "egg yolk strings with almonds and mint gelato" isn't a bad translation—they actually tease the yolks into thin strings and boil them in sugar syrup. Alongside the ice cream, it makes for quite the sugar rush.

i Entrées from €10; some gluten-free options; wheelchair accessible

NIGHTLIFE

✎ THREE MONKEYS

R. Lançarote de Freitas 26; 282 762 995; www.3monkeys.me.uk; open daily 1pm-2am

There are few better places in Lagos for monkeying around than at this popular bar just off the main square. Besides drinks like the Espresso Martini (Kahlua, vodka, espresso, coffee beans) or the Grenade Depthcharger (jager, tequila, and an entire Red Bull), Three Monkeys is known for their beer bongs. The staff takes count of everyone who completes this "booze Olympics" challenge, along with their nationality. If you stop by, help lead the US to victory! If you want to keep your wits about you, you can definitely take it easy and enjoy the international tunes. Or—if you're a Swedish female—they cordially invite you to partake in some wholesome "naked dwarf wrestling." On second thought, you might want to be drunk for that one.

i No cover, cocktails from €4.50, shots from €3; wheelchair accessible

MELLOW LOCO

R. do Ferrador 9; 913 458 627; open daily 9pm-2am

"Sometimes we're mellow, sometimes we're loco," shrugs the bartender at Mellow Loco. He points to some long-haired surfer bros, whose eyes are glued to a soccer game playing on the bar's flat screen TVs—very mellow, he explains. Later at night, however, you'd better believe this place turns into one of Lagos's most notorious party scenes. After knocking back a couple classic cocktails (Long Island iced tea, caipirinha, sex on the beach, etc.), you're likely to see partygoers pole dancing, jumping half-naked on the tables, or taking not-quite-PG selfies with the bar's cheesy photo booth. Just try not to end up looking like the Mellow Loco mascot by the end of the night (it's a disheveled goose with a smoke in one hand, a beer in the other, and both eyes x'ed out).

i No cover, cocktails from €4; wheelchair accessible

LISBON

Coverage by **Joseph Winters**

Not quite undiscovered, but still nowhere near as overrun as many other European capitals (no thank you, Paris), Lisbon is a historical, culinary, and cultural Shangri-La. With a history touched by the Romans, Moors, and several centuries of devout Catholicism (ultimately leading to a Portuguese Inquisition, yikes), the city boasts a mélange of traditions unlike any other city on the continent. It's got Medieval castles, massive cathedrals, retro trams and *elevadores,* and enough street art to make the whole city feel like one giant, urban museum. Walk through narrow cobblestoned streets following the scent of ultra-fresh *bacalhau* (cod) or *pastéis de nata* (egg pastries), or simply admiring the myriad Baroque, Gothic, and Islamic influences on the city's makeup.

ORIENTATION

Lisbon hugs the northern shore of the **Tagus River** *(Tejo* in Portuguese), and its most spacious square—**Praça do Comércio**—offers a grand view of the water. To the east are the maze-like streets of historical **Alfama, Mouraria,** and the impressive **Castelo São Jorge.** For a more modern experience, high-end shopping and gourmet eateries are located in the popular neighborhoods of **Baixa** and **Chiado,** just northwest of the Praça do Comércio. For nightlife and cheap eats, Lisboners flock to **Barrio Alto** (northwest and up the hill from Baixa, which includes the trendy and LGBT-friendly **Principe Real)** or **Cais do Sodré** (west along the water from the Praça do Comércio), although

Intendente (northeast of Baixa) has recently gained popularity among hipster-types. Going north, you'll travel along the luxurious **Avenida da Liberdade,** which starts in **Rossio Square** and goes to the **Marquês de Pombal** before branching off east and west. **Belém,** home to top-notch *pastéis de nata* (custard pastries), museums, and historical buildings, is a quick train or bus ride west of downtown—you'll pass through up-and-coming **Alcântara** to get there.

ESSENTIALS

GETTING THERE

By plane: Flights land in Lisbon at the Aeroporto de Madrid, just a couple of miles north of downtown. To get into the city, the easiest option is by metro. Take the green line to Alameda, and then change for your final destination is. You can also take an AeroBus. Line 1 runs from 7:30am-11pm and Line 2 operates between 7:45am and 10:45pm. The third option is taxi (from Departures) or Uber (from Terminal 1), but be forewarned of this method's high price tag.

By bus: The main bus terminal Sete Rios is just under 3mi. northwest of the city center, near a zoo. If you're coming from southern Portugal, this will likely be your stop. From here, the metro is your best bet for getting into town. If you're arriving from the north, your point of entry into Lisbon may be Gare do Oriente in the northeastern corner of the city. The terminal is connected to a metro station; hop on to reach your downtown destination. Prices vary from €15-20 for trips ranging from 2.5-4hr.

By train: Trains in Portugal are relatively reliable and more spacious than a typical bus. Options for entry include Gare do Oriente (if arriving from the north), Sete Rios, Entrecampos (between Gare do Oriente and Sete Rios), and Santa Apolónia (usually if you're arriving from the north). Any of these train stations offer easy metro access to downtown Lisbon. There are also two stations, Cais do Sodré and Rossio. Cais do Sodré services Lisbon-Cascais and -Estoril, Rossio goes between Lisbon and Sintra. Prices range from €20-45 depending on the origin city. For full timetables and to buy tickets, check www.cp.pt. If you book tickets in advance, you can receive a discount, and you can also save with a student card.

By boat: There is a boat option called the Transtejo, which offers transport from Cacilhas, Montijo, and Seixal (to Terminal Fluvial Cais do Sodré); from Barreiro (to Terminal Fluvial Terreiro do Paço); and from Trafaria and Porto Brandão (to Estação Fluvial de Belém). Check www.transtejo.pt for a full list of timetables and prices.

GETTING AROUND

Walking is the best way to familiarize yourself with Lisbon's streets. It's about 1.5mi. between the northwestern **Praça do Marquês de Pombal** and the riverfront **Praça do Comercio,** and 1mi. between easterly **Alfama** and the western **Pink Street.** Lisbon has a bike sharing program called Gira with 60 stations around the city. At only €2 a day, it's a good deal if you can plan your daily adventures around the docking stations. The metro is the easiest transit option, and stations are marked with a big letter M. Buy a Viva Viagem card at any metro station and load it up with rides for €1.45 each (tickets also work on the bus, with a 1hr re-entry period for the same ticket). You can buy extended passes within the metro as well (day passes €6.35). Pro tip: if you're planning on investing in a Lisboa Card (tourist card for reduced fare at museums and other sightseeing), you'll get free use of the metro, bus, and tram lines. Taxis are available in Lisbon and can easily be hailed from most of the busier city squares (starting at €3.25, extra for luggage or late-night trips). Uber is also available.

PRACTICAL INFORMATION

Tourist Offices: Lisbon runs a tourist information program called Ask Me Lisboa, with local offices scattered throughout the city, including one in the Lisbon airport. Look for the italic lowercase *i*, often in purple.

- Ask Me Lisboa, Lisboa Story Center: Praça do Comércio, 78-81; 91 408 13 66; www.visitlisboa.com; open daily 10am-10pm
- Ask Me Lisboa, Belém: Mosteiro dos Jerónimos; 91 051 79 81; www.visitlisboa.com; open daily 9am-6pm except 1st and 3rd Su of every month

Banks/ATMs/Currency Exchange: There are plenty of banks and ATMs throughout Lisbon. As a general rule, you should never have to walk more than a couple blocks before seeing a blue and white Multibanco sign.

- Deutsche Bank: Av. António Augusto de Aguiar 23 E/F; 21 780 34 00; www.db.com/portugal; open M-F 8:30am-3pm
- Banco do Portugal: R. do Comércio 148; 21 313 00 00; www.bportugal.pt

Post Offices: CTT, the national postal service, has an office in every Lisbon neighborhood. Check their website to find all locations and look for a red and white sign with a horseman on it.

- Estação dos Correios de Graça/Penha De França: Av. Gen. Roçadas 7A; 21 812 5160; www.ctt.pt; open M-F 9am-6pm
- Estação dos Correios De Arroios: R. Pascoal de Melo 64; 70 726 26 26; www.ctt.pt; open M-F 9am-6pm

Public Restrooms: Savvy Lisbon travelers can find restrooms in most of the city's neighborhoods—check grocery stores, tourist offices, and larger parks. If all else fails, plan your restroom use around your museum visits; they have cleaner bathrooms, anyway.

Internet: There is no city-wide Wi-Fi network in Lisbon, but you can buy nearly complete coverage from third-party Wi-Fi hotspot providers if you need consistent connectivity (from MEO: €10/day or €25/week; from NOS: €4/day or €24.90/30 days). Otherwise, look for free Internet access at any tourist office or nearly any shopping center, as well as passcode-locked Internet access in almost all cafés and restaurants.

BGLTQ+ Resources: ILGA Portugal is a Portuguese BGLTQ+ advocacy organization with headquarters in Lisbon. They offer education services, support for families and individuals, and help organize politically for BGLTQ causes. (ILGA Portugal: R. dos Fanqueiros, 40-1100-231 218 873 918; www.ilga-portugal.pt; open W-Sa 7pm-11pm)

EMERGENCY INFORMATION

Emergency Number: 112

Lisbon Police: The PSP (city police) or GNR (national police) have your back in case you find yourself in trouble.

- PSP: Av. de Moscavide 88, Edifício da PSP; 21 765 42 42; www.psp.pt
- GNR: Avenida do Mar e das Comunidades Madeirenses 13; 29 121 44 60; www.gnr.pt

US Embassy: Av. das Forças Armadas 133C; 21 727 33 00; pt.usembassy.gov/embassy-consulate/lisbon; open M-F 8am-5pm

Rape Crisis Center:

- APAV, Victim Support Portugal: Rua José Estêvão, 135 A, Level 1; 21 358 79 00; www.apav.pt; open M-F 10am-1pm and 2pm-5:30pm
- Associação de Mulheres contra a Violência – AMCV (Association of Women against Violence): R. João Villaret 9; 21 380 21 60; www.amcv.org.pt; open M-F 10am-6pm

Hospitals: Lisbon has several 24hr hospitals. Try these for emergency services:

- Hospital de Santa Maria: Av. Prof. Egas Moniz; 21 780 50 00; www.chln.pt; open daily 24hr
- Hospital da Luz Lisboa (private hospital): Av. Lusíada 100; 21 710 44 00; www.hospitaldaluz.pt/lisboa/en; open daily 24hr

Pharmacies: For all your ointment, salve, and emollient needs, check the streets of Baixa, Chiado, or any populated city square.

- Farmácia Cruz de Malta Lda.: R. Jardim do Tabaco 92-94-96; 21 886 61 26; open M-F 8:45am-7:30pm, Sa 9am-6pm
- Farmácia Nogueira: R. de Alcântara 5-A-B; 21 095 34 95; open M-F 8:30am-7:30pm, Sa 9am-6pm, Su 10am-6pm

ACCOMMODATIONS

🏨 THE INDEPENDENTE ($)

R. de São Pedro de Alcântara; 21 346 13 81; www.theindependente.pt; reception open 24hr

As you enter through the gargantuan arched doors, stepping onto black-and-white marbled tile and surrounded by marble pillars, you may wonder whether you're checking into a castle or a hostel. Besides the rustic bar (furnished with antique cookbooks and artsy chandeliers) and the *two* attached restaurants, the rooms are so spacious you could easily do an Olympic gymnastics routine inside them. While you're not cartwheeling across the room, enjoy a free game system and fully-loaded TV, or bury your nose in the hostel's mini library, located in the ground floor bar. The only thing prettier than the dorms at the Independente are the views you'll see while eating breakfast: airy common spaces offer breathtaking views of **Baixa** and **Bairro Alto.**

i Beds from €15; reservation recommended; max stay 14 nights; BGLTQ friendly; wheelchair accessible; Wi-Fi; breakfast, linens, computers, luggage storage, lockers, included; towels, laundry available; 18+ only

GSPOT HOSTEL ($)

Trav. do Fala-Só 24; 21 825 3344; reception open 24hr

"Once you've found the GSpot, you'll want to come again," is the GSpot's tongue-in-cheek slogan. In fact, everything about this party hostel toes the line between suggestive and explicit. Take the room names, for example: Teabag, Morning Wood, Rusty Trombone, etc. Jokes aside, the amenities are top-notch and include things like nightly family dinners (€7), a bar where you can try specialties like the G-Bomb (€5), and a free pancake breakfast. Plus, they're on track to becoming one of Lisbon's greenest hostels, with LED lighting, low-flow showerheads, and double-flush toilets. Apparently, this is what they tell guests who ask what the name GSpot comes from: "G stands for green," the owner says with wry smile as he softly shuts the door to the Meat Curtains room.

i Dorms from €15; reservation recommended; BGLTQ+ friendly; no wheelchair accessibility; Wi-Fi; breakfast, linens, luggage storage, lockers included; towels, laundry available

INN POSSIBLE LISBON HOSTEL ($)

R. Regedor 3; 21 886 1465; www.innpossiblelisbon.com; reception open 24hr

Get ready for stairs! Inn Possible is carved into a small vertical space on the hill just east of **Baixa,** and navigating it involves a bit of climbing. But despite its name, navigating the many staircases is not very inn-possible. Guests will enjoy a minimalist approach to hostel décor (read: clutter-free) and sparklingly clean facilities, as well as a host of highly thoughtful amenities. Trust us, after a couple of weeks on the road, you'll be grateful for gestures like flip-up charging tables at each bunk and big-enough roll-out lockers under each bed. There's also a chillout room with a kitchen and a third-story TV room with views overlooking the city. Although travelers don't really come here to party, we're not discounting the value of a high-octane game of Scrabble.

i Dorms from €17, privates from €80; reservation recommended; no wheelchair accessibility; Wi-Fi; breakfast, linens, lockers, kitchen, luggage storage included; towels €2, printing €0.20/page; airport transfers €5

URBAN GARDEN HOSTEL

R. Camilo Castelo Branco 2C; 21 193 3211; www.urbangardenhostel.com; reception open 24hr

Part urban garden, mostly party hostel, this single-story backpacker's haven is conveniently located just off the **Avenida da Liberdade,** uptown from the busier **Baixa** and **Chiado** neighborhoods. Since it's somewhat removed from the action of the city, Urban Garden Hostel brings the party to its visitors, offering nightly family dinners (€7) and weekend-ly all-you-can-drink booze fests (€10). Catch your breath between pub crawls and boat parties with the Netflix-connected TV or in the small patch of greenery, located in a small courtyard in the center of the hostel. Rooms are average, breakfast is quality, and the facilities are quite well-kept considering this hostel's low price tag.

i Dorms from €13.50; reservation recommended; BGLTQ+ friendly; no wheelchair accessibility; Wi-Fi; breakfast, linens, luggage storage, lockers included; towels for rent; laundry €10

SIGHTS
CULTURE

🏛 A VIDA PORTUGUESA (THE PORTUGUESE LIFE)

R. Anchieta 11; 213 465 073; www.avidaportuguesa.com; open M-Sa 10am-8pm, Su 11am-8pm

Step through A Vida Portuguesa's front doors and step back in time—nearly everything sold is charmingly vintage, from the handmade notebooks to the retro MiniBasketball kids toys (a bestseller, believe it or not). If you've been discouraged by the abundance of indistinguishable trinket shops in **Baixa** and **Chiado,** the "genuine and touching products of Portuguese origin and design" make for excellent souvenirs. There's a little bit of everything: porcelain swallows (the store's logo), pre-shave oils, artisanal *marmeladas,* infused chocolates, sardine tins, *azulejo* tiles, ceramics. Check out the original store in Chiado, or visit their newer spaces in **Intendente** and in the **Mercado da Ribeira.** (There's also one in **Porto,** if you're traveling out of town.)
i Prices vary; wheelchair accessible

EMBAIXADA – PORTUGUESE SHOPPING GALLERY

Pr. do Principe Real 26; 965 309 154; www.embaixadalx.pt; gallery open daily noon-3pm, restaurant open daily noon-midnight

If you forgot to pack your quinoa hydrating daily moisturizer or your calfskin monocle case, Embaixada's got your back. For just a few (dozen) euros, you can pick up these items and many, many more luxury goods in its **Principe Real** location, housed in a converted nineteenth-century Arabian palace. Embaixada hosts a variety of high-end retailers and two restaurants, all of which highlight Portuguese culture, food, design, and production. On the ground floor, sip Portuguese wine and dig into a hefty meat selection. Upstairs is an ultra-smooth gin bar offering over sixty brands of gin and a clientele whose outfits probably cost more than your roundtrip ticket to Portugal. Upon entering through the arched nooks and crannies of the surrounding rooms, you'll see made-to-measure men's apparel, babies' fashion accessories, luxury candles, fragrance sachets, and much more.
i Prices vary; wheelchair accessible

JARDIM BOTÂNICO DE LISBOA (LISBON BOTANICAL GARDEN)

R. da Escola Politécnica 54; 21 392 1800; www.museus.ulisboa.pt; open Tu-F 9am-5pm, Sa-Su 9am-8pm

Just steps away from trendy **Principe Real** is the Lisbon Botanical Garden, where you'll find yourself surrounded not by coffee shops and sardine-themed knick knacks, but by silk floss trees and European yews. Designed in the mid-nineteenth century as a scientific garden for the local university, a walk along the steep garden path takes visitors past an impressive collection of plants from around the world, including many in danger of extinction due to habitat loss. Check out the garden's chrysophyllum tree—only a handful are left in the wild, and this one has only once ever produced a single fruit with fertile seeds. Also notable is the Azorean dragon tree, whose red resin (called Dragon's Blood) has been used for everything from wood varnish to magic rituals, and was even featured in Hercules' eleventh labor.
i Garden admission €3, students €1.50; combined ticket (with Museu Nacional de História Natural e da Ciência), €6, students €3.50; Su free until 2pm; last entry 30min. before closing; wheelchair accessible

LX FACTORY

R. Rodrigues de Faria 103; 21 314 3399; www.lxfactory.com/en; open daily 6am-4am; individual shop hours vary

In a neighborhood that was once Lisbon's main manufacturing hub, you'll now find one of the city's trendiest boutiques, cafés, and startups. It's like a mini **Chiado,** only more hipster. Flanking a single cobblestoned street just perpendicular to the highway are vegan shoe stores, modular lighting showrooms, thin crust pizzerias, and *so* much street art. Fledgling entrepreneurs have offices above many of the shops, Among the most unique spaces is a warehouse turned bookstore-art gallery-café-bar (so you can educate, culture, caffeinate, and intoxicate yourself without crossing the street).

i *Prices vary; wheelchair accessible*

TIMEOUT MARKET

Av. 24 de Julho 49; 21 395 1274; www.timeoutmarket.com/lisboa/en/; open Su-W 10am-midnight, Th-Sa 10am-2am

Thanks to TimeOut Market, you no longer need to trek around all of Lisbon to feast on its finest culinary offerings; in this converted warehouse space you'll find no fewer than 24 restaurants, eight bars, and a dozen retail shops, all of which were handpicked by a panel of independent food experts. In one corner, there's a seafood smorgasbord, from high-end sushi to traditional grilled cod. Another section offers meaty pork bellies and pricey cuts of steak. An entire wall of the market is devoted to *cozinhas de chef* (chef's kitchens), each highlighting a different culinary superstar of Portugal. Of course, if you're in the mood for a cup of soup and a *pastel de nata,* TimeOut's perfect for that, too. Fair warning: you may need to fight for an empty seat in the food court-style communal tables.

i *Prices vary; wheelchair accessible*

LANDMARKS

▨ CASTELO DE SÃO JORGE (CASTLE OF ST. GEORGE)

Castelo de S. Jorge; 218 800 620; castelodesaojorge.pt; open daily 9am-9pm

The Castelo de São Jorge, Lisbon's most popular attraction, is obligatory. Part of a Medieval citadel, the Castelo's history goes deep—all the way back to the Iron Age (seventh to third century BCE). Past a former elite residential area with unparalleled panoramic views of downtown Lisbon and through huge stone archways, you'll finally enter the castle. Here, you can climb onto the walls and walk the castle's perimeter, oohing and aahing at the #views. The attached archeological site is also fantastic, showing you the layers of the Castelo's history—from excavated Iron Age construction to the ruins of Islamic houses that stood here in the years before Portuguese rule. There's also a museum—it's best to carve out an entire half-day, or at least two solid hours.

i *Admission €8.50, students €5; Câmara Oscura tour 10am-5pm, Núcleo Arqueológico tours 10:30am-5:30pm (both free); last entry 8:30pm; limited wheelchair accessibility*

ELEVADOR DE SANTA JUSTA (SANTA JUSTA LIFT)

R. do Ouro; 213 500 115; www.carris.pt/en/elevators; open daily Mar-Oct 7am-11pm, Nov-Feb 7am-9pm

Since 1902, the Elevador de Santa Justa has been helping Lisboners and weary tourists navigate the steep climb between lower **Baixa** and the **Largo do Carmo.** With wrought iron and wood and Gothic flourishes, it's one of the city's more artful forms of public transport. Today, the elevator ride is less about utility and more about #views, as it deposits riders at a delightful *miradouro* overlooking the **Praça Dom Pedro IV,** as well as all of Baixa. There's usually a long line of sweaty tourists at the entrance to the elevator, so if you want the viewpoint without the wait, you can reach it (for free!) from the Largo do Carmo via sky bridge (look for the Bellalisa Elevador restaurant).

i *Admission €5.15 (includes upper viewpoint access), upper viewpoint only €1.50; no wheelchair accessibility; included with Lisboa Card or day-pass to public transport (purchased within metro for €6.15)*

...the
fish
on
offer,
visit the
next-door restaurant.
...ned in 2018, it features fish
...es, as *petiscos,* or mashed into
...s recommendation: try the
...ortuguese curry sauce.
...t petiscos from €2, tinned fish
...e vegetarian option available;
...ccessible

...RIA ($)

...2; 21 347 1492; open daily
...ht

...mes to *pastéis de nata,* the
...d tarts ubiquitous at any
...ery, supermarket, or café,
...tions rule the foodscape.
...*astel* shop in **Belém** has an
...otees, but some would say
...a, a relative newcomer to the
...makes the superior pastries.
...or yourself at their tiny shop in
...here there's standing space only,
...en open enough for you to see
...f the *pastéis* production
...atch bakers roll the dough, stuff
...i muffin tins, and pop them
...nd shallow ovens, where the
...ds of each cup begin to bubble

...m €1, coffee from €0.70; vegetari-
...no wheelchair accessibility

MANTEIGARIA SILVA ($)

R. Dom Antão de Almada 1C/D; 213 424 905; www.manteigariasilva.pt; open M-Sa 9am-7:30pm

Although its name means "butter shop," there's so much more on offer at Manteigaria Silva than fancy slatherings for your morning toast. Serving Lisboners since 1890, this tiny shop just off the **Praça da Figueira** now sells the city's best selection of gourmet *bacalhau* (salted cod), cheeses, cured meats, sausages, wines, dried fruits, nuts—the list goes on. Stop by for a bit of *serra da estrela* or *azeitão* cheese during a daily tour (starting at €3.50), or snag some goods for a picnic in Rossio Square. Manteigaria Silva's products are also featured in chef José Ávillez's Bairro Alto, and there's now a second location in the **TimeOut Market.**

i Tastings and tours from €3.50; vegetarian options available; wheelchair accessible

PÃO PÃO QUEIJO QUEIJO ($)

R. de Belém 126; 21 362 6369; www.paopaoqueijoqueijo.com; open M-Sa 10am-midnight, Su 10am-8pm

This petit eatery near Starbucks (and the notorious **Pastéis de Belém**) might not be much of a looker, but that's not really the point. With a menu of over 50 kinds of baguette sandwiches (€3.75), around 30 salads (€3.95), and over a dozen pitas (also €3.95), Pão Pão Queijo Queijo is the budget backpacker's dream come true: cheap, tasty, and filling—a glorious trifecta. They're famous for their falafel, which some claim is the best in Lisbon. Go here to fill up on delicious Mediterranean food before joining the long line for a *pastel de nata* next door.

i Entrées from €3.75, combos from €6.95; gluten-free, vegan, and vegetarian options available; wheelchair accessible

TAPISCO ($$)

R. Dom Pedro V 81; 21 342 0681; www.tapisco.pt; open daily noon-midnight

If you were deterred by the €100 price tag at Henrique Sá Pessoa's Michelin-starred restaurant, **Alma,** Tapisco is one of the chef's more budget-friendly options for mere mortals. The restaurant's name is a word play between Spanish *tapas* and Portuguese *petiscos,* and Tapisco accordingly offers small plates featuring

MOSTEIRO DOS JERÓNIMOS (JERÓNIMOS MONASTERY)

Pr. do Império; open Oct-May Tu-Su 10am-5:30pm, June-Sept 10am-6:30pm

It took 100 years to build this behemoth of a monastery, with its gluttonous Manueline and Plateresque frills and flourishes. Commissioned by King Manuel I and funded by Portuguese voyages abroad, you'll find rich history at this monastery, where historical pictograms tell tales of the country's global explorations. Boasting sky-high ceilings and breathtaking stained glass, the Mosteiro dos Jerónimos is a showstopper, for sure. Admission to the church is free, but it's well worth the cash to visit the expansive cloister.

i Cloister admission €10, church entry free; wheelchair accessible; last entry 30 min. before closing

ROSSIO (PRAÇA DOM PEDRO IV) (PEDRO IV SQUARE)

Pr. Dom Pedro IV; open daily 24hr

Since the Middle Ages, Rossio has been one of Lisbon's top cultural spaces. Teeming with tourists and locals alike, visitors meet under the imposing gaze of Dom Pedro IV, perched on a 75-foot column in the middle of the square. Although the square officially bears his name (**Praça Dom Pedro IV**), it remains fondly known as Rossio Square to locals and tourists alike. Meet here for a coffee break in the surrounding cafés or snag some knicknacks in a streetside *loja.*

i Free; wheelchair accessible

TORRE DE BELÉM (TOWER OF BELÉM)

Av. de Brasília; 21 362 0034; www.torrebelem.pt; open Tu-Su 10am-6:30pm

Built in 1515 around the time of Portugal's prolific colonial shopping spree, the Torre de Belém is one of the neighborhood's most popular tourist attractions. There's no end to the photo ops—whether you're in the tower's *jardim* (garden), on the bulwark terrace, or on top of the tower, this emblem of Portuguese history is downright photogenic. Make sure to look for the stone rhino below the western tower—it signifies a failed gift attempt from King Manuel I to Pope Leo X. When the live rhino Manuel sent via ship drowned in a storm, its waterlogged body was recovered and Manuel proposed to give it

to the Pope as if nothing had happened. Needless to say, that plan didn't go well. At least it led to a charming bit of décor in an otherwise deathly piece of Gothic architecture.

i Admission €6; cash only; combined ticket (Mosteiro dos Jerónimos) €12; free with Lisboa card

MUSEUMS

⊠ MUSEU CALOUSTE GULBENKIAN (CALOUSTE GULBENKIAN MUSEUM)

Av. de Berna 45A; 217 823 461; gulbenkian.pt; open M 10am-6pm, W-Su 10am-6pm

Although it's a trek from downtown, the Museu Calouste Gulbenkian houses one of Lisbon's best collections of art. Reflecting Gulbenkian's desire to collect artwork representative of all genres, the *coleção do fundador* (collection of the founder) takes visitors chronologically through time, starting with Ancient Egyptian statuettes, leading you to Persian tapestries, Greco-Roman sculptures, seventeenth-century Asian pottery, and ends with a fabulous collection of nineteenth-century European art. Outside the museum is a sprawling park filled with ducks, turtles, and a tranquil interpretive garden where you can digest the hundreds of years of history you just traveled through. On the opposite side of the park is the *coleção moderna* (modern collection), home to Portuguese sculptures, paper-based art, and—of course—a healthy number of monochromatic paintings that could forgivably be mistaken for an elementary school art project.

i All-inclusive admission €12.50, founder's collection €10, exhibitions €5, under 29 50% off, free Su after 2pm; tours Su and M 10am (€12, includes access to modern collection), no booking required; last entry 5:30pm; wheelchair accessible

MUSEU COLEÇÃO BERARDO (BERARDO COLLECTION MUSEUM)

Pr. do Império; 21 361 2878; www.museu-berardo.pt; open daily 10am-7pm

Boasting works by **Picasso, Miró,** and **Warhol,** the Coleção Berardo is Lisbon's powerhouse modern art museum. Wrap yourself in a fancy scarf and don your biggest sunglasses and head towards **Belém** to take in Portugal's most-visited museum alongside other fashion-forward art fiends. The permanent exhibition starts at the beginning of the twentieth century with the abstract geometric shapes of Dadaism. Then there's Cubism, Surrealism, Informalism, kinetic art, *décollage, nouveaux-réalisme*—you get the idea. It's envelope-pushing and avant-garde in all the usual ways, whether that means a canvas with a single brush stroke on it or a slurry of seemingly random paint splatters. Once you get all the way through twenty-first-century American pop art, you can chill in the museum's lovely olive garden (not the restaurant, but an actual garden with olive trees).

i Admission €5, students €2.50; audio guide €5; last entry 6:30pm; wheelchair accessible; free on Sa, 30% off with Lisboa Card

MUSEU DE ARTE, ARQUITETURA, E TECNOLOGIA (MAAT) (MUSEUM OF ART, ARCHITECTURE, AND TECHNOLOGY)

Av. Brasília, Central Tejo; 21 002 8130; www.maat.pt/en; open W-Su 11am-7pm

The MAAT—one of Lisbon's newest museums (2017)—is also one of the city's most beautiful buildings. The exterior's fluid design evokes the **Tagus River** it overlooks, built into the riverbank as if it were a natural feature of the land. Stepping inside, visitors are immediately greeted by the cavernous Oval Room, where otherworldly orbs float mysteriously in the darkness. In the exhibition rooms, the museum hosts themed collections that aim to add to an international dialogue on contemporary problems. Aside from one other rotating exhibition, the MAAT is connected to a permanent collection housed in the **Central Tejo**, a former thermoelectric power plant where visitors can now explore the history of electricity generation on the banks of the Tagus. Be sure to plan ample time if you want to see everything—this museum's list of attractions is almost as long as its name.

i MAAT admission €5, Central Tejo €5, combined €9, students 50% off; check website for themed guided tours; wheelchair accessible; free first Su of every month or with Lisboa Card

MUSEU NACIONAL DE ARTE ANTIGUA (THE NATIONAL MUSEUM OF ANCIENT ART)

R. das Janelas Verdes; 21 391 2800; www.museudearteantiga.pt; open Tu-Su 10am-6pm

The first thing to know about the NMAA is that you'll never have time to truly appreciate everything. The Portuguese Painting and Sculpture room has enough history to last you a week, and that's just one floor. Other attractions include the room of Portuguese Discoveries, which features artwork "borrowed" from Portugal during its conquests abroad. Just make sure you check out the *Panels of St. Vincent*, a 1450 mural considered to be the greatest achievement of pre-modern Portuguese art; the *Belém Monstrance*, an ostentatious piece of religious metal work commissioned by King Manuel I and made of gold procured from Vasco da Gama's second voyage to India; and paintings by **Raphael** and **Dürer.** On a less academic note, there's also a room full of explicit art (read: nudes), which you may also want to explore.

i Admission €6, students €3; wheelchair accessible

OUTDOORS

PARKS OF LISBON

Hours typically dawn-dusk

Although Lisbon isn't renowned for its access to the outdoors, there are still a few city parks where you can get your daily dose of chlorophyll. The **Jardim da Estrela,** in the shadow of the basilica that shares its name, is a good option northwest of the city center. It sits on a hill overlooking the São Bento neighborhood, and it's a hotspot for families looking to entertain their young'uns at the duck pond. If you're visiting the **Calouste Gulbenkian Museum,** be sure to bask in the **Gulbenkian Gardens,** which features local and international sculptures, a turtle pond, and an interpretive garden. Just above the **Marquês de Pombal Square** (at the northernmost point of the **Av. da Liberdade**) is the enormous **Parque Eduardo VII,** which consists of a central manicured area filled with clean-cut hedges and neatly-paved walkways, with more natural, tree-covered paths on the hills to either side. Farther from downtown is the **Parque das Nações,** connecting the **Lisbon Oceanarium**

to the end of a waterfront walking and biking path (and a fun cable car for €3.95). This narrow patch of greenery takes you through public art installations, with the Tagus River on one side and warehouse-like shops and restaurants on the other. If none of these options are green enough for you, try the hillside **Parque Florestal de Monsanto:** 25 acres of eucalyptus forest broken up by the occasional garden, centered around an environmental interpretation center. You can get there by heading west from the city center. (Buses are the best option—take the 711 from Rossio, leaving every 15min.)

i Free; variable wheelchair accessibility

FOOD

CAFÉ DE SÃO BENTO ($$)

R. de São Bento 212; 21 395 2911; en.cafe-saobento.com; open M-F 12:30pm-2:30pm and 7pm-2am, Sa-Su 7pm-2am

Even when it opened in 1982, Café de São Bento was aiming for a throwback vibe. With its overwhelmingly red décor—from the walls to the tablecloths to the plush chairs—retro photography, and impeccably-dressed waiters, it's as if this steakhouse never left the 50s. The concise menu consists of a handful of steak preparations, from Portuguese style to São Bento style to just plain grilled or in a sandwich. Always serving filet mignon, Café de São Bento was recently declared the best steak in Lisbon by TimeOut magazine, and they even have their own coveted space in the waterfront **TimeOut Market.** Come hungry, leave a few kilos heavier—this is comfort food at its finest.

i Appetizers from €8.90, entrées from €16; one vegetarian option, gluten-free options available; no wheelchair accessibility

CERVEJARIA RAMIRO ($)

Av. Almirante Reis 1; 21 885 1024; www.cervejariaramiro.pt; open Tu-Su noon-12:30am

Despite looking like an unextraordinary Portuguese Denny's, locals and tourists alike flock to Cervejaria Ramiro for some of the best marine cuisine in town. Shrimp, giant red prawns, *percebes* (goose barnacles), lobster, and a whole host of other tantalizing dishes hold legendary status among regulars. Given Ramiro's cult status, prepare to wait for a table at flavors from across the Iberian Peninsula. Octopus salad: check. *Patatas bravas:* check. *La Bomba de Lisboa* ranks as one of their most popular dishes: meatballs stuffed with mashed potatoes and fried in panko bread crumbs. Reservations are highly recommended for lunch, as it can get quite busy. If you end up waiting in line, they'll offer you a complimentary glass of vermouth, so maybe queuing up isn't such a horrible fate after all.

i *Entrées from €7, drinks from €10; gluten-free and vegetarian options available; no wheelchair accessibility; lunch reservations only*

NIGHTLIFE

CASA INDEPENDENTE

Largo do Intendente Pina Manique 45; 21 887 2842; www.casaindependente.com; open Tu-Th 5pm-midnight, F-Sa 5pm-2am

With no sign or information marking the front door, it's easy to walk straight past this unassuming cocktail bar and nightclub. But they want it that way—it's part of Casa Independente's image as one of the city's premier underground hangouts, showcasing an eclectic mix of indie music artists from punk rock to electric to the Fanána of their resident band, Fogo Fogo. Inside the building, there are small rooms full of antique furniture, a streetside grand room with a makeshift stage, and a grape-covered patio where visitors can tuck into *tapiscos* and cocktails, or dance. A true Lisbon institution—try to make it to a weekend concert, when they open up the rooftop terrace, bringing the party into the open air and overlooking all of Intendente.

i *Concerts from €6, cocktails from €4.50, tapiscos from €4; cash only under €10; no wheelchair accessibility; resident band Fogo Fogo plays last Su every month*

CINCO LOUNGE

R. Ruben A. Leitão 17-A; 21 342 4033; www.cincolounge.com; open daily 9pm-2am

With its ultra-low lighting (where's my cocktail?), beyond-retro atmosphere (is it 1920?), and smoking-allowed policy (*hacking cough*), Cinco Lounge is about as authentic as it gets. Nestled in a quiet corner of the **Príncipe Real** neighborhood, this hazy haven harkens back to a time before the neighborhood's gentrification, when Portuguese businessmen could douse their stress in smoke, gin, and raspy conversation (forbidden topics include politics, religion, and—of course—*futebol*). Kick back in the lounge's plush, low-lying chairs and enjoy a classic cocktail or a long list of signature creations. Check out Cinco's famous Finder's Keepers cocktail; served in homemade cans with the recipe written on the back, they even have a can-sealing machine behind the bar counter that will seal your *bebida* right before your eyes.

i *No cover, cocktails from €7.50; no wheelchair accessibility*

DAMAS

R. da Voz do Operário 60; 964 964 416; open Tu 1pm-2am, W 6pm-2am, F 6pm-4am, Su 1pm-4am, Su 6pm-midnight

Lisbon's bohemian hotspot for alt music and counterculture. Damas is a restaurant by day, nightclub by night, and is a local favorite in historic **Alfama.** The "kamikaze kitchen" (as the chef calls it) churns out daily specials (local and mostly seasonal, of course) until nightfall, when students flood the tiny space for their daily dose of counterculture. Featuring a diverse array of genres from indie to congo to impressionistic folklore, there's always something going on at Damas. As an added bonus, free concerts mean you'll have plenty of money to spend on the cocktail menu.

i *No cover, free concerts, cocktails from €8; cash only; no wheelchair accessibility*

PENSÃO AMOR (LOVE GUESTHOUSE)

R. Alecrim 19; 21 314 3399; www.pensaoamor.pt; open Su-W 2pm-3am, Th-Sa 2pm-4am

They say this hostel's décor is a "wink" to the building's history as a brothel, but the bright red SEX sign above one of the arched doorways is more a slap in the face. The attached sex shop **(The Purple Rose),** the erotic library, and the photos of nude women on the wall aren't exactly what we'd call subtle. Come here for the raunchy vibe and enjoy specialty cocktails (like Bing Quin, a Chinesa—The Power of the Horizontal Vagina) while lounging on plush red sofas that look like they came straight from the 1920s.

i *No cover, cocktails from €8.50, snacks from €3.50; no wheelchair accessibility; food and drink prices increase at 10pm*

PORTO

Coverage by **Joseph Winters**

"Porto" or "Oporto"? The Portuguese call it "o Porto" (literally "the port"), so that's the root of all this lost-in-translation "Oporto" business. Rest assured that this northern Portuguese city—definitely called Porto—boasts history, opulence, and a healthy dose of grit that differentiates it from the country's larger capital city. Between baroque cathedrals, neoclassical palaces, and Romanesque ruins, Porto's history is inescapable. Records go as far back as the Celts who settled here near 300 BCE, and Roman influences are still visible in the catacombs and crypts of the city's oldest churches. In fact, the Latin name *Portus Cale* is the etymological root of the modern name Portugal. Today, the city's energy courses through its vertical streets and ancient alleys, along the River Douro, and into its striking array of glittering architecture, both old and new. Meander through Porto long enough and you'll run into an eclectic mix of UNESCO Heritage Sites, traditional corner stores, and newfangled coffee shops. As for food, expect no-frills dining and plenty of street foods like fried *bacalhau* (cod), *presunto* (sliced ham), and the gut-busting *francesinha* sandwich (four meats plus cheese and a fried egg smothered in gravy-like sauce). The only rule: finish each meal with a glass of the city's famous port wine, produced just steps across the river in the world-renowned cellars of Gaia.

ORIENTATION

In the center of Porto are the cosmopolitan neighborhoods of **Aliados** and **Bolhão.** Here, artisanal boutiques coexist alongside big-name fashion brands, traditional *lojas* and the city's sprawling municipal market. It's also home to the local university. Just down the hill is Ribeira, stretching from the fabulous **São Bento airport** to the **Douro River.** In between, there's all manner of taverns, wine tastings, and traditional Portuguese food—it's the lifeblood of touristic Porto. Directly across the river (cross the **Ponte Dom Luís I**) is **Vila Nova de Gaia.** It's actually another city, but the single street along the waterfront is constantly saturated by Porto tourists looking for tours (and tastes) at the dozens of wine cellars hugging the river. A few steps west is **Miragia.** Near the water is a formerly Jewish neighborhood that's a little calmer than its easterly neighbors, and up the hill along the **Rua da Cedofeita** is some of Porto's best nightlife. Even further west are Porto's residential areas in the neighborhoods of **Massarelos** and **Boavista,** although there's more to see than just apartment buildings here. Besides the stunning **Casa da Música, Jardim do Palácio de Cristal** humanizes Porto, reminding visitors that the city is about more than just old churches and UNESCO monuments. Keep going and you'll eventually reach **Serralves,** Porto's incredible center for contemporary arts. Porto's westernmost neighborhood is called **Foz do Douro,** along the mouth of the **Douro River.** Recommended only for travelers spending a handful of days in the city, Foz do Douro is laid-back, quiet, and greener than the inner city.

ESSENTIALS

GETTING THERE

Flights arrive from Lisbon and other major European cities northwest of Porto in the Francisco de Sá Carneiro Airport. From here, take the metro's purple line to the city center (€2, 45min.). Public buses run between the city center and the airport, as well, between 5:30am and 11:30pm (€2). Taxis can cost €25 for a ride that—depending on traffic—might take up to an hour. Buses from Lisbon (€19, 3.5hr) may arrive in one of several locations, but the most common is the Campo 24 de Agosto station, just east of the city center. If you have heavy luggage, there's a subway station connected to the bus terminal. Regional, urban, and interregional trains all arrive in the gorgeous São Bento train station, which is just about as central as you can get—your accommodations likely won't be a long walk from here. Arrivals from longer-distance origins like Lisbon (€25, 3hr) arrive in Campanhã, around 1.5mi. from the heart of Porto.

GETTING AROUND

Porto is a relatively small city; going from one end to the other on foot shouldn't take longer than an hour. Porto is far from Europe's most bike-friendly city, but many fearless travelers attempt to navigate the city's windy, uneven cobblestoned streets on two wheels. Look for bike rentals along the Largo São Domingos or the Douro—try Lopes and Lopinhos, Biclas and Triclas, or Vieguini for a more upscale experience. Rentals vary from €15-30 a day. It's also easy to hail a taxi from anywhere within the city center, with most trips costing under €7, although you'll be charged extra if your trip takes you outside city limits, or if you're traveling at night. General tip: if you plan on being a heavy user (of the public transportation system), the €7 24hr pass might be an economical pick. It's good for subways and buses, but not trams. The Porto metro is small but useful for getting around town in a jiffy. They're lettered A-F and also have corresponding colors. Andante tickets start at €1.20 for a two-zone ticket. The bus system in Porto, called STCP, is useful when trying to navigate between far-flung destinations without making a ton of transfers. A ticket onboard coasts €1.95, or €1.20 if you have an Andante ticket. Take the tram if you want to experience Porto in prime vintage fashion. For €3 a ride (or a two-day pass for €10), choose one of three tram lines that run every 30min.

PRACTICAL INFORMATION

Tourist Offices: Porto has many "fake" tourist offices that are really just tour companies trying to snare you into some day-tour of the city for more money than it's worth. The three official tourism offices are located at Aliados, just below the Catedral de Sé, and near the Campanhã train station. Look for the bluish-purple signs, but the words "Official Tourism Office" are also a dead giveaway.
- City center (Aliados): R. Clube dos Fenianos 25; 30 050 19 20; www.visitporto.travel; May-Oct open daily 9am-8pm, Aug open daily 9am-9pm, Nov-Apr open daily 9am-7pm
- Campanhã: Campanhã Train Station; 30 050 19 20; www.visitporto.travel; open daily 8am-midnight

Banks/ATMs/Currency Exchange: There are banks abound in Porto, with options including Novo Banco, Santander, Millennium Bcp, Banco BPI, and more.
- Santander Totta: Pr. da Batalha 120; 22 339 45 40; www.santandertotta.pt; open M-F 8:30am-3pm
- Banco BPI: R. de Santa Catarina 104; 22 204 6160; www.bancobpi.pt; open M-F 8:30am-3pm

Post Offices: The main CTT office in Porto is in Aliados, at the heart of the city center. Facing the big building up the hill, it's on the right. There's also an office at Batalha, just east of the São Bento train station.
- CTT Aliados: Praça General Humberto Delgado; 70 726 26 26; www.ct.pt; open M-F 8:30am-9pm, Sa 9am-6pm
- Batalha: R. Entreparedes S/N; 70 726 26 26; www.ct.pt; open M-F 9am-6pm

Public Restrooms: Good luck finding public restrooms in Porto. For desperate times, duck into the nearest mall, grocery store, or major bus or train station.

Internet: Amazingly, all public buses in Porto offer free Wi-Fi access; it only costs a €1.95 ride. Plus, if you happen to be in the city center (near Aliados), there's decent public Wi-Fi coverage. For students attending universities registered with eduroam, you can also log on to connect to Porto University's network when you're nearby (it's near Livraria Lello).

BGLTQ+ Resources: There is no BGLTQ+ resource center in Porto, but the national ILGA network is active in the city and can be contacted for support. Their main office is in Lisbon (R. dos Fanqueiros, 38; 218 873 918; ilga-portugal.pt; open M-F 10am-7pm).

EMERGENCY INFORMATION

Emergency Number: 112
Police: The local police (PSP) are your best bet if you find yourself in trouble. They're located in Aliados, to the left when facing up the hill. The GNR (national police) are a bit east of the city center.
- GNR: R. do Carmo; 22 339 96 00; www.gnr.pt
- PSP: R. Clube dos Fenianos 19; 22 208 18 33; www.psp.pt

US Embassy: The nearest US Embassy is in Lisbon (Av. das Forças Armadas 133C; 21 727 3300; pt.usembassy.gov; open M-F 8am-5pm).

Rape Crisis Center: The nearest rape crisis center is in Lisbon, a part of APAV, the Portuguese Association for Victim Support.
- GAV Oeiras: Esquadra de Oeiras da PSP, R. do Espargal 18; 21 454 02 57; apav.pt; open M-F 10am-6pm

Hospitals: A centrally-located option is the Hospital Geral de Santo António, just east of the University of Porto. Another option is the more westerly CUF hospital (part of a private chain).
- Hospital Geral de Santo António: Largo do Prof. Abel Salazar; 22 207 75 00; www.chporto.pt; open daily 24hr

Pharmacies: There aren't a lot of 24hr pharmacies in Porto, but many have decent hours, and a few are even open on Saturday. Check Via Santa Catarina or Rua dos Passos Manuel.
- Farmácia dos Clérigos: R. dos Clérigos 36; 22 339 23 70; www.farmaciados-clerigos.pt; open M-F 9am-7:30pm, Sa 9am-1pm

ACCOMMODATIONS

🎬 RIVOLI CINEMA HOSTEL ($)

R. do Dr. Magalhães Lemos 83; 22 017 46 34; www.rivolicinemahostel.com; reception open 24hr

The hostel experience isn't exactly known for being glamorous, but at the Rivoli Cinema Hostel, the walk to your dorm room actually involves a red carpet. At this hostel near the **Mercado do Bolhão**, everything is film-themed, from the Quentin Tarantino Room to the *Despicable Me* posters in the common space. Besides the spacious common areas and thematic rooms, Rivoli's amenities live up to its charm; the breakfast is generous, the dorms are comfortable, and the hostel organizes a variety of events like *francesinha* (a Portuguese sandwich from Porto) dinners followed by—of course—a movie. There's even a rooftop bar that opens to the public in the evenings, where you can sip a martini and look out over the city from the comfort of a fun-sized swimming pool.

i Dorms from €18, privates from €54; cash only; reservation recommended; BGLTQ+ friendly; no wheelchair accessibility; Wi-Fi; breakfast, linens, lockers, luggage storage, computers included; towels €2, laundry €6

GALLERY HOSTEL ($$)

R. Miguel Bombarda 222; 22 496 43 13; www.gallery-hostel.com; reception open 24hr

It isn't often your hostel doubles as a modern art gallery—true to its name, Gallery Hostel curates Portuguese and Spanish art, hanging it up throughout the building's common spaces for guests' perusal and changing the collection every two months. Even the hostel itself is a work of art: outdoor hallways are lined with greenery, there's a winter garden next to the bar, and some of the rooms' walls were painted by local artists. If that's not classy enough for you, try one of the hostel's Port wine tastings, followed by a film and dinner (€15). Well worth the short walk from downtown.

i Dorms from €25, privates from €75; reservation recommended; BGLTQ+ friendly; no wheelchair accessibility; Wi-Fi; breakfast, linens, lockers, luggage storage, towels included; laundry available

PORTO SPOT HOSTEL ($)

R. de Gonçalo Cristóvão 12; 22 408 52 05; www.spothostel.pt; reception open 24hr

The theme is "white" at this somewhat bland hostel far above the main hubbub of Porto's city center. What Porto Spot Hostel lacks in décor, however, it makes up for in cleanliness and a quality lineup of amenities like free walking tours and summertime BBQ parties. Particularly pleasing is the breakfast spread, which often includes peanut butter, a rarity at free hostel breakfasts. When you're not cartwheeling through your cavernous dorm room, there's a quiet garden with picnic tables and fruit trees, and the common room has plenty of cushy beanbags for a movie night in.

i Dorms from €20, privates from €80; reservation recommended; BGLTQ+ friendly; no wheelchair accessibility; Wi-Fi; breakfast, linens, lockers, luggage storage included; towels €2, laundry €7.50

MOSTEIRO DOS JERÓNIMOS (JERÓNIMOS MONASTERY)

Pr. do Império; open Oct-May Tu-Su 10am-5:30pm, June-Sept 10am-6:30pm

It took 100 years to build this behemoth of a monastery, with its gluttonous Manueline and Plateresque frills and flourishes. Commissioned by King Manuel I and funded by Portuguese voyages abroad, you'll find rich history at this monastery, where historical pictograms tell tales of the country's global explorations. Boasting sky-high ceilings and breathtaking stained glass, the Mosteiro dos Jerónimos is a showstopper, for sure. Admission to the church is free, but it's well worth the cash to visit the expansive cloister.

i Cloister admission €10, church entry free; wheelchair accessible; last entry 30 min. before closing

ROSSIO (PRAÇA DOM PEDRO IV) (PEDRO IV SQUARE)

Pr. Dom Pedro IV; open daily 24hr

Since the Middle Ages, Rossio has been one of Lisbon's top cultural spaces. Teeming with tourists and locals alike, visitors meet under the imposing gaze of Dom Pedro IV, perched on a 75-foot column in the middle of the square. Although the square officially bears his name (**Praça Dom Pedro IV**), it remains fondly known as Rossio Square to locals and tourists alike. Meet here for a coffee break in the surrounding cafés or snag some knicknacks in a streetside *loja*.

i Free; wheelchair accessible

TORRE DE BELÉM (TOWER OF BELÉM)

Av. de Brasília; 21 362 0034; www.torrebelem. pt; open Tu-Su 10am-6:30pm

Built in 1515 around the time of Portugal's prolific colonial shopping spree, the Torre de Belém is one of the neighborhood's most popular tourist attractions. There's no end to the photo ops—whether you're in the tower's *jardim* (garden), on the bulwark terrace, or on top of the tower, this emblem of Portuguese history is downright photogenic. Make sure to look for the stone rhino below the western tower—it signifies a failed gift attempt from King Manuel I to Pope Leo X. When the live rhino Manuel sent via ship drowned in a storm, its waterlogged body was recovered and Manuel proposed to give it

to the Pope as if nothing had happened. Needless to say, that plan didn't go well. At least it led to a charming bit of décor in an otherwise deathly piece of Gothic architecture.

i Admission €6; cash only; combined ticket (Mosteiro dos Jerónimos) €12; free with Lisboa card

MUSEUMS

🏛 MUSEU CALOUSTE GULBENKIAN (CALOUSTE GULBENKIAN MUSEUM)

Av. de Berna 45A; 217 823 461; gulbenkian. pt; open M 10am-6pm, W-Su 10am-6pm

Although it's a trek from downtown, the Museu Calouste Gulbenkian houses one of Lisbon's best collections of art. Reflecting Gulbenkian's desire to collect artwork representative of all genres, the *coleção do fundador* (collection of the founder) takes visitors chronologically through time, starting with Ancient Egyptian statuettes, leading you to Persian tapestries, Greco-Roman sculptures, seventeenth-century Asian pottery, and ends with a fabulous collection of nineteenth-century European art. Outside the museum is a sprawling park filled with ducks, turtles, and a tranquil interpretive garden where you can digest the hundreds of years of history you just traveled through. On the opposite side of the park is the *coleção moderna* (modern collection), home to Portuguese sculptures, paper-based art, and—of course—a healthy number of monochromatic paintings that could forgivably be mistaken for an elementary school art project.

i All-inclusive admission €12.50, founder's collection €10, exhibitions €5, under 29 50% off, free Su after 2pm; tours Su and M 10am (€12, includes access to modern collection), no booking required; last entry 5:30pm; wheelchair accessible

MUSEU COLEÇÃO BERARDO (BERARDO COLLECTION MUSEUM)

Pr. do Império; 21 361 2878; www.museu-berardo.pt; open daily 10am-7pm

Boasting works by **Picasso, Miró,** and **Warhol,** the Coleção Berardo is Lisbon's powerhouse modern art museum. Wrap yourself in a fancy scarf and don your biggest sunglasses and head towards **Belém** to take in Portugal's most-visited museum alongside other fashion-forward art fiends. The permanent exhibition starts at the beginning of the twentieth century with the abstract geometric shapes of Dadaism. Then there's Cubism, Surrealism, Informalism, kinetic art, *décollage, nouveaux-réalisme*—you get the idea. It's envelope-pushing and avant-garde in all the usual ways, whether that means a canvas with a single brush stroke on it or a slurry of seemingly random paint splatters. Once you get all the way through twenty-first-century American pop art, you can chill in the museum's lovely olive garden (not the restaurant, but an actual garden with olive trees).

i Admission €5, students €2.50; audio guide €5; last entry 6:30pm; wheelchair accessible; free on Sa, 30% off with Lisboa Card

MUSEU DE ARTE, ARQUITETURA, E TECNOLOGIA (MAAT) (MUSEUM OF ART, ARCHITECTURE, AND TECHNOLOGY)

Av. Brasília, Central Tejo; 21 002 8130; www. maat.pt/en; open W-Su 11am-7pm

The MAAT—one of Lisbon's newest museums (2017)—is also one of the city's most beautiful buildings. The exterior's fluid design evokes the **Tagus River** it overlooks, built into the riverbank as if it were a natural feature of the land. Stepping inside, visitors are immediately greeted by the cavernous Oval Room, where otherworldly orbs float mysteriously in the darkness. In the exhibition rooms, the museum hosts themed collections that aim to add to an international dialogue on contemporary problems. Aside from one other rotating exhibition, the MAAT is connected to a permanent collection housed in the **Central Tejo**, a former thermoelectric power plant where visitors can now explore the history of electricity generation on the banks of the Tagus. Be sure to plan ample time if you want to see everything—this museum's list of attractions is almost as long as its name.

i MAAT admission €5, Central Tejo €5, combined €9, students 50% off; check website for themed guided tours; wheelchair accessible; free first Su of every month or with Lisboa Card

MUSEU NACIONAL DE ARTE ANTIGUA (THE NATIONAL MUSEUM OF ANCIENT ART)

R. das Janelas Verdes; 21 391 2800; www. museudearteantiga.pt; open Tu-Su 10am-6pm

The first thing to know about the NMAA is that you'll never have time to truly appreciate everything. The Portuguese Painting and Sculpture room has enough history to last you a week, and that's just one floor. Other attractions include the room of Portuguese Discoveries, which features artwork "borrowed" from Portugal during its conquests abroad. Just make sure you check out the *Panels of St. Vincent*, a 1450 mural considered to be the greatest achievement of pre-modern Portuguese art; the *Belém Monstrance*, an ostentatious piece of religious metal work commissioned by King Manuel I and made of gold procured from Vasco da Gama's second voyage to India; and paintings by **Raphael** and **Dürer.** On a less academic note, there's also a room full of explicit art (read: nudes), which you may also want to explore.

i Admission €6, students €3; wheelchair accessible

OUTDOORS

PARKS OF LISBON

Hours typically dawn-dusk

Although Lisbon isn't renowned for its access to the outdoors, there are still a few city parks where you can get your daily dose of chlorophyll. The **Jardim da Estrela,** in the shadow of the basilica that shares its name, is a good option northwest of the city center. It sits on a hill overlooking the São Bento neighborhood, and it's a hotspot for families looking to entertain their young'uns at the duck pond. If you're visiting the **Calouste Gulbenkian Museum,** be sure to bask in the **Gulbenkian Gardens,** which features local and international sculptures, a turtle pond, and an interpretive garden. Just above the **Marquês de Pombal Square** (at the northernmost point of the **Av. da Liberdade**) is the enormous **Parque Eduardo VII,** which consists of a central manicured area filled with clean-cut hedges and neatly-paved walkways, with more natural, tree-covered paths on the hills to either side. Farther from downtown is the **Parque das Nações,** connecting the **Lisbon Oceanarium** to the end of a waterfront walking and biking path (and a fun cable car for €3.95). This narrow patch of greenery takes you through public art installations, with the Tagus River on one side and warehouse-like shops and restaurants on the other. If none of these options are green enough for you, try the hillside **Parque Florestal de Monsanto:** 25 acres of eucalyptus forest broken up by the occasional garden, centered around an environmental interpretation center. You can get there by heading west from the city center. (Buses are the best option—take the 711 from Rossio, leaving every 15min.)

i Free; variable wheelchair accessibility

FOOD

CAFÉ DE SÃO BENTO ($$)

R. de São Bento 212; 21 395 2911; en.cafe-saobento.com; open M-F 12:30pm-2:30pm and 7pm-2am, Sa-Su 7pm-2am

Even when it opened in 1982, Café de São Bento was aiming for a throwback vibe. With its overwhelmingly red décor—from the walls to the tablecloths to the plush chairs—retro photography, and impeccably-dressed waiters, it's as if this steakhouse never left the 50s. The concise menu consists of a handful of steak preparations, from Portuguese style to São Bento style to just plain grilled or in a sandwich. Always serving filet mignon, Café de São Bento was recently declared the best steak in Lisbon by TimeOut magazine, and they even have their own coveted space in the waterfront **TimeOut Market.** Come hungry, leave a few kilos heavier—this is comfort food at its finest.

i Appetizers from €8.90, entrées from €16; one vegetarian option, gluten-free options available; no wheelchair accessibility

CERVEJARIA RAMIRO ($)

Av. Almirante Reis 1; 21 885 1024; www.cervejariaramiro.pt; open Tu-Su noon-12:30am

Despite looking like an unextraordinary Portuguese Denny's, locals and tourists alike flock to Cervejaria Ramiro for some of the best marine cuisine in town. Shrimp, giant red prawns, *percebes* (goose barnacles), lobster, and a whole host of other tantalizing dishes hold legendary status among regulars. Given Ramiro's cult status, prepare to wait for a table at

peak hours. You can entertain yourself with a token-operated beer dispenser on the outside patio, just next to the display case of giant, squirming lobsters (your soon-to-be entrée?).

i Crustaceans from €40/kg, entrées from €11; wheelchair accessible; reservations accepted only after 7:30pm

FOOD TEMPLE ($)

Beco do Jasmim 18; 21 887 4397; www.thefoodtemple.com; open W-Su 7:30pm-midnight

The steak- and seafood-heavy cuisine of Lisbon is hardly ideal for the intrepid vegetarian—you can only order so many side salads and bread and olive plates before horrific boredom sets in. Thankfully, Alice Ming has you covered—her tiny Food Temple in Mouraria is 100% plant-based, satiating, and budget-friendly. There's an ever-changing daily menu of a soup, three *petiscos,* an entrée, and desserts. Sample dishes include fried "cod" sandwiches (made with jackfruit and seaweed for that fishy flavor), seitan and couscous salad with sweet potato, cabbage slaw, raw cheesecake—you never know what Ming will whip up on any given day. One thing's for sure: it could be one of your best meals in Lisbon, whether you're a meat-eater or a die-hard vegan. Inside seating is limited (although it's highly recommended, due to a cozy open kitchen), but they have some seating on the steep staircase just outside.

i Petiscos from €2.50, entrées from €10; Portuguese credit cards or cash only; all vegan, gluten-free options available; no wheelchair accessibility; reservations recommended

LOJA DAS CONSERVAS (PRESERVES SHOP) ($)

R. do Arsenal 130; 911 181 210; open M-Sa 10am-8pm, Su noon-8pm

The Loja das Conservas is the official retailer representing 19 factories of tinned fish production in Portugal—there isn't a square inch of wall space that isn't covered by a different brand of sardine, mackerel, or tuna. Whether you want them marinated in olive oil, with spices, with pickles, in tomato paste, in water, with skin, boneless, or some combination of these attributes—this shop probably has it. There's also an industrial-sized pedal seamer, which you can use to seal your own tin (€1.50), or lock a souvenir keychain inside of it (€12). For a taste of

the fish on offer, visit the next-door restaurant. Newly-opened in 2018, it features fish in sandwiches, as *petiscos,* or mashed into pâté. Chef's recommendation: try the tuna with Portuguese curry sauce.

i *Restaurant petiscos from €2, tinned fish from €2; one vegetarian option available; wheelchair accessible*

MANTEIGARIA ($)

R. do Loreto 2; 21 347 1492; open daily 8am-midnight

When it comes to *pastéis de nata,* the custard-filled tarts ubiquitous at any Lisbon bakery, supermarket, or café, two institutions rule the foodscape. A certain *pastel* shop in **Belém** has an army of devotees, but some would say Manteigaria, a relative newcomer to the *nata* game, makes the superior pastries. Come see for yourself at their tiny shop in **Chiado,** where there's standing space only, but a kitchen open enough for you to see each step of the the *pastéis* production process. Watch bakers roll the dough, stuff it into mini muffin tins, and pop them into long and shallow ovens, where the eggy innards of each cup begin to bubble and char.

i *Pastéis from €1, coffee from €0.70; vegetarian options; no wheelchair accessibility*

MANTEIGARIA SILVA ($)

R. Dom Antão de Almada 1C/D; 213 424 905; www.manteigariasilva.pt; open M-Sa 9am-7:30pm

Although its name means "butter shop," there's so much more on offer at Manteigaria Silva than fancy slatherings for your morning toast. Serving Lisboners since 1890, this tiny shop just off the **Praça da Figueira** now sells the city's best selection of gourmet *bacalhau* (salted cod), cheeses, cured meats, sausages, wines, dried fruits, nuts—the list goes on. Stop by for a bit of *serra da estrela* or *azeitão* cheese during a daily tour (starting at €3.50), or snag some goods for a picnic in Rossio Square. Manteigaria Silva's products are also featured in chef José Ávillez's Bairro Alto, and there's now a second location in the **TimeOut Market.**

i *Tastings and tours from €3.50; vegetarian options available; wheelchair accessible*

PÃO PÃO QUEIJO QUEIJO ($)

R. de Belém 126; 21 362 6369; www.paop-aoqueijoqueijo.com; open M-Sa 10am-midnight, Su 10am-8pm

This petit eatery near Starbucks (and the notorious **Pastéis de Belém**) might not be much of a looker, but that's not really the point. With a menu of over 50 kinds of baguette sandwiches (€3.75), around 30 salads (€3.95), and over a dozen pitas (also €3.95), Pão Pão Queijo Queijo is the budget backpacker's dream come true: cheap, tasty, and filling—a glorious trifecta. They're famous for their falafel, which some claim is the best in Lisbon. Go here to fill up on delicious Mediterranean food before joining the long line for a *pastel de nata* next door.

i *Entrées from €3.75, combos from €6.95; gluten-free, vegan, and vegetarian options available; wheelchair accessible*

TAPISCO ($$)

R. Dom Pedro V 81; 21 342 0681; www.tapisco.pt; open daily noon-midnight

If you were deterred by the €100 price tag at Henrique Sá Pessoa's Michelin-starred restaurant, **Alma,** Tapisco is one of the chef's more budget-friendly options for mere mortals. The restaurant's name is a word play between Spanish *tapas* and Portuguese *petiscos,* and Tapisco accordingly offers small plates featuring flavors from across the Iberian Peninsula. Octopus salad: check. *Patatas bravas:* check. *La Bomba de Lisboa* ranks as one of their most popular dishes: meatballs stuffed with mashed potatoes and fried in panko bread crumbs. Reservations are highly recommended for lunch, as it can get quite busy. If you end up waiting in line, they'll offer you a complimentary glass of vermouth, so maybe queuing up isn't such a horrible fate after all.

i Entrées from €7, drinks from €10; gluten-free and vegetarian options available; no wheelchair accessibility; lunch reservations only

NIGHTLIFE

CASA INDEPENDENTE

Largo do Intendente Pina Manique 45; 21 887 2842; www.casaindependente.com; open Tu-Th 5pm-midnight, F-Sa 5pm-2am

With no sign or information marking the front door, it's easy to walk straight past this unassuming cocktail bar and nightclub. But they want it that way—it's part of Casa Independente's image as one of the city's premier underground hangouts, showcasing an eclectic mix of indie music artists from punk rock to electric to the Fanána of their resident band, Fogo Fogo. Inside the building, there are small rooms full of antique furniture, a streetside grand room with a makeshift stage, and a grape-covered patio where visitors can tuck into *tapiscos* and cocktails, or dance. A true Lisbon institution—try to make it to a weekend concert, when they open up the rooftop terrace, bringing the party into the open air and overlooking all of Intendente.

i Concerts from €6, cocktails from €4.50, tapiscos from €4; cash only under €10; no wheelchair accessibility; resident band Fogo Fogo plays last Su every month

CINCO LOUNGE

R. Ruben A. Leitão 17-A; 21 342 4033; www.cincolounge.com; open daily 9pm-2am

With its ultra-low lighting (where's my cocktail?), beyond-retro atmosphere (is it 1920?), and smoking-allowed policy (*hacking cough*), Cinco Lounge is about as authentic as it gets. Nestled in a quiet corner of the **Principe Real** neighborhood, this hazy haven harkens back to a time before the neighborhood's

gentrification, when Portuguese businessmen could douse their stress in smoke, gin, and raspy conversation (forbidden topics include politics, religion, and—of course—*futebol).* Kick back in the lounge's plush, low-lying chairs and enjoy a classic cocktail or a long list of signature creations. Check out Cinco's famous Finder's Keepers cocktail; served in homemade cans with the recipe written on the back, they even have a can-sealing machine behind the bar counter that will seal your *bebida* right before your eyes.

i No cover, cocktails from €7.50; no wheelchair accessibility

DAMAS

R. da Voz do Operário 60; 964 964 416; open Tu 1pm-2am, W 6pm-2am, F 6pm-4am, Su 1pm-4am, Su 6pm-midnight

Lisbon's bohemian hotspot for alt music and counterculture. Damas is a restaurant by day, nightclub by night, and is a local favorite in historic **Alfama.** The "kamikaze kitchen" (as the chef calls it) churns out daily specials (local and mostly seasonal, of course) until nightfall, when students flood the tiny space for their daily dose of counterculture. Featuring a diverse array of genres from indie to congo to impressionistic folklore, there's always something going on at Damas. As an added bonus, free concerts mean you'll have plenty of money to spend on the cocktail menu.

i No cover, free concerts, cocktails from €8; cash only; no wheelchair accessibility

PENSÃO AMOR (LOVE GUESTHOUSE)

R. Alecrim 19; 21 314 3399; www.pensaoamor.pt; open Su-W 2pm-3am, Th-Sa 2pm-4am

They say this hostel's décor is a "wink" to the building's history as a brothel, but the bright red SEX sign above one of the arched doorways is more a slap in the face. The attached sex shop **(The Purple Rose),** the erotic library, and the photos of nude women on the wall aren't exactly what we'd call subtle. Come here for the raunchy vibe and enjoy specialty cocktails (like Bing Quin, a Chinesa—The Power of the Horizontal Vagina) while lounging on plush red sofas that look like they came straight from the 1920s.

i No cover, cocktails from €8.50, snacks from €3.50; no wheelchair accessibility; food and drink prices increase at 10pm

PORTO

Coverage by **Joseph Winters**

"Porto" or "Oporto"? The Portuguese call it "o Porto" (literally "the port"), so that's the root of all this lost-in-translation "Oporto" business. Rest assured that this northern Portuguese city—definitely called Porto—boasts history, opulence, and a healthy dose of grit that differentiates it from the country's larger capital city. Between baroque cathedrals, neoclassical palaces, and Romanesque ruins, Porto's history is inescapable. Records go as far back as the Celts who settled here near 300 BCE, and Roman influences are still visible in the catacombs and crypts of the city's oldest churches. In fact, the Latin name *Portus Cale* is the etymological root of the modern name Portugal. Today, the city's energy courses through its vertical streets and ancient alleys, along the River Douro, and into its striking array of glittering architecture, both old and new. Meander through Porto long enough and you'll run into an eclectic mix of UNESCO Heritage Sites, traditional corner stores, and newfangled coffee shops. As for food, expect no-frills dining and plenty of street foods like fried *bacalhau* (cod), *presunto* (sliced ham), and the gut-busting *francesinha* sandwich (four meats plus cheese and a fried egg smothered in gravy-like sauce). The only rule: finish each meal with a glass of the city's famous port wine, produced just steps across the river in the world-renowned cellars of Gaia.

ORIENTATION

In the center of Porto are the cosmopolitan neighborhoods of **Aliados** and **Bolhão.** Here, artisanal boutiques coexist alongside big-name fashion brands, traditional *lojas* and the city's sprawling municipal market. It's also home to the local university. Just down the hill is Ribeira, stretching from the fabulous **São Bento airport** to the **Douro River.** In between, there's all manner of taverns, wine tastings, and traditional Portuguese food—it's the lifeblood of touristic Porto. Directly across the river (cross the **Ponte Dom Luís I**) is **Vila Nova de Gaia.** It's actually another city, but the single street along the waterfront is constantly saturated by Porto tourists looking for tours (and tastes) at the dozens of wine cellars hugging the river. A few steps west is **Miragia.** Near the water is a formerly Jewish neighborhood that's a little calmer than its easterly neighbors, and up the hill along the **Rua da Cedofeita** is some of Porto's best nightlife. Even further west are Porto's residential areas in the neighborhoods of **Massarelos** and **Boavista,** although there's more to see than just apartment buildings here. Besides the stunning **Casa da Música, Jardim do Palácio de Cristal** humanizes Porto, reminding visitors that the city is about more than just old churches and UNESCO monuments. Keep going and you'll eventually reach **Serralves,** Porto's incredible center for contemporary arts. Porto's westernmost neighborhood is called **Foz do Douro,** along the mouth of the **Douro River.** Recommended only for travelers spending a handful of days in the city, Foz do Douro is laid-back, quiet, and greener than the inner city.

ESSENTIALS

GETTING THERE

Flights arrive from Lisbon and other major European cities northwest of Porto in the Francisco de Sá Carneiro Airport. From here, take the metro's purple line to the city center (€2, 45min.). Public buses run between the city center and the airport, as well, between 5:30am and 11:30pm (€2). Taxis can cost €25 for a ride that—depending on traffic—might take up to an hour. Buses from Lisbon (€19, 3.5hr) may arrive in one of several locations, but the most common is the Campo 24 de Agosto station, just east of the city center. If you have heavy luggage, there's a subway station connected to the bus terminal. Regional, urban, and interregional trains all arrive in the gorgeous São Bento train station, which is just about as central as you can get—your accommodations likely won't be a long walk from here. Arrivals from longer-distance origins like Lisbon (€25, 3hr) arrive in Campanhã, around 1.5mi. from the heart of Porto.

GETTING AROUND

Porto is a relatively small city; going from one end to the other on foot shouldn't take longer than an hour. Porto is far from Europe's most bike-friendly city, but many fearless travelers attempt to navigate the city's windy, uneven cobblestoned streets on two wheels. Look for bike rentals along the Largo São Domingos or the Douro—try Lopes and Lopinhos, Biclas and Triclas, or Vieguini for a more upscale experience. Rentals vary from €15-30 a day. It's also easy to hail a taxi from anywhere within the city center, with most trips costing under €7, although you'll be charged extra if your trip takes you outside city limits, or if you're traveling at night. General tip: if you plan on being a heavy user (of the public transportation system), the €7 24hr pass might be an economical pick. It's good for subways and buses, but not trams. The Porto metro is small but useful for getting around town in a jiffy. They're lettered A-F and also have corresponding colors. Andante tickets start at €1.20 for a two-zone ticket. The bus system in Porto, called STCP, is useful when trying to navigate between far-flung destinations without making a ton of transfers. A ticket onboard coasts €1.95, or €1.20 if you have an Andante ticket. Take the tram if you want to experience Porto in prime vintage fashion. For €3 a ride (or a two-day pass for €10), choose one of three tram lines that run every 30min.

PRACTICAL INFORMATION

Tourist Offices: Porto has many "fake" tourist offices that are really just tour companies trying to snare you into some day-tour of the city for more money than it's worth. The three official tourism offices are located at Aliados, just below the Catedral de Sé, and near the Campanhã train station. Look for the bluish-purple signs, but the words "Official Tourism Office" are also a dead giveaway.

- City center (Aliados): R. Clube dos Fenianos 25; 30 050 19 20; www.visitporto.travel; May-Oct open daily 9am-8pm, Aug open daily 9am-9pm, Nov-Apr open daily 9am-7pm
- Campanhã: Campanhã Train Station; 30 050 19 20; www.visitporto.travel; open daily 8am-midnight

Banks/ATMs/Currency Exchange: There are banks abound in Porto, with options including Novo Banco, Santander, Millennium Bcp, Banco BPI, and more.
- Santander Totta: Pr. da Batalha 120; 22 339 45 40; www.santandertotta.pt; open M-F 8:30am-3pm
- Banco BPI: R. de Santa Catarina 104; 22 204 6160; www.bancobpi.pt; open M-F 8:30am-3pm

Post Offices: The main CTT office in Porto is in Aliados, at the heart of the city center. Facing the big building up the hill, it's on the right. There's also an office at Batalha, just east of the São Bento train station.
- CTT Aliados: Praça General Humberto Delgado; 70 726 26 26; www.ct.pt; open M-F 8:30am-9pm, Sa 9am-6pm
- Batalha: R. Entreparedes S/N; 70 726 26 26; www.ct.pt; open M-F 9am-6pm

Public Restrooms: Good luck finding public restrooms in Porto. For desperate times, duck into the nearest mall, grocery store, or major bus or train station.

Internet: Amazingly, all public buses in Porto offer free Wi-Fi access; it only costs a €1.95 ride. Plus, if you happen to be in the city center (near Aliados), there's decent public Wi-Fi coverage. For students attending universities registered with eduroam, you can also log on to connect to Porto University's network when you're nearby (it's near Livraria Lello).

BGLTQ+ Resources: There is no BGLTQ+ resource center in Porto, but the national ILGA network is active in the city and can be contacted for support. Their main office is in Lisbon (R. dos Fanqueiros, 38; 218 873 918; ilga-portugal.pt; open M-F 10am-7pm).

EMERGENCY INFORMATION

Emergency Number: 112

Police: The local police (PSP) are your best bet if you find yourself in trouble. They're located in Aliados, to the left when facing up the hill. The GNR (national police) are a bit east of the city center.
- GNR: R. do Carmo; 22 339 96 00; www.gnr.pt
- PSP: R. Clube dos Fenianos 19; 22 208 18 33; www.psp.pt

US Embassy: The nearest US Embassy is in Lisbon (Av. das Forças Armadas 133C; 21 727 3300; pt.usembassy.gov; open M-F 8am-5pm).

Rape Crisis Center: The nearest rape crisis center is in Lisbon, a part of APAV, the Portuguese Association for Victim Support.
- GAV Oeiras: Esquadra de Oeiras da PSP, R. do Espargal 18; 21 454 02 57; apav.pt; open M-F 10am-6pm

Hospitals: A centrally-located option is the Hospital Geral de Santo António, just east of the University of Porto. Another option is the more westerly CUF hospital (part of a private chain).
- Hospital Geral de Santo António: Largo do Prof. Abel Salazar; 22 207 75 00; www.chporto.pt; open daily 24hr

Pharmacies: There aren't a lot of 24hr pharmacies in Porto, but many have decent hours, and a few are even open on Saturday. Check Via Santa Catarina or Rua dos Passos Manuel.
- Farmácia dos Clérigos: R. dos Clérigos 36; 22 339 23 70; www.farmaciadosclerigos.pt; open M-F 9am-7:30pm, Sa 9am-1pm

ACCOMMODATIONS

📰 RIVOLI CINEMA HOSTEL ($)

R. do Dr. Magalhães Lemos 83; 22 017 46 34; www.rivolicinemahostel.com; reception open 24hr

The hostel experience isn't exactly known for being glamorous, but at the Rivoli Cinema Hostel, the walk to your dorm room actually involves a red carpet. At this hostel near the **Mercado do Bolhão**, everything is film-themed, from the Quentin Tarantino Room to the *Despicable Me* posters in the common space. Besides the spacious common areas and thematic rooms, Rivoli's amenities live up to its charm: the breakfast is generous, the dorms are comfortable, and the hostel organizes a variety of events like *francesinha* (a Portuguese sandwich from Porto) dinners followed by—of course—a movie. There's even a rooftop bar that opens to the public in the evenings, where you can sip a martini and look out over the city from the comfort of a fun-sized swimming pool.

i Dorms from €18, privates from €54; cash only; reservation recommended; BGLTQ+ friendly; no wheelchair accessibility; Wi-Fi; breakfast, linens, lockers, luggage storage, computers included; towels €2, laundry €6

GALLERY HOSTEL ($$)

R. Miguel Bombarda 222; 22 496 43 13; www.gallery-hostel.com; reception open 24hr

It isn't often your hostel doubles as a modern art gallery—true to its name, Gallery Hostel curates Portuguese and Spanish art, hanging it up throughout the building's common spaces for guests' perusal and changing the collection every two months. Even then the hostel itself is a work of art: outdoor hallways are lined with greenery, there's a winter garden next to the bar, and some of the rooms' walls were painted by local artists. If that's not classy enough for you, try one of the hostel's Port wine tastings, followed by a film and dinner (€15). Well worth the short walk from downtown.

i Dorms from €25, privates from €75; reservation recommended; BGLTQ+ friendly; no wheelchair accessibility; Wi-Fi; breakfast, linens, lockers, luggage storage, towels included; laundry available

PORTO SPOT HOSTEL ($)

R. de Gonçalo Cristóvão 12; 22 408 52 05; www.spothostel.pt; reception open 24hr

The theme is "white" at this somewhat bland hostel far above the main hubbub of Porto's city center. What Porto Spot Hostel lacks in décor, however, it makes up for in cleanliness and a quality lineup of amenities like free walking tours and summertime BBQ parties. Particularly pleasing is the breakfast spread, which often includes peanut butter, a rarity at free hostel breakfasts. When you're not cartwheeling through your cavernous dorm room, there's a quiet garden with picnic tables and fruit trees, and the common room has plenty of cushy beanbags for a movie night in.

i Dorms from €20, privates from €80; reservation recommended; BGLTQ+ friendly; no wheelchair accessibility; Wi-Fi; breakfast, linens, lockers, luggage storage included; towels €2, laundry €7.50

SIGHTS
CULTURE

🖺 LIVRARIA LELLO (LELLO BOOKSTORE)

R. das Carmelitas 144; 22 200 20 37; www.livrarialello.pt; bookstore open M-F 10am-7:30pm, Sa-Su 10am-7pm; check-in open M-F 9:45am-7:30pm, Sa-Su 9:45am-7pm

More than a bookstore, the Livraria Lello is an architectural masterpiece in the heart of Porto, just next to the local university. The façade combines Gothic elements with Art Nouveau, and the interior's tiled ceiling and majestic central staircase introduce a little Art Deco. What really draws in the crowds, though, is the fact that JK Rowling was a frequent visitor from 1991-1993 while she was teaching English in Porto. The building is said to have inspired the author while she worked on the manuscript that would become *Harry Potter and the Sorcerer's Stone*.

i Admission €5; Wi-Fi; limited wheelchair accessibility; tickets available down the street at the "Check-In" or online

CASA DA MÚSICA (HOUSE OF MUSIC)

Av. da Boavista 604-610; 22 012 02 20; www.casadamusica.com; museum open M-Sa 9am-7pm, Su 9:30am-6pm; terrace and restaurant open M-Th 12:30pm-3pm and 7:30pm-11pm, F-Sa 12:30pm-3pm and 7:30pm-midnight

The Casa da Música simply doesn't fit into the Porto cityscape. As the Dutch architect intended, his colossal auditorium, a concrete dome-like building made of is nothing like the rest of the city's traditionalist style. Even the interior is unique: the concert hall is rectangular rather than circular, with glass walls at either end to let in the sunrise and sunset. Visitors hoping to explore this curious building must attend a guided tour, which lasts about an hour and also goes through five of the building's other quirky rooms, like a cyber music room where the walls are made of foam pyramids sprayed with liquid rubber. If you're tired of seventeenth-century cathedrals, you won't find anything more refreshing than the stunning Casa da Música.

i Admission €10, with Porto Card €5; limited wheelchair accessibility; mandatory guided tours; combined tickets available for Casa da Música, Serralves, and Teatro Nacional São José €20, or Casa da Música/Serralves €16

MERCADO DO BOLHÃO (BOLHÃO MARKET)

R. Formosa; 22 332 60 24; open M-F 7am-5pm, Sa 7am-1pm

Surrounded by H&Ms and Intimissimis, the Mercado do Bolhão is downtown Porto's down-to-earth oasis of Portuguese culture. Dating back to the mid-nineteenth century, the perimeter of the market is lined with butchers, bakers, fishermen, and more, while the inner circle is devoted to long rows of flower shops and greengrocers, whose vibrant products spill out onto narrow walkways. Veteran shop owners beckon visitors towards them, saying *"escolhe, escolhe!"* ("choose something!"). Fill a bag with fruits and cheeses, find some pork cheek to grill, or sip an espresso in one of the market's humble cafés. No frills—just fresh, quality food.

i Prices vary; limited wheelchair accessibility

PALÁCIO DA BOLSA (PALACE OF THE STOCK EXCHANGE)

R. Ferreira Borges; 22 339 90 13; www.palaciodabolsa.com; open daily Nov-Mar 9am-1pm and 2pm-5:30pm, Apr-Oct 9am-6:30pm

Formerly the seat of the Porto stock exchange, the Palácio da Bolsa is currently home to the city's Commerce Association and is a powerhouse of Portuguese culture. Each room includes details that were meticulously handcrafted exclusively by Portuguese artists, like the sumptuous granite detailing (which took forty years to complete), or an elaborate wooden table that took one artist three years to design with nothing more than a pocket knife. The big stunner is undoubtedly the magnificent Arab room, slathered in 20kg of gold leaf and covered in Arabic scrawl from the Quran. This room is still used today to receive foreign leaders and even royalty. Tours are mandatory, and help contextualize the palace's role in Porto's history.

i Admission €9, students €5.50; mandatory guided tours every 45min.; last entry 45min. before close; wheelchair accessible; guided tours mandatory for visitors

LANDMARKS

◪ TORRE DOS CLÉRIGOS (CLÉRIGOS TOWER)

R. de São Filipe de Nery; 22 014 54 89; www.torredosclerigos.pt; open daily 9am-7pm

Even though it's only 75.6 meters tall, the baroque Torre dos Clérigos soars above the rest of the Porto cityscape. It was designed by Nicolau Nasoni in the mid-1700s, quickly emerging as one of the main symbols of the city. Visitors can tour the museum's collection of sacred art, admire the church's neoclassical, rococo, and baroque interior from one of several unique vantage points, and culminate in climbing the 240 steps to the top of the tower. A narrow wraparound walkway offers incredible views but little elbow room.

i Admission €5, students €2.50; guided tour (pre-booked only) of museum, church, and tower €6.50; limited wheelchair accessibility

IGREJA DE SÃO FRANCISCO (SAN FRANCISCO CHURCH)

Pr. Infante Dom Henrique; 22 200 64 93; www.ordemsaofrancisco.pt; open daily Jul-Sept 9am-8pm, Mar-Jun 9am-7pm, Nov-Feb 9am-5:30pm

Nowhere in Porto is the gluttony of the Baroque more apparent than in this glittering hulk of a church, doused in almost 100kg of gold leaf and littered with sacred art. It started as your average Gothic cathedral, with a dingy interior and doom-and-gloom façade. But things really started to get out of hand in the eighteenth century, when Portuguese wood carvers began adding gilt woodwork to nearly every square inch of the interior. Be sure to check out the polychrome altarpiece known as the Jesse Tree, João Baptista Chapel, and the sculpture-lined catacombs, where prominent Porto natives were once buried.

i Admission €6, students €5; no wheelchair accessibility

PONTE DOM LUÍS I (DOM LUÍS I BRIDGE)

PTE Luiz I; open 24hr

Although Gustave Eiffel (yes, *that* Eiffel) would have loved to include the Ponte Dom Luís I in his architectural portfolio, his Douro-spanning bridge proposal was tragically rejected by the city of Porto in favor of the current double-decked metal design, put forward by a Belgian architecture society. At its construction in 1881, the 564-foot-long Ponte Dom Luís I was the longest arched bridge in the world. The bottom (for cars and pedestrians) connects the Porto riverbank to the wine cellars of **Gaia,** but the top deck offers much better views. Reserved for pedestrians and public transport, panos and selfies are highly recommended; it's one of the most photogenic spots in Porto.

i Free; wheelchair accessible; transport between the upper and lower decks available via funicular

SÉ DO PORTO (PORTO CATHEDRAL)

Terreiro da Sé; 22 205 90 28; www.diocese-porto.pt; church open daily Apr-Oct 9am-7pm, Nov-Mar 9am-6pm; cloisters open daily Apr-Oct 9am-6:30pm, Nov-Mar 9am-5:30pm

Completed in 1737, the Baroque façade of the Porto Cathedral is only one of many architectural themes you'll see in this behemoth of a church. Construction began sometime during the twelfth century, and much of the building—including the funerary chapel and cloister—reveal dramatic Gothic influences. In the eighteenth century, renovations by the tireless Nicholas Nasoni introduced Baroque flourishes like a spectacular silver altarpiece and several bronze bas-reliefs, all designed by Portuguese artists. Besides its 10/10 design, history has left its mark on Sé, as well: the church hosted King John I's wedding, and it's where his son Henry the Navigator would later be baptized.

i Cloisters admission €3, students €2; no wheelchair accessibility

MUSEUMS

◪ MUSEU DE SERRALVES (SERRALVES MUSEUM)

R. Dom João de Castro 210; 80 820 05 43; www.serralves.pt; open Apr-Sept M-F 10am-7pm, Sa-Su 10am-8pm; Oct-Mar M-F 10am-6pm, Sa-Su 10am-7pm

Running, yelling, lava lamps, Barbies performing sexual acts—the Serralves Museum knows no bounds when it comes to breaking artistic conventions. Despite being far from the city center, this cultural institution has become a destination in its own right, gracing Porto with some of the city's finest contemporary art since 1999.

Open your mind and wander through Serralves' ever-changing temporary exhibitions, commissions, and displays, and don't forget to visit to the connected park. It's divided into gorgeous glades, groves, and gardens, lined with hedges, and centered around a romantic duck pond. If you only visit one museum in Porto, make it this one.

i Admission €10, students €5; English tours at 4pm first Sa each month; limited wheelchair accessibility

CASA DO INFANTE (HOUSE OF THE PRINCE)

R. Alfândega 10; 22 206 04 00; www. cm-porto.pt; open Tu-Su 9:30am-1pm and 2pm-5:30pm

Despite 500 years of history as Porto's Customs House, 400 years since becoming one of the country's first money-minting establishments, and a 1600-year-old history of Roman occupation, the Casa do Infante is known for and named after a single guy: Prince Henry the Navigator. Born here in 1394, Henry went on to become one of fifteenth-century Portugal's most influential characters, leading and facilitating seagoing expeditions that led to the discovery of several islands off the coast of Africa. Half of the museum takes visitors chronologically through Henry's history, with another half exploring the historical significance of the building as one of Porto's most important hubs of trade and commerce.

i Admission €2.20, students €1.10; wheelchair accessible

MUSEU NACIONAL DE SOARES DOS REIS (SOARES DOS REIS NATIONAL MUSEUM)

R. de Dom Manuel II 44; 22 339 37 70; www. museodesoaresdosreis.gov.pt; open Tu-Su 10am-6pm

Founded in 1833, this is the country's oldest museum of Portuguese art. It features an extensive sculpture collection by its namesake (Soares dos Reis), as well as paintings and drawings by Henrique Pousão. Beginning with the relative stuffiness of the nineteenth century, the museum tour progresses chronologically to Portuguese modernism, culminating in abstract and impressionist paintings from recent decades. Upstairs is a collection highlighting Portuguese discoveries abroad, including Chinese porcelain and

Japanese Namban screens. There's still some homemade stuff, like an excellent collection of Portuguese *faïence* ceramics from the seventeenth century.

i Admission €5, students and Porto Card €2.50; last entry 5:30pm; wheelchair accessible

MUSEU DA MISERICÓRDIA DO PORTO (MISERICÓRDIA DO PORTO MUSEUM)

R. das Flores 15; 22 090 69 60; www.mipo.pt; open daily Apr 1-Sept 30 10am-6:30pm, Oct 1-Mar 31 open daily 10am-5:30pm

Combining art, history, and architecture, the Museu da Miséricordia do Porto is one of the city's most famous museums. The museum tour begins with a history of the Miséricordia, a charitable organization that has—since 1499—worked for the rights of Porto's underrepresented population by founding hospitals, sanitariums, and schools. The museum also has a stellar collection of sacred art from the sixteenth-eighteenth centuries, but the visit's highlight is undoubtedly the epic church, designed by the Italian architect Nicolau Nasoni (who also designed the nearby **Torre dos Clérigos**). Filled with blue and white *azulejos* and a golden neoclassical altarpiece, it contrasts starkly with the Gothic gloom of many Portuguese cathedrals.

i Admission €5, students €2.50; tours by pre-booking only (scheduled online); last entry 30min. before closing; limited wheelchair accessibility

OUTDOORS

🏞 JARDINS DO PALÁCIO DE CRISTAL (CRYSTAL PALACE GARDENS)

R. de Dom Manuel II 282; 22 209 70 00; www.cm-porto.pt; open daily Oct-Mar 8am-7pm, Apr-Sept 8am-9pm

Watch out for peacocks, swans, and roosters as you promenade through the elegant Jardins do Palácio de Cristal. Designed in the mid-nineteenth century by Berliner Emil David, the park's romantic charm is apparent in its shady groves, diverse flower beds, and an ivy-covered chalet that now houses a Romantic Museum. From the main entrance, meander beneath olive trees, palms and magnolias, on through Sycamore Avenue and arrive at a stunning collection of tiered gardens, each cascading farther downhill towards the

River Douro. The park is also home to a major branch of Porto's municipal library and an enormous domed sports complex, making it a popular destination for Porto locals.
i Free; limited wheelchair accessibility

FOOD

🍽 DATERRA ($)

R. de Mouzinho da Silveira 249; 22 319 92 57; www.daterra.pt; open Su-Th noon-11pm, F-Sa noon-11:30pm

In stark contrast to the meat and cheese-heavy cuisine of Porto is DaTerra, offering a buffet of fresh and tasty vegan dishes. It's not just salad, either; DaTerra likes playing with traditional Portuguese recipes, veganizing the *francesinha*,' de-meating *pica-pau*, and serving up animal-free *alheira* (bread sausage). At under €10, it's a steal, considering you can go back as many times as you want for extra helpings, although it's worth saving room for a the dairy-free *pastéis de nata* (not included in the buffet price). For the super-frugal, takeaway options start at €4.50 and you'd be surprised how much food you can cram into one of those paper boxes.
i Lunch buffet from €7.50, dinner buffet from €9.95; gluten-free, vegan, and vegetarian options available; wheelchair accessible

A PÉROLA DO BOLHÃO ($)

R. Formosa 279; 22 200 40 09; open M-F 9am-7:30pm, Sa 9am-1pm

There are many shops like A Pérola do Bolhão along the streets surrounding the **Mercado do Bolhão,** but few can boast a history as old or a selection as large. The building's intricate façade is a nod to Porto's art nouveau obsession, and the interior walls are coated with *azulejos* depicting Portugal's Age of Discoveries. Much of these blue tiles are covered by A Pérola's legendary selection of tinned fish, dried fruit, nuts, and candies. In display cases at the windows and in front of the counters are dozens of Portuguese cheeses and processed meats like *ovelheira* (dried pig ears) and regional blood sausage. Mix and match for the ultimate picnic basket and walk to **Aliados** or the **Jardim de S. Lázaro** for an excellent Portuguese snack al fresco.
i Prices vary; gluten-free, vegan, and vegetarian options available; wheelchair accessible

BRICK CLÉRIGOS ($$)

R. Campo dos Mártires da Pátria 103; 22 323 47 35; open W-F noon-4pm and 8pm-2am, Sa 1pm-4pm and 8pm-2am, Su noon-6pm

Old Portugal meets newfangled hipster at this Insta-worthy petiscos restaurant in the shadow of the **Torre dos Clérigos.** Air plants, pressed leaves, artisanal woodwork—the décor (and menu) conspires to provide an updated vibe to Portuguese food. Options include charcuterie platters, a variety of "toasties" (like pineapple and brie), or the popular pork cheek sandwich with garlic mayo and fresh fruits. In accordance with the restaurant's philosophy of friendship and interaction, guests at Brick Clérigos sit at a large communal table, rubbing shoulders with their neighbors and passing the salt to complete strangers. It's like a family meal, only without the family dynamics.
i Petiscos from €8; gluten-free, vegan, and vegetarian options available; no wheelchair accessibility

CAFÉ SANTIAGO ($)

R. de Passos Manuel 226; 22 205 57 97; www.porto.cafesantiago.pt; open M-Sa noon-11pm

Prepare your arteries, because—health concerns aside—you won't want to miss this Porto establishment's infamous *francesinha.* The city's patron sandwich, a francesinha is like a like a deluxe charcuterie platter, with a single bite involving *salchicha* (sausage), *linguiça* (another kind of sausage), *bife* (beef), *fiambre* (ham), and cheese all squished between two slices of thick white bread. Add the fried egg and drench it in gravy-like secret sauce, and you've got yourself one quality *francesinha*. Something about Café Santiago's preparation of this meat and cheese bomb has locals and tourists raving mad, so come prepared to wait in line for at least an hour during peak tourist season. Pro tip: Split it with a friend; your gut will thank you later.
i Francesinha from €8.75; no wheelchair accessibility; expect lines for lunch and dinner

NIGHTLIFE

☒ ESPAÇO 77

Trav. de Cedofeita 22; 22 321 88 93; open
M-F 11am-4am, Sa 6pm-4am

Entering Espaço 77 is like entering a
sacred shrine—to Super Bock. With
wall-to-wall lockers bearing the beer
company's logo and another wall with
framed bottles of the Portuguese booze,
Espaço 77 has made a name for itself by
selling €0.50 bottles of Mini Super Bock.
In 2017 alone, sales climbed to 582,000,
a number that has grown yearly since their
founding in 2010. Also popular is the
€2.50 Mini Super Bock plus *bifana* (beef
sandwich) combo, which can be enjoyed
between intermittent €1.50 shots (quite
the splurge). Sometimes, quantity really
is better than quality; for budget travelers
and penny-pinching college students,
Espaço 77 is an inexpensive godsend.
i Mini Super Bock from €0.50, other beers
from €1, food from €1.30; no wheelchair
accessibility

☒ MAUS HÁBITOS

R. de Passos Manuel 178; 93 720 29 18;
www.maushabitos.com; open Tu noon-midnight, W-Th noon-2am, F-Sa noon-4am, Su
noon-5pm

Branding themselves as an *espaço de
intervenção cultural* (space of cultural
intervention), Maus Hábitos's avant-garde
art exhibitions, inexpensive concerts,
and edgy DJ sets make it one of the
city's premier nightlife destinations. It's
on the fourth floor of an apartment on
the popular **Via Santa Catarina,** but it's
discreet enough to still feel somewhat
underground. Go for zany parties that
last into the early morning like the
Groove Ball or Monster Jinx, or go a bit
earlier to appreciate political artwork in
the space's rotating gallery. Even better,
scout things out beforehand at their
daytime restaurant, **Vícios de Mesa,**
where Instagram-ready dishes of the day
like Madonna pizza or avo toast are only
€5.50.
i No cover, tickets from €4, cocktails from €7;
limited wheelchair accessibility

PORTUGAL ESSENTIALS

MONEY

A 13% tax (known as value added tax) is included on all restaurants and
accommodations in Portugal. A 20% tip is never necessary, though Portuguese
restaurants may expect more from you than from a local if they deem you a
tourist.

SAFETY AND HEALTH

Police: Guarda Nacional Republicana (GNR) covers 98% of Portuguese territory,
especially urban areas. GNR are military personnel. Polícia de Segurança Pública
(PSP) is a civilian police force based in more populated areas. Not all officers speak
English.

Drugs and Alcohol: Using or possessing drugs is illegal in Portugal, but, in
2001, the charge was changed from criminal to administrative, meaning more
community service and less (usually no) jail time. The legal drinking age in
Portugal is 18.

SPAIN

Tapas or pintxos? What about *pinchos?* *¿Algo para picar?* Whatever you call Spain's favorite snack, the country's culture is as rich and varied as its gastronomy. From the brooding forests of the northeast to the sun-soaked Mediterranean coast, each region—and every city—offers a different flavor of Spain. And we're talking more than just *patatas bravas* and silky gazpacho; throughout its multi-millennial history, Spain has become a world-class potpourri of art, architecture, and culture. Boasting everything from metropolises like Madrid and Barcelona to hamlets dotting the Basque country, there are few nations on earth with such a diversity of delights. Run-ins with superstars like Goya, Picasso, and Dalí are daily occurrences. Moorish mosques, Gothic cathedrals, and Baroque palaces are routine sightseeing material. There's so much to do, to photograph, to eat: you'll almost certainly need that midday siesta if you plan on wading through everything the country has to offer. Whether you find yourself in sun-drenched Valencia or fiercely independent Bilbao, the Spain that welcomes you will do so loudly and proudly, most likely with an icy glass of sangria (or three). You couldn't resist if you tried—under the fuzzy spell of this spiced (and spiked) lemonade, savor the pull of Spain's mesmerizing embrace. In a blur, you'll be sipping your last drink, polishing off your last tapa, and crawling back from your final *fiesta*. Flights home from this dazzling country will always come far too soon.

541

BARCELONA

Coverage by **Austin Eder**

Known for its beaches, its *fútbol,* and its groundbreaking architecture, Barcelona is one of the most lively and vibrant places on Earth. Walking down its streets is drowning in a sea of color. Dining at its restaurants is being showered with the scents of seafood and sangria. Dancing at its clubs is to being pummeled into the earth with the deafening pulses of techno. But Barcelona, for all its beauty, is not without strife. Its role as Catalonia's capital has forced it into a pivotal position regarding the future of Spain. The country suffered a brief democratic crisis shortly after the Referendum of 2017—its leaders, confronted with an unfavorable outcome, dissolved parliament and called a snap election. Paradoxically, however, the country's future is clearer now than it was a year ago. Secession is a long way off, at least according to experts. So, what does this mean for you, eager backpacker? Well, the issue of Catalan independence aside, Barcelona is already laced with past remnants of political, social, and economic turmoil. Prior to becoming a tourist hotspot, Castell de Montjuïc served as a prison and torture facility. Until a few decades ago, the Bunkers of Carmel—a romantic viewpoint and local student hangout—functioned as a storage facility for weapons. Despite facing some grueling challenges, the city's citizens have proven to be extremely resilient. They've turned their frustrations into art, and now for every reminder of the city's turbulent past, there exists a beacon of a brighter future. Luckily for you, those beacons are open to the public and waiting to explored.

ORIENTATION

Barcelona is a sprawling metropolis with several different neighborhoods. From south to north along the coast lie **Montjuïc,** a hilly district that contains a castle, a botanical garden, a stadium, Barcelona's **Plaza de España,** and several different museums; **Poble-Sec,** a primarily residential neighborhood famed for its cheap restaurants and bars (check out **Carrer de Blai,** home to Barcelona's infamous €1 tapas); and **El Raval,** a grunge-chic area filled with cutting-edge exhibitions, bohemian bars, and street art. The **Gothic Quarter** is home to **La Rambla** and **Barcelona Cathedral**—two of the city's busiest attractions; south you'll find **Barceloneta,** a beachside neighborhood known for its clubs and cocktail bars, and to the east lies **La Ribera,** previously Barcelona's red-light district. Even further east is **El Poblenou,** which houses Barcelona's tech offices and design showrooms. Inland of these neighborhoods lie **Eixample** and **Gràcia,** which together constitute the majority of the city. **Plaça de Catalunya** serves as the city's de facto center. Important thoroughfares include **La Rambla, Passeig de Gràcia, Passeig de Colom,** and **Avinguda Diagonal,** which splices the city in half. Barcelona's metropolitan center lies south of Avinguda Diagonal and north of **Avinguda del Parallel.**

ESSENTIALS

GETTING THERE

Aeroport del Prat de Llobregat (El Prat Airport) harbors both domestic and international flights. From the airport, you can reach Barcelona's city center via bus, train, or taxi. The Aérobus is an express bus that connects both the international and domestic terminal to Plaça de Catalunya. It departs every 5min. and takes approximately 35min. (one way €5.90, round-trip €10.20).

City buses take slightly longer, but cost less (one way €2.15, round trip €4.50). Alternatively, you can take the metro from the airport to Estació Sants, Passeig de Gràcia, or El Clot. The ride lasts 40min. and costs €4.50. Trains to Estació Barcelona-Sants (domestic and international) and Estació de França (regional) depart from Terminal 1 of El Prat Airport. RENFE trains connect to Bilbao, Madrid, Seville, and Valencia. Barcelona's main bus station is called Estació d'Autobuses Barcelona Nord, and located close to the Arc de Triomf. Buses also depart from Estació Barcelona-Sants and El Prat Airport. Spain's main bus provider is ALSA. Taxis from the airport to the city center cost roughly €35.

GETTING AROUND

The fastest way to get around Barcelona is by metro. A single ride costs €2.15, while a T-10 Zone 1 ticket (10 rides) costs €9.90. Transfers on the Barcelona Metro are free and tickets are compatible with trams, trains, and buses. Metro lines are marked by an L before the line number and tram lines are marked with a T. Metros, trams, and trains run from 5am-midnight Su-Th, from 5am-2am on Friday, and 24hr on Saturday. Barcelona's buses travel to more remote places than the metro. The NitBus picks up the slack while the metro is closed, while BarriBuses (max 10 people) traverse the narrow streets of Barcelona's outer districts.

PRACTICAL INFORMATION

Tourist Offices: Plaça de Catalunya (Pl. de Catalunya; 932 853 834; barcelonaturisme.com; open daily 8:30am-9pm)

Banks/ATMs/Currency Exchange: ATMs abound in Barcelona and can be found on every other block in Eixample and Ciutat Vella. Passeig de Gràcia contains a high concentration of banks, including Deutsche Bank Filiale (Passeig de Gràcia, 112; 934 04 21 02; open M-F 8:30am-2pm).

Post Offices: Here's one in the Gothic Quarter (Plaça d'Antonio López; 934 86 83 02; correos.es; open M-F 8:30am-9:30pm, Sa 8:30am-2pm).

Internet: Free Wi-Fi is available at over 500 locations in Barcelona, including museums, parks, and beaches. Wi-Fi zones are marked by a blue "Barcelona Wi-Fi" sign. You can connect for free after accepting the terms and conditions through your browser.

Public Restrooms: Public toilets are few and far between in Barcelona, except near city beaches. Large shopping centres (or the El Corte Inglés department store) are an option, but restaurants are probably your best bet.

BGLTQ+ Resources: Gay Barcelona (gaybarcelona.com) provides up-to-date tips for finding BGLTQ+ friendly restaurants and bars. Casal Lambda is a Spanish non-profit that offers community spaces for socializing, a center for information and documentation, as well as counseling (Av. del Marquès de l'Argentera, 22; 933 19 55 50; open M-Sa 5pm-9pm).

EMERGENCY INFORMATION

Emergency Number: 112

Police: Police stations are dispersed throughout the city. This one is located on La Rambla (Carrer la Rambla, 43; 932 56 24 30).

US Embassy: Barcelona's US Consulate is located at Passeig de la Reina Elisenda de Montcada, 23 (932 80 22 27; open M-F 9am-1pm).

Rape Crisis Center: The Center for Assistance to Victims of Sexual Assault (CAVA) is located in Madrid, but can provide assistance to persons based in Barcelona (Carrer Alcalá, 124, Suite 1ºA; Madrid; 91 574 01 10).

Hospitals: Hospital Clínic de Barcelona is highly rated and open 24hr (Carrer de Villarroel, 170; 932 27 54 00).

Pharmacies: There are pharmacies located throughout Ciutat Vella and Eixample. Farmacia Clapés is open 24hr and located in the Gothic Quarter (Carrer la Rambla, 98; 933 01 28 43).

ACCOMMODATIONS

🏨 CASA GRACIA ($$)

Passeig de Gràcia, 116; 931 74 05 28; casagraciabcn.com; reception open 24hr

Stay here. Period. It's rare that we're fully sold on a single hostel, especially in a city as big as Barcelona, but Casa Gracia stole our heart—then squished it like a goddamn grape when they charged us. With dorms hovering right around €40, the uptick in price comes an uptick in service and comfort. From the outside, Casa Gracia looks more like a hotel than a hostel, blending seamlessly into the buildings in of the highest-end neighborhoods in Barcelona. After being greeted by a bellman on Casa Gracia's doorstep, you'll be corralled into a full-service cocktail bar that doubles as the hotel's—sorry, hostel's—reception. Two

100-year-old glass elevators connect the ground floor to the upper ones, which contain multiple common rooms, a trellis-covered patio the size of a basketball court, dozens of spacious dorms, and a handful of privates. Dorms feature en-suite baths, custom-designed bunk beds, floor-to-ceiling French doors, and a sprinkling of vintage furniture. Just book it already!

i *Dorms from €40; online reservation recommended; female-only dorms available; wheelchair accessible; Wi-Fi; full kitchen; free breakfast, towels, luggage storage; cocktail bar; lockers; linens provided; laundry available*

JAM HOSTEL ($)

Carrer de Montmany, 38-42; 933 15 53 38; jamhostelbarcelona.com; reception open 24hr

Located in **Gràcia,** Jam Hostel is a welcome change of pace and scenery from Barcelona's tourist-dense **Gothic Quarter.** Its main draw? A private terrace that's the size of a public square. Though the establishment itself is fairly small, it uses space wisely. Wide concrete hallways give way to spacious dorm rooms, spotless bathrooms, and a homey basement kitchen. Pockets of furniture are scattered wherever there's room, creating intimate spaces perfect for exchanging stories with other travelers or simply doing quiet work. Expect long, wine-fueled conversations that lead to meaningful friendships, not short, vodka-fueled pre-games that lead to grinding with sweaty strangers.

i *Dorms from €25; online reservation recommended; no wheelchair accessibility; Wi-Fi; kitchen; free beverages; free luggage storage; lockers; laundry €8; linens provided; towels €2; nightly salsa lessons and/or bar crawls*

360 HOSTEL BARCELONA ($)

Carrer de Bailèn, 7; 932 46 99 73; 360hostel. com; reception open 24hr

Must be something in the air. 360 Hostel hosts social expeditions daily that vary from walking tours to mojito tastings (read: poundings) to classic club nights, and its spacious common room offers many comfortable seating arrangements to converse with fellow travelers. While its colorful patterned floor tiles may be a little cracked, its doors a little worn, and its metal bunks a little wobbly, its other amenities are comfortable enough to fly under our radar of scrutiny. Upstairs, desktop computers clutter the desks that occupy a sun-drenched living space, and

each room comes equipped with a self-controlled AC unit. Dorms feature ample outlets, personal lamps, and lockers, and bathrooms are sizeable enough in number that you won't have to worry about standing in line.

i *Dorms from €30; female-only dorms available; no wheelchair accessibility; Wi-Fi; kitchen; free sangria; free luggage storage; lockers; linens provided; laundry €6*

HARMONY HOSTEL ($$$)

Carrer de Casanova, 52; 935 66 67 25; harmonyhostelbcn.com/hostel/; reception open 24hr

Quiet but not antisocial, Harmony Hostel is the place to stay if you're a fan of separating work and play. Made for the party attendees of the world, this homey hostel is a welcome pad to come back to after a long day of sightseeing or long night of bar-hopping. Though the dorms are dark, they're scrubbed down regularly. Bathrooms are spacious and reliable, and free community dinners are offered three times a week. The décor is what we like to call "eclectic Ikea"—as if Harmony Hostel's owner took an impromptu stroll through the Swedish superstore and, rather than purchasing a complete living room set, picked a single piece from every set on display. At the end of the day, however, the décor won't matter, especially since you'll be spending quite a bit of time getting to and from Barcelona's top attractions.

i *Dorms from €45; female-only dorms available; wheelchair accessible; Wi-Fi; lockers; linens included; laundry €7; free towels; kitchen; free dinner W, F, and Sa*

SIGHTS
CULTURE

BASILICA DE SANTA MARIA DEL MAR

Plaça de Santa Maria, 1; 933 10 23 90; santamariadelmarbarcelona.org/home/; open M-Sa 1pm-5pm, Su 2pm-5pm

Located in the metaphorical shadow of **Catedral de Barcelona,** Basilica de Santa Maria del Mar is not as grand in stature as its sister, but reigns supreme in experience. Built from the ground up by local townspeople during the early fourteenth century, it only took 54 years to build—take that, **Sagrada Família!** Like the great buildings of the Roman

Empire, this Basilica was constructed *ad quadratum,* meaning all of its features are based on the geometry of squares. Its side aisles are half the span of the central one and its columns are perfectly octagonal, lending the space an airiness typically absent from buildings this old. Sadly, the interiors aren't as impressively decorated as they used to be, due to a fire in 1936 that burned for 11 days straight. Still, the Basilica's most iconic architectural elements—the rose window and intricate reliefs—remain intact.

i Admission €10, reduced €8; rooftop tour €8, reduced €6.50; no wheelchair accessibility

🏛 GOTHIC QUARTER

North of La Rambla, west of Barceloneta, south of Via Laietana, east of Plaça de Catalunya; establishment hours vary

Soot-covered palms sway in the warm Mediterranean air, intermittently shading the tables that pepper **Plaça Reial.** Welcome to Barcelona's Gothic Quarter, the *barrio* immediately northeast of **La Rambla.** It's here that you'll find some of the city's oldest monuments, and here that you'll catch a glimpse of a past life in Spain. Originally the center of a Roman settlement, then the region's Jewish Quarter, and later a sombre lower-class neighborhood, the Gothic Quarter underwent a massive restoration project at the turn of the twentieth century. Today you'll find a hodgepodge of architectural styles, ranging from Medieval to Gothic to Flamboyant to Modernisme. Points of interest include the **Roman Walls,** which skirt Plaça Ramón Berenguer and date to the fourth century CE; the **Columbus Monument,** located at the intersection of Passeig de Colom and La Rambla; the **Catedral de Barcelona;** and of course, **La Rambla,** a tree-covered boulevard that doubles as a pedestrian mall.

i Free; limited wheelchair accessibility

🏛 VILLA DE GRÀCIA

Northwest of Avinguda Diagonal, northeast of Via Augusta, southeast of Parc Güell, and southwest of Carrer de Sardenya; establishment hours vary

Not to be confused with **Passeig de Gràcia,** a store-lined, intricately-paved boulevard that connects **Ciutat Vella** to **Eixample,** the district of Gràcia feels removed from the rest of the city, despite the fact that it's only a few metro stops

away. It is the atmospheric antithesis of Barcelona's **Gothic Quarter**—calm and cozy, not hectic and overbearing. Tourists are in the minority among the artists and young professionals who live here. Along with dread-locked youths, you'll encounter a ton of kids playing *fútbol* in plazas and grandmas chit-chatting on benches. At night, Gràcia's sloping streets come alive with patio restaurants serving traditional Catalan *pintxos.* Craft breweries, ethnic eateries, and galleries abound in this vibrant and diverse enclave of Catalan life—its intimate, close-packed streets and predominantly low-rise, Mediterranean buildings lending it a distinct, bohemian feel. We recommend taking a stroll down the lively **Carrer de Verdi** and turning right on **Carrer de Ros de Olano.** Eventually you'll arrive at **Plaça Del Sol,** where groups of students gather nightly to sit on the ground, drink, and be merry.

i Free; limited wheelchair accessibility

🏛 PALAU DE LA MÚSICA CATALANA

Carrer Palau de la Música, 4-6; 932 95 72 00; palaumusica.cat/en; tours daily 10am-6pm every 30min.

Though Antoni Gaudí gets most of the credit for making this city what it is today, he's not the only Spanish architect who left a lasting impression on Barcelona's skyline. **Lluís Domènech i Montaner,** designer of the Palau de la Música Catalana and **Hospital de la Santa Creu i Sant Pau,** hit a few home runs during his lifetime as well. Deemed a **UNESCO World Heritage Site,** this stunning concert hall is a masterpiece of Catalan modernist architecture. You can gawk at its intricate brick and mosaic exterior for free, but getting past the stone busts and glass columns will cost you a pretty penny (the interior is accessible via guided tour only). We'd typically dissuade you from emptying your pockets to listen to a half-there docent mumble for an hour, but in this case—take the tour. Get ready for an explosion of color and light unlike any you've seen before.

i Admission €20, students €11; guided tours in English, Spanish, French, and Catalan; English tours every hour 9am-6pm; wheelchair accessible with advance notice

MERCAT DE LA BOQUERIA

La Rambla, 91; 933 18 25 84; boqueria.
barcelona; open M-Sa 8am-8pm

Oooh, baby, have we got a treat for you!
Located at the end of **La Rambla,** lies
El Mercat de Sant Josep de la Boqueria.
This covered market has roots that stretch
back to 1217, making it one of the
oldest permanent exchanges in Europe.
It wasn't until 1840 that La Boqueria
started making a name for itself. The
dazzling display of nuts, spices, fruits,
vegetables, meat, cheese, and fish behind
its stained-glass facade will make your
head spin and your stomach rumble.
Apparently the market's name derives
from the word *boc,* meaning "goat" in
Catalan—the most popular meat sold
when La Boqueria first opened. Over
the centuries, it has expanded from just
meat to include fish, produce, and finally
today, fully-fledged restaurants.

i Free; food prices vary; limited wheelchair
accessibility

MERCAT SANTA CATALINA

Av. de Francesc Cambó, 16; 933 19 57
40; mercatsantacaterina.com; open M
7:30am-3:30pm, Tu 7:30am-8:30pm, W
7:30am-3:30pm, Th-F 7:30am-8:30pm, Sa
7:30am-3:30pm

This upscale produce market located a
block away from **Catedral de Barcelona**
is easily distinguished by its undulating,
honeycomb roof—a work of art in and
of itself—and easily covered in about
30 minutes. Unlike standard European
markets, Mercado de Santa Catalina's
stalls are organized in a spiderweb
pattern. Here you'll find a variety of
canned goods, smoked meats, fresh fish,
stinky cheeses, ripe fruit, and roasted
nuts—in other words, ideal snacks
to power you through your day in
the **Gothic Quarter.** Indoor-outdoor
restaurants spill onto the nearby avenue,
and a bustling bakery sends passerby
reeling with the pungent smell of bread.
Small olive trees and ivory-colored
umbrellas dot the patio on the market's
western side—perfect for lounging,
passing through, or shamelessly gorging
on the goodies you've just purchased.

i Prices vary; limited wheelchair accessibility

MERCAT FIRA DE BELLCAIRE ELS ENCANTS

Carrer de los Castillejos, 158; 932 46 30 30;
open M, W, F-Sa 9am-8pm

Mercat Fira de Bellcaire Els Encants, or
simply "Els Encants Vells," is a hoarder's
daydream and a neat-freak's worst
nightmare. Welcoming a whopping
100,000 new visitors each week, it's
Barcelona's largest flea market, and the
ideal venue to do some serious discount
damage. The stalls line one side of a
continuously-spiraling ramp that looks
like it continues forever. The real draw
is the market's pit, covered in everything
from rare books to used clothing to
overstock furniture to antiquities to
vinyls to toiletries to car parts to—shall
we go on? Finding treasures here involves
a combination of crawling, tip-toeing,
and leapfrogging over items that—in the
United States—would otherwise reside
comfortably on shelves. The vendors
here are more open to bartering than any
others in Barcelona, so slap on a smile,
load up on cash (but not too much;
pickpockets are everywhere), and get to
talkin'!

i Item prices vary; auctions M, W, and F at
8am; limited wheelchair accessibility

LANDMARKS

🏛 CASA BATLLÓ

Passeig de Gràcia, 43; 932 16 03 06; casa-
batllo.es; open daily 9am-9pm

A dominant silhouette on the **Passeig de
Gràcia** and one of the most emblematic
works by **Antoni Gaudí,** Casa Batlló was
constructed between 1904 and 1906 for
one of Barcelona's preeminent families.
True to the architect's style, this house
has almost no right angles or straight
lines, and is outfitted with walls that
undulate like waves. It is an ode to the
marine world, complete with decorative
elements that shimmer like fish scales
and turquoise stained glass windows
that look like bubbles. Nicknamed the
"House of Yawns" because of its gaping
iron balconies, its exterior is plastered
with lime mortar and sprinkled with
fragments of ceramic and colored
glass—a technique called *trencadís.*
Inside, a wooden stairwell resembling a
twisted spine leads guests to the **Noble
Floor,** offering a panoramic view of the
treetops and street below. Notice how

the windows get smaller and darker as you make your way upstairs. This was a conscious and ingenious design choice made by Gaudí to ensure that the home glows a consistent shade of blue throughout. Prepare yourself for an hour or so of being jostled around by an eager crowd of tourists, punctuated by the occasional *"¡Perdóneme!"*

i Admission €24.50, reduced €21.50; VR guide included; last entrance 8pm; limited wheelchair accessibility

CASTELL DE MONTJUÏC

Ctra. de Montjuïc, 66; 932 56 44 45; ajuntament.barcelona.cat/castelldemontjuic/ca; open daily Apr-Oct 10am-8pm, Nov-Mar 10am-6pm

Perched on the western face of Montjuïc, this palatial fortress dates back to the late seventeenth century, making it one of the oldest compounds in Barcelona. Its grounds are very *Alice in Wonderland,* which is surprising considering this place was used as a political prison for three centuries. Despite its tragic history, it is now one of Barcelona's top attractions because of its sweeping views of the sea and city. It's particularly beautiful in the early morning, before the hordes of tourists arrive and the attractions further west **(Jardí Botànic de Barcelona, Estadi Olímpic Lluís Companys, Fundació Joan Miró)** open their gates. You can get to the castle on foot, by taking the escalators near **Palau Nacional,** by riding the bus from **Plaza de España,** or by taking the funicular from Paral·lel station. Our favorite? The **Port Cable Car,** which connects **Barceloneta** to Montjuïc via air (€11 one way, €16.5 round trip).

i Admission €5, reduced €3; free every first Su and other Su after 3pm; last entry 7:30pm (Nov-Mar 5:30pm); no wheelchair accessibility

CATEDRAL DE BARCELONA

Pl. de la Seu; 933 428 262; catedralbcn.org; open M-F 12:30pm-7:45pm, Sa 12:30pm-5:30pm, Su 2pm-5:30pm

Located in the heart of the **Gothic Quarter,** the Catedral de la Santa Cruz y Santa Eulalia de Barcelona—or simply the Barcelona Cathedral—keeps watch over the city day and night. At both the front and back entrances, docents stand guard like bouncers. No, you won't have to recite a secret password to get in, but you will have to drop €7 and cover your shoulders with a shawl (free). During the afternoon, stained glass windows infuse the light with jewel-toned specks. One of the only choirs in Spain you can actually walk through, it's an impressive example of craftsmanship—each papal chair crowned with its own wooden spire. A dimly-lit crypt separates the aisle from the altar, and is flanked by multiple small chapels. Before departing through the southern courtyard, be sure to checkout its rooftop viewing platform, accessible via an elevator left of the nave.

i Admission €7; free rooftop access; last entry 30min. before closing; no shorts, no tank tops; wheelchair accessible entrance on Carrer del Bisbe

LA SAGRADA FAMILIA

Carrer de Mallorca, 401; 932 08 04 14; sagradafamilia.org/en/; open daily Apr-Sept 9am-8pm, Oct-May 9am-6pm, Dec 25-Jan 6 9am-2pm

Antoni Gaudí's life-long project, La Sagrada Familia was only 25 percent done when the architect died in 1926. By the time construction ceases in 2026, it will have taken longer to build than the Egyptian Pyramids. Why is it taking so long, you ask? The short answer: none of the interior surfaces are flat. Still left to build are 10 towers—six of which are larger than the existing ones, and one of which will reach a whopping 566 feet, making the edifice the largest religious building in Europe. As you move from north to south around its exterior, the stone reliefs emulate the story of the birth, life, and death of Jesus Christ. Inside, the transept depicts a parallel journey: that of the evolution of architecture from Medieval times to present. Particularly fascinating is the southern doorway, which is more "modern" than the world's most impressive skyscrapers. Massive white columns come alive each evening when the sun bursts through the stained glass windows. Whether you're in town for two weeks or two hours, it should be at the top of your priority list.

i Admission €15, with audio guide €22, with guided tour €24, with rooftop visit €29; reserve online at least a week in advance; last entry 30min. before closing; last elevator to Nativity Facade tower 15min. before close; last elevator to Passion Facade tower 15min. before closing; wheelchair accessible

PALAU GÜELL

Carrer Nou de la Rambla, 3-5; 934 72 57 75; alauguell.cat; open Apr-Oct Tu-Su 10am-8pm, Nov-Mar 10am-5:30pm

Gaudí left footprints all over the city, even in **El Raval,** which—until recently—qualified as a Spanish slum. One of his earliest works, Palau Güell lacks the whimsy of **Casa Battló** and **La Sagrada Familia,** but this urban palace is sophisticatedly understated; composed of stained wood, black limestone, and gilded iron. Hollow, echoey halls connect stately salons to dark living quarters—each of which is more impressive than the next. That

said, the highlight of Palau Güell is undoubtedly the **Central Hall.** Here, it's clear just how much of an impact Islamic architecture had on Gaudí's development as an artist. The oculus that rises above this multi-purposed room is riddled with holes. During the day, those holes flood the Central Hall with light, and as time passes, they mimic the night sky.

i Admission €12, reduced €9; free every first Su; audio guide included; last entry 1hr before closing; no wheelchair accessibility

ARC DE TRIOMF

Passeig de Lluís Companys; open daily 24hr

Located at the northern end of the promenade of the **Passeig de Lluís Companys,** the Arc de Triomf is an icon. Unlike its counterpart in Paris, you can walk right up to it without the fear of getting hit by a speeding bus on your way there. Designed in the **Neo-Mudéjar** style, its original purpose was to serve as the main access gate for the **1888 Barcelona World Fair.** Since then, millions of people have passed through it and continued down the palm-tree lined boulevard that extends east from its base. A frieze bearing the Catalan phrase *Barcelona rep les nacions* ("Barcelona welcomes all nations") glows above its archway. We interpret this as Barcelona saying, "We love tourists." So, the next time a local food vendor glares at you for saying, "I quiero esto sandwich," let the Arc de Triomf bring you some piece of mind.

i Free; wheelchair accessible

CASA MILÀ

Passeig de Gràcia, 92; 902 20 21 38; lapedrera.com; open M-Su 9am-8:30pm and 9pm-11pm

Casa Milà—popularly known as **La Pedrera**—was Gaudí's last civil work before he dedicated all of his time to **La Sagrada Familia.** Originally a private residence, it's now a **UNESCO World Heritage Site,** cultural center (did someone say jazz?), and home to a few lucky (read: very wealthy) families. Above several multi-million-dollar apartments lies **L'Espai Gaudí,** a mini-museum that contains small-scale models of the architect's most famous buildings and provides visitors with valuable insights into his life and creative process. The guided tour also includes a journey through Casa Milà's grand foyer and one of the apartments. In all honesty, though, the real magic of the building lives in its self-supporting, corrugated facade. Its undulating stones and iron balconies resemble a stone quarry, and together constitute a textbook example of Catalan modernism.

i Admission €22, students €16.50; day and night tour €41; audio guide included; last entry 30min. before closing; limited wheelchair accessibility

HOSPITAL DE LA SANTA CREU I SANT PAU

Carrer de Sant Quintí, 89; 932 91 90 00; open Nov-Mar M-Sa 9:30am-4:30pm, Su 9:30am-2:30pm; Apr-Oct M-Sa 9:30am-6:30pm, Su 9:30am-4:30pm

Just a short walk from **La Sagrada Familia,** this impressive Catalan modernisme complex houses several buildings—expansions of the original compound—that date to 1901. Its founding was 500 years earlier, when six medieval hospitals merged. Today, it's a tourist attraction and "knowledge center," where thinkers congregate to "tackle the challenges of twenty-first-century society." So, why the sudden shift of purpose? Perhaps the majestic façade, tiled domes, frescoe-covered ceilings, and white marble floors weren't being adequately appreciated by the ill. Ironically, it welcomes more visitors now than it did as a hospital.

i Admission €14, with audio guide €17, with guided tour €18, combined with Palau de la Música €25; free entry every first Su; guided tour in English daily 10:30am; wheelchair accessible

FONT MÀGICA DE MONTJUÏC

Plaça de Carles Buïgas, 1; open daily 24hr; shows Th-Sa Nov-Mar 8pm, Apr-Oct 9pm

Spectacular displays of light, color, music, and water acrobatics are what you're in for at the Font Màgica de Montjuïc. Located in front of the **Palau National** on the previous site of **The Four Columns,** this fountain was designed by **Carles Buïgas** in advance of the **1929 Barcelona International Exposition.** The 3,000 person-strong construction process lasted just over a year. Despite being ravaged in the

Spanish Civil War, it is as glorious today as it was nearly a century ago. For an hour each night, this bubbling cauldron of color captures the attention of thousands of pairs of eyes. Set to classical music playing from surround-sound speakers, these mesmerizing shows elicit *oohs* and *ahhs* with every crescendo, turning the audience into a choir.

i Free; limited wheelchair accessibility

MUSEUMS

FUNDACIÓ JOAN MIRÓ

Parc de Montjuïc; 934 43 94 70; mirobcn.org/en/; open Tu-Sa 10am-8pm except Th 10am-9pm, Su 10am-3pm

Carved into the side of **Montjuïc,** Fundació Joan Miró contains the single greatest collection of works produced by **Joan Miró.** It was designed by one of the artist's closest friends, **Josep Lluis Sert,** and looks a heck of a lot like a stack of white Legos. It's one of the most renowned artistic venues in the world, acclaimed for its airy interior and organic flow. Inside, you'll find the same curves and jagged edges of the foundation's roofline—embodied by the colorful subjects of Miró's paintings and sculptures. The museum also showcases a variety of pieces by other contemporary artists, including long-time legends like **Calder, Duchamp, Oldenburg,** and **Legern,** while the affiliated **Espai 13** focuses on this decade's emerging artists. The complex is expansive and jam-packed, so we recommend purchasing an audio guide and later relaxing in the shady garden to let the information sink in.

i Combined €12, reduced €7; temporary exhibition €7, reduced €5; Espai 13 €2.50; sculpture garden free; audio guide €5; Articket BCN €30; last entry 30min. before closing; wheelchair accessible

MUSEU NACIONAL D'ART DE CATALUNYA (MNAC)

Palau Nacional, Parc de Montjuïc; 93 622 03 60; museunacional.cat; open May-Sept Tu-Sa 10am-8pm, Su 10am-3pm; Oct-Apr Tu-Sa 10am-6pm, Su 10am-3pm

Perched on the slopes of **Montjuïc,** the **Palau Nacional** stands grandly over **Plaza de España.** The grounds, which include a cascading waterfall, never-ending flights of steps, and manicured garden, are worth a visit in and of themselves. Inside this Italian-style behemoth lies an outstanding collection of Romanesque church paintings and frescoes, as well as Catalan art from the late nineteenth and early twentieth centuries (read: a lot of modernisme and noucentisme; upstairs). MNAC also houses several niche pieces, such as **Gaudí's** handcrafted furniture and **Picasso's** cubist work. Palau Nacional's **Oval Hall** (typically closed to the public) is considered one of Europe's best venues to host large-scale events due to its magnificent classical architecture. If you happen to be in town during a poetry reading, concert, or some other kind of performance, it's worth trying to get inside.

i *Admission €12, reduced €8.40; temporary exhibition €4/€6; rooftop access €2; audio guide €4; limited wheelchair accessibility*

FUNDACIÓ ANTONI TÀPIES

Carrer d'Aragó,, 255; 934 870 315; fundaci-otapies.org; open Tu-Th 10am-7pm, F 10am-9pm, Sa 10am-7pm, Su 10am-3pm

Located in the heart of **Eixample,** Fundació Antoni Tàpies is a cultural center and museum dedicated primarily to showcasing the works of **Antoni Tàpies** (shocker!). If you don't know who he is, here's your chance: the guy's a modern art hot-shot known for his whacky 3D paintings, which incorporate waste paper, mud, sticks, and rags. Over time, his focus shifted from painting to furniture-making. The center houses several of these later works, in addition to abstract structures featuring several moving parts. The museum's permanent and temporary exhibitions are displayed in a Modernist building that dates back to 1882. It was the first structure in **Eixample** to integrate industrial typology and technology, combining exposed brick and iron to create stunning decorative landscapes. Today, the Fundació is distinguishable by its tall row of Art Nouveau rose windows and the massive wire cloud on its roof. Titled **Núvol i Cadira,** it was installed there by Tàpies himself.

i *Admission €7, reduced €5.60; last entrance 15min. before closing; wheelchair accessible*

MUSEO DEL FÚTBOL CLUB BARCELONA - CAMP NOU

Carrer d'Aristides Maillol; 902 18 99 00; fcbarcelona.com/tour/buy-tickets; open daily 9:30am-7:30pm

Ever wonder what it feels like to run onto the field of Camp Nou? Well, for €25, you can experience it for yourself—minus the 100,000 screaming painted fans, of course. Barça Museum is one of the most-visited sports museums in Europe. Here, you can get up close and personal with trophies, jerseys, and other significant memorabilia while gaining valuable insights about life on and off the field. The museum's interactive exhibits stress themes like effort, respect, ambition, teamwork, and humility, and are just as informative as they are engaging. Extras like audio guides (€5) and VR headsets (€5) are available to rent during your visit, and are highly recommended—especially the latter. If you consider yourself a die-hard soccer fan and are looking for an outlet to splurge, the **Players' Experience Tour** will grant you access to the field, bench, changing room, and—if you're super lucky—some face-to-face time with the players (€139).

i *Online €25, in person €27.50; stadium guided tour online €40, in person €42.50; limited wheelchair accessibility*

MUSEU D'ARQUEOLOGIA DE CATALUNYA (MAC)

Passeig de Santa Madrona, 39 - 41; 934 23 21 49; mac.cat; open Tu-Sa 9:30am-7pm, Sa 10am-2:30pm

With branches and excavation sites scattered across northern Spain, Barcelona's Archaeology Museum of Catalonia is part of a network dedicated to preserving the region's cultural and technological history. Its permanent collection consists of a variety of **Greek, Roman, and prehistoric artifacts,** and can be covered in about an hour. If you speak Catalan, your visit may last a little longer, but unfortunately for the rest of us, MAC lacks English translations. As you wind through the interactive exhibits on the lower floor, you'll be taken from the origins of man, through stone tool development, and finally to the Bronze and Iron ages. Most mornings, MAC's halls are about as dead as the human skulls in their display cases—great if you're into really old things, but a little too *Night at the Museum* for our taste. It's certainly worth a visit—for its historical significance, for its interesting traveling exhibits (read: entire rooms dedicated to the exploration of sex in the Roman Empire, magic in ancient Egypt, and other "taboo" topics), and for its air-conditioning.

i Admission €5.50, reduced €4.50; limited wheelchair accessibility

MUSEU D'ART CONTEMPORANI (MACBA)

Plaça dels Àngels, 1; 93 481 33 68; macba.cat; open M, W-F 11am-7:30pm, Sa 10am-8pm, Su 10am-3pm; library open M-Th 10am-7pm by appt only

Time to shove a stick up your ass and put in an order for a triple, soy, no foam, vegan latte— we're going to the contemporary art museum! Nah man, we're just messing with you. If you can put up with being frowned at by spectacle-wearing docents, it's an hour or two well-spent. Located on the same plaza as the **Centre de Cultura Contemporània (CCCB)** and **Església de Santa María de Montalegre,** MACBA has quickly risen to the top of Barcelona's museum scene since opening in 1995. Its stark minimalist interior is a far cry from the ribbed vaults and catenary arches that characterize the architecture of the city's major landmarks, making for a welcome change of pace and venue. Now a key player in the modern art world, MACBA harbors some amazing temporary exhibitions (calendar available online). While they vary in medium, explicitness, and immersiveness, it's safe to assume that they all critique contemporary culture.

i Combined €10, reduced €8; temporary exhibition €6, reduced €4.50; free first Su of month; guided tours in English M 6pm; wheelchair accessible

MUSEU PICASSO

Carrer Montcada, 15-23; 932 56 30 00; museupicasso.bcn.cat; open M 10am-5pm, Tu-Su 9am-8:30pm

Barcelona's Picasso Museum is one of the best in the world for two reasons. First, it's free to students. Second, it's located in a restored Medieval building that's so beautiful you'll be tempted to plop down on its central staircase and spend the afternoon staring at its courtyard. Picasso spent part of his youth in Barcelona, which was then undergoing a period of industrial growth. Museu Picasso displays a carefully-curated collection of works produced during his formative years, as well as highlights from his **Blue Period** and the preparatory sketches for Las Meninas, his 58-painting tribute to **Diego Velázquez.** The collection is organized temporally, so you can track Picasso's progression from a technical master to artistic rule-breaker. No assortment of paintings and sketches could better encapsulate the genius' iconic quote: "Learn the rules like a pro, so you can break them like an artist." Museu Picasso hosts over a million visitors each year, so it's best to arrive first thing in the morning.

i Combined €14, permanent collection €11, temporary exhibitions €6.50, students free; free first Su of every month 9am-7pm, free every other Su after 3pm; free guided tours; last entry 30 min before closing; wheelchair accessible

OUTDOORS

🏞 BUNKERS OF CARMEL

Carrer de Marià Labèrnia; 932 56 21 22; bunkers.cat/en/; open daily 24hr

The Bunkers of Carmel keep watch over the city from the top of **Turó de la Rovira,** a 262-meter-tall hill northeast of **Park Güell.** Contrary to its name, there are no bunkers below or around this world-renowned viewing platform. Instead, you'll find a network of abandoned military constructions connected by shantytowns. Now, the only thing preventing the Bunkers from being completely overrun by tourists is its distance from the city center. Once you make it, you'll be greeted with one of the most welcome sights on Earth: the Barcelona skyline. Groups of local twenty-somethings pepper the grounds, armed with picnic blankets, wine, baguettes, and cigarettes. Every night, the sky morphs from pink to purple to periwinkle blue and eventually indigo. On clear nights, the sparkling city below reflects the starry sky above.

i Free; no wheelchair accessibility

PARQUE GÜELL

Enter on Carrer d'Olot, Carretera del Carmel, n° 23 or Passatge de Sant Josep de la Muntanya; www.parkguell.cat; open daily May-Aug 8am-9:30pm, Sept-Oct, Mar-Apr 8am-8:30pm, Jan-Dec 8:30am-6:30pm

UNESCO World Heritage Site and life-size Candyland, Park Güell was designed in 1910 by architectural mastermind **Antoni Gaudí.** Despite the fact that it looks like it was designed to be photographed, this botanical will knock your socks off when you visit it in person. Park Güell's main entrance looks directly upon **La Escalinata del Dragón.** A masterpiece of mosaic and feat of engineering, it consists of two twin staircases flanked by checkered ceramic walls and split by **El Drac,** a colorful stone and glass salamander that shimmers in the Spanish sunlight. Behind the stairway, the columns of **Nature Square** sprout from the earth like great basalt beams. Take a few minutes to wander through **The Hypostyle Room,** a stunning mosaic colonnade. From the iconic benches above it, you can see all the way to the Mediterranean—past the spires of the two gingerbread-house-esque pavilions that together comprise **The Porter's Lodge.** Other highlights include **The Laundry Room Portico, The Austria Gardens, The Gaudí House Museum,** and the three organic **viaducts** that snake up Turó de Tres Creus. Pro tip: if you enter before 8am, the park's entirely yours to explore, take pictures in, and log roll around—for free!

i Admission €7.50; free before 8am; limited wheelchair accessibility

ROSALEDA DE CERVANTES

Av. Diagonal, 706; open daily 10am-9pm

It's a hike to get to, but this publicly-owned park located in the district of **Pedralbes** is home to over 10,000 rose bushes, remaining in full bloom from April to November. Every year, it hosts an international rose competition where new species are presented. Aside from the rose garden, the rest of the park consists of grassy plots and criss-crossing dirt pathways perfect for jogging, biking, or simply contemplating life's beauty. Take a break under a sculptural trellis or in the shade of a low tree to seek rare solace in a city this large. Since you're

already in the area, prolong your visit by checking out the **Royal Monastery of Santa Maria de Pedralbes,** one of Barcelona's most valuable examples of Gothic architecture.

i Free; wheelchair accessible

SANT SEBASTIÀ

Platja de Sant Sebastià; open daily 24hr

With 300 days of sunshine per year, it's no wonder beach-going is one of Barcelona's highest-rated daytime activities. The city's three-mile stretch of golden coastline bustles day and night, with new *chiringuitos* (beach bars) popping up each summer. San Sebastià is located near the end of the pedestrian promenade that parallels **Passeig de Joan de Borbó.** Still, it's quieter than its northern neighbor, **Playa de Sant Miguel.** Here, waves float over the tanned bodies and colorful towels that checker this piece of nature's carpet. The typical sounds of cars are drowned out by laughter and repeated volleyball spikes. Unfortunately, "secluded" beaches are few and far between in this region. If you're up for the trip, check out the beach's twin in **Sitges,** located 30 minutes south of Barcelona by train. Known as the "Spanish Saint-Tropez," Sitges' white sand beaches, turquoise water, and picturesque downtown are a welcome reprieve from the tourist frenzy of **La Barceloneta,** the seaside neighborhood where the Sant Sebastià Beach is located.

i Free; limited wheelchair accessibility; guard belongings at all times; nudity condoned

PARC DE LA CIUTADELLA

Passeig de Picasso, 21; 638 23 71 15; open daily 9am-9pm

New York has Central Park, Barcelona has Parc de la Ciutadella. A popular destination for picnicking, sunbathing, jogging, and drug deali—*wait, what?* Yes, you read that correctly. You'll encounter just as many young parents playing catch with their kids as you will red-eyed college students strumming on ukuleles. *A n y w a y s,* the park was Barcelona's first green space. Since opening to the public in the mid-nineteenth century, it has expanded to include the **Barcelona Zoo,** the **Parliament of Catalonia,** the **Museum** of Natural Science, the **Als Voluntaris Catalans,** and multiple modern sculptures. The **Cascada,** located on northern corner of the park opposite to the lake and rumored to be one of **Antoni Gaudí's** favorite fountains, is particularly beautiful, as are the manicured, flowering walkways near the **Umbracle.**

i *Free; limited wheelchair accessibility*

FOOD

🗺 EL PACHUCO ($)

Carrer de Sant Pau, 110; 931 79 68 05; open Su-Th 1:30pm-1:30am, F-Sa 1:30pm-3am

Take it from us: El Pachuco is the real deal. Although its Mexican tapas aren't what we would call "traditional," they hit the nail on the head when it comes to flavor. The tacos are juicy, the margaritas are generous, but the nachos—piled high with freshly-made toppings and big enough to share—are where El Pachuco really shines. It's a small establishment with a capacity of 30 people, tops. You'll know you're in the right place if you see a chalkboard sign that reads, "Keep Calm and Shut the Fuck Up," and a glass door that's perennially propped open by a hoard of hungry locals. Inside, liquor bottles and portraits of the Virgin Mary sit side by side on a wall of shelves, and parties of patrons huddle around wooden tables. El Pachuco has a strict no reservations and no credit card policy, so arrive an hour before standard meal times, cash in hand, if you want to score a table.

i *Nachos €11.80, 2 quesadillas €7.20, 5 tacos €8.80, beer from €3.20; cash preferred; vegetarian options available; no wheelchair accessibility*

🗺 GASTEREA ($)

Carrer de Verdi, 39; 932 37 23 43; open Th-Tu 7pm-1am

Gasterea's still got it. When we first recommended this place back in 2004, it was on the verge of its big break. Now, 15 years later, we can resolutely say that Gasterea serves the best *pinchos* in all of Barcelona. What initially drew us to this tiny bar was its comically low pricing. And though they've increased over the years due to an explosion in popularity, it remains one of the most inexpensive places to chow down on this side of town. Located on a bustling street in the otherwise quiet, residential neighborhood of **Gràcia,** Gasterea bursts at the seams at night. The hot *pinchos*—like the large plates—are made to order. If you're having trouble deciding where to start, just ask a bartender for some help. Multilingual and way more knowledgeable than we are, they'll be able to guide you in the right direction. Once you've gotten the ball rolling, feel free to gleefully swan-dive into the sea of fatty cheeses, cured meats, buttery fish, and smooth glazes that compose Gasterea's menu. There's truly no way to go wrong here.

i *All pinchos €1.90, casseroles €4.50, wine from €2.25; tap beer from €2.25; cash only; vegetarian options available; no wheelchair accessibility*

BO DE B ($)

Carrer de la Fusteria, 1; 936 67 49
45; open M-Th noon-11:30pm, F-Sa
noon-midnight, Su noon-7:30pm

Bookended by the **Catedral de
Barcelona** and **L'Aquàrium,**
Bo de B serves up scrumptious
Mediterranean sandwiches,
salads, platters, and plates for
a fraction of what they'd cost
on **Plaça Nova.** Though his
menu is Greek in theme and
in flavor, Bo de B's hands-on
owner rejects the construct of
nationality, frequently code-
switching to make sure his
guests feel welcome. Particularly
noteworthy is the Chicken
Tzatziki, served with roasted
peppers, spiced potatoes, sun-dried
tomatoes, chunks of feta cheese,
and yogurt sauce. Unfortunately,
plates and platters are only available
inside, and considering this hole-
in-the-wall joint has a capacity of
15, there's a good chance you'll have
to wait a while before sinking your
teeth into the most tender chicken
in Barcelona. If you're in a hurry, we
recommend ordering something para
llevar, and heading west to nearby
Plaça de l'Ictineo, a park and open-
air sculpture garden that offers great
views of the port.

i Salads from €7, hamburgers from €7;
cash only; vegetarian options available;
no wheelchair accessibility

BODEGA LA PENINSULAR ($$)

Carrer del Mar, 29; 932 21 40 89; taber-
naycafetin.es/la-peninsular/; open daily
1pm-midnight

Pricier than the neighboring local
tapas bars, but La Peninsular's *tapas
marines* (seafood tapas) are a must
if you find yourself in **Barceloneta.**
With a menu that ranges from grilled
cuttlefish and anchovies marinated in
vinegar (€6.90) to more traditional
tapas like *patatas bravas, tortillas
españolas,* and *chorizo,* you'd have to
go out of your way to leave empty-
bellied. Pro tip: Visit on Tuesday
through Saturday, when La Peninsular
purchases its seafood. Another pro tip:
Make a reservation, unless you want
to sit at the bar (which wouldn't be so
bad, considering all three are topped
with white marble). And a bonus one,

NABUCCO TIRAMISU ($)

Plaça de la Vila de Gràcia, 8; 932 17
61 01; nabuccotiramisu.com; open M-F
8:30am-9:30pm, Sa-Su 9am-9:30pm

On the hunt for a strong cup of
joe? Check out Nabucco Tiramisu,
a favorite among local young
professionals. Nabucco's espresso is
the drink equivalent of getting doused
by ice water—a single shot is potent
enough to power you through the rest
of your day. Chipped tables, metal
chairs, and lamps set the tone for
intimate conversation and quiet work.
Hours seem to fly by here, especially
if you fill them by alternating between
typing and chowing down on one of
Nabucco's refreshing fruit tarts, dense
cakes, or specialty tiramisu. If you're
craving something a little heavier,
Nabucco also offers a variety of
salads, pizzas, and sandwiches that are
equally mouthwatering.

i Drinks from €1, pastries from €3, pizza
slice €3, salads and sandwiches from €6;
vegetarian options available; wheelchair
accessible

for you, dear reader: La Peninsular only serves *paella* if you call ahead, so make that damn reservation already!

i Starters from €1.90, tapas from €6.90, wine from €3; reservation recommended; vegetarian options available; wheelchair accessible

CHÖK—THE CHOCOLATE KITCHEN ($$)

Carrer d'Astúries, 93; 933 487 616; chokbarcelona.com/en/; open daily 9am-10pm

You'll feel like a kid in a candy shop in Chök—it'd be hard not to, considering it's a literal candy shop. Of Chök's many locations, our favorite is in **Gràcia,** on the northeast corner of **Plaça de la Virreina.** Here, rows upon rows of chocolate-covered doughnuts, cronuts, cookies, truffles, beautiful little cakes, and other handcrafted delicacies fill sleek, dazzling displays. Our favorite? Chök's signature **cronuts.** These fluffy pastries are equal parts crispy, airy, and chewy, and coated in a thick chocolate shell. Atop this shell lies an impeccably-piped dollop of cream, as well as a sprinkling of sugar toppings. If you're not already bouncing off the walls, wash it all down with a lemonade slushy or other sweet drink, available for purchase at select locations, including this one.

i Truffles €0.50, pastries from €1.50, cronuts €3.95; vegetarian options available; limited wheelchair accessibility

FEDERAL CAFÉ ($$)

Passatge de la Pau, 11; 932 80 81 71; federalcafe.es/barcelona-gotic/; open M-Th 9am-11pm, F-Sa 9am-11:30pm, Su 9am-5:30pm

If you put an egg on something, does that make it brunch? Federal Café thinks so. Situated in the **Gothic Quarter,** Federal Café's **Passatge de la Pau** location looks more like a warehouse than a restaurant. Inside, shiny concrete floors reflect the light let in by a wall of east-facing windows, and carved drywall slabs double as art fixtures. Speaking of art, Federal Café's breakfast dishes could pass as miniature landscapes. Whole avocados—sliced thin, fanned out, and served with almost every savory

dish—resemble the vibrant green terraces of Machu Picchu. Particularly memorable was the build-your-own breakfast plate, which includes your choice of eggs, bacon, sausage, toast, roasted tomatoes, grilled asparagus, sauteed mushrooms, or Halloumi cheese. Each side is made with enough love to be a standalone dish. Put them all together = pure magic.

i Breakfast dishes from €7; toast and pastries from €2; vegan and vegetarian options available; wheelchair accessible

QUIMET & QUIMET ($$)

Carrer del Poeta Cabanyes, 25; 934 42 31 42; open M-F noon-4pm and 7pm-10:30pm

Located in **Poble-Sec,** known for its €1 tapas and cheap drinks, Quimet & Quimet's been leading the pack or five generations. It's so popular, in fact, that it's only open Monday through Friday—it's able to sustain business without working weekends. Each *bocadillo* on its menu is toasted to perfection, and slathered with the most sinful of toppings: anchovies, goat cheese, smoked salmon, truffle honey, tuna belly, sea urchin—the list goes on and on. We recommend starting with two or three, and ordering more once you figure out what you like. If you're not into finger food (though we can't imagine anyone *disliking* the kind offered here), Quimet & Quimet offers a variety of traditional Catalan dishes, as well as assortments of meat, cheese, and seafood. The restaurant itself consists of only a short bar and standing room only. We recommend paying Quimet & Quimet a visit during off hours so you can gorge on your *pintxos* in peace.

i Tapas from €2.50, beer from €5.75; vegetarian options available; limited wheelchair accessibility

NIGHTLIFE

LE JOURNAL

Carrer de Francisco Giner, 36; 933 68 41 37; open Su-Th 6pm-2am, F-Sa 6m-3am

Wickedly strong mojitos are the name of the game here. This quirky cocktail bar is a fantastic place to start an evening, and an equally good place to end it. Its location near **Passeig de Gràcia** makes it a prime launch pad no matter where you're headed, but for most, it's the first stop on a long trek towards the **Gothic Quarter,** home to Barcelona's most popular clubs and infamous underground piano bars. Inside, a small wooden bar gives way to a larger, sunken room. Le Journal's laid-back ambiance qualifies it as an ideal venue to tell stories, not necessarily to make them. As the evening unfolds, the bar's patrons steadily decrease in age. By midnight, Le Journal is stuffed to its wicker brim with young professionals and artistic types looking for an efficient way to kick off an evening of clubbing.

i Cocktails from €6, smoothies from €4.50; no wheelchair accessibility

▨ MARULA CAFÉ

Carrer dels Escudellers, 49; 933 18 76 90; open W-Th 11pm-5am, F-Sa 11:30pm-6am, Su 11pm-5am

Known for its alternative music scene and live performances, this is the place to go if the thought of bouncing around aimlessly to house music makes you squeamish. Behind several layers of red velvet curtains lies a fully-stocked bar, a dance floor, and an elevated stage, upon which local performers congregate to demonstrate their chops each evening; genres can range from funk to R&B to classic jazz in a single night. The clientele here verges on hipster—you'll see more flannel shirts and band tees than shimmery cocktail dresses and bicep-hugging button-ups. Coincidentally, this clandestine bar hosts fewer creeps than your standard nightclub, making it easy to kick back and actually enjoy the show. Still, we urge you to exercise caution; the area around **La Rambla** is notoriously sketchy at night (pickpockets and dealers congregate here to peddle drugs, alcohol, and club tickets), and is best traversed in groups.

i Cover from €10, shots €4; limited wheelchair accessibility

▨ OPIUM

Passeig Marítim, 34; 932 25 91 00; opiumbarcelona.com; open Su-W noon-5am, Th-Sa noon-6am

Famed as one of the best clubs in the world, Opium's lineups are up there. Its massive capacity, sleek decor, scantily-clad waitresses, and killer sound system attract DJs and artists from around the world, including **David Guetta, Bob Sinclar, Martin Solveig, Armin Van Buuren,** and **Jason Derulo.** This upscale bar-club combo offers stunning views of **Playa de la Barceloneta** and the Mediterranean Sea, making it popular among one-stoppers who roll up at sunset and party until the wee hours of the morning. Inside, mirrors reflect the multi colored spotlights that continually search Opium's crowded dance floor, and tall window panes bear sweat stains left by Brian, the underprepared, overeager frat bro who drunkenly mistook them for exits. If you're only in Barcelona for a night, we encourage you to give Opium a try (not the drug, ya dingo): this club never fails to deliver.

i Cover €20; ticket prices spike for big names; casual cocktail attire; limited wheelchair accessibility

JAMBOREE DANCE CLUB

Plaça Reial, 17; 933 04 12 10; masimas.com/jamboree; open daily 8pm-5am (schedule varies depending on performances)

For the uninitiated tourist, this premier dance club is a soft introduction to the hard-core clubbing promised to them by a Ibiza-frequenting older sibling. But, for those in-the-know, its a convenient place to let your guard down and dance the night away with your closest friends. The regular crowd is easy on the eyes, its concerts easy on the ears, and its drinks easy on the liver. A hike down a steep staircase leads you into the main room, which consists of a steamy brick cave below Barcelona's **Gothic Quarter.** Here, the music veers towards the mainstream, which—while frustrating to the die-hard Jazz fans out there—makes for some great communal moments. Upstairs, the music varies from indie rock to alternative—just depends on the night. Concerts typically take place at 8pm and 10pm (check online for specifications), after which Jamboree transforms into a fully-fledged club.

i Cover from €10, free if organized through hostel; drinks from €5; casual attire; no wheelchair accessibility

SALA APOLO

Carrer Nou de la Rambla, 113; 933 01 00 90; www.sala-apolo.com/en; open Su-Th midnight-5am, F-Sa 12:30am-6am

If an evening of reckless abandon is what you seek, look no further. This 75-year-old concert hall is one of the most visited in Europe, and the unequivocal center of nightlife in Barcelona. Its main floor features an aged, curtain-framed stage that—miraculously—keeps a very active mosh pit away from the on-call DJ. The club's original wood floors still bear the scuffs left by cinephiles who frequented this place decades ago. In addition to a single disco ball, gilded chandeliers hang luxuriously from the 50-foot ceiling. Outside of the pit, the bar and large lounge blur together, spinning in a medley of smoke and dim green light. Here, a refreshingly diverse crowd of angsty teens bobs slowly to the rhythm of reggae, and everyone over the age of 30 stands out like a sore thumb. Music ranges from hip hop to techno to Latin, varying by night.

i Cover from €13, drinks from €7; casual attire

GRANADA

Coverage by **Austin Eder**

Famed for the iconic Alhambra, an elaborate palatial fortification located atop a foothill of the Sierra Nevada Mountain Range, Granada's riches extend far beyond this one landmark. With history that dates back thousands of years, it's seen a lot (including three conquests, first by Romans, then by the Umayyad dynasty, and finally by Catholic monarchs!). Now, this city is more deliciously complex than any other in the south of Spain. Evidence of cultural exchange between Eastern and Western societies is apparent in everything from the cross-hatched beams that line several ceilings in the Nasrid Palaces—a quintessentially Moorish structure—to *flamenco*, the performance art whose origins trace back to the Gypsy caves of Sacromonte. Get lost in the winding maze of streets that is the Albaicín, Granada's Arabic quarter, and travel back in time to the Renaissance with a visit to the Capilla Real, under which rest Granada's final conquerors, Queen Isabella of Castile and King Ferdinand of Aragon. Here, daytime activities abound, such as admiring the graffiti art of El Niño de las Pinturas while strolling through el Realejo, or lounging on a hammock on a hostel rooftop. "Granada," meaning "pomegranate," is a unified whole larger than the sum of many sweet parts. Here, we've united some of the sweetest.

ORIENTATION

Tucked in a crook of the **Sierra Nevada Mountain Range,** Granada rests at the confluence of four rivers: the **Darro,** the **Genil,** the **Monachil,** and the **Beiro.** Its bus and train stations lie three kilometers northwest of the **Catedral de Granada,** which acts as the de facto city center. If you envisioned Granada as a letter "C," **la Alhambra**—the city's largest attraction—would fall in its center. Starting from the top of the C and curving around clockwise lie **Sacromonte,** Granada's cave community on the northern bank of the Río Darro; **el Albaicín,** its mountainous Arabic quarter; **Centro,** its modern, urban center; and **Realejo,** its graffiti-covered Jewish quarter. **Calle Gran Vía de Colón** runs diagonally (northwest-southeast) through the city center, splitting the Albaicín and el Centro, and intersects with **Calle Reyes Católicos** at **Plaza Isabel la Catolica. Plaza Nueva,** located near the gate of the Alhambra just north of the Catedral, is one of Granada's most famous gastronomic centers. As you move south, Granada grows increasingly more residential and industrial.

ESSENTIALS
GETTING THERE

The bus station is located at Carretera de Jaén (958 18 50 10). AISA buses (958 18 54 80; alsa.es) run throughout Andalucía and connect to the Madrid and Valencia-Barcelona lines. Transportes Rober runs regular services between the station and the city center. To get to the city center from the bus station, take bus SNI and get off at the Catedral stop. The main train station (958 27 12 72) is located at Av. de los Andaluces. RENFE trains (renfe.es) run to and from Barcelona, Seville, and several smaller cities. Aeropuerto Federico García Lorca is located about 15km outside of the city and services domestic and international budget airlines. A taxi will take you to the city center (€25) or directly to the Alhambra (€28). You can book a taxi in advance through Radio Taxi (963 70 33 33), but all major stations typically have queues. The bus company Autocares José González offers a direct service between the airport and the city center (€3; 958 39 01 64; autocaresjosegonzalez.com; every hour daily 5:20am-8pm).

GETTING AROUND

Transportes Rober runs almost 40 bus lines around the city as well as smaller direct buses to the Alhambra, the Albaicín, and Sacromonte (€1.20 per ride, €5 for 7 rides; 900 71 09 00; transportesrober.com). The tourist lines are #30, 31, 32, and 34. The circular lines (#11, 13, and 23) make full loops around the city. Rober also runs a special Feria line (€1.40) When most lines stop running at 11:30pm, the Búho lines pick up the slack (€1.30; #111 and 121; daily midnight-5:15am).

PRACTICAL INFORMATION

Tourist Offices: Granada's main tourist office is located at el Ayuntamiento, or the City Hall (Pl. del Carmen; 958 248 280; granadatur.com; open M-Sa 9am-8pm, Su 9am-2pm).

Banks/ATMs/Currency Exchange: Most ATMs are located in Granada's urban center, or the flat part of the city, specifically along Calle Gran Vía de Colón. Interchange is a money-exchange office that services for all major credit cards, including American Express (C. Reyes Católicos, 31; 958 22 45 12; open M-Sa 9am-10pm, Su 11am-3pm and 4pm-9pm).

Post Offices: Puerta Real (Puerta Real, 2, at the intersection of C. Reyes Católicos and Acera del Darro; 902 19 71 97; open M-F 8:30am-8:30pm, Sa 9:30am-2pm). Granada's postal code is 18005.

Public Restrooms: As far as free restrooms go, you're out of luck in Granada. Most establishments that have an entrance fee come equipped with clean restrooms, however.

Internet: Free public Wi-Fi is available at fast food chains and most cafés surrounding major monuments. Don't be afraid to ask waiters and waitresses for passwords: *¿Tiene Wi-Fi gratis?* Otherwise, Biblioteca de Andalucía has desktop computers that you can use for free for up to 1hr (C. Prof. Sainz Cantero, 6; 958 02 69 00; open M-F 9am-2pm). Idolos and Fans offers photocopying, fax, scanning, and Wi-Fi services (Camino de Ronda, 80; 958 52 14 96; open daily 10am-midnight).

BGLTQ+ Resources: Andalucía Diversidad offers information, social services, counseling, legal advice, and other resources to municipalities (C. Victoria, 8; 951 00 38 14; info@ andalucialgbt.org).

EMERGENCY INFORMATION

Emergency Number: 112

Police: The local police HQ is located at C. Huerta del Rasillo (958 20 68 78; open daily 9am-2pm). For major issues, head to the Granada Police Station (Pl. de los Campos (Realejo); 958 808 800; open daily 9am-2pm).

US Embassy: The nearest US Consulate is in Málaga (Av. Juan Gómez Juanito, 8; 952 47 48 91; open M-F 10am-2pm). Spain's US Embassy is located in Madrid (C. de Serrano, 75; 91 587 2200; es.usembassy.gov).

Rape Crisis Center: Call Granada Police Station at 958 808 800.

Hospitals: Hospital Universitario Vírgen de las Nieves (Av. de las Fuerzas Armadas, 2; 958 02 00 00; open daily 24hr)

Pharmacies: There are few 24hr pharmacies near the intersection of C. Reyes Católicos and Acera del Darro, including Farmácia Martín Valverde (C. Reyes Católicos, 5; 958 26 26 64).

ACCOMMODATIONS

🏨 MAKUTO BACKPACKERS HOSTEL ($$)

C. Tiña, 18; 958 80 58 76; makutohostel. com; reception open daily 8am-midnight; check in after 2pm, check out by 11am

Makuto Hostel is truly a backpacker's paradise—a claim supported by its amenities as well its guests, who often end up extending their stays (or even sign up to stay permanently as volunteers). Here, life centers around a lush, open-air courtyard that's decked out with a tiki bar, community dinner table, towering pomegranate tree, hammocks, and a zen nook, designed to serve as a reprieve from Makuto's social, verging on cult-like atmosphere. Ascend either of its terracotta staircases and you'll find smart, staggered, triple-decker bunks that stretch all the way up to the rafters, as well as several additional common spaces. The only downside to this hostel is the bathroom. More national park outhouse than indoor toilet, Makuto's singular station for relief is coed, crowded, and crustier than the toast served with free breakfast, despite the fact that it's cleaned daily.

i Dorms from €18; online reservation recommended; no wheelchair accessibility; Wi-Fi; kitchen; free breakfast; dinner €6; bar; linens included; towels and laundry for a fee; lockers in basement; free daily walking tour

CUEVAS COLORÁS ($)

C. Cuevas Coloradas, 23; 666 93 32 01; cuevascoloras.com; reception open by appt. only; check in 3pm-11pm, check out by 1pm

If we had to choose one word to describe Cuevas Colorás it would be… erotic? We hesitate to end that sentence with a period because, well, there's a cap to how romantic a cave can be. Yes, you read that correctly. *A cave.* Despite Cuevas Colorás' efforts to spruce the place up with splotches of deep red paint, bohemian tapestries, low couches piled high with colorful pillows, and countless paintings of naked women, it remains—at the end of the day—a damp, windowless hole in the ground. Structurally, this hilltop hostel consists of a crumbling stone and stucco facade, a subterranean common room and kitchen, a quaint private room (which, when we visited, was occupied by staff members who—how do we put this delicately?—were more keen on exploring each other's caves than the one they were (not) sleeping in. (You'd think solid earth would be more soundproof.) The hostel features a single bathroom, two shockingly-comfortable dorm rooms (one above ground one below), and a rooftop terrace—undoubtedly Cuevas Colorás' best feature. Situated on one of the highest streets in the **Albaicín,** this dwelling offers breathtaking views of **la Alhambra, la Sierra Nevada,** and the Granadan valley.

i Dorms from €15; online reservation recommended; no wheelchair accessibility; Wi-Fi; kitchenette; free breakfast; rooftop terrace; linens included; towels €2; laundry €4; lockers

SIGHTS
CULTURE

🏛 EL ALBAICÍN

Neighborhood open year-round

Though the Alhambra may draw you to Granada, the Albaicín might make you want to stay—it tends to have that effect on backpackers, who squat in this *barrio's* homey hostels for weeks, sometimes months longer than they initially anticipated. We recommend setting your map aside and following your feet through this web of winding cobblestone streets, crumbling stone walls, and vine-covered *carmens* (stucco-covered, open floor plan houses). Today, highlights of this **UNESCO world heritage site** include the **Mirador de San Nicolás; Puerta de Elvira,** an eleventh-century Moorish arch that originally served as one of the gates in the city walls; **Calle Elvira,** center of Granada's modern Moorish quarter and home to dozens of merchandise and souvenir shops; **el Mirador de la Placeta Álamo del Marqués,** a private viewpoint that offers the best westward-facing views of the city (open to the public daily 10am-8pm); and **Plaza Larga,** which transforms into a produce market most weekday mornings.

i Free; no wheelchair accessibility

LANDMARKS

🗺 CATEDRAL DE GRANADA (GRANADA CATHEDRAL)

C. Gran Vía de Colón, 5; 958 22 29 59; catedraldegranada.com; open M-Sa 10am-6:30pm, Su 3pm-6pm

The Cathedral of Granada was the first major undertaking of Ferdinand and Isabella after conquering the Nasrid Dynasty in 1492, and is the architectural equivalent of flipping the bird. A symbol of power and affluence, it boasts soaring Corinthian columns, a disorienting checkered floor, imposing Baroque organs, numerous chapels outfitted with **Renaissance, Gothic,** and **Rococo detailing,** and a boat-load of religious art and idolatry. If its white stucco walls haven't already drawn your eyes upward, take a gander at the ceiling and let your focus drift to the back of the nave. As far as stained glass, frescoes, and gilded reliefs go, it's truly one of the most impressive in Europe, rivaling that of the Sainte-Chapelle de Paris and St. Peter's Basilica in Rome. If you're crunched for time, we recommend listening to tracks on the audioguide 1, 4, 6, and 9 for an overview of the history of the cathedral's surroundings.

i Admission €5, students €3.50; wheelchair accessible

LA ALHAMBRA

C. Real de la Alhambra; 958 027 971; alhambradegranada.org; open Tu-Sa 9am-6pm, Su 9am-3:30pm

The Alhambra is kind of like Disneyland in that it is truly one of the most magical places on Earth, even though after spending four hours traipsing around this 142,000-square-meter wonderland, you'll begin seriously contemplating log-rolling down the hillside to escape the sun, hour-long lines between attractions, and screams of hungry children. (Read: pack a lunch, or you'll find yourself *internally screaming* as you savor every last crumb of the €3 bag of potato chips you purchased to avoid starvation.) To clarify, "Alhambra" refers to the entire collection of palaces, gardens, patios, baths, fortresses, and museums that sit atop a hill at the edge of the **Sierra Nevada Mountain Range,** not just a singular structure. Among the highlights of this royal city are the **Alcazaba,** a fourteenth-century Moorish fortress that offers a unique peek into Medieval military culture; the **Torre de la Vela,** one of four towers that flank the Alcazaba and the best viewpoint in all of Granada; the **Museo des Bellas Artes,** located in the **Palacio Carlos V,** a magnificent Renaissance building; the **Medina,** a plaza rimmed by public baths, ovens, workshops, and homes; the **Generalife Palace,** a royal mountain getaway, so to speak; and last, but certainly not least, the **Nasrid Palaces**—the permanent residence of Nasrid sultans and Catholic monarchs.

i Admission tickets (€7) include access to the Gardens, Alcazaba, and Nasrid Palaces; tickets available online, at Coral de Carbon, or at any La Caixa Bank ATM in Granada (€15.40); many parts of the Alhambra including the Plaza de los Aljibes can be accessed for free; advance tickets recommended; arrive at 5:30am if trying to buy a ticket day-of; 30min. tours meet at Nasrid Palaces; audio guides €6; limited wheelchair accessibility

MUSEUMS

CAPILLA REAL GRANADA (GRANA-DA ROYAL CHAPEL)

C. Oficios; 958 22 78 48; capillare-algranada.com; open Mar-Aug M-Sa 10:15am-1:30pm and 4pm-7:30pm, Su 11am-1:30pm and 2:30pm-6:30pm; Sep-Feb M-Sa 10:15am-1:30pm and 3:30pm-6:30pm

The Gothic counterpart to the **Catedral de Granada,** the Capilla Real Granada is one of the city's biggest draws and the official resting place of **Queen Isabella of Castile** and **King Ferdinand of Aragon.** The duo commissioned the construction of this chapel for just that purpose in 1504, but it wasn't completed until 1517—a year after Ferdinand kicked the proverbial bucket and thirteen after Isabella kicked hers. Upon entering, you'll be taken aback by the shrine's grandeur. An ornamented wrought-iron gate separates the aisle from the marble mausoleums above the crypt. At the back of the chapel, a gilded altarpiece stretches from floor to ceiling, and Renaissance paintings adorn the walls on either side. An adjacent room has since been converted to a small museum that houses some of Isabella's most prized possessions, including her crown and scepter.

i Admission €5, students €3.50; audio guides included; wheelchair accessible

MUSEO CUEVAS DEL SACROMON-TE (SACRAMONTE CAVES)

Barranco de los Negros; 958 21 51 20; sacromontegranada.com; open daily Mar 15-Oct 14 10am-8pm, Oct 15-Mar 14 10am-6pm

A scenic 30-minute walk is all that separates the Museo Cuevas del Sacromonte from the hustle and bustle of **Plaza Nueva,** yet it feels like an entirely different world. Set in a canyon amidst dry brush, cacti, and native wildlife, this open-air museum offers a refreshing take on the history of the region and its original inhabitants: Roma refugees who were expelled at the turn of the fifteenth century. Via a self-led tour through a series of refurbished caves, Museo Cuevas del Sacromonte zooms in on the domestic life of eighteenth- and nineteenth-century Gypsies. Duck and weave from one room to another as you learn about what daily life was like for members of this outcast community and about the Roma origins of Andalusia's iconic dance, **flamenco.** Museo Cuevas del Sacromonte is truly a treasure trove of information—information that's frequently overlooked by the city's more mainstream museums.

i Admission €5; no wheelchair accessibility

OUTDOORS

MIRADOR DE SAN NICOLÁS

C. Mirador de San Nicolás; open daily 24hr

The final destination of nearly every city walking tour, Mirador de San Nicolás is located in the heart of the **Albaicín** and is Granada's second-most popular attraction. Tourists congregate here to snap a picture of the **Alhambra**—now eye-level—and the snow-capped **Sierra Nevadas** that loom behind it. This cobblestone square is especially busy around 9pm, when street performers and local artisans flood its tree-canopied center and the hilltop fortress is spotlighted by horizontal beams of sunlight. TWe recommended paying the **Mirador** a visit at sunrise. If you arrive early enough, you'll have the place to yourself, save the locals that shuffle along **Callejón Atarazana** carrying heaping bags of groceries. Take a seat on the plaza's low, southern-facing wall—worn smooth by literal centuries of sweaty bottoms—and watch the sun ascend behind eight centuries of history.

i Free; no wheelchair accessibility

HIKING IN THE SIERRA NEVADAS

South of Granada

Not only does Granada's location at the base of the Sierra Nevada Mountain Range make it one of the most stunning urban landscapes on Earth, it also affords some killer hiking options. If you're feeling the need to get in some additional vertical, strap on your most supportive sneakers and take Bus #138 to **Monachil.** Though only 20 minutes from the city center, this European hiking hub feels as remote on its edges as it does in the park center. The trails that depart from Monachil will take you through dry, open plains as well as lush forests, and eventually connect to a small waterfall, where you can strip off, jump in, and cool down. Hostels often offer guided tours of the region, but the trails are easy to navigate, so no need to incur the expense if you're open to hiking alone.

i Bus €1.50; guided hostel tours from €10; bus runs hourly in both directions; no wheelchair accessibility

FOOD

🖾 BAR ÁVILA ($)

C. Verónica de la Virgen, 16; 685 42 49 06; open M-F 9am-midnight, Sa 9am-5pm

If you're on the hunt for tasty tapas, set your scope on Bar Ávila. This dive is a local favorite, frequented primarily by working couples and grandfatherly-types. In traditional Granadan fashion, every drink is served with a tapa. What's unique about Bar Ávila, however, is that *you* get to choose which one. The *carne en salsa* is dependably delicious and pairs wonderfully with a caña of Cerveza Alhambra, the city's local draft. As far as larger plates go, Bar Ávila's *calamares fritos* strikes a perfect balance between salty, spicy, and sour. Enjoy your meal at the dark granite counter or at a table around back—either way, you're sure to leave this bar's napkin-littered interior full and satisfied.

i Caña y tapa €2; vegetarian options available; no wheelchair accessibility

🖾 CAFÉ - BAR REINA MONICA ($$)

C. Panaderos, 20; 633 21 71 18; open daily noon-midnight

The five words you've been longing to hear ever since you left the States: all-you-can-eat buffet. Cheap food in the **Albaicín** is hard to come by, so we were shocked when we encountered a sign around the corner from the **Mirador de San Nicolás** that advertised a drink, bottomless tapas, and a dessert for just €10. With over 30 varieties of tapas, scrumptious paellas, roasted vegetables, and traditional *tostadas*, Café-Bar Reina Monica is the place to try out menu items you've been hesitant to sample out

elsewhere. If you don't like something, go back for something else—here, doing so won't send you into the red. Speaking of red, the stuffed tomatoes are an all-around win, as are the vibrant checked tablecloths that pop below the blue flower pots dangling from this restaurant's façade.

i Buffet from €10, bocadillos from €3; vegan and vegetarian options available; limited wheelchair accessibility; Wi-Fi

RESTAURANTE HICURI ART VEGAN ($$)

Pl. de los Girones, 4; 858 98 74 73; restaurantehicuriartvegan.com; open M-Sa noon-11pm

Perhaps the most common stereotype about veganism is that it perpetuates a lifestyle of deprivation. Restaurante Hicuri Art Vegan turns this stereotype on its head, serving up heaping plates of micronutrient-dense comfort food such as burgers, stir-fry, smoothies, tiramisu, and cheesecake. As for the other stereotypes, however, it leans into full-throttle. The restaurant's Birkenstock-wearing, Kombucha-sipping customers look as if they could spring from their wooden chairs, join hands, and sing Kumbaya. Similarly, the splattering of blossoming plants and floor-to-ceiling murals of children climbing trees under the contemplative gaze of a personified Mother Earth scream peace-loving hippie. The décor aside, Restaurante Hicuri Art Vegan's doing something right, as you'll be as hard-pressed as its juices to get a table without a reservation.

i Menú del día from €13.80, starters from €5, burgers from €7.50, smoothies from €4; caters to all dietary constraints; no wheelchair accessibility

NIGHTLIFE

🖾 BOHEMIA JAZZ CAFÉ

Pl. de los Lobos, 11; bohemiajazzcafe.negocio.site; open daily 3pm-2:45am

Arguably the coolest bar in Granada, there's enough eye fodder on Bohemia's walls, booze in Bohemia's cocktails, and soul in Bohemia's playlist to keep you occupied for *hours*. By day, it's an intimate hangout for artistic types and elderly locals, who sip on coffee concoctions topped with towers of whipped cream. By night, its curious ambiance is magnified by the low and rhythmic pulse of live jazz music. Here, wooden tables are surrounded by hundreds of photographs, frilly lamp shades, art deco posters, abstract art, and vintage knick-knacks. If you're coming for a show, be sure to check Bohemia's (very active) Facebook page for dates and times before arriving.

i Coffee from €2.50, sundaes from €4.50, cocktails from €6; no wheelchair accessibility

EL BAR DE ERIC

C. Escuelas, 8; 958 27 63 01; open daily 9am-2am

Owned by Eric Jiménez, lead drummer of Los Planetas, this rock-and-roll-themed bar in the center of Granada is decked out in funky black-and-white wallpaper and a smattering of photo art, posters, and tickets. Here, you can get a taste of trendy fusion food during the afternoon and of Granada's local music scene at night—once the clock strikes 10pm, this welcoming restaurant transforms into a poppin' venue for up-and-comers, attracting young people from across the city. Choose from a wide selection of wines and cocktails and kick back at a glossy white table for an acoustic performance you're sure to remember.

i Wine from €2.80, coffee from €1.30, raciones from €6; vegan and vegetarian options available; wheelchair accessible

BOOM BOOM ROOM

C. Cárcel Baja, 10; 608 66 66 10; boomboomroom.es; open Su-Th 3pm-6am, F-Sa 3pm-7am

Upon entering Boom Boom Room at 11pm on a Thursday, we thought we'd stepped into the foyer of an abandoned cruise ship. Turns out that in its previous life, this high-end discotec was a cinema, hence the grand entryway, towering ceilings, and split-level set up. According to its website, Boom Boom Room is committed to being Granada's number-one nightlife destination for the city's millennial population, and boy, does it deliver. Enter and you'll find yourself surrounded by overly-groomed men donning white button-ups that pucker around their biceps and ladies donning flashy dresses and strappy heels that echo the flashes of the multi-colored strobe lights dangling from the ceiling. On paper, BBR opens at 3pm; in reality, it opens at midnight. Arrive at 2am on a Friday for prime partying.

i Cover €10, drinks from €5; check Facebook page for drink promos; wheelchair accessible; cocktail attire

IBIZA

Coverage by **Austin Eder**

Though acclaimed for its nightlife, the White Isle—named for its abundance of white buildings—offers a ton of daytime activities. Whether you want to fill your time cooking like a lobster on a sandy beach or hiking Sa Talaiassa to work off a hangover, Ibiza has a little something for everyone. But who are we kidding? If you're reading this, odds are you're interested in one thing and one thing only: partying. Cut to Ibiza Town ("Eivissa"), the island's largest city. Here, time is seldom acknowledged, shots are sold in pairs, and the low rumble of bass plays deafeningly. Ibiza's true colors shine brightest against the pitch-black backdrop of the early morning, when the island's clubs flood with music lovers eager to experience the type of debauchery seen only in films. It'd be hard to run out of things to do on this well-endowed island, which boasts some of the world's most picturesque coves, rustic villages, imposing fortresses, and wildest locals. Sounds amazing, right? Well, for the most part, it is. But (and there's always a but), *Let's Go* would recommend that female travelers visit Ibiza as part of a group. Although Facebook groups and internet forums geared towards solo travel abound, they're not actively monitored and are—or were, when we last checked—filled with men looking for "female companions" to escort them on their island getaways. So, unless you're wanting to get a taste of the sugar-baby-slash-potential-murder-victim lifestyle, try to befriend your hostel roommates. Otherwise, it's time to mentally and physically prepare yourself for evenings of unwanted solicitations by drunken dude groups, which seem to keep on comin' no matter what you wear, where you are, or what time of night it is.

ORIENTATION

Ibiza is a Spanish island located approximately 185 kilometers southeast of **València.** At just 25 kilometers wide and 45 kilometers long, it's one of the smallest Balearic Islands. **Ibiza Town ("Eivissa"),** located on the southeast corner of the island, is Ibiza's largest city, followed by **San Antonio** (located on the western seaboard) and **Santa Eulària des Riu** (located on the eastern seaboard, north of Ibiza Town). Important thoroughfares to keep in mind while navigating Ibiza Town include **Avinguda de Santa Eulària des Riu,** which runs north-south and connects the **Port d'Eivissa** to **Dalt Vila,** Ibiza's historic walled town; and **Avenida d'Isidor Macabich,** which runs east-west through Ibiza Town's urban center and contains one of the city's most popular bus stops. **Avenida de Sant Jordi** leads southwest to **Playa d'en Bossa,** home to some of Ibiza's hottest clubs. Even further south lies **Aeroport d'Eivissa,** the island's primary airport. **Avinguda C-731** connects Ibiza Town to San Antonio. On the west side of the island, north-south **Avinguda del Doctor Fleming** and east-west **Passeig de la Mar** together skirt the **Port de Sant Antoni. Carrer de Madrid** cuts straight north from San Antonio's Balearia terminal into the center of the city. Ibiza's most frequented nightclubs are located in and around Ibiza Town, but San Antonio attracts a consistent crowd of young adults due to its slightly lower prices.

ESSENTIALS
GETTING THERE

There are two ways to get to Ibiza: by plane and by ferry. Flights out of Barcelona and Valencia are considerably cheaper than ferries if you book several weeks in advance. Aeroport d'Eivissa is located 6km south of Ibiza Town, and accepts major airlines as well as budget ones including Ryanair, Spanair, Iberia, Air Europa, and Vueling. To get to Eivissa from the airport, take Bus #10 (€3.50; payable on board) to Avinguda d'Espanya. Buses depart from the airport every 30min. and the average travel time is 20min. Alternatively, taxis to the city center cost €20 and take about 15min. Overnight ferries run between Barcelona/ Valencia and Ibiza daily, and are timed to arrive at daybreak. When purchasing your ferry ticket, remain cognizant of the destination name. Both Port d'Eivissa and Port de Sant Antoni, located in Ibiza Town and San Antonio respectively, harbor Balearia and Trasmediterránea ferries. Choose the port closest to your hotel or hostel, as traversing the island can be costly. The Balearia and Trasmediterránea terminals of the Port d'Eivissa are located about 1km east of Eivissa proper. Bus #10 swings by Delta Discos (Av. España 7), the stop closest to the terminals, every 30min. and will take you to the city center. Most restaurants, accommodations, and attractions in San Antonio are within walking distance of the Port de Sant Antoni.

GETTING AROUND

Despite being so small, Ibiza is difficult to navigate, especially if you're not willing or able to shell out a hefty chunk of cash for private transportation. All of Ibiza's cities can be crossed on foot in under 1hr. Travel between cities and to more remote clubs, coves, and villages is either cumbersome or costly. Most buses are operated by Alsa. Unfortunately, Ibiza's most scenic coves and quaint villages are inaccessible via public transportation. Bus #10 runs between the airport and the port, crossing through Ibiza Town, while bus #30 connects Ibiza Town to the San Antonio Bus Terminal (C. Londres, 7; 971 34 01 11). It departs every hour on the hour and the journey lasts approximately 50min. (€2; payable on board). Buses operate from 7am until midnight. After dark, services are taken over by the "Discobus," which shuttles around club-hoppers until 6am (€3.50; payable on board). If you find yourself in a transportation bind, taxis often loiter outside of clubs just after closing. During the summer months, expect to wait in a long line unless you try waving one down yourself.

PRACTICAL INFORMATION

Tourist Offices: Tourist offices are located at the airport, as well as the ferry terminals in Eivissa and San Antonio.
- Ibiza Town (Paseo de Vara de Rey, 1; 971301900; ibiza.travel; open M-Sa 9am-9pm, Su 9am-2pm)
- San Antonio (Passeig de Ses Fonts, 1; 971343363; visit.santantoni.net/es-es/)

Banks/ATMs/Currency Exchange: ATMs are dispersed throughout both Ibiza Town and San Antonio. Although most establishments in these cities accept electronic payment, it is important to keep cash on your person, especially when venturing to smaller, more remote towns. If you have needs that require the assistance of a teller, visit one of the following:
- Ibiza Town: CiaxaBank (Carrer d'Antoni Palau, 8; 971 80 98 00; caixabank.es; open M-F 8:15am-2pm)
- San Antonio: CiaxaBank (C. Santa Agnes, 1B; 971 80 97 30; caixabank.es; open M-F 8:15am-2pm)

Post Offices: Ibiza's main post office is located at Av. d'Isidor Macabich, 67 (902 19 71 97; correos.es; open M-F 8:30am-8:30pm, Sa 9:30am-1pm).

Public Restrooms: Public restrooms are few and far between in Ibiza Town (try the one located on Avinguda Santa Eulária des Riu near the Estación Maritima), and nonexistent in San Antonio. Most establishments that have an entrance fee—museums, clubs, or restaurants from which you purchase food or drink—come equipped with clean restrooms.

Water: Bottled water only, folks. In 2015, Ibiza's Ministry of Health deemed tap water "unfit for human consumption." Odds are a glass or two won't kill ya, but drink too much of it and you may end up with a hole in your stomach.

Internet: Free Wi-Fi is available at most restaurants and cafés, but seldom at or around monuments. Still, it never hurts to ask: *¿Tiene Wi-Fi gratis?*

BGLTQ+ Resources: Ibiza is a major BGLTQ+ summer destination with plenty of gay bars, festivals, and club nights including the long running La Troya party at Space and legendary woman-only weekend at Velvet Ibiza. More information about navigating the island can be found online at ellgeebe.com and iglta.org.

EMERGENCY INFORMATION

Emergency Number: 112
Police: Ibiza's police headquarters is located in Eivissa, although local branches are dispersed throughout the island.
- Ibiza Town (Comisaría de Policía; Avinguda de la Pau; 971 39 88 83)

US Embassy: The Palma de Mallorca Consular Agency covers all four Balearic Islands (including Ibiza) and is open on an appointment basis only (Carrer de Porto Pi, 8; 971 40 37 07; pmagency@state.gov).

Rape Crisis Center: In the event of an emergency, call 112 and contact the US Consulate. Though based in Palma, the officers can provide assistance filing reports with the police and seeking medical treatment.

Hospitals: Hospital Can Misses, located in Ibiza Town, is open daily 24hr (Carrer de Corona; 971 39 70 00). In the event of an emergency, call 112.

Pharmacies: Farmacia Escudero Rouppas, located northeast of Ibiza Town, is open daily 24hr (C. Atzaro, 8; 971 39 48 82).

ACCOMMODATIONS

◪ AMISTAT ISLAND HOSTEL IBIZA ($$$)

Carrer de Santa Rosalia, 25; San Antonio; 971 34 38 34; amistathostels.com; reception open 24hr

Amistat Island Ibiza *would* be the clear winner of best "budget" accommodation in Ibiza if it weren't on the opposite side of the island. Located in **San Antonio,** Amistat is an hour-long bus ride (or €50 taxi ride—choose your poison) from **Ushuaïa** and **Hï.** San Antonio knows how to throw down, and is home to some smaller, legendary nightclubs like **Es Paradis** and **Eden.** Plus, Amistat's amenities are unbeatable. A slew of daily activities, fingerprint-recognition locks, personal outlets, and air-conditioning are some of the highlights. The pleasantness of our stay at Amistat was amplified by its proximity to Ibiza's western coast, which offers seating to the island's best show: the San Antonio sunset.

i Dorms from €50; female-only dorms available; reservation recommended; wheelchair accessible; Wi-Fi; linens included; laundry; towels €3; luggage storage €4; lockers; kitchen; breakfast €6

GIRAMUNDO HOSTAL IBIZA ($$)

Carrer Ramon Muntaner, 55; Ibiza Town; 971 30 76 40; hostalgiramundoibiza.com; reception open 24hr; check in after 2pm, check out by 11am

Giramundo Hostal Ibiza is a long, staircase-laced trek from **Ibiza Town.** Once you make it over the last hill, however, you'll be greeted with one of the most beautiful sights on Earth: blue water, sailboats, and the rocky cliffs of **Illa de Ses Rates.** Behind Giramundo's humble stucco exterior you'll find a common room painted blue and filled with orange tables. Downstairs, a tight-knit group of twenty-somethings shuffle between a partially-stocked bar and somewhat-functional kitchen. See a trend here? Even though Giramundo's amenities may be—for lack of a better word—half-assed, it's got no shortage of community spirit. If you're traveling alone, or if you're traveling in a group but are open to meeting new people, Giramundo Hostal Ibiza is the place to stay. Nothing like close quarters to foster friendship.

i Dorms from €40, privates from €100; female-only dorms available; online reservation recommended; no wheelchair accessibility; Wi-Fi; linens included; kitchen; free breakfast, luggage storage; lockers; club passes available

SIGHTS

FOR THE HISTORY BUFF

DALT VILA

North of Ibiza Town

Designated as a **UNESCO World Heritage** site in 1999, Dalt Vila is the best-preserved coastal fortress on the Mediterranean and a magnificent example of Renaissance military architecture. To make the most of your visit, we recommend beginning at the **Portal de Ses Taules,** Dalt Vila's main gate, and continuing in a rough semicircle towards **Portal Nou,** located on the west side of the city. Continue up the steep cobbled ramp and you'll find yourself at the start of a truly magical journey, surrounded by white-washed residences, artisanal shops, climbing vines, flowering trees, and sweeping city-wide views. It's impossible to get lost here—continue walking upwards and

you'll eventually make it to the **Catedral de Eivissa,** visible from almost anywhere in Ibiza Town. Significant alleyways, plazas, portals, and buildings are marked with signs in Spanish, English, and French. If you're into archeology and aren't satisfied by the **Museum of Archaeology,** be sure to check out the ancient Phoenician ruins at **Sa Caleta** in Sant Josep and the Phoenician-Punic necropolis of **Puig des Molins.**

i Free; limited wheelchair accessibility

CATEDRAL DE EIVISSA

Pl. de la Catedral; Ibiza Town; 971 39 92 32; open Tu-Su 10am-2pm and 5pm-8pm

At the tippy top of **Dalt Vila** sits the Catedral de Eivissa, the most iconic silhouette on the Ibiza skyline. Despite looking so massive from the **Portal de Ses Taules,** it's teeny up close. Yet considering it's served only the residents of Dalt Vila's for the last six centuries, it's never really faced a capacity problem. The Catedral de Eivissa underwent a series of major refurbishments during the eighteenth century, and to say that the windows don't match the drapes would be an understatement. Its heavy flying buttresses and rectangular clock tower stand in stark contrast to the barrel ceilings and Baroque altarpiece inside.

i Free; limited wheelchair accessibility

MUSEO PUGET

Carrer Major, 12; Ibiza Town; 971 39 21 37; open Tu-F 10am-4:30pm, Sa-Su 10am-2pm

Located in a beautiful fifteenth-century mansion, Museo Puget houses 130 paintings, watercolors, and sketches by Ibizan artist **Narcís Puget Viñas** and his son, **Narcís Puget Riquer,** who donated all of his work to local government in 1981. Here, rooms are separated by medium, organized chronologically, and separated by low **Mudéjar arches.** On the first floor, a small **courtyard** is decorated in typical Cordoban fashion, with a cobblestone floor and lush potted plants. The building itself is worth a visit, but the art is icing on the cake.

i Free; no wheelchair accessibility

FOR THE BEACH BUM

CALA BASSA

Cala Bassa; Sant Josep de sa Talaia; open daily 8am-midnight

As tempting as the shoreline along **Avinguda del Doctor Fleming** may be, do yourself a favor hold out for Cala Bassa, one of the most scenic coves on Ibiza's western coast. Located only **11 kilometers southwest of San Antonio,** Cala Bossa seems worlds away from the contained frenzy of the city's day clubs. Here, families, couples, and solo travelers lounge along a horseshoe of golden sand, and yachters bob atop the turquoise water of the **Cap de Sa Serra.** Cala Bassa has exploded in popularity since the opening of the **Cala Bassa Beach Club,** a resort and restaurant planted 100 meters away amidst a forest of gnarled Sabina trees. While its presence here may prevent you from finding a plot of free sand after 1pm, it also means you'll have access to clean restrooms, cool drinks, and hearty—albeit overpriced—food during your stay. To reach Cala Bassa, take **Bus #7a** from the **San Antonio Bus Terminal.** The ride lasts approximately 25 minutes and costs €2.90.
i *Free, drinks from €3; limited wheelchair accessibility*

EL ARENAL

Ibiza Town (Eivissa)

El Arenal is a quirky, beachy neighborhood wedged between **Dalt Vila** and the **Port d'Eivissa.** It's here that you'll find Ibiza Town's trendiest boutiques, freshest markets, and fanciest restaurants. Pastel pink, yellow, and orange buildings are sprinkled with bright blue and green shutters, and linked together by canopies of dark pink bougainvillea. Points of interest include the **Estatua Vara de Rey,** a tribute to an Ibizan General who died in the 1898 Battle of El Caney, fought between Spain and the U.S. over Cuba; **Carrer Lluís Tur i Palau,** the restaurant-lined street that hugs the port; **Plaça de sa Riba,** a palm-covered plateau that looks northeast along the coast; and **Mercado Viejo,** an outdoor marketplace located at the base of the **Portal de Ses Taules.** The entire area is best traversed on foot.
i *Free; wheelchair accessible*

SUNSET IN SAN ANTONIO

Caló el Moro; San Antonio; arrive 30min. before sunset

Regardless of where you decide to watch it, experiencing a sunset on Ibiza's western coast—like exploring the streets of **Dalt Vila**—is absolutely non-negotiable. The sunset here is world-famous, and for a good reason. Every night around 9pm, the horizon is set ablaze with a profuse red glow. The waves settle, the sails calm, and the water begins to twinkle. The light cast by the receding sun is so powerful that virtually everything separating you from it—the passersby, the catamarans, the buoys, **Illa Sa Conillera**—is reduced to a stark silhouette. Our favorite place to watch the sunset? **Caló des Moro,** located on the northern fringes of **San Antonio.**
i *Free; wheelchair accessible*

FOR THE DARTIER

BOAT PARTIES

Playa d'en Bossa Pier; Ibiza Town; 628 944 809; oceanbeat.es/en/; boarding begins at 1pm, meet at Forever Bar (Camino 1002, 16) at 12:30pm for breakfast and ticket verification

Did you even go to Ibiza if you didn't go to a boat party? Parties range in quality and price, and typically the two go hand-in-hand. You can generally expect that the more you spend, the more fun you'll have. We found that the parties offered by **Oceanbeat** are the best bang for your buck. If you book online, €80 will buy you a champagne breakfast, four hours aboard a decked-out catamaran, free drinks the entire time you're on the water, a burlesque show, a six-hour after party at Bora Bora (Playa D'en Bossa; 971 30 19 06; open daily 9am-6am), and three free entrances to some of Ibiza's wildest nightclubs. Considering entrance alone to the likes of **Privilege, Sankeys, SWAG, and Es Paradis** run between €35 and €75 a pop, the **Oceanbeat Ibiza Boat Party** is—in our opinion—worth its price tag. (Be sure to check Oceanbeat's website for details regarding your trip prior to departure, as venues and times are subject to change.)
i *€80 per head, VIP pass €200; no refunds; no wheelchair accessibility; beach attire recommended*

SA COVA - WINE TASTING IN SANT MATEU D'ALBARCA

Diseminado Aubarca, 4; Sant Mateu d'Albarca; 971 187 046; open weekdays 10:30am-6pm, Sa 11am-2pm

As far as day drinking goes, it doesn't get much better than a private vineyard tour and wine tasting in **Sant Mateu,** a tiny town located about 20 kilometers north of Ibiza Town. **Sa Cova,** Ibiza's first for-profit winery, is open to visitors on a year-round basis. Tasting tours cost €17 and include four glasses of wine and tapas—a steal in Balearic terms. Though the appeal and intrigue of Ibiza's **Playa d'en Bossa** is unquestionable, the island's true beauty lies in its quiet, secluded villages. Spend an afternoon exploring Sant Mateu's cobblestone streets, bougainvillea-covered buildings, and long rows of grapevines. Neither you nor your palate will be disappointed. (Sa Cova Winery is accessible by taxi and by bus. From Ibiza Town, take **Bus #33** to Sant Mateu. The ride departs from Isidor Macabich, 54 and takes approximately 45 minutes. Sa Cova is a 20-minute walk north from the Sant Mateu bus stop.)
i €17 per head; tours must be arranged in advance; have cash on hand; no wheelchair accessibility

FOOD

🍽 S'ESCALINATA EIVISSA ($$)

Carrer Portal Nou, 10; Ibiza Town; 653 37 13 56; sescalinata.es/ibiza/; open daily 10:30am-2:30am

Certainly the coolest restaurant in **Dalt Vila** and a strong contender for the coolest restaurant in **Ibiza Town,** S'Escalinata Eivissa is an indoor-outdoor establishment where patrons dine on leather bean bag chairs under the shadows cast by D'Alt Vila's iconic white buildings. Considering its stellar ambiance, S'Escalinata Eivissa's offerings are surprisingly cheap. Food ranges from Mediterranean classics like seasoned hummus and pita bread to heartier dishes like burgers and warm wraps, and is sure to appease carnivores and

OCEAN BEACH IBIZA

Carrer des Molí, 12-14; San Antonio; 971 80 32 60; oceanbeachibiza.com; open daily noon-10pm (W noon-9pm)

All of the fun of a boat party, less of the claustrophobia. Ocean Beach Ibiza, located **just south of San Antonio,** is an all-day affair like no other. This hotel-club combo offers tourists the chance to remain plastered for as close to 24 hours as humanly possible. The party gets going around 2pm, and is a feast for the eyes and spirit. Bikini-clad waitresses weave between daybeds carrying bottles of Dom Pérignon, and people congregate around Ocean Beach's 600-square-meter pool sipping overpriced drinks. While the floaties may differ day by day, Ocean Beach's mission remains the same: to put on a hell of a show. When we visited, we were showered in champagne (last Friday of every month)—turns out the smell is hard to get rid of. If the thought of spending a day elbowing through a sea of oiled bodies to get a better view of the headliner doesn't appeal to you, check out **Pearl,** Ocean Beach's rooftop bar, for some of San Antonio's best craft cocktails.
i Entrance cost varies based on time of week and year; reserve tickets online at least 2 weeks in advance (€15 electronically + €20 at door); single lounger €70; two gin cocktails €10, individual cocktails from €8; Wi-Fi; limited wheelchair accessibility

herbivores alike. So kick your feet up on a refurbished produce-box-turned-coffee-table, breathe in the aroma of citrus, and get lost in the twists and turns of the succulents that line the small, sloping plaza around you. We recommend arriving just before sunset to secure a seat and ordering a glass of sangria (€5) or pint of beer (€5).

i Bocadillos from €7.50, tapas from €7, salads from €11, breakfast from €3.50; vegetarian options available; no wheelchair accessibility; Wi-Fi

CAN GOURMET ($)

Carrer de Guillem de Montgrí, 20; Ibiza Town; 635 26 66 66; can-gourmet.com/ibiza/; open M, W-Su 9:30am-10pm

Ibiza is famous for being a monetary black hole. Euros go flying in and never come out. It's difficult to find a meal for under €10, let alone a big ass sandwich—Can Gourmet's specialty. This iconic establishment is a sub shop through and through, serving up delectable and satisfying bocadillos for an eye-popping €6—cheaper than any cocktail you can find on this God-(un)forsaken island. Colorful potted plants and sombrero hats hang from the second floor balcony down to the pavement. Streetside, the "ham-mobile"—a bright green convertible truck stuffed with pig butts—displays the day's offerings, which vary slightly depending on what produce the owner decided to pick up that morning. Seating room in Can Gourmet's tiny interior is limited. We recommend ordering a *bocadillo* and bottle of craft beer *para llevar* and heading northeast to the port, which is just two blocks away. If you're overwhelmed by the number of tapas on Can Gourmet's menu, just ask for one of each of the restaurant's three most popular dishes.

i Sandwiches from €6; vegetarian options available; limited wheelchair accessibility

RESTAURANTE GOLDEN BUDDHA ($$)

Carrer de Santa Rosalia, 35; San Antonio; 971 34 56 33; goldenbuddhaibiza.com; open daily 10am-3:30am

Food's good; view's better. Restaurante Golden Buddha is the ultimate place to watch the sunset in Ibiza. Its menu boasts a wide array of breakfast, lunch, and dinner options that range from the types of dishes you'd find in a standard New York bistro to traditional Thai curry. What really sets Golden Buddha apart from the rest of the bars on the waterfront is its massive elevated patio, which is furnished with dozens of tables, low couches, and four-post gazebos designed for day-long lounging. Sailboats and catamarans float across an island-dotted harbor, and passerby stroll casually along **Passeig de Ponent.** If you're looking for something a little more upbeat, check out **Café del Mar,** a live music venue and neighborhood favorite located a couple blocks south. To secure a front-row seat at either of these establishments, arrive at least an hour before sunset.

i Salads from €9.50, burgers from €12.90, desserts from €4.50, beer from €3; vegetarian options available; limited wheelchair accessibility

NIGHTLIFE

▩ AMNESIA

Ctra. Ibiza a San Antonio, Km 5; San Rafael; 971 19 80 41; amnesia.es; open M-Sa midnight-6am

Conveniently located in the middle of fucking nowhere, Amnesia is—regrettably—an absolutely essential clubbing experience. Although the bumpy, 40-minute bus ride will test your patience, it will all feel worth it when you step foot inside Amnesia's packed interior. This 5,000-person capacity club is split into two sections, each with its own decor and lineups. The **Club Room**—a cavernous, stone-lined pit overflowing with raging, overly-perfumed twenty-somethings—is transformed daily. The **Terrace,** famous for its sunrise sessions, is guarded by the club's infamous ice canons and covered by a greenhouse-esque trellis. People naturally migrate here as the night drones on, eager to catch a glimpse of the light peeking through the windows above. Contrary to what its name suggests, every night at Amnesia is unforgettable—a fact attributable to its extremely diverse program. Sets vary from techno to house to bass to Latin, so make sure to check online before purchasing your ticket. Pro tip: drinks cost more upstairs than down.

i Cover from €35, water €9, cocktails from €15; no dress code

🏠 USHUAÏA

Platja d'en Bossa, 10; Ibiza Town; 971 39 67
10; theushuaiaexperience.com; open daily
4pm-midnight

An immediate hit upon opening in
2011, Ushuaïa (pronounced *ooh-sh-why-
ah*) blows the competition out of the
water as far as stage production goes. A
go-to location for a #darty, this luxury
hotel complex shuts down promptly at
midnight. Consequently, Ushuaïa's open-
air floor is a hotbed for "final-nighters,"
people who need to be sober enough to
make their 7am ferry but want to squeeze
every last ounce of enjoyment out of the
island beforehand. The result? Some of
the most incredible communal moments
in the history of clubbing. This open-air
venue is arguably the most enjoyable
place on the island to experience a lineup.
Of course, it helps that those lineups are
headlined by artists like **David Guetta**
and **Martin Garrix**. Against the backdrop
of a setting sun, Ushuaïa's massive stage
explodes in lights, fire, and confetti at all
the right moments, keeping the audience
in constant ecstasy. If the poolside
debauchery proves to be too much for
you, check out Ushuaïa Tower's **rooftop
lounge,** which offers stunning views of
the club and island below.

i *Cover from €40; beach attire recommended*

EDEN

Calle Salvador Espriu; San
Antonio; edenibiza.com;
open daily midnight-6am

Eden's proximity to
long-time competitor **Es
Paradis** has kept both
venues on their toes since
the early 90s. As a result,
they're frequently stepping
up their game, and now
boast reputations for being
two of the best clubs on the
island. But, of the two, Eden's
got the (five-inch-heeled) leg
up. It boasts the **island's best
sound system** and a beautiful,
garden-themed interior, making
it a favorite among die-hard house
fans and DJs alike. A night at Eden is
truly a religious experience, but not in
the biblical sense. On the spectrum of
holiness, where grandma's snowflake-
embroidered tracksuit lies on one end and
stripper's ruffled thong lies on another,
Eden skews heavily towards the latter.
Sets take place in the double-decker main
room, which is so chock-full of lights,
speakers, and people that you'll inevitably
find yourself disoriented, no matter your
degree of inebriation. Our advice? Give
in to the chaos. Let the chest-shattering
pulses of bass knock you to your knees—
where you'll inevitably find yourself
begging for mercy from your hangover
the next morning.

i *Cover from €25; casual cocktail attire; check
calendar before purchasing tickets*

PACHA

Avinguda d'Agost, 8; Ibiza Town; 971313600;
pachaibiza.com; open daily 11pm-6am

Stomping ground of Europe's rich and
famous, Pacha is held dearly in the hearts
of locals and considered a must-visit for
tourists making their clubbing rounds.
With over 45 years of party-planning
under its belt, Pacha boasts one of the
biggest talent rosters on Ibiza. Take your
pick from the cream of the electronic
music crop—with headliners like **David
Guetta, Calvin Harris, Martin Solveig,
Sven Väth,** and **Alesso** splattered across
the calendar, there's no way to go wrong.
That said, Pacha's known for two parties
in particular: **Flower Power** and **F***
Me I'm Famous.** If you score tickets to
either of those shows, you're golden. As its
name suggests, Flower Power is a blast to

the past on a scale so large it makes your bell bottoms look small. Expect soul, pop, funk, and other hits from the last four decades, set to the backdrop of exquisite and immersive handmade decorations. On other nights, Pacha's white, black, and red interior speaks for itself, brought to the life by the people within it.

i Cover from €40, €20 more at door; mixed drinks from €18, beer from €12; cocktail attire recommended; parties often fill up weeks in advance

MADRID

Coverage by **Joseph Winters**

Unlike other European cities, Madrid's identity can't be distilled into a single colossal monument. Instead, the spirit of Madrid is dispersed in the splendor of the smaller things: a Medieval alley here, a neoclassical palace there, all mishmashed into the city's more modern lilt. As the third-largest city in the European Union, visitors can expect a lot from Madrid—from architecture to gastronomy to nightlife, it delivers. For centuries, Spain has churned out world-class artists, and much of their work eventually finds its way back to the capital city. Madrid's so-called Golden Triangle of Art—the Museo del Prado, Centro de Arte Reina Sofía, and Museo Thyssen-Bornemisza—house thousands of works by Spanish legends like Goya, Picasso, Dalí, and Miró, as well as Flemish and Italian icons of the art world. And then there's the food. *Tapas* may be a worldwide phenomenon at this point, but there's no better place to *tapear* (literally "to go eat tapas") than Madrid. As the culinary crossroads of Spain, Madrid isn't limited by regional cuisine; visitors can find traditional flavors of Valencian *paella* or Madrileñan blood sausage in age-old taverns, right next to LA-esque health bars serving up cold-pressed juices. It's the late-night *churros con chocolate,* however, that capture our hearts every time. And they're only part of Madrid's nightlife situation— the city is notorious for insomnia. Once the sun sets and the temperature drops, the streets flood with bar-hoppers and party-goers, everyone scouting out that next glass of sangria. The wildest tourists inevitably find their way into Madrid's epic *teatros:* massive theaters-turned-concert venues, where world-class musicians and deejays flood the city's soundscape, impervious to the brightening skies of early morning.

ORIENTATION

Most of the city's action is bounded to the west by **Palacio Real** and its **Campo del Moro,** and to east by the **Parque del Buen Retiro** and the **Paseo del Prado,** an enormous thoroughfare that's home to the city's Golden Triangle of museums (**Museo del Prado, Museo Nacional Centro de Arte Reina Sofía,** and the **Museo Thyssen-Bornemisza**). The aptly-named **"Centro"** of Madrid is in—you guessed it—the center of the city, made of the commercial streets between the **Plaza Mayor** and the **Puerta del Sol** (known as **"Sol"**). East of the Centro is **Huertas** (the name of its main street), also called **Barrio de las Letras** (Neighborhood of the Letters). It's famous for having been home to writers like Lope de Vega and Cervantes. To the northeast, after crossing the ultra-highway known as the **Gran Vía,** visitors are welcomed into **Chueca,** Madrid's well-known BGLTQ+-friendly neighborhood. But perhaps "friendly" is an understatement; this neighborhood, with its gay bars and homoerotic fashion stores, is radically accepting. Chueca is popular for its trendy cafés and shopping, as well as for its nightlife. The other half of northern Madrid (northwest) is **Malasaña,** the Bohemian arts district, where you'll find an extraordinary concentration of concept stores, art supply shops, and Insta-ready dining options. If you keep going west, the **Plaza de España** and **Templo de Debod** are worth knowing about. South of Centro, the three neighborhoods of interest—from west to east—are **La Latina, Embajadores,** and **Lavapiés.** All three are less commercial than the northern half of Madrid, and everything from shopping to sleeping to tapas-ing is less expensive here. La Latina is known for traditional Spanish vibes and a killer flea market called **El Rastro** (every Sunday morning), and Lavapiés is particularly multicultural. Finally, in the southeasternmost corner of the city is the **Atocha Train Station.**

ESSENTIALS

GETTING THERE

By plane: Flights to Madrid arrive in the bustling Madrid-Barajas airport some 10mi. outside the city center. There are four terminals: most international flights will arrive in terminals 1-3, while flights operated by Iberia usually land in terminal 4. Each terminal offers connection to downtown via the metro's Line 8. It operates from 6:05am-1:30am, takes around 45min., and costs €4.50, not including the €2.50 one-time cost of a refillable refillable Tarjeta Multi public transport card. Taxis are also available, but are much more expensive. (€30, 30min.) There's a shuttle bus (Exprés Aeropuerto) going to Atocha Train Station every 20min. during the day and to Pl. de Cibeles every 35min. from 11:30pm-6am. Line 200 goes from terminals 1, 2, and 4 to the metro station at Avenida de América, where travelers will need to take another trip on the subway to get to downtown. Line 101 shuttles between terminals 1 and 2 to Canillejas. Either local bus runs from 6am-11:30pm and costs €4.50, including the airport fee.

By bus: There are two main bus stations in Madrid. The Intercambiador de Avenida de América is slightly north of downtown and is also a metro stop with connections to lines 6, 7, and 8. The more southerly station is called Estación Sur de Autobuses, also with a metro station—this one's called Méndez Álvaro and it connects to Line 6. Buses arrive at either station from Granada (€19, 5hr), Barcelona (€32, 8hr), Lisbon (€20, 9hr), Seville (€25, 6hr 30min), Bilbao (€32, 5hr), and other points of origin.

By train: Renfe is the national train operator, and trains arrive in Madrid from throughout the Iberian Peninsula, with many connections through France. AVE stands for Tren de Alta Velocidad Española, and they often break speeds of 200mph. AVE tickets are more expensive than regular trains, but they can cut travel time by more than half, depending on the journey. The main train station is the southeastern Puerta de Atocha. From here, it's not far to walk to most of downtown Madrid, but travelers with heavy luggage might want to hop on the metro (also called Atocha Station, part of Line 1). Madrid's northern train station is called Estació de Chamartín, and it features a metro station on Lines 1 and 10 with easy connections to downtown. Trains come in from Bilbao (€25, 5hr), Barcelona (€60, 3hr with AVE), Seville (€40, 2.5hr with AVE or 3hr without), Lisbon (€36, 10hr), and other origins.

GETTING AROUND

By foot: As with any city, the best way to dive into local culture is to walk. Everywhere. In all seriousness, it's worth thinking twice before taking the metro everywhere; Madrid is highly walkable, and it's the unexpected gems between points A and B that you're likely to remember most.

By bus: To take advantage of the bus and metro networks, travelers will need to pick up a Tarjeta Multi card at any metro station. It costs €2.50 and remains valid for 10 years—you refill it every time you need take another ride. Madrid's 200-line bus system (Empresa Municipal de Transporte, or EMT) shuttles through the city M-F 6am-11:30pm and Sa-Su 7am-11pm, with most buses passing a stop at least every 15min. Night buses are called *búhos*. There are fewer lines, and they run less frequently (every 35min Su-F and every 15min on Sa). Two daytime lines go to the airport: Line 200 goes from Av. de América to terminals 1, 2, and 4, and Line 101 goes from Canillejas to terminals 1 and 2. Note that to use your Tarjeta Multi card on the bus, you'll need to buy a 10-trip bundle (€12.20). Single bus tickets must be purchased on the bus (€1.50).

By metro: With more than 300 stations, Madrid's metro network is the second largest in Europe, and using it is highly intuitive. There are a dozen numbered lines crisscrossing the city from 6am-1:30am, and trains arrive at most stations every two minutes during rush hours. Line 8 routes through Nuevos Ministerios to the airport. Load up your Tarjeta Multi with ten trips (€12.20) or pay as you go (starting at €1.50/trip). Note the airport supplement for metro trips to and from Madrid Bajaras (€4.50 combined metro ticket and airport fee). Travelers planning on using the metro a lot may want to consider a Tourist Travel Pass, valid for unlimited travel over a set period of 1-7 days (€8.40-35.40).

By taxi: To hail a cab, look for the green light on the roof, indicating the taxi is available. Expect to pay around €2.50 plus €1.15 per kilometer for your route, along with some supplemental fees (like €5.50 extra if you're going to the airport). As a rule, the metro is always cheaper than a taxi.

By train: *Cercanías* trains run between the northern Nuevos Ministerios and the southern Atocha train station (and beyond). They're not too expensive and can be useful if you want a direct route with fewer stops than a metro journey.

By bike: There's a bike share program called BiciMAD offering over 1500 bikes at 120 stations around town. Each time you check out a bike, the session lasts two hours. There are also a number of more traditional bike rentals available offering sturdier bikes. Bikes are allowed on the subway all day Sa-Su, but not M-F from 7:30am-9:30am, 2pm-4pm, and 6pm-8pm.

PRACTICAL INFORMATION

Tourist Offices: The main tourist office is in Pl. Mayor, but there are a number of booths in Madrid's other main squares, including Sol. Look for the orange italic "i." They'll weigh you down with plenty of free maps, museum guides, event information, etc.
- Plaza Mayor: Pl. Mayor 27; 91 578 78 10; www.esmadrid.com; open daily 9:30am-9:30pm
- Sol: Pl. de Callao; 91 578 78 10; www.esmadrid.com; open daily 9:30am-8:30pm

Banks/ATMs/Currency Exchange: There are ATMs throughout the city, and plenty of banks along the east-west Gran Vía, as well as a bit further south in the area between Callao and Sol.
- Deutsche Bank (Centro): C. de Toledo 33; 913 64 20 24; www.db.com/spain; open M-Th 8:30am-4:30pm, F 8:30am-2:15pm
- Santander: C. de Carretas 14; 915 22 32 45; www.bancosantander.es; open M-F 8:30am-2:30pm

Post Offices: Correos is the national mail carrier, and they have a couple offices along the Gran Vía, one between Sol and Callao, and several more throughout the city center, including offices in Malasaña and northern Chueca.
- Correos (Puerta del Sol): C. de Preciados 3; 902 19 71 97; www.correos.es; open M-Sa 10am-10pm, Su 11am-9pm
- Correos (Tirso de Molina): Palos de la Frontera 6-10; 915 27 50 00; www.correos.es; open M-F 8:30am-8:30pm, Sa 9:30am-1pm

Public Restrooms: When nature calls, use a little ingenuity to find relief without paying for it. There are public restrooms in the city's many cultural centers and museums, many of which can be accessed without a ticket. Otherwise, El Corte Inglés, Spain's favorite department store, has locations throughout the city offering free public restrooms.

Internet: There is no official Wi-Fi network of Madrid, but between the city's countless restaurants, shopping malls, and cafés offering free Internet access, you should have no trouble finding a way to get online. If you're in a bind, locate the nearest McDonald's or Starbucks. If you're a student, you can use the eduroam network in many parts of the city, too.

BGLTQ+ Resources: The Federation of Lesbian, Gay, Trans and Bisexual people (FELGTB in Spanish) offers a directory of BGLTQ+-related events, information, and has a hotline for victims of discrimination (C. Infantas 40, Madrid; 913 604 605; www.felgtb.org; M-Th 8am-8pm, F 8am-3:30pm).

EMERGENCY INFORMATION

Emergency Number: 112
Police: Madrid's police regularly occupy the city's most crowded spaces like Callao, Sol, and just outside some of the classier hotels of Gran Vía. You can find their offices near the Paseo del Prado, but there are other locations on Gran Vía and in Malasaña and Chueca. In case of an emergency, dial 112 for quick police support.
- National Police (Centro): C. de Leganitos 19; 915 48 79 85; www.policia.es

US Embassy: C. de Serrano 75; 915 872 200; es.usembassy.gov; open M-F 8am-2pm

Hospitals: Madrid has several large hospitals east of Parque del Retiro, as well as some options to the north in the Chamartín neighborhood and beyond. In an emergency, dial 112 to be taken to the best location for your needs.
- Gregorio Marañón Hospital: C. del Dr. Esquerdo 46; 915 86 80 00; www.madrid.org; open daily 24hr
- Hospital Vithas Nuestra Señora de América: C. de Arturo Soria 103-107; 902 29 82 99; www.vithas.es; open daily 24hr

Pharmacies: Pharmacies and herbolarias are a dime a dozen in Madrid. Pretty much any major Madrid thoroughfare has a pharmacy on every few blocks. Here is one 24hr options:
- Farmacia Central 24 Horas: Paseo de Santa María de la Cabeza 64; 914 73 06 72; open daily 24hr

ACCOMMODATIONS

🏠 MAD4YOU HOSTEL ($)

C. Costanilla de San Vicente 4; 915 21 75 49; www.mad4youhostel.com; reception open 24hr

Situated in a sixteenth-century *corrala* (a courtyard-style residence that used to double as a theater), Mad4You is protected from alterations, listed by the city as a historically significant building. "We can pimp it up, but we can't change its character," they explain. Pimped up and old works just fine for us, though, especially when it means wood floors, a dazzlingly new kitchen, and a positively icy air-conditioning system running through nearly every room. Dorms line the balconies overlooking the central courtyard, and the bunks are all wood, with most rooms offering en-suite bathrooms. Add to that a summertime mojito bar and you've got yourself a primo hostel experience. It won't take long for you to be mad for this hostel, too.

i Dorms from €14, privates from €45; reservation recommended; BGLTQ+ friendly; no wheelchair accessibility; Wi-Fi; linens, breakfast, kitchen, luggage storage, lockers included; towels €2; laundry

2060 NEWTON HOSTEL ($)

C. de la Cabeza 11; 782 26 11 39; www.2060hostelandmarket.com; reception open 24hr

Based on a Newtonian prediction that the world will end in the year 2060, Newton Hostel brims with portentous charm. "Doomsday is coming, and it's going to be awesome," reads a sign leading to the first-floor dorms, as well as a room affectionately known as the "bunker." Those booking before the apocalypse will enjoy sparklingly modern facilities, including a hot tub and a rooftop terrace. Dorm beds are a little claustrophobic (some are time machine-like capsules with the only entrance at your feet) and showers are operated by an annoying button that releases seven seconds of water at a time, but other than that, Newton Hostel's not a bad final crash pad before the impending end of the world. As one of their walls sagely reminds us, "life is too short not to be the mushroom you want to be," or something. Just go with it; they're clearly trying.

i Dorms from €15, privates from €58; reservation recommended; BGLTQ+ friendly; wheelchair accessibility; Wi-Fi; linens, luggage storage, lockers, computer access, kitchen included; towels €2, laundry €7, sauna €5

BASTARDO HOSTEL ($)

C. de San Mateo 3; 682 519 535; www.bastardohoste.com; reception open 24hr

While the reception area looks more like a trendy gastropub than a budget backpacker's accommodations, we can confirm: Bastardo is, in fact, a hostel, although their cheeky neon *hotel ilegítimo* (illegitimate hotel) sign may describe it best. The ground floor's gorgeous wraparound windows enclose a restaurant called **Limbo** and a bar called **Pica Pica,** greeting guests with the smell of hops and finger food. On the upper floors, rooms can be opened with a QR code delivered straight to your smartphone, and each room comes with a private bathroom. Beds are equipped with reading lights, outlets (normal and USB), and a fold-out table where you can charge larger items like a laptop. Once you've finished gawking at the rooftop terrace and its plethora of hammocks, join an excursion to the microtheater, catch a drag show, or attend the ballet with the receptionist—all for free. As for us, we're considering moving in permanently.

i Dorms from €18, privates from €89; reservation recommended; max stay 14 nights; wheelchair accessible; Wi-Fi; linens, luggage storage, lockers, refrigerator included; breakfast €5, towels €2

OK HOSTEL MADRID ($)

C. Juanelo 24; 914 29 37 44; www.okhostels.com; reception open 24hr

Only one thing stands between OK Hostel and "hotel" status: a single letter S, which they say stands for "socializing and sharing." Other than that, OK spoils guests with a sleek lounge on the ground floor, games you'll actually want to play (i.e. a pool table, PlayStation, and organized drinking games), and newfangled room keys that can be worn around your wrist like a watch. Rooms are small, but bunks have wood frames and plenty of space to charge your entire collection of gadgetry. Signs throughout the hostel invite visitors to pass into dreamland on beds that (strangely) can be found in the hostel's common spaces. We'll stick to the dorms, but it wouldn't be hard to get comfy just about anywhere in this luxury hostel. No promises it'll make you as gleeful as the dancing pigs on the bar's tacky mural, but it's safe to say this hostel is significantly better than just OK.

i Dorms from €18, privates from €65; reservation recommended; max stay 7 nights; BGLTQ+ friendly; wheelchair accessible; Wi-Fi; linens, lockers, luggage storage, computer access included; breakfast €3, towels €2, laundry (wash €3, dry €3), locks €3; American Express not accepted

SUNGATE ONE ($)

C. Carmen 16; 910 236 806; www.sungatehostel.com; reception open 24hr

With a swath of accolades that includes Best Small Hostel in the World and Second Place overall for Europe (both from Hostelworld in 2018), you shouldn't need much convincing to get you into this gem of a hostel. There's thought behind every detail, from the instant you wake up (to free churros, of course) to the moment you drift off to dreamland in the comfort of your (non-

bunk) bed. The hours in between could be marked by free field trips to **Toledo** and **Segovia,** an excursion to the swimming pool, or a rowboat adventure and picnic at the **Parque del Retiro.** There's also free sangria nightly, in addition to events like Fuckin' Monday Cool Club (€8 for entrance and two drinks at a nearby bar). Of course, many guests choose to stay in for free community dinner (every night), often prepared by a fellow traveler (who shops on Sungate's dime for the ingredients of their choice). We could keep raving, but even now the clock is ticking; you'd better make reservations weeks in advance, because Sungate One offerings—and accolades—have made them wildly popular.

i Dorms from €17, privates from €88; reservation recommended; no wheelchair accessibility; Wi-Fi; linens, luggage storage, lockers, kitchen, computer access included; towels €2, laundry €7

SIGHTS

CULTURE

MERCADO EL RASTRO (EL RASTRO FLEA MARKET)

C. Ribera de Curtidores and surrounding streets; open Su 9am-3pm

Although it's officially capped out at 3500 vendors, El Rastro, Madrid's historic flea market, seems to go on forever, an endless sprawl of vintage stamps, Tibetan singing bowls, secondhand clothing, and who even knows what else. Founded over 400 years ago, *El Rastro* (the trail) refers to the tanneries that used to cover the area, and the trail of blood that followed animal carcasses as they were hauled here from the slaughterhouse. Things are a bit less gruesome today: explore themed streets specializing in used books and painting supplies, pick up some low-cost souvenirs for your family back home, and allow yourself to meander up and down the hill. There's no telling what treasure you might find buried within the junk.

i Prices vary; wheelchair accessible

CHUECA

Chueca; neighborhood open daily 24hr

Chueca is the LGBT epicenter of Madrid. Heck, it's the gayest place in Spain—if you're there during *orgullo* week (Madrid's gay pride celebration, usually at the beginning of July), the neighborhood takes on an almost aggressive vibe. Rainbows are everywhere; you can eat them (in gluten-free bakeries and cafés), wear them (as silken ponchos or risqué booty shorts), and photograph the heck out of them (flags, banners, and posters line every street). There's a ton of touristy variety, so allow time to duck into high-end boutiques and peruse some of Madrid's best fashion outlets. There's also a proliferation of erotic shops, if that's your thing. After dark, the neighborhood takes on a grittier feel, with hordes of locals and tourists bar-hopping well into the early morning, whether at Michelin-starred tapa joints or somewhat-sketchy "100% Gay" bar/sauna "experiences." Enjoy Madrid's pride and joy (but mostly pride).

i Prices vary; wheelchair accessible

CINE DORÉ

C. Santa Isabel 3; 913 693 225; www.mecd. gob.es; box office open Tu-Su 4:15pm-10pm, café open Tu-Su 5pm-12:15am, bookstore open Tu-Su 5:30pm-10pm

Unlike your typical neighborhood movie theater, you won't find *Avengers,* Hollywood rom coms, or Adam Sandler anywhere near the Cine Doré. Founded in 1922, this national Spanish theater specializes in avant-garde experimental films—think BGLTQ+ features, black and white Westerns, and silent movies from the national archives. There are three theaters, one of which is a recreation of the original, antique auditorium. Be sure to check if the outdoor rooftop cinema (with its own bar!) is open; it doesn't get much better than Spanish sangria and a show *en plein air.* Even if you don't end up watching anything, the building itself is worth checking out; it features a neoclassical facade and a vibrant art nouveau interior with a café and bookstore, covered head to toe with playful blue and white tiles.

i Tickets €2.50, students €2; limited wheelchair accessibility

EL TEATRO REAL (THE ROYAL THEATER)

Pl. de Isabel II; 91 516 06 00; www.te-atro-real.com; open for tours daily 10:30am-4:30pm

Posh tourists looking for a place to flash their fanciest getup should look no further than Madrid's Royal Theater. "El Real," as it is commonly known, was originally completed in 1850 under the auspices of Queen Isabella I, who dreamed of a theater to rival the rest of the continent's lavish opera houses. She certainly got it—the Teatro Real was one of Europe's premier performance venues for some 75 years before it closed in 1925 for safety reasons. Thankfully, it was nothing a few million euros couldn't fix (€100 million, actually)—and it again serves as the epicenter of Madrid's fine performing arts. Catch a concert by the **Spanish National Orchestra,** performances by the **National Ballet,** and of course the throaty warble of a good **Puccini, Verdi,** or **Händel** opera. Curious visitors can also tour the building (alone or with a guide), exploring the building's wraparound *rotonda,* which grants access to the stage's 28 boxes, including the royal boxes and state rooms. The whole place is strung with artwork from the **Museo del Prado** and the **National Heritage** art collections.

i Self-guided tour €7, students €6; General Tour (€8, students €6) daily at 10am, 11am, noon, 1pm; Technical Tour (€16, students €14) daily at 10am; Artistic Tour (€12, students €10) daily at 9:30am; Night Tour (€30) after performances; last entry 3:30pm; limited wheelchair accessibility; combined ticket with Palacio Real €15

MATADERO MADRID

Pl. de Legazpi 8; 915 177 309; www.mata-deromadrid.org; open Tu-F 4pm-9pm, Sa-Su 11am-9pm

What was once a disused slaughterhouse has gained new life as Matadero Madrid, a contemporary arts center just south of the city center. The complex is owned by the Madrid City Council, which uses the complex to host a constantly-rotating array of artists from across the artistic spectrum. Matadero's spaces include **Cineteca,** devoted exclusively to documentary films; the **Avant Garden,** featuring environmental exhibitions; and a graphic and interior design-focused **Central de Diseño.** Programming changes frequently, but past events have included poetry festivals, Muslim graphic novel expositions, circus performances, etc. Whatever the specifics, Matadero guarantees a place to "create, reflect, learn, and enjoy." The best part: they're proud to offer almost all of its spaces and events free of charge.

i Free; limited wheelchair accessibility; event information and tickets available online or at box office

MERCADO DE SAN ANTÓN (SAN ANTÓN MARKET)

C. Augusto Figueroa 24; 91 330 07 30; www. mercadosananton.com; open M-Sa 10am-10pm, Su 10am-midnight

Although they call themselves a "traditional market," we have trouble imagining Japanese takeout and a solar energy collector in Madrid's fifteenth-century food bazaars. Not that the upgrades are unappreciated; Mercado de San Antón's panoply of international tapas and artisanal nom noms makes it a delicious addition to the **Chueca** district. Built from the ground up in 2002, the interior is just as gorgeous as the rest of this trendy neighborhood, and the food is, too. Look for French macarons, *foie gras pintxos,* freshly-picked peaches, homemade sushi—it's a gourmet wonderland in there. The ground floor does to-go offerings and market staples (like fruits and veggies), while the second floor has ample seating with a view of the central courtyard. For stunning views outside the Mercado, head to the top floor, where there's a lovely terrace with its own chic restaurant.

i Eat-in prices vary; Wi-Fi; wheelchair accessible

MERCADO DE SAN MIGUEL (SAN MIGUEL MARKET)

Pl. de San Miguel; 915 42 49 36; www.mercadodesanmiguel.es; open Su-Th 10am-midnight, F-Sa 10am-1am

In stark contrast to much of Madrid's historic beauty, the Mercado de San Miguel's wraparound windows and iron infrastructure give it a stunningly modern vibe. That, plus a smorgasbord of Spain's best culinary creations—*pinchos, tortillas, bocadillo* sandwiches, and *tapas* galore—attract thousands of hungry, selfie stick-waving tourists on the daily. Originally built in 1916 and renovated in 2003, the Mercado de San Miguel's popularity is aided by its proximity to **Plaza Mayor,** which is only a few steps away. There's a central seating area with long, communal tables, crammed between some thirty food vendors offering everything from artisanal olives to froyo to mile-high burrata toasts. You'll definitely want to save your grocery shopping for elsewhere, but this is a great place to grab a midday bite or stock up on specialty picnic ingredients.

i Prices vary; wheelchair accessible

PLAZA DE TOROS DE LAS VENTAS

C. de Alcalá 237; plaza tours: 687 73 90 32, bullfights: 913 56 22 00; plaza tours: www. lasventastour.com; bullfights: www.las-ventas. com; open daily 10am-5:30pm

Seating as many as 25,000 spectators, Madrid's Las Ventas bullring is by far the largest in Spain, outdone only by one in Mexico City and another in Venezuela. It was designed in the decadent *Mudéjar* (Moorish) style by José Espeliú, with ornate arched windows, patterned ceramics every which way, and an imposing front door known colloquially as the "Gate of Glory." For aspiring *toreros* (bullfighters), exiting victorious through these doors is the ultimate goal. To see the plaza for yourself, the best way is to attend a fight—watching the sumptuously-clad bullfighters wrangle the bulls into submission is quite the hair-raising experience. Not to mention the fact that once the bull is killed, it's then eaten "as part of the rich and varied gastronomy of Spain." Tickets—which can be purchased online or at the gates—come at a variety of price points depending mostly on whether you sit in the *sol o sombra* (sun or shade). Otherwise, you can go on an audio-guided tour of the plaza during closing times, which gets you access to the ring itself, but also to normally off-limits places like the royal box or the **Puerta de Cuadrillas,** where the *torero* solemnly waits before entering the ring.

i Plaza tours €14.90, students €11.90, bullfights admission from €4.90-74.90 (depending on seats); guided tours must be pre-purchased (www.lasventastour.com); tours at 9:30am, 11:30am, and 3pm, duration 90min.; last entry at 5:30pm; limited wheelchair accessibility

TEATRO DE LA ZARZUELA (ZARZUELA THEATER)

C. de Jovellanos 4; 91 524 54 00; www.teatrodelazarzuela.mcu.es; box office open M-F noon-8pm, Sa-Su 2:30pm-8pm

Built specifically for the genre in 1856, this sumptuous theater is the prime place to watch a traditional Spanish *zarzuela*. Generally classified as operetta, it's a mélange of drama, music, and comedy that has captivated Spanish audiences since the 1600s, experiencing a golden age in the nineteenth century. The stage, which was modeled after Milan's La Scala theater, also hosts musical theater, concerts, traditional operas, and performances by Spain's **National Dance Company.** Visitors 35 and under get tickets 50 percent off, so don your finest Sunday clothes (or at least comb your hair) and treat yourself to a night of elevated Spanish culture.

i Tickets from €5-50, youth tickets 50% off (under 35 years old); free tours daily at 11am and noon; wheelchair accessible; box office closed for Aug; tickets purchased 2hr before showtime 60% off

LANDMARKS

⬛ TEMPLO DE DEBOD (TEMPLE OF DEBOD)

C. Ferraz 1; 913 66 74 15; www.templod-edebod.memoriademadrid.es.com; open Apr-Sept Tu-F 10am-2pm and 6pm-8pm, Sa-Su 10am-2pm; Oct-Mar Tu-F 9:45am-1:45pm and 4:15pm-6:15pm, Sa-Su 10am-2pm

Bet you weren't expecting to find an Egyptian temple in the heart of downtown Madrid, were you? Construction started in 2200 BCE under the auspices of King Adijalamani and completed over several centuries before being abandoned some 8000 years later. 1800 years later, Egypt decided to build a dam that would flood the temple, and they decided to donate the building to Madrid as a thank you to Spanish archeologists who had helped with its preservation. To this end, it was disassembled brick by brick, and the whole thing was painstakingly shipped to the Spanish capital, where it now rests atop a grassy hill next to **Plaza de España.** Bizarrely placed in the epicenter of urban

Madrid, it exudes a palpable mystique. Legend even has it that the goddess Isis gave birth to Horus in this very temple, but that was in Debod's pre-Spain days.

i Free; last entry 15min. before close; limited wheelchair accessibility; max visit duration 30min.

ANDÉN 0: ESTACIÓN MUSEO CHAMBERÍ (PLATFORM 0: CHAMBERÍ STATION MUSEUM)

Pl. de Chamberí; 902 444 403; www.metromadrid.es; open Th 10am-1pm, F 11am-7pm, Sa-Su 11am-3pm

Andén 0 offers a glimpse into Madrid's recent history; built in 1919, it was the city's first metro stop, connecting the neighborhood of **Chamberí** to **Bilbao** and **Iglesia** stations. It was designed by Antonio Palacios, inspired by the Parisian design and filled with blue and white cobalt tilework. During the **Spanish Civil War,** its underground tunnels were converted into warehouses and refugees—protection from air bombings. When the Madrid metro expanded in the 1960s, it had outgrown Chamberí and the station was retired for forty years, but a restoration project completed in 2008 saw it reopen to the public. Visitors are greeted with a short film about the station and can then descend the original metro steps to the main platform, which is decorated with tile advertisements for cafés of the 1920s and old-fashioned gadgets. Soft jazz fills the station, punctuated occasionally by the sound of trains whizzing by, en route to more modern destinations.

i Free; guided tours every hour; last entry 30min. before close; wheelchair accessible

BASILICA SAN FRANCISCO EL GRANDE (BASILICA OF SAN FRANCISCO EL GRANDE)

C. San Buenaventura 1; 91 365 38 00; www.esmadrid.com; open July-Aug Tu-Su 10:30am-1pm and 5pm-7pm, Sept-June Tu-Sa 10:30am-1pm and 4pm-6:30pm

Just down the street from the show-stopping **Royal Palace** and **Royal Theater** is yet another possession of the Spanish crown: the grandiose Royal Basilica. Featuring the largest dome in Spain, it was built in the eighteenth century by Francesco Sabatini, based on a design by Francisco Cabezas. The basilica's décor is just as magnificent as the architecture; hardly a square inch is free from gold, silver, or the brush strokes of Spanish masters. **Goya** is the main highlight—look for his work in the **Chapel of San Bernardino**. Admission to the basilica is free during morning mass, but to see the museum you'll need to attend a guided tour (Spanish only); ask the staff when the next one will begin.

i *Admission €5, students €3; last entry 30min. before close; limited wheelchair accessibility; admission free Sep-June Sa 10:30am-12:30pm, July-Aug Sa 5pm-7pm*

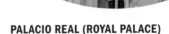

ESTADIO SANTIAGO BERNABÉU (SANTIAGO BERNABÉU STADIUM)

Av. de Concha Espina 1; 91 398 43 00; www.realmadrid.com; open M-Sa 10am-7pm, Su 10:30am-6:30pm

The uninitiated may be put off by the chintziness of the Bernabéu tour, but a stadium pilgrimage is non-negotiable for anyone with even a passing interest in the world of soccer. Bernabéu Stadium, built in 1947 and boasting a seating capacity of 80,000 spectators, is one of the world's most famous *fútbol* locales and home to the city's beloved Real Madrid team. The stadium has hosted a number of important matches through the years, most notably the 1982 FIFA World Cup (Italy won). Tours are a bit pricey, but they grant you access to otherwise off-limits places like the royal box, the players' dressing room, and the press room. The chintz comes in when you "make your dream come true" by having a photo of yourself taken against a green screen, onto which they project your favorite Real Madrid player. As always, exit through the gift shop, where you can deck yourself out in team merch.

i *Tours €25; audio guide €5; limited wheelchair accessibility; tours on game day only offer limited access to facilities starting 5hr before the match*

PALACIO REAL (ROYAL PALACE)

C. Bailén; 91 454 97 00; www.patrimonionacional.es; open daily Oct-Mar 10am-6pm, Apr-Sep 10am-8pm

King Felipe V's extravagant palace is one of Madrid's most stunning pieces of architecture. Even though it's called the Royal Palace, the royal family doesn't actually live there anymore; they live in the less-decadent **Palacio de la Zarzuela** outside the city center, reserving the Royal Palace for state events and ceremonies. Visitors can't visit all 3,400 rooms, but there's more than enough **Goya, Tiepolo,** and **Velázquez** in the 50 open rooms to kill a couple hours. Be on the lookout for the palace's collection of five **Stradivarius** violins, which are still used in occasional performances. Once you're done ogling the velvet-covered throne room and the silken Salón de Gasparini, head outside to the sweeping **Plaza de la Armería** to check out the royal pharmacy and armory (a strange combo, but why not?).

i *Admission €10, students under 25 €5; guided tours €4, audio guide €3; last entry 1hr before close; wheelchair accessible; free admission 2hr before close; combined ticket with royal kitchen €14, students €9; combined ticket with Teatro Real €15*

CENTROCENTRO PALACIO DE CIBELES AND PLAZA CIBELES

Pl. de Cibeles 1; 914 800 008; www.centrocentro.org; open Tu-Su 10am-8pm, observation deck open Tu-Su 10:30am-1:30pm and 4pm-7pm

A headquarters so central, they had to name it *Centro*Centro—the breathtaking, Neoclassical Palace of Cibeles used to serve a surprisingly mundane function: as the "Communications Cathedral," it was the headquarters of the National Postal Service. Ever since 2007, however, it's served as seat of the Madrid City Council, and currently hosts a plethora of cultural events, workshops, exhibitions, conferences, and even live performances. There's a bookshop, a café, tourist information, two restaurants, wide-open lounge areas—quite the multi-purpose cultural center. The eighth floor even has an observation deck with sweeping views of the city. Head here for a bit of R&R, a bite to eat, or a bombardment of tourist pamphlets and information packets. It's just up the street from the **Museo del Prado** on Madrid's largest boulevard.

i Free, observation deck admission €2; Wi-Fi; wheelchair accessible; free admission to the observation deck first W every month

PLAZA MAYOR

Pl. Mayor; www.madrid.es; open daily 24hr

Originally designed in 1617 in the Herrerian style by Juan Gómez de Mora, Plaza Mayor has been the epicenter of Madrid for some 400 years, although this urban confluence was an important meeting point long before then. Bullfights, weddings, the beatification of San Isidro Labrador—Madrid's patron saint—all occurred here, along with the more sinister *autos de fe,* hangings and burnings at the stake during the Spanish Inquisition. Today, it's a lively tourist hub lined with coffee shops, souvenirs, and Madrid's main tourist office. Be sure to check out the 237 wrought-iron balconies protruding from the surrounding buildings, as well as the gorgeous frescoes on the façade of the **Real Casa de la Panadería,** a royal bakery from the 1590s that was responsible for setting a city-wide price

on fresh bread so the poor could afford it. The square burned to the ground in 1790 and was reconstructed by Juan de Villanueva.

i Free; wheelchair accessible

REAL ERMITA DE SAN ANTONIO DE LA FLORIDA (ROYAL CHAPEL OF ST. ANTHONY OF LA FLORIDA)

Glorieta de San Antonio de la Florida 5; 915 420 722; www.madrid.es/ermita; open Tu-Su 9:30am-2pm and 3pm-7pm

The **Museo del Prado** may hold much more of **Goya**'s work, but this royal chapel is one of the few places where visitors can see his artwork in its natural habitat. The Baroque building was commissioned in 1792 by King Carlos IV, who asked Goya to paint the ceiling with a fresco honoring Saint Anthony of Padua. Goya's sprawling masterpiece, completed in 1798, depicts the saint resuscitating a murdered man so he can testify in defense of his father, who was wrongly accused of the murder. Cherubim surround Saint Anthony, straining to support the weight of the ceiling. Since 1919, the solemn chapel has been Goya's resting place, although apparently his skull is mysteriously missing. To help preserve the chapel, an identical one was built right next door to host the masses and celebrations that used to take place here.

i Free; guided tours Sa 1pm-1:50pm; wheelchair accessible

MUSEUMS

⊠ MUSEO CENTRO DE ARTE REINA SOFÍA

C. Santa Isabel 52; 91 774 1000; www.museoreinasofia.es; open M 10am-9pm, W-Sa 10am-9pm, Su 10am-7pm

Full of odd angles, geometric shapes, and paint splats, it isn't hard to guess the Museo Reina Sofía's genre. Spread over four floors, the collection is an ode to twentieth-century artwork, taking visitors on a fantastical tour from surrealism to movements like "situationist utopian urbanism." The most exciting part, however, is the second floor's cubism display. Beginning with the foundations of the movement at the beginning of the twentieth century, the museum has a superb collection of **Miró, Gris, Braque,** and more, all of which is a dramatic buildup to the most famous painting in the whole city: **Picasso's** *Guernica.* Painted for the Spanish State in 1937, this enormous cubist masterpiece—roughly 11 by 26 feet—condemns the bombing of the Basque town of Guernica by a Spanish rebel group. Since its debut at the Paris International Art Exhibition, it has become a world-famous symbol against oppression, violence, and war. Lining the *Guernica* room is ample documentation of the creative process, provided in large part by Picasso's partner at the time. If you can tear your eyes away from the museum's showstopper, look for more works by big-name Spanish masters like **Dalí, Barradas, Masson,** and **Gargallo.** The collection is arranged by theme rather than by artist, so you never know whose artwork may be around the corner.

i *Admission €10 at box office, online €8, students under 25 free; audio guides €4.50, students €3.50, guided tours by request; last entry 30min. before close; wheelchair accessible; Wi-Fi; admission free M 7pm-9pm, W-Sa 7pm-9pm, Su 1:30pm-7pm*

◪ MUSEO DEL PRADO

C. Ruiz de Alarcón 23; 91 330 2800; www. museodelprado.es; open M-Sa 10am-8pm, Su 10am-7pm

A Madrid visit sans Prado is basically a felony—it's the Louvre of Spain. Its collection of Spanish art is without a doubt the best in the world, and its colossal collection of 7,500 paintings, 4,800 prints, and 1000 sculptures from the twelfth to the twentieth century (of which some 1,300 works are on display) makes it one of the greatest museums in the world. Enter from the imposing **Plaza de Murillo** into a grand foyer and traverse through centuries of European masterpieces, with a particular emphasis on Spanish painters like **El Greco, Murillo, Velázaquez,** and—perhaps the museum's best-represented artist—**Goya.** Spread throughout the Palacio de Villanueva's three grand stories, visitors can also admire works by **Bosch, Botticelli, Raphael, Rembrandt,** and a deluge of other big-

name painters and sculptors. Even the least art-savvy will appreciate Goya's *Saturn Devouring His Son,* a famous self-portrait by **Dürer,** and Bosch's spellbinding *Garden of Earthly Delights.* Take your time but be realistic; a whole week wouldn't be enough to cover everything—plan to spend a minimum of two hours roving through this spectacular collection.

i *Admission €15, students under 25 free; permanent collection audio guides €4, each temporary exhibition €3.50, combined €6; last entry 30min. before close; wheelchair accessible; free admission to permanent collection and 50% off temporary exhibitions M-Sa 6pm-8pm, Su 5pm-7pm; no photos allowed*

MUSEO DE HISTORIA DE MADRID (MUSEUM OF HISTORY OF MADRID)

C. Fuencarral 78; 917 011 863; www.ma-drid.es/museodehistoria; collection open Tu-Su 10am-8pm, gardens and chapel open Tu-Su 10am-3pm

Housed in a **Baroque hospice** from the seventeenth century, this museum's collection chronicles Madrid's history entire history as the capital of Spain. Tours start in 1561, when **Felipe II** named Madrid the capital of a vast empire that stretched from Italy to the Netherlands. Moving into the eighteenth century, the next floor covers the Bourbon Dynasty, an emerging "enlightened" elite, and the beautification of the city by Charles III. A final section presents Madrid's industrialization and emergence as a modern world capital. Throughout the collection are enormous wall maps illustrating the city's growth, as well as a number of paintings you'll recognize from your own jaunts through Madrid. At the end of the visit is an impressive 1:814 scale model of the city as it looked at the end of King Ferdinand VIII's reign. A quality history lesson, to be sure, but the best part is that admission is always free.

i *Free; free tours from noon-5pm must be booked 48hr in advance; wheelchair accessible; no tours July-September*

MUSEO LÁZARO GALDIANO

C. Serrano 122; 91 561 60 84; www.
museodelazarogaldiano.es; open Tu-Sa
10am-4:30pm, Su 10am-3pm

Some people collect stamps or marbles,
but that was clearly too blasé for the
illustrious Lázaro Galdiano, who would
much rather collect masterpieces of
European art. Thanks to his expensive
hobby and his end-of-life donation to
the Spanish State, mere mortals can
now visit his astounding collection,
housed in the five stories of his
opulent estate a few blocks north of
the **Parque del Retiro.** Starting with
the ground floor, visitors can gawk
at the Galdiano's fabulous collection
of Italian, German, Flemish, Dutch,
French, and—of course—Spanish
paintings, which covers a period of
nearly 2500 years, from the fourth
century BCE to the first half of
the twentieth century. Frescoes by
Villamil, landscapes by **Bosch,**
portraits by **El Greco**—it's hard to
believe this stuff was sitting somewhere
as mundane as a living room for so
long. The highlight of the collection
lies in the **Goya** room: two small but
exquisite pieces titled *The Witches and
The Witches' Sabbath.* The entire top
floor (called "The Cabinet") showcases
most of the 13,000 other artifacts the
collector amassed during his lifetime,
from ivories to silverware to terracotta
figurines.
*i Admission €6, students €3; guided tours
by appointment only €8; limited wheelchair accessibility; admission free Tu-Sa
3:30pm-4:30pm, Su 2pm-3pm, first F
every month 5pm-9pm*

MUSEO NACIONAL THYSSEN BOR-
NEMISZA

Paseo del Prado 8; 917 911 370; www.
museothyssen.org; open Tu-Su 10am-7pm

What it lacks in size, it makes up for
in quality; this hard-to-pronounce
museum hosts a formidable
concentration of big-name artists, from
Gauguin to **Picasso** to **Miró.** Founded
in 1992 from the private stockpile
of a single German-Hungarian art
collector, the **Thyssen-Bornemisza**
collection moved to Madrid mostly by
circumstance, along with some gentle
nudging from the baron's Spanish wife,
Carmen Cervera (she was Miss Spain
in 1961). The collection doubled a

year after opening when the Spanish
government added 775 pieces of art
and grew even more when Cervera
loaned her own hoard of 429 works.
The result: a magnificent traipse
through artistic history from triptychs
of the thirteenth century all the way to
the early twentieth century. The visit
is an entourage of **Van Gogh, Renoir,
Kandinsky, Rembrandt, Dalí.** It's like
the red carpet but with dead painters.
As part of the Paseo del Prado's Golden
Triangle of Art (which also includes the
Prado and Reina Sofía), a visit is all but
obligatory for any Madrid tourist.
*i Admission €12, students €8; audio
guide €5, multimedia guide €6; last entry
1hr before close; wheelchair accessible;
free admission to permanent collection M
noon-4pm*

MUSEO DEL ROMANTICISMO

C. de San Mateo 13; 91 448 10 45; www.
mecd.gob.es; open Nov-Apr Tu-Sa 9:30am-
6:30pm, Su 10am-3pm; May-Oct Tu-Sa
9:30am-8:30pm, Su 10am-3pm

With its plush Isabelline furniture,
exotic *costumbrista* paintings, and
no fewer than fifteen mini grand
pianos, this museum conveys the
Romantic message loud and clear.
It's housed in the former palace of
the Marquis of Matallana, built in
1776 and inaugurated as a museum
in 1924. A tour of the building passes
through a number of thematic rooms,
all meticulously arranged to recall
Romantic themes. There are decked-
out antechambers, anterooms, great
halls, luxurious dining rooms—all of
which offer insight into nineteenth-
century Romantic life. The Lady's
Bedroom, for example, shows visitors
where the woman of the household
could "engage in all those mysterious
actions," according to the English
guidebook. Be sure to appreciate
the museum's impressive collection
of artwork, including a large **Goya**
painting in the chapel and a not-
so-serious "Satire of the Romantic
Lover's Suicide," which reveals a
self-deprecating side to this schmaltzy,
sentimentalist movement.
*i Admission €3, students under 25 free;
audio guides €2; wheelchair accessible;
free admission Sa 2pm-close*

MUSEO SOROLLA

Paseo del General Martínez Campos 37; 913 101 584; www.museosorolla.es; open Tu-Sa 9:30am-8pm, Su 10am-3pm

The Sorolla Museum offers far more than a peek into the artist's life— Sorolla lived here from 1911 to his death in 1923, filling the house with his own sketches, landscapes, portraits, and "color notes" (just for fun). Every inch of the mansion breathes Sorolla; besides the 1,294 paintings scattered throughout the interior, the estate itself was built from the ground up to his liking, based on sketches Sorolla had drawn for the architect Enrique María de Repullés y Vargas. Today, the house is stunningly preserved. Visits pass through a grand foyer with Valencian windows, an Andalusian courtyard with blue and white tilework, and Sorolla's cavernous study, where many of his most famous works were produced. You'll end up not in the gift shop, but in the gardens, which are filled with miniature hedges, fountains, and more gorgeous floral tilework.

i Admission €3, students under 25 free; audio guides €2.5, guided tour Tu-F 5pm €3; limited wheelchair accessibility; free admission on Sa, Su from 2pm-8pm

REAL ACADEMIA DE BELLAS ARTES DE SAN FERNANDO

C. Alcalá 13; 91 524 10 34; www.realac-ademiabellasartessanfernando.com; open Tu-Su 10am-3pm (closed Aug)

At various times in its history, this building has been a lavish residence, a royal art academy, one of Europe's first printmaking workshops, and now a fine arts museum and gallery. Despite being smack dab in the center of Madrid, it doesn't get nearly as many visitors as its bigger siblings on the Paseo del Prado, but its history as an art institute is rife with interesting Spanish culture. **Goya** himself was once a director of the academy, and there's an entire room dedicated to thirteen of his paintings, as well as his paint palette, made of dark walnut and framed in gilded laurel leaves. Other notable works include paintings by **Grís, Picasso, Zurburán,** and an unexpected portrait of George Washington, painted by **Giuseppe Pirovani** to celebrate the 1795 Treaty of Friendship between the US and

Spain. Separate from the art gallery is the **Calcografía Nacional** (free admission), where visitors can see selections from the 30,000-strong collection of engraved prints, including a massive Goya collection.

i Admission €8, students under 25 free; guided tours Tu, Th, F at 11am; last entry 15min. before close; wheelchair accessible; free entry to Calcografía Nacional, free entry to permanent collection on W

OUTDOORS

⬛ PARQUE DEL BUEN RETIRO

Pl. de la Independencia 7; www.esmadrid. com; open daily Apr-Sep 6am-midnight, Oct-Mar 6am-10pm

Aptly named "Park of the Pleasant Retreat," Madrid's most popular green space is the city's answer to its sticky, sweltering, let's-just-spend-the-day-inside-where-there's-air-conditioning midsummer days. But not even the best department store's AC can match the reinvigorating qualities of El Retiro's shaded walkways, rose gardens, and the great **Estanque Grande,** a huge man-made pool where visitors can splash around in their own rented rafts and kayaks. Boasting more than 300 acres and over 15,000 trees, Parque del Retiro was designed in the 1630s by the likes of **Cosimo Lotti** (the man behind Florence's famous Boboli Gardens) to be a royalty-only stomping ground and performance center. There was even a palace on the premises until the Peninsular War of 1807-14. Today, El Retiro is completely free and open to the public—after a few expansions and a bit of touching up, the park has become a symbol of Madrid, complete with an expansive rose garden, a "Forest of Remembrance," and endless walkways between its many monuments, fountains, and sculptures. It's worth checking out the three museums/exhibition centers in the park, too (they're all free): **Palacio de Velázquez, Casa de Vacas,** and the **Palacio de Cristal.** The latter is a breathtaking glass-and-steel building from the end of the nineteenth century.

i Free; limited wheelchair accessibility

CAMPO DEL MORO

Paseo Virgen del Puerto; 91 454 88 00; www.
esmadrid.com; open daily Oct-Mar 10am-
6pm, Apr-Sept 10am-8pm

Lying humbly in the imposing shadow of
the **Royal Palace,** the Moorish Gardens
got their name when a twelfth-century
troop of Muslims parked themselves here
before launching an (unsuccessful) attack
against Christian forces. More recently,
the gardens were a stomping ground
for Spanish royalty and their esteemed
visitors, finally being converted into an
open-access public park in the mid-
twentieth century. The grand, exquisitely-
manicured central Pradera was designed
with Versailles in mind—although
they don't quite match those gardens'
extravagance, there's something special
in the serenity of these gardens, hidden
from the swarm of tourists amassing at
the Royal Palace's façade. Shaded walking
paths cover the perimeter of the gardens,
passing through quiet glens, flocks of
peacocks, and a duck pond.
*i Free; park empties 30min. before close;
limited wheelchair accessibility*

REAL JARDÍN BOTÁNICO (ROYAL BOTANICAL GARDEN)

Paseo del Arte; 91 420 80 17; www.rjb.csic.es;
open daily Nov-Feb 10am-6pm, Mar 10am-
7pm, Apr 10am-8pm, May-Aug 10am-9pm,
Sept 10am-8pm, Oct 10am-7pm

Parque del Retiro not lush enough for
you? Next door, Madrid's Royal Botanical
Gardens have some 90,000 plants and
over 1,500 trees; more than enough
chlorophyll for all your herbivorous needs.
Founded in 1755, the gardens found their
current home near the **Museo del Prado**
in 1781 under the direction of Charles III.
Madrid's architectural all-stars **Sabatini**
and **Villanueva** are behind the gardens'
design, roughly dividing the gentle hillside
into four sections: the Terrace of Plots, of
Botanical Schools, the romantic Flower
Plan, and a Laurel Terrace. A self-guided
tour meanders past rhododendron
collections, Californian sequoias, Japanese
ornamentals, and more. There's a small
museum-bookstore-café at the top of
the hill, adorned with Mexican palms, a
reflective pond, and a statue of **Linnaeus,**
the esteemed Swedish naturalist.
*i Admission €4, students €2; last entry
30min. before close; wheelchair accessible;
admission free Tu after 5pm*

FOOD

🦐 SALA DE DESPIECE ($$)

C. de Ponzano 11; 917 52 61 06; www.
saladedespiece.com; open M-Th 1pm-5pm
and 7:30pm-12:30am, F 1pm-4:30pm and
7:30pm-1:30am, Sa 12:30pm-5:30pm and
7:30pm-1:30am, Su 12:30pm-5:30pm and
7:30pm-12:30am

Entering the Sala de Despiece is like
stumbling into a typical **Chamberí**
butcher shop. Everything is spotlessly
white, from the waiters' aprons to the
shiny wall tiles; a decorative austerity
inspired by the local butcheries and fish
markets. Unlike a typical restaurant,
guests don't sit at tables, but on bar stools
facing the butcher himself, where they can
watch their food as it is sliced, tenderized,
or julienned into an array of delicious
final products. Since ingredients are the
number one priority, the menu changes
frequently but is presented as a product
list, handwritten in blue, with different
categories for product name, origin,
preparation, and portion size. Anything
meaty is bound to be fantastic, but its
signature *Rolex* (pork belly and foie gras
with truffles) is to die for.
*i Entrées from €9; gluten-free and vegetarian
options available; no wheelchair accessibility;
no reservations except for Mesa de Despiece
(next door 12-seat restaurant, minimum
tasting menu €35)*

📧 CASA DANI ($)

Mercado de la Paz, C. Ayala 28; 915 75 59 25; www.casadani.es; open M-F 7am-7:30pm, Sa 7am-4:30pm

Tortillas españolas (Spanish tortillas) are a cross between a quiche, omelet, hash browns, and a tortilla. Potato-loaded and ham and cheese-studded, they're basically a miracle of Iberian cuisine, and Casa Dani has a special knack for preparing them. This sprawling restaurant is technically part of the **La Paz Market** north of the **Parque del Retiro,** but La Paz's other offerings feel like a sideshow to Casa Dani; the restaurant takes up around half of the place, with a fancy sit-down restaurant, a bar, a takeaway booth with its own food court-style seating area, and another sit-down restaurant (the outdoor terrace) just outside the market's entrance. Swarms of locals and tourists alike queue up around lunchtime for Spanish classics—if you're not going for the Spanish tortilla, try the marinated snails, *torreznos* (thinly-sliced bacon), or *salmorejo* (bread and tomato purée).

i Entrées from €9, menu of the day €11; cash only; gluten-free, vegan, and vegetarian options available; wheelchair accessible

CASA JULIO ($)

C. de la Madera 37; 915 22 72 74; open M-Sa 1pm-3:30pm and 6:30pm-11:30pm

Founded by—you guessed it—Julio, this tiny restaurant in **Malasaña** is now owned by his fourth-generation descendants, who faithfully continue their forefathers' mission to craft the best *croquetas* in Madrid. For the uninitiated, croquetas are fried dough balls stuffed with savory meats, cheeses, herbs, and veggies, and they're dangerously addictive. Since frying the first ones in 1921, Casa Julio has garnered quite a cult of followers, from celebrities to the humble, hungry tourist. Tradition mandates that you try a simple *jamón*-stuffed croqueta, but the most popular flavor involves a lip-smacking spinach and mushroom situation. Thankfully, you don't have to decide on just one; they come in groups of six (€6) or twelve if you're famished (€12). There are only five tables plus bar seating, so count on a wait if you're coming at peak mealtimes.

i Croquetas €7 for 6, tapas from €6; gluten-free and vegetarian options available; wheelchair accessible

CASA SALVADOR ($$)

C. Barbieri 12; 91 521 45 24; www.casa-salvadormadrid.com; open M 1:30pm-4pm, Tu-Th 1:30pm-4pm and 8:30pm-11pm, F-Sa 1:30pm-4pm and 8:30pm-11:30pm

Anthony Bourdain loved this place when he visited in 2010, although Ernest Hemingway had already granted Casa Salvador the golden seal of approval a few decades prior. Naturally, it's a required visit if you find yourself in the **Chueca** neighborhood. Unlike the hipster restaurants surrounding it, Casa Salvador harkens back to the good old days when Chueca was filled not with matcha lattes, but with bullfighting all-stars. Beginning in the 1940s, *toredores* could stop here for some pre-fight chopped veal, cod fritters, monkfish, and the house specialty: oxtail stew. Not exactly a light lunch, but maybe all that offal is the real secret to successful bullfighting. Regardless, guests can also appreciate the bullfighting legacy through the restaurant's impressive collection of drawings, photography, and sculpture devoted to the sport. Either that or a mouthful of tripe, you decide.

i Entrées from €12, menu of the day €25; gluten-free and vegetarian options available; wheelchair accessible

CASA TONI ($)

C. de la Cruz 14; 91 532 25 80; open daily noon-4pm and 7pm-midnight

Despite its central location in prime tourist trap territory, Casa Toni's cuisine is anything but watered-down for the finicky tourist's palate. Adventurous eaters will appreciate a simple, traditional menu with offerings like *zarajos* (braided lamb intestines) and *orejas a la plancha* (grilled pig ears). The whole menu, listed on a tall blackboard outside the restaurant, is an ode to scrap meat, featuring a wide range of animal odds and ends. Sautéed kidneys, lamb neck glands in sweet bread, blood sausage—this place isn't for the faint of heart, although they do have some more familiar offerings like garlicky mushrooms or fried eggplant. For the optimal experience, grab a pal and order a few dishes in typical tapas style.

i Tapas from €3.50, entrées from €7; gluten-free and vegetarian options available; no wheelchair accessibility

CHOCOLATERÍA SAN GINÉS ($)

Pasadizo San Ginés 5; 913 65 65 46; www.
chocolateriasangines.com; open daily 24hr

Pharmacies, sure. Hospitals, of course. But
a 24hr chocolate shop? At any time of the
day (since 1890!), Chocolatería San Ginés
is prepared to deliver its famous **churros-
and-chocolate** combo. And by chocolate,
we mean of hot cocoa variety—only the
drink they serve at San Ginés is nothing
like your run-of-the-mill Swiss Miss
packet. Thick, dark, and highly potent,
it's like a melted chocolate bar in a cup.
(Perfect for churro dipping.) Although
it's popular at all hours, things pick up
around 4am as weary party-goers wind
down at the chocolatería's iconic dark
green booths. Best hangover cure? Maybe
not, but good luck resisting the wafting
scent of molten chocolate as you stumble
out of the next-door **Joy Eslava** nightclub.
i *Chocolate €2, with six churros €4;
gluten-free, vegan, and vegetarian options
available; limited wheelchair accessibility*

CHUKA RAMEN ($$)

C. Echegaray 9; 640 65 13 46; www.chukara-
menbar.com; open Tu 8:30pm-11:30pm, W-Sa
1:30pm-3:30pm and 8:30pm-11:30pm

It might take some planning to get into
this elusive ramen bar hidden among
the taverns of **Huertas**—their hours are
limited and the place fills up fast—but
a single slurp of their shoyu ramen is
worth the fuss. Carefully crafted following
the Hokkaidō tradition and filled with
assari-style smoked fish, seafood, pork,
chicken, mushrooms, and seaweed,
the umami elixir is like a portal to the
Orient. The rest of the menu—a fusion
of Chinese and Japanese offerings—
features a similarly meticulous attention
to details, whether in the form of steam
buns, gyozas, or seasonal dishes like whole
roasted cauliflower and Iberian pork
barbecued à la Cantonese. It'll cost you
a few extra euros, but come on, this isn't
Panda Express.
i *Ramen from €15; gluten-free and vegetarian
options available; wheelchair accessible;
reservations recommended*

LA PECERA ($)

C. Velarde 2; 918 26 74 45; www.wearela-
pecera.com; open Tu-Su 2:30pm-10:30pm

Sure, Madrid's got plenty of *helado* (ice
cream). But a simple scoop on a sugar
cone would be way too vanilla (pun
intended) for an *heladería* straddling
Madrid's two trendiest neighborhoods,
Malasaña and **Chueca.** At La Pecera,
ice cream is served Japanese-style, from a
soft waffle "cone" shaped like a fish with
its mouth wide open (called a *taiyaki).*
The process is simple: choose vanilla or
chocolate for your doughy *taiyaki,* pick a
soft-serve flavor (options include matcha
and salted caramel), and top it with
powdered butter cookies, caramelized
almonds, or chocolate syrup. They don't
technically list step 4 (snap a photo for the
Insta), but the temptation is irresistible.
Despite being a relatively young Madrid
establishment, La Pecera has become so
popular that a sign outside the door has
to tell visitors which street to spill onto;
there's always a snaking queue of hipsters
at this hole-in-the-wall, especially just after
dinnertime.
i *Taiyaki €3.50, with toppings €4.50;
vegetarian options available; no wheelchair
accessibility*

LA TASQUERÍA ($$)

Duque de Sesto 48; 914 51 11 00; www.
latasqueria.com; open M-Sa 1:30pm-4pm
and 8:30pm-11pm, Su 1:30pm-4pm

The name of this classy but affordable
restaurant is a combination between *tasca*
(tavern) and *casquería* (a place serving
offal). Yes, offal. Chef Javi Estévez—who
was once a contestant on Top Chef—is
crazy about the stuff, offering a menu
stuffed with all manner of brains,
tongue, gizzards, tripe, tails, and more.
Somehow, Estévez manages to elevate
these unspeakable "scrap" meats to lofty,
mouth-watering heights, serving them in
a chic eatery you'd never expect from such
taboo cuisine. It takes an adventurous
spirit, but if there's ever a reliable place
to open your mid to offal, this is it; all
the dishes are masterfully executed. Try
some duck heart with raspberries, gizzards
with lettuce and anchovies, or test your
limits with the famous suckling pig head,
adorned with a side of tripe.
i *Entrées from €10, tasting menu €39;
gluten-free options available; no wheelchair
accessibility*

MERCADO ANTÓN MARTÍN ($)

C. de Santa Isabel 5; 91 369 06
20; www.mercadoantonmartin.com;
open M-F 9am-9pm, Sa 9am-3pm

Unlike many of Madrid's food
markets, recently retrofitted
with glistening interiors and
modern facilities, the Mercado
Antón Martín retains a quirky
throwback vibe (read: it's a
little dilapidated). Just like its
neighborhood of **Lavapies,** the
market caters to a more local,
international, and sometimes
countercultural audience—those
trendy Chueca tourists haven't made
their way down here yet. A stroll
through the market is enjoyably eclectic;
it's impossible to categorize Antón Martín
and its multifaceted vendors. There's a
vegan health bar alongside a *casquería*
(which sells offal), a fine cheese monger
next to a punk rock gastropub selling
tacos and beer. A *frutería* made to look
like a 50s diner. On the top floor is a
prestigious Spanish dance studio. Also
unlike the other Madrid markets, prices
at Antón Martín are quite fair; grocery
shopping here won't burn a hole through
your wallet.

i Restaurants $, bulk food $-$$; gluten-free,
vegan, and vegetarian options available;
wheelchair accessible

PANADERÍA PANIC ($)

C. Conde Duque 13; 910 86 22 01; open M-F
9:30am-9pm, Sa 9:30am-3pm

The malty aroma of yeast pours from this
boutique bakery like a beacon, beckoning
sourdough lovers from across Madrid to
the northwestern corner of **Malasaña.**
There are plenty of other bakeries in
the city offering daily-baked breads, but
Panadería Panic stands above the rest; it
started out as the pet project of a Javier
Marca, former art director at a Madrid
magazine, when in 2013 he finally
opened the doors at Panic, offering a small
selection of ciabattas, baguettes, and other
artisanal loaves. Everything is sourdough,
all the grains are organic, and the only
ingredients used in his bread are flour,
water, and salt; few ingredients equal big
flavor, according to Marca. His customers
agree—locals frequently clear out the
shelves well before closing hours, toting
baskets with loaves of 100% rye, spelt,
and oat flour. Of course, there's the classic
palo, which is Panic's best seller: just a very

long,
very
traditional
sourdough
baguette. Beauty in simplicity.

i Bread from €3.80/kg; cash only; gluten-free,
vegan, and vegetarian options available;
wheelchair accessible

PEZ TORTILLA ($)

C. Pez 36; 643 91 99 84; www.peztortilla.
com; open M-W 6pm-2am, Th noon-2am, F-Sa
noon-2:30am, Su noon-2am

Four amigos, a passion for beer, and a
hankering for the cheese-filled comfort of
a good *tortilla,* and you've got the perfect
recipe for Pez Tortilla, a trendy eatery
in the **Malasaña** neighborhood. At any
given time, there are some thirty or so
beers available (tap or in cans), including
quirky foreign ones like Extra Horny,
Hopulent IPA, and Northern Monk
Heathen, as well as their own house brew.
Obviously, you'll want to pair your pint
with a tortilla—the fifteen-strong menu
of flavors changes weekly, but a couple
stalwart options like brie with truffles and
jamón—their most popular tortilla—
are always on offer. Of course,
there's always the purist *clásico* with
caramelized onion: a divinely cheesy
experience that borders on religious.

i Tortilla pincho from €3, croquetas 2 for
€2; vegetarian options available; limited
wheelchair accessibility

RAYÉN VEGANO ($)

C. Lope de Vega 7; phone 675 38 20 72; www.rayenvegan.com; open M 1pm-4:30pm, W-F 1pm-4:30pm, Sa-Su 11am-4:30pm

Looking for lovingly-sourced, colorful, plant-based cuisine in the heart of meaty Madrid? Fittingly, you'll find it in the **Huertas** (gardens) district, in Rayén's adorably picnic-esque space. Founded by chefs Noemi (Kundalini yogi and astrologist) and Paulo (church organist who loves cats), Rayén has been dishing up organic and local veggies since 2013, based on a philosophy involving oneness with the world, compassion for all living things, and as much matcha as possible. Their creative menu features a handful of seasonal offerings, from polenta pizzas to marinated tempeh dishes. The best move, however, is to order a daily special: either a combo menu (two dishes) or a salad. "Salad" is a bit of an understatement, though, as the dish description is usually the length of a novelette; it takes a minute or so for the waiter to read through an epic ingredients list that includes six or seven raw and cooked veggies, a handful of grains and pulses, three dressings and marinades, crispy toppings, and—of course—an avocado. Served with your weight in bread and homemade hummus.

i Entrées from €10.90, menu of the day €12.90; gluten-free, vegan, and vegetarian options available; wheelchair accessible; menu of the day only available weekdays, kitchen closes 3:30pm

SUPERCHULO ($$)

C. de Manuela Malasaña 11; 910 232 706; www.superchulomadrid.com; open Su-Th 1pm-12:30am, F-Sa 1pm-2:30am

"Count colors, not calories" is the slogan of this on-trend **Malasaña** eatery, although we suspect they're also counting Insta likes—everything from the garden hanging from the ceiling to the veggie-filled earthenware bowls is drop-dead gorgeous. For tourists missing LA-style bistros where eating out is a chic fashion statement, this is your Madrid sanctuary. The menu is full of "rainbow food" and littered with hashtags, like a #pornfood section that includes guacamole bao stuffed with tempeh and peanuts, #sorrynotsorry nachos with four homemade sauces, and Flower Power pizza with creamed potato and edible flowers. And instead of salads, they offer—of course—Buddha bowls, all customizable with social media darlings like sweet potatoes, falafel, and the ubiquitous half avocado.

i Entrées from €10.50, menu of the day €11.90; gluten-free, vegan, and vegetarian options available; wheelchair accessible

TOMA CAFÉ ($)

C. de la Palma 49; 917 049 344; www.tomacafe.es; open M-F 8am-8pm, Sa-Su 10am-8pm

Caffeine fiends in Madrid were a sad bunch before Toma Café. Local roasters and single-origin beans are hard to come by in a city that hasn't really moved past its obsession for Nescafe. Toma, however, is like a slice of San Francisco, smack dab in the middle of Madrid's artsy **Malasaña** neighborhood. Every drink on the menu comes from beans they've roasted, ground, and brewed themselves, from plain old filter coffee to the froofier orange cappuccinos. The space is small but can accommodate a surprising number of computer-wielding coffee drinkers, so grab a cup, pair it with a light snack (all prepared/baked in-house!), and settle in for a restful afternoon. Coffee connoisseurs will be delighted to try the *ménage à trois:* a €6 selection of their featured roasts served as an espresso, a cortado, and a drip.

i Coffee from €1.50, light food from €4; gluten-free, vegan, and vegetarian options available; no wheelchair accessibility

NIGHTLIFE

🏴 FABRIK

Av. de la Industria 82; 902 93 03 22; www.grupo-kapital.com/fabrik; open Sa 11pm-6am, sometimes Su

Madrid has a thing for big nightlife venues, but Fabrik, a world-renowned party colossus, is on a whole different level. It's considered one of Europe's highest-quality nightlife locales, and for good reason. Apart from the converted warehouse's three-tiered stage and four dance areas, the outdoor terrace features sixteen bars and its own river. Yes, a river. Party-goers can expect big sound, lots of lasers, and freezing nitrogen fog machines to fill the club with smoke; they really don't hold back. Hosting a variety of the world's most famous DJs, many of Fabrik's parties are themed—

think "Mega Panic Water Party" or "Peace and Love" Fabrik. Sometimes they grant free entry to the first arrivals (up to 1000 people) who come in costume, so be sure to check the website before your pilgrimage.

i Cover €18 (1 drink included); no wheelchair accessibility; opening hours sometimes begin early in the afternoon, check website for event-specific information; to get there, take the metro to Fuenlabrada, followed by the 496 or 497 bus

🦎 SALMON GURU

C. Echegaray 21; 91 000 61 85; www.salmonguru.es; open Tu-Th 5pm-2am, F-Sa 5pm-2:30am, Su 5pm-2am

Those unfamiliar with the gastro-bartending world may not know about Diego Cabrera, but he's quite the mixology hotshot. Not only has he won recognition for being the country's best barman (2011 from the Spanish magazine "The Best of Gastronomy"), his first bar Le Cabrera was named best in the country in an international bartenders' convention. Salmon Guru is his latest pet project, and it's quickly become a shining star of the **Huertas** neighborhood. Surprisingly unpretentious despite the celebrity credentials, a playful pop-up menu offers quirky cocktails in a 50s-esque atmosphere lit by lots of neon. Choose from a small handful of featured creations—think spicy concoctions like Chipotle Chillón, with seven mysteries mescal and fiery chipotle syrup. They don't serve cocktails in fishbowls or anything like that, but you can order some actual fish if you're feeling peckish. The food menu also offers chicken chupa-chupas (like lollipops, but with poultry), mini burgers with foie gras, and other mischievous mashups.

i No cover, cocktails from €11; no wheelchair accessibility

CAFÉ CENTRAL

Pl. del Ángel 10; 91 369 41 43; www.cafecentralmadrid.com; open daily 11:30am-2:30am

For hep cats lookin' to get down with the world's best finger zingers, Café Central is undoubtedly Madrid's best jazz pad, you dig? In all seriousness, this small café near **Plaza Mayor** is known as the premier jazz venue in Spain. With nightly concerts since 1988, they've accumulated some 13000 performances, hosting big names from Wynton Marsalis to George Adams. The experience is unexpectedly intimate—a tiny stage sits mere feet away from the nearest diners, and there's only space for an audience of a few extra chairs. Reservations, which can be made over the phone or at the café starting at 6pm (concerts are at 9pm), are highly recommended.

i Events from €12, entrées from €7, cocktails from €7; limited wheelchair accessibility; MasterCard not accepted; reservations highly recommended

SIDRERÍA EL TIGRE

C. Infantas 30; 918 81 99 01; open M-Th 11:30am-1:30am, F-Sa 11:30am-2:30am

When hangriness strikes, you'll want to keep plenty of distance between yourself and **Chueca's** plentitude of €9 avocado toasts—that's where Sidrería El Tigre comes in. A far cry from the neighborhood's otherwise glitzy aesthetic, this tapas bar offers no frills and no nonsense, at least none of the avocado-slathered variety. They do have an enormous mounted boar head on the wall, accompanied by an adjacent mounted goat, but most visitors are just interested in the dirt-cheap tapas, provided for free when you order a drink. Think plates of ham and cheese-covered *tostas,* fried potatoes, creamy Spanish rice, all washed down with your €2 beer or sangria. Not exactly Michelin material, this is optimal for drunken nights out in Madrid's most fashionable *barrio.*

i No cover, cocktails from €6; cash only; wheelchair accessible

TABERNA DE ÁNGEL SIERRA

C. de Gravina 11; 915 310 126; www.tabernadeangelsierra.es; open Su-Th 10:30am-2:30am, F-Sa 10:30am-3am

The traditional time to down a glass of *vermut* (vermouth) may be before lunch, but try telling that to the crowds gathering within the Taberna de Ángel Sierra as the evening wears on. Having recently celebrated its 100th anniversary in 2017, this gorgeous tavern is all wood, embellished with gold detailing, stained glass, and some serious soccer paraphernalia. The tapas and *conservas* (mostly preparations of tinned fish) are great, but the Reus vermouth is what makes Ángel Sierra an integral part of the **Chueca** late-night pub crawl route. Hundreds of bottles line the walls, display cases, haphazardly lodged into every crevice within the building. Some are coated with inch-thick layers of dust, possibly relics of the tavern's opening in 1917. Treat yourself to a glass (or two), paired with codfish canapes or marinated anchovies.

i No cover, tapas from €1.70, drinks from €2; Wi-Fi; wheelchair accessible

TEATRO JOY ESLAVA

C. del Arenal 11; 913 66 54 39; www.joy-esla-va.com; open Su-Th midnight-5:30am, F-Su midnight-6am

Illuminating the backstreets of **Plaza Mayor** every single night since 1981, Joy Eslava is a legendary nightclub of Madrid. Housed in a grandiose half-acre theater with space for a thousand people on four stories, Joy Eslava emanates hip hop, reggaeton, pop, and more with a formidable 40,000-watt blast of sound. There's a weekly events list, each night with its own theme from "We Love Mondays" dance celebrations to "aggressive concept parties" on Sundays. Regular programming is punctuated (and often preceded) by special events from international celebrities like **Julio Iglesias** or **Vance Joy.** Even after some 13,000 performances, Joy Eslava manages to make each night memorable in its own way—and that's accounting for the inevitable booze-induced fog you're bound to experience.

i Cover (with 2 drinks) €16, events from €12; limited wheelchair accessibility; 18+

TEATRO KAPITAL

C. Atocha 125; 914 20 29 06; open W midnight-close, Th midnight-5:30am, F-Sa midnight-6am,

Housed in an alluring theater-turned-nightclub with seven floors, Teatro Kapital is by far central Madrid's largest club—the indubitable Goliath of the city's nightlife. Everything is centered around the building's main stage, which is your typical rager room/dance floor. What makes the place special are the themed rooms around the theater's perimeter—check out karaoke studios, a rooftop terrace, a Latin room called the "Mojito and Cuba Libre Area," and a Kissing Room with its own cocktail bar. There's something for nearly every mood—if you can get in. Apart from ID verifying your age (18+ only), plan on dressing to impress a bouncer at the entrance. Think elegant: your nicest shirt, dressier shoes (ditch the Tevas), and consider combing your hair, for goodness' sake. Arriving early (before 1am) also boosts your chances of getting in the door.

i Cover before 1:30am €17 with QR code discount (includes 2 drinks), after 1:30am Th €16 (1 drink), F €18 (1 drink), Sa €19 (1 drink), without QR code discount €25 (1 drink); no wheelchair accessibility; QR code available at www.discomadrid.com

PALMA DE MALLORCA

Coverage by **Austin Eder**

Jokingly referred to as the 17th German state, Mallorca is the largest of the four Balearic islands and a popular vacation destination for what seems like all Europeans, minus Spaniards. Walking around, you'll hear more German than Spanish, and if not for the quintessentially Spanish architecture, dry landscape, and turquoise water, it'd be difficult to differentiate Mallorca from a vibrant landlocked city in central Europe. Palma, the island's capital city, dates back to about 100 BCE. Here, homeless individuals and European moguls walk the same streets—share the same benches—without ever acknowledging one another. Palma is a city of striking contrasts. To explore its plazas, beaches, monuments, and restaurants is just as much a reawakening of the moral conscience as it is a reawakening of the senses.

ORIENTATION

Palma is located about 250 kilometers east of **Valencia,** on the southeastern tip of Mallorca. Ferries arrive at **Portopí,** a small neighborhood located on the southwestern corner of the **Puerto de Palma.** Just north of Portopí is the **Castell de Bellver**—a hilltop fortress that offers 360-degree views of Mallorca. **Avinguada de Gabriel Roca** begins at the Baleària terminal and traces the circumference of the port, connecting the waterfront barrios of **El Terreno, Son Armadams, Santa Catalina,** and **La Lonja** to the city center. The city center consists of the area corralled by Avinguda de Gabriel Roca to the south, **Avinguda de Gabriel Alomar** to the east, **Avenida de Alemanya** to the north, and the **Torrent de Sa Riera** to the west. Most museums and major landmarks are located in **La Seu,** the region just north of the **Parc de la Mar. Avenida d'Antoni Maura** is located just west of the Royal Palace and runs north-south, connecting the port to **Plaça de la Reina.** Two important pedestrian thoroughfares include **Carrer del Conquistador** and **Carrer de Colom,** the latter of which leads directly to **Plaça Major. Sindicat,** east of Plaça Major, is quieter and more residential than its western counterparts. Here you'll find many of Palma's bed-and-breakfast-style accommodations, as well as its most authentic restaurants.

ESSENTIALS

GETTING THERE

Palma is accessible by plane and by ferry. Palma de Mallorca Airport, located 8km east of the city center, services domestic and international flights. Bus #1 runs in a loop between the airport, the city center, and the port, departing every 15min. (€5; 971 214 444). Hours of operation depend on the time of year as well as whether you are traveling to or from the airport (Nov-Apr to city daily 6am-1:15am, Nov-Apr to airport daily 5:15am-1am; May-Oct to city daily 6am-1:45am, May-Oct to airport 5:15am-2am). Bus #21 connects the airport with S'Arenal, the beachside neighborhood south of the city. Taxis from the airport to the city center cost €25 and take about 20min. Baleària and Trasmediterranea ferries arrive at the Puerto de Palma de Mallorca, located 5km southwest of the city center. From the port, you can take Bus #1 or a taxi (€20; queued outside of the Baleària and Trasmediterránea terminals) to the city center. In the event that you are arriving by bus from another part of Mallorca, Palma's bus station is located at Carrer d'Eusebi Estada, 2, 1.6km north of La Seu.

GETTING AROUND

Palma is very well-connected as far as public transportation goes. Bus #2 runs in a loop connecting the city center with Santa Catalina and Balanguera. Buses are operated by EMT, which offers a helpful interactive map online at emtpalma.cat/en/lines-timetables. Taxis can sometimes be hard to track down, especially at obscure hours. If you have an early flight or ferry, it may be wise to make arrangements for within-city transportation beforehand (971 72 80 81). A single metro line runs between Plaça d'Espanya to the Universidad de las Islas Baleáres (€1.60 per trip). Renting a bike or scooter will allow you to access coves, beaches, and towns that are otherwise inaccessible via public transport.

PRACTICAL INFORMATION

Tourist Offices: Informació Turística de Mallorca (Plaça de la Reina, 2; 971 17 39 90; infomallorca.net; open M-Sa 8:30am-8pm)

Banks/ATMs/Currency Exchange: ATMs are dispersed about every fifth block within the bounds of Avinguda de Gabriel Alomar. Several banks are located on Passeig del Born, including BBVA, CaixaBank, and Santander.

Post Offices: Palma's main post office is located at C. Jaime III, 15, near El Corte Inglés (971 72 31 09; correos.es; open M-Sa 9:30am-9:30pm). Palma's postal code is 07001.

Public Restrooms: Public restrooms are few and far between in Palma. Most establishments that have an entrance fee come equipped with clean restrooms.

Internet: Free Wi-Fi is available near major monuments such as the Catedral de Santa Maria and Lonja de Mallorca. Some cafés offer access to Wi-Fi with the purchase of a drink. Don't be afraid to ask waiters and waitresses for passwords: *¿Tiene Wi-Fi gratis?*

BGLTQ+ Resources: In Mallorca, Palma is the natural epicenter of a thriving gay culture. The island's umbrella organization for LGBT resources is called Ben Amics (benamics.com). A complete map of certified BGTLQ+ friendly accommodations can be found online at guia.universogay.com/palmademallorca or mallorcagaymap.com.

EMERGENCY INFORMATION

Emergency Number: 112

Police: Comisaría De Distrito Centro (C. Ruiz De Alda, 8; 971 22 55 24)

US Embassy: Embajada de los Estados Unidos de América (Carrer de Porto Pi, 8; 971 40 37 07; pmagency@state.gov; appointment only)

Hospitals: Hospital General de Mallorca is open daily 24hr and located about 900m north of La Seu (Plaça de l'Hospital, 3; 971 21 21 46). Hospital Psiquiàtric de Palma de Mallorca is also an option, located 2km north of the city center (Camí de Jesús, 40; 971 21 23 00).

Pharmacies: Pharmacies, like ATMs, abound in Palma. Farmacia Balanguera, located between the two hospitals listed above, is open 24hr (Carrer de la Balanguera, 15; 971 45 87 88).

Rape Crisis Center: In the event of an emergency, call 112 and later contact the US Consulate. They can provide assistance filing a report with the police and seeking medical treatment.

ACCOMMODATIONS

☙ HOTEL BRICK ($$$)

Carrer Forn d'en Vila, 3; 871 03 18 94; brickpalma.com; check-in after 3pm, check out by 11am

The architectural version of teenage Johnny Depp, this upscale budget accommodation (note the lack of an "s" in its moniker) is equal parts angst and cool. It's located in what used to be a nineteenth-century pottery factory, and now houses several floors of dorms, a rooftop patio, and a full-service bar. On the ground floor, you'll find a roomy reception-bar combo that's been decked out with low leather couches, freestanding knick-knacks that range from shadeless lamps to retro record players, and an assortment of cocktail tables and bar stools that are just as great for working as they are for conversing. Dorms come equipped with earth-skimming, industrial-strength bunks, the most comfortable mattresses we encountered in Spain, spacious lockers, en-suite bathrooms, personal lamps, and outlets galore. Tall windows provide enough light (and #views) to remind you that you are, indeed, on one of the most beautiful islands in Europe.

i Dorms from €25; female-only dorms available; limited wheelchair accessibility; Wi-Fi; lockers, linens, and towels included; breakfast €2.50; full-service bar; rooftop deck

SIGHTS

CULTURE

PLAÇA MAJOR

Plaça Major; 971 71 94 07; plaza open daily 24hr, establishment hours vary

Day or night, this picturesque plaza buzzes with activity. It is the cultural heart of Mallorca's capital city, known for its craft market and assortment of cafés, bars, and artisanal shops. Here, yellow buildings with bright green shutters encase a large rectangle of grey pavers, atop which pigeons peck and children scamper. The area just southwest of Plaça Major— **Palma's Old Town**—is filled with tall

Eclectic buildings, Art Nouveau window casings, overpriced gelaterias, 100-year-old candy stores, upscale clothing boutiques, and the pearl factories for which Mallorca is famous. We recommend starting from **S'hort del Rei** and heading north along **Carrer del Conquistador,** then branching left on **Carrer de Sant Domingo.** From there, follow your feet down the narrow, sloping streets ahead.

i Free; limited wheelchair accessibility

SANTA CATALINA

North of Carrer de Sant Magí, east of Carrer de Joan Crespí; establishment hours vary

Ah, the wonders of gentrification. Located just inland of the **Puerto de Palma,** this hilly neighborhood is now home to some of Palma's tastiest restaurants, edgiest art galleries, trendiest boutique shops, and costliest real estate. Just ten years ago, however, such was not the case. According to some locals we spoke with during our time in Mallorca, Santa Catalina is still trying to escape its reputation as a shabby enclave for squatters, drug dealers, and misfits. Remnants of its previous identity are scattered about in the form of uncleared heaps of litter, vacant ground-floor apartments, and facades ornamented with impassioned anti-tourist messages. Don't come by yourself after dark, but Santa Catalina is one of the only areas in Palma that has yet to be fully overtaken by the tourism industry. **Mercat de Santa Catalina** (Plaça de la Navegació; 971 73 07 10; open M-F 9am-4pm, Sa 8am-4pm) serves as this neighborhood's de facto center, while most restaurants are located on **Carrer de Sant Magí.**

i Free; limited wheelchair accessibility

LANDMARKS

CATEDRAL DE SANTA MARIA DE PALMA

Plaça de la Seu; 902 02 24 45; catedralde-mallorca.org; open Apr-May M-F 10am-5:15pm, Jun-Sep M-F 10am-6:15pm, Oct M-F 10am-5:15pm, Nov-Mar M-F 10am-3:15pm, all Sa 10am-2:15pm

If you weren't knocked on your ass by the short urban hike up to La Seu (or by the €7 entrance fee), you will be once you step foot into this quintessentially Gothic cathedral. There's so much stained glass, it's like a disco ball was taken apart and repurposed. While many of the cathedral's

original features—the massive flying buttresses, the ornamented stone facades, the rose windows and stained glass that lines the central aisle, the soaring 44-meter nave—remain intact, several cosmetic changes were undertaken during this time, including moving the choir closer to the altar. Odds are if you arrive at opening or just before closing, you'll have the entire place to yourself.

i Combined admission to cathedral and Museo Diocesà €7; wheelchair accessible

LONJA DE MALLORCA

Plaça de la Llotja, 5; 672 23 35 55; open Tu-Su 10:30am-1:30pm and 5:30pm-11pm

With soaring ribbed vaults and spiraling stone columns that resemble palm trees, this civil building was designed during the fifteenth century, and long served as a center of mercantile activity during Spain's Golden Age. As the centuries passed and trade declined, however, the building's function changed according to need. Today, it stands empty—a single, expansive room that's free for you to explore, to touch, and to lounge about. The area immediately surrounding this Gothic monument is known as **La Lonja,** a vibrant after-dark destination for locals and tourists alike.

i Free; wheelchair accessible

MUSEUMS

ES BALUARD

Plaça de la Porta de Santa Catalina, 10; 71 90 82 00; esbaluard.org; open Tu-Su 10am-8pm

Located within the walls of the **Sant Pere,** a sixteenth-century building on Palma's bay, this art museum lays special emphasis on the artistic currents of the second half of the twentieth century. The permanent collection consists of works made exclusively by Balearic artists, or artists somehow related to this stunning Spanish archipelago, and covers the entire spectrum of contemporary expression: painting, sculpture, drawing, photography, video—you name it! Es Baluard has housed temporary collections by hot-shots like **Picasso, Miró, Léger, Magritte,** and **Picabia** (among others). Even if you're not of the artistic persuasion, this complex of contrasts is worth a visit for the grounds alone. Kick back and sip on a glass of sangria at Es

Baluard's small restaurant, or head towards the southern wall for a spectacular view of La Seu and the Puerto de Palma.

i *Admission €6, reduced €4.50, grounds free; wheelchair accessible*

OUTDOORS

CALA COMTESSA

Carrer de les Nanses; open daily 24hr

As enticing as **Playa de Can Pere Antoni** might be, do yourself a favor and head 9km southwest to Cala Comtessa. Here, a small stretch of spotless sand is bookended by shallow tide pools, and offers a spectacular view of **Illa de Sa Caleta,** a tiny uninhabitable island located some 200 meters offshore. A stretch of warm, turquoise water connects the two and is so clear you can see your reflection in it. If amenities—snacks, restrooms, and rentable loungers—are what you're looking for, we recommend heading to the neighboring **Playa de Illetes,** located 400 meters northeast via Passeig Illetes. (To access these beaches, take bus #3 from 53-Plaça del Rei Joan Carles I to 93-Passeig d'Illetes 57. The ride takes approximately 40 minutes and costs €1.50, payable on board.)

i *Free; limited wheelchair accessibility*

S'HORT DEL REI

Av. d'Antoni Maura, 18; open daily 24hr

This manicured garden located at the base of the **Royal Palace of La Almudaina** serves as a welcome reprieve from both the heat of the unrelenting Spanish sun and an‐near‐endless tourist frenzy occuring on the Plaça de la Reina. Here, the air is 10 degrees cooler and 10 decibels quieter, stirred only by the occasional squawk of a seagull flying overhead or gust of Mediterranean wind floating inland. Take a seat on a wooden bench or low stone planter and gaze at the water archways that criss-cross before you. Bearing many a fallen flower petal and many a glob of melted gelato, the S'hort del Rei is as much a place for people-watching as plant-watching. Continue south towards the **Parc de la Mar,** a seafront plaza with a man-made lake, and you'll encounter the **Arco de la Drassana,** a tenth-century arch that spans a swan-filled pond.

i *Free; no wheelchair accessibility*

FOOD

EL PERRITO ($$)

Carrer d'Anníbal, 20; 971 68 85 69; open M-F 8am-8pm, Sa 8am-4:30pm

Located in the up-and-coming neighborhood of **Santa Catalina,** El Perrito serves up scrumptious brunch options from dawn until dusk. Take a seat outside at one of four marble tables or inside in El Perrito's canine-themed salon and choose from a variety of morning classics such as eggs benedict with crispy serrano ham, bagel with cured salmon, avocado, and cream cheese, or fruit salad with nuts, yogurt, chia, and muesli. Because this kitchy hangout is one of the most affordable breakfast options in Palma, it attracts a lot of other young travelers. Especially around lunch-time, you'll find the dark grey, succulent-filled interior overflowing with locals (and their pets). Arrive before 11am to score a table.

i *Breakfast items from €2; vegetarian options available; limited wheelchair accessibility*

LA CUADRA DEL MAÑO ($$$)

Carrer del Miracle, 8; 636 04 07 40; open Tu 7pm-midnight, W-Sa 7pm-12:30am, Su 1pm-5:30pm

Even though it's located in Palma's most tourist-dense area, La Cuadra del Maño is the antithesis of a tourist trap. Its small, rustic interior is decked out with dark wooden beams, long rectangular tables, and an assortment of knickknacks so obscure it'd leave an antiques auctioneer scratching his head. Here, everyone knows everyone; bartenders slap patrons on their backs upon entering, and the owner and grill master kisses guests on their cheeks upon taking each of their orders. The menu is a vegetarian's worst nightmare, consisting of only four items: steak, steak, steak, and more steak. Each piece comes from a different part of the cow, and is served with two heaping sides of perfectly-seasoned potatoes and corn. If you're looking for a place to splurge, this is the place to do it.

i *Entrées from €15; reservation recommended for parties larger than 2; limited wheelchair accessibility*

YOU BUY WE COOK ($$)

Mercado del Olivar, Plaça de l'Olivar, 4; 691 35 10 35; eltenedor.es; open Tu-Th 11:30am-4pm, F-Sa 11:30am-4:30pm

Located on the second floor of the **Mercado del Olivar,** You Buy We Cook will prepare anything—and we're talking anything—you purchase downstairs for a flat rate of €3.50. Craving freshly-grilled salmon? Ready in two minutes. Need some help shelling oysters? A waiter will crack 'em open at your table. Just found out your hostel doesn't have an oven after impulse-buying a chicken? They can whole-roast it for you. Although its décor is nothing special, this was undoubtedly one of the coolest gastronomic experiences we've ever encountered. The market is so close you can smell the citrus, aged cheese, and cured ham from your cloth-covered table. Here, the cost of your meal will ultimately come down to how well you barter for it.

i *Flat cooking fee €3.50, wine from €2.50; cash only; vegetarian options available; no wheelchair accessibility*

NIGHTLIFE

🦑 LAB COCKTAIL BAR

Carrer de Sant Magí, 22; 649 54 78 16; bar-labacademy.com; open Su-Th 7pm-2:30am, F-Sa 7pm-3am

As its name suggests, LAB's specialty is craft cocktails, but it also offers a variety of bottled wines, expensive champagnes, and beers on tap. Cocktails range from the classics to unique creations with names like "Take Off Your Cool" and "Fuckin' Around," and are accompanied by handy graphs that pit alcohol content against sweetness, bitterness, and acidity. We recommend the "Hootie Hoo," which consists of Bacardi rum shaken with fresh lime juice and sweetened with sugar. To give you a sense of how potent these concoctions truly are, ours was served in a studded iron teapot that you must pour out carefully into a shot glass, limiting consumption to one small gulp at a time.

i *Cocktails from €9, wine from €4; no wheelchair accessibility*

BLUE JAZZ CLUB

Paseo Mallorca, 6, 8th floor; 971 72 72 40; bluejazz.es/carta; open M-W 5pm-midnight, Th 5pm-1am, F-Sa 11am-2am, Su 11am-midnight

You! Yes, you! Time to take a shower and coif that hair because visiting this rooftop club involves passing as a guest at a five star hotel. Located eight stories above **Hotel Saratoga's** spotless, shimmery lobby lies Blue Jazz Club, a lounge and live music venue that offers spectacular views of the **Puerto de Palma** and **Catedral de Santa Maria.** Here, a sea of white and black leather chairs gives way to a square blue bar, which in turn opens up to a small scenic patio. You'll also find a rooftop pool, sleek tan loungers, and a few thatch umbrellas. We recommend heading straight to the rooftop at 9pm to watch the sunset behind the **Bellver Castle,** then going downstairs for some long-lasting cocktails and soulful tunes. Because of the venue and the clientele, Blue Jazz Club attracts some pretty stellar headliners, especially during the summer months. Concerts take place every Thursday, Friday, and Saturday at 10pm, 11pm, and 11pm, respectively, and occasionally on Mondays at 9pm.

i *Cocktails from €9, beer from €3, wine from €4, soda from €2.50; limited wheelchair accessibility*

PAMPLONA

Coverage by **Joseph Winters**

Pamplona is famous for two things: Ernest Hemingway and bulls. The former fixation—sparked by the city's important role in *The Sun Also Rises*—manifests in the name of just about every half of Pamplona's business establishments. Only in this city can you sip coffee at the Hemingway Café, get a haircut at the Hemingway *peluquería,* and then grab shawarma at Hemingway Döner Kebab. As for the bulls, those visiting during San Fermín (July 6-14) are in for a wild spectacle involving bullfights, more than a million visitors, and, of course, the lunatic Running of the Bulls. For a city obsessed with fleeing from angry bovine, Pamplona is otherwise surprisingly pleasant. As a major stop along the Camino de Santiago, its hostels and cafés are often brimming with pilgrims en route to northwestern Spain, sporting backpacks the size of their bodies and keychains featuring the blue and yellow shell of Saint James. In Pamplona's *Casco Viejo* (Old Town), there are many stocky churches and military fortifications, fantastically-preserved relics of the interminable threat of enemy invasion. The fortress-like Cathedral of Pamplona is a particularly impressive example of the city's architecture, with elements dating as far back as the fourteenth century, and a mausoleum containing the remains of all the kings of Navarre since 1134. Visit for history, for the thrill of the bullfight, for an official Hemingway mani-pedi. Even during the non-San Fermín season, when the dust clears ever so slightly, the vigor of the *torero* runs strong through the heart of the city, permeating bustling bars and stylish cafés.

ORIENTATION

The heart of Pamplona lies within its **Casco Viejo** (Old Town), inside the central **Plaza del Castillo.** The cobblestone streets surrounding this plaza zigzag between fourteenth-century cathedrals, hostels, and plenty of restaurants bearing the Hemingway name. In the past, this area was made of three neighborhoods intersecting in the modern-day **Ayuntamiento de Pamplona** (Town Hall). In the northeast corner is the gargantuan **Pamplona Cathedral.** Heading south from the Plaza del Castillo, the Old Town gives way to a vibrant shopping district, roughly demarcated by the wide-open **Paseo de Sarasate** and flanked to the east by the **Plaza de Toros** (bullring). Further south are more shops and hostel options. Historic Pamplona is lined with an ancient wall that remains remarkably intact, hundreds of years after its latest reconstruction between the sixteenth and eighteenth centuries. Most impressive is the **Ciudadela,** a star-shaped military fortification meant to keep the French from pestering the Pamplonans. At the westernmost edge of the historic downtown, Ciudadela is now a park and contemporary art space. It also houses the **underground bus terminal.** The **train terminal** is about 1.5 miles north of the city, across the **Arga River.** Frequent buses run between the station and downtown, or it's a pleasant half-hour walk into downtown.

ESSENTIALS
GETTING THERE

Flights to Pamplona arrive 4mi. south of the city. From here, it's an easy bus ride into the city center, although you'll have to walk about a 0.5mi. to catch Line 16 at Noáin bus stop. Taxis are also an option, but it'll cost you up to €20. The bus terminal is located in the southwest corner of the city, near La Ciudadela. Frequent buses run from Bilbao, (€18, 2hr), San Sebastián (€8, 1.5hr), Estella (€6, 1hr), Olite (€4, 45min), and other origins within Navarra. In addition, trains connect Pamplona to many of the same places as the bus network, but they often take longer. The train station is north of the city center, and travelers can catch the Line 9 bus from Paseo de Sarasate to make it to downtown. Trains arrive from Madrid (€50, 3hr), San Sebastián (€20, 2hr), Vitoria/Gasteiz (€6.10, 1hr) Barcelona (€50, 4hr) and elsewhere.

GETTING AROUND

The simplest way to navigate Pamplona is by foot. If you get tired, however, you can take the bus. The green and yellow buses prowling Pamplona are called *villavesas* by locals (named after a 1920s bus company). There are 28 daytime routes crisscrossing the city, including the A Line, which goes to the airport, and Line 14, which passes monuments like the Pamplona Cathedral. A single journey costs €1.35 (note that prices increase to €1.60 during San Fermín from July 6-15).

PRACTICAL INFORMATION

Tourist Offices: The main tourist office is located in the new town on Calle San Saturnino (C. San Saturnino 2; 948 42 07 00; www.turismo.navarra.es; open daily 9am-2pm and 3pm-8pm). Look for the statue of bulls just across the street. There are also info booths throughout the city (look for the lowercase "i" symbol).

Banks/ATMs/Currency Exchange:
Banks and ATMs abound, particularly
near the church of San Nicolás (in the
Old Town) and along the more urban
Avenida de Carlos III el Noble.
- Deutsche Bank: C. Paulino Caballero 3; 948 22 89 36; www.db.com/spain; open M 8:30am-4:30pm, Tu 8:30am-3pm, W-Th 8:30am-4:30pm, F 8:30am-2:15pm
- Santander: Paseo de Pablo Sarasate Pasealekua 3; 948 21 03 37; www.bancosantander.es; open M-Th 8:30am-2pm and 4pm-6:30pm, F 8:30am-2pm

Post Offices: There are several Correos
offices in Pamplona. One is next to
a candy store on the Paseo de Pablo
Sarasate, another is on the southwestern
side of the La Ciudadela park. Hust look
for a blue and yellow sign with a French
horn-esque logo.
- C. Pablo Sarasate 9; 902 19 71 97; www.correos.es; open M-F 8:30am-8:30pm, Sa 9:30am-1pm
- Av. de Sancho el Fuerte 69; 902 19 71 97; www.correos.es; open M-F 8:30am-2:30pm and 4:30pm-8pm, Sa 9:30am-1pm

Public Restrooms: There are public
bathrooms in the Plaza del Castillo, near
the Monument to the Running of the
Bulls, along Avenida Carlos III el Noble,
and in the Plaza Fueros de Navarra.
In a pinch, try Dia, BM, or Eroski
supermarket, or buy an espresso at any
café.

Internet: Fortunately, there is a small
public Wi-Fi network in Pamplona.
It isn't exactly lithe or supple, but
it'll update your Facebook feed every
few minutes or so. Access points are
somewhat sparse—look for a connection
in Cidadela, Avenida Carlos III el Noble,
and in the Plaza del Castillo. Check www.
pamplona.es for a complete map of the
hotspots.

BGLTQ+ Resources: Their office is
in Madrid, but the State Federation of
Lesbian, Gay, Trans and Bisexual People
(FELGTB in Spanish) offers a directory
of BGLTQ+-related events, information,
and has a hotline for victims of
discrimination (C. Infantas 40, Madrid;
913 604 605; www.felgtb.org; open
M-Th 8am-8pm, F 8am-3:30pm).

EMERGENCY INFORMATION

Emergency Number: general emergency
112; national police emergency number
091; national health emergency number:
061

Police: Your two options are the local
police and the national police. If you're
unsure whom to contact in an emergency,
dial 091 for quick access to the national
guys.
- Policía Municipal: C. Monasterio de Irache 2; 948 42 06 40; www.policia-municipal.pamplona.es
- Policía Nacional: C. Beloso Alto 3-5; 091; www.policia.es

US Embassy: The US Embassy is in
Madrid, but you can call if you have a
specific question (C. de Serrano 75; 915
872 200; es.usembassy.gov; open M-F
8am-2pm).

Rape Crisis Center: The Rape Crisis
Network Europe recommends CAVAS, a
center for victims of sexual assault, whose
main office is in Madrid (C. Alcalá 124;
91 574 01 10; www.cavascv.org).

Hospitals: In case of an emergency, dial
112 or 061 and an ambulance will take
you to the nearest hospital. If you need a
walk-in visit, try the Clinica Universidad
de Navarra, located in the southwestern
corner of the city.
- Virgen del Camino Hospital: C. de Irunlarrea 4; 848 42 22 22; www.pamplona.es; open daily 24hr
- Clinica Universidad de Navarra: Av. de Pío XII 36; 948 25 54 00; www.cun.es; open daily 8am-10pm

Pharmacies: Due to the siesta, most
Pamplona pharmacies close down in the
midafternoon. There's a 24hr one near
the bus terminal (Farmacia Yanguas), but
otherwise you'll just have to wait to get
that antifungal crème. Check Avenida de
la Baja Navarra or Avenida de Carlos III
el Noble for plenty of options.
- Farmacia Yanguas: C. Yanguas y Miranda 17; 948 24 50 30; www.farmaciayanguas24h.com; open daily 24hr
- Farmacia L. Maeztu: C. Nueva 1; open M-F 9am-2pm and 4:30pm-8pm, Sa 9am-2pm

ACCOMMODATIONS

🏨 HOSTEL HEMINGWAY ($)

C. Amaya 26; 948 98 38 84; www.hostelhem-ingway.com; reception open daily 8am-11pm

If Hemingway himself were staying in Pamplona, he'd stay in this decked-out, generous hostel just south of historic downtown. Well, maybe—he'd certainly be tempted by Hostel Hemingway's international theme; each colorful room is centered around a world culture: one has sketches of the Great Pyramids, another has Moroccan floor mats, and the common room is plastered with photos donated by pilgrims who are in the thick of their pilgrimage to Santiago de Compostela. Adding to the quirkiness, the hostel's seven rooms are named after a song celebrating seven "steps" to July 7's San Fermín (January 1, February 2, March 3, etc.). We're not sure how Hemingway would feel about being the hostel's cartoon-sized mascot, but T-shirts bearing his bull-riding, cigar-smoking caricature sure are adorable.

i Dorms from €16, privates from €44; reservation recommended; BGLTQ+ friendly; wheelchair accessible; Wi-Fi; breakfast, linens, towels, luggage storage, lockers, kitchen, pad-locks included; laundry; pilgrims €13 per night

PLAZA CATEDRAL ALBERGUE ($)

C. Navarrería 35; 620 91 39 68; www.alber-gueplazacatedral.com; reception open daily summer 11am-9pm during the summer, winter noon-8pm

Located one block from the **Camino de Santiago** and directly facing Pamplona's massive cathedral, the hostel is well-loved by tourists and pilgrims alike. The combines a cushy common area with a modern kitchen and dining room, and although the rooms are sparse, the windows open onto a gorgeous garden of linden trees and rose bushes. Other quirks include a medieval-style well in the bathroom (to fill the toilets), and rooms named after the surrounding mountains of Navarre. Most guests hardly notice these subtleties, their heads buried in the hostel's board game collection.

i Dorms from €15; reservation recommended; BGLTQ+ friendly; wheelchair accessible; Wi-Fi; breakfast, linens, lockers, luggage storage kitchen included

XARMA HOSTEL ($)

Av. de la Baja Navarra 23; 948 04 64 49; www.xarmahostel.com; reception open daily 1pm-11pm

Picturesque window seats, origami cranes, and community dining tables give Xarma a homey feel. Popular with families and slightly older travelers, it's not your typical post-pub crawl crash pad. The backyard patio is particularly alluring, especially when the massive magnolia is in bloom. Guests are welcome to use the BBQ facilities, help the owners water their many flower pots, or simply admire the greenery. Xarma is very popular with Camino-walkers—be sure to book in advance to secure a room.

i Dorms from €20, privates from €22; reservation recommended; BGLTQ+ friendly; wheelchair accessible; Wi-Fi; breakfast, linens, luggage storage, lockers, kitchen included; laundry

SIGHTS
CULTURE

IGLESIA DE SAN LORENZO

C. Mayor 74; 948 225 371; www.capilla-sanfermin.com; open M-Sa 8:30am-12:30pm and 5:30pm-8pm, Su 8:30am-1:45pm and 5:30pm-8pm

On July 7 of each year, the world-famous **San Fermín** festivities begin at the doorstep of this sacred cathedral. Although the building isn't as ancient as its neighboring churches (it's a 1901 construction built with a mixed neoclassical-Baroque style), it holds a special place in the hearts of many Pamplonans, particularly because of its **Chapel of San Fermín.** Inside sits a magnificent polychrome wood and silver effigy of the dark-skinned San Fermín, who leaves his sumptuous hideout just once each year, joining the fray of visitors crowding Pamplona's streets in a procession that officially kicks off the world-famous bullfighting festival. The rest of the week, the church and its chapel serve as the religious epicenter of the celebrations, with devout party-goers stopping by to praise the venerable saint.

i Free; July 6-7 open 8:30am-8pm; July 8-13 open 8:30am-12:30pm and 5:30pm-8pm

PLAZA DE TOROS DE PAMPLONA (BULLRING OF PAMPLONA)

Paseo de Hemingway; 948 22 53 89; www. feriadeltoro.com; open Tu-Sa 10:30am-7pm, Su 10:30am-2pm

Nine days a year, from July 6-14, Pamplona's bullring opens up its doors to one of the dramatic man-versus-beast spectacle that is bullfighting. The best way to experience the the crazy spectacle is to snag a ticket to one of the actual fights, but if you happen to arrive in the offseason, you can still tour the stadium, which is the third largest in the world (behind Mexico City and Madrid) and is the largest reinforced concrete building in all of Spain. The route begins at the **Callejón**, the ring's entrance, and passes through several films detailing the elaborate preparations made for the **San Fermín** festivities before opening up into the stadium itself. With seating for 20,000, it's quite a sight to behold. This is where bulls—and *toreros*—have given their lives for this crazy sport (does it count as a sport?) since Medieval times. The visit ends in a chapel that serves as a waiting room for bullfighters as they wait to enter the ring. As the exhibition notes, truly a "place of silence and fear." Thankfully, your next destination is the gift shop rather than face-to-face with a 2,200-pound hunk of angry beef.
i *Admission €6, students €4; guided tours Tu-Sa 11am, noon, 1pm, 4pm, 5pm, 6pm, Su 11am, noon, 1pm; last entry 30min. before close; limited wheelchair accessibility; exhibitions closed June 16-July 28; tickets available online*

LANDMARKS

📰 CATEDRAL DE SANTA MARÍA LA REAL (PAMPLONA CATHEDRAL)

C. Curia; 948 21 25 94; www.catedralde-pamplona.com; open autumn-winter M-Sa 10:30am-5pm, spring-summer M-Sa 10:30am-7pm

This colossal cathedral has a way of sneaking up on visitors. Its neoclassical façade appears out of nowhere behind Pamplona's crowded streets, with the left tower holding a 25,000-pound bell named María, the largest one in Spain still used today. The church was built on the ruins of a Roman edifice when the city was founded in the year 74 BCE by the general Pompey. From then, buildings

came and went up to the fourteenth century, when the current foundation was completed—albeit without any clear architectural unity. Despite the exterior's elegant Corinthian symmetry, the inside is pure gothic. Check out those flying buttresses, the flamboyant polychrome tracery, and in the central nave, the alabaster tomb of **Carlos III El Noble,** King of Navarre. It's the cloister that really turns heads; the decorative graffiti coating its walls is astoundingly well-preserved, one of the best-kept pieces of Gothic architecture in existence. There's also a museum attached to the cathedral, showcasing the ongoing archeological efforts to uncover the history's ancient past.
i *Admission €5, students €4, free entrance M-F 9am-10:30am and 7pm-8:15pm, Sa 9am-10:30am and 7pm-9pm; tours by appointment; last ticket sold 1hr before closing; limited wheelchair accessibility; to climb the bell tower, arrive at 11:15am M-Sa*

PLAZA DEL CASTILLO (CASTLE PLAZA)

Pl. del Castillo; 948 420 100; www.pamplona. es; open daily 24hr

Affectionately known as "Pamplona's living room," the 14,000-square meter Plaza del Castillo lies at the heart of the city's *Casco Viejo* **(Old Town).** Unlike your typical living room, this one has hosted bullfights (until 1844), political demonstrations, and military parades since its founding in the sixteenth century. It's surrounded by a number of historic cafés and hotels (including **Café Iruña** of Hemingway fame), a couple of casinos, and lots of souvenir shops. Families, pilgrims, and backpackers kick back with ice cream cones and *bocadillos* on the plaza's many park benches. In the center is a bandstand from the 1940s, where speakers often address crowds numbering in the thousands—especially during the peak of **San Fermín.**
i *Free; wheelchair accessible; free public restrooms available*

MUSEUMS

◾ MUSEO DE NAVARRA (MUSEUM OF NAVARRE)

C. de Santo Domingo 47; 848 42 64 93; www.turismo.navarra.es; open Tu-Su 9:30am-2pm and 5pm-9pm, Su 11am-2pm

For anyone with questions about Navarrese history, this five-story museum probably has more answers than you bargained for. Housed in a former medieval hospital and attached to a sixteenth-century plateresque chapel, the permanent collection takes visitors on a journey from prehistory to the twentieth century, complete with archeological finds, Medieval triptychs, and Renaissance masterpieces. As you ascend staircase after staircase of religious iconography, oil paintings, and massive tilework mosaics, don't miss a particularly stunning hispano-arabic ivory chest from the year 1005. The museum also proudly features **Goya's portrait of the Marquis de San Adrián,** said to be world-famous for the "velvety texture of the trousers."

i Admission €2, students €1, free Sa evening and all day Su; free tours by appointment only; wheelchair accessible

MUSEO UNIVERSIDAD DE NAVARRA (UNIVERSITY OF NAVARRE MUSEUM)

Campus Universitario; 948 302 912; www.museo.unav.edu; open Sept-June Tu-Sa 10am-8pm, Su noon-2pm, July-Aug Tu-Su 11am-2pm, closed July 6-July 14

Although it's a mile or so away from historic Pamplona, the University of Navarre's stellar collection is well worth the walk or bus fare. Featuring a surprising lineup of big-name artists **(Palazuelo, Tàpies, Chillido,** and that **Picasso** dude), the permanent collection spans three floors, with a large exhibition hall for avant-garde contemporary artists, primarily having to do with social upheaval. There's sculpture and photography aplenty, but you'll probably want to beeline it to *Le Tricorne,* a study of London's Alhambra Theater done by Picasso.

i Admission €4.50, students €3; free guided tours T-F at 6pm and Sa at noon; wheelchair accessible

OUTDOORS

◾ CIUDADELA DE PAMPLONA (PAMPLONA CITADEL)

Av. Ejercito; 948 420 975; www.pamplona.es; park open M-F 7:30am-9:30pm, Sa 8am-9:30pm, Su 9am-9:30pm

Formerly one of the most outstanding military complexes in all of Europe, Pamplona's star-shaped Ciudadela is now home to a **lush urban park:** "the lungs of Pamplona," as it's affectionately known. The citadel was commissioned in the seventeenth century by **King Felipe II,** who was annoyed at France's constant incursions on the city. He named the five bastions of the citadel after the city's most beloved saints: **San Antón, la Victoria, Santiago, Santa María,** and **San Felipe la real.** Apparently the first two weren't that beloved because they would later be demolished to accommodate Pamplona's expanding city center. Today, military structures within the citadel have been converted into contemporary art exhibitions, so visitors can enjoy a 5km loop through the park, interrupted by cubism in the gunpowder room or pointillism in the Sala de Armas.

i Free; limited wheelchair accessibility; closed for San Fermín July 4-21

PARQUE DE YAMAGUCHI (YAMAGUCHI PARK)

Av. Barañain; 948 420 100; www.pamplona.es; open 24hr

In an unexpected bit of Japanese-Spanish synergism, the towns of Yamaguchi and Pamplona teamed up in 1997 to create Yamaguchi Park, a tiny slice of the Far East in the heart of urban Pamplona. A few footpaths and bike lanes crisscross the park's 21 acres, converging on a central duck pond with a cozy pavilion in the center. The park's largest tree, a magnificent Japanese **Koinobori,** was donated at the park's inception "in the hopes that the friendship between our two cities continues forever," reads a plaque written by the former mayor of Yamaguchi. A perfect spot for a picnic, a bit of fresh air, or just a change of scenery from the cobblestones and cathedrals. It's adjacent to the **Pamplona Planetarium,** too, with its own Garden of the Galaxy.

i Free; wheelchair accessible

FOOD

🔖 KANTINA KATAKRAK ($)

C. Mayor 54; 948 225 520; www.katakrak.net; open M-W 10am-11pm, Th-Sa 10am-1am

For those who like their scrambled eggs with a side of political activism, there's Katakrak. Part of a three-business collaboration also including a bookstore and an art collective, Katakrak's cantina uses food as a vehicle for political action. The menu features things like the "Refugees Welcome" salmon burger, or a "Black Lives Matter" olive pâté with grilled vegetables. They walk the walk, too, sourcing from local providers, buying organic ingredients, and serving exclusively fair trade coffee. Since opening in 2013, they've helped transform an otherwise neglected Pamplona backstreet into a thriving cultural space: "Project Bye-Bye Ghetto," as they say. All in a day's work at Katakrak—go grab yourself a Black Panther Breakfast Special and help solve the world's problems.

i Entrées from €6, menu of the day €13; gluten-free, vegan, and vegetarian options available; wheelchair accessible

BAR GAUCHO ($)

C. Espoz y Mina 7; 948 22 50 73; www.cafebargaucho.com; open daily 9am-3pm and 6:30pm-11pm

Gaucho is fussy about its *pintxos,* but that's about it. The no-frills interior isn't elaborately decorated, spacious, or even that comfortable, sending a clear message: it's about the food. Since its founding in 1968, Gaucho has been regaled with many awards for their "miniature haute cuisine," including elaborate delicacies like smoked sturgeon with ginger and flower petals. The star dish? *Foie fresco a la plancha:* fresh-grilled foie gras. Expand your horizons with these extravagant eats, or opt for something a little more familiar, like the array of croquettes, fritas, and *lasañitas* (little lasagnas) prepared daily. Thankfully, none of the prices are as haute as the cuisine. To drink, go for a specialty gin and tonic; Gaucho boasts a gin menu featuring over 30 different brands.

i Pintxos from €2; gluten-free and vegetarian options available; wheelchair accessible

CAFÉ IRUÑA ($$)

Pl. del Castillo 44; 948 222 064; www.cafeiruna.com; open M-Th 8am-2am, F-Su 9am-2am

Ernest Hemingway's *The Sun Also Rises* helped put Pamplona on the map, and—most importantly—the tourist's itinerary. One of his favorite haunts was this gilded, Arabesque café in the **Plaza del Castillo,** where nearly 100 years later, little has changed. "Except forty thousand tourists have been added," Hemingway once noted wistfully. Café Iruña still exudes an alluring mystique that initially attracted the American writer, with gilded columns, ornate metalwork, and wall-length mirrors topped with Navarran coats of arms. "The Iruña," as Hemingway refers to it in his writing, offers typical Pamplonan fare—espresso drinks, an array of meaty *pintxos,* rich seafood dishes. The real draw is the history, where you can dine with the spirit of Hemingway (almost literally: there's a glowering statue of the author in a side room).

i Raciones from €7, menu of the day €15.90, pintxos from €2; gluten-free and vegetarian options available; wheelchair accessible

RESTAURANTE SARASATE ($)

C. San Nicolás 19-21; 948 22 57 27; www.restaurantesaraste.es; open Su-Th 1pm-5pm, F-Sa 1pm-5pm and 8:30pm-11pm

From its loft above the Calle San Nicolás, Restaurante Sarasate has been gracing the people of Pamplona with vegetarian vittles since 1979: "the oldest in all of Spain," a waiter assured us. We're not so sure, but it's clear Sarasate has had plenty of time to garner a loyal following of veg-heads, who come back time and again for the killer *menu del día,* which is (very) loosely inspired by the cuisine of Navarre. Special dishes include chestnut soup, mushroom-stuffed pumpkins, or the simple but wildly popular veggie and mushroom lasagna. Their fruit-filled desserts are on point, as well—the pear flan and banana pudding are to die for. The perfect counter to Pamplona's otherwise *jamón*-heavy cuisine.

i Entrées from €6, menu of the day €11.50; gluten-free, vegan, and vegetarian options available; no wheelchair accessibility

NIGHTLIFE

⬛ MANNEKEN BEER

C. Iñigo Artista 9; 948 25 81 04; www.
facebook.com/mannekenbeer; open M-F
5pm-midnight, Sa noon-3pm and 6pm-2am,
Su noon-3pm and 6pm-midnight

The logo of a winking dwarf peeing
into a beer mug isn't exactly classy, but
guests don't visit Manneken for refined
elegance; they come for beer. With an
enormous menu including over 200
brands at any given time, Manneken
Beer is indisputably Pamplona's premier
alehouse. It's a bit of a hike from **Casco
Viejo,** but the walk will work up your
thirst for quirky offerings like Natural
Born Chillers, Toothless Unicorn, or
Berserk Llama Syndrome. In fact, the
menu is so bloated it has to be displayed
on a giant, ever-changing digital screen. If
you need help deciding, ask the bartender
for a taste, but you may need to resort to
the eeny, meeny, miny, mo method for
this one.

*i No cover, beer from €2.50; no wheelchair
accessibility*

CERVECERÍA LA ESTAFETA

C. Estafeta 54; open daily 11am-1am

With a beer-swinging, alpine hat-wearing
mascot, the mounted head of a bull, and
religious figurines honoring the city's
patron saints, La Estafeta comes as a
somewhat bizarre Bavarian-Pamplonan
cocktail of cultures. Tourists don't seem
to mind, though, as the pub is constantly
jam-packed with folks eager to taste
some decadent *pintxos*. There are about

six options, each a variation on the
tower of meat concept so popular in
Pamplona—a single tosta may come with
jamón, sausage, prosciutto, *and* a fried
quail egg (because why not?). Alternately,
satisfy your late-night munchies with
their popular fried cheese bites, which are
stuffed with beef and chili peppers before
being bathed in *béchamel.* For a *cervería,*
the beer selection isn't anything to get
excited about unless you're a Heineken
fan; La Estafeta's strong suits are its stellar
location and its laid-back vibe.

*i No cover, drinks from €5; wheelchair
accessible*

INFERNU TABERNA

C. San Augustín 4; open Th-Su 11pm-4am

If the words "Roots of Evil" or "KILL
US" excite you, you'll love Bar Infernu.
They've been bringing high-octane music
to the heart of Pamplona's city center for
the past ten years, whether it's hard rock,
heavy metal, or some sort of combination
called "metalcore." Regardless, they
themselves may have described it best
with their simple advertisement: *mucho
ruido!* ("A lot of noise!"). The concert
space is small but mighty; the makeshift
stage puts attendees and performers nearly
face-to-face, although biggest raves end
up spilling out onto the street. A word to
the wise: easy on the head-banging; you'll
want to save your throat for some pale
ales. Bar Infernu recently got into the craft
beer game, partnering with a few select
Navarran breweries like Brew and Roll.

*i Events from €8, drinks from €5; cash only;
no wheelchair accessibility; check Facebook
page for varying hours*

SALAMANCA

Coverage by **Joseph Winters**

From the soaring heights of the Catedral Nueva to the city's intimate city squares,
Salamanca's plateresque sandstone and Renaissance architecture make it a treasure of
northern Spain. As the region's most popular tourism destination, it offers a wealth
of monuments, museums, and convents, although the entire historic center—a
UNESCO World Heritage Site—is an attraction in its own right. Salamanca's history
is indelibly entwined in the University of Salamanca, the fourth-oldest western
university and the first to be officially recognized by the Pope (Alexander IV). Students
populate the streets in and around the historic center, scarfing down *bocadillos* and
sipping espressos along the Calle de los Libreros. In the scorching heat of summer, the
Salamancan *siesta* becomes an indispensable part of daily life. Best to save your energy
for the late evening, when the Plaza Mayor comes alive with the rest of the city, its
burnt yellow façade turned to gold by hundreds of dazzling spotlights.

SPAIN SALAMANCA

ORIENTATION

Roughly ovular in shape, historic Salamanca is bordered by the **Rio Tormes** to the south and by two major roads to the east (**Paseo de Canalejas**) and west (**Paseo San Vicente**). Smack dab in the city center is the splendid **Plaza Mayor**, with six arched doorways branching outwards in every direction. The area south of the Plaza is where you'll find most of Salamanca's history, including the university buildings and the city's glorious cathedrals. West, past the **Calle de la Gran Via,** things get a bit more residential, although there are still plenty of dining options to be found. Immediately north of the Plaza Mayor is Salamanca's luxe shopping district and prime hunting ground for those in need of a bank, ATM, or hostel. The northwest quarter is home to a mini international district full of cheap eats and bohemian coffee joints, perfect for budget bites and late-night options. Beyond the boundaries of the historic city center, to the north is a vibrant shopping district, as well as Salamanca's biggest mall, **El Corte Inglés.** Side streets in this area house local restaurants and bars that are less popular among tourists. To the south, cross the **Puente Romano** to find yourself in a delightful tree-lined park with pedestrian and bike paths, a peaceful respite from the sandstone jungle of the main city.

ESSENTIALS

GETTING THERE

The Salamanca train station lies just a few minutes' walk northeast of the city center. Journeys from Madrid cost around €24 (1.5hr to 4.5hr). From Ávila you're looking at €12.25 (just over 1hr), and Portuguese destinations often connect from Valladolid for €12.25 (1.5hr). Arrivals by bus end at a northwestern terminal, also very walkable from the city center. From Madrid it's €17 (2.5hr), it's €8 from Ávila (1.5hr), and €10 from Valladolid (1.5hr).

GETTING AROUND

Salamanca is entirely walkable. There is also an urban bus network, with single trips costing €1.05 (valid for 45min. once you begin a trip). Line 4 runs between the bus station to the edge of the historic city center. To get there from the train station, try Line 1.

PRACTICAL INFORMATION

Tourist Offices: You can't miss the Salamanca tourist office, found in the Plaza Mayor near the southwestern entrance (Pl. Mayor 32; 923 21 83 42; www.salamanca.es; open M-F 9am-7pm, Sa 10am-7pm, Su 10am-2pm).
Banks/ATMs/Currency Exchange: Look for banks along the Calle Toro running north from the Plaza Mayor—options abound, from Santander to Deutsche Bank to BBVA. There are plenty of ATMs throughout the city, most of them blue and yellow EuroBanks.

- Deutsche Bank: C. Concejo 21; 923 28 04 00; www.deutsche-bank.es; open M-Th 8:30am-4:30pm, F 8:30am-2:15pm
- Santander: C. Toro 33; 923 29 90 00; www.bancosantander.es; open M-F 8:30am-2:30pm

Post Offices: Look for the bright yellow Correos logo—Salamanca's main post office is behind a wall covered in Italian-style porticos (Gran Via 25-29; 902 19 71 97; www.correos.es; open M-F 8:30am-8:30pm, Sa 9:30am-1pm).
Public Restrooms: Although public toilets are scarce in Salamanca, there's one in the Mercado Central de Abastos (next to the Plaza Mayor), and all museums and coffee shops have their own attached bathrooms. In a pinch, you can also check most Dia supermarkets or the occasional Carrefour.
Internet: There is no free internet network in Salamanca, although university students with access to Eduroam may be able to connect to the University of Salamanca's Wi-Fi network. Other than that, use a coffee shop's network, or walk north to the shopping mall called El Corte Inglés for storewide free Wi-Fi.
BGLTQ+ Resources: There's no BGLTQ+ center in Salamanca—your best bet is in Madrid at the Colectivo LGTB+ de Madrid. They offer a free information service on sexual orientation, health, HIV and STDs, family, marriage, homophobia, asylum, etc. All free and confidential, reachable by phone or email (C. Puebla 9; 91 523 00 70; www.cogam.es; open M-F 5pm-9pm).

EMERGENCY INFORMATION

Emergency Number: 112

Police: Both the national and the local police have offices outside the city center, just east of the Paseo de Canalejas. The Policía Nacional are closer in case of an emergency.

- Policía Nacional: C. Jardines; 92 312 77 00; www.policia.es
- Policía Local de Salamanca: Av. De la Aldehuela 43-63; 92 319 44 33; www.policialocal.aytosalamanca.es

US Embassy: The US Embassy is in Madrid (C. de Serrano 75; 915 87 22 00; es.usembassy.gov; open M-F 8am-2pm), but you can call if you have a specific question.

Rape Crisis Center: The Rape Crisis Network Europe recommends CAVAS, a center for victims of sexual assault, whose main office is in Madrid (C. Alcalá 124; 91 574 01 10; www.cavascv.org).

Hospitals: In a medical emergency, dial 112 and ask for an ambulance.

- Hospital General de la Santísima Trinidad: Paseo de Carmelitas 74-94; 923 269 300; www.fhgst.es; open daily 24hr
- Hospital Virgen de la Vega: Paseo de San Vicente 58-182; 92 329 12 00; www.saludcastillayleon.es; open daily 24hr

Pharmacies: Most pharmacies in Salamanca take the siesta, so hopefully you don't need some extra meds between 1pm and 4pm. If you do, there are a couple options in the city center offering extended hours, and even a 24hr pharmacy on the Calle Toro.

- Farmacia Amador Felipe Conde: C. Toro 25; 90 287 68 24; www.farmacialiceo.com; open daily 24hr
- Farmacia del Corrillo: Pl. del Corrillo; 92 321 34 10; www.farmaciaelcorrillo.com; open daily 9:30am-10pm

ACCOMMODATIONS

🏨 HOSTEL ERASMUS HOME ($)

C. Jesús, 18; 92 37 10 257; www.erasmushome.com; reception open 24hr

No animals were harmed in the decorating of Erasmus Hostel: the mounted heads on the walls are toy stuffed animals, 100% cotton and machine-washable (on a cold cycle). Besides these cuddly critters, this chipper hostel is dotted with flower boxes, foosball tables, and a sticky note wall of fame where guests have left messages and drawings for future hostellers. Rooms are bright and spacious, but the "kitchen" is relatively useless (just a fridge and microwave); you'll definitely want to visit the attached restaurant and beer garden, where guests get 20 percent off at breakfast and ten percent off the rest of the day.

i Dorms from €16, 2-bed privates from €36; reservation recommended; BGLTQ+ friendly; limited wheelchair accessibility; Wi-Fi; linens, lockers, luggage storage, computer access included; laundry

HOSTAL ESCALA LUNA ($$$)

C. Melendez 13, 1A; 923 21 87 49; www.hostalescalalunasalamanca.com; reception open Su-Th 8am-midnight, F-Sa 24hr

Hostal Escala Luna may not be typical hostel material, but neither are the amenities: in-room refrigerators, bathrooms, and beds; even bike repair stations. On top of that, some rooms have air-conditioning, which is a godsend in the Salamancan heat. Those niceties don't encourage a lot of socializing, but Escala Luna's adorable common room—done up to look like a train carriage breezing through the countryside—may entice you away from your private room. Splurge on a night here and feel refreshed: the memory of Escala Luna will tide you through another week of sleep-deprivation, sweaty dorms, and that couple making noise on the bunk below.

i Privates from €38; reservation recommended; no wheelchair accessibility; Wi-Fi; linens, towels, toiletries, lockers, luggage storage included; laundry €10

HOSTEL ESCAPA2 ($)

Paseo de Canalejas, 14-16; 633 96 15 97; reception open M-F 9am-8pm, Sa-Su 10am-6pm

We're not sure what happened to Escapa1, but Escapa2 is a cheery hostel offering quiet rooms and a mighty reputation for bachelor parties. four-bed dorms are popular among Spanish visitors from Madrid or elsewhere, who book a whole room and descend upon Salamanca's nightlife in full hooligan mode. For non-partiers, Hostel Escapa2 doesn't organize any events, but they have a smattering of attractive amenities like in-room showers and baths and a fully-equipped kitchen.

They'll also change your sheets daily if you're feeling extra grimy from the broiling Salamancan summer.

i Dorms from €25, privates from €99; reservation recommended; no wheelchair accessibility; Wi-Fi; breakfast, linens, towels, lockers, luggage storage, parking included; laundry €4

HOSTAL TORMES ($)

C. de Rua Mayor 20; 692 611 819; www.hostaltormes.es; reception open daily 9am-9pm

Live like a real-life Salamanca University student in this dormitory-turned-hostel! It's about as luxurious as it sounds: cubby-like rooms, itty bitty windows, wooden desks, sterile atmosphere. There are, however, some fun Pac-Man wall paintings, as well as sinks and a closet in every room, but other than that, Hostal Tormes' greatest asset is its super-central location. From the building's doorstep, it's about a twenty-second walk to **Plaza Mayor** or two minutes to the cathedrals of Salamanca. There's no breakfast, but good eats are easy to come by in the maze-like streets just outside the hostel.

i Dorms from €25, 2-bed privates from €55; reservation recommended; no wheelchair accessibility; Wi-Fi; linens, towels, closets, luggage storage included

REVOLUTUM HOSTEL ($)

C. Sánchez Barbero 7; 923 21 76 56; www.revolutumhoste.com; reception open daily 9am-1am

Rather than a living room or café, Revolutum has a "living café" where croissants and cheese tarts harmoniously coexist with plush sofas and feathery lampshades. Between that, the garden patio, and the wall murals painted to look like they belong in the Louvre, the hardest part about staying in Revolutum may be packing your bags to leave. Expect hotel-level amenities like free toiletries, towels, and a breakfast spread that actually has something other than packaged toast and off-brand Nutella. Plus, thanks to its central location three minutes from **Plaza Mayor,** Revolutum provides easy access to Salamanca's main attractions without ever leaving you too far from your "chill out" bungalow.

i Dorms from €20, privates from €40; reservation recommended; wheelchair accessible; Wi-Fi; breakfast, linens, toiletries, kitchen access included

ROOMIN HOSTEL ($)

C. Cristo de los Milagros 6; 628 92 46 22; www.roominhostel.com

Part hostel, part university residence, the Roomin building reaches five floors high, and the heat accumulates with each story. Despite the clammy nights, Roomin Hostel offers two tidy common rooms, jumbo bottles of shampoo, and hot cocoa all day—what more could you ask for? Maybe a sangria from the hostel receptionist—not guaranteed, but it's been known to happen. There's also a fully-equipped kitchen. Plus, its central location (just ten minutes from the train station and five from **Plaza Mayor**) makes Roomin Hostel a great home base for a night of Salamancan bar hopping (or cathedral hopping, for the nightlife-averse).

i Dorms from €13, privates from €19; reservation recommended; no wheelchair accessibility; Wi-Fi; breakfast, linens, lockers included; luggage storage €2, towels €2, laundry €5

SIGHTS
CULTURE

🏛 IERONIMUS

Pl. Juan XXIII; 923 266 701; www.ieronimus.es; open daily 10am-8pm

If the vantage point from inside the **Catedral Nueva** wowed you, the view from Ieronimus is a step above—actually many steps above, as it culminates in the cathedral's 100m tall belltower. After twisting in and around the cathedral's central knave and onto its roof, some 200 steps lead visitors into the belfry, the uppermost vantage point of the city and the second highest tower in all of Spain (second to Giralda Tower in Seville). From here, views open up at large windows in each direction—to the north is the old town and **Plaza Mayor,** to the east and west are sandstone facades and red shingles of Salamancan residences, and to the south is the gentle **Rio Tormes.** In two words: postcard Salamanca. Unlike many of the region's historical towers, this one is roomy enough for a crowd, allowing visitors to catch their breath and spend a few more minutes appreciating the landscape.

i Admission €3.75; last 45min. before closing; wheelchair accessible; Wi-Fi

CASA MUSEO UNAMUNO (UNAMUNO RESIDENCE MUSEUM)

C. Libreros 25; 923 294 400; www.unamuno.usal.es; open M-F 10am-2pm

A giant of Spanish literary history, **Miguel de Unamuno** was part of the infamous Generation of '98, a group of Spanish authors who were active during the social crisis caused by Spain's defeat in the Spanish-American war, as well as the loss of many of its colonies including Cuba, Puerto Rico, the Phillippines, and Guam. While Unamuno taught at the **University of Salamanca** (1900-1914), he lived in this building, and much of it has been preserved in his honor. Lively guides begin the tour with a rapid-fire history lesson, followed by an orientation video, and—finally—visitors ascend the stairs to the author's living quarters. Lining the hallways are photos of Unamuno, as well as drawings from his sketchbook and a timeline of milestones in his life. Notable rooms to admire are Unamuno's library and office; the former has a beautiful collection of antique books in 16 languages (eleven of which Unamuno could understand), and the latter is arranged just as Unamuno might have left it, with half-written letters scattered across the same table where the master composed some of his most famous works like "San Manuel Bueno, mártir."

i *Admission €4, students €2; mandatory tours at 10am, 11am, noon, 1pm; last entry 1pm; no wheelchair accessibility; Spanish tours only*

CIELO DE SALAMANCA (SKY OF SALAMANCA)

Pl. Fray Luis de León 3; open Apr-Sept M-Sa 10am-2pm and 4pm-8pm, Oct-Mar M-F 10am-2pm and 4pm-7pm

Painted in 1473 by Salamanca native **Fernando Gallego,** the Cielo de Salamanca is like a low-tech version of a planetarium. Visitors enter via the patio of **Escuelas Menores,** where there's a courtyard lined with Italian style porticos. A small door to the left opens into a very dimly-lit room with a ramp towards the center of the monument. Tilt your head back to admire the domed fresco, with artistic renderings of northern hemisphere constellations. Cancer, Capricorn, Sagittarius, Aquarius, Pisces—they detail in the curved painting is an astrological feat, and it's astonishingly well-preserved to the present.

i *Free; wheelchair accessible*

ESCUELAS MAYORES

C. Libreros 19; www.museo.usal.es; open Sept 16-Mar 31 M-Sa 10am-7pm; open Apr-Sept 15 M-Sa 10am-8pm, Su 10am-2pm

Founded in 1218 and only completed in the mid-1400s, the Escuelas Mayores—and particularly the Universidad Civil—are the crown jewel of the **University of Salamanca.** Tours begin by meandering through real university classrooms where famous professors have given lectures. Then it's on to the building's churchlike cloister, where original university documents are on display alongside an interesting array of didactic instruments. The artifacts are interesting, but the building itself is the real looker; be sure to note the Plateresque façade of the at the lower cloister, which opens onto Gothic vaults, lined with decorative floral designs and crowned with the university's coat of arms. Oh, and there's also the university library, which happens to be the oldest on the continent, home to over 2800 medieval manuscripts.

i *Admission €10, students €5; no wheelchair accessibility; audio guides €2*

LA GALATEA

C. de los Libreros 28; 923 26 91 63; www.lagalatea.es; open Tu-Sa 10:30am-2pm and 4:30pm-8pm

Although most windows on this street are now shuttered, private, or university owned, the "Street of the Booksellers" used to house over fifty used, new, vintage, and antique bookshops. Students from the **University of Salamanca** would flock here to buy textbooks, novels, and newspapers from the many competing vendors. La Galatea has been bringing tradition back for some twenty years, striving day by day to respect tradition and modernity by meeting "the needs of a new public that wants to fill themselves with beauty and understanding." There's a prodigious collection of rare books and first editions, an unexpected supply of vinyl LPs, and a bargain table where you can find everything from biographies of the Dalai Lama to the **Dummy's Guide to Soil Fertilization.**

i *Books from €1; no wheelchair accessibility*

MERCADO CENTRAL DE ABASTOS

Pl. del Mercado; 923 213 000; www.merca-docentralsalamanca.com; open M 8am-2pm and 4pm-7pm, Tu-F 8am-2pm and 4pm-8pm, Sa 8am-2pm

At the Mercado Central de Abastos, shoppers can stock up on pig ears, wide-eyed fish heads, cow tongues, octopus tentacles; you know, the basics. Located in a warehouse next to **Plaza Mayor,** this public market offers all the bulk culinary wonders of Salamanca. The perimeter is lined with *pescaterías* (fish shops), florists, and *fruterías* (fruit shops), and the smell of cured pork wafts in from the *carnicería* stalls in the basement. You'll see plenty of tourists and locals side-by-side, eyeing options and sniffing out the best deals. The market also has a few grab-and-go *bocadillo* options, like mini sandwiches or—our favorite—churros, as cheap as 10 for €2.

i Bulk goods prices vary; wheelchair accessible

LANDMARKS

🏛 CATEDRAL VIEJA, CATEDRAL NUEVA, CLAUSTRO, Y MUSEO (OLD CATHEDRAL, NEW CATHEDRAL, CLOISTER, AND MUSEUM)

C. Benedicto XVI; 923 217 476; www.cate-dralsalamanca.org; open Oct-Mar 10am-6pm, Apr-Sept 10am-8pm

Get ready for a history lesson; with artifacts accumulated over a thousand years, over 16 chapels (each named after a different saint), and countless paintings and sculptures dedicated to hundreds of religious figures, there's no way to retain the entire opus of epic history that is the Catedral de Salamanca audio guide. Tours begin in the breathtaking new cathedral, a Goliath of gothic architecture with three knaves and around a dozen thematic chapels. The amount of religious iconography is overwhelming, but visitors should keep an eye out for gilded polychrome wood carvings, an eleventh-century crucifix that was once carried into medieval battle, and a "ferociously realistic" representation of death in the Capilla Dorada. A blast of cool air welcomes visitors into the Romanesque old cathedral, dating back to the twelfth century and thankfully left intact after the construction of the new one. As you wander through this haunting historical treasure, save time to put the audio guide down and let its immensity soak through the silence.

i Admission €5, students €4; last entry 45min. before closing; limited wheelchair accessibility; audioguides included

CASA DE LAS CONCHAS (HOUSE OF SHELLS)

C. Compañía 2; 923 26 93 17; www.salaman-ca.es; open July-Aug M-F 9am-3pm, Sa 9am-2pm; Sept-June M-F 9am-9pm, Sa 9am-2pm

Despite being 150 miles (as the crow flies) from the nearest beach, Don Rodrigo Arias Maldonado decided to decorate this gothic building's facade with over 300 seashells. He commissioned it in the fifteenth century, probably out of respect for the symbol of the Order of the Santiago de Compostela, of which Maldonado was a proud member. Inside the building is a gargoyle-lined courtyard and a public library, as well as an exhibition room hosting concerts and cultural events, mostly in Spanish. There isn't much to do other than snap a couple of photos—the façade really is splendid—unless, of course, you're down for a Spanish-language *psicoanálisis* conference.

i Free; no wheelchair accessibility

PLAZA MAYOR (MAIN PLAZA)

Pl. Mayor; 923 21 83 42; www.salamanca.es; open daily 24hr

The name's boring, but the plaza itself is quite a stunner; with 88 baroque arches and 247 balconies, it's the city's prized focal point. Until the mid-1800s it was used for bullfighting, but the only bovines you'll find here now are the steaks served in the upscale restaurants and cafés lining the perimeter of the plaza. In the center of the plaza is a plaque honoring the 1988 naming of Salamanca as a **UNESCO World Heritage Site.** To see Plaza Mayor's sandstone facades really shine (literally), check it out at night; the entire square glows gold, warmly lit by hundreds of lanterns and spotlights. In fact, it's so dazzling you'd never notice how none of the facades are quite the same height.

i Free; wheelchair accessible

C. de la Compañia; 923 27 71 00; www.salamanca. es; San Marcos open M-F 9am-3pm and 4pm-7pm, Sa 10am-2pm and 4pm-7pm; Scala Coeli open daily 10am-7:15pm

Give yourself a break from Gothic and Plateresque architecture and get a taste of the baroque at La Clerecía. Built between the seventeenth and eighteenth centuries, its bright white interior and glittering gold altarpiece are a jarring departure from the somber aura of other churches. Mandatory guided tours last about 45min. and are only offered in Spanish, but climbing the 166 steps of the Scala Coeli can be done at your leisure—it isn't quite as high as Ieronimus, but unlike the **Catedral Nueva's belltower,** this one offers true panoramic views of the city.

i *San Marcos admission €3, Scala Coeli €3.75, combined €6; Scala Coeli free Tu 10am-2pm; mandatory tours every 45min.; no wheelchair accessibility*

MUSEUMS

⊠ MUSEO ART NOUVEAU Y ART DECÓ (ART NOUVEAU AND ART DECO MUSEUM)

C. Gibraltar 14; 923 12 14 25; www. museocasalis.org; open Apr-July Tu-Su 11am-8pm; daily Aug 11am-8pm; Sept Tu-Su 11am-8pm; Oct-Mar Tu-F 11am-2pm and 4pm-7pm, Sa-Su 11am-8pm

Starkly contrasting with melancholy of looming **Catedral Nueva** is this cheerful twentieth-century palace, originally built by a Salamancan merchant who had a penchant for Art Nouveau. Enter through the foyer into an opulent ovular room and look up; the terrace windows and the entire ceiling are modern stained glass, plunging the entire space into soft blue light. Besides the building itself, the museum collection covers the nineteenth and early twentieth centuries, featuring sumptuous furniture, jewelry, gold and ivory chryselephantine, and other niche

PUENTE ROMANO (ROMAN BRIDGE)

Puente Romano; www.salamancaturistica. com; open daily 24hr

Although only 15 out of its 26 arches actually date from Roman times, we'll cut it some slack; Puente Romano has survived disastrous floods, a war against Napoleonic troops, and heavy traffic into the early 1990s. The bridge was probably built in the first century AD and remained the only southern access point to Salamanca for nearly 2000 years. Clearly, it's a big deal, important enough to take up a full half of Salamanca's coat of arms. The bridge has minimal signage, but visitors can walk its length and look out over the ambling **Rio Tormes,** with the **Catedral Nueva** looming large in the background. On the opposite side of the river is a pleasant walking path through tree-lined park. After crossing, head left to reenter Salamanca via the **Puente de Enrique Estevan** for even more stunning views of the Catedral Nueva.

i *Free; wheelchair accessible*

SPAIN SALAMANCA

collector's items of the times. Check out the iridescent glass work by Art Nouveau titan **Rene Lalique,** as well as their prized collection of French porcelain dolls.

i Admission €4, students €2; free admission Th 11am-2pm; no wheelchair accessibility

MUSEO DE HISTORIA DE LA AUTO-MOCIÓN (AUTOMOTIVE HISTORY MUSEUM)

Pl. de Mercado Viejo; 923 26 02 93; www.museoautomocion.com; open July-Aug Tu-Su 10am-2pm and 5:30pm-8:30pm; Sept-June Tu-Su 10am-2pm and 5pm-8pm

Forget cathedrals and sacred vestments; this museum is a whole new world brimming with over 100 vehicles and thousands of car parts, ranging from the first century BC to the present "and future" (whatever that means). With three stories and a 4000 square meter exhibition space, the collection is unexpectedly impressive—there are tricycles from the 1880s, swanky Renault Clio Super 1600 racecars, and even Cadillacs that were driven by Spanish heads of state. If HS-21 GTS means anything to you, you'll love this niche museum. Strike up a conversation with the young car buffs polishing the Model T's, or just marvel at the bug-eyed wonders that used to cruise the streets of Europe.

i Admission €4, students €2; tours by appointment only €1; last entry 10min. before closing; limited wheelchair accessibility; free first Tu afternoon each month

MUSEO DE SALAMANCA (SALAMANCA MUSEUM)

Patio de Escuela 2; 923 212 235; www.turismocastillayleon.com; open Oct-Jun M-Sa 10am-2pm and 4pm-7pm, Su 10am-2pm; July-Sept Tu-Sa 10am-2pm and 5pm-8pm, Su 10am-2pm

From stone age archaeology to abstract modern art, the Museo de Salamanca paints a detailed history of the city. Founded in 1848, it moved to the medieval **Álvarez Albarca Palace** a century later, and the collection is dispersed throughout the rooms surrounding its gothic courtyard. Starting from protohistoria, visitors work their way through Roman rubble, coffered ceilings from the Middle

Ages, and onto religious artwork from the sixteenth-eighteenth centuries. Some of the museum's prized artifacts include John Flanders's *Panels of Saint Andrew* and a famous portrait of **Miguel de Unamuno,** painted by Juan de Echevarría. The visit ends in the contemporary period, showcasing art by Salamanca locals—be sure to check out the sculpted hippo: "undoubtedly the main attraction," the museum guidebook assures us.

i Admission €1.20, students €0.60; thematic tours by appointment only

MUSEO TAURINO (BULLFIGHTING MUSEUM)

Doctor Piñuela 507; 923 21 94 25; www.museotaurinosalamanca.es; open Tu-Sa 10:30am-1:30pm and 5:30pm-8pm, Su 10:30am-1:30pm

According to the Museo Taurino, some 200,000 people around the world are currently employed in the bullfighting business—a shockingly large number, given the amount of people we've met who have ever seen a match. Since as early as the 1400s and until the mid-nineteenth century, Salamanca was a bullfighting hub, known for raising husky steeds and gallant matadors. Dressed in elaborate costumes and flailing ridiculous red capes through the air, these men of Salamancan legend would prance through **Plaza Mayor,** irking their hulking bovine into tiredness and eventually killing them. Explore the history of this bizarre sport (theatrical performance?) in the Museo Taurino, admire the nine mounted bull heads, and watch a video of a modern-day bullfight.

i Admission €3, students €2; wheelchair accessible

MUSEO Y CONVENTO DE SAN ESTEBAN (SAINT ESTEBAN CONVENT AND MUSEUM)

Pl. del Concilio de Trento; 923 215 000; www.turismocastillayleon.com; open Nov 6-Mar 16 Tu-Sa 10am-2pm and 4pm-6pm, Su 10am-2pm; Mar 17-Nov 5 Tu-Sa 10am-2pm and 4pm-8pm, Su 10am-2pm

Gothic cloisters, Renaissance arches, Baroque doorways, and Italian porticos conspire to give the Convent of San Esteban a grandiose appearance. It was finished in 1610 and served as an important burying place for many theologians of the **University of Salamanca.** In the ghostly Pantheon of the Theologians, visitors walk directly above their tombstones while spooky music emanates from the walls. The museum is tiny, featuring a medieval apothecary collection and sculptures from the sixteenth century. The church is the convent's biggest draw, with a single gothic knave and a gilded baroque altarpiece from the late 1600s. Be sure to snap a photo from the upper choir, which seats exactly 118 monks in elaborately hand-carved wooden booths.

i Admission €3.50, students €2.50; tours included with ticket, F 5pm, Sa noon and 5pm (1.5hr, groups of 12 or more); last entry 15min. before close; no wheelchair accessibility

OUTDOORS

RIO TORMES (TORMES RIVER)

Rio Tormes; open daily 24hr

Across from historic Salamanca, there's a small, unnamed park with a walking path, a bike lane, and a petite Catholic church. If you're planning on crossing **Puente Romano,** the greenway meanders through an outdoor track and children's playground before ending connecting with the **Puente de Enrique Estevan.** The loop takes less than 20 minutes, but it feels refreshingly removed from the downtown hustle. There's also a great view of **Catedral Nueva** from the Puente de Enrique Estevan.

i Free; wheelchair accessible

FOOD

🍴 CAFÉ BAR MANDALA ($)

C. Serranos 9-11; 923 123 342; www.mandalasalamanca.com; open daily 8am-11pm

Between sacred Tibetan Buddhist mandalas, a Mediterranean-inspired menu, and décor reminiscent of a Middle Eastern mosque, Mandala gives off a hodgepodge vibe that's a little hippie, a little touristy, and very delicious. Providing the ultimate combination of quality *and* quantity, the menu includes over 100 milkshakes and juices. That's not to mention crêpes, sandwiches, salads, quesadillas, and a case full of *postres caseros*—house-made

desserts. If you're famished, try the set menu for lunch or dinner, including options like stuffed pumpkin au gratin or black rice with calamari and lobster, as well as salads, bottomless bread, and coffee or dessert.

i Entrées from €8; gluten-free, vegan, vegetarian options available; no wheelchair accessibility; menu of the day M-F lunch €12.90, F dinner and Sa-Su €14.90

BRUIN CAFÉ ERASMUS ($$)

C. Meléndez 7; 923 265 742; www.erasmushome.com; open daily 9am-2am

Whether you're homesick for German beers, yearning for Italian risottos, or craving American hamburgers, Erasmus has you covered; their internationally-inspired menu spreads the gamut of non-Spanish comfort food, although there are a few good *bocadillos* on offer. In fact, Erasmus hosts weekly international nights, where guests practice foreign language skills and compete in the Erasmus Pub Quiz (Spanish or English). The prize: a free meal at the restaurant! Even if you go home empty-handed, the café is a fun hangout spot, with its outdoor biergarten, an impressive collection of crusty paper money, and two strange mannequins dressed as strippers and locked in large glass cages.

i Entrées from €9; gluten-free and vegetarian options available; no wheelchair accessibility; menu of the day €14.95

DON COCHINILLO ($)

C. Van Dyck 55; 923 60 06 78; www. restaurantedoncochinillo.es; open Tu-Su 1pm-11:30pm

Save your Insta aspirations for later; the Don Cochinillo aesthetic hasn't really entered the twenty-first century yet, with a cartoon logo and a no-frills interior just begging for an air plant, terrarium, or at least something with a bird on it. Thankfully, the food is another story altogether—Don Cochinillo is well-loved by locals for their *tapas exquisitas*, served here since 1904. Top choices include just about any kind of grilled meat, Salamanca's famous *farinato* (erstwhile "sausage of the poor" gets a gourmet makeover), and Don Cochinillo's specialty: *cochinillo asado* (roasted and fried piglet, often served horrifyingly whole). You may end up elbowing your neighbor at their long communal tables, but don't let that stop you from digging in to this true Salamancan establishment.

i Entrées from €5.50, menu of the day €12; gluten-free and vegetarian options available; no wheelchair accessibility

EL LAUREL COCINA VEGETARIANA ($)

C. San Pablo 49; 923 260 601; open Tu-Sa 1:30pm-4pm and 9pm-12:30am, Su 1:30pm-4pm

Banana spirulina chlorella milkshake, anyone? There are greens, beans, and grains galore at this vegetarian haven in the heart of meat-crazy Salamanca. But with a menu of the day for only €10.90, it's quite promising for carnivorous travelers, as well. A few blocks south of the city's busiest streets, El Laurel is always bustling with diners tucking in to guacamole nachos, stuffed peppers, and "carnitas" crepes. The house specialty is veggie moussaka, a veritable mountain of vegetables that come bathed in a rich tomato sauce. If you're not feeling the chlorella milkshake, finish with a slice of decadent, house-made tiramisu.

i Entrées from €7.75, menu of the day €10.90 (lunch M-F, dinner Tu-Th only); gluten-free, vegan, and vegetarian options available; wheelchair accessible

EL MINUTEJO ($)

C. Van Dyck 55; 654 95 26 01; open M-Th 7pm-12:15am, F 7pm-1am, Sa-Su 1pm-4pm and 7pm-1am

Although it's a couple blocks removed from the historical city center, El Minutejo's history with local Salamancans goes way back. Its décor is pretty austere, but the food is mind-bogglingly good, and the prices even better. Cover your table with an array of tortas—just €1.40 each—salmon, cured meat from León with garlic mushrooms, Iberian ham with bacon queso. Add a salad and a ración or two (try the cheesy chicken breast), and you've got a top-notch sampler of Salamanca's finest. It gets crowded around 9pm on, so large groups should come earlier or plan to wait.

i Appetizers from €1.50, raciones from €3.50; cash only; gluten-free and vegetarian options available; no wheelchair accessibility

SERENDIPITY ($)

C. Serranos 35; 687 735 368; www. serendipitycoworking.es; open M-Th 9am-10pm, F 9am-11pm, Sa 10:30am-11pm, Su 4:30pm-11pm

Describing themselves as a place to "uncork dreams" and "weave friendships," Serendipity is aptly named: a lucky find in the heart of historic Salamanca. It's technically part of a coworking collaborative, but visitors are welcomed with open arms (literally—hugs are listed on the menu, free of charge). Seated in an eclectic array of armchairs, sofas, loveseats, and benches covered in fake grass, guests sprawl out in Serendipity's café, getting comfy with their computers and a glass of house kombucha. There aren't many food options, but everything is homemade daily and democratically priced, like *tostas* starting at €1.50 and their famous *empanadillas* for only €2.20. There's also a special breakfast option called *Mucho Más que Té* (Much More than Tea) with toast, OJ, and coffee. They'll even throw in a mystical fortune-telling rock if you ask nicely. The perfect place for some quiet you time.

i Snacks and coffee from €1.50; cash only; gluten-free, vegan, and vegetarian options available; limited wheelchair accessibility

ZAZU BISTRO ($$)

Pl. Libertad, 8; 923 26 16 90; www.restau-rantezazu.com; open daily 2pm-4pm and 9pm-midnight

Normally we wouldn't consider duck confit tagliatelle to be the ideal budget traveler's food, but this charming bistro in the heart of Salamanca is our blue moon exception. The menu of the day is only €15.90 and includes a starter, a main, bread, a drink, and dessert or coffee—not bad for an occasional splurge. Situated in a 200 year-old residence, Zazu's *castaño* wood floors are still the originals, as are the stone walls and cozy furniture in the upstairs dining room. It's all the hominess of grandma's house, but with crabcakes and French cheeses instead of mystery meat casserole. To finish your meal, Zazu's gourmet cupcakes are strongly recommended.

i Entrées from €11; gluten-free and vegetarian options available; no wheelchair accessibility; menu of the day €15.90

NIGHTLIFE

⬛ LA MALHABLADA ($)

C. Meléndez 27; gallery open daily 6:30pm-11pm, microtheater open Su-Th 8pm-9:45pm, F-Sa 9pm-1:35am

There's food, art, drinks, a "microtheater"—La Malhablada is everything we want in a night out and more. From their unconventional space in a 1908 residence filled with all the original, mismatched furniture, they promote cultural activities and artistic experiences through a constantly-rotating exhibition space and a quirky café. Their most intriguing offering by far is, however, their microtheater roulette: a handful of fifteen-minute comedies, tragedies, documentaries, or otherwise live performances that may or may not revolve around a central theme. At times hysterical, at other times gripping, this rapid-fire experience never fails to be at least a little bit dizzying.

i Shows from €3.50, drinks from €3.50; no wheelchair accessibility; microtheater tickets available in the café (reservations for groups of 10+)

THE DOCTOR COCKTAIL BAR ($)

C. Dr. Piñuela 5; 923 263 151; open Su-W 4pm-1:30am, Th-Sa 4pm-2:30am

We wish every trip to the doctor involved this cocktail bar's whisky, rum, and tequila concoctions; they're not joking when they say their bartenders have earned their MDs in mixology. From just a few steps outside **Plaza Mayor,** the Doctor Cocktail Bar has an extensive eight-page menu of tongue-tingling brews inspired by international drinking habits. Depending on your diagnosis, the Doctor may prescribe the Zombie (three kinds of rum, two of brandy, with OJ and pineapple juice), the French Japan (limey tequila with sake and umeshu liqueur), or even an espresso spiked with Grand Marnier, cacao liqueur, brandy, and cream. Whatever ails you, the Doctor will make you well again.

i No cover, drinks from €6.50; no wheelchair accessibility

KANDHAVIA ($)

C. Bermejeros 16; phone 637 538 165; www.kandhavia.com; open M-W 11pm-4:30am, Th 11pm-5:30am, F-Sa 11pm-6:30am, Su 2am-6:30am

One of the city's highest-energy rave locales, Kandhavia offers disco, lasers, and plenty of tipsy college students. Fusing reggae, electronica, R&B, and a couple of genres we'd never heard of like "Drum&Bass" and "Dancehall," the music's nearly as messy as the mosh pit, housed in a warehouse-like space near the historical city center. Enter the fray and join crowds of students from the **University of Salamanca,** who like to kick back at Kandhavia, whether it's the end of exams season or just another Thursday night. Check Kandhavia's Instagram page to see if there's anything special glowing on; they host occasional beer pong tournaments and holiday parties.

i No cover; drinks from €3.50; cash only; no wheelchair accessibility

SEVILLE

Coverage by **Austin Eder**

Seville is one of Europe's most significant cultural hubs, and evidence of its turbulent past can be found in everything from its buildings to its food to its dance. Walking down the broad Avenida de Constitución, you'll question how such opulence could be created without the aid of the technological luxuries we enjoy today. A stroll down the narrow streets of Santa Cruz transports you to an entirely different era—even here, in the quarter with the darkest history, the city's riches are reflected in the delicate marble and iron window casings that cling to pastel walls. You'll notice that Seville truly comes to life just before nightfall, when its shaded alleyways are illuminated by the sinking Mediterranean sun and rooftop mosaics begin to glisten. Getting lost in Casco Antiguo is as crucial a component of a trip to Seville as is a visit to the magnificent Plaza de España or towering Catedral de Sevilla. Don't be afraid to set down your map and get walking—in the event you really do get lost, we'll be here to guide you back.

ORIENTATION

Seville's city center spans both the eastern and western banks of the **Guadalquivir,** with the bulk of tourist activity occurring in **Casco Antiguo** on the western side. Here, you'll find the city's major landmarks, museums, and nightlife. **Santa Cruz** extends roughly from the southernmost tip of Parque de María Luisa to a few blocks north of the Catedral. Northwest of Santa Cruz lies **El Arenal,** which contains **Plaza de Toros** and some upscale options for nightlife. Northeast of Santa Cruz lies **San Bartolomé,** a less picture-perfect, arguably more authentic version of its southern neighbor. Immediately north of Santa Cruz is **Alfalfa,** a popular nightlife destination among students and young professionals (and coincidentally, where you'll find most of the city's hostels). West of Alfalfa is **Museo,** home to—you guessed it—a boat load of museums, and further north still lie **Feria** and **Macarena.** Across the river lies **Triana,** Santa Cruz's eastern counterpart, and **Los Robles,** a vibrant residential neighborhood.

ESSENTIALS

GETTING THERE

Aeropuerto de Sevilla is located 10km from Seville and taxis or pre-arranged cars will drive you to Casco Antiguo—the city center—for a flat rate that hovers around €30. Alternatively, buses to Plaza de Armas, the city's main bus station, depart from the airport from 5:20am to 12:50am daily and take approximately 35min. You can buy your ticket on board for €4 (€6 returning). Aeropuerto de Sevilla is the main airport serving Andalucía, and is a base for budget airlines such as TAP Portugal, Ryanair, and Vueling. The airport connects to dozens of destinations in Europe and Northern Africa, but can only be accessed by connecting flight from North America. Seville Santa Justa is the city's main train station, and provides trains to stations throughout Spain. You can book train and bus tickets online or at each respective station.

GETTING AROUND

Seville is a fairly well-connected city with integrated metro, bus, and tram systems, but you can traverse the city center on foot from north to south in under an hour. Most buses depart from Puerta de Jerez (south of Casco Antiguo) or Plaza Ponce de Leon (east of Casco Antiguo), and operate daily from 6am to 11:30pm (night buses run from midnight to 2am and depart from the Prado). The circular buses, C3 and C4, trace a ring around the city center, while a smaller line, C5, follows a circular route inside of it (tickets €1.50, purchase on board). More affordable options include the Tarjeta Multiviaje (card €1.50, €0.76 for each subsequent trip, compatible with both buses and trams) and one or three-day

passes (€5 and €10, respectively). Seville Metro (tickets from €1.30) consists of one line with 22 stops that runs 18km throughout the greater metropolitan area. MetroCentro, Seville's tram network, travels south from Plaza Nueva, the centre of the city, and has four stops, covering a total distance of 1.4km (€1.20, purchased at stations).

PRACTICAL INFORMATION

Tourist Offices: Tourist offices are dispersed throughout the city. Seville's main tourist office is called Oficina Sevilla Centro (Pl. de San Francisco, 19; 955 471 232; open M-F 9am-7:30pm, Sa-Su 10am-2pm)

Banks/ATMs/Currency Exchange: Like pharmacies, you can find ATMs sprinkled throughout the city. Make sure you have enough cash on you to cover the cost of transportation into the city before departing, as taxis only take cash.

Post Offices: Some hostels will hold packages for you, but don't count on it. To send mail, visit Correos, the city's main post office (Av. de la Constitución, 32; 902 19 71 97; correos.es; open M-F 8:30am-8:30pm, Sa 9:30am-1pm).

Public Restrooms: As far as free restrooms go, you're out of luck in Seville. In total, there are two, both located near Plaza de España. Most establishments that have an entrance fee come equipped with clean restrooms.

Internet: Free public Wi-Fi is available at Starbucks, McDonald's, and most cafés surrounding major monuments such as the Catedral de Sevilla and Alcázar de Sevilla. Don't be afraid to ask waiters and waitresses for passwords: *¿Tiene Wi-Fi gratis?*

BGLTQ+ Resources: Seville lacks specific, in-person resources; however, more information about navigating Spain's BGLTQ+ culture can be found online at gayiberia.com and gayinspain.com.

EMERGENCY INFORMATION

Emergency Number: 112

Police: Officers are stationed near most attractions and actively monitor for petty crime and protests during the day. The headquarters closest to Casco Antiguo is located in Triana on Calle Betis, a popular street for nightlife (C. Betis, 40; 954 28 95 06).

US Embassy: Seville's US Consulate is located at Pl. Nueva, 8 (954 218 751; open M-F 10am-1pm by appointment, email sevillecons@state.gov).

Rape Crisis Center: The Assistance Center for Victims of Sexual Assault (CAVAS) offers free services to individuals who have suffered some type of sexual aggression, including emergency accompaniment to hospitals, legal help, and psychological support (+34 91 574 01 10; +34 91 574 32 64; rcne.com/contact/countries/spain/).

Hospitals: The following are open 24hr. In the event of a medical emergency, call 112.
- Hospital Victoria Eugenia of Spanish Red Cross (Ronda de Capuchinos, 11; 954 35 14 00; hospitalveugenia.com)
- Hospital San Juan de Dios (Av. Eduardo Dato, 42; 954 93 93 00; sjd. es/Seville/?q=hospital-san-juan-de-di-os-Seville/)

Pharmacies: Pharmacies are prolific in Seville. Farmacia Republica Argentina is open 24hr, located in Triana, a 20-minute walk from Casco Antiguo (Av. de la República Argentina, 10; 954 27 66 87).

ACCOMMODATIONS

🏨 LA BANDA ROOFTOP HOSTEL

C. Dos de Mayo, 16; 955 22 81 18; labandahostel.com; reception open 24hr; check in after 2pm, check out by 11am

Whether you're in Seville for a single night or for several weeks, booking a bed at La Banda should be your top priority. Few hostels successfully strike a balance between comfort and fun—La Banda Rooftop Hostel, despite some of its quirks (read: few common toilets, many guests), is a master tightrope walker. Its spacious rooms feature sturdy wooden bunks equipped with privacy curtains, lights, and ample outlets to charge your devices, as well as updated bathrooms with overhead showers, free soap, and floors that don't pool. Four stories above La Banda's pillow-heavy, tastefully-postered foyer, you'll find a outdoor bar with long wooden benches, low couches, and a killer view of the **Catedral** and **Giralda.** Enjoy €3 cocktails and a hearty home-cooked meal (fixed price) at sunset, and watch the city come alive from above to the tune of smooth jazz or an open mic performance.

i Dorms from €26; BGLTQ+ friendly; no wheelchair accessibility; Wi-Fi; kitchen; free luggage storage; linens, towel, daily walking tour included; breakfast €3; dinner €6; cocktails €3 daily from 6pm-8pm; pub crawls; discount gym pass; food tours

🏨 FOR YOU HOSTEL SEVILLA

Calle Bailén, 15; 954 32 15 30; foryouhostel-Seville.zenithoteles.com/es/; reception open 24hr; check in after 1pm, check out at 11am

Forget living large—at For You Hostel Sevilla, you can live, sleep, and drink *super-sized.* For You's got all the fixings of a five-star hotel, and, if it weren't for its moniker, dorm set-up, and price tag (dorms start at €16, making it one of the most affordable options in Seville), it could easily pass for one. Behind the sun-drenched, marble-tiled lobby stands a fully-stocked bar, comfortable common room, and outdoor patio, whose top-notch wood furnishings match those of the tranquil roof deck four flights up. Sandwiched between the two are dozens of spacious rooms, each equipped with custom bunk beds featuring double-sized mattresses, USB outlets, lights, and sound-proof privacy curtains. The lockers themselves also have outlets (ingenious!) and can easily store a 55L backpack. With such luxuries, however, comes a dearth of social options—we nearly thought we were going to be thrown out on the street after asking what time the (nonexistent) pub crawl starts.

i Dorms from €16; privates, family rooms, and female-only dorms available; Wi-Fi; wheelchair accessible; linens, towels, luggage storage included; kitchen

OASIS BACKPACKERS PALACE SEVILLA

C. Compañía, 1; 955 22 82 87; oasisSeville.
com; reception open 24hr; check-in after 2pm,
check out at 11:30am

Oasis Backpackers Palace Sevilla is as
social as hostels get. Yes, we know—the
atmosphere of a hostel is highly dependent
on its guests. But *this* hostel is set up
such that it is *dependably* social, no matter
the exact composition of its clientele.
Among its numerous amenities are a pool,
rooftop bar with sweeping views of the
city, large common rooms that link the
dorms together, and nightly pub crawls
(€15). For these reasons, the hostel tends
to attract more groups than solo travelers.
Despite its party atmosphere, the rooms
are clean and comfortable—that is, unless
you're assigned to a top bunk, in which
case you'll be left lampless and powerless
with a tedious climb.

i *Dorms from €20 Nov 2-February 27, €24
Feb 28-Nov 1; online reservation recommended; privates and female-only dorms available;
BGLTQ+ friendly; wheelchair accessible; Wi-Fi;
laundry; linens, luggage storage, lockers,
kitchen, pool included; pool*

SEVILLA INN BACKPACKERS

C. Ángeles, 11; 954 21 95 41; innhostels.
com/Seville/; reception open 24hr

Located 190 meters northeast of
the **Catedral de Sevilla,** Sevilla Inn
Backpackers has got the rest of the city's
hostels beat in terms of location. At the
expense of being so close to the major
attractions, however, expect the dorms to
be smaller, the floors a little creakier, and
the outlets fewer and farther between.
The owners of Sevilla Inn Backpackers
have done a good job of sprucing up the
place—the entryway-turned-common
room is cozy, featuring eclectic décor, a
kitchenette, and several places to kick back
and relax during the day. This hostel tends
to attract more couples and middle-aged
travelers than students or large groups.
That's not to say there is a shortage of
nightlife here—exit the glass front door
and you'll find yourself on **Calle Mateos
Gago,** one of the city's highest-rated
locales for fine wining and dining.

i *Dorms from €14; online reservation recommended; female-only dorms available; Wi-Fi;
no wheelchair accessibility; laundry; linens,
kitchen, luggage storage, lockers, breakfast
included*

SIGHTS
CULTURE

🖼 SANTA CRUZ Y SAN BARTOLOMÉ

Pl. de Santa Cruz; establishment hours vary

Taking a winding stroll through the
colorful neighborhood of Santa Cruz will
likely be the highlight of your sightseeing
experience in Seville—it certainly was for
us. Previously the city's **Jewish Quarter,**
Santa Cruz is corralled by **Jardines de
Murillo** to the south and **Alfalfa** to the
north, and consists of blocks upon blocks
of tightly-spaced residences, restaurants,
and flamenco theaters. We recommend
departing from **Plaza de Santa Cruz**—
home to a manicured garden and several
small ceramic shops—at around 6pm and
heading northwest.

i *Free; limited wheelchair accessibility*

🖼 CASA DE PILATOS

Pl. de Pilatos, 1; 954 22 52 98; fundacionme-
dinaceli.org/monumentos/pilatos/; open daily
9am-7pm

Constructed at the turn of the sixteenth
century, the Casa de Pilatos is the most
important residence in Seville behind
the **Alcázar.** It features one of the largest
azulejo—or Spanish painted, tin-glazed
tilework—collections in the world. The
house and gardens, a mixture of Italian
Renaissance and Spanish Mudéjar
styles, are more impressive than any
other compound in the region, Alcázar
included. Dark gilded rooms are
interspersed with bright open courtyards,
and Greco-Roman statues, artifacts, and
imagery are littered throughout. Purchase
your tickets online or in person—a
worthwhile splurge despite the hefty
entrance fee.

i *Admission €8 for ground floor, €10 for entire
grounds; free for children under 10 and EU
residents on M from 3pm-7pm; audio guide
included; limited wheelchair accessibility*

PALACIO DE LA CONDESA DE LEBRIJA

C. Cuna, 8; 954 22 78 02; palaciodelebrija.
com; open M-F 10:30am-7:30pm, Sa 10am-
2pm and 4pm-6pm, Su 10am-2pm

The Palace of the Countess of Lebrija,
possesses the same grandeur and
opulence as the **Alcázar,** just on a smaller
scale—almost as if someone shrunk it
by 50 percent, then copied and pasted it
between a tapas bar and flower shop on
Calle Cuna. Today, the palace houses
an impressive, intimate, and interactive
exhibit of Grecian, Roman, and Moorish
art. Gawk at the impressive carvings that
adorn the marble columns around the
central courtyard, swerve between the
massive Chinese and Persian pots that
obscure its long tiled walkways, and and
tiptoe around the millennium-old mosaics
that pave the ground floor—all so close
you could practically touch them.
i Ground floor admission €6, entire grounds
€9; limited wheelchair accessibility

IGLESIA DEL SALVADOR

Pl. del Salvador, 3; 954 21 16 79; catedral-
deSeville.es/iglesia-de-el-salvador/; open
Sep-June M-Sa 11am-6pm, Su 3pm-7:30pm;
July-Aug M-Sa 10:30am-5:30pm, Su 3pm-
7:30pm

Seville's got no shortage of churches.
If you're struggling to decide which to
visit, take our word and cut straight to
Iglesia del Salvador, where you're sure
to get your fill of religious idolatry and
baroque architecture. From the outside,
this thirteenth-century behemoth
could pass for a secular building. Its
brick façade blends seamlessly with the
terracotta-colored paint of the clothing
manufacturing plant next door, and if not
for its large rose window and tiled dome,
you might mistake it for an upscale hotel.
As you walk from the back to the front
of the church, details grow more ornate:
corinthian columns give way to finely-
carved, hand-painted abutments; white
stucco ceilings transition into graphic
frescoes; and eye-level shrines bloom
into three-dimensional altarpieces that
seemingly stretch into the heavens.
i Admission €4, joint ticket to Iglesia del
Salvador y Catedral de Seville €9; limited
wheelchair accessibility

MERCADO DE TRIANA

C. San Jorge, 6; open M-F 9am-early afternoon, Sa 10am-early afternoon, Su noon-5pm

Mercado de Triana is one of two
markets open daily in Seville, the other
being **Mercado Lonja del Barranco,**
which is located on the east side of the
Guadalquivir. Upon entering, you'll
be bombarded with the scents of fresh
seafood, cheese, herbs, wine, and cured
meats. Wind through this dimly-lit,
humid maze, tasting as you go. *Unlike*
Mercado Lonja del Barranco, the goods
are not astronomically-priced; *like*
Mercado Lonja del Barranco, you can
watch as booth owners prepare your
meal directly in front of you. Beyond
produce, this market includes several
stalls of hand-thrown ceramic cookware.
If you're looking to explore handmade
crafts further, exit through the doors on
the north side of the complex, which are
carved into the walls of an ancient castle,
and make a right on **Calle Jon de la
Inquisición.** On summer Sundays from
9am-2pm, the cobblestone street on the
banks of the Guadalquivir transforms
into "**Paseo des Artes,**" where local artists
congregate to showcase beautiful jewelry,
woodwork, and leatherwork. **Centro
Cerámica Triana,** located at Calle Callao
16, is also worth a visit.
i Prices vary; limited wheelchair accessibility;
best time to visit is around noon Th-Sa

LANDMARKS

CATEDRAL DE SEVILLA (Y LA GIRALDA)

Av. de la Constitución; catedraldeSeville.
es; Cathedral open M 11am-3:30pm, T-Sa
11am-5pm, Su 2:30pm-6pm; Giralda open
Sep-June M 11am-3:30pm, T-Sa 11am-5pm,
Su 2:30pm-6pm, July-Aug M 9:30am-3:30pm,
Tu-Sa 9:30am-4pm, Su 2:30pm-6pm

Completed in the sixteenth century,
Seville Cathedral is the world's third
largest church behind Catedral Basílica
Santuário Nacional de Nossa Senhora
Aparecida in Brazil and St. Peter's Basilica
in Rome. It is truly the Redwood Forest
of religious structures—upon walking
inside, you'll feel dwarfed by its massive
corinthian columns and soaring 140-foot
ceiling, which is decorated with intricate
stone decals and complemented by
gilded altarpieces. Oh, also, the remains
of **Christopher Columbus** are housed

here, which is pretty cool. *The Giralda,* or bell tower, stretches 343 feet into the air and can be ascended free of charge. To avoid an hour-long queue, purchase your ticket to the Cathedral at the **Iglesia del Salvador** (combined entrance €8).

i Admission €9, students €4; with audioguide €12, students €7; purchase in advance online or in person; wheelchair accessible

◫ PLAZA DE ESPAÑA

Av. de Isabel la Católica; open daily 24hrs

Upon stepping foot in the square, you'll feel as if you've been transported to a different era—a different world even. Soaring towers flank both ends of the semicircular complex, serving as visual counterpoints to the **Vicente Traver** fountain and primary entryway that stands behind it. Separating the paved plaza from the buildings that surround it is a shallow moat, upon which ducks paddle and rowboats (€6 per half hour) glide. The building's tiled alcoves, decorated in the **Art Deco** style, bring life and color to the Plaza de España, and are great places to put your feet up after exploring the surrounding **Parque de María Luisa.** Although much of the compound is occupied by the Spanish government, you can explore the marvelous interior by climbing the grand staircase on the southern rim.

i Free; limited wheelchair accessibility

ALCÁZAR DE SEVILLE

Patio de Banderas; 954 50 23 24; AlcázarSeville.org; open daily 9:30am-5pm

The Alcázar is Seville's biggest tourist attraction, and consists of a maze of tiled courtyards, soaring archways, and lush gardens. Built on the remains of an Abbasid Muslim residential fortress for Peter of Castile, the compound has been deemed "the preeminent example" of Mudéjar architecture on the Iberian peninsula. The Alcázar's age can be seen in its slight imperfections—here an archway is a bit off center, there a window tilts slightly to the left. It was, along with the Catedral de Seville and General Archive of the Indies, designated a **UNESCO World Heritage Site** in 1987, and remains Europe's oldest palace still in use (the royal family lives upstairs!).

i Admission €9.5, students €2; book tickets online at least a day in advance; limited wheelchair accessibility

PLAZA DE TOROS (MAESTRANZA)

Paseo de Cristóbal Colón, 12; 954 22 45 77; realmaestranza.com; open daily 9.30am-7 pm, except on bullfighting days until 3pm

This magnificent yellow and white stadium was constructed in 1761 and holds up to 12,000 spectators each Sunday between April and September. It's one of the most challenging environments for matadors not only because of its lofty history, but also because of the viewing public, which is considered one of the most unforgiving in all of bullfighting fandom. Each tour begins with a trek through a succinct historical exhibit that traces bullfighting's evolution from a horseback sport to the performance art. When you exit, be sure to stop by **Museo Naval Torre del Oro,** where you'll get a second dose of Seville's bloody history.

i Admission €8, students €5; free M 3pm-7pm; audio guides included; limited wheelchair accessibility

REAL FÁBRICA DE TOBACOS DE SEVILLE (UNIVERSIDAD DE SEVILLE)

C. San Fernando, 4; us.es; open M-F 8am-9pm, Sa 9am-2pm

The Royal Tobacco Factory is a massive stone building that currently serves as the seat of the rectorate of the **University of Seville.** Prior to that, it was, as its name suggests, a tobacco factory, which has since packed up shop and moved to the nearby neighborhood of **Los Robles.** Although much of the interior has been altered for use by the university, the exterior remains largely the same—an exemplar of eighteenth-century industrial architecture. If you continue walking towards the back of the building, through its two grand courtyards and up the second set of marble staircases, you'll find a beautiful, naturally-lit study area where students work and mingle.

i Free; limited wheelchair accessibility; free restrooms upstairs

MUSEUMS

🖾 CENTRO ANDALUZ DE ARTE CONTEMPORÁNEO (CAAC)

Av. Américo Vespucio, 2; 955 03 70 70; caac.es; open Tu-Sa 11am-9pm, Su 10am-3:30pm

Located on the west side of the **Guadalquivir** north of **Triana,** Centro Andaluz de Arte Contemporáneo one of the city's furthest attractions. Don't let CAAC's distance deter you: housed in a refurbished monastery, CAAC's permanent collection pays special attention to the history of contemporary Andalusian creativity in the context of the international artistic environment through media including (but not limited to) painting, sculpture, photography, and video. The museum includes a small restaurant and bar, which hosts local performance artists most weekend afternoons.

i Admission €1.80 for temporary exhibitions, €3 for entire museum; free Tu-F 7pm-9pm, all day Sa; limited wheelchair accessibility; advisable not to walk alone from Casco Antiguo

MUSEO DEL BAILE FLAMENCO

C. Manuel Rojas Marcos, 3; 954 34 03 11; museodelbaileflamenco.com; open daily 10am-7pm

Museo del Baile Flamenco is a one-stop-shop for all things flamenco, offering a digestible take on the history, practice, and allure of this unique dance form. It is a performance venue, museum, and gallery all in one, and upon entering, you'll be handed a card with summaries of the contents of each room, making it easy to prioritize what you'd like to see. We recommend visiting the museum, attending a performance, then meandering through the gallery (in that order). Shows begin at 5pm, 7pm, 9:45pm, and 10:15pm daily; arrive at least 15 minutes early to snag a seat in the front row and experience the athleticism and grace first-hand.

i Admission €10, students €8; show tickets €20, students €14; combined €24, students €18; limited wheelchair accessibility

MUSEO DE BELLAS ARTES

Pl. del Museo, 9; 955 54 29 31; juntade-andalucia.es/cultura/museos/MBASE/?l-ng=es; open Tu-Sa 9am-8pm, Su 9am-3pm

The Museo de Bellas Artes is Seville's premier art museum, housing millions of dollars of paintings, sculptures, and furniture from the fifteenth through early twentieth centuries (think lots of winged babies) in a cathedral that dates back to 1594. High ceilings, ornate frescoes, and white marble staircases characterize the interior of this building—in and of itself a piece of art. There's enough here to keep visitors engaged and entertained for days, but for the less artistically-inclined, the entire museum can be covered in just under two hours. We recommend arriving when it opens, before the sun is high and the rest of the tourists arrive.

i Admission €1.50; wheelchair accessible

OUTDOORS

🖾 PARQUE DE MARÍA LUISA

Paseo de las Delicias; 955 47 32 32; open daily 8am-10pm

New York has Central Park, Seville has Parque de María Luisa. Although this expansive, lush plot of greenery, fountains, paved boulevards, tiled courtyards, monuments, and exedras has existed since the seventeenth century, it wasn't until 1911, under the skilled eye of landscape architect **Jean-Claude Nicolas Forestier** (who also designed the gardens of Champ-de-Mars in Paris), that it assumed its present shape. This botanical garden's main complexes include the **Plaza de España, Costurero de la Reina,** and the **Plaza America,** all of which deserve a visit both for their design and their contents. Between stops, take a breather in the shade of an orange tree, or, perhaps, go for a quick bike ride—a great way to cover a lot of ground in a short amount of time.

i Free; bikes available to rent near the Plaza de España; limited wheelchair accessibility

SPAIN SEVILLE

JARDINES DE MURILLO

Av. de Menéndez Pelayo; open daily
7am-midnight

The Jardines de Murillo were
overhauled at the same time
as **Parque de María Luisa**
as a part of an initiative to
improve transportation within
and around the **Santa Cruz**
neighborhood. This highly-
manicured, quiet park consists
of a network of dirt pathways,
palm trees, low shrubbery, and
ceramic courtyards, with most
activity centering around five
roundabouts. Though located
parallel to **Avenida de Menéndez
Pelayo,** one of the city's busiest
streets, Jardines de Murillo feels like a
little slice of paradise, secluded from
the tourist frenzy occurring just on
the other side of **the Alcázar's** exterior
walls.

i Free; limited wheelchair accessibility

METROPOL PARASOL (LAS SETAS)

Pl. de la Encarnación; open M-F 10am-
11pm, Sa-Su 10am-11:30pm

See Seville from a different perspective
and ascend the Metropol Parasol, a
massive wooden sculpture (at 490 by
230 feet, it claims to be the largest
freestanding wood structure in the
world!) whose latticed frame shades
the bustling **Plaza de Encarnación.**
The base of the structure houses
a small, upscale market, as well as
several restaurants and a popular
underground exhibit that showcases
Roman ruins and artifacts excavated
on-site. As much of the **Antiquarum**
can be viewed through the floor-to-
ceiling glass panes that encase it, we
recommend strolling right by to the
elevator. Sunset is by far the most
popular time to visit, but get there a
little earlier to avoid waiting in line.
Apart from **the Giralda**, the Metropol
Parasol offers the best 360-degree view
of Seville.

i Lift to top €3, admission to Antiquarum
€2.10, cocktails from €5; limited wheelchair accessibility

FOOD

🍽 LA BRUNILDA TAPAS ($)

Calle Galeria, 5; 954 22 04 81; labrunil-
datapas.com; open Tu-Sa 1pm-4pm and
8:30pm-11:30pm, Su 1pm-4pm; closed
Aug

Hands-down *the* best (affordable)
tapas in Seville. La Brunilda has a
reputation— there was already a line
when we arrived at 1pm on a Sunday.
Upon entering, you'll be greeted by
an attentive waitstaff, a cavernous
but updated interior, and a small
but thoughtfully-curated menu of
omnivorous starters and large plates
such as *Risoto de Idiazábal y setas*. We
particularly enjoyed the cod fritters
with pear aioli, a dense fish patty fried
crisp to the touch and served with a
light, semi-sweet glob of cream. Arrive
a half hour before opening to ensure
that you score a table.

i Starters from €3.20, meats from €4.50,
seafood from €3.20; beer €1.40, wine
€2.60, mixed drinks €4.50; vegetarian
options available; limited wheelchair accessibility; no reservations accepted

🍽 LA CACHERRERÍA ($)

C. Carlos Cañal, 14; 954 21 21 66; open M-Th 8:30am-10pm, F 8:30am-midnight, Sa 9am-3am, Su 10am-10pm

With nothing but a couple of tables and a sun-worn awning outside of its narrow front door, La Cacherrería is easy to miss. But right past it and you'll be missing out on one (or three) of the best mojitos of your life, not to mention some stellar food and an unparalleled dining experience. La Cacherrería's interior can best be described as *witches'-den-meets-junkyard-chic-meets-grandpa's-last-garage-sale.* Among other things, globes, evil eyes, cuckoo clocks, accordions, Nepali flags, and a couple of miniature phonographs hang from its ceiling, and hundreds of pennies are stacked perilously on the bricks that compose its northern wall. Serving up scrumptious bagel sandwiches, fresh wraps, and large parfaits, La Cacherrería is the closest you'll get—food wise, at least—to an American brunch.

i Bagels, wraps, salads, and toasts from €4.50; smoothies, milkshakes, and parfaits from €2.50; Cruzcampo on tap €1, wine from €2.50; cocktails from €3; vegetarian options available; no wheelchair accessibility

🍽 ALMAZEN CAFÉ ($)

C. San Esteban, 15; 955 35 97 64; open Tu-W 9am-8pm, Th-Sa 9am-11pm, Su 9am-2pm

Almazen is a jewel of a café, located in the hip, artistic neighborhood of **San Bartolomé.** Ample seating, free Wi-Fi, an easily-navigable menu, and a bilingual staff make dining here *easy.* Almazen Café is particularly popular for its homemade breakfast, which includes decadent parfaits, fruit tartlets, and a variety of cakes and coffees. Highlights from the afternoon menu include Chorizo Criollo and Empanadas Porteñas—rich, meaty dishes that pair wonderfully with a glass of red wine, craft beer, or blended iced tea. Enjoy your meal inside surrounded by original artwork or outside on a covered patio; either way, you'll leave full, happy, and ready to take on the day.

i Tapas from €3; drinks from €1; vegan and vegetarian options available; Wi-Fi; limited wheelchair accessibility

FILO SANDWICHERÍA PIJA ($)

Hernando Colón, 19; 955 186 892; filoSeville.es; open M-F 8am-10pm, Sa-Su 9am-10pm

One word: vegetables—fresh ones in heaping quantities, no less. If the produce and pastries in the front window don't lure you in, Filo's dimly-lit interior, decorated with hand-tossed ceramic bowls and wicker baskets, will. Take your pick from a variety of sandwiches, salads, and freshly-squeezed juices; if nothing fits your fancy, opt for a Frankenstein varietal and choose your own base and toppings for a couple euros extra. Not only is the food delicious, but at the same price as a McDonald's combo meal, it's well worth your money.

i Breakfast from €4.90, sandwiches from €6.50, salads from €6.50, drinks from €1.90; dairy-free, gluten-free, vegan, and vegetarian options available; wheelchair accessible

NIGHTLIFE

🍽 LA CARBONERÍA

C. Levíes, 8; 954 21 44 60; open daily 7am-2am

Every evening at 9:30pm and midnight, something akin to magic happens at La Carbonería. The locals lounging on the tree-covered garden patio extinguish their cigarettes, the lights inside begin to dim, and the cacophony of multilingual chatter, clinking glasses, and creaking of wooden benches begins to quiet down. The flamenco performance is one of the most authentic in the city, and lasts between 30 minutes and a full hour. The bar itself is tucked away in one of the quietest parts of the city, between **Santa Cruz** and **San Bartolomé,** so don't fret if you find yourself walking in what may seem like the wrong direction. You'll know you've made it when you spot the small black lettering on its doorway—"La Carbonería," lit by the soft glow of the lights that line the courtyard.

i Mojitos €5, liter of sangria €9, cocktails €6; food from €11; free flamenco shows daily; wheelchair accessible

🍽 LA BICICLETERIA

Feria 36; 608 73 48 06; open daily between 10pm-midnight, closes whenever the party dies down

Knock slow, knock hard. Entrance is not guaranteed to all at this clandestine bar, but you'll increase your chances of getting if you approach its graffitied door confidently and speaking the language (or are attached to the hips of people who do). A visit to La Bicicleteria will reveal a side of Seville very few tourists get to experience. Inside, a small sunken room pulses with the smooth sounds of jazz, reggae, and old rock and smoke twirls in the yellow cones of light cast by lamps that hang low to the ground. The décor, like the clientele, is bohemian and non-conformist, and on a good night, it feels more like an attending intimate house party than anything else.

i No wheelchair accessibility; weekdays are as popular as weekends; preferable not to attend or walk home alone

BODEGA SANTA CRUZ

Calle Rodrigo Caro, 1A; 954 21 16 94; open M-Sa 8am-midnight, Su 8:30am-midnight

A bustling bar located steps from the **Catedral**, Bodega Santa Cruz—or *Las Columnas* as locals call it—is steeped in character and authenticity. Don't let the boisterous crowd outside of its tall double doors frighten you off; if you manage to squeeze through to Bodega Santa Cruz's long mahogany bar, you'll be rewarded with cheap beer and tasty tapas, all served within a matter of seconds. On weekend evenings, flamenco musicians gather on the front porch for free performances.

i Tapas from €2, cheap beer on tap; cash only; limited vegetarian options available

SPAIN ESSENTIALS

VISAS

Spain is a member of the European Union and is part of the Schengen Area, so US citizens can stay in Sweden for up to 90 days without a visa.

MONEY

Tipping and Bargaining: Native Spaniards rarely tip more than their spare change, even at expensive restaurants. Don't feel like you have to tip, as the servers' pay is almost never based on tips. Bargaining is common and necessary in open-air and street markets. Do not barter in malls or established shops.

Taxes: Spain has a 10% value added tax (IVA) on all means and accommodations. The prices listed in Let's Go include IVA. Retail goods bear a much higher 21% IVA, although the listed prices generally include this tax. Non-EU citizens who have stayed in the EU fewer than 180 days can claim back the tax paid on purchases at the airport.

SAFETY AND HEALTH

Drugs and Alcohol: Recreational drugs are illegal in Spain, and police take these laws seriously. the legal drinking age is 16 in Asturias and 18 elsewhere. In Asturias, it is still illegal for stores to sell alcohol to those under the age of 18.

Local Laws and Police: There are several types of police in Spain. The policía local wear blue or black uniforms, deal more with local issues, and report to the mayor or town hall in each municipality. The guardia civil wear olive-green uniforms and are responsible for issues more relevant to travelers: customs, crowd control, and national security. Catalonia also has its own police force, the Mossos d'Esquadra. Officers generally wear blue and occasionally sport berets. This police force is often used for crowd control and to deal with riots.

SWEDEN

Many things that people traditionally associate with Scandinavia, like ABBA, IKEA, and Swedish Fish, are actually Swedish. And if you have to pick a Scandinavian country, Sweden is the one to see. It's Scandinavia's most populous country; it contains its largest city, boasts its tallest skyscraper, and houses the largest scale model of the solar system in the entire world. Sweden lies near Norway and Denmark geographically, but also ideologically. Sweden is laid-back enough to just suck it up and join the European Union (unlike Norway), but not so laid-back that drinking in the streets is commonplace (unlike Denmark). It will come as no surprise that Sweden isn't cheap, but given all it has going for it, you might want to shell out a little extra cash. There are museums dedicated to everything from ancient ships to liquor, palaces and gardens fit to rival any in Europe, and the hostels you've always dreamed of (you know, the ones where the kitchen is just as rowdy as most of the bars in the area). Sweden is a country of paradoxes. Everyone rides a bicycle, but no one wears a helmet. The tobacco use is high, but so is life expectancy. And for a country who brands itself as neutral, it certainly exports a lot of weapons. So, what is the real Sweden like? Pack up your IKEA bag—you might have to assemble it first—and find out.

MALMÖ

Coverage by **Eric Chin**

Sweden and Denmark have fought each other throughout history with the frequency of you and your roommate fighting over who gets the shower. Though not official, it's widely believed that no two countries have gone to war as often as these, and Malmö was right in the thick of it all. Positioned just across Oresund from Copenhagen, the city has changed hands multiple times, eventually falling under Swedish control for the long haul. The resulting city is diverse and independent with visible reminders of its Danish past such as Malmöhus Castle and the occasional *smørrebrød* restaurant. It's also increasingly modern, especially since the completion of the Öresund Bridge, which connects Malmö to Copenhagen. From ancient Gothic churches to Scandinavia's tallest skyscraper, American-style burger joints to New Nordic Cuisine, and swing dancing bars to hard-charging nightclubs, Malmö has it all. The small city vibe is real here, but, if you ever get bored, Copenhagen is just a short, border control-free (how civilized!), train ride away. Malmö has sights ranging from brick-building-lined squares to absolutely baffling modern art exhibitions. And if you're regretting not buying a ticket to Majorca, fear not: there are beaches here, and two of them are nude. That's Malmö for you.

ORIENTATION

Though Malmö doesn't have the vast, diverse neighborhoods of a city like Stockholm, there are still distinct areas. The heart of the city is **Gamla Staden,** which contains **Malmö C,** as well as most of the city's cultural and historical landmarks, like **Malmöhus Castle** and **Lilla Torg.** To the west is **Ribersborg,** home of Malmö's main beach and open-air bathhouse, **Ribersborgs Kallbadhus.** North of the city center is the exclusive neighborhood of Västra Hamnen, which claims to be Europe's first entirely carbon-neutral district. It's also home of Turning Torso. Things get a bit more residential south of Gamla Staden, but no less fun. **Möllevången,** known by the cool kids (and you want to be a cool kid around here) as **Möllan,** is Malmö's hip, no-hands-bike-riding, polaroid-wielding, beanie-wearing neighborhood. Catch a live show at **Folkets Park,** choose from a huge variety of international cuisines, or just head out for a stroll through the cultural spectrum that is Malmö.

ESSENTIALS

GETTING THERE

Malmö Airport (MMX), sometimes called by its old name, Sturup, is a small airport about 30km east of the city center. It connects to a number of major cities in Europe, especially in central Europe. Flygbussarna Airport Coaches travel regularly between the airport and city center, and can be purchased online (www.flygbussarna.se) for SEK 105. Also consider Copenhagen Airport (CPH), which flies to far more cities, including a few in North America. Malmö's train station is Malmö Central Station (Malmö C). Trains to destinations throughout Sweden are operated by SJ.

GETTING AROUND

Malmö is super walkable. If you want to use public transportation, your best bet is to buy a Jojo card (available at Malmö C), which can be used on buses and trains (1-day pass SEK 65, 3-day pass SEK 165). You can also load money onto the card, in which case (single-fare SEK 17). Malmö is another bike-friendly Scandinavian city, and city bike stations can be found all over the city center (1-day pass SEK 80, 3-day pass SEK 165). They can be purchased online (www.malmobybike.se). Rentals are for 1hr each.

PRACTICAL INFORMATION

Tourist Offices: Malmö has no dedicated tourist office. Instead, maps, information can be found at "InfoPoints" around the city. Look for a green "i" logo in shop windows. The closest InfoPoint to Malmö Central Station is Travel Shop (Carlsgatan 4; 040 330 570; open M-F 9am-5pm, Sa-Su 10am-5pm).

Banks/ATMs/Currency Exchange: Credit and debit cards can be used almost everywhere in Malmö. If you need cash, ATMs (Bankomat in Sweden) can be found on the street, and currency exchange is possible at banks like Forex (Malmö Central Station; 10 211 1664; open M-F 7am-8pm, Sa-Su 10am-6pm).

Post Offices: PostNord Postombud at ICA Malmborgs Caroli (Stora Kvarngatan 59; 020 23 22 21; open M-F 8am-8pm, Sa 8am-6pm, Su 11am-6pm)

Internet: Free Wi-Fi is available at most cafés, including independent shops and chains like Espresso House. Malmö Central Station and the City Library also offer free Wi-Fi.

BGLTQ+ Resources: RFSL is the Swedish Federation for Lesbian, Gay, Bisexual, Transgender, and Queer Rights (Stora Nygatan 18; www.malmo.rfsl.se).

EMERGENCY INFORMATION

Emergency Number: 112
Police: Malmö Porslinsgatan (Porslinsgatan 4B; 77 114 14 00; open M-F 7am-10pm, Sa-Su 8am-5pm)
Hospitals: Skåne University Hospital (Södra Förstadsgatan 101; 040 33 10 00)
Pharmacies: Apoteket Gripen (Bergsgatan 48; 0771 450 450; open daily 8am-11pm)

ACCOMMODATIONS

RUT & RAGNARS VANDRARHEM ($)

Nobelvägen 113; 406 116 060; www.rutochragnars.se; reception open 9am-1pm

Though the name makes it sound more like a Viking alehouse, Rut & Ragnars is the cheapest hostel you'll find in Malmö. The street entrance is unassuming, but inside there are definitely some features that elevate this place above your normal budget hostel. Check out the two kitchens, a lounge with TV, and free coffee and tea. The dorm rooms have couches and wall decorations to keep them from feeling too prison-like, and beds are equipped with privacy curtains to maximize your personal space. Don't expect anything too fancy, like a five-star breakfast buffet, but Rut & Ragnars is a solid choice for its asking price.

i Dorms from SEK 200, students SEK 180, singles SEK 430, doubles SEK 590; reservation recommended; max stay 7 nights; BGLTQ+ friendly; wheelchair accessible; Wi-Fi; linen SEK 50; laundry facilities SEK 50

STF VANDRARHEM MALMÖ CITY ($$)

Rönngatan 1; 406 116 220; www.swedish-touristassociation.com/facilities/stf-malmo-city-hostel

Small cities often don't have great hosteling culture, and Malmö is no exception. It just doesn't draw the hordes of backpackers required to sustain vibrant hostels. With that in mind, STF Vandrarhem is definitely your best bet in the city. While it's not a continuous party like you'll find in Stockholm, it definitely has a social atmosphere, especially on the weekends, and the facilities, including a kitchen and outdoor courtyard. The breakfast buffet, though a bit expensive for non-STF/HI members, is an excellent way to start the day.

i Dorms from SEK 270, privates from SEK 560, additional SEK 50 per night for non-STF/HI members; reservation recommended; max stay 5 nights; BGLTQ+ friendly; wheelchair accessible; Wi-Fi; linens included; lockers provided; breakfast SEK 65 for members, SEK 80 for non-members

SIGHTS
CULTURE

FOLK Å ROCK

Lilla Torg, Skomakaregatan 11; 40 781 03; www.folkarock.se; open M-Sa 10am-10pm, Su noon-6pm

Like that kid in high school whose parents told him he could be whatever he wanted, Folk å Rock is a little bit like Jeff Goldblum—part café, part bar, and part record store. Its abundance of indoor and outdoor seating is great for a steaming latte on a rainy afternoon or a cold beer on a sunny evening, but the upstairs music store is good for browsing all the time. Shelves of CDs and vinyl skew heavily towards your dad's favorites (Hendrix, Aerosmith, the Grateful Dead, you name it), but poke around a bit and you'll find timeless classics from **ABBA** to the Beatles, and even some contemporary artists, like Adele and Lana Del Rey.

i *Coffee and espresso drink from SEK 20, pastries and cakes from SEK 20, beer from SEK 60; wheelchair accessible*

RIBERSBORGS KALLBADHUS

Limhamnsvägen, Brygga 1; 040 260 366; www.ribersborgskallbadhus.se; open M-Tu 9am-8pm, W 9am-9pm, Th-F 9am-8pm, Sa-Su 9am-6pm

For the full Swedish spa experience, Ribersborgs Kallbadhus is the go-to. This open-air bathhouse pokes out into the sea on its own pier, giving it an exclusive and private feel, which is good, considering that clothes are banned here. That's right, this place is completely nude. With separate areas for men and women, each side features an enclosed swimming area and saunas of varying temperatures. With ample deck space, you're guaranteed not only to snag a place to get your perfect tan, but also to see way more old man/lady parts than you've ever wanted. Don't worry, though; much like Planet Fitness, this is a judgment-free zone.

i *Admission SEK 65; swimwear prohibited in the sauna*

LANDMARKS

HARBOR SCULPTURES

Posthusplatsen

The entire city of Malmö is overrun with sculptures (admittedly, there are worse things with which to be overrun), depicting everything from the classic old man on a horse, to a slightly cartoonish marching band headed down one of the main streets. But some of the most interesting statues can be found along the harbor right next to **Malmö Central Station.** Here, you'll find works ranging from straightforward, but poignant, like *Non-Violence* (a large, bronze revolver with its muzzle twisted in a knot), to

the absolutely psychedelic, like *Spectral Self Container* (a mind-bending rainbow piece that looks more like it belongs in a college-level topology textbook).

i *Free; wheelchair accessible*

LILLA TORG

Lilla Torg; open daily 24hr

Its name may literally translate to "Small Square" but don't tell that to Lilla Torg; this little square has a big personality and big-time bragging rights. Surrounded by old-looking brick and wooden buildings, the cobblestone streets are packed from dawn to dusk on most nights. These buildings house everything from the kind of rock and roll club/bar your dad and his buddies would love to steakhouses frequented by Italian men with chihuahuas. Ample outdoor seating makes Lilla Torg the perfect place to get a good dose of sun and people-watching at any time of day.

i *Prices vary; wheelchair accessible*

TURNING TORSO

Lilla Varvsgatan 14; open daily 24hr

Turning Torso is Scandinavia's tallest skyscraper that towers like an enormous middle finger to the rest of the world's conventional, straight-sided buildings. The building itself is composed of nine cubes with curved edges, stacked one on top of the next, each offset slightly from the one below. The result is an elegant tower that looks more like it belongs in Dubai than in the third-largest city in Sweden. Don't bother going inside as it's mostly residential, but the Turning Torso Gallery next door has a natural, Whole Foods-y kind of market, and the whole neighborhood is a nice place for a wander.

i *Free; wheelchair accessible*

MUSEUMS

SCIENCE AND MARITIME HOUSE

Malmöhusvägen; 40 344 438; www.malmo. se; open daily 10am-5pm

This is a fun museum geared towards children, but that doesn't mean you can't enjoy it, too. But that doesn't mean you can't enjoy it too, right? You're probably young at heart, and that's what counts. Check out the explanation about the future of nanotechnology and seriously silly rooms full of simple games, like a hydrogen rocket, to help illustrate complex concepts. The star of the show, though, is the **U3 submarine** on display in the courtyard. Visitors can go inside the sub to view the cramped quarters, endless dials, and tiny control room. There are guided tours led by some of the sub's original crew members.

i Admission to Malmö Museum and Science and Maritime House adults SEK 40, students SEK 20, free 19 and under; U3 submarine tours Tu and Su 1pm-4pm; wheelchair accessible

MALMÖ MUSEUM

Malmöhusvägen; 40 344 437; www.malmo. se; open daily 10am-5pm

Denmark and Sweden fought constantly in the Middle Ages, and Malmö was often right in the thick of it. Thus, it needed a castle, which was cleverly named **Malmöhus Castle**. Today, the castle serves not only as a historical building, but also as the city's museum. Some castle rooms have been preserved, but you'll also find temporary exhibits, art galleries, and even a natural history museum and aquarium. It sounds like a lot, but none of the exhibits are particularly long..

i Admission to Malmö Museum and Science and Maritime House SEK 40, students SEK 20, 19 and under free; Malmöhus Castle tours July 5-August 27 W-Su 3pm; wheelchair accessible

OUTDOORS

RIBERSBORGSSTRANDEN

Open daily 24hr

Ribersborgsstranden is the place to take dip in the Scandinavian sea. It's a long stretch of beach and green space just west of the city center that provides numerous swimming options for the general public, as well as a pier designed specifically for visitors with disabilities. There's also a nude beach (how European), in case you just can't resist the call of the wild, but **Ribersborgs Kallbadhus** is too gentrified for you.

i Free; wheelchair accessible

FOOD

🗹 SALTIMPORTEN CANTEEN ($$)

Grimsbygatan 24; 706 518 426; www. saltimporten.com; open M-F noon-2pm

Saltimporten Canteen may just be Malmö's best lunch spot. They only use the freshest ingredients, the atmosphere is upbeat, and, at SEK 95 for an entrée, the price is tough to beat. So what's the catch? It's only open weekdays noon-2pm. The rotating menu features a single dish each day; some examples include beef tartare with mushrooms and hazelnuts or lamb with new potatoes and fennel. But no matter what's being served, you can bet it will be elegant and executed to perfection. The restaurant itself is bright and modern with exposed ventilation ducts and an aggressive number of windows. Perfect for the solo traveler, the long communal tables bring together people who would venture all the way out to this pier to eat pretentious food.

i Lunch SEK 95; vegetarian options available; wheelchair accessible

🗹 SURF SHACK ($$)

Västergatan 9; 761 764 080; www.surf-shacksmashburgers.com; open M-Th 11am-9pm, F-Sa 11am-10pm; Su noon-8pm

It's a bit gimmicky to open a surf-themed burger joint when you're closer to the Arctic Circle than the equator, but there are so many dudes in Sweden with long blond hair that it works. Surf Shack draws a hungry crowd at mealtimes, and it's easy to see why: these burgers are massive. The "Mini Burger" weighs in at 115g and constitutes a meal in itself, but, if you're feeling ravenous, make it a double with the "Surf Burger"—a tower so high, it has to be held together with a skewer. Keep it classic with free toppings like grilled onions and mayo, or go full Hawaiian with pineapple and teriyaki sauce. Surf Shack even features milkshakes spiked with whiskey or rum.

i Single burgers from SEK 70, doubles from SEK 95, fries SEK 25, spiked milkshakes SEK 110; gluten-free, vegan, and vegetarian options available; limited wheelchair accessibility

LILLA KAFFEROSTERIET ($$)

Baltzarsgatan 24; 40 482 000; www.lillakaf-feriosteriet.se

The concept of size in Malmö must be a bit different than in the rest of the world, because, like **Lilla Torg,** Lilla Kafferosteriet, (literally "small coffee roasters"), is anything but small. This café sprawls across multiple rooms on two floors, an outdoor patio, and a courtyard. The décor is rustic, with exposed beams, peeling paint (it's charming...somehow), and rough-cut wooden counters that look like they were placed by Paul Bunyan himself. Lilla Kafferosteriet draws everyone from businesspeople to grumpy children.

i Coffee and espresso drinks from SEK 20, pastries from SEK 20

NIGHTLIFE
MALMÖ BREWING CO. & TAPROOM

Bergsgatan 33; 733 921 966; www.malmo-brewing.com; open M-Th 4pm-midnight, F 4pm-3am, Sa noon-3am, Su 2pm-10pm

This is it: Malmö's only microbrewery, and hasn't grown complacent in its monopoly. Downstairs in the rustic brick basement that houses the bar is a board listing over 30 different beers on tap, with clever (or maybe just ridiculous) names like **"Janky Stout"** and **"Kitten in Trance."** The atmosphere is casual, with laid-back hip hop and R&B, and the crowd a mix of older guys who would probably say they "dabble" in brewing, and young people getting a cold beer while their tastes are still discerning enough to appreciate it. If you get here early, don't miss the BBQ menu with classics like ribs, brisket, and pulled pork so good you'll forget that you're thousands of miles from the American Midwest.

i Beer from SEK 70, entrées from SEK 100; BGLTQ+ friendly; no wheelchair accessibility

STOCKHOLM

Coverage by **Eric Chin**

Congratulations, you've made it to Stockholm: the biggest, baddest, and brightest city in the north. You've seen the fjords in Bergen and joined the hordes of cyclists in Copenhagen, but now it's time to move up to a true metropolis (or, at least, a city with a real subway system). Stockholm is a Scandinavia-traveler's dream. It's a bustling city where oxford-clad businessmen in Östermalm rub elbows with hipsters in Söder, where the museums range from old-fashioned (The Nordic Museum) to positively psychedelic (ABBA: The Museum), and where the world's first bar made from ice coexists with a luminescent tiki bar. Spend some time in one of the city's numerous hostels (which are the best in Scandinavia), and you'll meet every kind of traveler from backpackers who packed three pairs of socks to child millionaires with more suitcases than can fit under a dorm bed. No matter where you fall in the duffel bag vs. three suitcase debate, you'll find something in Stockholm. Foodies can choose between gourmet coffee and pickled herring, history buffs from crown jewels and ancient cannons, and outdoor adventurers from kayaks and bicycles.

ORIENTATION

Stockholm is the biggest city in Scandinavia and is truly urban with an extensive, highly efficient public transportation system and many neighborhoods with distinct character. At the center of it all is the bustling **Norrmalm district,** where you'll find **Stockholm Central Station** and the busy shopping street, **Drottninggatan.** Norrmalm is flanked to the west by **Kungsholmen,** a growing residential area home to City Hall, and to the east by Östermalm, Stockholm's most extravagant neighborhood. Östermalm is filled with expensive stores, Ferrari dealerships, and cafés rampant with suit-clad men who carry briefcases (not only because they're

European, but also because they're rich). To the south are several notable islands, which house **Gamla Stan, Södermalm,** and **Djurgården.** Djurgården has many interesting museums and cultural sights like **ABBA The Museum, Gröna Lund, the Vasa Museum,** and **Skansen.** Gamla Stan, just south of Norrmalm, is the **Old Town,** where you'll find narrow, cobblestone streets packed with tourists, restaurants for tourists, and shops for tourists (as well as the **Royal Palace**). Finally, just south of Gamla Stan is Södermalm (usually shortened to Söder), an old working class neighborhood turned hipster hangout spot.

ESSENTIALS

GETTING THERE

Stockholm's main airport is Stockholm Arlanda, located about 40km north of the city with flights to most major European cities, as well as to a few airports in North America and Asia. The easiest way to travel between Arlanda and Stockholm Central Station is the Arlanda Express, a 20min. train ride with departures every 15min. most of the day. One-way tickets cost SEK 280 for adults (26 and older), SEK 150 for people 25 and under, and SEK 140 for students, and can be booked online at www.arlandaexpress.com. Stockholm Central Station (Stockholm C) is the main train station in Stockholm. Trains to destinations around Sweden are operated by SJ. The main hall is open daily 5am-1:15am, though parts of the station open earlier.

GETTING AROUND

Public transportation in Stockholm includes buses, a metro system (called Tunnelbana), trams, and ferries around the city. Tickets can be purchased on the SL app or at ticket kiosks. Tickets cannot be purchased on-board buses or trams. If you plan on using public transportation more than a few times, it makes sense to purchase a travel card for SEK 20. With the card, you can buy a pass for 24hr (SEK 120, SEK 80 discounted), 72hr (SEK 240, SEK 160 discounted), or one week (SEK 315, SEK 210 discounted). Stockholm has a city bike program with over 100 stations across the city. A 3-day rental costs SEK 165 and can be purchased at most tourist centers. Bikes can be taken from any stand and returned to any stand, but each individual bike must be returned within three hours.

Tourist Offices: Stockholm Visitor Center (Kulturhuset, Sergels Torg 3-5, 8 508 28 508; open May 1-Sept 15 M-F 9am-7pm, Sa 9am-4pm, Su 10am-4pm; Sept 16-Apr 30 M-F 9am-6pm, Sa 9am-4pm, Su 10am-4pm)

Banks/ATMs/Currency Exchange: If you need hard currency (unlikely), exchanges are available at Arlanda Airport and Stockholm Central Station, but you may be better off just finding an ATM (Bankomat in Swedish) on the street.

Post Offices: Sweden's postal service is called PostNord, and doesn't have many brick-and-mortar locations. Letters can be mailed on the street, or at private mail centers like Mail Boxes Etc (Torsgatan 2; 8 124 494 00; open June 26-Aug 21 M-F 10am-6pm, Sa 10am-2pm; Aug 22-June 25 M-F 8am-7pm, Sa 10am-2pm).

Internet: The Stockholm Visitor Center, Arlanda Airport, and Stockholm Central Station also have Wi-Fi.

BGLTQ+ Resources: RFSL is the Swedish Federation for Lesbian, Gay, Bisexual, and Transgender Rights (Sveavägen 59; 08 501 62 950; www.rfslstockholm.com).

EMERGENCY INFORMATION

Emergency Number: 112. For 24-hour non-emergency health advice, call 1177.

Police: Norrmalm Police Station (Kungsholmsgatan 43; 114 14; open daily 24hr)

US Embassy: There is a US Embassy in Stockholm (Dag Hammarskjölds Väg 31; 08 783 53 00; open M-F 8am-4:30pm).

Rape Crisis Center: Södersjukhuset, one of Stockholm's main hospitals, has a 24hr telephone hotline and an emergency clinic for rape victims on the second floor (Sjukhusbacken 10; 08 616 46 70).

Hospitals: Södersjukhuset (SÖS) (Sjukhusbacken 10; 8 616 10 00; open daily 24hr)

Pharmacies: Pharmacies in Stockholm (called apotek) are widely available and generally open between 10am and 6pm. There is a 24hr pharmacy right across the street from Stockholm Central Station.

ACCOMMODATIONS

🏨 CITY BACKPACKERS HOSTEL ($$)

Upplandsgatan 2a; 8 206 920; www.cityback-packers.org; reception open 8am-midnight

There are only two reasons that you should ever consider a hostel in Stockholm other than City Backpackers: either it's absolutely booked or you hate friendship, chocolate, weekends, and everything good in the world. The beds are soft as clouds and the décor looks like it was picked out by a hipster from the 1950s—complete with cartoon posters of snowboarding monks and retro TV sets—and the guests are overwhelmingly young and outgoing. The kitchen and common room are often so full on Friday and Saturday nights that the party sometimes never even leaves the hostel, though it may move upstairs into the outdoor courtyard and bar.

i Dorms from SEK 300, privates from SEK 820; reservation recommended; BGLTQ+ friendly; no wheelchair accessibility; Wi-Fi; linens SEK 24; laundry SEK 50; breakfast SEK 65, SEK 55 if booked at check-in

CITY HOSTEL ($)

Fleminggatan 19; 8 410 038 30; www.cityhostel.se/en; reception open 9am-6pm

City Hostel is a solid choice, with a prime location downtown and a slew of amenities, including an enormous kitchen, and bathrooms fitted with speakers blaring The Strokes all night long. The clientele falls all over the age spectrum, but it shouldn't be hard to find other young travelers happy to check out the long list of nightlife recommendations posted by the staff. Alcohol isn't permitted in the hostel, though, so don't expect any of the debauchery you'll find down the street at City Backpackers.

i Dorms from SEK 240, privates from SEK 495; reservation recommended; BGLTQ+ friendly; no wheelchair accessibility; Wi-Fi; linens included; laundry SEK 30

SKANSTULLS HOSTEL ($)

Ringvägen 135; 8 643 03 04; www.skanstulls.se/en; reception open 9am-8pm

You simply can't go wrong hosteling in Stockholm, and Skanstulls certainly lives up to the hype. Its prime location in **Söder** means you're never far from some of the city's best (and cheapest) bars. The kitchen and lounge are decked out with plush chairs and plenty of cooking space, and free pasta means you'll never go hungry, even as a backpacker on a budget. It's also right next to the **Skanstulls subway station,** keeping you connected to **Gamla Stan** and the city center.

i Dorms from SEK 235, privates from 540; reservation recommended; max stay 7 nights; BGLTQ+ friendly; Wi-Fi; linen SEK 50; lockers; breakfast SEK 75

SIGHTS
CULTURE

🏨 STOCKHOLM PALACE

Slottsbacken 1; 8 402 60 00; www.kungahuset.se; open daily July-Aug 9am-5pm, May-June/Sept 10am-5pm, Oct-Apr Tu-Su 10am-4pm

Now before you jump up and rush over here to meet the king and queen, there are two things you might want to know: the royal family doesn't actually live here and this isn't the original palace (that one, you'll be surprised to hear, burned down in 1697). But it's not as boring as it sounds. Since the royals aren't around, much of the palace is open to the public. Guided tours of the **Royal Apartments** are available several times daily through the summer, and the treasury houses, well, treasures, like **Gustav Vasa's** sword of state and **Erik XIV's** orb.

i Admission SEK 160, students SEK 80, guided tour SEK 20; tours daily May-Sept: Royal Apartments 10:30am, 1:30pm, 3:30pm; Treasury 11:30am; limited wheelchair accessibility; different parts of the palace complex have different hours, so check online; ticket valid for one week

DROTTNINGHOLM

178 02 Drottningholm; www.kungahuset.se; open daily Jan 1-Jan 7 noon-3:30pm, Jan 8-March Sa-Su noon-3pm, Apr 11am-3:30pm, May-Sept 10am-4:30pm, Oct F-Su 11am-3:30pm, Nov-Dec 10 Sa-Su noon-3:30pm, Dec 31 noon-3:30pm

Drottningholm is the reason the royals abandoned the **Royal Palace,** and it's not hard to see why. This palace is just as impressive, but everything is quieter since it's outside the city. Drottningholm, a **UNESCO World Heritage site,** has a proper garden that the Swedes proudly describe as their "answer to Versailles," though that seems a bit presumptuous. FFor a fee, you can visit the **Chinese Pavilion,** a gift from an eighteenth-century king to his queen. Apparently, the offering of a small Chinese palace was a pleasant surprise.

i Palace admission SEK 130, students SEK 65; palace and Chinese Pavilion admission SEK 190, students SEK 90; guided tour SEK 30; check website for seasonal tour times; no wheelchair accessibility

GRÖNA LUND

Lilla Allmänna Gränd 9; 010 708 91 00; www.gronalund.com; open daily 10am-11pm

Gröna Lund is Stockholm's answer to Six Flags, Lake Compounce, or whatever your local version of a hot, sweaty amusement park packed with too many strollers, ill-fitting tank tops, and screaming kids happens to be called. It has all your vomit-inducing favorites, like the carousel and teacups, but it also has real roller coasters. Multiple streets are lined with carnival games and food stands, and the park even hosts concerts through the summer, with big-time artists like the 1975 and Zara Larsson, as well as your dad's washed up favorites like Elton John and Alice Cooper.

i Admission SEK 115, rides from SEK 25, all-day pass SEK 330; wheelchair accessible

CITY HALL

Hantverkargatan 1; 8 508 290 58; www.international.stockholm.se/the-city-hall; open daily 9am-4pm

Much like you during your freshman year of college, Stockholm's City Hall has a bit of an identity crisis. It has a garden filled with fountains and marble statues and an area surrounded by columns and painted with symbols from Roman mythology in the style of a grand palace—an idea only slightly undercut by the fact that the rest of the building is made of red brick. Regardless, its garden is a great spot to relax and enjoy views of Stockholm's skyline.

i Guided tours Apr-Oct SEK 110, students SEK 90, Nov-Mar SEK 90, students SEK 70; tower ticket SEK 50; guided tours every 30min. from 9am-3:30pm (last tour at 4pm from June 7-Aug 27), tower tours every 40min. from 9:10am-5:10pm (last tour 3:50pm May-Sept); wheelchair accessible

FREE TOUR STOCKHOLM

Sergels torg; www.freetourstockholm.com

Imagine you've just arrived in Stockholm after touring some of Scandinavia's quieter towns. All of a sudden, you're overwhelmed. Stockholm is big; it has multiple neighborhoods—multiple islands even! Be honest, you probably haven't planned very much, but your solution is simple: a free tour. Free Tour Stockholm offers tours every day to three different parts of the city, perfect for getting your bearings. The City tour hits all the basics: **Hötorget** (the open-air market), the **Concert Hall,** and the main shopping streets. The **Old Town tour** dives a bit more into history, with stops at the **Royal Palace** and several old buildings of note. If you're too trendy for that, the **Söder tour** takes you to the area sometimes called "Stockholm's Brooklyn." You can be the judge of that.

i Free, but tip the guide; city tour 10am, Södermalm tour 1pm, Old Town tour 4pm; only city tour is wheelchair accessible; tours are 2hr

UPPSALA

Today, Uppsala is Sweden's fourth-largest city but doesn't get as much tourist love as its history would suggest it deserves. But until relatively recently, the city held a few very important distinctions. It was the site of the coronations of Swedish kings and queens until the eighteenth century, and today its cathedral is the center of Church of Sweden. Aside from its cultural significance, Uppsala is also one of the original college towns. Uppsala University was founded in 1477 and has influence over the city like a coal mining operation over the company town. It runs a number of museums and gardens around Uppsala and even accounts for a substantial portion of the population during the year with its enrollment of over 40,000. With that many students around, you can expect an abundance of coffee shops, cheap lunch deals, and a more relaxed atmosphere. Uppsala is a sleepy town, especially in the summer, but that could be just what you need after a few exhausting days in Stockholm.

Uppsala is a compact city. The **Centrum district** contains **Uppsala Central Station** as well as much of the city's shopping and restaurants. Most of the cultural sights and landmarks, along with **Uppsala University,** are across the river to the west. Here you'll find **Uppsala Castle, Uppsala Cathedral, Gustavianum,** and the **Botanical Garden.**

GETTING THERE

Uppsala is less than 45min. from Stockholm by train. Trains between Stockholm and Uppsala, operated mostly by SJ, are frequent throughout the day, and round-trip tickets can often be purchased for less than SEK 200 either online (www.sj.com) or at Stockholm C and Uppsala Central Station (Uppsala C).

GETTING AROUND

Uppsala is easily walkable from one end to the other. There is a bus system called UL that covers the city center. Single tickets cost SEK 28 if purchased in advance, or you can buy a 24hr pass for SEK 88.

Swing by...

UPPSALA CATHEDRAL
Domkyrkoplan; 1 84 30 36 30; www.uppsaladomkyrka.se; open daily 8am-6pm
Okay, it's a church. Surely, you've seen enough churches, right? Wrong. Uppsala Cathedral is the most important church in Sweden, as the seat of the **Archbishop of Uppsala,** and the tallest House of Jesus in all of Scandinavia. It's also probably the most interesting and recognizable building in the whole city, with its unusual combination of Gothic architecture and brick materials. Under the vaulted ceilings, frescoes, and stained-glass windows, the cathedral houses a huge collection of artifacts, as well as tombs of famous Swedes. The legendary king **Gustav Vasa** is buried here, and if you're at all familiar with royal egos, it won't surprise you to learn that his tomb is decorated with a thank you letter to himself.
i Admission and cathedral tour free, tower and treasury admission SEK 50; summer tours Cathedral tour M-Sa 10am and 2pm, Su 3pm, treasury tour daily 4pm; wheelchair accessible

Check out...

GUSTAVIANUM
Akademigatan 3; 1 847 175 71; www.gustavianum.uu.se; open June-Aug Tu-Su
10am-4pm, Sept-May Tu-Su 11am-5pm

You guessed it: this museum is named after a King Gustav. You probably shouldn't be surprised at this point. The building has served a number of purposes for Uppsala University over the years, including dorm and classroom space, but today it functions as the university's history museum. The eclectic collection includes exhibits about ancient Egypt, Vikings, and a room full of heavy duty scientific artifacts from physics, chemistry, and astronomy. But the centerpiece of the museum is the university's old anatomical theater, a steep, octagonal amphitheater where pre-meds of old would observe dissections of human cadavers.

i *Admission adult SEK 50, students SEK 40; tours daily 1pm; wheelchair accessible*

Grab a bite at...

DYLAN'S GRILL ($)
Vaksalagatan 10; www.dylansgrill.se; open M-Tu 11am-8pm, W-Sa 11am-10pm, Su 11am-8pm

With so many college students in such a small town, you're pretty much guaranteed a cheap burger joint, and Dylan's fills the void, with options like the Cowboy (with jalapeños and barbecue sauce) and the Farmer (with a fried egg). A double burger and fries cost less than SEK 100, so the broke student vibe is real here, especially with the cheap-but-charming orange and blue plastic furniture.

i *Single burgers from SEK 60, doubles from SEK 75, fries SEK 20, shakes SEK 45; gluten-free and vegetarian options available; wheelchair accessible*

Don't miss...

BOTANICAL GARDEN
Villavägen 6-8; The Park open daily May-Oct 7am-9pm, Nov-Apr 7am-7pm; Tropical Greenhouse June-Aug M-F 9am-3pm, Sa-Su 11am-4pm, Sept-May Tu-F 9am-3pm, Sa-Su noon-3pm

It's tough to make it big as a botanical garden in Europe; you have to compete with Versailles and the Kew Gardens, just to name two. Uppsala's answer? A rainforest. That's right; even though this dark horse of a garden may not have the fountains and peacocks of some of its southern counterparts, Uppsala's Botanical Garden has an entire greenhouse that mimics a tropical climate, in order to grow all sorts of plants that wouldn't last up north. In the unlikely event that you just can't get enough of that fine Swedish weather, another outdoor park has a wide variety of native plants and plenty of hidden benches where you can sit and contemplate life.

i *Tropical Greenhouse SEK 50; park and garden tours June-Aug Sa-Sun 2pm; limited wheelchair accessibility*

SWEDEN STOCKHOLM

GLOBEN

77 131 00 00; www.stockholmlive.com/
en; open daily July 3-Aug 13 10am-8pm;
Aug 14-July 2 M-F 10am-6pm, Sa-Su
10am-4pm

Next time you're at a Sweden-themed
trivia night, remember Globen. It's
the world's largest hemispherical
building, and it also represents the sun
in the **Sweden Solar System,** a scale
model of the solar system (also the
world's largest) that stretches across
the entire country. Surely everyone's
favorite narcissist, **Gustav Vasa,** would
be happy to learn that Stockholm is
indeed at the center of the universe.
Globen is mainly used as a concert
venue, but it's popular with travelers
because of **SkyView:** a ride in a glass-
walled gondola that travels up and over
the top of the dome, providing some of
the best aerial views of Stockholm.
i Admission SEK 150; last ride leaves
10min. before closing; wheelchair accessible

RIKSDAGSHUSET (PARLIAMENT HOUSE)

Riksgatan 1; 8 786 40 00; www.riksdagen.
se

This is where all the magic happens,
folks. Here, that 25% value-added
tax is levied, the socialist safety net
constructed, and the blond-hair-
and-blue-eyes mandate enacted.
The Riksdagshuset's **Public Gallery**
is open whenever the Riksdag is in
session, so that Swedes and visitors
alike can directly observe the political
process. Guided tours provide more
information about the political
workings of the Riksdag and about the
history of the buildings themselves.
i Free; tours June 26-Aug 18 M-F noon,
1pm, 2pm, 3pm; wheelchair accessible

MUSEUMS

⬛ ABBA THE MUSEUM

Djurgårdsvägen 68; 7 717 575 75; www.
abbathemuseum.com/en; open daily May
29-Sept 3 9am-7pm; Sept 4-Oct 1 M-Tu
10am-6pm, W-Th 10am-7pm, F-Sa 10am-
6pm; Oct 2-Oct 29 M-Tu noon-6pm, W-Th
10am-7pm, F-Su 10am-6pm; Oct 30-Nov
5 M-Tu 10am-6pm, W-Th 10am-7pm, F-Su
10am-6pm; Nov 6-Dec 31 M-Tu noon-6pm,
W-Th 10am-7pm, F-Su 10am-6pm

ABBA: performers of "Dancing
Queen," source for *Mamma Mia!*, and
that thing that happens when your
parents get ahold of the aux cord.
The museum is masterfully designed
to make your heart ache for the days
of bedazzled bodysuits and platform
boots, regardless of whether or not you
lived through them in the first place.
See stage outfits worn in concert, a
complete replica of ABBA's recording
studio, and all sorts of authentic
props and instruments from a more
flamboyant time in music history. Get
in on the action by hopping on the
stage and singing along to an ABBA
classic, alongside holograms of the
bandmates.
i Admission SEK 250; last entry 90min.
before closing; wheelchair accessible; card
only; advance online booking recommended

NORDIC MUSEUM

Djurgårdsvägen 6-16; 8 519 546 00; www.
nordiskamuseet.se/en; open daily June-
Aug 9am-6pm; Sept-May M-Tu 10am-5pm,
W 10am-8pm, Th-Su 10am-5pm

Despite being called the Nordic
Museum, this museum focuses almost
exclusively on Sweden. It covers over
500 years of Swedish history and
looks at many different aspects of
life, like furniture in the *Homes and
Interiors* exhibit, the contemporary
section of which is basically a giant
temple to IKEA. *Table Settings* depicts
the transition of Swedish cuisine
from lowly dishes like the pinnacle
of cuisine: meatballs. Another object
of interest is a collection of Sweden's
oldest dollhouses, which were
apparently meant for adults.
i Admission SEK 120; free audio guide;
tours daily at 11am and 2pm; wheelchair
accessible

VASA MUSEUM

Galärvarvsvägen 14; 8 519
548 00; www.vasamuseet.
se/en; open daily June-Aug
8:30am-6pm, Sept-May
M-Tu 10am-5pm, W 10am-
8pm, Th-Su 10am-5pm

Many Scandinavian
museums follow a similar
plan: take a boat, build
a house around it, and
voila, museum. The ship in
question is the *Vasa,* named
by and for one of those kings
of the most egotistical Vasa
dynasty, **Gustavus Adolphus.**
Unfortunately for him, it turned
out that the *Vasa* wasn't something
you wanted to have your name on;
it capsized and sank just 30 minutes
into its maiden voyage. Today, you
can learn about everything from its
construction, to how it was sailed
(briefly) and how it (would have)
performed in battle. Vasa is the most
visited museum in Scandinavia, so
anticipate crowds.

*i Admission SEK 130, students SEK 110;
tours daily June-Aug every 30min. from
9:30am-4:30pm; wheelchair accessible;
free audio guide*

OUTDOORS

ARCHIPELAGO BOAT TOUR

Strandvägen Berth 15-16; 8 120 040 45;
www.stromma.se

You've probably seen a few of the main
archipelagos, like **Djurgården** and
Södermalm, but the islands extend far
to east, all the way out into the Baltic
Sea. In all, the Stockholm Archipelago
consists of about 30,000 islands. You'll
never come close to seeing them all,
but a good place to start is with a boat
tour. Sit back and relax as you cruise
out of Stockholm and into the islands.
Your guide will explain the history of
certain buildings, as well as how some
of the sillier names came about, like
a group of islands named Monday,
Tuesday, Wednesday, etc.

*i Tours from SEK 280; 2.5-3hr tours run at
10:30am, noon, 1:30pm, and 3pm; limited
wheelchair accessibility*

SJÖCAFÉET KAYAK AND BIKE RENTAL

Galärvarvsvägen 2; 8 660 57 57; www.sjo-
cafeet.se; open daily Apr-Sept 9am-9pm

Tour agencies like to call Stockholm
the "Venice of the North" due to the
large network of canals and islands
that make up the city. That moniker
may be a bit of an overstatement,
but if you want to get closer to the
water than possible on a big motor
boat or cruise ship, kayaking is a great
option. Sjöcaféet is a café located
conveniently on the north shore of the
island Djurgården that offers kayak,
bicycle, and even peddle boat rentals
for anyone who can't decide between
the two.

*i Bicycle SEK 80 per hour, SEK 275 per
day; kayak SEK 125 per hour, SEK 400 per
day; no wheelchair accessibility*

SWEDEN STOCKHOLM

FOOD

⚿ KAJSAS FISK ($$)

Hötorgshallen 3; 8 20 72 62; www.kajsas-fisk.se; open M-Th 11am-6pm, F 11am-7pm, Sa 11am-4pm

Kajsas Fisk is located in the basement of **Hötorgshallen food hall,** surrounded by artisanal butchers and fish vendors selling things that look more like ET than fish. Most of the other restaurants around are too expensive to consider, but Kajsas Fisk has one of the better deals in the city with its fish soup: a big, steaming bowl chock-full of fish, mussels, spices, shrimp, and a dollop of secret sauce. Plus, help yourself to unlimited bread and salad.

i Entrées SEK from 100, beer from SEK 55; wheelchair accessible

JOHAN & NYSTRÖM ($$)

Swedenborgsgatan 7; 8 702 20 40; www.johanochnystrom.se; open M-F 7am-8pm, Sa-Su 8am-7pm

In a neighborhood like **Södermalm,** it takes a lot to stand out as a coffee shop. "Hip, young café," describes just about every establishment around, but Johan & Nyström is one of the best. An apron-clad barista will fix you up a cappuccino from the rainbow-striped espresso machine or a cup of coffee so smooth that even the most devoted Starbucks latte-lover will think twice before asking for milk and sugar. The outdoor seating area is shaded, so you can break out your denim overalls, Södermalm style, without breaking a sweat, even on the sunniest Stockholm day.

i Brewed coffee SEK 40, espresso drinks, tea, and tea-based drinks from SEK 30

NIGHTLIFE

⚿ AIFUR

Västerlånggatan 68b; 8 20 10 55; www.aifur.se; open M-Th 5pm-11pm, F-Sa 5pm-1am

Aifur is a restaurant and bar designed completely in the Viking tradition with replicas of spears and shields and proudly serving mead from earthenware mugs. There's live music, even on weeknights, from a variety of performers on fiddles and hand drums, all dressed the part. To top it all off,

the whole place is in a vaulted cellar designed to look like an ancient mead hall. The place couldn't be more Nordic even if Thor himself was lounging in the corner.

i Mead from SEK 90, beer from SEK 70; BGLTQ+ friendly; wheelchair accessible

⚿ BREWDOG

Ringvägen 149b; www.brewdog.com; open M-Th 4pm-midnight, F-Sa 2pm-1am, Su 2pm-11pm

The quality of the beer is not up for debate at BrewDog, a hip microbrewery in an even hipper neighborhood: Söder. Pick from a rotating carousel of house and guest brews with the inventive names you've come to expect. Forgot your overalls and man bun? Get the same effect with a glass of the Colonial Hipster, a New England IPA. Looking for something familiar? You can't go wrong with the PBR (Perhaps Blue Ribbon; get your head out of the frat house). BrewDog has a casual atmosphere perfect for nights when you want to drink, chat, and not be hungover in the morning.

i Beer SEK 70; BGLTQ+ friendly; no wheelchair accessibility

ICEBAR

Vasaplan 4; 8 505 635 20; www.icebar-stockholm.com; open M-Th 11:15am-midnight, F-Sa 11:15am-1am

You'd think that the novelty of a bar entirely made of ice would be somewhat lost in a place like Sweden, but apparently it isn't. In fact, Icebar was the world's first such establishment, and it's still going strong. The dress code is very strict: a furry poncho with attached gloves (don't worry, it looks equally ridiculous on everyone), and a glass made of ice (don't break it, or you'll have to pay for a replacement). As advertised, the walls, bar, and seats are all hewn straight from the ice, and the temperature is maintained at a positively balmy 19 degrees Farenheit. Gimmicky? Definitely a little, but that doesn't mean you can't still have a good time.

i Admission (includes first cocktail) SEK 199 pre-booked, SEK 210 at the door, cocktails SEK 95, shots SEK 75; BGLTQ+ friendly; wheelchair accessible; last entry 45min. before closing

SWEDEN ESSENTIALS

VISAS

Sweden is a member of the European Union and is part of the Schengen Area, so US citizens can stay in Sweden for up to 90 days without a visa.

MONEY

Sweden's currency is the Swedish krona, officially abbreviated SEK and locally used interchangeably with kr.

Tipping: Tipping in Sweden is neither expected nor required; a gratuity is often included in the service charge at restaurants. If there is no service charge, or if you received particularly excellent service, feel free to tip 5-10%, or to round the bill to the nearest SEK 10.

Taxes: Sweden's standard VAT rate is a steep 25%, and is included in all posted prices. Some stores in Sweden, specifically those with Global Blue stickers, will refund the VAT for goods leaving the country with you. Be sure to ask at the counter for specifics, and to save receipts for any goods for which you are claiming a refund.

SAFETY AND HEALTH

BGLTQ+ Travel: Like the rest of Scandinavia, Sweden is very progressive when it comes to BGLTQ+ rights. Hostels, restaurants, and nightlife establishments are very friendly towards the BGLTQ+ community, and many Swedish cities have dedicated BGLTQ+ nightlife venues.

Drugs and Alcohol: There is technically no purchasing age for beverages under 2.25% ABV, though stores will often set their own age limits. Alcohol stronger than 2.25% ABV is strictly regulated. It is sold in bars and restaurants, where it cannot leave the premises and the purchasing age is 18. In government-owned stores called Systembolaget, the purchasing age is 20.

SWITZERLAND

**Switzerland jams to a different beat
than the rest of Europe.** A collection of
Confederate states in the middle of the
European continent, it's surprisingly diverse,
both culturally and linguistically: you'll
find yourself speaking English, French,
German, and possibly Italian during your
stay here… maybe even during the same
day! Switzerland's cultural diversity lies, in
part, in the interplay of religions between
neighboring lands. The Zwingli Protestant
Reformation and the Calvinist movement
took place in Zürich and Geneva,
respectively. Visiting Switzerland comes
with a hefty price tag, as it happens to be
one of the most expensive countries in
Europe. But, if we had to pick a place to
cash out, this is it.

Of course, the country has more
to its name than just cheese, watches,
chocolate, skiing, and Roger Federer.
It boasts a kind of natural beauty that's
hard to find elsewhere in Europe. Your
visit to Switzerland will, without a
doubt, be heightened by breathtaking
views of pristine lakes and snow-capped
mountains.

Whether you're visiting in the summer
to paraglide in Gimmelwald or in the
winter to ski on Jungfrau, you've come
to the right place. Hike the cow-covered
trails in the mountains. Watch majestic
glaciers crash, a spectacle impossible to
make up. Take to the streets and explore the
Lac Léman area in the student-filled city of
Lausanne. Pretend to be a United Nations
diplomat in Geneva and admire one of the
grandest mountain ranges on the planet. We
can't guarantee that Switzerland will be easy
on your wallet, but we can guarantee a trip to
remember.

GENEVA

Coverage by **Alejandro Lampell**

A cosmopolitan city with a vibrant international community, Geneva is the indisputable belle of Switzerland. Situated on the shore of Lac Léman (Lake Geneva), the city is surrounded by towering, stately French Alps on all fronts, meaning you'll have unparalleled view at all times. Geneva was originally established as a Roman outpost and the city has a strong historical significance. The cathedral, a European heritage site, served as a refuge for Jean Calvin; it was here that he professed his Calvinist ideas of austerity and advocated for returning to basic interpretations of the Bible itself. Geneva's proximity to France resulted in an influx of Counter-Reformation ideas into the city, which in turn led to a mix of culture and belief still present today. Home to more than 22 international organizations including the International Committee of the Red Cross, the World Health Organization, and—how could we forget—the United Nations, the city has established itself as a powerhouse on the international stage.

ORIENTATION

The city of Geneva is located in the westernmost region of Switzerland on the southwestern shore of **Lac Léman** (Lake Geneva), with suburbs extending into neighboring France. The city is split by the **Rhône River** into **Rive Gauche,** the left bank, and **Rive Droite,** the right bank. The Rive Droite is the area of the city north of the Rhône River; here you'll find the main train station, the headquarters of several international organizations, and the airport. The nearby **Pâquis District** is filled with international restaurants and upscale hotels, and is where the city's prostitution and drug markets are most concentrated. **Vieille Ville** (Old Town), whose center is the picturesque **Place du Bourg-de-Four,** is located on the Rive Gauche. **Rue du Rhône** is one of the main shopping streets in the city, filled with upscale shops and the equivalent of Swiss shopping malls. To the northeast of the city center is **Collonge-Bellerive,** Geneva's most expensive residential area. In this neighborhood stands the **Villa Diodati,** where Mary Shelley worked on her seminal work, *Frankenstein.*

ESSENTIALS

GETTING THERE

Geneva has the second-largest international airport in Switzerland after Zürich. The airport is located 4km from the city center and is easily accessible via the public transportation system. Upon arrival at the airport, you can collect a free, 80min. public transportation ticket that covers Zone 10, Tout Genève. In order to use this ticket, you have to provide a valid plane ticket. Take the tram to the main train station, Gare de Cornavin. The main bus station is Gare Routière de Genève, located a 5min. walk from the Gare de Cornavin. This station serves both domestic and international travel. Buses are typically cheaper than trains but may not be as reliable.

GETTING AROUND

Most of Geneva can be covered on foot or bike. Rent a bike from the Genève Roule stops for 4hr of free bike-riding with a 2CHF deposit. There are six stations around the city. Geneva has a fairly efficient public transportation system (Transports Public Genevois) that includes buses, trams, and boats. Download the TP app to view the bus and tram schedule. The public transportation system is divided into different zones. Zone 10 is the zone for Tout Genève, the proper city of Geneva and suburbs. You will receive a Geneva Transport Card, which is valid for the duration of your stay (maximum 15 days). If you are planning to use the public transport system and do not have the Geneva Transport Card, then you must buy a Tout Genève pass. A one-hour ticket costs 3CHF.

PRACTICAL INFORMATION

Tourist Offices: Geneva Tourist Information Office (Rue du Mont-Blanc 18; 022 909 70 00; open M-W 9am-6pm, Th 10am-6pm, F-S 9am-6pm, Su/ public holidays 10am-4pm)

Banks/ATMs/Currency Exchange: There are banks and ATMs all over the city. One of the best currency exchange houses is Migros Change (Rue du Mont-Blanc 16; 058 573 29 40; open M-F 8:30am-6:30pm, Sa 9am-6pm).

Post Offices: There are many different post offices throughout the city, but the largest one is located by the main train station (Rue des Gares 16; 0848 888 888; open M-F 9am-7pm, Sa 9am-noon).

Internet: The city of Geneva boasts more than 78 spots with free Wi-Fi. You can get a map at the Tourist Information Office with all of the locations. You can also rent out a Wi-Fi router at the Tourist Information Center (3 days 39.90CHF, 7 days 64.90CHF, 15 days 129.90CHF).

BLGTQ+ Resources: The main BGLTQ+ helpline in Switzerland is 080 013 31 33.

EMERGENCY INFORMATION

Emergency Numbers: General (112); police (117); fire department (118); ambulance (144); Swiss Helicopter Rescue Service (1414)

Police: Fondation Privée de secours du Syndicat de la Police Judiciaire (Blvd. Carl-Vogt 17; 022 427 81 11; open M-F 9am-4pm)

US Embassy: Consular Agency in Geneva (Rue Versonnex 7; 22 840 51 60; open M-F 10am-1pm, by appointment only)

Rape Crisis Center: Rape Centre (Pl. des Charmilles 3; 022 345 20 20; information for different hotlines in Geneva can be found at www.angloinfo.com/how-to/switzerland/geneva/healthcare/support-groups).

Hospitals: Geneva University Hospital (Rue Gabrielle-Perret-Gentil 4; 022 372 33 11; open daily 24hr)

Pharmacies: Pharmacie Amavita Gare Cornavin (Gare Cornavin; 058 878 10 00; open M-Sa 7am-11pm, Su 9am-11pm)

ACCOMMODATIONS

GENEVA HOSTEL ($$)

Rue Rothschild 28-30; 022 732 62 60; www.genevahostel.ch; reception open 24hr

Wedged between the lake and a collection of international organization headquarters, Geneva Hostel has a lean look and boasts all of the amenities required while on the road: spacious rooms, sturdy wooden bunks, an attentive and welcoming staff. The modern, cubic lounge chairs in the lobby are consistently occupied, as is the upstairs terrace, which provides a stunning view of the city.

i *Dorm 36CHF; reservation recommended; max stay 6 nights; wheelchair accessible; Wi-Fi; linens included; laundry 8CHF*

CITY HOSTEL GENEVA ($$)

Rue Ferrier 2; 022 901 15 00; www.cityhostel.ch; reception open 7:30am-noon and 1pm-midnight

City Hostel Geneva provides some of the only affordable housing in this city and is usually full. It attracts a diverse community of travelers, from students on class trips to retirees celebrating dipping into their life savings. Don't let City Hostel's dilapidated block façade fool you; the inside of the hostel is very modern, boasting several useful amenities such as a laundry room, a TV room (which tends to be underutilized), and free Wi-Fi. The hostel provides a free city transportation card for the duration of your stay and the friendly staff will eagerly provide recommendations for things to do in the surrounding area.

i *Dorms from 37CHF, privates from 90CHF; nightly parking 11CHF; reservation recommended; max stay for dorms 8 days, max for privates 21 days; BGLTQ+ friendly; no wheelchair accessibility; Wi-Fi; laundry*

SIGHTS
CULTURE

PLACE DU BOURG-DE-FOUR

Pl. du Bourg-de-Four; open daily 24hr

Formerly a cattle marketplace and a Roman forum, the Place du Bourg-de-Four is now a lively square in the middle of **Old Town.** Enjoy an espresso on the patio of one of various cafés and relax in the shadows cast by eighteenth-century buildings, squeezed tightly together along the perimeter of the square. At night, the square glows a pale yellow—lit up by vintage bistro lights and the laughter of patrons.
i *Restaurant prices vary; limited wheelchair accessibility*

LANDMARKS

🔾 JET D'EAU

Central Lake Geneva (corner of Quai Gustave Ador and Rue du 31); open daily Jan 2-Mar 5 10am-4pm; Mar 6-Apr 30 M-Th 10am-sunset, F-Su 10am-10:30pm; daily May 1-Sept 10 9am-11:15pm; Sept 11-Oct 29 M-Th 10am-sunset, F-Su 10am-10:30pm; daily Nov 16-Mar 4 10am-4pm

Originally built to control the excess pressure from a hydraulic plant, this fountain has become a symbol of innovation and progress. Situated right at the harbor where the **River Rhône** meets the lake, the enormous stream is visible from almost anywhere in the city. After sunset, lights illuminate the water and create a surreal display of colors. Make sure to bring a bathing suit if you plan to get up close and personal; the wind tends to change quickly by the waterfront, and what appear to be dry docks could become soaking wet in a matter of seconds.
i *Free; wheelchair accessible*

🔾 PALAIS DES NATIONS

Pregny Gate (Av. de la Paix 14); 022 917 12 34; www.unog.ch/visits; open Sep-Mar M-F 10am-noon and 2pm-4pm, Apr-Aug M-Sa 10am-noon and 2pm-4pm

At the Palais des Nations, the only thing keeping you from the paradise of tangible social progress is an airport-style security checkpoint. Contrary to what one might assume, tours of this complex begin at the back of the palace, not the flag-lined main entrance. If you visit during a conference, you may have the rare opportunity of sitting in on an actual **United Nations** meeting. If your timing doesn't line up, rest assured that you'll still be able to explore the very same rooms that have hosted some of the greatest debates in human history. Make sure to check out the **Broken Chair Sculpture,** a monument imagined and constructed in the adjacent plaza by Swiss artist **Daniel Berset** after the passing of the **Ottawa Treaty,** on your way out.
i *Admission adult 12CHF, students 10CHF, children 7CHF; wheelchair accessible; tours at 10:30am, noon, 2:30pm, and 4pm; visitors must check luggage and large personal items*

CATHÉDRALE ST. PIERRE

Place du Bourg-de-Four 24; 022 311 75 75; www.cathedrale-geneve.ch; open June 1-Sept 30 M-F 9:30am-6:30pm, Sa 9:30am-5pm, Su noon-6:30pm (bell ringing 5pm, organ concert 6pm); Jan 10-May 31 M-Sa 10am-5:30pm, Su noon-5:30pm

The place of **John Calvin's** revolutionary sermons, St. Pierre's Cathedral—a **European Heritage Site**—is located in the heart of Geneva's old city. The building's ornate façades contrast sharply with its simple Protestant interior—a physical testament to the city's diverse cultural composition. Two towers jut from the roof of the church: the southern-facing one holds five bells, while the northern one boasts a stunning panoramic view of the city and of the **Jet d'Eau** in the distance.
i *Church entrance free, entrance to tower 5CHF, children (6-16) 2CHF; last entry to tower 30min. before closing; limited wheelchair accessibility*

MUSEUMS

🔾 MUSÉE INTERNATIONAL DE LA CROIX-ROUGE ET DU CROIS-SANT-ROUGE

Avenue de la Paix 17; 022 748 95 11; www.redcrossmuseum.ch; open Nov-Mar Tu-Su 10am-5pm, Apr-Oct Tu-Su 10am-6pm

This museum addresses three problems facing modern society: the defense of human dignity, reconstruction of family links, and reduction of natural risks— all through a series of eye-opening exhibits and testimonials from those suffering from different forms of marginalization or displacement. Appropriately located near the headquarters of the **Red Cross Organization,** this museum is a necessary and worthwhile stop on any tour of Geneva.

i Adults 15CHF, students and seniors (65+) 7CHF; wheelchair accessible

MICROCOSM MUSEUM (CERN)

Route de Meyrin 385; 022 767 84 84; www.microcosm.web.cern.ch; open M-F 8:30am-5:30pm, Sa 9am-5pm (closed May 1st, May 25th, June 5th); Universe of Particles exhibition open M-Sa 10am-pm

At the edge of the Swiss country lies the CERN Large Hadron Collider, one of the largest research institutes in the world. At the Microcosm Museum, you'll learn all about the technology behind the equipment, the discoveries, and life at CERN from video testimonials. Just across the French border is the **Universe of Particles,** an interactive exhibit that describes the beginning of the universe and the composition of matter in a futuristic-style room. The 30-minute ride from the city might seem long, but these fun—and most importantly free—museums can keep people of all ages entertained the whole day.

i Free; limited wheelchair accessibility; guided tours at 11am and 1pm

OUTDOORS

JARDIN D'ANGLAIS

Quai du Général-Guisan 34; www.ville-geneve.ch/plan-ville/parcs-jardins-plages-bains-publics/jardin-anglais; open daily 24hr

Inspired by the landscape architecture characteristic of English gardens, this small park overlooking Lake Geneva and the famous Jet d'Eau provides a respite from the city. Highlights include

the **Flower Clock,** which consists of more than 12,000 individual plantings, and the **National Monument,** which honors Geneva's incorporation into the Swiss confederation.

i Free; wheelchair accessible

FOOD

BIRDIE ($$)

Rue des Bains 40; 022 320 29 00; www.birdiecoffee.com; open Tu-F 8am-6pm, Sa-Su 10am-6pm

A small coffee shop that offers all of the staples—cappuccinos, lattes, macchiatos, espressos—Birdie was one of our favorite hubs of grub-workplace-caffeination stations in Geneva. Brunch-style meals are offered every day between 8:30am and 2:30pm, and if you don't happen to like the beans Birdie keeps in stock, you can ask a barista to grind your own beans for you. Sip away to the tune of smooth jazz and indulge in even smoother Wi-Fi.

i Coffee from 4CHF, entrées from 16CHF; vegetarian options available; wheelchair accessible

BOKY ($)

Rue des Alpes 21; 022 738 37 94; open M-Sa 11am-11pm

Boky does Chinese comfort food and does it well. With heaping plates and prices geared towards a backpacking budget, this is a great place to come with friends and

sample several dishes. Swing by on weekdays at noon for all-you-can-eat buffet (22.50CHF) of fried noodles, dumplings, and Beijing duck.

i *Appetizers 8CHF, entrées 16CHF; vegetarian options available; wheelchair accessible*

INGLEWOOD ($)

Blvd. du Pont-d'Arve 44; 022 320 38 66; www.inglewood.ch; open M-Sa 11:30am-2:30pm and 7pm-10pm

Why someone would want to name a restaurant after the city of Inglewood escapes us. What doesn't escape us is the memory of sinking our teeth into Pasadena for the first time. *No, not the city, silly. The burger!* Inglewood's menu consists primarily of burgers named after cities in California. Unlike the drought-stricken state, these puppies are *juicy*—no dryness here. Like the Golden State, however, Inglewood's buns are smooth and tan, grilled to perfection before functioning as the capstones to each delicious package. Flash your student ID for a free drink.

i *Burger meal from 15CHF; vegetarian options available; wheelchair accessible*

NIGHTLIFE

BARBERSHOP

Blvd. Georges-Favon 14; 022 320 71 92; open M-W 11:30am-midnight, Th 11:30am-1am, F 11:30am-2am, Sa 6:30pm-2am

This bar is decorated with objects you're likely find in any American frat house: empty liquor bottles, inflatable objects, signposts, and posters line the walls. An obvious favorite among students, Barbershop is the place to go if you're looking to meet locals and try some out-of-the-box cocktail concoctions.

i *Beers from 5CHF, shots 5CHF, cocktails 15CHF; BGLTQ+ friendly; wheelchair accessible*

LE KRAKEN

Rue de l'École-de-Médecine 8; 022 321 59 41; www.lekrakenbar.ch; open M-Th 11am-1am, F 11am-2am, Sa 1pm-2am

With mahogany walls, velvet chairs, and the aroma of aged whiskey, Le Kraken looks more like a CEO's study than a bar. Tattoo-clad bartenders move quickly behind the large bar, serving up classic and novel concoctions like piña coladas and spiked ginger lemonade. If nothing on the menu is to your liking, a bartender will whip up something satisfying on the spot. Grab your drink and head out back, where you'll find a small secret garden.

i *Shots from 5CHF, cocktails 15CHF, beer from 5CHF*

L'ELÉPHANT DANS LA CANETTE

Av. du Mail 18; 022 321 70 70; www.elephantdanslacanette.ch; open M-Tu 11am-1am, W 7am-1am, Th 11am-1am, F 11am-2am, Sa 7am-2am, Su 4pm-midnight

Ever thought about what would happen if you downed a hundred shots in a single night? Well, you could theoretically find out the answer to that question at L'Eléphant (100 shots, 300CHF), but after conducting our own research, we strongly advise against it. Whether you're looking to party or kick back with a pitcher of beer (1.5L, 14CHF) and a couple friends, L'Eléphant dans la Canette, with its wide variety of cocktails, relaxed ambiance, and dirt-cheap booze, is sure to fulfill your nightlife needs.

i *Beer from 3CHF, cocktails from 8CHF, shots 5CHF; BGLTQ+ friendly; no wheelchair accessibility*

GIMMELWALD

Coverage by **Alejandro Lampell**

"You're going to Gimmelwald? You probably mean 'Grindelwald!'"
"No, *Gim-mel-wald.*"
"Are you sure?"
This is the default conversation you will have with most Swiss people, who are convinced that you want to go visit Dumbledore's childhood friend-turned-nemesis. Stand your ground and tell them proudly it is, without a doubt, Gimmelwald that you seek. This is a small village, and, when we say small, we mean that locals are

outnumbered by livestock. Together with the neighboring village of Mürren, these gems are some of the last traffic-free towns in Switzerland, situated a mile off the ground at the base of the Bernese Alps.

With miles and miles of hiking trails and countless activities from paragliding to biking to climbing, Gimmelwald is the perfect getaway for the adventurous backpacker. During the winter, these towns double as ski resorts—picturesque wooden cabins are blanketed with a thick layer of powdery snow. It puts the renowned ski destinations of the United States to shame; Colorado and Vermont look like washed out waterways in comparison to the pristine slopes of the Jungfrau ski region. Granted, the trek to get here might be difficult, but the views, wide array of outdoor activities, and culture justify the trip.

ORIENTATION

Gimmelwald and Mürren are on the area known as the **Berner Oberland** (Bernese Highlands), which are the highest mountains in the canton of **Bern**, south of **Interlaken**. The mountain on which these two towns are located—**Schilthorn**—is southwest of the **Jungfrau, Eiger,** and **Mönch,** facing the valley where **Stechelberg** is located. Gimmelwald and Mürren are located approximately 45 minutes apart by foot, with an altitude increase of 1000 feet between the two, respectively (facing Schilthorn, Mürren is located upwards to the right of Gimmelwald). The Schwarzmönch mountain blocks the view of the Jungfrau, Eiger, and Monch; however, if you take a hike towards **Grütschalp,** they soon come into view. The **James Bond Museum** and **Piz Gloria** are located at the top of the Schilthorn.

ESSENTIALS

GETTING THERE

Getting to Gimmelwald is a worthy trek. The Bernese Oberland region is accessed almost exclusively from Interlaken, the closest major city. Many cities around Switzerland and neighboring countries connect Interlaken via train. From Interlaken Ost (there are two train stations in Interlaken, one in the eastern part of the city and the other in the west) take a 20min. regional train ride to Lauterbrunnen. From here, take a train to Grütschalp and a cable car to Mürren. To reach Gimmelwald, you can take a subsequent cable car or hike downhill 45min. Another way to get there involves taking a 10min. bus ride from Lauterbrunnen to Stechelberg. The bus is located outside the train station and there are instructions to the bus area, which is usually in front of a bakery. Once you have made it to Stechelberg, take the cable car up to Gimmelwald (10min.). If you are driving, you can park your car in Lauterbrunnen or Stechelberg at one of the designated car parking spots and then follow the aforementioned steps. Mürren and Gimmelwald are not accessible by car or any other conventional method not listed here.

GETTING AROUND

The primary way to get around is by hiking. From Gimmelwald to Mürren, it is a 45min. uphill hike. Trails go all the way to Schilthorn or down to Stechelberg, but they are difficult, so exercise caution if you attempt them. Cable car is the most convenient method of transportation. Gimmelwald has only one cable car station whereas Mürren has both a cable car station and a train station *(Bahnstation)*. The cable car follows the Stechelberg-Gimmelwald-Mürren-Birg-Schilthorn route, so you must get off at each station and board a different cable car. There are connections every 30min. from Stechelberg, with departures from 7:25am-4:25pm. Departures to the peak from the valley occur every 25 and 55min. past the hour. Departures to the valley from the peak are every three and 33min. past the hour. The last ride departs at 5:55pm. Last departure for Stechelberg-Gimmelwald-Mürren is at 11:45pm on Su-Th and at 12:55pm F-Sa. There are extended sunrise and sunset times during July and August. For an adult, the Stechelberg-Schilthorn roundtrip is 84CHF and Mürren-Schilthorn roundtrip is 66CHF. For children (6-16) the Stechelberg-Schilthorn roundtrip is 42CHF and the Mürren-Schilthorn roundtrip is 33CHF. The cable car is occasionally closed for maintenance during the spring and fall seasons, so make sure to check beforehand.

A train connects Mürren, Winteregg, and Grütschalp. From Grütschalp, a cable car can be taken to Lauterbrunnen. The train travels through towns in the mountain, whereas, in the other path, you should take a bus to cross the valley. A ticket from Lauterbrunnen to Mürren costs 25.20CHF roundtrip, while that from Interlaken Ost to Mürren costs 40.40CHF.

In this region of Switzerland, transportation is more expensive than you would think, so you should consider the different options available at the SBB train company. You might consider getting a half-fare card for one month for 120CHF (applies to all public transport) or the Swiss Travel Pass (216-458CHF depending on duration), which provides free access to public transport (often including funiculars and boats) and free entrance to museums. Another option is the Tell Pass, which is great for this region as it includes travel on all trains, buses, boats and aerial cable ways for 2 days (180CHF), 3 days (210CHF), 4 days (230CHF), 5 days (220CHF), or 10 days (300CHF).

Besides those options, there are some more particular to the region. You can get the Ferienpass Mürren-Schilthorn, which allows as many trips as desired on Schilthornbahn Cable Car, bus line Lauterbrunnen-Isenfluh, and cableway Isenfluh-Sulwald, 4 days (adults 140CHF, kids 93CHF) or 6 days (adults 160CHF, kids 103CHF). Alternatively, the Regionalpass Berner Oberland includes tickets for transportation by train, boat, bus and cable car on selected routes in Bernese Oberland 4 days (250CHF), 6 days (310CHF), 8 days (350CHF), 10 days (390CHF). The Swiss Travel Pass and half-fare card will decrease these costs.

PRACTICAL INFORMATION

Tourist Offices: The nearest tourist information center is in Mürren, a 45min. hike north of Gimmelwald (3825 Mürren; 033 856 86 86; open mid-June to mid-Oct 8:30am-6:45pm, daily mid-Oct to mid-Dec 8:30am-noon and 1pm-5pm, daily mid-Dec to mid-Apr 8:30am-7:45pm, daily mid-Apr to mid June 8:30am-noon, 1pm-5pm).

Banks/ATMs/Currency Exchange: The nearest ATM is located at the cable car station in Mürren (Schilthornbahn). The closest bank is in Lauterbrunnen (Bank EKI Cooperative; Railway station 473a; 033 855 36 55; open M-F 8am-noon, only M and F 2pm-5pm).

Post Offices: Post agency in Coop store (Dorfstrasse 1032; 033 225 29 70; open M-F 8am-noon and 1:45pm-6:30pm, Sa 8am-noon and 1:45pm-5pm)

Internet: There is free Wi-Fi in the Tourist Information Center in Mürren and in the cable car station in Mürren (Schilthornbahn). Visitors can rent pocket Wi-Fi hotspots at Mürren for 3 days (39.90CHF), 7 days (64.90CHF), 10 days (83.40CHF), or 15 days (129.90CHF).

EMERGENCY INFORMATION

Emergency Numbers: General (112); police (117); fire department (118); ambulance (144); Swiss Helicopter Rescue Service (1414)

Police: Lauterbrunnen (Stutzli 466; 033 356 85 01; "appointment agreement by telephone")

US Embassy: The nearest US Embassy is located in Switzerland's capital, Bern (Sulgeneckstrasse 19; 031 357 70 11; appointments are available M-F 9am-11:30am, speak to representative M-F 2pm-4pm).

Hospitals: The closest doctor is in Lauterbrunnen and the closest hospital is in Interlaken.
- Caremed Praxis (doctor) (Dokterhuus, Lauterbrunnen; 033 856 26 26)
- Regionalspital Interlaken Hospital (Weissenaustrasse 27, Unterseen; 033 826 26 26; open daily 24hr for emergencies)

Pharmacies: Wengen Apotheke (Wengiboden 1412E; 033 855 12 46; open M-F 8am-noon and 2-6:30pm, Sa 8am-noon and 2pm-6pm, Su 4-6pm)

ACCOMMODATIONS

🏚 MOUNTAIN HOSTEL ($$)

Nidrimatten, Gimmelwald; 338551704; www.mountainhostel.com; hostel open Dec 1-Mar 30, mid-Apr-Oct 31; reception open daily 8:30am-10pm

Rise and shine to stunning views of the **Bernese Alps** in this hidden gem of a hostel. You would be hard-pressed to find a homier place that attracts more genuine and down-to-earth people passionate about the outdoors. It's a little surprising that the hostel doesn't have keys, but *no keys, no problem,* we say! This is an extremely safe area. Live carefree in the mountains with incredibly helpful staff who help you make the most of your time in Gimmelwald.

i Bunks 45CHF; reservation recommended; BGLTQ+ friendly; no wheelchair accessibility; Wi-Fi; linens included; laundry 5CHF; cleaning lockout 9:30am-11am including the bathroom; quiet hours begin at midnight

EIGER GUESTHOUSE ($$$)

Aegerta 1079E; 338565460; www.eigerguesthouse.com; reception open 8am-11:30pm

Striking a fine, middle-ground line between an upper-tier hostel and lower-tier hotel, the Eiger Guesthouse boasts a prime location and stellar amenities. Situated directly in front of the train station, Eiger Guesthouse, not to be confused with its next-door neighbor, Eiger Hotel, has a diverse guest community. The classic wooden façade gives way to colorful green walls, yellow doors, and different images of the typical Alp outdoor activities: paragliding, skiing, air balloon rides. The four-bunk bedrooms are clean and have patios that offer breathtaking views. If you're looking to upgrade your stay, select a "superior room" with a television.

i Budget room 60CHF, double 160CHF; reservation recommended; BGLTQ+ friendly; no wheelchair accessibility; Wi-Fi; linens included

SIGHTS

CULTURE

UNTERSEEN

Unterseen; open daily 24hr

Situated on the eastern bank of **Lake Thun,** Unterseen (meaning Lower Lake) is the historic old town area of Interlaken, filled with classic timber-framed, flower-covered buildings. Stroll along the aqua-colored **River Aare,** passing by a thirteenth-century church and bell tower, and make a trip to the **Tourism Museum,** where you can discover how much tourism has influenced Interlaken (spoiler alert: a lot).

i Restaurant and store prices vary; free walking tours of Interlaken; tours most days at 5:45pm; limited wheelchair accessibility

LANDMARKS

🏚 SCHILTHORN AND BIRG

Schlithorn; 338260007; www.schilthorn.ch/en/welcome; daily ascents every half hour from Mürren to Schilthorn 7:25am to 4:25pm, last descent 5:55pm; cable car maintenance Nov 13-Dec 8, Apr 23-Apr 27, Nov 12-Dec 10

"The name's Bond. James Bond." Venture to Blofeld's Research Museum, hidden at the top of Schilthorn, with nothing other than an expensive cable-car ride, long wait, and crowds of tourists to slow your ascent. The top of the mountain was the set of some of the most iconic scenes of *On Her Majesty's Secret Service* (1969), one of the classic Bond movies. Apart from access to **Bond World 007,** a museum that describes the film's production in tremendous detail, the expensive cable car ride gives you access to Birg, which is close to the summit and includes a "thrill walk" over a glass bridge and down a fenced path that hugs the mountain. Above the clouds, Schilthorn and Birg provide superb views of the Bernese Alps.

i Stechelberg-Schilthorn roundtrip 105CHF, Mürren-Schilthorn roundtrip 82.20CHF; limited wheelchair accessibility

OUTDOORS

🏴 PARAGLIDING

Company headquarters in Fuhren, for paragliding, meet at the Mürren train station; 792478463; www.airtime-paragliding.ch; book appointments online

Sometimes you skip things to save money. Sometimes you splurge for worthwhile experiences. Do you cash out for a potentially life-changing adventure? It's a difficult question to answer, but we can settle this one for you: Cash. Out. *Now.* From Mürren, lift off and embark on a paragliding journey, gliding from side to side (and upside-down) as you experience the valleys and mountains of the Alps—Eiger, Mönch, and Jungfrau included—from a completely different perspective. The guide who accompanies you (and keeps you safe) will take pictures and video during your flight for a hefty price tag, but let's be real, you'll want to document it. It's exhilarating, thrilling, and unparalleled; imagine feeling simply weightless mid-air. At the end of the day, you'll remember how it felt to fly, not how it felt when money flew out of your pocket.

i *Summer paragliding 170CHF from Mürren, 180CHF winter from Mürren, 280CHF from Birg or Schilthorn; photos with GoPro 30CHF, photos and videos 40CHF; no wheelchair accessibility*

VIA FERRATA

Lower part of Mürren; 338568686; www.klettersteig-muerren.ch/index.php/en; open mid-June-mid-Oct

For the thrill-seekers not satisfied with hiking, follow the Via Ferrata, which translates to "the way of the iron" in Italian. You'll follow a protected climbing route while being harnessed on to an iron rope on a mountainside. Unlike most "iron ways," this one travels downward instead of upwards, from its starting point in Mürren down to Gimmelwald, and covers over 2.2 kilometers. Be warned: this is not an easy trail and, for first-timers, it's best to book a guided tour at the Tourist Office.

i *Free admission; equipment rental at Intersport Stäger Sport 25 CHF or Alfred's Sporthaus 22CHF; book guided tours with Schweizer Bergsportschule Grindelwald-SPORTS (33 854 12 80); no wheelchair accessibility*

MOUNTAIN VIEW TRAIL

www.gimmelwald.ch/e/activities/summer/hiking.htm

Baby, *this* is what you came for. After countless hours of travel and expensive transportation, you've made it and, now, you can enjoy nature's beauty at no cost whatsoever. There are over 800 kilometers of footpaths in the **Jungfrau** mountain region, many of which are easily accessible from Gimmelwald and Mürren. Whether you're a novice or a well-worn expert, you'll find a path suited to your ability, each with its individually breathtaking view. We recommend the Mountain View Trail, which departs from Mürren, travels along the ridge of the mountain, and winds through meadows and forests.

i *Free; no wheelchair accessibility*

TRÜMMELBACHFÄLLE

Trümmelbachfälle, CH-3824 Trümmelbach; 338553232; www.truemmelbachfaelle.ch; open daily mid-Apr-June 9am-5pm, July-Aug 8:30am-6pm, Sept-early Nov 9am-5pm

Feel tiny and powerless at this **UNESCO World Natural Heritage site** as 20,000 liters (per second) of melted glacier come crashing down in front of you. The Trümmelbach Falls is a set of ten waterfalls that exclusively drain the water coming down from the glaciers on the **Eiger, Mönch,** and **Jungfrau** mountains. The rails and tunnels that meander through the mountains provide astounding views of the crashing water. Not down for hiking but still up for the views? Take the elevator up to the sixth waterfall and walk your way down.

i *Adult admission 11CHF, children (6-16years) 4CHF; last elevator ride 30min before closing; limited wheelchair accessibility*

FOOD

EIGER GUESTHOUSE RESTAURANT ($$$)

Aegerta 1079E, Mürren; 338565460; www.eigerguesthouse.com; open daily from 11:30am-10pm

Located in front of the main train station, this locale offers a wide variety of food—from pasta and pizza to Swiss specialties and *bratwurst*—for reasonable prices. Opt for the 23.50CHF per person fondue, arguably the best quality-quantity ratio in Mürren.

i *Entrées from 18CHF; card min of 20CHF; vegetarian options available; wheelchair accessible*

RESTAURANT MOUNTAIN HOSTEL ($)

Nidrimatten, Gimmelwald; 338551704; www.mountainhostel.com; open daily 11am-8pm

Why leave the comfort of your hostel when it offers delicious pizza right downstairs? Call ahead and order a basic margherita pizza (16CHF) or a pie with mixed toppings (19CHF), both of which are big enough to feed two hungry hikers. If you're not in the mood for pizza, the daily specials range from a big plate of spaghetti to a Swiss specialty of *raclette* with potatoes. Sit at the familial picnic tables inside or, if the weather permits, the ones outside with a clear view of the **Schwarzmönch mountain** up ahead.

i *Pizza from 16CHF, entrées from 18CHF; vegetarian options available; no wheelchair accessibility*

SNACKBAR BERRY ($$)

Bir Schiir 1056, Mürren; 077 496 14 36; open M-Tu, Th-Su 7:30am-5:30pm

Snackbar Berry is a do-it-all store, complete with strong coffee, scrumptious noodles, juicy hamburgers, Dutch delicacies called stroopwafel, and complimentary Wi-Fi.

i *Dishes from 10CHF; cash only; vegetarian options available; limited wheelchair accessibility*

THAM CHINESE RESTAURANT ($$$)

Rouft 1067A CH-3825, Mürren; 338560110; www.tham.ch/chinesisches-restaurant/chinese-food.html; open daily noon-9pm

Up in the Alps, where livestock outnumber humans and mountains tower above you, the last thing you expect to find is a Chinese restaurant. Tham serves typical Chinese fare from fried rice to Szechuan beef and duck, all for a reasonable price tag. A family business, this small locale has comfortable wooden tables and chairs and an open kitchen. Let the swinging paws of the doll cats lure you in and stay for the comfort food.

i *Entrées from 18CHF; vegetarian options available; wheelchair accessible*

NIGHTLIFE

MOUNTAIN HOSTEL BAR

Nidrimatten, Gimmelwald; 338551704; www.mountainhostel.com; open daily 11am-10pm

The options for nightlife are limited in a village of 130 people, but fear not, dear backpacker, there are ways to turn up even here. Pop by the reception-turned-bar at Mountain Hostel, where weary backpackers gather to kick back, share a brew, and recount crazy stories. The bar has two different tap beers, dark and light, and shots from bottles hung wrong-side-up from the ceiling. If you are up for the challenge, ask for the 1-liter beer boot or, if you really dare, its big-footed 2-liter sibling.

i *Beer 5.50CHF, shots 5CHF; BGLTQ+ friendly; no wheelchair accessibility*

TÄCHI BAR (HOTEL EIGER)

Aegerten; 338565454; www.hoteleiger.
com/en/taechi-bar; open M-Th 11:30am-
11:30pm, F-Sa 11:30am-noon

Below one of Mürren's most prestigious
hotels, Hotel Eiger, Tächi Bar looks like
an upscale ski cabin and is the closest
you will get to nightlife in Mürren. An
illuminated bar stocked with the likes
of Grey Goose and Bombay lines the
back wall and is attended to by friendly
bartenders in red vests and bowties.
With decorations of skiing equipment
and seating around a fireplace, the
mountain cabin feel permeates this
joint. On weekends, Tächi hosts DJs
and opens up the speckled dancefloor,
attracting a slightly younger clientele
than it would on the weekdays.

i *Beer from 4.50CHF, shots 6.50CHF, mixed
drinks from 12CHF; BGLTQ+ friendly; wheelchair accessible*

LAUSANNE

Coverage by **Alejandro Lampell**

Usually overlooked by the neighboring Geneva, "Lausanne-geles," as the young locals
jokingly call it, is a university town with a bustling cultural life and fascinating history.
Lausanne, originally called Lousonna, was founded as a Roman military camp built
over a Celtic settlement in 15BCE and has seen large amounts of structural and
cultural changes throughout the ages. Most of the changes come from the influence
of the Zwingli Protestant Reformation and the Counter-Reformation; the former is
more prominent in the eastern part of the city while the later manifests in the French-
speaking regions. Lausanne's Ouchy district, located on the shores of beautiful Lac
Léman, has served as the headquarters for the International Olympic Committee since
1915, and the Flon district boasts a vibrant nightlife scene and is the hub of the first
fully automated metro in Switzerland.

ORIENTATION

Lausanne, on the northeast shores of **Lac Léman,** is in Switzerland's western, French-
speaking region. Centuries ago, affluent residents owned homes on the plateau to
avoid diseases, which is why you'll find most of the main tourist attractions, including
the **Cathédrale,** on a hillside overlooking the rest of the city. The center of the city
covers part of an ancient river called the **Flon** upon which the **Rue Centrale** now
runs. This is especially confusing because maps do not show the different levels, so you
can get lost trying to determine whether to stay on the lower road or take an upper
bridge connecting different neighborhoods. The city is divided into different districts.
The **Vieille Ville** district (Old Town) is where you'll find the **Cathédrale, St. Francis
Church,** and the **Rue de Bourg,** a major shopping area. To the south of Vieille Ville
is the **Flon District,** which has recently undergone major renovations and now houses
the city's nightlife and different cultural events. The two metro lines intersect at the
Flon stop. The **Ouchy District,** home to the renowned **Olympic Museum** and is
the most scenic part of the town, located adjacent to the lake. Just inland of the **Plage
de Vidy** lies the **Université de Lausanne** and the **École Polytechnique Fédérale de
Lausanne.**

ESSENTIALS
GETTING THERE

Most travelers travel to Lausanne via
the Swiss Federal Rail System (SBB).
The main train station (Lausanne Gare)
connects to Geneva, Zürich, Bern,
and several other cities (both domestic
and international) with trains running
between 4:45am and 1:30am every
30min. There are direct trains from
Geneva Airport to Lausanne (45 min.).
Check out super-saver tickets, which offer
reduced fares (50%-off) for SBB train
rides. The closest international airport to
Lausanne is in Geneva, which has daily
international connecting flights to the

United States. Although uncommon, you can take a boat ride from Geneva to Lausanne during high season, which costs around 45CHF and takes 4hr. Buses connect Lausanne to major Swiss, French, and Spanish cities. These are usually cheaper but take longer than a train ride. If you manage to score a deal on a train ticket, opt for that over a bus.

GETTING AROUND

Lausanne is easily walkable. Since much of the city is located on a hillside, there are different levels to streets. Almost all accommodations give out the Lausanne Transport card, which grants free public transport (bus, train, and metro for a maximum of 15 days) in zones 11, 12, 15, 16, and 18 and discounts on museums tickets and boat rides. Lausanne has a small subway system with two metro lines, both of which intersect at the Flon station. The M1 line runs to the west towards University of Lausanne and the Ecole Polytechnique Fédérale de Lausanne, while the M2 line runs north-south, from Epalinges to Ouchy, right next to Lac Léman. You can buy tickets (1hr 3.60CHF, 1 day 9.30CHF) at blue machines in bus/train/metro stations; remember to validate your ticket before riding. Buses run from 5am-midnight. There are additional late-night buses on F, Sa, and Su from 1am-4am.

PRACTICAL INFORMATION

Tourist Offices: Tourist Information Center (Pl. de la Navigation 6; 021 613 73 21; high season open daily from 9am-7pm, low season 9am-6pm)

Banks/ATMs/Currency Exchange: ATMs are easily accessible throughout the city. Here's the information for one bank: Cembra Money Bank AG Lausanne (Av. Louis-Ruchonnet 1; 21 310 40 50; open M-F 9am-6pm).

Post Offices: Av. de la Gare 43B; 0848 888 888; open M-F 8am-8pm, Sa 8am-4pm, Su 4pm-7pm

Internet: Wi-Fi is available throughout the main train station, but you need a Swiss number to access it. Free Wi-Fi is available at tourist information centers, in front of the lake, and in the main areas of the city.

BGLTQ+ Resources: The main BGLTQ+ helpline in Switzerland is 080 013 31 33.

EMERGENCY INFORMATION

Emergency Numbers: General (112); police (117); fire department (118); ambulance (144); Swiss Helicopter Rescue Service (1414)

Police: There is a city and a canton police. The city police are easily accessible (Hôtel de Police de Lausanne; Rue Saint-Martin 33; 021 315 15 15; open daily from 6am-9pm; 24hr emergency services available).

US Embassy: The closest Consular Agency in located in Geneva (Rue Versonnex 7; 22 840 51 60; open M-F 10am-1pm, by appointment only).

Rape Crisis Center: The domestic abuse hotline for all of Switzerland is 147.

Hospitals: Centre Hospitalier Universitaire Vaudois (Rue du Bugnon 46; 021 314 11 11; open daily 24hr)

Pharmacies: Pharmacie 24 (Av. de Montchoisi 1; 021 613 12 24; open daily 8am-midnight)

ACCOMMODATIONS

YOUTH HOSTEL - JEUNOTEL ($$)

Chemin du Bois-de-Vaux 36; 021 626 02 22; www.youthhostel.ch/en/hostels/lausanne; reception open 24hr

Away from the bustle of **Vieille Ville** and just steps from the very popular **Plage de Vidy,** Youth Hostel Jeunotel practically skims the water of **Lac Léman.** This concrete and glass behemoth seems more like a hotel than a hostel as it's frequented by a wide range of people: families, school groups, and everything in between. Jeunotel lacks a backpacking culture. But, if you're just looking for a place to kick back, work on your tan, and figure out Lausanne's map system, Youth Hostel Jeunotel may be the option for you.

i Dorms from 46CHF, doubles from 107CHF; reservation recommended; max stay 7 nights; BGLTQ+ friendly; limited wheelchair accessibility; Wi-Fi; linens included; laundry; breakfast included

SIGHTS

LANDMARKS

CATHÉDRALE DE LAUSANNE

Pl. de la Cathédrale; 021 316 71 60; www.cathedrale-lausanne.ch; open daily Oct-Mar 9am-5:30pm, Apr-Sept M-Sa 9am-7pm, Su 10am-6pm; prayer service M-F 7:30am; tower visit open M-Sa 9:30am-5:30pm, Su 1pm-5pm

On a hilltop overlooking the city, the Cathédrale de Lausanne stands tall as the religious hub of Switzerland's French-speaking region. The stalls, located in what used to be the main entrance, display fading colored sculptures, a sign of the Catholic roots of the Cathédrale before the influence of Zwingli's Reformation struck. Take the set of winding stone steps to the top of the tower for a stunning view of the city, lake region, and collection of bells that dates back to the thirteenth-century.

i Free; tower admission adult 5CHF, students 3CHF; last entry 30min. before closing; limited wheelchair accessibility

CHÂTEAU SAINTE MARIE

Rie du Port-Franc 18; 021 316 40 40; exterior open daily 24hr

The Château Sainte Marie is a beautiful medieval castle commissioned by the Bishops of Lausanne in the fifteenth century and has undergone a series of refurbishments in recent years. The bishops chose this location (atop a massive hill) to dissuade peasants from squatting on its doorstep. Today, it does just the opposite, attracting tens of thousands of tourists each year. Unfortunately, the interior is still not open to the public, so you won't be able to catch a glimpse of the pristine frescoes nor the members of the cantonal government, who use the castle as a meeting place. You will, however, be greeted by some seriously impressive architecture and sweeping views of the city below.

i Free; interior closed to the public; limited wheelchair accessibility

ÉGLISE SAINT-FRANCOIS (CHURCH OF ST. FRANCIS)

Pl. St-Francois; 021 331 56 38; www.sainf.ch; open Tu-F 10am-noon and 4pm-6:40pm

You'll find this large Franciscan-monastery-turned-Protestant-church tucked among the chic boutiques of the **Place St-Francois.** Dating back to the thirteenth century, the Church of St. Francis has undergone countless renovations; it currently serves as a hub for concerts and art exhibitions. Attend one of the **St. Francis Concerts** (every Saturday) to hear the organ boom, and swing by the outdoor market on your way out.

i Free; no wheelchair accessibility

MUSEUMS

COLLECTION DE L'ART BRUT

Av. des Bergières 11; 021 315 25 70; www.artbrut.ch; open Sept-June Tu-Su 11am-6pm, daily July-Aug 11am-6pm

"Art Brut is art brut and it is well understood everywhere. Not that well? Well, that is why we are curious to go and see for ourselves," said **Jean Dubuffet,** the creator of the **Art Brut** movement. This quote, plastered on the outside of the museum, describes a movement composed of art created by historically marginalized individuals. The works are distinguishable by their use of bright colors, abstract images, and incomprehensible symbols. They typically touch upon themes of loss, hospitalization, and abandonment.

i Adult 10CHF, students 5CHF, groups of 6 5CHF per person, children under 16 free, first Sa of the month free; last entry 5:30pm; no wheelchair accessibility

MUSÉE DE L'ELYSÉE

Av. de l'Elysée 18; 021 316 99 11; www.elysee.ch; open Tu-Su 11am-6pm

In a dark room illuminated with projections of photographs and filled with the sounds of acoustic music, images switch in sync with each strum of a guitar. This is the scene at Musée de l'Elysée, Lausanne's only museum dedicated entirely to photography. New exhibitions pop up every few months and delve into the art, incorporating key aspects of history and interpretation. In the attic, the museum has an interactive station that offers you a chance to listen to professionals' interpretations of the photographs and a chance for you to test your hand with a camera.

i *Combined entrance and magazine 15CHF, entrance to museum 8CHF, seniors 6CHF, students 4CHF; free for art students, kids under 16, and everyone the first Sa of every month; last entry 5:30pm; free tour first Sa of month at 4pm; limited wheelchair accessibility*

OUTDOORS

ESPLANADE DE MONTBENON

Allée Ernest-Ansermet 3; open daily 24hr

Pristine green lawns, well-kept bushes, and blossoming flowers make up the Esplanade de Montbenon, which boasts a view of the houses next to the lake below. An unkempt vineyard in the fourteenth century, this (now) public park has developed with the city: the introductions of the **Palais de Justice** and the Casino in the nineteenth and twentieth centuries, respectively, brought with them the introduction of flower patches and chestnut trees. This is a popular hangout for students and families alike, so if you find yourself in need of a break from monument-hopping, make like a local and plant yourself in the shade of a tree for some well-deserved R&R.

i *Free; limited wheelchair accessibility*

FOOD

BLACKBIRD ($$)

Rue Cheneau-de-Bourg 1; 021 323 76 76; www.blackbirdcafé.ch; open M-F 7:30am-3pm, Sa 8am-4pm, Su 9am-3:30pm

Breakfast all day, every day—exactly the way it should be. Blackbird is the "Breakfast Club" of Lausanne. Antique bottles and black and white paintings of black birds give this locale an alternative feel. Enjoy culinary classics from around the world: a spicy breakfast burrito, pancakes and eggs, and even Nordic smoked salmon.

i *Entrées from 14CHF; vegetarian options available; limited wheelchair accessibility*

CARROUSEL BURGER ($)

1006 Lausanne; open daily 10am-midnight in summer, shorter hours in winter

Named after the iconic children's **Carrousel d'Ouchy,** this small restaurant offers a wide variety of fair fare to enjoy next to the aqua-colored **Lac Léman.** A favorite among families and students, the menu includes an array of ice cream flavors and "granite" (flavored shredded ice), perfect for a hot summer day. In the mood for a larger meal? Enjoy a cheeseburger on a baguette or a classic croque-monsieur. If you're anything like us, you'll gobble it up within minutes of receiving it, if not out of hunger then out of the desire to avoid the predatory glances of the ducks and birds swarming around your feet.

i *Entrées from 10CHF; vegetarian options available; wheelchair accessible*

PZ PIZZA ($$)

Rue Grand-St-Jean 5; 021 312 82 82; www.pzpizza.ch; open M-Sa 11:30am-10:30pm

The periodic table is missing an element: Pz. The restaurant plays on the element theme by asking you to pick a basic base (type of sauce, type of cheese) and toppings designated by chemical symbols. The toppings are even divided into groups much like a periodic table. Would you like an alkili or a halogen today?

i *Entrées from 12CHF; vegetarian options available; limited wheelchair accessibility*

NIGHTLIFE

LES ARCHES

Route de Bel-Air; www.lesarches.ch; open M-W 11am-midnight, Th 11am-1am, F-Sa 11am-2am, Su 1pm-midnight

Located under the **Grand Pont,** Les Arches is open all day, so you can slowly transition from enjoying a powerful espresso to a smooth mojito without ever leaving the comfort of your chair. At night, the understaffed bartenders tend to be attacked from all sides by thirsty customers, so make sure to get there early, order a drink, and reserve a good seat to enjoy the cool night breeze and live music in the **Place de l'Europe.**

i *Shots 6CHF, beer from 5CHF, cocktails from 9CHF; wheelchair accessible*

XOXO BAR

R. des Côtes-de-Montbenon 20; 021 311 29 55; open Tu-W 11:45am-2pm and 6pm-midnight, Th 11:45am-2pm and 6pm-1am, F 11:45am-2pm and 6pm-2am, Sa 6pm-2am

Located on a rooftop and outfitted with chic lounge chairs and cream-colored patio umbrellas, Xoxo Bar is the place to be whether you want to enjoy a coffee during the day or a cocktail at night. With cocktail pitchers large enough to satisfy up to five people, the locale is perfect for lounging with friends and watching the sun set over the Lausanne skyline. If you're looking to drink underground, visit the basement's dimly-lit bistro—perfect for a low-key night with friends.

i Beer from 4.50CHF, cocktails 15CHF, cocktail pitchers 38CHF

LUCERNE

Coverage by **Alejandro Lampell**

In the heart of Switzerland, skirting a pristine lake and nestled into the foothills of the Alps, is the city of Lucerne. A lot smaller and less chaotic than other major Swiss cities, it has historically been used as a stop on the way to the impressive peaks of Pilatus, Rigi, and Stanserhorn. Its impressive legacy—the myths and legends of the surrounding area and the beauty of the city—has made the city a popular destination for tourists looking for that one-with-nature Swiss experience. Lucerne, along with Uri, Schwyz, and Unterwalden, was one of the Swiss cantons that formed the "eternal" Swiss Confederacy. History, like the gushing Reuss River, flows through the city—the current is particularly strong in the Altstadt (Old Town), which has the oldest wooden bridge in Europe, Kapellbrücke, and one of the best preserved medieval fortifications in Switzerland, Museggmauer. Like Zürich, Lucerne is a large cultural hub, that host several major music and art festivals as well as a poppin' nightlife scene. The city is also famous for Fasnacht, an annual carnival held before the start of Lent.

ORIENTATION

An hour train ride southwest of Zürich, Lucerne is smack in the middle of Switzerland, on the northwestern shore of Lake Lucerne. River Reuss cuts through the city of Lucerne on a northwest-to-east trajectory. The **Altstadt** (Old Town) is right at the mouth of the river with the Kapellbrücke crossing the Reuss diagonally. To the north of the city is **Museggmauer,** the old city's fortifications. The major mountains **Pilatus, Stanserhorn,** and **Rigi** are located south and east of the city, respectively. To visit **Mt. Pilatus,** the closest mountain, take a boat to **Alpnachstad,** a train to its summit, and a cable car to Kriens.

ESSENTIALS

GETTING THERE

The closest international airport to Lucerne is located in Zürich. From the Zürich Airport, you can take a direct train to Lucerne main train station. This train runs at least once an hour and takes around 1hr. You can also rent a car and drive down to Zürich (50min.); available parking spots are few and far between. The most common way to arrive at the city is via train. You can see whether there is a train from different cities to Lucerne at www.fahrplan.sbb.ch.

GETTING AROUND

Most of the old city can be explored on foot and lends itself to very scenic walks—the distance from the historic city wall to the train station and Kapellbrücke area is less than 1km. Within the city, the public transport is dominated by buses and local trains. The regional area is divided into zones and the city of Lucerne proper is Zone 10, which is where you will probably spend the most time. Travel within the city limits is included a Zone 10 ticket. A day-pass for zone 10 is 8.20CHF, and a single ticket for 1hr is 4.10CHF. Short-distance tickets valid for up to six stops (or 30min.) are 2.50CHF. Public transport runs roughly 5am-

12:30am, and night buses *(Nachtstern)* run F and Sa nights. As with other Swiss transport, you must validate your ticket either at the stop prior to boarding or on the bus itself.

The state-run SBB train company is exorbitantly priced, so it's worthwhile to purchase SuperSaver tickets—these are up to 50% off popular routes at off-peak times. Select the SuperSaver option at sbb. ch. If you're traveling around Switzerland a lot, you might want to consider getting a half-fare card for one month (120CHF, applies to all public transport) or the Swiss Travel pass (216-458CHF, depending on duration). If you're visiting the Alps as well as central Switzerland, consider the Tell Pass—it includes travel on all trains, buses, boats, and aerial cable ways (including Pilatus, Rigi and Titlis) for 2 (180CHF), 3 (210CHF), 4 (230CHF), 5 (220CHF), or 10 (300CHF) days. This is the best deal for traveling through the Lucerne Lake area. Boat travel ranges from 3-45CHF, bike travel about 20CHF per day, and taxis 3.50CHF/km.

Tickets for boat rides on the vast Lake Lucerne range from 3-45CHF, depending on duration. Get tickets at the blue stand at Schwanenplatz, across from the train station.

PRACTICAL INFORMATION

Tourist Offices: Several tourist offices are located in Lucerne's central train station (Zentralstrasse 5; 0 41 227 17 17; summer M-F 8:30am-7pm, Sa 9am-7pm, Su 9am-5pm; winter M-F 8:30am-5:30pm, Sa 9am-5pm, Su 9am-1pm; Apr M-F 8:30am-5:30pm, Sa-Su 9am-5pm).

Banks/ATMs/Currency Exchange: ATMs can be found outside of and near banks. Closest to the station are UBS and Credit Suisse, both just across the bridge and on the left. Use CHF to avoid poor exchange rates.

Post Offices: There are many post offices around the city. Postselle Universität has longer hours (Frohburgstrasse 3; M-F 9am-9pm, Sa 9am-4pm, Su 1:30pm-5:30pm).

Internet: Wi-Fi, "WLAN," is free in the train station and around the city center for 1hr; look for network Luzern. Register with a phone number. Many cafés, bars, and restaurants offer free Wi-Fi.

BGLTQ+ Resources: BGLTQ+ Helpline of Switzerland (Located in Bern, Monbijoustrasse 73; 080 013 31 33; hello@lgbt-helpline.ch; www. lgbt-helpline.ch/en); Queer Office hosts weekly meetings every Tuesday at Neubad to address issues affecting the BGLTQ+ community (hallo@queeroffice.ch, www. queeroffice.ch).

EMERGENCY INFORMATION

Emergency Numbers: General (112); police (117); fire department (118); ambulance (144); Swiss Helicopter Rescue Service (1414)

Police: Station Hirschengraben 17a; 041 248 86 17; open daily 7am-7pm

US Embassy: Nearest is US Consular Agency in Zürich. The US Embassy is in Bern.

Rape Crisis Center: Rape Crisis Network Europe in Switzerland, based in Geneva (3 des Charmilles; 022 345 20 20).

Hospitals: For most non-emergency problems, it is recommended that you set up an appointment at a Permanence with a doctor. There is one at Lucerne main station, open M-Th 7am-11pm, F 7am until Su 11pm nonstop (Medical Center Luzern AG; 041 211 14 44; www. permanence-luzern.ch).
• Hospital Kantonsspital Luzern (Spitalstrasse 16; 041 205 11 11; www.luks. ch; 24hr emergency services available)

Pharmacies: Pharmacies in German are called *Apotheken*. The one with the longest opening hours is in Benu, in main train station.
• Benu Bahnof Luzern (M-Sa 7:30am-10pm, Su 10am-8pm; 041 220 13 13)

ACCOMMODATIONS

🏨 BELLPARK HOSTEL ($)

Luzernerstrasse 23; 413102515; www.bell-parkhostel.ch; reception open 7:45am-10am and 4pm-11pm

Located in the small town of **Kriens**—mostly a stomping ground for people on their way back to Lucerne from **Mt. Pilatus**—Bellpark Hostel provides serenity for the weary traveler. With its eggshell white and sapphire blue façade, this welcoming hostel looks transplanted directly from the rocky cliffs of Santorini. The ground floor houses the reception, lounge area, and dining room, where backpackers sit around long wooden tables and plan the best attack on their Alp of choice. A buffet-style breakfast is included in the nightly fare and so are bus rides for the duration of your stay.

i Dorms from 27CHF, doubles from 80CHF; reservation recommended; max stay 14 days; BGLTQ+ friendly; no wheelchair accessibility; Wi-Fi; linens included; laundry 8CHF

BACKPACKERS HOSTEL ($$)

Alpenquai 42; 413600420; www.backpackerslucerne.ch/index_en.php; reception open 4:30am-10am and 4-11pm

A little off the beaten track, Backpackers Hostel is located on the southernmost tip of **Lake Lucerne** in a mostly suburban setting, among private residences and primary schools. With the nearest tram stop a five-minute walk away, it feels a bit secluded, but it's actually only a ten-minute tram ride away from the city center. The views from the ensuite balconies are serene, and if you visit during the summer, you'll be spending a good deal of your time outside, as the rooms lack air-conditioning. The hostel itself is very clean, has a friendly staff, and boasts a penthouse common room with grand open spaces and a great view of the lake.

i Dorms from 33CHF, doubles 84CHF; reservation recommended; BGLTQ+ friendly; limited wheelchair accessibility; Wi-Fi; linens included; laundry 4.50CHF

SIGHTS

CULTURE

🏛 LUCERNE RATHAUS

Kornmarkt 3; 412271717

Recently renovated and ornamented with the Swiss and Lucerne canton flags, the **Rathaus' maroon clock tower** is a prominent sublimity in the Reuss River skyline. Although not open to the public, the building, as the meeting place of the **Grand Council of the City,** buzzes with political energy. Every Saturday the Rathaus hosts an open-air market, which envelops you with the smell of fresh herbs, farmer's cheese, warm bread, and ripe berries. The market is also a great place to meet locals. Stop by to experience the Rathaus's Renaissance architecture and *Emmentaler*-style roof, fill your belly, and learn more about the people who make Lucerne the vibrant city that it is today.

i Free entry; market stand prices vary

LANDMARKS

KAPELLBRÜCKE

Kapellbrücke; 412271717; www.luzern.com/en/chapel-bridge

Kapellbrücke is the oldest surviving wooden bridge in Europe. During the summer time Kapellbrücke is particularly busy—the arrival of swans and honeybees brings with it the arrival of swarms of tourists. Chapel Bridge has become an emblem of the city with paintings along the bridge depicting its complex history. Sadly, a fire in 1993 destroyed most of these paintings, but the bridge itself stands strong today. The looming **Wasserturm** (water tower) next to the bridge was a dungeon back in the day but is no longer accessible to visitors.

i Free; wheelchair accessible

LÖWENDENKMAL

Denkmalstrasse 4; 412271717; www.luzern.com/en/lion-monument; open daily 24hr

Mark Twain considered Löwendenkmal "the most mournful and moving piece of stone in the world," and we agree... with half of that statement. While the monument—an image of a dying lion chiseled out of a massive slab of marble—is quite moving, it's not as mournful as Twain says it is. This sculpture commemorates the death of the Swiss mercenaries that served under **King Louis XVI** and has since become a symbol of both Lucerne and of the larger Swiss resistance. A keen eye might notice the outline of a pig encompassing the lion—a sly jab by the artist to the city that didn't pay him for his work.

i Free; wheelchair accessible

MUSEGGMAUER

Schirmertorweg; 793566979; www.museggmauer.ch; open Apr 1-Nov 2 8am-7pm

Standing the test of time, Museggmauer consists of the remnants of the city's exterior fortifications dating back to the fifteenth century. With nine intact towers connected along the defense line, four of which are accessible to visitors, Museggmauer provides a breathtaking view of the city, the lake, and the mountains. Make sure to climb up **Zytturm clocktower** to see the large pendulum clock that strikes a minute before the hour and **Männliturm tower,** which is topped with an iron soldier.

i Free; no wheelchair accessibility

MUSEUMS

🏛 SWISS MUSEUM OF TRANSPORT

Lidostrasse 5; 413704444; www.verkehrshaus.ch/en; open daily 10am-6pm

This museum teems with kids of all ages who usually come on organized outings and is the most popular museum in all of Switzerland. For a hefty price, you can gain access to an in-depth description of the development of transportation and communication systems in Switzerland from the building of the **Gotthard railway** to the latest race cars and airplane models. With interactive models, railway simulations, and some expansive grounds, the museum is great for families seeking to keep children entertained for hours on end. It also includes a planetarium, film theatre, and "Swiss chocolate adventure."

i Adult 30CHF, students 26CHF; last entry to complex 2hr before closing; last entry to museum 15min. before closing; limited wheelchair accessibility

GLETSCHERGARTEN

Denkmalstrasse 4; 414104340; www.gletschergarten.ch/en; summer daily 9am-6pm, winter daily 10am-5pm

The Gletschergarten (Glacier Garden) tends to be overlooked. Access includes the museum and a mirror maze with convoluted and treacherous paths. Although the Gletschergarten in itself is not extremely entertaining, the observation tower towards the back is worth the trek and provides a stunning view of Lucerne. The museum covers the life and work of **Joseph Wilhelm Amrein-Troller,** one of the garden's discoverers, and includes interactive exhibits demonstrating the geological timeline of the land where Lucerne currently stands.

i Adults 15CHF, students and seniors 12CHF, children 8CHF; last entry 30min. before closing,adult price drops to 10CHF 45min. before closing; adult price drops to 7.50CHF 30min. before closing; limited wheelchair accessibility; private tours by reservation only

FOOD

🏨 ALPINEUM KAFFEEHAUS BAR ($$$)

Denkmalstrasse 11; 774249098; open
M-F 8am-12:30am, Sa 9am-12:30am, Su
noon-6pm

Despite being within walking distance
of several major monuments and
museums, Alpineum Kaffeehaus has
yet to be overrun by tourists. Upon
arriving on the premises (which are
beautiful, might we add) it was clear
that this was a more authentic local
restaurant and bar than some of those
we'd visited, and we weren't sure how we
would be received. We were welcomed
warmly and handed a drink menu that
(presumably) used to be a book about
alpine skiing. Standouts include the
classic cappuccino and the Sama Sama,
a shot of house-made ginger liquor.
During the weekdays, Alpineum offers
a set menu (vegetarian 18.50CHF, meat
19.50CHF), the contents of which
are subject to the whims of the chef.
During the weekend, Alpineum hosts
themed "food events" such as Big Bang
Burger Sunday.
i Entrées from 18CHF; vegetarian options
available; limited wheelchair accessibility

DEAN AND DAVID ($$)

Morgartenstrasse 4; 412200222; www.
deananddavid.de; open M-F 11am-9pm, Sa
11am-8pm, Su closed

Clean, fresh, eco-friendly. This Munich-
based company provides healthy
alternatives for travelers hoping to ditch
the carbs and get their daily dose of
greens. According to Dean and David's
website, the menu was inspired by the
cookshops of southeast Asia, juice bars
of Australia, and salad culture of New
York—a combination more apparent
in the restaurant's leafy décor than the
food itself. Create your own salad, wrap,
or pressed juice, and tack on a tasty
dessert to complete a meal that will
leave your hungry, aching body feeling
full and refreshed.
i Entrées from 12CHF; vegetarian options
available; limited wheelchair accessibility

NIGHTLIFE

BAR59

Industriestrasse 5; 413605200; www.
bar59.ch; open W-Sa 8pm-4am

The street name says it all. An
underground bar-club combo located
in Lucerne's industrial district, Bar59
is known for its affordable drinks and
grungy charm. If you manage to make
it past the bouncer, you'll be greeted
by postered walls, old-school sofas, and
hundreds of sweaty twenty-somethings
trying to catch a breath before venturing
into Bar59's back room. When you're
ready, follow them through the large
black door at the rear of the bar to
experience what very well may be your
best night in Lucerne.
i Beer from 5CHF, pitcher of beer 19CHF,
shots 5CHF, drinks 13CHF; BGLTQ+ friendly

FRANKY BAR LOUNGE

Frankenstrasse 6; 412101073; bar open
M-Th 5pm-12:30am, F-Sa 5pm-4am; club
open Th-Sa 10pm-4am

Dim light cast by artisanal bulbs
reflects off of the glass bottles stacked
from floor to ceiling on the rear wall;
the low thump of R&B fills the lulls
in conversation between patrons;
bartenders donning all-black attire
run sprints behind the large wooden
bar. Welcome to Franky's, one of the
coolest lounges in Lucerne. Located a
mere five minutes from the main train
station, FBL's got a little for everyone:
a lively upstairs bar area conducive
to mingling, an underground club
conducive to raging, and an outdoor
patio conducive to chilling. The drinks
aren't exactly cheap, but what you lose
in drunkenness you make up for in
suavity.
i No cover, shots 5CHF, beer 5CHF, drinks
14CHF; BGLTQ+ friendly

ZÜRICH

Coverage by **Alejandro Lampell**

What do you get when you combine the financial prowess of New York with the rich cultural history of a European city at a crossroads and set it against the scintillating backdrop of the Swiss Alps? Zürich. Founded as a customs post by the Romans in 58 BCE, Zürich is now the most populous city in Switzerland and one of the most significant financial and industrial centers in the world. As the birthplace of the Swiss Protestant Reformation and the Dada movement, it also retains significant cultural importance as the home to over 50 museums and some of the largest music festivals in Europe. Zürich is a manageable size and has an impressive public transport system, but most sights, restaurants, and clubs close to the city center are accessible by foot. While it's true that trips to Zürich (like the rest of Switzerland's cities) do get pricey, don't worry, fearless traveler. With our help, you can go in and get out with money left in your pocket.

ORIENTATION

Zürich is located on the northwest tip of **Lake Zürich** in the central region of Switzerland. Southwest of the city, hugging the boundaries of the suburbs, lie the **Albis Mountains.** The city consists of 12 different districts, which are colloquially referred to as neighborhoods. Zürich's **Old Town** is split in two by the **River Limmat,** which flows into Lake Zürich. The eastern part of the Old Town, **Niederdorf,** is a winding network of medieval streets and tight alleyways. On the other hand, the western part of the Old Town is relatively commercial. **Bahnhofstrasse,** one of the most famous shopping streets in the world, constantly buzzes with tourists. This street leads straight to **Paradeplatz,** the financial district, housing major banks such as UBS and Credit Suisse. The major neighborhoods follow the river as it comes down from the northwest and winds along the northern portion of Lake Zürich. Just north of the old city is **Hauptbahnhof,** the main train station. **Zürich West** and **Langstrasse,** both located in the northwestern part of the city, are home to numerous entertainment venues and bars and are frequented mostly by students and locals.

ESSENTIALS

GETTING THERE

The Zürich International Airport is easily accessible from almost anywhere, with connections to over 150 destinations. It is located 10km away from the city center and you need only take a one-way, 10min. tram ride to Hauptbahnhof (single ticket 6.80CHF), the main railway station in the center of Zürich. When you land in the airport, exit the arrival area and go across to a building that houses a big shopping center. The train station is on the lower floor of this center; try not to confuse it with the tram system, which is located on the upper floor. Hauptbahnhof connects Zürich to many other Swiss cities and major European cities such as Paris, Milan, Hamburg, and others. Carparkplatz Sihlquai is the main bus station that connects Zürich to other European cities. Both the railway station and the bus station are located in the center of the city, which is a couple minutes south of Old Town.

GETTING AROUND

The Zürich Transport Network (ZVV) controls all the transportation in the canton of Zürich and includes tram, bus, boat, and train. The three former options are used to get around the city and Lake Zürich, and they run from 5am-12:30am. On Friday and Saturday, the night network *(Nachtnetze)* runs from 1am-5am and requires 2 tickets: a normal transport ticket and a night supplement ticket (1 for 5CHF, or 6 for 27CHF, discounts and ZürichCARD not applicable). Text "NZ" to (988) to purchase the supplement. Buy tickets at blue machines located at every stop (most take credit cards or coins only, no bills). For all purchased tickets, you must validate them once at a blue machine.

The public transport network is divided into zones. Zürich is zone 110, which includes the old city and most of the sights. Short-distance tickets (2.60CHF) are valid for 30min. in zones 110 (Zürich) and 120 (Winterthur), but usually span only 5 or 6 stops, so check the listing on the ticket machine at purchase. A day-pass for zone 110 is 8.60CHF (river boat included) while a 1hr pass is 4.30CHF. It costs an additional 2CHF per zone to travel through multiple zones. Travelers under 25 get a reduced price for multi-day passes, multiple-journey tickets, and group tickets. Carry ID in case of inspection.

Save money with the ZürichCARD (24CHF for 24hr, 4CHF for 72hr), which provides access to public transport for zone 110 and to and from the airport, as well as discounts or free entrance to many museums and clubs, and free sides or desserts at participating restaurants with purchases of an entrée. These are sold at most ticket machines and the tourist office in the main train station, where you can pick up a pamphlet for a complete list of benefits. Before using, validate once at a blue ticket machine or orange validator on one of the platforms.

Taxis are clean and safe but expensive (initial fee 6-8CHF, then 3.80-5CHF/km or 80CHF/hour). Taxis around the train station are especially exorbitant. Bicycle rentals are free but require ID and a 20CHF deposit. Stations are located just outside train station, near tracks 3 (M-F 8am-9:30pm) and 18 (M-F 9am-7:30pm). More information available at www.zuerirollt.ch.

PRACTICAL INFORMATION

Tourist Offices: Zürich Tourist Information, located in the main train station.
- Hauptbahnhof Zürich (Main Train Station; 044 215 40 00; open May 1-Oct 31 M-Sa 8am-8:30pm, Su 8:30am-6:30pm; Nov 1-Apr 31 M-Sa 8:30am-7pm, Su 9am-6pm

Banks/ATMs/Currency Exchange: ATMs are available at banks. Banking hours M-F 8:30am-4:30pm; closed on major holidays. You can exchange

money at any Swiss bank, the airport, the main railway station, and major hostels. Exchange houses are less common and usually do not have great rates, especially the ones in the airport. Usually the best option is to withdraw money from an ATM.

Post Offices: Central post office is Sihlpost (Kasernenstrasse 97 (Sihlpost tram stop); 084 888 88 88; open M-F 6:30am-10:30pm, Sa 6:30am-8pm, Su 10am-10:30pm)

Internet: The first hour of Wi-Fi is free in all Swiss train stations, but you'll need to register the first time with a phone number. The Zürich airport offers 2hr of free Wi-Fi; you must register using your phone number. At the tourist office, you can rent a Wi-Fi router, which provides unlimited 4G/LTE Internet (40CHF for 3 days, 65CHF for 7 days, 83CHF for 10 days, 130CHF for 15 days)

Public Toilets: There are free public toilets throughout the city, but you must pay 1CHF at major tram stops (open Apr-Oct 6:30am –9:45pm, Nov-Mar 6:30am-8:45pm).

BGLTQ+ Resources: BGLTQ+ Helpline of Switzerland (Located in Bern; Monbijoustrasse 73; 080 013 31 33; hello@lgbt-helpline.ch; www.lgbt-helpline.ch/en/).

EMERGENCY INFORMATION

Emergency Numbers: General (112); police (117); fire department (118); ambulance (144); Swiss Helicopter Rescue Service (1414)

Police: The Cantonal Police Zürich takes responsibility for the canton of Zürich (Kasernenstrasse 29; 044 247 22 11). The Zürich City Police (Bahnhofquai 3; 044 411 71 17). In an emergency, call 117.

US Embassy: Consular Agency in Zürich (Dufourstrasse 101 third floor; open M-F 10am-1pm (by appointment only), closed on US and Swiss/Local holidays; 043 499 29 60).

Rape Crisis Center: Zürich Frauenzentrale (women's center) (Schanzengraben 29; 044 206 30 20)

Hospitals: For most non-emergency problems, it is recommended that you set up an appointment at a Permanence with a doctor. There is one at Zürich main station, open all year from 7am-

10pm (Bahnhofplatz 15; 044 215 44 44; www.permanence.ch).
- Universitätsspital (Rämistrasse 100; 044 255 11 11; open daily 24hr)
- Stadtspital Triemli (Birmensdorfer-strasse 497, 044 466 11 11; open daily 24hr)
- Stadtspital Waid (Tièchestrasse 99, 044 366 20, 55; open daily 24hr)

Pharmacies: On Sundays, the only shops allowed open are located in railway stops and petrol stations. Some groceries with pharmacies inside are open until 11pm. The large Coop supermarket next to the main railway station is open M-Sa 7am-10pm.
- Bahnhof Apotheke im Hauptbahn-hof (044 225 42 42)
- Bellevue Apotheke (044 266 62 22)
- Apotheke-Drogerie Bahnhof Enge (044 201 21 41)

ACCOMMODATIONS

🛏 YOUTH HOSTEL ZÜRICH ($$)

Mutschellenstrasse 114; 433997800; www.youthhostel.ch/Zürich; reception open 24hr, door locks at 11pm

Tired of the city's rapid pace? Take a 15-minute tram ride to the suburbs where you'll find this friendly hostel. The clientele ranges from young children to older couples; the diversity makes for some fun and engaging conversations. The lobby, outfitted with air hockey and ping pong tables, seems like an attempt at a "teen section" for a cruise, but, who are we kidding, we all love those sections. With linens included, lockers provided, and ensuite sinks, Youth Hostel Zürich is a good bargain.

i Dorms from 50CHF; reservation recommended; BGLTQ+ friendly; wheelchair accessible; Wi-Fi; linens included; laundry

CITY BACKPACKER – HOTEL BIBER ($)

Niederdorfstrasse 5; 442519015; www.city-backpacker.ch; reception open 8am-noon and 3pm-10pm

Follow the cartoon beaver—hidden in an alley of the **Old Town**—up four flights of stairs to the reception of this centrally located and popular hostel. As its name suggests, City Backpacker is frequented mostly by backpackers and students attracted by the low prices. The building is old and quite cramped,

but the rooms are clean (some with kitchens) and there is a great rooftop upstairs where most travelers hang around.

i Dorms from 37CHF, singles from 77CHF, doubles from 118CHF, triples from 159CHF; reservation recommended; max 7 nights; BGLTQ+ friendly; no wheelchair accessibility; Wi-Fi; linens 3CHF; laundry 10 CHF

HOSTEL OTTER OLD TOWN ($$)

Oberdorfstrasse 7; 442512207; www.oldtownZürich.com; reception open 7:30am-10pm

Tucked in among boutiques and restaurants in the heart of the **Old Town,** Hostel Otter Old Town is frequented by a wide variety of people due to its prime location and excellent prices. Located above the brightly colored **Wuste Bar,** the hostel has rooms ranging from dorms to themed private suites. A five-minute walk from main attractions **Grossmünster** and **Fraumünster,** Hostel Otter Old Town is also equipped with common rooms that are conducive to mingling.

i Dorms from 40CHF, doubles from 140CHF; reservation recommended; max stay 7 nights; BGLTQ+ friendly; wheelchair accessible; linens included; laundry 10 CHF; dorms include budget breakfast, private rooms include continental breakfast (dorm upgrade 7CHF)

SIGHTS
CULTURE

LÖWENBRÄUKUNST

Oberdorfstrasse 2; 443077900; www.lowenbraukunst.ch; museums open T, W, F 11am-6pm, Th 11am-8pm

If you enjoy wandering through large empty spaces, staring at piercingly white walls, and finding meaning in absurd combinations of mundane objects, consider Löwenbräukunst an essential stop during your tour of Zürich. A brewery-turned-arts-complex, it's home to two of the most important contemporary art museums in Switzerland, **Migros** and **Kunsthalle Zürich,** and contains many small galleries for local artists. Löwenbräukunst is the kind of place where it's difficult to differentiate between what is and what isn't art—we learned the hard way and recommend refraining from sitting on anything, no matter how heavy your pack may feel. Galleries are dispersed throughout the complex and open to the public; some are "working galleries" where you can watch the artists in live-time as they refine their masterpieces.

i Free admission, single museum 12CHF, reduced 8CHF, both museums 20CHF, reduced 12CHF, free on Th 5pm-8pm; tours given twice a month, look online for details; last entry 15 min. before closing; wheelchair accessible

SCHIFFBAU

Schiffbaustrasse 6; 442655858; www. schauspielhaus.ch/de; open M-F 11am-7pm, Sa 2pm-7pm

Reuse, reduce, recycle. Switzerland's eco-friendly approach to reusing old buildings has led to the creation of trendy new cultural centers. One such center, Schiffbau, was transformed from a derelict shipbuilding edifice to an expansive complex that houses a three-theater stage, restaurant LaSalle, and Moods Jazz Club. Tickets for the theater start at 10CHF, and shows, which range from classics to regionally specific originals, are performed almost exclusively in German. The complex is also used for different events throughout the year. Right behind the former shipbuilding yard is *Turbinenplatz,* a large concrete garden where you can sit on a wooden bench and watch it light up at night.

i Free; theatre tickets half-priced on M; wheelchair accessible

LANDMARKS
. . . .

🖼 OLD TOWN

Open daily 24hr

Follow the beautiful church steeples through narrow cobblestone roads and you'll always find yourself in the heart of Zürich, the Old Town. Start off on **Lindenhof Hill,** a former Roman fort which provides an amazing view of the city center and the **River Limmat** passing through it. A walk around the winding streets is a treat for a history buff, as it offers views of the medieval churches Grossmünster, Fraumünster, and St. Peter, as well as Lenin's apartment during his exile. For those more interested in the present, Old Town provides some of the best shopping along **Bahnhofstrasse** (best for looking unless you are into small, unknown brands like Gucci or Chanel) and a vibrant nightlife.

i Free; free city tour daily 11am, meets next to UBS at Paradeplatz

GROSSMÜNSTER

Grossmünsterplatz; 442513860; www.grossmuenster.ch; open daily summer 10am-6pm, winter 10am-5pm; Karlsturm open summer M-Sa 10am-5pm, Su 12:30am-5:30pm, winter M-Sa 10am-4:30pm, Su 12:30am-4:30pm

Two stunning church towers with views overlooking a city and the surrounding mountain range—*yawn.* Typical for a European city. Yet Grossmünster is no typical church. It's the birthplace of Switzerland's Protestant Reformation, when in the sixteenth century **Huldrych Zwingli** served as the parishioner. Grossmünster's history is deeply intertwined with local folklore, for Grossmünsterplatz is the plot to which Felix and Regula, the patron saints of Zürich, decided to carry their severed heads and die. If you're up to the task, we recommend taking the 187 narrow stairs up to the top of one of the towers (**Karlstrum**) for a sweeping panorama of Zürich.

i Church free; Karlstrum adult 4CHF, students 2CHF, groups of 10 3CHF per person; tours 180CHF; tours without guide run M, W-F with reservation

MUSEUMS
. . . .

🖼 LANDESMUSEUM ZÜRICH (SWISS NATIONAL MUSEUM)

Museumstrasse 2; 442186511; www. nationalmuseum.ch; open Tu-W 10am-5pm, Th 10am-7pm, F-Su 10am-5pm

Want to learn about the rise and fall of a combination of European cantons? Look no further, young Herodotus, and head over to the Swiss National Museum located adjacent to the main train station in a chateau of a building. You'll encounter an extensive display of Swiss history from the time of the settlers to the present. We loved the exhibits describing the influx of Greco-Roman culture and Germanic tribes. With entertaining exhibitions such as miniature replicas of major battles and rotating displays, history has never been so tantalizing.

i Adult 10CHF, students 8CHF, children up to 16 free; last entry 15min. before closing; guided tours available; wheelchair accessible

FIFA WORLD MUSEUM

Seestrasse 27; 433882500; www.fifamuseum.com; open Tu-Sa 10am-7pm, Su 9am-6pm

Recent corruption scandals have left FIFA branded with labels such as fraudulent, corporate, and strictly money-driven. The sport it represents—soccer—is still, however, associated with beauty, grace, athleticism, and passionate fans. The FIFA World Museum, although a little pricey, is the mecca of any avid soccer fan and, even if you don't know the difference between the EPL or La Liga it's still entertaining for those who prefer slam dunks, home runs, and touchdowns. The lower level contains soccer memorabilia and the complete history of the World Cup, while the upper level is decked out with foosball, and **FIFA video games.**

i Admission 24CHF, children 0-6 free, children (7-15) 14CHF, students 18 CHF; last entry 30min. before closing; wheelchair accessible; free audio guide by downloading app

KUNSTHAUS

Heimplatz 1; 442538497; www.kunsthaus. ch; open Tu 10am-6pm, W-Th 10am-8pm, F-Su 10am-6pm, closed major holidays

From the outside, Kunsthaus is nothing special. It's big, rectangular, and to be honest, pretty bland. Don't let its unassuming exterior fool you though. Housed within its walls are some of the world's most prized pieces of two-dimensional art—works by **Monet, Picasso, Chagall, Pollock,** among others. As you climb from floor to floor, you travel through a timeline spanning from the Medieval Ages to contemporary art. Temporary exhibitions are usually located near the entrance along with free audio guides.

i Admission 11CHF; last entry 15min. before closing; wheelchair accessible

OUTDOORS

UETLIBERG MOUNTAIN

8143 Uetliberg; 444576666; www.uetliberg. ch; open daily 24 hr (restaurant open M-Sa 9am-11pm, Su 9am-6pm)

The Uetliberg is a mountain in the Swiss plateau, part of the **Albis chain,** that offers stunning views of the entire city of Zürich and a prime opportunity to fulfill your yodeling dreams. We recommend skipping the train and hiking to **Uto Kulm** (the summit); the trails are well-marked yet isolated. At the top, you'll find a viewing tower (2CHF) and a restaurant that overlooks the mountain range. Although its prices are on the higher end of the spectrum, consider stopping by to grab a drink. Considering all the yodeling you've been doing, you're probably parched.

i Free, train 50CHF, children under 16 25CHF; trains run every 30min. and take approximately 20min.

FOOD

🍴 ÄSS BAR ($)

Stüssihofstatt 6; 435480544; aess-bar.ch; open M-Sa 9am-6:30pm

Go ahead, laugh a little. No, Äss Bar is not bacon-themed. The word "äss" translates to "eatable" and ties into the idea of sustainability. Not what you expected? Neither did we. Rather than discard excess pastries, this small bakery sells them at a discounted price (half-off). Grab a hazelnut croissant (1.50CHF) and a sandwich (3CHF) to-go and head towards the river, where you'll be greeted with a shockingly-impressive view of **Uetliberg.**

i Pastries from 1.50CHF; cash only; vegetarian options available; no wheelchair accessibility

🍴 WURST AND MORITZ ($$)

Hardstrasse 318; 435404147; www. wurstundmoritz-zuerich.ch; open M-W 11am-10pm, Th-Sa 11am-11:45pm, Su 11am-10pm

While in the German-speaking region of Switzerland, you might find yourself wondering, "To wurst or not to wurst?" The answer, might we tell you, is *always* "to wurst," and there's no better place to do so in Zürich than

Wurst and Moritz. Frequented mostly by locals and students, W&M's combo meals (16CHF) include your choice of sausage, lightly-salted fries, and a pint of beer. Take at one of the high tables or outside on the expansive street-side patio and relish in the greasy goodness in front of you. You deserve it.

i Entrées from 12CHF; vegan and vegetarian options available; limited wheelchair accessibility

RACLETTE FACTORY ($$)

Rindermarkt 1; 2610410; www.raclette-factory.ch; open Su-Th 11am-10pm, F-Sa 11am-11pm

As you've already probably discovered, Swiss cuisine, like the rest of the country, is expensive. Enter the hero, Raclette Factory—known for its Swiss décor, fresh bread, melted cheese, and large wine collection, and your window into the Swiss culinary experience. We recommend skipping over the half-platter (80g) and going straight to the full-platter (160g); you'll receive more bang for your buck.

i Platters from 12CHF; vegetarian options available; no wheelchair accessibility

NIGHTLIFE

▨ BQM

Leonhardstrasse 34; 446327503; www.bqm-bar.ch; open term time M-Th 11:45am-11pm, open during final exams M-F 11:45am-10pm

Being back on a college campus will inevitably bring back a flood of emotions, including nostalgia for cheap alcohol. (Just us? Cool.) BQM, located under the same roof as the **University of Zürich's** cafeteria, is your best bet for meeting youngish individuals and securing a liter and a half of beer for less than 20CHF. Outside you'll find a beautiful panorama of **Old Town,** with **Fraumunster, St. Peter's,** and **Grossmunster** in direct view. Because campus policy requires bars to shut down by 11pm during term time, BQM a good first stop.

i No cover, shots from 5CHF, 1.5L beer 18CHF

▨ CABARET VOLTAIRE

Spiegelgasse 1; 432685720; www.cabaret-voltaire.ch; open Tu-Th 6pm-midnight, F 6pm-2am, Sa 4pm-2am, Su 4pm-midnight

The ground floor houses a bookstore and art gallery. On the upper level, share a beer with old poet types staring blankly into the ether and ask yourself, as does the black-and-white wall print, "to be da-da or not DaDa?" On certain nights, unintelligible-but-fascinating live performances ensue in the back room, which is ever-permeated by the synthetic smell of the in-house fog machine.

i Beer from 6CHF, drinks 13CHF; minimum card charge; BGLTQ+ friendly

ZÜRI BAR ($)

Niederdorfstrasse 24; 442618874; open M-Th 4pm-midnight, F 4pm-1am, Sa noon-1am

For a 70-year-old, Züri keeps things tight. It's famed as one of the oldest bars in Zürich's **Old Town** and attracts its clientele accordingly. Find yourself conversing with a local who has been around longer than the bar itself or enjoying a scotch solo in a small, cushy booth. The friendly staff and reasonably-priced alcohol have drawn the pool of regulars as well as the hoard of tourists that frequents the establishment.

i Drinks 14.50CHF, beer from 5CHF

NELSON'S PUB

Beatengasse 11; 442126016; www.nelson-pubZürich.ch; open M-Th 11:30am-2am, F 11:30am-4:30am, Sa 2pm-4:30am

Simply put, Nelson's Pub is where 30-year-old Zürchers go to get sloshed. This nautical-themed bar is the perfect place to spend the wee hours of the morning broadcasting your sorrows. The bartenders, like the diverse clientele, are eager to help talk things through, and by the time you've resolved your issues, Nelson's will have filled up enough for you to not look like a total whacko when you start passionately lip syncing Taylor Swift's "We Are Never Ever Getting Back Together" in the middle of the dance floor.

i Beer from 6CHF, hard liquor 15CHF

SWITZERLAND ESSENTIALS

ELECTRICITY

The standard voltage in Switzerland is 220V, and the power sockets used are of type J, particular to only Switzerland, Liechtenstein, and Rwanda. Type C plugs that are used throughout most of Europe fit into the type J socket, but double check to make sure the adapter you are taking works.

MONEY

Tipping: Do not feel obligated to tip in Switzerland as a federal law replaced tips with an all-inclusive bill back in the '70s. If you are very happy with your service, you can round your bill up to the nearest five or ten francs. However, waiters do not expect this tip, so don't feel bad if you're spending on a backpacker's budget and cannot afford to tip at every single establishment.

HEALTH AND SAFETY

Intra-city travel operates such that you are expected to have the proper ticket with you when riding public transportation. From time to time authorities will hop aboard to check tickets. If you are caught without a valid ticket, you will incur a hefty fine (90CHF).

Drugs and Alcohol: In Switzerland, the legal drinking age for beer and wine is 16 years old and 18 years old for all other drinks. Public drinking is legal for everybody of age, except in certain public spaces, which are determined by cantons.

INDEX

ACKNOWLEDGMENTS

First, we'd like to thank the Researcher-Writers who wrote, and wrote, and wrote, and wrote, countless pages of copy. Thank you to Margaret for your amazing Instagram DMs and cheerful FaceTime calls; Joseph for your reliable vegan-sustainable-food-ethically-sourced-grass-fed-meat restaurant listings and sprinkling of ~interesting~ nightlife locales; Austin for your elegant and impossible-to-trim-down copy; Lucy for your encounters with local UK people and hilarious stories—and to all of last year's Researcher-Writers. We are so proud of all the work you have done—from researching it, writing it, to sharing it with us. You made our summer fun-filled and never boring: we regularly read parts aloud to each other during the editing process because it was just that good. And, of course, to Graham and Daphne, our USA and Canada Researcher-Writers whose writing is not featured in this book, but who deserve their own shoutouts for being two inexpressibly lovely people. This year's team could not have been better.

Thank you to Emily at Placepass for supporting us and for using our content on your website. We are so grateful for the opportunities you have given us, and for a now two-year partnership that makes our work possible.

Thank you to Michael, Nathaniel, Sara, and Kristine. When things were bleak, your emails and constant support helped ground us and reassure us that we were headed in the right direction. Nathaniel, thank you for supporting Cassandra as she wrote the Bookplan and puzzled out the task that is book production. Michael, you're known among us as the InDesign wizard—and it's true! Thank you for working with Cassandra to implement template changes that she would never have been able to do herself. Sara, thank you for the vast amount of marketing knowledge you gave to Laura when we just started out, and for your incredibly honest advice. Kristine, thank you for all the random tips, late-night texting conversations, the constant moral support, and initiative (read: volunteering as tribute) you took when it came to proofing. The team owes more to y'all than we can express, and we are so grateful that you were willing to help us out through each step of the process. Most of all, thank you for giving us the tools to figure things out for ourselves—a skill that came in handy many a late night in the office.

Thank you to the team at Dev: Noah, Olivia, Kyle, and Bliss. We've gushed in person many times about how wonderful your work is, but we will never really be able to express how grateful we are for your reboot of Sandbox. Your contribution to this year's final product is immeasurable: there is no way production would have run as smoothly as it did this summer. Thank you for meeting with us and taking our feedback—all with a crazy-fast turnaround. You guys rock.

Thank you to the team at Campus Insights: James, Akanksha, Amy, Dhruv, and Jared. Your research on our behalf is invaluable. The blank invoice was the best thing to happen to us all summer—we love you to death and we love the never-ending jokes and strange things we hear from the pod next door.

Thank you to our families who struggled to understand what it is we do on a daily basis yet who checked in and worried in the classic helicopter-parent fashion. Thank you to our friends and blockmates who told us to go home when we sent 10pm Snapchats from the office, and who offered to help us in any way they could. (Food. Mostly food.)

Finally, thank you to everyone at HSA who supported us as we valiantly forged ahead in the journey that is book production. To Ali and Rameen, who have been with us since the beginning. To Jim, for your advice and thoughtful questions as we worked through typical publishing problems. To the business office, for your invaluable help and experience. And, of course, to all the managers who were there as we yelled about copy, blasted weird music, and who supported us in any way we could as we worked towards producing the book now in your hands.

PUBLISHING DIRECTOR, Laura Wilson

EDITOR IN CHIEF, Cassandra Luca

ASSOCIATE EDITOR, Danielle Eisenman

PRESIDENT, HARVARD STUDENT AGENCIES, Ali Dastjerdi

GENERAL MANAGER, HARVARD STUDENT AGENCIES, Jim McKellar

ABOUT US

THE STUDENT TRAVEL GUIDE

Let's Go publishes travel guides written by its team of Researcher-Writers, who are all students at Harvard College. Armed with pens, notebooks, and laptops (hopefully, with chargers), our student researchers travel across Europe on pre-planned itineraries, hopping from city to city to seek out invaluable travel experiences for our readers. Because we are a completely student-run company, we have a unique perspective on how students travel, where they want to go, and what they're looking for when they get there. Whether you want to venture into the crater of Mount Etna, kayak in Lagos, or museum-hop in London, our guides have got you covered. We write for readers on a budget who know that there's more to travel than tour buses.

FIFTY-NINE YEARS OF WISDOM

Let's Go has been on the road for 59 years and counting. We started in 1960 with a small, 20-page pamphlet that included travel tips and food, accommodation, and activity recommendations for Europe's major cities. Over the last six decades, however, our Researcher-Writers have written guides covering almost every corner of the planet. Europe? Check. Australia? You betcha. India? Been there, done that. And despite the growth, our witty, candid guides are still researched and written entirely by Harvard students on shoestring budgets who know how to deal with everything from debit card fraud to stolen phones to bad cuttlefish. This year's guide is the second in full-color, and features a content architecture that allows readers to easily pinpoint reviews of hostels, sights, restaurants, and food in any given city. And, of course, like all other Let's Go guides, the one in your hand still features the same witty and irreverent voice that has been carried by *Let's Go* teams for decades.

THE *LET'S GO* COMMUNITY

More than just a travel guide company, Let's Go is a community that reaches from our headquarters in Cambridge, MA all across the globe. Our staff of dedicated student editors, designers, writers, and tech nerds is united by a shared passion for travel and desire to help other travelers get the most out of their experiences. We love it when our readers become part of the Let's Go community as well—when you travel, drop us a postcard (67 Mt. Auburn St., Cambridge, MA 02138, USA), send us an email (webmaster@letsgo.com), or sign up on our website (www.letsgo.com) to tell us about your adventures and discoveries.

GET INVOLVED! If you want to share your discoveries, suggestions, or corrections, please drop us a line. We appreciate every piece of correspondence, whether a postcard, a 10-page email, or a coconut. Visit *Let's Go* at **www.letsgo.com** or send an email to **webmaster@letsgo.com**, subject: Let's Go Europe 2019."

Address mail to:

Let's Go
67 Mount Auburn St.
Cambridge, MA 02138, USA

In addition to the invaluable travel advice our readers share with us, many are kind enough to offer their services as researchers or editors. Unfortunately, our charter enables us to employ only currently enrolled Harvard students.

Distributed by **Publishers Group West.**
Printed in Canada by **Friesens Corp.**

Let's Go Europe Copyright © 2019 by Let's Go, Inc. All rights reserved. No part of this book may be used or reproduced in any manner whatsoever without written permission except in the case of brief quotations embodied in critical articles or reviews. *Let's Go* is available for purchase in bulk by institutions and authorized resellers.

ISBN-13: 978-1-61237-053-8
Fifty-ninth edition
10 9 8 7 6 5 4 3 2 1

Let's Go Europe is written by Let's Go Publications, 67 Mt. Auburn St., Cambridge, MA 02138, USA.

Let's Go and the LG Logo are trademarks of Let's Go, Inc.

LEGAL DISCLAIMER. For 59 years, *Let's Go* has published the world's favorite budget travel guides, written entirely by students and updated periodically based on the personal anecdotes and travel experiences of our student writers. Although every effort was made to ensure that the information was correct at the time of going to press, the author and publisher do not assume and hereby disclaim any liability to any party for any loss or damage caused by errors, omissions, or any potential travel disruption due to labor or financial difficulty, whether such errors or omissions result from negligence, accident, or any other cause.

QUICK REFERENCE

EMERGENCY PHONE NUMBERS (POLICE)

Austria	133	Ireland	999
Belgium	101	Italy	113
Croatia	192	The Netherlands	911
Czechia	158	Norway	112
Denmark	114	Poland	997
France	17	Portugal	112
Germany	110	Spain	092
Great Britain	999	Sweden	112
Greece	100	Switzerland	117
Hungary	107	General Emergency (Europe)	112

USEFUL PHRASES

ENGLISH	FRENCH	GERMAN	ITALIAN	SPANISH
Hello/Hi	Bonjour/Salut	Hallo/Tag	Ciao	Hola
Goodbye/Bye	Au revoir	Auf Wiedersehen/Tschüss	Arrivederci/Ciao	Adiós/Chau
Yes	Oui	Ja	Sì	Sí
No	Non	Nein	No	No
Excuse me!	Pardon!	Entschuldigen Sie!	Scusa!	¡Perdón!
Thank you	Merci	Danke	Grazie	Gracias
Go away!	Allez-y!	Geh weg!	Vattene via!	¡Váyase!
Help!	Au secours!	Hilfe!	Aiuto!	¡Ayude!
Call the police!	Appelez la police!	Ruf die Polizei!	Chiamare la polizia!	¡Llame a la policía!
Get a doctor!	Cherchez un médecin!	Hol einen Arzt!	Chiamare un medico!	¡Llame a un médico!
I don't understand	Je ne comprends pas	Ich verstehe nicht	Non capisco	No comprendo
Do you speak English?	Parlez-vous anglais?	Sprechen Sie Englisch?	Lei parla inglese?	¿Habla inglés?
Where is...?	Où est...?	Wo ist...?	Dov' è...?	¿Dónde está...?

TEMPERATURE CONVERSIONS

°CELSIUS	-5	0	5	10	15	20	25	30	35	40
°FAHRENHEIT	23	32	41	50	59	68	77	86	95	104

MEASUREMENT CONVERSIONS

1 inch (in.) = 25.4mm	1 millimeter (mm) = 0.039 in.
1 foot (ft.) = 0.305m	1 meter (m) = 3.28 ft.
1 mile (mi.) = 1.609km	1 kilometer (km) = 0.621 mi.
1 pound (lb.) = 0.454kg	1 kilogram (kg) = 2.205 lb.
1 gallon (gal.) = 3.785L	1 liter (L) = 0.264 gal.